Crafting and Executing Strategy

THE QUEST FOR COMPETITIVE ADVANTAGE

Concepts and Cases

Crafting and Executing Strategy

THE QUEST FOR COMPETITIVE ADVANTAGE

Concepts and Cases

EIGHTEENTH EDITION

Arthur A. Thompson
The University of Alabama

Margaret A. Peteraf
Dartmouth College

John E. Gamble
University of South Alabama

A. J. Strickland III
The University of Alabama

McGraw-Hill Irwin

CRAFTING AND EXECUTING STRATEGY: THE QUEST FOR COMPETITIVE ADVANTAGE: CONCEPTS AND CASES

ISBN 978-0-07-811272-0
MHID 0-07-811272-9

Vice president and editor-in-chief: *Brent Gordon*
Editorial director: *Paul Ducham*
Executive editor: *Michael Ablassmeir*
Executive director of development: *Ann Torbert*
Development editor II: *Laura Griffin*
Editorial assistant: *Andrea Heirendt*
Vice president and director of marketing: *Robin J. Zwettler*
Marketing director: *Amee Mosley*
Executive marketing manager: *Anke Braun Weekes*
Vice president of editing, design, and production: *Sesha Bolisetty*
Manager of editing, design, and production: *Lori Koetters*
Manager of photo, design & publishing tools: *Mary Conzachi*

Lead project manager: *Harvey Yep*
Senior buyer: *Michael R. McCormick*
Cover and interior designer: *Cara Hawthorne, cara david DESIGN*
Senior photo research coordinator: *Keri Johnson*
Photo researcher: *Bill Van Werden*
Executive producer, Media technology: *Mark Christianson*
Senior media project manager: *Susan Lombardi*
Media project manager: *Cathy L. Tepper*
Cover image: *© MIPAN/Veer*
Typeface: *10.5/12 Times New Roman MT Std*
Compositor: *Laserwords Private Limited*
Printer: *R. R. Donnelley*

Library of Congress Cataloging-in-Publication Data

Crafting and executing strategy : the quest for competitive advantage : concepts and cases.—18th ed./Arthur A. Thompson . . . [et al.].
    p. cm.
    Rev. ed. of: Crafting and executing strategy/Arthur A. Thompson. 17th ed. 2010.
    Includes index.
    ISBN-13: 978-0-07-811272-0 (alk. paper)
    ISBN-10: 0-07-811272-9 (alk. paper)
    1. Strategic planning. 2. Strategic planning—Case studies. I. Thompson, Arthur A., 1940-
II. Thompson, Arthur A., 1940- Crafting and executing strategy.
HD30.28.T53 2012
658.4′012—dc22

                                                                    2010050276

www.mhhe.com

To our families and especially our spouses:
Hasseline, Paul, and Kitty.

Arthur A. Thompson, Jr., earned his B.S. and Ph.D. degrees in economics from The University of Tennessee, spent three years on the economics faculty at Virginia Tech, and served on the faculty of The University of Alabama's College of Commerce and Business Administration for 24 years. In 1974 and again in 1982, Dr. Thompson spent semester-long sabbaticals as a visiting scholar at the Harvard Business School.

His areas of specialization are business strategy, competition and market analysis, and the economics of business enterprises. In addition to publishing over 30 articles in some 25 different professional and trade publications, he has authored or co-authored five textbooks and six computer-based simulation exercises. His textbooks and strategy simulations have been used at well over 1,000 college and university campuses worldwide.

Dr. Thompson and his wife of 49 years have two daughters, two grandchildren, and a Yorkshire Terrier.

Margaret A. Peteraf is the Leon E. Williams Professor of Management at the Tuck School of Business at Dartmouth College. She is an internationally recognized scholar of strategic management, with a long list of publications in top management journals. She has earned myriad honors and prizes for her contributions, including the 1999 Strategic Management Society Best Paper Award recognizing the deep influence of her work on the field of Strategic Management. Professor Peteraf is on the Board of Directors of the Strategic Management Society and has been elected as a Fellow of the Society. She served previously as a member of the Academy of Management's Board of Governors and as Chair of the Business Policy and Strategy Division of the Academy. She has also served in various editorial roles and is presently on 9 editorial boards, including the *Strategic Management Journal,* the *Academy of Management Review,* and *Organization Science*. She has taught in Executive Education programs in various programs around the world and has won teaching awards at the MBA and Executive level.

Professor Peteraf earned her Ph.D., M.A., and M.Phil. at Yale University and held previous faculty appointments at Northwestern University's Kellogg Graduate School of Management and at the University of Minnesota's Carlson School of Management.

John E. Gamble is currently a Professor of Management in the Mitchell College of Business at the University of South Alabama. His teaching specialty at USA is strategic management and he also conducts a course in strategic management in Germany, which is sponsored by the University of Applied Sciences in Worms.

Dr. Gamble's research interests center on strategic issues in entrepreneurial, health care, and manufacturing settings. His work has been published in various scholarly journals and he is the author or co-author of more than 50 case studies published in an assortment of strategic management and strategic marketing texts. He has done consulting on industry and market analysis for clients in a diverse mix of industries.

Professor Gamble received his Ph.D. in management from The University of Alabama in 1995. Dr. Gamble also has a Bachelor of Science degree and a Master of Arts degree from The University of Alabama.

Dr. A. J. (Lonnie) Strickland is the Thomas R. Miller Professor of Strategic Management at the Culverhouse School of Business at The University of Alabama. He is a native of North Georgia, and attended the University of Georgia, where he received a Bachelor of Science degree in math and physics; Georgia Institute of Technology, where he received a Master of Science in industrial management; and Georgia State University, where he received his Ph.D. in business administration.

Lonnie's experience in consulting and executive development is in the strategic management arena, with a concentration in industry and competitive analysis. He has developed strategic planning systems for numerous firms all over the world. He served as Director of Marketing and Strategy at Bell-South, has taken two companies to the New York Stock Exchange, is one of the founders and directors of American Equity Investment Life Holding (AEL), and serves on numerous boards of directors. He is a very popular speaker in the area of Strategic Management.

Lonnie and his wife, Kitty, have been married for 44 years; they have two children, and two grandchildren. Each summer Lonnie and his wife live on their private game reserve in South Africa where they enjoy taking their friends on safaris.

The defining trait of this 18th edition is an invigorated and much sharpened presentation of the material in each of the 12 chapters, with an as up-to-date and engaging discussion of the core concepts and analytical tools as you will find anywhere. Complementing the text chapters is a fresh, engrossing collection of 28 cases with unusual ability to work magic in the classroom. We are confident you will find the text chapters in this edition squarely on target, clearly written, peppered with fresh examples, and compelling. Together with a power-house lineup of high-interest cases, this is a text sure to ignite your students' interest in strategy, translate their enthusiasm into learning achievements, and enable you to shine in the classroom.

This edition represents one of our most important and thoroughgoing revisions ever. The newest member of the author team, Margie Peteraf, led a thorough reexamination of every paragraph on every page of the 17th-edition chapters. The overriding objectives were to inject new perspectives and the best academic thinking, strengthen linkages to the latest research findings, modify the coverage and exposition as needed to ensure squarely on-target content, and give every chapter a major facelift. While this 18th edition retains the 12-chapter structure of the prior edition, every chapter has been totally refreshed. Coverage was trimmed in some areas and expanded in others. New material has been added here and there. The presentations of some topics were recast, others fine-tuned, and still others left largely intact. As with past editions, scores of new examples have been added, along with fresh Illustration Capsules, to make the content come alive and to provide students with a ringside view of strategy in action. The result is a major step forward in terms of punch, up-to-date coverage, clarity, and classroom effectiveness. But none of the changes have altered the fundamental character that has driven the text's success over three decades. The chapter content continues to be solidly mainstream and balanced, mirroring *both* the penetrating insight of academic thought and the pragmatism of real-world strategic management. And, as always, we have taken great care to keep the chapters very reader-friendly and exceptionally teachable.

A differentiating feature of this text has always been the tight linkage between the content of the chapters and the cases. The lineup of cases that accompany the 18th edition is outstanding in this respect—a truly appealing mix of strategically relevant and thoughtfully crafted cases, certain to engage students and sharpen their skills in applying the concepts and tools of strategic analysis. Many involve high-profile companies that the students will immediately recognize and relate to; all are framed around key strategic issues and serve to add depth and context to the topical content of the chapters. We are confident that you will be impressed with how well these cases work in the classroom and the amount of student interest they will spark.

For some years now, growing numbers of strategy instructors at business schools worldwide have been transitioning from a purely text-case course structure to a more robust and energizing text-case-simulation course structure.

Incorporating a competition-based strategy simulation has the strong appeal of providing class members with *an immediate and engaging opportunity to apply the concepts and analytical tools covered in the chapters and to become personally involved in crafting and executing a strategy for a virtual company that they have been assigned to manage and that competes head-to-head with companies run by other class members.* Two widely used and pedagogically effective online strategy simulations, *The Business Strategy Game* and *GLO-BUS,* are optional companions for this text. Both simulations were created by this text's senior author and, like the cases, are closely linked to the content of each chapter in the text. The Exercises for Simulation Participants, found at the end of each chapter, provide clear guidance to class members in applying the concepts and analytical tools covered in the chapters to the issues and decisions that they have to wrestle with in managing their simulation company.

Through our experiences as business school faculty members, we fully understand the assessment demands on faculty teaching strategic management and business policy courses. In many institutions, capstone courses have emerged as the logical home for assessing student achievement of program learning objectives. The 18th edition includes a set of Assurance of Learning Exercises at the end of each chapter that link to the specific learning objectives appearing at the beginning of each chapter and highlighted throughout the text. *An important new instructional feature of the 18th edition is the linkage of selected chapter-end Assurance of Learning Exercises and seven cases to the publisher's Web-based assignment and assessment platform called Connect.* Your students will be able to use the online Connect supplement to (1) complete two or three of the Assurance of Learning Exercises appearing at the end of each of the 12 chapters, (2) complete chapter-end quizzes, and (3) enter their answers to a select number of the suggested assignment questions for 7 of the 28 cases in this edition. All of the Connect exercises are automatically graded, thereby enabling you to easily assess the learning that has occurred.

In addition, both of the companion strategy simulations have a built-in Learning Assurance Report that quantifies how well each member of your class performed on nine skills/learning measures *versus tens of thousands of other students worldwide* who completed the simulation in the past 12 months. We believe the chapter-end Assurance of Learning Exercises, the all-new online and automatically graded Connect exercises, and the Learning Assurance Report generated at the conclusion of *The Business Strategy Game* and *GLO-BUS* simulations provide you with easy-to-use, empirical measures of student learning in your course. All can be used in conjunction with other instructor-developed or school-developed scoring rubrics and assessment tools to comprehensively evaluate course or program learning outcomes and measure compliance with AACSB accreditation standards.

Taken together, the various components of the 18th-edition package and the supporting set of instructor resources provide you with enormous course design flexibility and a powerful kit of teaching/learning tools. We've done our very best to ensure that the elements constituting the 18th edition will work well for you in the classroom, help you economize on the time needed to be well prepared for each class, and cause students to conclude that your course is one of the very best they have ever taken—from the standpoint of both enjoyment and learning.

REVITALIZED AND EFFECTIVE CONTENT: THE SIGNATURE OF THE 18TH EDITION

Our objective in undertaking a major revision of this text was to ensure that its content was current, with respect to both scholarship and managerial practice, and was presented in as clear and compelling a fashion as possible. We established five criteria for meeting this objective, namely, that the final product must:

- Explain core concepts in language that students can grasp and provide first-rate examples of their relevance and use by actual companies.
- Thoroughly describe the tools of strategic analysis, how they are used, and where they fit into the managerial process of crafting and executing strategy.
- Incorporate the latest developments in the theory and practice of strategic management in every chapter to keep the content solidly in the mainstream of contemporary strategic thinking.
- Focus squarely on what every student needs to know about crafting, implementing, and executing business strategies in today's market environments.
- Provide an attractive set of contemporary cases that involve headline strategic issues and give students ample opportunity to apply what they've learned from the chapters.

We believe the 18th edition measures up on all five criteria. Chapter discussions cut straight to the chase about what students really need to know. At the same time, our explanations of core concepts and analytical tools are covered in enough depth to make them understandable and usable, since a shallow explanation carries little punch and almost no instructional value. Chapter content is driven by the imperative of including well-settled strategic management principles, fresh examples that illustrate the principles through the practices of real-world companies, recent research findings and contributions to the literature on strategic management, and the latest thinking of prominent academics and practitioners. There's a logical flow from one chapter to the next, as well as an unparalleled set of cases with which to drive the lessons home. And we have worked hard to hammer home the whys and hows of successfully crafting and executing strategy in an engaging, cogent, and convincing fashion.

Six standout features strongly differentiate this text and the accompanying instructional package from others in the field:

1. *Our coverage of the resource-based theory of the firm in the 18th edition is unsurpassed by any other leading strategy text.* RBV principles and concepts are prominently and comprehensively integrated into our coverage of crafting both single-business and multibusiness strategies. In Chapters 3 through

8 it is repeatedly emphasized that a company's strategy must be matched *not only* to its external market circumstances *but also* to its internal resources and competitive capabilities. Moreover, an RBV perspective is thoroughly integrated into the presentation on strategy execution (Chapters 10, 11, and 12) to make it unequivocally clear how and why the tasks of assembling intellectual capital and building core competencies and competitive capabilities are absolutely critical to successful strategy execution and operating excellence.

2. *Our coverage of the relational view, which focuses on cooperative strategies and the role that interorganizational activity can play in the pursuit of competitive advantage, is similarly unsurpassed by other leading texts.* The topics of alliances, joint ventures, franchising, and other types of cooperative and collaborative relationships are featured prominently in a number of chapters and are integrated into other material throughout the text as well. We show how strategies of this nature can contribute to the success of single business companies as well as multibusiness enterprises. And while we begin with coverage of such topics with respect to firms operating in domestic markets, we extend our discussion of this material to the international realm as well.

3. *Our coverage of business ethics, core values, social responsibility, and environmental sustainability is unsurpassed by any other leading strategy text.* In this new edition, we have embellished the highly important chapter "Ethics, Corporate Social Responsibility, Environmental Sustainability, and Strategy" with fresh content so that it can better fulfill the important functions of (1) alerting students to the role and importance of ethical and socially responsible decision making and (2) addressing the accreditation requirement of the AACSB International that business ethics be visibly and thoroughly embedded in the core curriculum. Moreover, discussions of the roles of values and ethics are integrated into portions of other chapters to further reinforce why and how considerations relating to ethics, values, social responsibility, and sustainability should figure prominently into the managerial task of crafting and executing company strategies.

4. *The caliber of the case collection in the 18th edition is truly top-notch* from the standpoints of student appeal, teachability, and suitability for drilling students in the use of the concepts and analytical treatments in Chapters 1 through 12. The 28 cases included in this edition are the very latest, the best, and the most on target that we could find. The ample information about the cases in the Instructor's Manual makes it effortless to select a set of cases each term that will capture the interest of students from start to finish.

5. *The text is paired with the publisher's trailblazing Web-based assignment and assessment platform called Connect.* This will enable professors to gauge class members' prowess in accurately completing (a) selected chapter-end exercises, (b) chapter-end quizzes, and (c) the creative author-developed exercises for seven of the cases in this edition.

6. *Two cutting-edge and widely used strategy simulations—The Business Strategy Game and GLO-bus—are optional companions to the 18th edition.* These give you unmatched capability to employ a text-case-simulation model of course delivery.

ORGANIZATION, CONTENT, AND FEATURES OF THE 18TH-EDITION TEXT CHAPTERS

The following rundown summarizes the noteworthy features and topical emphasis in this new edition:

- Although Chapter 1 continues to focus on the central questions of "*What is strategy?*" and "*Why is it important?*" the presentation of this material has been sharpened considerably, with more concise definitions of the key concepts and significant updating to improve the currency of the material. We introduce students to the primary approaches to building competitive advantage and the key elements of business-level strategy. Following Henry Mintzberg's process approach, we explain why a company's strategy is partly planned and partly reactive and why a strategy and its environment tend to co-evolve over time. We discuss the importance of a viable business model that outlines the company's customer value proposition and its profit formula, framing this discussion in terms of key elements of value, price, and cost. We show how the mark of a winning strategy is its ability to pass three tests: (1) the *fit test* (for internal and external fit), (2) the *competitive advantage test,* and (3) the *performance test.* And we explain why good company performance depends upon good strategy execution as well as a sound strategy. In short, this brief chapter is a perfect accompaniment for your opening-day lecture on what the course is all about and why it matters.

- Chapter 2 delves more deeply into the managerial process of actually crafting and executing a strategy—it makes a great assignment for the second day of class and provides a smooth transition into the heart of the course. The focal point of the chapter is the five-step managerial process of crafting and executing strategy: (1) forming a strategic vision of where the company is headed and why, (2) developing strategic as well as financial objectives with which to measure the company's progress, (3) crafting a strategy to achieve these targets and move the company toward its market destination, (4) implementing and executing the strategy, and (5) monitoring progress and making corrective adjustments as needed. Students are introduced to such core concepts as strategic visions, mission statements and core values, the balanced scorecard, strategic intent, and business-level versus corporate-level strategies. There's a robust discussion of why *all managers are on a company's strategy-making, strategy-executing team* and why a company's strategic plan is a collection of strategies devised by different managers at different levels in the organizational hierarchy. The chapter winds up with a section on how to exercise good corporate governance and examines the conditions that led to recent high-profile corporate governance failures.

- Chapter 3 sets forth the now-familiar analytical tools and concepts of industry and competitive analysis and demonstrates the importance of tailoring strategy to fit the circumstances of a company's industry and competitive environment. The standout feature of this chapter is a presentation of Michael Porter's "five-forces model of competition" *that has long been the clearest, most straightforward discussion of any text in the field.* This edition also provides expanded coverage of a company's macro-environment to enable students to conduct what some call *Pestel analysis* of *p*olitical, *e*conomic, *s*ocial, *t*echnological, *e*nvironmental, and *l*egal factors.

- Chapter 4 presents the resource-based view of the firm and convincingly argues why a company's strategy must be built around its most competitively valuable resources and capabilities. We provide students with a simple taxonomy for identifying a company's resources and capabilities and frame our discussion of how a firm's resources and capabilities can provide a sustainable competitive advantage with the *VRIN model.* We introduce the notion of a company's *dynamic capabilities* and cast SWOT analysis as a simple, easy-to-use way to assess a company's overall situation in terms of its ability to seize market opportunities and ward off external threats. There is solid coverage of value chain analysis, benchmarking, and competitive strength assessments—standard tools for appraising a company's relative cost position and customer value proposition vis-à-vis rivals. *An important feature of this chapter is a table showing how key financial and operating ratios are calculated and how to interpret them;* students will find this table handy in doing the number crunching needed to evaluate whether a company's strategy is delivering good financial performance.

- Chapter 5 deals with the basic approaches used to compete successfully and gain a competitive advantage over market rivals. This discussion is framed around the five generic competitive strategies—low-cost leadership, differentiation, best-cost provider, focused differentiation, and focused low cost. We emphasize that regardless of a company's choice, competitive success depends upon a company's capacity to deliver more customer value—one way or another. We provide a fuller treatment of *cost drivers* and *uniqueness drivers* as the keys to bringing down a company's cost and enhancing its differentiation, respectively, in support of this overall goal.

- Chapter 6 continues the theme of competitive strategies for single-business firms with its spotlight on *strategic actions (offensive and defensive) and their timing,* including blue-ocean strategies and first-mover advantages and disadvantages. It also serves to segue into the material covered in the next two chapters (on international and diversification strategies) by introducing the topic of *strategies that alter a company's scope of operations.* The chapter features sections on the strategic benefits and risks of horizontal mergers and acquisitions, vertical integration, and outsourcing of certain value chain activities. The concluding section of this chapter covers the advantages and drawbacks of using strategic alliances and cooperative arrangements to alter a company's scope of operations, with some pointers on how to make strategic alliances work.

- Chapter 7 explores the full range of strategy options for expanding a company's geographic scope and competing in foreign markets: export strategies, licensing, franchising, establishing a wholly owned subsidiary via acquisition or "greenfield" venture, and alliance strategies. In the 18th edition, we've added new coverage of topics such as Porter's *Diamond of National Advantage;* the choice between *multidomestic, global, and transnational strategies; profit sanctuaries* and cross-border strategic moves; and *the quest for competitive advantage via sharing, transferring, or accessing valuable resources and capabilities across national borders.* The chapter concludes with a discussion of the special issues of competing in the markets of developing countries and the strategies that local companies can use to defend against global giants.

- Chapter 8 introduces the topic of corporate-level strategy—a topic of concern for multibusiness companies pursuing diversification. This chapter begins by explaining why successful diversification strategies must create shareholder value and lays out the three essential tests that a strategy must pass to achieve this goal *(the industry attractiveness, cost-of-entry, and better-off tests)*. We discuss alternative means of entering new businesses (acquisition, internal start-up, or joint venture) and offer a method for discerning which choice is a firm's best option. Then we turn our attention to a comparison of related versus unrelated diversification strategies, showing that they differ in terms of the nature of their critical resources *(specialized versus general parenting capabilities)* and whether they can exploit cross-business strategic fit for competitive gain. The chapter's analytical spotlight is trained on the techniques and procedures for assessing the strategic attractiveness of a diversified company's business portfolio—the relative attractiveness of the various industries the company has diversified into, the company's competitive strength in each of its lines of business, and the extent to which there is *strategic fit* and *resource fit* among its different businesses. The chapter concludes with a brief survey of a company's four main postdiversification strategy alternatives: (1) sticking closely with the existing business lineup, (2) broadening the diversification base, (3) divesting some businesses and retrenching to a narrower diversification base, and (4) restructuring the makeup of the company's business lineup.

- Chapter 9 reflects the very latest in the literature on (1) a company's duty to operate according to ethical standards, (2) a company's obligation to demonstrate socially responsible behavior and corporate citizenship, and (3) why more companies are limiting strategic initiatives to those that meet the needs of consumers in a manner that protects natural resources and ecological support systems needed by future generations. The discussion includes approaches to ensuring consistent ethical standards for companies with international operations. The contents of this chapter will definitely give students some things to ponder and will help to make them more *ethically aware* and conscious of *why all companies should conduct their business in a socially responsible and sustainable manner.* Chapter 9 has been written as a stand-alone chapter that can be assigned in the early, middle, or late part of the course.

- Chapter 10 begins a three-chapter module on executing strategy (Chapters 10 to 12), anchored around a pragmatic, compelling conceptual framework. Chapter 10 presents an overview of this 10-step framework and then develops the first three pieces of it: (1) *staffing the organization* with capable managers and employees, (2) *marshaling the resources and building the organizational capabilities* required for successful strategy execution, and (3) *creating a strategy-supportive organizational structure* and structuring the work effort. We discuss three approaches to building and strengthening a company's capabilities, ranging from internal development to acquisitions to collaborative arrangements, and consider outsourcing as an option for structuring the work effort. We argue for matching a company's organizational structure to its strategy execution requirements, describe four basic types of organizational structures (simple, functional, multidivisional, and matrix), and discuss centralized versus decentralized decision making. We conclude with some further perspectives on facilitating collaboration with external partners and structuring the company's work effort.

- Chapter 11 covers five important topics concerning strategy execution: (1) *allocating ample resources* to strategy-critical activities, (2) ensuring that *policies and procedures* facilitate rather than impede strategy execution, (3) employing *process management tools* and adopting *best practices* to drive continuous improvement in the performance of value chain activities, (4) installing *information and operating systems* that enable company personnel to better carry out their strategic roles proficiently, and (5) tying *rewards and incentives* directly to good strategy execution and the achievement of performance targets.

- Chapter 12 concludes the text with a discussion of corporate culture and leadership in relation to good strategy execution. The recurring theme throughout the final three chapters is that implementing strategy entails figuring out the specific actions, behaviors, and conditions that are needed for a smooth strategy-supportive operation and then following through to get things done and deliver results. The goal here is to ensure that students understand that the strategy-executing phase is a make-things-happen and make-them-happen-right kind of managerial exercise—one that is critical for achieving operating excellence and reaching the goal of strong company performance.

We have done our best to ensure that the 12 chapters convey the best thinking of academics and practitioners in the field of strategic management and hit the bull's-eye in topical coverage for senior- and MBA-level strategy courses. The ultimate test of the text, of course, is the positive pedagogical impact it has in the classroom. If this edition sets a more effective stage for your lectures and does a better job of helping you persuade students that the discipline of strategy merits their rapt attention, then it will have fulfilled its purpose.

THE CASE COLLECTION

The 28-case lineup in this edition is flush with interesting companies and valuable lessons for students in the art and science of crafting and executing strategy. There's a good blend of cases from a length perspective—close to one-fifth are under 15 pages yet offer plenty for students to chew on; about one-fourth are medium-length cases; and the remainder are detail-rich cases that call for more sweeping analysis.

At least 25 of the 28 cases involve companies, products, people, or activities that students will have heard of, know about from personal experience, or can easily identify with. The lineup includes at least nine cases that will provide students with insight into the special demands of competing in industry environments where technological developments are an everyday event, product life cycles are short, and competitive maneuvering among rivals comes fast and furious. Twenty of the cases involve situations in which company resources and competitive capabilities play as large a role in the strategy-making, strategy-executing scheme of things as industry and competitive conditions do. Scattered throughout the lineup are eight cases concerning non-U.S. companies, globally competitive industries, and/or cross-cultural situations; these cases, in conjunction with the globalized content of the text chapters, provide abundant material for linking the study of strategic management tightly to the ongoing globalization of the world economy. You'll also find 8 cases dealing with the strategic problems of family-owned or relatively small entrepreneurial businesses and 20 cases involving public companies and situations on which students can do further research on the Internet.

A handful of cases will have accompanying videotape segments on the DVD.

THE TWO STRATEGY SIMULATION SUPPLEMENTS: *THE BUSINESS STRATEGY GAME* AND *GLO-BUS*

The Business Strategy Game and *GLO-BUS: Developing Winning Competitive Strategies*—two competition-based strategy simulations that are delivered online and that feature automated processing and grading of performance—are being marketed by the publisher as companion supplements for use with the 18th edition (and other texts in the field).

- *The Business Strategy Game* is the world's most popular strategy simulation, having been used in courses involving over 600,000 students at more than 700 university campuses in over 40 countries.
- *GLO-BUS,* a somewhat simpler strategy simulation introduced in 2004, has been used at more than 400 university campuses worldwide in courses involving over 120,000 students.

How the Strategy Simulations Work

In both *The Business Strategy Game (BSG)* and *GLO-BUS,* class members are divided into teams of one to five persons and assigned to run a company that competes head-to-head against companies run by other class members.

- In *BSG,* team members run an athletic footwear company, producing and marketing both branded and private-label footwear.
- In *GLO-BUS,* team members operate a digital camera company that designs, assembles, and markets entry-level digital cameras and upscale, multifeatured cameras.

In both simulations, companies compete in a global market arena, selling their products in four geographic regions—Europe-Africa, North America, Asia-Pacific, and Latin America. Each management team is called upon to craft a strategy for their company and make decisions relating to plant operations, workforce compensation, pricing and marketing, social responsibility/citizenship, and finance.

Company co-managers are held accountable for their decision making. Each company's performance is scored on the basis of earnings per share, return on equity investment, stock price, credit rating, and image rating. Rankings of company performance, along with a wealth of industry and company statistics, are available to company co-managers after each decision round to use in making strategy adjustments and operating decisions for the next competitive round. You can be certain that the market environment, strategic issues, and operating challenges that company co-managers must contend with are *very tightly linked* to what your class members will be reading about in the text chapters. The circumstances that co-managers face in running their simulation company embrace the very concepts, analytical tools, and strategy options they encounter in the text chapters (this is something you can quickly confirm by skimming through some of the Exercises for Simulation Participants that appear at the end of each chapter).

We suggest that you schedule 1 or 2 practice rounds and anywhere from 4 to 10 regular (scored) decision rounds (more rounds are better than fewer rounds). Each decision round represents a year of company operations and will entail roughly two hours of time for company co-managers to complete. In traditional 13-week, semester-long courses, there is merit is scheduling one decision round per week. In courses that run 5 to 10 weeks, it is wise to schedule two decision rounds per week for the last several weeks of the term (sample course schedules are provided for courses of varying length and varying numbers of class meetings).

When the instructor-specified deadline for a decision round arrives, the simulation server automatically accesses the saved decision entries of each company, determines the competitiveness and buyer appeal of each company's product offering relative to the other companies being run by students in your class, and then awards sales and market shares to the competing companies, geographic region by geographic region. The unit sales volumes awarded to each company *are totally governed by:*

- How its prices compare against the prices of rival brands.
- How its product quality compares against the quality of rival brands.
- How its product line breadth and selection compare.
- How its advertising effort compares.
- And so on, for a total of 11 competitive factors that determine unit sales and market shares.

The competitiveness and overall buyer appeal of each company's product offering *in comparison to the product offerings of rival companies* is all-decisive— this algorithmic feature is what makes *BSG* and *GLO-BUS* "competition-based" strategy simulations. Once each company's sales and market shares are awarded based on the competitiveness of its respective overall product offering, the various company and industry reports detailing the outcomes of the decision round are then generated. Company co-managers can access the results of the decision round 15 to 20 minutes after the decision deadline.

The Compelling Case for Incorporating Use of a Strategy Simulation

There are *three exceptionally important benefits* associated with using a competition-based simulation in strategy courses taken by seniors and MBA students:

- *A three-pronged text-case-simulation course model delivers significantly more teaching-learning power than the traditional text-case model.* Using *both* cases and a strategy simulation to drill students in thinking strategically and applying what they read in the text chapters is a stronger, more effective means of helping them connect theory with practice and develop better business judgment. What cases do that a simulation cannot is give class members broad exposure to a variety of companies and industry situations and insight into the kinds of strategy-related problems managers face. But what a competition-based strategy simulation does far better than case analysis is thrust class members squarely into *an active, hands-on managerial role* where they are totally responsible for assessing market conditions, determining how to respond to the actions of competitors, forging a long-term direction and strategy for their company, and making all kinds of operating decisions. Because they are held fully accountable for their decisions and their company's performance, *co-managers are strongly motivated* to dig deeply into company operations, probe for ways to be more cost-efficient and competitive, and ferret out strategic moves and decisions calculated to boost company performance. *Consequently, incorporating both case assignments and a strategy simulation to develop the skills of class members in thinking strategically and applying the concepts and tools of strategic analysis turns out to be more pedagogically powerful than relying solely on case assignments—there's stronger retention of the lessons learned and better achievement of course learning objectives.*

To provide you with quantitative evidence of the learning that occurs with using *The Business Strategy Game* or *GLO-BUS*, there is a built-in Learning Assurance Report showing how well each class member performs on nine skills/learning measures versus tens of thousands of students worldwide who have completed the simulation in the past 12 months.

- *The competitive nature of a strategy simulation arouses positive energy and steps up the whole tempo of the course by a notch or two.* Nothing sparks class excitement quicker or better than the concerted efforts on the part of class members at each decision round to achieve a high industry ranking and avoid the perilous consequences of being outcompeted by other class members. Students really enjoy taking on the role of a manager, running their own company, crafting strategies, making all kinds of operating decisions, trying to outcompete rival companies, and getting immediate feedback on the resulting company performance. Lots of back-and-forth chatter occurs when the results of the latest simulation round become available and co-managers renew their quest for strategic moves and actions that will strengthen company performance. Co-managers become *emotionally invested* in running their company and figuring out what strategic moves to make to boost their company's performance. Interest levels climb. All this stimulates learning and causes students to see the practical relevance of the subject matter and the benefits of taking your course.

    As soon as your students start to say "Wow! Not only is this fun but I am learning a lot," *which they will,* you have won the battle of engaging students in the subject matter and moved the value of taking your course to a much higher plateau in the business school curriculum. This translates into *a livelier, richer learning experience from a student perspective and better instructor-course evaluations.*

- *Use of a fully automated online simulation reduces the time instructors spend on course preparation, course administration, and grading.* Since the simulation exercise involves a 20- to 30-hour workload for student teams (roughly 2 hours per decision round times 10 to 12 rounds, plus optional assignments), simulation adopters often compensate by trimming the number of assigned cases from, say, 10 to 12 to perhaps 4 to 6. This significantly reduces the time instructors spend reading cases, studying teaching notes, and otherwise getting ready to lead class discussion of a case or grade oral team presentations. Course preparation time is further cut because you can use several class days to have students meet in the computer lab to work on upcoming decision rounds or a three-year strategic plan (in lieu of lecturing on a chapter or covering an additional assigned case). Not only does use of a simulation permit assigning fewer cases, but it also permits you to eliminate at least one assignment that entails considerable grading on your part. Grading one less written case or essay exam or other written assignment saves enormous time. With *BSG* and *GLO-BUS,* grading is effortless and takes only minutes; once you enter percentage weights for each assignment in your online grade book, a suggested overall grade is calculated for you. You'll be pleasantly surprised—and quite pleased—at how little time it takes to gear up for and to administer *The Business Strategy Game* or *GLO-BUS*.

In sum, incorporating use of a strategy simulation turns out to be *a win-win proposition for both students and instructors.* Moreover, a very convincing argument can be made that a competition-based strategy simulation is *the single most effective teaching/learning tool that instructors can employ to teach the discipline of business and competitive strategy, to make learning more enjoyable, and to promote better achievement of course learning objectives.*

A Bird's-Eye View of *The Business Strategy Game*

The setting for *The Business Strategy Game (BSG)* is the global athletic footwear industry (there can be little doubt in today's world that a globally competitive strategy simulation is *vastly superior* to a simulation with a domestic-only setting). Global market demand for footwear grows at the rate of 7 to 9 percent annually for the first five years and 5 to 7 percent annually for the second five years. However, market growth rates vary by geographic region—North America, Latin America, Europe-Africa, and Asia-Pacific.

Companies begin the simulation producing branded and private-label footwear in two plants, one in North America and one in Asia. They have the option to establish production facilities in Latin America and Europe-Africa, either by constructing new plants or by buying previously constructed plants that have been sold by competing companies. Company co-managers exercise control over production costs on the basis of the styling and quality they opt to manufacture, plant location (wages and incentive compensation vary from region to region), the use of best practices and Six Sigma programs to reduce the production of defective footwear and to boost worker productivity, and compensation practices.

All newly produced footwear is shipped in bulk containers to one of four geographic distribution centers. All sales in a geographic region are made from footwear inventories in that region's distribution center. Costs at the four regional distribution centers are a function of inventory storage costs, packing and shipping fees, import tariffs paid on incoming pairs shipped from foreign plants, and exchange rate impacts. At the start of the simulation, import tariffs average $4 per pair in Europe-Africa, $6 per pair in Latin America, and $8 in the Asia-Pacific region. However, the Free Trade Treaty of the Americas allows tariff-free movement of footwear between North America and Latin America. Instructors have the option to alter tariffs as the game progresses.

Companies market their brand of athletic footwear to footwear retailers worldwide and to individuals buying online at the company's Web site. Each company's sales and market share in the branded footwear segments hinge on its competitiveness on 11 factors: attractive pricing, footwear styling and quality, product line breadth, advertising, use of mail-in rebates, appeal of celebrities endorsing a company's brand, success in convincing footwear retailers to carry its brand, number of weeks it takes to fill retailer orders, effectiveness of a company's online sales effort at its Web site, and customer loyalty. Sales of private-label footwear hinge solely on being the low-price bidder.

All told, company co-managers make as many as 53 types of decisions each period that cut across production operations (up to 10 decisions per plant, with a maximum of four plants), plant capacity additions/sales/upgrades (up to 6 decisions per plant), worker compensation and training (3 decisions per plant), shipping (up to 8 decisions per plant), pricing and marketing (up to 10 decisions in four geographic regions), bids to sign celebrities (2 decision entries per bid), financing of company operations (up to 8 decisions), and corporate social responsibility and environmental sustainability (up to 6 decisions).

Each time company co-managers make a decision entry, an assortment of on-screen calculations instantly shows the projected effects on unit sales, revenues, market shares, unit costs, profit, earnings per share, ROE, and other operating statistics. The on-screen calculations help team members evaluate the relative merits of one decision entry versus another and put together a promising strategy.

Companies can employ any of the five generic competitive strategy options in selling branded footwear—low-cost leadership, differentiation, best-cost provider, focused low cost, and focused differentiation. They can pursue essentially the same strategy worldwide or craft slightly or very different strategies for the Europe-Africa, Asia-Pacific, Latin America, and North America markets. They can strive for competitive advantage based on more advertising, a wider selection of models, more appealing styling/quality, bigger rebates, and so on.

Any well-conceived, well-executed competitive approach is capable of succeeding, provided it is not overpowered by the strategies of competitors or defeated by the presence of too many copycat strategies that dilute its effectiveness. The challenge for each company's management team is to craft and execute a competitive strategy that produces good performance on five measures: earnings per share, return on equity investment, stock price appreciation, credit rating, and brand image.

All activity for *The Business Strategy Game* takes place at www.bsg-online.com.

A Bird's-Eye View of *GLO-BUS*

The industry setting for *GLO-BUS* is the digital camera industry. Global market demand grows at the rate of 8 to 10 percent annually for the first five years and 4 to 6 percent annually for the second five years. Retail sales of digital cameras are seasonal, with about 20 percent of consumer demand coming in each of the first three quarters of each calendar year and 40 percent coming during the big fourth-quarter retailing season.

Companies produce entry-level and upscale, multifeatured cameras of varying designs and quality in a Taiwan assembly facility and ship assembled cameras directly to retailers in North America, Asia-Pacific, Europe-Africa, and Latin America. All cameras are assembled as retail orders come in and are shipped immediately upon completion of the assembly process—companies maintain no finished-goods inventories, and all parts and components are delivered on a just-in-time basis (which eliminates the need to track inventories and simplifies the accounting for plant operations and costs). Company co-managers exercise control over production costs on the basis of the designs and components they specify for their cameras, workforce compensation and training, the length of warranties offered (which affects warranty costs), the amount spent for technical support provided to buyers of the company's cameras, and their management of the assembly process.

Competition in each of the two product market segments (entry-level and multifeatured digital cameras) is based on 10 factors: price, camera performance and quality, number of quarterly sales promotions, length of promotions in weeks, size of the promotional discounts offered, advertising, number of camera models, size of retail dealer network, warranty period, and amount/caliber of technical support provided to camera buyers. Low-cost leadership, differentiation strategies, best-cost provider strategies, and focus strategies are all viable competitive options. Rival companies can strive to be the clear market leader in either entry-level cameras or upscale multifeatured cameras or both. They can focus on one or two geographic regions or strive for geographic balance. They can pursue essentially the same strategy worldwide or craft slightly or very different strategies for the Europe-Africa, Asia-Pacific, Latin America, and North America markets. Just as with *The Business Strategy Game,* almost any well-conceived, well-executed competitive approach is capable of succeeding, *provided it is not overpowered by the strategies of competitors or defeated by the presence of too many copycat strategies that dilute its effectiveness.*

Company co-managers make 49 types of decisions each period, ranging from R&D, camera components, and camera performance (10 decisions) to production operations and worker compensation (15 decisions) to pricing and marketing (15 decisions) to the financing of company operations (4 decisions) to corporate social responsibility (5 decisions). *Each time participants make a decision entry, an assortment of on-screen calculations instantly shows the projected effects on unit sales, revenues, market shares, unit costs, profit, earnings per share, ROE, and other operating statistics. These on-screen calculations help team members evaluate the relative merits of one decision entry versus another and stitch the separate decisions into a cohesive and promising strategy.* Company performance is judged on five criteria: earnings per share, return on equity investment, stock price, credit rating, and brand image.

All activity for *GLO-BUS* occurs at www.glo-bus.com.

Administration and Operating Features of the Two Simulations

The Internet delivery and user-friendly designs of both *BSG* and *GLO-BUS* make them incredibly easy to administer, even for first-time users. And the menus and controls are so similar that you can readily switch between the two simulations or use one in your undergraduate class and the other in a graduate class. If you have not yet used either of the two simulations, you may find the following of particular interest:

- Setting up the simulation for your course is done online and takes about 10 to 15 minutes. Once setup is completed, no other administrative actions are required beyond those of moving participants to a different team (should the need arise) and monitoring the progress of the simulation (to whatever extent desired).

- Participant's Guides are delivered electronically to class members at the Web site—students can read the guide on their monitors or print out a copy, as they prefer.

- There are 2- to 4-minute Video Tutorials scattered throughout the software (including each decision screen and each page of each report) that provide on-demand guidance to class members who may be uncertain about how to proceed.

- Complementing the Video Tutorials are detailed and clearly written Help sections explaining "all there is to know" about (a) each decision entry and the relevant cause-effect relationships, (b) the information on each page of the

Industry Reports, and (c) the numbers presented in the Company Reports. *The Video Tutorials and the Help screens allow company co-managers to figure things out for themselves, thereby curbing the need for students to ask the instructor "how things work."*

- Built-in chat capability on each screen enables company co-managers to collaborate online in the event that a face-to-face meeting to review results and make decision entries is not convenient (or feasible, as is usually the case for class members taking an online course). Company co-managers can also use their cell phones to talk things over while online looking at the screens.

- Both simulations are quite suitable for use in distance-learning or online courses (and are currently being used in such courses on numerous campuses).

- Participants and instructors are notified via e-mail when the results are ready (usually about 15 to 20 minutes after the decision round deadline specified by the instructor/game administrator).

- Following each decision round, participants are provided with a complete set of reports—a six-page Industry Report, a one-page Competitive Intelligence report for each geographic region that includes strategic group maps and bulleted lists of competitive strengths and weaknesses, and a set of Company Reports (income statement, balance sheet, cash flow statement, and assorted production, marketing, and cost statistics).

- Two "open-book" multiple-choice tests of 20 questions are built into each simulation. The quizzes, which you can require or not as you see fit, are taken online and automatically graded, with scores reported instantaneously to participants and automatically recorded in the instructor's electronic grade book. Students are automatically provided with three sample questions for each test.

- Both simulations contain a three-year strategic plan option that you can assign. Scores on the plan are automatically recorded in the instructor's online grade book.

- At the end of the simulation, you can have students complete online peer evaluations (again, the scores are automatically recorded in your online grade book).

- Both simulations have a Company Presentation feature that enables each team of company co-managers to easily prepare PowerPoint slides for use in describing their strategy and summarizing their company's performance in a presentation to either the class, the instructor, or an "outside" board of directors.

- *A Learning Assurance Report provides you with hard data concerning how well your students performed vis-à-vis students playing the simulation worldwide over the past 12 months.* The report is based on nine measures of student proficiency, business know-how, and decision-making skill and can also be used in evaluating the extent to which your school's academic curriculum produces the desired degree of student learning insofar as accreditation standards are concerned.

For more details on either simulation, please consult Section 2 of the Instructor's Manual accompanying this text or register as an instructor at the simulation Web sites (**www.bsg-online.com** and **www.glo-bus.com**) to access even more comprehensive information. You should also consider signing up for one of the webinars that the simulation authors conduct several times each month (sometimes several times weekly) to demonstrate how the software works, walk you through the various features and menu options, and answer any questions. You have an open invitation to call the senior author of this text at (205) 722-9145 to arrange a personal demonstration or talk about how one of the simulations might work in one of your courses. We think you'll be quite impressed with the cutting-edge capabilities that have been programmed into *The Business Strategy Game* and *GLO-BUS,* the simplicity with which both simulations can be administered, and their exceptionally tight connection to the text chapters, core concepts, and standard analytical tools.

RESOURCES AND SUPPORT MATERIALS FOR THE 18TH EDITION

For Students

Key Points Summaries   At the end of each chapter is a synopsis of the core concepts, analytical tools, and other key points discussed in the chapter. These chapter-end synopses, along with the core concept definitions and margin notes scattered throughout each chapter, help students focus on basic strategy principles, digest the messages of each chapter, and prepare for tests.

Two Sets of Chapter-End Exercises   Each chapter concludes with two sets of exercises. The *Assurance of Learning Exercises* can be used as the basis for class discussion, oral presentation assignments, short written reports, and substitutes for case assignments. The *Exercises for Simulation Participants* are designed expressly for use by adopters who have incorporated use of a simulation and want to go a step further in tightly and explicitly connecting the chapter content to the simulation company their students are running. The questions in both sets of exercises (along with those Illustration Capsules that qualify as "mini-cases") can be used to round out the rest of a 75-minute class period should your lecture on a chapter last for only 50 minutes.

A Value-Added Web Site   The student section of the Online Learning Center (OLC) at Web site www.mhhe.com/thompson contains a number of helpful aids:

- Ten-question self-scoring chapter tests that students can take to measure their grasp of the material presented in each of the 12 chapters.
- The "Guide to Case Analysis," containing sections on what a case is, why cases are a standard part of courses in strategy, preparing a case for class discussion, doing a written case analysis, doing an oral presentation, and using financial ratio analysis to assess a company's financial condition. We suggest having students read this guide before the first class discussion of a case.
- PowerPoint slides for each chapter.
- Selected Case Video clips.

The *Connect*™ *Management* Web-Based Assignment and Assessment Platform   Beginning with this edition, we have taken advantage of the publisher's innovative *Connect*™ assignment and assessment platform

and created several features that simplify the task of assigning and grading three types of exercises for students:

- There are self-scoring chapter tests consisting of 20 to 25 multiple-choice questions that students can take to measure their grasp of the material presented in each of the 12 chapters.

- There are one to two author-developed Interactive Application exercises for each of the 12 chapters that drill students in the use and application of the concepts and tools of strategic analysis.

- The *Connect*™ platform also includes author-developed Interactive Application exercises for 7 of the 28 cases in this edition that require students to work through answers to a select number of the assignment questions for the case; these exercises have multiple components and include calculating assorted financial ratios to assess a company's financial performance and balance sheet strength, identifying a company's strategy, doing five-forces and driving-forces analysis, doing a SWOT analysis, and recommending actions to improve company performance. The content of these case exercises is tailored to match the circumstances presented in each case, calling upon students to do whatever strategic thinking and strategic analysis are called for to arrive at pragmatic, analysis-based action recommendations for improving company performance.

All of the *Connect*™ exercises are automatically graded (with the exception of a few exercise components that entail student entry of essay answers), thereby simplifying the task of evaluating each class member's performance and monitoring the learning outcomes. The progress-tracking function built into the *Connect*™ *Management* system enables you to:

- View scored work immediately and track individual or group performance with assignment and grade reports.

- Access an instant view of student or class performance relative to learning objectives.

- Collect data and generate reports required by many accreditation organizations, such as AACSB.

For Instructors

Online Learning Center (OLC)   In addition to the student resources, the instructor section of **www.mhhe.com/thompson** includes an Instructor's Manual and other support materials. Your McGraw-Hill representative can arrange delivery of instructor support materials in a format-ready Standard Cartridge for Blackboard, WebCT, and other Web-based educational platforms.

Instructor's Manual   The accompanying IM contains:

- A section on suggestions for organizing and structuring your course.
- Sample syllabi and course outlines.
- A set of lecture notes on each chapter.
- Answers to the chapter-end Assurance of Learning Exercises.
- A copy of the test bank.
- A comprehensive case teaching note for each of the 28 cases. These teaching notes are filled with suggestions for using the case effectively, have very thorough, analysis-based answers to the suggested assignment questions for the case, and contain an epilog detailing any important developments since the case was written.

Test Bank and EZ Test Online   There is a test bank containing over 900 multiple-choice questions and short-answer/essay questions. It has been tagged with AACSB and Bloom's Taxonomy criteria. All of the test bank questions are also accessible within a computerized test bank powered by McGraw-Hill's flexible electronic testing program EZ Test Online (www.eztestonline.com). Using EZ Test Online allows you to create paper and online tests or quizzes. With EZ Test Online, instructors can select questions from multiple McGraw-Hill test banks or author their own and then either print the test for paper distribution or give it online.

PowerPoint Slides   To facilitate delivery preparation of your lectures and to serve as chapter outlines, you'll have access to approximately 500 colorful and professional-looking slides displaying core concepts, analytical procedures, key points, and all the figures in the text chapters.

Instructor's Resource CD   All of our instructor supplements are available on disk; the disk set includes the complete Instructor's Manual, computerized test bank (EZ Test), accompanying PowerPoint slides, and the Digital Image Library with all of the figures from the text. It is a useful aid for compiling a syllabus and daily course schedule, preparing customized lectures, and developing tests on the text chapters.

The Business Strategy Game and GLO-BUS Online Simulations
Using one of the two companion simulations is a powerful and constructive way of emotionally connecting students to the subject matter of the course. We know of no more effective way to arouse the competitive energy of students and prepare them for the challenges of real-world business decision making than to have them match strategic wits with classmates in running a company in head-to-head competition for global market leadership.

ACKNOWLEDGMENTS

We heartily acknowledge the contributions of the case researchers whose case-writing efforts appear herein and the companies whose cooperation made the cases possible. To each one goes a very special thank-you. We cannot overstate the importance of timely, carefully researched cases in contributing to a substantive study of strategic management issues and practices. From a research standpoint, strategy-related cases are invaluable in exposing the generic kinds of strategic issues that companies face, in forming hypotheses about strategic behavior, and in drawing experience-based generalizations about the practice of strategic management. From an instructional standpoint, strategy cases give students essential practice in diagnosing and evaluating the strategic situations of companies and organizations, in applying the concepts and tools of strategic analysis, in weighing strategic options and crafting strategies, and in tackling the challenges of successful strategy execution. Without a continuing stream of fresh, well-researched, and well-conceived cases, the discipline of strategic management would lose its close ties to the very institutions whose strategic actions and behavior it is aimed at explaining. There's no question, therefore, that first-class case research constitutes a valuable scholarly contribution to the theory and practice of strategic management.

A great number of colleagues and students at various universities, business acquaintances, and people at McGraw-Hill provided inspiration, encouragement, and counsel during the course of this project. Like all text authors in the strategy field, we are intellectually indebted to the many academics whose research and writing have blazed new trails and advanced the discipline of strategic management. In addition, we'd like to thank the following reviewers who provided seasoned advice and splendid suggestions for improving the chapters in this 18th edition:

Joan H. Bailar, Lake Forest Graduate School of Management
David Blair, University of Nebraska at Omaha
Jane Boyland, Johnson & Wales University
William J. Donoher, Missouri State University
Stephen A. Drew, Florida Gulf Coast University
Jo Ann Duffy, Sam Houston State University
Alan Ellstrand, University of Arkansas
Susan Fox-Wolfgramm, Hawaii Pacific University
Rebecca M. Guidice, University of Nevada–Las Vegas
Mark Hoelscher, Illinois State University
Sean D. Jasso, University of California–Riverside
Xin Liang, University of Minnesota–Duluth
Paul Mallette, Colorado State University
Dan Marlin, University of South Florida–St. Petersburg
Raza Mir, William Paterson University
Mansour Moussavi, Johnson & Wales University
James D. Spina, University of Maryland
Monica A. Zimmerman, West Chester University

We also express our thanks to Dennis R. Balch, Jeffrey R. Bruehl, Edith C. Busija, Donald A. Drost, Randall Harris, Mark Lewis Hoelscher, Phyllis Holland, James W. Kroeger, Sal Kukalis, Brian W. Kulik, Paul Mallette, Anthony U. Martinez, Lee Pickler, Sabine Reddy, Thomas D. Schramko, V. Seshan, Charles Strain, Sabine Turnley, S. Stephen Vitucci, Andrew Ward, Sibin Wu, Lynne Patten, Nancy E. Landrum, Jim Goes, Jon Kalinowski, Rodney M. Walter, Judith D. Powell, Seyda Deligonul, David Flanagan, Esmerlda Garbi, Mohsin Habib, Kim Hester, Jeffrey E. McGee, Diana J. Wong, F. William Brown, Anthony F. Chelte, Gregory G. Dess, Alan B. Eisner, John George, Carle M. Hunt, Theresa Marron-Grodsky, Sarah Marsh, Joshua D. Martin, William L. Moore, Donald Neubaum, George M. Puia, Amit Shah, Lois M. Shelton, Mark Weber, Steve Barndt, J. Michael Geringer, Ming-Fang Li, Richard Stackman, Stephen Tallman, Gerardo R. Ungson, James Boulgarides, Betty Diener, Daniel F. Jennings, David Kuhn, Kathryn Martell, Wilbur Mouton, Bobby Vaught, Tuck Bounds, Lee Burk, Ralph Catalanello, William Crittenden, Vince Luchsinger, Stan Mendenhall, John Moore, Will Mulvaney, Sandra Richard, Ralph Roberts, Thomas Turk, Gordon Von Stroh, Fred Zimmerman, S. A. Billion, Charles Byles, Gerald L. Geisler, Rose Knotts, Joseph Rosenstein, James B. Thurman, Ivan Able, W. Harvey Hegarty, Roger Evered, Charles B. Saunders, Rhae M. Swisher, Claude I. Shell, R. Thomas Lenz, Michael C. White, Dennis Callahan, R. Duane Ireland, William E. Burr II, C. W. Millard, Richard Mann, Kurt Christensen, Neil W. Jacobs, Louis W. Fry, D. Robley Wood, George J. Gore, and William R. Soukup. These reviewers provided valuable guidance in steering our efforts to improve earlier editions.

We owe a special debt of gratitude to Catherine Maritan, for her detailed comments on a number of chapters, and to Richard S. Shreve and Anant K. Sundaram, who gave us sage advice regarding the material in Chapter 9. We'd like to thank the following students of the Tuck School of Business for their assistance with the chapter revisions: C. David Morgan, Amy E. Florentino, John R. Moran, Mukund Kulashakeran, Jeffrey L. Boyink, Jonathan D. Keith, Anita Natarajan, Alison F. Connolly, and Melissa E. Vess. And we'd like to acknowledge the help of Dartmouth students Catherine Wu, Jack McNeily, and Jenna Pfeffer, as well as Feldberg librarians Karen Sluzenski and Sarah J. Buckingham and Tuck staff members Annette Lyman, Mary Biathrow, Doreen Aher, and Karen H. Summer.

As always, we value your recommendations and thoughts about the book. Your comments regarding coverage and contents will be taken to heart, and we always are grateful for the time you take to call our attention to printing errors, deficiencies, and other shortcomings. Please e-mail us at athompso@cba.ua.edu, margaret.a.peteraf@tuck.dartmouth.edu, jgamble@usouthal.edu, or astrickl@cba.ua.edu.

Arthur A. Thompson

Margaret A. Peteraf

John E. Gamble

A. J. Strickland

Chapter Structure and Organization

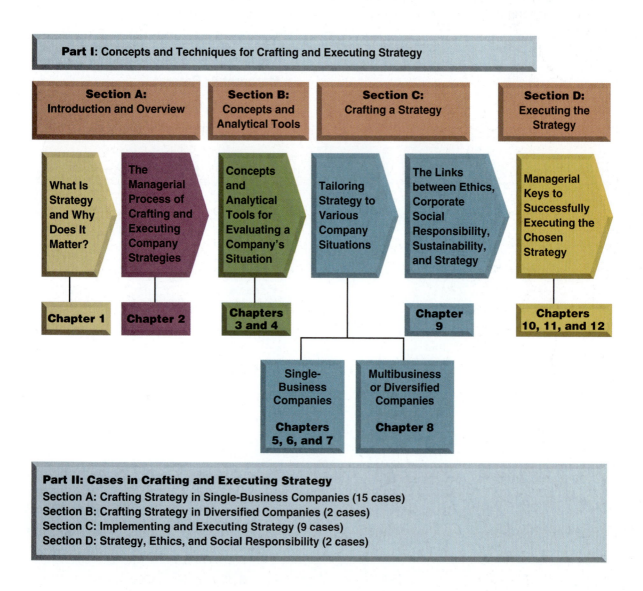

Part I: Concepts and Techniques for Crafting and Executing Strategy

Section A: Introduction and Overview

Section B: Concepts and Analytical Tools

Section C: Crafting a Strategy

Section D: Executing the Strategy

What Is Strategy and Why Does It Matter?

The Managerial Process of Crafting and Executing Company Strategies

Concepts and Analytical Tools for Evaluating a Company's Situation

Tailoring Strategy to Various Company Situations

The Links between Ethics, Corporate Social Responsibility, Sustainability, and Strategy

Managerial Keys to Successfully Executing the Chosen Strategy

Chapter 1

Chapter 2

Chapters 3 and 4

Chapter 9

Chapters 10, 11, and 12

Single-Business Companies

Chapters 5, 6, and 7

Multibusiness or Diversified Companies

Chapter 8

Part II: Cases in Crafting and Executing Strategy

Section A: Crafting Strategy in Single-Business Companies (15 cases)
Section B: Crafting Strategy in Diversified Companies (2 cases)
Section C: Implementing and Executing Strategy (9 cases)
Section D: Strategy, Ethics, and Social Responsibility (2 cases)

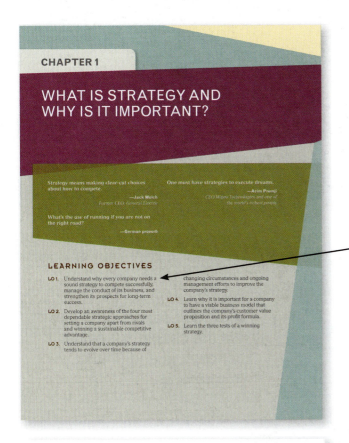

CHAPTER 1

WHAT IS STRATEGY AND WHY IS IT IMPORTANT?

Strategy means making clear-cut choices about how to compete.

—Jack Welch
Former CEO, General Electric

What's the use of running if you are not on the right road?

—German proverb

One must have strategies to execute dreams.

—Azim Premji
CEO Wipro Technologies and one of the world's richest people

LEARNING OBJECTIVES

LO 1. Understand why every company needs a sound strategy to compete successfully, manage the conduct of its business, and strengthen its prospects for long-term success.

LO 2. Develop an awareness of the four most dependable strategic approaches for setting a company apart from rivals and winning a sustainable competitive advantage.

LO 3. Understand that a company's strategy tends to evolve over time because of

changing circumstances and ongoing management efforts to improve the company's strategy.

LO 4. Learn why it is important for a company to have a viable business model that outlines the company's customer value proposition and its profit formula.

LO 5. Learn the three tests of a winning strategy.

Learning Objectives are listed at the beginning of each chapter; corresponding numbered indicators in the margins show where learning objectives are covered in the text.

ILLUSTRATION CAPSULE 2.3
Examples of Company Objectives

NORDSTROM

Increase same store sales by 2–4%. Expand credit revenue by $25–$35 million while also reducing associated expenses by $10–$20 million as a result of lower bad debt expenses. Continue moderate store growth by opening three new Nordstrom stores, relocating one store and opening 17 Nordstrom Racks. Find more ways to connect with customers on a multi-channel basis, including plans for an enhanced online experience, improved mobile shopping capabilities and better engagement with customers through social networking. Improve customer focus: "Most important, we continue to do everything in our power to elevate our focus on the customer. Our challenge is to keep building on this momentum. Our number one goal firmly remains improving customer service" (Blake Nordstrom, CEO).

MICROSOFT

On a broad level, deliver end-to-end experiences that connect users to information, communications, entertainment, and people in new and compelling ways across their lives at home, at work, and the broadest-possible range of mobile scenarios. Given the dramatic changes in the way people interact with technology, as touch, gestures, handwriting, and speech recognition become a normal part of how we control devices, focus on making technology more accessible and simpler to use, which will create opportunities to reach new markets and deliver new kinds of computing experiences.

More specifically, grow revenue in the PC Division slightly faster than the overall PC market fueled especially by emerging market trends.

Launch Office 2010 for the business market and promote adoption followed by a 2011 launch of the WindowsPhone 7 in the Entertainment and Devices Division. Grow annuity revenue between 4–6% in the Server and Tools Business segment. Target overall gross margin increases of 1% fueled in part by improved operational efficiency. Operating expenses are targeted at $26.1–$26.3 billion for the year with projected capital spending at $2 billion.

MCDONALD'S

Reinvest $2.4 billion in the business; 50% of this will be spent on opening 1,000 new restaurants around the world, including roughly 500 in Asia Pacific, 250 in Europe, and 150 in the U.S. The other half will be allocated toward "re-imagining" the décor and menu of over 2,000 existing locations. Re-imagining has a direct positive impact on sales as market share increases after re-imagining restaurants in the U.S., France and Australia demonstrate. Continue to expand refranchising; 80% of restaurants have been refranchised and this will be augmented by 200–300 restaurants in the next year. Focus on menu choice with a balance of familiar and popular core products as well as new items to keep products relevant.

Illustration Capsules appear in boxes throughout each chapter to provide in-depth examples, connect the text presentation to real-world companies, and convincingly demonstrate "strategy in action." Some are appropriate for use as mini-cases.

Margin Notes define core concepts and call attention to important ideas and principles.

---

pany. The answer to the question "*Where do we want to go from here?*" lies within management's vision of the company's future direction—what new customer groups and customer needs to endeavor to satisfy and what new capabilities to build or acquire. The question "*How are we going to get there?*" challenges managers to craft and execute a strategy capable of moving the company in the intended direction.

Developing clear answers to the question "*How are we going to get there?*" is the essence of managing strategically. Rather than relying on the status quo as a road map and dealing with new opportunities or threats as they emerge, managing strategically involves developing a full-blown game plan that spells out the competitive moves and business approaches that will be employed to compete successfully, attract and please customers, conduct operations, achieve targeted levels of performance, and grow the business. Thus, a company's strategy is all about *how:*

- *How* to outcompete rivals.
- *How* to respond to changing economic and market conditions and capitalize on growth opportunities.
- *How* to manage each functional piece of the business (e.g., R&D, supply chain activities, production, sales and marketing, distribution, finance, and human resources).
- *How* to improve the company's financial and market performance.

The specific elements that constitute management's answer to the question "*How are we going to get there?*" define a company's business strategy. Thus, a company's **strategy** is management's *action plan* for competing successfully and operating profitably, based on an integrated array of considered choices.[1] The crafting of a strategy represents a managerial commitment to pursuing a particular set of actions. In choosing a strategy, management is in effect saying, "Among all the many different business approaches and ways of competing we could have chosen, we have decided to employ this particular combination of approaches in moving the company in the intended direction, strengthening its market position and competitiveness, and boosting performance." The strategic choices a company

CORE CONCEPT

A company's **strategy** consists of the competitive moves and business approaches that managers are employing to compete successfully, improve performance, and grow the business.

---

22   **Part 1** Concepts and Techniques for Crafting and Executing Strategy

Figure 2.1   The Strategy-Making, Strategy-Executing Process

Figure 2.1 displays this five-stage process, which we examine next in some detail.

STAGE 1: DEVELOPING A STRATEGIC VISION, A MISSION, AND A SET OF CORE VALUES

Figures scattered throughout the chapters provide conceptual and analytical frameworks.

KEY POINTS

The strategic management process consists of five interrelated and integrated stages:

1. *Developing a strategic vision* of the company's future, *mission* that defines the company's current purpose, and a set of *core values* to guide the pursuit of the vision and mission. This managerial step provides direction for the company, motivates and inspires company personnel, aligns and guides actions throughout the organization, and communicates to stakeholders management's aspirations for the company's future.

2. *Setting objectives* to convert the vision and mission into performance targets and using the targeted results as yardsticks for measuring the company's performance. Objectives need to spell out *how much* of *what kind* of performance *by when.* Two broad types of objectives are required: *financial objectives* and *strategic objectives* A *balanced-scorecard* approach provides a popular method for linking financial objectives to specific, measurable strategic objectives.

3. *Crafting a strategy* to achieve the objectives and move the company along the strategic course that management has charted. Crafting deliberate strategy calls for strategic analysis, based on the business model. Crafting emergent strategy is a learning-by-doing process involving experimentation. Who participates in the process of crafting strategy depends on (1) whether the process is emergent or deliberate and (2) the level of strategy concerned. Deliberate strategies are mostly top-down, while emergent strategies are bottom-up, although both cases require two-way interaction between different types of managers. In large, diversified companies, there are four levels of strategy, each of which involves a corresponding level of management: corporate strategy (multibusiness strategy), business strategy (strategy for individual businesses that compete in a single industry), functional-area strategies within each business (e.g., marketing, R&D, logistics), and operating strategies (for key operating units, such as manufacturing plants). Thus, strategy making is an inclusive, collaborative activity involving not only senior company executives but also the heads of major business divisions, functional-area managers, and operating managers on the frontlines. The larger and more diverse the operations of an enterprise, the more points of strategic initiative it has and the more levels of management that play a significant strategy-making role.

Key Points at the end of each chapter provide a handy summary of essential ideas and things to remember.

LO 1, LO 3

2. Based on the strategic group map in Illustration Capsule 3.1, who are Nordstrom's closest competitors? Between which two strategic groups is competition the strongest? Why do you think no retail chains are positioned in the upper right corner of the map? Which company/strategic group faces the weakest competition from the members of other strategic groups?

LO 1, LO 4

3. Using your knowledge as a snack-food consumer and your analysis of the five forces in that industry (from question 1), describe the key success factors for the snack-food industry. Your list should contain no more than six industry KSFs. In deciding on your list, it's important to distinguish between factors critical for the success of *any* firm in the industry and factors that pertain only to specific companies.

EXERCISES FOR SIMULATION PARTICIPANTS

LO 1

1. Which of the five competitive forces is creating the strongest competitive pressures for your company?
2. What are the "competitive weapons" that rival companies in your industry can use to gain sales and market share? See Table 3.2 to help you identify possible competitive tactics. (You may be able to think of others.)
3. What are the factors affecting the intensity of rivalry in the industry in which your company is competing. Use Figure 3.4 and the accompanying discussion to help you pinpoint the specific factors most affecting competitive intensity. Would you characterize the rivalry among the companies in your industry as brutal, strong, moderate, or relatively weak? Why?

LO 2

4. Are there any factors driving change in the industry in which your company is competing? What impact will these drivers of change have? How will they change demand or supply? Will they cause competition to become more or less intense? Will they act to boost or squeeze profit margins? List at least two actions your company should consider taking in order to combat any negative impacts of the factors driving change.

LO 3

5. Draw a strategic group map showing the market positions of the companies in your industry. Which companies do you believe are in the most attractive position on the map? Which companies are the most weakly positioned? Which companies do you believe are likely to try to move to a different position on the strategic group map?

LO 4

6. What do you see as the key factors for being a successful competitor in your industry? List at least three.

Exercises at the end of each chapter, linked to learning objectives, provide a basis for class discussion, oral presentations, and written assignments. Several chapters have exercises that qualify as mini-cases.

Twenty-eight cases detail the strategic circumstances of actual companies and provide practice in applying the concepts and tools of strategic analysis.

CASE 1

Mystic Monk Coffee

David L. Turnipseed
University of South Alabama

As Father Daniel Mary, the Prior of the Carmelite Order of monks in Clark, Wyoming, walked to chapel to preside over Mass, he noticed the sun glistening across the four-inch snowfall from the previous evening. Snow in June was not unheard of in Wyoming, but the late snowfall and the bright glow of the rising sun made him consider the opposing forces accompanying change and how he might best prepare his monastery to achieve his vision of creating a new Mount Carmel in the Rocky Mountains. His vision of transforming the small brotherhood of 13 monks living in a small home used as makeshift rectory into a 500-acre monastery that would include accommodations for 30 monks, a Gothic church, a convent for Carmelite nuns, a retreat center for lay visitors, and a hermitage presented a formidable challenge. However, as a former high school football player, boxer, bull rider, and man of great faith, Father Prior Daniel Mary was unaccustomed to shrinking from a challenge.

Father Prior had identified a nearby ranch that met the requirements of his vision perfectly, but its current listing price of $8.9 million presented a financial obstacle to creating a place of prayer, worship, and solitude in the Rockies. The Carmelites had received a $250,000 donation that could be used toward the purchase, and the monastery had earned nearly $75,000 during the first year of its Mystic Monk coffee-roasting operations, but more money would be needed. The coffee roaster used to produce packaged coffee sold to Catholic consumers at the Mystic Monk Coffee website was reaching its capacity, but a larger roaster could be purchased for $35,000. Also, local Cody, Wyoming, business owners had begun a foundation for those wishing to donate to the monks' cause. Father Prior Daniel Mary did not have a great deal of experience in business matters but considered to what extent the monastery could rely on its Mystic Monk Coffee operations to fund the purchase of the ranch. If Mystic Monk Coffee was capable of making the vision a reality, what were the next steps in turning the coffee into land?

THE CARMELITE MONKS OF WYOMING

Carmelites are a religious order of the Catholic Church that was formed by men who came to the Holy Land as pilgrims and crusaders and had chosen to remain near Jerusalem to seek God. The men established their hermitage at Mount Carmel because of its beauty, seclusion, and Biblical importance as the site where Elijah stood against King Ahab and the false prophets of Jezebel to prove Jehovah to be the one true God. The Carmelites led a life of solitude, silence, and prayer at Mount Carmel before eventually returning to Europe and becoming a recognized order of the Catholic Church. The size of the Carmelite Order varied widely throughout the centuries with its peak coming

FOR STUDENTS: An Assortment of Support Materials

Web site: www.mhhe.com/thompson The student portion of the Web site features the "Guide to Case Analysis," with special sections on what a case is, why cases are a standard part of courses in strategy, preparing a case for class discussion, doing a written case analysis, doing an oral presentation, and using financial ratio analysis to assess a company's financial condition. In addition, there are 10-question self-scoring chapter tests and a select number of PowerPoint slides for each chapter.

The Business Strategy Game or *GLO-BUS* **Simulation Exercises** Either one of these text supplements involves teams of students managing companies in a head-to-head contest for global market leadership. Company co-managers have to make decisions relating to product quality, production, workforce compensation and training, pricing and marketing, and financing of company operations. The challenge is to craft and execute a strategy that is powerful enough to deliver good financial performance despite the competitive efforts of rival companies. Each company competes in America, Latin America, Europe-Africa, and Asia-Pacific.

BRIEF CONTENTS

TABLE OF CONTENTS

Section C: Crafting a Strategy

ILLUSTRATION CAPSULES

9 ETHICS, CORPORATE SOCIAL RESPONSIBILITY, ENVIRONMENTAL SUSTAINABILITY, AND STRATEGY 292

Section D: Executing the Strategy

10 BUILDING AN ORGANIZATION CAPABLE OF GOOD STRATEGY EXECUTION: PEOPLE, CAPABILITIES, AND STRUCTURE   328

ILLUSTRATION CAPSULES

PART TWO Cases in Crafting and Executing Strategy

Section A: Crafting Strategy in Single-Business Companies

PART 1

Concepts and Techniques for Crafting and Executing Strategy

CHAPTER 1

WHAT IS STRATEGY AND WHY IS IT IMPORTANT?

> Strategy means making clear-cut choices about how to compete.
>
> **—Jack Welch**
> *Former CEO, General Electric*

> What's the use of running if you are not on the right road?
>
> **—German proverb**

> One must have strategies to execute dreams.
>
> **—Azim Premji**
> *CEO Wipro Technologies and one of the world's richest people*

LEARNING OBJECTIVES

LO 1. Understand why every company needs a sound strategy to compete successfully, manage the conduct of its business, and strengthen its prospects for long-term success.

LO 2. Develop an awareness of the four most dependable strategic approaches for setting a company apart from rivals and winning a sustainable competitive advantage.

LO 3. Understand that a company's strategy tends to evolve over time because of changing circumstances and ongoing management efforts to improve the company's strategy.

LO 4. Learn why it is important for a company to have a viable business model that outlines the company's customer value proposition and its profit formula.

LO 5. Learn the three tests of a winning strategy.

In any given year, a group of companies will stand out as the top performers, in terms of metrics such as profitability, sales growth, or growth in shareholder value. Some of these companies will find that their star status fades quickly, due to little more than a fortuitous constellation of circumstances, such as being in the right business at the right time. But other companies somehow manage to rise to the top and stay there, year after year, pleasing their customers, shareholders, and other stakeholders alike in the process. Companies such as Apple, Google, Coca-Cola, Procter & Gamble, McDonald's, and Microsoft come to mind—but long-lived success is not just the province of U.S. companies. Diverse kinds of companies, both large and small, from many different countries have been able to sustain strong performance records, including Sweden's IKEA (in home furnishings), Australia's BHP Billiton (in mining), Korea's Hyundai Heavy Industries (in shipbuilding and construction), Mexico's America Movil (in telecommunications), and Japan's Nintendo (in video game systems).

What can explain the ability of companies like these to beat the odds and experience prolonged periods of profitability and growth? Why is it that some companies, like Southwest Airlines and Walmart, continue to do well even when others in their industry are faltering? Why can some companies survive and prosper even through economic downturns and industry turbulence?

Many factors enter into a full explanation of a company's performance, of course. Some come from the external environment; others are internal to the firm. But only one thing can account for the kind of long-lived success records that we see in the world's greatest companies—and that is a cleverly crafted and well executed *strategy*, one that facilitates the capture of emerging opportunities, produces enduringly good performance, is adaptable to changing business conditions, and can withstand the competitive challenges from rival firms.

In this opening chapter, we define the concept of strategy and describe its many facets. We will explain what is meant by a competitive advantage, discuss the relationship between a company's strategy and its business model, and introduce you to the kinds of competitive strategies that can give a company an advantage over rivals in attracting customers and earning above-average profits. We will look at what sets a winning strategy apart from others and why the caliber of a company's strategy determines whether it will enjoy a competitive advantage over other firms or be burdened by competitive disadvantage. By the end of this chapter, you will have a clear idea of why the tasks of crafting and executing strategy are core management functions and why excellent execution of an excellent strategy is the most reliable recipe for turning a company into a standout performer over a long-term horizon.

WHAT DO WE MEAN BY *STRATEGY*?

LO 1

Understand why every company needs a sound strategy to compete successfully, manage the conduct of its business, and strengthen its prospects for long-term success.

In moving a company forward, managers of all types of organizations—small family-owned businesses, rapidly growing entrepreneurial firms, not-for-profit organizations, and the world's leading multinational corporations—face the same three central questions:

- What is our present situation?
- Where do we want to go from here?
- How are we going to get there?

The first question, *"What is our present situation?"* prompts managers to evaluate industry conditions, the company's current financial performance and market standing, its resources and capabilities, its competitive strengths and weaknesses, and changes taking place in the business environment that might affect the company. The answer to the question *"Where do we want to go from here?"* lies within management's vision of the company's future direction—what new customer groups and customer needs to endeavor to satisfy and what new capabilities to build or acquire. The question *"How are we going to get there?"* challenges managers to craft and execute a strategy capable of moving the company in the intended direction.

Developing clear answers to the question *"How are we going to get there?"* is the essence of managing strategically. Rather than relying on the status quo as a road map and dealing with new opportunities or threats as they emerge, managing strategically involves developing a full-blown game plan that spells out the competitive moves and business approaches that will be employed to compete successfully, attract and please customers, conduct operations, achieve targeted levels of performance, and grow the business. Thus, a company's strategy is all about *how:*

- *How* to outcompete rivals.
- *How* to respond to changing economic and market conditions and capitalize on growth opportunities.
- *How* to manage each functional piece of the business (e.g., R&D, supply chain activities, production, sales and marketing, distribution, finance, and human resources).
- *How* to improve the company's financial and market performance.

CORE CONCEPT

A company's **strategy** consists of the competitive moves and business approaches that managers are employing to compete successfully, improve performance, and grow the business.

The specific elements that constitute management's answer to the question *"How are we going to get there?"* define a company's business strategy. Thus, a company's **strategy** is management's *action plan* for competing successfully and operating profitably, based on an integrated array of considered choices.[1] The crafting of a strategy represents a managerial commitment to pursuing a particular set of actions. In choosing a strategy, management is in effect saying, "Among all the many different business approaches and ways of competing we could have chosen, we have decided to employ this particular combination of approaches in moving the company in the intended direction, strengthening its market position and competitiveness, and boosting performance." The strategic choices a company makes are seldom easy decisions and often involve difficult trade-offs—but that does not excuse failure to pursue a concrete course of action.[2]

In most industries, there are many different avenues for outcompeting rivals and boosting company performance, thus giving managers considerable freedom in choosing the specific elements of their company's strategy.[3] Consequently, some companies strive to improve their performance by employing strategies aimed at achieving lower costs than rivals, while others pursue strategies aimed at achieving product superiority or personalized customer service or quality dimensions that rivals cannot match. Some companies opt for wide product lines, while others concentrate their energies on a narrow product lineup. Some position themselves in only one part of the industry's chain of production/distribution activities (preferring to be just in manufacturing or wholesale distribution or retailing), while others are partially or fully integrated, with operations ranging from components production to manufacturing and assembly to wholesale distribution and retailing. Some competitors deliberately confine their operations to local or regional markets; others opt to compete nationally, internationally (several countries), or globally (all or most of the major country markets worldwide). Some companies decide to operate in only one industry, while others diversify broadly or narrowly into related or unrelated industries.

There is no shortage of opportunity to fashion a strategy that both tightly fits a company's own particular situation and is discernibly different from the strategies of rivals. In fact, competitive success requires a company's managers to make strategic choices about the key building blocks of its strategy that differ from the choices made by competitors—not 100 percent different but at least different in several important respects. A strategy stands a better chance of succeeding when it is predicated on actions, business approaches, and competitive moves aimed at appealing to buyers *in ways that set a company apart from rivals*. Simply trying to mimic the strategies of the industry's successful companies rarely works. Rather, every company's strategy needs to have some distinctive element that draws in customers and produces a competitive edge. Strategy, at its essence, is about competing differently—doing what rival firms *don't* do or what rival firms *can't* do.[4]

A company's strategy provides direction and guidance, in terms of not only what the company *should* do but also what it *should not* do. Knowing what not to do can be as important as knowing what to do, strategically. At best, making the wrong strategic moves will prove a distraction and a waste of company resources. At worst, it can bring about unintended long-term consequences that put the company's very survival at risk.

Figure 1.1 illustrates the broad types of actions and approaches that often characterize a company's strategy in a particular business or industry. For a more concrete example of the specific actions constituting a firm's strategy, see Illustration Capsule 1.1, describing McDonald's strategy in the quick-service restaurant industry.

Strategy and the Quest for Competitive Advantage

The heart and soul of any strategy is the actions and moves in the marketplace that managers are taking to gain a competitive edge over rivals. A creative, distinctive strategy that sets a company apart from rivals and

> Strategy is about competing differently from rivals—doing what competitors *don't* do or, even better, doing what they *can't* do! Every strategy needs a distinctive element that attracts customers and produces a competitive edge.

CORE CONCEPT

A company achieves **sustainable competitive advantage** when it can meet customer needs more effectively or efficiently than rivals and when the basis for this is durable, despite the best efforts of competitors to match or surpass this advantage.

Figure 1.1   Identifying a Company's Strategy—What to Look For

Actions to gain sales and market share via more performance features, more appealing design, better quality or customer service, wider product selection, or other such actions

Actions to strengthen the firm's bargaining position with suppliers, distributors, and others

Actions to gain sales and market share with lower prices based on lower costs

Actions to upgrade, build, or acquire competitively important resources and capabilities

THE PATTERN OF ACTIONS AND BUSINESS APPROACHES THAT DEFINE A COMPANY'S STRATEGY

Actions to enter new product or geographic markets or to exit existing ones

Actions and approaches used in managing R&D, production, sales and marketing, finance, and other key activities

Actions to capture emerging market opportunities and defend against external threats to the company's business prospects

Actions to strengthen competitiveness via strategic alliances and collaborative partnerships

Actions to strengthen market standing and competitiveness by acquiring or merging with other companies

provides a competitive advantage is a company's most reliable ticket for earning above-average profits. Competing in the marketplace on the basis of a competitive advantage tends to be more profitable than competing with no advantage. And a company is almost certain to earn significantly higher profits when it enjoys a competitive advantage as opposed to when it is hamstrung by competitive disadvantage.

LO 2

Develop an awareness of the four most-dependable strategic approaches for setting a company apart from rivals and winning a sustainable competitive advantage.

Competitive advantage comes from an ability to meet customer needs more *effectively,* with products or services that customers value more highly, or more *efficiently,* at lower cost. Meeting customer needs more effectively can translate into the ability to command a higher price (e.g., Godiva chocolate), which can improve profits by boosting revenues. Meeting customer needs more cost-effectively can translate into being able to charge lower prices and achieve higher sales volumes (e.g., Walmart), thereby improving profits on the revenue side as well as the cost side. Furthermore, if a company's competitive edge holds promise for being sustainable (as opposed to just temporary), then so much the better for both the strategy and the company's future profitability. What makes a competitive advantage **sustainable** (or durable), as opposed to temporary, are elements of the strategy that give buyers *lasting reasons to prefer* a company's products or services over those of competitors—reasons that competitors are unable to nullify or overcome despite their best efforts.

ILLUSTRATION CAPSULE 1.1

McDonald's Strategy in the Quick-Service Restaurant Industry

In 2010, McDonald's was setting new sales records despite a global economic slowdown and declining consumer confidence in the United States. More than 60 million customers visited one of McDonald's 32,000 restaurants in 117 countries each day, which allowed the company to record 2009 revenues and earnings of more than $22.7 billion and $6.8 billion, respectively. McDonald's performance in the marketplace made it one of only two companies listed on the Dow Jones Industrial Average (the other was Walmart Stores, Inc.) that actually increased in share value in spite of the economic meltdown. The company's sales were holding up well amid the ongoing economic uncertainty in early 2010, with global sales as measured in constant currencies increasing by more than 4 percent in the first quarter. Its combined operating margin had risen to nearly 30 percent. The company's success was a result of its well-conceived and executed Plan-to-Win strategy that focused on "being better, not just bigger." Key initiatives of the Plan-to-Win strategy included:

- *Improved restaurant operations.* McDonald's global restaurant operations improvement process involved employee training programs ranging from on-the-job training for new crew members to college-level management courses offered at the company's Hamburger University. The company also sent nearly 200 high-potential employees annually to its McDonald's Leadership Institute to build the leadership skills needed by its next generation of senior managers. McDonald's commitment to employee development earned the company a place on *Fortune*'s list of Top 25 Global Companies for Leaders in 2010. The company also trained its store managers to closely monitor labor, food, and utility costs.

- *Affordable pricing.* In addition to tackling operating costs in each of its restaurants, McDonald's kept its prices low by closely scrutinizing administrative costs and other corporate expenses. McDonald's saw the poor economy in the United States as an opportunity to renegotiate its advertising contracts with newspapers and television networks in early 2009. The company also began

to replace its company-owned vehicles with more fuel-efficient models when gasoline prices escalated dramatically in the United States during 2008. However, McDonald's did not choose to sacrifice product quality in order to offer lower prices. The company implemented extensive supplier monitoring programs to ensure that its suppliers did not change product specifications to lower costs. For example, the company's chicken breasts were routinely checked for weight when arriving from suppliers' production facilities. The company's broad approach to minimizing non-value-adding expenses allowed it to offer more items on its Dollar Menu in the United States, its Ein Mal Eins menu in Germany, and its 100 Yen menu in Japan.

- *Wide menu variety and beverage choices.* McDonald's has expanded its menu beyond the popular-selling Big Mac and Quarter Pounder to include such new, healthy quick-service items as grilled chicken salads, chicken snack wraps, and premium chicken sandwiches in the United States, Lemon Shrimp Burgers in Germany, and Ebi shrimp wraps in Japan. The company has also added an extensive line of premium coffees that include espressos,

(continued)

cappuccinos, and lattes sold in its McCafe restaurant locations in the United States, Europe, and the Asia/Pacific region. McDonald's latte was judged "as good [as] or better" than lattes sold by Starbucks or Dunkin' Donuts in a review by the *Chicago Tribune*'s Good Eating and Dining staff in December 2008.

- *Convenience and expansion of dining opportunities.* The addition of McCafes helped McDonald's increase same store sales by extending traditional dining hours. Customers wanting a midmorning coffee or an afternoon snack helped keep store traffic high after McDonald's had sold its last Egg McMuffin, McGriddle, or chicken biscuit and before the lunch crowd arrived to order Big Macs, Quarter Pounders, chicken sandwiches, or salads. The company also extended its drive-thru hours to 24 hours in more than 25,000 locations in cities around the world where consumers tended to eat at all hours of the day and night. At many high-traffic locations in the United States, double drive-thru lanes were added to serve customers more quickly.

- *Ongoing restaurant reinvestment and international expansion.* With more than 14,000 restaurants in the United States, the focus of McDonald's expansion of units was in rapidly growing emerging markets such as Russia and China. The company opened 125 new restaurants in China and 40 new restaurants in Russia in 2008. The company also refurbished about 10,000 of its locations in the United States between 2004 and 2008 as a part of its McCafe rollout and as a way to make its restaurants pleasant places for both customers to dine and employees to work.

Sources: Janet Adamy, "McDonald's Seeks Way to Keep Sizzling," *Wall Street Journal Online,* March 10, 2009; various annual reports; various company press releases.

Four of the most frequently used and dependable strategic approaches to setting a company apart from rivals, building strong customer loyalty, and winning a competitive advantage are:

1. *Striving to be the industry's low-cost provider, thereby aiming for a cost-based competitive advantage over rivals.* Walmart and Southwest Airlines have earned strong market positions because of the low-cost advantages they have achieved over their rivals and their consequent ability to underprice competitors. These advantages in meeting customer needs *efficiently* have translated into volume advantages, with Walmart as the world's largest discount retailer and Southwest as the largest U.S. air carrier, based on the number of domestic passengers.[5]

2. *Outcompeting rivals on the basis of differentiating features, such as higher quality, wider product selection, added performance, value-added services, more attractive styling, and technological superiority.* Successful adopters of differentiation strategies include Apple (innovative products), Johnson & Johnson in baby products (product reliability), Rolex (top-of-the-line prestige), and Mercedes (engineering design). These companies have achieved a competitive advantage because of their ability to meet customer needs more effectively than rivals can, thus driving up their customers' willingness to pay higher prices. One way to sustain this type of competitive advantage is to be sufficiently innovative to thwart the efforts of clever rivals to copy or closely imitate the product offering.

3. *Focusing on a narrow market niche and winning a competitive edge by doing a better job than rivals of serving the special needs and tastes of buyers in the niche.* Firms using a focus strategy can achieve an advantage through either greater efficiency in serving the niche or greater effectiveness in meeting the special needs. Prominent companies that enjoy competitive success in a specialized market niche include eBay in online auctions, Jiffy Lube International

in quick oil changes, McAfee in virus protection software, and The Weather Channel in cable TV.

4. *Aiming to offer the lowest (best) prices for differentiated goods that at least match the features and performance of higher-priced rival brands.* This is known as a *best-cost provider strategy,* and it rests on the ability to be the most cost-effective provider of an upscale product or service. This option is a hybrid strategy that blends elements of the previous approaches. Target is an example of a company that is known for its hip product design (a reputation it built by featuring cheap-chic designers such as Isaac Mizrahi), as well as a more appealing shopping ambience than other "big-box" discounters, such as Walmart and Kmart. It offers the perfect illustration of a best-cost provider strategy.

Winning a *sustainable* competitive edge over rivals with any of the above four strategies generally hinges as much on building competitively valuable expertise and capabilities that rivals cannot readily match as it does on having a distinctive product offering. Clever rivals can nearly always copy the attributes of a popular product or service, but for rivals to match the experience, know-how, and specialized capabilities that a company has developed and perfected over a long period of time is substantially harder to do and takes much longer. FedEx, for example, has superior capabilities in next-day delivery of small packages. Walt Disney has hard-to-beat capabilities in theme park management and family entertainment. In recent years, Apple has demonstrated impressive product innovation capabilities in digital music players, smart phones, and e-readers. Hyundai has become the world's fastest-growing automaker as a result of its advanced manufacturing processes and unparalleled quality control system. Ritz Carlton and Four Seasons have uniquely strong capabilities in providing their hotel guests with an array of personalized services. Each of these capabilities has proved hard for competitors to imitate or best.

The tight connection between competitive advantage and profitability means that the quest for sustainable competitive advantage always ranks center stage in crafting a strategy. The key to successful strategy making is to come up with one or more strategy elements that act as a magnet to draw customers and that produce a lasting competitive edge over rivals. Indeed, what separates a powerful strategy from a run-of-the-mill or ineffective one is management's ability to forge a series of moves, both in the marketplace and internally, that sets the company apart from its rivals, tilts the playing field in the company's favor by giving buyers reason to prefer its products or services, and produces a sustainable competitive advantage over rivals. The bigger and more sustainable the competitive advantage, the better are a company's prospects for winning in the marketplace and earning superior long-term profits relative to its rivals. Without a strategy that leads to competitive advantage, a company risks being outcompeted by stronger rivals and locked into mediocre financial performance.

Why a Company's Strategy Evolves over Time

The appeal of a strategy that yields a sustainable competitive advantage is that it offers the potential for an enduring edge over rivals. However, managers of every company must be willing and ready to modify the strategy in response to changing market conditions, advancing technology, the fresh moves of competitors, shifting buyer needs, emerging market opportunities, and new ideas for improving the strategy. In some industries, conditions change at a fairly slow pace, making it feasible for the major components of a good strategy to remain in place for long

LO 3

Understand that a company's strategy tends to evolve over time because of changing circumstances and ongoing management efforts to improve the company's strategy.

periods. But in industries where industry and competitive conditions change frequently and in sometimes dramatic ways, the life cycle of a given strategy is short. Industry environments characterized by high-velocity change require companies to repeatedly adapt their strategies.[6] For example, companies in industries with rapid-fire advances in technology like medical equipment, electronics, and wireless devices often find it essential to adjust key elements of their strategies several times a year, sometimes even finding it necessary to "reinvent" their approach to providing value to their customers.

Regardless of whether a company's strategy changes gradually or swiftly, the important point is that the task of crafting strategy is not a one-time event but always a work in progress. Adapting to new conditions and constantly evaluating what is working well enough to continue and what needs to be improved are normal parts of the strategy-making process, resulting in an *evolving strategy*.[7]

> Changing circumstances and ongoing management efforts to improve the strategy cause a company's strategy to evolve over time—a condition that makes the task of crafting strategy *a work in progress,* not a one-time event.

A Company's Strategy Is Partly Proactive and Partly Reactive

The evolving nature of a company's strategy means that the typical company strategy is a blend of (1) *proactive* actions to improve the company's financial performance and secure a competitive edge and (2) *adaptive* reactions to unanticipated developments and fresh market conditions. In most cases, much of a company's current strategy flows from previously initiated actions and business approaches that are working well enough to merit continuation and from newly launched initiatives aimed at boosting financial performance and edging out rivals. This part of management's action plan for running the company is its **deliberate strategy,** consisting of strategy elements that are both planned and realized as planned (while other planned strategy elements may not work out).

> A company's strategy is shaped partly by management analysis and choice and partly by the necessity of adapting and learning by doing.

But managers must always be willing to supplement or modify the proactive strategy elements with as-needed reactions to unanticipated conditions. Inevitably, there will be occasions when market and competitive conditions take an unexpected turn that calls for some kind of strategic reaction or adjustment. Hence, *a portion of a company's strategy is always developed on the fly,* coming as a response to fresh strategic maneuvers on the part of rival firms, unexpected shifts in customer requirements, fast-changing technological developments, newly appearing market opportunities, a changing political or economic climate, or other unanticipated happenings in the surrounding environment. Under conditions of high uncertainty, strategy elements are more likely to emerge from experimentation, trial-and-error, and adaptive learning processes than from a proactive plan. These unplanned, reactive, and adaptive strategy adjustments make up the firm's **emergent strategy,** consisting of the new strategy elements that emerge as changing conditions warrant. A company's strategy in toto (its *realized* strategy) thus tends to be a *combination* of proactive and reactive elements, with certain strategy elements being *abandoned* because they have become obsolete or ineffective—see Figure 1.2.[8] A company's realized strategy can be observed in the pattern of its actions over time—a far better indicator than any of its strategic plans on paper or public pronouncements about its strategy.

CORE CONCEPTS

> A company's **proactive (or deliberate) strategy** consists of strategy elements that are both planned and realized as planned; its **reactive (or emergent) strategy** consists of new strategy elements that emerge as changing conditions warrant.

Figure 1.2   **A Company's Strategy Is a Blend of Proactive Initiatives and Reactive Adjustments**

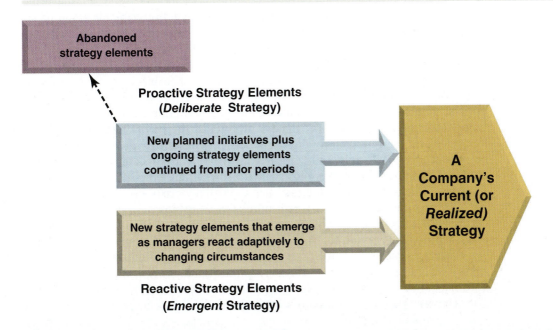

THE RELATIONSHIP BETWEEN A COMPANY'S STRATEGY AND ITS BUSINESS MODEL

Closely related to the concept of strategy is the company's **business model.** A company's business model is management's blueprint for delivering a valuable product or service to customers in a manner that will generate ample revenues to cover costs and yield an attractive profit.[9] It is management's story line for how the strategy will be a moneymaker. Without the ability to deliver good profitability, the strategy is not viable and the survival of the business is in doubt.

The two crucial elements of a company's business model are (1) its *customer value proposition* and (2) its *profit formula.* The customer value proposition lays out the company's approach to satisfying buyer wants and needs at a price customers will consider a good value. The greater the value provided (V) and the lower the price (P), the more attractive the value proposition is to customers. The profit formula describes the company's approach to determining a cost structure that will allow for acceptable profits, given the pricing tied to its customer value proposition. More specifically, a company's profit formula depends on three basic elements: V—the *value* provided to customers, in terms of how effectively the goods or services of the company meet customers' wants and needs; P—the *price* charged to customers; and C—the company's *costs.* The lower the costs (C), given the customer value proposition ($V - P$), the greater the ability of the business model to be a moneymaker. Thus the profit formula reveals how efficiently a company can meet customer wants and needs and deliver on the value proposition.

Magazines and newspapers employ a business model keyed to delivering information and entertainment they believe readers will find valuable and a profit formula aimed at securing sufficient revenues from subscriptions and advertising to more than cover the costs of producing and delivering their products to readers. Mobile phone providers, satellite radio companies, and broadband providers also employ a subscription-based business model. The business model of network TV and radio broadcasters entails providing free programming to audiences but charging advertising fees based on audience size. Gillette's business model in razor blades involves selling a "master product"—the razor—at an attractively low price and then making money on repeat purchases of razor blades that can be produced very cheaply and sold at high profit margins. Printer manufacturers like Hewlett-Packard, Lexmark, and Epson pursue much the same business model as Gillette—selling printers at a low (virtually break-even) price and making large profit margins on the repeat purchases of printer supplies, especially ink cartridges.

The nitty-gritty issue surrounding a company's business model is whether it can execute its customer value proposition profitably. Just because company managers have crafted a strategy for competing and running the business, this does not automatically mean that the strategy will lead to profitability—it may or it may not. The relevance of a company's business model is to clarify *how the business will (1) provide customers with value and (2) generate revenues sufficient to cover costs and produce attractive profits.*[10] Illustration Capsule 1.2 describes two contrasting business models in radio broadcasting.

WHAT MAKES A STRATEGY A WINNER?

Three tests can be applied to determine whether a strategy is a *winning strategy:*

1. ***The Fit Test:*** *How well does the strategy fit the company's situation?* To qualify as a winner, a strategy has to be well matched to industry and competitive conditions, a company's best market opportunities, and other pertinent aspects of the business environment in which the company operates. No strategy can work well unless it exhibits good *external fit* and is in sync with prevailing market conditions. At the same time, a winning strategy has to be tailored to the company's resources and competitive capabilities and be supported by a complementary set of functional activities (i.e., activities in the realms of supply chain management, operations, sales and marketing, and so on). That is, it must also exhibit *internal fit* and be compatible with a company's ability to execute the strategy in a competent manner. Unless a strategy exhibits good fit with both the external and internal aspects of a company's overall situation, it is likely to be an underperformer and fall short of producing winning results. Winning strategies also exhibit *dynamic fit* in the sense that they evolve over time in a manner that maintains close and effective alignment with the company's situation even as external and internal conditions change.[11]

A **winning strategy** must pass three tests:

1. The Fit Test
2. The Competitive Advantage Test
3. The Performance Test

ILLUSTRATION CAPSULE 1.2

Sirius XM and Over-the-Air Broadcast Radio: Two Contrasting Business Models

	Sirius XM	Over-the-Air Radio Broadcasters
Customer value proposition	Digital music, news, national and regional weather, traffic reports in limited areas, and talk radio programming provided for a monthly subscription fee. Programming was interrupted only by brief, occasional ads.	Free-of-charge music, national and local news, local traffic reports, national and local weather, and talk radio programming. Listeners could expect frequent programming interruption for ads.
Profit formula	*Revenue generation:* Monthly subscription fees, sales of satellite radio equipment, and advertising revenues. *Cost structure:* Fixed costs associated with operating a satellite-based music delivery service. Fixed and variable costs related to programming and content royalties, marketing, and support activities.	*Revenue generation:* Advertising sales to national and local businesses. *Cost structure:* Fixed costs associated with terrestrial broadcasting operations. Fixed and variable costs related to local news reporting, advertising sales operations, network affiliate fees, programming and content royalties, commercial production activities, and support activities.
	Profit margin: Sirius XM's profitability was dependent on attracting a sufficiently large number of subscribers to cover its costs and provide attractive profits.	*Profit margin:* The profitability of over-the-air radio stations was dependent on generating sufficient advertising revenues to cover costs and provide attractive profits.

2. ***The Competitive Advantage Test:*** *Can the strategy help the company achieve a sustainable competitive advantage?* Strategies that fail to achieve a durable competitive advantage over rivals are unlikely to produce superior performance for more than a brief period of time. Winning strategies enable a company to

achieve a competitive advantage over key rivals that is long-lasting. The bigger and more durable the competitive advantage, the more powerful it is.

3. ***The Performance Test: Is the strategy producing good company performance?*** The mark of a winning strategy is strong company performance. Two kinds of performance indicators tell the most about the caliber of a company's strategy: (1) profitability and financial strength and (2) competitive strength and market standing. Above-average financial performance or gains in market share, competitive position, or profitability are signs of a winning strategy.

Strategies that come up short on one or more of the above tests are plainly less appealing than strategies passing all three tests with flying colors. Managers should use the same questions when evaluating either proposed or existing strategies. New initiatives that don't seem to match the company's internal and external situations should be scrapped before they come to fruition, while existing strategies must be scrutinized on a regular basis to ensure they have good fit, offer a competitive advantage, and are contributing to above-average performance or performance improvements.

WHY CRAFTING AND EXECUTING STRATEGY ARE IMPORTANT TASKS

Crafting and executing strategy are top-priority managerial tasks for a very big reason. A clear and reasoned strategy is management's prescription for doing business, its road map to competitive advantage, its game plan for pleasing customers, and its formula for improving performance. High-achieving enterprises are nearly always the product of astute, creative, proactive strategy making. Companies don't get to the top of the industry rankings or stay there with illogical strategies, copy-cat strategies, or timid attempts to try to do better. Only a handful of companies can boast of hitting home runs in the marketplace due to lucky breaks or the good fortune of having stumbled into the right market at the right time with the right product. And even then, unless they subsequently craft a strategy that capitalizes on their luck, building in what's working and discarding the rest, success of this sort will be fleeting. So there can be little argument that a company's strategy matters—and matters a lot.

The chief executive officer of one successful company put it well when he said:

> In the main, our competitors are acquainted with the same fundamental concepts and techniques and approaches that we follow, and they are as free to pursue them as we are. More often than not, the difference between their level of success and ours lies in the relative thoroughness and self-discipline with which we and they develop and execute our strategies for the future.

Good Strategy + Good Strategy Execution = Good Management

Crafting and executing strategy are thus core management functions. Among all the things managers do, nothing affects a company's ultimate success or failure more fundamentally than how well its management team charts the company's direction, develops competitively effective strategic moves and business approaches, and pursues what needs to be done internally to produce good day-in, day-out strategy execution and operating excellence. Indeed, *good strategy and good strategy execution are the most telling signs of good management.* Managers don't deserve a gold star for designing a potentially brilliant strategy but failing to put the organizational means in place to carry it out in high-caliber fashion. Competent execution of a mediocre strategy scarcely merits enthusiastic applause for management's efforts either. The rationale for using the twin standards of good strategy making and good strategy execution to determine whether a company is well managed is therefore compelling: *The better conceived a company's strategy and the more competently it is executed, the more likely that the company will be a standout performer in the marketplace.* In stark contrast, a company that lacks clear-cut direction, has a flawed strategy, or can't execute its strategy competently is a company whose financial performance is probably suffering, whose business is at long-term risk, and whose management is sorely lacking.

> How well a company performs is directly attributable to the caliber of its strategy and the proficiency with which the strategy is executed.

THE ROAD AHEAD

Throughout the chapters to come and the accompanying case collection, the spotlight is trained on the foremost question in running a business enterprise: *What must managers do, and do well, to make a company a winner in the marketplace?* The answer that emerges, and that becomes the message of this book, is that doing a good job of managing inherently requires good strategic thinking and good management of the strategy-making, strategy-executing process.

The mission of this book is to provide a solid overview of what every business student and aspiring manager needs to know about crafting and executing strategy. We will explore what good strategic thinking entails, describe the core concepts and tools of strategic analysis, and examine the ins and outs of crafting and executing strategy. The accompanying cases will help build your skills both in diagnosing how well the strategy-making, strategy-executing task is being performed and in prescribing actions for how the strategy in question or its execution can be improved. In the process, we hope to convince you that first-rate capabilities in crafting and executing strategy are basic to managing successfully and are skills every manager needs to possess.

As you tackle the following pages, ponder the following observation by the essayist and poet Ralph Waldo Emerson: "Commerce is a game of skill which many people play, but which few play well." If the content of this book helps you become a savvy player and equips you to succeed in business, then your journey through these pages will indeed be time well spent.

KEY POINTS

The tasks of crafting and executing company strategies are the heart and soul of managing a business enterprise and winning in the marketplace. The key points to take away from this chapter include the following:

1. A company's strategy is the *game plan* management is using to stake out a market position, conduct its operations, attract and please customers, compete successfully, and achieve the desired performance targets.

2. The central thrust of a company's strategy is undertaking moves to build and strengthen the company's long-term competitive position and financial performance by *competing differently* from rivals and gaining a sustainable competitive advantage over them.

3. A company achieves a sustainable competitive advantage when it can meet customer needs more effectively or efficiently than rivals and when the basis for this is durable, despite the best efforts of competitors to match or surpass this advantage.

4. A company's strategy typically evolves over time, emerging from a blend of (1) proactive and deliberate actions on the part of company managers to improve the strategy and (2) reactive, as-needed adaptive responses to unanticipated developments and fresh market conditions.

5. A company's business model is management's story line for how the strategy will be a moneymaker. It contains two crucial elements: (1) the *customer value proposition*—a plan for satisfying customer wants and needs at a price customers will consider good value, and (2) the *profit formula*—a plan for a cost structure that will enable the company to deliver the customer value proposition profitably. In effect, a company's business model sets forth the economic logic for making money in a particular business, given the company's current strategy.

6. A winning strategy will pass three tests: (1) *Fit* (external, internal, and dynamic consistency), (2) *Competitive Advantage* (durable competitive advantage), and (3) *Performance* (outstanding financial and market performance).

7. Crafting and executing strategy are core management functions. How well a company performs and the degree of market success it enjoys are directly attributable to the caliber of its strategy and the proficiency with which the strategy is executed.

ASSURANCE OF LEARNING EXERCISES

LO 1, LO 2

1. Go to www.bestbuy.com, click on the investor relations section, and explore Best Buy's latest annual reports and 10-K filings to see if you can identify the key elements of Best Buy's strategy. Use the framework provided in Figure 1.1 to help identify these key elements. What approach toward winning a competitive advantage does Best Buy seem to be pursuing?

LO 1, LO 2, LO 5

2. On the basis of what you know about the quick-service restaurant industry, does McDonald's strategy as described in Illustration Capsule 1.1 seem to be well matched to industry and competitive conditions? Does the strategy seem to be keyed to having a cost-based advantage, offering differentiating features, serving the unique needs of a narrow market niche, or being the best-cost provider? What is there about the action elements of McDonald's strategy that is consistent with its approach to competitive advantage? From the information provided, which tests of a winning strategy does McDonald's strategy pass?

LO 4, LO 3

3. Go to www.nytco.com/investors and check whether the New York Times Company's recent financial reports indicate that its business model is working. Can the company's business model remain sound as more consumers go to the Internet to find general information and stay abreast of current events and news stories? Is its revenue stream from advertisements growing or declining? Are its subscription fees and circulation increasing or declining? Read the company's latest press releases. Is there evidence that the company's business model is evolving? To what degree does its strategic response to changing industry conditions seem proactive and deliberate versus reactive and adaptive (emergent)?

EXERCISE FOR SIMULATION PARTICIPANTS

This chapter discusses three questions that must be answered by managers of organizations of all sizes:

- What is our present situation?
- Where do we want to go from here?
- How are we going to get there?

After you read the Participant's Guide or Player's Manual for the strategy simulation exercise that you will participate in this academic term, you and your co-managers should come up with brief one- or two-paragraph answers to these three questions *before* entering your first set of decisions. While the management team's answer to the first of the three questions can be developed from your reading of the manual, the second and third questions will require a collaborative discussion among the members of your company's management team about how you intend to manage the company you have been assigned to run.

LO 1, LO 2

1. *What is our company's current situation?* A substantive answer to this question should cover the following issues:

    - Is your company in a good, average, or weak competitive position vis-à-vis rival companies?
    - Does your company appear to be in sound financial condition?
    - What problems does your company have that need to be addressed?

LO 3, LO 5

2. *Where do we want to take the company during the time we are in charge?* A complete answer to this question should say something about each of the following:

    - What goals or aspirations do you have for your company?
    - What do you want the company to be known for?
    - What market share would you like your company to have after the first five decision rounds?

- By what amount or percentage would you like to increase total profits of the company by the end of the final decision round?
- What kinds of performance outcomes will signal that you and your co-managers are managing the company in a successful manner?

LO 3, LO 4

3. *How are we going to get there?* Your answer should cover these issues:

- Which of the basic strategic and competitive approaches discussed in this chapter do you think makes the most sense to pursue?
- What kind of competitive advantage over rivals will you try to achieve?
- How would you describe the company's business model?
- What kind of actions will support these objectives?

ENDNOTES

[1] Jan Rivkin, "An Alternative Approach to Making Strategic Choices," Harvard Business School, 9-702-433, 2001.

[2] Costas Markides, "What Is Strategy and How Do You Know If You Have One?" *Business Strategy Review* 15, no. 2 (Summer 2004), pp. 5–6. See also David J. Collis and Michael F. Rukstad, "Can You Say What Your Strategy Is?" *Harvard Business Review* 86, no. 4 (April 2008), pp. 82–90.

[3] For a discussion of the different ways that companies can position themselves in the marketplace, see Michael E. Porter, "What Is Strategy?" *Harvard Business Review* 74, no. 6 (November–December 1996), pp. 65–67.

[4] Ibid.

[5] Walmartstores.com/download/2230.pdf; Southwest Airlines Fact Sheet, July 16, 2009.

[6] For more on the strategic challenges posed by high-velocity changes, see Shona L. Brown and Kathleen M. Eisenhardt, *Competing on the Edge: Strategy as Structured Chaos* (Boston, MA: Harvard Business School Press, 1998), chap. 1.

[7] For an excellent discussion of strategy as a dynamic process involving continuous, unending creation and re-creation of strategy, see Cynthia A. Montgomery, "Putting Leadership Back into Strategy," *Harvard Business Review* 86, no. 1 (January 2008), pp. 54–60.

[8] See Henry Mintzberg and Joseph Lampel, "Reflecting on the Strategy Process," *Sloan Management Review* 40, no. 3 (Spring 1999), pp. 21–30; Henry Mintzberg and J. A. Waters, "Of Strategies, Deliberate and Emergent," *Strategic Management Journal* 6 (1985), pp. 257–72; Costas Markides, "Strategy as Balance: From 'Either-Or' to 'And,'" *Business Strategy Review* 12, no. 3 (September 2001), pp. 1–10.

[9] Mark W. Johnson, Clayton M. Christensen, and Henning Kagermann, "Reinventing Your Business Model," *Harvard Business Review* 86, no. 12 (December 2008), pp. 52–53; Joan Magretta, "Why Business Models Matter," *Harvard Business Review* 80, no. 5 (May 2002), p. 87.

[10] For further discussion of the meaning and role of a company's customer value proposition and profit proposition, see W. Chan Kim and Renée Mauborgne, "How Strategy Shapes Structure," *Harvard Business Review* 87, no. 9 (September 2009), pp. 74–75.

[11] For a discussion of the three types of fit, see Rivkin, "An Alternative Approach to Making Strategic Choices." For an example of managing internal fit dynamically, See M. Peteraf and R. Reed, "Managerial Discretion and Internal Alignment under Regulatory Constraints and Change," *Strategic Management Journal* 28 (2007), pp. 1089–1112.

CHAPTER 2

CHARTING A COMPANY'S DIRECTION: VISION AND MISSION, OBJECTIVES, AND STRATEGY

> The vision we have . . . determines what we do and the opportunities we see or don't see.
>
> **—Charles G. Koch**
> *CEO of Koch Industries, the second-largest privately held company in the U.S.*

> A good goal is like a strenuous exercise—it makes you stretch.
>
> **—Mary Kay Ash**
> *Founder of Mary Kay Cosmetics*

> If you don't know where you are going, any road will take you there.
>
> **—Cheshire Cat to Alice**
> *Lewis Carroll, Alice in Wonderland*

LEARNING OBJECTIVES

LO 1. Grasp why it is critical for company managers to have a clear strategic vision of where a company needs to head and why.

LO 2. Understand the importance of setting both strategic and financial objectives.

LO 3. Understand why the strategic initiatives taken at various organizational levels must be tightly coordinated to achieve companywide performance targets.

LO 4. Become aware of what a company must do to achieve operating excellence and to execute its strategy proficiently.

LO 5. Become aware of the role and responsibility of a company's board of directors in overseeing the strategic management process.

Crafting and executing strategy are the heart and soul of managing a business enterprise. But exactly what is involved in developing a strategy and executing it proficiently? What are the various components of the strategy-making, strategy-executing process and to what extent are company personnel—aside from senior management—involved in the process? In this chapter we present an overview of the ins and outs of crafting and executing company strategies. Special attention will be given to management's direction-setting responsibilities—charting a strategic course, setting performance targets, and choosing a strategy capable of producing the desired outcomes. We will also explain why strategy making is a task for a company's entire management team and discuss which kinds of strategic decisions tend to be made at which levels of management. The chapter concludes with a look at the roles and responsibilities of a company's board of directors in the strategy-making, strategy-executing process and how good corporate governance protects shareholder interests and promotes good management.

WHAT DOES THE STRATEGY-MAKING, STRATEGY-EXECUTING PROCESS ENTAIL?

The process of crafting and executing a company's strategy consists of five interrelated managerial stages:

1. *Developing a strategic vision* of the company's long-term direction, a *mission* that describes the company's purpose, and a set of *values* to guide the pursuit of the vision and mission.
2. *Setting objectives* and using them as yardsticks for measuring the company's performance and progress.
3. *Crafting a strategy* to achieve the objectives and move the company along the strategic course that management has charted.
4. *Executing the chosen strategy* efficiently and effectively.
5. *Monitoring developments, evaluating performance, and initiating corrective adjustments* in the company's vision and mission, objectives, strategy, or execution in light of actual experience, changing conditions, new ideas, and new opportunities.

Figure 2.1   **The Strategy-Making, Strategy-Executing Process**

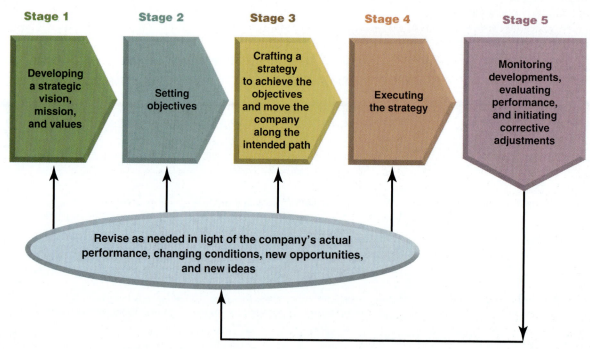

Figure 2.1 displays this five-stage process, which we examine next in some detail.

STAGE 1: DEVELOPING A STRATEGIC VISION, A MISSION, AND A SET OF CORE VALUES

LO 1

Grasp why it is critical for company managers to have a clear strategic vision of where a company needs to head and why.

Very early in the strategy-making process, a company's senior managers must wrestle with the issue of what directional path the company should take. Can the company's prospects be improved by changing its product offerings and/or the markets in which it participates and/or the customers it caters to and/or the technologies it employs? Deciding to commit the company to one path versus another pushes managers to draw some carefully reasoned conclusions about whether the company's present strategic course offers attractive opportunities for growth and profitability or whether changes of one kind or another in the company's strategy and long-term direction are needed.

Developing a Strategic Vision

Top management's views and conclusions about the company's long-term direction and what product-customer-market-technology mix seems optimal for the road ahead constitute a **strategic vision** for the company. A strategic vision delineates management's aspirations for the business, providing a panoramic view of "where we are going" and a convincing rationale for why this makes good business sense for the company. A strategic vision thus points an organization in a particular direction, charts a strategic path for it to follow in preparing for the future, and builds commitment to the future course of action. A clearly articulated strategic vision communicates management's aspirations to stakeholders and helps steer the energies of company personnel in a common direction.

Well-conceived visions are *distinctive* and *specific* to a particular organization; they avoid generic, feel-good statements like "We will become a global leader and the first choice of customers in every market we serve"—which could apply to hundreds of organizations.[1] And they are not the product of a committee charged with coming up with an innocuous but well-meaning one-sentence vision that wins consensus approval from various stakeholders. Nicely worded vision statements with no specifics about the company's product-market-customer-technology focus fall well short of what it takes for a vision to measure up.

A sampling of vision statements currently in use shows a range from strong and clear to overly general and generic. A surprising number of the vision statements found on company Web sites and in annual reports are vague and unrevealing, saying very little about the company's future direction. Some could apply to almost any company in any industry. Many read like a public relations statement—high-sounding words that someone came up with because it is fashionable for companies to have an official vision statement.[2] But the real purpose of a vision statement is to serve as a management tool for giving the organization a sense of direction. Like any tool, it can be used properly or improperly, either clearly conveying a company's future strategic path or not.

For a strategic vision to function as a valuable managerial tool, it must convey what management wants the business to look like and provide managers with a reference point in making strategic decisions and preparing the company for the future. It must say something definitive about how the company's leaders intend to position the company beyond where it is today. Table 2.1 provides some dos and don'ts in composing an effectively worded vision statement. Illustration Capsule 2.1 provides a critique of the strategic visions of several prominent companies.

Communicating the Strategic Vision

Effectively communicating the strategic vision down the line to lower-level managers and employees is as important as the strategic soundness of the long-term direction top management has chosen. Company personnel can't be expected to unite behind managerial efforts to get the organization moving in the intended direction until they understand why the strategic course that management has charted is reasonable and beneficial. It is particularly important for executives to provide a compelling rationale for a dramatically *new* strategic vision and company direction. When company personnel don't understand or accept the need for redirecting organizational efforts, they are prone to resist change. Hence, reiterating the basis for the new direction, addressing employee concerns head-on, calming fears, lifting spirits, and providing updates and progress reports as events unfold all become part of the task in mobilizing support for the vision and winning commitment to needed actions.

Winning the support of organization members for the vision nearly always means putting "where we are going and why" in writing, distributing the statement organizationwide, and having executives personally explain the vision and its

Table 2.1   Wording a Vision Statement—the Dos and Don'ts

The Dos	The Don'ts
Be graphic. Paint a clear picture of where the company is headed and the market position(s) the company is striving to stake out.	**Don't be vague or incomplete.** Never skimp on specifics about where the company is headed or how the company intends to prepare for the future.
Be forward-looking and directional. Describe the strategic course that management has charted and the kinds of product-market-customer-technology changes that will help the company prepare for the future.	**Don't dwell on the present.** A vision is not about what a company once did or does now; it's about "where we are going."
Keep it focused. Be specific enough to provide managers with guidance in making decisions and allocating resources.	**Don't use overly broad language.** All-inclusive language that gives the company license to head in almost any direction, pursue almost any opportunity, or enter almost any business must be avoided.
Have some wiggle room. Language that allows some flexibility is good. The directional course may have to be adjusted as market-customer-technology circumstances change, and coming up with a new vision statement every one to three years signals rudderless management.	**Don't state the vision in bland or uninspiring terms.** The best vision statements have the power to motivate company personnel and inspire shareholder confidence about the company's direction and business outlook.
Be sure the journey is feasible. The path and direction should be within the realm of what the company can pursue and accomplish; over time, a company should be able to demonstrate measurable progress in achieving the vision.	**Don't be generic.** A vision statement that could apply to companies in any of several industries (or to any of several companies in the same industry) is incapable of giving a company its own unique identity.
Indicate why the directional path makes good business sense. The directional path should be in the long-term interests of stakeholders (especially shareowners, employees, and customers).	**Don't rely on superlatives only.** Visions that claim the company's strategic course is one of being the "best" or "the most successful" or "a recognized leader" or the "global leader" usually shortchange the essential and revealing specifics about the path the company is taking to get there.
Make it memorable. To give the organization a sense of direction and purpose, the vision needs to be easily communicated. Ideally, it should be reducible to a few choice lines or a memorable "slogan" (like Henry Ford's famous vision of "a car in every garage").	**Don't run on and on.** Vison statements that are overly long tend to be unfocused and meaningless. A vision statement that is not short and to-the-point will tend to lose its audience.

Sources: John P. Kotter, *Leading Change* (Boston: Harvard Business School Press, 1996), p. 72; Hugh Davidson, *The Committed Enterprise* (Oxford: Butterworth Heinemann, 2002), chap. 2; and Michel Robert, *Strategy Pure and Simple II* (New York: McGraw-Hill, 1992), chaps. 2, 3, and 6.

> Strategic visions become real only when the vision statement is imprinted in the minds of organization members and then translated into hard objectives and strategies.

rationale to as many people as feasible. *A strategic vision can usually be stated adequately in one to two paragraphs, and managers should be able to explain it to company personnel and outsiders in 5 to 10 minutes.* Ideally, executives should present their vision for the company in a manner that reaches out and grabs people. An engaging and convincing strategic vision has enormous motivational value—for the same reason that a stonemason is more inspired by building a great cathedral for the ages than simply laying stones to create floors and walls. When managers articulate a vivid and compelling case for where the company is headed, organization members begin to say "This is interesting and has a lot of merit. I want to be involved and do my part to help make it happen." The more that a vision evokes positive support and excitement, the greater its impact in terms of arousing a committed organizational effort and getting company personnel to move in a common direction.[3] Thus executive ability to paint a convincing and inspiring picture of a company's journey and destination is an important element of effective strategic leadership.

Examples of Strategic Visions—How Well Do They Measure Up?

Vision Statement	Effective Elements	Shortcomings
Coca-Cola Our vision serves as the framework for our Roadmap and guides every aspect of our business by describing what we need to accomplish in order to continue achieving sustainable, quality growth.  • People: Be a great place to work where people are inspired to be the best they can be. • Portfolio: Bring to the world a portfolio of quality beverage brands that anticipate and satisfy people's desires and needs. • Partners: Nurture a winning network of customers and suppliers; together we create mutual, enduring value. • Planet: Be a responsible citizen that makes a difference by helping build and support sustainable communities. • Profit: Maximize long-term return to shareowners while being mindful of our overall responsibilities. • Productivity: Be a highly effective, lean and fast-moving organization.	• Graphic • Focused • Flexible • Makes good business sense	• Long • Not forward-looking
UBS We are determined to be the best global financial services company. We focus on wealth and asset management, and on investment banking and securities businesses. We continually earn recognition and trust from clients, shareholders, and staff through our ability to anticipate, learn and shape our future. We share a common ambition to succeed by delivering quality in what we do. Our purpose is to help our clients make financial decisions with confidence. We use our resources to develop effective solutions and services for our clients. We foster a distinctive, meritocratic culture of ambition, performance and learning as this attracts, retains and develops the best talent for our company. By growing both our client and our talent franchises, we add sustainable value for our shareholders.	• Focused • Feasible • Desirable	• Not forward-looking • Bland or uninspiring • Hard to communicate
Walmart Saving People Money So They Can Live Better	• Focused • Memorable • Feasible • Makes good business sense	• Dwells on the present

Sources: Company documents and Web sites (accessed April 23, 2010, and June 6, 2010).

Expressing the Essence of the Vision in a Slogan   The task of effectively conveying the vision to company personnel is assisted when management can capture the vision of where to head in a catchy or easily remembered slogan. A number of organizations have summed up their vision in a brief phrase:

- Levi Strauss & Company: "We will clothe the world by marketing the most appealing and widely worn casual clothing in the world."
- Nike: "To bring innovation and inspiration to every athlete in the world."
- Mayo Clinic: "The best care to every patient every day."
- Scotland Yard: "To make London the safest major city in the world."
- Greenpeace: "To halt environmental abuse and promote environmental solutions."

Creating a short slogan to illuminate an organization's direction and purpose helps rally organization members to hurdle whatever obstacles lie in the company's path and maintain their focus.

The Payoffs of a Clear Vision Statement   A well-conceived, forcefully communicated strategic vision pays off in several respects: (1) It crystallizes senior executives' own views about the firm's long-term direction; (2) it reduces the risk of rudderless decision making; (3) it is a tool for winning the support of organization members for internal changes that will help make the vision a reality; (4) it provides a beacon for lower-level managers in setting departmental objectives and crafting departmental strategies that are in sync with the company's overall strategy; and (5) it helps an organization prepare for the future. When management is able to demonstrate significant progress in achieving these five benefits, the first step in organizational direction setting has been successfully completed.

Crafting a Mission Statement

The defining characteristic of a strategic vision is what it says about the company's *future strategic course*—"the direction we are headed and our aspirations for the future." In contrast, a **mission statement** describes the enterprise's *current business and purpose*—"who we are, what we do, and why we are here." The mission statements that one finds in company annual reports or posted on company Web sites are typically quite brief; some do a better job than others of conveying what the enterprise is all about. Consider, for example, the mission statement of Trader Joe's (a specialty grocery chain):

> The mission of Trader Joe's is to give our customers the best food and beverage values that they can find anywhere and to provide them with the information required for informed buying decisions. We provide these with a dedication to the highest quality of customer satisfaction delivered with a sense of warmth, friendliness, fun, individual pride, and company spirit.

Note that Trader Joe's mission statement does a good job of conveying "who we are, what we do, and why we are here," but it says nothing about the company's long-term direction.

Another example of a well-stated mission statement with ample specifics about what the organization does is that of the Occupational Safety and Health Administration (OSHA): "to assure the safety and health of America's workers by setting and enforcing standards; providing training, outreach, and education; establishing partnerships; and encouraging

> The distinction between a strategic vision and a mission statement is fairly clear-cut: A **strategic vision** portrays a company's aspirations for its *future* ("where we are going"), whereas a company's **mission** describes its *purpose* and its *present* business ("who we are, what we do, and why we are here").

continual improvement in workplace safety and health." Microsoft's grandiloquent mission statement—"To help people and businesses throughout the world realize their full potential"—says so little about the customer needs it is satisfying that it could be applied to almost any firm. A well-conceived mission statement should employ language specific enough to give the company its own identity.

Ideally, a company mission statement is sufficiently descriptive to:

- Identify the company's product or services.
- Specify the buyer needs it seeks to satisfy.
- Identify the customer groups or markets it is endeavoring to serve.
- Specify its approach to pleasing customers.
- Give the company its own identity.

Not many company mission statements fully reveal *all* these facets of the business or employ language specific enough to give the company an identity that is distinguishably different from those of other companies in much the same business or industry. A few companies have worded their mission statements so obscurely as to mask what they are all about. Occasionally, companies couch their mission in terms of making a profit. This is misguided. Profit is more correctly an *objective* and a *result* of what a company does. Moreover, earning a profit is the obvious intent of every commercial enterprise. Such companies as BMW, McDonald's, Shell Oil, Procter & Gamble, Nintendo, and Nokia are each striving to earn a profit for shareholders; but plainly the fundamentals of their businesses are substantially different when it comes to "who we are and what we do." It is management's answer to "make a profit doing what and for whom?" that reveals the substance of a company's true mission and business purpose.

Linking the Vision and Mission with Company Values

The **values** of a company (sometimes called *core values*) are the beliefs, traits, and behavioral norms that management has determined should guide the pursuit of its vision and mission. They relate to such things as fair treatment, integrity, ethical behavior, innovativeness, teamwork, top-notch quality, superior customer service, social responsibility, and community citizenship. Many companies have developed a statement of values to emphasize the expectation that the values be reflected in the conduct of company operations and the behavior of company personnel.

Most companies have identified four to eight core values. At FedEx, the six core values concern people (valuing employees and promoting diversity), service (putting customers at the heart of all it does), innovation (inventing services and technologies to improve what it does), integrity (managing with honesty, efficiency, and reliability), and loyalty (earning the respect of the FedEx people, customers, and investors every day, in everything it does). Home Depot embraces eight values—entrepreneurial spirit, excellent customer service, giving back to the community, respect for all people, doing the right thing, taking care of people, building strong relationships, and creating shareholder value—in its quest to be the world's leading home improvement retailer.

Do companies practice what they preach when it comes to their professed values? Sometimes no, sometimes yes—it runs the gamut. At one extreme are

---

CORE CONCEPT

A well-conceived **mission statement** conveys a company's *purpose* in language specific enough to give the company its own identity.

CORE CONCEPT

A company's **values** are the beliefs, traits, and behavioral norms that company personnel are expected to display in conducting the company's business and pursuing its strategic vision and mission.

companies with window-dressing values; the values are given lip service by top executives but have little discernible impact on either how company personnel behave or how the company operates. Such companies have value statements because they are in vogue and make the company look good. At the other extreme are companies whose executives are committed to infusing the company with the desired character, traits, and behavioral norms so that they are ingrained in the company's corporate culture—the core values thus become an integral part of the company's DNA and what makes it tick. At such value-driven companies, executives "walk the talk" and company personnel are held accountable for displaying the stated values.

At companies where the stated values are real rather than cosmetic, managers connect values to the pursuit of the strategic vision and mission in one of two ways. In companies with long-standing values that are deeply entrenched in the corporate culture, senior managers are careful to craft a vision, mission, and strategy that match established values; they also reiterate how the value-based behavioral norms contribute to the company's business success. If the company changes to a different vision or strategy, executives take care to explain how and why the core values continue to be relevant. In new companies or companies having unspecified values, top management has to consider what values, behaviors, and business conduct should characterize the company and then draft a value statement that is circulated among managers and employees for discussion and possible modification. A final value statement that incorporates the desired behaviors and traits and that connects to the vision and mission is then officially adopted. Some companies combine their vision, mission, and values into a single statement or document, circulate it to all organization members, and in many instances post the vision, mission, and value statement on the company's Web site. Illustration Capsule 2.2 describes how core values drive the company's mission at the Zappos Family of Companies, a widely known and quite successful online shoe and apparel retailer that was acquired recently by Amazon (but will continue to operate separately).

STAGE 2: SETTING OBJECTIVES

LO 2

Understand the importance of setting both strategic and financial objectives.

The managerial purpose of setting **objectives** is to convert the vision and mission into specific performance targets. Well-stated objectives are *specific, quantifiable* or *measurable,* and contain a *deadline for achievement.* As Bill Hewlett, cofounder of Hewlett-Packard, shrewdly observed, "You cannot manage what you cannot measure. . . . And what gets measured gets done."[4] Concrete, measurable objectives are managerially valuable for three reasons: (1) They focus efforts and align actions throughout the organization, (2) they serve as *yardsticks* for tracking a company's performance and progress, and (3) they provide motivation and inspire employees to greater levels of effort. Ideally, managers should develop challenging yet achievable objectives that *stretch* an organization to perform at its full potential.

What Kinds of Objectives to Set

Two very distinct types of performance targets are required: those relating to financial performance and those relating to strategic performance. **Financial objectives** communicate management's targets for financial

CORE CONCEPT

Objectives are an organization's performance targets—the specific results management wants to achieve.

ILLUSTRATION CAPSULE 2.2

Zappos Family Mission and Core Values

We've been asked by a lot of people how we've grown so quickly, and the answer is actually really simple. . . . We've aligned the entire organization around one mission: *to provide the best customer service possible.* Internally, we call this our **WOW** philosophy.

These are the ten core values that we live by:

Deliver Wow through Service. At the Zappos Family of Companies, anything worth doing is worth doing with WOW. WOW is such a short, simple word, but it really encompasses a lot of things. To WOW, you must differentiate yourself, which means doing something a little unconventional and innovative. You must do something that's above and beyond what's expected. And whatever you do must have an emotional impact on the receiver. We are not an average company, our service is not average, and we don't want our people to be average. We expect every employee to deliver WOW.

Embrace and Drive Change. Part of being in a growing company is that change is constant. For some people, especially those who come from bigger companies, the constant change can be somewhat unsettling at first. If you are not prepared to deal with constant change, then you probably are not a good fit for the company.

Create Fun and a Little Weirdness. At Zappos, We're Always Creating Fun and A Little Weirdness! One of the things that makes our company different from a lot of other companies is that we value being fun and being a little weird. We don't want to become one of those big companies that feels corporate and boring. We want to be able to laugh at ourselves. We look for both fun and humor in our daily work.

Be Adventurous, Creative, and Open Minded. We think it's important for people and the company as a whole to be bold and daring (but not reckless). We do not want people to be afraid to take risks and make mistakes. We believe if people aren't making mistakes, then that means they're not taking enough risks. Over time, we want everyone to develop his/her gut about business decisions. We want people to develop and improve their decision-making skills. We encourage people to make mistakes as long as they learn from them.

Pursue Growth and Learning. We think it's important for employees to grow both personally and professionally. It's important to constantly challenge and stretch yourself

and not be stuck in a job where you don't feel like you are growing or learning.

Build Open and Honest Relationships With Communication. Fundamentally, we believe that openness and honesty make for the best relationships because that leads to trust and faith. We value strong relationships in all areas: with managers, direct reports, customers (internal and external), vendors, business partners, team members, and co-workers.

Build a Positive Team and Family Spirit. At our company, we place a lot of emphasis on our culture because we are both a team and a family. We want to create an environment that is friendly, warm, and exciting. We encourage diversity in ideas, opinions, and points of view.

Do More with Less. The Zappos Family of Companies has always been about being able to do more with less. While we may be casual in our interactions with each other, we are focused and serious about the operations of our business. We believe in working hard and putting in the extra effort to get things done.

Be Passionate and Determined. Passion is the fuel that drives us and our company forward. We value passion, determination, perseverance, and the sense of urgency. We are inspired because we believe in what we are doing and where we are going. We don't take "no" or "that'll never work" for an answer because if we had, then our company would have never started in the first place.

Be Humble. While we have grown quickly in the past, we recognize that there are always challenges ahead to tackle. We believe that no matter what happens we should always be respectful of everyone.

Source: Information posted at www.zappos.com (accessed June 6, 2010). Copyright © 2011 Zappos.com, Inc.

29

performance. **Strategic objectives** are related to a company's marketing standing and competitive vitality. Examples of commonly used financial and strategic objectives include the following:

Financial Objectives	Strategic Objectives
• An *x* percent increase in annual revenues • Annual increases in after-tax profits *of x* percent • Annual increases in earnings per share of *x* percent • Annual dividend increases of *x* percent • Profit margins of *x* percent • An *x* percent return on capital employed (ROCE) or return on shareholders' equity investment (ROE) • Increased shareholder value—in the form of an upward-trending stock price • Bond and credit ratings of *x* • Internal cash flows of *x* dollars to fund new capital investment	• Winning an *x* percent market share • Achieving lower overall costs than rivals • Overtaking key competitors on product performance or quality or customer service • Deriving *x* percent of revenues from the sale of new products introduced within the past five years • Having broader or deeper technological capabilities than rivals • Having a wider product line than rivals • Having a better-known or more powerful brand name than rivals • Having stronger national or global sales and distribution capabilities than rivals • Consistently getting new or improved products to market ahead of rivals

The importance of setting and achieving financial objectives is intuitive. Without adequate profitability and financial strength, a company's long-term health and ultimate survival are jeopardized. Furthermore, subpar earnings and a weak balance sheet alarm shareholders and creditors and put the jobs of senior executives at risk. However, good financial performance, by itself, is not enough.

The Balanced Scorecard: Improved Strategic Performance Fosters Better Financial Performance

A company's financial performance measures are really *lagging indicators* that reflect the results of past decisions and organizational activities.[5] But a company's past or current financial performance is not a reliable indicator of its future prospects—poor financial performers often turn things around and do better, while good financial performers can fall upon hard times. The best and most reliable *leading indicators* of a company's future financial performance and business prospects are strategic outcomes that indicate whether the company's competitiveness and market position are stronger or weaker. The accomplishment of strategic objectives signals that the company is well positioned to sustain or improve its performance. For instance, if a company is achieving ambitious strategic objectives such that its competitive strength and market position are on the rise, then there's reason to expect that its *future* financial performance will be better than its current or past performance. If a company begins to lose competitive strength and fails to achieve important strategic objectives, then its ability to maintain its present profitability is highly suspect.

Consequently, utilizing a performance measurement system that strikes a *balance* between financial objectives and strategic objectives is optimal.[6] Just tracking a company's financial performance overlooks the fact that what ultimately enables a company to deliver better financial results from its operations is the achievement of strategic objectives that improve its competitiveness and market strength. Indeed, *the surest path to boosting company profitability* quarter after quarter and year after year *is to relentlessly pursue strategic outcomes* that strengthen the company's market position and produce a growing competitive advantage over rivals.

The most widely used framework for balancing financial objectives with strategic objectives is known as the **Balanced Scorecard**.[7] This is a method for linking financial performance objectives to specific strategic objectives that derive from a company's business model. It provides a company's employees with clear guidelines about how their jobs are linked to the overall objectives of the organization, so they can contribute most productively and collaboratively to the achievement of these goals. In 2008, nearly 60 percent of global companies used a balanced-scorecard approach to measuring strategic and financial performance.[8] Examples of organizations that have adopted a balanced-scorecard approach to setting objectives and measuring performance include UPS, Ann Taylor Stores, UK Ministry of Defense, Caterpillar, Daimler AG, Hilton Hotels, Duke University Hospital, and Siemens AG.[9] Illustration Capsule 2.3 provides selected strategic and financial objectives of four prominent companies.

The Merits of Setting Stretch Objectives

Ideally, managers ought to use the objective-setting exercise as a tool for *stretching an organization to perform at its full potential and deliver the best possible results.* Challenging company personnel to go all out and deliver "stretch" gains in performance pushes an enterprise to be more inventive, to exhibit more urgency in improving both its financial performance and its business position, and to be more intentional and focused in its actions. Stretch objectives spur exceptional performance and help build a firewall against contentment with modest gains in organizational performance. As Mitchell Leibovitz, former CEO of the auto parts and service retailer Pep Boys, once said, "If you want to have ho-hum results, have ho-hum objectives." *There's no better way to avoid unimpressive results than by setting stretch objectives and using compensation incentives to motivate organization members to achieve the stretch performance targets.*

Why Both Short-Term and Long-Term Objectives Are Needed

A company's set of financial and strategic objectives should include both near-term and longer-term performance targets. Short-term (quarterly or annual) objectives focus attention on delivering performance improvements in the current period and satisfy shareholder expectations for near-term progress. Longer-term targets (three to five years off) force managers to consider what to do *now* to put the company in position to perform better later. Long-term objectives are critical for achieving optimal long-term performance and stand as a barrier to a nearsighted management philosophy and an undue focus on short-term results. When trade-offs have to be made between achieving long-run objectives and achieving short-run objectives, long-run objectives should take precedence (unless the achievement of one or more short-run performance targets has unique importance).

The Need for Objectives at All Organizational Levels

Objective setting should not stop with top management's establishing of company-wide performance targets. Company objectives need to be broken down into

ILLUSTRATION CAPSULE 2.3
Examples of Company Objectives

NORDSTROM

Increase same store sales by 2–4%. Expand credit revenue by $25–$35 million while also reducing associated expenses by $10–$20 million as a result of lower bad debt expenses. Continue moderate store growth by opening three new Nordstrom stores, relocating one store and opening 17 Nordstrom Racks. Find more ways to connect with customers on a multi-channel basis, including plans for an enhanced online experience, improved mobile shopping capabilities and better engagement with customers through social networking. Improve customer focus: "Most important, we continue to do everything in our power to elevate our focus on the customer. Our challenge is to keep building on this momentum. Our number one goal firmly remains improving customer service" (Blake Nordstrom, CEO).

MICROSOFT

On a broad level, deliver end-to-end experiences that connect users to information, communications, entertainment, and people in new and compelling ways across their lives at home, at work, and the broadest-possible range of mobile scenarios. Given the dramatic changes in the way people interact with technology, as touch, gestures, handwriting, and speech recognition become a normal part of how we control devices, focus on making technology more accessible and simpler to use, which will create opportunities to reach new markets and deliver new kinds of computing experiences.

More specifically, grow revenue in the PC Division slightly faster than the overall PC market fueled especially by emerging market trends.

Launch Office 2010 for the business market and promote adoption followed by a 2011 launch of the WindowsPhone 7 in the Entertainment and Devices Division. Grow annuity revenue between 4–6% in the Server and Tools Business segment. Target overall gross margin increases of 1% fueled in part by improved operational efficiency. Operating expenses are targeted at $26.1–$26.3 billion for the year with projected capital spending at $2 billion.

MCDONALD'S

Reinvest $2.4 billion in the business; 50% of this will be spent on opening 1,000 new restaurants around the world, including roughly 500 in Asia Pacific, 250 in Europe, and 150 in the U.S. The other half will be allocated toward "re-imagining" the décor and menu of over 2,000 existing locations. Re-imagining has a direct positive impact on sales as market share increases after re-imagining restaurants in the U.S., France and Australia demonstrate. Continue to expand refranchising; 80% of restaurants have been refranchised and this will be augmented by 200–300 restaurants in the next year. Focus on menu choice with a balance of familiar and popular core products as well as new items to keep products relevant.

Developed with C. David Morgan.

Sources: "Nordstrom 2009 Annual Report," http://phx.corporate-ir.net/phoenix.zhtml?c=93295&p=irol-irhome, https://materials.proxyvote.com/Approved/655664/20100312/AR_57243/images/Nordstrom-AR2009.pdf (accessed April 4, 2010); "Nordstrom Fourth Quarter and Fiscal Year 2009 Earning, February 22, 2010," http://phx.corporate-ir.net/phoenix.zhtml?c=93295&p=irol-newsArticle&ID=1393755&highlight= (accessed April 30, 2010); Nordstrom "4Q 2009 Financial Results," http://investor.nordstrom.com/phoenix.zhtml?c=93295&p=irol-audioArchives (accessed April 30, 2010); Thompson Reuters Street Events, "JWN – Q4 2009 Nordstrom Earnings Conference Call," www.streetevents.com, February 2010 (transcribed version of Webcast accessed April 30, 2010, through InvesText database); "Microsoft Annual Report" www.microsoft.com/msft/reports/default.mspx (accessed April 23, 2010); "Microsoft Third Quarter Earnings Call," www.microsoft.com/msft/earnings/fy10/earn_rel_q3_10.mspx (accessed April 30, 2010); Thompson Reuters Street Events, "MCD – Q4 2009 McDonald's Corporate Earnings Conference Call," www.streetevents.com, January 2010 (transcribed version of Webcast accessed April 30, 2010, through InvesText database).

performance targets for each of the organization's separate businesses, product lines, functional departments, and individual work units. Company performance can't reach full potential unless each organizational unit sets and pursues performance targets that contribute directly to the desired companywide outcomes and results. Objective-setting is thus a *top-down process* that must extend to the lowest organizational levels. And it means that each organizational unit must take care to set performance targets that support—rather than conflict with or negate—the achievement of companywide strategic and financial objectives.

The ideal situation is a team effort in which each organizational unit strives to produce results in its area of responsibility that contribute to the achievement of the company's performance targets and strategic vision. Such consistency signals that organizational units know their strategic role and are on board in helping the company move down the chosen strategic path and produce the desired results.

STAGE 3: CRAFTING A STRATEGY

The task of stitching a strategy together entails addressing a series of hows: *how* to grow the business, *how* to please customers, *how* to outcompete rivals, *how* to respond to changing market conditions, *how* to manage each functional piece of the business, *how* to develop needed capabilities, and *how* to achieve strategic and financial objectives. It also means choosing among the various strategic alternatives—proactively searching for opportunities to do new things or to do existing things in new or better ways.[10] The faster a company's business environment is changing, the more critical it becomes for its managers to be good entrepreneurs in diagnosing the direction and force of the changes under way and in responding with timely adjustments in strategy. Strategy makers have to pay attention to early warnings of future change and be willing to experiment with dare-to-be-different ways to establish a market position in that future. When obstacles appear unexpectedly in a company's path, it is up to management to adapt rapidly and innovatively. *Masterful strategies come from doing things differently from competitors where it counts—out-innovating them, being more efficient, being more imaginative, adapting faster—rather than running with the herd.* Good strategy making is therefore inseparable from good business entrepreneurship. One cannot exist without the other.

Strategy Making Involves Managers at All Organizational Levels

A company's senior executives obviously have important strategy-making roles. The chief executive officer (CEO), as captain of the ship, carries the mantles of chief direction setter, chief objective setter, chief strategy maker, and chief strategy implementer for the total enterprise. Ultimate responsibility for *leading* the strategy-making, strategy-executing process rests with the CEO. In some enterprises the CEO or owner functions as strategic visionary and chief architect of strategy, personally deciding what the key elements of the company's strategy will be, although others may well assist with data gathering and analysis and the CEO may seek the advice of senior executives or board members. A CEO-centered approach

LO 3

Understand why the strategic initiatives taken at various organizational levels must be tightly coordinated to achieve companywide performance targets.

to strategy development is characteristic of small owner-managed companies and sometimes large corporations that were founded by the present CEO or that have a CEO with strong strategic leadership skills. Steve Jobs at Apple, Andrea Jung at Avon, and Howard Schultz at Starbucks are prominent examples of corporate CEOs who have wielded a heavy hand in shaping their company's strategy.

Even here, however, it is a mistake to view strategy making as a *top* management function, the exclusive province of owner-entrepreneurs, CEOs, other senior executives, and board members. The more a company's operations cut across different products, industries, and geographic areas, the more that headquarters executives have little option but to delegate considerable strategy-making authority to down-the-line managers in charge of particular subsidiaries, divisions, product lines, geographic sales offices, distribution centers, and plants. On-the-scene managers who oversee specific operating units can be reliably counted on to have more detailed command of the strategic issues and choices for the particular operating unit under their supervision—knowing the prevailing market and competitive conditions, customer requirements and expectations, and all the other relevant aspects affecting the several strategic options available. Managers with day-to-day familiarity of, and authority over, a specific operating unit thus have a big edge over headquarters executives in making wise strategic choices for their operating unit.

> **CORE CONCEPT**
>
> In most companies, crafting and executing strategy is a *collaborative team effort* in which every manager has a role for the area he or she heads. It is flawed thinking to view crafting and executing strategy as something only high-level managers do.

Take, for example, a company like General Electric, a \$183 billion global corporation with 325,000 employees, operations in some 100 countries, and businesses that include jet engines, lighting, power generation, electric transmission and distribution equipment, housewares and appliances, medical equipment, media and entertainment, locomotives, security devices, water purification, and financial services. While top-level headquarters executives may well be personally involved in shaping GE's *overall* strategy and fashioning *important* strategic moves, it doesn't follow that a few senior executives in GE's headquarters have either the expertise or a sufficiently detailed understanding of all the relevant factors to wisely craft all the strategic initiatives taken for hundreds of subsidiaries and thousands of products. They simply cannot know enough about the situation in every GE organizational unit to decide on every strategy detail and direct every strategic move made in GE's worldwide organization. Rather, it takes involvement on the part of GE's whole management team—top executives, business group heads, the heads of specific business units and product categories, and key managers in plants, sales offices, and distribution centers—to craft the thousands of strategic initiatives that end up constituting the whole of GE's strategy.

The *level* of strategy also has a bearing on who participates in crafting strategy. In diversified companies, where multiple businesses have to be managed, the strategy-making task involves four distinct levels of strategy. Each of these involves different facets of the company's overall strategy and calls for the participation of different types of managers, as shown in Figure 2.2.

1. *Corporate strategy* is strategy at the multibusiness level—how to achieve a competitive edge through a multibusiness, multimarket strategy. It concerns how to boost the combined performance of *the set of businesses* the company has diversified into and the means of capturing cross-business synergies and turning them into competitive advantage. It addresses the questions of what businesses to hold or divest, which new markets to enter, and what mode of

Figure 2.2   A Company's Strategy-Making Hierarchy

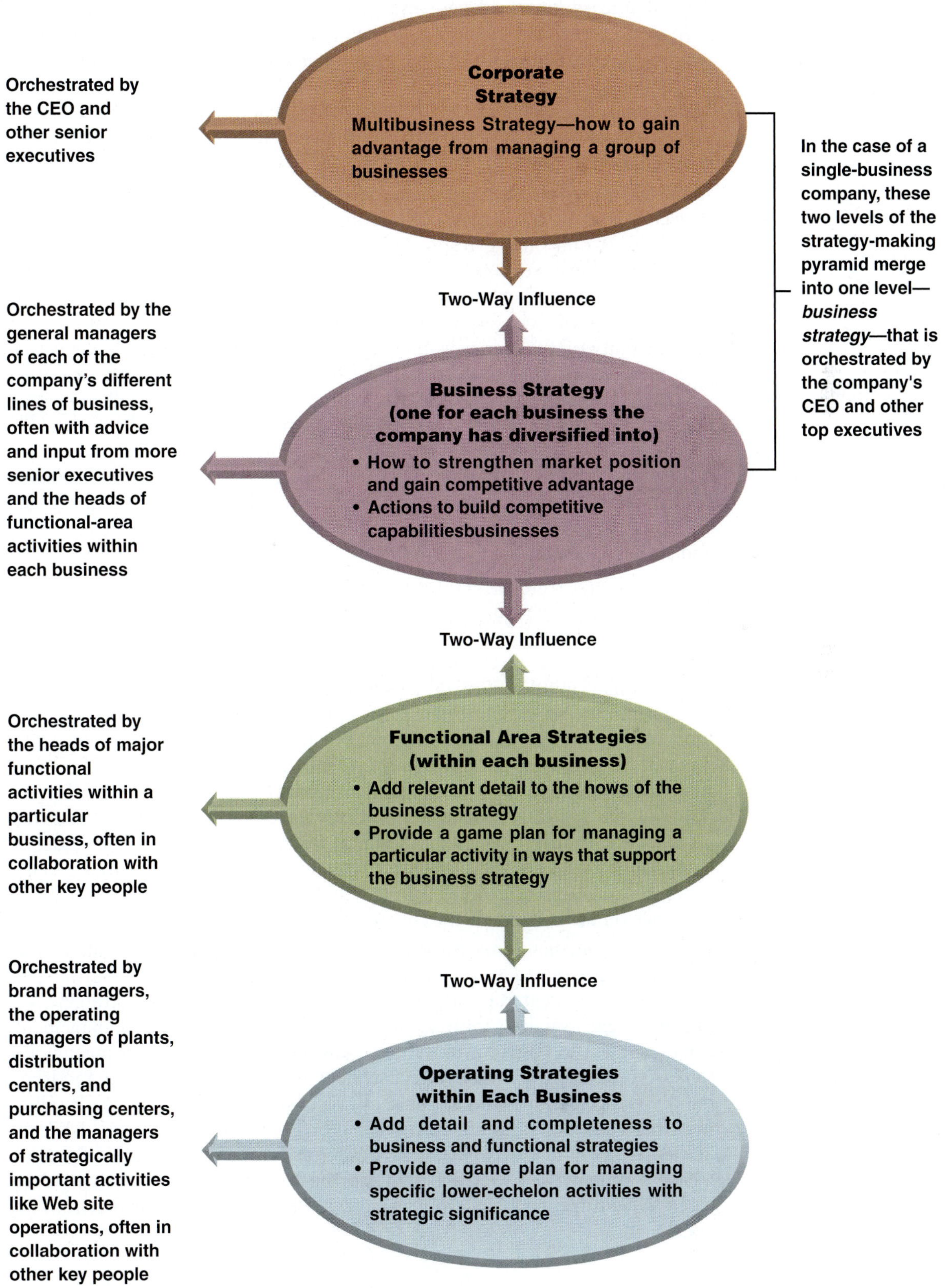

Orchestrated by
the CEO and
other senior
executives

**Corporate
Strategy**

Multibusiness Strategy—how to gain
advantage from managing a group of
businesses

In the case of a
single-business
company, these
two levels of the
strategy-making
pyramid merge
into one level—
*business
strategy*—that is
orchestrated by
the company's
CEO and other
top executives

Two-Way Influence

Orchestrated by the
general managers
of each of the
company's different
lines of business,
often with advice
and input from more
senior executives
and the heads of
functional-area
activities within
each business

**Business Strategy
(one for each business the
company has diversified into)**
• How to strengthen market position
  and gain competitive advantage
• Actions to build competitive
  capabilitiesbusinesses

Two-Way Influence

Orchestrated by
the heads of major
functional
activities within a
particular
business, often in
collaboration with
other key people

**Functional Area Strategies
(within each business)**
• Add relevant detail to the hows of the
  business strategy
• Provide a game plan for managing a
  particular activity in ways that support
  the business strategy

Two-Way Influence

Orchestrated by
brand managers,
the operating
managers of plants,
distribution
centers, and
purchasing centers,
and the managers
of strategically
important activities
like Web site
operations, often in
collaboration with
other key people

**Operating Strategies
within Each Business**
• Add detail and completeness to
  business and functional strategies
• Provide a game plan for managing
  specific lower-echelon activities with
  strategic significance

entry to employ (e.g., through an acquisition, strategic alliance, or franchising). It concerns the *scope* of the firm and thus includes diversification strategies, vertical integration strategies, and geographic expansion strategies. Senior corporate executives normally have lead responsibility for devising corporate strategy and for choosing among whatever recommended actions bubble up from the organization below. Key business-unit heads may also be influential regarding issues related to the businesses they head. Major strategic decisions are usually reviewed and approved by the company's board of directors. We will look deeper into crafting corporate strategy in Chapter 8.

2.   *Business strategy* is strategy at the level of a single line of business—one that competes in a relatively well-defined industry or market domain. The key focus is on crafting responses to changing market circumstances and initiating actions to develop strong competitive capabilities, build competitive advantage, strengthen market position, and enhance performance. Orchestrating the development of business-level strategy is typically the responsibility of the manager in charge of the business, although corporate-level managers may be influential. The business head has at least two other strategy-related roles: (1) seeing that lower-level strategies are well conceived, consistent, and adequately matched to the overall business strategy and (2) getting major business-level strategic moves approved by corporate-level officers and keeping them informed of emerging strategic issues. In diversified companies, business-unit heads have the additional obligation of making sure business-level objectives and strategy conform to corporate-level objectives and strategy themes.

3.   *Functional-area strategies* concern the actions and approaches employed in managing particular functions within a business—like R&D, production, sales and marketing, customer service, and finance. A company's marketing strategy, for example, represents the managerial game plan for running the sales and marketing part of the business. A company's product development strategy represents the game plan for keeping the company's product lineup in tune with what buyers are looking for. The primary role of functional strategies is to flesh out the details of a company's business strategy. Lead responsibility for functional strategies within a business is normally delegated to the heads of the respective functions, with the general manager of the business having final approval. Since the different functional-level strategies must be compatible with the overall business strategy and with one another to have beneficial impact, the general business manager may at times exert stronger influence on the content of the functional strategies.

4.   *Operating strategies* concern the relatively narrow strategic initiatives and approaches for managing key operating units (e.g., plants, distribution centers, purchasing centers) and specific operating activities with strategic significance (e.g., quality control, materials purchasing, brand management, Internet sales). A distribution center manager of a company promising customers speedy delivery must have a strategy to ensure that finished goods are rapidly turned around and shipped out to customers once they are received from the company's manufacturing facilities. Operating strategies, while of limited scope, add further detail to functional strategies and to the overall business strategy. Lead responsibility for operating strategies is usually delegated to frontline managers, subject to review and approval by higher-ranking managers.

Even though operating strategy is at the bottom of the strategy-making hierarchy, its importance should not be downplayed. A major plant that fails in its strategy to achieve production volume, unit cost, and quality targets can damage the company's reputation for quality products and undercut the achievement of company sales and profit objectives. Frontline managers are thus an important part of an organization's strategy-making team. One cannot reliably judge the strategic importance of a given action simply by the strategy level or location within the managerial hierarchy where it is initiated.

In single-business enterprises, the corporate and business levels of strategy making merge into one level—business strategy—because the strategy for the whole company involves only one distinct line of business. Thus a single-business enterprise has three levels of strategy: business strategy for the company as a whole, functional-area strategies for each main area within the business, and operating strategies undertaken by lower-echelon managers to flesh out strategically significant aspects of the company's business and functional-area strategies. Proprietorships, partnerships, and owner-managed enterprises may have only one or two strategy-making levels since their strategy-making process can be handled by just a few key people. The larger and more diverse the operations of an enterprise, the more points of strategic initiative it has and the more levels of management that have a significant strategy-making role.

The overall point is this: Regardless of the type of enterprise and whether the strategy is primarily deliberate or primarily emergent, crafting strategy involves managers in various positions and at various organizational levels. And while managers farther down in the managerial hierarchy obviously have a narrower, more specific strategy-making role than managers closer to the top, the important understanding is that in most of today's companies *every company manager typically has a strategy-making role—ranging from minor to major—for the area he or she heads.* Hence any notion that an organization's strategists are at the top of the management hierarchy and that midlevel and frontline personnel merely carry out the strategic directives of senior managers needs to be cast aside. In companies with wide-ranging operations, it is far more accurate to view strategy making as a *collaborative team effort* involving managers (and sometimes other key employees) down through the whole organizational hierarchy. A valuable strength of collaborative strategy making is that the team of people charged with crafting the strategy include the very people who will also be charged with implementing and executing it. Giving people an influential stake in crafting the strategy they must later help execute not only builds motivation and commitment but also enhances accountability at multiple levels of management—the excuse of "It wasn't my idea to do this" won't fly.

> In most companies, crafting strategy is a *collaborative team effort* that includes managers in various positions and at various organizational levels. Crafting strategy is rarely something only high-level executives do.

A Strategic Vision + Objectives + Strategy = A Strategic Plan

Developing a strategic vision and mission, setting objectives, and crafting a strategy are basic direction-setting tasks. They map out where a company is headed, its purpose, the targeted strategic and financial outcomes, the basic business model, and the competitive moves and internal action approaches to be used in achieving the desired business results. Together, they constitute a **strategic plan** for coping with industry conditions, outcompeting rivals, meeting objectives, and making progress toward the strategic vision.[11] Typically, a strategic plan includes a commitment to allocate resources to the plan and specifies a time period for achieving goals (usually three to five years).

In some companies, the strategic plan is focused around achieving exceptionally bold strategic objectives—stretch goals requiring resources that are well beyond the current means of the company. This type of strategic plan is more the expression of a **strategic intent** to rally the organization through an *unshakable—often obsessive—commitment* to do whatever it takes to acquire the resources and achieve the goals. Nike's strategic intent during the 1960s was to overtake Adidas—an objective far beyond Nike's means at the time. Starbucks strategic intent is to make the Starbucks brand the world's most recognized and respected brand.

In companies that do regular strategy reviews and develop explicit strategic plans, the strategic plan usually ends up as a written document that is circulated to most managers and perhaps selected employees. Near-term performance targets are the part of the strategic plan most often spelled out explicitly and communicated to managers and employees. A number of companies summarize key elements of their strategic plans in the company's annual report to shareholders, in postings on their Web sites, or in statements provided to the business media, whereas others, perhaps for reasons of competitive sensitivity, make only vague, general statements about their strategic plans.[12] In small, privately owned companies, it is rare for strategic plans to exist in written form. Small-company strategic plans tend to reside in the thinking and directives of owners/executives, with aspects of the plan being revealed in meetings and conversations with company personnel, and in the understandings and commitments among managers and key employees about where to head, what to accomplish, and how to proceed.

STAGE 4: EXECUTING THE STRATEGY

Managing the implementation of a strategy is an operations-oriented, make-things-happen activity aimed at performing core business activities in a strategy-supportive manner. It is easily the most demanding and time-consuming part of the strategy management process. Converting strategic plans into actions and results tests a manager's ability to direct organizational action, motivate people, build and strengthen company competencies and competitive capabilities, create and nurture a strategy-supportive work climate, and meet or beat performance targets. Initiatives to put the strategy in place and execute it proficiently have to be launched and managed on many organizational fronts.

Management's action agenda for executing the chosen strategy emerges from assessing what the company will have to do to achieve the targeted financial and strategic performance. Each company manager has to think through the answer to "What has to be done in my area to execute my piece of the strategic plan, and what actions should I take to get the process under way?" How much internal change is needed depends on how much of the strategy is new, how far internal practices and competencies deviate from what the strategy requires, and how well the present work climate/culture supports good strategy execution. Depending on the amount of internal change involved, full implementation and proficient execution of company strategy (or important new pieces thereof) can take several months to several years.

In most situations, managing the strategy execution process includes the following principal aspects:

- Staffing the organization with the needed skills and expertise.
- Building and strengthening strategy-supporting resources and competitive capabilities.
- Organizing the work effort along the lines of best practice.
- Allocating ample resources to the activities critical to strategic success.
- Ensuring that policies and procedures facilitate rather than impede effective strategy execution.
- Installing information and operating systems that enable company personnel to carry out their roles effectively and efficiently.
- Motivating people and tying rewards and incentives directly to the achievement of performance objectives.
- Creating a company culture and work climate conducive to successful strategy execution.
- Exerting the internal leadership needed to propel implementation forward and drive continuous improvement of the strategy execution processes.

Good strategy execution requires diligent pursuit of operating excellence. It is a job for a company's whole management team. Success hinges on the skills and cooperation of operating managers who can push for needed changes in their organizational units and consistently deliver good results. Management's handling of the strategy implementation process can be considered successful if things go smoothly enough that the company meets or beats its strategic and financial performance targets and shows good progress in achieving management's strategic vision.

STAGE 5: EVALUATING PERFORMANCE AND INITIATING CORRECTIVE ADJUSTMENTS

The fifth component of the strategy management process—monitoring new external developments, evaluating the company's progress, and making corrective adjustments—is the trigger point for deciding whether to continue or change the company's vision and mission, objectives, strategy, and/or strategy execution methods.[13] As long as the company's strategy continues to pass the three tests of a winning strategy (good fit, competitive advantage, strong performance), company executives may well decide to stay the course. Simply fine-tuning the strategic plan and continuing with efforts to improve strategy execution are sufficient.

However, whenever a company encounters disruptive changes in its environment, questions need to be raised about the appropriateness of its direction and strategy. If a company experiences a downturn in its market position or persistent shortfalls in performance, then company managers are obligated to ferret out the causes—do they relate to poor strategy, poor strategy execution, or both?—and take timely corrective action. A company's direction, objectives, and strategy have to be revisited anytime external or internal conditions warrant. It is to be expected that a company will modify its strategic vision, direction, objectives, and strategy over time.

Likewise, it is not unusual for a company to find that one or more aspects of its strategy execution are not going as well as intended. Proficient strategy execution is always the product of much organizational learning. It is achieved unevenly—coming quickly in some areas and proving nettlesome in others. It is both normal and desirable to periodically assess strategy execution to determine which aspects are working well and which need improving. Successful strategy execution entails vigilantly searching for ways to improve and then making corrective adjustments whenever and wherever it is useful to do so.

> A company's vision and mission, objectives, strategy, and approach to strategy execution are never final; managing strategy is an ongoing process.

CORPORATE GOVERNANCE: THE ROLE OF THE BOARD OF DIRECTORS IN THE STRATEGY-CRAFTING, STRATEGY-EXECUTING PROCESS

LO 5

Become aware of the role and responsibility of a company's board of directors in overseeing the strategic management process.

Although senior managers have *lead responsibility* for crafting and executing a company's strategy, it is the duty of a company's board of directors to exercise strong oversight and see that the five tasks of strategic management are conducted in a manner that is in the best interests of shareholders and other stakeholders.[14] A company's board of directors has four important obligations to fulfill:

1. *Critically appraise the company's direction, strategy, and business approaches.* Board members must ask probing questions and draw on their business acumen to make independent judgments about whether strategy proposals have been adequately analyzed and whether proposed strategic actions appear to have greater promise than alternatives. Asking incisive questions is usually sufficient to test whether the case for management's proposals is compelling and to exercise vigilant oversight. However, when the company's strategy is failing or is plagued with faulty execution, and certainly when there is a precipitous collapse in profitability, board members have a duty to be more proactive, expressing their concerns about the validity of the strategy and/or operating methods, initiating debate about the company's strategic path, having one-on-one discussions with key executives and other board members, and perhaps directly intervening as a group to alter the company's executive leadership and, ultimately, its strategy and business approaches.

2. *Evaluate the caliber of senior executives' strategic leadership skills.* The board is always responsible for determining whether the current CEO is doing a good job of strategic leadership.[15] The board must also evaluate the leadership skills of other senior executives, since the board must elect a successor when the incumbent CEO steps down, either going with an insider

or deciding that an outsider is needed. Evaluation of senior executives' skills is enhanced when outside directors visit company facilities and talk with company personnel to personally evaluate whether the strategy is on track, how well the strategy is being executed, and how well issues and problems are being addressed. Independent board members at GE visit operating executives at each major business unit once a year to assess the company's talent pool and stay abreast of emerging strategic and operating issues affecting the company's divisions.

3. *Institute a compensation plan for top executives that rewards them for actions and results that serve stakeholder interests—especially those of shareholders.* A basic principle of corporate governance is that the owners of a corporation (the shareholders) delegate managerial control to a team of executives who are compensated for their efforts on behalf of the owners. In their role as an *agent* of shareholders, corporate managers have a clear and unequivocal duty to make decisions and operate the company in accord with shareholder interests. (This does not mean disregarding the interests of other stakeholders—employees, suppliers, the communities in which the company operates, and society at large.) Most boards of directors have a compensation committee, composed entirely of directors from *outside* the company, to develop a salary and incentive compensation plan that rewards senior executives for boosting the company's *long-term* performance and growing the economic value of the enterprise on behalf of shareholders; the compensation committee's recommendations are presented to the full board for approval. But during the past 10 to 15 years, many boards of directors have done a poor job of ensuring that executive salary increases, bonuses, and stock option awards are tied tightly to performance measures that are truly in the long-term interests of shareholders. Rather, compensation packages at many companies have increasingly rewarded executives for short-term performance improvements that led to undue risk taking and compensation packages that, in the view of many people, were obscenely large. This has proved damaging to long-term company performance and has worked against shareholder interests—witness the huge loss of shareholder wealth that occurred at many financial institutions in 2008–2009 because of executive risk taking in subprime loans, credit default swaps, and collateralized mortgage securities in 2006–2007. As a consequence, the need to overhaul and reform executive compensation has become a hot topic in both public circles and corporate boardrooms. Illustration Capsule 2.4 discusses how weak governance at the mortgage companies Fannie Mae and Freddie Mac allowed opportunistic senior managers to boost their compensation while making decisions that imperiled the futures of the companies they managed.

4. *Oversee the company's financial accounting and financial reporting practices.* While top executives, particularly the company's CEO and CFO (chief financial officer), are primarily responsible for seeing that the company's financial statements fairly and accurately report the results of the company's operations, board members have a fiduciary duty to protect shareholders by exercising oversight of the company's financial practices. In addition, corporate boards must ensure that generally acceptable accounting principles (GAAP) are properly used in preparing the company's financial statements

Corporate Governance Failures at Fannie Mae and Freddie Mac

Executive compensation in the financial services industry during the mid-2000s ranks high among examples of failed corporate governance. Corporate governance at the government-sponsored mortgage giants Fannie Mae and Freddie Mac was particularly weak. The politically appointed boards at both enterprises failed to understand the risks of the subprime loan strategies being employed, did not adequately monitor the decisions of the CEO, did not exercise effective oversight of the accounting principles being employed (which led to inflated earnings), and approved executive compensation systems that allowed management to manipulate earnings to receive lucrative performance bonuses. The audit and compensation committees at Fannie Mae were particularly ineffective in protecting shareholder interests, with the audit committee allowing the company's financial officers to audit reports prepared under their direction and used to determine performance bonuses. Fannie Mae's audit committee also was aware of management's use of questionable accounting practices that reduced losses and recorded one-time gains to achieve financial targets linked to bonuses. In addition, the audit committee failed to investigate formal charges of accounting improprieties filed by a manager in the Office of the Controller.

Fannie Mae's compensation committee was equally ineffective. The committee allowed the company's CEO, Franklin Raines, to select the consultant employed to design the mortgage firm's executive compensation plan and agreed to a tiered bonus plan that would permit Raines and other senior managers to receive maximum bonuses without great difficulty. The compensation plan allowed Raines to earn performance-based bonuses of $52 million and total compensation of $90 million between 1999 and 2004. Raines was forced to resign in December 2004 when the Office of Federal Housing Enterprise Oversight found that Fannie Mae executives had fraudulently inflated earnings to receive bonuses linked to financial performance. Securities and Exchange Commission investigators also found evidence of improper accounting at Fannie Mae and required the company to restate its earnings between 2002 and 2004 by $6.3 billion.

Poor governance at Freddie Mac allowed its CEO and senior management to manipulate financial data to receive performance-based compensation as well. Freddie Mac CEO Richard Syron received 2007 compensation of $19.8 million while the mortgage company's share price declined from a high of $70 in 2005 to $25 at year-end 2007. During Syron's tenure as CEO, the company became embroiled in a multibillion-dollar accounting scandal, and Syron personally disregarded internal reports dating to 2004 that cautioned of an impending financial crisis at the company. Forewarnings within Freddie Mac and by federal regulators and outside industry observers proved to be correct, with loan underwriting policies at Freddie Mac and Fannie Mae leading to combined losses at the two firms in 2008 of more than $100 billion. The price of

(continued)

Freddie Mac's shares had fallen to below $1 by the time of Syron's resignation in September 2008.

Both organizations were placed into a conservatorship under the direction of the U.S. government in September 2008 and were provided bailout funds of nearly $60 billion by April 2009. In May 2009, Fannie Mae requested another $19 billion of the $200 billion committed by the U.S. government to cover the operating losses of the two government-sponsored mortgage firms. By June 2010, the bill for bailing out the two enterprises had risen to $145 billion, with the expectation that still more aid would be required to get them back on sound financial footing.

Sources: "Adding Up the Government's Total Bailout Tab," *New York Times Online,* February 4, 2009; Eric Dash, "Fannie Mae to Restate Results by $6.3 Billion because of Accounting," *New York Times Online,* December 7, 2006; Annys Shin, "Fannie Mae Sets Executive Salaries," *Washington Post,* February 9, 2006, p. D4; Scott DeCarlo, Eric Weiss, Mark Jickling, James R. Cristie, *Fannie Mae and Freddie Mac: Scandal in U.S. Housing* (Nova, 2006), pp. 266–86; "Chaffetz, Conyers, Smith, Issa and Bachus Call for FOIA to Apply to Fannie-Freddie," June 17, 2010 (June 2010 Archives), http://chaffetz.house.gov/2010/06/ (accessed June 24, 2010).

and that proper financial controls are in place to prevent fraud and misuse of funds. Virtually all boards of directors have an audit committee, always composed entirely of *outside directors* (*inside directors* hold management positions in the company and either directly or indirectly report to the CEO). The members of the audit committee have lead responsibility for overseeing the decisions of the company's financial officers and consulting with both internal and external auditors to ensure that financial reports are accurate and that adequate financial controls are in place. Faulty oversight of corporate accounting and financial reporting practices by audit committees and corporate boards during the early 2000s resulted in the federal investigation of more than 20 major corporations between 2000 and 2002. The investigations of such well-known companies as Global Crossing, Enron, Qwest Communications, and WorldCom found that upper management had employed fraudulent or unsound accounting practices to artificially inflate revenues, overstate assets, and reduce expenses. The scandals resulted in the conviction of a number of corporate executives and the passage of the Sarbanes-Oxley Act of 2002, which tightened financial reporting standards and created additional compliance requirements for public boards.

Every corporation should have a strong, independent board of directors that (1) is well informed about the company's performance, (2) guides and judges the CEO and other top executives, (3) has the courage to curb management actions the board believes are inappropriate or unduly risky, (4) certifies to shareholders that the CEO is doing what the board expects, (5) provides insight and advice to management, and (6) is intensely involved in debating the pros and cons of key decisions and actions.[16] Boards of directors that lack the backbone to challenge a strong-willed or "imperial" CEO or that rubber-stamp almost anything the CEO recommends without probing inquiry and debate (perhaps because the board is stacked with the CEO's cronies) abdicate their duty to represent and protect shareholder interests.

Effective corporate governance requires the board of directors to oversee the company's strategic direction, evaluate its senior executives, handle executive compensation, and oversee financial reporting practices.

KEY POINTS

The strategic management process consists of five interrelated and integrated stages:

1. *Developing a strategic vision* of the company's future, a *mission* that defines the company's current purpose, and a set of *core values* to guide the pursuit of the vision and mission. This managerial step provides direction for the company, motivates and inspires company personnel, aligns and guides actions throughout the organization, and communicates to stakeholders management's aspirations for the company's future.

2. *Setting objectives* to convert the vision and mission into performance targets and using the targeted results as yardsticks for measuring the company's performance. Objectives need to spell out *how much* of *what kind* of performance *by when.* Two broad types of objectives are required: *financial objectives* and *strategic objectives.* A *balanced-scorecard* approach provides a popular method for linking financial objectives to specific, measurable strategic objectives.

3. *Crafting a strategy* to achieve the objectives and move the company along the strategic course that management has charted. Crafting deliberate strategy calls for strategic analysis, based on the business model. Crafting emergent strategy is a learning-by-doing process involving experimentation. Who participates in the process of crafting strategy depends on (1) whether the process is emergent or deliberate and (2) the level of strategy concerned. Deliberate strategies are mostly top-down, while emergent strategies are bottom-up, although both cases require two-way interaction between different types of managers. In large, diversified companies, there are four levels of strategy, each of which involves a corresponding level of management: corporate strategy (multibusiness strategy), business strategy (strategy for individual businesses that compete in a single industry), functional-area strategies within each business (e.g., marketing, R&D, logistics), and operating strategies (for key operating units, such as manufacturing plants). Thus, strategy making is an inclusive, collaborative activity involving not only senior company executives but also the heads of major business divisions, functional-area managers, and operating managers on the frontlines. The larger and more diverse the operations of an enterprise, the more points of strategic initiative it has and the more levels of management that play a significant strategy-making role.

4. *Executing the chosen strategy* and converting the strategic plan into action. Managing the execution of strategy is an operations-oriented, make-things-happen activity aimed at shaping the performance of core business activities in a strategy-supportive manner. Management's handling of the strategy implementation process can be considered successful if things go smoothly enough that the company meets or beats its strategic and financial performance targets and shows good progress in achieving management's strategic vision.

5. *Monitoring developments, evaluating performance, and initiating corrective adjustments* in light of actual experience, changing conditions, new ideas, and new opportunities. This stage of the strategy management process is the trigger point for deciding whether to continue or change the company's vision and mission, objectives, strategy, and/or strategy execution methods.

The sum of a company's strategic vision and mission, objectives, and strategy constitutes a *strategic plan* for coping with industry conditions, outcompeting rivals, meeting objectives, and making progress toward the strategic vision. A company whose strategic plan is based around ambitious *stretch goals* that require an unwavering commitment to do whatever it takes to achieve them is said to have *strategic intent.*

Boards of directors have a duty to shareholders to play a vigilant role in overseeing management's handling of a company's strategy-making, strategy-executing process. This entails four important obligations: (1) Critically appraise the company's direction, strategy, and strategy execution, (2) evaluate the caliber of senior executives' strategic leadership skills, (3) institute a compensation plan for top executives that rewards them for actions and results that serve stakeholder interests—*especially those of shareholders,* and (4) ensure that the company issues accurate financial reports and has adequate financial controls.

ASSURANCE OF LEARNING EXERCISES

LO 1

1. Using the information in Table 2.1, critique the adequacy and merit of the following vision statements, listing effective elements and shortcomings. Rank the vision statements from best to worst once you complete your evaluation.

Vision Statement	Effective Elements	Shortcomings
Wells Fargo We want to satisfy all of our customers' financial needs, help them succeed financially, be the premier provider of financial services in every one of our markets, and be known as one of America's great companies.		
Hilton Hotels Corporation Our vision is to be the first choice of the world's travelers. Hilton intends to build on the rich heritage and strength of our brands by: • Consistently delighting our customers • Investing in our team members • Delivering innovative products and services • Continuously improving performance • Increasing shareholder value • Creating a culture of pride • Strengthening the loyalty of our constituents		
The Dental Products Division of 3M Corporation Become THE supplier of choice to the global dental professional markets, providing world-class quality and innovative products. [*Note:* All employees of the division wear badges bearing these words, and whenever a new product or business procedure is being considered, management asks "Is this representative of THE leading dental company?"]		

(continued)

Vision Statement	Effective Elements	Shortcomings
H. J. Heinz Company Be the world's premier food company, offering nutritious, superior tasting foods to people everywhere. Being the premier food company does not mean being the biggest but it does mean being the best in terms of consumer value, customer service, employee talent, and consistent and predictable growth.		
Chevron To be *the* global energy company most admired for its people, partnership and performance. Our vision means we: • provide energy products vital to sustainable economic progress and human development throughout the world; • are people and an organization with superior capabilities and commitment; • are the partner of choice; • deliver world-class performance; • earn the admiration of all our stakeholders—investors, customers, host governments, local communities and our employees—not only for the goals we achieve but how we achieve them.		

Source: Company Web sites and annual reports.

LO 2

2. Go to the company Web sites for Home Depot (http://corporate.homedepot.com/wps/portal); Avon (www.avoncompany.com/); and Yum Brands, a restaurant company that includes KFC, Pizza Hut, and Taco Bell (www.yum.com), to find some examples of strategic and financial objectives. Make a list of four objectives for each company, and indicate which of these are strategic and which are financial.

LO 5

3. Go to www.dell.com/leadership, and read the sections dedicated to Dell's board of directors and corporate governance. Is there evidence of effective governance at Dell in regard to (1) accurate financial reports and controls, (2) a critical appraisal of strategic action plans, (3) evaluation of the strategic leadership skills of the CEO, and (4) executive compensation?

EXERCISES FOR SIMULATION PARTICIPANTS

LO 1, LO 2, LO 3

1. Meet with your co-managers and prepare a strategic vision statement for your company. It should be at least one sentence long and no longer than a brief paragraph. When you are finished, check to see if your vision statement is in compliance with the dos and don'ts set forth in Table 2.1. If not, revise it accordingly. What would be a good slogan that captures the essence of your strategic vision and that could be used to help communicate the vision to company personnel, shareholders, and other stakeholders?

2. What is your company's strategic intent? Write a sentence that expresses your company's strategic intent.

3. What are your company's financial objectives?

4. What are your company's strategic objectives?

5. What are the three or four key elements of your company's strategy?

ENDNOTES

[1] For a more in-depth discussion of the challenges of developing a well-conceived vision, as well as some good examples, see Hugh Davidson, *The Committed Enterprise: How to Make Vision and Values Work* (Oxford: Butterworth Heinemann, 2002), chap. 2; W. Chan Kim and Renée Mauborgne, "Charting Your Company's Future," *Harvard Business Review* 80, no. 6 (June 2002), pp. 77–83; James C. Collins and Jerry I. Porras, "Building Your Company's Vision," *Harvard Business Review* 74, no. 5 (September–October 1996), pp. 65–77; Jim Collins and Jerry Porras, *Built to Last: Successful Habits of Visionary Companies* (New York: HarperCollins, 1994), chap. 11; Michel Robert, *Strategy Pure and Simple II: How Winning Companies Dominate Their Competitors* (New York: McGraw-Hill, 1998), chaps. 2, 3 and 6.

[2] Davidson, *The Committed Enterprise,* pp. 20 and 54.

[3] Ibid., pp. 36, 54.

[4] As quoted in Charles H. House and Raymond L. Price, "The Return Map: Tracking Product Teams," *Harvard Business Review* 60, no. 1 (January–February 1991), p. 93.

[5] Robert S. Kaplan and David P. Norton, *The Strategy-Focused Organization* (Boston: Harvard Business School Press, 2001), p. 3. Also see Robert S. Kaplan and David P. Norton, *The Balanced Scorecard: Translating Strategy into Action* (Boston: Harvard Business School Press, 1996), chap. 1.

[6] Kaplan and Norton, p.7. Also see Kevin B. Hendricks, Larry Menor, and Christine Wiedman, "The Balanced Scorecard: To Adopt or Not to Adopt," *Ivey Business Journal* 69, no. 2 (November–December 2004), pp. 1–7; Sandy Richardson, "The Key Elements of Balanced Scorecard Success," *Ivey Business Journal* 69, no. 2 (November–December 2004), pp.7–9.

[7] Kaplan and Norton, *The Balanced Scorecard.*

[8] Information posted on the Web site of Bain and Company, www.bain.com (accessed May 27, 2009).

[9] Information posted on the Web site of Balanced Scorecard Institute, http://www.balancedscorecard.org/ (accessed May 27, 2009).

[10] For a fuller discussion of strategy as an entrepreneurial process, see Henry Mintzberg, Bruce Ahlstrand, and Joseph Lampel, *Strategy Safari: A Guided Tour through the Wilds of Strategic Management* (New York: Free Press, 1998), chap. 5. Also see Bruce Barringer and Allen C. Bluedorn, "The Relationship between Corporate Entrepreneurship and Strategic Management," *Strategic Management Journal* 20 (1999), pp. 421–44; Jeffrey G. Covin and Morgan P. Miles, "Corporate Entrepreneurship and the Pursuit of Competitive Advantage," *Entrepreneurship: Theory and Practice* 23, no. 3 (Spring 1999), pp. 47–63; David A. Garvin and Lynned C. Levesque, "Meeting the Challenge of Corporate Entrepreneurship," *Harvard Business Review* 84, no. 10 (October 2006), pp. 102–12.

[11] For an excellent discussion of why a strategic plan needs to be more than a list of bullet points and should in fact tell an engaging, insightful, stage-setting story that lays out the industry and competitive situation as well as the vision, objectives, and strategy, see Gordon Shaw, Robert Brown, and Philip Bromiley, "Strategic Stories: How 3M Is Rewriting Business Planning," *Harvard Business Review* 76, no. 3 (May–June 1998), pp. 41–50.

[12] In many companies, there is often confusion or ambiguity about exactly what a company's strategy is; see David J. Collis and Michael G. Rukstad, "Can You Say What Your Strategy Is?" *Harvard Business Review* 86, no. 4 (April 2008), pp. 82–90.

[13] For an excellent discussion of why effective strategic leadership on the part of senior executives involves continuous re-creation of a company's strategy, see Cynthia A. Montgomery, "Putting Leadership Back into Strategy," *Harvard Business Review* 86, no. 1 (January 2008), pp. 54–60.

[14] For a timely and insightful discussion of the strategic and leadership functions of a company's board of directors, see Jay W. Lorsch and Robert C. Clark, "Leading from the Boardroom," *Harvard Business Review* 86, no. 4 (April 2008), pp. 105–11.

[15] For a deeper discussion of this function, see Stephen P. Kaufman, "Evaluating the CEO," *Harvard Business Review* 86, no. 10 (October 2008), pp. 53–57.

[16] For a discussion of what it takes for the corporate governance system to function properly, see David A. Nadler, "Building Better Boards," *Harvard Business Review* 82, no. 5 (May 2004), pp. 102–5; Cynthia A. Montgomery and Rhonda Kaufman, "The Board's Missing Link," *Harvard Business Review* 81, no. 3 (March 2003), pp. 86–93; John Carver, "What Continues to Be Wrong with Corporate Governance and How to Fix It," *Ivey Business Journal* 68, no. 1 (September–October 2003), pp. 1–5. See also Gordon Donaldson, "A New Tool for Boards: The Strategic Audit," *Harvard Business Review* 73, no. 4 (July–August 1995), pp. 99–107.

CHAPTER 3

EVALUATING A COMPANY'S EXTERNAL ENVIRONMENT

Analysis is the critical starting point of strategic thinking.

—Kenichi Ohmae
Consultant and Author

Things are always different—the art is figuring out which differences matter.

—Laszlo Birinyi
Investments Manager

In essence, the job of a strategist is to understand and cope with competition.

—Michael Porter
Harvard Business School professor and Cofounder of Monitor Consulting

LEARNING OBJECTIVES

LO 1. Gain command of the basic concepts and analytical tools widely used to diagnose the competitive conditions in a company's industry.

LO 2. Learn how to diagnose the factors shaping industry dynamics and to forecast their effects on future industry profitability.

LO 3. Become adept at mapping the market positions of key groups of industry rivals.

LO 4. Understand why in-depth evaluation of a business's strengths and weaknesses in relation to the specific industry conditions it confronts is an essential prerequisite to crafting a strategy that is well-matched to its external situation.

In Chapter 1, we learned that one of the three central questions that managers must address in evaluating their business prospects is "What's the company's present situation?" Two facets of a company's situation are especially pertinent: (1) competitive conditions in the industry in which the company operates—its external environment; and (2) the company's resources and organizational capabilities—its internal environment.

Insightful diagnosis of a company's external and internal environments is a prerequisite for managers to succeed in crafting a strategy that is an excellent *fit* with the company's situation—the first test of a winning strategy. As depicted in Figure 3.1, the task of crafting a strategy should always begin with an appraisal of the company's external environment and internal environment (as a basis for deciding on a long-term direction and developing a strategic vision), then move toward an evaluation of the most promising alternative strategies and business models, and culminate in choosing a specific strategy.

This chapter presents the concepts and analytical tools for zeroing in on those aspects of a company's external environment that should be considered in making strategic choices about where and how to compete. Attention centers on the competitive arena in which a company operates, the drivers of market change, the market positions of rival companies, and the factors that determine competitive success. In Chapter 4 we explore the methods of evaluating a company's internal circumstances and competitive capabilities.

Figure 3.1   **From Thinking Strategically about the Company's Situation to Choosing a Strategy**

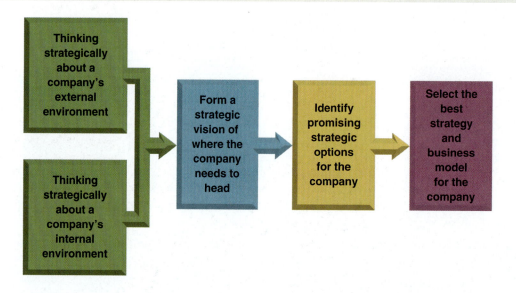

THE STRATEGICALLY RELEVANT COMPONENTS OF A COMPANY'S MACRO-ENVIRONMENT

CORE CONCEPT

The **macro-environment** encompasses the broad environmental context in which a company's industry is situated.

Every company operates in a larger environment that goes well beyond just the industry in which it operates; this **"macro-environment"** includes seven principal components: population demographics; societal values and lifestyles; political, legal, and regulatory factors; the natural environment and ecological factors; technological factors; general economic conditions; and global forces. Each of these components has the potential to affect the firm's more immediate industry and competitive environment, although some are likely to have a more important effect than others (see Figure 3.2). Since macroeconomic factors affect different industries in different ways and to different degrees, it is important for managers to determine which of these represent the most *strategically relevant factors* outside the firm's industry boundaries. By *strategically relevant,* we mean important enough to have a bearing on the decisions the company ultimately makes about its direction, objectives, strategy, and business model. Strategically relevant influences coming from the outer ring of the external environment can sometimes have a high impact on a company's business situation and have a very significant impact on the company's direction and strategy. For example, the strategic opportunities of cigarette producers to grow their businesses are greatly reduced by antismoking ordinances, the decisions of governments to impose higher cigarette taxes, and the growing cultural stigma attached to smoking. Motor vehicle companies must adapt their strategies to customer concerns about high gasoline prices and to environmental concerns about

Figure 3.2   The Components of a Company's Macro-Environment

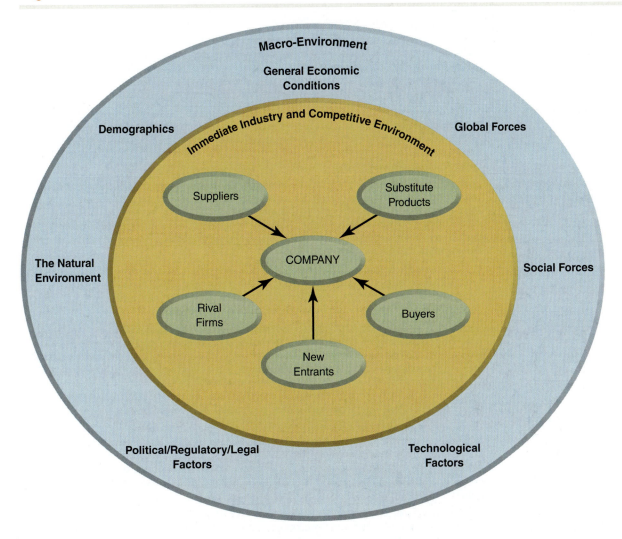

carbon emissions. Companies in the food processing, restaurant, sports, and fitness industries have to pay special attention to changes in lifestyles, eating habits, leisure-time preferences, and attitudes toward nutrition and fitness in fashioning their strategies. Table 3.1 provides a brief description of the components of the macro-environment and some examples of the industries or business situations that they might affect.

Happenings in the outer ring of the environment may occur rapidly or slowly, with or without advance warning. As company managers scan the external environment, they must be alert for potentially important outer-ring developments, assess their impact and influence, and adapt the company's direction and strategy as needed. However, the factors and forces in a company's environment having the *biggest* strategy-shaping impact typically pertain to the company's immediate industry and competitive environment—competitive pressures, the actions of rival firms, buyer behavior, supplier-related considerations, and so on. Consequently, it is on a company's industry and competitive environment that we concentrate the bulk of our attention in this chapter.

Table 3.1   The Seven Components of the Macro-Environment

Component	Description
Demographics	Demographics includes the size, growth rate, and age distribution of different sectors of the population. It includes the geographic distribution of the population, the distribution of income across the population, and trends in these factors. Population demographics can have large implications for industries such as health care, where costs and service needs vary with demographic factors such as age and income distribution.
Social forces	Social forces include the societal values, attitudes, cultural factors, and lifestyles that impact businesses. Social forces vary by locale and change over time. An example includes the attitudes toward gender roles and diversity in the workforce. Another example is the trend toward healthier lifestyles, which can shift spending toward exercise equipment and health clubs and away from alcohol and snack foods.
Political, legal, and regulatory factors	These factors include political policies and processes, as well as the regulations and laws with which companies must comply. Examples include labor laws, antitrust laws, tax policy, regulatory policies, the political climate, and the strength of institutions such as the court system. Some political factors, such as banking deregulation, are industry-specific. Others, such as minimum wage legislation, affect certain types of industries (low-wage, labor-intensive industries) more than others.
Natural environment	This includes ecological and environmental forces such as weather, climate, climate change, and associated factors like water shortages. These factors can directly impact industries such as insurance, farming, energy production, and tourism. They may have an indirect but substantial effect on other industries such as transportation and utilities.
Technological factors	Technological factors include the pace of technological change and technical developments that have the potential for wide-ranging effects on society, such as genetic engineering, the rise of the Internet, and changes in communication technologies. They include activities and institutions involved in creating new knowledge and controlling the use of technology, such as R&D consortia, university-sponsored technology incubators, patent and copyright laws, and government control over the Internet. Technological change can encourage the birth of new industries, such as those based on nanotechnology, and disrupt others, such as the recording industry.
Global forces	Global forces include conditions and changes in global markets, including political events and policies toward international trade. They also include sociocultural practices and the institutional environment in which global markets operate. Global forces influence the degree of international trade and investment through such mechanisms as trade barriers, tariffs, import restrictions, and trade sanctions. Their effects are often industry-specific, such as import restrictions on steel.
General economic conditions	General economic conditions include economic factors at the local, state, national, or international level that affect firms and industries. These include the rate of economic growth, unemployment rates, inflation rates, interest rates, trade deficits or surpluses, savings rates, and per capita domestic product. Economic factors also include conditions in the markets for stocks and bonds, which can affect consumer confidence and discretionary income. Some industries, such as construction, are particularly vulnerable to economic downturns but are positively affected by factors such as low interest rates. Others, such as discount retailing, may benefit when general economic conditions weaken, as consumers become more price-conscious.

THINKING STRATEGICALLY ABOUT A COMPANY'S INDUSTRY AND COMPETITIVE ENVIRONMENT

To gain a deep understanding of a company's industry and competitive environment, managers do not need to gather all the information they can find and spend lots of time digesting it. Rather, they can focus more directly on using some well-defined concepts and analytical tools to get clear answers to seven questions:

1. Does the industry offer attractive opportunities for growth?
2. What kinds of competitive forces are industry members facing, and how strong is each force?
3. What factors are driving changes in the industry, and what impact will these changes have on competitive intensity and industry profitability?
4. What market positions do industry rivals occupy—who is strongly positioned and who is not?
5. What strategic moves are rivals likely to make next?
6. What are the key factors for competitive success in the industry?
7. Does the industry offer good prospects for attractive profits?

Analysis-based answers to these seven questions provide managers with the understanding needed to craft a strategy that fits the company's external situation and positions the company to best meet its competitive challenges. The remainder of this chapter is devoted to describing the methods of obtaining solid answers to the seven questions and explaining how the nature of a company's industry and competitive environment weighs upon the strategic choices of company managers.

QUESTION 1: DOES THE INDUSTRY OFFER ATTRACTIVE OPPORTUNITIES FOR GROWTH?

Answering the question of whether or not an industry will offer the prospect of attractive profits begins with a consideration of whether it offers good opportunities for growth. Growth, of course, cannot guarantee profitability—a lesson that too many firms that have pursued growth for growth's sake have learned the hard way. But it is an indicator of how much customers value the industry's products (or services) and whether the industry demand is strong enough to support profitable sales growth.

Key economic indicators of an industry's growth prospects include market size, in terms of overall unit sales and sales volume, as well as the industry growth rate. Assessing the market size and growth rate will depend, however, on whether the industry is defined broadly or narrowly, in terms of its product or service characteristics. For example, the freight transport industry is far more inclusive than the air freight industry, and market size will vary accordingly. Market size and growth rates will also depend on where the geographic boundary lines are drawn (local, regional, national, or global). In addition, market size and growth rates often vary markedly by region (e.g., Europe versus Asia) and by demographic market segment (e.g., Gen Y versus baby boomers). Looking at the market in a variety of ways can help managers assess the various opportunities for growth and its limits.

One reason for differences among industries in the size of the market and the rate of growth stems from what is known as the "industry life cycle." This is the notion that industries commonly follow a general pattern of development and maturation, consisting of four stages: emergence, rapid growth, maturity, and decline.[1] The size of a market and its growth rate, then, depend on which stage of the life cycle best characterizes the industry in question.

QUESTION 2: WHAT KINDS OF COMPETITIVE FORCES ARE INDUSTRY MEMBERS FACING, AND HOW STRONG ARE THEY?

LO 1

Gain command of the basic concepts and analytical tools widely used to diagnose the competitive conditions in a company's industry.

The character and strength of the competitive forces operating in an industry are never the same from one industry to another. Far and away the most powerful and widely used tool for systematically diagnosing the principal competitive pressures in a market is the *five-forces model of competition.*[2] This model holds that the competitive forces affecting industry profitability go beyond rivalry among competing sellers and include pressures stemming from four coexisting sources. As depicted in Figure 3.3, the five competitive forces include (1) competition from *rival sellers,* (2) competition from *potential new entrants* to the industry, (3) competition from producers of *substitute products,* (4) *supplier* bargaining power, and (5) *customer* bargaining power.

Using the five-forces model to determine the nature and strength of competitive pressures in a given industry involves building the picture of competition in three steps:

- *Step 1:* For each of the five forces, identify the different parties involved, along with the specific factors that bring about competitive pressures.
- *Step 2:* Evaluate how strong the pressures stemming from each of the five forces are (strong, moderate to normal, or weak).
- *Step 3:* Determine whether the strength of the five competitive forces, overall, is conducive to earning attractive profits in the industry.

Competitive Pressures Created by the Rivalry among Competing Sellers

The strongest of the five competitive forces is often the market maneuvering for buyer patronage that goes on among rival sellers of a product or service. In effect, *a market is a competitive battlefield* where the contest among competitors is ongoing and dynamic. Each competing company endeavors to deploy whatever means in its business arsenal it believes will attract and retain buyers, strengthen its market position, and yield good profits. The challenge is to craft a competitive strategy that, at the very least, allows a company to hold its own against rivals and that, ideally, *produces a competitive edge over rivals.* But when one firm deploys a strategy or makes a new strategic move that produces good results, its rivals typically respond with offensive or defensive countermoves of their own. This pattern of action and reaction, move and countermove, produces a continually evolving competitive landscape where the market battle ebbs and flows, sometimes takes unpredictable twists and turns, and produces winners and losers.[3]

Competitive battles among rival sellers can assume many forms that extend well beyond lively price competition. For example, rivalrous firms may resort to such marketing tactics as special sales promotions, heavy advertising, rebates, or low-interest-rate financing to drum up additional sales. Active rivals may race one another to differentiate their products by offering better performance

Figure 3.3   The Five-Forces Model of Competition: A Key Analytical Tool

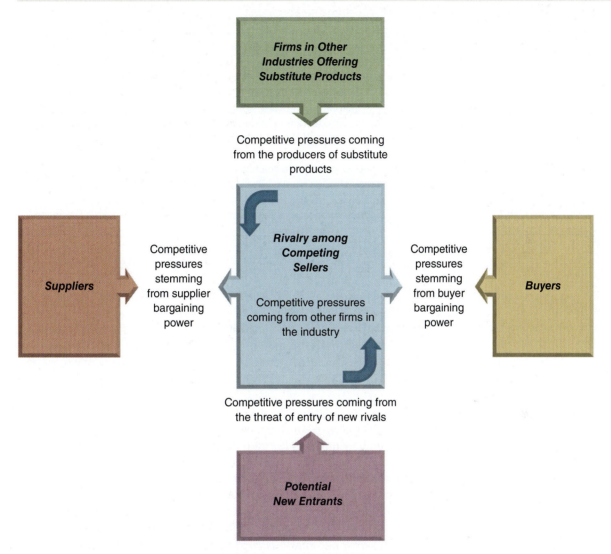

Sources: Adapted from Michael E. Porter, "How Competitive Forces Shape Strategy," *Harvard Business Review* 57, no. 2 (March–April 1979), pp. 137–45, and Michael E. Porter, "The Five Competitive Forces That Shape Strategy," *Harvard Business Review* 86, no. 1 (January 2008), pp. 80–86.

features or higher quality or improved customer service or a wider product selection. Rivals may also compete through the rapid introduction of next-generation products, frequent introduction of new or improved products, and efforts to build stronger dealer networks, establish positions in foreign markets, or otherwise expand distribution capabilities and market presence. Table 3.2 provides a sampling of the types of competitive weapons available to rivals, along with their primary effects.

The intensity of rivalry varies from industry to industry and depends on a number of identifiable factors. Figure 3.4 summarizes these factors, identifying those that intensify or weaken rivalry among direct competitors in an industry. A brief explanation of why these factors affect the degree of rivalry is in order:[4]

Table 3.2   Common "Weapons" for Competing with Rivals

Types of Competitive Weapons	Primary Effects
Price discounting, clearance sales, "blowout" sales	Lowers price (P), acts to boost total sales volume and market share, lowers profit margins per unit sold when price cuts are big and/or increases in sales volume are relatively small
Couponing, advertising items on sale	Acts to increase unit sales volume and total revenues, lowers price (P), increases unit costs (C), may lower profit margins per unit sold ($P - C$)
Advertising product or service characteristics, using ads to enhance a company's image or reputation	Boosts buyer demand, increases product differentiation and perceived value (V), acts to increase total sales volume and market share, may increase unit costs (C) and/or lower profit margins per unit sold
Innovating to improve product performance and quality	Acts to increase product differentiation and value (V), boosts buyer demand, acts to boost total sales volume, likely to increase unit costs (C)
Introducing new or improved features, increasing the number of styles or models to provide greater product selection	Acts to increase product differentiation and value (V), strengthens buyer demand, acts to boost total sales volume and market share, likely to increase unit costs (C)
Increasing customization of product or service	Acts to increase product differentiation and value (V), increases switching costs, acts to boost total sales volume, often increases unit costs (C)
Building a bigger, better dealer network	Broadens access to buyers, acts to boost total sales volume and market share, may increase unit costs (C)
Improving warranties, offering low-interest financing	Acts to increase product differentiation and value (V), increases unit costs (C), increases buyer costs to switch brands, acts to boost total sales volume and market share

- *Rivalry is stronger in markets where buyer demand is growing slowly or declining, and it is weaker in fast-growing markets.* Rapidly expanding buyer demand produces enough new business for all industry members to grow without using volume-boosting sales tactics to draw customers away from rival enterprises. But in markets where buyer demand is growing only 1 to 2 percent or is shrinking, companies anxious (or perhaps desperate) to gain more business typically employ price discounts, sales promotions, and other tactics to boost their sales volumes, sometimes to the point of igniting a fierce battle for market share.

- *Rivalry increases as it becomes less costly for buyers to switch brands.* The less expensive it is for buyers to switch their purchases from the seller of one brand to the seller of another brand, the easier it is for sellers to steal customers away from rivals. But the higher the costs buyers incur to switch brands, the less prone they are to brand switching. Switching costs include not only monetary costs but also the time, inconvenience, and psychological costs involved in switching brands. For example distributors and retailers may not switch to the brands of rival manufacturers because they are hesitant to sever long-standing supplier relationships, incur any technical support costs or retraining expenses in making the switchover, go to the trouble of testing the quality and reliability of the rival brand, or devote resources to marketing the new brand (especially if the brand is not well known).

- *Rivalry increases as the products of rival sellers become more alike, and it diminishes as the products of industry rivals become more strongly differentiated.* When the offerings of rivals are identical or weakly differentiated, buyers have less reason to be brand-loyal—a condition that makes it easier for rivals to convince

Figure 3.4 Factors Affecting the Strength of Rivalry

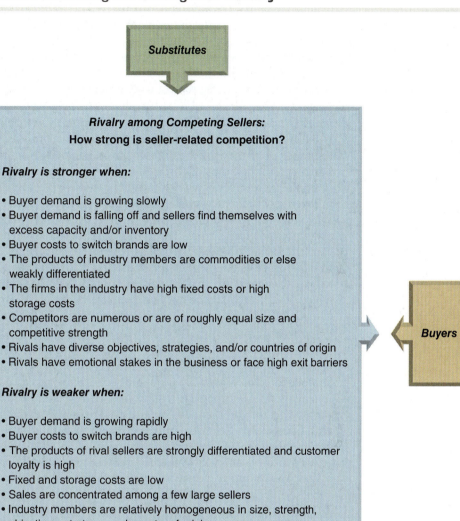

Substitutes

Suppliers

Buyers

Rivalry among Competing Sellers:
How strong is seller-related competition?

Rivalry is stronger when:

- Buyer demand is growing slowly
- Buyer demand is falling off and sellers find themselves with excess capacity and/or inventory
- Buyer costs to switch brands are low
- The products of industry members are commodities or else weakly differentiated
- The firms in the industry have high fixed costs or high storage costs
- Competitors are numerous or are of roughly equal size and competitive strength
- Rivals have diverse objectives, strategies, and/or countries of origin
- Rivals have emotional stakes in the business or face high exit barriers

Rivalry is weaker when:

- Buyer demand is growing rapidly
- Buyer costs to switch brands are high
- The products of rival sellers are strongly differentiated and customer loyalty is high
- Fixed and storage costs are low
- Sales are concentrated among a few large sellers
- Industry members are relatively homogeneous in size, strength, objectives, strategy, and country of origin
- Exit barriers are low

New Entrants

buyers to switch to their offerings. And since the brands of different sellers have comparable attributes, buyers can shop the market for the best deal and switch brands at will. On the other hand, strongly differentiated product offerings among rivals breed high brand loyalty on the part of buyers—because many buyers view the attributes of certain brands as more appealing or better suited to their needs. Strong brand attachments make it tougher for sellers to draw customers away from rivals. Unless meaningful numbers of buyers are open to considering new or different product attributes being offered by rivals, the high degree of brand loyalty that accompanies strong product differentiation works against fierce rivalry among competing sellers. *The degree of product differentiation also affects switching costs.* When the offerings of rivals are identical or weakly differentiated, it is usually easy and inexpensive for buyers to switch their purchases from one seller to another. But in the case of strongly differentiated brands with quite different features and functionality (like rival brands of cell phones), buyers may be reluctant to go through the brand-switching hassle.

- *Rivalry is more intense when there is unused production capacity, especially if the industry's product has high fixed costs or high storage costs.* Whenever a market is oversupplied (such that sellers have unutilized production capacity and/or too much inventory), the result is a "buyer's market" that intensifies rivalry perhaps even to the point of threatening the survival of competitively weak firms. A similar effect occurs when a product is perishable, seasonal, or costly to hold in inventory, since firms often engage in aggressive price cutting to ensure that they are not left with unwanted or costly inventories. Likewise, whenever fixed costs account for a large fraction of total cost so that unit costs are significantly lower at full capacity, firms come under significant pressure to cut prices to boost sales whenever they are operating below full capacity. Unused capacity imposes a significant cost-increasing penalty because there are fewer units over which to spread fixed costs. The pressure of high fixed or high storage costs can push rival firms into price concessions, special discounts, rebates, and other volume-boosting competitive tactics.

- *Rivalry intensifies as the number of competitors increases and as competitors become more equal in size and competitive strength.* The greater the number of competitors, the higher the probability that one or more companies will be busily engaged in a strategic offensive intended to enhance their market standing, thereby heating up competition and putting new pressures on rivals to respond with offensive or defensive moves of their own. In addition, when rivals are of comparable size and competitive strength, they can usually compete on a fairly equal footing—an evenly matched contest tends to be fiercer than a contest in which one or more industry members have commanding market shares and substantially greater resources and capabilities than their much smaller rivals.

- *Rivalry often becomes more intense—as well as more volatile and unpredictable—as the diversity of competitors increases in terms of long-term directions, objectives, strategies, and countries of origin.* A diverse group of sellers often contains one or more mavericks willing to try novel or rule-breaking market approaches, thus generating a livelier and less predictable competitive environment. Globally competitive markets usually boost the intensity of rivalry, especially when aggressors having lower costs or products with more attractive features are intent on gaining a strong foothold in new country markets.

- *Rivalry is stronger when high exit barriers keep unprofitable firms from leaving the industry.* In industries where the assets cannot easily be sold or transferred to other uses, where workers are entitled to job protection, or where owners are committed to remaining in business for personal reasons, failing firms tend to hold on longer than they might otherwise—even when they are bleeding red ink. This increases rivalry in two ways. Firms that are losing ground or in financial trouble often resort to deep price discounting that can trigger a price war and destabilize an otherwise attractive industry. In addition, high exit barriers result in an industry being more overcrowded than it would otherwise be, and this boosts rivalry and forces the weakest companies to scramble (often pushing them into desperate maneuvers of all kinds) to win sufficient sales and revenues to stay in business.

Rivalry can be characterized as *cutthroat* or *brutal* when competitors engage in protracted price wars or habitually undertake other aggressive strategic moves that prove mutually destructive to profitability. Rivalry can be considered *fierce* to *strong* when the battle for market share is so vigorous that the profit margins of most industry members are squeezed to bare-bones levels. Rivalry can be characterized as *moderate* or *normal* when the maneuvering among industry members, while lively and healthy, still allows most industry members to earn acceptable profits. Rivalry is *weak* when most companies in the industry are relatively well satisfied with their sales growth and market shares, rarely undertake offensives to steal customers away from one another, and—because of weak competitive forces—earn consistently good profits and returns on investment.

Competitive Pressures Associated with the Threat of New Entrants

New entrants to a market bring new production capacity, the desire to establish a secure place in the market, and sometimes substantial resources. Just how serious the competitive threat of entry is in a particular market depends on two classes of factors: *barriers to entry* and the *expected reaction of incumbent firms to new entry.*[5]

Industry incumbents that are willing and able to launch strong defensive maneuvers to maintain their positions can make it hard for a new entrant to gain a sufficient market foothold to survive and eventually become profitable. Entry candidates may have second thoughts if they conclude that existing firms are likely to give newcomers a hard time by offering price discounts (especially to the very customer groups a newcomer is seeking to attract), spending more on advertising, running frequent sales promotions, adding attractive new product features (to match or beat the newcomer's product offering), or providing additional services to customers. Such defensive maneuvers on the part of incumbents raise an entrant's costs and risks and have to be considered likely if one or more incumbents have previously tried to strongly contest the entry of new firms into the marketplace.

A barrier to entry exists whenever it is hard for a newcomer to break into the market and/or the economics of the business put a potential entrant at a disadvantage. The most widely encountered such barriers that entry candidates must hurdle include the following:[6]

- *Sizable economies of scale in production, distribution, advertising, or other areas of operation.* When incumbent companies enjoy cost advantages associated with large-scale operations, outsiders must either enter on a large scale (a costly and perhaps risky move) or accept a cost disadvantage and consequently lower profitability.
- *Significant cost advantages held by existing firms due to experience and learning curve effects.* In many industries, incumbent firms are favored by learning-based cost savings that accrue from experience in performing certain activities such as manufacturing or new product development or inventory management. This gives incumbent firms a first-mover advantage over new entrants that may be difficult to overcome.

- *Other cost advantages enjoyed by industry incumbents.* Existing industry members may also have other types of cost advantages that are hard for a newcomer to replicate. These can stem from (1) preferential access to raw materials, components, or other inputs, (2) cost savings accruing from patents or proprietary technology, (3) favorable locations, and (4) low fixed costs (because they have older facilities that have been mostly depreciated). The bigger the cost advantages of industry incumbents, the more risky it becomes for outsiders to attempt entry (since they will have to accept thinner profit margins or even losses until the cost disadvantages can be overcome).

- *Strong brand preferences and high degrees of customer loyalty.* The stronger the attachment of buyers to established brands, the harder it is for a newcomer to break into the marketplace. In such cases, a new entrant must have the financial resources to spend enough on advertising and sales promotion to overcome customer loyalties and build its own clientele. Establishing brand recognition and building customer loyalty can be a slow and costly process. In addition, if it is difficult or costly for a customer to switch to a new brand, a new entrant may have to offer buyers a discounted price or an extra margin of quality or service. Such barriers discourage new entry because they act to boost financial requirements and lower expected profit margins for new entrants.

- *Strong "network effects" in customer demand.* In industries where buyers are more attracted to a product when there are many other users of the product, there are said to be "network effects," since demand is higher the larger the network of users. Video game systems are an example, since users prefer to have the same systems as their friends so that they can play together on systems they all know and share games. When incumbents have a larger base of users, new entrants with comparable products face a serious disadvantage in attracting buyers.

- *High capital requirements.* The larger the total dollar investment needed to enter the market successfully, the more limited the pool of potential entrants. The most obvious capital requirements for new entrants relate to manufacturing facilities and equipment, introductory advertising and sales promotion campaigns, working capital to finance inventories and customer credit, and sufficient cash to cover start-up costs.

- *The difficulties of building a network of distributors or dealers and securing adequate space on retailers' shelves.* A potential entrant can face numerous distribution channel challenges. Wholesale distributors may be reluctant to take on a product that lacks buyer recognition. Retailers must be recruited and convinced to give a new brand ample display space and an adequate trial period. When existing sellers have strong, well-functioning distributor-dealer networks, a newcomer has an uphill struggle in squeezing its way into existing distribution channels. Potential entrants sometimes have to "buy" their way into wholesale or retail channels by cutting their prices to provide dealers and distributors with higher markups and profit margins or by giving them big advertising and promotional allowances. As a consequence, a potential entrant's own profits may be squeezed unless and until its product gains enough consumer acceptance that distributors and retailers are anxious to carry it.

- *Restrictive government policies.* Regulated industries like cable TV, telecommunications, electric and gas utilities, radio and television broadcasting, liquor retailing, and railroads entail government-controlled entry. Government agencies can also limit or even bar entry by requiring licenses and permits, such as the medallion required to drive a taxicab in New York City. Government-mandated safety regulations and environmental pollution standards also create entry barriers because they raise entry costs. In international markets, host governments commonly limit foreign entry and must approve all foreign investment applications. National governments commonly use tariffs and trade restrictions (antidumping rules, local content requirements, quotas, etc.) to raise entry barriers for foreign firms and protect domestic producers from outside competition.

The threat of entry changes as the industry's prospects grow brighter or dimmer and as entry barriers rise or fall. For example, in the pharmaceutical industry the expiration of a key patent on a widely prescribed drug virtually guarantees that one or more drug makers will enter with generic offerings of their own. Use of the Internet for shopping is making it much easier for e-tailers to enter into competition against some of the best-known retail chains. Moreover, new strategic actions by incumbent firms to increase advertising, strengthen distributor-dealer relations, step up R&D, or improve product quality can erect higher roadblocks to entry.

> High entry barriers and weak entry threats today do not always translate into high entry barriers and weak entry threats tomorrow.

Additional Entry Threat Considerations

There are two additional factors that need to be considered in evaluating whether the threat of entry is strong or weak. The first concerns how attractive the growth and profit prospects are for new entrants. *Rapidly growing market demand and high potential profits act as magnets, motivating potential entrants to commit the resources needed to hurdle entry barriers.*[7] When growth and profit opportunities are sufficiently attractive, certain types of entry barriers are unlikely to provide an effective entry deterrent. At most, they limit the pool of candidate entrants to enterprises with the requisite competencies and resources and with the creativity to fashion a strategy for competing with incumbent firms. Hence, *the best test of whether potential entry is a strong or weak competitive force in the marketplace is to ask if the industry's growth and profit prospects are strongly attractive to potential entry candidates with sufficient expertise and resources to hurdle prevailing entry barriers.* When the answer is no, potential entry is a weak competitive force. When the answer is yes, then potential entry adds significantly to competitive pressures in the marketplace.

A second factor concerns the pool of potential entrants and their capabilities in relation to the particular entry barriers in place. Companies with sizable financial resources, proven competitive capabilities, and a respected brand name may be able to marshal the resources to hurdle certain types of entry barriers rather easily, while small start-up enterprises may find the same entry barriers insurmountable. Thus, how hard it will be for potential entrants to compete on a level playing field is always relative to the financial resources and competitive capabilities of likely entrants. The big take-away is this: *Whether an industry's entry barriers ought to be considered high or low depends on the resources and capabilities possessed by the pool of potential entrants.*[8] As a rule, the bigger the pool of entry candidates that have what it takes, the stronger is the threat of entry.

> The threat of entry is stronger when entry barriers are low, when incumbent firms are unable or unwilling to vigorously contest a newcomer's entry, and when there's a sizable pool of entry candidates with resources and capabilities well suited for competing in the industry.

For example, when Honda opted to enter the U.S. lawn mower market in competition against Toro, Snapper, Craftsman, John Deere, and others, it was easily able to hurdle entry barriers that would have been formidable to other newcomers because it had long-standing expertise in gasoline engines; its well-known reputation for quality and durability in automobiles gave it instant credibility with homeowners. In fact, the strongest competitive pressures associated with potential entry frequently come not from outsiders but from current industry participants with strong capabilities looking for growth opportunities. *Existing industry members are often strong candidates to enter market segments or geographic areas where they currently do not have a market presence.* Companies already well established in certain product categories or geographic areas often possess the resources, competencies, and competitive capabilities to hurdle the barriers of entering a different market segment or new geographic area.

Figure 3.5 summarizes the factors that cause the overall competitive threat from potential new entrants to be strong or weak.

Figure 3.5   Factors Affecting the Threat of Entry

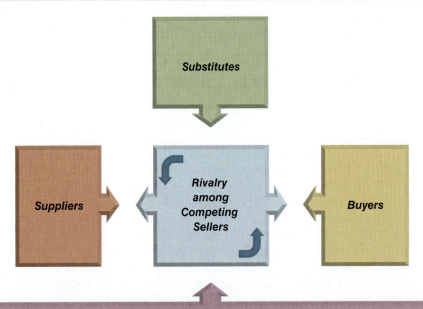

Potential New Entrants

How strong are the competitive pressures coming from the threat of entry of new rivals?

Entry threats are stronger when:
- Entry barriers are low
- Industry members are unwilling or unable to strongly contest the entry of newcomers
- There is a large pool of potential entrants, some of which have the capabilities to overcome high entry barriers
- Existing industry members are looking to expand their market reach by entering product segments or geographic areas where they do not have a presence
- Buyer demand is growing rapidly and newcomers can expect to earn attractive profits without inviting a strong reaction from incumbents

Entry threats are weaker when:
- Entry barriers are high
  - High economies of scale
  - Significant experience-based cost advantages
  - Other cost advantages held by industry members (e.g., access to inputs, technology, favorable location) or low fixed costs
  - Strong product differentiation and brand loyalty
  - Strong network effects
  - High capital requirements
  - Limited new access to distribution channels
  - Restrictive government policies
- Industry members are willing and able to contest new entry
- Industry outlook is risky and uncertain, discouraging entry

Competitive Pressures from the Sellers of Substitute Products

Companies in one industry come under competitive pressure from the actions of companies in a closely adjoining industry whenever buyers view the products of the two industries as good substitutes. For instance, the producers of sugar experience competitive pressures from the sales and marketing efforts of the makers of Equal, Splenda, and Sweet'N Low. Newspapers are struggling to maintain their relevance to subscribers who can watch the news on any of numerous TV channels and use Internet sources to get information about sports results, stock quotes, and job opportunities. The retailers of music CDs are experiencing competitive pressure from downloadable digital music on sites such as iTunes.

As depicted in Figure 3.6, whether the competitive pressures from substitute products are strong, moderate, or weak depends on three factors:

1. *Whether substitutes are readily available.* The presence of readily available substitutes creates competitive pressure by placing a ceiling on the prices industry members can charge without giving customers an incentive to switch to substitutes and risking sales erosion.[9] This price ceiling, at the same time, puts a lid on the profits that industry members can earn unless they find ways to cut costs.

2. *Whether buyers view the substitutes as attractively priced in relation to their quality, performance, and other relevant attributes.* In deciding whether to switch to a substitute product, customers compare its performance, features, ease of use, and other attributes as well as price to see if the substitute offers more value for the money than the industry's product. The users of paper cartons constantly weigh the price/performance trade-offs with plastic containers and metal cans, for example.

3. *Whether the costs that buyers incur in switching to the substitutes are low or high.* Low switching costs make it easier for the sellers of attractive substitutes to lure buyers to their offerings; high switching costs deter buyers from purchasing substitute products.[10] Typical switching costs include the time and inconvenience involved in switching, payments for technical help in making the changeover, the cost of any additional equipment needed, employee retraining costs, the cost of testing the quality and reliability of the substitute, and the psychological costs of severing old supplier relationships and establishing new ones.

Before assessing the competitive pressures coming from substitutes, company managers must identify the substitutes, which is less easy than it sounds since it involves (1) determining where the industry boundaries lie and (2) figuring out which other products or services can address the same basic customer needs as those produced by industry members. Deciding on the industry boundaries is necessary for determining which firms are direct rivals and which produce substitutes. This is a matter of perspective—there are no hard-and-fast rules, other than to say that other brands of the same basic product constitute rival products and not substitutes.

As a rule, *the lower the price of substitutes, the higher their quality and performance; and the lower the user's switching costs, the more intense the competitive pressures posed by substitute products.* Other market indicators of the competitive strength of substitute products include (1) whether the sales of substitutes are growing faster than the sales of the industry being analyzed (a sign that the

Figure 3.6   **Factors Affecting Competition from Substitute Products**

Firms in Other Industries Offering Substitute Products

How strong are competitive pressures coming from substitute products from outside the industry?

Competitive pressures from substitutes are stronger when:

- Good substitutes are readily available or new ones are emerging
- Substitutes are attractively priced
- Substitutes have comparable or better performance features
- Buyers have low costs in switching to substitutes

Competitive pressures from substitutes are weaker when:

- Good substitutes are not readily available or don't exist
- Substitutes are higher-priced relative to the performance they deliver
- Buyers have high costs in switching to substitutes

Signs That Competition from Substitutes Is Strong

- Sales of substitutes are growing faster than sales of the industry being analyzed
- Producers of substitutes are moving to add new capacity
- Profits of the producers of substitutes are on the rise

Suppliers

Rivalry among Competing Sellers

Buyers

New Entrants

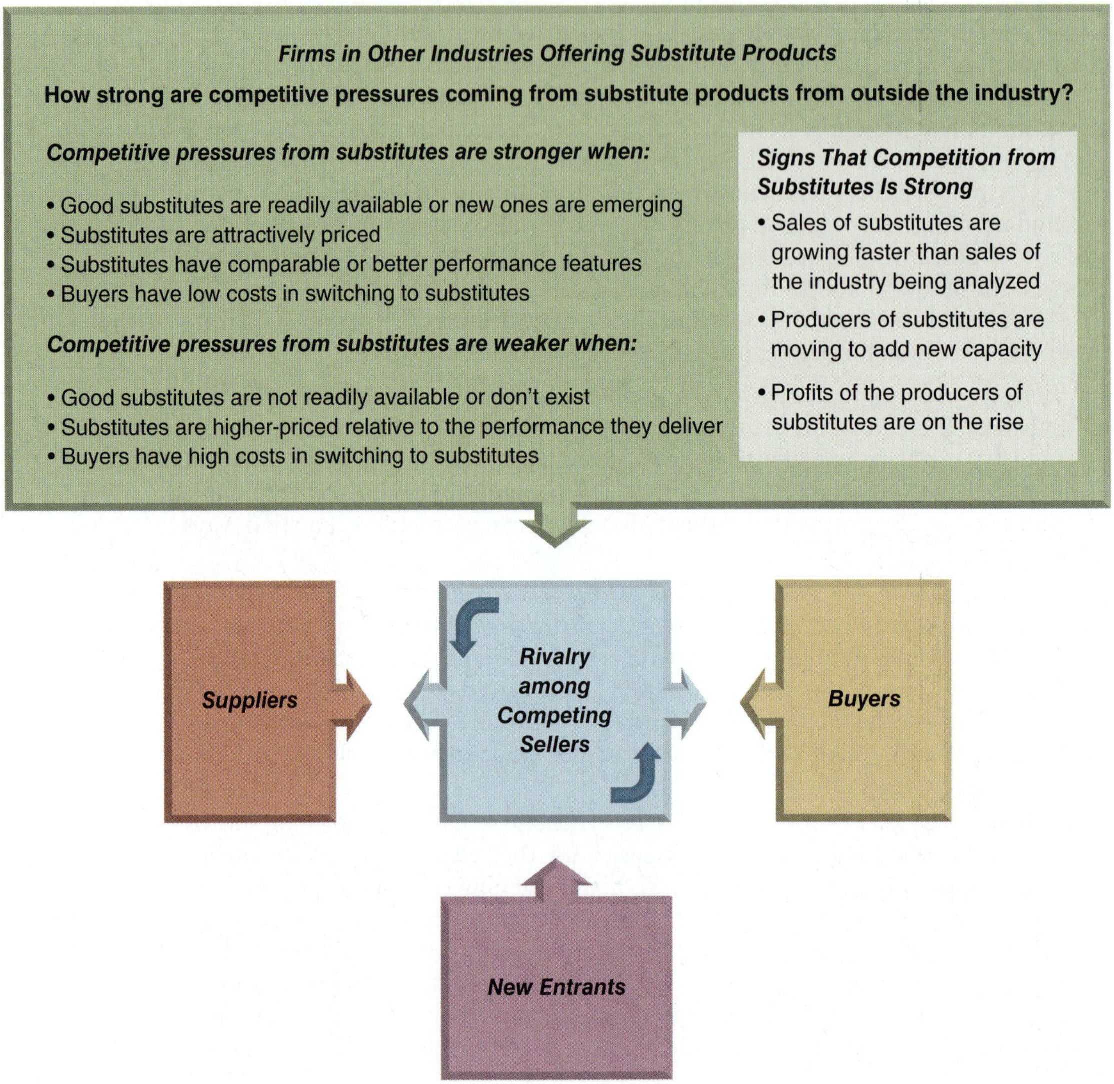

sellers of substitutes may be drawing customers away from the industry in question), (2) whether the producers of substitutes are moving to add new capacity, and (3) whether the profits of the producers of substitutes are on the rise.

Competitive Pressures Stemming from Supplier Bargaining Power

Whether the suppliers of industry members represent a weak or strong competitive force depends on the degree to which suppliers have sufficient *bargaining power* to influence the terms and conditions of supply in their favor. Suppliers with strong bargaining power can erode industry profitability by charging industry members higher prices, passing costs on to them, and limiting their opportunities to find better deals. For instance, Microsoft and Intel, both of whom supply PC makers with essential components, have been known to use their dominant market status not only to charge PC makers premium prices but also to leverage PC makers in other ways. The bargaining power of these two companies over their customers is so great that both companies have faced antitrust charges on numerous occasions. Before a legal agreement ending the practice, Microsoft pressured PC makers to load only Microsoft products on the screens of new computers that come with factory-loaded software. Intel has also defended against antitrust charges but continues to give PC makers who use the biggest percentages of Intel chips in their PC models top priority in filling orders for newly introduced Intel chips. Being on Intel's list of preferred customers helps a PC maker get an allocation of the first production runs of Intel's latest chips and thus get new PC models to market ahead of rivals. Microsoft's and Intel's pressuring of PC makers has helped them maintain their dominant positions in their industries.

Small-scale retailers often must contend with the power of manufacturers whose products enjoy well-known brand names, since consumers expect to find these products on the shelves of the retail stores where they shop. This provides the manufacturer with a degree of pricing power and often the ability to push hard for favorable shelf displays. Similarly, the operators of franchised units of such chains as McDonald's, Dunkin' Donuts, Pizza Hut, Sylvan Learning Centers, and Hampton Inns must frequently agree to source some of their supplies from the franchisor at prices and terms favorable to that franchisor. Supplier bargaining power is also a competitive factor in industries where unions have been able to organize the workforce (which supplies labor). Air pilot unions, for example, have employed their bargaining power to increase pilots' wages and benefits in the air transport industry.

As shown in Figure 3.7, a variety of factors determines the strength of suppliers' bargaining power:[11]

- *Whether suppliers' products are in short supply.* Suppliers of items in short supply have pricing power and bargaining leverage, whereas a surge in the available supply of particular items shifts the bargaining power to the industry members.

- *Whether suppliers provide a differentiated input that enhances the performance or quality of the industry's product.* The more differentiated and valuable a particular input is in terms of enhancing the performance or quality of the products of industry members, the more bargaining leverage and pricing power suppliers have.

- *Whether the item being supplied is a standard item or a commodity that is readily available from a host of suppliers.* The suppliers of commodities (like copper or steel reinforcing rods or shipping cartons) are in a weak position to demand a premium price or insist on other favorable terms because industry members can readily obtain essentially the same item at the same price from many other suppliers eager to win their business.

- *Whether it is difficult or costly for industry members to switch their purchases from one supplier to another.* The higher the switching costs of industry members, the stronger the bargaining power of their suppliers. Low switching costs limit supplier bargaining power by enabling industry members to change suppliers if any one supplier attempts to raise prices by more than the costs of switching.

- *Whether there are good substitutes available for the suppliers' products.* The ready availability of substitute inputs lessens the bargaining power of suppliers by reducing the dependence of industry members on the suppliers. The better

Figure 3.7   Factors Affecting the Bargaining Power of Suppliers

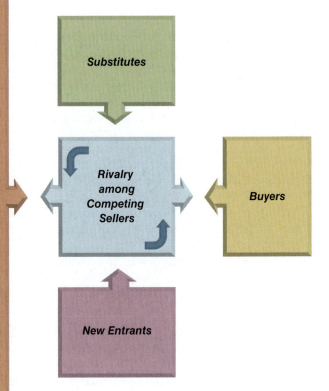

Suppliers

How strong are the competitive pressures stemming from supplier bargaining power?

Supplier bargaining power is stronger when:

- Supplier products/services are in short supply (which gives suppliers leverage in setting prices)
- Supplier products/services are differentiated
- Supplier products/services are critical to industry members' production processes
- Industry members incur high costs in switching their purchases to alternative suppliers
- There are no good substitutes for what the suppliers provide
- Suppliers are not dependent on the industry for a large portion of their revenues
- The supplier industry is more concentrated than the industry it sells to and is dominated by a few large companies

Supplier bargaining power is weaker when:

- There is a surge in the availability of supplies
- The item being supplied is a "commodity" that is readily available from many suppliers at the going market price
- Industry members' switching costs to alternative suppliers are low
- Good substitutes for supplier products/services exist
- Industry members account for a big fraction of suppliers' sales
- The number of suppliers is large relative to the number of industry members and there are no suppliers with large market shares
- Industry members have the potential to integrate backward into the business of suppliers and to self-manufacture their own requirements

the price and performance characteristics of the substitute inputs, the weaker the bargaining power of suppliers.

- *Whether industry members account for a sizable fraction of suppliers' total sales.* As a rule, suppliers have less bargaining leverage when their sales to members of the industry constitute a big percentage of their total sales. In such cases, the well-being of suppliers is closely tied to the well-being of their major customers. Suppliers have a big incentive to protect and enhance the competitiveness of their major customers via reasonable prices, exceptional quality, and ongoing advances in the technology of the items supplied.
- *Whether the supplier industry is dominated by a few large companies and whether it is more concentrated than the industry it sells to.* Suppliers with sizable market

shares and strong demand for the items they supply generally have sufficient bargaining power to charge high prices and deny requests from industry members for lower prices or other concessions.

- *Whether it makes good economic sense for industry members to integrate backward and self-manufacture items they have been buying from suppliers.* The make-or-buy issue generally boils down to whether suppliers who specialize in the production of particular parts or components and make them in volume for many different customers have the expertise and scale economies to supply as-good or better components at a lower cost than industry members could achieve via self-manufacture. Frequently, it is difficult for industry members to self-manufacture parts and components more economically than they can obtain them from suppliers who specialize in making such items. For instance, most producers of outdoor power equipment (lawn mowers, rotary tillers, leaf blowers, etc.) find it cheaper to source the small engines they need from outside manufacturers that specialize in small-engine manufacture than to make their own engines, because the quantity of engines they need is too small to justify the investment in manufacturing facilities, master the production process, and capture scale economies. Specialists in small-engine manufacture, by supplying many kinds of engines to the whole power equipment industry, can obtain a big-enough sales volume to fully realize scale economies, become proficient in all the manufacturing techniques, and keep costs low. As a rule, suppliers are safe from the threat of self-manufacture by their customers *until* the volume of parts a customer needs becomes large enough for the customer to justify backward integration into self-manufacture of the component.

In identifying the degree of supplier power in an industry, it is important to recognize that different types of suppliers are likely to have different amounts of bargaining power. Thus, the first step is for managers to identify the different types of suppliers, paying particular attention to those that provide the industry with important inputs. The next step is to assess the bargaining power of each type of supplier separately. Figure 3.7 summarizes the conditions that tend to make supplier bargaining power strong or weak.

Competitive Pressures Stemming from Buyer Bargaining Power and Price Sensitivity

Whether buyers are able to exert strong competitive pressures on industry members depends on (1) the degree to which buyers have bargaining power and (2) the extent to which buyers are price-sensitive. Buyers with strong bargaining power can limit industry profitability by demanding price concessions, better payment terms, or additional features and services that increase industry members' costs. Buyer price sensitivity limits the profit potential of industry members by restricting the ability of sellers to raise prices without losing revenue.

The strength of buyers as a competitive force depends on a set of factors that predict the degree of bargaining power and price sensitivity, which may vary according to buyer group (e.g., wholesalers, large retail chains, small retailers, consumers). Retailers tend to have greater bargaining power over industry sellers if they have influence over the purchase decisions of the end user or if they are critical in providing sellers with access to the end user. For example, large retail chains like Walmart, Best Buy, Staples, Home Depot, and Kroger typically have considerable negotiating leverage in purchasing products from manufacturers because of manufacturers' need for broad retail exposure and the most appealing shelf locations. Retailers may stock two or three competing brands of a product but rarely all competing brands, so competition among rival manufacturers for visibility on the shelves of popular multistore retailers gives such retailers significant bargaining strength. Major supermarket chains like Kroger, Safeway, Food Lion, and Publix have sufficient bargaining power to demand promotional allowances and lump-sum payments (called slotting fees) from food products manufacturers in return for stocking certain brands or putting them in the best shelf locations. Motor vehicle manufacturers have strong bargaining power in negotiating to buy original-equipment tires from Goodyear, Michelin, Bridgestone/Firestone, Continental, and Pirelli not only because they buy in large quantities but also because tire makers believe they gain an advantage in supplying replacement tires to vehicle owners if their tire brand is original equipment on the vehicle.

In contrast, individual consumers rarely have any real bargaining power in negotiating price concessions or other favorable terms with sellers. While an individual with other purchase options may refuse to buy a high-priced item, her actions will have no discernible effect on industry profitability. As a buyer group, however, consumers can limit the profit potential of an industry for the same reasons that other buyer groups exert competitive pressure. These reasons are discussed below and summarized in Figure 3.8:[12]

- *Buyers' bargaining power is greater when their costs of switching to competing brands or substitutes are relatively low.* Buyers who can readily switch brands have more leverage than buyers who have high switching costs. Switching costs limit industry profitability, in essence, by putting a cap on how much producers can raise price or reduce quality before they will lose the buyer's business.

- *Buyer power increases when industry goods are standardized or differentiation is weak.* In such circumstances, buyers make their selections on the basis of price, which increases price competition among vendors. When products are differentiated, buyers' options are more limited and they are less focused on obtaining low prices, which may signal poor quality.

- *Buyers have more power when they are large and few in number relative to the number of sellers.* The smaller the number of buyers, the more sellers have to compete for their business and the less easy it is for sellers to find alternative buyers when a customer is lost to a competitor. The prospect of losing a customer not easily replaced often makes a seller more willing to grant concessions of one kind or another. The larger the buyer, the more important their business is to the seller and the more sellers will be willing to grant concessions.

- *Buyer power increases when buyer demand is weak and industry members are scrambling to sell more units.* Weak or declining demand creates a "buyers' market," in which bargain-hunting buyers are able to press for better deals and special treatment; conversely, strong or rapidly growing demand creates a "sellers' market" and shifts bargaining power to sellers.

- *Buyers gain leverage if they are well informed about sellers' products, prices, and costs.* The more information buyers have, the better bargaining position they are in. The mushrooming availability of product information on the Internet is giving added bargaining power to consumers. Buyers can easily use the Internet to compare prices and features of vacation packages, shop for the best interest rates on mortgages and loans, and find the best prices on big-ticket items such as digital cameras. Bargain hunters can shop around for the best deal on the Internet and use that information to negotiate better deals

Figure 3.8   Factors Affecting the Bargaining Power of Buyers

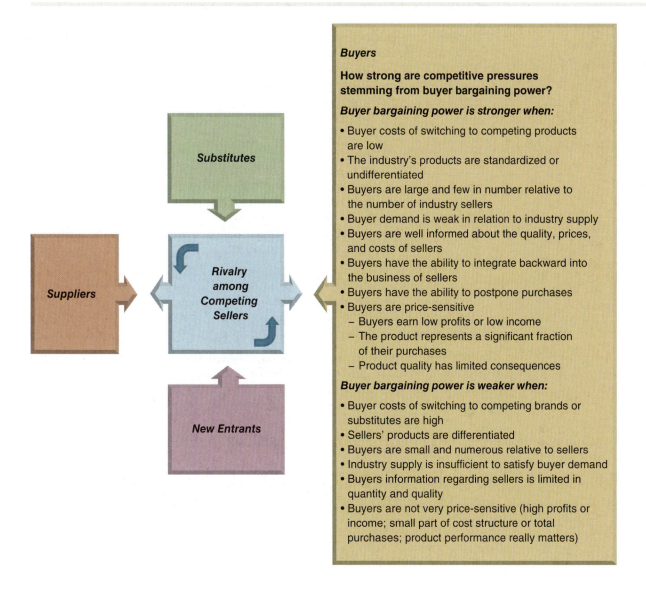

Buyers

How strong are competitive pressures stemming from buyer bargaining power?

Buyer bargaining power is stronger when:

- Buyer costs of switching to competing products are low
- The industry's products are standardized or undifferentiated
- Buyers are large and few in number relative to the number of industry sellers
- Buyer demand is weak in relation to industry supply
- Buyers are well informed about the quality, prices, and costs of sellers
- Buyers have the ability to integrate backward into the business of sellers
- Buyers have the ability to postpone purchases
- Buyers are price-sensitive
  - Buyers earn low profits or low income
  - The product represents a significant fraction of their purchases
  - Product quality has limited consequences

Buyer bargaining power is weaker when:

- Buyer costs of switching to competing brands or substitutes are high
- Sellers' products are differentiated
- Buyers are small and numerous relative to sellers
- Industry supply is insufficient to satisfy buyer demand
- Buyers information regarding sellers is limited in quantity and quality
- Buyers are not very price-sensitive (high profits or income; small part of cost structure or total purchases; product performance really matters)

from local retailers; this method is becoming commonplace in buying new and used motor vehicles.

- *Buyers' bargaining power is greater when they pose a credible threat of integrating backward into the business of sellers.* Companies like Anheuser-Busch, Coors, and Heinz have integrated backward into metal can manufacturing to gain bargaining power in obtaining the balance of their can requirements from otherwise powerful metal can manufacturers. Retailers gain bargaining power by stocking and promoting their own private-label brands alongside manufacturers' name brands.

- *Buyer leverage increases if buyers have discretion to delay their purchases or perhaps even not make a purchase at all.* Consumers often have the option to delay purchases of durable goods, such as major appliances, or discretionary goods, such as hot tubs and home entertainment centers, if they are not happy with the prices offered. Business customers may also be able to defer their purchases of certain items, such as plant equipment or maintenance services. This puts pressure on sellers to provide concessions to buyers so that the sellers can keep their sales numbers from dropping off.

- *Buyer price sensitivity increases when buyers are earning low profits or have low income.* Price is a critical factor in the purchase decisions of low-income consumers and companies that are barely scraping by. In such cases, their high price sensitivity limits the ability of sellers to charge high prices.

- *Buyers are more price-sensitive if the product represents a large fraction of their total purchases.* When a purchase eats up a large portion of a buyer's budget or represents a significant part of his or her cost structure, the buyer cares more about price than might otherwise be the case. When the item is a small fraction of total purchases, buyers are less likely to feel that negotiating or shopping for a better deal is worth the time and trouble.

- *Buyers are more price-sensitive if product performance has limited consequences.* When product performance has limited consequences for the buyer, then purchase decisions are based mostly on price. On the other hand, when product quality is important, such as when it materially affects the quality of an intermediate buyer's goods, then price becomes a less important factor. Price is particularly unimportant to intermediate buyers when a good has the potential to pay for itself by reducing a buyer's other production costs.

The starting point for the analysis of buyers as a competitive force is to identify the different types of buyers along the value chain—then proceed to analyzing the bargaining power and price sensitivity of each type separately. Overall, buyers exert strong competitive pressures and force industry profitability downward if the majority of industry member sales are made to buyer groups that have either strong bargaining power or high price sensitivity. Buyers are able to exert only moderate competitive pressures on sellers when the majority of sellers' revenues come from buyers with intermediate levels of power or price sensitivity. Competitive pressures exerted by buyers are weak when a big portion of sellers' sales revenues comes from buyers with weak bargaining power and price sensitivity.

Is the Collective Strength of the Five Competitive Forces Conducive to Good Profitability?

Assessing whether each of the five competitive forces gives rise to strong, moderate, or weak competitive pressures sets the stage for evaluating whether, overall, the strength of the five forces is conducive to good profitability. Is the state of competition in the industry stronger than "normal"? Can companies in this industry reasonably expect to earn decent profits in light of the prevailing competitive forces? Are some of the competitive forces sufficiently powerful to undermine industry profitability?

The most extreme case of a "competitively unattractive" industry occurs when all five forces are producing strong competitive pressures: Rivalry among sellers is vigorous, low entry barriers allow new rivals to gain a market foothold, competition from substitutes is intense, and both suppliers and buyers are able to exercise considerable leverage. Fierce to strong competitive pressures coming from all five directions drive industry profitability to unacceptably low levels, frequently producing losses for many industry members and forcing some out of business. But an industry can be competitively unattractive without all five competitive forces being strong. In fact, intense competitive pressures *from just one or two* of the five forces may suffice to destroy the conditions for good profitability and prompt some companies to exit the business.

As a rule, *the strongest competitive forces determine the extent of the competitive pressure on industry profitability.*[13] Thus, in evaluating the strength of the five forces overall and their effect on industry profitability, managers should look to the strongest forces. Having more than one strong force will not worsen the effect on industry profitability, but it does mean that the industry has multiple competitive challenges with which to cope. In that sense, an industry with three to five strong forces is even more "unattractive" as a place to compete. Especially intense competitive conditions seem to be the norm in tire manufacturing, apparel, and commercial airlines, three industries where profit margins have historically been thin.

> **CORE CONCEPT**
>
> The strongest of the five forces determines how strong the forces of competition are overall and the extent of the downward pressure on an industry's level of profitability.

In contrast, when the overall impact of the five competitive forces is moderate to weak, an industry is "attractive" in the sense that the *average* industry member can reasonably expect to earn good profits and a nice return on investment. The ideal competitive environment for earning superior profits is one in which both suppliers and customers are in weak bargaining positions, there are no good substitutes, high barriers block further entry, and rivalry among present sellers generates only limited competitive pressures. Weak competition is the best of all possible worlds for also-ran companies because even they can usually eke out a decent profit—if a company can't make a decent profit when competition is weak, then its business outlook is indeed grim.

In most industries, the collective strength of the five competitive forces is somewhere near the middle of the two extremes of very intense and very weak, typically ranging from slightly stronger than normal to slightly weaker than normal and typically allowing well-managed companies with sound strategies to earn moderately attractive profits.

Matching Company Strategy to Competitive Conditions

Working through the five-forces model step by step not only aids strategy makers in assessing whether the intensity of competition allows good profitability but also promotes sound strategic thinking about how to better match company strategy to the specific competitive character of the marketplace. Effectively matching a company's business strategy to prevailing competitive conditions has three aspects:

> A company's strategy is increasingly effective the more it provides some insulation from competitive pressures, shifts the competitive battle in the company's favor, and positions firms to take advantage of attractive growth opportunities.

1. Pursuing avenues that shield the firm from as many of the different competitive pressures as possible.
2. Initiating actions calculated to shift the competitive forces in the company's favor by altering the underlying factors driving the five forces.
3. Spotting attractive arenas for expansion, where competitive pressures in the industry are somewhat weaker.

But making headway on these three fronts first requires identifying competitive pressures, gauging the relative strength of each of the five competitive forces, and gaining a deep enough understanding of the state of competition in the industry to know which strategy buttons to push.

QUESTION 3: WHAT FACTORS ARE DRIVING INDUSTRY CHANGE, AND WHAT IMPACTS WILL THEY HAVE?

LO 2

Learn how to diagnose the factors shaping industry dynamics and to forecast their effects on future industry profitability.

While it is critical to understand the nature and intensity of the competitive forces in an industry, it is just as important to understand that the intensity of these forces and the level of an industry's attractiveness are fluid and subject to change. All industries are affected by new developments and ongoing trends that alter industry conditions, some more speedily than others. Many of these changes are important enough to require a strategic response. Since the five competitive forces have such significance for an industry's profit potential, it is critical that managers remain alert to the changes most likely to affect the strength of the five forces. Environmental scanning for changes of this nature will enable managers to forecast changes in the expected profitability of the industry and to adjust their company's strategy accordingly.

Changes that affect the competitive forces in a positive manner may present opportunities for companies to reposition themselves to take advantage of these forces. Changes that affect the five forces negatively may require a defensive strategic response. Regardless of the direction of change, managers will be able to react in a more timely fashion, with lower adjustment costs, if they have advance notice of the coming changes. Moreover, with early notice, managers may be able to influence the direction or scope of environmental change and improve the outlook.

Analyzing Industry Dynamics

CORE CONCEPT

Dynamic industry analysis involves determining how the **drivers of change** are affecting industry and competitive conditions.

Managing under changing conditions begins with a strategic analysis of the industry dynamics. This involves three steps: (1) identifying the **drivers of change,** (2) assessing whether the drivers of change are, individually or collectively, acting to make the industry more or less attractive, and (3) determining what strategy changes are needed to prepare for the impacts of the anticipated change. All three steps merit further discussion.

Identifying an Industry's Drivers of Change

While many types of environmental change can affect industries in one way or another, it is important to focus on the most powerful agents of change—those with the biggest influence in reshaping the industry landscape and altering competitive conditions. Many drivers of change originate in the outer ring of the company's external environment (see Figure 3.2), but others originate in the company's more immediate industry and competitive environment. Although some drivers of change are unique and specific to a particular industry situation, most drivers of industry and competitive change fall into one of the following categories:[14]

- *Changes in an industry's long-term growth rate.* Shifts in industry growth up or down are a key driver of industry change, affecting the balance between industry supply and buyer demand, entry and exit, and the character and strength of competition. Whether demand is growing or declining is one of the key factors influencing the intensity of rivalry in an industry, as explained earlier. But the strength of this effect will depend on how changes in the industry growth rate affect entry and exit in the industry. If entry barriers are low, then growth in demand will attract new entrants, increasing the number of industry rivals. If exit barriers are low, then shrinking demand will induce exit, resulting in fewer remaining rivals. Since the numbers of firms in an industry also affects the strength of rivalry, these secondary effects via entry and exit would counteract the more direct effects of the change in demand on rivalry. Depending on how much entry or exit takes place, the net result might be that the overall force of rivals remains the same. A change in the long-term growth rate may affect industry conditions in other ways as well. For example, if growth prospects induce the entry of a large, established firm with ambitious growth goals, the intensity of rivalry may increase markedly due to the added diversity or changes in the size mix of incumbents. The exact effect of growth rate changes will vary depending on the specific industry situation. In analyzing the effects of any change driver, managers need to keep in mind the various factors that influence the five forces.

- *Increasing globalization.* Globalization can be precipitated by the blossoming of consumer demand in more and more countries and by the actions of government officials in many countries to reduce trade barriers or open up once-closed markets to foreign competitors, as is occurring in many parts of Europe, Latin America, and Asia. Significant differences in labor costs among countries give manufacturers a strong incentive to locate plants for labor-intensive products in low-wage countries and use these plants to supply market demand across the world. Wages in China, India, Singapore, Mexico, and Brazil, for example, are about one-fourth those in the United States, Germany, and Japan. Because globalization is a complex phenomenon that affects different industries in different ways, analyzing its effects on industry dynamics is a challenging task that requires a consideration of how each of the five forces may be affected. For example, globalization increases the diversity and number of competitors, and this in turn increases the force of rivalry in an industry. At the same time, the lowering of trade barriers increases the threat of entry, putting further pressure on industry profitability. On the other hand, globalization is likely to weaken supplier power by increasing the number of suppliers and increasing the possibility of substituting cheap labor for other inputs. The specific effects vary by industry and will impact some industries more than others. Globalization is very much a driver of industry change in such industries as motor vehicles, steel, petroleum, personal computers, video games, public accounting, and textbook publishing.

- *Changes in who buys the product and how they use it.* Shifts in buyer demographics and the ways products are used can greatly alter industry and competitive conditions. Longer life expectancies and growing percentages of relatively well-to-do retirees, for example, are driving demand growth in such industries as health care, prescription drugs, recreational living, and vacation travel. This is the most common effect of changes in buyer demographics, and it affects industry rivalry, as observed above. But other effects are possible as well. Dell's "buy direct" strategy lessened the buyer power of big-box middlemen in the PC industry by cutting out the intermediate buyers and selling directly to end users. Buyer power increased in the pharmaceutical industry when large HMOs created lists of approved drugs, reducing the role of individual (powerless) doctors in the choice process.

- *Technological change.* Advances in technology can cause disruptive change in an industry by introducing substitutes that offer buyers an irresistible price/performance combination. At the least, this increases the power of substitutes; it may change the business landscape in more fundamental ways if it has a devastating effect on demand. Technological change can also impact the manufacturing process in an industry. This might lead to greater economies of scale, for example, which would increase industry entry barriers. Or it could lead to greater product differentiation, as did the introduction of "mass-customization" techniques. Increasing product differentiation tends to lower buyer power, increase entry barriers, and reduce rivalry—all of which have positive implications for industry profitability.

- *Emerging new Internet capabilities and applications.* The emergence of high-speed Internet service and Voice-Over-Internet-Protocol technology, along with an ever-growing series of Internet applications, provides a special case of technological change that has been a major driver of change in industry after industry. It has reshaped many aspects of the business landscape and can affect the five forces in various ways. The ability of companies to reach consumers via the Internet increases the number of rivals a company faces and often escalates rivalry by pitting pure online sellers against combination brick-and-click sellers against pure brick-and-mortar sellers (increasing diversity and size mix). The Internet gives buyers increasing power through unprecedented ability to research the product offerings of competitors and shop the market for the best value (making buyers better informed). Widespread use of e-mail has forever eroded the business of providing fax services and the first-class-mail delivery revenues of government postal services worldwide (substitute power). Video-conferencing via the Internet erodes the demand for business travel (increasing rivalry in the travel market). The Internet of the future will feature faster speeds, dazzling applications, and over a billion connected gadgets performing an array of functions, thus driving further industry and competitive changes. But Internet-related impacts vary from industry to industry. The challenges here are to assess precisely how emerging Internet developments are altering a particular industry's landscape and to factor these impacts into the strategy-making equation.

- *Product and marketing innovation.* An ongoing stream of product innovations tends to alter the pattern of competition in an industry by attracting more first-time buyers, rejuvenating industry growth, and/or increasing product differentiation, with concomitant effects on rivalry, entry threat, and buyer power. Product innovation has been a key driving force in such industries as digital cameras, golf clubs, video games, toys, and prescription drugs. Similarly, when firms are successful in introducing *new ways* to market their products, they can spark a burst of buyer interest, widen industry demand, increase or lower entry barriers, and increase product differentiation—any or all of which can alter the competitiveness of an industry.

- *Entry or exit of major firms.* The entry of one or more foreign companies into a geographic market once dominated by domestic firms nearly always changes the balance between demand and supply and shakes up competitive conditions by adding diversity. Likewise, when an established domestic firm from another industry attempts entry either by acquisition or by launching its own start-up venture, it usually applies its skills and resources in some innovative fashion that pushes competition in new directions. Entry by a major firm thus often produces a new ball game, with greater rivalry as the result. Similarly, exit of a major firm changes the competitive structure by reducing the number of market leaders and increasing the dominance of the leaders who remain. The primary effect is on the degree of rivalry in the industry, through changes in industry concentration.

- *Diffusion of technical know-how across more companies and more countries.* As knowledge about how to perform a particular activity or execute a particular manufacturing technology spreads, products tend to become more commodity-like. This increases the intensity of rivalry, buyer power, and the threat of entry into an industry, as described earlier.

- *Improvements in cost and efficiency in closely adjoining markets.* Big changes in the costs of substitute producers can dramatically alter the state of competition by changing the price/performance trade-off between an industry's products and that of substitute goods. For example, lower production costs and longer-life products have allowed the makers of super-efficient, fluorescent-based spiral lightbulbs to cut deeply into the sales of incandescent lightbulbs. This has occurred because the spiral lightbulbs, despite being priced two to three times higher than incandescent bulbs, are still far cheaper to use because of their energy-saving efficiency (as much as $50 per bulb) and longer lives (up to eight years between replacements).

- *Reductions in uncertainty and business risk.* Many companies are hesitant to enter industries with uncertain futures or high levels of business risk, and firms already in these industries may be cautious about making aggressive capital investments to expand—often because it is unclear how much time and money it will take to overcome various technological hurdles and achieve acceptable production costs (as is the case in the infant solar power industry). Likewise, firms entering foreign markets where demand is just emerging or where political conditions are volatile may be cautious and limit their downside exposure by using less risky strategies. Over time, however, diminishing risk levels and uncertainty tend to stimulate new entry and capital investments on the part of growth-minded companies seeking new opportunities. This can dramatically alter industry and competitive conditions by increasing rivalry, as the numbers of firms in the industry and their diversity increases.

- *Regulatory influences and government policy changes.* Changes in regulations and government policies can affect competitive conditions in industries in a variety of ways. For example, regulatory actions can affect barriers to entry directly, as they have in industries such as airlines, banking, and broadcasting. Regulations regarding product quality, safety, and environmental protection can affect entry barriers more indirectly, by altering capital requirements or economies of scale. Government actions can also affect rivalry through antitrust policies, as they have in soft-drink bottling, where exclusive territorial rights were granted, and in automobile parts, where a loosening of restrictions led to increasing supplier power.[15] In international markets, host governments can affect industry rivalry or supplier and buyer power by opening their domestic markets to foreign participation or closing them to protect domestic companies.

- *Changing societal concerns, attitudes, and lifestyles.* Emerging social issues and changing attitudes and lifestyles can be powerful instigators of industry change. Growing concerns about global warming have emerged as a major driver of change in the energy industry, changing the rate of industry growth in different sectors. The greater attention and care being given to household pets has driven growth across the whole pet industry. Changes in the industry growth rate, as we have seen, can affect the intensity of industry rivalry and entry conditions.

Table 3.3 lists these 12 most common drivers of change. That there are so many different *potential* drivers of change explains why a full understanding of all types of change drivers is a fundamental part of analyzing industry dynamics. However, for each industry no more than three or four of these drivers are likely to be powerful enough to qualify as the *major determinants* of why and how an industry's competitive conditions are changing. The true analytical task is to evaluate the forces of industry and competitive change carefully enough to separate major factors from minor ones.

Assessing the Impact of the Factors Driving Industry Change

Just identifying the factors driving industry change is not sufficient, however. The second, and more important, step in dynamic industry analysis is to determine whether the prevailing change drivers, on the whole, are acting to make the industry environment more or less attractive. Answers to three questions are needed:

1. Overall, are the factors driving change causing demand for the industry's product to increase or decrease?
2. Is the collective impact of the drivers of change making competition more or less intense?
3. Will the combined impacts of the change drivers lead to higher or lower industry profitability?

Getting a handle on the collective impact of the factors driving industry change requires looking at the likely effects of each factor separately, since the drivers of change may not all be pushing change in the same direction. For example, one change driver may be acting to spur demand for the industry's product while

Table 3.3   The Most Common Drivers of Industry Change

1. Changes in the long-term industry growth rate
2. Increasing globalization
3. Changes in who buys the product and how they use it
4. Technological change
5. Emerging new Internet capabilities and applications
6. Product and marketing innovation
7. Entry or exit of major firms
8. Diffusion of technical know-how across companies and countries
9. Improvements in efficiency in adjacent markets
10. Reductions in uncertainty and business risk
11. Regulatory influences and government policy changes
12. Changing societal concerns, attitudes, and lifestyles

another is working to curtail demand. Whether the net effect on industry demand is up or down hinges on which driver of change is the more powerful. Similarly, the effects of the drivers of change on each of the five forces should be looked at individually first, and then collectively, to view the overall effect. In summing up the overall effect of industry change on the five forces, it is important to recall that it is the *strongest* of the five forces that determines the degree of competitive pressure on industry profitability and therefore the industry's profit potential. The key question, then, is whether a new strong force is emerging or whether forces that are strong presently are beginning to weaken.

> The most important part of dynamic industry analysis is to determine whether the collective impact of the change drivers will be to increase or decrease market demand, make competition more or less intense, and lead to higher or lower industry profitability.

Developing a Strategy That Takes the Changes in Industry Conditions into Account

The third step in the strategic analysis of industry dynamics—where the real payoff for strategy making comes—is for managers to draw some conclusions about *what strategy adjustments will be needed to deal with the impacts of the changes in industry conditions.* The value of analyzing industry dynamics is to gain better understanding of what strategy adjustments will be needed to cope with the drivers of industry change and the impacts they are likely to have on competitive intensity and industry profitability. Indeed, without understanding the forces driving industry change and the impacts these forces will have on the character of the industry environment and on the company's business over the next one to three years, managers are ill-prepared to craft a strategy tightly matched to emerging conditions. To the extent that managers are unclear about the drivers of industry change and their impacts, or if their views are off-base, the chances of making astute and timely strategy adjustments are slim. So dynamic industry analysis is not something to take lightly; it has practical value and is basic to the task of thinking strategically about where the industry is headed and how to prepare for the changes ahead.

> Dynamic industry analysis, when done properly, pushes company managers to think about what's around the corner and what the company needs to be doing to get ready for it.

QUESTION 4: HOW ARE INDUSTRY RIVALS POSITIONED—WHO IS STRONGLY POSITIONED AND WHO IS NOT?

Since competing companies commonly sell in different price/quality ranges, emphasize different distribution channels, incorporate product features that appeal to different types of buyers, have different geographic coverage, and so on, it stands to reason that some companies enjoy stronger or more attractive market positions than other companies. Understanding which companies are strongly positioned and which are weakly positioned is an integral part of analyzing an industry's competitive structure. The best technique for revealing the market positions of industry competitors is **strategic group mapping.**[16]

LO 3

Become adept at mapping the market positions of key groups of industry rivals.

Using Strategic Group Maps to Assess the Market Positions of Key Competitors

A **strategic group** consists of those industry members with similar competitive approaches and positions in the market.[17] Companies in the same strategic group can resemble one another in any of several ways: They may have comparable product-line breadth, sell in the same price/quality range, emphasize the same distribution channels, use essentially the same product attributes to appeal to similar types of buyers, depend on identical technological approaches, or offer buyers similar services and technical assistance.[18] An industry contains only one strategic group when all sellers pursue essentially identical strategies and have similar market positions. At the other extreme, an industry may contain as many strategic groups as there are competitors when each rival pursues a distinctively different competitive approach and occupies a substantially different market position.

The procedure for constructing a *strategic group map* is straightforward:

- Identify the competitive characteristics that differentiate firms in the industry. Typical variables are price/quality range (high, medium, low), geographic coverage (local, regional, national, global), product-line breadth (wide, narrow), degree of service offered (no frills, limited, full), use of distribution channels (retail, wholesale, Internet, multiple), degree of vertical integration (none, partial, full), and degree of diversification into other industries (none, some, considerable).

- Plot the firms on a two-variable map using pairs of these differentiating characteristics.

- Assign firms occupying about the same map location to the same strategic group.

- Draw circles around each strategic group, making the circles proportional to the size of the group's share of total industry sales revenues.

This produces a two-dimensional diagram like the one for the retail chain store industry in Illustration Capsule 3.1.

Several guidelines need to be observed in creating strategic group maps.[19] First, the two variables selected as axes for the map should *not* be highly correlated; if they are, the circles on the map will fall along a diagonal and reveal nothing more about the relative positions of competitors than would be revealed by comparing the rivals on just one of the variables. For instance, if companies with broad product lines use multiple distribution channels while companies with narrow lines use a single distribution channel, then looking at broad versus narrow product lines reveals just as much about industry positioning as looking at single versus multiple distribution channels; that is, one of the variables is redundant.

Second, the variables chosen as axes for the map should reflect key approaches to offering value to customers and expose big differences in how rivals position themselves to compete in the marketplace. This, of course, means analysts must identify the characteristics that differentiate rival firms and use these differences as variables for the axes and as the basis for deciding which firm belongs in which strategic group. Third, the variables used as axes don't have to be either quantitative or continuous; rather, they can be discrete variables, defined in terms of distinct classes and combinations. Fourth, drawing the sizes of the circles on the map proportional to the combined sales of the firms in each strategic group allows the map to reflect the relative sizes of each strategic

ILLUSTRATION CAPSULE 3.1

Comparative Market Positions of Selected Retail Chains: A Strategic Group Map Example

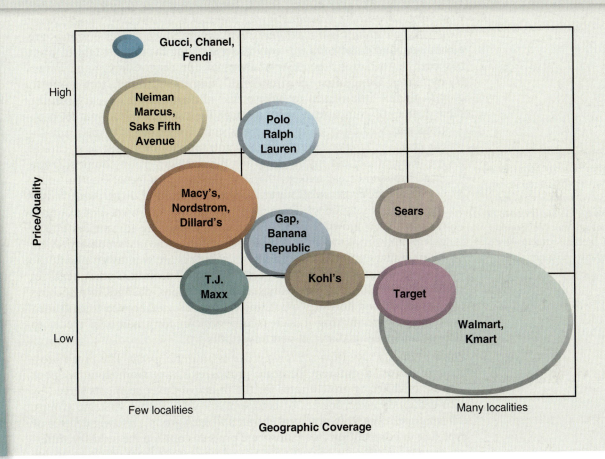

Note: Circles are drawn roughly proportional to the sizes of the chains, based on revenues.

group. Fifth, if more than two good variables can be used as axes for the map, then it is wise to draw several maps to give different views of the relationships among the competitive positions present in the industry's structure—there is not necessarily one best map for portraying how competing firms are positioned.

What Can Be Learned from Strategic Group Maps?

Strategic group maps are revealing in several respects. The most important has to do with identifying which industry members are close rivals and which are distant rivals. Firms in the same strategic group are the closest rivals; the next closest rivals are in the immediately adjacent groups. Often, firms in strategic groups that are far apart on the map hardly compete at all. For instance, Walmart's clientele, merchandise selection, and pricing points are much too different to justify calling Walmart a close

> Strategic group maps reveal which companies are close competitors and which are distant competitors.

competitor of Neiman Marcus or Saks Fifth Avenue. For the same reason, Timex is not a meaningful competitive rival of Rolex.

The second thing to be gleaned from strategic group mapping is that *not all positions on the map are equally attractive.*[20] Two reasons account for why some positions can be more attractive than others:[21]

1. *Prevailing competitive pressures in the industry and drivers of change favor some strategic groups and hurt others.* Discerning which strategic groups are advantaged and disadvantaged requires scrutinizing the map in light of what has been learned from the prior analyses of competitive forces and industry dynamics. Quite often the strength of competition varies from group to group—there's little reason to believe that all firms in an industry feel the same degrees of competitive pressure, since their strategies and market positions may well differ in important respects. For instance, in the ready-to-eat cereal industry, there are significantly higher entry barriers (capital requirements, brand loyalty, etc.) for the strategic group comprising the large branded-cereal makers than for the group of generic-cereal makers or the group of small natural-cereal producers. Furthermore, industry dynamics may affect different groups in different ways. For example, the long-term growth in demand may be increasing for some strategic groups and shrinking for others—as is the case in the news industry, where Internet news services and cable news networks are gaining ground at the expense of newspapers and network television. The industry driving forces of emerging Internet capabilities and applications, changes in who buys the product and how they use it, and changing societal concerns, attitudes, and lifestyles are making it increasingly difficult for traditional media to increase audiences and attract new advertisers.

2. *Profit prospects vary from strategic group to strategic group.* The profit prospects of firms in different strategic groups can vary from good to poor because of differing growth rates for the principal buyer segments served by each group, differing degrees of competitive rivalry within strategic groups, differing pressures from potential entrants to each group, differing degrees of exposure to competition from substitute products outside the industry, differing degrees of supplier or customer bargaining power from group to group, and differing impacts from the industry's drivers of change.

> Some strategic groups are more favorably positioned than others because they confront weaker competitive forces and/or because they are more favorably impacted by the drivers of industry change.

Thus, part of strategic group map analysis always entails drawing conclusions about where on the map is the "best" place to be and why. Which companies/strategic groups are destined to prosper because of their positions? Which companies/strategic groups seem destined to struggle because of their positions? What accounts for why some parts of the map are better than others?

QUESTION 5: WHAT STRATEGIC MOVES ARE RIVALS LIKELY TO MAKE NEXT?

Unless a company pays attention to the strategies and situations of competitors and has some inkling of what moves they will be making, it ends up flying blind into competitive battle. As in sports, scouting the opposition is an essential part of game plan development. **Competitive intelligence** about rivals' strategies, their latest actions and announcements, their financial performance, their strengths and weaknesses, and the thinking and leadership styles of their executives is valuable for anticipating the strategic moves competitors are likely to make next. Having good information about the strategic direction and likely moves of key competitors allows a company to prepare defensive countermoves, to craft its own strategic moves with some confidence about what market maneuvers to expect from rivals in response, and to exploit any openings that arise from competitors' missteps.

Good **competitive intelligence** helps managers avoid the damage to sales and profits that comes from being caught napping by the surprise moves of rivals.

One indicator of the types of moves a rival is likely to make is its financial performance—how much pressure it is under to improve. Rivals with good financial performance are likely to continue their present strategy with only minor fine-tuning. Poorly performing rivals are virtually certain to make fresh strategic moves. Ambitious rivals looking to move up in the industry ranks are strong candidates for launching new strategic offensives to pursue emerging market opportunities and exploit the vulnerabilities of weaker rivals.

Other good clues about what actions a specific company is likely to undertake can often be gleaned from what its management is saying in company press releases, information posted on the company's Web site (especially the presentations management has recently made to securities analysts), and such public documents as annual reports and 10-K filings. (Figure 1.1 in Chapter 1 indicates what to look for in identifying a company's strategy.) Company personnel may be able to pick up useful information from a rival's exhibits at trade shows and from conversations with a rival's customers, suppliers, and former employees. (See Illustration Capsule 3.2 for a discussion of the ethical limits to gathering competitive intelligence.)[22] Many companies have a competitive intelligence unit that sifts through the available information to construct up-to-date strategic profiles of rivals—their current strategies, resources, competitive capabilities, and competitive shortcomings. Such profiles are typically updated regularly and made available to managers and other key personnel.

There are several useful questions that company managers can pose to help predict the likely actions of important rivals:

1. Which competitors have strategies that are producing good results—and thus are likely to make only minor strategic adjustments?
2. Which competitors are losing ground in the marketplace or otherwise struggling to come up with a good strategy—and thus are strong candidates for altering their prices, improving the appeal of their product offerings, moving to a different part of the strategic group map, and otherwise adjusting important elements of their strategy?
3. Which competitors are poised to gain market share, and which ones seem destined to lose ground?
4. Which competitors are likely to rank among the industry leaders five years from now? Do the up-and-coming competitors have strong ambitions and the resources needed to overtake the current industry leader?
5. Which rivals badly need to increase their unit sales and market share? What strategic options are they most likely to pursue: lowering prices, adding new models and styles, expanding their dealer networks, entering additional geographic markets, boosting advertising to build better brand-name awareness, acquiring a weaker competitor, or placing more emphasis on direct sales via their Web sites?

ILLUSTRATION CAPSULE 3.2
Business Ethics and Competitive Intelligence

Those who gather competitive intelligence on rivals can sometimes cross the fine line between honest inquiry and unethical or even illegal behavior. For example, calling rivals to get information about prices, the dates of new product introductions, or wage and salary levels is legal, but misrepresenting one's company affiliation during such calls is unethical. Pumping rivals' representatives at trade shows is ethical only if one wears a name tag with accurate company affiliation indicated.

Avon Products at one point secured information about its biggest rival, Mary Kay Cosmetics (MKC), by having its personnel search through the garbage bins outside MKC's headquarters.[23] When MKC officials learned of the action and sued, Avon claimed it did nothing illegal, since a 1988 Supreme Court case had ruled that trash left on public property (in this case, a sidewalk) was anyone's for the taking. Avon even produced a videotape of its removal of the trash at the MKC site. Avon won the lawsuit—but Avon's action, while legal, scarcely qualifies as ethical.

6. Which rivals are likely to enter new geographic markets or make major moves to substantially increase their sales and market share in a particular geographic region?

7. Which rivals are strong candidates to expand their product offerings and enter new product segments where they do not currently have a presence?

8. Which rivals are good candidates to be acquired? Which rivals may be looking to make an acquisition and are financially able to do so?

To succeed in predicting a competitor's next moves, company strategists need to have a good understanding of each rival's situation, its pattern of behavior in the past, how its managers think, and what the rival's best strategic options are. Doing the necessary detective work can be time-consuming, but scouting competitors well enough to anticipate their next moves allows managers to prepare effective countermoves (perhaps even beat a rival to the punch) and to take rivals' probable actions into account in crafting their own best course of action.

QUESTION 6: WHAT ARE THE KEY FACTORS FOR FUTURE COMPETITIVE SUCCESS?

An industry's **key success factors (KSFs)** are those competitive factors that affect industry members' ability to survive and prosper in the marketplace—the particular strategy elements, product attributes, operational approaches, resources, and competitive capabilities that spell the difference between being a strong competitor and a weak competitor—and between profit and loss. KSFs by their very nature are so important to competitive success that *all firms* in the industry must pay close attention to them or risk becoming an industry laggard or failure. To indicate the significance of KSFs another way, how well the elements of a company's strategy measure up against an industry's KSFs determines just how financially and competitively successful that company will be. Identifying KSFs, in light of the prevailing and anticipated industry and competitive conditions, is therefore always a top priority in analytical and strategy-making considerations. Company strategists need to understand the industry landscape well enough to separate the factors most important to competitive success from those that are less important.

Key success factors vary from industry to industry, and even from time to time within the same industry, as drivers of change and competitive conditions change. But regardless of the circumstances, an industry's key success factors can always be deduced by asking the same three questions:

1. On what basis do buyers of the industry's product choose between the competing brands of sellers? That is, what product attributes and service characteristics are crucial?

2. Given the nature of competitive rivalry and the competitive forces prevailing in the marketplace, what resources and competitive capabilities must a company have to be competitively successful?

3. What shortcomings are almost certain to put a company at a significant competitive disadvantage?

Only rarely are there more than five key factors for competitive success. When there appear to be more, usually some are of greater importance than others. Managers should therefore bear in mind the purpose of identifying key success factors—to determine which factors are most important to competitive success—and resist the temptation to label a factor that has only minor importance as a KSF. Compiling a list of every factor that matters even a little bit defeats the purpose of concentrating management attention on the factors truly critical to long-term competitive success.

In the beer industry, for example, although there are many types of buyers (wholesale, retail, end consumer), it is most important to understand the preferences and buying behavior of the beer drinkers. Their purchase decisions are driven by price, taste, convenient access, and marketing. Thus the KSFs include a *strong network of wholesale distributors* (to get the company's brand stocked and favorably displayed in retail outlets, bars, restaurants, and stadiums, where beer is sold) and *clever advertising* (to induce beer drinkers to buy the company's brand and thereby pull beer sales through the established wholesale/retail channels). Because there is a potential for strong buyer power on the part of large distributors and retail chains, competitive success depends on some mechanism to offset that power, of which advertising (to create demand pull) is one. Thus the KSFs also include *superior product differentiation* (as in microbrews) or *superior firm size and branding capabilities* (as in national brands). The KSFs also include *full utilization of brewing capacity* (to keep manufacturing costs low and offset the high advertising, branding, and product differentiation costs).

Correctly diagnosing an industry's KSFs raises a company's chances of crafting a sound strategy. The key success factors of an industry point to those things that every firm in the industry needs to attend to in order to retain customers and weather the competition. If the company's strategy cannot deliver on the key success factors of its industry, it is unlikely to earn enough profits to remain a viable business. The goal of strategists, however, should be to do more than just meet the KSFs, since all firms in the industry need to clear this bar to survive. The goal of company strategists should be to design a strategy that allows it to compare favorably vis-à-vis rivals on each and every one of the

CORE CONCEPT

Key success factors are the strategy elements, product and service attributes, operational approaches, resources, and competitive capabilities with the greatest impact on competitive success in the marketplace.

LO 4

Understand why in-depth evaluation of a business's strengths and weaknesses in relation to the specific industry conditions it confronts is an essential prerequisite to crafting a strategy that is well-matched to its external situation.

industry's KSFs and that aims at being *distinctively better* than rivals on one (or possibly two) of the KSFs.

QUESTION 7: DOES THE INDUSTRY OFFER GOOD PROSPECTS FOR ATTRACTIVE PROFITS?

The final step in evaluating the industry and competitive environment is to use the results of the analyses performed in answering Questions 1 to 6 to determine whether the industry presents the company with strong prospects for attractive profits. The important factors on which to base a conclusion include:

- The industry's growth potential.
- Whether strong competitive forces are squeezing industry profitability to sub-par levels.
- Whether industry profitability will be favorably or unfavorably affected by the prevailing drivers of change in the industry (i.e., whether the industry growth potential and competition appear destined to grow stronger or weaker).
- Whether the company occupies a stronger market position than rivals (one more capable of withstanding negative competitive forces) and whether this is likely to change in the course of competitive interactions.
- How well the company's strategy delivers on the industry key success factors.

As a general proposition, if a company can conclude that its overall profit prospects are above average in the industry, then the industry environment is basically attractive *(for that company)*; if industry profit prospects are below average, conditions are unattractive *(for the company)*. However, it is a mistake to think of a particular industry as being equally attractive or unattractive to all industry participants and all potential entrants.[24] Attractiveness is relative, not absolute, and conclusions one way or the other have to be drawn from the perspective of a particular company. For instance, a favorably positioned competitor may see ample opportunity to capitalize on the vulnerabilities of weaker rivals even though industry conditions are otherwise somewhat dismal. And even if an industry has appealing potential for growth and profitability, a weak competitor (one that may be part of an unfavorably positioned strategic group) may conclude that having to fight a steep uphill battle against much stronger rivals holds little promise of eventual market success or good return on shareholder investment. Similarly, industries attractive to insiders may be unattractive to outsiders because of the difficulty of challenging current market leaders with their particular resources and competencies or because they have more attractive opportunities elsewhere.

> The degree to which an industry is attractive or un-attractive is not the same for all industry participants and all potential entrants.

When a company decides an industry is fundamentally attractive and presents good opportunities, a strong case can be made that it should invest aggressively to capture the opportunities it sees and to improve its long-term competitive position in the business. When a strong competitor concludes an industry is becoming less attractive, it may elect to simply protect its present position, investing cautiously if at all and looking for opportunities in other industries. A competitively weak company in an unattractive industry may see its best option as finding a buyer, perhaps a rival, to acquire its business.

KEY POINTS

Thinking strategically about a company's external situation involves probing for answers to the following seven questions:

1. *Does the industry offer attractive opportunities for growth?* Industries differ significantly on such factors as market size and growth rate, geographic scope, life-cycle stage, the number and sizes of sellers, industry capacity, and other conditions that describe the industry's demand-supply balance and opportunities for growth. Identifying the industry's basic economic features and growth potential sets the stage for the analysis to come, since they play an important role in determining an industry's potential for attractive profits.

2. *What kinds of competitive forces are industry members facing, and how strong is each force?* The strength of competition is a composite of five forces: (1) competitive pressures stemming from the competitive jockeying among industry rivals, (2) competitive pressures associated with the market inroads being made by the sellers of substitutes, (3) competitive pressures associated with the threat of new entrants into the market, (4) competitive pressures stemming from supplier bargaining power, and (5) competitive pressures stemming from buyer bargaining. The nature and strength of the competitive pressures have to be examined force by force and their collective strength must be evaluated. The strongest forces, however, are the ultimate determinant of the intensity of the competitive pressure on industry profitability. Working through the five-forces model aids strategy makers in assessing how to insulate the company from the strongest forces, identify attractive arenas for expansion, or alter the competitive conditions so that they offer more favorable prospects for profitability.

3. *What factors are driving changes in the industry, and what impact will these changes have on competitive intensity and industry profitability?* Industry and competitive conditions change because of a variety of forces, some coming from the industry's macro-environment and others originating within the industry. The most common change drivers include changes in the long-term industry growth rate, increasing globalization, changing buyer demographics, technological change, Internet-related developments, product and marketing innovation, entry or exit of major firms, diffusion of know-how, efficiency improvements in adjacent markets, reductions in uncertainty and business risk, government policy changes, and changing societal factors. Once an industry's change drivers have been identified, the analytical task becomes one of determining whether they are acting, individually and collectively, to make the industry environment more or less attractive. Are the change drivers causing demand for the industry's product to increase or decrease? Are they acting to make competition more or less intense? Will they lead to higher or lower industry profitability?

4. *What market positions do industry rivals occupy—who is strongly positioned and who is not?* Strategic group mapping is a valuable tool for understanding the similarities, differences, strengths, and weaknesses inherent in the market positions of rival companies. Rivals in the same or nearby strategic groups

are close competitors, whereas companies in distant strategic groups usually pose little or no immediate threat. The lesson of strategic group mapping is that some positions on the map are more favorable than others. The profit potential of different strategic groups varies due to strengths and weaknesses in each group's market position. Often, industry competitive pressures and change drivers favor some strategic groups and hurt others.

5. *What strategic moves are rivals likely to make next?* Scouting competitors well enough to anticipate their actions can help a company prepare effective countermoves (perhaps even beating a rival to the punch) and allows managers to take rivals' probable actions into account in designing their own company's best course of action. Managers who fail to study competitors risk being caught unprepared by the strategic moves of rivals.

6. *What are the key factors for competitive success?* An industry's key success factors (KSFs) are the particular strategy elements, product attributes, operational approaches, resources, and competitive capabilities that all industry members must have in order to survive and prosper in the industry. KSFs vary by industry and may vary over time as well. For any industry, however, they can be deduced by answering three basic questions: (1) On what basis do buyers of the industry's product choose between the competing brands of sellers, (2) what resources and competitive capabilities must a company have to be competitively successful, and (3) what shortcomings are almost certain to put a company at a significant competitive disadvantage? Correctly diagnosing an industry's KSFs raises a company's chances of crafting a sound strategy.

7. *Does the outlook for the industry present the company with sufficiently attractive prospects for profitability?* The last step in industry analysis is summing up the results from answering questions 1 to 6. If the answers reveal that a company's overall profit prospects in that industry are above average, then the industry environment is basically attractive *for that company;* if industry profit prospects are below average, conditions are unattractive for them. What may look like an attractive environment for one company may appear to be unattractive from the perspective of a different company.

Clear, insightful diagnosis of a company's external situation is an essential first step in crafting strategies that are well matched to industry and competitive conditions. To do cutting-edge strategic thinking about the external environment, managers must know what questions to pose and what analytical tools to use in answering these questions. This is why this chapter has concentrated on suggesting the right questions to ask, explaining concepts and analytical approaches, and indicating the kinds of things to look for.

ASSURANCE OF LEARNING EXERCISES

LO 1, LO 2

1. Prepare a brief analysis of the snack-food industry using the information provided on industry trade association Web sites. On the basis of information provided on these Web sites, draw a five-forces diagram for the snack-food industry and briefly discuss the nature and strength of each of the five competitive forces. What factors are driving change in the industry?

LO 1, LO 3

2. Based on the strategic group map in Illustration Capsule 3.1, who are Nordstrom's closest competitors? Between which two strategic groups is competition the strongest? Why do you think no retail chains are positioned in the upper right corner of the map? Which company/strategic group faces the weakest competition from the members of other strategic groups?

LO 1, LO 4

3. Using your knowledge as a snack-food consumer and your analysis of the five forces in that industry (from question 1), describe the key success factors for the snack-food industry. Your list should contain no more than six industry KSFs. In deciding on your list, it's important to distinguish between factors critical for the success of *any* firm in the industry and factors that pertain only to specific companies.

EXERCISES FOR SIMULATION PARTICIPANTS

LO 1

1. Which of the five competitive forces is creating the strongest competitive pressures for your company?

2. What are the "competitive weapons" that rival companies in your industry can use to gain sales and market share? See Table 3.2 to help you identify possible competitive tactics. (You may be able to think of others.)

3. What are the factors affecting the intensity of rivalry in the industry in which your company is competing. Use Figure 3.4 and the accompanying discussion to help you pinpoint the specific factors most affecting competitive intensity. Would you characterize the rivalry among the companies in your industry as brutal, strong, moderate, or relatively weak? Why?

LO 2

4. Are there any factors driving change in the industry in which your company is competing? What impact will these drivers of change have? How will they change demand or supply? Will they cause competition to become more or less intense? Will they act to boost or squeeze profit margins? List at least two actions your company should consider taking in order to combat any negative impacts of the factors driving change.

LO 3

5. Draw a strategic group map showing the market positions of the companies in your industry. Which companies do you believe are in the most attractive position on the map? Which companies are the most weakly positioned? Which companies do you believe are likely to try to move to a different position on the strategic group map?

LO 4

6. What do you see as the key factors for being a successful competitor in your industry? List at least three.

ENDNOTES

[1] For a more extended discussion of the problems with the life-cycle hypothesis, see Michael E. Porter, *Competitive Strategy: Techniques for Analyzing Industries and Competitors* (New York: Free Press, 1980), pp. 157–62.
[2] The five-forces model of competition is the creation of Professor Michael Porter of the Harvard Business School. See Michael E. Porter, "How Competitive Forces Shape Strategy," *Harvard Business Review* 57, no. 2 (March–April 1979), pp. 137–45; Porter, *Competitive Strategy*, chap. 1; and Porter's most recent discussion of the model, "The Five Competitive Forces That Shape Strategy," *Harvard Business Review* 86, no. 1 (January 2008), pp. 78–93.
[3] For a discussion of how a company's actions to counter the moves of rival firms tend to escalate competitive pressures, see Pamela J. Derfus, Patrick G. Maggitti, Curtis M.Grimm, and Ken G. Smith, "The Red Queen Effect: Competitive Actions and Firm Performance," *Academy of Management Journal* 51, no. 1 (February 2008), pp. 61–80.
[4] Many of these indicators of whether rivalry produces intense competitive pressures are based on Porter, *Competitive Strategy*, pp. 17–21.
[5] Porter, *Competitive Strategy*, p. 7; Porter, "The Five Competitive Forces That Shape Strategy," p. 81.
[6] The role of entry barriers in shaping the strength of competition in a particular market has long been a standard topic in the literature of microeconomics. For a discussion of how entry barriers affect competitive pressures associated with potential entry, see J. S. Bain, *Barriers to New Competition* (Cambridge, MA: Harvard University Press, 1956); F. M. Scherer, *Industrial Market Structure and Economic Performance* (Chicago: Rand McNally, 1971), pp. 216–20, 226–33; Porter, *Competitive Strategy*, pp. 7–17; Porter, "The Five Competitive Forces That Shape Strategy," pp. 80–82.
[7] For a good discussion of this point, see George S. Yip, "Gateways to Entry," *Harvard Business Review* 60, no. 5 (September–October 1982), pp. 85–93.
[8] C. A. Montgomery and S. Hariharan, "Diversified Expansion by Large Established Firms," *Journal of Economic Behavior & Organization* 15, no. 1 (January 1991), pp. 71–89.
[9] Porter, "How Competitive Forces Shape Strategy," p. 142; Porter, *Competitive Strategy*, pp. 23–24.
[10] Porter, *Competitive Strategy*, p. 10.
[11] Ibid., pp. 27–28.
[12] Ibid., pp. 24–27.
[13] Porter, "The Five Competitive Forces That Shape Strategy," p. 80.
[14] Most of the candidate driving forces described here are based on the discussion in Porter, *Competitive Strategy*, pp. 164–83.
[15] D. Yoffie, "Cola Wars Continue: Coke and Pepsi in 2006," Harvard Business School case 9-706-447, rev. April 2, 2007; B. C. Lynn, "How Detroit Went Bottom-Up," *American Prospect*, October 2009, pp. 21–24.
[16] Porter, *Competitive Strategy*, chap. 7.
[17] Ibid., pp. 129–30.
[18] For an excellent discussion of how to identify the factors that define strategic groups, see Mary Ellen Gordon and George R. Milne, "Selecting the Dimensions That Define Strategic Groups: A Novel Market-Driven Approach," *Journal of Managerial Issues* 11, no. 2 (Summer 1999), pp. 213–33.
[19] Porter, *Competitive Strategy*, pp. 152–54.
[20] For other benefits of strategic group analysis, see Avi Fiegenbaum and Howard Thomas, "Strategic Groups as Reference Groups: Theory, Modeling and Empirical Examination of Industry and Competitive Strategy," *Strategic Management Journal* 16 (1995), pp. 461–76; S. Ade Olusoga, Michael P. Mokwa, and Charles H. Noble, "Strategic Groups, Mobility Barriers, and Competitive Advantage," *Journal of Business Research* 33 (1995), pp. 153–64.
[21] Porter, *Competitive Strategy*, pp. 130, 132–38, and 152–55.
[22] For further discussion of legal and ethical ways of gathering competitive intelligence on rival companies, see Larry Kahaner, *Competitive Intelligence* (New York: Simon & Schuster, 1996).
[23] Ibid., pp. 84–85.
[24] B. Wernerfelt and C. Montgomery, "What Is an Attractive Industry?" *Management Science* 32, no. 10 (October 1986), pp. 1223–30.

CHAPTER 4

EVALUATING A COMPANY'S RESOURCES, CAPABILITIES, AND COMPETITIVENESS

> Before executives can chart a new strategy, they must reach common understanding of the company's current position.
>
> **—W. Chan Kim and Renée Mauborgne**
> *Consultants and INSEAD Professors*

> You have to learn to treat people as a resource ... you have to ask not what do they cost, but what is the yield, what can they produce?
>
> **—Peter F. Drucker**
> *Business Thinker and Management Consultant*

> Organizations succeed in a competitive marketplace over the long run because they can do certain things their customers value better than can their competitors.
>
> **—Robert Hayes, Gary Pisano, and David Upton**
> *Harvard Business School Professors*

> Only firms who are able to continually build new strategic assets faster and cheaper than their competitors will earn superior returns over the long term.
>
> **—C. C. Markides and P. J. Williamson**
> *London Business School Professors and Consultants*

LEARNING OBJECTIVES

LO 1. Learn how to take stock of how well a company's strategy is working.

LO 2. Understand why a company's resources and capabilities are central to its strategic approach and how to evaluate their potential for giving the company a competitive edge over rivals.

LO 3. Discover how to assess the company's strengths and weaknesses in light of market opportunities and external threats.

LO 4. Grasp how a company's value chain activities can affect the company's cost structure, degree of differentiation, and competitive advantage.

LO 5. Understand how a comprehensive evaluation of a company's competitive situation can assist managers in making critical decisions about their next strategic moves.

In Chapter 3 we described how to use the tools of industry analysis to assess the profit potential and key success factors of a company's external environment. This laid the groundwork for matching a company's strategy to its external situation. In this chapter we discuss techniques for evaluating a company's internal situation, including its collection of resources and capabilities and the activities it performs along its value chain. Internal analysis enables managers to determine whether their strategy has appealing prospects for giving the company a significant competitive edge over rival firms. Combined with external analysis, it facilitates an understanding of how to reposition a firm to take advantage of new opportunities and to cope with emerging competitive threats. The analytical spotlight will be trained on six questions:

1. How well is the company's present strategy working?

2. What are the company's competitively important resources and capabilities?

3. Is the company able to take advantage of market opportunities and overcome external threats to its external well-being?

4. Are the company's prices and costs competitive with those of key rivals, and does it have an appealing customer value proposition?

5. Is the company competitively stronger or weaker than key rivals?

6. What strategic issues and problems merit front-burner managerial attention?

In probing for answers to these questions, five analytical tools—resource and capability analysis, SWOT analysis, value chain analysis, benchmarking, and competitive strength assessment—will be used. All five are valuable techniques for revealing a company's competitiveness and for helping company managers match their strategy to the company's own particular circumstances.

QUESTION 1: HOW WELL IS THE COMPANY'S PRESENT STRATEGY WORKING?

LO 1

Learn how to take stock of how well a company's strategy is working.

In evaluating how well a company's present strategy is working, the best way to start is with a clear view of what the strategy entails. Figure 4.1 shows the key components of a single-business company's strategy. The first thing to examine is the company's competitive approach. What moves has the company made recently to attract customers and improve its market position—for instance, has it cut prices, improved the design of its product, added new features, stepped up advertising, entered a new geographic market (domestic or foreign), or merged with a competitor? Is it striving for a competitive advantage based on low costs or an appealingly different or better product offering? Is it concentrating on serving a broad spectrum of customers or a narrow market niche? The company's functional strategies in R&D, production, marketing, finance, human resources, information technology, and so on further characterize company strategy, as do any efforts to establish competitively valuable alliances or partnerships with other enterprises.

The two best indicators of how well a company's strategy is working are (1) whether the company is achieving its stated financial and strategic objectives and (2) whether the company is an above-average industry performer. Persistent shortfalls in meeting company performance targets and weak performance relative to rivals are reliable warning signs that the company has a weak strategy or suffers from poor strategy execution or both. Other indicators of how well a company's strategy is working include:

- Whether the firm's sales are growing faster than, slower than, or about the same pace as the market as a whole, thus resulting in a rising, eroding, or stable market share.
- Whether the company is acquiring new customers at an attractive rate as well as retaining existing customers.
- Whether the firm's profit margins are increasing or decreasing and how well its margins compare to rival firms' margins.
- Trends in the firm's net profits and return on investment and how they compare to the same trends for other companies in the industry.
- Whether the company's overall financial strength and credit rating are improving or declining.
- How shareholders view the company on the basis of trends in the company's stock price and shareholder value (relative to the stock price trends at other companies in the industry).
- Whether the firm's image and reputation with its customers are growing stronger or weaker.
- How well the company stacks up against rivals on technology, product innovation, customer service, product quality, delivery time, price, getting newly developed products to market quickly, and other relevant factors on which buyers base their choices.
- Whether key measures of operating performance (such as days of inventory, employee productivity, unit cost, defect rate, scrap rate, order-filling accuracy, delivery times, and warranty costs) are improving, remaining steady, or deteriorating.

Figure 4.1   Identifying the Components of a Single-Business Company's Strategy

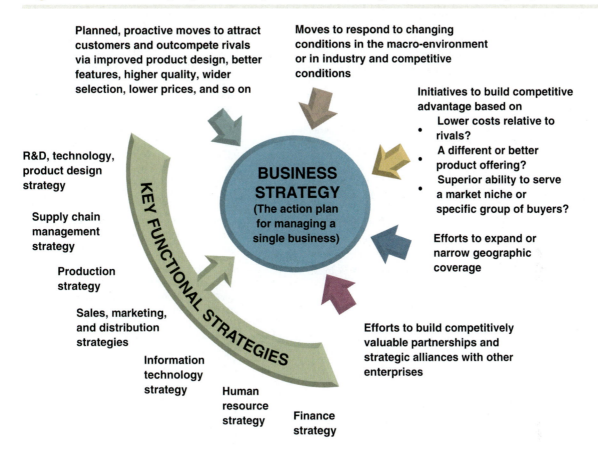

Planned, proactive moves to attract customers and outcompete rivals via improved product design, better features, higher quality, wider selection, lower prices, and so on

Moves to respond to changing conditions in the macro-environment or in industry and competitive conditions

Initiatives to build competitive advantage based on
- **Lower costs relative to rivals?**
- **A different or better product offering?**
- **Superior ability to serve a market niche or specific group of buyers?**

R&D, technology, product design strategy

Supply chain management strategy

Production strategy

Sales, marketing, and distribution strategies

Information technology strategy

Human resource strategy

Finance strategy

KEY FUNCTIONAL STRATEGIES

BUSINESS STRATEGY (The action plan for managing a single business)

Efforts to expand or narrow geographic coverage

Efforts to build competitively valuable partnerships and strategic alliances with other enterprises

The stronger a company's current overall performance, the less likely the need for radical changes in strategy. The weaker a company's financial performance and market standing, the more its current strategy must be questioned. Weak performance is almost always a sign of weak strategy, weak execution, or both.

Evaluating how well a company's strategy is working should include quantitative as well as qualitative assessments. Table 4.1 provides a compilation of the financial ratios most commonly used to evaluate a company's financial performance and balance sheet strength.

> The stronger a company's financial performance and market position, the more likely it has a well-conceived, well-executed strategy.

QUESTION 2: WHAT ARE THE COMPANY'S COMPETITIVELY IMPORTANT RESOURCES AND CAPABILITIES?

Regardless of how well the strategy is working, it is important for managers to understand the underlying reasons. Clearly, this is critical if strategy changes are needed. But even when the strategy is working well, this can help managers to bolster a

Table 4.1   **Key Financial Ratios: How to Calculate Them and What They Mean**

Ratio	How Calculated	What It Shows
Profitability Ratios		
1. Gross profit margin	$$\dfrac{\text{Revenues} - \text{Cost of goods sold}}{\text{Revenues}}$$	Shows the percentage of revenues available to cover operating expenses and yield a profit. Higher is better, and the trend should be upward.
2. Operating profit margin (or return on sales)	$$\dfrac{\text{Revenues} - \text{Operating expenses}}{\text{Revenues}}$$ *or* $$\dfrac{\text{Operating income}}{\text{Revenues}}$$	Shows how much profit is earned on each dollar of sales, before paying interest charges and income taxes. Earnings before interest and taxes is known as *EBIT* in financial and business accounting. Higher is better, and the trend should be upward.
3. Net profit margin (or net return on sales)	$$\dfrac{\text{Profits after taxes}}{\text{Revenues}}$$	Shows after-tax profits per dollar of sales. Higher is better, and the trend should be upward.
4. Return on total assets	$$\dfrac{\text{Profits after taxes } + \text{ Interest}}{\text{Total assets}}$$	A measure of the return on total investment in the enterprise. Interest is added to after-tax profits to form the numerator, since total assets are financed by creditors as well as by stockholders. Higher is better, and the trend should be upward.
5. Return on stockholder's equity	$$\dfrac{\text{Profits after taxes}}{\text{Total stockholders' equity}}$$	Shows the return stockholders are earning on their investment in the enterprise. A return in the 12% to 15% range is "average," and the trend should be upward.
6. Return on invested capital	$$\dfrac{\text{Profits after taxes}}{\text{Long-term debt} + \text{total equity}}$$	Shows how effectively a company uses the monetary capital invested in its operations and the returns to those investments. Higher is better, and the trend should be upward.
7. Earnings per share	$$\dfrac{\text{Profits after taxes}}{\substack{\text{Number of shares of common} \\ \text{stock outstanding}}}$$	Shows the earnings for each share of common stock outstanding. The trend should be upward, and the bigger the annual percentage gains, the better.
Liquidity Ratios		
1. Current ratio	$$\dfrac{\text{Current assets}}{\text{Current liabilities}}$$	Shows a firm's ability to pay current liabilities using assets that can be converted to cash in the near term. The ratio should definitely be higher than 1.0; a ratio of 2.0 or higher is better still.
2. Working capital	Current assets − Current liabilities	Shows the cash available for a firm's day-to-day operations. Bigger amounts are better because the company has more internal funds available to (1) pay its current liabilities on a timely basis and (2) finance inventory expansion, additional accounts receivable, and a larger base of operations without resorting to borrowing or raising more equity capital.

(Continued)

Ratio	How Calculated	What It Shows
Leverage Ratios		
1. Debt-to-assets ratio	$$\frac{\text{Total debt}}{\text{Total assets}}$$	Measures the extent to which borrowed funds have been used to finance the firm's operations. A low fraction or ratio is better—a high fraction indicates overuse of debt and greater risk of bankruptcy.
2. Long-term debt-to-capital ratio	$$\frac{\text{Long-term debt}}{\text{Long-term debt } + \text{Total stockholders' equity}}$$	An important measure of creditworthiness and balance sheet strength. It indicates the percentage of capital investment that has been financed by creditors and bondholders. A ratio below 0.25 is usually preferable since monies invested by stockholders account for 75% or more of the company's total capital. The lower the ratio, the greater the capacity to borrow additional funds. A debt-to capital ratio above 0.50 and certainly above 0.75 indicates a heavy and perhaps excessive reliance on debt, lower creditworthiness, and weak balance sheet strength.
3. Debt-to-equity ratio	$$\frac{\text{Total debt}}{\text{Total stockholders' equity}}$$	Should usually be less than 1.0. A high ratio (especially above 1.0) signals excessive debt, lower creditworthiness, and weaker balance sheet strength.
4. Long-term debt-to-equity ratio	$$\frac{\text{Long-term debt}}{\text{Total stockholders' equity}}$$	Shows the balance between debt and equity in the firm's *long-term* capital structure. A low ratio indicates greater capacity to borrow additional funds if needed.
5. Times-interest-earned (or coverage) ratio	$$\frac{\text{Operating income}}{\text{Interest expenses}}$$	Measures the ability to pay annual interest charges. Lenders usually insist on a minimum ratio of 2.0, but ratios above 3.0 signal better creditworthiness.
Activity Ratios		
1. Days of inventory	$$\frac{\text{Inventory}}{\text{Cost of goods sold} \div 365}$$	Measures inventory management efficiency. Fewer days of inventory are usually better.
2. Inventory turnover	$$\frac{\text{Cost of goods sold}}{\text{Inventory}}$$	Measures the number of inventory turns per year. Higher is better.
3. Average collection period	$$\frac{\text{Accounts receivable}}{\text{Total sales} \div 365}$$ *or* $$\frac{\text{Accounts receivable}}{\text{Average daily sales}}$$	Indicates the average length of time the firm must wait after making a sale to receive cash payment. A shorter collection time is better.
Other Important Measures of Financial Performance		
1. Dividend yield on common stock	$$\frac{\text{Annual dividends per share}}{\text{Current market price per share}}$$	A measure of the return to owners received in the form of dividends.

(Continued)

Ratio	How Calculated	What It Shows
2. Price-earnings ratio	$$\frac{\text{Current market price per share}}{\text{Earnings per share}}$$	A P/E ratio above 20 indicates strong investor confidence in a firm's outlook and earnings growth. Firms whose future earnings are at risk or likely to grow slowly typically have ratios below 12.
3. Dividend payout ratio	$$\frac{\text{Annual dividends per share}}{\text{Earnings per share}}$$	Indicates the percentage of after-tax profits paid out as dividends.
4. Internal cash flow	After tax profits + Depreciation	A quick and rough estimate of the cash a company's business is generating after payment of operating expenses, interest, and taxes. Such amounts can be used for dividend payments or funding capital expenditures.
5. Free cash flow	After tax profits + Depreciation − Capital Expenditures − Dividends	A quick and rough estimate of the cash a company's business is generating after payment of operating expenses, interest, taxes, dividends, and desirable reinvestments in the business. The larger a company's free cash flow, the greater is its ability to internally fund new strategic initiatives, repay debt, make new acquisitions, repurchase shares of stock, or increase dividend payments.

CORE CONCEPT

A company's resources and capabilities represent its **competitive assets** and are big determinants of its competitiveness and ability to succeed in the marketplace.

LO 2

Understand why a company's resources and capabilities are central to its strategic approach and how to evaluate their potential for giving the company a competitive edge over rivals.

successful strategy and avoid harmful missteps. How well a strategy works depends a great deal on the relative strengths and weaknesses of a company's resources and capabilities. A company's resources and capabilities are its **competitive assets** and determine whether its competitive power in the marketplace will be impressively strong or disappointingly weak. Companies with minimal or only ordinary competitive assets nearly always are relegated to a trailing position in the industry.

Resource and capability analysis provides managers with a powerful tool for sizing up the company's competitive assets and determining whether they can provide the foundation necessary for competitive success in the marketplace. This is a two step process. The first step is for managers to identify the company's resources and capabilities so that they have a better idea of what they have to work with in crafting the company's competitive strategy. The second step is to examine the company's resources and capabilities more closely to ascertain which of them are the most competitively valuable and to determine whether the best of them can help the firm attain a sustainable competitive advantage over rival firms.[1] This step involves applying the *four tests of a resource's competitive power*.

Identifying the Company's Resources and Capabilities

A firm's resources and capabilities are the fundamental building blocks of its competitive strategy. In crafting strategy, it is essential for managers to be able to recognize a resource or an organizational capability for what it is and to know how to take stock of the company's full complement of resources and capabilities.

To do a good job with this, managers and strategists need to start with a basic understanding of what these terms mean.

In brief, a **resource** is a productive input or competitive asset that is owned or controlled by the firm. Firms have many different types of resources at their disposal that vary not only in kind but in quality as well. Some are higher-quality than others, and some are more competitively valuable, having greater potential to give a firm a competitive advantage over its rivals. For example, a company's brand is a resource, as is an R&D team—yet some brands such as Coca-Cola and Kleenex are well known, with enduring value, while others have little more name recognition than generic products. In similar fashion, some R&D teams are far more innovative and productive than others due to the outstanding talents of the individual team members, the team's composition, and its chemistry.

A **capability** is the capacity of a firm to perform some activity proficiently. Capabilities also vary in form, quality, and competitive importance, with some being more competitively valuable than others. Apple's product innovation capabilities are widely recognized as being far superior to those of its competitors; Nordstrom is known for its superior incentive management capabilities; PepsiCo is admired for its marketing and brand management capabilities.

Resource and capability analysis is a powerful tool for sizing up a company's competitive assets and determining if they can support a sustainable competitive advantage over market rivals.

CORE CONCEPT

A **resource** is a competitive asset that is owned or controlled by a company; a **capability** is the capacity of a firm to perform some activity proficiently.

Types of Company Resources A useful way to identify a company's resources is to look for them within categories, as shown in Table 4.2. Broadly speaking, resources can be divided into two main categories:

Table 4.2 Types of Company Resources

Tangible Resources

- *Physical resources:* ownership of or access rights to natural resources (such as mineral deposits); state-of-the-art manufacturing plants, equipment, and/or distribution facilities; land and real estate; the locations of stores, manufacturing plants, or distribution centers, including the overall pattern of their physical locations
- *Financial resources:* cash and cash equivalents; marketable securities; other financial assets such as the borrowing capacity of the firm (as indicated from its balance sheet and credit rating)
- *Technological assets:* patents, copyrights, and trade secrets; production technology, stock of other technologies, technological processes
- *Organizational resources:* IT and communication systems (servers, workstations, etc.); other planning, coordination, and control systems; the company's organizational design and reporting structure

Intangible Resources

- *Human assets and intellectual capital:* the experience, cumulative learning, and tacit knowledge of employees; the education, intellectual capital, and know-how of specialized teams and work groups; the knowledge of key personnel concerning important business functions (e.g., skills in keeping operating costs low, improving product quality, and providing customer service); managerial talent; the creativity and innovativeness of certain personnel
- *Brands, company image, and reputational assets:* brand names, trademarks, product image, buyer loyalty and goodwill; company image, reputation for quality, service, and reliability; reputation with suppliers and partners for fair dealing
- *Relationships:* alliances or joint ventures that provide access to technologies, specialized know-how, or geographic markets; partnerships with suppliers that reduce costs and/or enhance product quality and performance; networks of dealers or distributors; the trust established with various partners
- *Company culture and incentive system:* the norms of behavior, business principles, and ingrained beliefs within the company; the attachment of personnel to the company's ideals; the compensation system and the motivation level of company personnel

tangible and **intangible** resources. Although *human resources* make up one of the most important parts of a company's resource base, we include them in the intangible category to emphasize the role played by the skills, talents, and knowledge of a company's human resources.

Tangible resources are the most easily identified, since tangible resources are those that can be touched or quantified readily. Obviously, they include various types of *physical resources* such as manufacturing facilities and mineral resources, but they also include a company's *financial resources, technological resources,* and *organizational resources* such as the company's communication and control systems.

Intangible resources are harder to discern, but they are often among the most important of a firm's competitive assets. They include various sorts of *human assets and intellectual capital,* as well as a company's *brands, image, and reputational assets.* While intangible resources have no material existence on their own, they are often embodied in something material. Thus the skills and knowledge resources of a firm are embodied in its managers and employees; a company's brand name is embodied in the company logo or product labels. Other important kinds of intangible resources include a company's *relationships* with suppliers, buyers, or partners of various sorts, and the *company's culture and incentive system.* A more detailed listing of the various types of tangible and intangible resources is provided in Table 4.2.

Listing a company's resources category by category can prevent managers from inadvertently overlooking some company resources that might be competitively important. At times, it can be difficult to decide exactly how to categorize certain types of resources. For example, resources such as a work group's specialized expertise in developing innovative products can be considered to be technological assets or human assets or intellectual capital and knowledge assets; the work ethic and drive of a company's workforce could be included under the company's human assets or its culture and incentive system. In this regard, it is important to remember that *it is not exactly how a resource is categorized that matters but, rather, that all of the company's different types of resources are included in the inventory.* The real purpose of using categories in identifying a company's resources is to ensure that none of a company's resources go unnoticed when sizing up the company's competitive assets.

Identifying Capabilities

Organizational capabilities are more complex entities than resources; indeed, they are built up through the use of resources and draw on some combination of the firm's resources as they are exercised.[2] Virtually all organizational capabilities are *knowledge-based, residing in people and in a company's intellectual capital or in organizational processes and systems, which embody tacit knowledge.* For example, General Mill's brand management capabilities draw on the knowledge of the company's brand managers, the expertise of its marketing department, and the company's relationships with retailers, since brand building is a cooperative activity requiring retailer support. The capability in video game design for which Electronic Arts is known derives from the creative talents and technological expertise of its highly talented game developers, the company's culture of creativity, and a compensation system that generously rewards talented developers for creating best-selling video games.

Because of their complexity, capabilities are harder to categorize than resources and more challenging to search for as a result. There are, however, two approaches that can make the process of uncovering and identifying a firm's capabilities more systematic. The first method takes the completed listing of a firm's resources as its starting point. Since capabilities are built from resources and utilize resources as they are exercised, a firm's resources can provide a strong set of clues about the types of capabilities the firm is likely to have accumulated. This approach simply involves looking over the firm's resources and considering whether (and to what extent) the firm has built up any related capabilities. So, for example, a fleet of trucks, the latest RFID tracking technology, and a set of large automated distribution centers may be indicative of sophisticated capabilities in logistics and distribution. R&D teams composed of top scientists with expertise in genomics may suggest organizational capabilities in developing new gene therapies or in biotechnology more generally.

The second method of identifying a firm's capabilities takes a functional approach. Many capabilities relate to fairly specific functions; these draw on a limited set of resources and typically involve a single department or organizational unit. Capabilities in injection molding or continuous casting or metal stamping are manufacturing-related; capabilities in direct selling, promotional pricing, or database marketing all connect to the sales and marketing functions; capabilities in basic research, strategic innovation, or new product development link to a company's R&D function. This approach requires managers to survey the various functions a firm performs to find the different capabilities associated with each function.

A problem with this second method is that many of the most important capabilities of firms are inherently *cross-functional*. Cross-functional capabilities draw on a number of different kinds of resources and are generally multidisciplinary in nature—they spring from the effective collaboration among people with different expertise working in different organizational units. An example is the capability for fast-cycle, continuous product innovation that comes from teaming the efforts of groups with expertise in market research, new product R&D, design and engineering, advanced manufacturing, and market testing. Cross-functional capabilities and other complex capabilities involving numerous linked and closely integrated competitive assets are sometimes referred to as **resource bundles.** Although resource bundles are not as easily pigeonholed as other types of resources and capabilities, they can still be identified by looking for company activities that link different types of resources, functions, and departmental units. It is important not to miss identifying a company's resource bundles, since they can be the most competitively important of a firm's competitive assets. Unless it includes a company's cross-functional capabilities and resource bundles, no identification of a company's resources and capabilities can be considered complete.

> **CORE CONCEPT**
>
> A **resource bundle** is a linked and closely integrated set of competitive assets centered around one or more cross-functional capabilities.

Determining Whether a Company's Resources and Capabilities Are Potent Enough to Produce a Sustainable Competitive Advantage

To determine the strategic relevance and competitive power of a firm's resources and capabilities, it is necessary to go beyond merely identifying a company's resources and capabilities. The second step in resource and capability analysis is designed to ascertain which of a company's resources and capabilities are competitively valuable and to what extent they can support a company's quest for a sustainable competitive advantage over market rivals. This involves probing the *caliber* of a firm's competitive assets relative to those of its competitors.[3] When a company has competitive assets that are central to its strategy and superior to those of rival firms, it has a competitive advantage over other firms. If this advantage proves durable despite the best efforts of competitors to overcome it, then the company is said to have a *sustainable* **competitive advantage.** While it may be difficult for a company to achieve a sustainable competitive advantage, it is an important strategic objective because it imparts a potential for attractive and long-lived profitability.

The Four Tests of a Resource's Competitive Power

The competitive power of a resource or capability is measured by how many of the following four tests it can pass.[4] The first two tests determine whether a resource or capability can support a competitive advantage. The last two determine whether the competitive advantage can be sustained in the face of active competition.

1. *Is the resource (or capability) competitively valuable?* To be competitively valuable, a resource or capability must be directly relevant to the company's strategy, making the company a more effective competitor, able to exploit market opportunities and ward off external threats. Unless the resource contributes to the effectiveness of the company's strategy, it cannot pass this first test. An indicator of its effectiveness is whether the resource enables the company to strengthen its business model through a better customer value proposition and/or profit formula. Companies have to guard against contending that something they do well is necessarily competitively valuable. Apple's operating system for its PCs is by most accounts a world beater (compared to Windows Vista and Windows 7), but Apple has failed miserably in converting its strength in operating system design into competitive success in the global PC market—it is an also-ran with a paltry 3 to 5 percent market share worldwide.

2. *Is the resource rare—is it something rivals lack?* Resources and capabilities that are common among firms and widely available cannot be a source of competitive advantage. All makers of branded cereals have valuable marketing capabilities and brands, since the key success factors in the ready-to-eat cereal industry demand this. They are not rare. The brand strength of Cheerios, however, is uncommon and has provided General Mills with greater market share as well as the opportunity to benefit from brand extensions like Honey Nut Cheerios. A resource or capability is considered rare if it is held by only a small number of firms in an industry or specific competitive domain. Thus, while general management capabilities are not rare in an absolute sense, they are relatively rare in some of the less developed regions of the world and in some business domains.

3. *Is the resource hard to copy?* If a resource or capability is both valuable and rare, it will be competitively superior to comparable resources of rival firms. As such, it is a source of competitive advantage for the company. The more difficult and more costly it is for competitors to imitate, the more likely that it can also provide a *sustainable* competitive advantage. Resources tend to be difficult to copy when they are unique (a fantastic real estate location, patent-protected technology, an unusually talented and motivated labor force), when they must be built over time in ways that are difficult to imitate (a well-known brand name, mastery of a complex process technology, a global network of dealers and distributors), and when they entail financial outlays or large-scale operations that few industry members can undertake. Imitation is also difficult for resources that reflect a high level of *social complexity* (company culture, interpersonal

relationships among the managers or R&D teams, trust-based relations with customers or suppliers) and *causal ambiguity,* a term that signifies the hard-to-disentangle nature of the complex resources, such as a web of intricate processes enabling new drug discovery. Hard-to-copy resources and capabilities are important competitive assets, contributing to the longevity of a company's market position and offering the potential for sustained profitability.

4. *Can the resource be trumped by different types of resources and capabilities—are there good substitutes available for the resource?* Even resources and capabilities that are valuable, rare, and hard to copy can lose much of their competitive power if rivals have other types of resources and capabilities that are of equal or greater competitive power. A company may have the most technologically advanced and sophisticated plants in its industry, but any efficiency advantage it enjoys may be nullified if rivals are able to produce equally good products at lower cost by locating their plants in countries where wage rates are relatively low and a labor force with adequate skills is available.

> **CORE CONCEPTS**
>
> **Social complexity** and **causal ambiguity** are two factors that inhibit the ability of rivals to imitate a firm's most valuable resources and capabilities. Causal ambiguity makes it very hard to figure out how a complex resource contributes to competitive advantage and therefore exactly what to imitate.

The vast majority of companies are not well endowed with standout resources or capabilities, capable of passing all four tests with high marks. Most firms have a mixed bag of resources—one or two quite valuable, some good, many satisfactory to mediocre. Resources and capabilities that are valuable pass the first of the four tests. As key contributors to the efficiency and effectiveness of the strategy, they are relevant to the firm's competitiveness but are no guarantee of competitive advantage. They may offer no more than competitive parity with competing firms.

Passing both of the first two tests requires more—it requires resources and capabilities that are not only valuable but also rare. This is a much higher hurdle that can be cleared only by resources and capabilities that are *competitively superior.* Resources and capabilities that are competitively superior are the company's true strategic assets.[5] They provide the company with a competitive advantage over its competitors, if only in the short run.

To pass the last two tests, a resource must be able to maintain its competitive superiority in the face of competition. It must be resistant to imitative attempts and efforts by competitors to find equally valuable substitute resources. Assessing the availability of substitutes is the most difficult of all the tests since substitutes are harder to recognize, but the key is to look for resources or capabilities held by other firms that *can serve the same function* as the company's core resources and capabilities.[6]

Very few firms have resources and capabilities that can pass these tests, but those that do enjoy a sustainable competitive advantage with far greater profit potential. Walmart is a notable example, with capabilities in logistics and supply chain management that have surpassed those of its competitors for over 30 years. Lincoln Electric Company, less well known but no less notable in its achievements, has been the world leader in welding products for over 100 years as a result of its unique piecework incentive system for compensating production workers and the unsurpassed worker productivity and product quality that this system has fostered.

A Company's Resources and Capabilities Must Be Managed Dynamically
Even companies like Walmart and Lincoln Electric cannot afford to rest on their laurels. Rivals that are initially unable to replicate a key resource may develop better and better substitutes over time. Resources and

capabilities can depreciate like other assets if they are managed with benign neglect. Disruptive environmental change can also destroy the value of key strategic assets, turning resources and capabilities "from diamonds to rust."[7] Some resources lose their clout quickly when there are rapid changes in technology, customer preferences, distribution channels, or other competitive factors.

> A company requires a dynamically evolving portfolio of resources and capabilities to sustain its competitiveness and help drive improvements in its performance.

For a company's resources and capabilities to have *durable* value, they must be continually refined, updated, and sometimes augmented with altogether new kinds of expertise. Not only are rival companies endeavoring to sharpen and recalibrate their capabilities, but customer needs and expectations are also undergoing constant change. Organizational capabilities grow stale unless they are kept freshly honed and on the cutting edge.[8] A company's resources and capabilities are far more competitively potent when they are (1) in sync with changes in the company's own strategy and its efforts to achieve a resource-based competitive advantage and (2) fully supportive of company efforts to attract customers and combat competitors' newly launched offensives to win bigger sales and market shares. Management's challenge in managing the firm's resources and capabilities dynamically has two elements: attending to ongoing recalibration of existing competitive assets and casting a watchful eye for opportunities to develop totally new kinds of capabilities.

The Role of Dynamic Capabilities   Companies that know the importance of recalibrating and upgrading their most valuable resources and capabilities ensure that these activities are done on a continual basis. By incorporating these activities into their routine managerial functions, they gain the experience necessary to be able to do them consistently well. At that point, their ability to freshen and renew their competitive assets becomes a capability in itself—a **dynamic capability.** A dynamic capability is the ability to modify or augment the company's existing resources and capabilities.[9] This includes the capacity to improve existing resources and capabilities incrementally, in the way that 3M continually upgrades the R&D resources driving its product innovation strategy. It also includes the capacity to add new resources and capabilities to the company's competitive asset portfolio. An example is Pfizer's acquisition capabilities, which have enabled it to replace degraded resources such as expiring patents with newly acquired capabilities in biotechnology.

QUESTION 3: IS THE COMPANY ABLE TO SEIZE MARKET OPPORTUNITIES AND NULLIFY EXTERNAL THREATS?

An essential element in evaluating a company's overall situation entails examining the company's resources and competitive capabilities in terms of the degree to which they enable it to pursue its best market opportunities and defend against the external threats to its future well-being. The simplest and most easily applied tool for conducting this examination is widely known as *SWOT analysis,* so named because it zeros in on a company's internal <u>S</u>trengths and <u>W</u>eaknesses, market <u>O</u>pportunities, and external <u>T</u>hreats. Just as important, a first-rate SWOT analysis provides the basis for crafting a strategy that capitalizes on the company's resource strengths, overcomes its resource weaknesses, aims squarely at capturing the company's best opportunities, and defends against the threats to its future well-being.

Identifying a Company's Internal Strengths

A *strength* is something a company is good at doing or an attribute that enhances its competitiveness in the marketplace. A company's strengths depend on the quality of its resources and capabilities. Resource and capability analysis provides a way for managers to assess the quality objectively. While resources and capabilities that pass the four tests of sustainable competitive advantage are among the company's greatest strengths, other types can be counted among the company's strengths as well. A capability that is not potent enough to produce a sustainable advantage over rivals may yet enable a series of temporary advantages if used as a basis for entry into a new market or market segment. A resource bundle that fails to match those of top-tier competitors may still allow a company to compete successfully against the second tier.

Assessing a Company's Competencies—What Activities Does It Perform Well?
One way to appraise the degree of a company's strengths has to do with the company's competence level in performing key pieces of its business—such as supply chain management, R&D, production, distribution, sales and marketing, and customer service. Which activities does it perform especially well? And are there any activities it performs better than rivals? A company's proficiency in conducting different facets of its operations can range from a mere competence in performing an activity to a core competence to a distinctive competence.

A **competence** is an internal activity an organization performs with proficiency—a capability, in other words. A **core competence** is a proficiently performed internal activity that is *central* to a company's strategy and competitiveness. Ben & Jerry's Ice Cream, a subsidiary of Unilever, has a core competence in creating unusual flavors of ice cream and marketing them with catchy names like Chunky Monkey, Chubby Hubby, Cherry Garcia, Karamel Sutra, Imagine Whirled Peace, and Phish Food. A core competence is a more competitively valuable company strength than a competence because of the activity's key role in the company's strategy and the contribution it makes to the company's market success and profitability. Often, core competencies can be leveraged to create new markets or new product demand, as the engine behind a company's growth. 3M Corporation has a core competence in product innovation—its record of introducing new products goes back several decades and new product introduction is central to 3M's strategy of growing its business.

A **distinctive competence** is a competitively valuable activity that a company *performs better than its rivals*. A distinctive competence thus signifies greater proficiency than a core competence. Because a distinctive competence represents a level of proficiency that rivals do not have, it qualifies as a *competitively superior strength* with competitive advantage potential. This is particularly true when the distinctive competence enables

---

LO 3

Discover how to assess the company's strengths and weaknesses in light of market opportunities and external threats.

SWOT analysis is a simple but powerful tool for sizing up a company's strengths and weaknesses, its market opportunities, and the external threats to its future well-being.

Basing a company's strategy on its most competitively valuable resource and capability strengths gives the company its best chance for market success.

CORE CONCEPT

A **competence** is an activity that a company has learned to perform with proficiency—a capability, in other words.

a company to deliver standout value to customers (in the form of lower prices, better product performance, or superior service). For instance, Apple has a distinctive competence in product innovation, as exemplified by its iPod, iPhone, and iPad products.

The conceptual differences between a competence, a core competence, and a distinctive competence draw attention to the fact that a company's strengths and competitive assets are not all equal.[10] Some competencies merely enable market survival because most rivals have them—indeed, not having a competence or capability that rivals have can result in competitive disadvantage. If an apparel company does not have the competence to produce its apparel items very cost-efficiently, it is unlikely to survive given the intensely price-competitive nature of the apparel industry. Every Web retailer requires a basic competence in designing an appealing and user-friendly Web site. Core competencies are *competitively* more important strengths than competencies because they are central to the company's strategy. Distinctive competencies are even more competitively important. Because a distinctive competence is a competitively valuable capability that is unmatched by rivals, it can propel the company to greater market success and profitability. A distinctive competence is thus potentially the mainspring of a company's success—unless it is trumped by other, even more powerful types of competencies that rivals hold.

Identifying Company Weaknesses and Competitive Deficiencies

A **weakness,** or *competitive deficiency,* is something a company lacks or does poorly (in comparison to others) or a condition that puts it at a competitive disadvantage in the marketplace. A company's internal weaknesses can relate to (1) inferior or unproven skills, expertise, or intellectual capital in competitively important areas of the business; (2) deficiencies in competitively important physical, organizational, or intangible assets; or (3) missing or competitively inferior capabilities in key areas. *Company weaknesses are thus internal shortcomings that constitute competitive liabilities.* Nearly all companies have competitive liabilities of one kind or another. Whether a company's internal weaknesses make it competitively vulnerable depends on how much they matter in the marketplace and whether they are offset by the company's strengths.

Table 4.3 lists many of the things to consider in compiling a company's strengths and weaknesses. Sizing up a company's complement of strengths and deficiencies is akin to constructing a *strategic balance sheet,* where strengths represent *competitive assets* and weaknesses represent *competitive liabilities.* Obviously, the ideal condition is for the company's competitive assets to outweigh its competitive liabilities by an ample margin—a 50-50 balance is definitely not the desired condition!

Identifying a Company's Market Opportunities

Market opportunity is a big factor in shaping a company's strategy. Indeed, managers can't properly tailor strategy to the company's situation without first identifying its market opportunities and appraising the growth and profit potential each one holds. Depending on the prevailing circumstances, a company's opportunities can be plentiful or scarce, fleeting or lasting, and can range from wildly attractive (an absolute "must" to pursue) to marginally interesting (because of the high risks or questionable profit potentials) to unsuitable (because the company's strengths are ill-suited to successfully capitalizing on the opportunities). A sampling of potential market opportunities is shown in Table 4.3.

Newly emerging and fast-changing markets sometimes present stunningly big or "golden" opportunities, but it is typically hard for managers at one company to peer into "the fog of the future" and spot them much ahead of managers at other companies.[11] But as the fog begins to clear, golden opportunities are nearly always seized rapidly— and the companies that seize them are usually those that have been actively waiting, staying alert with diligent market reconnaissance, and preparing themselves to capitalize on shifting market conditions by patiently assembling an arsenal of competitively valuable resources— talented personnel, technical know-how, strategic partnerships, and a war chest of cash to finance aggressive action when the time comes.[12] In mature markets, unusually attractive market opportunities emerge sporadically, often after long periods of relative calm—but future market conditions may be more predictable, making emerging opportunities easier for industry members to detect.

> A company is well advised to pass on a particular market opportunity unless it has or can acquire the competencies needed to capture it.

In evaluating a company's market opportunities and ranking their attractiveness, managers have to guard against viewing every *industry* opportunity as a *company* opportunity. Not every company is equipped with the competencies to successfully pursue each opportunity that exists in its industry. Some companies are more capable of going after particular opportunities than others, and a few companies may be hopelessly outclassed. *The market opportunities most relevant to a company are those that match up well with the company's competitive assets, offer the best growth and profitability, and present the most potential for competitive advantage.*

Identifying the Threats to a Company's Future Profitability

Often, certain factors in a company's external environment pose *threats* to its profitability and competitive well-being. Threats can stem from the emergence of cheaper or better technologies, rivals' introduction of new or improved products, the entry of lower-cost foreign competitors into a company's market stronghold, new regulations that are more burdensome to a company than to its competitors, vulnerability to a rise in interest rates or tight credit conditions, the potential of a hostile takeover, unfavorable demographic shifts, adverse changes in foreign exchange rates, political upheaval in a foreign country where the company has facilities, and the like. A list of potential threats to a company's future profitability and market position is shown in Table 4.3.

External threats may pose no more than a moderate degree of adversity (all companies confront some threatening elements in the course of doing business), or they may be so imposing as to make a company's situation and outlook quite tenuous. On rare occasions, market shocks can give birth to a *sudden-death* threat that throws a company into an immediate crisis and a battle to survive. Many of the world's major airlines were plunged into an unprecedented financial crisis by the perfect storm of 9/11, rising prices for jet fuel, mounting competition

Table 4.3   What to Look For in Identifying a Company's Strengths, Weaknesses, Opportunities, and Threats

Potential Strengths and Competitive Assets	Potential Weaknesses and Competitive Deficiencies
• Competencies that are well matched to industry key success factors • Strong financial condition; ample financial resources to grow the business • Strong brand-name image/company reputation • Attractive customer base • Proprietary technology/superior technological skills/important patents • Superior intellectual capital • Skills in advertising and promotion • Strong bargaining power over suppliers or buyers • Product innovation capabilities • Proven capabilities in improving production processes • Good supply chain management capabilities • Good customer service capabilities • Superior product quality • Wide geographic coverage and/or strong global distribution capability • Alliances/joint ventures that provide access to valuable technology, competencies, and/or attractive geographic markets • A product that is strongly differentiated from those of rivals • Cost advantages over rivals • Core competencies in _____ • A distinctive competence in _____ • Resources that are hard to copy and for which there are no good substitutes	• Competencies that are not well-matched to industry key success factors • In the wrong strategic group • Losing market share because _____ • Lack of attention to customer needs • Weak balance sheet, short on financial resources to grow the firm, too much debt; • Higher overall unit costs relative to those of key competitors • Weak or unproven product innovation capabilities • A product/service with ho-hum attributes or features inferior to the offerings of rivals • Too narrow a product line relative to rivals • Weak brand image or reputation • Weaker dealer network than key rivals and/or lack of adequate global distribution capability • Behind on product quality, R&D, and/or technological know-how • Lack of management depth • Inferior intellectual capital relative to rivals • Plagued with internal operating problems or obsolete facilities • Too much underutilized plant capacity • No well-developed or proven core competencies • No distinctive competencies or competitively superior resources • Resources that are readily copied or for which there are good substitutes • No clear strategic direction
Potential Market Opportunities	Potential External Threats to a Company's Future Profitability
• Openings to win market share from rivals • Sharply rising buyer demand for the industry's product • Serving additional customer groups or market segments • Expanding into new geographic markets • Expanding the company's product line to meet a broader range of customer needs • Utilizing existing company skills or technological know-how to enter new product lines or new businesses • Online sales via the Internet • Integrating forward or backward • Falling trade barriers in attractive foreign markets • Acquiring rival firms or companies with attractive technological expertise or capabilities • Entering into alliances or joint ventures to expand the firm's market coverage or boost its competitive capability • Openings to exploit emerging new technologies	• Increasing intensity of competition among industry rivals—may squeeze profit margins • Slowdowns in market growth • Likely entry of potent new competitors • Loss of sales to substitute products • Growing bargaining power of customers or suppliers • Vulnerability to industry driving forces • Shift in buyer needs and tastes away from the industry's product • Adverse demographic changes that threaten to curtail demand for the industry's product • Adverse economic conditions that threaten critical suppliers or distributers • Changes in technology—particularly disruptive technology that can undermine the company's distinctive competencies • Restrictive foreign trade policies • Costly new regulatory requirements • Tight credit conditions • Rising prices on energy or other key inputs

from low-fare carriers, shifting traveler preferences for low fares as opposed to lots of in-flight amenities, and higher labor costs. Similarly, the global economic crisis that began with the mortgage lenders, banks, and insurance companies has produced shock waves from which few industries have been insulated, causing even strong performers like General Electric to falter. While not all crises can be anticipated, it is management's job to identify the threats to the company's future prospects and to evaluate what strategic actions can be taken to neutralize or lessen their impact.

What Do the SWOT Listings Reveal?

SWOT analysis involves more than making four lists. The two most important parts of SWOT analysis are *drawing conclusions* from the SWOT listings about the company's overall situation and *translating these conclusions into strategic actions* to better match the company's strategy to its internal strengths and market opportunities, to correct important weaknesses, and to defend against external threats. Figure 4.2 shows the steps involved in gleaning insights from SWOT analysis.

> Simply making lists of a company's strengths, weaknesses, opportunities, and threats is not enough; the payoff from SWOT analysis comes from the conclusions about a company's situation and the implications for strategy improvement that flow from the four lists.

Figure 4.2   The Steps Involved in SWOT Analysis: Identify the Four Components of SWOT, Draw Conclusions, Translate Implications into Strategic Actions

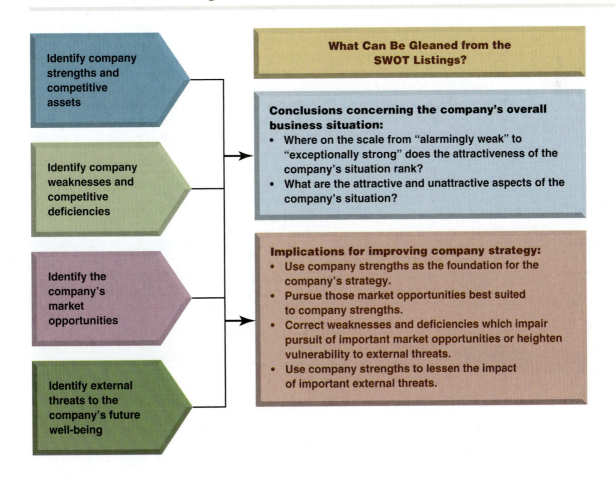

Identify company strengths and competitive assets

Identify company weaknesses and competitive deficiencies

Identify the company's market opportunities

Identify external threats to the company's future well-being

What Can Be Gleaned from the SWOT Listings?

Conclusions concerning the company's overall business situation:
- Where on the scale from "alarmingly weak" to "exceptionally strong" does the attractiveness of the company's situation rank?
- What are the attractive and unattractive aspects of the company's situation?

Implications for improving company strategy:
- Use company strengths as the foundation for the company's strategy.
- Pursue those market opportunities best suited to company strengths.
- Correct weaknesses and deficiencies which impair pursuit of important market opportunities or heighten vulnerability to external threats.
- Use company strengths to lessen the impact of important external threats.

Just what story the SWOT listings tell about the company's overall situation is often revealed in the answers to the following set of questions:

- What aspects of the company's situation are particularly attractive?
- What aspects are of the most concern?
- All things considered, where on a scale of 1 to 10 (where 1 is alarmingly weak and 10 is exceptionally strong) do the company's overall situation and future prospects rank?
- Are the company's internal strengths and competitive assets powerful enough to enable it to compete successfully?
- Are the company's weaknesses and competitive deficiencies mostly inconsequential and readily correctable, or could one or more prove fatal if not remedied soon?
- Do the company's strengths and competitive assets outweigh its weaknesses and competitive liabilities by an attractive margin?
- Does the company have attractive market opportunities that are well suited to its internal strengths? Does the company lack the competitive assets to pursue any of the most attractive opportunities?
- Are the threats alarming, or are they something the company appears able to deal with and defend against?

The final piece of SWOT analysis is to translate the diagnosis of the company's situation into actions for improving the company's strategy and business prospects. *A company's internal strengths should always serve as the basis of its strategy—placing heavy reliance on a company's best competitive assets is the soundest route to attracting customers and competing successfully against rivals.*[13] As a rule, strategies that place heavy demands on areas where the company is weakest or has unproven competencies are suspect and should be avoided. Plainly, managers have to look toward correcting competitive weaknesses that make the company vulnerable, hold down profitability, or disqualify it from pursuing an attractive opportunity. Furthermore, strategy has to be aimed squarely at capturing those market opportunities that are most attractive and suited to the company's collection of competencies. How much attention to devote to defending against external threats to the company's market position and future performance hinges on how vulnerable the company is, whether there are attractive defensive moves that can be taken to lessen their impact, and whether the costs of undertaking such moves represent the best use of company competitive assets.

QUESTION 4: ARE THE COMPANY'S PRICES AND COSTS COMPETITIVE WITH THOSE OF KEY RIVALS, AND DOES IT HAVE AN APPEALING CUSTOMER VALUE PROPOSITION?

Company managers are often stunned when a competitor cuts its price to "unbelievably low" levels or when a new market entrant comes on strong with a very low price. The competitor may not, however, be "dumping" (an economic term for selling at prices that are below cost), buying its way into the market with a super-low price, or waging a desperate move to gain sales—it may simply have substantially lower costs. One of the most telling signs of whether a company's business position is strong or precarious is whether its prices and costs can remain competitive with industry rivals. For a company to retain its market share, its costs must be *in line* with those of close rivals selling similar quality products.

While less common, new entrants can also storm the market with a product that ratchets the quality level up so high that customers will abandon competing sellers even if they have to pay more for the new product. With its vastly greater storage capacity and lightweight, cool design, Apple's iPod left other makers of portable digital music players in the dust when it was first introduced. By introducing new models with even more attractive features, Apple has continued its worldwide dominance of this market. Apple's new iPad appears to be doing the same in the market for e-readers and tablet PCs.

Regardless of where on the quality spectrum a company competes, it must also remain competitive in terms of its customer value proposition in order to stay in the game. Tiffany's value proposition, for example, remains attractive to customers who want customer service, the assurance of quality, and a high-status brand despite the availability of cut-rate diamond jewelry online. Target's customer value proposition has withstood the Walmart low-price juggernaut by attention to product design, image, and attractive store layouts in addition to efficiency.

The value provided to the customer depends on how well a customer's needs are met for the price paid. How well customer needs are met depends on the perceived quality of a product or service as well as other, more tangible attributes. The greater the amount of customer value that the company can offer profitably compared to its rivals, the less vulnerable it will be to competitive attack. For managers, the key is to keep close track of how *cost effectively* the company can deliver value to customers relative to its competitors. If they can deliver the same amount of value with lower expenditures (or more value at the same cost), they will maintain a competitive edge.

Two analytical tools are particularly useful in determining whether a company's prices, costs, and customer value proposition are competitive: value chain analysis and benchmarking.

The Concept of a Company Value Chain

Every company's business consists of a collection of activities undertaken in the course of designing, producing, marketing, delivering, and supporting its product or service. All the various activities that a company performs internally combine to form a **value chain**—so called because the underlying intent of a company's activities is to do things that ultimately *create value for buyers.*

As shown in Figure 4.3, a company's value chain consists of two broad categories of activities: the *primary activities* that are foremost in creating value for customers and the requisite *support activities* that facilitate and enhance the performance of the primary activities.[14] The exact nature of the primary and secondary activities that make up a company's value chain

LO 4

Grasp how a company's value chain activities can affect the company's cost structure, degree of differentiation, and competitive advantage.

The higher a company's costs are above those of close rivals, the more competitively vulnerable it becomes.

The greater the amount of customer value that a company can offer profitably relative to close rivals, the less competitively vulnerable it becomes.

CORE CONCEPT

A company's **value chain** identifies the primary activities that create customer value and the related support activities.

vary according to the specifics of a company's business; hence, the listing of the primary and support activities in Figure 4.3 is illustrative rather than definitive. For example, the primary value-creating activities for a manufacturer of bakery goods, such as Pepperidge Farm, include supply chain management, baking and packaging operations, distribution, and sales and marketing but are unlikely to include service. Its support activities include quality control as well as product R&D, human resource management, and administration. For a department store retailer, such as Macy's, customer service is included among its primary activities, along with merchandise selection and buying, store layout and product display, and advertising; its support activities include site selection, hiring and training, and store maintenance, plus the usual assortment of administrative activities. For a hotel chain like Marriot, the primary activities and costs are in site selection and construction, reservations, operation of its hotel properties, and marketing; principal support activities include accounting, hiring and training hotel staff, supply chain management, and general administration.

With its focus on value-creating activities, the value chain is an ideal tool for examining how a company delivers on its customer value proposition. It permits a deep look at the company's cost structure and ability to offer low prices. It reveals the emphasis that a company places on activities that enhance differentiation and support higher prices, such as service and marketing. Note that there is also a profit margin component to the value chain; this is because profits are necessary to compensate the company's owners/shareholders and investors, who bear risks and provide capital. Tracking the profit margin along with the value-creating activities is critical because unless an enterprise succeeds in delivering customer value profitably (with a sufficient return on invested capital), it can't survive for long. This is the essence of a sound business model.

Illustration Capsule 4.1 shows representative costs for various activities performed by Just Coffee, a cooperative producer and roaster of fair-trade organic coffee.

Comparing the Value Chains of Rival Companies   The primary purpose of value chain analysis is to facilitate a comparison, activity-by-activity, of how effectively and efficiently a company delivers value to its customers, relative to its competitors. Segregating the company's operations into different types of primary and secondary activities is the first step in this comparison. The next is to do the same for the company's most significant competitors.

Even rivals in the same industry may differ significantly in terms of the activities they perform. For instance, the "operations" component of the value chain for a manufacturer that makes all of its own parts and components and assembles them into a finished product differs from the "operations" of a rival producer that buys the needed parts and components from outside suppliers and only performs assembly operations. How each activity is performed may affect a company's relative cost position as well as its capacity for differentiation. Thus, even a simple comparison of how the activities of rivals' value chains differ can be revealing of competitive differences.

A Company's Primary and Secondary Activities Identify the Major Components of Its Internal Cost Structure   Each activity in the value chain gives rise to costs and ties up assets. For a company to remain competitive, it is critical for it to perform its activities cost-effectively,

Figure 4.3   A Representative Company Value Chain

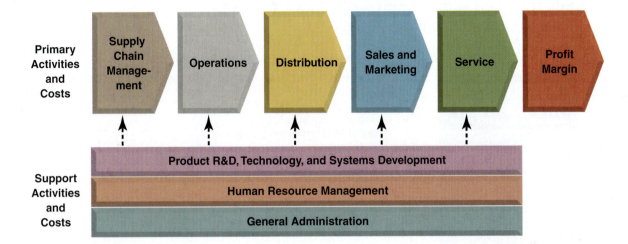

PRIMARY ACTIVITIES

- **Supply Chain Management**—Activities, costs, and assets associated with purchasing fuel, energy, raw materials, parts and components, merchandise, and consumable items from vendors; receiving, storing, and disseminating inputs from suppliers; inspection; and inventory management.

- **Operations**—Activities, costs, and assets associated with converting inputs into final product form (production, assembly, packaging, equipment maintenance, facilities, operations, quality assurance, environmental protection).

- **Distribution**—Activities, costs, and assets dealing with physically distributing the product to buyers (finished goods warehousing, order processing, order picking and packing, shipping, delivery vehicle operations, establishing and maintaining a network of dealers and distributors).

- **Sales and Marketing**—Activities, costs, and assets related to sales force efforts, advertising and promotion, market research and planning, and dealer/distributor support.

- **Service**—Activities, costs, and assets associated with providing assistance to buyers, such as installation, spare parts delivery, maintenance and repair, technical assistance, buyer inquiries, and complaints.

SUPPORT ACTIVITIES

- **Product R&D, Technology, and Systems Development**—Activities, costs, and assets relating to product R&D, process R&D, process design improvement, equipment design, computer software development, telecommunications systems, computer-assisted design and engineering, database capabilities, and development of computerized support systems.

- **Human Resources Management**—Activities, costs, and assets associated with the recruitment, hiring, training, development, and compensation of all types of personnel; labor relations activities; and development of knowledge-based skills and core competencies.

- **General Administration**—Activities, costs, and assets relating to general management, accounting and finance, legal and regulatory affairs, safety and security, management information systems, forming strategic alliances and collaborating with strategic partners, and other "overhead" functions.

Source: Based on the discussion in Michael E. Porter, *Competitive Advantage* (New York: Free Press, 1985), pp. 37–43.

The Value Chain for Just Coffee, a Producer of Fair-Trade Organic Coffee

Value Chain Activities and Costs in Producing, Roasting, and Selling a Pound of Fair-Trade Organic Coffee	
1. Average cost of procuring the coffee from coffee-grower cooperatives	$2.30
2. Import fees, storage costs, and freight charges	.73
3. Labor cost of roasting and bagging	.89
4. Cost of labels and bag	.45
5. Average overhead costs	3.03
6. Total company costs	$7.40
7. Average retail markup over company costs (company operating profit)	2.59
8. Average price to consumer at retail	$9.99

Source: Developed by the authors with help from Jonathan D. Keith from information on Just Coffee's Web site, www.justcoffee.coop/the_coffee_dollar_breakdown (accessed June 16, 2010).

regardless of which it chooses to emphasize. Once the major value chain activities are identified, the next step is to evaluate the company's cost competitiveness using what accountants call *activity-based costing* to determine the costs of performing each value chain activity (and assets required, including working capital).[15] The degree to which a company's costs should be disaggregated into specific activities depends on how valuable it is to develop cost data for narrowly defined activities as opposed to broadly defined activities. Generally speaking, cost estimates are needed at least for each broad category of primary and secondary activities, but finer classifications may be needed if a company discovers that it has a cost disadvantage vis-à-vis rivals and wants to pin down the exact source or activity causing the disadvantage. Quite often, there are links between activities such that the manner in which one activity is done can affect the costs of performing other activities. For instance, how an automobile is designed has a huge impact on the number of different parts and components, their respective manufacturing costs, and the expense of assembling the various parts and components into a finished product.

The combined costs of all the various activities in a company's value chain define the company's internal cost structure. Further, the cost of each activity contributes to whether the company's overall cost position relative to rivals is favorable or unfavorable. But a company's own internal costs are insufficient to assess whether its costs are competitive with those of rivals. Cost and price differences among competing companies can have their origins in activities performed by suppliers or by distribution allies involved in getting the product to the final customer or end user of the product, in which case the company's entire value chain system becomes relevant.

The Value Chain System for an Entire Industry

A company's value chain is embedded in a larger system of activities that includes the value chains of its suppliers and the value chains of whatever wholesale distributors and retailers it utilizes in getting its product or service to end users. This *value chain system* has implications that extend far beyond the company's costs. It can affect attributes like product quality that enhance differentiation and have importance for the company's customer value proposition as well as its profitability.[16] Suppliers' value chains are relevant because suppliers perform activities and incur costs in creating and delivering the purchased inputs utilized in a company's own value-creating activities. The costs, performance features, and quality of these inputs influence a company's own costs and product differentiation capabilities. Anything a company can do to help its suppliers' drive down the costs of their value chain activities or improve the quality and performance of the items being supplied can enhance its own competitiveness—a powerful reason for working collaboratively with suppliers in managing supply chain activities.[17]

> A company's cost competitiveness depends not only on the costs of internally performed activities (its own value chain) but also on costs in the value chains of its suppliers and distribution channel allies.

Similarly, the value chains of a company's distribution channel partners are relevant because (1) the costs and margins of a company's distributors and retail dealers are part of the price the ultimate consumer pays and (2) the activities that distribution allies perform affect sales volumes and customer satisfaction. For these reasons, companies normally work closely with their distribution allies (who are their direct customers) to perform value chain activities in mutually beneficial ways. For instance, motor vehicle manufacturers have a competitive interest in working closely with their automobile dealers to promote higher sales volumes and better customer satisfaction with dealers' repair and maintenance services. Producers of bathroom fixtures are heavily dependent on the sales and promotional activities of their distributors and building supply retailers and on whether distributors/retailers operate cost-effectively enough to be able to sell at prices that lead to attractive sales volumes.

As a consequence, *accurately assessing a company's competitiveness entails scrutinizing the nature and costs of value chain activities throughout the entire value chain system for delivering its products or services to end-use customers.* A typical industry value chain system that incorporates the value chains of suppliers and forward channel allies (if any) is shown in Figure 4.4. As was the case with company value chains, the specific activities constituting industry value chains also vary significantly. The primary value chain system activities in the pulp and paper industry (timber farming, logging, pulp mills, and papermaking) differ from the primary value chain system activities in the home appliance industry (parts and components manufacture, assembly, wholesale distribution, retail sales). The value chain system in the soft-drink industry (syrup manufacture, bottling and can filling, wholesale distribution, advertising, and retail merchandising) differs from that in the computer software industry (programming, disk loading, marketing, distribution).

Figure 4.4   Representative Value Chain System for an Entire Industry

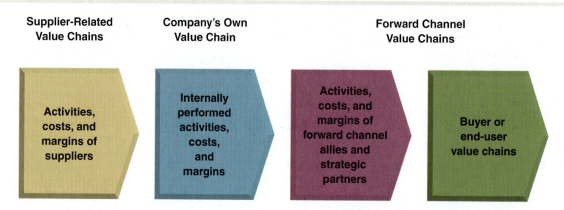

Source: Based in part on the single-industry value chain displayed in Michael E. Porter, *Competitive Advantage* (New York: Free Press, 1985), p. 35.

Benchmarking: A Tool for Assessing Whether the Costs and Effectiveness of a Company's Value Chain Activities Are in Line

Once a company has developed good estimates for the costs and effectiveness of each of the major activities in its own value chain and has sufficient data relating to the value chain activities of suppliers and distribution allies, then it is ready to explore how it compares on these dimensions with key rivals. This is where benchmarking comes in. **Benchmarking** entails comparing how different companies perform various value chain activities—how inventories are managed, how products are assembled, how fast the company can get new products to market, how customer orders are filled and shipped—and then making cross-company comparisons of the costs and effectiveness of these activities.[18] The objectives of benchmarking are to identify the best practices in performing an activity, to learn how other companies have actually achieved lower costs or better results in performing benchmarked activities, and to take action to improve a company's competitiveness whenever benchmarking reveals that its costs and results of performing an activity are not on a par with what other companies have achieved.

Xerox became one of the first companies to use benchmarking in 1979 when Japanese manufacturers began selling midsize copiers in the United States for $9,600 each—less than Xerox's production costs.[19] Xerox management suspected its Japanese competitors were dumping, but it sent a team of line managers to Japan, including the head of manufacturing, to study competitors' business processes and costs. With the aid of Xerox's joint venture partner in Japan, Fuji-Xerox, which knew the competitors well, the team found that Xerox's costs were excessive due to gross inefficiencies in the company's manufacturing processes and business practices. The findings triggered a major internal effort at Xerox to become cost-competitive and prompted Xerox to begin benchmarking 67 of its key work processes against companies identified as employing the best

CORE CONCEPT

Benchmarking is a potent tool for improving a company's own internal activities that is based on learning how other companies perform them and borrowing their "best practices."

practices. Xerox quickly decided not to restrict its benchmarking efforts to its office equipment rivals but to extend them to any company regarded as "world class" in performing *any activity* relevant to Xerox's business. Other companies quickly picked up on Xerox's approach. Toyota managers got their idea for just-in-time inventory deliveries by studying how U.S. supermarkets replenished their shelves. Southwest Airlines reduced the turnaround time of its aircraft at each scheduled stop by studying pit crews on the auto racing circuit. Over 80 percent of Fortune 500 companies reportedly use benchmarking for comparing themselves against rivals on cost and other competitively important measures.

The tough part of benchmarking is not whether to do it but rather how to gain access to information about other companies' practices and costs. Sometimes benchmarking can be accomplished by collecting information from published reports, trade groups, and industry research firms or by talking to knowledgeable industry analysts, customers, and suppliers. Sometimes field trips to the facilities of competing or noncompeting companies can be arranged to observe how things are done, ask questions, compare practices and processes, and perhaps exchange data on productivity, staffing levels, time requirements, and other cost components—but the problem here is that such companies, even if they agree to host facilities tours and answer questions, are unlikely to share competitively sensitive cost information. Furthermore, comparing one company's costs to another's costs may not involve comparing apples to apples if the two companies employ different cost accounting principles to calculate the costs of particular activities.

> Benchmarking the costs of company activities against rivals provides hard evidence of whether a company is cost-competitive.

However, a third and fairly reliable source of benchmarking information has emerged. The explosive interest of companies in benchmarking costs and best practices has prompted numerous consulting firms and business organizations (e.g., Accenture, A.T. Kearney, Benchnet—The Benchmarking Exchange, Best Practices LLC, and the Strategic Planning Institute's Council on Benchmarking and Best Practices, LLC) to gather benchmarking data, distribute information about best practices, and provide comparative cost data without identifying the names of particular companies. Having an independent group gather the information and report it in a manner that disguises the names of individual companies protects competitively sensitive data and lessens the potential for unethical behavior on the part of company personnel in gathering their own data about competitors. Illustration Capsule 4.2 presents a widely recommended code of conduct for engaging in benchmarking.

Strategic Options for Remedying a Disadvantage in Costs or Effectiveness

Examining the costs of a company's own value chain activities and comparing them to rivals' indicates who has how much of a cost advantage or disadvantage and which cost components are responsible. Similarly, much can be learned by comparisons at the activity level of how effectively a company delivers on its value proposition relative to its competitors and which elements in its value chain system are responsible. Such information is vital in strategic actions to eliminate a cost disadvantage, deliver more customer value, enhance differentiation, and improve profitability. Such information can also help a company to recognize and reinforce activities in which it has a comparative advantage and to find

ILLUSTRATION CAPSULE 4.2

Benchmarking and Ethical Conduct

Because discussions between benchmarking partners can involve competitively sensitive data, conceivably raising questions about possible restraint of trade or improper business conduct, many benchmarking organizations urge all individuals and organizations involved in benchmarking to abide by a code of conduct grounded in ethical business behavior. One of the most widely used codes of conduct is the one developed by APQC (formerly the American Productivity and Quality Center) and advocated by the Qualserve Benchmarking Clearinghouse; it is based on the following principles and guidelines:

- Avoid discussions or actions that could lead to or imply an interest in restraint of trade, market and/or customer allocation schemes, price fixing, dealing arrangements, bid rigging, or bribery. Don't discuss costs with competitors if costs are an element of pricing.

- Refrain from the acquisition of trade secrets from another by any means that could be interpreted as improper, including the breach of any duty to maintain secrecy. Do not disclose or use any trade secret that may have been obtained through improper means or that was disclosed by another in violation of duty to maintain its secrecy or limit its use.

- Be willing to provide to your benchmarking partner the same type and level of information that you request from that partner.

- Communicate fully and early in the relationship to clarify expectations, avoid misunderstanding, and establish mutual interest in the benchmarking exchange.

- Be honest and complete with the information submitted.

- The use or communication of a benchmarking partner's name with the data obtained or practices observed requires the prior permission of the benchmarking partner.

- Honor the wishes of benchmarking partners regarding how the information that is provided will be handled and used.

- In benchmarking with competitors, establish specific ground rules up front. For example, "We don't want to talk about things that will give either of us a competitive advantage, but rather we want to see where we both can mutually improve or gain benefit."

- Check with legal counsel if any information-gathering procedure is in doubt. If uncomfortable, do not proceed. Alternatively, negotiate and sign a specific nondisclosure agreement that will satisfy the attorneys representing each partner.

- Do not ask competitors for sensitive data or cause benchmarking partners to feel they must provide data to continue the process.

- Use an ethical third party to assemble and "blind" competitive data, with inputs from legal counsel in direct competitor sharing. (Note: When cost is closely linked to price, sharing cost data can be considered to be the same as sharing price data.)

- Any information obtained from a benchmarking partner should be treated as internal, privileged communications. If "confidential" or proprietary material is to be exchanged, then a specific agreement should be executed to specify the content of the material that needs to be protected, the duration of the period of protection, the conditions for permitting access to the material, and the specific handling requirements necessary for that material.

Sources: APQC, www.apqc.org; Qualserve Benchmarking Clearinghouse, www.awwa.org (accessed October 8, 2010).

new avenues for enhancing its competitiveness through lower costs, greater differentiation, or a more attractive customer value proposition. There are three main areas in a company's total value chain system where company managers can try to improve its efficiency and effectiveness: (1) a company's own activity segments, (2) suppliers' part of the overall value chain, and (3) the distribution channel portion of the chain.

Improving the Efficiency and Effectiveness of Internally Performed Value Chain Activities

Managers can pursue any of several strategic approaches to reduce the costs of internally performed value chain activities and improve a company's cost competitiveness:[20]

1. Implement the use of best practices throughout the company, particularly for high-cost activities.
2. Redesign the product and/or some of its components to eliminate high-cost components or facilitate speedier and more economical manufacture or assembly—computer chip makers regularly design around the patents held by others to avoid paying royalties; automakers have substituted lower-cost plastic and rubber for metal at many exterior body locations.
3. Relocate high-cost activities (such as manufacturing) to geographic areas like Southeast Asia or Latin America or eastern Europe where they can be performed more cheaply.
4. See if certain internally performed activities can be outsourced from vendors or performed by contractors more cheaply than they can be done in-house.
5. Shift to lower-cost technologies and/or invest in productivity-enhancing, cost-saving technological improvements (robotics, flexible manufacturing techniques, state-of-the-art information systems).
6. Stop performing activities that add little or no customer value. Examples include seldom-used customer services, employee training programs that are of marginal value, and maintaining large raw-material or finished-goods inventories.

How successfully a company competes depends on more than low costs. It also depends on how effectively it delivers value to the customer and on its ability to differentiate itself from rivals. To improve the effectiveness of its customer value proposition and enhance differentiation, there are several approaches a manager can take:[21]

1. Implement the use of best practices for quality throughout the company, particularly for high-value activities (those that are important for creating value for the customer).
2. Adopt best practices and technologies that spur innovation, improve design, and enhance creativity.
3. Implement the use of best practices in providing customer service.
4. Reallocate resources to devote more to activities that will have the biggest impact on the value delivered to the customer and that address buyers' most important purchase criteria.
5. For intermediate buyers (distributors or retailers, for example), gain an understanding of how the activities the company performs impact the buyer's value chain. Improve the effectiveness of company activities that have the greatest impact on the efficiency or effectiveness of the buyer's value chain.
6. Adopt best practices for signaling the value of the product and for enhancing customer perceptions.

Improving the Efficiency and Effectiveness of Supplier-Related Value Chain Activities

Improving the efficiency and effectiveness of the value chain activities of suppliers can also address a company's competitive weaknesses with respect to costs and differentiation. On the cost side, a company can gain savings in suppliers' part of the overall value chain by pressuring suppliers for lower prices, switching to lower-priced substitute inputs, and collaborating closely with suppliers to identify mutual cost-saving opportunities.[22] For example, just-in-time deliveries from suppliers can lower a company's inventory and internal logistics costs and may also allow suppliers to economize on their warehousing, shipping, and production scheduling costs—a win-win outcome for both. In a few instances, companies may find that it is cheaper to integrate backward into the business of high-cost suppliers and make the item in-house instead of buying it from outsiders.

Similarly, a company can enhance its differentiation by working with or through its suppliers to do so. Some methods include selecting and retaining suppliers who meet higher-quality standards, coordinating with suppliers to enhance design or other features desired by customers, providing incentives to encourage suppliers to meet higher-quality standards, and assisting suppliers in their efforts to improve. Fewer defects in parts from suppliers not only improve quality and enhance differentiation throughout the value chain system but can lower costs as well since there is less waste and disruption to the production processes.

Improving the Efficiency and Effectiveness of Distribution-Related Value Chain Activities   Taking actions aimed at improvements with respect to the forward or downstream portion of the value chain system can also help to remedy a company's competitive disadvantage with respect to either costs or differentiation. Any of three means can be used to achieve better cost competitiveness in the forward portion of the industry value chain: (1) Pressure distributors, dealers, and other forward channel allies to reduce their costs and markups so as to make the final price to buyers more competitive with the prices of rivals; (2) collaborate with forward channel allies to identify win-win opportunities to reduce costs—a chocolate manufacturer, for example, learned that by shipping its bulk chocolate in liquid form in tank cars instead of as 10-pound molded bars, it could not only save its candy-bar manufacturing customers the costs associated with unpacking and melting but also eliminate its own costs of molding bars and packing them; and (3) change to a more economical distribution strategy, including switching to cheaper distribution channels (perhaps direct sales via the Internet) or perhaps integrating forward into company-owned retail outlets.

The means to enhance differentiation through activities at the forward end of the value chain system include (1) engaging in cooperative advertising and promotions with forward allies (dealers, distributors, retailers, etc.), (2) creating exclusive arrangements with downstream sellers or other mechanisms that increase their incentives to enhance delivered customer value, and (3) creating and enforcing standards for downstream activities and assisting in training channel partners in business practices. Harley-Davidson, for example, enhances the shopping experience and perceptions of buyers by selling through retailers that sell Harley-Davidson motorcycles exclusively and meet Harley-Davidson standards.

Translating Proficient Performance of Value Chain Activities into Competitive Advantage

Value chain analysis and benchmarking are not only useful for identifying and remedying competitive disadvantages; they can also be used to uncover and strengthen competitive advantages. A company's value-creating activities can offer a competitive advantage in one of two ways: (1) They can contribute to greater efficiency and lower costs relative to competitors, or (2) they can provide a basis for differentiation, so customers are willing to pay relatively more for the company's goods and services. A company that does a *first-rate job* of managing its value chain activities *relative to competitors* stands a good chance of profiting from its competitive advantage.

Achieving a cost-based competitive advantage requires determined management efforts to be cost-efficient in performing value chain activities. Such efforts have to be ongoing and persistent, and they have to involve each and every value chain activity. The goal must be continuous cost reduction, not a one-time or on-again–off-again effort. Companies whose managers are truly committed to low-cost performance of value chain activities and succeed in engaging company personnel to discover innovative ways to drive costs out of the business have a real chance of gaining a durable low-cost edge over rivals. It is not as easy as it seems to imitate a company's low-cost practices. Companies like Dollar General, Nucor Steel, Irish airline Ryanair, Greyhound Lines, and French discount retailer Carrefour have been highly successful in managing their values chains in a low-cost manner.

Ongoing and persistent efforts are also required for a competitive advantage based on differentiation. Superior reputations and brands are built up slowly over time, through continuous investment and activities that deliver consistent, reinforcing messages. Differentiation based on quality requires vigilant management of activities for quality assurance throughout the value chain. While the basis for differentiation (e.g., status, design, innovation, customer service, reliability, image) may vary widely among companies pursuing a differentiation advantage, companies that succeed do so on the basis of a commitment to coordinated value chain activities aimed purposefully at this objective. Examples include Grey Goose Vodka (status), IKEA (design), FedEx (reliability), 3M (innovation), Body Shop (image), and Nordstrom (customer service).

How Activities Relate to Resources and Capabilities   There is a close relationship between the value-creating activities that a company performs and its resources and capabilities. An organizational capability or competence implies a *capacity* for action; in contrast, a value-creating activity *is* the action. With respect to resources and capabilities, activities are "where the rubber hits the road." When companies engage in a value-creating activity, they do so by drawing on specific company resources and capabilities that underlie and enable the activity. For example, brand-building activities depend on human resources, such as experienced brand managers (including their knowledge and expertise in this arena), as well as organizational capabilities in advertising and marketing. Cost-cutting activities may derive from organizational capabilities in inventory management, for example, and resources such as inventory tracking systems.

Because of this correspondence between activities and supporting resources and capabilities, value chain analysis can complement resource and capability analysis as tools for assessing a company's competitive advantage. Resources and capabilities that are *both valuable and rare* provide a company with *what it takes* for competitive advantage. For a company with competitive assets of this sort, the potential is there. When these assets are deployed in the form of a value-creating activity, that potential is realized due to their competitive superiority. Resource analysis is one tool for identifying competitively superior resources and capabilities. But their value and the competitive superiority of that value can only be assessed objectively *after* they are deployed. Value chain analysis and benchmarking provide the type of data needed to make that objective assessment.

There is also a dynamic relationship between a company's activities and its resources and capabilities. Value-creating activities are more than just the embodiment of a resource's or capability's potential. They also contribute to the formation and development of capabilities. The road to competitive advantage begins with management efforts to build organizational expertise in performing certain competitively important value chain activities. With consistent practice and continuous investment of company resources, these activities rise to the level of a reliable organizational capability or a competence. To the extent that top management makes the growing capability a cornerstone of the company's strategy, this capability becomes a core competence for the company. Later, with further organizational learning and gains in proficiency, the core competence may evolve into a distinctive competence, giving the company superiority over rivals in performing an important value chain activity. Such superiority, if it gives the company significant competitive clout in the marketplace, can produce an attractive competitive edge over rivals. Whether the resulting competitive advantage is on the cost side or on the differentiation side (or both) will depend on the company's choice of which types of competence-building activities to engage in over this time period, as shown in Figure 4.5.

> Performing value chain activities in ways that give a company the capabilities to either outmatch rivals on differentiation or beat them on costs will help the company to secure a competitive advantage.

QUESTION 5: IS THE COMPANY COMPETITIVELY STRONGER OR WEAKER THAN KEY RIVALS?

LO 5

Understand how a comprehensive evaluation of a company's competitive situation can assist managers in making critical decisions about their next strategic moves.

Resource and capability analysis together with value chain analysis and benchmarking will reveal whether a company has a competitive advantage over rivals on the basis of *individual* resources, capabilities, and activities. These tools can also be used to assess the competitive advantage attributable to a *bundle* of resources and capabilities. Resource bundles can sometimes pass the four tests of a resource's competitive power even when the individual components of the resource bundle cannot. For example, although Callaway Golf Company's engineering capabilities and market research capabilities are matched relatively well by rivals Cobra Golf and Ping Golf, the company's bundling of resources used in its product development process (including cross-functional development systems, technological capabilities, knowledge of consumer preferences, and a collaborative organizational culture) gives it a competitive advantage that has allowed it to remain the largest seller of golf equipment for more than a decade.

Resource analysis and value chain/benchmarking analysis of the company's resources, capabilities, and activities (both as individual entities and as bundles) are necessary for determining whether the company is competitively stronger or weaker than key rivals. But they are not sufficient for gaining a complete picture

Figure 4.5 Translating Company Performance of Value Chain Activities into Competitive Advantage

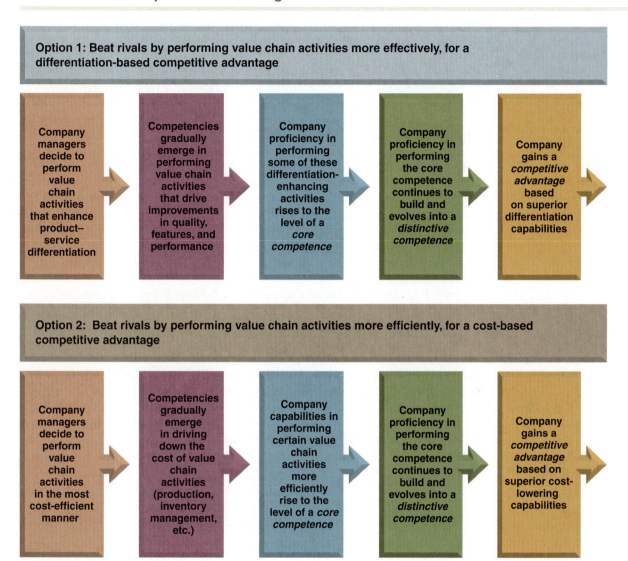

Option 1: Beat rivals by performing value chain activities more effectively, for a differentiation-based competitive advantage

Company managers decide to perform value chain activities that enhance product–service differentiation	Competencies gradually emerge in performing value chain activities that drive improvements in quality, features, and performance	Company proficiency in performing some of these differentiation-enhancing activities rises to the level of a *core competence*	Company proficiency in performing the core competence continues to build and evolves into a *distinctive competence*	Company gains a *competitive advantage* based on superior differentiation capabilities

Option 2: Beat rivals by performing value chain activities more efficiently, for a cost-based competitive advantage

Company managers decide to perform value chain activities in the most cost-efficient manner	Competencies gradually emerge in driving down the cost of value chain activities (production, inventory management, etc.)	Company capabilities in performing certain value chain activities more efficiently rise to the level of a *core competence*	Company proficiency in performing the core competence continues to build and evolves into a *distinctive competence*	Company gains a *competitive advantage* based on superior cost-lowering capabilities

of a company's competitive situation. A more comprehensive assessment needs to be made of the company's *overall* competitive strengths and weaknesses since a competitive advantage along one part of its value chain can be overwhelmed by competitive disadvantages along other parts of the chain. In making an overall assessment of a company's competitiveness, the answers to two questions are of particular interest: First, how does the company rank relative to competitors on each of the important factors that determine market success? Second, all things considered, does the company have a *net* competitive advantage or disadvantage versus major competitors?

An easy-to-use method for answering these two questions involves developing quantitative strength ratings for the company and its key competitors on each industry key success factor and each competitively pivotal resource and capability. Much of the information needed for doing a competitive strength assessment comes from previous analyses. Industry and five-forces analyses reveal the key success factors and competitive forces that separate industry winners from losers. Analyzing benchmarking data and scouting key competitors provide a basis for judging the competitive strength of rivals on such factors as cost, key product attributes, customer service, image and reputation, financial strength, technological skills, distribution capability, and other resources and capabilities. Resource and capability analysis reveals which factors are competitively important, given the external situation. Together with value chain analysis, it also shines a light on the competitive strengths of the company. That is, it reveals whether the company or its rivals have the advantage with respect to competitively important resources, capabilities, and activities. The four tests of a resource's competitive power indicate, further, whether any of these advantages are sustainable. SWOT analysis provides a more comprehensive and forward-looking picture of the company's overall situation by surveying the entire set of its strengths and weaknesses in relation to rivals and the external environment.

Step 1 in doing a competitive strength assessment is to make a list of the industry's key success factors and most telling measures of competitive strength or weakness (6 to 10 measures usually suffice). Step 2 is to assign weights to each of the measures of competitive strength based on their perceived importance—it is highly unlikely that the different measures are equally important. In an industry where the products/services of rivals are virtually identical, for instance, having low unit costs relative to rivals is nearly always the most important determinant of competitive strength. In an industry with strong product differentiation, the most significant measures of competitive strength may be brand awareness, brand image and reputation, product attractiveness, and distribution capability. A weight could be as high as 0.75 (maybe even higher) in situations where one particular competitive variable is overwhelmingly decisive, or a weight could be as low as 0.20 when two or three strength measures are more important than the rest. Lesser competitive strength indicators can carry weights of 0.05 or 0.10. Whether the differences between the importance weights are big or little, *the sum of the weights must add up to 1.*

Step 3 is to rate the firm and its rivals on each competitive strength measure. Numerical rating scales (e.g., from 1 to 10) are best to use, although ratings of stronger (+), weaker (–), and about equal (=) may be appropriate when information is scanty and assigning numerical scores conveys false precision. Step 4 is to multiply each strength rating by its importance weight to obtain weighted strength scores (a strength rating of 4 times a weight of 0.20 gives a weighted strength score of 0.80). Step 5 is to sum the weighted scores on each measure to get overall weighted competitive strength ratings for each company. Step 6 is to use the overall strength ratings to draw conclusions about the size and extent of the company's net competitive advantage or disadvantage and to take specific note of areas of strength and weakness.

Table 4.4 provides an example of competitive strength assessment in which a hypothetical company (ABC Company) competes against two rivals. In the

Table 4.4   A Representative Weighted Competitive Strength Assessment

Key Success Factor/Strength Measure	Importance Weight	Competitive Strength Assessment (Rating scale: 1 = very weak; 10 = very strong)					
		ABC Co.		Rival 1		Rival 2	
		Strength Rating	Weighted Score	Strength Rating	Weighted Score	Strength Rating	Weighted Score
Quality/product performance	0.10	8	0.80	5	0.50	1	0.10
Reputation/image	0.10	8	0.80	7	0.70	1	0.10
Manufacturing capability	0.10	2	0.20	10	1.00	5	0.50
Technological skills	0.05	10	0.50	1	0.05	3	0.15
Dealer network/distribution capability	0.05	9	0.45	4	0.20	5	0.25
New product innovation capability	0.05	9	0.45	4	0.20	5	0.25
Financial resources	0.10	5	0.50	10	1.00	3	0.30
Relative cost position	0.30	5	1.50	10	3.00	1	0.30
Customer service capabilities	0.15	5	0.75	7	1.05	1	0.15
Sum of importance weights	1.00						
Overall weighted competitive strength rating			**5.95**		**7.70**		**2.10**

example, relative cost is the most telling measure of competitive strength, and the other strength measures are of lesser importance. The company with the highest rating on a given measure has an implied competitive edge on that measure, with the size of its edge reflected in the difference between its weighted rating and rivals' weighted ratings. For instance, Rival 1's 3.00 weighted strength rating on relative cost signals a considerable cost advantage versus ABC Company (with a 1.50 weighted score on relative cost) and an even bigger cost advantage against Rival 2 (with a weighted score of 0.30). The measure-by-measure ratings reveal the competitive areas where a company is strongest and weakest, and against whom.

The overall competitive strength scores indicate how all the different strength measures add up—whether the company is at a net overall competitive advantage or disadvantage against each rival. The higher a company's *overall weighted strength rating,* the stronger its *overall competitiveness* versus rivals. The bigger the difference between a company's overall weighted rating and the scores of *lower-rated* rivals, the greater is its implied *net competitive advantage.* Thus, Rival 1's overall weighted score of 7.70 indicates a greater net competitive advantage over Rival 2 (with a score of 2.10) than over ABC Company (with a score of 5.95). Conversely, the bigger the difference between a company's overall rating and the scores of *higher-rated* rivals, the greater its implied *net competitive disadvantage.* Rival 2's score of 2.10 gives it a smaller net competitive disadvantage against ABC Company (with an overall score of 5.95) than against Rival 1 (with an overall score of 7.70).

High weighted competitive strength ratings signal a strong competitive position and possession of competitive advantage; low ratings signal a weak position and competitive disadvantage.

Strategic Implications of Competitive Strength Assessments

Competitive strength assessments provide useful conclusions about a company's competitive situation. The ratings show how a company compares against rivals, factor by factor (or capability by capability), thus revealing where it is strongest and weakest, and against whom. Moreover, the overall competitive strength score indicates how all the different factors add up—whether the company is at a net competitive advantage or disadvantage against each rival. The firm with the largest overall competitive strength rating enjoys the strongest competitive position, with the size of its net competitive advantage reflected by how much its score exceeds the scores of rivals.

In addition, the strength ratings provide guidelines for designing wise offensive and defensive strategies. For example, if ABC Co. wants to go on the offensive to win additional sales and market share, such an offensive probably needs to be aimed directly at winning customers away from Rival 2 (which has a lower overall strength score) rather than Rival 1 (which has a higher overall strength score). Moreover, while ABC has high ratings for technological skills (a 10 rating), dealer network/distribution capability (a 9 rating), new product innovation capability (a 9 rating), quality/product performance (an 8 rating), and reputation/image (an 8 rating), these strength measures have low importance weights—meaning that ABC has strengths in areas that don't translate into much competitive clout in the marketplace. Even so, it outclasses Rival 2 in all five areas, plus it enjoys substantially lower costs than Rival 2 (ABC has a 5 rating on relative cost position versus a 1 rating for Rival 2)—and relative cost position carries the highest importance weight of all the strength measures. ABC also has greater competitive strength than Rival 3 as concerns customer service capabilities (which carries the second-highest importance weight). Hence, because ABC's strengths are in the very areas where Rival 2 is weak, ABC is in a good position to attack Rival 2—it may well be able to persuade a number of Rival 2's customers to switch their purchases over to ABC's product.

> A company's competitive strength scores pinpoint its strengths and weaknesses against rivals and point directly to the kinds of offensive/defensive actions it can use to exploit its competitive strengths and reduce its competitive vulnerabilities.

But ABC should be cautious about cutting price aggressively to win customers away from Rival 2, because Rival 1 could interpret that as an attack by ABC to win away Rival 1's customers as well. And Rival 1 is in far and away the best position to compete on the basis of low price, given its high rating on relative cost in an industry where low costs are competitively important (relative cost carries an importance weight of 0.30). Rival 1's very strong relative cost position vis-à-vis both ABC and Rival 2 arms it with the ability to use its lower-cost advantage to thwart any price cutting on ABC's part; clearly ABC is vulnerable to any retaliatory price cuts by Rival 1—Rival 1 can easily defeat both ABC and Rival 2 in a price-based battle for sales and market share. If ABC wants to defend against its vulnerability to potential price cutting by Rival 1, then it needs to aim a portion of its strategy at lowering its costs.

The point here is that a competitively astute company should utilize the strength scores in deciding what strategic moves to make—what strengths to exploit in winning business away from rivals, which rivals to attack, and which competitive weaknesses to try to correct. When a company has important competitive strengths in areas where one or more rivals are weak, it makes sense to consider offensive moves to exploit rivals' competitive weaknesses. When a company has important competitive weaknesses in areas where one or more rivals are strong, it makes sense to consider defensive moves to curtail its vulnerability.

QUESTION 6: WHAT STRATEGIC ISSUES AND PROBLEMS MERIT FRONT-BURNER MANAGERIAL ATTENTION?

The final and most important analytical step is to zero in on exactly what strategic issues company managers need to address—and resolve—for the company to be more financially and competitively successful in the years ahead. This step involves drawing on the results of both industry analysis and the evaluations of the company's own competitiveness. The task here is to get a clear fix on exactly what strategic and competitive challenges confront the company, which of the company's competitive shortcomings need fixing, what obstacles stand in the way of improving the company's competitive position in the marketplace, and what specific problems merit front-burner attention by company managers.

> Zeroing in on the strategic issues a company faces and compiling a "worry list" of problems and roadblocks creates a strategic agenda of problems that merit prompt managerial attention.

The "worry list" of issues and problems that have to be wrestled with can include such things as:

- *How* to stave off market challenges from new foreign competitors.
- *How* to combat the price discounting of rivals.
- *How* to reduce the company's high costs and pave the way for price reductions.
- *How* to sustain the company's present rate of growth in light of slowing buyer demand.
- *Whether* to expand the company's product line.
- *Whether* to correct the company's competitive deficiencies by acquiring a rival company with the missing strengths.
- *Whether* to expand into foreign markets rapidly or cautiously.
- *Whether* to reposition the company and move to a different strategic group.
- *What to do* about growing buyer interest in substitute products.
- *What to do* to combat the aging demographics of the company's customer base.

The worry list thus always centers on such concerns as "how to … ," "what to do about … ," and "whether to… ." The purpose of the worry list is to identify the specific issues/problems that management needs to address, not to figure out what specific actions to take. Deciding what to do—which strategic actions to take and which strategic moves to take—comes later (when it is time to craft the strategy and choose among the various strategic alternatives).

> Actually deciding on a strategy and what specific actions to take is what comes *after* developing the list of strategic issues and problems that merit front-burner management attention.

If the items on the worry list are relatively minor—which suggests that the company's strategy is mostly on track and reasonably well matched to the company's overall situation, company managers seldom need to go much beyond fine-tuning the present strategy. If, however, the issues and problems confronting the company are serious and indicate the present strategy is not well suited for the road ahead, the task of crafting a better strategy has got to go to the top of management's action agenda.

> A good strategy must contain ways to deal with all the strategic issues and obstacles that stand in the way of the company's financial and competitive success in the years ahead.

KEY POINTS

There are six key questions to consider in evaluating a company's ability to compete successfully against market rivals:

1. *How well is the present strategy working?* This involves evaluating the strategy from a qualitative standpoint (completeness, internal consistency, rationale, and suitability to the situation) and also from a quantitative standpoint (the strategic and financial results the strategy is producing). The stronger a company's current overall performance, the less likely the need for radical strategy changes. The weaker a company's performance and/or the faster the changes in its external situation (which can be gleaned from industry and competitive forces analysis), the more its current strategy must be questioned.

2. *Do the company's resources and capabilities have sufficient competitive power to give it a sustainable advantage over competitors?* The answer to this question comes from conducting the four tests of a resource's competitive power. If a company has resources and capabilities that are competitively valuable and rare, the firm will have a competitive advantage over market rivals. If its resources and capabilities are also hard to copy, with no good substitutes, then the firm may be able to sustain this advantage even in the face of active efforts by rivals to overcome it.

3. *Is the company able to seize market opportunities and overcome external threats to its future well-being?* The answer to this question comes from performing a SWOT analysis. The two most important parts of SWOT analysis are (1) drawing conclusions about what story the compilation of strengths, weaknesses, opportunities, and threats tells about the company's overall situation and (2) acting on the conclusions to better match the company's strategy to its internal strengths and market opportunities, to correct the important internal weaknesses, and to defend against external threats. A company's strengths and competitive assets are strategically relevant because they are the most logical and appealing building blocks for strategy; internal weaknesses are important because they may represent vulnerabilities that need correction. External opportunities and threats come into play because a good strategy necessarily aims at capturing a company's most attractive opportunities and at defending against threats to its well-being.

4. *Are the company's prices, costs, and value proposition competitive?* One telling sign of whether a company's situation is strong or precarious is whether its prices and costs are competitive with those of industry rivals. Another sign is how it compares with rivals in terms of differentiation—how effectively it delivers on its customer value proposition. Value chain analysis and benchmarking are essential tools in determining whether the company is performing particular functions and activities efficiently and effectively, learning whether its costs are in line with competitors, whether it is differentiating in ways that really enhance customer value, and deciding which internal activities and business processes need to be scrutinized for improvement. They complement resource and capability analysis by providing data at the level of individual activities that provides more objective evidence of whether individual resources and capabilities, or bundles of resources and linked activity sets, are competitively superior.

5. *On an overall basis, is the company competitively stronger or weaker than key rivals?* The key appraisals here involve how the company matches up against key rivals on industry key success factors and other chief determinants of competitive success and whether and why the company has a *net* competitive advantage or disadvantage. Quantitative competitive strength assessments, using the method presented in Table 4.4, indicate where a company is competitively strong and weak and provide insight into the company's ability to defend or enhance its market position. As a rule, a company's competitive strategy should be built around its competitive strengths and should aim at shoring up areas where it is competitively vulnerable. When a company has important competitive strengths in areas where one or more rivals are weak, it makes sense to consider offensive moves to exploit rivals' competitive weaknesses. When a company has important competitive weaknesses in areas where one or more rivals are strong, it makes sense to consider defensive moves to curtail its vulnerability.

6. *What strategic issues and problems merit front-burner managerial attention?* This analytical step zeros in on the strategic issues and problems that stand in the way of the company's success. It involves using the results of industry analysis as well as resource and value chain analysis of the company's competitive situation to identify a "worry list" of issues to be resolved for the company to be financially and competitively successful in the years ahead. The worry list always centers on such concerns as "how to ... ," "what to do about ... ," and "whether to ... "—the purpose of the worry list is to identify the specific issues/problems that management needs to address. Actually deciding on a strategy and what specific actions to take is what comes after the list of strategic issues and problems that merit front-burner management attention is developed.

Solid analysis of the company's competitive situation vis-à-vis its key rivals, like good industry analysis, is a valuable precondition for good strategy making. A competently done evaluation of a company's resources, capabilities, and competitive strengths exposes strong and weak points in the present strategy and how attractive or unattractive the company's competitive position is and why. Managers need such understanding to craft a strategy that is well suited to the company's competitive circumstances.

ASSURANCE OF LEARNING EXERCISES

LO 2, LO 3, LO 4

1. Review the information in Illustration Capsule 4.1 concerning the average costs of producing and selling fair-trade coffee. Then answer the following questions:

   a. Companies that do not sell fair-trade coffee can buy coffee direct from small farmers for as little as $0.75 per pound. By paying substandard wages, they can also reduce their labor costs of roasting and bagging coffee to $0.70 per pound and reduce their overhead by 20 percent. If they sell their coffee at the same average price as Just Coffee, what would their profit margin be and how would this compare to Just Coffee's?

b. How can Just Coffee respond to this type of competitive threat? Does it have any valuable competitive assets that can help it respond, or will it need to acquire new ones. Would your answer change the company's value chain in any way?

LO 1

2. Using the information in Table 4.1 and the financial statement information for Avon Products below, calculate the following ratios for Avon for both 2008 and 2009:

a. Gross profit margin

b. Operating profit margin

c. Net profit margin.

d. Times interest earned coverage

e. Return on shareholders' equity

f. Return on assets

g. Debt-to-equity ratio

h. Days of inventory

i. Inventory turnover ratio

j. Average collection period

Based on these ratios, did Avon's financial performance improve, weaken, or remain about the same from 2008 to 2009?

Consolidated Statements of Income for Avon Products, Inc., 2008–2009 (in millions, except per-share data)

	Years ended December 31	
	2009	2008
Net sales	$10,284.7	$10,588.9
Other revenue	98.1	101.2
Total revenue	10,382.8	10,690.1
Costs, expenses, and other:		
Cost of sales	3,888.3	3,949.1
Selling, general and administrative expenses	5,476.3	5,401.7
Operating profit	1,018.2	1,339.3
Interest expense	104.8	100.4
Interest income	(20.2)	(37.1)
Other expense, net	7.1	37.7
Total other expenses	91.7	101.0
Income before taxes	926.5	1,238.3
Income taxes	298.3	362.7
Net income	628.2	875.6

(Continued)

	Years ended December 31	
	2009	2008
Net income attributable to noncontrolling interests	(2.4)	(.3)
Net income attributable to Avon	$ 625.8	$ 875.3
Earnings per share:		
Basic	$ 1.45	$ 2.04
Diluted	$ 1.45	$ 2.03

Consolidated Balance Sheets for Avon Products, Inc., 2008–2009 (in millions, except per-share data)

	As of Dec. 31, 2009	As of Dec. 31, 2008
Assets		
Cash and cash equivalents	$ 1,311.6	$ 1,104.7
Accounts receivable (less allowances of $165.5 and $127.9)	779.7	687.8
Inventories	1,067.5	1,007.9
Prepaid expenses and other	1,030.5	756.5
Total current assets	4,189.3	3,556.9
Property, plant, and equipment, at cost		
Land	144.3	85.3
Buildings and improvements	1,048.1	1,008.1
Equipment	1,506.9	1,346.5
Total property, plant, and equipment, at cost	2,699.3	2,439.9
Less accumulated depreciation	(1,169.7)	(1,096.0)
Net property, plant, and equipment	1,529.6	1,343.9
Other assets	1,113.8	1,173.2
Total assets	$ 6,832.7	$ 6,074.0
Liabilities and Shareholders' Equity		
Debt maturing within 1 year	$ 138.1	$1,031.4
Accounts payable	754.7	724.3
Accrued compensation	291.0	234.4
Other accrued liabilities	697.1	581.9
Sales and taxes other than income	259.2	212.2
Income taxes	134.7	128.0
Total current liabilities	2,274.8	2,912.2
Long-term debt	2,307.8	1,456.2
Employee benefit plans	588.9	665.4
Long-term income taxes	173.8	168.9
Other liabilities	174.8	159.0
Total liabilities	$ 5,520.1	$ 5,361.7
Commitments and contingencies		

(Continued)

Shareholders' equity

Common stock, par value $.25—authorized 1,500 shares; issued 740.9 and 739.4 shares	$ 186.1	$ 185.6
Additional paid-in capital	1,941.0	1,874.1
Retained earnings	4,383.9	4,118.9
Accumulated other comprehensive loss	(692.6)	(965.9)
Treasury stock, at cost (313.4 and 313.1 shares)	(4,545.8)	(4,537.8)
Total Avon shareholders' equity	1,272.6	674.9
Noncontrolling interest	40.0	37.4
Total shareholders' equity	**$ 1,312.6**	**$ 712.3**
Total liabilities and shareholders' equity	**$ 6,832.7**	**$ 6,074.0**

Source: Avon Products, Inc., 2009 10-K.

EXERCISES FOR SIMULATION PARTICIPANTS

LO 1

1. Using the formulas in Table 4.1 and the data in your company's latest financial statements, calculate the following measures of financial performance for your company:

   a. Operating profit margin

   b. Return on total assets

   c. Current ratio

   d. Working capital

   e. Long-term debt-to-capital ratio

   f. Price-earnings ratio

LO 1

2. On the basis of your company's latest financial statements and all the other available data regarding your company's performance that appear in the Industry Report, list the three measures of financial performance on which your company did "best" and the three measures on which your company's financial performance was "worst."

LO 1, LO 2, LO 3, LO 4, LO 5

3. What hard evidence can you cite that indicates your company's strategy is working fairly well (or perhaps not working so well, if your company's performance is lagging that of rival companies)?

LO 3

4. What internal strengths and weaknesses does your company have? What external market opportunities for growth and increased profitability exist for

your company? What external threats to your company's future well-being and profitability do you and your co-managers see? What does the preceding SWOT analysis indicate about your company's present situation and future prospects—where on the scale from "exceptionally strong" to "alarmingly weak" does the attractiveness of your company's situation rank?

LO 2, LO 3

5. Does your company have any core competencies? If so, what are they?

LO 4

6. What are the key elements of your company's value chain? Refer to Figure 4.3 in developing your answer.

LO 5

7. Using the methodology presented in Table 4.4, do a weighted competitive strength assessment for your company and two other companies that you and your co-managers consider to be very close competitors.

ENDNOTES

[1] In recent years, considerable research has been devoted to the role a company's resources and competitive capabilities play in determining its competitiveness, shaping its strategy, and impacting its profitability. Following the trailblazing article by Birger Wernerfelt, "A Resource-Based View of the Firm," *Strategic Management Journal* 5, no. 5 (September–October 1984), pp. 171–80, the findings and conclusions have merged into what is now referred to as the resource-based view of the firm. Other very important contributions include Jay Barney, "Firm Resources and Sustained Competitive Advantage," *Journal of Management* 17, no. 1 (1991), pp. 99–120; Margaret A. Peteraf, "The Cornerstones of Competitive Advantage: A Resource-Based View," *Strategic Management Journal* 14, no. 3 (March 1993), pp. 179–91; Birger Wernerfelt, "The Resource-Based View of the Firm: Ten Years After," *Strategic Management Journal* 16, no. 3 (March 1995), pp. 171–74. A full-blown overview of the resource-based view of the firm, in its most current form, is presented in Jay B. Barney and Delwyn N. Clark, *Resource-Based Theory: Creating and Sustaining Competitive Advantage* (New York: Oxford University Press, 2007).
[2] A more detailed explanation of the relationship between resources and capabilities can be found in R. Amit and P. Schoemaker, "Strategic Assets and Organizational Rent," *Strategic Management Journal* 14 (1993), pp. 33–46.
[3] See, for example, Jay B. Barney, "Looking Inside for Competitive Advantage," *Academy of Management Executive* 9, no. 4 (November 1995), pp. 49–61; Christopher A. Bartlett and Sumantra Ghoshal, "Building Competitive

Advantage through People," *MIT Sloan Management Review* 43, no. 2 (Winter 2002), pp. 34–41; Danny Miller, Russell Eisenstat, and Nathaniel Foote, "Strategy from the Inside Out: Building Capability-Creating Organizations," *California Management Review* 44, no. 3 (Spring 2002), pp. 37–54.
[4] See Barney, "Firm Resources and Sustained Competitive Advantage," pp. 105–9; M. Peteraf and J. Barney, "Unraveling the Resource-Based Tangle," *Managerial and Decision Economics* 24, no. 4 (June–July 2003), pp. 309–23.
[5] See Amit and Schoemaker, Strategic Assets and Organizational Rent, for more on the power of strategic assets to improve a company's profitability.
[6] For a discussion of how to recognize powerful substitute resources, see Margaret A. Peteraf and Mark E. Bergen, "Scanning Dynamic Competitive Landscapes: A Market-Based and Resource-Based Framework," *Strategic Management Journal* 24 (2003), pp. 1027–42.
[7] See C. Montgomery, "Of Diamonds and Rust: A New Look at Resources," in C. Montgomery (ed.), *Resource-Based and Evolutionary Theories of the Firm* (Boston: Kluwer Academic, 1995), pp. 251–68.
[8] For a good discussion of what happens when a company's capabilities grow stale and obsolete, see D. Leonard-Barton, "Core Capabilities and Core Rigidities: A Paradox in Managing New Product Development," *Strategic Management Journal* 13 (Summer 1992), pp. 111–25; Montgomery, "Of Diamonds and Rust."
[9] The concept of dynamic capabilities was introduced by D. Teece, G. Pisano, and A. Shuen, "Dynamic Capabilities and Strategic Management," *Strategic Management*

Journal 18, no. 7 (1997), pp. 509–33. Other important contributors to the concept include K. Eisenhardt and J. Martin, "Dynamic Capabilities: What Are They?" *Strategic Management Journal* 21, nos. 10–11 (2000), pp. 1105–21; M. Zollo and S. Winter, "Deliberate Learning and the Evolution of Dynamic Capabilities," *Organization Science* 13 (2002), pp. 339–51; C. Helfat et al., *Dynamic Capabilities: Understanding Strategic Change in Organizations* (Malden, MA: Blackwell, 2007).
[10] For a more extensive discussion of how to identify and evaluate the competitive power of a company's capabilities, see David W. Birchall and George Tovstiga, "The Strategic Potential of a Firm's Knowledge Portfolio," *Journal of General Management* 25, no. 1 (Autumn 1999), pp. 1–16; Nick Bontis, Nicola C. Dragonetti, Kristine Jacobsen, and Goran Roos, "The Knowledge Toolbox: A Review of the Tools Available to Measure and Manage Intangible Resources," *European Management Journal* 17, no. 4 (August 1999), pp. 391–401. Also see David Teece, "Capturing Value from Knowledge Assets: The New Economy, Markets for Know-How, and Intangible Assets," *California Management Review* 40, no. 3 (Spring 1998), pp. 55–79.
[11] Donald Sull, "Strategy as Active Waiting," *Harvard Business Review* 83, no. 9 (September 2005), pp. 121–22.
[12] Ibid., pp. 124–26.
[13] See M. Peteraf, "The Cornerstones of Competitive Advantage: A Resource-Based View," *Strategic Management Journal,* March 1993, pp. 179–91.
[14] The value chain concept was developed and articulated by Michael Porter in his 1985

best-seller, *Competitive Advantage* (New York: Free Press).

[15] For discussions of the accounting challenges in calculating the costs of value chain activities, see John K. Shank and Vijay Govindarajan, *Strategic Cost Management* (New York: Free Press, 1993), especially chaps. 2–6, 10, and 11; Robin Cooper and Robert S. Kaplan, "Measure Costs Right: Make the Right Decisions," *Harvard Business Review* 66, no. 5 (September–October 1988), pp. 96–103; Joseph A. Ness and Thomas G. Cucuzza, "Tapping the Full Potential of ABC," *Harvard Business Review* 73, no. 4 (July–August 1995), pp. 130–38.

[16] Porter, *Competitive Advantage,* p. 34.

[17] The strategic importance of effective supply chain management is discussed in Hau L. Lee, "The Triple-A Supply Chain," *Harvard Business Review* 82, no. 10 (October 2004), pp. 102–12.

[18] For more details, see Gregory H. Watson, *Strategic Benchmarking: How to Rate Your Company's Performance Against the World's Best* (New York: Wiley, 1993); Robert C. Camp, *Benchmarking: The Search for Industry Best Practices That Lead to Superior Performance* (Milwaukee: ASQC Quality Press, 1989); Dawn Iacobucci and Christie Nordhielm, "Creative Benchmarking," *Harvard Business Review* 78 no. 6 (November–December 2000), pp. 24–25.

[19] Jeremy Main, "How to Steal the Best Ideas Around," *Fortune,* October 19, 1992, pp. 102–3.

[20] Some of these options are discussed in more detail in Porter, *Competitive Advantage,* chap. 3.

[21] Porter discusses options such as these in *Competitive Advantage,* chap. 4.

[22] An example of how Whirlpool Corporation transformed its supply chain from a competitive liability to a competitive asset is discussed in Reuben E. Stone, "Leading a Supply Chain Turnaround," *Harvard Business Review* 82, no. 10 (October 2004), pp. 114–21.

CHAPTER 5

THE FIVE GENERIC COMPETITIVE STRATEGIES

Which One to Employ?

> I'm spending my time trying to understand our competitive position and how we're serving customers.
>
> **—Lou Gerstner**
> *Former CEO credited with IBM's turnaround*

> Competitive strategy is about being different. It means deliberately choosing to perform activities differently or to perform different activities than rivals to deliver a unique mix of value.
>
> **—Michael E. Porter**
> *Harvard Business School professor and Cofounder of Monitor Consulting*

> The essence of strategy lies in creating tomorrow's competitive advantages faster than competitors mimic the ones you possess today.
>
> **—Gary Hamel and C. K. Prahalad**
> *Professors, authors, and consultants*

LEARNING OBJECTIVES

LO 1. Understand what distinguishes each of the five generic strategies and why some of these strategies work better in certain kinds of industry and competitive conditions than in others.

LO 2. Gain command of the major avenues for achieving a competitive advantage based on lower costs.

LO 3. Learn the major avenues to a competitive advantage based on differentiating a company's product or service offering from the offerings of rivals.

LO 4. Recognize the attributes of a best-cost provider strategy and the way in which some firms use a hybrid strategy to go about building a competitive advantage and delivering superior value to customers.

There are several basic approaches to competing successfully and gaining a competitive advantage over rivals, but they all involve the capacity to deliver more customer value than rivals can. Superior value can mean a good product at a lower price, a superior product that is worth paying more for, or a best-value offering that represents an attractive combination of price, features, quality, service, and other appealing attributes. But whatever form delivering superior value takes, it nearly always requires performing value chain activities differently than rivals and building competitively valuable resources and capabilities that rivals cannot readily match or trump.

This chapter describes the five *generic competitive strategy options*. Which of the five to employ is a company's first and foremost choice in crafting an overall strategy and beginning its quest for competitive advantage.

THE FIVE GENERIC COMPETITIVE STRATEGIES

A company's competitive strategy *deals exclusively with the specifics of management's game plan for competing successfully*—its specific efforts to please customers, its offensive and defensive moves to counter the maneuvers of rivals, its responses to shifting market conditions, its initiatives to strengthen its market position, and the specific kind of competitive advantage it is trying to achieve. The chances are remote that any two companies—even companies in the same industry—will employ competitive strategies that are exactly alike in every detail. Why? Because managers at different companies always have a slightly different spin on how best to deal with competitive pressures and industry driving forces, what future market conditions will be like, and what strategy specifics make the most sense for their particular company in light of the company's strengths and weaknesses, its most promising market opportunities, and the external threats to its future well-being.

LO 1

Understand what distinguishes each of the five generic strategies and why some of these strategies work better in certain kinds of industry and competitive conditions than in others.

However, when one strips away the details to get at the real substance, the two factors that most distinguish one competitive strategy from another boil down to (1) whether a company's market target is broad or narrow and (2) whether the company is pursuing a competitive advantage linked to low costs or product differentiation. As shown in Figure 5.1, these two factors give rise to five competitive strategy options for staking out a market position, operating the business, and delivering value to customers:[1]

1. *A low-cost provider strategy:* striving to achieve lower overall costs than rivals on products that attract a broad spectrum of buyers.
2. *A broad differentiation strategy:* seeking to differentiate the company's product offering from rivals' with attributes that will appeal to a broad spectrum of buyers.
3. *A focused (or market niche) low-cost strategy:* concentrating on a narrow buyer segment and outcompeting rivals on costs, thus being in position to win buyer favor by means of a lower-priced product offering.
4. *A focused (or market niche) differentiation strategy:* concentrating on a narrow buyer segment and outcompeting rivals with a product offering that meets the specific tastes and requirements of niche members better than the product offerings of rivals.
5. *A best-cost provider strategy:* giving customers *more value for the money* by offering upscale product attributes at a lower cost than rivals. Being the "best-cost" producer of an upscale product allows a company to underprice rivals whose products have similar upscale attributes. This option is a *hybrid* strategy that *blends elements of differentiation and low-cost strategies* in a unique way.

The remainder of this chapter explores the ins and outs of these five generic competitive strategies and how they differ.

Figure 5.1 The Five Generic Competitive Strategies: Each Stakes Out a Different Market Position

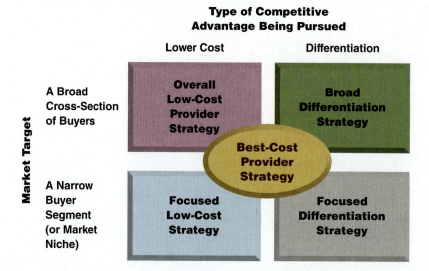

Source: This is an author-expanded version of a three-strategy classification discussed in Michael E. Porter, *Competitive Strategy* (New York: Free Press, 1980), pp. 35–40.

LOW-COST PROVIDER STRATEGIES

Striving to be the industry's overall low-cost provider is a powerful competitive approach in markets with many price-sensitive buyers. A company achieves **low-cost leadership** when it becomes the industry's lowest-cost provider rather than just being one of perhaps several competitors with comparatively low costs. A low-cost provider's strategic target is to have lower costs than rivals on products of comparable quality. In striving for a cost advantage over rivals, company managers must take care to incorporate features and services that buyers consider essential—*a product offering that is too frills-free sabotages the attractiveness of the company's product and can turn buyers off even if it is cheaper than competing products.* For maximum effectiveness, a low-cost provider needs to pursue cost-saving approaches that are difficult for rivals to copy. When it is relatively easy or inexpensive for rivals to imitate the low-cost firm's methods, then any resulting cost advantage evaporates too quickly to gain a very valuable edge in the marketplace.

A low-cost advantage over rivals has enormous competitive power, sometimes enabling a company to achieve faster rates of growth (by using price cuts to draw customers away from rivals) and frequently helping to boost a company's profitability. A company can translate a low-cost advantage over rivals into attractive profit performance in either of two ways:

1. By using its lower-cost edge to underprice competitors and attract price-sensitive buyers in great enough numbers to increase total profits.
2. By refraining from using price cuts to steal sales away from rivals (which runs the risk of starting a price war) and, instead, charging a price roughly equal to those of other low-priced rivals. While this strategy will not increase the company's market share, it will enable the company to earn a bigger profit margin per unit sold (because the company's costs per unit are below the unit costs of rivals) and thereby propel it to higher total profits and return on investment than rivals are able to earn.

While many companies are inclined to exploit a low-cost advantage by attacking rivals with lower prices (in hopes that the expected gains in sales and market share will lead to higher total profits), this strategy can backfire if rivals respond with retaliatory price cuts of their own (in order to protect their customer base) and the aggressor's price cuts fail to produce sales gains that are big enough to offset the profit erosion associated with charging a lower price. The bigger the risk that rivals will respond with matching price cuts, the more appealing it becomes to employ the second option for using a low-cost advantage to achieve higher profitability.

The Two Major Avenues for Achieving a Cost Advantage

To achieve a low-cost edge over rivals, a firm's cumulative costs across its overall value chain must be lower than competitors' cumulative costs. There are two ways to accomplish this:[2]

> **LO 2**
>
> Gain command of the major avenues for achieving a competitive advantage based on lower costs.

> **CORE CONCEPT**
>
> A **low-cost leader's** basis for competitive advantage is lower overall costs than competitors. Successful low-cost leaders are exceptionally good at finding ways to drive costs out of their businesses and still provide a product or service that buyers find acceptable.

> A low-cost advantage over rivals can translate into better profitability than rivals attain.

1. Do a better job than rivals of performing value chain activities more cost-effectively.

2. Revamp the firm's overall value chain to eliminate or bypass some cost-producing activities.

Let's look at each of the two approaches to securing a cost advantage.

Cost-Efficient Management of Value Chain Activities

For a company to do a more cost-efficient job of managing its value chain than rivals, managers must launch a concerted, ongoing effort to ferret out cost-saving opportunities in every part of the value chain. No activity can escape cost-saving scrutiny, and all company personnel must be expected to use their talents and ingenuity to come up with innovative and effective ways to keep costs down. All avenues for performing value chain activities at a lower cost than rivals have to be explored. Particular attention, however, needs to be paid to a set of factors known as **cost drivers,** which have an especially strong effect on a company's costs and which managers can use as levers to push costs down. (Figure 5.2 provides a list of important cost drivers.) Cost-cutting methods that demonstrate an effective use of the cost drivers include:

1. *Striving to capture all available economies of scale.* Economies of scale stem from an ability to lower unit costs by increasing the scale of operation, and they can affect the unit costs of many activities along the value chain, including manufacturing, R&D, advertising, distribution, and general administration. For example, PepsiCo and Anheuser-Busch have the ability to afford the $3 million cost of a 30-second Super Bowl ad because the cost of such an ad can be spread out over the hundreds of millions of units they sell. In contrast, a small company with a sales volume of only 1 million units would find the $3 million cost of a Super Bowl ad prohibitive—just one ad would raise costs over $2 per unit even if the ad was unusually effective and caused sales volume to jump 25 percent, to 1.25 million units. Similarly, a large manufacturing plant can be more economical to operate than a smaller one. In global industries, making separate products for each country market instead of selling a mostly standard product worldwide tends to boost unit costs because of lost time in model changeover, shorter production runs, and inability to reach the most economic scale of production for each country model.

2. *Taking full advantage of experience and learning-curve effects.* The cost of performing an activity can decline over time as the learning and experience of company personnel build. Learning/experience economies can stem from debugging and mastering newly introduced technologies, using the experiences and suggestions of workers to install more efficient plant layouts and assembly procedures, and the added speed and effectiveness that accrues from repeatedly picking sites for and building new plants, retail outlets, or distribution centers. Aggressively managed low-cost providers pay diligent attention to capturing the benefits of learning and experience and to keeping these benefits proprietary to whatever extent possible.

3. *Trying to operate facilities at full capacity.* Whether a company is able to operate at or near full capacity has a big impact on units costs when

Figure 5.2   Cost Drivers: The Keys to Driving Down Company Costs

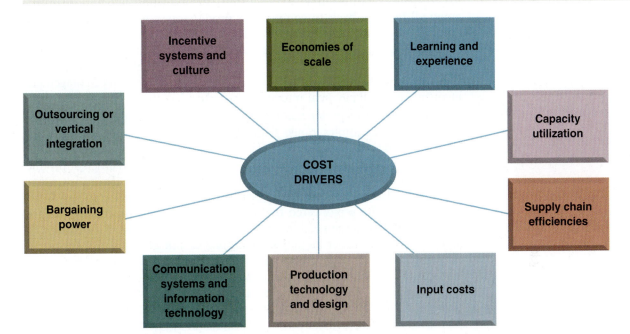

Sources: Adapted by the authors from M. Porter, *Competitive Advantage: Creating and Sustaining Competitive Advantage* (New York: Free Press, 1985).

its value chain contains activities associated with substantial fixed costs. Higher rates of capacity utilization allow depreciation and other fixed costs to be spread over a larger unit volume, thereby lowering fixed costs per unit. The more capital-intensive the business and the higher the fixed costs relative to total costs, the greater the unit-cost penalty for underutilizing existing capacity.

4. *Improving supply chain efficiency.* Partnering with suppliers to streamline the ordering and purchasing process, to reduce inventory carrying costs via just-in-time inventory practices, to economize on shipping and materials handling, and to ferret out other cost-saving opportunities is a much-used approach to cost reduction. A company with a distinctive competence in cost-efficient supply chain management can sometimes achieve a sizable cost advantage over less adept rivals.

5. *Using lower cost inputs wherever doing so will not entail too great a sacrifice in quality.* Some examples include lower-cost raw materials or component parts, nonunion labor "inputs," and lower rental fees due to differences in location. If the costs of certain factors are "too high," a company may even design the high-cost inputs out of the product altogether.

6. *Using the company's bargaining power vis-à-vis suppliers or others in the value chain system to gain concessions.* Home Depot, for example, has sufficient bargaining clout with suppliers to win price discounts on large-volume purchases. PepsiCo similarly uses its bargaining power to win concessions from supermarkets, mass merchandisers, and other forward channel allies.

7. *Using communication systems and information technology to achieve operating efficiencies.* For example, data sharing, starting with customer orders and going all the way back to components production, coupled with the use of enterprise resource planning (ERP) and manufacturing execution system (MES) software, can greatly reduce production times and labor costs. Numerous companies now have online systems and software that turn formerly time-consuming and labor-intensive tasks like purchasing, inventory management, invoicing, and bill payment into speedily performed mouse clicks.

8. *Employing advanced production technology and process design to improve overall efficiency.* Examples range from highly automated robotic production technology to computer-assisted design (CAD) techniques to design for manufacture (DFM) procedures that enable more integrated and efficient production. Dell's highly automated PC assembly plant in Austin, Texas, is a prime example of the use of advanced product and process technologies. Other manufacturers have pioneered the use of production or processing technology that eliminates the need for costly investments in facilities or equipment and that requires fewer employees. Companies can also achieve substantial efficiency gains through process innovation or through approaches such as business process management, business process reengineering, and total quality management that aim to coordinate production activities and drive continuous improvement in productivity and quality.[3] Procter & Gamble is an example of a company known for its successful application of business process reengineering techniques.

9. *Being alert to the cost advantages of outsourcing or vertical integration.* Outsourcing the performance of certain value chain activities can be more economical than performing them in-house if outside specialists, by virtue of their expertise and volume, can perform the activities at lower cost. Indeed, outsourcing has, in recent years, become a widely used cost reduction approach. On the other hand, there can be times when integrating into the activities of either suppliers or distribution channel allies can lower costs through greater production efficiencies, reduced transaction costs, or a better bargaining position.

10. *Motivating employees through incentives and company culture.* A company's incentive system can encourage not only greater worker productivity but also cost-saving innovations that come from worker suggestions. The culture of a company can also spur worker pride in productivity and continuous improvement. Companies that are well known for their cost-reducing incentive systems and culture include Nucor Steel, which characterizes itself as a company of "11,900 teammates," Southwest Airlines, and Walmart.

In addition to the above means of performing value chain activities more efficiently than rivals, managers can also achieve important cost savings by deliberately opting for an inherently economical strategy. For instance, a company can often open up a significant cost advantage over rivals by:

- Having lower specifications for purchased materials, parts, and components than do rivals. Thus, a maker of personal computers can use the cheapest hard drives, microprocessors, monitors, and other components so as to end up with lower production costs than rival PC makers.

- Stripping frills and features from its product offering that are not highly valued by price-sensitive or bargain-hunting buyers. Deliberately restricting the company's product offering to "the essentials" can help a company cut costs associated with snazzy attributes and a full lineup of options and extras. Activities and costs can also be eliminated by offering buyers fewer services.

- Offering a limited product line as opposed to a full product line. Pruning slow-selling items from the product lineup and being content to meet the needs of most buyers rather than all buyers can eliminate activities and costs associated with numerous product versions and wide selection.
- Distributing the company's product only through low-cost distribution channels and avoiding high-cost distribution channels.
- Choosing to use the most economical method for delivering customer orders (even if it results in longer delivery times).

The point here is that a low-cost provider strategy entails not only performing value chain activities cost-effectively but also judiciously choosing cost-saving strategic approaches.

Revamping the Value Chain System to Lower Costs   Dramatic cost advantages can often emerge from redesigning the company's value chain system in ways that eliminate costly work steps and entirely bypass certain cost-producing value chain activities. While using communication technologies and information systems or business process reengineering to drive down costs often involves activities that span the value chain system, other approaches to revamping the value chain system can include:

- *Selling direct to consumers and bypassing the activities and costs of distributors and dealers.* To circumvent the need for distributors-dealers, a company can (1) create its own direct sales force (which adds the costs of maintaining and supporting a sales force but which may well be cheaper than utilizing independent distributors and dealers to access buyers) and/or (2) conduct sales operations at the company's Web site (incurring costs for Web site operations and shipping may be a substantially cheaper way to make sales to customers than going through distributor-dealer channels). Costs in the wholesale/retail portions of the value chain frequently represent 35 to 50 percent of the price final consumers pay, so establishing a direct sales force or selling online may offer big cost savings.
- *Coordinating with suppliers to bypass the need to perform certain value chain activities, speed up their performance, or otherwise increase overall efficiency.* Examples include having suppliers combine particular parts and components into preassembled modules, thus permitting a manufacturer to assemble its own product in fewer work steps and with a smaller workforce, and sharing real-time sales information to lower costs through improved inventory management. At Walmart, some items supplied by manufacturers are delivered directly to retail stores rather than being routed through Walmart's distribution centers and delivered by Walmart trucks; in other instances, Walmart unloads incoming shipments from manufacturers' trucks arriving at its distribution centers directly onto outgoing Walmart trucks headed to particular stores without ever moving the goods into the distribution center. Many supermarket chains have greatly reduced in-store meat butchering and cutting activities by shifting to meats that are cut and packaged at the meatpacking plant and then delivered to their stores in ready-to-sell form.
- *Reducing materials handling and shipping costs by having suppliers locate their plants or warehouses close to the company's own facilities.* Having suppliers locate their plants or warehouses very close to a company's own plant facilitates just-in-time deliveries of parts and components to the exact work station where they will

be utilized in assembling the company's product. This not only lowers incoming shipping costs but also curbs or eliminates the need for a company to build and operate storerooms for incoming parts and components and have plant personnel move the inventories to the work stations as needed for assembly.

Illustration Capsule 5.1 describes how Walmart has managed its value chain in the retail grocery portion of its business to achieve a dramatic cost advantage over rival supermarket chains and become the world's biggest grocery retailer.

Examples of Companies That Revamped Their Value Chains to Reduce Costs   Nucor Corporation, the most profitable steel producer in the United States and one of the largest steel producers worldwide, drastically revamped the value chain process for manufacturing steel products by using relatively inexpensive electric arc furnaces where scrap steel and directly reduced iron ore are melted and then sent to a continuous caster and rolling mill to be shaped into steel bars, steel beams, steel plate, and sheet steel. Using electric arc furnaces to make new steel products by recycling scrap steel eliminated many of the steps used by traditional steel mills that made their steel products from iron ore, coke, limestone, and other ingredients using costly coke ovens, basic oxygen blast furnaces, ingot casters, and multiple types of finishing facilities—plus Nucor's value chain system required far few employees. As a consequence, Nucor was able to make steel with a far lower capital investment, a far smaller workforce, and far lower operating costs than traditional steel mills. Nucor's strategy to replace the traditional steelmaking value chain with its simpler, quicker value chain approach has made it one of the lowest-cost producers of steel in the world and enabled Nucor to take huge volumes of sales and market share away from traditional steel companies and earn attractive profits. (Nucor has reported profits for every quarter in every year during the 1966–2008 period—a remarkable accomplishment in a mature and cyclical industry notorious for poor profitability.) While the recession-plagued year of 2009 was not a good one for Nucor, it returned to profits quickly in 2010.

Southwest Airlines has achieved considerable cost savings by reconfiguring the traditional value chain of commercial airlines, thereby allowing it to offer travelers dramatically lower fares. Its mastery of fast turnarounds at the gates (about 25 minutes versus 45 minutes for rivals) allows its planes to fly more hours per day. This translates into being able to schedule more flights per day with fewer aircraft, allowing Southwest to generate more revenue per plane on average than rivals. Southwest does not offer assigned seating, baggage transfer to connecting airlines, or first-class seating and service, thereby eliminating all the cost-producing activities associated with these features. The company's fast and user-friendly online reservation system facilitates e-ticketing and reduces staffing requirements at telephone reservation centers and airport counters. Its use of automated check-in equipment reduces staffing requirements for terminal check-in.

The Keys to Being a Successful Low-Cost Provider

To succeed with a low-cost provider strategy, company managers have to scrutinize each cost-creating activity and determine what factors cause costs to be high or low. Then they have to use this knowledge to streamline or reengineer how activities are performed, exhaustively pursuing cost efficiencies throughout the value chain. Normally, low-cost producers try to engage all company personnel in continuous cost improvement efforts, and they strive to operate with exceptionally small corporate staffs to keep administrative costs to a minimum. Many successful low-cost

How Walmart Managed Its Value Chain to Achieve a Huge Low-Cost Advantage over Rival Supermarket Chains

Walmart has achieved a very substantial cost and pricing advantage over rival supermarket chains both by revamping portions of the grocery retailing value chain and by outmanaging its rivals in efficiently performing various value chain activities. Its cost advantage stems from a series of initiatives and practices:

- Instituting extensive information sharing with vendors via online systems that relay sales at its checkout counters directly to suppliers of the items, thereby providing suppliers with real-time information on customer demand and preferences (creating an estimated 6 percent cost advantage). It is standard practice at Walmart to collaborate extensively with vendors on all aspects of the purchasing and store delivery process to squeeze out mutually beneficial cost savings. Procter & Gamble, Walmart's biggest supplier, went so far as to integrate its enterprise resource planning (ERP) system with Walmart's.

- Pursuing global procurement of some items and centralizing most purchasing activities so as to leverage the company's buying power (creating an estimated 2.5 percent cost advantage).

- Investing in state-of-the-art automation at its distribution centers, efficiently operating a truck fleet that makes daily deliveries to Walmart's stores, and putting other assorted cost-saving practices into place at its headquarters, distribution centers, and stores (resulting in an estimated 4 percent cost advantage).

- Striving to optimize the product mix and achieve greater sales turnover (resulting in about a 2 percent cost advantage).

- Installing security systems and store operating procedures that lower shrinkage rates (producing a cost advantage of about 0.5 percent).

- Negotiating preferred real estate rental and leasing rates with real estate developers and owners of its store sites (yielding a cost advantage of 2 percent).

- Managing and compensating its workforce in a manner that produces lower labor costs (yielding an estimated 5 percent cost advantage).

Altogether, these value chain initiatives give Walmart an approximately 22 percent cost advantage over Kroger, Safeway, and other leading supermarket chains. With such a sizable cost advantage, Walmart has been able to underprice its rivals and rapidly become the world's leading supermarket retailer.

Sources: Developed by the authors from information at www.walmart.com and in Marco Iansiti and Roy Levien, "Strategy as Ecology," *Harvard Business Review* 82, no. 3 (March 2004), p. 70.

leaders also use benchmarking to keep close tabs on how their costs compare with those of rivals and firms performing comparable activities in other industries.

But while low-cost providers are champions of frugality, they seldom hesitate to spend aggressively on resources and capabilities *that promise to drive costs out of the business.* Indeed, having resources or capabilities of this type and ensuring that they remain competitively superior is essential for achieving competitive advantage as a low-cost provider. Walmart, one of the world's foremost low-cost providers, has been an early adopter of state-of-the-art technology throughout its operations—its distribution facilities are an automated showcase, it has developed sophisticated online systems to order goods from suppliers and manage inventories, it equips its stores with cutting-edge sales-tracking and checkout systems, and it sends daily point-of-sale data to 4,000 vendors, *but Walmart carefully estimates the cost savings of new technologies before it rushes to invest in them.* By continuously investing in complex technologies that are hard for rivals to match, Walmart has sustained its competitive advantage for over 30 years.

Other companies noted for their successful use of low-cost provider strategies include Vizio in big-screen TVs, Briggs & Stratton in small gasoline engines, Bic in ballpoint pens, Stride Rite in footwear, Poulan in chain saws, and General Electric and Whirlpool in major home appliances.

When a Low-Cost Provider Strategy Works Best

A low-cost provider strategy becomes increasingly appealing and competitively powerful when:

1. *Price competition among rival sellers is vigorous.* Low-cost providers are in the best position to compete offensively on the basis of price, to use the appeal of lower price to grab sales (and market share) from rivals, to win the business of price-sensitive buyers, to remain profitable despite strong price competition, and to survive price wars.

2. *The products of rival sellers are essentially identical and readily available from many eager sellers.* Look-alike products and/or overabundant product supply set the stage for lively price competition; in such markets, it is the less efficient, higher-cost companies whose profits get squeezed the most.

3. *There are few ways to achieve product differentiation that have value to buyers.* When the differences between product attributes or brands do not matter much to buyers, buyers are nearly always very sensitive to price differences and market share winners will tend to be those with the lowest-priced brands.

4. *Most buyers use the product in the same ways.* With common user requirements, a standardized product can satisfy the needs of buyers, in which case low selling price, not features or quality, becomes the dominant factor in causing buyers to choose one seller's product over another's.

5. *Buyers incur low costs in switching their purchases from one seller to another.* Low switching costs give buyers the flexibility to shift purchases to lower-priced sellers having equally good products or to attractively priced substitute products. A low-cost leader is well positioned to use low price to induce its customers not to switch to rival brands or substitutes.

6. *Buyers are large and have significant power to bargain down prices.* Low-cost providers have partial profit-margin protection in bargaining with high-volume buyers, since powerful buyers are rarely able to bargain price down past the survival level of the next most cost-efficient seller.

7. *Industry newcomers use introductory low prices to attract buyers and build a customer base.* A low-cost provider can use price cuts of its own to make it harder for a new rival to win customers. Moreover, the pricing power of a low-cost provider acts as a barrier for new entrants.

As a rule, the more price-sensitive buyers are, the more appealing a low-cost strategy becomes. A low-cost company's ability to set the industry's price floor and still earn a profit erects protective barriers around its market position.

Pitfalls to Avoid in Pursuing a Low-Cost Provider Strategy

Perhaps the biggest mistake a low-cost provider can make to spoil the profitability of its low-cost advantage is getting carried away with overly aggressive price cutting to win sales and market share away from rivals. *Higher unit sales and market shares do not automatically translate into higher total profits.* A low-cost/low-price advantage results in superior profitability only if (1) prices are cut by less than the size of the unit cost advantage or (2) the added gains in unit sales are large enough to bring in a bigger total profit despite lower margins per unit sold. A company with a 5 percent per-unit cost advantage cannot cut prices 20 percent, end up with a volume gain of only 10 percent, and still expect to earn higher profits!

A lower price improves total profitability only if the price cuts lead to total revenues that are big enough to *more than cover* all the added costs associated with selling more units. When the incremental gains in total revenues flowing from a lower price exceed the incremental increases in total costs associated with a higher sales volume, then cutting price is a profitable move. But if a lower selling price results in revenue gains that are smaller than the increases in total costs, company profits end up lower than before and the price cut ends up reducing profits rather than raising them.

A second pitfall of a low-cost provider strategy is failing to emphasize avenues of cost advantage that can be kept proprietary or that relegate rivals to playing catch-up. The real value of a cost advantage depends on its sustainability. Sustainability, in turn, hinges on whether the company achieves its cost advantage in ways difficult for rivals to copy or otherwise overcome.

A third pitfall is becoming too fixated on cost reduction. Low cost cannot be pursued so zealously that a firm's offering ends up being too features-poor to generate buyer appeal. Furthermore, a company driving hard to push its costs down has to guard against misreading or ignoring increased buyer interest in added features or service, declining buyer sensitivity to price, or new developments that start to alter how buyers use the product. Otherwise, it risks losing market ground if buyers start opting for more upscale or feature-rich products.

Even if these mistakes are avoided, a low-cost provider strategy still entails risk. An innovative rival may discover an even lower-cost value chain approach. Important cost-saving technological breakthroughs may suddenly emerge. And if a low-cost provider has heavy investments in its present means of operating, then it can prove very costly to quickly shift to the new value chain approach or a new technology.

> A low-cost provider is in the best position to win the business of price-sensitive buyers, set the floor on market price, and still earn a profit.

> Reducing price does not lead to higher total profits unless the incremental gain in total revenues exceeds the incremental increase in total costs.

> A low-cost provider's product offering must always contain enough attributes to be attractive to prospective buyers—low price, by itself, is not always appealing to buyers.

BROAD DIFFERENTIATION STRATEGIES

Differentiation strategies are attractive whenever buyers' needs and preferences are too diverse to be fully satisfied by a standardized product offering. Successful product differentiation requires careful study of buyers' needs and behaviors to learn what buyers consider important, what they think has value, and what they are willing to pay for.[4] Then the trick is for a company to incorporate certain buyer-desired attributes into its product offering such that its offering will not only appeal to a broad range of buyers but also be different enough to stand apart from the product offerings of rivals—in regard to the latter, a strongly differentiated product offering is always preferable to a weakly differentiated one. A differentiation strategy calls for a customer value proposition that is *unique*. The strategy achieves its aim when an attractively large number of buyers find the customer value proposition appealing and become strongly attached to a company's differentiated attributes.

Successful differentiation allows a firm to do one or more of the following:

- Command a premium price for its product.
- Increase unit sales (because additional buyers are won over by the differentiating features).
- Gain buyer loyalty to its brand (because some buyers are strongly bonded to the differentiating features of the company's product offering).

Differentiation enhances profitability whenever a company's product can command a sufficiently higher price or produce sufficiently bigger unit sales *to more than cover the added costs of achieving the differentiation.* Company differentiation strategies fail when buyers don't value the brand's uniqueness and/or when a company's approach to differentiation is easily copied or matched by its rivals.

Companies can pursue differentiation from many angles: a unique taste (Dr Pepper, Listerine); multiple features (Microsoft Office, the iPhone); wide selection and one-stop shopping (Home Depot, Amazon.com); superior service (FedEx); engineering design and performance (Mercedes, BMW); prestige and distinctiveness (Rolex); product reliability (Johnson & Johnson in baby products); quality manufacture (Karastan in carpets, Michelin in tires, Honda in automobiles); technological leadership (3M Corporation in bonding and coating products); a full range of services (Charles Schwab in stock brokerage); wide product selection (Campbell's soups); and high fashion design (Gucci and Chanel).

Managing the Value Chain to Create the Differentiating Attributes

Differentiation is not something hatched in marketing and advertising departments, nor is it limited to the catchalls of quality and service. Differentiation opportunities can exist in activities all along an industry's value chain. The most systematic approach that managers can take, however, involves focusing on the **uniqueness drivers,** a set of factors—analogous to cost drivers—that are particularly effective in creating differentiation. Figure 5.3 contains a list of important uniqueness drivers. Ways that managers can enhance differentiation based on these drivers include the following:

1. *Striving to create superior product features, design, and performance.* This applies to the physical and well as functional attributes of a product, including features such as expanded end uses and applications, added user safety, greater recycling capability, or enhanced environmental protection. Design features can be important in enhancing the aesthetic appeal of a product. Ducati's motorcycles, for example, are prized for their designs and have been exhibited in the Guggenheim art museum in New York City.[5]

Figure 5.3 Uniqueness Drivers: The Keys to Creating a Differentiation Advantage

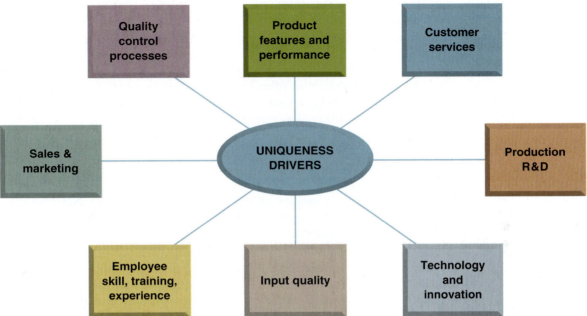

Source: Adapted from M. Porter, *Competitive Advantage: Creating and Sustaining Competitive Advantage* (New York: Free Press, 1985).

2. *Improving customer service or adding additional services.* Better customer services, in areas such as delivery, returns, and repair, can be as important in creating differentiation as superior product features. Examples include superior technical assistance to buyers, higher-quality maintenance services, more and better product information provided to customers, more and better training materials for end users, better credit terms, quicker order processing, or greater customer convenience.

3. *Pursuing production R&D activities.* Engaging in production R&D may permit custom-order manufacture at an efficient cost, provide wider product variety and selection through product "versioning," improve product quality, or make production methods safer for the environment. Many manufacturers have developed flexible manufacturing systems that allow different models and product versions to be made on the same assembly line. Being able to provide buyers with made-to-order products can be a potent differentiating capability.

4. *Striving for innovation and technological advances.* Successful innovation is the route to more frequent first-on-the-market victories and is a powerful differentiator. If the innovation proves hard to replicate, through patent protection or other means, it can provide a company with a first mover advantage that is sustainable.

5. *Pursuing continuous quality improvement.* Perceived quality differences can be an important differentiator in the eyes of customers. Quality control processes can be applied throughout the value chain, including postsale customer service activities. They can reduce product defects, prevent premature product failure, extend product life, make it economical to offer longer warranty

coverage, improve economy of use, result in more end-user convenience, or enhance product appearance. Companies whose quality management systems meet certification standards, such as the ISO 9001 standards, can enhance their reputation for quality with customers.

6. *Increasing the intensity of marketing and sales activities.* Marketing and advertising can have a tremendous effect on the value perceived by buyers and therefore their willingness to pay more for the company's offerings. They can create differentiation even when little tangible differentiation exists otherwise. For example, blind taste tests show that even the most loyal Pepsi or Coke drinkers have trouble telling one cola drink from another.[6] Brands create customer loyalty, which increases the perceived "cost" of switching to another product. Brand management activities are therefore also important in supporting differentiation.

7. *Seeking out high-quality inputs.* Input quality can ultimately spill over to affect the performance or quality of the company's end product. Starbucks, for example, gets high ratings on its coffees partly because it has very strict specifications on the coffee beans purchased from suppliers.

8. *Improving employee skill, knowledge, and experience through human resource management activities.* Hiring, training, and retaining highly skilled and experienced employees is important since such employees are often the source of creative, innovative ideas that are behind new product development. Moreover, they are essential to performing differentiating activities such as design, engineering, marketing, and R&D. Company culture and reward systems can help unleash the potential contribution of high-value employees to a differentiation strategy.

Managers need keen understanding of the sources of differentiation and the activities that drive uniqueness to evaluate various differentiation approaches and design durable ways to set their product offering apart from rival brands.

Revamping the Value Chain System to Increase Differentiation   Just as pursuing a cost advantage can involve the entire value chain system, the same is true for a differentiation advantage. Activities performed upstream by suppliers or downstream by distributors and retailers can have a meaningful effect on customers' perceptions of a company's offerings and its value proposition. Approaches to enhancing differentiation through changes in the value chain system include:[7]

- *Coordinating with channel allies to enhance customer perceptions of value.* Coordinating with downstream partners such as distributors, dealers, brokers, and retailers can contribute to differentiation in a variety of ways. Methods that companies use to influence the value chain activities of their channel allies include setting standards for downstream partners to follow, providing them with templates to standardize the selling environment or practices, training channel personnel, or cosponsoring promotions and advertising campaigns. Coordinating with retailers is important for enhancing the buying experience and building a company's image. Coordinating with distributors or shippers can mean quicker delivery to customers, more accurate order filling, and/or lower shipping costs. The Coca-Cola Company considers coordination with its bottler/distributors so important that it has at times taken over a troubled bottler for the purpose of improving its management and upgrading its plant and equipment before releasing the product to the market.[8]

- *Coordinating with suppliers to better address customer needs.* Collaborating with suppliers can also be a powerful route to a more effective differentiation strategy. Coordinating and collaborating with suppliers can improve many dimensions affecting product features and quality. This is particularly true for companies that only engage in assembly operations, such as Dell in PCs and Ducati in motorcycles. Close coordination with suppliers can also enhance differentiation by speeding up new product development cycles or speeding delivery to end customers. Strong relationships with suppliers can also mean that the company's supply requirements are prioritized when industry supply is insufficient to meet overall demand.

Delivering Superior Value via a Broad Differentiation Strategy

Differentiation strategies depend on meeting customer needs in unique ways or creating new needs, through activities such as innovation or persuasive advertising. The objective is to offer customers something that rivals can't—at least in terms of the level of satisfaction. There are four basic routes to achieving this aim.

The first route is to incorporate product attributes and user features that *lower the buyer's overall costs* of using the company's product. This is the least obvious and most overlooked route to a differentiation advantage. It is a differentiating factor since it can help business buyers be more competitive in their markets and more profitable. Producers of materials and components often win orders for their products by reducing a buyer's raw-material waste (providing cut-to-size components), reducing a buyer's inventory requirements (providing just-in-time deliveries), using online systems to reduce a buyer's procurement and order processing costs, and providing free technical support. This route to differentiation can also appeal to individual consumers who are looking to economize on their overall costs of consumption. Making a company's product more economical for a buyer to use can be done by incorporating energy-efficient features (energy-saving appliances and lightbulbs help cut buyers' utility bills; fuel-efficient vehicles cut buyer costs for gasoline) and/or by increasing maintenance intervals and product reliability so as to lower buyer costs for maintenance and repairs.

A second route is to incorporate *tangible* features that increase customer satisfaction with the product, such as product specifications, functions, and styling. This can be accomplished by including attributes that add functionality, enhance the design, expand the range of uses, save time for the user, are more reliable, or make the product cleaner, safer, quieter, simpler to use, portable, more convenient, or longer-lasting than rival brands. Cell phone manufacturers are in a race to introduce next-generation devices capable of being used for more purposes and having simpler menu functionality.

A third route to a differentiation-based competitive advantage is to incorporate *intangible* features that enhance buyer satisfaction in noneconomic ways. Toyota's Prius appeals to environmentally conscious motorists not only because these drivers want to help reduce global carbon dioxide emissions but also because they identify with the image conveyed. Rolls-Royce, Ralph Lauren, Tiffany, Rolex, and Prada have differentiation-based competitive advantages linked to buyer desires for status, image, prestige, upscale fashion, superior craftsmanship, and the finer things in life.

> Differentiation can be based on *tangible* or *intangible* attributes.

Intangibles that contribute to differentiation can extend beyond product attributes to the reputation of the company and to customer relations or trust.

The fourth route is to *signal the value* of the company's product offering to buyers. Typical signals of value include a high price (in instances where high price implies high quality and performance), more appealing or fancier packaging than competing products, ad content that emphasizes a product's standout attributes, the quality of brochures and sales presentations, the luxuriousness and ambience of a seller's facilities (important for high-end retailers and for offices or other facilities frequented by customers). They make potential buyers aware of the professionalism, appearance, and personalities of the seller's employees and/or make potential buyers realize that a company has prestigious customers. Signaling value is particularly important (1) when the nature of differentiation is based on intangible features and is therefore subjective or hard to quantify, (2) when buyers are making a first-time purchase and are unsure what their experience with the product will be, and (3) when repurchase is infrequent and buyers need to be reminded of a product's value.

Regardless of the approach taken, achieving a successful differentiation strategy requires, first, that the company have strengths in capabilities, such as customer service, marketing, brand management, and technology, that can create and support differentiation. That is, the resources, competencies, and value chain activities of the company must be well matched to the requirements of the strategy. For the strategy to result in competitive advantage, the company's competencies must also be sufficiently unique in delivering value to buyers that they help set its product offering apart from those of rivals. They must be competitively superior. There are numerous examples of companies that have differentiated themselves on the basis of distinctive competencies and capabilities. Apple has set itself apart from rivals on the basis of its capabilities to develop innovative new products and speed next-generation products to market ahead of competitors. When a major new event occurs, many people turn to Fox News and CNN because they have the capability to devote more airtime to breaking news stories and get reporters on the scene very quickly. Avon and Mary Kay Cosmetics have differentiated themselves from other cosmetics and personal care companies by assembling a sales force numbering in the hundreds of thousands that gives them a direct sales capability—their sales associates personally demonstrate products to interested buyers, take their orders on the spot, and deliver the items to buyers' homes.

The most successful approaches to differentiation are those that are hard or expensive for rivals to duplicate. Indeed, this is the route to a sustainable differentiation advantage. While resourceful competitors can, in time, clone almost any tangible product attribute, socially complex intangible attributes, such as company reputation, long-standing relationships with buyers, and image are much harder to imitate. Differentiation that creates switching costs that lock in buyers also provides a route to sustainable advantage. For example, if a buyer makes a substantial investment in learning to use one type of system, that buyer is less likely to switch to a competitor's system. (This has kept many users from switching away from Microsoft Office products, despite the fact that there are other applications with superior features.) As

> Easy-to-copy differentiating features cannot produce sustainable competitive advantage.

a rule, differentiation yields a longer-lasting and more profitable competitive edge when it is based on a well-established brand image, patent-protected product innovation, complex technical superiority, a reputation for superior product quality and reliability, relationship-based customer service, and unique competitive capabilities. Such differentiating attributes are generally tougher and take longer for rivals to match, and buyers widely perceive them as offering superior value.

When a Differentiation Strategy Works Best

Differentiation strategies tend to work best in market circumstances where:

- *Buyer needs and uses of the product are diverse.* Diverse buyer preferences present competitors with a bigger window of opportunity to do things differently and set themselves apart with product attributes that appeal to particular buyers. For instance, the diversity of consumer preferences for menu selection, ambience, pricing, and customer service gives restaurants exceptionally wide latitude in creating a differentiated product offering. Similar opportunities exist for the publishers of magazines, the makers of motor vehicles, and the manufacturers of cabinetry and countertops.

- *There are many ways to differentiate the product or service that have value to buyers.* There's plenty of room for retail apparel competitors to stock different styles and quality of apparel merchandise but very little room for the makers of paper clips or copier paper or sugar to set their products apart. Likewise, the sellers of different brands of gasoline or orange juice have little differentiation opportunity compared to the sellers of high-definition TVs or patio furniture or breakfast cereal. Basic commodities, such as chemicals, mineral deposits, and agricultural products, provide few opportunities for differentiation.

- *Few rival firms are following a similar differentiation approach.* The best differentiation approaches involve trying to appeal to buyers on the basis of attributes that rivals are not emphasizing. A differentiator encounters less head-to-head rivalry when it goes its own separate way in creating uniqueness and does not try to outdifferentiate rivals on the very same attributes. When many rivals are all claiming "ours tastes better than theirs" or "ours gets your clothes cleaner than theirs," the most likely result is weak brand differentiation and "strategy overcrowding"— competitors end up chasing much the same buyers with much the same product offerings.

- *Technological change is fast-paced and competition revolves around rapidly evolving product features.* Rapid product innovation and frequent introductions of next-version products not only provide space for companies to pursue separate differentiating paths but also heighten buyer interest. In video game hardware and video games, golf equipment, PCs, cell phones, and MP3 players, competitors are locked into an ongoing battle to set themselves apart by introducing the best next-generation products; companies that fail to come up with new and improved products and distinctive performance features quickly lose out in the marketplace. In U.S. network TV broadcasting, NBC, ABC, CBS, Fox, and several others are always scrambling to develop a lineup of TV shows that will win higher audience ratings and pave the way for charging higher advertising rates and boosting ad revenues.

Pitfalls to Avoid in Pursuing a Differentiation Strategy

Differentiation strategies can fail for any of several reasons. *A differentiation strategy is always doomed when competitors are able to quickly copy most or all of the appealing product attributes a company comes up with.* Rapid imitation means that no rival achieves differentiation, since whenever one firm introduces some aspect of uniqueness that strikes the fancy of buyers, fast-following copycats quickly reestablish similarity. This is

> Any differentiating feature that works well is a magnet for imitators, although imitation attempts are not always successful.

why a firm must seek out sources of uniqueness that are time-consuming or burdensome for rivals to match if it hopes to use differentiation to win a lasting competitive edge over rivals.

A second pitfall is that *the company's attempt at differentiation produces an unenthusiastic response on the part of buyers.* Thus even if a company succeeds in setting its product apart from those of rivals, its strategy can result in disappointing sales and profits if buyers find other brands more appealing. Any time many potential buyers look at a company's differentiated product offering and conclude "so what," the company's differentiation strategy is in deep trouble.

The third big pitfall of a differentiation strategy is *overspending on efforts to differentiate the company's product offering, thus eroding profitability.* Company efforts to achieve differentiation nearly always raise costs, often substantially since marketing and R&D are expensive undertakings. The trick to profitable differentiation is either to keep the unit cost of achieving differentiation below the price premium that the differentiating attributes can command in the marketplace (thus increasing the profit margin per unit sold) or to offset thinner profit margins per unit by selling enough additional units to increase total profits. If a company goes overboard in pursuing costly differentiation efforts and then unexpectedly discovers that buyers are unwilling to pay a sufficient price premium to cover the added costs of differentiation, it ends up saddled with unacceptably thin profit margins or even losses. The need to contain differentiation costs is why many companies add little touches of differentiation that add to buyer satisfaction but are inexpensive to institute. Upscale restaurants often provide valet parking. Laundry detergent and soap manufacturers add pleasing scents to their products. Ski resorts provide skiers with complimentary coffee or hot apple cider at the base of the lifts in the morning and late afternoon.

Other common mistakes in crafting a differentiation strategy include:[9]

- *Being timid and not striving to open up meaningful gaps in quality, service, or performance features vis-à-vis the products of rivals.* Tiny differences between rivals' product offerings may not be visible or important to buyers. If a company wants to generate the fiercely loyal customer following needed to earn superior profits and open up a differentiation-based competitive advantage over rivals, then its strategy must result in *strong rather than weak product differentiation.* In markets where differentiators do no better than achieve weak product differentiation (because the attributes of rival brands are fairly similar in the minds of many buyers), customer loyalty to any one brand is weak, the costs of brand switching are fairly low, and no one company has enough of a market edge that it can get by with charging a price premium over rival brands.

- *Adding so many frills and extra features that the product exceeds the needs and use patterns of most buyers.* A dazzling array of features and options not only drives up costs (and therefore product price) but also runs the risk that many buyers will conclude that a less deluxe and lower-priced brand is a better value since they have little occasion or reason to use some of the deluxe attributes.

  - *Charging too high a price premium.* While buyers may be intrigued by a product's deluxe features, they may nonetheless see it as being overpriced relative to the value delivered by the differentiating attributes. A company must guard against turning off would-be buyers with what is perceived as "price gouging." Normally, the bigger the price premium for the differentiating extras, the harder it is to keep buyers from switching to the lower-priced offerings of competitors.

Overdifferentiating and overcharging can be fatal strategy mistakes.

A low-cost provider strategy can defeat a differentiation strategy when buyers are satisfied with a basic product and don't think "extra" attributes are worth a higher price.

FOCUSED (OR MARKET NICHE) STRATEGIES

What sets focused strategies apart from low-cost provider and broad differentiation strategies is concentrated attention on a narrow piece of the total market. The target segment, or niche, can be defined by geographic uniqueness, by specialized requirements in using the product, or by special product attributes that appeal only to niche members. Community Coffee, the largest family-owned specialty coffee retailer in the United States, has a geographic focus on the state of Louisiana and communities across the Gulf of Mexico. Community holds only a 1.1 percent share of the national coffee market but has recorded sales in excess of $100 million and has won a 50 percent share of the coffee business in the 11-state region where it is distributed. Examples of other firms that concentrate on a well-defined market niche keyed to a particular product or buyer segment include Animal Planet and the History Channel (in cable TV); Cannondale (in top-of-the-line mountain bikes); Enterprise Rent-a-Car (a specialist in providing rental cars to repair garage customers); Bandag (a specialist in truck tire recapping that promotes its recaps aggressively at over 1,000 truck stops); CGA, Inc. (a specialist in providing insurance to cover the cost of lucrative hole-in-one prizes at golf tournaments); and Match.com (the world's largest online dating service). Microbreweries, bed-and-breakfast inns, and local owner-managed retail boutiques have also scaled their operations to serve narrow or local customer segments.

A Focused Low-Cost Strategy

A focused strategy based on low cost aims at securing a competitive advantage by serving buyers in the target market niche at a lower cost and lower price than those of rival competitors. This strategy has considerable attraction when a firm can lower costs significantly by limiting its customer base to a well-defined buyer segment. The avenues to achieving a cost advantage over rivals also serving the target market niche are the same as those for low-cost leadership: outmanage rivals in keeping the costs of value chain activities contained to a bare minimum and search for innovative ways to bypass certain value chain activities. The only real difference between a low-cost provider strategy and a focused low-cost strategy is the size of the buyer group that a company is trying to appeal to—the former involves a product offering that appeals broadly to almost all buyer groups and market segments, whereas the latter aims at just meeting the needs of buyers in a narrow market segment.

Focused low-cost strategies are fairly common. Producers of private-label goods are able to achieve low costs in product development, marketing, distribution, and advertising by concentrating on making generic items imitative of name-brand merchandise and selling directly to retail chains wanting a low-priced store brand. The Perrigo Company has become a leading manufacturer of over-the-counter health care products, with 2010 sales of more than $2.2 billion, by focusing on producing private-label brands for retailers such as Walmart, CVS, Walgreens, Rite-Aid, and Safeway. Budget motel chains, like Motel 6, cater to price-conscious travelers who just want to pay for a clean, no-frills place to spend the night. Redbox has established a low-cost network of more than 15,000 vending machines in high-traffic shopping locations that enable it to rent movie DVDs for $1 and sell used movie DVDs for $7. Illustration Capsule 5.2 describes how Vizio's low costs and focus on big-box retailers has allowed it to become the largest seller of flat-panel HDTVs in the United States in less than six years from its startup.

A Focused Differentiation Strategy

A focused strategy keyed to differentiation aims at securing a competitive advantage with a product offering carefully designed to appeal to the unique preferences and needs of a narrow, well-defined group of buyers (as opposed to a broad differentiation strategy aimed at many buyer groups and market segments). Successful use of a focused differentiation strategy depends on the existence of a buyer segment that is looking for special product attributes or seller capabilities and on a firm's ability to stand apart from rivals competing in the same target market niche.

Companies like Godiva Chocolates, Rolls-Royce, Haägen-Dazs, and W. L. Gore (the maker of Gore-Tex) employ successful differentiation-based focused strategies targeted at upscale buyers wanting products and services with world-class attributes. Indeed, most markets contain a buyer segment willing to pay a big price premium for the very finest items available, thus opening the strategic window for some competitors to pursue differentiation-based focused strategies aimed at the very top of the market pyramid. Ferrari markets its 1,500 cars sold in North America each year to a list of just 20,000 highly affluent car enthusiasts. Only the highest echelon of this exclusive group were contacted by Ferrari for a chance to put their names on the waiting list for one of the 29 $1.9 million FXX models planned for sale in North America.

Another successful focused differentiator is "fashion food retailer" Trader Joe's, a 300-store, 25-state chain that is a combination gourmet deli and food warehouse. Customers shop Trader Joe's as much for entertainment as for conventional grocery items—the store stocks out-of-the-ordinary culinary treats like raspberry salsa, salmon burgers, and jasmine fried rice, as well as the standard goods normally found in supermarkets. What sets Trader Joe's apart is not just its unique combination of food novelties and competitively priced grocery items but also its capability to turn an otherwise mundane grocery excursion into a whimsical treasure hunt that is just plain fun. Illustration Capsule 5.3 describes Progressive Insurance's focused differentiation strategy.

When a Focused Low-Cost or Focused Differentiation Strategy Is Attractive

A focused strategy aimed at securing a competitive edge based either on low cost or differentiation becomes increasingly attractive as more of the following conditions are met:

- The target market niche is big enough to be profitable and offers good growth potential.
- Industry leaders do not see that having a presence in the niche is crucial to their own success—in which case focusers can often escape battling head to head against some of the industry's biggest and strongest competitors.

ILLUSTRATION CAPSULE 5.2

Vizio's Focused Low-Cost Strategy

California-based Vizio, Inc., designs flat-panel LCD and plasma TVs that range in size from 20 to 55 inches and are sold only by big-box discount retailers such as Walmart, Sam's Club, Costco Wholesale, and Best Buy. If you've shopped for a flat-panel TV recently, you've probably noticed that Vizio is among the lowest-priced brands and that its picture quality is surprisingly good considering the price. The company is able to keep its cost low by only designing TVs and then sourcing its production to a limited number of contract manufacturers in Taiwan. In fact, 80 percent of its production is handled by a company called AmTran Technology. Such a dependence on a supplier can place a buyer in a precarious situation by making it vulnerable to price increases or product shortages, but Vizio has countered this possible threat by making AmTran a major stockholder. AmTran Technology owns a 23 percent stake in Vizio and earns about 80 percent of its revenues from its sales of televisions to Vizio. Vizio's close relationship with its major supplier and its focus on a single product category sold through limited distribution channels allows it to offer its customers deep price discounts.

Vizio's first major account was landed in 2003 when it approached buyers for Costco with a 46-inch plasma TV whose wholesale price was half that of the next lowest-price competitor. Within two months, Costco was carrying Vizio flat-panel TVs in 320 of its warehouse stores in the United States. In October 2007, Vizio approached buyers for Sam's Club with a 20-inch LCD TV that could be sold at retail for under $350. The price and quality of the 20-inch TV led Sam's Club buyers to place an order for 20,000 TVs for March 2008 delivery. By 2009, Vizio had become the largest seller of flat-panel HDTVs in the United States, with a market share of 21.6 percent.

Sources: "Picture Shift: U.S. Upstart Takes On TV Giants in Price War," *Wall Street Journal,* April 15, 2008, p. A1; Vizio, Inc., "Vizio Achieves #1 LCD HDTV Ranking in North America and #1 Ranking in U.S. Flat Panel HDTV Shipments," press release, May 11, 2009.

- It is costly or difficult for multisegment competitors to put capabilities in place to meet the specialized needs of buyers constituting the target market niche and at the same time satisfy the expectations of their mainstream customers.
- The industry has many different niches and segments, thereby allowing a focuser to pick a competitively attractive niche suited to its most valuable resources and capabilities. Also, with more niches there is more room for focusers to avoid each other in competing for the same customers.
- Few, if any, other rivals are attempting to specialize in the same target segment—a condition that reduces the risk of segment overcrowding.
- The focuser has a reservoir of customer goodwill and loyalty (accumulated from having catered to the specialized needs and preferences of niche members over many years) that it can draw on to help stave off ambitious challengers looking to horn in on its business.

The advantages of focusing a company's entire competitive effort on a single market niche are considerable, especially for smaller and medium-size companies that may lack the breadth and depth of resources to tackle going after a broad customer base with a "something for everyone" lineup of models, styles,

Progressive Insurance's Focused Differentiation Strategy in Auto Insurance

Progressive Insurance has fashioned a strategy in auto insurance focused on people with a record of traffic violations who drive high-performance cars, drivers with accident histories, motorcyclists, teenagers, and other so-called high-risk categories of drivers that most auto insurance companies steer away from. Progressive discovered that some of these high-risk drivers are affluent and pressed for time, making them less sensitive to paying premium rates for their car insurance. Management learned that it could charge such drivers premiums high enough to cover the level of risk they presented, plus the company differentiated itself from other car insurers by expediting the process of obtaining insurance and decreasing the annoyance that high-risk drivers faced in obtaining insurance coverage. In addition, Progressive pioneered the low-cost direct sales model of allowing customers to purchase insurance online and over the phone.

Progressive also studied the market segments for insurance carefully enough to discover that some motorcycle owners were not especially risky (middle-aged suburbanites who sometimes commuted to work or used their motorcycles mainly for recreational trips with their friends). Progressive's strategy allowed it to become a leader in providing car insurance to the owners of high-value vehicles who appreciated Progressive's streamlined approach to doing business.

In further differentiating and promoting Progressive's policies, management created teams of roving claims adjusters who would arrive at accident scenes to assess claims and issue checks for repairs on the spot. Progressive introduced 24-hour claims reporting, now an industry standard. In addition, it developed a sophisticated pricing system so that it could quickly and accurately assess each customer's risk and weed out unprofitable customers.

By being creative and excelling at the nuts and bolts of its business, Progressive has won a 7.6 percent share of the $150 billion market for auto insurance and has the highest underwriting margins in the auto insurance industry.

Sources: www.progressiveinsurance.com; I. McMillan, A. van Putten, and R. McGrath, "Global Gamesmanship," *Harvard Business Review* 81, no. 5 (May 2003), p. 68; *Fortune,* May 16, 2005, p. 34; "Motorcyclists Age, Affluence Trending Upward," *BestWire,* July 24, 2007.

and product selection. YouTube has become a household name by concentrating on short video clips posted online. Papa John's and Domino's Pizza have created impressive businesses by focusing on the home delivery segment. Porsche and Ferrari have done well catering to wealthy sports car enthusiasts.

The Risks of a Focused Low-Cost or Focused Differentiation Strategy

Focusing carries several risks. One is the chance that competitors will find effective ways to match the focused firm's capabilities in serving the target niche—perhaps by coming up with products or brands specifically designed to appeal to buyers in the target niche or by developing expertise and capabilities that offset the focuser's strengths. In the lodging business, large chains like Marriott have launched multi-brand strategies that allow them to compete effectively in several lodging segments simultaneously. Marriott has flagship J.W. Marriot and Ritz-Carlton hotels with deluxe accommodations for business travelers and resort vacationers; its Courtyard by Marriott and SpringHill Suites brands cater to business travelers looking for moderately priced lodging; Marriott Residence Inns and TownePlace Suites are designed as a "home away from home" for travelers staying five or more nights; and the 535 Fairfield Inn locations are intended to appeal to travelers looking for quality lodging at an "affordable" price. Multibrand strategies are attractive to large companies like Marriott precisely because they enable a company to enter a market niche and siphon business away from companies that employ a focused strategy.

A second risk of employing a focused strategy is the potential for the preferences and needs of niche members to shift over time toward the product attributes desired by the majority of buyers. An erosion of the differences across buyer segments lowers entry barriers into a focuser's market niche and provides an open invitation for rivals in adjacent segments to begin competing for the focuser's customers. A third risk is that the segment may become so attractive that it is soon inundated with competitors, intensifying rivalry and splintering segment profits.

BEST-COST PROVIDER STRATEGIES

Best-cost provider strategies stake out a middle ground between pursuing a low-cost advantage and a differentiation advantage and between appealing to the broad market as a whole and a narrow market niche—see Figure 5.1. Such a middle ground allows a company to aim squarely at the sometimes great mass of value-conscious buyers looking for a good to very good product or service at an economical price. Value-conscious buyers frequently shy away from both cheap low-end products and expensive high-end products, but they are quite willing to pay a "fair" price for extra features and functionality they find appealing and useful. The essence of a best-cost provider strategy is giving customers more *value for the money* by satisfying buyer desires for appealing features/performance/quality/service and charging a lower price for these attributes compared to rivals with similar caliber product offerings.[10] From a competitive-positioning standpoint, best-cost strategies are thus a *hybrid,* balancing a strategic emphasis on low cost against a strategic emphasis on differentiation (desirable features delivered at a relatively low price).

To profitably employ a best-cost provider strategy, a company *must have the resources and capabilities to incorporate attractive or upscale attributes into its product offering at a lower cost than rivals.* When a company can incorporate appealing features, good to excellent product performance or quality, or more satisfying customer service into its product offering *at a lower cost than rivals,* then it enjoys "best-cost" status—it is the low-cost provider of a product or service with *desirable attributes.* A best-cost provider can use its low-cost advantage to underprice

> **CORE CONCEPT**
>
> **Best-cost provider strategies** are a *hybrid* of low-cost provider and differentiation strategies that aim at providing desired quality/features/performance/service attributes while beating rivals on price.

rivals whose products or services have similarly desirable attributes and still earn attractive profits. It is usually not difficult to entice buyers away from rivals with an equally good product at a more economical price.

Being a best-cost provider is different from being a low-cost provider because the additional attractive attributes entail additional costs (which a low-cost provider can avoid by offering buyers a basic product with few frills). Moreover, the two strategies aim at a distinguishably different market target. *The target market for a best-cost provider is value-conscious buyers*—buyers who are looking for appealing extras and functionality at an appealingly low price. Value-hunting buyers (as distinct from *price-conscious buyers* looking for a basic product at a bargain-basement price) often constitute a very sizable part of the overall market. Normally, value-conscious buyers are willing to pay a "fair" price for extra features, but they shy away from paying top dollar for items having all the bells and whistles. It is the desire to cater to *value-conscious buyers* as opposed to *budget-conscious buyers* that sets a best-cost provider apart from a low-cost provider—the two strategies aim at distinguishably different market targets.

LO 4

Recognize the attributes of a best-cost provider strategy and the way in which some firms use a hybrid strategy to go about building a competitive advantage and delivering superior value to customers.

When a Best-Cost Provider Strategy Works Best

A best-cost provider strategy works best in markets where product differentiation is the norm and there is an attractively large number of value-conscious buyers who prefer midrange products to cheap, basic products or expensive top-of-the-line products. A best-cost provider needs to position itself near the middle of the market with either a medium-quality product at a below-average price or a high-quality product at an average or slightly higher price. The objective is to provide the *best value* for better-quality, differentiated products. Best-cost provider strategies also work well in recessionary times when great masses of buyers become value-conscious and are attracted to economically priced products and services with appealing attributes. *But unless a company has the resources, know-how, and capabilities to incorporate upscale product or service attributes at a lower cost than rivals, adopting a best-cost strategy is ill-advised*—a winning strategy must always be matched to a company's most valuable resources and capabilities.

Illustration Capsule 5.4 describes how Toyota has applied the principles of the best-cost provider strategy in producing and marketing its Lexus brand.

The Big Risk of a Best-Cost Provider Strategy

A company's biggest vulnerability in employing a best-cost provider strategy is getting squeezed between the strategies of firms using low-cost and high-end differentiation strategies. Low-cost providers may be able to siphon customers away with the appeal of a lower price (despite less appealing product attributes). High-end differentiators may be able to steal customers away with the appeal of better product attributes (even though their products carry a higher price tag). Thus, to be successful, a best-cost provider must offer buyers *significantly* better product attributes in order to justify a price above what low-cost leaders are charging. Likewise, it has to achieve significantly lower costs in providing upscale features so that it can outcompete high-end differentiators on the basis of a *significantly* lower price.

Toyota Motor Company is widely regarded as a low-cost producer among the world's motor vehicle manufacturers. Despite its emphasis on product quality, Toyota has achieved low-cost leadership because it has developed considerable skills in efficient supply chain management and low-cost assembly capabilities and because its models are positioned in the low-to-medium end of the price spectrum, where high production volumes are conducive to low unit costs. But when Toyota decided to introduce its new Lexus models to compete in the luxury-car market segment, it employed a classic best-cost provider strategy. Toyota took the following four steps in crafting and implementing its Lexus strategy:

- Designing an array of high-performance characteristics and upscale features into the Lexus models to make them comparable in performance and luxury to other high-end models and attractive to Mercedes, BMW, Audi, Jaguar, Cadillac, and Lincoln buyers.

- Transferring its capabilities in making high-quality Toyota models at low cost to making premium-quality Lexus models at costs below other luxury-car makers. Toyota's supply chain capabilities and low-cost assembly know-how allowed it to incorporate high-tech performance features and upscale quality into Lexus models at substantially less cost than Mercedes, BMW, and other luxury-vehicle makers have been able to achieve in producing their models.

- Using its relatively lower manufacturing costs to underprice comparable Mercedes, BMW, Audi, and Jaguar models. Toyota believed that with its cost advantage it could price

attractively equipped Lexus cars low enough to draw price-conscious buyers away from comparable high-end brands. Toyota's pricing policy also allowed it to induce Toyota, Honda, Ford, or GM owners desiring more luxury to switch to a Lexus. Lexus's pricing advantage has typically been quite significant. For example, in 2009 the Lexus RX 350, a midsize SUV, carried a sticker price in the $38,000 to $48,000 range (depending on how it was equipped), whereas comparable Mercedes M-class SUVs had price tags in the $45,000 to $63,000 range and a comparable BMW X5 SUV could range anywhere from $47,000 to $65,000.

- Establishing a new network of Lexus dealers, separate from Toyota dealers, dedicated to providing a level of personalized, attentive customer service unmatched in the industry.

Toyota's best-cost strategy has resulted in growing sales of Lexus models (now over 400,000 vehicles annually). Lexus has consistently ranked first in the widely watched J. D. Power & Associates quality survey, and Lexus owners enjoy both top-notch dealer service and product quality.

THE CONTRASTING FEATURES OF THE FIVE GENERIC COMPETITIVE STRATEGIES: A SUMMARY

Deciding which generic competitive strategy should serve as the framework on which to hang the rest of the company's strategy is not a trivial matter. Each of the five generic competitive strategies *positions* the company differently in its market and competitive environment. Each establishes a central theme for how the company will endeavor to outcompete rivals. Each creates some boundaries or guidelines for maneuvering as market circumstances unfold and as ideas for improving the strategy are debated. Each points to different ways of experimenting and tinkering with the basic strategy—for example, employing a low-cost leadership strategy means experimenting with ways that costs can be cut and value chain activities can be streamlined, whereas a broad differentiation strategy means exploring ways to add new differentiating features or to perform value chain activities differently if the result is to add value for customers in ways they are willing to pay for. Each entails differences in terms of product line, production emphasis, marketing emphasis, and means of maintaining the strategy, as shown in Table 5.1.

Thus a choice of which generic strategy to employ spills over to affect many aspects of how the business will be operated and the manner in which value chain activities must be managed. Deciding which generic strategy to employ is perhaps the most important strategic commitment a company makes—it tends to drive the rest of the strategic actions a company decides to undertake.

Table 5.1   Distinguishing Features of the Five Generic Competitive Strategies

	Low-Cost Provider	Broad Differentiation	Focused Low-Cost Provider	Focused Differentiation	Best-Cost Provider
Strategic target	• A broad cross-section of the market.	• A broad cross-section of the market.	• A narrow market niche where buyer needs and preferences are distinctively different.	• A narrow market niche where buyer needs and preferences are distinctively different.	• Value-conscious buyers. • A middle market range.
Basis of competitive strategy	• Lower overall costs than competitors.	• Ability to offer buyers something attractively different from competitors' offerings.	• Lower overall cost than rivals in serving niche members.	• Attributes that appeal specifically to niche members.	• Ability to offer better goods at attractive prices.
Product line	• A good basic product with few frills (acceptable quality and limited selection).	• Many product variations, wide selection; emphasis on differentiating features.	• Features and attributes tailored to the tastes and requirements of niche members.	• Features and attributes tailored to the tastes and requirements of niche members.	• Items with appealing attributes; assorted features; better quality, not best.
Production emphasis	• A continuous search for cost reduction without sacrificing acceptable quality and essential features.	• Build in whatever differentiating features buyers are willing to pay for; strive for product superiority.	• A continuous search for cost reduction for products that meet basic needs of niche members.	• Small-scale production or custom-made products that match the tastes and requirements of niche members.	• Build in appealing features and better quality at lower cost than rivals.

(Continued)

	Low-Cost Provider	Broad Differentiation	Focused Low-Cost Provider	Focused Differentiation	Best-Cost Provider
Marketing emphasis	• Low prices, good value. • Try to make a virtue out of product features that lead to low cost.	• Tout differentiating features. • Charge a premium price to cover the extra costs of differentiating features.	• Communicate attractive features of a budget-priced product offering that fits niche buyers' expectations.	• Communicate how product offering does the best job of meeting niche buyers' expectations.	• Tout delivery of *best* value. • Either deliver comparable features at a lower price than rivals or else match rivals on prices and provide better features.
Keys to maintaining the strategy	• Economical prices, good value. • Strive to manage costs down, year after year, in every area of the business.	• Stress constant innovation to stay ahead of imitative competitors. • Concentrate on a few key differentiating features.	• Stay committed to serving the niche at the lowest overall cost; don't blur the firm's image by entering other market segments or adding other products to widen market appeal.	• Stay committed to serving the niche better than rivals; don't blur the firm's image by entering other market segments or adding other products to widen market appeal.	• Unique expertise in simultaneously managing costs down while incorporating upscale features and attributes.
Resources and capabilities required	• Capabilities for driving costs out of the value chain system. • *Examples:* large-scale automated plants, an efficiency-oriented culture, bargaining power.	• Capabilities concerning quality, design, intangibles, and innovation. • *Examples:* marketing capabilities, R&D teams, technology.	• Capabilities to lower costs on niche goods. • *Examples:* lower input costs for the specific product desired by the niche, batch production capabilities.	• Capabilities to meet the highly specific needs of niche members. • *Examples:* custom production, close customer relations.	• Capabilities to simultaneously deliver lower cost and higher-quality/differentiated features. • *Examples:* TQM practices, mass customization.

Successful Competitive Strategies Are Resource-Based

For a company's competitive strategy to succeed in delivering good performance and the intended competitive edge over rivals, it has to be underpinned by an appropriate set of resources, know-how, and competitive capabilities. To succeed in employing a low-cost provider strategy, a company has to have the resources and capabilities needed to keep its costs below those of its competitors; this means having the expertise to cost-effectively manage value chain activities better than rivals and/or having the innovative capability to bypass certain value chain activities being performed by rivals. Successful focused strategies require the capability to do an outstanding job of satisfying the needs and expectations of niche

A company's competitive strategy is unlikely to succeed unless it is predicated on leveraging a competitively valuable collection of resources and capabilities that match the strategy.

buyers. Success in employing a best-cost strategy requires the resources and capabilities to simultaneously incorporate desirable product or service attributes and deliver them at a lower cost than rivals. To succeed in strongly differentiating its product in ways that are appealing to buyers, a company must have the resources and capabilities to incorporate unique attributes into its product offering that a broad range of buyers will find appealing and worth paying for, This is easier said than done because, given sufficient time, competitors can clone almost any product feature buyers find quite appealing. Hence, long-term differentiation success is usually dependent on having a hard-to-imitate portfolio of resource capabilities (like patented technology; strong, socially complex skills in product innovation; expertise in relationship-based customer service) that allow a company to sustain its differentiation-based competitive advantage. Likewise, sustaining the competitive edge inherent in any generic strategy depends on resources, capabilities, and competences that rivals have a hard time duplicating and for which there are no good substitutes.

KEY POINTS

The key points to take away from this chapter include the following:

1. Deciding which of the five generic competitive strategies to employ—overall low-cost, broad differentiation, focused low-cost, focused differentiation, or best-cost—is perhaps the most important strategic commitment a company makes. It tends to drive the remaining strategic actions a company undertakes and sets the whole tone for pursuing a competitive advantage over rivals.

2. In employing a low-cost provider strategy and trying to achieve a low-cost advantage over rivals, a company must do a better job than rivals of cost-effectively managing value chain activities and/or it must find innovative ways to eliminate cost-producing activities. Low-cost provider strategies work particularly well when the products of rival sellers are virtually identical or very weakly differentiated and supplies are readily available from eager sellers, when there are not many ways to differentiate that have value to buyers, when many buyers are price-sensitive and shop the market for the lowest price, and when buyer switching costs are low.

3. Broad differentiation strategies seek to produce a competitive edge by incorporating tangible and intangible attributes that set a company's product/service offering apart from rivals in ways that buyers consider valuable and worth paying for. Successful differentiation allows a firm to (1) command a premium price for its product, (2) increase unit sales (because additional buyers are won over by the differentiating features), and/or (3) gain buyer loyalty to its brand (because some buyers are strongly attracted to the differentiating features and bond with the company and its products). Differentiation strategies work best when diverse buyer preferences open up windows of opportunity to strongly differentiate a company's product offering from those of rival brands, in situations where few other rivals are pursuing a similar differentiation approach, and in circumstances where companies are racing to bring out the most appealing next-generation product. A differentiation strategy is doomed when competitors are able to quickly copy most or all of the appealing product attributes a company comes up with, when a company's differentiation efforts fail to interest many buyers, and when a company overspends

on efforts to differentiate its product offering or tries to overcharge for its differentiating extras.

4. A focused strategy delivers competitive advantage either by achieving lower costs than rivals in serving buyers constituting the target market niche or by developing a specialized ability to offer niche buyers an appealingly differentiated offering that meets their needs better than rival brands do. A focused strategy based on either low cost or differentiation becomes increasingly attractive when the target market niche is big enough to be profitable and offers good growth potential, when it is costly or difficult for multisegment competitors to put capabilities in place to meet the specialized needs of the target market niche and at the same time satisfy the expectations of their mainstream customers, and when few other rivals are attempting to specialize in the same target segment.

5. Best-cost provider strategies combine a strategic emphasis on low cost with a strategic emphasis on more than minimal quality, service, features, or performance. The aim is to create competitive advantage by giving buyers *more value for the money for midrange products*—an approach that entails (1) matching close rivals on key quality/service/features/performance attributes, (2) beating them on the costs of incorporating such attributes into the product or service, and (3) charging a more economical price. A best-cost provider strategy works best in markets with large numbers of value-conscious buyers desirous of purchasing appealingly good products and services for less money.

6. In all cases, competitive advantage depends on having competitively superior resources and capabilities that are a good match for the chosen generic strategy. A sustainable advantage depends on maintaining that competitive superiority with resources, capabilities, and value chain activities that rivals have trouble matching and for which there are no good substitutes.

ASSURANCE OF LEARNING EXERCISES

LO 1, LO 2, LO 3, LO 4

1. Best Buy is the largest consumer electronics retailer in the United States, with 2009 sales of nearly $45 billion. The company competes aggressively on price with such rivals as Costco Wholesale, Sam's Club, Walmart, and Target, but it is also known by consumers for its first-rate customer service. Best Buy customers have commented that the retailer's sales staff is exceptionally knowledgeable about the company's products and can direct them to the exact location of difficult-to-find items. Best Buy customers also appreciate that demonstration models of PC monitors, MP3 players, and other electronics are fully powered and ready for in-store use. Best Buy's Geek Squad tech support and installation services are additional customer service features that are valued by many customers. How would you characterize Best Buy's competitive strategy? Should it be classified as a low-cost provider strategy? A differentiation strategy? A best-cost strategy? Explain your answer.

LO 3

2. Stihl is the world's leading manufacturer and marketer of chain saws, with annual sales exceeding $2 billion. With innovations dating to its 1929

invention of the gasoline-powered chain saw, the company holds over 1,000 patents related to chain saws and outdoor power tools. The company's chain saws, leaf blowers, and hedge trimmers sell at price points well above competing brands and are sold only by its network of over 8,000 independent dealers. The company boasts in its advertisements that its products are rated number one by consumer magazines and are *not* sold at Lowe's or Home Depot. How does Stihl's choice of distribution channels and advertisements contribute to its differentiation strategy?

LO 3

3. Explore BMW's Web site (www.bmw.com), and then click on the link for www.bmwgroup.com. The site you find provides an overview of the company's key functional areas, including research and development and production activities (see the page headings). Under Research and Development, click on Innovation & Technology and explore the links at the sidebar to better understand the types of resources and capabilities that underlie BMW's approach to innovation. Also review the statements under Production focusing on automobile production worldwide and sustainable production. How do the resources, capabilities, and activities of BMW contribute to its differentiation strategy and the unique position in the industry that it has achieved?

EXERCISES FOR SIMULATION PARTICIPANTS

LO 1, LO 2, LO 3, LO 4

1. Which one of the five generic competitive strategies best characterizes your company's strategic approach to competing successfully?
2. Which rival companies appear to be employing a low-cost provider strategy?
3. Which rival companies appear to be employing a broad differentiation strategy?
4. Which rival companies appear to be employing some type of focused strategy?
5. Which rival companies appear to be employing a best-cost provider strategy?
6. What is your company's action plan to achieve a sustainable competitive advantage over rival companies? List at least three (preferably more) specific kinds of decision entries on specific decision screens that your company has made or intends to make to win this kind of competitive edge over rivals.

ENDNOTES

[1] This classification scheme is an adaptation of a narrower three-strategy classification presented in Michael E. Porter, *Competitive Strategy: Techniques for Analyzing Industries and Competitors* (New York: Free Press, 1980). For a discussion of the different ways that companies can position themselves in the marketplace, see Michael E. Porter, "What Is Strategy?" *Harvard Business*

Review 74, no. 6 (November–December 1996), pp. 65–67.
[2] M. Porter, *Competitive Advantage: Creating and Sustaining Superior Performance* (New York: Free Press, 1985), p. 97.
[3] Michael Hammer and James Champy were the main proponents of business process reengineering. See M. Hammer and J. Champy, *Reengineering the Corporation: A*

Manifesto for Business Revolution, rev. and updated (New York: HarperBusiness, 2003).
[4] For a discussion of how unique industry positioning and resource combinations are linked to consumers' perspectives of value and their willingness to pay more for differentiated products or services, see Richard L. Priem, "A Consumer Perspective on Value Creation," *Academy of Management Review* 32, no. 1 (2007), pp. 219–35.

[5] G. Gavetti, "Ducati," Harvard Business School case 9-701-132, rev. March 8, 2002.

[6] http://jrscience.wcp.muohio.edu/nsfall01/FinalArticles/Final-IsitWorthitBrandsan.html.

[7] This section expands on the section on value chain linkages found in Porter, *Competitive Advantage,* p. 125.

[8] D. Yoffie, "Cola Wars Continue: Coke and Pepsi in 2006," Harvard Business School case 9-706-447.

[9] Porter, *Competitive Advantage,* pp. 160–62.

[10] For an excellent discussion of best-cost provider strategies, see Peter J. Williamson and Ming Zeng, "Value-for-Money Strategies for Recessionary Times," *Harvard Business Review* 87, no. 3 (March 2009), pp. 66–74.

CHAPTER 6

STRENGTHENING A COMPANY'S COMPETITIVE POSITION

Strategic Moves, Timing, and Scope of Operations

Competing in the marketplace is like war. You have injuries and casualties, and the best strategy wins.

—John Collins
NHL executive

It was our duty to expand.

—Ingvar Kamprad
Founder of IKEA

In the virtual economy, collaboration is a new competitive imperative.

—Michael Dell
CEO of Dell Inc.

In this new wave of technology, you can't do it all yourself, you have to form alliances.

—Carlos Slim
CEO of Telmex, Telcel and América Móvil and the . wealthiest person in the world

LEARNING OBJECTIVES

LO 1. Learn whether and when to pursue offensive or defensive strategic moves to improve a company's market position.

LO 2. Recognize when being a first mover or a fast follower or a late mover is most advantageous.

LO 3. Become aware of the strategic benefits and risks of expanding a company's horizontal scope through mergers and acquisitions.

LO 4. Learn the advantages and disadvantages of extending the company's scope of operations via vertical integration.

LO 5. Become aware of the conditions that favor farming out certain value chain activities to outside parties.

LO 6. Understand when and how strategic alliances can substitute for horizontal mergers and acquisitions or vertical integration and how they can facilitate outsourcing.

Once a company has settled on which of the five generic competitive strategies to employ, attention turns to how strategic choices along several other dimensions can complement its competitive approach and maximize the power of its overall strategy. The first dimension concerns competitive actions—both offensive and defensive; the second concerns competitive dynamics and the timing of strategic moves; and the third concerns the breadth of a company's activities (or its *scope* of operations along an industry's entire value chain). All in all, the following measures to strengthen a company's competitive position and create a full-blown business strategy have to be considered:

- Whether and when to go on the offensive and initiate aggressive strategic moves to improve the company's market position.

- Whether and when to employ defensive strategies to protect the company's market position.

- When to undertake strategic moves—whether advantage or disadvantage lies in being a first mover, a fast follower, or a late mover.

- Whether to bolster the company's market position by merging with or acquiring another firm in the same industry.

- Whether to integrate backward or forward into more stages of the vertical chain of activities that (typically) begins with raw-material production and ends with sales to the end consumer.

- Whether to outsource certain value chain activities or perform them in-house.

- Whether to enter into strategic alliances or partnership arrangements with other enterprises.

This chapter presents the pros and cons of each of these strategy-enhancing measures.

GOING ON THE OFFENSIVE—STRATEGIC OPTIONS TO IMPROVE A COMPANY'S MARKET POSITION

No matter which one of the five generic competitive strategies a firm employs, there are times when it makes sense for the company to *go on the offensive* to strengthen its market position and improve its overall business performance. Strategic offensives are called for when a company spots opportunities to gain profitable market share at the expense of rivals or when a company has no choice but to try to whittle away at a strong rival's competitive advantage. Companies like Walmart, Apple, and Google play hardball, aggressively pursuing competitive advantage and trying to reap the benefits of a leading market share, superior profit margins, and more rapid growth, as well as the reputational rewards of being known as a winning company on the move.[1] The best offensives tend to incorporate several principles: (1) focusing relentlessly on building competitive advantage and then striving to convert it into sustainable advantage (as described in Chapter 4), (2) creating and deploying company resources in ways that cause rivals to struggle to defend themselves, (3) employing the element of surprise as opposed to doing what rivals expect and are prepared for, and (4) displaying a strong bias for swift, decisive, and overwhelming actions to overpower rivals.[2]

Choosing the Basis for Competitive Attack

As a rule, challenging rivals on competitive grounds where they are strong is an uphill struggle.[3] Offensive initiatives that exploit competitor weaknesses stand a far better chance of succeeding than do those that challenge competitor strengths, especially if the weaknesses represent important vulnerabilities and if weak rivals can be caught by surprise with no ready defense.[4]

> The best offensives use a company's most competitively potent resources to attack rivals in the areas where they are weakest.

Strategic offensives should, as a general rule, be based on exploiting a company's strongest strategic assets—its most valuable resources and capabilities, such as a better-known brand name, a more efficient production or distribution system, greater technological capability, or a superior reputation for quality. But a consideration of the company's strengths should not be made without also considering the rival's strengths and weaknesses. A strategic offensive should be based on those areas of strength where the company has its greatest competitive advantage over the targeted rivals. If a company has especially good customer service capabilities, it can make special sales pitches to the customers of those rivals that provide subpar customer service. Aggressors with a recognized brand name and strong marketing skills can launch efforts to win customers away from rivals with weak brand recognition. There is considerable appeal in emphasizing sales to buyers in geographic regions where a rival has a weak market share or is exerting less competitive effort. Likewise, it may be attractive to pay special attention to buyer segments that a rival is neglecting or is weakly equipped to serve.

> Sometimes a company's best strategic option is to seize the initiative, go on the attack, and launch a strategic offensive to improve its market position.

Ignoring the need to tie a strategic offensive to a company's resources where they are competitively stronger than rivals' is like going to war with a popgun—the prospects for success are dim. For instance, it is foolish for a company with relatively high costs to employ a price-cutting offensive—price-cutting offensives are best left to financially strong companies whose costs are relatively low in comparison to those of the companies being attacked. Likewise, it is ill-advised to pursue a product innovation offensive without having competitively superior expertise in R&D, new product development, and speeding new products to market.

The principal offensive strategy options include the following:

1. *Using a cost-based advantage to attack competitors on the basis of price or value.* A price-cutting offensive can involve offering customers an equally good or better product at a lower price or offering a low-priced, lower-quality product that gives customers more value for the money. This is the classic offensive for improving a company's market position vis-à-vis rivals, but it works well only

under certain circumstances. Lower prices can produce market share gains if competitors don't respond with price cuts of their own and if the challenger convinces buyers that its product offers them a better value proposition. However, such a strategy increases total profits only if the gains in additional unit sales are enough to offset the impact of lower prices and thinner margins per unit sold. Price-cutting offensives are generally successful only when a company *first achieves a cost advantage and then hits competitors with a lower price.*[5] Walmart's rise to dominance in discount retailing and supermarkets was based on just this type of strategic offensive. Ryanair also used this strategy successfully against rivals such as British Air and Aer Lingus, by first cutting costs to the bone and then targeting leisure passengers who care more about low price than in-flight amenities and service.[6] While some companies have used price-cutting offensives as a means of obtaining the cost advantages associated with greater market share (economies of scale or experience), this has proved to be a highly risky strategy. More often than not, such price-cutting offensives are met with retaliatory attacks that can mire the entire industry in a costly price war.

2. *Leapfrogging competitors by being the first adopter of next-generation technologies or being first to market with next-generation products.* In technology-based industries, the opportune time to overtake an entrenched competitor is when there is a shift to the next generation of the technology. Microsoft got its next-generation Xbox 360 to market a full 12 months ahead of Sony's PlayStation 3 and Nintendo's Wii, helping it convince video gamers to buy an Xbox rather than wait for the new PlayStation 3 and Wii to hit the market. This type of offensive strategy is high-risk, however, since it requires costly investment at a time when consumer reactions to the new technology are yet unknown.

3. *Pursuing continuous product innovation to draw sales and market share away from less innovative rivals.* Ongoing introductions of new and improved products can put rivals under tremendous competitive pressure, especially when rivals' new product development capabilities are weak. But such offensives can be sustained only if a company has sufficient product innovation skills to keep its pipeline full and maintain buyer enthusiasm for its new and better product offerings.

4. *Adopting and improving on the good ideas of other companies (rivals or otherwise).*[7] The idea of warehouse-type home improvement centers did not originate with Home Depot cofounders Arthur Blank and Bernie Marcus; they got the "big-box" concept from their former employer Handy Dan Home Improvement. But they were quick to improve on Handy Dan's business model and take Home Depot to the next plateau in terms of product line breadth and customer service. Casket maker Hillenbrand greatly improved its market position by adapting Toyota's production methods to casket making. Offense-minded companies are often quick to take any good idea (not nailed down by a patent or other legal protection), make it their own, and then aggressively apply it to create competitive advantage for themselves.

5. *Using hit-and-run or guerrilla warfare tactics to grab sales and market share from complacent or distracted rivals.* Options for "guerrilla offensives" include occasional lowballing on price (to win a big order or steal a key account from a rival), surprising key rivals with sporadic but intense bursts of promotional activity (offering a special trial offer for new customers to draw them away

from rival brands), or undertaking special campaigns to attract buyers away from rivals plagued with a strike or problems in meeting buyer demand.[8] Guerrilla offensives are particularly well suited to small challengers that have neither the resources nor the market visibility to mount a full-fledged attack on industry leaders and that may not merit a full retaliatory response from larger rivals.[9]

6. *Launching a preemptive strike to secure an advantageous position that rivals are prevented or discouraged from duplicating.*[10] What makes a move preemptive is its one-of-a-kind nature—whoever strikes first stands to acquire competitive assets that rivals can't readily match. Examples of preemptive moves include (1) securing the best distributors in a particular geographic region or country; (2) obtaining the most favorable sites in terms of customer demographics, cost characteristics, or access to transportation, raw-material supplies, or low-cost inputs; (3) tying up the most reliable, high-quality suppliers via exclusive partnerships, long-term contracts, or acquisition; and (4) moving swiftly to acquire the assets of distressed rivals at bargain prices. To be successful, a preemptive move doesn't have to totally block rivals from following; it merely needs to give a firm a prime position that is not easily replicated or circumvented.

How long it takes for an offensive to yield good results varies with the competitive circumstances.[11] It can be short if buyers respond immediately (as can occur with a dramatic cost-based price cut, an imaginative ad campaign, or an especially appealing new product). Securing a competitive edge can take much longer if winning consumer acceptance of an innovative product will take some time or if the firm may need several years to debug a new technology, put new production capacity in place, or develop and perfect new competitive capabilities. But how long it takes for an offensive move to improve a company's market standing (and whether it can do so) also depends on whether market rivals recognize the threat and begin a counterresponse. And whether rivals will respond depends on whether they are capable of making an effective response and if they believe that a counterattack is worth the expense and the distraction.[12]

Choosing Which Rivals to Attack

Offensive-minded firms need to analyze which of their rivals to challenge as well as how to mount the challenge. The following are the best targets for offensive attacks:[13]

* *Market leaders that are vulnerable.* Offensive attacks make good sense when a company that leads in terms of size and market share is not a true leader in terms of serving the market well. Signs of leader vulnerability include unhappy buyers, an inferior product line, a weak competitive strategy with regard to low-cost leadership or differentiation, strong emotional commitment to an aging technology the leader has pioneered, outdated plants and equipment, a preoccupation with diversification into other industries, and mediocre or declining profitability. Toyota's massive product recalls in 2009 and 2010 due to safety concerns presented other car companies with a prime opportunity to attack a vulnerable and distracted market leader. GM and Ford used incentives and low-financing offers aimed at winning over Toyota buyers to increase their market share during this period. Offensives to erode the positions of vulnerable market leaders have real promise when the challenger is also able to revamp

its value chain or innovate to gain a fresh cost-based or differentiation-based competitive advantage.[14] To be judged successful, attacks on leaders don't have to result in making the aggressor the new leader; a challenger may "win" by simply becoming a stronger runner-up. Caution is well advised in challenging strong market leaders—there's a significant risk of squandering valuable resources in a futile effort or precipitating a fierce and profitless industrywide battle for market share.

- *Runner-up firms with weaknesses in areas where the challenger is strong.* Runner-up firms are an especially attractive target when a challenger's resources and capabilities are well suited to exploiting their weaknesses.

- *Struggling enterprises that are on the verge of going under.* Challenging a hard-pressed rival in ways that further sap its financial strength and competitive position can weaken its resolve and hasten its exit from the market. In this type of situation, it makes sense to attack the rival in the market segments where it makes the most profits, since this will threaten its survival the most.

- *Small local and regional firms with limited capabilities.* Because small firms typically have limited expertise and resources, a challenger with broader and/or deeper capabilities is well positioned to raid their biggest and best customers—particularly those that are growing rapidly, have increasingly sophisticated requirements, and may already be thinking about switching to a supplier with more full-service capability.

Blue-Ocean Strategy—A Special Kind of Offensive

A **blue-ocean strategy** seeks to gain a dramatic and durable competitive advantage by abandoning efforts to beat out competitors in existing markets and, instead, inventing a new industry or distinctive market segment that renders existing competitors largely irrelevant and allows a company to create and capture altogether new demand.[15] This strategy views the business universe as consisting of two distinct types of market space. One is where industry boundaries are defined and accepted, the competitive rules of the game are well understood by all industry members, and companies try to outperform rivals by capturing a bigger share of existing demand; in such markets, lively competition constrains a company's prospects for rapid growth and superior profitability since rivals move quickly to either imitate or counter the successes of competitors. The second type of market space is a "blue ocean" where the industry does not really exist yet, is untainted by competition, and offers wide-open opportunity for profitable and rapid growth if a company can come up with a product offering and strategy that allows it to create new demand.

> **CORE CONCEPT**
>
> A **blue-ocean strategy** is based on discovering or inventing new industry segments that create altogether new demand, thereby positioning the firm in uncontested market space offering superior opportunities for profitability and growth.

A terrific example of such wide-open or blue-ocean market space is the online auction industry that eBay created and now dominates. Other examples of companies that have achieved competitive advantages by creating blue-ocean market spaces include Starbucks in the coffee shop industry, Dollar General in extreme discount retailing, FedEx in overnight package delivery, and Cirque du Soleil in live entertainment. Cirque du Soleil "reinvented the circus" by creating a distinctively different market space for its performances (Las Vegas nightclubs and theater-type settings) and pulling in a whole new group of customers—adults and corporate clients—who were willing to pay several times more than the price of a conventional circus ticket to have an "entertainment experience" featuring sophisticated clowns and star-quality acrobatic acts in a comfortable atmosphere. Companies that create blue-ocean market spaces can usually sustain their initial competitive advantage without encountering a major competitive challenge for 10 to 15 years because of high barriers to imitation and the strong brand-name awareness that a blue-ocean strategy can produce.

Zipcar Inc. is presently using a blue-ocean strategy to compete against entrenched rivals in the rental-car industry. It rents cars by the hour or day (rather than by the week) to members who pay a yearly fee for access to cars parked in designated spaces located conveniently throughout large cities. By allowing drivers under 25 years of age to rent cars and by targeting city dwellers who need to supplement their use of public transportation with short-term car rentals, Zipcar entered uncharted waters in the rental-car industry, growing rapidly in the process. Founded in 2000, Zipcar filed to go public in mid-2010.

DEFENSIVE STRATEGIES—PROTECTING MARKET POSITION AND COMPETITIVE ADVANTAGE

> Good defensive strategies can help protect a competitive advantage but rarely are the basis for creating one.

In a competitive market, all firms are subject to offensive challenges from rivals. The purposes of defensive strategies are to (1) lower the risk of being attacked, (2) weaken the impact of any attack that occurs, and (3) influence challengers to aim their efforts at other rivals. While defensive strategies usually don't enhance a firm's competitive advantage, they can definitely help fortify the firm's competitive position, protect its most valuable resources and capabilities from imitation, and defend whatever competitive advantage it might have. Defensive strategies can take either of two forms: actions to block challengers and actions to signal the likelihood of strong retaliation.

Blocking the Avenues Open to Challengers

The most frequently employed approach to defending a company's present position involves actions that restrict a challenger's options for initiating a competitive attack. There are any number of obstacles that can be put in the path of would-be challengers.[16] A defender can participate in alternative technologies as a hedge against rivals attacking with a new or better technology. A defender can introduce new features, add new models, or broaden its product line to close off

> There are many ways to throw obstacles in the path of would-be challengers.

gaps and vacant niches to opportunity-seeking challengers. It can thwart the efforts of rivals to attack with a lower price by maintaining economy-priced options of its own. It can try to discourage buyers from trying competitors' brands by lengthening warranties, offering free training and support services, developing the capability to deliver spare parts to users faster than rivals can, providing coupons and sample giveaways to buyers most prone to experiment, and making early announcements about impending new products or price changes to induce potential buyers to postpone switching. It can challenge the quality or safety of rivals' products. Finally, a defender can grant volume discounts or better financing terms to dealers and distributors to discourage them from experimenting with other suppliers, or it can convince them to handle its product line *exclusively* and force competitors to use other distribution outlets.

Signaling Challengers That Retaliation Is Likely

The goal of signaling challengers that strong retaliation is likely in the event of an attack is either to dissuade challengers from attacking at all or to divert them to less threatening options. Either goal can be achieved by letting challengers know the battle will cost more than it is worth. Signals to would-be challengers can be given by:[17]

- Publicly announcing management's commitment to maintaining the firm's present market share.
- Publicly committing the company to a policy of matching competitors' terms or prices.
- Maintaining a war chest of cash and marketable securities.
- Making an occasional strong counterresponse to the moves of weak competitors to enhance the firm's image as a tough defender.

Signaling is most likely to be an effective defensive strategy if the signal is accompanied by a credible commitment to follow through.

TIMING A COMPANY'S OFFENSIVE AND DEFENSIVE STRATEGIC MOVES

When to make a strategic move is often as crucial as *what* move to make. Timing is especially important when **first-mover advantages** or **disadvantages** exist.[18] Under certain conditions, being first to initiate a strategic move can have a high payoff in the form of a competitive advantage that later movers can't dislodge. Moving first is no guarantee of success, however, since first movers also face some significant disadvantages. Indeed, there are circumstances in which it is more advantageous to be a fast follower or even a late mover. Because the timing of strategic moves can be consequential, it is important for company strategists to be aware of the nature of first-mover advantages and disadvantages and the conditions favoring each type.[19]

The Potential for First-Mover Advantages

Market pioneers and other types of first movers typically bear greater risks and greater development costs than firms that move later. If the market responds well to its initial move, the pioneer will benefit from a monopoly position (by virtue of being first to market) that enables it to recover its investment costs and make an attractive profit. If the firm's pioneering move gives it a competitive advantage that can be sustained even after other firms enter the market space, its first-mover advantage will be greater still. The extent of this type of advantage, however, will

LO 2

Recognize when being a first mover or a fast follower or a late mover is most advantageous.

depend on whether and how fast follower firms can piggyback on the pioneer's success and either imitate or improve on its move.

The conditions that favor first-mover advantages, then, are those that slow the moves of follower firms or prevent them from imitating the success of the first mover. There are six such conditions in which first-mover advantages are most likely to arise:

1. *When pioneering helps build a firm's reputation with buyers and creates brand loyalty.* A firm's reputation can insulate it from competition when buyer uncertainty about product quality keeps the firm's customers from trying competitors' offerings and when new buyers minimize their risk by choosing on the basis of reputation. Similarly, customer loyalty to an early mover's brand can create a tie that binds, limiting the success of later entrants' attempts to poach from the early mover's customer base and steal market share.

2. *When a first mover's customers will thereafter face significant switching costs.* Switching costs limit the ability of late movers to lure away the customers of early movers by making it expensive for a customer to switch to another company's product or service. Switching costs can arise for a number of reasons. They may be due to the time a consumer invests in learning how to use a specific company's product. They may arise from an investment in complementary products that are also brand-specific. They can also arise from certain types of loyalty programs or long-term contracts that give customers greater incentives to remain with an initial provider.

3. *When property rights protections thwart rapid imitation of the initial move.* In certain types of industries, property rights protections in the form of patents, copyrights, and trademarks prevent the ready imitation of an early mover's initial moves. First-mover advantages in pharmaceuticals, for example, are heavily dependent on patent protections, and patent races in this industry are common. In other industries, however, patents provide limited protection and can frequently be circumvented. Property rights protections also vary among nations, since they are dependent on a country's legal institutions and enforcement mechanisms.

4. *When an early lead enables the first mover to move down the learning curve ahead of rivals.* When there is a steep learning curve and when learning can be kept proprietary, a first mover can benefit from volume-based cost advantages that grow ever larger as its experience accumulates and its scale of operations increases. This type of first-mover advantage is self-reinforcing and, as such, can preserve a first mover's competitive advantage over long periods of time. Honda's advantage in small multiuse motorcycles has been attributed to such an effect, as has the long-lived advantage of Lincoln Electric Company in arc welders, which are used in industries such as construction and shipbuilding.

5. *When a first mover can set the technical standard for the industry.* In many technology-based industries, the market will converge around a single technical standard. By establishing the industry standard, a first mover can gain a powerful advantage that, like experienced-based advantages, builds over time. The greater the importance of technical standards in an industry, the greater the advantage of being the one to set the standard and the more firmly the first mover will be entrenched. The lure of such an advantage, however, can result in standard wars among early movers, as each strives to set the industry standard. The key to winning such wars is to enter early on the

basis of strong fast-cycle product development capabilities, gain the support of key customers and suppliers, employ penetration pricing, and make allies of the producers of complementary products.

To sustain any advantage that may initially accrue to a pioneer, a first mover needs to be a fast learner and continue to move aggressively to capitalize on any initial pioneering advantage. It helps immensely if the first mover has deep financial pockets, important competitive capabilities, and astute managers. What makes being a first mover strategically important is not being the first company to do something but, rather, being the first competitor to put together the precise combination of features, customer value, and sound revenue/cost/profit economics that gives it an edge over rivals in the battle for market leadership.[20] If the marketplace quickly takes to a first mover's innovative product offering, the first mover must have large-scale production, marketing, and distribution capabilities if it is to take full advantage of its market lead. If technology is advancing at a torrid pace, a first mover cannot hope to sustain its lead without having strong capabilities in R&D, design, and new product development, along with the financial strength to fund these activities.

Illustration Capsule 6.1 describes how Amazon.com achieved a first-mover advantage in online retailing.

The Potential for First-Mover Disadvantages or Late-Mover Advantages

There are circumstances when first movers face significant disadvantages and when it is actually better to be an adept follower than a first mover. First-mover disadvantages *(or late-mover advantages)* arise in the following four instances:

1. *When pioneering is more costly than imitating, and only negligible experience or learning-curve benefits accrue to the leader.* Such conditions allow a follower to end up with lower costs than the first mover and either win customers away with lower prices or benefit from more profitable production.

2. *When the products of an innovator are somewhat primitive and do not live up to buyer expectations.* In this situation, a clever follower can study customers' reactions to the pioneer's products and win disenchanted buyers away from the leader with better-performing products. Moreover, the first mover may find itself saddled with a negative reputation that retards its ability to recover from its early missteps.

3. *When rapid market evolution gives fast followers the opening to leapfrog a first mover's products with more attractive next-version products.* Industries characterized by fast-paced changes in either technology or buyer needs and expectations may present opportunities for second movers to improve on the pioneer's products and offer customers a more attractive value proposition as a result.

4. *When market uncertainties make it difficult to ascertain what will eventually succeed.* Under these conditions, first movers are likely to make numerous mistakes that later movers can avoid and learn from. Even if the pioneer manages to please early adopters, it may turn out that the needs of early adopters are very different from mass-market needs. Late movers may find it far more advantageous to wait until these needs are clarified and then focus on satisfying the mass market's demand.

ILLUSTRATION CAPSULE 6.1

Amazon.com's First-Mover Advantage in Online Retailing

Amazon.com's path to becoming the world's largest online retailer began in 1994 when Jeff Bezos, a Manhattan hedge fund analyst at the time, noticed that the number of Internet users was increasing by 2,300 percent annually. Bezos saw the tremendous growth as an opportunity to sell products online that would be demanded by a large number of Internet users and could be easily shipped. Bezos launched the online bookseller Amazon.com in 1995. The start-up's revenues soared to $148 million in 1997, $610 million in 1998, and $1.6 billion in 1999. Bezos' business plan—hatched while on a cross-country trip with his wife in 1994—made him *Time* magazine's Person of the Year in 1999.

The volume-based and reputational benefits of Amazon.com's early entry into online retailing had delivered a first-mover advantage, but between 2000 and 2009 Bezos undertook a series of additional strategic initiatives to solidify the company's number-one ranking in the industry. Bezos undertook a massive building program in the late-1990s that added five new warehouses and fulfillment centers totaling $300 million. The additional warehouse capacity was added years before it was needed, but Bezos wanted to move preemptively against potential rivals and ensure that, as demand continued to grow, the company could continue to offer its customers the best selection, the lowest prices, and the cheapest and most convenient delivery. The company also expanded its product line to include sporting goods, tools, toys, grocery items, electronics, and digital music downloads, giving it another means of maintaining its experience and scale-based advantages. Amazon.com's 2008 revenues of $19.2 billion made it the world's largest Internet retailer; Jeff Bezos' shares in Amazon.com made him the 110th-wealthiest person in the world in 2009, with an estimated net worth of $8.2 billion.

Moving down the learning curve in Internet retailing was not an entirely straightforward process for Amazon.com. Bezos commented in a *Fortune* article profiling the company, "We were investors in every bankrupt, 1999-vintage e-commerce startup. Pets.com, living.com, kozmo.com. We invested in a lot of high-profile flameouts." He went on to specify that although the ventures were a "waste of money," they "didn't take us off our own mission." Bezos also suggested that gaining advantage as a first mover is "taking a million tiny steps—and learning quickly from your missteps."

Sources: Mark Brohan, "The Top 500 Guide," *Internet Retailer,* June 2009 (accessed at www.internetretailer.com on June 17, 2009); Josh Quittner, "How Jeff Bezos Rules the Retail Space," *Fortune,* May 5, 2008, pp. 126–34.

To Be a First Mover or Not

In weighing the pros and cons of being a first mover versus a fast follower versus a late mover, it matters whether the race to market leadership in a particular industry is a marathon or a sprint. In marathons, a slow mover is not unduly penalized—first-mover advantages can be fleeting, and there's ample time for fast followers and sometimes even late movers to play catch-up.[21] Thus the speed at which the pioneering innovation is likely to catch on matters considerably as companies struggle with whether to pursue a particular emerging market opportunity aggressively (as a first mover or fast follower) or cautiously (as a late mover). For instance, it took 18 months for 10 million users to sign up for Hotmail, 5.5 years for worldwide mobile phone use to grow from 10 million to 100 million, and close to 10 years for the number of at-home broadband subscribers to reach 100 million worldwide. The lesson here is that there is a market penetration curve for every emerging opportunity; typically, the curve has an inflection point at which all the pieces of the business model fall into place, buyer demand explodes, and the market takes off. The inflection point can come early on a fast-rising curve (as with use of e-mail) or farther on up a slow-rising curve (as with the use of broadband). Any company that seeks competitive advantage by being a first mover thus needs to ask some hard questions:

- Does market takeoff depend on the development of complementary products or services that currently are not available?
- Is new infrastructure required before buyer demand can surge?
- Will buyers need to learn new skills or adopt new behaviors? Will buyers encounter high switching costs in moving to the newly introduced product or service?
- Are there influential competitors in a position to delay or derail the efforts of a first mover?

When the answers to any of these questions are yes, then a company must be careful not to pour too many resources into getting ahead of the market opportunity—the race is likely going to be more of a 10-year marathon than a 2-year sprint.[22] On the other hand, if the market is a winner-take-all type of market, where powerful first-mover advantages insulate early entrants from competition and prevent later movers from making any headway, then it may be best to move quickly despite the risks.

STRENGTHENING A COMPANY'S MARKET POSITION VIA ITS SCOPE OF OPERATIONS

Apart from considerations of competitive moves and their timing, there is another set of managerial decisions that can affect the strength of a company's market position. These decisions concern the scope of a company's operations—the breadth of its activities and the extent of its market reach. Decisions regarding the **scope of the firm** focus on which activities a firm will perform internally and which it will not. For example, should Panera Bread Company produce the fresh dough that its company-owned and franchised bakery-cafés use in making baguettes, pastries, bagels, and other types of bread, or should it obtain its dough from outside suppliers? Scope decisions also concern which segments of the market to serve—decisions that can include geographic market segments as well as product and service segments. Should Panera expand its menu to include light dinner entrees? Should it offer delivery or drive-through service? Should it expand into all 50 states or concentrate on strengthening its market presence regionally?

Decisions such as these, in essence, determine where the boundaries of a firm lie and the degree to which the operations within those boundaries cohere. They also have much to do with the direction and extent of a business's growth. In this chapter, we introduce the topic of company scope and discuss different types of

> **CORE CONCEPT**
>
> The **scope of the firm** refers to the range of activities which the firm performs internally, the breadth of its product and service offerings, the extent of its geographic market presence, and its mix of businesses.

scope decisions in relation to a company's business-level strategy. In the next two chapters, we develop two additional dimensions of a firm's scope. Chapter 7 focuses on international expansion—a matter of extending the company's geographic scope into foreign markets. Chapter 8 takes up the topic of corporate strategy, which concerns diversifying into a mix of different businesses. Scope issues are at the very heart of corporate-level strategy.

Several dimensions of firm scope have relevance for business-level strategy in terms of their capacity to strengthen a company's position in a given market. These include the firm's **horizontal scope,** which is the range of product and service segments that the firm serves within its market. Mergers and acquisitions involving other market participants provide a means for a company to expand its horizontal scope. Expanding the firm's vertical scope by means of vertical integration can also affect the success of its market strategy. **Vertical scope** is the extent to which the firm engages in the various activities that make up the industry's entire value chain system, from initial activities such as raw-material production all the way to retailing and after-sales service activities. Outsourcing decisions concern another dimension of scope since they involve narrowing the firm's boundaries with respect to its participation in value chain activities. We discuss the pros and cons of each of these options in the sections that follow. Since strategic alliances and partnerships provide an alternative to vertical integration and acquisition strategies and are sometimes used to facilitate outsourcing, we conclude this chapter with a discussion of the benefits and challenges associated with cooperative arrangements of this sort.

HORIZONTAL MERGER AND ACQUISITION STRATEGIES

Mergers and acquisitions are much-used strategic options; for example, the total worldwide value of mergers and acquisitions completed in 2008 and 2009 was approximately $5 trillion.[23] A *merger* is the combining of two or more companies into a single corporate entity, with the newly created company often taking on a new name. An *acquisition* is a combination in which one company, the acquirer, purchases and absorbs the operations of another, the acquired. The difference between a merger and an acquisition relates more to the details of ownership, management control, and financial arrangements than to strategy and competitive advantage. The resources and competitive capabilities of the newly created enterprise end up much the same whether the combination is the result of acquisition or merger.

Horizontal mergers and acquisitions, which involve combining the operations of firms within the same general industry, provide an effective means for firms to rapidly increase the scale and horizontal scope of their core business. For example, Microsoft has used an aggressive acquisition strategy to extend its software business into new segments and strengthen its technological capabilities in this domain. Mergers between airlines, such as the 2010 United-Continental merger, have increased their scale of operations and extended their reach geographically. Companies from developing economies are increasingly expanding their businesses through cross-border acquisitions, as we discuss in the following chapter on international strategy.

Combining the operations of two companies, via merger or acquisition, is an attractive strategic option for strengthening the resulting company's competitiveness and opening up avenues of new market opportunity. Increasing a company's horizontal scope can strengthen its business and increase its profitability in five ways: (1) by improving the efficiency of its operations, (2) by heightening its product differentiation, (3) by reducing market rivalry, (3) by increasing the company's bargaining power over suppliers and buyers, and (5) by enhancing its flexibility and dynamic capabilities (discussed in Chapter 4).

To achieve these benefits, horizontal merger and acquisition strategies typically are aimed at any of five outcomes:[24]

1. *Increasing the company's scale of operations and market share.* Many mergers and acquisitions are undertaken with the objective of transforming two or more high-cost companies into one lean competitor with significantly lower costs. When a company acquires another company in the same industry, there's usually enough overlap in operations that less efficient plants can be closed or distribution and sales activities partly combined and downsized. Likewise, it is usually feasible to squeeze out cost savings in administrative activities, again by combining and downsizing such administrative activities as finance and accounting, information technology, human resources, and so on. The combined companies may also be able to reduce supply chain costs because of greater bargaining power over common suppliers and closer collaboration with supply chain partners. By helping to consolidate the industry and remove excess capacity, such combinations can also reduce industry rivalry and improve industry profitability.

2. *Expanding a company's geographic coverage.* One of the best and quickest ways to expand a company's geographic coverage is to acquire rivals with operations in the desired locations. If there is some geographic overlap, then one benefit is being able to reduce costs by eliminating duplicate facilities in those geographic areas where undesirable overlap exists. Since a company's size increases with its geographic scope, another benefit is increased bargaining power with the company's suppliers or buyers. For companies whose business customers require national or international coverage, a broader geographic scope can provide differentiation benefits while also enhancing the company's bargaining power. Food products companies like Nestlé, Kraft, Unilever, and Procter & Gamble have made acquisitions an integral part of their strategies to expand internationally in order to serve key customers such as Walmart on a global basis. Greater geographic coverage can also contribute to product differentiation by enhancing a company's name recognition and brand awareness. Banks like Wells Fargo and Bank of America have used acquisition strategies to establish a market presence and gain name recognition in an ever-growing number of states and localities.

3. *Extending the company's business into new product categories.* Many times a company has gaps in its product line that need to be filled in order to offer customers a more effective product bundle or the benefits of one-stop-shopping.[25] For example, customers might prefer to acquire a suite of software applications from a single vendor that can offer more integrated solutions to the company's problems. Acquisition can be a quicker and more potent way to broaden a company's product line than going through the exercise of introducing a company's own new product to fill the gap. Expanding

into additional market segments or product categories can offer companies benefits similar to those gained by expanding geographically: greater product differentiation, bargaining power, and efficiencies. It can also reduce rivalry by helping to consolidate an industry. Coca-Cola has increased the effectiveness of the product bundle it provides to retailers by acquiring Minute Maid (juices and juice drinks), Odwalla (juices), Hi-C (ready-to-drink fruit beverages), and GlaceauWater, the maker of VitaminWater. By entering the low-cost segment of the rental-car industry with its 2010 acquisition of Dollar Thrifty (whose brands include Dollar Rent a Car and Thrifty Rent a Car), Hertz can benefit from greater scale and stronger bargaining power over its suppliers.

4. *Gaining quick access to new technologies or complementary resources and capabilities.* By making acquisitions to bolster a company's technological know-how or to expand its skills and capabilities, a company can bypass a time-consuming and expensive internal effort to build desirable new resources and organizational capabilities. From 2000 through April 2009, Cisco Systems purchased 85 companies to give it more technological reach and product breadth, thereby enhancing its standing as the world's biggest provider of hardware, software, and services for building and operating Internet networks. By acquiring technologies and other resources and capabilities that complement its own set, a company can gain many of the types of benefits available from extending its horizontal scope. Among them is the greater flexibility and dynamic capabilities that spring from greater innovativeness and the ability to compete on the basis of a more effective bundle of resources.

5. *Leading the convergence of industries whose boundaries are being blurred by changing technologies and new market opportunities.* In fast-cycle industries or industries whose boundaries are changing, companies can use acquisition strategies to hedge their bets about the direction that an industry will take, increase their capacity to meet changing demands, and respond flexibly to changing buyer needs and technological demands. Such acquisitions add to a company's dynamic capabilities by bringing together the resources and products of several different companies and enabling the company to establish a strong position in the consolidating markets. Microsoft has made a series of acquisitions that have enabled it to launch Microsoft TV Internet Protocol Television (IPTV). Microsoft TV allows broadband users to use their home computers or Xbox game consoles to watch live programming, see video on demand, view pictures, and listen to music. News Corporation has also prepared for the convergence of media services with the purchase of satellite TV companies to complement its media holdings in TV broadcasting (the Fox network and TV stations in various countries), cable TV (Fox News, Fox Sports, and FX), filmed entertainment (Twentieth Century Fox and Fox studios), newspapers, magazines, and book publishing.

Numerous companies have employed a horizontal acquisition strategy to catapult themselves from the ranks of the unknown into positions of market leadership. In 1998, Wells Fargo & Company became the 10th-largest bank in the United States as a result of the merger between Wells Fargo and Norwest Corporation. Although it was still only a network of small midwestern banks at that time, it continued to grow via acquisition over the next decade, pursuing a business model based on selling a full range of financial services to an ever-larger base of customers. New opportunity presented itself, however, in the wake of the 2008 financial crisis. By acquiring troubled Wachovia Bank (which operated primarily in the Southeast and parts of the Atlantic Coast), Wells Fargo & Company was able to double its size and transform itself into a nationwide bank with global presence. By 2010, it was the fourth-largest bank in the United States, with $1.2 trillion in assets and over 10,000 branch banks. Moreover, its reputation had grown along with it; it was listed by *Fortune* magazine as the world's 14th "Most Admired Company in 2009," was among *Barron's* "World's 25 Most Respected Companies," and was on *Forbes's* list of the "Top 100 Best Companies in the World."

Illustration Capsule 6.2 describes how Clear Channel Worldwide has used acquisitions to build a leading global position in radio broadcasting.

Why Mergers and Acquisitions Sometimes Fail to Produce Anticipated Results

All too frequently, mergers and acquisitions do not produce the hoped-for outcomes.[26] Cost savings may prove smaller than expected. Gains in competitive capabilities may take substantially longer to realize or, worse, may never materialize at all. Efforts to mesh the corporate cultures can stall due to formidable resistance from organization members. Managers and employees at the acquired company may argue forcefully for continuing to do things the way they were done before the acquisition. Key employees at the acquired company can quickly become disenchanted and leave; the morale of company personnel who remain can drop to disturbingly low levels because they disagree with newly instituted changes. Differences in management styles and operating procedures can prove hard to resolve. The managers appointed to oversee the integration of a newly acquired company can make mistakes in deciding which activities to leave alone and which activities to meld into their own operations and systems.

A number of mergers/acquisitions have been notably unsuccessful. Ford's $2.5 billion acquisition of Jaguar was a failure, as was its $2.5 billion acquisition of Land Rover (both were sold to India's Tata Motors in 2008 for $2.3 billion). Daimler AG, the maker of Mercedes-Benz and Smart cars, entered into a high-profile merger with Chrysler only to dissolve it in 2007, taking a loss of $30 billion. A number of recent mergers and acquisitions have yet to live up to expectations—prominent examples include Oracle's acquisition of Sun Microsystems, the Fiat-Chrysler deal, Bank of America's acquisition of Merrill Lynch, and the merger of Sprint and Nextel in the mobile phone industry. Antitrust concerns on the part of regulatory authorities have prevented the successful conclusion of other mergers and acquisitions. Coca-Cola, for example, failed to win approval in 2009 for its proposed $2.4 billion acquisition of Huiyuan Juice Group under China's new antimonopoly law.

VERTICAL INTEGRATION STRATEGIES

Expanding the firm's vertical scope by means of a vertical integration strategy provides another way to strengthen the company's position in its core market. A **vertically integrated firm** is one that participates in multiple segments or stages of an industry's overall value chain. A good example of a vertically integrated

Clear Channel Communications: Using Mergers and Acquisitions to Become a Global Market Leader in Radio Broadcasting

In 2009, Clear Channel Communications was among the worldwide leaders in radio broadcasting. Clear Channel owned and operated more than 1,000 radio stations in the United States and operated an additional 240 radio stations in Australia, New Zealand, and Mexico. The company, which was founded in 1972 by Lowry Mays and Billy Joe McCombs, got its start by acquiring an unprofitable country-music radio station in San Antonio, Texas. Over the next 10 years, Mays learned the radio business and slowly bought other radio stations in a variety of states. Going public in 1984 helped the company raise the equity capital needed to continue acquiring radio stations in additional geographic markets.

By 1998, Clear Channel had used acquisitions to build a leading position in radio stations. Domestically, it owned, programmed, or sold airtime for 69 AM radio stations and 135 FM stations in 48 local markets in 24 states. Clear Channel's big move was to begin expanding internationally by acquiring interests in radio station properties in a variety of countries. In October 1999, Clear Channel made a major acquisition that expanded its horizontal scope significantly: It acquired AM-FM, Inc., and changed its name to Clear Channel Communications. The AM-FM, Inc., acquisition gave Clear Channel operations in 32 countries, including 830 radio stations.

Additional acquisitions were completed during the 2000–2003 period. The emphasis was on buying radio broadcasting properties with operations in many of the same local markets, which made it feasible to (1) cut costs by sharing facilities and staffs, (2) improve programming, and (3) sell advertising to customers in packages that not only helped Clear Channel's advertising clients distribute their messages more effectively but also allowed the company to combine its sales activities, achieving significant cost savings and boosting profit margins. In 2008, Clear Channel sought a buyer for 288 of its 1,005 radio stations that operated in small markets. Its remaining 717 radio stations all operated in the top-100 markets in the United States.

Sources: www.clearchannel.com (accessed May 2008); *BusinessWeek,* October 19, 1999, p. 56.

LO 4

Learn the advantages and disadvantages of extending the company's scope of operations via vertical integration.

firm is Maple Leaf Foods, a major Canadian producer of fresh and processed meats whose best-selling brands include Maple Leaf and Schneiders. Maple Leaf Foods participates in hog and poultry production, with company-owned hog and poultry farms; it has its own meat-processing and -rendering facilities; it packages its products and distributes them from company-owned distribution centers; and it conducts marketing, sales, and customer service activities for its wholesale and retail buyers but does not otherwise participate in the final stage of the meat processing vertical chain—the retailing stage.

A vertical integration strategy can expand the firm's range of activities *backward* into sources of supply and/or *forward* toward end users. When Tiffany & Co, a manufacturer and retailer of fine jewelry, began sourcing, cutting, and polishing its own diamonds, it integrated backward along the diamond supply chain. Mining giant De Beers Group and Canadian miner Aber Diamond integrated forward when they entered the diamond retailing business.

A firm can pursue vertical integration by starting its own operations in other stages of the vertical activity chain, by acquiring a company already performing the activities it wants to bring in-house, or by entering into a strategic alliance or joint venture. Vertical integration strategies can aim at *full integration* (participating in all stages of the vertical chain) or *partial integration* (building positions in selected stages of the vertical chain). Firms can also engage in *tapered integration* strategies, which involve a mix of in-house and outsourced activity in any given stage of the vertical chain. Oil companies, for instance, supply their refineries with oil from their own wells as well as with oil that they purchase from other producers—they engage in tapered backward integration. Since Boston Beer Company, the maker of Samuel Adams, sells most of its beer through distributors but also operates brew-pubs, it practices tapered forward integration.

The Advantages of a Vertical Integration Strategy

Under the right conditions, a vertical integration strategy can add materially to a company's technological capabilities, strengthen the firm's competitive position, and boost its profitability.[27] But it is important to keep in mind that vertical integration has no real payoff strategywise or profitwise unless it produces cost savings and/or differentiation benefits sufficient to justify the extra investment.

Integrating Backward to Achieve Greater Competitiveness   It is harder than one might think to generate cost savings or improve profitability by integrating backward into activities such as parts and components manufacture (which could otherwise be purchased from suppliers with specialized expertise in making these parts and components). For backward integration to be a cost-saving and profitable strategy, a company must be able to (1) achieve the same scale economies as outside suppliers and (2) match or beat suppliers' production efficiency with no drop-off in quality. Neither outcome is a slam dunk. To begin with, a company's in-house requirements are often too small to reach the optimum size for low-cost operation—for instance, if it takes a minimum production volume of 1 million units to achieve mass-production economies and a company's in-house requirements are just 250,000 units, then it falls far short of being able to capture the scale economies of outside suppliers (which may readily find buyers for 1 million or more units). Furthermore, matching the production efficiency of suppliers is fraught with problems when suppliers have considerable production experience of their own, when the technology they employ has elements that are hard to master, and/or when substantial R&D expertise is required to develop next-version parts and components or keep pace with advancing technology in parts/components production.

But that said, there are still occasions when a company can improve its cost position and competitiveness by performing a broader range of vertical chain activities in-house rather than having certain of these activities performed by outside suppliers. When the item being supplied is a major cost component, when there is a sole supplier, or when suppliers have outsized profit margins, vertical integration can lower costs by limiting supplier power. Vertical integration can also lower costs by facilitating the coordination of production flows and avoiding bottleneck problems. Furthermore, when a company has proprietary know-how that it wants to keep from rivals, then in-house performance of value-adding activities related to this know-how is beneficial even if such activities could be performed by outsiders. Apple recently decided to integrate backward

> **CORE CONCEPT**
>
> A **vertically integrated firm** is one that performs value chain activities along several portions or stages of an industry's overall value chain, which begins with the production of raw materials or initial inputs and culminates in final sales and service to the end consumer.

> **CORE CONCEPT**
>
> **Backward integration** involves performing industry value chain activities previously performed by suppliers or other enterprises engaged in earlier stages of the industry value chain; **forward integration** involves performing industry value chain activities closer to the end user.

into producing its own chips for iPhones, chiefly because chips are a major cost component, they have big profit margins, and in-house production would help coordinate design tasks and protect Apple's proprietary iPhone technology. International Paper Company backward integrates into pulp mills that it sets up nearby its paper mills (outside suppliers are generally unwilling to make a site-specific investment for a buyer) and reaps the benefits of coordinated production flows, energy savings, and transportation economies.

Backward vertical integration can produce a differentiation-based competitive advantage when performing activities internally contributes to a better-quality product/service offering, improves the caliber of customer service, or in other ways enhances the performance of the final product. On occasion, integrating into more stages along the vertical added-value chain can add to a company's differentiation capabilities by allowing it to build or strengthen its core competencies, better master key skills or strategy-critical technologies, or add features that deliver greater customer value. Spanish clothing maker Inditex has backward integrated into fabric making, as well as garment design and manufacture, for its successful Zara brand. By tightly controlling the process and postponing dyeing until later stages, Zara can respond quickly to changes in fashion trends and supply its customers with the hottest items. NewsCorp backward integrated into film studios (Twentieth Century Fox) and TV program production to ensure access to high-quality content for its TV stations (and to limit supplier power).

Integrating Forward to Enhance Competitiveness
Like backward integration, forward integration can lower costs by increasing efficiency and bargaining power. In addition, it can allow manufacturers to gain better access to end users, strengthen brand awareness, and increase product differentiation. Automakers, for example, have forward integrated into the lending business in order to exercise more control and make auto loans a more attractive part of the car-buying process. Forward integration can also enable companies to make the end users' purchasing experience a differentiating feature. For example, Ducati and Harley motorcycles both have company-owned retail stores that are essentially little museums, filled with iconography, that provide an environment conducive to selling not only motorcycles and gear but memorabilia, clothing, and other items featuring the brand. Insurance companies and brokerages have the ability to make consumers' interactions with local agents and office personnel a differentiating feature by focusing on building relationships.

In many industries, independent sales agents, wholesalers, and retailers handle competing brands of the same product; having no allegiance to any one company's brand, they tend to push whatever earns them the biggest profits. An independent insurance agency, for example, represents a number of different insurance companies and tries to find the best match between a customer's insurance requirements and the policies of alternative insurance companies. Under this arrangement, it's possible for an agent to develop a preference for one company's policies or underwriting practices and neglect other represented insurance companies. An insurance company may conclude, therefore, that it is better off integrating forward and setting up its own local offices, as State Farm and Allstate have done. Likewise, some tire manufacturers (such as Goodyear) have integrated forward into tire retailing to exert better control over sales force/customer interactions. A number of consumer-goods manufacturers, like Coach, Pepperidge Farm, and Samsonite, have integrated forward into retailing so as to move seconds, overstocked items, and slow-selling merchandise through their own branded factory outlet stores.

Some producers have opted to integrate forward by selling directly to customers at the company's Web site. Bypassing regular wholesale/retail channels in favor of direct sales and Internet retailing can have appeal if it reinforces the brand and enhances consumer satisfaction or if it lowers distribution costs, produces a relative cost advantage over certain rivals, and results in lower selling prices to end users. In addition, sellers are compelled to include the Internet as a retail channel when a sufficiently large number of buyers in an industry prefer to make purchases online. However, a company that is vigorously pursuing online sales to consumers at the same time that it is also heavily promoting sales to consumers through its network of wholesalers and retailers is competing directly against its distribution allies. Such actions constitute *channel conflict* and create a tricky route to negotiate. A company that is actively trying to expand online sales to consumers is signaling *a weak strategic commitment to its dealers* and *a willingness to cannibalize dealers' sales and growth potential.* The likely result is angry dealers and loss of dealer goodwill. Quite possibly, a company may stand to lose more sales by offending its dealers than it gains from its own online sales effort. Consequently, in industries where the strong support and goodwill of dealer networks is essential, companies may conclude that it is important to avoid channel conflict and that their Web sites should be designed to partner with dealers rather than compete against them.

The Disadvantages of a Vertical Integration Strategy

Vertical integration has some substantial drawbacks beyond the potential for channel conflict.[28] The most serious drawbacks to vertical integration include the following concerns:

- Vertical integration raises a firm's capital investment in the industry, *increasing business risk.* What if industry growth and profitability go sour?

- Vertically integrated companies are often *slow to embrace technological advances* or more efficient production methods when they are saddled with older technology or facilities. A company that obtains parts and components from outside suppliers can always shop the market for the latest and best parts and components, whereas a vertically integrated firm that is saddled with older technology or facilities that make items it no longer needs is looking at the high costs of premature abandonment.

- Integrating backward into parts and components manufacture *can impair a company's operating flexibility* when it comes to changing out the use of certain parts and components. It is one thing to design out a component made by a supplier and another to design out a component being made in-house (which can mean laying off employees and writing off the associated investment in equipment and facilities). Most of the world's automakers, despite their expertise in automotive technology and manufacturing, have concluded that purchasing many of their key parts and components from manufacturing specialists results in higher quality, lower costs, and greater design flexibility than does the vertical integration option.

- Vertical integration potentially results in *less flexibility in accommodating shifting buyer preferences* when a new product design doesn't include parts and components that the company makes in-house. Integrating forward or backward locks a firm into relying on its own in-house activities and sources of supply.

- Vertical integration *may not enable a company to realize economies of scale* if its production levels are below the minimum efficient scale. Small companies in particular are likely to suffer a cost disadvantage by producing in-house when suppliers of many small companies can realize scale economies that a small company cannot attain on its own.

- Vertical integration poses all kinds of *capacity matching problems*. In motor vehicle manufacturing, for example, the most efficient scale of operation for making axles is different from the most economic volume for radiators and different yet again for both engines and transmissions. Building the capacity to produce just the right number of axles, radiators, engines, and transmissions in-house—and doing so at the lowest unit costs for each—is much easier said than done. If internal capacity for making transmissions is deficient, the difference has to be bought externally. If internal capacity for radiators proves excessive, customers need to be found for the surplus. And if by-products are generated—as occurs in the processing of many chemical products—they require arrangements for disposal. Consequently, integrating across several production stages in ways that achieve the lowest feasible costs can be a monumental challenge.

- Integration forward or backward often calls for *radical new skills and business capabilities*. Parts and components manufacturing, assembly operations, wholesale distribution and retailing, and direct sales via the Internet represent different kinds of businesses, operating in different types of industries, with different key success factors. Managers of a manufacturing company should consider carefully whether it makes good business sense to invest time and money in developing the expertise and merchandising skills to integrate forward into wholesaling or retailing. Many manufacturers learn the hard way that company-owned wholesale/retail networks present many headaches, fit poorly with what they do best, and don't always add the kind of value to their core business they thought they would.

In today's world of close working relationships with suppliers and efficient supply chain management systems, *very few businesses can make a case for integrating backward into the business of suppliers* to ensure a reliable supply of materials and components or to reduce production costs. The best materials and components suppliers stay abreast of advancing technology and are adept in improving their efficiency and keeping their costs and prices as low as possible. A company that pursues a vertical integration strategy and tries to produce many parts and components in-house is likely to find itself very hard-pressed to keep up with technological advances and cutting-edge production practices for each part and component used in making its product

Weighing the Pros and Cons of Vertical Integration

All in all, therefore, a strategy of vertical integration can have both important strengths and weaknesses. The tip of the scales depends on (1) whether vertical integration can enhance the performance of strategy-critical activities in ways that lower cost, build expertise, protect proprietary know-how, or increase differentiation; (2) the impact of vertical integration on investment costs, flexibility and response times, and the administrative costs of coordinating operations across more vertical chain activities; and (3) how difficult it will be for the company to acquire the set of skills and capabilities needed to operate in another stage of the vertical chain. *Vertical integration strategies have merit according to which capabilities and value-adding activities truly need to be performed in-house and which can be performed better or cheaper by outsiders.* Without solid benefits, integrating forward or backward is not likely to be an attractive strategy option.

American Apparel, the largest U.S. clothing manufacturer, has made vertical integration a central part of its strategy, as described in Illustration Capsule 6.3.

OUTSOURCING STRATEGIES: NARROWING THE SCOPE OF OPERATIONS

In contrast to vertical integration strategies, outsourcing strategies narrow the scope of a business's operations (and the firm's boundaries, in terms of what activities are performed internally). **Outsourcing** involves a conscious decision to forgo attempts to perform certain value chain activities internally and instead to farm them out to outside specialists.[29] Many PC makers, for example, have shifted from assembling units in-house to outsourcing the entire assembly process to manufacturing specialists because enterprises that assemble many brands of PCs are better able to bargain down the prices of PC components (by buying in very large volumes) and because they have greater expertise in performing assembly tasks more cost-effectively. Nike has outsourced most of its manufacturing-related value chain activities so that it can concentrate on marketing and managing its brand.

Outsourcing certain value chain activities can be advantageous whenever:

- *An activity can be performed better or more cheaply by outside specialists.* A company should generally *not* perform any value chain activity internally that can be performed more efficiently or effectively by outsiders—the chief exception occurs when a particular activity is strategically crucial and internal control over that activity is deemed essential.

- *The activity is not crucial to the firm's ability to achieve sustainable competitive advantage and won't hollow out its core competencies.* Outsourcing of support activities such as maintenance services, data processing and data storage, fringe-benefit management, and Web site operations has become commonplace. Colgate-Palmolive, for instance, has been able to reduce its information technology operational costs by more than 10 percent per year through an outsourcing agreement with IBM. A number of companies have outsourced their call center operations to foreign-based contractors that have access to lower-cost labor supplies and can employ lower-paid call center personnel to respond to customer inquiries or requests for technical support.

- *It streamlines company operations in ways that improve organizational flexibility and speed time to market.* Outsourcing gives a company the flexibility to switch suppliers in the event that its present supplier falls behind competing suppliers. To the extent that its suppliers can speedily get next-generation parts and components into production, then a company can get its own next-generation product offerings into the marketplace quicker. Moreover, seeking out new suppliers with the needed capabilities already in place is frequently quicker,

ILLUSTRATION CAPSULE 6.3

American Apparel's Vertical Integration Strategy

American Apparel, known for its hip line of basic garments and its provocative advertisements, is no stranger to the concept of "doing it all." The Los Angeles–based casual wear company has made both forward and backward vertical integration a central part of its strategy, making American Apparel a rarity in the U.S. fashion industry. Not only does it do all its own fabric cutting and sewing, but it also owns several knitting and dyeing facilities in southern California, as well as a distribution warehouse, a wholesale operation, and over 270 retail stores in 20 countries. American Apparel even does its own clothing design, marketing, and advertising, often using its employees as photographers and clothing models.

Founder and CEO Dov Charney claims that the company's vertical integration strategy lets American Apparel respond more quickly to rapid market changes, allowing the company to bring an item from design to its stores worldwide in the span of a week. End-to-end coordination also improves inventory control, helping prevent common problems in the fashion business such as stockouts and steep markdowns. The company capitalizes on its California-based vertically integrated operations by using taglines such as "Sweatshop Free. Made in the USA" to bolster its "authentic" image.

However, this strategy is not without risks and costs. In an industry where 97 percent of goods are imported, American Apparel pays its workers wages and benefits above the relatively high mandated American minimum. Furthermore, operating in so many key vertical chain activities makes it impossible to be expert in all of them and creates optimal scale and capacity mismatches—problems with which the firm has partly dealt by tapering its backward integration into knitting and dyeing. Lastly, while the company can respond quickly to new fashion trends, its vertical integration strategy may make it more difficult for the company to scale back in an economic downturn or respond to radical change in the industry environment. Ultimately, only time will tell whether American Apparel will dilute or capitalize on its vertical integration strategy in its pursuit of profitable growth.

Developed with John R. Moran.

Sources: American Apparel Web site, www.americanapparel.net (accessed June 16, 2010); American Apparel investor presentation, June 2009, http://files.shareholder.com/downloads/APP/938846703x0x300331/3dd0b7ca-e458-45b8-8516-e25ca272016d/NYC%20JUNE%202009.pdf; Dov Charney. "American Apparel—Dov Charney Interview," *YouTube,* 2007, http://youtube.com/watch?v=hYqR8Ull8A4; Christopher Palmeri, "Living on the Edge at American Apparel," *BusinessWeek,* June 27, 2005.

easier, less risky, and cheaper than hurriedly retooling internal operations to replace obsolete capabilities or trying to install and master new technologies.

- *It reduces the company's risk exposure to changing technology and/or buyer preferences.* When a company outsources certain parts, components, and services, its suppliers must bear the burden of incorporating state-of-the-art technologies and/or undertaking redesigns and upgrades to accommodate a company's plans to introduce next-generation products. If what a supplier provides falls out of favor with buyers, or is designed out of next-generation products, or rendered unnecessary by technological change, it is the supplier's business that suffers rather than a company's own internal operations.

- *It allows a company to assemble diverse kinds of expertise speedily and efficiently.* A company can nearly always gain quicker access to first-rate capabilities and expertise by employing suppliers who already have them in place than it can by trying to build them from scratch with its own company personnel.

- *It allows a company to concentrate on its core business, leverage its key resources, and do even better what it already does best.* A company is better able to heighten its own competitively valuable capabilities when it concentrates its full resources and energies on performing those activities internally that it can perform better than outsiders and/or that it needs to have under its direct control. Coach, for example, devotes its energy to designing new styles of ladies handbags and leather accessories, opting to outsource handbag production to 40 contract manufacturers in 15 countries. Hewlett-Packard, IBM, and others have sold manufacturing plants to suppliers and then contracted to purchase the output.

The Big Risk of Outsourcing Value Chain Activities

The biggest danger of outsourcing is that a company will farm out too many or the wrong types of activities and thereby hollow out its own capabilities.[30] For example, in recent years, companies anxious to reduce operating costs have opted to outsource such strategically important activities as product development, engineering design, and sophisticated manufacturing tasks—the very capabilities that underpin a company's ability to lead sustained product innovation. While these companies may have been able to lower their operating costs by outsourcing these functions to outsiders that can perform them more cheaply, *their ability to lead the development of innovative new products has been weakened in the process.* For example, nearly every U.S. brand of laptop and cell phone (with the notable exception of Apple) is not only manufactured but designed in Asia.[31] It is strategically dangerous for a company to be dependent on outsiders for competitive capabilities that over the long run determine its market success. Companies like IBM, Dell, American Express, and Bank of America are alert to the danger of farming out the performance of strategy-critical value chain activities and generally only outsource relatively mundane functions: IBM outsources customer support operations, Dell outsources manufacturing, American Express outsources IT functions, and BoA outsources human resource management.

> A company must guard against outsourcing activities that hollow out the resources and capabilities that it needs to be a master of its own destiny.

Another risk of outsourcing comes from the lack of direct control. It may be difficult to monitor, control, and coordinate the activities of outside parties by mean of contracts and arm's-length transactions alone; unanticipated problems may arise that cause delays or cost overruns and become hard to resolve amicably. Moreover, contract-based outsourcing can be problematic because outside parties lack incentives to make investments specific to the needs of the outsourcing company's value chain.

STRATEGIC ALLIANCES AND PARTNERSHIPS

Strategic alliances and cooperative partnerships provide one way to gain some of the benefits offered by vertical integration, outsourcing, and horizontal mergers and acquisitions while minimizing the associated problems. Companies frequently engage in cooperative strategies as an alternative to vertical integration or horizontal mergers and acquisitions. Increasingly, companies are also employing strategic alliances and partnerships to extend their scope of operations via international expansion and diversification strategies, as we describe in Chapters 7 and 8. Strategic alliances and cooperative arrangements are now a common means of narrowing a company's scope of operations as well, serving as a useful way to manage outsourcing (in lieu of traditional, purely price-oriented contracts).

For example, oil and gas companies engage in considerable vertical integration—but Shell Oil Company and Pemex (Mexico's state-owned petroleum company) have found that joint ownership of their Deer Park Refinery in Texas lowers their investment costs and risks in comparison to going it alone. The colossal failure of the Daimler-Chrysler merger formed an expensive lesson for Daimler AG about what can go wrong with horizontal mergers and acquisitions; its 2010 strategic alliance with Renault-Nissan may allow the two companies to achieve jointly the global scale required for cost competitiveness in cars and trucks while avoiding the type of problems that so plagued Daimler-Chrysler. Many companies employ strategic alliances to manage the problems that might otherwise occur with outsourcing—Cisco's system of alliances guards against loss of control, protects its proprietary manufacturing expertise, and enables the company to monitor closely the assembly operations of its partners while devoting its energy to designing new generations of the switches, routers, and other Internet-related equipment for which it is known.

Companies in all types of industries and in all parts of the world have elected to form strategic alliances and partnerships to complement their own strategic initiatives and strengthen their competitiveness in domestic and international markets—the very same goals that motivate vertical integration, horizontal mergers and acquisitions, and outsourcing initiatives. This is an about-face from times past, when the vast majority of companies were content to go it alone, confident that they already had or could independently develop whatever resources and know-how were needed to be successful in their markets. But in today's world, large corporations—even those that are successful and financially strong—have concluded that it doesn't always make good strategic and economic sense to be *totally independent* and *self-sufficient* with regard to each and every skill, resource, and capability they may need. When a company needs to strengthen its competitive position, whether through greater differentiation, efficiency improvements, or a stronger bargaining position, the fastest and most effective route may be to partner with other enterprises having similar goals and complementary capabilities; moreover, partnering offers greater flexibility should a company's resource requirements or goals later change.

A **strategic alliance** is a formal agreement between two or more separate companies in which there is strategically relevant collaboration of some sort, joint contribution of resources, shared risk, shared control, and mutual dependence. Often, alliances involve cooperative marketing, sales or distribution, joint production, design collaboration, or projects to jointly develop new technologies or products. They can vary in terms of their duration and the extent of the collaboration; some are intended as long-term arrangements, involving an extensive set of cooperative activities, while others are designed to accomplish more limited, short-term objectives.

Collaborative arrangements may entail a contractual agreement, but they commonly stop short of formal ownership ties between the partners (although sometimes an alliance member will secure minority ownership of another member). A special type of strategic alliance involving ownership ties is the **joint venture.** A joint venture entails forming a new corporate entity that is jointly owned by two or more companies that agree to share in the revenues, expenses, and control of the newly formed entity. Since joint ventures involve setting up a mutually owned business, they tend to be more durable but also riskier than other arrangements. In other types of strategic alliances, the collaboration between the partners involves a much less rigid structure in which the partners retain their independence from one another. If a strategic alliance is not working out, a partner can choose to simply walk away or reduce its commitment to collaborating at any time.

> **CORE CONCEPT**
>
> A **joint venture** is a type of strategic alliance in which the partners set up an independent corporate entity that they own and control jointly, sharing in its revenues and expenses.

Five factors make an alliance "strategic," as opposed to just a convenient business arrangement:[32]

1. It helps build, sustain, or enhance a core competence or competitive advantage.

2. It helps block a competitive threat.

3. It increases the bargaining power of alliance members over suppliers or buyers.

4. It helps open up important new market opportunities.

5. It mitigates a significant risk to a company's business.

Strategic cooperation is a much-favored approach in industries where new technological developments are occurring at a furious pace along many different paths and where advances in one technology spill over to affect others (often blurring industry boundaries). Whenever industries are experiencing high-velocity technological advances in many areas simultaneously, firms find it virtually essential to have cooperative relationships with other enterprises to stay on the leading edge of technology and product performance even in their own area of specialization.

It took a $3.2 billion joint venture involving the likes of Sprint-Nextel, Clearwire, Intel, Time Warner Cable, Google, Comcast, and Bright House Networks to roll out next-generation 4G wireless services based on Sprint's and Clearwire's WiMax mobile networks, with the objective of reaching 100 metropolitan areas and 120 million people by the end of 2010. WiMax was an advanced Wi-Fi technology that allowed people to browse the Internet at speeds as great as 10 times faster than other cellular Wi-Fi technologies. The venture was a necessity for Sprint-Nextel and Clearwire since they lacked the financial resources to handle the rollout on their own. The appeal of the partnership for Time Warner, Comcast, and Bright House was the ability to bundle the sale of wireless services to their cable customers, while Intel had the chip sets for WiMax and hoped that WiMax would become the dominant wireless Internet format. Google's interest in the alliance was to strengthen its lead in desktop search on wireless devices.

Clear Channel Communications has entered into a series of partnerships to provide a multiplatform launchpad for artists like Taylor Swift, Phoenix, and Sara Bareilles. In 2008, they launched iHeartRadio on the iPhone, leveraging their relationships with record labels, artists, TV music channels, and media companies to rake in $175 million in digital revenue as compared to $50 million earned by Pandora in the same period. In 2010, they partnered with MySpace, Hulu, and the artist management company 19 Entertainment for "If I Can Dream," an original reality series where unsigned musicians and actors share a "Real World"-style house in Los Angeles and document their attempts at stardom. Clear Channel has helped promote the show by conducting exclusive radio interviews and performances with the talent, which in turn has helped the show become a top-30 weekly program on Hulu.[33]

Since 2003, Samsung Electronics, a global electronics company headquartered in South Korea, has entered into more than 30 major strategic alliances involving such companies as Sony, Nokia, Intel, Microsoft, Dell, Toshiba, Lowe's, IBM, Hewlett-Packard, and Disney Automation; the alliances involved joint investments, technology transfer arrangements, joint R&D projects, and agreements to supply parts and components—all of which facilitated Samsung's strategic efforts to globalize its business and secure its position as a leader in the worldwide electronics industry. Microsoft collaborates very closely with independent software developers to ensure that their programs will run on the next-generation versions of Windows. Genentech, a leader in biotechnology and human genetics, has formed R&D alliances with over 30 companies to boost its prospects for developing new cures for various diseases and ailments. United Airlines, American Airlines, Continental, Delta, and Northwest created an alliance to form Orbitz, an Internet travel site that enabled them to compete head to head against Expedia and Travelocity and, further, gave them more economical access to travelers and vacationers shopping online for airfares, rental cars, lodging, cruises, and vacation packages.

Toyota has forged long-term strategic partnerships with many of its suppliers of automotive parts and components, both to achieve lower costs and to improve the quality and reliability of its vehicles. In 2008, when Chrysler found itself unable to build hybrid SUVs and trucks using its Two Mode technological innovation (because it lacked the economies of scale necessary to produce proprietary components at a reasonable cost), it entered into a strategic alliance with Nissan whereby Nissan would build Chrysler vehicles with the hybrid technology and Chrysler would take over the production of certain Nissan truck models. Daimler AG has been entering a variety of alliances to lower its risks and improve its prospects in electric cars, where it lacks key capabilities. Its equity-based strategic partnership with Tesla Motors, for example, will allow Daimler to use proven technology to bring its electric vehicles to market quickly, while helping Tesla learn how to mass produce its electric cars. Daimler's 2010 joint venture with Chinese car maker BYD is intended to help Daimler make and sell electric cars for the Chinese market.

Studies indicate that large corporations are commonly involved in 30 to 50 alliances and that a number have hundreds of alliances. One study estimated that corporate revenues coming from activities involving strategic alliances have more than doubled since 1995.[34] Another study reported that the typical large corporation relied on alliances for 15 to 20 percent of its revenues, assets, or income.[35] Companies that have formed a host of alliances have a need to manage their alliances like a portfolio—terminating those that no longer serve a useful purpose or that have produced meager results, forming promising new alliances, and restructuring certain existing alliances to correct performance problems and/or redirect the collaborative effort.[36]

Company use of alliances is quite widespread.

Why and How Strategic Alliances Are Advantageous

The most common reasons companies enter into strategic alliances are to expedite the development of promising new technologies or products, to overcome deficits in their own technical and manufacturing expertise, to bring together the personnel and expertise needed to create desirable new skill sets and capabilities, to improve supply chain efficiency, to share the risks of high-stake, risky ventures, to gain economies of scale in production and/or marketing, and to acquire or improve market access through joint marketing agreements.[37] Manufacturers frequently pursue alliances with parts and components suppliers to gain the efficiencies of better supply chain management and to speed new products to market. By joining forces in components production and/or final assembly, companies may be able to realize cost savings not achievable with their own small volumes. Allies can learn much from one another in performing joint research, sharing technological know-how, and collaborating on complementary new technologies and products—sometimes enough to enable them to pursue other new opportunities on their own.[38] In industries where technology is advancing rapidly, alliances are all about fast cycles of learning, staying abreast of the latest developments, gaining quick access to the latest round of technological know-how, and developing dynamic capabilities. In bringing together firms with different skills and knowledge bases, alliances open up learning opportunities that help partner firms better leverage their own resources and capabilities.[39]

The best alliances are highly selective, focusing on particular value-creating activities, whether within or across industry boundaries, and on obtaining a specific competitive benefit. They enable a firm to build on its strengths and to learn.

There are several other instances in which companies find strategic alliances particularly valuable. As we explain in the next chapter, a company that is racing for *global market leadership* needs alliances to:[40]

- *Get into critical country markets quickly* and accelerate the process of building a potent global market presence.
- *Gain inside knowledge about unfamiliar markets and cultures through alliances with local partners.* For example, U.S., European, and Japanese companies wanting to build market footholds in the fast-growing Chinese market have pursued partnership arrangements with Chinese companies to help get products through the customs process, to help guide them through the maze of government regulations, to supply knowledge of local markets, to provide guidance on adapting their products to better match the buying preferences of Chinese consumers, to set up local manufacturing capabilities, and to assist in distribution, marketing, and promotional activities.
- *Access valuable skills and competencies* that are concentrated in particular geographic locations (such as software design competencies in the United States, fashion design skills in Italy, and efficient manufacturing skills in Japan and China).

A company that is racing to *stake out a strong position in an industry of the future* needs alliances to:[41]

- *Establish a stronger beachhead* for participating in the target industry.
- *Master new technologies and build new expertise and competencies* faster than would be possible through internal efforts.
- *Open up broader opportunities* in the target industry by melding the firm's own capabilities with the expertise and resources of partners.

Capturing the Benefits of Strategic Alliances

The extent to which companies benefit from entering into alliances and partnerships seems to be a function of six factors:[42]

1. *Picking a good partner.* A good partner must bring complementary strengths to the relationship. To the extent that alliance members have nonoverlapping strengths, there is greater potential for synergy and less potential for coordination problems and conflict. In addition, a good partner needs to share the company's vision about the overall purpose of the alliance and to have specific goals that either match or complement those of the company. Strong partnerships also depend on good chemistry among key personnel and compatible views about how the alliance should be structured and managed.

2. *Being sensitive to cultural differences.* Cultural differences among companies can make it difficult for their personnel to work together effectively. Cultural differences can be problematic among companies from the same country, but when the partners have different national origins, the problems are often magnified. Unless there is respect among all the parties for company cultural differences, including those stemming from different local cultures and local business practices, productive working relationships are unlikely to emerge.

3. *Recognizing that the alliance must benefit both sides.* Information must be shared as well as gained, and the relationship must remain forthright and trustful. Many alliances fail because one or both partners grow unhappy with what they are learning. Also, if either partner plays games with information or tries to take advantage of the other, the resulting friction can quickly erode the value of further collaboration. Open, trustworthy behavior on both sides is essential for fruitful collaboration.

4. *Ensuring that both parties live up to their commitments.* Both parties have to deliver on their commitments for the alliance to produce the intended benefits. The division of work has to be perceived as fairly apportioned, and the caliber of the benefits received on both sides has to be perceived as adequate. Such actions are critical for the establishment of trust between the parties; research has shown that trust is an important factor in fostering effective strategic alliances.[43]

5. *Structuring the decision-making process so that actions can be taken swiftly when needed.* In many instances, the fast pace of technological and competitive changes dictates an equally fast decision-making process. If the parties get bogged down in discussions or in gaining internal approval from higher-ups, the alliance can turn into an anchor of delay and inaction.

6. *Managing the learning process and then adjusting the alliance agreement over time to fit new circumstances.* One of the keys to long-lasting success is adapting the nature and structure of the alliance to be responsive to shifting market conditions, emerging technologies, and changing customer requirements. Wise allies are quick to recognize the merit of an evolving collaborative arrangement, where adjustments are made to accommodate changing market conditions and to overcome whatever problems arise in establishing an effective working relationship. Most alliances encounter troubles of some kind within a couple of years—those that are flexible enough to evolve are better able to recover.[44]

Most alliances that aim at sharing technology or providing market access turn out to be temporary, lasting only a few years. This is not necessarily an indicator of failure, however. Strategic alliances can be terminated after a few years simply because they have fulfilled their purpose; indeed, many alliances are intended to be of limited duration, set up to accomplish specific short-term objectives. Longer-lasting collaborative arrangements, however, may provide even greater strategic benefits. Alliances are more likely to be long-lasting when (1) they involve collaboration with partners that do not compete directly, (2) a trusting relationship has been established, and (3) both parties conclude that continued collaboration is in their mutual interest, perhaps because new opportunities for learning are emerging.

The Drawbacks of Strategic Alliances and Partnerships

While strategic alliances provide a way of obtaining the benefits of vertical integration, mergers and acquisitions, and outsourcing, they also suffer from some of the same drawbacks. Culture clash and integration problems due to different management styles and business practices can interfere with the success of an alliance, just as they can with vertical integration or horizontal mergers and acquisitions. Anticipated gains may fail to materialize due to an overly optimistic view of the synergies or a poor fit in terms of the combination of resources and capabilities. When outsourcing is conducted via alliances, there is no less risk of becoming dependent on other companies for essential expertise and capabilities— indeed, this may be the Achilles' heel of such alliances.

Moreover, there are additional pitfalls to collaborative arrangements. The greatest danger is that a partner will gain access to a company's proprietary knowledge base, technologies, or trade secrets, enabling the partner to match the company's core strengths and costing the company its hard-won competitive advantage. This risk is greatest when the alliance is among industry rivals or when the alliance is for the purpose of collaborative R&D, since this type of partnership requires an extensive exchange of closely held information.

The question for managers is when to engage in a strategic alliance and when to choose an alternative means of meeting their objectives. The answer to this question depends on the relative advantages of each method and the circumstances under which each type of organizational arrangement is favored.

The principle advantages of strategic alliances over vertical integration or horizontal mergers/acquisitons are threefold:

1. They lower investment costs and risks for each partner by facilitating resource pooling and risk sharing. This can be particularly important when investment needs and uncertainty are high, such as when a dominant technology standard has not yet emerged.
2. They are more flexible organizational forms and allow for a more adaptive response to changing conditions. Flexibility is key when environmental conditions or technologies are changing rapidly. Moreover, strategic alliances under such circumstances may enable the development of each partner's dynamic capabilities.
3. They are more rapidly deployed—a critical factor when speed is of the essence. Speed is of the essence when there is a winner-take-all type of competitive situation, such as the race for a dominant technological design or a race down a steep experience curve, where there is a large first-mover advantage.

The key advantages of using strategic alliances rather than arm's-length transactions to manage outsourcing are (1) the increased ability to exercise control over the partners' activities and (2) a greater willingness for the partners to make relationship-specific investments. Arm's-length transactions discourage such investments since they imply less commitment and do not build trust.

On the other hand, there are circumstances when other organizational mechanisms are preferable to partnering. Mergers and acquisitions are especially suited for situations in which strategic alliances or partnerships do not go far enough in providing a company with access to needed resources and capabilities.[45] Ownership ties are more permanent than partnership ties, allowing the operations of the merger/acquisition participants to be tightly integrated and creating more in-house control and autonomy. Other organizational mechanisms are also preferable to alliances when there is limited property rights protection for valuable know-how and when companies fear being taken advantage of by opportunistic partners.

While it is important for managers to understand when strategic alliances and partnerships are most likely (and least likely) to prove useful, it is also important to know how to manage them.

How to Make Strategic Alliances Work

A surprisingly large number of alliances never live up to expectations. A recent article reported that even though the number of strategic alliances increases by about 25 percent annually, about 60 to 70 percent of alliances continue to fail each year.[46] The success of an alliance depends on how well the partners work together, their capacity to respond and adapt to changing internal and external conditions, and their willingness to renegotiate the bargain if circumstances so warrant. A successful alliance requires real in-the-trenches collaboration, not merely an arm's-length exchange of ideas. Unless partners place a high value on the skills, resources, and contributions each brings to the alliance and the cooperative arrangement results in valuable win-win outcomes, it is doomed.

While the track record for strategic alliances is poor on average, many companies have learned how to manage strategic alliances successfully and routinely defy these averages. Samsung Group, which includes Samsung Electronics and had worldwide sales of $117.8 billion in 2009, successfully manages an ecosystem of over 1,300 partnerships that enable productive activities from global procurement to local marketing to collaborative R&D. Samsung Group takes a systematic approach to managing its partnerships and devotes considerable resources to this enterprise. In 2008, for example, it established a Partner Collaboration and Enhancement Office under the direct control of its CEO. Samsung Group supports its partners with financial help as well as training and development resources to ensure that its alliance partners' technical, manufacturing, and management capabilities remain globally competitive. As a result, some of its equipment providers have emerged as the leading firms in their industries while contributing to Samsung's competitive advantage in the global TV market.

Companies that have greater success in managing their strategic alliances and partnerships often credit the following factors:

- *They create a system for managing their alliances.* Companies need to manage their alliances in a systematic fashion, just as they manage other functions.

This means setting up a process for managing the different aspects of alliance management from partner selection to alliance termination procedures. To ensure that the system is followed on a routine basis by all company managers, many companies create a set of explicit procedures, process templates, manuals, or the like.

- *They build relationships with their partners and establish trust.* Establishing strong interpersonal relationships is a critical factor in making strategic alliances work since they facilitate opening up channels of communication, coordinating activity, aligning interests, and building trust. Cultural sensitivity is a key part of this, particularly for cross-border alliances. Accordingly, many companies include cultural sensitivity training for their managers as a part of their alliance management program.

- *They protect themselves from the threat of opportunism by setting up safeguards.* There are a number of means for preventing a company from being taken advantage of by an untrustworthy partner or unwittingly losing control over key assets. Contractual safeguards, including noncompete clauses, can provide some protection. But if the company's core assets are vulnerable to being appropriated by partners, it may be possible to control their use and strictly limit outside access. Cisco Systems, for example, does not divulge the source code for its designs to its alliance partners, thereby controlling the initiation of all improvements and safeguarding its innovations from imitation.

- *They make commitments to their partners and see that their partners do the same.* When partners make credible commitments to a joint enterprise, they have stronger incentives for making it work and are less likely to "free-ride" on the efforts of other partners. Because of this, equity-based alliances tend to be more successful than nonequity alliances.[47]

- *They make learning a routine part of the management process.* There are always opportunities for learning from a partner, but organizational learning does not take place automatically. Moreover, whatever learning takes place cannot add to a company's knowledge base unless the learning is incorporated into the company's routines and practices. Particularly when the purpose of an alliance is to improve a company's knowledge assets and capabilities, it is important for the company to learn thoroughly and rapidly about its partners' technologies, business practices, and organizational capabilities and then transfer valuable ideas and practices into its own operations promptly.

Finally, managers should realize that alliance management is an organizational capability, much like any other. It develops over time, out of effort, experience, and learning. For this reason, it is wise to begin slowly, with simple alliances, designed to meet limited, short-term objectives. Short-term partnerships that are successful often become the basis for much more extensive collaborative arrangements. Even when strategic alliances are set up with the hope that they will become long-term engagements, they have a better chance of succeeding if they are phased in so that the partners can learn how they can work together most fruitfully.

KEY POINTS

1. Once a company has settled on which of the five generic competitive strategies to employ, attention turns to how strategic choices regarding (1) competitive actions, (2) timing, and (3) scope of operations can complement its competitive approach and maximize the power of its overall strategy.

2. Strategic offensives should, as a general rule, be grounded in a company's strategic assets. The best offensives use a company's resource and capability strengths to attack rivals in the competitive areas where they are comparatively weakest.

3. Companies have a number of offensive strategy options for improving their market positions: using a cost-based advantage to attack competitors on the basis of price or value, leapfrogging competitors with next-generation technologies, pursuing continuous product innovation, adopting and improving the best ideas of others, using hit-and-run tactics to steal sales away from unsuspecting rivals, and launching preemptive strikes. A blue-ocean type of offensive strategy seeks to gain a dramatic and durable competitive advantage by abandoning efforts to beat out competitors in existing markets and, instead, inventing a new industry or distinctive market segment that renders existing competitors largely irrelevant and allows a company to create and capture altogether new demand.

4. The purposes of defensive strategies are to lower the risk of being attacked, weaken the impact of any attack that occurs, and influence challengers to aim their efforts at other rivals. Defensive strategies to protect a company's position usually take one of two forms: (1) actions to block challengers and (2) actions to signal the likelihood of strong retaliation.

5. The timing of strategic moves also has competitive relevance and is especially important when first-mover advantages or disadvantages exist. Company managers are obligated to carefully consider the advantages or disadvantages that attach to being a first mover versus a fast follower versus a wait-and-see late mover.

6. Decisions concerning the scope of a company's operations—which activities a firm will perform internally and which it will not—can also affect the strength of a company's market position. The *scope of the firm* refers to the range of its activities, the breadth of its product and service offerings, the extent of its geographic market presence, and its mix of businesses. Companies can expand their scope horizontally (more broadly within their focal market) or vertically (up or down the chain of value-adding activities that start with raw-material production and end with sales and service to the end consumer). Horizontal mergers and acquisitions (combinations of market rivals) provide a means for a company to expand its horizontal scope. Vertical integration expands a firm's vertical scope.

7. Horizontal mergers and acquisitions can strengthen a firm's competitiveness in five ways: (1) by improving the efficiency of its operations, (2) by heightening its product differentiation, (3) by reducing market rivalry, (3) by increasing the company's bargaining power over suppliers and buyers, and (5) by enhancing its flexibility and dynamic capabilities.

8. Vertical integration, forward or backward, makes strategic sense only if it strengthens a company's position via either cost reduction or creation of a differentiation-based advantage. Otherwise, the drawbacks of vertical integration (increased investment, greater business risk, increased vulnerability to technological changes, less flexibility in making product changes, and the potential for channel conflict) are likely to outweigh any advantages.

9. Outsourcing involves farming out pieces of the value chain formerly performed in-house to outside vendors, thereby narrowing the scope of the firm. Outsourcing can enhance a company's competitiveness whenever (1) an activity can be performed better or more cheaply by outside specialists; (2) having the activity performed by others won't hollow out the outsourcing company's core competencies; (3) it streamlines company operations in ways that improve organizational flexibility, speed decision making, and cut cycle time; (4) it reduces the company's risk exposure; (5) it allows a company to access capabilities more quickly and improves its ability to innovate; and (6) it permits a company to concentrate on its core business and focus on what it does best.

10. Strategic alliances and cooperative partnerships provide one way to gain some of the benefits offered by vertical integration, outsourcing, and horizontal mergers and acquisitions while minimizing the associated problems. They serve as an alternative to vertical integration and mergers and acquisitions; they serve as a supplement to outsourcing, allowing more control relative to outsourcing via arm's-length transactions.

11. Companies that manage their alliances well generally (1) create a system for managing their alliances, (2) build relationships with their partners and establish trust, (3) protect themselves from the threat of opportunism by setting up safeguards, (4) make commitments to their partners and see that their partners do the same, and (5) make learning a routine part of the management process.

ASSURANCE OF LEARNING EXERCISES

LO 3

1. Using your university library's subscription to Lexis-Nexis, EBSCO, or a similar database, perform a search on "acquisition strategy." Identify at least two companies in different industries that are using acquisitions to strengthen their market positions. How have these acquisitions enhanced the acquiring companies' competitive capabilities?

LO 4

2. Go to www.bridgestone.co.jp/english/ir, and review information about Bridgestone Corporation's tire and raw-material operations under the About Bridgestone and IR Library links. To what extent is the company vertically integrated? What segments of the vertical chain has the company chosen to enter? What are the benefits and liabilities of Bridgestone's vertical integration strategy?

LO 5, LO 6

3. Go to www.google.com, and do a search on "outsourcing." Identify at least two companies in different industries that have entered into outsourcing agreements with firms with specialized services. In addition, describe what value chain activities the companies have chosen to outsource. Do any of these outsourcing agreements seem likely to threaten any of the companies' competitive capabilities? Are the companies using strategic alliances to manage their outsourcing?

EXERCISES FOR SIMULATION PARTICIPANTS

LO 1

1. What offensive strategy options does your company have? Identify at least two offensive moves that your company should seriously consider to improve the company's market standing and financial performance.

LO 2

2. What options for being a first mover does your company have? Do any of these first-mover options hold competitive advantage potential?

LO 1

3. What defensive strategy moves should your company consider in the upcoming decision round? Identify at least two defensive actions that your company has taken in a past decision round.

LO 3

4. Does your company have the option to merge with or acquire other companies? If so, which rival companies would you like to acquire or merge with?

LO 4

5. Is your company vertically integrated? Explain.

LO 5, LO 6

6. Is your company able to engage in outsourcing? If so, what do you see as the pros and cons of outsourcing? Are strategic alliances involved? Explain.

ENDNOTES

[1] An insightful discussion of aggressive offensive strategies is presented in George Stalk, Jr., and Rob Lachenauer, "Hardball: Five Killer Strategies for Trouncing the Competition," *Harvard Business Review* 82, no. 4 (April 2004), pp. 62–71. For a discussion of offensive strategies to enter attractive markets where existing firms are making above-average profits, see David J. Bryce and Jeffrey H. Dyer, "Strategies to Crack Well-Guarded Markets," *Harvard Business Review* 85, no. 5 (May 2007), pp. 84–92. A discussion of offensive strategies particularly suitable for industry leaders is presented in Richard D'Aveni, "The Empire Strikes Back: Counterrevolutionary Strategies for Industry Leaders," *Harvard Business Review* 80, no. 11 (November 2002), pp. 66–74.

[2] George Stalk, "Playing Hardball: Why Strategy Still Matters," *Ivey Business Journal* 69, no.2 (November–December 2004), pp. 1–2. See K. G. Smith, W. J. Ferrier, and C. M. Grimm, "King of the Hill: Dethroning the Industry Leader," *Academy of Management Executive* 15, no. 2 (May 2001), pp. 59–70; also see W. J. Ferrier, K. G. Smith, and C. M. Grimm, "The Role of Competitive Action

in Market Share Erosion and Industry Dethronement: A Study of Industry Leaders and Challengers," *Academy of Management Journal* 42, no. 4 (August 1999), pp. 372–88.

[3] For a discussion of how to wage offensives against strong rivals, see David B. Yoffie and Mary Kwak, "Mastering Balance: How to Meet and Beat a Stronger Opponent," *California Management Review* 44, no. 2 (Winter 2002), pp. 8–24.

[4] Stalk, "Playing Hardball," pp. 1–2.

[5] Ian C. MacMillan, Alexander B. van Putten, and Rita Gunther McGrath, "Global Gamesmanship," *Harvard Business Review* 81, no. 5 (May 2003), pp. 66–67; also see Ashkay R. Rao, Mark E. Bergen, and Scott Davis, "How to Fight a Price War," *Harvard Business Review* 78, no. 2 (March–April 2000), pp. 107–16.

[6] D. B. Yoffie and M. A. Cusumano, "Judo Strategy—The Competitive Dynamics of Internet Time," *Harvard Business* Review 77, no. 1 (January–February 1999), pp. 70–81.

[7] Stalk and Lachenauer, "Hardball: Five Killer Strategies," p. 64.

[8] For an interesting study of how small firms can successfully employ guerrilla-style tactics, see Ming-Jer Chen and Donald C. Hambrick, "Speed, Stealth, and Selective Attack: How Small Firms Differ from Large Firms in Competitive Behavior," *Academy of Management Journal* 38, no. 2 (April 1995), pp. 453–82. Other discussions of guerrilla offensives can be found in Ian MacMillan, "How Business Strategists Can Use Guerrilla Warfare Tactics," *Journal of Business Strategy* 1, no. 2 (Fall 1980), pp. 63–65; William E. Rothschild, "Surprise and the Competitive Advantage," *Journal of Business Strategy* 4, no. 3 (Winter 1984), pp. 10–18; Kathryn R. Harrigan, *Strategic Flexibility* (Lexington, MA: Lexington Books, 1985), pp. 30–45; Liam Fahey, "Guerrilla Strategy: The Hit-and-Run Attack," in Liam Fahey (ed.), *The Strategic Management Planning Reader* (Englewood Cliffs, NJ: Prentice Hall, 1989), pp. 194–97.

[9] Yoffie and Cusumano, "Judo Strategy." See also D. B. Yoffie and M. Kwak, "Mastering Balance: How to Meet and Beat a Stronger Opponent," *California Management Review* 44, no. 2 (Winter 2002), pp. 8–24.

[10] The use of preemptive strike offensives is treated comprehensively in Ian MacMillan, "Preemptive Strategies," *Journal of Business Strategy* 14, no. 2 (Fall 1983), pp. 16–26.

[11] Ian C. MacMillan, "How Long Can You Sustain a Competitive Advantage?" in Liam Fahey (ed.), *The Strategic Planning Management Reader* (Englewood Cliffs, NJ: Prentice Hall, 1989), pp. 23–24.

[12] For a discussion of competitors' reactions, see Kevin P. Coyne and John Horn, "Predicting Your Competitor's Reactions," *Harvard Business Review* 87 no. 4 (April 2009), pp. 90–97.

[13] Philip Kotler, *Marketing Management,* 5th ed. (Englewood Cliffs, NJ: Prentice Hall, 1984), p. 400.

[14] Michael E. Porter, *Competitive Advantage* (New York: Free Press, 1985), p. 518.

[15] W. Chan Kim and Renée Mauborgne, "Blue Ocean Strategy," *Harvard Business Review* 82, no. 10 (October 2004), pp. 76–84.

[16] Porter, *Competitive Advantage,* pp. 489–94.

[17] Ibid., pp. 495–97. The list here is selective; Porter offers a greater number of options.

[18] Ibid., pp. 232–33.

[19] For research evidence on the effects of pioneering versus following, see Jeffrey G. Covin, Dennis P. Slevin, and Michael B. Heeley, "Pioneers and Followers: Competitive Tactics, Environment, and Growth," *Journal of Business Venturing* 15, no. 2 (March 1999), pp. 175–210; Christopher A. Bartlett and Sumantra Ghoshal, "Going Global: Lessons from Late-Movers," *Harvard Business Review* 78, no. 2 (March–April 2000), pp. 132–45.

[20] Gary Hamel, "Smart Mover, Dumb Mover," *Fortune,* September 3, 2001, p. 195.

[21] Ibid., p.192; Costas Markides and Paul A. Geroski, Racing to be 2nd: Conquering the Industries of the Future," *Business Strategy Review* 15, no. 4 (Winter 2004), pp. 25–31.

[22] For a more extensive discussion, see Fernando Suarez and Gianvito Lanzolla, "The Half-Truth of First-Mover Advantage," *Harvard Business Review* 83, no. 4 (April 2005), pp. 121–27.

[23] Henry Gibbon, "Worldwide M&A Declines 28% to US$2trn," *Acquisitions Monthly,* January 2010 (issue 303), pp. 4–11.

[24] For an excellent review of the strategic objectives of various types of mergers and acquisitions and the managerial challenges that different kinds of mergers and acquisitions present, see Joseph L. Bower, "Not All M&As Are Alike—and That Matters," *Harvard Business Review* 79, no. 3 (March 2001), pp. 93–101.

[25] O. Chatain and P. Zemsky, "The Horizontal Scope of the Firm: Organizational Tradeoffs vs. Buyer-Supplier Relationships," *Management Science* 53, no. 4 (April 2007), pp. 550–65.

[26] For a more expansive discussion, see Jeffrey H. Dyer, Prashant Kale, and Harbir Singh, "When to Ally and When to Acquire," *Harvard Business Review* 82, no. 4 (July–August 2004), pp. 109–10.

[27] See Kathryn R. Harrigan, "Matching Vertical Integration Strategies to Competitive Conditions," *Strategic Management Journal* 7, no. 6 (November–December 1986), pp. 535–56; for a more extensive discussion of the advantages and disadvantages of vertical integration, see John Stuckey and David White, "When and When Not to Vertically Integrate," *Sloan Management Review* (Spring 1993), pp. 71–83.

[28] The resilience of vertical integration strategies despite the disadvantages is discussed in Thomas Osegowitsch and Anoop Madhok, "Vertical Integration Is Dead, or Is It?" *Business Horizons* 46, no. 2 (March–April 2003), pp. 25–35.

[29] For a good overview of outsourcing strategies, see Ronan McIvor, "What Is the Right Outsourcing Strategy for Your Process?" *European Management Journal* 26, no. 1 (February 2008), pp. 24–34.

[30] For a good discussion of the problems that can arise from outsourcing, see Gary P. Pisano and Willy C. Shih, "Restoring American Competitiveness," *Harvard Business Review* 87, no. 7–8 (July–August 2009), pp. 114–25; Jérôme Barthélemy, "The Seven Deadly Sins of Outsourcing," *Academy of Management Executive* 17, no. 2 (May 2003), pp. 87–100.

[31] Pisano and Shih, "Restoring American Competitivness," pp. 116–17.

[32] Jason Wakeam, "The Five Factors of a Strategic Alliance," *Ivey Business Journal* 68, no 3 (May–June 2003), pp. 1–4.

[33] *Advertising Age,* May 24, 2010, p. 14.

[34] Salvatore Parise and Lisa Sasson, "Leveraging Knowledge Management across Strategic Alliances," *Ivey Business Journal* 66, no. 4 (March–April 2002), p. 42.

[35] David Ernst and James Bamford, "Your Alliances Are Too Stable," *Harvard Business Review* 83, no. 6 (June 2005), p.133.

[36] An excellent discussion of the portfolio approach to managing multiple alliances and how to restructure a faltering alliance is presented in Ernst and Bamford, "Your Alliances Are Too Stable," pp. 133–41.

[37] Michael E. Porter, *The Competitive Advantage of Nations* (New York: Free Press, 1990), p. 66. For a discussion of how to realize the advantages of strategic partnerships, see Nancy J. Kaplan and Jonathan Hurd, "Realizing the Promise of Partnerships," *Journal of Business Strategy* 23, no. 3 (May–June 2002), pp. 38–42; Parise and Sasson, "Leveraging Knowledge Management across Strategic Alliances," pp. 41-47; Ernst and Bamford, "Your Alliances Are Too Stable," pp. 133–41; and Jonathan Hughes and Jeff Weiss, "Simple Rules for Making Alliances Work," *Harvard Business Review* 85, no. 11 (November 2007), pp. 122–31.

[38] For a discussion of how to raise the chances that a strategic alliance will produce strategically important outcomes, see M. Koza and A. Lewin, "Managing Partnerships and Strategic Alliances: Raising the Odds of Success," *European Management Journal* 18, no. 2 (April 2000), pp. 146–51.

[39] A. Inkpen, "Learning, Knowledge Acquisition, and Strategic Alliances," *European Management Journal* 16, no. 2 (April 1998), pp. 223–29.

[40] Yves L. Doz and Gary Hamel, *Alliance Advantage: The Art of Creating Value through Partnering* (Boston: Harvard Business School Press), chap. 1.

[41] Ibid.

[42] Ibid., chaps. 4–8; Patricia Anslinger and Justin Jenk, "Creating Successful Alliances," *Journal of Business Strategy* 25, no. 2 (2004), pp. 18–23; Rosabeth Moss Kanter, "Collaborative Advantage: The Art of the Alliance," *Harvard Business Review* 72, no. 4 (July–August 1994), pp. 96–108; Joel Bleeke and David Ernst, "The Way to Win in

Cross-Border Alliances," *Harvard Business Review* 69, no. 6 (November–December 1991), pp. 127–35; Gary Hamel, Yves L. Doz, and C. K. Prahalad, "Collaborate with Your Competitors—and Win," *Harvard Business Review* 67, no. 1 (January–February 1989), pp. 133–39; Hughes and Weiss, "Simple Rules for Making Alliances Work."

[43] J. B. Cullen, J. L. Johnson, and T. Sakano, "Success through Commitment and Trust: The Soft Side of Strategic Alliance Management," *Journal of World Business* 35, no. 3 (Fall 2000), pp. 223–40; T. K. Das and B. S. Teng, "Between Trust and Control: Developing Confidence in Partner Cooperation in Alliances," *Academy of Management Review* 23, no. 3 (July 1998), pp. 491–512.

[44] K. M. Eisenhardt and C. B. Schoonhoven, "Resource-Based View of Strategic Alliance Formation: Strategic and Social Effects in Entrepreneurial Firms," *Organization Science* 7, no. 2 (March–April 1996), pp. 136–50; M. Zollo, J. J. Reuer, and H. Singh, "Interorganizational Routines and Performance in Strategic Alliances," *Organization Science* 13, no. 6 (November–December 2002), pp. 701–13.

[45] The pros and cons of mergers/acquisitions versus strategic alliances are described in Dyer, Kale, and Singh, "When to Ally and When to Acquire," pp. 109–15.

[46] Hughes and Weiss, "Simple Rules for Making Alliances Work," p. 122.

[47] Y. G. Pan and D. K. Tse, "The Hierarchical Model of Market Entry Modes," *Journal of International Business Studies* 31, no. 4 (2000), pp. 535–54.

CHAPTER 7

STRATEGIES FOR COMPETING IN INTERNATIONAL MARKETS

> We're not going global because we want to or because of any megalomania, but because it's really necessary. . . . The costs are so enormous today that you really need to have worldwide revenues to cover them.
>
> **—Rupert Murdoch**
> *CEO of the media conglomerate News Corporation*

> Globalization [provides] a long-lasting competitive advantage. If we build a new gas turbine, in 18 months our competitors also have one. But building a global company is not so easy to copy.
>
> **—Percy Barnevik**
> *Former CEO of the Swiss-Swedish industrial corporation ABB*

> Capital, technology, and ideas flow these days like quicksilver across national boundaries.
>
> **—Robert H. Waterman, Jr.**
> *Internationally recognized expert on management practices*

LEARNING OBJECTIVES

LO 1. Develop an understanding of the primary reasons companies choose to compete in international markets.

LO 2. Learn how and why differing market conditions across countries and industries make crafting international strategy a complex undertaking.

LO 3. Learn about the major strategic options for entering and competing in foreign markets.

LO 4. Gain familiarity with the three main strategic approaches for competing internationally.

LO 5. Understand how international companies go about building competitive advantage in foreign markets.

Any company that aspires to industry leadership in the 21st century must think in terms of global, not domestic, market leadership. The world economy is globalizing at an accelerating pace as ambitious growth-minded companies race to build stronger competitive positions in the markets of more and more countries, as countries previously closed to foreign companies open up their markets, as companies in developing countries gain competitive strength, and as advances in information technology and communication shrink the importance of geographic distance. The forces of globalization are changing the competitive landscape in many industries, offering companies attractive new opportunities but at the same time introducing new competitive threats. Companies in industries where these forces are greatest are therefore under considerable pressure to come up with a strategy for competing successfully in foreign markets.

This chapter focuses on strategy options for expanding beyond domestic boundaries and competing in the markets of either a few or a great many countries. In the process of exploring these issues, we will introduce such concepts as multidomestic, global, and transnational strategies; the Porter diamond of national advantage; and cross-country differences in cultural, demographic, and market conditions. The chapter also includes sections on strategy options for entering and competing in foreign markets; the importance of locating value chain operations in the most advantageous countries; and the special circumstances of competing in such developing markets as China, India, Brazil, Russia, and eastern Europe.

WHY COMPANIES DECIDE TO ENTER FOREIGN MARKETS

LO 1

Develop an understanding of the primary reasons companies choose to compete in international markets.

A company may opt to expand outside its domestic market for any of five major reasons:

1. *To gain access to new customers.* Expanding into foreign markets offers potential for increased revenues, profits, and long-term growth and becomes an especially attractive option when a company's home markets are mature and nearing saturation levels. Companies often expand internationally to extend the life cycle of their products, as Honda has done with its classic 50-cc motorcycle, the Honda cub (which is still selling well in developing markets, more than 50 years after it was first introduced in Japan). A larger target market also offers companies the opportunity to earn a return on large investments more rapidly. This can be particularly important in R&D-intensive industries, where development is fast-paced or competitors imitate innovations rapidly.

2. *To achieve lower costs through economies of scale, experience, and increased purchasing power.* Many companies are driven to sell in more than one country because domestic sales volume alone is not large enough to fully capture economies of scale in product development, manufacturing, or marketing. Similarly, firms expand internationally to increase the rate at which they accumulate experience and move down the learning curve. International expansion can also lower a company's input costs through greater pooled purchasing power. The relatively small size of country markets in Europe and limited domestic volume explains why companies like Michelin, BMW, and Nestlé long ago began selling their products all across Europe and then moved into markets in North America and Latin America.

3. *To further exploit its core competencies.* A company with competitively valuable resources and capabilities can often extend a market-leading position in its home market into a position of regional or global market leadership by leveraging these resources further. Nokia's competencies and capabilities in mobile phones have propelled it to global market leadership in the wireless telecommunications business. Walmart is capitalizing on its considerable expertise in discount retailing to expand into China, Latin America, Japan, South Korea, and the United Kingdom; Walmart executives believe the company has tremendous growth opportunities in China. Companies can often leverage their resources internationally by replicating a successful business model, using it as a basic blueprint for international operations, as Starbucks and McDonald's have done.[1]

4. *To gain access to resources and capabilities located in foreign markets.* An increasingly important motive for entering foreign markets is to acquire resources and capabilities that cannot be accessed as readily in a company's home market. Companies often enter into cross-border alliances or joint ventures, for example, to gain access to resources and capabilities that complement their own or to learn from their partners.[2] Cross-border acquisitions are commonly made for similar reasons.[3] In other cases, companies choose to establish operations in other countries to utilize local distribution networks, employ low-cost human resources, or acquire technical knowledge. In a few

cases, companies in industries based on natural resources (e.g., oil and gas, minerals, rubber, and lumber) find it necessary to operate in the international arena because attractive raw-material supplies are located in many different parts of the world.

5. *To spread its business risk across a wider market base.* A company spreads business risk by operating in many different countries rather than depending entirely on operations in a few countries. Thus, when a company with operations across much of the world encounters economic downturns in certain countries, its performance may be bolstered by buoyant sales elsewhere.

In addition, companies that are the suppliers of other companies often expand internationally when their major customers do so, to meet their needs abroad and retain their position as a key supply chain partner. Automotive parts suppliers, for example, have followed automobile manufacturers abroad, and retail goods suppliers have followed large retailers into foreign markets.

WHY COMPETING ACROSS NATIONAL BORDERS MAKES STRATEGY MAKING MORE COMPLEX

Crafting a strategy to compete in one or more countries of the world is inherently more complex because of (1) factors that affect industry competitiveness that vary from country to country, (2) the potential for location-based advantages in certain countries, (3) different government policies and economic conditions that make the business climate more favorable in some countries than in others, (4) the risks of adverse shifts in currency exchange rates, and (5) cross-country differences in cultural, demographic, and market conditions.

LO 2

Learn how and why differing market conditions across countries and industries make crafting international strategy a complex undertaking.

Cross-Country Variation in Factors That Affect Industry Competitiveness

Certain countries are known for their strengths in particular industries. For example, Chile has competitive strengths in industries such as copper, fruit, fish products, paper and pulp, chemicals, and wine. Japan is known for competitive strength in consumer electronics, automobiles, semiconductors, steel products, and specialty steel. Where industries are more likely to develop competitive strength depends on a set of factors that describe the nature of each country's business environment and vary across countries. Because strong industries are made up of strong firms, the strategies of firms that expand internationally are usually grounded in one or more of these factors. The four major factors are summarized in a framework known as the *Diamond of National Advantage* (see Figure 7.1).[4]

Demand Conditions
The demand conditions in an industry's home market include the relative size of the market and the nature of domestic buyers' needs and wants. Industry sectors that are larger and more important in their home market tend to attract more resources and grow faster than others. Demanding domestic buyers for an industry's products spur greater innovativeness and improvements in quality. Such conditions foster the development of stronger

Figure 7.1   The Diamond of National Advantage

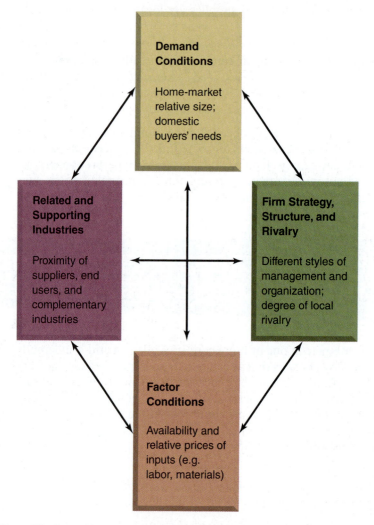

Source: Adapted from M. Porter, "The Competitive Advantage of Nations," *Harvard Business Review*, March–April 1990, pp. 73–93.

industries, with firms that are capable of translating a home-market advantage into a competitive advantage in the international arena.

Factor Conditions   Factor conditions describe the availability, quality, and cost of raw materials and other inputs (called *factors*) that firms in an industry require to produce their products and services. The relevant factors vary from industry to industry but can include different types of labor, technical or managerial knowledge, land, financial capital, and natural resources. Elements of a country's infrastructure may be included as well, such as its transportation, communication, and banking system. For instance, in India there are efficient, well-developed national channels for distributing trucks, scooters, farm equipment, groceries, personal care items, and other packaged products to the country's 3 million retailers, whereas in China distribution is primarily local and there is a limited national network for distributing most products. Competitively strong industries and firms develop where relevant factor conditions are favorable.

Related and Supporting Industries   Robust industries often develop as part of a cluster of related industries, including suppliers of components and capital equipment, end users, and the makers of complementary products, including those that are technologically related. The sports car makers Ferrari and Maserati, for example, are located in an area of Italy known as the "engine technological district" that includes other firms involved in racing, such as Ducati Motorcycles, along with hundreds of small suppliers. The advantage to firms that develop as part of a related-industry cluster comes from the close collaboration with key suppliers and the greater knowledge sharing throughout the cluster, resulting in greater efficiency and innovativeness.

Firm Strategy, Structure, and Rivalry   Different country environments foster the development of different styles of management, organization, and strategy. For example, strategic alliances are a more common strategy for firms from Asian or Latin American countries, which emphasize trust and cooperation in their organizations, than for firms from North American, where individualism is more influential. In addition, countries vary in terms of the competitiveness of their industries. Fierce competitive conditions in home markets tend to hone domestic firms' competitive capabilities and ready them for competing internationally.

For an industry in a particular country to become competitively strong, all four factors must be favorable for that industry. When they are, the industry is likely to contain firms that are capable of competing successfully in the international arena. Thus the diamond framework can be used to reveal the answers to several questions that are important for competing on an international basis. First, it can help predict where foreign entrants into an industry are most likely to come from. This can help managers prepare to cope with new foreign competitors, since the framework also reveals something about the basis of the new rivals' strengths. Second, it can reveal the countries in which foreign rivals are likely to be weakest and thus help managers decide which foreign markets to enter first. And third, because it focuses on the attributes of a country's business environment that allow firms to flourish, it reveals something about the advantages of conducting particular business activities in that country. Thus the diamond framework is an aid to deciding where to locate different value chain activities most beneficially—a topic that we address next.

Locating Value Chain Activities for Competitive Advantage

Increasingly, companies are locating different value chain activities in different parts of the world to exploit location-based advantages that vary from country to country. This is particularly evident with respect to the location of manufacturing activities. Differences in wage rates, worker productivity, energy costs, environmental regulations, tax rates, inflation rates, and the like, create sizable variations in manufacturing costs from country to country. By locating its plants in certain countries, firms in some industries can reap major manufacturing cost advantages because of lower input costs (especially labor), relaxed government regulations, the proximity of suppliers and technologically related industries, or unique natural resources. In such cases, the low-cost countries become principal production sites, with most of the output being exported to markets in other parts of the world. Companies that build production facilities in low-cost countries (or that source their products from contract manufacturers in these countries) gain a competitive advantage over rivals with plants in countries where costs are higher. The competitive role of low manufacturing costs is most evident in low-wage countries like China, India, Pakistan, Cambodia, Vietnam, Mexico, Brazil, Guatemala, the Philippines, and several countries in Africa and eastern Europe that have become production havens for manufactured goods with high labor content (especially textiles and apparel). Hourly compensation for production workers in 2007 averaged about $0.81 in China versus about $1.10 in the Philippines, $2.92 in Mexico, $5.96 in Brazil, $6.58 in Taiwan, $7.91 in Hungary, $8.27 in Portugal, $19.75 in Japan, $24.59 in the United States, $28.91 in Canada, $37.66 in Germany, and $48.56 in Norway.[5] China is fast becoming the manufacturing capital of the world—virtually all of the world's major manufacturing companies now have facilities in China.

For other types of value chain activities, input quality or availability are more important considerations. Tiffany entered the mining industry in Canada to access diamonds that could be certified as "conflict free" and not associated with either the funding of African wars or unethical mining conditions. Many U.S. companies locate call centers in countries such as India and Ireland, where English is spoken and the workforce is well educated. Other companies locate R&D activities in countries where there are prestigious research institutions and well-trained scientists and engineers. Likewise, concerns about short delivery times and low shipping costs make some countries better locations than others for establishing distribution centers.

The Impact of Government Policies and Economic Conditions in Host Countries

Cross-country variations in government policies and economic conditions affect both the opportunities available to a foreign entrant and the risks of operating within that country. The governments of some countries are anxious to attract foreign investments and go all out to create a business climate that outsiders will view as favorable. A good example is Ireland, which has one of the world's most pro-business environments. Ireland offers companies very low corporate tax rates, has a government that is responsive to the needs of industry, and aggressively recruits high-tech manufacturing facilities and international companies. Ireland's policies were a major factor in Intel's decision to locate a $2.5 billion chip manufacturing plant in Ireland that employs over 4,000 people. Governments anxious to spur economic growth, create more jobs, and raise living standards for their citizens usually enact policies aimed at stimulating business innovation and capital investment. They may provide incentives such as reduced taxes, low-cost loans, site location and site development assistance, and government-sponsored training for workers to encourage companies to construct production and distribution facilities. When new business-related issues or developments arise, pro-business governments make a practice of seeking advice and counsel from business leaders. When tougher business-related regulations are deemed appropriate, they endeavor to make the transition to more costly and stringent regulations somewhat business-friendly rather than adversarial.

On the other hand, governments sometimes enact policies that, from a business perspective, make locating facilities within a country's borders less attractive. For example, the nature of a company's operations may make it particularly costly to achieve compliance with a country's environmental regulations. Some governments, desirous of discouraging foreign imports, provide subsidies and low-interest loans to domestic companies (to enable them to better compete against foreign companies), enact deliberately burdensome procedures and requirements for imported goods to pass customs inspection (to make it harder for imported goods to compete against the products of local businesses), and impose tariffs or quotas on the imports of certain goods (also to help protect local businesses from foreign competition). They may also specify that a certain percentage of the parts and components used in manufacturing a product be obtained from local suppliers, require prior approval of capital spending projects, limit withdrawal of funds from the country, and require minority (sometimes majority) ownership of foreign company operations by local companies or investors. Sometimes foreign companies wanting only to sell their products in a country face a web of regulations regarding technical standards and product certification. Political leaders in some countries may be openly hostile to or suspicious of companies from certain foreign countries operating within their borders. Moreover, there are times when a government may place restrictions on exports to ensure adequate local supplies and regulate the prices of imported and locally produced goods. Such government actions make a country's business climate less attractive and in some cases may be sufficiently onerous as to discourage a company from locating production or distribution facilities in that country or maybe even selling its products in that country.

The decision about whether to enter a particular country must take into account the degree of political and economic risk. **Political risks** stem from government hostility to foreign business, weak governments, and political instability. In industries that a government deems critical to the national welfare, there is sometimes a risk that the government will nationalize the industry and expropriate the assets of foreign companies. In 2010, for example, Ecuador threatened to expropriate the holdings of all foreign oil companies that refused to sign new contracts giving the state control of all production. Other political risks include the loss of investments due to war or political unrest, regulatory changes that create operating uncertainties, security risks due to terrorism, and corruption. **Economic risks** are intertwined with political risks but also stem from factors such as inflation rates and the stability of a country's monetary system. The threat of piracy and lack of protection for intellectual property are important sources of economic risk. Another is fluctuations in the value of different currencies—a factor that we discuss in more detail next.

The Risks of Adverse Exchange Rate Shifts

When companies produce and market their products and services in many different countries, they are subject to the impacts of sometimes favorable and sometimes unfavorable changes in currency exchange rates. The rates of exchange between different currencies can vary by as much as 20 to 40 percent annually, with the changes occurring sometimes gradually and sometimes swiftly. Sizable shifts in exchange rates, which tend to be hard to predict because of the variety of factors involved and the uncertainties surrounding when and by how much these factors will change, shuffle the global cards of which countries represent the low-cost manufacturing locations and which rivals have the upper hand in the marketplace.

To understand the economic risks associated with fluctuating exchange rates, consider the case of a U.S. company that has located manufacturing facilities in Brazil (where the currency is reals—pronounced "ray-alls") and that exports most of the Brazilian-made goods to markets in the European Union (where the currency is euros). To keep the numbers simple, assume that the exchange rate is 4 Brazilian reals for 1 euro and that the product being made in Brazil has a manufacturing cost of 4 Brazilian reals (or 1 euro). Now suppose that for some reason the exchange rate shifts from 4 reals per euro to 5 reals per euro (meaning that the real has declined in value and that the euro is stronger). Making the product in Brazil is now more cost-competitive because a Brazilian good costing 4 reals to produce has fallen to only 0.8 euro at the new exchange rate (4 reals divided by 5 reals per euro = 0.8 euro) and this clearly puts the producer of the Brazilian-made good *in a better position to compete* against the European makers of the same good. On the other hand, should the value of the Brazilian real grow stronger in relation to the euro—resulting in an exchange rate of 3 reals to 1 euro—the same Brazilian-made good formerly costing 4 reals (or 1 euro) to produce now has a cost of 1.33 euros (4 reals divided by 3 reals per euro = 1.33 euros) and this puts the producer of the Brazilian-made good in a weaker competitive position vis-à-vis European producers of the same good. Clearly, the attraction of manufacturing a good in Brazil and selling it in Europe is far greater when the euro is strong (an exchange rate of 1 euro for 5 Brazilian reals) than when the euro is weak and exchanges for only 3 Brazilian reals.

But there is one more piece to the story. When the exchange rate changes from 4 reals per euro to 5 reals per euro, not only is the cost competitiveness of the Brazilian manufacturer stronger relative to European manufacturers of the same item but the Brazilian-made good that formerly cost 1 euro and now costs only 0.8 euro can also be sold to consumers in the European Union for a lower euro price than before. In other words, the combination of a stronger euro and a weaker real acts to *lower the price of Brazilian-made goods* in all the countries that are members of the European Union, and this is likely to *spur sales of the Brazilian-made good in Europe and boost Brazilian exports to Europe.* Conversely, should the exchange rate shift from 4 reals per euro to 3 reals per euro—which makes the Brazilian manufacturer less cost competitive with European manufacturers of the same item—the Brazilian-made good that formerly cost 1 euro and now costs 1.33 euros will sell for a higher price in euros than before, thus weakening the demand of European consumers for Brazilian-made goods and acting to reduce Brazilian exports to Europe. Thus *Brazilian exporters are likely to experience (1) rising demand for their goods in Europe whenever the Brazilian real grows weaker relative to the euro and (2) falling demand for their goods in Europe whenever the real grows stronger relative to the euro.*

> Fluctuating exchange rates pose significant economic risks to a company's competitiveness in foreign markets. Exporters are disadvantaged when the currency of the country where goods are being manufactured grows stronger relative to the currency of the importing country.

Insofar as U.S.-based manufacturers are concerned, declines in the value of the U.S. dollar against foreign currencies act to reduce or eliminate whatever cost advantage foreign manufacturers might have over U.S. manufacturers and can even prompt foreign companies to establish production plants in the United States. Likewise, a weak euro versus other currencies enhances the cost competitiveness of companies manufacturing goods in Europe for export to foreign markets; a strong euro versus other currencies weakens the cost competitiveness of

European plants that manufacture goods for export. The growing strength of the euro relative to the U.S. dollar has encouraged a number of European manufacturers such as Volkswagen, Fiat, and Airbus to shift production from European factories to new facilities in the United States. Also, the weakening dollar caused Chrysler to discontinue its contract manufacturing agreement with an Austrian firm for assembly of minivans and Jeeps sold in Europe. Beginning in 2008, Chrysler's vehicles sold in Europe were exported from its factories in Illinois and Missouri. The weak dollar was also a factor in Ford's and GM's recent decisions to begin exporting U.S.-made vehicles to China and Latin America.

> Domestic companies facing competitive pressure from lower-cost imports are benefited when their government's currency grows *weaker* in relation to the currencies of the countries where the lower-cost goods are being made.

It is important to note that *currency exchange rates are rather unpredictable,* swinging first one way and then another way, so the competitiveness of any company's facilities in any country is partly dependent on whether exchange rate changes over time have a favorable or unfavorable cost impact. Companies producing goods in one country for export abroad always improve their cost competitiveness when the country's currency grows weaker relative to currencies of the countries where the goods are being exported to, and they find their cost competitiveness eroded when the local currency grow stronger. On the other hand, domestic companies that are under pressure from lower-cost imported goods become more cost competitive when their currency grows weaker in relation to the currencies of the countries where the imported goods are made—in other words, a U.S. manufacturer views a weaker U.S. dollar as a *favorable exchange rate shift* because such shifts help make its costs more competitive than those of foreign rivals.

Cross-Country Differences in Demographic, Cultural, and Market Conditions

Differing population sizes, income levels, and other demographic factors give rise to considerable differences in market size and growth rates from country to country. Less than 20 percent of the populations of Brazil, India, and China have annual purchasing power equivalent to $25,000. Middle-class consumers represent a much smaller portion of the population in these and other developing countries than in North America, Japan, and much of western Europe—China's middle class numbers about 300 million out of a population of 1.35 billion.[6] At the same time, in developing markets like India, China, Brazil, and Malaysia, market growth potential is far higher than it is in the more mature economies of Britain, Denmark, Canada, and Japan. The potential for market growth in automobiles is explosive in China, where 2009 sales of new vehicles amounted to 13.6 million, surpassing U.S. sales of 10 million and making China the world's largest market.[7] Owing to widely differing population demographics and income levels, there is a far bigger market for luxury automobiles in the United States and Germany than in Argentina, India, Mexico, China, and Thailand.

Buyer tastes for a particular product or service sometimes differ substantially from country to country. In France consumers prefer top-loading washing machines, while in most other European countries consumers prefer front-loading machines. Soups that appeal to Swedish consumers are not popular in Malaysia. Italian coffee drinkers prefer espressos, but in North America the preference is for mild-roasted coffees. Sometimes, product designs suitable in one country are inappropriate in another because of differing local standards—for example, in the United States electrical devices run on 110-volt electric systems, but in some

European countries the standard is a 240-volt electric system, necessitating the use of different electrical designs and components. Cultural influences can also affect consumer demand for a product. For instance, in South Korea, many parents are reluctant to purchase PCs even when they can afford them because of concerns that their children will be distracted from their schoolwork by surfing the Web, playing PC-based video games, and becoming Internet "addicts."[8]

Consequently, companies operating in an international marketplace have to wrestle with *whether and how much to customize their offerings in each different country market to match the tastes and preferences of local buyers or whether to pursue a strategy of offering a mostly standardized product worldwide.* While making products that are closely matched to local tastes makes them more appealing to local buyers, customizing a company's products country by country may have the effect of raising production and distribution costs due to the greater variety of designs and components, shorter production runs, and the complications of added inventory handling and distribution logistics. Greater standardization of a multinational company's product offering, on the other hand, can lead to scale economies and learning curve effects, thus contributing to the achievement of a low-cost advantage. *The tension between the market pressures to localize a company's product offerings country by country and the competitive pressures to lower costs is one of the big strategic issues that participants in foreign markets have to resolve.*

THE CONCEPTS OF MULTIDOMESTIC COMPETITION AND GLOBAL COMPETITION

In crafting a strategy to compete on an international basis, it is essential for managers to recognize that the pattern of international competition varies in important ways from industry to industry.[9] At one extreme is **multidomestic competition,** in which there's so much cross-country variation in market conditions and in the companies contending for leadership that the market contest among rivals in one country is localized and not closely connected to the market contests in other countries. The standout features of multidomestic competition are that (1) buyers in different countries are attracted to different product attributes, (2) sellers vary from country to country, and (3) industry conditions and competitive forces in each national market differ in important respects. Take the banking industry in Poland, Mexico, and Australia as an example—the requirements and expectations of banking customers vary among the three countries, the lead banking competitors in Poland differ from those in Mexico or Australia, and the competitive battle going on among the leading banks in Poland is unrelated to the rivalry taking place in Mexico or Australia. Thus, with multidomestic competition, rival firms battle for national championships and winning in one country does not necessarily signal the ability to fare well in other countries. In multidomestic competition, the power of a company's strategy and capabilities in one country has little impact on its competitiveness in other countries where it operates. Moreover, any competitive advantage a company secures in one country is largely confined to that country; the spillover effects to other countries are minimal to nonexistent.

CORE CONCEPT

Multidomestic competition exists when the competition among rivals in each country market is localized and not closely connected to the competition in other country markets—there is no world market, just a collection of self-contained local markets.

Industries characterized by multidomestic competition include radio and TV broadcasting, consumer banking, life insurance, apparel, metals fabrication, many types of food products (coffee, cereals, breads, canned goods, frozen foods), and retailing.

At the other extreme is **global competition,** in which prices and competitive conditions across country markets are strongly linked and the term *global* has true meaning. In a globally competitive industry, much the same group of rival companies competes in many different countries but especially in countries where sales volumes are large and where having a competitive presence is strategically important to building a strong global position in the industry. Thus, a company's competitive position in one country both affects and is affected by its position in other countries. In global competition, a firm's overall competitive advantage grows out of its entire worldwide operations; the competitive advantage it creates at its home base is supplemented by advantages growing out of its operations in other countries (having plants in low-wage countries, being able to transfer expertise from country to country, having the capability to serve customers that also have multinational operations, and having brand-name recognition in many parts of the world). Rival firms in globally competitive industries vie for worldwide leadership. Global competition exists in motor vehicles, television sets, tires, cell phones, personal computers, copiers, watches, digital cameras, bicycles, and commercial aircraft.

An industry can have segments that are globally competitive and segments in which competition is country by country.[10] In the hotel/motel industry, for example, the low- and medium-priced segments are characterized by multidomestic competition—competitors mainly serve travelers within the same country. In the business and luxury segments, however, competition is more globalized. Companies like Nikki (owned by Japan Airlines), Marriott, Sheraton, and Hilton have hotels at many international locations, use worldwide reservation systems, and establish common quality and service standards to gain marketing advantages in serving businesspeople and other travelers who make frequent international trips. In lubricants, the marine engine segment is globally competitive—ships move from port to port and require the same oil everywhere they stop. Brand reputations in marine lubricants have a global scope, and successful marine engine lubricant producers (ExxonMobil, BP Amoco, and Shell) operate globally. In automotive motor oil, however, multidomestic competition dominates—countries have different weather conditions and driving patterns, production of motor oil is subject to limited scale economies, shipping costs are high, and retail distribution channels differ markedly from country to country. Thus, domestic firms—like Quaker State and Pennzoil in the United States and Castrol in Great Britain—can be leaders in their home markets without competing globally.

It is also important to recognize that an industry can be in transition from multidomestic competition to global competition. In a number of today's industries—beer and major home appliances are prime examples—leading domestic competitors have begun expanding into more and more foreign markets, often acquiring local companies or brands and integrating them into their operations. As some industry members start to build global brands and a global presence, other industry members find themselves pressured to follow the same strategic path—especially if establishing multinational operations results in important scale economies and a powerhouse brand name. As the industry consolidates to fewer players, such that many of the same companies find themselves in head-to-head

CORE CONCEPT

Global competition exists when competitive conditions across national markets are linked strongly enough to form a true world market and when leading competitors compete head to head in many different countries.

competition in more and more country markets, global competition begins to replace multidomestic competition.

At the same time, consumer tastes in a number of important product categories are converging across the world. Less diversity of tastes and preferences opens the way for companies to create global brands and sell essentially the same products in almost all countries of the world. Even in industries where consumer tastes remain fairly diverse, companies are learning to use "custom mass production" to economically create different versions of a product and thereby satisfy the tastes of people in different countries.

In addition to taking the obvious cultural and political differences between countries into account, a company must shape its strategic approach to competing in foreign markets according to whether its industry is characterized by multidomestic competition, global competition, or some combination, depending on differences among industry sectors and on how the industry is evolving.

STRATEGIC OPTIONS FOR ENTERING AND COMPETING IN INTERNATIONAL MARKETS

LO 3

Learn about the major strategic options for entering and competing in foreign markets.

Once a company decides to expand beyond its domestic borders it must consider the question of how to enter foreign markets. There are six primary strategic options for doing so:

1. Maintain a national (one-country) production base and export goods to foreign markets.
2. License foreign firms to produce and distribute the company's products abroad.
3. Employ a franchising strategy.
4. Establish a wholly owned subsidiary in the foreign market by acquiring a foreign company.
5. Create a wholly owned foreign subsidiary from the ground up via a "greenfield" venture.
6. Rely on strategic alliances or joint ventures to partner with foreign companies.

Which option to employ depends on a variety of factors, including the nature of the firm's strategic objectives, whether the firm has the full range of resources and capabilities needed to operate abroad, country-specific factors such as trade barriers, and the transaction costs involved (the costs of contracting with a partner and monitoring its compliance with the terms of the contract, for example). The options vary considerably regarding the level of investment required and the associated risks, but higher levels of investment and risk generally provide the firm with the benefits of greater ownership and control.

Export Strategies

Using domestic plants as a production base for exporting goods to foreign markets is an excellent initial strategy for pursuing international sales. It is a conservative way to test the international waters. The amount of capital needed to begin exporting is often quite minimal; existing production capacity may well be sufficient to make goods for export. With an export strategy, a manufacturer can limit its involvement in foreign markets by contracting with foreign wholesalers experienced in importing to handle the entire distribution and marketing function in their countries or regions of the world. If it is more advantageous to maintain control over these functions, however, a manufacturer can establish its own distribution and sales organizations in some or all of the target foreign markets. Either way, a home-based production and export strategy helps the firm minimize its direct investments in foreign countries. Such strategies have been favored traditionally by Chinese, Korean, and Italian companies—products are designed and manufactured at home and then distributed through local channels in the importing countries; the primary functions performed abroad relate chiefly to establishing a network of distributors and perhaps conducting sales promotion and brand awareness activities.

Whether an export strategy can be pursued successfully over the long run hinges on whether its advantages for the company continue to outweigh its disadvantages. This depends in part on the relative cost competitiveness of the home-country production base. In some industries, firms gain additional scale economies and learning curve benefits from centralizing production in one or several giant plants whose output capability exceeds demand in any one country market; exporting is one obvious way to capture such economies. However, an export strategy is vulnerable when (1) manufacturing costs in the home country are substantially higher than in foreign countries where rivals have plants, (2) the costs of shipping the product to distant foreign markets are relatively high, or (3) adverse shifts occur in currency exchange rates. The disadvantages of export strategies can also swell due to high tariffs and other trade barriers, inadequate control over marketing or distribution, and an inability to tap into location advantages available elsewhere, such as skilled low-cost labor.

Licensing Strategies

Licensing makes sense when a firm with valuable technical know-how, an appealing brand, or a unique patented product has neither the internal organizational capability nor the resources to enter foreign markets. Licensing also has the advantage of avoiding the risks of committing resources to country markets that are unfamiliar, politically volatile, economically unstable, or otherwise risky. By licensing the technology, trademark, or production rights to foreign-based firms, the firm does not have to bear the costs and risks of entering foreign markets on its own, yet it is able to generate income from royalties. The big disadvantage of licensing is the risk of providing valuable technological know-how to foreign companies and thereby losing some degree of control over its use; monitoring licensees and safeguarding the company's proprietary know-how can prove quite difficult in some circumstances. But if the royalty potential is considerable and the companies to whom the licenses are being granted are trustworthy and reputable, then licensing can be a very attractive option. Many software and pharmaceutical companies use licensing strategies.

Franchising Strategies

While licensing works well for manufacturers and owners of proprietary technology, franchising is often better suited to the international expansion efforts of service and retailing enterprises. McDonald's, Yum! Brands (the parent of Pizza Hut,

KFC, and Taco Bell), the UPS Store, Jani-King International (the world's largest commercial cleaning franchisor), Roto-Rooter, 7-Eleven, and Hilton Hotels have all used franchising to build a presence in foreign markets. Franchising has much the same advantages as licensing. The franchisee bears most of the costs and risks of establishing foreign locations; a franchisor has to expend only the resources to recruit, train, support, and monitor franchisees. The big problem a franchisor faces is maintaining quality control; foreign franchisees do not always exhibit strong commitment to consistency and standardization, especially when the local culture does not stress the same kinds of quality concerns. Another problem that can arise is whether to allow foreign franchisees to make modifications in the franchisor's product offering so as to better satisfy the tastes and expectations of local buyers. Should McDonald's allow its franchised units in Japan to modify Big Macs slightly to suit Japanese tastes? Should the franchised Pizza Hut units in China be permitted to substitute spices that appeal to Chinese consumers? Or should the same menu offerings be rigorously and unvaryingly required of all franchisees worldwide?

Acquisition Strategies

Acquisition strategies have the advantages of a high level of control as well as speed, which can be a significant factor when a firm wants to enter a foreign market at a relatively large scale. When a strong presence in the market or local economies of scale are a significant competitive factor in the market, these advantages may make acquiring a large local firm preferable to most other entry modes. Similarly, when entry barriers are high—whether in the form of trade barriers, access to a local distribution network, or building key relationships with local constituents and officials—an acquisition may be the only route to overcoming such hurdles. Acquisition may also be the preferred entry strategy if the strategic objective is to gain access to the core capabilities or well-guarded technologies of a foreign firm.

At the same time, acquisition strategies have their downside as a foreign entry strategy. Acquisition strategies are always costly, since it is necessary to pay a premium over the share-price value of a company in order to acquire control. This can saddle the acquiring company with a good deal of debt, increasing its risk of bankruptcy and limiting its other investment options. Acquiring a foreign firm can be particularly tricky due to the challenge of international negotiations, the burden of foreign legal and regulatory requirements, and the added complexity of postacquisition integration efforts when companies are separated by distance, culture, and language.[11] While the potential benefits of a cross-border acquisition can be high, the risk of failure is high as well.

Greenfield Venture Strategies

A **greenfield venture** strategy is one in which the company creates a subsidiary business in the foreign market by setting up the entire operation (plants, distribution system, etc.) from the ground up. Like acquisition strategies, greenfield ventures have the advantage of high control, but to an even greater degree since starting from scratch allows the company to set up every aspect of the operation to its specifications. Since organizational change is notoriously difficult and hampered by a variety of inertial factors, it is much harder to fine-tune the operations of an acquired firm to this degree—particularly a foreign firm. Entering a foreign market from the ground up provides a firm with another potential advantage: It enables the company to *learn by doing* how to operate in the foreign market and how to best serve local needs, navigate the local politics, and compete most effectively against local rivals. This is not to say, however, that the company needs to acquire all the knowledge and experience needed from the ground up; in building its operation, the company can avail itself of local managerial talent and know-how by simply hiring experienced local managers who understand the local market conditions, local buying habits, local competitors, and local ways of doing business. By assembling a management team that also includes senior managers from the parent company (preferably with considerable international experience), the parent company can transfer technology, business practices, and the corporate culture into the new foreign subsidiary and ensure that there is a conduit for the flow of information between the corporate office and local operations.

Greenfield ventures in foreign markets also pose a number of problems, just as other entry strategies do. They represent a costly capital investment, subject to a high level of risk. They require numerous other company resources as well, diverting them from other uses. They do not work well in countries without strong, well-functioning markets and institutions that protect the rights of foreign investors and provide other legal protections.[12] Moreover, an important disadvantage of greenfield ventures relative to other means of international expansion is that they are the slowest entry route—particularly if the objective is to achieve a sizable market share. On the other hand, successful greenfield ventures may offer higher returns to compensate for their high risk and slower path.

Alliance and Joint Venture Strategies

Collaborative agreements with foreign companies in the form of strategic alliances or joint ventures are widely used as a means of entering foreign markets.[13] Often they are used in conjunction with another entry strategy, such as exporting, franchising, or establishing a greenfield venture. Historically, firms in industrialized nations that wanted to export their products and market them in less developed countries sought alliances with local companies in order to do so—such arrangements were often necessary to win approval for entry from the host country's government. Companies wanting to set up a manufacturing operation abroad often had to do so via a joint venture with a foreign firm. Over the last 20 years, those types of restrictions have been lifted in countries such as India and China, and companies have been able to enter these markets via more direct means.[14]

Today, a more important reason for using strategic alliances and joint ventures as a vehicle for international expansion is that they facilitate resource and risk sharing. When firms need access to complementary resources to succeed abroad, when the venture requires substantial investment, and when the risks are high, the attraction of such strategies grows. A company can benefit immensely from a foreign partner's familiarity with local government regulations, its knowledge of the buying habits and product preferences of consumers, its distribution channel relationships, and so on. Both Japanese and American companies are actively forming alliances with European companies to better compete in the 27-nation European Union and to capitalize on emerging but risky opportunities in the countries of eastern Europe. Similarly, many U.S. and European companies

> Collaborative strategies involving alliances or joint ventures with foreign partners are a popular way for companies to edge their way into the markets of foreign countries.

are allying with Asian companies in their efforts to enter markets in China, India, Thailand, Indonesia, and other Asian countries where they lack local knowledge and uncertainties abound. Many foreign companies, of course, are particularly interested in strategic partnerships that will strengthen their ability to gain a foothold in the U.S. market.

Another potential benefit of a collaborative strategy is the learning and added expertise that come from performing joint research, sharing technological know-how, studying one another's manufacturing methods, and understanding how to tailor sales and marketing approaches to fit local cultures and traditions. Indeed, by learning from the skills, technological know-how, and capabilities of alliance partners and implanting the knowledge and know-how of these partners in its own personnel and organization, a company can upgrade its capabilities and become a stronger competitor in its home market. DaimlerChrysler's strategic alliance with Mitsubishi, for example, was motivated by a desire to learn from Mitsubishi's technological strengths in small-size vehicles in order to improve the performance of its loss-making "smart car" division.[15]

> Cross-border alliances enable a growth-minded company to widen its geographic coverage and strengthen its competitiveness in foreign markets; at the same time, they offer flexibility and allow a company to retain some degree of autonomy and operating control.

Many companies believe that cross-border alliances and partnerships are a better strategic means of gaining the above benefits (as compared to acquiring or merging with foreign-based companies to gain much the same benefits) because they allow a company to preserve its independence (which is not the case with a merger), retain veto power over how the alliance operates, and avoid using scarce financial resources to fund acquisitions. Furthermore, an alliance offers the flexibility to readily disengage once its purpose has been served or if the benefits prove elusive, whereas an acquisition is a more permanent sort of arrangement (although the acquired company can, of course, be divested).[16]

Illustration Capsule 7.1 provides four examples of cross-border strategic alliances.

The Risks of Strategic Alliances with Foreign Partners   Alliances and joint ventures with foreign partners have their pitfalls, however. Cross-border allies typically have to overcome language and cultural barriers and figure out how to deal with diverse operating practices. The transaction costs of working out a mutually agreeable arrangement and monitoring partner compliance with the terms of the arrangement can be high. The communication, trust building, and coordination costs are not trivial in terms of management time.[17] Often, partners soon discover they have conflicting objectives and strategies, deep differences of opinion about how to proceed, and/or important differences in corporate values and ethical standards. Tensions build up, working relationships cool, and the hoped-for benefits never materialize.[18] It is not unusual for there to be little personal chemistry among some of the key people on whom success or failure of the alliance depends—the rapport such personnel need to work well together may never emerge. And even if allies are able to develop productive personal relationships, they can still have trouble reaching mutually agreeable ways to deal with key issues or resolve differences. Occasionally, the egos of corporate executives can clash. An alliance between Northwest Airlines and KLM Royal Dutch Airlines resulted in a bitter feud among both companies' top officials (who, according to some reports, refused to speak to each other).[19] Plus there is the thorny problem of getting alliance partners to sort through issues and reach decisions fast enough to stay abreast of rapid advances in technology or fast-changing market conditions.

1. The engine of General Motors' growth strategy in Asia is its three-way joint venture with Wulung, a Chinese producer of mini-commercial vehicles, and SAIC (Shanghai Automotive Industrial Corporation), China's largest automaker. The success of the SAIC-GM-Wulung Automotive Company is also GM's best hope for financial recovery since it emerged from bankruptcy on July 10, 2009. While GM lost $4.8 billion overall before interest and taxes during the last six months of 2009, its international operations (everything except North America and Europe) earned $1.2 billion. Its Chinese joint ventures accounted for approximately one-third of that profit, due in part to the roaring success of the no-frills Wulung Sunshine, a lightweight minivan that has become China's best-selling vehicle. In 2010, General Motors' sales in China topped its U.S. sales—the first time that sales in a foreign market have done so in the 102-year history of the company. GM is now positioning its Chinese joint venture to serve as a springboard for the company's expansion in India, with the possibility of launching a product to rival the Tata Nano there. When GM's president of international operations, Timothy E. Lee, was asked about GM's ability to compete in India, he replied, "When you harvest from your partnerships the collective wisdom of other cultures, it's incredible what you can do."

2. The European Aeronautic Defense and Space Company (EADS) was formed by an alliance of aerospace companies from Britain, Spain, Germany, and France that included British Aerospace, Daimler-Benz Aerospace, and Aerospatiale. The objective of the alliance was to create a European aircraft company capable of competing with U.S.-based Boeing Corp. The alliance has proved highly successful, infusing its commercial airline division, Airbus, with the know-how and resources needed to compete head to head with Boeing for world leadership in large commercial aircraft (those designed for over 100 passengers). The company also established an alliance with U.S. military aircraft manufacturer Northrop Grumman to develop a highly sophisticated refueling tanker based on the A330 airliner for the U.S. Air Force.

3. Cisco, the worldwide leader in networking components, entered into a strategic alliance with Finnish telecommunications firm Nokia Siemens Networks to develop communications networks capable of transmitting data either across the Internet or by mobile technologies. Nokia Siemens Networks itself was created through a 2006 international joint venture between German-based Siemens AG and the Finnish communications giant Nokia. The Cisco–Nokia Siemens alliance was created to better position both companies for convergence among Internet technologies and wireless communication devices that was expected to dramatically change how both computer networks and wireless telephones would be used.

4. Verio, a subsidiary of Japan-based NTT Communications and one of the leading global providers of Web hosting services and IP data transport, operates with the philosophy that in today's highly competitive and challenging technology market, companies must gain and share skills, information, and technology with technology leaders across the world. Believing that no company can be all things to all customers in the Web hosting industry, Verio executives have developed an alliance-oriented business model that combines the company's core competencies with the skills and products of best-of-breed technology partners. Verio's strategic partners include Accenture, Cisco Systems, Microsoft, Sun Microsystems, Oracle, Arsenal Digital Solutions (a provider of worry-free tape backup, data restore, and data storage services), Internet Security Systems (a provider of firewall and intrusion detection systems), and Mercantec (which develops storefront and shopping cart software). Verio's management believes that its portfolio of strategic alliances allows it to use innovative, best-of-class technologies in providing its

(Continued)

customers with fast, efficient, accurate data transport and a complete set of Web hosting services. An independent panel of 12 judges recently selected Verio as the winner of the Best Technology Foresight Award for its efforts in pioneering new technologies.

Developed with Mukund Kulashekaran.

Sources: Company Web sites and press releases; Yves L. Doz and Gary Hamel, *Alliance Advantage: The Art of Creating Value through Partnering* (Boston: Harvard Business School Press, 1998); Joanne Muller, "Can China Save GM?" *Forbes.com,* May 10, 2010, www.forbes.com/forbes/2010/0510/global-2000-10-automobiles-china-detroit-whitacre-save-gm.html; "GM's First-Half China Sales Surge Past the U.S.," *Bloomberg Businessweek,* July 2, 2010, www.businessweek.com/news/2010-07-02/gm-s-first-half-china-sales-surge-past-the-u-s-.html; Nandini Sen Gupta, "General Motors May Drive in Nano Rival with Chinese Help," *Economic Times,* May 31, 2010, http://economictimes.indiatimes.com/articleshow/5992589.cms.

One worrisome problem with alliances or joint ventures is that a firm may risk losing some of its competitive advantage if an alliance partner is given full access to its proprietary technological expertise or other unique and competitively valuable capabilities. There is a natural tendency for allies to struggle to collaborate effectively in competitively sensitive areas, thus spawning suspicions on both sides about forthright exchanges of information and expertise. It requires many meetings of many people working in good faith over a period of time to iron out what is to be shared, what is to remain proprietary, and how the cooperative arrangements will work.

Even if a collaborative arrangement proves to be a win-win proposition for both parties, a company has to guard against becoming overly dependent on foreign partners for essential expertise and competitive capabilities. If a company is aiming for global market leadership and needs to develop capabilities of its own, then at some juncture a cross-border merger or acquisition may have to be substituted for cross-border alliances and joint ventures. One of the lessons about cross-border alliances is that they are more effective in helping a company establish a beachhead of new opportunity in world markets than they are in enabling a company to achieve and sustain global market leadership.

When a Cross-Border Alliance May Be Unnecessary Experienced multinational companies that market in 50 to 100 or more countries across the world find less need for entering into cross-border alliances than do companies in the early stages of globalizing their operations.[20] Multinational companies make it a point to develop senior managers who understand how "the system" works in different countries, plus they can avail themselves of local managerial talent and know-how by simply hiring experienced local managers and thereby detouring the hazards of collaborative alliances with local companies. If a multinational enterprise with considerable experience in entering the markets of different countries wants to detour the hazards of allying with local businesses, it can simply assemble a capable management team consisting of both senior managers with considerable international experience and local managers. The role of its own in-house managers with international business savvy is to transfer technology, business practices, and the corporate culture into the company's operations in the new country market and to serve as conduits for the flow of information between the corporate office and local operations. The role of local managers is to contribute needed understanding of the local market conditions, local buying habits, and local ways of doing business and, often, to head up local operations.

Hence, one cannot automatically presume that a company needs the wisdom and resources of a local partner to guide it through the process of successfully entering the markets of foreign countries. Indeed, experienced multinationals often discover that local partners do not always have adequate local market knowledge—much of the so-called experience of local partners can predate the emergence of current market trends and conditions and sometimes their operating practices can be archaic.[21]

COMPETING INTERNATIONALLY: THE THREE MAIN STRATEGIC APPROACHES

Broadly speaking, a firm's **international strategy** is simply its strategy for competing in two or more countries simultaneously. Typically, a company will start to compete internationally by entering just one or perhaps a select few foreign markets, selling its products or services in countries where there is a ready market for them. But as it expands further internationally, it will have to confront head-on the conflicting pressures of local responsiveness versus efficiency gains from standardizing and integrating operations globally. Moreover, it will have to consider whether the markets abroad are characterized by multidomestic competition, global competition, or some mix. The issue of whether and how to vary the company's competitive approach to fit specific market conditions and buyer preferences in each host country or whether to employ essentially the same strategy in all countries is perhaps the foremost strategic issue that companies must address when they operate in two or more foreign markets.[22] Figure 7.2 shows a company's three options for resolving this issue: a *multidomestic, global,* or *transnational* strategy.

Multidomestic Strategy—Think Local, Act Local

A **multidomestic strategy** is one based on differentiating products and services on a country-by-country or regional basis to meet differing buyer needs and to address divergent local market conditions. It is a good choice for companies that compete primarily in industries characterized by multidomestic competition. This type of strategy involves having plants produce different product versions for different local markets and adapting marketing and distribution to fit local customs, cultures, regulations, and market requirements. Castrol, a specialist in oil lubricants, produces over 3,000 different formulas of lubricants to meet the requirements of different climates, vehicle types and uses, and equipment applications that characterize different country markets. In the food products industry, it is common for companies to vary the ingredients in their products and sell the localized versions under local brand names to cater to country-specific tastes and eating preferences.

In essence, a multidomestic strategy represents a **think-local, act-local** approach to international strategy. A think-local, act-local approach is possible only when decision making is decentralized, giving local managers considerable latitude for crafting and executing strategies for the country markets they are responsible for. Giving local managers

LO 4

Gain familiarity with the three main strategic approaches for competing internationally.

CORE CONCEPT

An **international strategy** is a strategy for competing in two or more countries simultaneously.

CORE CONCEPT

A **multidomestic strategy** is one in which a company varies its product offering and competitive approach from country to country in an effort to be responsive to differing buyer preferences and market conditions. It is a **think-local, act-local** type of international strategy, facilitated by decision making decentralized to the local level.

Figure 7.2   Three Approaches for Competing Internationally

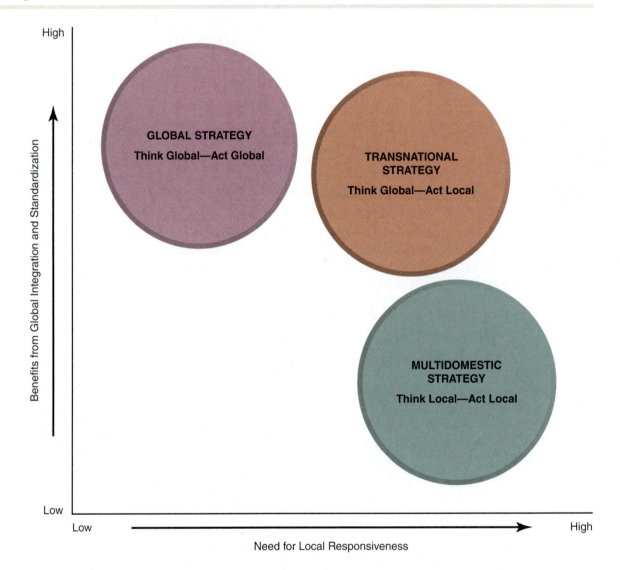

decision-making authority allows them to address specific market needs and respond swiftly to local changes in demand. It also enables them to focus their competitive efforts, stake out attractive market positions vis-à-vis local competitors, react to rivals' moves in a timely fashion, and target new opportunities as they emerge.

A think-local, act-local approach to strategy making is most appropriate when the need for local responsiveness is high due to significant cross-country differences in demographic, cultural, and market conditions and when the potential for efficiency gains from standardization is limited, as depicted in Figure 7.2. Consider, for example, the wide variation in refrigerator usage and preference around the world. Northern Europeans want large refrigerators because they tend to shop once a week in supermarkets; southern Europeans prefer small refrigerators because they shop daily. In parts of Asia refrigerators are a status symbol and may be placed in the living room, leading to preferences for stylish designs and colors—in India bright blue and red are popular colors. In other Asian countries household space is constrained, and many refrigerators are only 4 feet high so that the top can be used for storage. If the minimum efficient scale for producing refrigerators is relatively low, there would be little reason to forgo the benefits of meeting these varying needs precisely in favor of a standardized, one-size-fits-all approach to production.

Despite their obvious benefits, think-local, act-local strategies have three big drawbacks:

1. They hinder transfer of a company's capabilities, knowledge, and other resources across country boundaries, since the company's efforts are not integrated or coordinated across country boundaries. This can make the company less innovative overall.

2. They raise production and distribution costs due to the greater variety of designs and components, shorter production runs for each product version, and complications of added inventory handling and distribution logistics.

3. They are not conducive to building a single, worldwide competitive advantage. When a company's competitive approach and product offering vary from country to country, the nature and size of any resulting competitive edge also tends to vary. At the most, multidomestic strategies are capable of producing a group of local competitive advantages of varying types and degrees of strength.

Global Strategy—Think Global, Act Global

A **global strategy** contrasts sharply with a multidomestic strategy in that it takes a standardized, globally integrated approach to producing, packaging, selling, and delivering the company's products and services worldwide. Companies employing a global strategy sell the same products under the same brand names everywhere, utilize much the same distribution channels in all countries, and compete on the basis of the same capabilities and marketing approaches worldwide. Although the company's strategy or product offering may be adapted in very minor ways to accommodate specific situations in a few host countries, the company's fundamental competitive approach (low cost, differentiation, best cost, or focused) remains very much intact worldwide and local managers stick close to the global strategy.

A **think-global, act-global** strategic theme prompts company managers to integrate and coordinate the company's strategic moves worldwide and to expand into most, if not all, nations where there is significant buyer demand. It puts considerable strategic emphasis on building a *global* brand name and aggressively pursuing opportunities to transfer ideas, new products, and capabilities from one country to another.[23] Global strategies are characterized by relatively centralized value chain activities, such as production and distribution. While there may be more than one manufacturing plant and distribution center to minimize transportation costs, for example, they tend to be few in number. Achieving the efficiency potential of a global strategy requires that resources and best practices be shared, value chain activities be integrated, and capabilities be transferred from one location to another as they are developed. These objectives are best facilitated through centralized decision making and strong headquarters control.

Because a global strategy cannot accommodate varying local needs, it is an appropriate strategic choice when there are pronounced efficiency benefits from standardization and when buyer needs are relatively homogeneous across countries and regions. A globally standardized and integrated approach is

> **CORE CONCEPT**
>
> A **global strategy** is one in which a company employs the same basic competitive approach in all countries where it operates, sells much the same products everywhere, strives to build global brands, and coordinates its actions worldwide with strong headquarters control. It represents a **think-global, act-global** approach.

especially beneficial when high volumes significantly lower costs due to economies of scale or added experience (moving the company further down a learning curve). It can also be advantageous if it allows the firm to replicate a successful business model on a global basis efficiently or engage in higher levels of R&D by spreading the fixed costs and risks over a higher-volume output. It is a fitting response to industry conditions marked by global competition.

The drawbacks of global strategies are several: (1) They do not enable firms to address local needs as precisely as locally based rivals can, (2) they are less responsive to changes in local market conditions, either in the form of new opportunities or competitive threats, (3) they raise transportation costs and may involve higher tariffs, and (4) they involve higher coordination costs due to the more complex task of managing a globally integrated enterprise.

Transnational Strategy—Think Global, Act Local

A **transnational strategy** (sometimes called *glocalization*) incorporates elements of both a globalized and a localized approach to strategy making. This type of middle-ground strategy is called for when there are relatively high needs for local responsiveness as well as appreciable benefits to be realized from standardization, as Figure 7.2 suggests. A transnational strategy encourages a company to **think global, act local** to balance these competing objectives.

Often, companies implement a transnational strategy with mass-customization techniques that enable them to address local preferences in an efficient, semistandardized manner. Both McDonald's and KFC have discovered ways to customize their menu offerings in various countries without compromising costs, product

> **CORE CONCEPT**
>
> A **transnational strategy** is a **think-global, act-local** approach that incorporates elements of both multidomestic and global strategies.

quality, and operating effectiveness. When it first opened Disneyland Paris, Disney learned the hard way that a global approach to its international theme parks would not work; it has since adapted elements of its strategy to accommodate local preferences even though much of its strategy still derives from a globally applied formula. Otis Elevator found that a transnational strategy delivers better results than a global strategy when competing in countries like China where local needs are highly differentiated. In 2000, it switched from its customary single-brand approach to a multibrand strategy aimed at serving different segments of the market. By 2009, it had doubled its market share in China and increased its revenues sixfold.[24]

A transnational strategy is far more conducive than other strategies to transferring and leveraging subsidiary skills and capabilities. But, like other approaches to competing internationally, transnational strategies also have significant drawbacks:

1. They are the most difficult of all international strategies to implement due to the added complexity of varying the elements of the strategy to situational conditions.
2. They place large demands on the organization due to the need to pursue conflicting objectives simultaneously.
3. Implementing the strategy is likely to be a costly and time-consuming enterprise, with an uncertain outcome.

Table 7.1 provides a summary of the pluses and minuses of the three approaches to competing internationally.

Table 7.1   Advantages and Disadvantages of Multidomestic, Global, and Transnational Approaches

	Advantages	Disadvantages
Multidomestic (think local, act local)	• Can meet the specific needs of each market more precisely • Can respond more swiftly to localized changes in demand • Can target reactions to the moves of local rivals • Can respond more quickly to local opportunities and threats	• Hinders resource and capability sharing or cross-market transfers • Higher production and distribution costs • Not conducive to a worldwide competitive advantage
Transnational (think global, act local)	• Offers the benefits of both local responsiveness and global integration • Enables the transfer and sharing of resources and capabilities across borders • Provides the benefits of flexible coordination	• More complex and harder to implement • Conflicting goals may be difficult to reconcile and require trade-offs • Implementation more costly and time-consuming
Global (think global, act global)	• Lower costs due to scale and scope economies • Greater efficiencies due to the ability to transfer best practices across markets • More innovation from knowledge sharing and capability transfer • The benefit of a global brand and reputation	• Unable to address local needs precisely • Less responsive to changes in local market conditions • Higher transportation costs and tariffs • Higher coordination and integration costs

THE QUEST FOR COMPETITIVE ADVANTAGE IN THE INTERNATIONAL ARENA

There are three important ways in which a firm can gain competitive advantage (or offset domestic disadvantages) by expanding outside its domestic market.[25] First, it can use location to lower costs or achieve greater product differentiation. Second, it can transfer competitively valuable resources, competencies, and capabilities from one country to another or share them across international borders to extend and deepen its competitive advantages. And third, it can benefit from cross-border coordination in ways that a domestic-only competitor cannot.

LO 5

Understand how international companies go about building competitive advantage in foreign markets.

Using Location to Build Competitive Advantage

To use location to build competitive advantage, a company must consider two issues: (1) whether to concentrate each activity it performs in a few select countries or to disperse performance of the activity to many nations, and (2) in which countries to locate particular activities.[26]

When to Concentrate Activities in a Few Locations

It is advantageous for a company to concentrate its activities in a limited number of locations when:

- *The costs of manufacturing or other activities are significantly lower in some geographic locations than in others.* For example, much of the world's athletic footwear is manufactured in Asia (China and Korea) because of low labor costs; much of the production of circuit boards for PCs is located in Taiwan because of both low costs and the high-caliber technical skills of the Taiwanese labor force.

- *There are significant scale economies in production or distribution.* The presence of significant economies of scale in components production or final assembly means that a company can gain major cost savings from operating a few ultra-efficient plants as opposed to a host of small plants scattered across the world. Achieving low-cost provider status often requires a company to have the largest worldwide manufacturing share (as distinct from brand share or market share), with production centralized in one or a few world-scale plants. Some companies even use such plants to manufacture units sold under the brand names of rivals to further boost production-related scale economies. Makers of digital cameras and LCD TVs located in Japan, South Korea, and Taiwan have used their scale economies to establish a low-cost advantage. Likewise, a company may be able to reduce its distribution costs by capturing scale economies associated with establishing large-scale distribution centers to serve major geographic regions of the world market (for example, North America, Latin America, Europe–Middle East, and Asia-Pacific).

> Companies that compete internationally can pursue competitive advantage in world markets by locating their value chain activities in whatever nations prove most advantageous.

- *There are sizable learning and experience benefits associated with performing an activity in a single location.* In some industries, a manufacturer can lower unit costs, boost quality, or master a new technology more quickly by concentrating production in a few locations. The greater the cumulative volume of production at a plant, the faster the buildup of learning and experience of the plant's workforce, thereby enabling quicker capture of the learning/experience benefits.

- *Certain locations have superior resources, allow better coordination of related activities, or offer other valuable advantages.* A research unit or a sophisticated production facility may be situated in a particular nation because of its pool of technically trained personnel. Samsung became a leader in memory chip technology by establishing a major R&D facility in Silicon Valley and transferring the know-how it gained back to its operations in South Korea. Companies also locate activities to benefit from proximity to a cluster of related and supporting industries, as discussed earlier. Cisco Systems, an international firm that sells networking and communications technology, such as routers, restricts its acquisitions to companies located in one of three well-known clusters of high-tech activity.[27] Where just-in-time inventory practices yield big cost savings and/or where an assembly firm has long-term partnering arrangements with its key suppliers, parts manufacturing plants may be located close to final assembly plants. A customer service center or sales office may be opened in a particular country to help cultivate strong relationships with pivotal customers located nearby.

When to Disperse Activities across Many Locations

There are several instances when dispersing activities is more advantageous than concentrating them. Buyer-related activities—such as distribution to dealers, sales and advertising, and after-sale service—usually must take place close to buyers. This means physically locating the capability to perform such activities in every country market where a firm has major customers (unless buyers in several adjoining countries can be served quickly from a nearby central location). For example, firms that make mining and oil-drilling equipment maintain operations in many locations around the world to support customers' needs for speedy equipment repair and technical assistance. The four biggest public accounting firms have offices in numerous countries to serve the foreign operations of their international corporate clients. Dispersing activities to many locations is also competitively advantageous when high transportation costs, diseconomies of large size, and trade barriers make it too expensive to operate from a central location. Many companies distribute their products from multiple locations to shorten delivery times to customers. In addition, it is strategically advantageous to disperse activities to hedge against the risks of fluctuating exchange rates, supply interruptions (due to strikes, mechanical failures, and transportation delays), and adverse political developments. Such risks are usually greater when activities are concentrated in a single location.

As discussed earlier, there are a variety of reasons for locating different value chain activities in different countries—all having to do with location-based advantages that vary from country to country. While the classic reason for locating an activity in a particular country is low cost, input quality and availability are also important considerations.[28] Such activities as materials procurement, parts manufacture, finished-goods assembly, technology research, and new product development can frequently be decoupled from buyer locations and performed wherever advantage lies. Components can be made in Mexico; technology research done in Frankfurt; new products developed and tested in Phoenix; and assembly plants located in Spain, Brazil, Taiwan, or South Carolina. Capital can be raised in whatever country it is available on the best terms.

Sharing and Transferring Resources and Capabilities across Borders to Build Competitive Advantage

When a company has competitively valuable resources and capabilities, it may be able to mount a resource-based strategic offensive to enter additional country markets. If a company's resources retain their value in foreign contexts, then entering new markets can extend the company's resource-based competitive advantage over a broader domain. For example, companies have used powerful brand names such as Rolex, Chanel, and Tiffany to extend their differentiation-based competitive advantages into markets far beyond their home-country origins. In each of these cases, the luxury brand name represents a valuable resource that is *shared among all of the company's international operations* and allows the company to command a higher willingness to pay from its customers in each country.

Transferring resources and capabilities across borders provides another means to extend a company's competitive advantage internationally. For example, if a firm learns how to assemble its product more efficiently at its Brazilian plant, the accumulated expertise can be quickly communicated to assembly plants in other world locations. Whirlpool, the leading global manufacturer of home appliances, with 69 manufacturing and technology research centers around the world and sales in nearly every country, uses an online global information technology platform to quickly and effectively transfer key product innovations and improved production techniques both across national borders and across its various appliance brands.

Sharing or transferring resources and capabilities across borders provides a way for a company to leverage its core competencies more fully and extend its competitive advantages into a wider array of geographic markets. Thus a technology-based competitive advantage in one country market may provide a similar basis for advantage in other country markets (depending on local market conditions). But since sharing or transferring valuable resources across borders is a very cost-effective means of extending a company's competitive advantage, these activities can also contribute to a company's competitive advantage on the costs side, giving multinational companies a powerful edge over domestic-only rivals. Since valuable resources and capabilities (such as brands, technologies, and production capabilities) are often developed at very high cost, deploying them abroad spreads the fixed development cost over greater output, thus lowering the company's unit costs. The cost of transferring already developed resources and capabilities is low by comparison. And even if the resources and capabilities need to be fully replicated in the foreign market or adapted to local conditions, this can usually be done at low additional cost relative to the initial investment in capability building.

Consider the case of Walt Disney's theme parks as an example. The success of the theme parks in the United States derives in part from core resources such as the Disney brand name and characters like Mickey Mouse that have universal appeal and worldwide recognition. These resources can be freely shared with new theme parks as Disney expands internationally. Disney can replicate its theme parks in new countries cost-effectively since it has already borne the costs of developing its core resources, park attractions, basic park design, and operating capabilities. The cost of replicating its theme parks abroad should be relatively low, even if they need to be adapted to a variety of local country conditions. By expanding internationally, Disney is able to enhance its competitive advantage over local theme park rivals. It does so by leveraging the differentiation advantage conferred by resources such as the Disney name and the park attractions. And by moving into new foreign markets, it augments its competitive advantage worldwide through the efficiency gains that come from cross border resource sharing and low-cost capability transfer and business model replication.

Sharing and transferring resources and capabilities across country borders may also contribute to the development of broader or deeper competencies and capabilities—ideally helping a company achieve *dominating depth* in some competitively valuable area. For example, an international company that consistently incorporates the same differentiating attributes in its products worldwide has enhanced potential to build a global brand name with significant power in the marketplace. The reputation for quality that Honda established worldwide began in motorcycles but enabled the company to command a position in both automobiles and outdoor power equipment in multiple-country markets. A one-country customer base is often too small to support the resource buildup needed to achieve such depth; this is particularly true when the market is developing or protected and sophisticated resources have not been required. By deploying capabilities across a larger international domain, a company can gain the experience needed to upgrade them to a higher performance standard. And by facing a more challenging set of international competitors, a company may be spurred to develop a stronger set of competitive capabilities. Moreover, by entering international markets, firms may be able to augment their capability set by learning from international rivals, cooperative partners, or acquisition targets.

However, sharing and transferring resources and capabilities across borders cannot provide a guaranteed recipe for competitive success. Because lifestyles and buying habits differ internationally, resources that are valuable in one country may not have value in another. For example, brands that are popular in one country may not transfer well or may lack recognition in the new context and thus offer no advantage against an established local brand. In addition, whether a resource or capability can confer a competitive advantage abroad depends on the conditions of rivalry in each particular market. If the rivals in a foreign country market have superior resources and capabilities, then an entering firm may find itself at a competitive disadvantage even if it has a resource-based advantage domestically and can transfer the resources at low cost.

Using Cross-Border Coordination for Competitive Advantage

Companies that compete on an international basis have another source of competitive advantage relative to their purely domestic rivals: They are able to benefit from coordinating activities across different countries' domains.[29] For example, an international manufacturer can shift production from a plant in one country to a plant in another to take advantage of exchange rate fluctuations, to cope with components shortages, or to profit from changing wage rates or energy costs. Production schedules can be coordinated worldwide; shipments can be diverted from one distribution center to another if sales rise unexpectedly in one place and fall in another. By coordinating their activities, multinational companies may also be able to enhance their leverage with host-country governments or respond adaptively to changes in tariffs and quotas.

Efficiencies can also be achieved by shifting workloads from where they are unusually heavy to locations where personnel are underutilized. Whirlpool's efforts to link its product R&D and manufacturing operations in North America, Latin America, Europe, and Asia allowed it to accelerate the discovery of innovative appliance features, coordinate the introduction of these features in the appliance products marketed in different countries, and create a cost-efficient worldwide supply chain. Whirlpool's conscious efforts to integrate and coordinate its various operations around the world have helped it become a low-cost producer and also speed product innovations to market, thereby giving Whirlpool an edge over rivals worldwide.

PROFIT SANCTUARIES AND CROSS-BORDER STRATEGIC MOVES

Profit sanctuaries are country markets (or geographic regions) in which a company derives substantial profits because of its protected market position or unassailable competitive advantage. Japan, for example, is the chief profit sanctuary for most Japanese companies because trade barriers erected by the Japanese government effectively block foreign companies from competing for a large share of Japanese sales. Protected from the threat of foreign competition in their home market, Japanese companies can safely charge somewhat higher prices to their Japanese customers and thus earn attractively large profits on sales made in Japan. Other profit sanctuaries may be protected because a company has an unassailable market position due to unrivaled and inimitable capabilities. In most cases, a company's biggest and most strategically crucial profit sanctuary is its home market, but multinational companies may also enjoy profit sanctuary status in other nations where they have a strong position based on some type of competitive advantage. Companies that compete worldwide are likely to have more profit sanctuaries than companies that compete in just a few country markets; a domestic-only competitor, of course, can have only one profit sanctuary at most (see Figure 7.3).

Figure 7.3   Profit Sanctuary Potential of Domestic-only, International, and Global Competitors

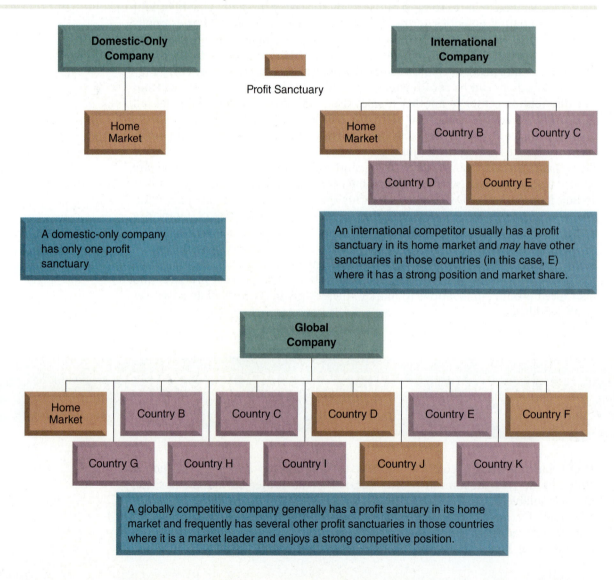

Using Cross-Market Subsidization to Wage a Strategic Offensive

Profit sanctuaries are valuable competitive assets, providing the financial strength to support strategic offensives in selected country markets and fuel a company's race for world-market leadership. The added financial capability afforded by multiple profit sanctuaries gives an international competitor the financial strength to wage a market offensive against a domestic competitor whose only profit sanctuary is its home market. The international company has the flexibility of lowballing its prices or launching high-cost marketing campaigns in the domestic company's home market and grabbing market share at the domestic company's expense. Razor-thin margins or even losses in these markets can be subsidized with the healthy profits earned in its profit sanctuaries—a practice called **cross-market subsidization.** The international company can adjust the depth of its price cutting to move in and capture market share quickly, or it can shave prices slightly to make gradual market inroads (perhaps over a decade or more) so as not to threaten domestic firms precipitously and trigger protectionist government actions. If the domestic company retaliates with matching price cuts or increased marketing expenses, it exposes its entire revenue stream and profit base to erosion; its profits can be squeezed substantially and its competitive strength sapped, even if it is the domestic market leader.

> **CORE CONCEPT**
>
> **Cross-market subsidization**—supporting competitive offensives in one market with resources and profits diverted from operations in another market—can be a powerful competitive weapon.

When taken to the extreme, cut-rate pricing attacks by international competitors may draw charges of unfair dumping. A company is said to be dumping when it sells its goods in foreign markets at prices that are (1) well below the prices at which it normally sells in its home market or (2) well below its full costs per unit. Companies that engage in dumping usually keep their selling prices high enough to cover variable costs per unit, thereby limiting their losses on each unit to some percentage of fixed costs per unit.

Dumping can be a tempting strategy in either of two instances: (1) when selling goods abroad at below-market prices can allow a firm to avoid the high costs of idling plants, and (2) when temporary below-cost pricing can allow a company to make lasting market share gains by driving weak firms from the market. The first may be justified as a legitimate competitive practice, while the latter is usually viewed to be predatory in nature. A charge of unfair dumping is more easily defended when a company with unused production capacity discovers that it is cheaper to keep producing (as long as the selling prices cover average variable costs per unit) than it is to incur the costs associated with idle plant capacity. By keeping its plants operating at or near capacity, not only may a company be able to cover variable costs and earn a contribution to fixed costs, but it also may be able to use its below-market prices to draw price-sensitive customers away from foreign rivals. It is wise for companies pursuing such an approach to court these new customers and retain their business when prices later begin a gradual rise back to normal market levels.

Alternatively, a company may use below-market pricing to drive down the price so far in the targeted country that domestic firms are quickly put in dire financial straits or in danger of being driven out of business. However, using below-market pricing in this way *runs a high risk of host-government retaliation on behalf of the adversely affected domestic companies.* Almost all governments can be expected to retaliate against perceived dumping practices by imposing special tariffs on goods being imported from the countries of the guilty companies.

Indeed, as the trade among nations has mushroomed over the past 10 years, most governments have joined the World Trade Organization (WTO), which promotes fair-trade practices among nations and actively polices dumping. Companies based in France and China were recently found guilty of dumping laminate flooring at unreasonably low prices in Canada to the detriment of Canadian producers.[30] Companies deemed guilty of dumping frequently come under pressure from their government to cease and desist, especially if the tariffs adversely affect innocent companies based in the same country or if the advent of special tariffs raises the specter of an international trade war.

Using Cross-Border Tactics to Defend against International Rivals

Cross-border tactics can also be used as a means of defending against the strategic moves of strong international rivals with multiple profit sanctuaries of their own. If a company finds itself under competitive attack by an international rival in one country market, one way to respond is with a counterattack against one of the rival's key markets in a different country—preferably where the rival is least protected and has the most to lose. This is a possible option when rivals compete against one another in much the same markets around the world.

For companies with at least one profit sanctuary, having a presence in a rival's key markets can be enough to deter the rival from making aggressive attacks. The reason for this is that the combination of some market presence (even at small scale) and a profit sanctuary elsewhere can send a signal to the rival that the company could quickly ramp up production (funded by the profit sanctuary) to mount a competitive attack in that market if the rival attacks one of the company's key markets in another country.

When international rivals compete against one another in multiple-country markets, this type of deterrence effect can restrain them from taking aggressive action against one another due to the fear of a retaliatory response that might escalate the battle into a cross-border competitive war. **Mutual restraint** of this sort tends to stabilize the competitive position of multimarket rivals against one another. And while it may prevent each firm from making any major market share gains at the expense of its rival, it also prevents costly competitive battles that would be likely to erode the profitability of both companies without any compensating gain.

CORE CONCEPT

When the same companies compete against one another in multiple geographic markets, the threat of cross-border counterattacks may be enough to deter aggressive competitive moves and encourage **mutual restraint** among international rivals.

STRATEGIES FOR COMPETING IN THE MARKETS OF DEVELOPING COUNTRIES

Companies racing for global leadership have to consider competing in developing-economy markets like China, India, Brazil, Indonesia, Thailand, Poland, Russia, and Mexico—countries where the business risks are considerable but where the opportunities for growth are huge, especially as their economies develop and living standards climb toward levels in the industrialized world.[31]

With the world now comprising nearly 7 billion people—fully 40 percent of whom live in India and China, and hundreds of millions more live in other, less developed countries in Asia and Latin America—a company that aspires to world market leadership (or to sustained rapid growth) cannot ignore the market opportunities or the base of technical and managerial talent such countries offer. For example, in 2010 China was the world's second-largest economy (behind the United States), as measured by purchasing power. Its population of 1.4 billion people now consumes a quarter of the world's luxury products, due to the rapid growth of a wealthy class.[32] China is also the world's largest consumer of many commodities. China's growth in demand for consumer goods had made it the world's largest market for vehicles by 2009 and put it on track to become the world's largest market for luxury goods by 2014.[33] Thus, no company that aspires to global market leadership can afford to ignore the strategic importance of establishing competitive market positions in China, India, other parts of the Asia-Pacific region, Latin America, and eastern Europe. Illustration Capsule 7.2 describes Yum! Brands' strategy to increase its sales and market share in China.

Tailoring products to fit market conditions in a developing country like China, however, often involves more than making minor product changes and becoming more familiar with local cultures.[34] Ford's attempt to sell a Ford Escort in India at a price of $21,000—a luxury-car price, given that India's best-selling Maruti-Suzuki model sold at the time for $10,000 or less and that fewer than 10 percent of Indian households had an annual purchasing power greater than $20,000—met with a less-than-enthusiastic market response. McDonald's has had to offer vegetable burgers in parts of Asia and to rethink its prices, which are often high by local standards and affordable only by the well-to-do. Kellogg has struggled to introduce its cereals successfully because consumers in many less developed countries do not eat cereal for breakfast and changing habits is difficult and expensive. Single-serving packages of detergents, shampoos, pickles, cough syrup, and cooking oils are very popular in India because they allow buyers to conserve cash by purchasing only what they need immediately. Thus, many companies find that trying to employ a strategy akin to that used in the markets of developed countries is hazardous.[35] Experimenting with some, perhaps many, local twists is usually necessary to find a strategy combination that works.

Strategy Options for Competing in Developing-Country Markets

There are several options for tailoring a company's strategy to fit the sometimes unusual or challenging circumstances presented in developing-country markets:

- *Prepare to compete on the basis of low price.* Consumers in developing markets are often highly focused on price, which can give low-cost local competitors the edge unless a company can find ways to attract buyers with bargain prices as well as better products.[36] For example, when Unilever entered the market for laundry detergents in India, it realized that 80 percent of the population could not afford the brands it was selling to affluent consumers there. To compete against a very low-priced detergent made by a local company, Unilever developed a low-cost detergent (named Wheel), constructed new low-cost production facilities, packaged the detergent in single-use amounts so that it could be sold at a very low unit price, distributed the product to local merchants by handcarts, and crafted an economical marketing campaign that

ILLUSTRATION CAPSULE 7.2

Yum! Brands' Strategy for Becoming the Leading Food Service Brand in China

In 2010, Yum! Brands operated more than 37,000 restaurants in more than 110 countries. Its best-known brands were KFC, Taco Bell, Pizza Hut, A&W, and Long John Silver's. In 2009, its fastest growth in revenues came from its 3,369 restaurants in China, which recorded operating profits of $602 million during the year. KFC was the largest quick-service chain in China, with 2,870 units in 2009, while Pizza Hut was the largest casual-dining chain, with 450 units. Yum! Brands planned to open at least 500 new restaurant locations annually in China, including new Pizza Hut Home delivery units and East Dawning units, which had a menu offering traditional Chinese food. All of Yum! Brands' menu items for China were developed in its R&D facility in Shanghai.

In addition to adapting its menu to local tastes and adding new units at a rapid pace, Yum! Brands also adapted the restaurant ambience and decor to appeal to local consumer preferences and behavior. The company changed its KFC store formats to provide educational displays that supported parents' priorities for their children and to make KFC a fun place for children to visit. The typical KFC outlet in China averaged two birthday parties per day.

In 2009, Yum! Brands operated 60 KFC, Taco Bell, Pizza Hut, A&W, and Long John Silver's restaurants for every 1 million Americans. The company's more than 3,300 units in China represented only 2 restaurants per 1 million Chinese. Yum! Brands management believed that its strategy keyed to continued expansion in the number of units in China and additional menu refinements

would allow its operating profits from restaurants located in China to account for 40 percent of systemwide operating profits by 2017.

Sources: Yum! Brands 2009 10-K and other information posted at www.yum.com.

included painted signs on buildings and demonstrations near stores. The new brand quickly captured $100 million in sales and was the number-one detergent brand in India in 2008 based on dollar sales. Unilever later replicated the strategy in India with low-priced packets of shampoos and deodorants and in South America with a detergent brand named Ala.

- *Be prepared to modify aspects of the company's business model or strategy to accommodate local circumstances (but not to such an extent that the company loses the advantage of global scale and branding).*[37] For instance, when Dell entered China, it discovered that individuals and businesses were not accustomed to placing orders through the Internet (whereas over 50 percent of Dell's sales in North America were online). To adapt, Dell modified its direct sales model to rely more heavily on phone and fax orders and decided to be patient in getting Chinese customers to place Internet orders. Further, because numerous Chinese government departments and state-owned enterprises insisted that hardware vendors make their bids through distributors and systems integrators (as opposed to dealing directly with Dell salespeople, as did large enterprises in other countries), Dell opted to use third parties in marketing its products to this buyer segment (although it did sell through its own sales force where it could). But Dell was careful not to abandon the parts of its business model that gave it a competitive edge over rivals. Similarly, when McDonald's moved into Russia in the 1990s, it was forced to alter its practice of obtaining needed supplies from outside vendors because capable local suppliers were not available; to supply its Russian outlets and stay true to its core principle of serving consistent-quality fast food, McDonald's set up its own vertically integrated supply chain—cattle were imported from Holland and russet potatoes were imported from the United States. McDonald's management also worked with a select number of Russian bakers for its bread, brought in agricultural specialists from Canada and Europe to improve the management practices of Russian farmers, built its own 100,000-square-foot McComplex to produce hamburgers, French fries, ketchup, mustard, and Big Mac sauce, and set up a trucking fleet to move supplies to restaurants.

- *Try to change the local market to better match the way the company does business elsewhere.*[38] An international company often has enough market clout to drive major changes in the way a local country market operates. When Hong Kong–based STAR launched its first satellite TV channel in 1991, it generated profound impacts on the TV marketplace in India. The Indian government lost its monopoly on TV broadcasts, several other satellite TV channels aimed at Indian audiences quickly emerged, and the excitement of additional TV channels in India triggered a boom in TV manufacturing in India. When Japan's Suzuki entered India, it triggered a quality revolution among Indian auto parts manufacturers. Local component suppliers teamed up with Suzuki's vendors in Japan and worked with Japanese experts to produce higher-quality products. Over the next two decades, Indian companies became proficient in making top-notch components for vehicles, won more prizes for quality than companies in any country other than Japan, and broke into the global market as suppliers to many automakers in Asia and other parts of the world. Mahindra and Mahindra, one of India's premier automobile manufacturers, has been recognized by a number of organizations for its product quality. Among its most noteworthy awards was its number-one ranking by J.D. Power Asia Pacific in 2007 for new vehicle overall quality.

- *Stay away from developing markets where it is impractical or uneconomic to modify the company's business model to accommodate local circumstances.*[39] Home Depot expanded into Mexico in 2001 and China in 2006, but it has avoided entry into other developing countries because its value proposition of good quality, low prices, and attentive customer service relies on (1) good highways and logistical systems to minimize store inventory costs, (2) employee stock ownership to help motivate store personnel to provide good customer service, and (3) high labor costs for housing construction and home repairs that encourage homeowners to engage in do-it-yourself projects. Relying on these factors in the U.S. and Canadian markets has worked spectacularly for

Home Depot, but the company has found that it cannot count on these factors in nearby Latin America.

Company experiences in entering developing markets like China, India, Russia, and Brazil indicate that profitability seldom comes quickly or easily. Building a market for the company's products can often turn into a long-term process that involves re-education of consumers, sizable investments in advertising and promotion to alter tastes and buying habits, and upgrades of the local infrastructure (transportation systems, distribution channels, etc.). In such cases, a company must be patient, work within the system to improve the infrastructure, and lay the foundation for generating sizable revenues and profits once conditions are ripe for market takeoff.

> Profitability in developing markets rarely comes quickly or easily—new entrants have to adapt their business models and strategies to local conditions and be patient in earning a profit.

DEFENDING AGAINST GLOBAL GIANTS: STRATEGIES FOR LOCAL COMPANIES IN DEVELOPING COUNTRIES

If opportunity-seeking, resource-rich multinational companies are looking to enter developing-country markets, what strategy options can local companies use to survive? As it turns out, the prospects for local companies facing global giants are by no means grim. Studies of local companies in developing markets have disclosed five strategies that have proved themselves in defending against globally competitive companies.[40] Illustration Capsule 7.3 discusses how a travel agency in China used a combination of these strategies to become that country's largest travel consolidator and online travel agent.

1. *Develop business models that exploit shortcomings in local distribution networks or infrastructure.* In many instances, the extensive collection of resources possessed by the global giants is of little help in building a presence in developing markets. The lack of well-established wholesaler and distributor networks, telecommunication systems, consumer banking, or media necessary for advertising makes it difficult for large internationals to migrate business models proved in developed markets to developing countries. Such markets sometimes favor local companies whose managers are familiar with the local language and culture and are skilled in selecting large numbers of conscientious employees to carry out labor-intensive tasks. Shanda, a Chinese producer of massively multiplayer online role-playing games (MMORPG), has overcome China's lack of an established credit card network by selling prepaid access cards through local merchants. The company's focus on online games also addresses shortcomings in China's software piracy laws. Emerge Logistics has used its understanding of China's extensive government bureaucracy and fragmented network of delivery services to deliver goods for international companies doing business in China. Many foreign firms have found it difficult to get their goods to market since the average Chinese trucking company owns only one or two trucks. An India-based electronics company has been able to carve out a market niche for itself by developing an all-in-one business machine designed especially for India's 1.2 million small shopkeepers that tolerates the frequent power outages in that country.[41]

ILLUSTRATION CAPSULE 7.3

How Ctrip Successfully Defended against International Rivals to Become China's Largest Online Travel Agency

Ctrip has utilized a business model tailored to the Chinese travel market, its access to low-cost labor, and its unique understanding of customer preferences and buying habits to build scale rapidly and defeat foreign rivals such as Expedia and Travelocity in becoming the largest travel agency in China. The company was founded in 1999 with a focus on business travelers, since corporate travel accounts for the majority of China's travel bookings. The company also placed little emphasis on online transactions, since at the time there was no national ticketing system in China, most hotels did not belong to a national or international chain, and most consumers preferred paper tickets to electronic tickets. To overcome this infrastructure shortcoming, the company established its own central database of 5,600 hotels located throughout China and flight information for all major airlines operating in China. Ctrip set up a call center of 3,000 representatives that could use its proprietary database to provide travel information for up to 100,000 customers per day. Because most of its transactions were not done over the Internet, the company hired couriers in all major cities in China to ride by bicycle or scooter to collect payments and deliver tickets to Ctrip's corporate customers. Ctrip also initiated a loyalty program that provided gifts and incentives to the administrative personnel who arranged travel for business executives. By 2009, Ctrip.com held 60 percent of China's online travel market and planned to enter the Taiwanese tourism market, having just acquired EzTravel, Taiwan's largest online travel site.* By April 2010, its market cap reached $5.34 billion and was creeping up rapidly on Expedia's market cap of $7.23 billion.**

*"Ctrip.com Acquires ezTravel," *China Hospitality News,* August 11, 2009, www.chinahospitalitynews.com/en/2009/08/11/12859-ctrip-com-acquires-eztravel/. ** Dennis Schaal, "Online Travel Powerhouses—Priceline, Expedia . . . and Ctrip?" *Tnooz.co: Talking Travel Tech,* April 1, 2010, www.tnooz.com/2010/04/01/news/online-travel-powerhouses-priceline-expedia-and-ctrip/.

Source: Based on information in Arindam K. Bhattacharya and David C. Michael, "How Local Companies Keep Multinationals at Bay," *Harvard Business Review 86,* no. 3 (March 2008), pp. 85–95.

2. *Utilize keen understanding of local customer needs and preferences to create customized products or services.* When developing-country markets are largely made up of customers with strong local needs, a good strategy option is to concentrate on customers who prefer a local touch and to accept the loss of the customers attracted to global brands.[42] A local company may be able to astutely exploit its local orientation—its familiarity with local preferences, its expertise in traditional products, its long-standing customer relationships. A small Middle Eastern cell phone manufacturer competes successfully against industry giants Nokia, Samsung, and Motorola by selling a model designed especially for Muslims—it is loaded with the Koran, alerts people at prayer times, and is equipped with a compass that points them toward Mecca. Shenzhen-based Tencent has become the leader in instant messaging in China through its unique understanding of Chinese behavior and culture.

3. *Take advantage of aspects of the local workforce with which large multinational companies may be unfamiliar.* Local companies that lack the technological capabilities of foreign entrants may be able to rely on their better

understanding of the local labor force to offset any disadvantage. Focus Media is China's largest outdoor advertising firm and has relied on low-cost labor to update its 130,000 LCD displays and billboards in 90 cities in a low-tech manner, while multinational companies operating in China use electronically networked screens that allow messages to be changed remotely. Focus uses an army of employees who ride to each display by bicycle to change advertisements with programming contained on a USB flash drive or DVD. Indian information technology firms such as Infosys Technologies and Satyam Computer Services have been able to keep their personnel costs lower than those of international competitors EDS and Accenture because of their familiarity with local labor markets. While the large internationals have focused recruiting efforts in urban centers like Bangalore and Delhi, driving up engineering and computer science salaries in such cities, local companies have shifted recruiting efforts to second-tier cities that are unfamiliar to foreign firms.

4. *Use acquisition and rapid-growth strategies to better defend against expansion-minded internationals.* With the growth potential of developing markets such as China, Indonesia, and Brazil obvious to the world, local companies must attempt to develop scale and upgrade their competitive capabilities as quickly as possible to defend against the stronger international's arsenal of resources. Most successful companies in developing markets have pursued mergers and acquisitions at a rapid-fire pace to build first a nationwide and then an international presence. Hindalco, India's largest aluminum producer, has followed just such a path to achieve its ambitions for global dominance. By acquiring companies in India first, it gained enough experience and confidence to eventually acquire much larger foreign companies with world-class capabilities.[43] When China began to liberalize its foreign trade policies, Lenovo (the Chinese PC maker) realized that its long-held position of market dominance in China could not withstand the onslaught of new international entrants such as Dell and HP. Its acquisition of IBM's PC business allowed Lenovo to gain rapid access to IBM's globally recognized PC brand, its R&D capability, and its existing distribution in developed countries. This has allowed Lenovo not only to hold its own against the incursion of global giants into its home market but to expand into new markets around the world.[44]

5. *Transfer company expertise to cross-border markets and initiate actions to contend on an international level.* When a company from a developing country has resources and capabilities suitable for competing in other country markets, launching initiatives to transfer its expertise to foreign markets becomes a viable strategic option.[45] Televisa, Mexico's largest media company, used its expertise in Spanish culture and linguistics to become the world's most prolific producer of Spanish-language soap operas. Jollibee Foods, a family-owned company with 56 percent of the fast-food business in the Philippines, combated McDonald's entry first by upgrading service and delivery standards and then by using its expertise in seasoning hamburgers with garlic and soy sauce and making noodle and rice meals with fish to open outlets catering to Asian residents in Hong Kong, the Middle East, and California. By continuing to upgrade its capabilities and learn from its experience in foreign markets, a company can sometimes transform itself into one capable of competing on a worldwide basis, as an emerging global giant.[46] Sundaram Fasteners of India began its foray into foreign markets as a supplier of radiator caps to

GM—an opportunity it pursued when GM first decided to outsource the production of this part. As a participant in GM's supplier network, the company learned about emerging technical standards, built its capabilities, and became one of the first Indian companies to achieve QS 9000 quality certification. With the expertise it gained and its recognition for meeting quality standards, Sundaram was then able to pursue opportunities to supply automotive parts in Japan and Europe.

KEY POINTS

1. Competing in international markets allows companies to (1) gain access to new customers, (2) achieve lower costs through greater scale economies, learning curve effects, or purchasing power, (3) leverage core competencies developed domestically in additional country markets, (4) gain access to resources and capabilities located outside a company's domestic market, and (5) spread business risk across a wider market base.

2. Companies electing to expand into international markets must consider five factors when evaluating strategy options: (1) cross-country variation in factors that affect industry competitiveness, (2) location-based drivers regarding where to conduct different value chain activities, (3) varying political and economic risks, (4) potential shifts in exchange rates, and (5) differences in cultural, demographic, and market conditions.

3. The strategies of firms that expand internationally are usually grounded in home-country advantages concerning demand conditions, factor conditions, related and supporting industries, and firm strategy, structure, and rivalry, as described by the Diamond of National Advantage framework.

4. The pattern of international competition varies in important ways from industry to industry. At one extreme is *multidomestic competition,* in which the market contest among rivals in one country is not closely connected to the market contests in other countries—there is no world market, just a collection of self-contained country (or maybe regional) markets. At the other extreme is *global competition,* in which competitive conditions across national markets are linked strongly enough to form a true world market, wherein leading competitors compete head to head in many different countries.

5. There are six strategic options for entering foreign markets. These include (1) maintaining a national (one-country) production base and exporting goods to foreign markets, (2) licensing foreign firms to produce and distribute the company's products abroad, (3) employing a franchising strategy, (4) establishing a wholly owned subsidiary by acquiring a foreign company, (5) creating a wholly owned foreign subsidiary from the ground up via a greenfield venture, and (6) using strategic alliances or other collaborative partnerships to enter a foreign market.

6. A company must choose among three alternative approaches for competing internationally: (1) a *multidomestic strategy,* which is a *think-local, act-local* approach to crafting international strategy; (2) a *global strategy*—a *think-global, act-global* approach; and (3) a combination *think-global, act-local* approach, known as a *transnational strategy.* A think-local, act-local, or multidomestic, strategy is appropriate for industries or companies that must vary

their product offerings and competitive approaches from country to country in order to accommodate different buyer preferences and market conditions. The think-global, act-global approach that characterizes a global strategy works best when there are substantial cost benefits to be gained from taking a standardized and globally integrated approach and little need for local responsiveness. A transnational approach (think global, act local) is called for when there is a high need for local responsiveness as well as substantial benefits from taking a globally integrated approach. While this is the most challenging international strategy to implement, it can be used when it is feasible for a company to employ essentially the same basic competitive strategy in all markets but still customize its product offering and some aspect of its operations to fit local market circumstances.

7. There are three general ways in which a firm can gain competitive advantage (or offset domestic disadvantages) in international markets. One way involves locating various value chain activities among nations in a manner that lowers costs or achieves greater product differentiation. A second way draws on an international competitor's ability to extend or deepen its competitive advantage by cost-effectively sharing, replicating, or transferring its most valuable resources and capabilities across borders. A third concerns benefiting from cross-border coordination in ways that are unavailable to domestic-only competitors.

8. Profit sanctuaries are country markets in which a company derives substantial profits because of its protected market position. They are valuable competitive assets, providing companies with the financial strength to mount strategic offensives in selected country markets or to support defensive moves that can ward off mutually destructive competitive battles. They may be used to wage strategic offenses in international markets through *cross-subsidization*—a practice of supporting competitive offensives in one market with resources and profits diverted from operations in another market. They may be used defensively to encourage *mutual restraint* among competitors when there is international *multimarket competition* by signaling that each company has the financial capability for mounting a strong counterattack if threatened. For companies with at least one profit sanctuary, having a presence in a rival's key markets can be enough to deter the rival from making aggressive attacks.

9. Companies racing for global leadership have to consider competing in developing markets like China, India, Brazil, Indonesia, and Mexico—countries where the business risks are considerable but the opportunities for growth are huge. To succeed in these markets, companies often have to (1) compete on the basis of low price, (2) be prepared to modify aspects of the company's business model or strategy to accommodate local circumstances (but not so much that the company loses the advantage of global scale and global branding), and/or (3) try to change the local market to better match the way the company does business elsewhere. Profitability is unlikely to come quickly or easily in developing markets, typically because of the investments needed to alter buying habits and tastes, the increased political and economic risk, and/or the need for infrastructure upgrades. And there may be times when a company should simply stay away from certain developing markets until conditions for entry are better suited to its business model and strategy.

10. Local companies in developing-country markets can seek to compete against large multinational companies by (1) developing business models that exploit shortcomings in local distribution networks or infrastructure, (2) utilizing superior understanding of local customer needs and preferences or local relationships, (3) taking advantage of competitively important qualities of the local workforce with which large multinational companies may be unfamiliar, (4) using acquisition strategies and rapid-growth strategies to better defend against expansion-minded multinational companies, or (5) transferring company expertise to cross-border markets and initiating actions to compete on a global level.

ASSURANCE OF LEARNING EXERCISES

LO 2, LO 3, LO 4

1. Harley-Davidson has chosen to compete in various country markets in Europe and Asia using an export strategy. Go to the Investor Relations section at www.harley-davidson.com and read the sections of its latest annual report related to its international operations. Why does it seem that the company has avoided developing production facilities outside the United States?

LO 3, LO 5

2. The Hero Group is among the 10 largest corporations in India, with 20 business segments and annual revenues of $3.2 billion in fiscal 2006. Many of the corporation's business units have utilized strategic alliances with foreign partners to compete in new product and geographic markets. Review the company's statements concerning its alliances and international business operations at www.herogroup.com/alliance.htm, and prepare a two-page report that outlines the group's successful use of international strategic alliances.

LO 2, LO 4, LO 5

3. Assume you are in charge of developing the strategy for an international company selling products in 50 different countries around the world. One of the issues you face is whether to employ a multidomestic strategy, a global strategy, or a transnational strategy.

    a. If your company's product is mobile phones, do you think it would make better strategic sense to employ a multidomestic strategy, a global strategy, or a transnational strategy? Why?

    b. If your company's product is dry soup mixes and canned soups, would a multidomestic strategy seem to be more advisable than a global strategy? Why?

    c. If your company's product is large home appliances such as washing machines, ranges, ovens, and refrigerators, would it seem to make more sense to pursue a multidomestic strategy, a global strategy, or a transnational strategy? Why?

    d. If your company's product is apparel and footwear, would a multidomestic strategy, a global strategy, or a transnational strategy seem to have more appeal? Why?

EXERCISES FOR SIMULATION PARTICIPANTS

The questions below are for simulation participants whose companies operate in an international market arena. If your company competes only in a single country, then skip the questions in this section.

LO 2

1. Does your company compete in a world-market arena characterized by multidomestic competition or global competition? Explain why.

LO 3, LO 4, LO 5

2. Which one of the following best describes the strategic approach your company is taking in trying to compete successfully on an international basis?

   - Think local, act local
   - Think global, act local
   - Think global, act global

   Explain your answer, and indicate two or three chief elements of your company's strategic approach to competing in two or more different geographic regions.

LO 2

3. To what extent, if any, have you and your co-managers adapted your company's strategy to take shifting exchange rates into account? In other words, have you undertaken any actions to try to minimize the impact of adverse shifts in exchange rates?

LO 2

4. To what extent, if any, have you and your co-managers adapted your company's strategy to take geographic differences in import tariffs or import duties into account?

ENDNOTES

[1] Sidney G. Winter and Gabriel Szulanski, "Replication as Strategy," *Organization Science* 12, no. 6 (November–December 2001), pp. 730–43; Sidney G. Winter and Gabriel Szulanski, "Getting It Right the Second Time," *Harvard Business Review* 80, no. 1 (January 2002), pp. 62–69.

[2] A. C. Inkpen and A. Dinur, "Knowledge Management Processes and International Joint Ventures," *Organization Science* 9, no. 4 (July–August 1998), pp. 454–68; P. Dussauge, B. Garrette, and W. Mitchell, "Learning from Competing Partners: Outcomes and Durations of Scale and Link Alliances in Europe, North America and Asia," *Strategic Management Journal* 21, no. 2 (February 2000), pp. 99–126; C. Dhanaraj, M. A. Lyles, H. K. Steensma et al., "Managing Tacit and Explicit Knowledge Transfer in IJVs: The Role of Relational Embeddedness and the Impact on

Performance," *Journal of International Business Studies* 35, no. 5 (September 2004), pp. 428–42; K. W. Glaister and P. J. Buckley, "Strategic Motives for International Alliance Formation," *Journal of Management Studies* 33, no. 3 (May 1996), pp. 301–32.

[3] J. Anand and B. Kogut, "Technological Capabilities of Countries, Firm Rivalry and Foreign Direct Investment," *Journal of International Business Studies* 28, no. 3 (1997), pp. 445–65; J. Anand and A. Delios, "Absolute and Relative Resources as Determinants of International Acquisitions," *Strategic Management Journal* 23, no. 2 (February 2002), pp. 119–35; A. Seth, K. Song, and A. Pettit, "Value Creation and Destruction in Cross-Border Acquisitions: An Empirical Analysis of Foreign Acquisitions of U.S. Firms," *Strategic Management Journal* 23, no. 10 (October 2002), pp. 921–40; J. Anand, L. Capron, and W. Mitchell, "Using

Acquisitions to Access Multinational Diversity: Thinking beyond the Domestic versus Cross-Border M&A Comparison," *Industrial & Corporate Change* 14, no. 2 (April 2005), pp. 191–224.

[4] M. Porter, "The Competitive Advantage of Nations," *Harvard Business Review*, March–April 1990, pp. 73–93.

[5] U.S. Department of Labor, "International Comparisons of Hourly Compensation Costs in Manufacturing in 2007," *Bureau of Labor Statistics Newsletter*, March 26, 2009, p. 8.

[6] "China's Middle Class Found Wanting for Happiness," *The Independent*, March 19, 2010, www.independent.co.uk/life-style/house-and-home/chinas-middle-class-found-wanting-for-happiness-1924180.html.

[7] "China Car Sales 'Overtook the US' in 2009," *BBC News*, January 11, 2010, http://news.bbc.co.uk/2/hi/8451887.stm.

[8] Sangwon Yoon, "South Korea Targets Internet Addicts; 2 Million Hooked," *Valley News,* April 25, 2010, p. C2.

[9] Michael E. Porter, *The Competitive Advantage of Nations* (New York: Free Press, 1990), pp. 53–54.

[10] Ibid., p. 61.

[11] K.E. Meyer, M. Wright, and S. Pruthi, "Institutions, Resources, and Entry Strategies in Emerging Economies," *Strategic Management Journal* 30, no. 5 (2009), pp. 61–80; E. Pablo, "Determinants of Cross-Border M&As in Latin America," *Journal of Business Research* 62, no. 9 (2009), pp. 861–67; R. Olie, "Shades of Culture and Institutions in International Mergers," *Organization Studies* 15, no. 3 (1994), pp. 381–406.

[12] Meyer et al., "Institutions, Resources, and Entry Strategies in Emerging Economies."

[13] See Yves L. Doz and Gary Hamel, *Alliance Advantage* (Boston: Harvard Business School Press, 1998), especially chaps. 2–4; Joel Bleeke and David Ernst, "The Way to Win in Cross-Border Alliances," *Harvard Business Review* 69, no. 6 (November –December 1991), pp. 127–33; Gary Hamel, Yves L. Doz, and C. K. Prahalad, "Collaborate with Your Competitors—and Win," *Harvard Business Review* 67, no. 1 (January–February 1989), pp. 134–35; Porter, *The Competitive Advantage of Nations,* p. 66.

[14] N. Kumar and A. Chadha, "India's Outward Foreign Direct Investments in Steel Industry in a Chinese Comparative Perspective," *Industrial and Corporate Change* 18, no. 2 (2009), pp. 249–67; R. Chittoor, S. Ray, P. Aulakh, and M. B. Sarkar, "Strategic Responses to Institutional Changes: 'Indigenous Growth' Model of the Indian Pharmaceutical Industry," *Journal of International Management* 14 (2008), pp. 252–69.

[15] F. Froese and L. Goeritz, "Integration Management of Western Acquisitions in Japan," *Asian Business and Management* 6 (2007) pp. 95–114.

[16] For a discussion of the pros and cons of alliances versus acquisitions, see Jeffrey H. Dyer, Prashant Kale, and Harbir Singh, "When to Ally and When to Acquire," *Harvard Business Review* 82, no. 7–8 (July–August 2004), pp. 109–15.

[17] For additional discussion of company experiences with alliances and partnerships, see Doz and Hamel, *Alliance Advantage,* chaps. 2–7; and Rosabeth Moss Kanter, "Collaborative Advantage: The Art of the Alliance," *Harvard Business Review* 72, no. 4 (July–August 1994), pp. 96–108.

[18] Jeremy Main, "Making Global Alliances Work," *Fortune,* December 19, 1990, p. 125.

[19] Details are reported in Shawn Tully, "The Alliance from Hell," *Fortune,* June 24, 1996, pp. 64–72.

[20] C. K. Prahalad and K. Lieberthal, "The End of Corporate Imperialism," *Harvard Business Review,* 81, no. 8 (August 2003), pp.109–117.

[21] Ibid.

[22] For an in-depth discussion of the challenges of crafting strategies suitable for a world in which both production and markets are globalizing, see Pankaj Ghemawat, "Managing Differences: The Central Challenge of Global Strategy," *Harvard Business Review* 85, no. 3 (March 2007), pp. 59–68.

[23] For more details on the merits of and opportunities for cross-border transfer of successful strategy experiments, see C. A. Bartlett and S. Ghoshal, *Managing across Borders: The Transnational Solution,* 2nd ed. (Boston: Harvard Business School Press, 1998), pp. 79–80 and chap. 9. Also see Pankaj Ghemawat, "Managing Differences: The Central Challenge of Global Strategy," *Harvard Business Review* 85, no. 3 (March 2007), pp. 58–68.

[24] Lynn S. Paine, "The China Rules," *Harvard Business Review* 88, no. 6 (June 2010) pp. 103–8.

[25] Porter, *The Competitive Advantage of Nations,* pp. 53–55.

[26] Ibid., pp. 55–58.

[27] A. Inkpen, A. Sundaram, and K. Rockwood, "Cross-Border Acquisitions of U.S. Technology Assets," *California Management Review* 42, no. 3 (Spring 2000), pp. 50–71.

[28] Porter, *The Competitive Advantage of Nations,* p. 57.

[29] C. K. Prahalad and Yves L. Doz, *The Multinational Mission* (New York: Free Press, 1987), pp. 58–60; Ghemawat, "Managing Differences," pp. 58–68.

[30] Canadian International Trade Tribunal, findings issued June 16, 2005, and posted at www.citt-tcce.gc.ca (accessed September 28, 2005).

[31] This point is discussed at greater length in Prahalad and Lieberthal, "The End of Corporate Imperialism," pp. 68–79; also see David J. Arnold and John A. Quelch, "New Strategies in Emerging Markets," *Sloan Management Review* 40, no. 1 (Fall 1998), pp. 7–20. For a more extensive discussion of strategy in emerging markets, see C. K. Prahalad, *The Fortune at the Bottom of the Pyramid: Eradicating Poverty through Profits* (Upper Saddle River, NJ: Wharton, 2005), especially chaps. 1–3.

[32] "Is a Luxury Good Consumption Tax Useful?" *Beijing Review.com.cn,* June 18, 2010, www.bjreview.com.cn/print/txt/2010-06/18/content_280191.htm; "GM's First-Half China Sales Surge Past the U.S.," *Bloomberg Businessweek,* July 2, 2010, http://businessweek.com/news/2010-07-02/gm-s-first-half-china-sales-surge-past-the-u-s-.html.

[33] Joanne Muller, "Can China Save GM?" *Forbes.com,* May 10, 2010, www.forbes.com/forbes/2010/0510/global-2000-10-automobiles-china-detroit-whitacre-save-gm.html; "Is a Luxury Good Consumption Tax Useful?"

[34] Prahalad and Lieberthal, "The End of Corporate Imperialism," pp. 72–73.

[35] Tarun Khanna, Krishna G. Palepu, and Jayant Sinha, "Strategies That Fit Emerging Markets," *Harvard Business Review* 83, no. 6 (June 2005), p. 63; Arindam K. Bhattacharya and David C. Michael, "How Local Companies Keep Multinationals at Bay," *Harvard Business Review* 86, no. 3 (March 2008), pp. 94–95.

[36] Prahalad and Lieberthal, "The End of Corporate Imperialism," p. 72.

[37] Khanna, Palepu, and Sinha, "Strategies That Fit Emerging Markets," pp. 73–74.

[38] Ibid., p. 74.

[39] Ibid., p. 76.

[40] The results and conclusions from a study of 134 local companies in 10 emerging markets are presented in Tarun Khanna and Krishna G. Palepu, "Emerging Giants: Building World-Class Companies in Developing Countries," *Harvard Business Review* no. 10 (October 2006), pp. 60–69; also, an examination of strategies used by 50 local companies in emerging markets is discussed in Arindam K. Bhattacharya and David C. Michael, "How Local Companies Keep Multinationals at Bay," pp. 85–95.

[41] Steve Hamm, "Tech's Future," *BusinessWeek,* September 27, 2004, p. 88.

[42] Niroj Dawar and Tony Frost, "Competing with Giants: Survival Strategies for Local Companies in Emerging Markets," *Harvard Business Review* 77, no. 1 (January–February 1999), p. 122; see also Guitz Ger, "Localizing in the Global Village: Local Firms Competing in Global Markets," *California Management Review* 41, no. 4 (Summer 1999), pp. 64–84; Khanna and Palepu, "Emerging Giants," pp. 63–66.

[43] N. Kumar, "How Emerging Giants Are Rewriting the Rules of M&A," *Harvard Business Review,* May 2009, pp. 115–21.

[44] H. Rui and G. Yip, "Foreign Acquisitions by Chinese Firms: A Strategic Intent Perspective," *Journal of World Business* 43 (2008), pp. 213–26.

[45] Dawar and Frost, "Competing with Giants," p. 124.

[46] Ibid., p. 126; Khanna and Palepu, "Emerging Giants," pp. 60–69.

CHAPTER 8

CORPORATE STRATEGY

Diversification and the Multibusiness Company

> Fit between a parent and its businesses is a two-edged sword: A good fit can create value; a bad one can destroy it.
>
> **—Andrew Campbell,**
> *Michael Gould, and Marcus Alexander*

> We are quite pragmatic. If a business does not contribute to our overall vision, it has to go.
>
> **—Richard Wambold**
> *CEO, Pactiv*

> Make winners out of every business in your company. Don't carry losers.
>
> **—Jack Welch**
> *Former CEO, General Electric*

> I think our biggest achievement to date has been bringing back to life an inherent Disney synergy that enables each part of our business to draw from, build upon, and bolster the others.
>
> **—Michael Eisner**
> *Former CEO, Walt Disney Company*

LEARNING OBJECTIVES

LO 1. Understand when and how business diversification can enhance shareholder value.

LO 2. Gain an understanding of how related diversification strategies can produce cross-business strategic fit capable of delivering competitive advantage.

LO 3. Become aware of the merits and risks of corporate strategies keyed to unrelated diversification.

LO 4. Gain command of the analytical tools for evaluating a company's diversification strategy.

LO 5. Understand a diversified company's four main corporate strategy options for solidifying its diversification strategy and improving company performance.

n this chapter, we move up one level in the strategy-making hierarchy, from strategy making in a single-business enterprise to strategy making in a diversified enterprise. Because a diversified company is a collection of individual businesses, the strategy-making task is more complicated. In a one-business company, managers have to come up with a plan for competing successfully in only a single industry environment—the result is what we labeled in Chapter 2 as *business strategy* (or *business-level strategy*). But in a diversified company, the strategy-making challenge involves assessing multiple industry environments and developing a *set* of business strategies, one for each industry arena in which the diversified company operates. And top executives at a diversified company must still go one step further and devise a companywide or *corporate strategy* for improving the attractiveness and performance of the company's overall business lineup and for making a rational whole out of its diversified collection of individual businesses.

In most diversified companies, corporate-level executives delegate considerable strategy-making authority to the heads of each business, usually giving them the latitude to craft a business strategy suited to their particular industry and competitive circumstances and holding them accountable for producing good results. But the task of crafting a diversified company's overall or corporate strategy falls squarely in the lap of top-level executives and involves four distinct facets:

1. *Picking new industries to enter and deciding on the mode of entry.* The first concerns in diversifying are what new industries to get into and whether to enter by starting a new business from the ground up, acquiring a company already in the target industry, or forming a joint venture or strategic alliance with another company.

2. *Pursuing opportunities to leverage cross-business value chain relationships and strategic fit into competitive advantage.* A company that diversifies into businesses with competitively important value chain matchups (pertaining to common technology, supply chain logistics, production, distribution channels, and/or customers) gains competitive advantage potential not open to a company that diversifies into businesses whose value chains are totally unrelated and that require totally different resources and capabilities. Capturing this competitive advantage potential requires capitalizing on such cross-business opportunities as transferring skills or technology from one business to another, reducing costs via sharing common facilities and resources, utilizing the company's well-known brand names and distribution muscle to increase the sales of newly acquired products, and encouraging knowledge-sharing and collaborative activity among the businesses.

3. *Establishing investment priorities and steering corporate resources into the most attractive*

business units. A diversified company's different businesses are usually not equally attractive from the standpoint of investing additional funds. It is incumbent on corporate management to (a) decide on the priorities for investing capital in the company's different businesses, (b) channel resources into areas where earnings potentials are higher and away from areas where they are lower, and (c) divest business units that are chronically poor performers or are in an increasingly unattractive industry. Divesting poor performers and businesses in unattractive industries frees up unproductive investments either for redeployment to promising business units or for financing attractive new acquisitions.

4. *Initiating actions to boost the combined performance of the corporation's collection of businesses.* Corporate strategists must craft moves to improve the overall performance of the corporation's business lineup and sustain increases in shareholder value. Strategic options for diversified corporations include (a) sticking closely with the existing business lineup and pursuing opportunities presented by these businesses, (b) broadening the scope of diversification by entering additional industries, (c) divesting some businesses and retrenching to a narrower collection of diversified businesses with better overall performance prospects, and (d) restructuring the entire company by divesting some businesses and acquiring others so as to put a whole new face on the company's business lineup.

The demanding and time-consuming nature of these four tasks explains why corporate executives generally refrain from becoming immersed in the details of crafting and executing business-level strategies, preferring instead to delegate lead responsibility for business strategy and business-level operations to the heads of each business unit.

In the first portion of this chapter we describe the various means a company can use to become diversified, and we explore the pros and cons of related versus unrelated diversification strategies. The second part of the chapter looks at how to evaluate the attractiveness of a diversified company's business lineup, decide whether the company has a good diversification strategy, and identify ways to improve its future performance. In the chapter's concluding section, we survey the strategic options open to already diversified companies.

WHEN TO DIVERSIFY

As long as a company has its hands full trying to capitalize on profitable growth opportunities in its present industry, there is no urgency to pursue diversification. But the opportunities for profitable growth are often limited in mature industries and declining markets. A company may also encounter diminishing market opportunities and stagnating sales if its industry becomes competitively unattractive and unprofitable. A company's growth prospects may dim quickly if demand for the industry's product is eroded by the appearance of alternative technologies, substitute products, or fast-shifting buyer preferences. Consider, for example, how digital cameras have virtually destroyed the business of companies dependent on making camera film and doing film processing, how iPods and other brands of digital music players (as well as online music stores) have affected the revenues of retailers of music CDs, and how the mushrooming use of cell phones and Internet-based voice communication have diminished demand for landline-based telecommunication services and eroded the revenues of such once-dominant long-distance providers as AT&T, British Telecommunications, and NTT in Japan. Under conditions such as these, diversification into new industries always merits strong consideration—particularly if the resources and capabilities of a company can be employed more fruitfully in other industries.[1]

A company becomes a prime candidate for diversifying under the following four circumstances:[2]

1. When it spots opportunities for expanding into industries whose technologies and products complement its present business.

2. When it can leverage its collection of resources and capabilities by expanding into businesses where these resources and capabilities are valuable competitive assets.

3. When diversifying into additional businesses opens new avenues for reducing costs via cross-business sharing or transfer of competitively valuable resources and capabilities.

4. When it has a powerful and well-known brand name that can be transferred to the products of other businesses and thereby used as a lever for driving up the sales and profits of such businesses.

BUILDING SHAREHOLDER VALUE: THE ULTIMATE JUSTIFICATION FOR DIVERSIFYING

Diversification must do more for a company than simply spread its business risk across various industries. In principle, diversification cannot be considered a success unless it results in *added long-term economic value for shareholders*—value that shareholders cannot capture on their own by purchasing stock in companies in different industries or investing in mutual funds so as to spread their investments across several industries.

For there to be reasonable expectations of producing added long-term shareholder value, a move to diversify into a new business must pass three tests:[3]

1. *The industry attractiveness test.* The industry to be entered must be attractive enough to yield consistently good returns on investment. Whether an industry is attractive depends chiefly on the presence of industry and competitive conditions that are conducive to earning as-good or better profits and return on investment than the company is earning in its present business(es). It is hard to justify diversifying into an industry where profit expectations are *lower* than those in the company's present businesses.

2. *The cost-of-entry test.* The cost of entering the target industry must not be so high as to erode the potential for good profitability. Industry attractiveness is not a sufficient reason for a firm to diversify into an industry. In fact, the more attractive an industry's prospects are for growth and long-term profitability, the more expensive the industry can be to get into. Entry barriers for start-up companies are likely to be high in attractive industries; were barriers

LO 1

Understand when and how business diversification can enhance shareholder value.

low, a rush of new entrants would soon erode the potential for high profitability. And buying a well-positioned company in an appealing industry often entails a high acquisition cost that makes passing the cost-of-entry test less likely. Since the owners of a successful and growing company usually demand a price that reflects their business's profit prospects, it's easy for such an acquisition to fail the cost-of-entry test.

3. *The better-off test.* Diversifying into a new business must offer potential for the company's existing businesses and the new business to perform better together under a single corporate umbrella than they would perform operating as independent, stand-alone businesses—an effect known as **synergy.** For example, let's say that company A diversifies by purchasing company B in another industry. If A and B's consolidated profits in the years to come prove no greater than what each could have earned on its own, then A's diversification won't provide its shareholders with added value. Company A's shareholders could have achieved the same $1 + 1 = 2$ result by merely purchasing stock in company B. Diversification does not result in added long-term value for shareholders unless it produces a $1 + 1 = 3$ effect where the businesses *perform better together* as part of the same firm than they could have performed as independent companies.

> ## CORE CONCEPT
>
> Creating added value for shareholders via diversification requires building a multibusiness company where the whole is greater than the sum of its parts—an outcome known as **synergy.**

Diversification moves must satisfy all three tests to grow shareholder value over the long term. Diversification moves that can pass only one or two tests are suspect.

STRATEGIES FOR ENTERING NEW BUSINESSES

The means of entering new businesses can take any of three forms: acquisition, internal start-up, or joint ventures with other companies.

Acquisition of an Existing Business

Acquisition is a popular means of diversifying into another industry. Not only is it quicker than trying to launch a brand-new operation, but it also offers an effective way to hurdle such entry barriers as acquiring technological know-how, establishing supplier relationships, becoming big enough to match rivals' unit costs, having to spend large sums on introductory advertising and promotions, and securing adequate distribution. Acquisitions are also commonly employed to access resources and capabilities that are complementary to those of the acquiring firm and that cannot be developed readily internally. Buying an ongoing operation allows the acquirer to move directly to the task of building a strong market position in the target industry, rather than getting bogged down in trying to develop the knowledge, experience, scale of operation, and market reputation necessary for a start-up entrant to become an effective competitor.

However, acquiring an existing business can prove quite expensive. The costs of acquiring another business include not only the acquisition price but also the costs of negotiating and completing the purchase transaction and the costs of integrating the business into the diversified company's portfolio. If the company to be acquired is a successful company, the acquisition price will include a hefty *premium* over the preacquisition value of the company. For example, the $5.8 billion that Xerox paid to acquire Affiliated Computer Services in 2010 included a 38 percent premium over the service company's market value.[4] Premiums are paid in order to convince the shareholders and managers of the target company that it is in their financial interests to approve the deal. The average premium in deals between U.S. companies rose to 56 percent in 2009, but it is more often in the 30 to 40 percent range.[5]

> **CORE CONCEPT**
>
> An **acquisition premium** is the amount by which the price offered exceeds the preacquisition market value of the target company.

The big dilemma an acquisition-minded firm faces is whether to pay a premium price for a successful company or to buy a struggling company at a bargain price.[6] If the buying firm has little knowledge of the industry but ample capital, it is often better off purchasing a capable, strongly positioned firm—even if its current owners demand a premium price. However, when the acquirer sees promising ways to transform a weak firm into a strong one and has the resources, the know-how, and the patience to do it, a struggling company can be the better long-term investment.

While acquisitions offer an enticing means for entering a new business, many fail to deliver on their promise.[7] Realizing the potential gains from an acquisition requires a successful integration of the acquired company into the culture, systems, and structure of the acquiring firm. This can be a costly and time-consuming operation. Acquisitions can also fail to deliver long-term shareholder value if the acquirer overestimates the potential gains and pays a premium in excess of the realized gains. High integration costs and excessive price premiums are two reasons that an acquisition might fail the cost-of-entry test. Firms with significant experience in making acquisitions are better able to avoid these types of problems.[8]

Internal Development

Internal development of new businesses has become an increasingly important means for companies to diversify and is often referred to as **corporate venturing** or *new venture development.* It involves building a new business from scratch. Although building a new business from the ground up is generally a time-consuming and uncertain process, it avoids the pitfalls associated with entry via acquisition and may allow the firm to realize greater profits in the end. It may offer a viable means of entering a new or emerging industry where there are no good acquisition candidates.

> **CORE CONCEPT**
>
> **Corporate venturing** (or *new venture development*) is the process of developing new businesses as an outgrowth of a company's established business operations. It is also referred to as *corporate entrepreneurship* or *intrapreneurship* since it requires entrepreneurial-like qualities within a larger enterprise.

Entering a new business via internal development also poses some significant hurdles. An internal new venture not only has to overcome industry entry barriers but also has to invest in new production capacity, develop sources of supply, hire and train employees, build channels of distribution, grow a customer base, and so on. The risks associated with internal start-ups are substantial, and the likelihood of failure is often high. Moreover, the culture, structures, and organizational systems of some companies may impede innovation and make it difficult for corporate entrepreneurship to flourish.

Generally, internal development of a new business has appeal only when (1) the parent company already has in-house most or all of the skills and resources it needs to piece together a new business and compete effectively; (2) there is ample time to launch the business; (3) the internal cost of entry is lower than the cost of entry via acquisition; (4) the targeted industry is populated with many relatively small firms such that the new start-up does not have to compete head to head against larger, more powerful rivals; (5) adding new production capacity will not adversely impact the supply-demand balance in the industry; and (6) incumbent firms are likely to be slow or ineffective in responding to a new entrant's efforts to crack the market.[9]

Joint Ventures

Joint ventures entail forming a new business that is owned jointly by two or more companies. Entering a new business via joint venture can be useful in at least three types of situations.[10] First, a joint venture is a good vehicle for pursuing an opportunity that is too complex, uneconomical, or risky for one company to pursue alone. Second, joint ventures make sense when the opportunities in a new industry require a broader range of competencies and know-how than a company can marshal. Many of the opportunities in satellite-based telecommunications, biotechnology, and network-based systems that blend hardware, software, and services call for the coordinated development of complementary innovations and the tackling of an intricate web of financial, technical, political, and regulatory factors simultaneously. In such cases, pooling the resources and competencies of two or more companies is a wiser and less risky way to proceed. Third, companies sometimes use joint ventures to diversify into a new industry when the diversification move entails having operations in a foreign country—several governments require foreign companies operating within their borders to have a local partner that has minority, if not majority, ownership in the local operations. Aside from fulfilling host-government ownership requirements, companies usually seek out a local partner with expertise and other resources that will aid the success of the newly established local operation.

However, as discussed in Chapters 6 and 7, partnering with another company—in the form of either a joint venture or a collaborative alliance—has significant drawbacks due to the potential for conflicting objectives, disagreements over how to best operate the venture, culture clashes, and so on. Joint ventures are generally the least durable of the entry options, usually lasting only until the partners decide to go their own ways.

Choosing a Mode of Entry

The choice of how best to enter a new business—whether through internal development, acquisition, or joint venture—depends on the answers to four important questions:

- Does the company have all of the resources and capabilities it requires to enter the business through internal development or is it lacking some critical resources?
- Are there entry barriers to overcome?
- Is speed an important factor in the firm's chances for successful entry?
- Which is the least costly mode of entry, given the company's objectives?

The Question of Critical Resources and Capabilities   If a firm has all the resources it needs to start up a new business or will be able to easily purchase or lease any missing resources, it may choose to enter the business via internal development. However, if missing critical resources cannot be easily purchased or leased, a firm wishing to enter a new business must obtain these missing resources through either acquisition or joint venture. Bank of America acquired Merrill Lynch in 2008 to obtain critical investment banking resources and capabilities that it lacked. The acquisition of these additional capabilities complemented Bank of America's strengths in corporate banking and opened up new business opportunities for Bank of America. Firms often acquire other companies as a way to enter foreign markets where they lack local marketing knowledge, distribution capabilities, and relationships with local suppliers or customers. McDonald's acquisition of Burghy, Italy's only national hamburger chain, offers an example.[11] If there are no good acquisition opportunities or if the firm wants to avoid the high cost of acquiring and integrating another firm, it may choose to enter via joint venture. This type of entry mode has the added advantage of spreading the risk of entering a new business, which is particularly attractive when uncertainty is high. DeBeers's joint venture with the luxury goods company LVMH provided DeBeers with the complementary marketing capabilities it needed to enter the diamond retailing business, as well as partner to share the risk.

The Question of Entry Barriers The second question to ask is whether entry barriers would prevent a new entrant from gaining a foothold and succeeding in the industry. If entry barriers are low and the industry is populated by small firms, internal development may be the preferred mode of entry. If entry barriers are high, the company may still be able to enter with ease if it has the requisite resources and capabilities for overcoming high barriers. For example, entry barriers due to reputational advantages may be surmounted by a diversified company with a widely known and trusted corporate name. But if the entry barriers cannot be overcome readily, then the only feasible entry route may be through acquisition of a well-established company. While entry barriers may also be overcome with a strong complementary joint venture, this mode is the more uncertain choice due to the lack of industry experience.

The Question of Speed Speed is another determining factor in deciding how to go about entering a new business. Acquisition is a favored mode of entry when speed is of the essence, as is the case in rapidly changing industries where fast movers can secure long-term positioning advantages. Speed is important in industries where early movers gain experience-based advantages that grow ever larger over time as they move down the learning curve and in technology-based industries where there is a race to establish an industry standard or leading technological platform. But in other cases it can be better to enter a market after the uncertainties about technology or consumer preferences have been resolved and learn from the missteps of early entrants. In these cases, joint venture or internal development may be preferred.

The Question of Comparative Cost The question of which mode of entry is most cost-effective is a critical one, given the need for a diversification strategy to pass the cost-of-entry test. Acquisition can be a high-cost mode of entry due to the need to pay a premium over the share price of the target company. When the premium is high, the price of the deal will exceed the worth of the acquired company as a stand-alone business by a substantial amount. Moreover, the true cost of an acquisition must include the *transaction costs* of identifying and evaluating potential targets, negotiating a price, and completing other aspects of deal making. In addition, the true cost must take into account the costs of integrating the acquired company into the parent company's portfolio of businesses.

Strategic alliances and other types of partnerships may provide a way to conserve on such entry costs. But even here, there are organizational coordination costs and transaction costs that must be considered, including settling on the terms of the arrangement. If the partnership doesn't proceed smoothly and is not founded on trust, these costs may be significant. In making the choice about how to proceed, the firm should also consider the possibility of even simpler arrangements. If the objective is simply to leverage a brand name and company logo, for example, a strategic alliance centered on licensing may be the lowest-cost alternative. Licensing is particularly attractive if the company lacks other resources and capabilities that are needed for an entry move. Harley-Davidson, for example, has chosen to license its brand name to makers of apparel as an alternative to entering the apparel industry, for which it is ill suited.

CHOOSING THE DIVERSIFICATION PATH: RELATED VERSUS UNRELATED BUSINESSES

Once a company decides to diversify, it faces the choice of whether to diversify into **related businesses, unrelated businesses,** or some mix of both. Businesses are said to be *related* when their value chains exhibit competitively important cross-business relationships. By this, we mean that there is a close correspondence between the businesses in terms of how they perform *key* value chain activities and the resources and capabilities each needs to perform those activities. The big appeal of related diversification is to build shareholder value by leveraging these cross-business relationships into competitive advantages, thus allowing the company as a whole to perform better than just the sum of its individual businesses. Businesses are said to be *unrelated* when the resource requirements and key value chain activities are so dissimilar that no competitively important cross-business relationships exist.

The next two sections explore the ins and outs of related and unrelated diversification.

STRATEGIC FIT AND DIVERSIFICATION INTO RELATED BUSINESSES

A related diversification strategy involves building the company around businesses where there is *strategic fit with respect to key value chain activities and competitive assets.* **Strategic fit** exists whenever one or more activities constituting the value chains of different businesses are sufficiently similar as to present opportunities for cross-business sharing or transferring of the resources and capabilities that enable these activities.[12] Prime examples of such opportunities include:

LO 2

Gain an understanding of how related diversification strategies can produce cross-business strategic fit capable of delivering competitive advantage.

- *Transferring specialized expertise, technological know-how, or other competitively valuable capabilities from one business's value chain to another's.*

- *Combining the related value chain activities of separate businesses into a single operation to achieve lower costs.* For instance, it is often feasible to manufacture the products of different businesses in a single plant, use the same warehouses for shipping and distribution, or have a single sales force for the products of different businesses (because they are marketed to the same types of customers).

- *Exploiting common use of a well-known brand name that connotes excellence in a certain type of product range.* For example, Yamaha's name in motorcycles gave the company instant credibility and recognition in entering the personal-watercraft business, allowing it to achieve a significant market share without spending large sums on advertising to establish a brand identity for the WaveRunner. Sony's name in consumer electronics made it easier for Sony to enter the market for video games with its PlayStation console and lineup of PlayStation video games. Apple's well-known and highly popular iPods gave the firm instant credibility and name recognition in launching its iPhones and iPads.

- *Sharing other resources that support corresponding value chain activities of the businesses, such as relationships with suppliers or a dealer network.* After acquiring Marvel Comics in 2009, the Walt Disney Company saw to it that Marvel's iconic characters, such as Spiderman, Iron Man, and the Black Widow, were shared with many of the other Disney businesses, including its theme parks, retail stores, and video game business. (Disney's characters, starting with Mickey Mouse, have always been among the most valuable of its resources.)

- *Engaging in cross-business collaboration and knowledge sharing to create new competitively valuable resources and capabilities.*

CORE CONCEPT

Strategic fit exists when the value chains of different businesses present opportunities for cross-business resource transfer, lower costs through combining the performance of related value chain activities or resource sharing, cross-business use of a potent brand name, and cross-business collaboration to build stronger competitive capabilities.

Related diversification is based on value chain matchups with respect to *key* value chain activities—those that play a central role in each business's strategy and that link to its industry's key success factors. Such matchups facilitate the sharing or transfer of the competitively important resources and capabilities that enable the performance of these activities and underlie each business's quest for competitive advantage. By facilitating the sharing or transferring of such important competitive assets, related diversification can boost each business's prospects for competitive success.

The resources and capabilities that are leveraged in related diversification are *specialized resources and capabilities.* By this, we mean that they have very *specific* applications; their use is restricted to a limited range of business contexts in which these applications are competitively relevant. Because they are adapted for particular applications, specialized resources and capabilities must be utilized by certain kinds of businesses operating in specific types of industries to have value; they have limited utility outside this specific range of industry and business applications. This is in contrast to *generalized resources and capabilities* (such as general management capabilities, human resource management capabilities, and general accounting services), which can be applied usefully across a wide range of industry and business types.

L'Oréal is the world's largest beauty products company, with more than $25 billion in revenues and a successful strategy of related diversification built upon leveraging a highly specialized set of resources and capabilities. These include 18 dermatologic and cosmetic research centers, R&D capabilities and scientific knowledge concerning skin and hair care, patents and secret formulas for hair and skin care products, and robotic applications developed specifically for testing the safety of hair and skin care products. These resources and capabilities are highly valuable for businesses focused on products for human skin and hair—they are *specialized* to such applications, and, in consequence, they are of little or no value beyond this restricted range of applications. To leverage these resources in a way that maximizes their potential value, L'Oréal has diversified into cosmetics, hair care products, skin care products, and fragrances (but not food, transportation, industrial services, or any application area far from the narrow domain in which its specialized resources are competitively relevant). L'Oréal's businesses are related to one another on the basis of its value-generating specialized resources and capabilities and the cross-business linkages among the value chain activities that they enable.

Corning's most competitively valuable resources and capabilities are specialized to applications concerning fiber optics and specialty glass and ceramics. Over the course of its 150-year history, it has developed an unmatched understanding of fundamental glass science and related technologies in the field of optics. Its capabilities now span a variety of sophisticated technologies and include expertise in domains such as custom glass composition, specialty glass melting and forming, precision optics, high-end transmissive coatings, and opto-mechanical materials. Corning has leveraged these specialized capabilities into a position of global leadership in five related market segments: display technologies based on glass substrates, environmental technologies using ceramic substrates and filters, optical fibers and cables for telecommunications, optical biosensors for drug discovery, and specialty materials employing advanced optics and specialty glass solutions. The market segments into which Corning has diversified are all related by their reliance on Corning's specialized capability set and by the many value chain activities that they have in common as a result.

General Mills has diversified into a closely related set of food businesses on the basis of its capabilities in the realm of "kitchen chemistry" and food production technologies. Its businesses include General Mills cereals, Pillsbury and Betty Crocker baking products, yogurts, organic foods, dinner mixes, canned goods, and snacks. Earlier it had diversified into restaurant businesses on the mistaken notion that all food businesses were related. As a result of exiting these businesses in the mid-1990s, the company was able to improve its overall profitability and strengthen its position in its remaining businesses. The lesson from its experience—and a takeaway for the managers of any diversified company—is that it is not product relatedness that defines a well-crafted related diversification strategy. Rather, the businesses must be related in terms of their key value chain activities and the specialized resources and capabilities that enable these activities.[13] An example is Citizen Holdings Company, whose products appear to be different (watches, miniature card calculators, handheld televisions) but are related in terms of their common reliance on miniaturization know-how and advanced precision technologies.[14]

While companies pursuing related diversification strategies may also have opportunities to share or transfer their *generalized* resources and capabilities (e.g. information systems; human resource management practices; accounting and tax services; budgeting, planning, and financial reporting systems; expertise in legal and regulatory affairs; and fringe-benefit management systems), the most competitively valuable opportunities for resource sharing or transfer always come from leveraging their specialized resources and capabilities. The reason for this is that specialized resources and capabilities drive the key value-creating activities that both connect the businesses (at points where there is strategic fit) and link to the key success factors in the markets where they are competitively relevant. Figure 8.1 illustrates the range of opportunities to share and/or transfer specialized resources and capabilities among the value chain activities of related businesses. It is important to recognize that even though generalized resources and capabilities may be shared by multiple business units, such resource sharing alone cannot form the backbone of a strategy keyed to related diversification.

CORE CONCEPT

Related diversification involves sharing or transferring *specialized* resources and capabilities. **Specialized resources and capabilities** have very specific applications and their use is limited to a restricted range of industry and business types, in contrast to **generalized resources and capabilities** that can be widely applied and can be deployed across a broad range of industry and business types.

Figure 8.1   Related Businesses Provide Opportunities to Benefit from Competitively Valuable Strategic Fit

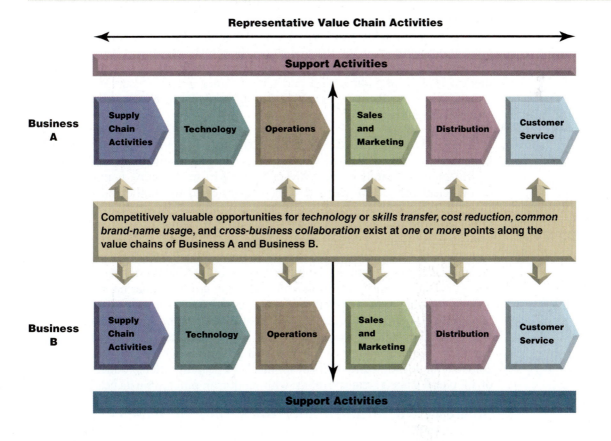

Identifying Cross-Business Strategic Fit along the Value Chain

Cross-business strategic fit can exist anywhere along the value chain—in R&D and technology activities, in supply chain activities and relationships with suppliers, in manufacturing, in sales and marketing, in distribution activities, or in customer service activities.[15]

Strategic Fit in Supply Chain Activities Businesses that have strategic fit with respect to supply chain activities can perform better together because of the potential for skills transfer in procuring materials, the sharing of capabilities in logistics, the benefits of added collaboration with common supply chain partners, and/or added leverage with shippers in securing volume discounts on incoming parts and components. Dell Computer's strategic partnerships with leading suppliers of microprocessors, circuit boards, disk drives, memory chips, flat-panel displays, wireless capabilities, long-life batteries, and other PC-related components have been an important element of the company's strategy to diversify into servers, data storage devices, networking components, and LCD TVs—products that include many components common to PCs and that can be sourced from the same strategic partners that provide Dell with PC components.

Strategic Fit in R&D and Technology Activities Businesses with technology-sharing benefits can perform better together than apart because of potential cost savings in R&D, potentially shorter times in getting new products to market, and more innovative products or processes. Moreover, technological advances in one business can lead to increased sales for both. Technological innovations have been the driver behind the efforts of cable TV companies to diversify into high-speed Internet access (via the use of cable modems) and, further, to explore providing local and long-distance telephone service to residential and commercial customers either through a single wire or by means of VoIP (voice over Internet protocol) technology.

Manufacturing-Related Strategic Fit Cross-business strategic fit in manufacturing-related activities can represent an important source of competitive advantage in situations where a diversifier's expertise in quality manufacture and cost-efficient production methods can be transferred to another business. When Emerson Electric diversified into the chain-saw business, it transferred its expertise in low-cost manufacture to its newly acquired Beaird-Poulan business division; the transfer drove Beaird-Poulan's new strategy—to be the low-cost provider of chain-saw products—and fundamentally changed the way Beaird-Poulan chain saws were designed and manufactured. Another benefit of production-related value chain matchups is the ability to consolidate production into a smaller number of plants and significantly reduce overall production costs. When snowmobile maker Bombardier diversified into motorcycles, it was able to set up motorcycle assembly lines in the same manufacturing facility where it was assembling snowmobiles. When Smucker's acquired Procter & Gamble's Jif peanut butter business, it was able to combine the manufacture of its own Smucker's peanut butter products with those of Jif, plus it gained greater leverage with vendors in purchasing its peanut supplies.

Strategic Fit in Sales and Marketing Activities Various cost-saving opportunities spring from diversifying into businesses with closely related sales and marketing activities. When the products are sold directly to the same customers, sales costs can often be reduced by using a single sales force and avoiding having two different salespeople call on the same customer. The products of related businesses can be promoted at the same Web site and included in the same media ads and sales brochures. After-sale service and repair organizations for the products of closely related businesses can often be consolidated into a single operation. There may be opportunities to reduce costs by consolidating order processing and billing and using common promotional tie-ins. When global power-tool maker Black & Decker acquired Vector Products, it was able to use its own global sales force and distribution facilities to sell and distribute the newly acquired Vector power inverters, vehicle battery chargers, and rechargeable spotlights because the types of customers that carried its power tools (discounters like Walmart and Target, home centers, and hardware stores) also stocked the types of products produced by Vector.

A second category of benefits arises when different businesses use similar sales and marketing approaches; in such cases, there may be competitively valuable opportunities to transfer selling, merchandising, advertising, and product differentiation skills from one business to another. Procter & Gamble's product lineup includes Folgers coffee, Tide laundry detergent, Crest toothpaste, Ivory soap, Charmin toilet tissue, Gillette razors and blades, Duracell batteries, Oral-B toothbrushes, and Head & Shoulders shampoo. All of these have different competitors and different supply chain and production requirements, but they all move through the same wholesale distribution systems, are sold in common retail settings to the same shoppers, are advertised and promoted in much the same ways, and require the same marketing and merchandising skills.

Distribution-Related Strategic Fit   Businesses with closely related distribution activities can perform better together than apart because of potential cost savings in sharing the same distribution facilities or using many of the same wholesale distributors and retail dealers to access customers. When Conair Corporation acquired Allegro Manufacturing's travel bag and travel accessory business in 2007, it was able to consolidate its own distribution centers for hair dryers and curling irons with those of Allegro, thereby generating cost savings for both businesses. Likewise, since Conair products and Allegro's neck rests, ear plugs, luggage tags, and toiletry kits were sold by the same types of retailers (discount stores, supermarket chains, and drugstore chains), Conair was able to convince many of the retailers not carrying Allegro products to take on the line.

Strategic Fit in Customer Service Activities   Opportunities for cost savings from sharing resources or for greater differentiation through skills transfer can come from strategic fit with respect to customer service activities, just as they do along other points of the value chain. For example, cost savings may come from consolidating after-sale service and repair organizations for the products of closely related businesses into a single operation. Likewise, different businesses can often use the same customer service infrastructure. For instance, an electric utility that diversifies into natural gas, water, appliance sales and repair services, and home security services can use the same customer data network, the same customer call centers and local offices, the same billing and customer accounting systems, and the same customer service infrastructure to support all of its products and services. Through the transfer of best practices in customer service across a set of related businesses or through sharing resources such as proprietary information about customer preferences, a multibusiness company can create a differentiation advantage through higher-quality customer service.

Strategic Fit, Economies of Scope, and Competitive Advantage

What makes related diversification an attractive strategy is the opportunity to convert cross-business strategic fit into a competitive advantage over business rivals whose operations do not offer comparable strategic-fit benefits. The greater the relatedness among a diversified company's businesses, the bigger a company's window for converting strategic fit into competitive advantage via (1) transferring skills or knowledge, (2) combining related value chain activities to achieve lower costs, (3) leveraging the use of a well-respected brand name or other differentiation-enhancing resources, and (4) using cross-business collaboration and knowledge sharing to create new resources and capabilities and drive innovation.

The Path to Competitive Advantage and Economies of Scope

Sharing or transferring valuable specialized assets among the company's businesses can help each business perform its value chain activities more proficiently. This translates into competitive advantage for the businesses in one or two basic ways: (1) The businesses can contribute to greater efficiency and lower costs relative to their competitors, and/or (2) they can provide a basis for differentiation so that customers are willing to pay relatively more for the businesses' goods and services. In either or both of these ways, a firm with a well-executed related diversification strategy can boost the chances of its businesses attaining a competitive advantage.

Related businesses often present opportunities to eliminate or reduce the costs of performing certain value chain activities; such cost savings are termed **economies of scope**—a concept distinct from *economies of scale.* Economies of *scale* are cost savings that accrue directly from a larger-size operation; for example, unit costs may be lower in a large plant than in a small plant, lower in a large distribution center than in a small one, lower for large-volume purchases of network advertising than for small-volume purchases. Economies of *scope,* however, stem directly from resource sharing, facilitated by strategic fit along the value chains of related businesses. Such economies are open only to a multibusiness enterprise that enables its businesses to share technology, perform R&D together, use common manufacturing or distribution facilities, share a common sales force or distributor-dealer network, use the same established brand name, and/or share other commonly employed resources and capabilities. *The greater the cross-business economies associated with resource sharing and strategic fit, the greater the potential for a related diversification strategy to yield a competitive advantage based on lower costs than those of rivals.*

From Competitive Advantage to Added Profitability and Gains in Shareholder Value

The competitive advantage potential that flows from economies of scope and the capture of other strategic-fit benefits is what enables a company pursuing related diversification to achieve $1 + 1 = 3$ financial performance and the hoped-for gains in shareholder value. The strategic and business logic is compelling: Capturing the benefits of strategic fit along the value chains of its related businesses gives a diversified company a clear path to achieving competitive advantage over undiversified competitors and competitors whose own diversification efforts don't offer equivalent strategic-fit benefits.[16] Such competitive advantage potential provides a company with a dependable basis for earning profits and a return on investment that exceeds what the company's businesses could earn as stand-alone enterprises. Converting the competitive advantage potential into greater profitability is what fuels $1 + 1 = 3$ gains in shareholder value—the necessary outcome for satisfying the better-off test and proving the business merit of a company's diversification effort.

There are four things to bear in mind here:

1. Capturing cross-business strategic-fit benefits via a strategy of related diversification builds shareholder value in ways that shareholders cannot undertake by simply owning a portfolio of stocks of companies in different industries.
2. The capture of cross-business strategic-fit benefits is possible only via a strategy of related diversification.
3. The benefits of cross-business strategic fit come from the transferring or sharing of competitively valuable resources and capabilities among the businesses—resources and capabilities that are *specialized* to certain applications and have value only in specific types of industries and businesses.
4. The benefits of cross-business strategic fit are not automatically realized when a company diversifies into related businesses; *the benefits materialize only after management has successfully pursued internal actions to capture them.*

> Diversifying into related businesses where competitively valuable strategic-fit benefits can be captured puts a company's businesses in position to perform better financially as part of the company than they could have performed as independent enterprises, thus providing a clear avenue for boosting shareholder value.

DIVERSIFICATION INTO UNRELATED BUSINESSES

An unrelated diversification strategy discounts the merits of pursuing cross-business strategic fit and, instead, focuses squarely on entering and operating businesses in industries that allow the company as a whole to increase its earnings. Companies that pursue a strategy of unrelated diversification generally exhibit a willingness to diversify into *any industry* where senior managers see an opportunity to realize consistently good financial results. Such companies are frequently labeled *conglomerates* because their business interests range broadly across diverse industries. Companies that pursue unrelated diversification nearly always enter new businesses by acquiring an established company rather than by forming a start-up subsidiary within their own corporate structures or participating in joint ventures.

With a strategy of unrelated diversification, the emphasis is on satisfying the attractiveness and cost-of-entry tests and each business's prospects for good financial performance. Thus, with an unrelated diversification strategy, company managers spend much time and effort screening acquisition candidates and evaluating the pros and cons of keeping or divesting existing businesses, using such criteria as:

- Whether the business can meet corporate targets for profitability and return on investment.
- Whether the business is in an industry with attractive growth potential.
- Whether the business is big enough to contribute *significantly* to the parent firm's bottom line.

> **LO 3**
>
> Become aware of the merits and risks of corporate strategies keyed to unrelated diversification.

But the key to successful unrelated diversification is to go beyond these considerations and ensure that the strategy passes the better-off test as well. This test requires more than just growth in revenues; it requires *growth in profits*—beyond what could be achieved by a mutual fund or a holding company that owns the businesses without adding any value. Unless the different businesses are more profitable together under the corporate umbrella than they are apart as independent businesses, *the strategy cannot create economic value for shareholders.* And unless it does so, there is *no real justification for unrelated diversification,* since top executives have a fiduciary responsibility to maximize long-term shareholder value.

Building Shareholder Value via Unrelated Diversification

Given the absence of cross-business strategic fit with which to create competitive advantages, building economic shareholder value via unrelated diversification ultimately hinges on the ability of the parent company to improve its businesses via other means. Critical to this endeavor is the role that the parent company plays *as a corporate parent.* To the extent that a company has strong *parenting capabilities*—capabilities that involve nurturing, guiding, grooming, and governing constituent businesses—a corporate parent can propel its businesses forward and help them gain ground over their market rivals. Corporate parents also contribute to the competitiveness of their unrelated businesses by sharing or transferring *generalized resources and capabilities* across the businesses—competitive assets that have utility in any type of industry and that can be leveraged across a wide range of business types as a result. Examples of the kinds of generalized resources that a corporate parent leverages in unrelated diversification include the corporation's reputation, credit rating, and access to financial markets; governance mechanisms; a corporate ethics program; a central data and communications center; shared administrative resources such as public relations and legal services; and common systems for functions such as budgeting, financial reporting, and quality control.

The three principal ways in which a parent company can further the prospects of its unrelated businesses and increase long-term economic shareholder value are discussed below.

Astute Corporate Parenting   An effective way for a diversified company to improve the performance of its otherwise unrelated businesses is through astute corporate parenting. *Corporate parenting* refers to the role that a diversified corporation plays in nurturing its component businesses through the provision of top management expertise, disciplined control, financial resources, and other types of generalized resources and capabilities such as long-term planning systems, business development skills, management development processes, and incentive systems.[17]

One of the most important ways that corporate parents contribute to the success of their businesses is by offering high-level oversight and guidance.[18] The top executives of a large diversified corporation have among them many years of accumulated experience in a variety of business settings and can often contribute expert problem-solving skills, creative strategy suggestions, and first-rate advice and guidance on how to improve competitiveness and financial performance to the heads of the company's various business subsidiaries; this is especially true in the case of newly acquired businesses. Particularly astute high-level guidance from corporate executives can help the subsidiaries perform better than they would otherwise be able to do through the efforts of the business-unit heads alone.[19]

The outstanding leadership of Royal Little, the founder of Textron, was a major reason that the company became an exemplar of the unrelated diversification strategy while he was CEO. Little's bold moves transformed the company from its origins as a small textile manufacturer into a global powerhouse known for its Bell helicopters, Cessna aircraft, and host of other strong brands in a wide array of industries. Norm Wesley, CEO of the conglomerate Fortune Brands from 1999 to 2007, is similarly credited with driving the sharp rise in the company's stock price while he was at the helm. Fortune Brands is now the $7 billion maker of products ranging from spirits (e.g., Jim Beam bourbon and rye, Gilbey's gin and vodka, Courvoisier cognac) to golf products (e.g., Titleist golf balls and clubs, FootJoy golf shoes and apparel, Scotty Cameron putters) to hardware (e.g., Moen faucets, American Lock security devices, Therma-Tru doors).

Corporate parents can also create added value for their businesses by providing them with other types of generalized or parenting resources that lower the operating costs of the individual businesses or that enhance their operating effectiveness. The administrative resources located at a company's corporate headquarters are a prime example. They typically include legal services, accounting expertise and tax services, and other elements of the administrative infrastructure, such as risk management capabilities, information technology resources, and resources concerning public relations and corporate communications. Providing individual business with such types of generalized and support resources and capabilities creates value by lowering companywide overhead costs, since each business would otherwise have to duplicate the centralized activities.

Corporate brands that do not connote any specific type of product are another type of generalized corporate resource that can be shared among unrelated businesses. GE's brand is an example, having been applied to businesses as diverse as financial services (GE Capital), medical imaging (GE medical diagnostics), and lighting (GE lightbulbs). Corporate brands that are applied in this fashion are sometimes called *umbrella brands*. Utilizing a well-known corporate name (GE) in a diversified company's individual businesses has potential not only to lower costs (by spreading the fixed cost of developing and maintaining the brand over many businesses) but also to enhance each business's customer value proposition by linking its products to a name that consumers trust. In similar fashion, a corporation's reputation for well-crafted products, for product reliability, or for trustworthiness can lead to greater customer willingness to purchase the products of a wider range of a diversified company's businesses. Incentive systems, financial control systems, and a company's culture are other types of generalized corporate resources that may prove useful in enhancing the daily operations of a diverse set of businesses.

Judicious Cross-Business Allocation of Financial Resources

Widely diversified firms may also be able to create added value by serving as an internal capital market and allocating surplus cash flows from some businesses to fund the capital requirements of other businesses. This can be particularly important when interest rates are high or credit is unusually tight (such as in the wake of the worldwide banking crisis that began in 2008) or in economies with less well developed capital markets. Under these conditions, an unrelated diversifier with strong financial resources can add value by shifting funds from business units generating excess cash (more than they need to fund their own operating requirements and new capital investment opportunities) to other, cash-short businesses with appealing growth prospects. A parent company's ability to function as its own internal capital market enhances overall corporate performance and boosts shareholder value to the extent that its top managers have better access to information about investment opportunities internal to the firm than do external financiers and can avoid the costs of external borrowing.

Acquiring and Restructuring Undervalued Companies

One way for parent companies to add value to unrelated businesses is by acquiring weakly performing companies at a bargain price and then *restructuring* their operations (and perhaps their strategies) in ways that produce sometimes dramatic increases in profitability. **Restructuring** refers to overhauling and streamlining the operations of a business—combining plants with excess capacity, selling off redundant or underutilized assets, reducing unnecessary expenses, revamping its product offerings, instituting new sales and marketing approaches, consolidating administrative functions to reduce overhead costs, instituting new financial controls and accounting systems, and otherwise improving the operating efficiency and profitability of a company. Restructuring sometimes involves transferring seasoned managers to the newly acquired business, either to replace the top layers of management or to step in temporarily until the business is returned to profitability or is well on its way to becoming a major market contender.

Restructuring is often undertaken when a diversified company acquires a new business that is performing well below levels that the corporate parent believes are achievable. Diversified companies that have capabilities in restructuring (sometimes called *turnaround capabilities*) are often able to significantly boost the performance of weak businesses in a relatively wide range of industries. Newell Rubbermaid (whose diverse product line includes Sharpie pens, Levolor window treatments, Bernzomatic propane torches, Goody hair accessories, Aprica strollers and car seats, Calphalon cookware, and Lenox power and hand tools) developed such a strong set of turnaround capabilities that the company was said to "Newellize" the businesses it acquired.

Successful unrelated diversification strategies based on restructuring require the parent company to have considerable expertise in identifying underperforming target companies and in negotiating attractive acquisition prices so that each acquisition passes the cost-of-entry test. The capabilities in this regard of Lords James Hanson and Gordon White, who headed up the storied British conglomerate Hanson Trust, played a large part in Hanson's impressive record of profitability through the early 1990s.

The Path to Greater Shareholder Value through Unrelated Diversification

For a strategy of unrelated diversification to produce companywide financial results above and beyond what the businesses could generate operating as stand-alone entities, corporate executives must:

- Do a superior job of diversifying into new businesses that can produce consistently good earnings and returns on investment (to satisfy the attractiveness test).
- Do an excellent job of negotiating favorable acquisition prices (to satisfy the cost-of-entry test).
- Do a superior job of corporate parenting via high-level managerial oversight and resource sharing, financial resource allocation and portfolio management, or restructuring underperforming businesses (to satisfy the better-off test).

The best corporate parents understand the nature and value of the kinds of resources at their command and know how to leverage them effectively across their businesses. Those that are able to create more value in their businesses than other diversified companies have what is called a **parenting advantage**.[20] When a corporation has a parenting advantage, its top executives have the best chance of being able to craft and execute an unrelated diversification strategy that can satisfy all three tests and truly enhance long-term economic shareholder value.

The Drawbacks of Unrelated Diversification

Unrelated diversification strategies have two important negatives that undercut the pluses: very demanding managerial requirements and limited competitive advantage potential.

Demanding Managerial Requirements Successfully managing a set of fundamentally different businesses operating in fundamentally different industry and competitive environments is a very challenging and exceptionally difficult proposition.[21] Consider, for example, that corporations like General Electric and Berkshire Hathaway have dozens of business subsidiaries making hundreds and sometimes thousands of products. While headquarters executives can glean information about the industry from third-party sources, ask lots of questions when making occasional visits to the operations of the different businesses, and do their best to learn about the company's different businesses, they still remain heavily dependent on briefings from business-unit heads and on "managing by the numbers"—that is, keeping a close track on the financial and operating results of each subsidiary. Managing by the numbers works well enough when business conditions are normal and the heads of the various business units are capable of consistently meeting their numbers. But the problem comes when things start to go awry in a business due to exceptional circumstances and corporate management has to get deeply involved in the problems of a business it does not know all that much about. Because every business tends to encounter rough sledding at some juncture, unrelated diversification is thus a somewhat risky strategy from a managerial perspective.[22] Just one or two unforeseen problems or big strategic mistakes (like misjudging the importance of certain competitive forces, not recognizing that a newly acquired business has some serious resource deficiencies and/or competitive shortcomings, or being too optimistic about turning around a struggling subsidiary) can cause a precipitous drop in corporate earnings and crash the parent company's stock price.

Hence, competently overseeing a set of widely diverse businesses can turn out to be much harder than it sounds. In practice, comparatively few companies have proved that they have top management capabilities that are up to the task. There are far more companies whose corporate executives have failed at delivering consistently good financial results with an unrelated diversification strategy than there are companies with corporate executives who have been successful.[23] Unless a company truly has a parenting advantage, the odds are that the result of unrelated diversification will be 1 + 1 = 2 or less.

Limited Competitive Advantage Potential The second big negative is that *unrelated diversification offers a limited potential for competitive advantage beyond what each individual business can generate on its own.* Unlike

> Relying solely on the expertise of corporate executives to wisely manage a set of unrelated businesses is *a much weaker foundation for enhancing shareholder value* than is a strategy of related diversification.

a related diversification strategy, unrelated diversification provides no cross-business strategic-fit benefits that allow each business to perform its key value chain activities in a more efficient and effective manner. A cash-rich corporate parent pursuing unrelated diversification can provide its subsidiaries with much-needed capital, may achieve economies of scope in activities relying on generalized corporate resources, and may even offer some managerial know-how to help resolve problems in particular business units, but otherwise it has little to offer in the way of enhancing the competitive strength of its individual business units. In comparison to the highly specialized resources that facilitate related diversification, the generalized resources that support unrelated diversification tend to be relatively low value, for the simple reason that they are more common. Unless they are of exceptionally high quality (such as GE's world-renowned general management capabilities), resources and capabilities that are generalized in nature are less likely to provide a source of competitive advantage for diversified companies. *Without the competitive advantage potential of strategic fit in strategically important value chain activities, consolidated performance of an unrelated group of businesses stands to be little more than the sum of what the individual business units could achieve if they were independent, in most circumstances.*

Inadequate Reasons for Pursuing Unrelated Diversification

When firms pursue an unrelated diversification strategy for the wrong reasons, the odds are that the result will be 1 + 1 = 2 or less. Rationales for unrelated diversification that are not likely to increase shareholder value include the following:

- *Risk reduction.* Managers sometimes pursue unrelated diversification in order to reduce risk by spreading the company's investments over a set of truly diverse industries whose technologies and markets are largely disconnected. But this cannot create long-term shareholder value since the company's shareholders can more flexibly (and more efficiently) reduce their exposure to risk by investing in a diversified portfolio of stocks and bonds.
- *Growth.* While unrelated diversification may enable a company to achieve rapid or continuous growth, firms that pursue growth for growth's sake are unlikely to maximize shareholder value. While growth can bring more attention and prestige to a firm from greater visibility and higher industry rankings, only profitable growth—the kind that comes from creating added value for shareholders—can justify a strategy of unrelated diversification.
- *Stabilization.* In a broadly diversified company, there's a chance that market downtrends in some of the company's businesses will be partially offset by cyclical upswings in its other businesses, thus producing somewhat less earnings volatility. In actual practice, however, there's no convincing evidence that the consolidated profits of firms with unrelated diversification strategies are more stable or less subject to reversal in periods of recession and economic stress than the profits of firms with related diversification strategies.
- *Managerial motives.* Unrelated diversification can provide benefits to managers such as higher compensation (which tends to increase with firm size and degree of diversification) and reduced employment risk. Diversification for these reasons is far more likely to reduce shareholder value than to increase it.

Because unrelated diversification strategies *at their best* have only a limited potential for creating long-term economic value for shareholders, it is essential that managers not compound this problem by taking a misguided approach toward unrelated diversification, in pursuit of objectives that are more likely to destroy shareholder value than create it.

COMBINATION RELATED-UNRELATED DIVERSIFICATION STRATEGIES

There's nothing to preclude a company from diversifying into both related and unrelated businesses. Indeed, in actual practice the business makeup of diversified companies varies considerably. Some diversified companies are really *dominant-business enterprises*—one major "core" business accounts for 50 to 80 percent of total revenues and a collection of small related or unrelated businesses accounts for the remainder. Some diversified companies are *narrowly diversified* around a few (two to five) related or unrelated businesses. Others are *broadly diversified* around a wide-ranging collection of related businesses, unrelated businesses, or a mixture of both. And a number of multibusiness enterprises have diversified into unrelated areas but have a collection of related businesses within each area—thus giving them a business portfolio consisting of *several unrelated groups of related businesses.* There's ample room for companies to customize their diversification strategies to incorporate elements of both related and unrelated diversification, as may suit their own competitive asset profile and strategic vision. *Combination related-unrelated diversification strategies have particular appeal for companies with a mix of valuable competitive assets, covering the spectrum from generalized to specialized resources and capabilities.*

Figure 8.2 shows the range of alternatives for companies pursuing diversification.

EVALUATING THE STRATEGY OF A DIVERSIFIED COMPANY

Strategic analysis of diversified companies builds on the concepts and methods used for single-business companies. But there are some additional aspects to consider and a couple of new analytical tools to master. The procedure for evaluating the pluses and minuses of a diversified company's strategy and deciding what actions to take to improve the company's performance involves six steps:

LO 4

Gain command of the analytical tools for evaluating a company's diversification strategy.

1. Assessing the attractiveness of the industries the company has diversified into, both individually and as a group.
2. Assessing the competitive strength of the company's business units and determining which are strong contenders in their respective industries.

Figure 8.2   Strategy Alternatives for a Company Pursuing Diversification

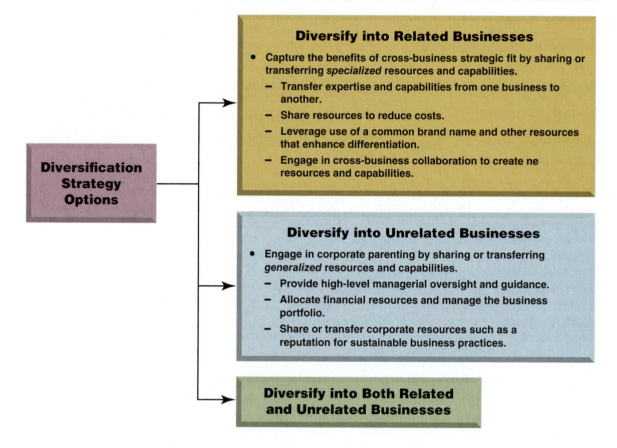

3. Checking the competitive advantage potential of cross-business strategic fit among the company's various business units.

4. Checking whether the firm's resources fit the requirements of its present business lineup.

5. Ranking the performance prospects of the businesses from best to worst and determining what the corporate parent's priority should be in allocating resources to its various businesses.

6. Crafting new strategic moves to improve overall corporate performance.

The core concepts and analytical techniques underlying each of these steps merit further discussion.

Step 1: Evaluating Industry Attractiveness

A principal consideration in evaluating a diversified company's business makeup and the caliber of its strategy is the attractiveness of the industries in which it has business operations. Answers to several questions are required:

1. *Does each industry the company has diversified into represent a good market for the company to be in?* Ideally, each industry in which the firm operates will pass the attractiveness test.

2. *Which of the company's industries are most attractive, and which are least attractive?* Comparing the attractiveness of the industries and ranking them

from most to least attractive is a prerequisite to wise allocation of corporate resources across the various businesses.

3. *How appealing is the whole group of industries in which the company has invested?* The answer to this question points to whether the group of industries holds promise for attractive growth and profitability. A company whose revenues and profits come chiefly from businesses in relatively unattractive industries probably needs to look at divesting businesses in unattractive industries and entering industries that qualify as highly attractive.

The more attractive the industries (both individually and as a group) a diversified company is in, the better its prospects for good long-term performance.

Calculating Industry Attractiveness Scores for Each Industry into Which the Company Has Diversified   A simple and reliable analytical tool involves calculating quantitative industry attractiveness scores, which can then be used to gauge each industry's attractiveness, rank the industries from most to least attractive, and make judgments about the attractiveness of all the industries as a group.

Assessing industry attractiveness involves a consideration of the conditions of each business's macro-environment as well as its competitive environment—the very same factors that are used to evaluate the strategy of a single-business company, as discussed in Chapter 3. Key indicators of industry attractiveness thus include:

- Social, political, regulatory, and environmental factors
- Seasonal and cyclical factors
- Industry uncertainty and business risk
- Market size and projected growth rate
- Industry profitability
- The intensity of competition (five forces)
- Emerging opportunities and threats

In addition, it is critically important to consider those aspects of industry attractiveness that pertain *specifically* to a company's diversification strategy. This involves looking at all the industries in which the company has invested to assess their resource requirements and to consider whether there is good cross-industry strategic fit. The following measures are typically used to gauge industry attractiveness from this multibusiness perspective:

- *The presence of cross-industry strategic fit.* The more an industry's value chain and resource requirements match up well with the value chain activities of other industries in which the company has operations, the more attractive the industry is to a firm pursuing related diversification.
- *Resource requirements.* Industries having resource requirements that match those of the parent company or are otherwise within the company's reach are more attractive than industries in which capital and other resource requirements could strain corporate financial resources and organizational capabilities.

After a set of attractiveness measures that suit a diversified company's circumstances has been identified, each attractiveness measure is assigned a weight reflecting its relative importance in determining an industry's attractiveness—it is weak methodology to assume that the various attractiveness measures are equally important. The intensity of competition in an industry should nearly always carry a high weight (say, 0.20 to 0.30). Strategic-fit considerations should be assigned a high weight in the case of companies with related diversification strategies; but for companies with an unrelated diversification strategy, strategic fit with other industries may be dropped from the list of attractiveness measures altogether. The importance weights must add up to 1.

Next, each industry is rated on each of the chosen industry attractiveness measures, using a rating scale of 1 to 10 (where a *high* rating signifies *high* attractiveness and a *low* rating signifies *low* attractiveness). *Keep in mind here that the more intensely competitive an industry is, the lower the attractiveness rating for that industry.* Likewise, the more the resource requirements associated with being in a particular industry are beyond the parent company's reach, the lower the attractiveness rating. On the other hand, the presence of good cross-industry strategic fit should be given a very high attractiveness rating, since there is good potential for competitive advantage and added shareholder value. Weighted attractiveness scores are then calculated by multiplying the industry's rating on each measure by the corresponding weight. For example, a rating of 8 times a weight of 0.25 gives a weighted attractiveness score of 2.00. The sum of the weighted scores for all the attractiveness measures provides an overall industry attractiveness score. This procedure is illustrated in Table 8.1.

Interpreting the Industry Attractiveness Scores   Industries with a score much below 5 probably do not pass the attractiveness test. If a company's industry attractiveness scores are all above 5, it is probably fair to conclude that the group of industries the company operates in is attractive as a whole. But the group of industries takes on a decidedly lower degree of attractiveness as the number of industries with scores below 5 increases, especially if industries with low scores account for a sizable fraction of the company's revenues.

Table 8.1   Calculating Weighted Industry Attractiveness Scores*

Industry Attractiveness Measure	Importance Weight	Industry A Rating/ Score	Industry B Rating/ Score	Industry C Rating/ Score	Industry D Rating/ Score
Market size and projected growth rate	0.10	8/0.80	5/0.50	7/0.70	3/0.30
Intensity of competition	0.25	8/2.00	7/1.75	3/0.75	2/0.50
Emerging opportunities and threats	0.10	2/0.20	9/0.90	4/0.40	5/0.50
Cross-industry strategic fit	0.20	8/1.60	4/0.80	8/1.60	2/0.40
Resource requirements	0.10	9/0.90	7/0.70	10/1.00	5/0.50
Seasonal and cyclical influences	0.05	9/0.45	8/0.40	10/0.50	5/0.25
Societal, political, regulatory, and environmental factors	0.05	10/0.50	7/0.35	7/0.35	3/0.15
Industry profitability	0.10	5/0.50	10/1.00	3/0.30	3/0.30
Industry uncertainty and business risk	0.05	5/0.25	7/0.35	10/0.50	1/0.05
Sum of the assigned weights	1.00				
Overall weighted industry attractiveness scores		**7.20**	**6.75**	**5.10**	**2.95**

*Rating scale: 1 = very unattractive to company; 10 = very attractive to company.

For a diversified company to be a strong performer, a substantial portion of its revenues and profits must come from business units with relatively high attractiveness scores. It is particularly important that a diversified company's principal businesses be in industries with a good outlook for growth and above-average profitability. Having a big fraction of the company's revenues and profits come from industries with slow growth, low profitability, or intense competition tends to drag overall company performance down. Business units in the least attractive industries are potential candidates for divestiture, unless they are positioned strongly enough to overcome the unattractive aspects of their industry environments or they are a strategically important component of the company's business makeup.

The Difficulties of Calculating Industry Attractiveness Scores There are two hurdles to using this method of evaluating industry attractiveness. One is deciding on appropriate weights for the industry attractiveness measures, since they have a subjective component; different analysts may have different views about which weights are appropriate for the different attractiveness measures. The second hurdle is gaining sufficient command of the industry to assign more accurate and objective ratings. Generally, a company can come up with the statistical data needed to compare its industries on such factors as market size, growth rate, seasonal and cyclical influences, and industry profitability. Cross-industry fit and resource requirements are also fairly easy to judge. But the attractiveness measure on which judgment weighs most heavily is intensity of competition. It is not always easy to conclude whether competition in one industry is stronger or weaker than in another industry because of the different types of competitive influences that prevail and the differences in their relative importance. In the event that the available information is too skimpy to confidently assign a rating value to an industry on a particular attractiveness measure, then it is usually best to use a score of 5, which avoids biasing the overall attractiveness score either up or down.

But despite the hurdles, calculating industry attractiveness scores is a systematic and reasonably reliable method for ranking a diversified company's industries from most to least attractive—numbers like those shown for the four industries in Table 8.1 help pin down the basis for judging which industries are more attractive and to what degree.

Step 2: Evaluating Business-Unit Competitive Strength

The second step in evaluating a diversified company is to appraise how strongly positioned each of its business units is in its respective industry. Doing an appraisal of each business unit's strength and competitive position in its industry not only reveals its chances for industry success but also provides a basis for ranking the units from competitively strongest to competitively weakest and sizing up the competitive strength of all the business units as a group.

Calculating Competitive Strength Scores for Each Business Unit Quantitative measures of each business unit's competitive strength can be calculated using a procedure similar to that for measuring industry attractiveness.

The following factors are used in quantifying the competitive strengths of a diversified company's business subsidiaries:

- Relative market share. A business unit's *relative market share* is defined as the ratio of its market share to the market share held by the largest rival firm in the industry, with market share measured in unit volume, not dollars. A 10 percent market share, for example, does not signal much competitive strength if the leader's share is 50 percent (a 0.20 relative market share), but a 10 percent share is actually quite strong if the leader's share is only 12 percent (a 0.83 relative market share)—this why a company's relative market share is a better measure of competitive strength than a company's market share based on either dollars or unit volume.
- Costs relative to competitors' costs.
- Ability to match or beat rivals on key product attributes.
- Brand image and reputation.
- Other competitively valuable resources and capabilities.
- Ability to benefit from strategic fit with the company's other businesses.
- Ability to exercise bargaining leverage with key suppliers or customers.
- Caliber of alliances and collaborative partnerships with suppliers and/or buyers.
- Profitability relative to competitors. Above-average profitability is a signal of competitive advantage, while below-average profitability usually denotes competitive disadvantage.

After settling on a set of competitive strength measures that are well matched to the circumstances of the various business units, weights indicating each measure's importance need to be assigned. A *case can be made for using different weights* for different business units whenever the importance of the strength measures differs significantly from business to business, but otherwise it is simpler just to go with a single set of weights and avoid the added complication of multiple weights. As before, the importance weights must add up to 1. Each business unit is then rated on each of the chosen strength measures, using a rating scale of 1 to 10 (where a *high* rating signifies competitive *strength* and a *low* rating signifies competitive *weakness*). In the event that the available information is too skimpy to confidently assign a rating value to a business unit on a particular strength measure, then it is usually best to use a score of 5, which avoids biasing the overall score either up or down. Weighted strength ratings are calculated by multiplying the business unit's rating on each strength measure by the assigned weight. For example, a strength score of 6 times a weight of 0.15 gives a weighted strength rating of 0.90. The sum of the weighted ratings across all the strength measures provides a quantitative measure of a business unit's overall market strength and competitive standing. Table 8.2 provides sample calculations of competitive strength ratings for four businesses.

Interpreting the Competitive Strength Scores   Business units with competitive strength ratings above 6.7 (on a scale of 1 to 10) are strong market contenders in their industries. Businesses with ratings in the 3.3-to-6.7 range have moderate competitive strength vis-à-vis rivals. Businesses with ratings below 3.3 are in competitively weak market positions. If a diversified company's business units all have competitive strength scores above 5, it is fair to conclude that its business units are all fairly strong market contenders in their respective industries.

Table 8.2 **Calculating Weighted Competitive Strength Scores for a Diversified Company's Business Units***

Competitive Strength Measure	Importance Weight	Business A in Industry A Rating/ Score	Business B in Industry B Rating/ Score	Business C in Industry C Rating/ Score	Business D in Industry D Rating/ Score
Relative market share	0.15	10/1.50	1/0.15	6/0.90	2/0.30
Costs relative to competitors' costs	0.20	7/1.40	2/0.40	5/1.00	3/0.60
Ability to match or beat rivals on key product attributes	0.05	9/0.45	4/0.20	8/0.40	4/0.20
Ability to benefit from strategic fit with company's other businesses	0.20	8/1.60	4/0.80	8/0.80	2/0.60
Bargaining leverage with suppliers/ buyers; caliber of alliances	0.05	9/0.45	3/0.15	6/0.30	2/0.10
Brand image and reputation	0.10	9/0.90	2/0.20	7/0.70	5/0.50
Competitively valuable capabilities	0.15	7/1.05	2/0.30	5/0.75	3/0.45
Profitability relative to competitors	0.10	5/0.50	1/0.10	4/0.40	4/0.40
Sum of the assigned weights	1.00				
Overall weighted competitive strength scores		**7.85**	**2.30**	**5.25**	**3.15**

*Rating scale: 1 = very weak; 10 = very strong.

But as the number of business units with scores below 5 increases, there's reason to question whether the company can perform well with so many businesses in relatively weak competitive positions. This concern takes on even more importance when business units with low scores account for a sizable fraction of the company's revenues.

Using a Nine-Cell Matrix to Simultaneously Portray Industry Attractiveness and Competitive Strength
The industry attractiveness and business strength scores can be used to portray the strategic positions of each business in a diversified company. Industry attractiveness is plotted on the vertical axis and competitive strength on the horizontal axis. A nine-cell grid emerges from dividing the vertical axis into three regions (high, medium, and low attractiveness) and the horizontal axis into three regions (strong, average, and weak competitive strength). As shown in Figure 8.3, high attractiveness is associated with scores of 6.7 or greater on a rating scale of 1 to 10, medium attractiveness to scores of 3.3 to 6.7, and low attractiveness to scores below 3.3. Likewise, high competitive strength is defined as scores greater than 6.7, average strength as scores of 3.3 to 6.7, and low strength as scores below 3.3. *Each business unit is plotted on the nine-cell matrix according to its overall attractiveness score and strength score, and then it is shown as a "bubble."* The size of each bubble is scaled to the percentage of revenues the business generates relative to total corporate revenues. The bubbles in Figure 8.3 were located on the grid using the four industry attractiveness scores from Table 8.1 and the strength scores for the four business units in Table 8.2.

The locations of the business units on the attractiveness-strength matrix provide valuable guidance in deploying corporate resources to the various business units. In general, *a diversified company's prospects for good overall performance are*

Figure 8.3   **A Nine-Cell Industry Attractiveness–Competitive Strength Matrix**

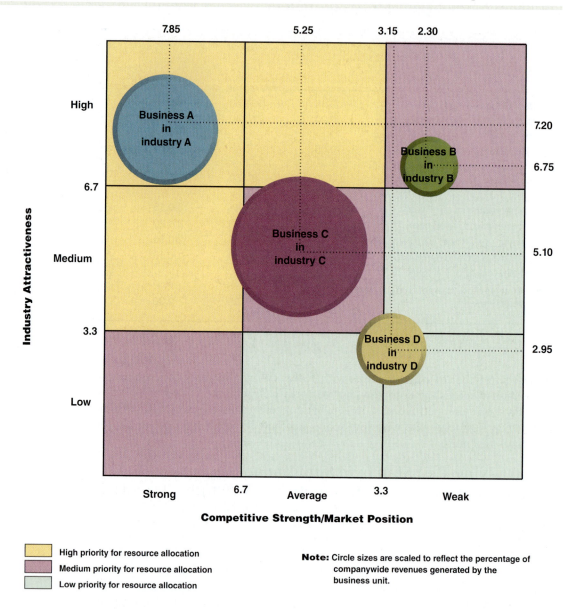

High priority for resource allocation
Medium priority for resource allocation
Low priority for resource allocation

Note: Circle sizes are scaled to reflect the percentage of companywide revenues generated by the business unit.

enhanced by concentrating corporate resources and strategic attention on those business units having the greatest competitive strength and positioned in highly attractive industries—specifically, businesses in the three cells in the upper left portion of the attractiveness-strength matrix, where industry attractiveness and competitive strength/market position are both favorable. The general strategic prescription for businesses falling in these three cells (for instance, business A in Figure 8.3) is "grow and build," with businesses in the high-strong cell standing first in line for resource allocations by the corporate parent.

Next in priority come businesses positioned in the three diagonal cells stretching from the lower left to the upper right (businesses B and C in Figure 8.3). Such businesses usually merit medium or intermediate priority in the parent's resource allocation ranking. However, some businesses in the medium-priority diagonal cells may have brighter or dimmer prospects than others. For example, a small business in the upper right cell of the matrix (like business B), despite being in a highly attractive industry, may occupy too weak a competitive position in its industry to justify the investment and resources needed to turn it into a strong market contender and shift its position leftward in the matrix over time. If, however, a business in the upper right cell has attractive opportunities for rapid growth and a good potential for winning a much stronger market position over time, it may merit a high claim on the corporate parent's resource allocation ranking and be given the capital it needs to pursue a grow-and-build strategy—the strategic objective here would be to move the business leftward in the attractiveness-strength matrix over time.

Businesses in the three cells in the lower right corner of the matrix (like business D in Figure 8.3) typically are weak performers and have the lowest claim on corporate resources. Most such businesses are good candidates for being divested (sold to other companies) or else managed in a manner calculated to squeeze out the maximum cash flows from operations—the cash flows from low-performing/low-potential businesses can then be diverted to financing expansion of business units with greater market opportunities. In exceptional cases where a business located in the three lower right cells is nonetheless fairly profitable (which it might be if it is in the low-average cell) or has the potential for good earnings and return on investment, the business merits retention and the allocation of sufficient resources to achieve better performance.

The nine-cell attractiveness-strength matrix provides clear, strong logic for why a diversified company needs to consider both industry attractiveness and business strength in allocating resources and investment capital to its different businesses. A good case can be made for concentrating resources in those businesses that enjoy higher degrees of attractiveness and competitive strength, being very selective in making investments in businesses with intermediate positions on the grid, and withdrawing resources from businesses that are lower in attractiveness and strength unless they offer exceptional profit or cash flow potential.

Step 3: Checking the Competitive Advantage Potential of Cross-Business Strategic Fit

While this step can be bypassed for diversified companies whose businesses are all unrelated (since, by design, strategic fit is lacking), a high potential for converting strategic fit into competitive advantage is central to concluding just how good a company's related diversification strategy is. Checking the competitive advantage potential of cross-business strategic fit involves searching for and evaluating how much benefit a diversified company can gain from cross-business resource and value chain matchups.

But more than just strategic-fit identification is needed. The real test is what competitive value can be generated from strategic fit. To what extent can cost savings be realized? How much competitive value will come from cross-business transfer of skills, technology, or intellectual capital? Will transferring a potent brand name to the products of other businesses increase sales significantly? Will cross-business collaboration to create or strengthen competitive capabilities lead to significant gains in the marketplace or in financial performance? Without significant strategic fit and

> The greater the value of cross-business strategic fit in enhancing a company's performance in the marketplace or on the bottom line, the more competitively powerful is its strategy of related diversification.

Figure 8.4   Identifying the Competitive Advantage Potential of Cross-Business Strategic Fit

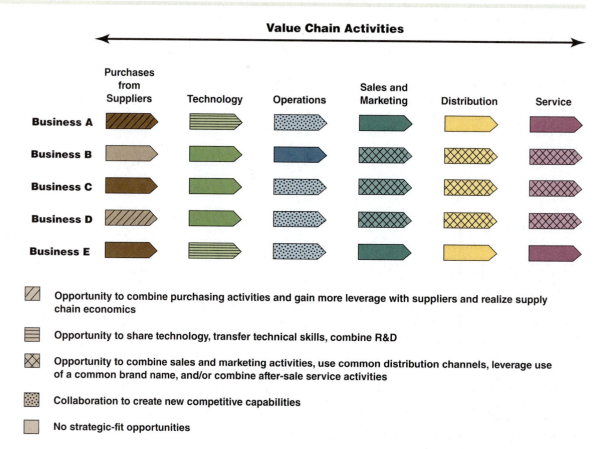

Opportunity to combine purchasing activities and gain more leverage with suppliers and realize supply chain economics

Opportunity to share technology, transfer technical skills, combine R&D

Opportunity to combine sales and marketing activities, use common distribution channels, leverage use of a common brand name, and/or combine after-sale service activities

Collaboration to create new competitive capabilities

No strategic-fit opportunities

dedicated company efforts to capture the benefits, one has to be skeptical about the potential for a diversified company's businesses to perform better together than apart.

Figure 8.4 illustrates the process of comparing the value chains of a company's businesses and identifying opportunities to exploit competitively valuable cross-business strategic fit.

Step 4: Checking for Resource Fit

The businesses in a diversified company's lineup need to exhibit good **resource fit.** In firms with a related diversification strategy, resource fit exists when the firm's businesses strengthen its overall mix of resources and capabilities and when the businesses have matching resource requirements at points along their value chains that are critical for the businesses' market success. In companies pursuing unrelated diversification, resource fit exists when the parent company has capabilities *as a corporate parent* of unrelated businesses, resources of a general nature that it can share or transfer to its component businesses, and corporate resources sufficient to support its entire group of businesses without being spread too thin. Resource fit in terms of a sufficiency of corporate resources to manage and support the entire enterprise is also relevant for related diversifiers and companies pursuing a mixed diversification strategy; Firms pursuing related diversification can also benefit from leveraging the resources of the corporate parent.

Financial Resource Fit One dimension of resource fit concerns whether a diversified company can generate the internal cash flows sufficient to fund the capital requirements of its businesses, pay its dividends, meet its debt obligations, and otherwise remain financially healthy. While additional capital can usually be raised in financial markets, it is important for a diversified firm to have a healthy **internal capital market** that can support the financial requirements of its business lineup. The greater the extent to which a diversified company is able to fund investment in its businesses through internally generated cash flows rather than from equity issues or borrowing, the more powerful its financial resource fit and the less dependent the firm is on external financial resources. This can provide an important competitive advantage over single business rivals when credit market conditions are tight, as they have been in the United States and abroad in recent years.

A *portfolio approach* to ensuring financial fit among a firm's businesses is based on the fact that different businesses have different cash flow and investment characteristics. For example, business units in rapidly growing industries are often **cash hogs**—so labeled because the cash flows they are able to generate from internal operations aren't big enough to fund their expansion. To keep pace with rising buyer demand, rapid-growth businesses frequently need sizable annual capital investments—for new facilities and equipment, for new product development or technology improvements, and for additional working capital to support inventory expansion and a larger base of operations. A business in a fast-growing industry becomes an even bigger cash hog when it has a relatively low market share and is pursuing a strategy to become an industry leader.

In contrast, business units with leading market positions in mature industries may be **cash cows**—businesses that generate substantial cash surpluses over what is needed to adequately fund their operations. Market leaders in slow-growth industries often generate sizable positive cash flows *over and above what is needed for growth and reinvestment* because their industry-leading positions tend to enable them to earn attractive profits and because the slow-growth nature of their industry often entails relatively modest annual investment requirements. Cash cows, although not always attractive from a growth standpoint, are valuable businesses from a financial resource perspective. The surplus cash flows they generate can be used to pay corporate dividends, finance acquisitions, and provide funds for investing in the company's promising cash hogs.

Viewing a diversified group of businesses as a collection of cash flows and cash requirements (present and future) is a major step forward in understanding what the financial ramifications of diversification are and why having businesses with good financial resource fit can be important. For instance, *a diversified company's businesses exhibit good financial resource fit when the excess cash generated by its cash cow businesses is sufficient to fund the investment requirements of*

CORE CONCEPT

A strong **internal capital market** allows a diversified company to add value by shifting capital from business units generating *free cash flow* to those needing additional capital to expand and realize their growth potential.

CORE CONCEPT

A **cash hog** business generates cash flows that are too small to fully fund its operations and growth and requires cash infusions to provide additional working capital and finance new capital investment.

CORE CONCEPT

A **cash cow** business generates cash flows over and above its internal requirements, thus providing a corporate parent with funds for investing in cash hog businesses, financing new acquisitions, or paying dividends.

promising cash hog businesses. Ideally, investing in promising cash hog businesses over time results in growing the hogs into self-supporting *star businesses* that have strong or market-leading competitive positions in attractive, high-growth markets and high levels of profitability. Star businesses are often the cash cows of the future—when the markets of star businesses begin to mature and their growth slows, their competitive strength should produce self-generated cash flows more than sufficient to cover their investment needs. The "success sequence" is thus cash hog to young star (but perhaps still a cash hog) to self-supporting star to cash cow. While the practice of viewing a diversified company in terms of cash cows and cash hogs has declined in popularity, it illustrates one approach to analyzing financial resource fit and allocating financial resources across a portfolio of different businesses.

Aside from cash flow considerations, there are two other factors to consider in assessing whether a diversified company's businesses exhibit good financial fit:

- *Does the company have adequate financial strength to fund its different businesses and maintain a healthy credit rating?* A diversified company's strategy fails the resource-fit test when the company's financial resources are stretched across so many businesses that its credit rating is impaired. Severe financial strain sometimes occurs when a company borrows so heavily to finance new acquisitions that it has to trim way back on capital expenditures for existing businesses and use the big majority of its financial resources to meet interest obligations and to pay down debt. Many of the world's largest banks (e.g., Royal Bank of Scotland, Citigroup, HSBC) recently found themselves so undercapitalized and financially overextended that they were forced to sell off some of their business assets to meet regulatory requirements and restore public confidence in their solvency.

- *Do any of the company's individual businesses not contribute adequately to achieving companywide performance targets?* A business exhibits poor financial fit with the company if it soaks up a disproportionate share of the company's financial resources, makes subpar bottom-line contributions, is too small to make a material earnings contribution, or is unduly risky (such that the financial well-being of the whole company could be jeopardized in the event it falls on hard times).

Nonfinancial Resource Fit   Just as a diversified company must have adequate financial resources to support its various individual businesses, it must also have a big-enough and deep-enough pool of managerial, administrative, and competitive capabilities to support all of its different businesses. The following two questions help reveal whether a diversified company has sufficient nonfinancial resources:

- *Does the company have (or can it develop) the specific resources and capabilities needed to be successful in each of its businesses?*[24] Sometimes a diversified company's resources and capabilities are poorly matched to the resource requirements of one or more businesses it has diversified into. For instance, BTR, a multibusiness company in Great Britain, discovered that the company's resources and managerial skills were quite well suited for parenting its industrial manufacturing businesses but not for parenting its distribution businesses (National Tyre Services and Texas-based Summers Group). As a result, BTR decided to divest its distribution businesses and focus exclusively on diversifying around small industrial manufacturing.[25] For companies pursuing related diversification strategies, a mismatch between the company's competitive assets and the key success factors of an industry can be serious enough to warrant divesting businesses in that industry or not acquiring a new business. In contrast, when a company's resources and capabilities are a good match with the key success factors of industries it is not presently in, it makes sense to take a hard look at acquiring companies in these industries and expanding the company's business lineup.

- *Are the company's resources being stretched too thinly by the resource requirements of one or more of its businesses?* A diversified company must guard against overtaxing its resources and capabilities, a condition that can arise when (1) it goes on an acquisition spree and management is called on to assimilate and oversee many new businesses very quickly or (2) it lacks sufficient resource depth to do a creditable job of transferring skills and competencies from one of its businesses to another. The broader the diversification, the greater the concern about whether the company has sufficient managerial depth to cope with the diverse range of operating problems its wide business lineup presents. Plus, the more a company's diversification strategy is tied to transferring its existing know-how or technologies to new businesses, the more it has to develop a big-enough and deep-enough resource pool to supply these businesses with sufficient capability to create competitive advantage.[26] Otherwise, its competitive assets end up being thinly spread across many businesses, and the opportunity for competitive advantage slips through the cracks.

Step 5: Ranking the Performance Prospects of Business Units and Assigning a Priority for Resource Allocation

Once a diversified company's strategy has been evaluated from the perspective of industry attractiveness, competitive strength, strategic fit, and resource fit, the next step is to rank the performance prospects of the businesses from best to worst and determine which businesses merit top priority for resource support and new capital investments by the corporate parent.

The most important considerations in judging business-unit performance are sales growth, profit growth, contribution to company earnings, and return on capital invested in the business. Sometimes, cash flow is a big consideration. As a rule, the prior analyses, taken together, signal which business units are likely to be strong performers on the road ahead and which are likely to be laggards. And it is a short step from ranking the prospects of business units to drawing conclusions about whether the company as a whole is capable of strong, mediocre, or weak performance in upcoming years.

The rankings of future performance generally determine what priority the corporate parent should give to each business in terms of resource allocation. *Business subsidiaries with the brightest profit and growth prospects and solid strategic and resource fit generally should head the list for corporate resource support.* More specifically, corporate executives must be diligent in steering resources out of low-opportunity areas into high-opportunity areas. Divesting marginal businesses is one of the best ways of freeing unproductive assets for redeployment. Surplus funds from cash cows also can be used to finance the range of chief strategic and financial options shown in Figure 8.5. Ideally, a company will have enough funds to do what is needed, both strategically and financially. If not,

Figure 8.5   **The Chief Strategic and Financial Options for Allocating a Diversified Company's Financial Resources**

strategic uses of corporate resources should usually take precedence unless there is a compelling reason to strengthen the firm's balance sheet or divert financial resources to pacify shareholders.

Step 6: Crafting New Strategic Moves to Improve Overall Corporate Performance

LO 5

Understand a diversified company's four main corporate strategy options for solidifying its diversification strategy and improving company performance.

The diagnosis and conclusions flowing from the five preceding analytical steps set the agenda for crafting strategic moves to improve a diversified company's overall performance. Corporate strategy options once a company has diversified boil down to four broad categories of actions (see Figure 8.6):

1. Sticking closely with the existing business lineup and pursuing the opportunities these businesses present.
2. Broadening the company's business scope by making new acquisitions in new industries.
3. Divesting some businesses and retrenching to a narrower base of business operations.
4. Restructuring the company's business lineup with a combination of divestitures and new acquisitions to put a whole new face on the company's business makeup.

Sticking Closely with the Existing Business Lineup   The option of sticking with the current business lineup makes sense when the company's present businesses offer attractive growth opportunities and can be counted on to create economic value for shareholders. As long as the company's set of existing businesses puts it in good position for the future and these businesses

Figure 8.6 **A Company's Four Main Strategic Alternatives After It Diversifies**

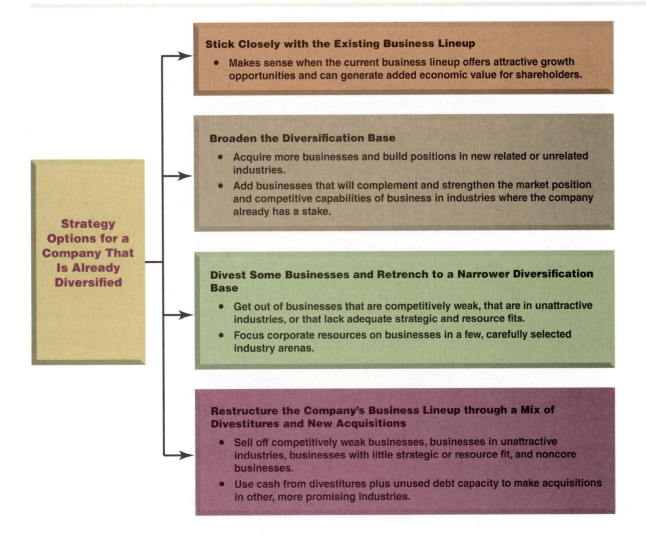

Strategy Options for a Company That Is Already Diversified

Stick Closely with the Existing Business Lineup
- Makes sense when the current business lineup offers attractive growth opportunities and can generate added economic value for shareholders.

Broaden the Diversification Base
- Acquire more businesses and build positions in new related or unrelated industries.
- Add businesses that will complement and strengthen the market position and competitive capabilities of business in industries where the company already has a stake.

Divest Some Businesses and Retrench to a Narrower Diversification Base
- Get out of businesses that are competitively weak, that are in unattractive industries, or that lack adequate strategic and resource fits.
- Focus corporate resources on businesses in a few, carefully selected industry arenas.

Restructure the Company's Business Lineup through a Mix of Divestitures and New Acquisitions
- Sell off competitively weak businesses, businesses in unattractive industries, businesses with little strategic or resource fit, and noncore businesses.
- Use cash from divestitures plus unused debt capacity to make acquisitions in other, more promising industries.

have good strategic and resource fit, then rocking the boat with major changes in the company's business mix is unnecessary. Corporate executives can concentrate their attention on getting the best performance from each of the businesses, steering corporate resources into areas of greatest potential and profitability. The specifics of "what to do" to wring better performance from the present business lineup have to be dictated by each business's circumstances and the preceding analysis of the corporate parent's diversification strategy.

However, in the event that corporate executives are not entirely satisfied with the opportunities they see in the company's present set of businesses and conclude that changes in the company's direction and business makeup are in order, they can opt for any of the three other strategic alternatives that follow.

Broadening a Diversified Company's Business Base Diversified companies sometimes find it desirable to build positions in new industries, whether related or unrelated. There are several motivating factors. One is the potential for transferring resources and capabilities to other related or complementary businesses. A second is rapidly changing conditions in one or more of a company's core businesses brought on by technological, legislative, or new product innovations that alter buyer preferences and resource requirements. For instance, the passage of legislation in the United States allowing banks, insurance companies, and stock brokerages to enter each other's businesses spurred a raft of acquisitions and mergers to create full-service financial enterprises capable of meeting the multiple financial needs of customers.

A third, and often very important, motivating factor for adding new businesses is to complement and strengthen the market position and competitive capabilities of one or more of the company's present businesses. Procter & Gamble's acquisition of Gillette strengthened and extended P&G's reach into personal care and household products—Gillette's businesses included Oral-B toothbrushes, Gillette razors and razor blades, Duracell batteries, and Braun shavers and small appliances. Cisco Systems built itself into a worldwide leader in networking systems for the Internet by making 130 technology-based acquisitions between 1993 and 2008 to extend its market reach from routing and switching into IP telephony, home networking, wireless LAN, storage networking, network security, broadband, and optical and broadband systems.

Another important avenue for expanding the scope of a diversified company is to grow by extending the operations of existing businesses into additional country markets. Expanding a company's geographic scope may offer an exceptional competitive advantage potential by facilitating the full capture of economies of scale and learning/experience curve effects. In some businesses, the volume of sales needed to realize full economies of scale and/or benefit fully from experience and learning curve effects exceeds the volume that can be achieved by operating within the boundaries of just one or several country markets, especially small ones.

Illustration Capsule 8.1 describes how Johnson & Johnson has used acquisitions to diversify far beyond its well-known Band-Aid and baby care businesses and become a major player in pharmaceuticals, medical devices, and medical diagnostics.

Divesting Some Businesses and Retrenching to a Narrower Diversification Base
Retrenching to a narrower diversification base is usually undertaken when top management concludes that its diversification strategy has ranged too far afield and that the company can improve long-term performance by concentrating on building stronger positions in a smaller number of core businesses and industries. Hewlett-Packard spun off its testing and measurement businesses into a stand-alone company called Agilent Technologies so that it could better concentrate on its PC, workstation, server, printer and peripherals, and electronics businesses.

But there are other important reasons for divesting one or more of a company's present businesses. Sometimes divesting a business has to be considered because market conditions in a once-attractive industry have badly deteriorated. A business can become a prime candidate for divestiture because it lacks adequate strategic or resource fit, because it is a cash hog with questionable long-term potential, or because it is weakly positioned in its industry with little prospect the corporate parent can realize a decent return on its investment in the business. Sometimes a company acquires businesses that, down the road, just do not work out as expected even though management has tried all it can think of to make them profitable. Subpar performance by some business units is bound to occur,

Managing Diversification at Johnson & Johnson: The Benefits of Cross-Business Strategic Fit

Johnson & Johnson (J&J), once a consumer products company known for its Band-Aid line and its baby care products, has evolved into a $61 billion diversified enterprise consisting of some 250-plus operating companies organized into three divisions: pharmaceuticals, medical devices and diagnostics, and consumer health care products. Over the past decade J&J has made acquisitions totaling more than $50 billion; about 10 to 15 percent of J&J's annual growth in revenues has come from acquisitions. Much of the company's recent growth has been in the pharmaceutical division, which in 2009 accounted for 36 percent of J&J's revenues and 41 percent of its operating profits.

While each of J&J's business units sets its own strategies and operates with its own finance and human resource departments, corporate management strongly encourages cross-business cooperation and collaboration, believing that many of the advances in 21st-century medicine will come from applying advances in one discipline to another. J&J's drug-coated stent grew out of a discussion between a drug researcher and a researcher in the company's stent business. The innovative product helps prevent infection after cardiac procedures. (When stents are inserted to prop open arteries following angioplasty, the drug coating helps prevent infection.) A gene technology database compiled by the company's gene research lab was shared with personnel from the diagnostics division, who developed a test that the drug researchers used to predict which patients would most benefit from an experimental cancer therapy. J&J's liquid Band-Aid product (a liquid coating applied to hard-to-cover places like fingers and knuckles) is based on a material used in a wound-closing product sold by the company's hospital products company. Scientists from three separate business units worked collaboratively toward the development of an absorbable patch that would stop bleeding on contact. The development of the instant clotting patch was expected to save the lives of thousands of accident victims since uncontrolled bleeding was the number-one cause of death due to injury.

J&J's corporate management maintains that close collaboration among people in its diagnostics, medical devices, and pharmaceutical businesses—where numerous examples of cross-business strategic fit exist—gives J&J an edge on competitors, most of whom cannot match the company's breadth and depth of expertise.

Sources: Amy Barrett, "Staying on Top," *BusinessWeek,* May 5, 2003, pp. 60–68; Johnson & Johnson 2007 Annual Report; www. jnj.com (accessed July 29, 2010).

thereby raising questions of whether to divest them or keep them and attempt a turnaround. Other business units, despite adequate financial performance, may not mesh as well with the rest of the firm as was originally thought. For instance, PepsiCo divested its group of fast-food restaurant businesses to focus its resources on its core soft-drink and snack-food businesses, where their resources and capabilities could add more value.

On occasion, a diversification move that seems sensible from a strategic-fit standpoint turns out to be a poor *cultural fit.*[27] Several pharmaceutical companies had just this experience. When they diversified into cosmetics and perfume, they discovered their personnel had little respect for the "frivolous" nature of such products compared to the far nobler task of developing miracle drugs to cure the ill. The absence of shared values and cultural compatibility between the medical research and chemical-compounding expertise of the pharmaceutical companies and the fashion/marketing orientation of the cosmetics business was the undoing of what otherwise was diversification into businesses with technology-sharing potential, product-development fit, and some overlap in distribution channels.

There's evidence indicating that pruning businesses and narrowing a firm's diversification base improves corporate performance.[28] A useful guide to determine whether or when to divest a business subsidiary is to ask, "If we were not in this business today, would we want to get into it now?"[29] When the answer is no or probably not, divestiture should be considered. Another signal that a business should become a divestiture candidate is whether it is worth more to another company than to the present parent; in such cases, shareholders would be well served if the company sells the business and collects a premium price from the buyer for whom the business is a valuable fit.[30]

Selling a business outright to another company is far and away the most frequently used option for divesting a business. But sometimes a business selected for divestiture has ample resources and capabilities to compete successfully on its own. In such cases, a corporate parent may elect to spin the unwanted business off as a financially and managerially independent company, either by selling shares to the investing public via an initial public offering or by distributing shares in the new company to existing shareholders of the corporate parent.

> Diversified companies need to divest low-performing businesses or businesses that don't fit in order to concentrate on expanding existing businesses and entering new ones where opportunities are more promising.

Restructuring a Diversified Company's Business Lineup through a Mix of Divestitures and New Acquisitions

If there is a serious mismatch between the company's resources and the type of diversification it has pursued, then a **companywide restructuring** effort may be called for. Restructuring a diversified company on a companywide basis *(corporate restructuring)* involves divesting some businesses and acquiring others so as to put a whole new face on the company's business lineup.[31] Performing radical surgery on a company's group of businesses may also be an appealing strategy alternative when its financial performance is being squeezed or eroded by:

CORE CONCEPT

Companywide restructuring *(corporate restructuring)* involves divesting some businesses and acquiring others so as to put a whole new face on the company's business lineup.

- Too many businesses in slow-growth, declining, low-margin, or otherwise unattractive industries (a condition indicated by the number and size of businesses with industry attractiveness ratings below 5 and located on the bottom half of the attractiveness-strength matrix—see Figure 8.3).
- Too many competitively weak businesses (a condition indicated by the number and size of businesses with competitive strength ratings below 5 and located on the right half of the attractiveness-strength matrix).
- Ongoing declines in the market shares of one or more major business units that are falling prey to more market-savvy competitors.
- An excessive debt burden with interest costs that eat deeply into profitability.
- Ill-chosen acquisitions that haven't lived up to expectations.

Companywide restructuring can also be mandated by the emergence of new technologies that threaten the survival of one or more of a diversified company's

ILLUSTRATION CAPSULE 8.2

VF's Corporate Restructuring Strategy That Made It the Star of the Apparel Industry

VF Corporation's corporate restructuring, which includes a mix of divestitures and acquisitions, has provided its shareholders with returns that are more than five times greater than shareholder returns provided by competing apparel manufacturers. Its total return to investors in 2009 (a year in which the economy was down and many manufacturers were struggling) was 38.7 percent. VF's growth in revenue and earnings made it number 310 on *Fortune*'s list of the 500 largest U.S. companies in 2009. In 2010, it earned a spot on *Fortune*'s "World's Most Admired Companies" list.

The company's corporate restructuring began in 2000 when it divested its slow-growing businesses, including its namesake Vanity Fair brand of lingerie and sleepwear. The company's $136 million acquisition of North Face in 2000 was the first in the series of many acquisitions of "lifestyle brands" that connected with the way people lived, worked, and played. Since the acquisition and turnaround of North Face, VF has spent $2.8 billion to acquire 18 additional businesses. New apparel and lifestyle brands acquired by VF Corporation include Vans skateboard shoes, Nautica, Eagle Creek, John Varvatos, 7 For All Mankind sportswear, Reef surf wear, and Lucy athletic wear. The company also acquired a variety of apparel companies specializing in apparel segments such as uniforms for professional baseball and football teams and law enforcement personnel.

VF Corporation's acquisitions came after years of researching each company and developing a relationship with an acquisition candidate's chief managers before closing the deal. The company made a practice of leaving management of acquired companies in place, while bringing in new managers only when necessary talent and skills were lacking. In addition, companies acquired by VF were allowed to keep long-standing traditions that shaped culture and spurred creativity. For example, the Vans headquarters in Cypress, California, retained its half-pipe and concrete floor so that its employees could skateboard to and from meetings.

In 2009, VF Corporation was among the most profitable apparel firms in the industry, with net earnings of $461 million. The company expected new acquisitions that would push VF's revenues to $11 billion by 2012.

Sources: Suzanne Kapner, "How a 100-Year Old Apparel Firm Changed Course," *Fortune,* April 9, 2008, online edition; www.vfc.com (accessed July 29, 2010).

important businesses. On occasion, corporate restructuring can be prompted by special circumstances—such as when a firm has a unique opportunity to make an acquisition so big and important that it has to sell several existing business units to finance the new acquisition or when a company needs to sell off some businesses in order to raise the cash for entering a potentially big industry with wave-of-the-future technologies or products.

Candidates for divestiture in a corporate restructuring effort typically include not only weak performers or those in unattractive industries but also business units that lack strategic fit with the businesses to be retained, businesses that are cash hogs or that lack other types of resource fit, and businesses incompatible with the company's revised diversification strategy (even though they may be profitable or in an attractive industry). As businesses are divested, corporate restructuring generally involves aligning the remaining business units into groups with the best strategic fit and then redeploying the cash flows from the divested business to either pay down debt or make new acquisitions to strengthen the parent company's business position in the industries it has chosen to emphasize.[32]

Over the past decade, corporate restructuring has become a popular strategy at many diversified companies, especially those that had diversified broadly into many different industries and lines of business. In 2008, GE's CEO Jeffrey Immelt announced that GE would spin off its industrial division, which included GE appliances, lighting, and various industrial businesses. Earlier, he had led GE's withdrawal from the insurance business by divesting several companies and spinning off others. He further restructured GE's business lineup with two other major initiatives: (1) spending $10 billion to acquire British-based Amersham and extend GE's Medical Systems business into diagnostic pharmaceuticals and biosciences, thereby creating a $15 billion business designated as GE Healthcare, and (2) acquiring the entertainment assets of debt-ridden French media conglomerate Vivendi Universal Entertainment and integrating its operations into GE's NBC division, thereby creating a broad-based $13 billion media business positioned to compete against Walt Disney, Time Warner, Fox, and Viacom. Illustration Capsule 8.2 discusses how VF Corporation shareholders have benefited through the company's large-scale restructuring program.

KEY POINTS

1. The purpose of diversification is to build shareholder value. Diversification builds shareholder value when a diversified group of businesses can perform better under the auspices of a single corporate parent than they would as independent, stand-alone businesses—the goal is to achieve not just a $1 + 1 = 2$ result but, rather, to realize important $1 + 1 = 3$ performance benefits. Whether getting into a new business has potential to enhance shareholder value hinges on whether a company's entry into that business can pass the attractiveness test, the cost-of-entry test, and the better-off test.

2. Entry into new businesses can take any of three forms: acquisition, internal start-up, or joint venture/strategic partnership. The choice of which is best depends on the firm's resources and capabilities, the industry's entry barriers, the importance of speed, and the relative costs.

3. There are two fundamental approaches to diversification—into related businesses and into unrelated businesses. The rationale for *related* diversification is to benefit from *strategic fit:* Diversify into businesses with matchups along their respective value chains, and then capitalize on the strategic fit by sharing or transferring the resources and capabilities that enable the matching value chain activities in order to gain competitive advantage.

4. *Unrelated* diversification strategies surrender the competitive advantage potential of strategic fit at the value chain level in return for the potential that can be realized from superior corporate parenting. An outstanding corporate parent can benefit its businesses through (1) providing high-level oversight and making available other corporate resources, (2) allocating financial resources across the business portfolio, and (3) restructuring underperforming acquisitions.

5. Related diversification provides a stronger foundation for creating shareholder value than unrelated diversification, since the *specialized resources and*

capabilities that are leveraged in related diversification tend to be more valuable competitive assets than the *generalized resources and capabilities* underlying unrelated diversification, which in most cases are relatively common and easier to imitate.

6. Analyzing how good a company's diversification strategy is consists of a six-step process:

Step 1: *Evaluate the long-term attractiveness of the industries into which the firm has diversified.* Industry attractiveness needs to be evaluated from three angles: the attractiveness of each industry on its own, the attractiveness of each industry relative to the others, and the attractiveness of all the industries as a group.

Step 2: *Evaluate the relative competitive strength of each of the company's business units.* The purpose of rating the competitive strength of each business is to gain a clear understanding of which businesses are strong contenders in their industries, which are weak contenders, and the underlying reasons for their strength or weakness. The conclusions about industry attractiveness can be joined with the conclusions about competitive strength by drawing an industry attractiveness–competitive strength matrix that helps identify the prospects of each business and what priority each business should be given in allocating corporate resources and investment capital.

Step 3: *Check for cross-business strategic fit.* A business is more attractive strategically when it has value chain relationships with the company's other business units that offer potential to (1) realize economies of scope or cost-saving efficiencies, (2) transfer technology, skills, know-how, or other resource capabilities from one business to another, (3) leverage use of a trusted brand name or other resources that enhance differentiation, and (4) build new resources and competitive capabilities via cross-business collaboration. Cross-business strategic fit represents a significant avenue for producing competitive advantage beyond what any one business can achieve on its own.

Step 4: *Check whether the firm's resource mix fits the resource requirements of its present business lineup.* In firms with a related diversification strategy, resource fit exists when the company's businesses add to its overall resource position and when they have matching resource requirements at the value chain level. In companies pursuing unrelated diversification, resource fit exists when the parent company has generalized resources that can add value to its component businesses and when it has corporate resources sufficient to support its entire group of businesses without spreading itself too thin. When there is financial resource fit among the businesses of any type of diversified company, the company can generate internal cash flows sufficient to fund the capital requirements of its businesses, pay its dividends, meet its debt obligations, and otherwise remain financially healthy.

Step 5: *Rank the performance prospects of the businesses from best to worst, and determine what the corporate parent's priority should be in allocating resources to its various businesses.* The most important considerations in judging business-unit performance are sales growth, profit growth, contribution to company earnings, and the return on capital invested in the business. Normally, strong business units in attractive industries have significantly better performance prospects than weak businesses or businesses in unattractive industries. Business subsidiaries with the brightest profit and growth prospects and solid strategic and resource fit generally should head the list for corporate resource support.

Step 6: *Crafting new strategic moves to improve overall corporate performance.* This step entails using the results of the preceding analysis as the basis for devising actions to strengthen existing businesses, make new acquisitions, divest weak-performing and unattractive businesses, restructure the company's business lineup, expand the scope of the company's geographic reach into new markets around the world, and otherwise steer corporate resources into the areas of greatest opportunity.

7. Once a company has diversified, corporate management's task is to manage the collection of businesses for maximum long-term performance. There are four different strategic paths for improving a diversified company's performance: (1) sticking with the existing business lineup, (2) broadening the firm's business base by diversifying into additional businesses or geographic markets, (3) retrenching to a narrower diversification base by divesting some of its present businesses, and (4) restructuring the company's business lineup with a combination of divestitures and new acquisitions to put a whole new face on the company's business makeup.

ASSURANCE OF LEARNING EXERCISES

LO 1, LO 2

1. See if you can identify the value chain relationships that make the businesses of the following companies related in competitively relevant ways. In particular, you should consider whether there are cross-business opportunities for (1) transferring skills/technology, (2) combining related value chain activities to achieve economies of scope, and/or (3) leveraging the use of a well-respected brand name or other resources that enhance differentiation.

OSI Restaurant Partners

*   Outback Steakhouse
*   Carrabba's Italian Grill
*   Roy's Restaurant (Hawaiian fusion cuisine)
*   Bonefish Grill (market-fresh fine seafood)
*   Fleming's Prime Steakhouse & Wine Bar

L'Oréal

*   Maybelline, Lancôme, Helena Rubinstein, Kiehl's, Garner, and Shu Uemura cosmetics
*   L'Oréal and Soft Sheen/Carson hair care products
*   Redken, Matrix, L'Oréal Professional, and Kerastase Paris professional hair care and skin care products
*   Ralph Lauren and Giorgio Armani fragrances
*   Biotherm skincare products
*   La Roche–Posay and Vichy Laboratories dermocosmetics

Johnson & Johnson

- Baby products (powder, shampoo, oil, lotion)
- Band-Aids and other first-aid products
- Women's health and personal care products (Stayfree, Carefree, Sure & Natural)
- Neutrogena and Aveeno skin care products
- Nonprescription drugs (Tylenol, Motrin, Pepcid AC, Mylanta, Monistat)
- Prescription drugs
- Prosthetic and other medical devices
- Surgical and hospital products
- Acuvue contact lenses

LO 1, LO 3

2. A defining characteristic of unrelated diversification is few cross-business commonalities in terms of key value chain activities. Peruse the business group listings for Lancaster Colony shown below, and see if you can confirm that it has diversified into unrelated business groups.

Lancaster Colony's business lineup

- Specialty food products: Cardini, Marzetti, Girard's, and Pheiffer salad dressings; T. Marzetti and Chatham Village croutons; Jack Daniels mustards; Inn Maid noodles; New York and Mamma Bella garlic breads; Reames egg noodles; Sister Schubert's rolls; and Romanoff caviar
- Candle-lite brand candles marketed to retailers and private-label customers chains
- Glassware, plastic ware, coffee urns, and matting products marketed to the food service and lodging industry

If need be, visit the company's Web site (www.lancastercolony.com) to obtain additional information about its business lineup and strategy.

LO 1, LO 2, LO 3

3. The Walt Disney Company is in the following businesses:

- Theme parks
- Disney Cruise Line
- Resort properties
- Movie, video, and theatrical productions (for both children and adults)
- Television broadcasting (ABC, Disney Channel, Toon Disney, Classic Sports Network, ESPN and ESPN2, E!, Lifetime, and A&E networks)
- Radio broadcasting (Disney Radio)
- Musical recordings and sales of animation art
- Anaheim Mighty Ducks NHL franchise
- Anaheim Angels major-league baseball franchise (25 percent ownership)
- Books and magazine publishing

- Interactive software and Internet sites
- The Disney Store retail shops

Based on the above listing, would you say that Walt Disney's business lineup reflects a strategy of related diversification, unrelated diversification, or a combination of related and unrelated diversification? Be prepared to justify and explain your answer in terms of the nature of Disney's shared or transferred resources and capabilities and the extent to which the value chains of Disney's different businesses seem to have competitively valuable cross-business relationships.

If need be, visit the company's Web site (http://corporate.disney.go.com/index.html?ppLink=pp_wdig) to obtain additional information about its business lineup and strategy.

EXERCISES FOR SIMULATION PARTICIPANTS

LO 1, LO 2, LO 3

1. In the event that your company had the opportunity to diversify into other products or businesses of your choosing, would you opt to pursue related diversification, unrelated diversification, or a combination of both? Explain why.

LO 1, LO 2

2. What specific resources and capabilities does your company possess that would make diversifying into related businesses attractive? Indicate what kinds of strategic-fit benefits could be captured by transferring these resources and competitive capabilities to newly acquired related businesses.

LO 1, LO 2

3. If your company opted to pursue a strategy of related diversification, what industries or product categories could it diversify into that would allow it to achieve economies of scope? Name at least two or three such industries or product categories, and indicate the specific kinds of cost savings that might accrue from entry into each.

LO 1, LO 2

4. If your company opted to pursue a strategy of related diversification, what industries or product categories could it diversify into that would allow it to capitalize on using its present brand name and corporate image to good advantage in the newly entered businesses or product categories? Name at least two or three such industries or product categories, and indicate *the specific benefits* that might be captured by transferring your company's brand name to each.

ENDNOTES

1 For a more detailed discussion of when diversification makes good strategic sense, see Constantinos C. Markides, "To Diversify or Not to Diversify," *Harvard Business Review* 75, no. 6 (November–December 1997), pp. 93–99.

2 For a discussion of how hidden opportunities within a corporation's existing asset base may offer growth to corporations with declining core businesses, see Chris Zook, "Finding Your Next Core Business," *Harvard Business Review* 85, no. 4 (April 2007), pp. 66–75.

3 Michael E. Porter, "From Competitive Advantage to Corporate Strategy," *Harvard Business Review* 45, no. 3 (May–June 1987), pp. 46–49.

4 Rita Nazareth, "CEOs Paying 56% M&A Premium Shows Stocks May Be Cheap (Update3)," *Bloomberg.com,* December 21, 2009, www.bloomberg.com/apps/news?pid=20603037&sid=ahPolYY.zgQ.

5 Ibid.

6 Michael E. Porter, *Competitive Strategy: Techniques for Analyzing Industries and Competitors* (New York: Free Press, 1980), pp. 354–55.

7 A. Shleifer and R. Vishny, "Takeovers in the 60s and the 80s—Evidence and Implications," *Strategic Management Journal* 12 (Winter 1991), pp. 51–59; T. Brush, "Predicted Change in Operational Synergy and Post-Acquisition Performance of Acquired Businesses," *Strategic Management Journal* 17, no. 1(1996), pp. 1–24; J. P. Walsh, "Top Management Turnover Following Mergers and Acquisitions," *Strategic Management Journal* 9, no. 2 (1988), pp. 173–83; A. Cannella and D. Hambrick, "Effects of Executive Departures on the Performance of Acquired Firms," *Strategic Management Journal* 14 (Summer 1993), pp.137–52; R. Roll, "The Hubris Hypothesis of Corporate Takeovers," *Journal of Business* 59, no. 2 (1986), pp. 197–216; P. Haspeslagh and D. Jemison, *Managing Acquisitions* (New York: Free Press, 1991).

8 M. L. A. Hayward, "When Do Firms Learn from Their Acquisition Experience? Evidence from 1990–1995," *Strategic Management Journal* 23, no. 1 (2002), pp. 21–29; G. Ahuja and R. Katila, "Technological Acquisitions and the Innovation Performance of Acquiring Firms: A Longitudinal Study," *Strategic Management Journal* 22, no. 3 (2001), pp. 197–220; H. Barkema and F. Vermeulen, "International Expansion through Start-Up or Acquisition: A Learning Perspective," *Academy of Management Journal* 41, no. 1 (1998), pp. 7–26.

9 Haspeslagh and Jemison, *Managing Acquisitions,* pp. 344–45.

10 Yves L. Doz and Gary Hamel, *Alliance Advantage: The Art of Creating Value through Partnering* (Boston: Harvard Business School Press, 1998), chaps. 1 and 2.

11 J. Glover, "The Guardian," March 23, 1996, www.mcspotlight.org/media/press/guardpizza_23mar96.html.

12 Michael E. Porter, *Competitive Advantage* (New York: Free Press, 1985), pp. 318–19 and pp. 337–53; Porter, "From Competitive Advantage to Corporate Strategy," pp. 53–57. For an empirical study supporting the notion that strategic fit enhances performance (provided the resulting combination is competitively valuable and difficult to duplicate by rivals), see Constantinos C. Markides and Peter J. Williamson, "Corporate Diversification and Organization Structure: A Resource-Based View," *Academy of Management Journal* 39, no. 2 (April 1996), pp. 340–67.

13 David J. Collis and Cynthia A. Montgomery, "Creating Corporate Advantage," *Harvard Business Review* 76, no. 3 (May–June 1998), pp. 72–80; Markides and Williamson, "Corporate Diversification and Organization Structure."

14 Markides and Williamson, "Corporate Diversification and Organization Structure."

15 For a discussion of the strategic significance of cross-business coordination of value chain activities and insight into how the process works, see Jeanne M. Liedtka, "Collaboration across Lines of Business for Competitive Advantage," *Academy of Management Executive* 10, no. 2 (May 1996), pp. 20–34.

16 For a discussion of what is involved in actually capturing strategic-fit benefits, see Kathleen M. Eisenhardt and D. Charles Galunic, "Coevolving: At Last, a Way to Make Synergies Work," *Harvard Business Review* 78, no. 1 (January–February 2000), pp. 91–101; Constantinos C. Markides and Peter J. Williamson, "Related Diversification, Core Competences and Corporate Performance," *Strategic Management Journal* 15 (Summer 1994), pp. 149–65.

17 A. Campbell, M. Goold, and M. Alexander, "Corporate Strategy: The Quest for Parenting Advantage," *Harvard Business Review* 73, no. 2 (March–April 1995), pp. 120–32.

18 C. Montgomery and B. Wernerfelt, "Diversification, Ricardian Rents, and Tobin-Q," *RAND Journal of Economics* 19, no. 4 (1988), pp. 623–32.

19 Ibid.

20 Ibid.

21 For a review of the experiences of companies that have pursued unrelated diversification successfully, see Patricia L. Anslinger and Thomas E. Copeland, "Growth through Acquisitions: A Fresh Look," *Harvard Business Review* 74, no. 1 (January–February 1996), pp. 126–35.

22 Of course, management may be willing to assume the risk that trouble will not strike before it has had time to learn the business well enough to bail it out of almost any difficulty. But there is research that shows this is very risky from a financial perspective; see, for example, M. Lubatkin and S. Chatterjee, "Extending Modern Portfolio Theory," *Academy of Management Journal* 37, no.1(February 1994), pp. 109–36.

23 For research evidence of the failure of broad diversification and trend of companies to focus their diversification efforts more narrowly, see Lawrence G. Franko, "The Death of Diversification? The Focusing of the World's Industrial Firms, 1980–2000," *Business Horizons* 47, no. 4 (July–August 2004), pp. 41–50.

24 For an excellent discussion of what to look for in assessing this type of strategic fit, see Campbell, Goold, and Alexander, "Corporate Strategy: The Quest for Parenting Advantage."

25 Ibid., p. 128.

26 A good discussion of the importance of having adequate resources, as well as upgrading corporate resources and capabilities, can be found in David J. Collis and Cynthia A. Montgomery, "Competing on Resources: Strategy in the 90s," *Harvard Business Review* 73, no. 4 (July–August 1995), pp. 118–28.

27 Peter F. Drucker, *Management: Tasks, Responsibilities, Practices,* (New York: Harper & Row, 1974), p. 709.

28 See, for example, Constantinos C. Markides, "Diversification, Restructuring, and Economic Performance," *Strategic Management Journal* 16 (February 1995), pp. 101–18.

29 Drucker, *Management: Tasks, Responsibilities, Practices,* p. 94.

30 Collis and Montgomery, "Creating Corporate Advantage."

31 For a discussion of why divestiture needs to be a standard part of any company's diversification strategy, see Lee Dranikoff, Tim Koller, and Anton Schneider, "Divestiture: Strategy's Missing Link," *Harvard Business Review* 80, no. 5 (May 2002), pp. 74–83.

32 Evidence that restructuring strategies tend to result in higher levels of performance is contained in Markides, "Diversification, Restructuring, and Economic Performance."

CHAPTER 9

ETHICS, CORPORATE SOCIAL RESPONSIBILITY, ENVIRONMENTAL SUSTAINABILITY, AND STRATEGY

Business is the most important engine for social change in our society.

—Lawrence Perlman
Former CEO of Ceridian Corporation

It takes many good deeds to build a good reputation and only one bad one to lose it.

—Benjamin Franklin
American Statesman, Inventor, and Philosopher

Corporations are economic entities, to be sure, but they are also social institutions that must justify their existence by their overall contribution to society.

—Henry Mintzberg, Robert Simons, and Kunal Basu
Professors

Companies have to be socially responsible or shareholders pay eventually.

—Warren Shaw
Former CEO of LGT Asset Management

LEARNING OBJECTIVES

LO 1. Understand how the standards of ethical behavior in business relate to the ethical standards and norms of the larger society and culture in which a company operates.

LO 2. Recognize conditions that can give rise to unethical business strategies and behavior.

LO 3. Gain an understanding of the costs of business ethics failures.

LO 4. Gain an understanding of the concepts of corporate social responsibility and environmental sustainability and of how companies balance these duties with economic responsibilities to shareholders.

Clearly, a company has a responsibility to make a profit and grow the business—in capitalistic or market economies, management's fiduciary duty to create value for shareholders is not a matter for serious debate. Just as clearly, a company and its personnel also have a duty to obey the law and play by the rules of fair competition. But does a company have a duty to go beyond legal requirements and operate according to the ethical norms of the societies in which it operates—should all company personnel be held to some standard of ethical conduct? And does a company have a duty or obligation to contribute to the betterment of society independent of the needs and preferences of the customers it serves? Should a company display a social conscience and devote a portion of its resources to bettering soci-

ety? How far should a company go in protecting the environment, conserving natural resources for use by future generations, and ensuring that its operations do not ultimately endanger the planet?

The focus of this chapter is to examine what link, if any, there should be between a company's efforts to craft and execute a winning strategy and its duties to (1) conduct its activities in an ethical manner, (2) demonstrate socially responsible behavior by being a committed corporate citizen and directing corporate resources to the betterment of employees, the communities in which it operates, and society as a whole, and (3) adopt business practices that conserve natural resources, protect the interests of future generations, and preserve the well-being of the planet.

WHAT DO WE MEAN BY *BUSINESS ETHICS*?

Ethics concerns principles of right or wrong conduct. **Business ethics** is the application of ethical principles and standards to the actions and decisions of business organizations and the conduct of their personnel.[1] Ethical principles in business are not materially different from ethical principles in general because business actions have to be judged in the context of society's standards of right and wrong. There is not a special set of ethical standards applicable only to business situations. If dishonesty is considered unethical and immoral, then dishonest behavior in business— whether it relates to customers, suppliers, employees, shareholders, competitors, government, or society—qualifies as equally unethical and immoral. If being ethical entails not deliberately harming others, then recalling a defective or unsafe product is ethically necessary. If society deems bribery unethical, then it is unethical for company personnel to make payoffs to government officials or bestow gifts and other favors on prospective customers to win or retain business. In short, ethical behavior in business situations requires adhering to generally accepted norms about right or wrong conduct. As a consequence, company managers have an obligation—indeed, a duty—to observe ethical norms when crafting and executing strategy.

WHERE DO ETHICAL STANDARDS COME FROM—ARE THEY UNIVERSAL OR DEPENDENT ON LOCAL NORMS?

LO 1

Understand how the standards of ethical behavior in business relate to the ethical standards and norms of the larger society and culture in which a company operates.

Notions of right and wrong, fair and unfair, ethical and unethical are present in all societies and cultures. But there are three distinct schools of thought about the extent to which ethical standards travel across cultures and whether multinational companies can apply the same set of ethical standards in any and all locations where they operate. Illustration Capsule 9.1 describes the difficulties Apple has faced in trying to enforce a common set of ethical standards across its vast global supplier network.

The School of Ethical Universalism

According to the school of **ethical universalism,** the most important concepts of what is right and what is wrong are *universal* and transcend culture, society, and religion.[2] For instance, being truthful (or not being deliberately deceitful) strikes a chord of what's right in the peoples of all nations. Likewise, demonstrating integrity of character, not cheating, and treating people with courtesy and respect are concepts that resonate with people of virtually all cultures and religions. In most societies, people would concur that it is unethical for companies to knowingly expose workers to toxic chemicals and hazardous materials or to sell products known to be unsafe or harmful to the users.

CORE CONCEPT

The school of **ethical universalism** holds that common understandings across multiple cultures and countries about what constitutes right and wrong give rise to universal ethical standards that apply to members of all societies, all companies, and all businesspeople.

Common moral agreement about right and wrong actions and behaviors across multiple cultures and countries gives rise to universal ethical standards that apply to members of all societies, all companies, and all businesspeople. These universal ethical principles set forth the traits and behaviors that are considered virtuous and that a good person is supposed to believe in and to display. Thus, adherents of the school of ethical universalism maintain it is entirely appropriate to expect all businesspeople to conform to these universal ethical standards.[3]

The strength of ethical universalism is that it draws on the collective views of multiple societies and cultures to put some clear boundaries on what constitutes ethical business behavior and what constitutes unethical business behavior regardless of the country or culture in which a company's personnel are conducting activities. This means that in those instances where basic moral standards really do not vary significantly according to local cultural beliefs, traditions, or religious convictions, a multinational company can develop a code

ILLUSTRATION CAPSULE 9.1

Many of Apple's Suppliers Flunk the Ethics Test

Apple requires its suppliers to comply with the company's Supplier Code of Conduct as a condition of being awarded contracts. To ensure compliance, Apple has a supplier monitoring program that includes audits of supplier factories, corrective action plans, and verification measures. In the company's 24-page 2010 Progress Report on Supplier Responsibility, Apple reported that in 2009 it conducted 102 audits of supplier facilities in such countries as China, the Czech Republic, Malaysia, the Philippines, Singapore, South Korea, Taiwan, Thailand, and the United States; 80 of these audits were first-time audits and 22 were repeat audits.

Apple distinguishes among the seriousness of infractions, designating "core violations" as those that go directly against the core principles of its Supplier Code of Conduct and must be remedied immediately. During the 2009 audits, 17 such violations were discovered, including 3 cases of underage labor, 8 cases involving excessive recruitment fees, 3 cases of improper hazardous waste disposal, and 3 cases of deliberately falsified audit records. Apple responded by ensuring that immediate corrective actions were taken, placing violators on probation, and planning to audit them again in a year's time.

While all six of Apple's final assembly manufacturers had high compliance scores—on average, registering well above 90 percent compliance on all issues—other suppliers did not fare so well on the 2009 audits. At 60 of the audited facilities, workers were required to work more than 60 hours per week more than 50 percent of the time—Apple sets a maximum of 60 hours per week (except in unusual or emergency circumstances). In 65 of the audited facilities, workers were found to have been required to work more than six consecutive days a week at least once per month—Apple requires at least one day of rest per seven days of work (except in unusual or emergency circumstances).

At 48 facilities, Apple found that overtime wages had been calculated improperly, resulting in underpayment of overtime compensation. Apple auditors discovered that at 24 facilities workers were being paid less than the specified minimum wage and that at 45 facilities wage deductions were used to discipline employees. At 57 of the audited facilities, worker benefits (for such things as retirement, sick leave, or maternity leave) were below the legally required amounts.

Apple requires suppliers to provide a safe working environment and to eliminate physical hazards to employees where possible. But the 2009 audits revealed that workers were not wearing appropriate protective personal equipment at 49 facilities. Violations were found at 70 facilities where workers were improperly trained, where unlicensed workers were operating equipment, and where required inspections of equipment were not being conducted. Apple auditors found that 44 facilities had failed to conduct environmental impact assessments, 11 facilities did not have permits for air emissions, and 4 facilities did not meet the conditions specified in their emission permits. Moreover, the audits revealed that 55 supplier facilities did not have any personnel assigned to ensuring compliance with Apple's Supplier Code of Conduct.

For Apple, the audits represent a starting point for bringing its suppliers into compliance, through greater scrutiny, education and training of suppliers' personnel, and incentives. Apple collects quarterly data to hold its suppliers accountable for their actions and makes procurement decisions based, in part, on these numbers. Suppliers that are unable to meet Apple's high standards of conduct ultimately end up losing Apple's business.

Sources: Apple's 2010 Progress Report on Supplier Responsibility; Dan Moren, "Apple Releases 2010 Report on Supplier Responsibility," *Macworld.com,* February 23, 2010, www.macworld.com/article/146653/2010/02/suppliers_2010.htm (accessed July 1, 2010); Andrew Morse and Nick Wingfield, "Apple Audits Labor Practices: Company Says Suppliers Hired Underage Workers, Violated Other Core Policies," *Wall Street Journal Online,* March 1, 2010, http://online.wsj.com/article/SB10001424 052748704231304575091920704104154.html (accessed July 1, 2010); Nicholas Kolakowski, "Apple Finds Violations during 2009 Supplier and Manufacturer Audit," *eWeek.com,* March 1, 2010, www.eweek.com/c/a/Mobile-and-Wireless/Apple-Finds-Violations-During-2009-Supplier-and-Manufacturer-Audit-522622/ (accessed July 1, 2010).

of ethics that it applies more or less evenly across its worldwide operations.[4] It can avoid the slippery slope that comes from having different ethical standards for different company personnel depending on where in the world they are working.

The School of Ethical Relativism

Apart from a select set of universal moral prescriptions—like being truthful and trustworthy—that apply in every society and business circumstance, there are meaningful variations in the ethical standards by which different societies judge the conduct of business activities. Indeed, differing religious beliefs, social customs, traditions, and behavioral norms frequently give rise to different standards about what is fair or unfair, moral or immoral, and ethically right or wrong. The school of **ethical relativism** holds that when there are cross-country or cross-cultural differences in what is deemed ethical or unethical in business situations, it is appropriate for local moral standards to take precedence over what the ethical standards may be in a company's home market. The thesis is that what constitutes ethical or unethical behavior on the part of local businesspeople is properly governed by local ethical standards rather than the standards that prevail in other locations.[5] Consider the following examples.

> **CORE CONCEPT**
>
> The school of **ethical relativism** holds that differing religious beliefs, customs, and behavioral norms across countries and cultures give rise to *multiple sets of standards concerning what is ethically right or wrong.* These differing standards mean that whether business-related actions are right or wrong depends on the prevailing local ethical standards.

The Use of Underage Labor   In industrialized nations, the use of underage workers is considered taboo. Social activists are adamant that child labor is unethical and that companies should neither employ children under the age of 18 as full-time employees nor source any products from foreign suppliers that employ underage workers. Many countries have passed legislation forbidding the use of underage labor or, at a minimum, regulating the employment of people under the age of 18. However, in India, Bangladesh, Botswana, Sri Lanka, Ghana, Somalia, and more than 100 other countries, it is customary to view children as potential, even necessary, workers.[6] Many poverty-stricken families cannot subsist without the income earned by young family members; sending their children to school instead of having them work is not a realistic option. In 2006, the International Labor Organization estimated that 191 million children ages 5 to 14 were working around the world.[7] If such children are not permitted to work—due to pressures imposed by activist groups in industrialized nations—they may be forced to go out on the streets begging or to seek work in parts of the "underground" economy such as drug trafficking and prostitution.[8] So if all businesses in countries where employing underage workers is common succumb to the pressures of activist groups and government organizations to stop employing underage labor, then have they served the best interests of the underage workers, their families, and society in general?

The Payment of Bribes and Kickbacks   A particularly thorny area facing multinational companies is the degree of cross-country variability in paying bribes.[9] In many countries in eastern Europe, Africa, Latin America, and Asia, it is customary to pay bribes to government officials in order to win a government contract, obtain a license or permit, or facilitate an administrative ruling.[10] Likewise, in many countries it is normal to make payments to prospective customers in order to win or retain their business. In some developing nations, it is difficult for any company, foreign or domestic, to move goods through customs without paying off low-level officials.[11] A *Wall Street Journal* article reported that

30 to 60 percent of all business transactions in eastern Europe involved paying bribes and the costs of bribe payments averaged 2 to 8 percent of revenues.[12] Some people stretch to justify the payment of bribes and kickbacks on grounds that bribing government officials to get goods through customs or giving kickbacks to customers to retain their business or win new orders is simply a payment for services rendered, in the same way that people tip for service at restaurants.[13] But while this is a clever rationalization, it rests on moral quicksand.

Companies that forbid the payment of bribes and kickbacks in their codes of ethical conduct and that are serious about enforcing this prohibition face a particularly vexing problem in countries where bribery and kickback payments are an entrenched local custom.[14] Refusing to pay bribes or kickbacks in these countries (so as to comply with the company's code of ethical conduct) is very often tantamount to losing business to competitors willing to make such payments—an outcome that penalizes ethical companies and ethical company personnel (who may suffer lost sales commissions or bonuses). On the other hand, the payment of bribes or kickbacks not only undercuts the company's code of ethics but also risks breaking the law. U.S. companies are prohibited by the Foreign Corrupt Practices Act (FCPA) from paying bribes to government officials, political parties, political candidates, or others in all countries where they do business. The Organization for Economic Cooperation and Development (OECD) has antibribery standards that criminalize the bribery of foreign public officials in international business transactions—as of 2009, the 30 OECD members and 8 nonmember countries had adopted these standards.[15] In 2008, Siemens, one of the world's largest corporations and headquartered in Munich, Germany, was fined $1.6 billion by the U.S. and German governments for bribing foreign officials to help it secure huge public works contracts around the world. Investigations revealed that Siemens created secret offshore bank accounts and used middlemen posing as consultants to deliver suitcases filled with cash, paying an estimated $1.4 billion to over 4,000 well-placed government officials in Asia, Africa, Europe, the Middle East, and Latin America between 2001 and 2007. An estimated 300 Siemens sales employees, executives, and board members were being investigated in 2009 for their roles in the scheme. The evidence gathered indicated that such bribes were a core element of Siemens' strategy and business model.

Penalizing companies for overseas bribes is becoming more widespread internationally. The Serious Fraud Office (SFO) in London held a landmark investigation in December 2009 of DePuy International, a subsidiary of Johnson & Johnson, for bribing Greek officials to purchase products. This comes after DePuy was fined over $311 million by the U.S. government for kickbacks to U.S. surgeons in 2007.[16]

Ethical Relativism Equates to Multiple Sets of Ethical Standards The existence of varying ethical norms such as those cited above explains why the adherents of ethical relativism maintain that there are few absolutes when it comes to business ethics and thus few ethical absolutes for consistently judging a company's conduct in various countries and markets. Indeed, ethical relativists argue that while there are some general moral prescriptions that apply regardless of the business circumstance, there are plenty of situations where ethical norms must be contoured to fit the local customs, traditions, and notions of fairness shared by the parties involved. They argue that a "one-size-fits-all" template for judging the ethical appropriateness of business actions and the behaviors of company personnel simply does not exist—in other

Under ethical relativism, there can be no one-size-fits-all set of authentic ethical norms against which to gauge the conduct of company personnel.

words, ethical problems in business cannot be fully resolved without appealing to the shared convictions of the parties in question.[17] While European and American managers may want to impose standards of business conduct that give heavy weight to such core human rights as personal freedom, individual security, political participation, and the ownership of property, managers in China may have a much weaker commitment to these kinds of human rights. Japanese managers may prefer ethical standards that show respect for the collective good of society. Muslim managers may wish to apply ethical standards compatible with the teachings of Mohammed. Clearly, there is some merit in the school of ethical relativism's view that what is deemed right or wrong, fair or unfair, moral or immoral, ethical or unethical in business situations depends partly on the context of each country's local customs, religious traditions, and societal norms. Hence, there is a kernel of truth in the argument that businesses need some room to tailor their ethical standards to fit local situations. A company has to be very cautious about exporting its home-country values and ethics to foreign countries where it operates—"photocopying" ethics is disrespectful of other cultures and neglects the important role of moral free space (in which there is room to accommodate local ethical standards).

Pushed to the Extreme, Ethical Relativism Breaks Down

While the ethical relativism rule of "When in Rome, do as the Romans do" appears reasonable, it nonetheless presents a big problem—when the envelope starts to be pushed, as will inevitably be the case, *it is tantamount to rudderless ethical standards.* Consider, for instance, the following example: In 1992, the owners of the *SS United States,* an aging luxury ocean liner constructed with asbestos in the 1940s, had the liner towed to Turkey, where a contractor had agreed to remove the asbestos for $2 million (versus a far higher cost in the United States, where asbestos removal safety standards were much more stringent).[18] When Turkish officials blocked the asbestos removal because of the dangers to workers of contracting cancer, the owners had the liner towed to the Black Sea port of Sevastopol, in the Crimean Republic, where the asbestos removal standards were quite lax and where a contractor had agreed to remove more than 500,000 square feet of carcinogenic asbestos for less than $2 million. There are no moral grounds for arguing that exposing workers to carcinogenic asbestos is ethically correct, regardless of what a country's law allows or the value the country places on worker safety.

A company that adopts the principle of ethical relativism and holds company personnel to local ethical standards necessarily assumes that what prevails as local morality is an adequate guide to ethical behavior. This can be ethically dangerous—it leads to the conclusion that if a country's culture is accepting of bribery or environmental degradation or exposing workers to dangerous conditions (toxic chemicals or bodily harm), then so much the worse for honest people and environmental protection and safe working conditions. Such a position is morally unacceptable. Even though bribery of government officials in China is a common practice, when Lucent Technologies found that managers in its Chinese operations had bribed government officials, it fired the entire senior management team.[19]

Moreover, from a global markets perspective, ethical relativism results in a maze of conflicting ethical standards for multinational companies wanting to address the very real issue of which ethical standards to enforce companywide. It is a slippery slope indeed to resolve such ethical diversity without any kind of higher-order moral compass. Imagine, for example, that a multinational company (in the name of ethical relativism) permits company personnel to pay bribes and kickbacks in countries where such payments are customary but forbids them to make such payments in countries where bribes and kickbacks are considered unethical or illegal. Or that the company says it is appropriate to use child labor in its plants in countries where underage labor is acceptable but inappropriate to employ child labor at the remainder of its plants. Having thus adopted conflicting ethical standards for operating in different countries, company managers have little moral basis for enforcing any ethical standards companywide— rather, the clear message to employees would be that the company has no ethical standards or principles of its own. This is scarcely strong moral ground to stand on.

> Codes of conduct based on ethical relativism can be *ethically dangerous* for multinational companies by creating a maze of conflicting ethical standards.

Ethics and Integrative Social Contracts Theory

Social contract theory provides a middle position between the opposing views of universalism (that the same set of ethical standards should apply everywhere) and relativism (that ethical standards vary according to local custom).[20] According to **integrated social contracts theory,** universal ethical principles or norms based on the collective views of multiple cultures and societies combine to form a "social contract" that all individuals, groups, organizations and businesses in all situations have a duty to observe. *Within the boundaries of this social contract,* local cultures or groups can specify what other actions may or may not be ethically permissible. While this system leaves some "moral free space" for the people in a particular country (or local culture or even a company) to make specific interpretations of what other actions may or may not be permissible, universal ethical norms always take precedence. Thus, local ethical standards can be *more* stringent than the universal ethical standards, but never less so.

> **CORE CONCEPT**
>
> According to **integrated social contracts theory,** universal ethical principles based on the collective views of multiple societies form a "social contract" that all individuals and organizations have a duty to observe in all situations. *Within the boundaries of this social contract,* local cultures or groups can specify what additional actions may or may not be ethically permissible.

Hence, while firms, industries, professional associations, and other business-relevant groups are "contractually obligated" to society to observe universal ethical norms, they have the discretion to go beyond these universal norms and specify other behaviors that are out of bounds and place further limitations on what is considered ethical. For example, both the legal and medical professions have standards regarding what kinds of advertising are ethically permissible that extend beyond the universal norm that advertising not be false or misleading. Similarly, food products companies are beginning to establish ethical guidelines for judging what is and is not appropriate advertising for food products that are inherently unhealthy and may cause dietary or obesity problems for people who eat them regularly or consume them in large quantities.

The strength of integrated social contracts theory is that it accommodates the best parts of ethical universalism and ethical relativism. It is indisputable that cultural differences impact how business is conducted in various parts of the world and that these cultural differences sometimes give rise to different ethical norms. But it is just as indisputable that some ethical norms are more authentic or universally applicable than others, meaning that in many instances of cross-country differences one side may be more "ethically correct" than another. In such instances, resolving cross-cultural differences over what is ethically permissible entails applying the rule that *universal or "first-order" ethical norms override the local or "second-order" ethical norms.* A good example is the payment of bribes and kickbacks. Yes, bribes and kickbacks seem to be common in some countries, but does this justify paying them? Just because bribery flourishes in a country does not mean it is an authentic or legitimate ethical norm. Virtually all of the world's major religions (e.g., Buddhism, Christianity, Confucianism, Hinduism, Islam, Judaism, Sikhism, and Taoism) and all moral schools of thought condemn bribery and corruption.[21] Therefore, a multinational company might reasonably conclude that the right ethical standard is one of refusing to condone bribery and kickbacks on the part of company personnel no matter what the local custom is and no matter what the sales consequences are.

Granting an automatic preference to local-country ethical norms presents vexing problems to multinational company managers when the ethical standards followed in a foreign country are lower than those in its home country or are in conflict with the company's code of ethics. Sometimes—as with bribery and kickbacks—there can be no compromise on what is ethically permissible and what is not. *This is precisely what integrated social contracts theory maintains—adherence to universal or "first-order" ethical norms should always take precedence over local or "second-order" norms.* Consequently, integrated social contracts theory offers managers in multinational companies clear guidance in resolving cross-country ethical differences: Those parts of the company's code of ethics that involve universal ethical norms must be enforced worldwide, but *within* these boundaries there is room for ethical diversity and opportunity for host-country cultures to exert *some* influence in setting their own moral and ethical standards. Such an approach avoids the discomforting case of a self-righteous multinational company trying to operate as the standard bearer of moral truth and imposing its interpretation of its code of ethics worldwide no matter what. And it avoids the equally disturbing case for a company's ethical conduct to be no higher than local ethical norms in situations where local ethical norms permit practices that are generally considered immoral or when local norms clearly conflict with a company's code of ethical conduct.

> According to integrated social contracts theory, adherence to universal or "first-order" ethical norms should always take precedence over local or "second-order" norms.

HOW AND WHY ETHICAL STANDARDS IMPACT THE TASKS OF CRAFTING AND EXECUTING STRATEGY

Many companies have acknowledged their ethical obligations in official codes of ethical conduct and statements of company values. In the United States, for example, the Sarbanes-Oxley Act, passed in 2002, requires that companies whose stock is publicly traded have a code of ethics or else explain in writing to the Securities and Exchange Commission (SEC) why they do not. But there's a big difference between having a code of ethics that serves merely as public window dressing and having ethical standards that truly paint the white lines for a company's actual strategy and business conduct.[22] *The litmus test of whether a company's code of ethics is cosmetic is the extent to which it is embraced in crafting strategy and in operating the business day to day.*

It is up to senior executives to walk the talk and make a point of considering three sets of questions whenever a new strategic initiative is under review:

- Is what we are proposing to do fully compliant with our code of ethical conduct? Are there any areas of ambiguity that may be of concern?

- Is it apparent that this proposed action is in harmony with our core values? Are any conflicts or potential problems evident?

- Is there anything in the proposed action that could be considered ethically objectionable? Would our stakeholders, our competitors, the SEC, or the media view this action as ethically objectionable?

Unless questions of this nature are posed—either in open discussion or by force of habit in the minds of strategy makers—there's room for strategic initiatives to become disconnected from the company's code of ethics and stated core values. If a company's executives believe strongly in living up to the company's ethical standards, they will unhesitatingly reject strategic initiatives and operating approaches that don't measure up. However, in companies with a cosmetic approach to ethics, any strategy-ethics-values linkage stems mainly from a desire to avoid the risk of embarrassment and possible disciplinary action should strategy makers be held accountable for approving a strategic initiative that is deemed by society to be unethical and perhaps illegal.

While most company managers are careful to ensure that a company's strategy is within the bounds of what is legal, evidence indicates they are not always so careful to ensure that all elements of their strategies and operating activities are within the bounds of what is considered ethical. In recent years, there have been revelations of ethical misconduct on the part of managers at such companies as Enron, Tyco International, HealthSouth, Adelphia, Royal Dutch/Shell, Parmalat (an Italy-based food products company), Rite Aid, Mexican oil giant Pemex, AIG, Citigroup, several leading brokerage houses, mutual fund companies, investment banking firms, and a host of mortgage lenders. Much of the crisis in residential real estate that emerged in the United States in 2007–2008 stemmed from consciously unethical strategies at certain banks and mortgage companies to boost the fees they earned on processing home mortgage applications by deliberately lowering lending standards and finding ways to secure mortgage approvals for home buyers who lacked sufficient income to make their monthly mortgage payments. Once these lenders earned their fees on the so-called subprime loans (a term used for high-risk mortgage loans to home buyers with dubious qualifications to repay the loans), they secured the assistance of investment banking firms to bundle those and other mortgages into collateralized debt obligations (CDOs), found means of having the CDOs assigned triple-A bond ratings, and auctioned them to unsuspecting investors, who later suffered huge losses when the high-risk borrowers began to default on their loan payments (government authorities later forced some of the firms that auctioned off these CDOs to repurchase them at the auction price and bear the losses themselves).

The consequences of crafting strategies that cannot pass the test of moral scrutiny are manifested in sizable fines, devastating public relations hits, sharp drops in stock prices that cost shareholders billions of dollars, and criminal indictments and convictions of company executives. The fallout from all these scandals has resulted in heightened management attention to legal and ethical considerations in crafting strategy.

WHAT ARE THE DRIVERS OF UNETHICAL STRATEGIES AND BUSINESS BEHAVIOR?

LO 2

Recognize conditions that can give rise to unethical business strategies and behavior.

Confusion over conflicting ethical standards may suggest one reason for the lack of an effective moral compass in business dealings and why certain elements of a company's strategy may be unethical. But apart from this, three main drivers of unethical business behavior stand out:[23]

- Faulty oversight that implicitly allows the overzealous pursuit of personal gain, wealth, and self-interest.

- Heavy pressures on company managers to meet or beat short-term performance targets.

- A company culture that puts profitability and business performance ahead of ethical behavior.

Faulty Oversight and the Overzealous Pursuit of Personal Gain, Wealth, and Self-Interest   People who are obsessed with wealth accumulation, greed, power, status, and their own self-interest often push ethical principles aside in their quest for personal gain. Driven by their ambitions, they exhibit few qualms in skirting the rules or doing whatever is necessary to achieve their goals. A general disregard for business ethics can prompt all kinds of unethical strategic maneuvers and behaviors at companies. According to a civil complaint filed by the Securities and Exchange Commission, the chief executive officer (CEO) of Tyco International, a well-known $35.6 billion manufacturing and services company, conspired with the company's chief financial officer (CFO) to steal more than $170 million, including a company-paid $2 million birthday party for the CEO's wife held on an island off the coast of Italy, a $7 million Park Avenue apartment for his wife, and secret interest-free loans to finance personal investments and purchase lavish artwork, yachts, estate jewelry, and vacation homes. Tyco's CEO and CFO were further charged with conspiring to reap more than $430 million from sales of stock, using questionable accounting to hide their actions, and engaging in deceptive accounting practices to distort the company's financial condition from 1995 to 2002. In 2005, both Tyco executives were convicted on multiple counts of looting the company and sent to jail.

Responsible corporate governance and oversight by the company's corporate board is necessary to guard against self-dealing and the manipulation of information to disguise such actions by a company's managers. **Self-dealing** occurs when managers take advantage of their position to further their own private interests rather than those of the firm. As discussed in Chapter 2, the duty of the corporate board (and its compensation and audit committees in particular) is to guard against such actions. A strong, independent board is necessary to have proper oversight of the company's financial practices and to hold top managers accountable for their actions.

A particularly egregious example of the lack of proper oversight is the case of Enron Corporation, a former diversified energy company that has become a symbol of corporate corruption and fraud. Andrew Fastow, Enron's chief financial officer (CFO), set himself up as the manager of one of Enron's off-the-books partnerships and as the part-owner of another, allegedly earning extra compensation of $30 million for his owner-manager roles in the two partnerships; Enron's board of directors agreed to suspend the company's conflict-of-interest rules designed to protect the company from this very kind of executive self-dealing. Although *Fortune* magazine had named Enron "America's Most Innovative Company" for six years running, in the end it turned out that Enron's real creativity was in its accounting practices. Enron's eventual downfall resulted not only in the company's bankruptcy in 2001 but also in the dissolution of its auditor, Arthur Andersen, which was one of the top-five accounting firms at the time.

> **CORE CONCEPT**
>
> **Self-dealing** occurs when managers take advantage of their position to further their own private interests rather than those of the firm.

Illustration Capsule 9.2 discusses the more recent multibillion-dollar Ponzi schemes perpetrated at Bernard L. Madoff Investment Securities and alleged at Stanford Financial Group.

Heavy Pressures on Company Managers to Meet or Beat Short-Term Earnings Targets

Performance expectations of Wall Street analysts and investors create enormous pressure on management to do whatever it takes to deliver good financial results each and every quarter. Executives at high-performing companies know that investors will see the slightest sign of a slowdown in earnings growth as a red flag and drive down the company's stock price. In addition, slowing growth or declining profits could lead to a downgrade of the company's credit rating if it has used lots of debt to finance its growth. The pressure to "never miss a quarter"—so as not to upset the expectations of analysts, investors, and creditors—prompts nearsighted managers to engage in short-term maneuvers to make the numbers, regardless of whether these moves are really in the best long-term interests of the company. Sometimes the pressure induces company personnel to continue to stretch the rules until the limits of ethical conduct are overlooked.[24] Once ethical boundaries are crossed in efforts to "meet or beat their numbers," the threshold for making more extreme ethical compromises becomes lower.

Several top executives at the former telecommunications company WorldCom were convicted of concocting a fraudulent $11 billion accounting scheme to hide costs and inflate revenues and profit over several years; the scheme was said to have helped the company keep its stock price propped up high enough to make additional acquisitions, support its nearly $30 billion debt load, and allow executives to cash in on their lucrative stock options. HealthSouth's chief financial managers were convicted of overstating the company's earnings by $1.4 billion between 1996 and 2002 in an attempt to hide the company's slowing growth from investors. A 2007 internal investigation at Dell Computer found that executives had engaged in a scheme to manipulate the company's accounting data to meet investors' quarterly earnings expectations. The fraudulent accounting practices inflated the company's earnings by $150 million between 2002 and 2006. The executives were terminated by Dell Computer in 2007.

Company executives often feel pressured to hit financial performance targets because their compensation depends heavily on the company's performance. During the late 1990s, it became fashionable for boards of directors to grant lavish bonuses, stock option awards, and other compensation benefits to executives for meeting specified performance targets. So outlandishly large were these rewards that executives had strong personal incentives to bend the rules and engage in behaviors that allowed the targets to be met. Much of the accounting manipulation at the root of recent corporate scandals has entailed situations in which executives benefited enormously from misleading accounting or other shady activities that

Investment Fraud at Bernard L. Madoff Investment Securities and Stanford Financial Group

Bernard Madoff engineered the largest investment scam in history to accumulate a net worth of more than $800 million and build a reputation as one of Wall Street's most savvy investors—he was appointed to various Securities and Exchange Commission panels, invited to testify before Congress on investment matters, made chairman of Nasdaq, and befriended by some of the world's most influential people. Madoff deceived Wall Street and investors with a simple Ponzi scheme that promised investors returns that would beat the market by 400 to 500 percent. The hedge funds, banks, and wealthy individuals that sent Bernard L. Madoff Investment Securities billions to invest on their behalf were quite pleased when their statements arrived showing annual returns as high as 45 percent. But, in fact, the portfolio gains shown on these statements were fictitious. Funds placed with Bernard Madoff were seldom, if ever, actually invested in any type of security—the money went to cover losses in his legitimate stock-trading business, fund periodic withdrawals of investors' funds, and support Madoff's lifestyle (including three vacation homes, a $7 million Manhattan condominium, yachts, and luxury cars).

For decades, the Ponzi scheme was never in danger of collapse because most Madoff investors were so impressed with the reported returns that they seldom made withdrawals from their accounts, and when they did withdraw funds Madoff used the monies being deposited by new investors to cover the payments. Madoff's deception came to an end in late 2008 when the dramatic drop in world stock prices caused so many of Madoff's investors to request withdrawals of their balances that there was not nearly enough new money coming in to cover the amounts being withdrawn. As with any Ponzi scheme, the first investors to ask Madoff for their funds were paid, but those asking later were left empty-handed. All told, more than 1,300 account holders lost about $65 billion when Bernard Madoff admitted to the scam in December 2008. As of late October 2009, investigators had located assets of only about $1.4 billion to return to Madoff account holders. Madoff was sentenced to 150 years in prison for his crimes.

Increased oversight at the Securities and Exchange Commission after the December 2008

Madoff confession led to the June 2009 indictment of R. Allen Stanford and five others who were accused of running an investment scheme similar to that perpetrated by Bernard Madoff. Stanford was alleged to have defrauded more than 30,000 Stanford Financial Group account holders out of $7 billion through the sale of spurious certificates of deposit (CDs). The CDs marketed by Stanford Financial Group were issued by the company's Antiguan subsidiary, Stanford International Bank, and carried rates that were as much as three to four times greater than the CD rates offered by other financial institutions. Stanford claimed that the Stanford International Bank was able to provide such exceptional yields because of its investment in a globally diversified portfolio of stocks, bonds, commodities, and alternative investments and because of the tax advantages provided by the bank's location in Antigua. All the investments made by Stanford International Bank were said to be safe and liquid financial instruments monitored by more than 20 analysts and audited by Antiguan regulators. In fact, the deposits were invested in much riskier private equity placements and real estate investments and were subject to severe fluctuations in value. The statements provided to CD holders were alleged by prosecutors to be based on fabricated performance and phony financial statements.

Federal prosecutors also alleged that deposits of at least $1.6 billion were diverted into undisclosed personal loans to Allen Stanford. At the time of Stanford's indictment, he ranked 605th on *Forbes* magazine's list of the world's wealthiest persons, with an estimated net worth of

(Continued)

$2.2 billion. Stanford was a notable sports enthusiast and philanthropist—he supported a cricket league in Antigua and professional golf tournaments in the United States and contributed millions to the St. Jude Children's Research Hospital and museums in Houston and Miami.

Stanford also pledged $100 million to support programs aimed at slowing global warming. In May 2009, Stanford Investment Bank disclosed that it owed $7.2 billion to about 28,000 account holders. Its total assets at the time stood at $1 billion, including $46 million in cash.

Developed with C. David Morgan.

Sources: James Bandler, Nicholas Varchaver, and Doris Burke, "How Bernie Did It," *Fortune Online,* April 30, 2009 (accessed July 7, 2009); Duncan Greenberg, "Billionaire Responds to SEC Probe," *Forbes Online,* February 13, 2009 (accessed July 9, 2009); Katie Benner, "Stanford Scandal Sets Antigua on Edge," *Fortune Online,* February 25, 2009 (accessed July 9, 2009); Alyssa Abkowitz, "The Investment Scam-Artist's Playbook," *Fortune Online,* February 25, 2009 (accessed July 9, 2009); Kathryn Glass, "Stanford Bank Assets Insufficient to Repay Depositors," *Fox Business.com,* May 15, 2009 (accessed July 9, 2009); Bill McQuillen, Justin Blum, and Laurel Brubaker Calkins, "Allen Stanford Indicted by U.S. in $7 Billion Scam," *Bloomberg.com,* June 19, 2009 (accessed July 9, 2009); Jane J. Kim, "The Madoff Fraud: SIPC Sets Payouts in Madoff Scandal," *Wall Street Journal* (Eastern Edition), October 29, 2009, p. C4.

allowed them to hit the numbers and receive incentive awards ranging from $10 million to $100 million.

The fundamental problem with **short-termism**—the tendency for managers to focus excessive attention on short-term performance objectives—is that it doesn't create value for customers or improve the firm's competitiveness in the marketplace; that is, it sacrifices the activities that are the most reliable drivers of higher profits and added shareholder value in the long run. Cutting ethical corners in the name of profits carries exceptionally high risk for shareholders—the steep stock price decline and tarnished brand image that accompany the discovery of scurrilous behavior leave shareholders with a company worth much less than before—and the rebuilding task can be arduous, taking both considerable time and resources.

> **CORE CONCEPT**
>
> **Short-termism** is the tendency for managers to focus excessively on short-term performance objectives at the expense of longer-term strategic objectives. It has negative implications for the likelihood of ethical lapses as well as company performance in the longer run.

A Company Culture That Puts Profitability and Business Performance Ahead of Ethical Behavior

When a company's culture spawns an ethically corrupt or amoral work climate, people have a company-approved license to ignore "what's right" and engage in any behavior or employ any strategy they think they can get away with.[25] At such companies, unethical people are given free reign, and otherwise honorable people may succumb to the many opportunities around them to engage in unethical practices. A perfect example of a company culture gone awry on ethics is Enron.[26]

Enron's leaders encouraged company personnel to focus on the current bottom line and to be innovative and aggressive in figuring out how to grow current earnings—regardless of the methods. Enron's annual "rank and yank" performance evaluation process, in which the lowest-ranking 15 to 20 percent of employees were let go, made it abundantly clear that bottom-line results were what mattered most. The name of the game at Enron became devising clever ways to boost revenues and earnings, even if this sometimes meant operating outside established policies. In fact, outside-the-lines behavior was celebrated if it generated profitable new business.

A high-performance/high-rewards climate came to pervade the Enron culture, as the best workers (determined by who produced the best bottom-line results) received impressively large incentives and bonuses (amounting to as much as

$1 million for traders and even more for senior executives). On Car Day at Enron, an array of luxury sports cars arrived for presentation to the most successful employees. Understandably, employees wanted to be seen as part of Enron's star team and partake in the benefits granted to Enron's best and brightest employees. The high monetary rewards, the ambitious and hard-driving people whom the company hired and promoted, and the competitive, results-oriented culture combined to give Enron a reputation not only for trampling competitors at every opportunity but also for internal ruthlessness. The company's super-aggressiveness and win-at-all-costs mindset nurtured a culture that gradually and then more rapidly fostered the erosion of ethical standards, eventually making a mockery of the company's stated values of integrity and respect. When it became evident in fall 2001 that Enron was a house of cards propped up by deceitful accounting and a myriad of unsavory practices, the company imploded in a matter of weeks—one of the biggest bankruptcies of all time, costing investors $64 billion in losses.

More recently, a team investigating an ethical scandal at oil giant Royal Dutch/ Shell Group that resulted in the payment of $150 million in fines found that an ethically flawed culture was a major contributor to why managers made rosy forecasts that they couldn't meet and why top executives engaged in maneuvers to mislead investors by overstating Shell's oil and gas reserves by 25 percent (equal to 4.5 billion barrels of oil). The investigation revealed that top Shell executives knew that a variety of internal practices, together with unrealistic and unsupportable estimates submitted by overzealous, bonus-conscious managers in Shell's exploration and production group, were being used to overstate reserves. An e-mail written by Shell's top executive for exploration and production (who was caught up in the ethical misdeeds and later forced to resign) said, "I am becoming sick and tired of lying about the extent of our reserves issues and the downward revisions that need to be done because of our far too aggressive/optimistic bookings."[27]

In contrast, when high ethical principles are deeply ingrained in the corporate culture of a company, culture can function as a powerful mechanism for communicating ethical behavioral norms and gaining employee buy-in to the company's moral standards, business principles, and corporate values. In such cases, the ethical principles embraced in the company's code of ethics and/or in its statement of corporate values are seen as integral to the company's identity, self-image, and ways of operating. Stories of former and current moral heroes are kept in circulation, and the deeds of company personnel who display ethical values and are dedicated to walking the talk are celebrated at internal company events. The message that ethics matters—and matters a lot—resounds loudly and clearly throughout the organization and in its strategy and decisions. Illustration Capsule 9.3 discusses GE's approach to building a culture that combines demands for high performance with expectations for ethical conduct.

WHY SHOULD COMPANY STRATEGIES BE ETHICAL?

There are two reasons why a company's strategy should be ethical: (1) because a strategy that is unethical is morally wrong and reflects badly on the character of the company personnel and (2) because an ethical strategy can be good business and serve the self-interest of shareholders.

How General Electric's Top Management Built a Culture That Fuses High Performance with High Integrity

GE's CEO, Jeffrey Immelt, has made it a priority to foster a culture built on high ethical standards. The company's heavy reliance on financial controls and performance-based reward systems—which are necessary because of GE's broad multinational diversification—could easily tempt managers at all levels to cut corners, engage in unethical sales tactics, inaccurately record revenues or expenses, or participate in corrupt practices prevalent in the many emerging markets where GE competes. Immelt and GE's other top managers clearly recognize that without a strong ethical culture, there would be little to deter the company's thousands of managers across the globe from pursuing the many types of unethical behavior that would, on the surface, boost performance.

The first step in establishing an ethical culture at GE was for its top management to forcefully communicate the company's principles that should guide decision making. Jeffrey Immelt begins and ends each annual meeting of the company's 220 officers and 600 senior managers with a recitation of the company's fundamental ethical principles. Immelt and GE's other managers are careful to not violate these principles themselves or give implied consent for others to skirt these principles, since human nature makes subordinates at all levels ever vigilant for the signs of hypocrisy in the actions of higher-ups. The importance of walking the talk justifies GE's "one strike and you're out" standard for its top management. For example, a high-level manager in an emerging market was terminated for failing to conduct required diligence on a third-party vendor known for its shady business practices, including the payment of bribes to local officials. Another executive was fired from GE for agreeing to a large and important Asian customer's request to falsify supplier documents that were used by regulatory agencies.

With so many ethical standards prevailing in the more than 100 countries where GE operates, the company has turned to global ethical standards rather than allowing local cultures to shape business behavior. The company's global standards cover such topics as how to best evaluate suppliers' environmental records

and working conditions in its manufacturing businesses and how to avoid money-laundering schemes or aiding and abetting financial services customers engaged in tax evasion or accounting fraud. Operating-level managers are formally responsible for ensuring ethical compliance in their divisions and are required to submit quarterly tracking reports to GE's corporate offices on key indicators such as spills, accident rates, and violation notices. Managers of operating units falling in the bottom quartile on the quarterly assessments are required to submit plans for improving the ethical shortcomings. GE also evaluates the ethical performance of its 4,000 managers who are responsible for profit centers or are key contributors on business teams.

GE's approach to culture building also includes instilling such principles into the behavior of the company's 300,000-plus employees with no managerial responsibility. Employees are provided training to help them understand the company's ethical principles and how those principles can help them make decisions in the ethical gray areas that arise while making everyday decisions. In Immelt's words, "At a time when many people are more cynical than ever about business, GE must seek to earn this high level of trust every day, employee by employee."* GE also allows employees to lodge anonymous complaints about ethics compliance; the complaints are evaluated by more than 500 employees around the world with either full-time or part-time ombudsperson capacity. About 20 percent of the

(Continued)

307

1,500 concerns lodged annually lead to serious discipline. Hourly employees are also included in annual assessments of ethical performance and are rewarded through bonuses, promotions, or recognition for identifying or resolving ethical issues at the operating level.

* *General Electric,* "The Spirit and the Letter," January 2008, www.ge.com/citizenship/reporting/spirit_and_letter.jsp.

Developed with C. David Morgan.

Source: Based on the discussion of GE's culture-building process by the company's former legal counsel in Ben W. Heineman, Jr., "Avoiding Integrity Land Mines," *Harvard Business Review* 85, no. 4 (April 2007), pp. 100–8.

The Moral Case for an Ethical Strategy

Managers do not dispassionately assess what strategic course to steer. Ethical strategy making generally begins with managers who themselves have strong moral character (i.e., who are trustworthy, have integrity, and truly care about conducting the company's business in an honorable manner). Managers with high ethical principles are usually advocates of a corporate code of ethics and strong ethics compliance, and they are genuinely committed to upholding corporate values and ethical business principles. They demonstrate their commitment by displaying the company's stated values and living up to its business principles and ethical standards. They understand there's a big difference between adopting value statements and codes of ethics and ensuring that they are followed strictly in a company's actual strategy and business conduct. As a consequence, ethically strong managers consciously opt for strategic actions that can pass the strictest moral scrutiny—they display no tolerance for strategies with ethically controversial components.

LO 3

Gain an understanding of the costs of business ethics failures.

The Business Case for Ethical Strategies

In addition to the moral reasons for adopting ethical strategies, there may be solid business reasons. Pursuing unethical strategies and tolerating unethical conduct not only damages a company's reputation but also may result in a wide-ranging set of other costly consequences. Figure 9.1 shows the types of costs a company can incur when unethical behavior on its part is discovered, the wrongdoings of company personnel are headlined in the media, and it is forced to make amends for its behavior. The more egregious are a company's ethical violations, the higher the costs and the bigger the damage to its reputation (and to the reputations of the company personnel involved). In high-profile instances, the costs of ethical misconduct can easily run into the hundreds of millions and even billions of dollars, especially if they provoke widespread public outrage and many people were harmed. The penalties levied on executives caught in wrongdoing can skyrocket as well, as the 150-year prison term sentence of financier Bernie Madoff illustrates.

The fallout of ethical misconduct on the part of a company goes well beyond the costs of making amends for the misdeeds. Rehabilitating a company's shattered reputation is time-consuming and costly. Customers shun companies known for their shady behavior. Companies known to have engaged in unethical conduct have difficulty in recruiting and retaining talented employees; indeed, many people take a company's ethical reputation into account when deciding whether to accept a job

Conducting business in an ethical fashion is not only morally right—it is in a company's enlightened self-interest.

Figure 9.1 The Costs Companies Incur When Ethical Wrongdoing Is Found Out

Visible Costs	Internal Administrative Costs	Intangible or Less Visible Costs
• Government fines and penalties • Civil penalties arising from class-action lawsuits and other litigation aimed at punishing the company for its offense and the harm done to others • The costs to shareholders in the form of a lower stock price (and possibly lower dividends)	• Legal and investigative costs incurred by the company • The costs of providing remedial education and ethics training to company personnel • Costs of taking corrective actions • Administrative costs associated with ensuring future compliance	• Customer defections • Loss of reputation • Lost employee morale and higher degrees of employee cynicism • Higher employee turnover • Higher recruiting costs and difficulty in attracting talented employees • Adverse effects on employee productivity • The costs of complying with often harsher government regulations

Source: Adapted from Terry Thomas, John R. Schermerhorn, and John W. Dienhart, "Strategic Leadership of Ethical Behavior," *Academy of Management Executive* 18, no. 2 (May 2004), p. 58.

offer.[28] Most ethically upstanding people are repulsed by a work environment where unethical behavior is condoned; they don't want to get entrapped in a compromising situation, nor do they want their personal reputations tarnished by the actions of an unsavory employer. Creditors are usually unnerved by the unethical actions of a borrower because of the potential business fallout and subsequent risk of default on loans.

All told, a company's unethical behavior risks doing considerable damage to shareholders in the form of lost revenues, higher costs, lower profits, lower stock prices, and a diminished business reputation. To a significant degree, therefore, ethical strategies and ethical conduct are *good business.* Most companies understand the value of operating in a manner that wins the approval of suppliers, employees, investors, and society at large. Most businesspeople recognize the risks and adverse fallout attached to the discovery of unethical behavior. Hence, companies have an incentive to employ strategies that can pass the test of being ethical. Even if a company's managers are not of strong moral character and personally committed to high ethical standards, they have good reason to operate within ethical bounds, if only to (1) avoid the risk of embarrassment, scandal, and possible disciplinary action for unethical conduct on their part and (2) escape being held accountable for unethical behavior by personnel under their supervision and their own lax enforcement of ethical standards.

> Shareholders suffer major damage when a company's unethical behavior is discovered. Making amends for unethical business conduct is costly, and it takes years to rehabilitate a tarnished company reputation.

STRATEGY, CORPORATE SOCIAL RESPONSIBILITY, AND EVIRONMENTAL SUSTAINABILITY

The idea that businesses have an obligation to foster social betterment, a much-debated topic in the past 50 years, took root in the 19th century when progressive companies in the aftermath of the industrial revolution began to provide workers with housing and other amenities. The notion that corporate executives should balance the interests of all stakeholders—shareholders, employees, customers, suppliers, the communities in which they operated, and society at large—began to blossom in the 1960s. Some years later, a group of chief executives of America's 200 largest corporations, calling themselves the Business Roundtable, came out in strong support of the concept of **corporate social responsibility:**[29]

> Balancing the shareholder's expectations of maximum return against other priorities is one of the fundamental problems confronting corporate management. The shareholder must receive a good return but the legitimate concerns of other constituencies (customers, employees, communities, suppliers and society at large) also must have the appropriate attention. . . . [Leading managers] believe that by giving enlightened consideration to balancing the legitimate claims of all its constituents, a corporation will best serve the interest of its shareholders.

Today, corporate social responsibility (CSR) is a concept that resonates in western Europe, the United States, Canada, and such developing nations as Brazil and India.

CORE CONCEPT

Corporate social responsibility (CSR) refers to a company's *duty* to operate in an honorable manner, provide good working conditions for employees, encourage workforce diversity, be a good steward of the environment, and actively work to better the quality of life in the local communities where it operates and in society at large.

What Do We Mean by *Corporate Social Responsibility?*

The essence of socially responsible business behavior is that a company should balance strategic actions to benefit shareholders against the *duty* to be a good corporate citizen. The underlying thesis is that company managers should display a *social conscience* in operating the business and specifically take into account how management decisions and company actions affect the well-being of employees, local communities, the environment, and society at large.[30] Acting in a socially responsible manner thus encompasses more than just participating in community service projects and donating monies to charities and other worthy social causes. Demonstrating social responsibility also entails undertaking actions that earn trust and respect from all stakeholders—operating in an honorable and ethical manner, striving to make the company a great place to work, demonstrating genuine respect for the environment, and trying to make a difference in bettering society. As depicted in Figure 9.2, corporate responsibility programs commonly include the following elements:

- *Making efforts to employ an ethical strategy and observe ethical principles in operating the business.* A sincere commitment to observing ethical principles is a necessary component of a CSR strategy simply because unethical conduct is incompatible with the concept of good corporate citizenship and socially responsible business behavior.

Figure 9.2   The Five Components of a Corporate Social Responsibility Strategy

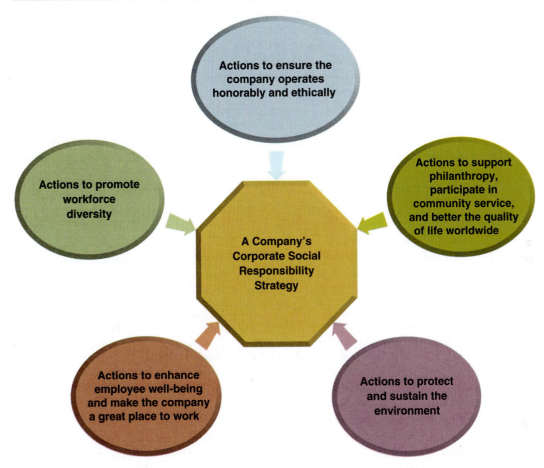

Source: Adapted from material in Ronald Paul Hill, Debra Stephens, and Iain Smith, "Corporate Social Responsibility: An Examination of Individual Firm Behavior," *Business and Society Review* 108, no. 3 (September 2003), p. 348.

- *Making charitable contributions, supporting community service endeavors, engaging in broader philanthropic initiatives, and reaching out to make a difference in the lives of the disadvantaged.* Some companies fulfill their philanthropic obligations by spreading their efforts over a multitude of charitable and community activities—for instance, Microsoft and Johnson & Johnson support a broad variety of community, art, and social welfare programs. Others prefer to focus their energies more narrowly. McDonald's, for example, concentrates on sponsoring the Ronald McDonald House program (which provides a home away from home for the families of seriously ill children receiving treatment at nearby hospitals). British Telecom gives 1 percent of its profits directly to communities, largely for education—teacher training, in-school workshops, and digital technology. Leading prescription drug maker GlaxoSmithKline and other pharmaceutical companies either donate or heavily discount medicines for distribution in the least developed nations. Companies frequently reinforce their philanthropic efforts by encouraging employees to support charitable causes and participate in community affairs, often through programs that match employee contributions.

- *Taking actions to protect the environment and, in particular, to minimize or eliminate any adverse impact on the environment stemming from the company's own business activities.* Social responsibility as it applies to environmental protection entails actively striving to be a good steward of the environment. This means using the best available science and technology to reduce environmentally harmful aspects of the company's operations *below the levels required by prevailing environmental regulations.* It also means putting time and money into improving the environment in ways that extend past a company's own industry boundaries—such as participating in recycling projects, adopting energy conservation practices, and supporting efforts to clean up local water supplies. Retailers like Walmart and Home Depot in the United States and B&Q in the United Kingdom have pressured their suppliers to adopt stronger environmental protection practices in order to lower the carbon footprint of their entire supply chains.[31]

- *Taking actions to create a work environment that enhances the quality of life for employees.* Numerous companies exert extra effort to enhance the quality of life for their employees, both at work and at home. This can include on-site day care, flexible work schedules, workplace exercise facilities, special leaves for employees to care for sick family members, work-at-home opportunities, career development programs and education opportunities, special safety programs, and the like.

- *Taking actions to build a workforce that is diverse with respect to gender, race, national origin, and other aspects that different people bring to the workplace.* Most large companies in the United States have established workforce diversity programs, and some go the extra mile to ensure that their workplaces are attractive to ethnic minorities and inclusive of all groups and perspectives. At some companies, the diversity initiative extends to suppliers—sourcing items from small businesses owned by women or ethnic minorities, for example. The pursuit of workforce diversity can be good business. At Coca-Cola, where strategic success depends on getting people all over the world to become loyal consumers of the company's beverages, efforts to build a public persona of inclusiveness for people of all races, religions, nationalities, interests, and talents have considerable strategic value.

The particular combination of socially responsible endeavors a company elects to pursue defines its **corporate social responsibility (CSR) strategy.** Illustration Capsule 9.4 describes John Deere's approach to corporate social responsibility—an approach that corresponds closely to the description in Figure 9.2. But the specific components emphasized in a CSR strategy vary from company to company and are typically linked to a company's core values. General Mills, for example, builds its CSR strategy around the theme of "nourishing lives" to emphasize its commitment to good nutrition as well as philanthropy, community building, and environmental protection.[32] Starbucks' CSR strategy includes four main elements (ethical sourcing, community service, environmental stewardship, and farmer support), all of which have touch points with the way that the company procures its coffee—a key aspect of its product differentiation strategy.[33] Some companies use other terms, such as *corporate citizenship, corporate responsibility,* or *sustainable responsible business (SRB)* to characterize their CSR initiatives.

ILLUSTRATION CAPSULE 9.4

John Deere's Approach to Corporate Social Responsibility

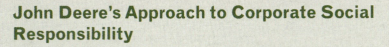

Principal Components of John Deere's Corporate Social Responsibility Strategy	Specific Actions to Execute the Strategy
Adhering to the core values of integrity, quality commitment, and innovation *Integrity* means telling the truth, keeping our word, and treating others with fairness and respect. *Quality* means delivering the value customers, employees, shareholders, and other business partners expect every day. *Commitment* means doing our best to meet expectations over the long run. *Innovation* means inventing, designing, and developing breakthrough products and services that customers want to buy from John Deere.	• Committing to ethical behavior and fair dealing in all relationships • Providing Business Conduct Guidelines that show employees how they are expected to carry out company business • Creating an Office of Corporate Compliance to ensure ethical and fair business practices are maintained throughout global operations • Instituting a 24-hour hotline for confidential anonymous reporting of ethical violations • Offering employees professional guidance when they feel they are operating in complicated or ambiguous business and cultural situations
Engaging in philanthropy and community betterment	• Supporting agricultural development in resource-poor countries • Providing increased access to financing for the rural poor in Africa (in partnership with Opportunity International) • Helping start *BackPack* programs in the U.S. to supply supplemental food for school-age children • Supporting a variety of higher educational programs and such programs as Junior Achievement, FFA, and the National 4-H Council • Instituting an employee matching gift program
Conserving resources and sustaining the environment	• Establishing ambitious greenhouse-gas reduction goals to be achieved over the next 5 to 10 years • Mandating the use of recycling and waste reduction practices across all company operations • Implementing a worldwide Environmental Management System geared to ISO14001 standards • Helping to develop long-term comprehensive climate change strategies through EPS's Climate Leaders Program • Designing products to conserve water, encourage biofuel development, and support sustainable agriculture
Supporting and enhancing the workforce	• Maintaining effective workplace safety programs—more than 1,000 awards from the U.S. National Safety Council • Providing programs to promote employee health and wellness and work-life balance • Establishing global occupational health programs keyed to local health issues and infrastructure

(Continued)

Principal Components of John Deere's Corporate Social Responsibility Strategy	Specific Actions to Execute the Strategy
	• Helping employees with career development through mentoring, coaching, and a programmatic approach • Creating a continuous learning environment with extensive training opportunities and a tuition reimbursement program
Promoting diversity and inclusiveness	• Creating an inclusive culture in which employees of all backgrounds can develop their leadership potential • Providing training and tools designed to make work teams more diverse, productive, and effective • Sponsoring employee networks that bring together people from around the world with shared interests, gender, ethnicity, or skills • Encouraging diversity within the company's dealer and supplier base • Supporting minority education programs and collegiate diversity initiatives

Source: Information posted at www.deere.com (accessed July 8, 2010).

Although there is wide variation in how companies devise and implement a CSR strategy, communities of companies concerned with corporate social responsibility (such as CSR Europe) have emerged to help companies share best CSR practices. Moreover, a number of reporting standards have been developed, including ISO 26000—a new internationally recognized standard for social responsibility produced by the International Standards Organization (ISO).[34] Companies that exhibit a strong commitment to corporate social responsibility are often recognized by being included on lists such as *Corporate Responsibility* magazine's "100 Best Corporate Citizens" or *Corporate Knights* magazine's "Global 100 Most Sustainable Corporations."

Corporate Social Responsibility and the Triple Bottom Line
CSR initiatives undertaken by companies are frequently directed at improving the company's "triple bottom line"—a reference to three types of performance metrics: *economic, social, environmental.* The goal is for a company to succeed simultaneously in all three dimensions, as illustrated in Figure 9.3.[35] The three dimensions of performance are often referred to in terms of the "three pillars" of "people, planet, and profit." The term *people* refers to the various social initiatives that make up CSR strategies, such as corporate giving, community involvement, and company efforts to improve the lives of its internal and external stakeholders. *Planet* refers to a firm's ecological impact and environmental practices. The term *profit* has a broader meaning with respect to the triple bottom line than it does otherwise. It encompasses not only the profit a firm earns for its shareholders but also the economic impact that the company has on society more generally, in terms of the overall value that it creates and the overall costs that it imposes on society. For example, Procter & Gamble's Swiffer cleaning system, one of the company's best-selling products, not only offers an earth-friendly design but also outperforms less ecologically friendly alternatives in terms of its broader economic impact: It

Figure 9.3   **The Triple Bottom Line: Excelling on Three Measures of Company Performance**

Source: Developed with help from Amy E.Florentino.

reduces demands on municipal water sources, saves electricity that would be needed to heat mop water, and doesn't add to the amount of detergent making its way into waterways and waste treatment facilities. Nike sees itself as bringing people, planet, and profits into balance by producing innovative new products in a more sustainable way, recognizing that sustainability is key to its future profitability.

Many companies now make a point of citing the beneficial outcomes of their CSR strategies in press releases and issue special reports for consumers and investors to review. Staples, the world's largest office products company, makes reporting an important part of its commitment to corporate responsibility; the company posts a "Staples Soul Report" on its Web site that describes its initiatives and accomplishments in the areas of diversity, environment, community, and ethics. Triple-bottom-line (TBL) reporting is emerging as an increasingly important way for companies to make the results of their CSR strategies apparent to stakeholders and for stakeholders to hold companies accountable for their impact on society. The use of standard reporting frameworks and metrics, such as those developed by the Global Reporting Initiative, promotes greater transparency and facilitates benchmarking CSR efforts across firms and industries.

Investment firms have created mutual funds comprising companies that are excelling on the basis of the triple bottom line in order to attract funds from environmentally and socially aware investors. The Dow Jones Sustainability World Index is made up of the top 10 percent of the 2,500 companies listed in the Dow Jones World Index in terms of economic performance, environmental performance, and social performance. Companies are evaluated in these three performance areas, using indicators such as corporate governance, climate change mitigation, and labor practices. Table 9.1 shows a sampling of the companies selected for the Dow Jones Sustainability World Index in 2009 and 2010.

Table 9.1   **A Selection of Companies Recognized for Their Triple Bottom Line Performance in 2009 and 2010**

Name	Market Sector	Country
Johnson & Johnson	Health care and pharmaceuticals	United States
PepsiCo	Food and beverages	United States
adidas	Athletic footwear, apparel, and equipment	Germany
Intel	Technology	United States
Unilever	Food and beverages	Netherlands
Samsung	Electronics	Korea
Nokia	Technology	Finland
Caterpillar	Machinery and equipment	United States
Roche AG	Health care	Switzerland
Air France–KLM	Travel and leisure	France
3M	Adhesives and abrasives	United States
Procter & Gamble	Consumer goods	United States
Sony	Electronics	Japan
BMW	Automobiles and parts	Germany
Novartis	Health care	Switzerland
IBM	Technology	United States
CEMIG	Utilities	Brazil
Cisco Systems	Technology	United States
General Electric	Technology	United States
Coca-Cola	Beverages	United States

Sources: Dow Jones indexes, STOXX Limited, and SAM Group, www.sustainability-indexes.com/07_htmle/indexes/djsiworld_ supersectorleaders.html, www.sustainability-indexes.com/07_htmle/publications/factsheets.html (accessed July 5, 2010).

What Do We Mean by *Sustainability* and *Sustainable Business Practices?*

The term *sustainability* is used in a variety of ways. In many firms, it is synonymous with corporate social responsibility; it is seen by some as a term that is gradually replacing CSR in the business lexicon. Indeed, sustainability reporting and TBL reporting are often one and the same, as illustrated by the Dow Jones Sustainability Index, which tracks the same three types of performance measures that constitute the triple bottom line.

More often, however, the term takes on a more focused meaning, concerned with the relationship of a company to its *environment* and its use of *natural resources,* including land, water, air, plants, animals, minerals, fossil fuels, and biodiversity. It is widely recognized that the world's natural resources are finite and are being consumed and degraded at rates that threaten their capacity for renewal. Since corporations are the biggest users of natural resources, managing and maintaining these resources is critical for the long-term economic interests of corporations.

For some companies, this issue has direct and obvious implications for the continued viability of their business model and strategy. Pacific Gas and Electric has begun measuring the full carbon footprint of its supply chain to become not only "greener" but a more efficient energy producer.[36] Beverage companies such as Coca-Cola and PepsiCo are having to rethink their business models because of the prospect of future worldwide water shortages. For other companies, the connection is less direct, but all companies are part of a business ecosystem whose economic health depends on the availability of natural resources. In response, most major companies have begun to change *how* they do business, emphasizing the use of **sustainable business practices,** defined as those capable of meeting the needs of the present without compromising the ability to meet the needs of the future.[37] Many have also begun to incorporate a consideration of environmental sustainability into their strategy-making activities.

Environmental sustainability strategies entail deliberate and concerted actions to operate businesses in a manner that protects natural resources and ecological support systems, guards against outcomes that will ultimately endanger the planet, and is therefore sustainable for centuries.[38] One aspect of environmental sustainability is keeping use of the Earth's natural resources within levels that can be replenished via the use of sustainable business practices. In the case of some resources (like crude oil, fresh water, and the harvesting of edible fish from the oceans), scientists say that use levels either are already unsustainable or will be soon, given the world's growing population and propensity to consume additional resources as incomes and living standards rise. Another aspect of sustainability concerns containing the adverse effects of greenhouse gases and other forms of air pollution so as to reduce global warming and other undesirable climate and atmospheric changes. Other aspects of sustainability include greater reliance on sustainable energy sources, greater use of recyclable materials, the use of sustainable methods of growing foods (so as to reduce topsoil depletion and the use of pesticides, herbicides, fertilizers, and other chemicals that may be harmful to human health or ecological systems), habitat protection, environmentally sound waste management practices, and increased attempts to decouple environmental degradation and economic growth (according to many scientists, economic growth has historically been accompanied by declines in the well-being of the environment).

Unilever, a diversified producer of processed foods, personal care, and home cleaning products, is among the many committed corporations pursuing sustainable business practices. The company tracks 11 sustainable agricultural indicators in its processed-foods business and has launched a variety of programs to improve the environmental performance of its suppliers. Examples of such programs include special low-rate financing for tomato suppliers choosing to switch to water-conserving irrigation systems and training programs in India that have allowed contract cucumber growers to reduce pesticide use by 90 percent while improving yields by 78 percent. Unilever has also reengineered many internal processes to improve the company's overall performance on sustainability measures. For example, the company's factories have reduced water usage by 63 percent and total waste by 67 percent since 1995 through the implementation of sustainability initiatives. Unilever has also redesigned packaging for many of

> **CORE CONCEPT**
>
> **Sustainable business practices** are those that meet the needs of the present without compromising the ability to meet the needs of the future.

> **CORE CONCEPT**
>
> A company's **environmental sustainability strategy** consists of its deliberate actions to protect the environment, provide for the longevity of natural resources, maintain ecological support systems for future generations, and guard against ultimate endangerment of the planet.

its products to conserve natural resources and reduce the volume of consumer waste. For example, the company's Suave shampoo bottles were reshaped to save almost 150 tons of plastic resin per year, which is the equivalent of 15 million fewer empty bottles making it to landfills annually. As the producer of Lipton Tea, Unilever is the world's largest purchaser of tea leaves; the company has committed to sourcing all of its tea from Rainforest Alliance Certified farms by 2015, due to their comprehensive triple-bottom-line approach toward sustainable farm management.

Crafting Corporate Social Responsibility and Sustainability Strategies

While CSR and environmental sustainability strategies take many forms, those that both provide valuable social benefits *and* fulfill customer needs in a superior fashion may also contribute to a company's competitive advantage.[39] For example, while carbon emissions may be of some concern for financial institutions such as Wells Fargo, Toyota's sustainability strategy for reducing carbon emissions has produced both competitive advantage and environmental benefits. Its Prius hybrid electric- and gasoline-powered automobile is not only among the least polluting automobiles but is also the best-selling hybrid vehicle in the United States; it has earned the company the loyalty of fuel-conscious buyers and given Toyota a green image. Green Mountain Coffee Roasters' commitment to protect the welfare of coffee growers and their families (in particular, making sure they receive a fair price) also meets its customers' wants and needs. In its dealings with suppliers at small farmer cooperatives in Peru, Mexico, and Sumatra, Green Mountain pays "fair-trade" prices for coffee beans (in 2009, the fair-trade prices were a minimum of $1.26 per pound for conventional coffee versus market prices of $0.65 per pound). Green Mountain also purchases about 29 percent of its coffee directly from farmers so as to cut out intermediaries and see that farmers realize a higher price for their efforts—coffee is the world's second most heavily traded commodity after oil, requiring the labor of some 20 million people, most of whom live at the poverty level.[40] Its consumers are aware of these efforts and purchase Green Mountain coffee, in part, to encourage such practices.

CSR strategies and environmental sustainability strategies are more likely to contribute to a company's competitive advantage if they are linked to a company's competitively important resources and capabilities or value chain activities. Thus, it is common for companies engaged in natural resource extraction, electric power production, forestry and paper products, motor vehicles, and chemical production to place more emphasis on addressing environmental concerns than, say, software and electronics firms or apparel manufacturers. Companies whose business success is heavily dependent on high employee morale or attracting and retaining the best and brightest employees are somewhat more prone to stress the well-being of their employees and foster a positive, high-energy workplace environment that elicits the dedication and enthusiastic commitment of employees, thus putting real meaning behind the claim "Our people are our greatest asset." Ernst & Young, one of the four largest global accounting firms, stresses its "People First" workforce diversity strategy that is all about respecting differences, fostering individuality, and promoting inclusiveness so that its more than 144,000 employees in 140 countries

> CSR strategies and environmental sustainability strategies that both provide valuable social benefits *and* fulfill customer needs in a superior fashion can lead to competitive advantage. Corporate social agendas that address only social issues may help boost a company's reputation for corporate citizenship but are unlikely to improve its competitive strength in the marketplace.

can feel valued, engaged, and empowered in developing creative ways to serve the firm's clients. As a service business, Marriot's most competitively important resource is also people. Thus its social agenda includes providing 180 hours of paid classroom and on-the-job training to the chronically unemployed. Ninety percent of the graduates from the job training program take jobs with Marriott, and about two-thirds of those remain with Marriott for more than a year. At Whole Foods Market, an $8 billion supermarket chain specializing in organic and natural foods, its environmental sustainability strategy is evident in almost every segment of its company value chain and is a big part of its differentiation strategy. The company's procurement policies encourage stores to purchase fresh fruits and vegetables from local farmers and screen processed-food items for more than 400 common ingredients that the company considers unhealthy or environmentally unsound. Spoiled food items are sent to regional composting centers rather than landfills, and all cleaning products used in its stores are biodegradable. The company also has created the Animal Compassion Foundation to develop natural and humane ways of raising farm animals and has converted all of its vehicles to run on biofuels.

Not all companies choose to link their corporate environmental or social agendas to their value chain, their business model, or their industry. For example, Chick-Fil-A, an Atlanta-based fast-food chain with over 1,400 outlets in 38 states, has a charitable foundation that funds two scholarship programs and supports 12 foster homes as well as a summer camp for some 1,900 campers.[41] However, unless a company's social responsibility initiatives become part of the way it operates its business every day, the initiatives are unlikely to catch fire and be fully effective. As an executive at Royal Dutch/Shell put it, corporate social responsibility "is not a cosmetic; it must be rooted in our values. It must make a difference to the way we do business."[42] The same is true for environmental sustainability initiatives.

The Moral Case for Corporate Social Responsibility and Environmentally Sustainable Business Practices

The moral case for why businesses should act in a manner that benefits all of the company's stakeholders—not just shareholders—boils down to "It's the right thing to do." Ordinary decency, civic-mindedness, and contributions to the well-being of society should be expected of any business.[43] In today's social and political climate, most business leaders can be expected to acknowledge that socially responsible actions are important and that businesses have a duty to be good corporate citizens. But there is a complementary school of thought that business operates on the basis of an implied social contract with the members of society. According to this contract, society grants a business the right to conduct its business affairs and agrees not to unreasonably restrain its pursuit of a fair profit for the goods or services it sells. In return for this "license to operate," a business is obligated to act as a responsible citizen, do its fair share to promote the general welfare, and avoid doing any harm. Such a view clearly puts a moral burden on a company to take corporate citizenship into consideration and do what's best for shareholders within the confines of discharging its duties to operate honorably, provide good working conditions to employees, be a good environmental steward, and display good corporate citizenship.

> Every action a company takes can be interpreted as a statement of what it stands for.

The Business Case for Corporate Social Responsibility and Environmentally Sustainable Business Practices

Whatever the moral arguments for socially responsible business behavior and environmentally sustainable business practices, it has long been recognized that it is in the enlightened self-interest of companies to be good citizens and devote some of their energies and resources to the betterment of employees, the communities in which they operate, and society in general. In short, there are reasons why the exercise of social and environmental responsibility may be good business:

- *Such actions can lead to increased buyer patronage.* A strong visible social responsibility or environmental sustainability strategy may give a company an edge in differentiating itself from rivals and in appealing to consumers who prefer to do business with companies that are good corporate citizens. Ben & Jerry's, Whole Foods Market, Stonyfield Farm, and the Body Shop have definitely expanded their customer bases because of their visible and well-publicized activities as socially conscious companies. More and more companies are also recognizing the cash register payoff of social responsibility strategies that reach out to people of all cultures and demographics (women, retirees, and ethnic groups).

- *A strong commitment to socially responsible behavior reduces the risk of reputation-damaging incidents.* Companies that place little importance on operating in a socially responsible manner are more prone to scandal and embarrassment. Consumer, environmental, and human rights activist groups are quick to criticize businesses whose behavior they consider to be out of line, and they are adept at getting their message into the media and onto the Internet. Pressure groups can generate widespread adverse publicity, promote boycotts, and influence like-minded or sympathetic buyers to avoid an offender's products. Research has shown that product boycott announcements are associated with a decline in a company's stock price.[44] When a major oil company suffered damage to its reputation on environmental and social grounds, the CEO repeatedly said that the most negative impact the company suffered—and the one that made him fear for the future of the company—was that bright young graduates were no longer attracted to working for the company.[45] For many years, Nike received stinging criticism for not policing sweatshop conditions in the Asian factories that produced Nike footwear, causing Nike cofounder and former CEO Phil Knight to observe that "Nike has become synonymous with slave wages, forced overtime, and arbitrary abuse."[46] In 1997, Nike began an extensive effort to monitor conditions in the 800 factories of the contract manufacturers that produced Nike shoes. As Knight said, "Good shoes come from good factories and good factories have good labor relations." Nonetheless, Nike has continually been plagued by complaints from human rights activists that its monitoring procedures are flawed and that it is not doing enough to correct the plight of factory workers. As this suggests, a damaged reputation is not easily repaired.

- *Socially responsible actions and sustainable business practices can lower costs and enhance employee recruiting and workforce retention.* Companies with

> The higher the public profile of a company or its brand, the greater the scrutiny of its activities and the higher the potential for it to become a target for pressure group action.

deservedly good reputations for social responsibility and sustainable business practices are better able to attract and retain employees, compared to companies with tarnished reputations. Some employees just feel better about working for a company committed to improving society.[47] This can contribute to lower turnover, better worker productivity, and lower costs for staff recruitment and training. For example, Starbucks is said to enjoy much lower rates of employee turnover because of the company's socially responsible practices as well as superior employee benefits and management efforts to make Starbucks a great place to work. Making a company a great place to work pays dividends in recruitment of talented workers, more creativity and energy on the part of workers, higher worker productivity, and greater employee commitment to the company's business mission/vision and success in the marketplace. Sustainable business practices are often concomitant with greater operational efficiencies. For example, when a U.S. manufacturer of recycled paper, taking eco-efficiency to heart, discovered how to increase its fiber recovery rate, it saved the equivalent of 20,000 tons of waste paper—a factor that helped the company become the industry's lowest-cost producer.[48]

- *Opportunities for revenue enhancement may also come from CSR and environmental sustainability strategies.* The drive for sustainability and social responsibility can spur innovative efforts that in turn lead to new products and opportunities for revenue enhancement. Electric cars such as the Chevy Volt and the Tesler Roadster are one example. In many cases, the revenue opportunities are tied to a company's core products. PepsiCo and Coca-Cola, for example, have expanded into the juice business to offer a healthier alternative to their carbonated beverages. GE has created a profitable new business in wind turbines. In other cases, revenue enhancement opportunities come from innovative ways to reduce waste and use the by-products of a company's production. Tyson Foods now produces jet fuel for B52 bombers from the vast amount of animal waste resulting from its meat product business. Staples has become one of the largest nonutility corporate producers of renewable energy in the United States due to its installation of solar power panels in all of its outlets (and sale of what it does not consume in renewable energy credit markets).

- *Well-conceived CSR strategies and sustainable business practices are in the best long-term interest of shareholders.* Social responsibility strategies and strategies to promote environmental sustainability can work to the advantage of shareholders in several ways. They help avoid or preempt legal and regulatory actions that could prove costly and otherwise burdensome. In addition, when CSR and sustainability strategies increase buyer patronage, offer revenue-enhancing opportunities, lower costs, increase productivity, and reduce the risk of reputation-damaging incidents, they contribute to the total value created by a company and improve its profitability. In this manner, well-conceived socially and environmentally responsible strategies can enhance shareholder value even as they address the needs of other company stakeholders. While some question whether addressing social needs is truly in the interest of a company's shareholders, the answer depends on how well such strategies are crafted and whether they contribute to the success of the company's business model. A review of 135 studies indicated there is a positive, but small, correlation between good corporate behavior and good financial

> Socially responsible strategies that create value for customers and lower costs can improve company profits and shareholder value at the same time that they address other stakeholder interests.

performance; only 2 percent of the studies showed that dedicating corporate resources to social responsibility harmed the interests of shareholders.[49] Another indicator is the performance of mutual funds dedicated to socially responsible investments (SRIs) relative to other types of funds. The longest-running SRI index, the Domini 400, has continued to perform competitively, slightly outperforming the S&P 500 (the top-500 firms in the Standard and Poor's Index).[50] Similarly, the Dow Jones Sustainability Index has performed comparably to the Dow Jones Large Cap and Total Market Indexes.[51]

In sum, companies that take social responsibility and environmental sustainability seriously can improve their business reputations and operational efficiency while also reducing their risk exposure and encouraging loyalty and innovation. Overall, companies that take special pains to protect the environment (beyond what is required by law), are active in community affairs, and are generous supporters of charitable causes and projects that benefit society are more likely to be seen as good investments and as good companies to work for or do business with. Shareholders are likely to view the business case for social responsibility as a strong one, particularly when it results in the creation of more customer value, greater productivity, lower operating costs, and lower business risk—all of which should increase firm profitability and enhance shareholder value even as the company's actions address broader stakeholder interests.

> There's little hard evidence indicating shareholders are disadvantaged in any meaningful way by a company's actions to be socially responsible.

Companies are, of course, sometimes rewarded for bad behavior—a company that is able to shift environmental and other social costs associated with its activities onto society as a whole can reap large short-term profits. The major cigarette producers for many years were able to earn greatly inflated profits by shifting the health-related costs of smoking onto others and escaping any responsibility for the harm their products caused to consumers and the general public. Only recently have they been facing the prospect of having to pay high punitive damages for their actions. Unfortunately, the cigarette makers are not alone in trying to evade paying for the social harms of their operations for as long as they can. Calling a halt to such actions usually hinges on (1) the effectiveness of activist social groups in publicizing the adverse consequences of a company's social irresponsibility and marshaling public opinion for something to be done, (2) the enactment of legislation or regulations to correct the inequity, and (3) widespread actions on the part of socially conscious buyers to take their business elsewhere.

KEY POINTS

1. Ethics concerns standards of right and wrong. Business ethics concerns the application of ethical principles and standards to the actions and decisions of business organizations and the conduct of their personnel. Ethical principles in business are not materially different from ethical principles in general.

2. There are three schools of thought about ethical standards for companies with international operations:

   - According to the *school of ethical universalism,* common understandings across multiple cultures and countries about what constitutes right and wrong behaviors give rise to universal ethical standards that apply to members of all societies, all companies, and all businesspeople.

- According to the *school of ethical relativism,* different societal cultures and customs have divergent values and standards of right and wrong. Thus, what is ethical or unethical must be judged in the light of local customs and social mores and can vary from one culture or nation to another.

- According to the *integrated social contracts theory,* universal ethical principles or norms based on the collective views of multiple cultures and societies combine to form a "social contract" that all individuals in all situations have a duty to observe. Within the boundaries of this social contract, local cultures or groups can specify what additional actions are not ethically permissible. However, when local ethical norms are more permissive than the universal norms, universal norms always take precedence.

3. Confusion over conflicting ethical standards may provide one reason why some company personnel engage in unethical strategic behavior. But three other factors prompt unethical business behavior: (1) faulty oversight that implicitly sanctions the overzealous pursuit of wealth and personal gain, (2) heavy pressures on company managers to meet or beat short-term earnings targets, and (3) a company culture that puts profitability and good business performance ahead of ethical behavior. In contrast, culture can function as a powerful mechanism for promoting ethical business conduct when high ethical principles are deeply ingrained in the corporate culture of a company.

4. Business ethics failures can result in three types of costs: (1) visible costs, such as fines, penalties, and lower stock prices, (2) internal administrative costs, such as legal costs and costs of taking corrective action, and (3) intangible costs, such as customer defections and damage to the company's reputation.

5. The term *corporate social responsibility* concerns a company's *duty* to operate in an honorable manner, provide good working conditions for employees, encourage workforce diversity, be a good steward of the environment, and support philanthropic endeavors in local communities where it operates and in society at large. The particular combination of socially responsible endeavors a company elects to pursue defines its corporate social responsibility (CSR) strategy.

6. The triple bottom line refers to company performance in three realms: economic, social, environmental. Increasingly, companies are reporting their performance with respect to all three performance dimensions.

7. *Sustainability* is a term that is used in various ways, but most often it concerns a firm's relationship to the environment and its use of natural resources. Sustainable business practices are those capable of meeting the needs of the present without compromising the world's ability to meet future needs. A company's environmental sustainability strategy consists of its deliberate actions to protect the environment, provide for the longevity of natural resources, maintain ecological support systems for future generations, and guard against ultimate endangerment of the planet.

8. CSR strategies and environmental sustainability strategies that both provide valuable social benefits *and* fulfill customer needs in a superior fashion can lead to competitive advantage.

9. The moral case for social responsibility boils down to a simple concept: It's the right thing to do. There are also solid reasons why CSR and environmental sustainability strategies may be good business—they can be conducive to greater buyer patronage, reduce the risk of reputation-damaging incidents, provide opportunities for revenue enhancement, and lower costs. Well-crafted CSR and environmental sustainability strategies are in the best long-term interest of shareholders, for the reasons above and because they can avoid or preempt costly legal or regulatory actions.

ASSURANCE OF LEARNING EXERCISES

LO 1, LO 2, LO 3, LO 4

1. Assume that you are the sales manager at a European company that makes sleepwear products for children. Company personnel discover that the chemicals used to flameproof the company's line of children's pajamas might cause cancer if absorbed through the skin. After this discovery, the pajamas are banned from sale in the European Union and the United States, but senior executives of your company learn that the children's pajamas in inventory and the remaining flameproof material can be sold to sleepwear distributors in certain East European countries where there are no restrictions against the material's use. Your superiors instruct you to make the necessary arrangements to sell the inventories of banned pajamas and flameproof materials to East European distributors. How would you handle this situation?

LO 4

2. Review Microsoft's statements about its corporate citizenship programs at www.microsoft.com/about/corporatecitizenship. How does the company's commitment to global citizenship provide positive benefits for its stakeholders? How does Microsoft plan to improve social and economic empowerment in developing countries through its Unlimited Potential program? Why is this important to Microsoft shareholders?

LO4

3. Go to www.nestle.com, and read the company's latest sustainability report. What are Nestlé's key sustainable environmental policies? How is the company addressing social needs? How do these initiatives relate to the company's principles, values, and culture and its approach to competing in the food industry?

EXERCISES FOR SIMULATION PARTICIPANTS

LO 1

1. Is your company's strategy ethical? Why or why not? Is there anything that your company has done or is now doing that could legitimately be considered "shady" by your competitiors?

LO 4

2. In what ways, if any, is your company exercising corporate social responsibility and good corporate citizenship? What are the elements of your company's CSR strategy? Are there any changes to this strategy that you would suggest?

LO 3, LO 4

3. If some shareholders complained that you and your co-managers have been spending too little or too much on corporate social responsibility, what would you tell them?

LO 4

4. Is your company striving to conduct its business in an environmentally sustainable manner? What specific *additional* actions could your company take that would make an even greater contribution to environmental sustainability?

LO4

5. In what ways is your company's environmental sustainability strategy in the best long-term interest of shareholders? Does it contribute to your company's competitive advantage or profitability?

ENDNOTES

[1] James E. Post, Anne T. Lawrence, and James Weber, *Business and Society: Corporate Strategy, Public Policy, Ethics,* 10th ed. (Burr Ridge, IL: McGraw-Hill Irwin, 2002), p. 103.

[2] For research on what are the universal moral values (six are identified—trustworthiness, respect, responsibility, fairness, caring, and citizenship), see Mark S. Schwartz, "Universal Moral Values for Corporate Codes of Ethics," *Journal of Business Ethics* 59, no. 1 (June 2005), pp. 27–44.

[3] See Mark. S. Schwartz, "A Code of Ethics for Corporate Codes of Ethics," *Journal of Business Ethics* 41, nos. 1–2 (November–December 2002), pp. 27–43.

[4] Ibid., pp. 29–30.

[5] T. L. Beauchamp and N. E. Bowie, *Ethical Theory and Business* (Upper Saddle River, NJ: Prentice-Hall, 2001), p. 8.

[6] Based on information in U.S. Department of Labor, "The Department of Labor's 2002 Findings on the Worst Forms of Child Labor," 2003, accessible at www.dol.gov/ILAB/media/reports.

[7] U.S. Department of Labor, "The Department of Labor's 2006 Findings on the Worst Forms of Child Labor," 2006, www.dol.gov/ilab/programs/ocft/PDF/2006OCFTreport.pdf; ibid., p. 17.

[8] W. M. Greenfield, "In the Name of Corporate Social Responsibility," *Business Horizons* 47, no. 1 (January–February 2004), p. 22.

[9] For a study of why such factors as low per-capita income, lower disparities in income

distribution, and various cultural factors are often associated with a higher incidence of bribery, see Rajib Sanyal, "Determinants of Bribery in International Business: The Cultural and Economic Factors," *Journal of Business Ethics* 59, no. 1 (June 2005), pp. 139–45.

[10] For data relating to bribe-paying frequency in 30 countries, see Transparency International, *2007 Global Corruption Report,* p. 332, and *2008 Global Corruption Report,* p. 306, www.globalcorruptionreport.org.

[11] Thomas Donaldson and Thomas W. Dunfee, "When Ethics Travel: The Promise and Peril of Global Business Ethics," *California Management Review* 41, no. 4 (Summer 1999), p. 53.

[12] John Reed and Erik Portanger, "Bribery, Corruption Are Rampant in Eastern Europe, Survey Finds," *Wall Street Journal,* November 9, 1999, p. A21.

[13] For a study of "facilitating" payments to obtain a favor (such as expediting an administrative process, obtaining a permit or license, or avoiding an abuse of authority), which are sometimes condoned as unavoidable or are excused on grounds of low wages and lack of professionalism among public officials, see Antonio Argandoña, "Corruption and Companies: The Use of Facilitating Payments," *Journal of Business Ethics* 60, no. 3 (September 2005), pp. 251–64.

[14] Donaldson and Dundee, "When Ethics Travel," p. 59.

[15] See "OECD Convention on Combating Bribery of Foreign Public Officials in

International Business Transactions," www.oecd.org/document/21/0,3343,en_2649_34859_2017813_1_1_1_1,00.html (accessed May 22, 2009).

[16] Michael Peel, "Landmark Bribery Case Goes to Trial," *Financial Times,* December 2, 2009, p. 4 (retrieved December 27, 2009, from ABI/INFORM Global, document ID:1913325051).

[17] Thomas Donaldson and Thomas W. Dunfee, *Ties That Bind: A Social Contracts Approach to Business Ethics* (Boston: Harvard Business School Press, 1999), pp. 35 and 83.

[18] Based on a report in M. J. Satchell, "Deadly Trade in Toxics," *U.S. News & World Report,* March 7, 1994, p. 64, and cited in Donaldson and Dunfee, "When Ethics Travel," p. 46.

[19] R. Chen and C. Chen, "Chinese Professional Managers and the Issue of Ethical Behavior," *Ivey Business Journal* 69, no. 5 (May/June 2005), pp. 1–5.

[20] Two of the definitive treatments of integrated social contracts theory as applied to ethics are Thomas Donaldson and Thomas W. Dunfee, "Towards a Unified Conception of Business Ethics: Integrative Social Contracts Theory," *Academy of Management Review* 19, no. 2 (April 1994), pp. 252–84, and Donaldson and Dunfee, *Ties That Bind,* especially chaps. 3, 4, and 6. See also Andrew Spicer, Thomas W. Dunfee, and Wendy J. Bailey, "Does National Context Matter in Ethical Decision Making? An Empirical Test of Integrative Social Contracts Theory," *Academy of Management Journal* 47, no. 4 (August 2004), p. 610.

[21] P. M. Nichols, "Outlawing Transnational Bribery through the World Trade Organization," *Law and Policy in International Business* 28, no. 2 (1997), pp. 321–22.

[22] For an overview of widely endorsed guidelines for creating codes of conduct, see Lynn Paine, Rohit Deshpandé, Joshua D. Margolis, and Kim Eric Bettcher, "Up to Code: Does Your Company's Conduct Meet World-Class Standards?" *Harvard Business Review* 83, no. 12 (December 2005), pp. 122–33.

[23] For survey data on what managers say about why they sometimes behave unethically, see John F. Veiga, Timothy D. Golden, and Kathleen Dechant, "Why Managers Bend Company Rules," *Academy of Management Executive* 18, no. 2 (May 2004), pp. 84–89.

[24] For more details, see Ronald R. Sims and Johannes Brinkmann, "Enron Ethics (Or: Culture Matters More than Codes)," *Journal of Business Ethics* 45, no. 3 (July 2003), pp. 244–46.

[25] Veiga, Golden, and Dechant, "Why Managers Bend Company Rules," p. 36.

[26] The following account is based largely on the discussion and analysis in Sims and Brinkmann, "Enron Ethics," pp. 245–52. Perhaps the definitive book-length account of the corrupt Enron culture is Kurt Eichenwald, *Conspiracy of Fools: A True Story* (New York: Broadway Books, 2005).

[27] Chip Cummins and Almar Latour, "How Shell's Move to Revamp Culture Ended in Scandal," *Wall Street Journal,* November 2, 2004, p. A14.

[28] Archie B. Carroll, "The Four Faces of Corporate Citizenship," *Business and Society Review* 100/101 (September 1998), p. 6.

[29] Business Roundtable, "Statement on Corporate Responsibility," October 1981, p. 9.

[30] For an argument that the concept of corporate social responsibility is not viable because of the inherently conflicted nature of a corporation, see Timothy M. Devinney, "Is the Socially Responsible Corporation a Myth? The Good, the Bad, and the Ugly of Corporate Social Responsibility," *Academy of Management Perspectives* 23, no. 2 (May 2009), pp. 44–56.

[31] Sarah Roberts, Justin Keeble, and David Brown, "The Business Case for Corporate Citizenship" (study conducted by Arthur D. Little for the World Economic Forum), p. 3, www.afic.am (accessed June 9, 2009). A revised and more wide-ranging version of this study can be found at www.bitc.org.uk/document.rm?id = 5253.

[32] "General Mills' 2010 Corporate Social Responsibility Report Highlights New and Longstanding Achievements in the Areas of Health, Community, and Environment" (CSR press release), *CSRwire,* April 15, 2010, www.csrwire.com/press_releases/29347-General-Mills-2010- Corporate-Social-Responsibility-report-now-available.html.

[33] Arthur A. Thompson and Amit J. Shah, "Starbucks' Strategy and Internal Initiatives to Return to Profitable Growth," a case study appearing in the Cases section of this text.

[34] Adrian Henriques, "ISO 26000: A New Standard for Human Rights?" Institute for Human Rights and Business, March 23, 2010, www.institutehrb.org/blogs/guest/iso_26000_a_new_standard_for_human_rights.html?gclid = CJih7NjN2aICFVs65Qo-drVOdyQ (accessed July 7, 2010).

[35] Gerald I. J. M. Zetsloot and Marcel N. A. van Marrewijk, "From Quality to Sustainability," *Journal of Business Ethics* 55 (2004), pp. 79–82.

[36] Tilde Herrera, "PG&E Claims Industry First with Supply Chain Footprint Project," *GreenBiz.com,* June 30, 2010, www.greenbiz.com/news/2010/06/30/pge-claims-industry-first-supply-chain-carbon-footprint-project.

[37] This definition is based on the Brundtland Commission's report, which described sustainable development in a like manner: United Nations General Assembly, "Report of the World Commission on Environment and Development: Our Common Future," 1987, www.un-documents.net/wced-ocf.htm, transmitted to the General Assembly as an annex to document A/42/427—"Development and International Co-operation: Environment" (retrieved February 15, 2009).

[38] See, for example, Robert Goodland, "The Concept of Environmental Sustainability," *Annual Review of Ecology and Systematics* 26 (1995), pp. 1–25; J. G. Speth, *The Bridge at the End of the World: Capitalism, the Environment, and Crossing from Crisis to Sustainability* (New Haven, CT: Yale University Press, 2008).

[39] For an excellent discussion of crafting corporate social responsibility strategies capable of contributing to a company's competitive advantage, see Michael E. Porter and Mark R. Kramer, "Strategy & Society: The Link between Competitive Advantage and Corporate Social Responsibility," *Harvard Business Review* 84, no. 12 (December 2006), pp. 78–92.

[40] World Business Council for Sustainable Development, "Corporate Social Responsibility: Making Good Business Sense," January 2000, p. 7, www.wbscd.ch (accessed October 10, 2003). For a discussion of how companies are connecting social initiatives to their core values, see David Hess, Nikolai Rogovsky, and Thomas W. Dunfee, "The Next Wave of Corporate Community Involvement: Corporate Social Initiatives," *California Management Review* 44, no. 2 (Winter 2002), pp. 110–25. See also Susan Ariel Aaronson, "Corporate Responsibility in the Global Village: The British Role Model and the American Laggard," *Business and Society Review* 108, no. 3 (September 2003), p. 323.

[41] www.chick-fil-a.com (accessed June 1, 2009).

[42] N. Craig Smith, "Corporate Responsibility: Whether and How," *California Management Review* 45, no. 4 (Summer 2003), p. 63.

[43] For an excellent discussion of the social responsibilities that corporations have in emerging countries where many people live in poverty, see Jeb Brugmann and C. K. Pralahad, "Cocreating Business's New Social Compact," *Harvard Business Review* 85, no. 2 (February 2007), pp. 80–90.

[44] Wallace N. Davidson, Abuzar El-Jelly, and Dan L. Worrell, "Influencing Managers to Change Unpopular Corporate Behavior through Boycotts and Divestitures: A Stock Market Test," *Business and Society* 34, no. 2 (1995), pp. 171–96.

[45] Ibid., p. 3.

[46] Tom McCawley, "Racing to Improve Its Reputation: Nike Has Fought to Shed Its Image as an Exploiter of Third-World Labor Yet It Is Still a Target of Activists," *Financial Times,* December 2000, p. 14; Smith, "Corporate Responsibility," p. 61.

[47] Smith, "Corporate Responsibility," p. 63; see also World Economic Forum, "Findings of a Survey on Global Corporate Leadership," www.weforum.org/corporatecitizenship (accessed October 11, 2003).

[48] Roberts, Keeble, and Brown, "The Business Case for Corporate Citizenship," p. 6.

[49] Joshua D. Margolis and Hillary A. Elfenbein, "Doing Well by Doing Good: Don't Count on It," *Harvard Business Review* 86, no. 1 (January 2008), pp. 19–20. Of some 80 studies that examined whether a company's social performance is a good predictor of its financial performance, 42 concluded yes, 4 concluded no, and the remainder reported mixed or inconclusive findings. See Smith, "Corporate Responsibility," p. 65; Lee E. Preston and Douglas P. O'Bannon, "The Corporate Social-Financial Performance Relationship," *Business and Society* 36, no. 4 (December 1997), pp. 419–29; Ronald M. Roman, Sefa Hayibor, and Bradley R. Agle, "The Relationship between Social and Financial Performance: Repainting a Portrait," *Business and Society* 38, no. 1 (March 1999), pp. 109–25; Joshua D. Margolis and James P. Walsh, *People and Profits* (Mahwah, NJ: Lawrence Erlbaum, 2001).

[50] "Performance and Socially Responsible Investments," *The Social Investment Forum,* 2009, www.socialinvest.org/resources/performance.cfm (accessed November 15, 2009).

[51] Glenn Cheney, "Sustainability Looms as a Bigger Issue," *Accounting Today,* May 18, 2009, www.accessmylibrary.com/article-1G1-199972817/sustainability-looms-bigger-issue.html (accessed November 15, 2009).

CHAPTER 10

BUILDING AN ORGANIZATION CAPABLE OF GOOD STRATEGY EXECUTION

People, Capabilities, and Structure

> Strategies most often fail because they aren't executed well.
>
> **—Larry Bossidy and Ram Charan**
> *CEO Honeywell International, author and consultant*

> People are not your most important asset. The right people are.
>
> **—Jim Collins**
> *Professor and author*

> Of all the things I've done, the most vital is coordinating the talents of those who work for us and pointing them toward a certain goal.
>
> **—Walt Disney**
> *Founder of the Disney Company*

LEARNING OBJECTIVES

LO 1. Gain an understanding of what managers must do to execute strategy successfully.

LO 2. Learn why hiring, training, and retaining the right people constitute a key component of the strategy execution process.

LO 3. Understand that good strategy execution requires continuously building and upgrading the organization's resources and capabilities.

LO 4. Gain command of what issues to consider in establishing a strategy-supportive organizational structure and organizing the work effort.

LO 5. Become aware of the pros and cons of centralized and decentralized decision making in implementing the chosen strategy.

Once managers have decided on a strategy, the emphasis turns to converting it into actions and good results. Putting the strategy into place and getting the organization to execute it well call for different sets of managerial skills. Whereas crafting strategy is largely a market-driven and resource-driven activity, executing strategy is an operations-driven activity revolving around the management of people and business processes. Whereas successful strategy making depends on strategic vision, solid industry and competitive analysis, and shrewd market positioning, successful strategy execution depends on doing a good job of working with and through others; allocating resources; building and strengthening competitive capabilities; creating an appropriate organizational structure; instituting strategy-supportive policies, processes, and systems; motivating and rewarding people; and instilling a discipline of getting things done. Executing strategy is an action-oriented, make-things-happen task that tests a manager's ability to direct organizational change, achieve continuous improvement in operations and business processes, create and nurture a strategy-supportive culture, and consistently meet or beat performance targets.

Experienced managers are emphatic in declaring that it is a whole lot easier to develop a sound strategic plan than it is to execute the plan and achieve the desired outcomes. According to one executive, "It's been rather easy for us to decide where we wanted to go. The hard part is to get the organization to act on the new priorities."[1] In a recent study of 1,000 companies, government agencies, and not-for-profit organizations in over 50 countries, 60 percent of employees rated their organizations poor in terms of strategy implementation.[2] *Just because senior managers announce a new strategy doesn't mean that organization members will embrace it and move forward enthusiastically to implement it.* Senior executives cannot simply direct immediate subordinates to abandon old ways and take up new ways, and they certainly cannot expect the needed actions and changes to occur in rapid-fire fashion and still lead to the desired outcomes. Some managers and employees may be skeptical about the merits of the strategy, seeing it as contrary to the organization's best interests, unlikely to succeed, or threatening to their departments or careers. Moreover, employees may have misconceptions about the new strategy or have different ideas about what internal changes are needed to execute it. Long-standing attitudes, vested interests, inertia, and ingrained organizational practices don't melt away when managers decide on a new strategy and begin efforts to implement it—especially if only a few people have been involved in crafting the strategy or if the rationale for strategic change requires quite a bit of salesmanship. It takes adept managerial leadership to convincingly communicate a new strategy and the reasons for it, overcome pockets of doubt and disagreement, secure the commitment and enthusiasm of key personnel, gain agreement on how to implement the strategy, and move forward to get all the pieces into place. Company personnel must understand—in their heads and hearts—why a new strategic direction is necessary and where the new strategy is taking them.[3] Instituting change is, of course, easier when the problems with the old strategy have become obvious and/or the company has spiraled into a financial crisis.

But the challenge of successfully implementing new strategic initiatives goes well beyond managerial adeptness in overcoming resistance to change. What really makes executing strategy a tougher, more time-consuming management challenge than crafting strategy are the wide array of managerial activities that must be attended to and the number of bedeviling issues that must be worked out. It takes first-rate "managerial smarts" to zero in on what exactly needs to be done to put new strategic initiatives in place and, further, how best to get these things done in a timely manner that yields good results. Demanding people-management skills and perseverance are required to get a variety of initiatives launched and moving and to integrate the efforts of many different work groups into a smoothly functioning whole. Depending on how much consensus building and organizational change is involved, the process of implementing strategy changes can take several months to several years. To achieve *real proficiency* in executing the strategy can take even longer.

Like crafting strategy, *executing strategy is a job for a company's whole management team, not just a few senior managers.* While the chief executive officer and the heads of major units (business divisions, functional departments, and key operating units) are ultimately responsible for seeing that strategy is executed successfully, the process typically affects every part of the firm—all value chain activities and all work groups. Top-level managers must rely on the active support and cooperation of middle and lower managers to institute whatever new operating practices are needed in the various functional areas and operating units to achieve proficient strategy execution. It is middle and lower-level managers who ultimately must ensure that work groups and frontline employees do a good job of performing strategy-critical value chain activities and produce operating results that allow companywide performance targets to be met. In consequence, strategy execution requires every manager to think through the answer to the question: *"What does my area have to do to implement its part of the strategic plan, and what should I do to get these things accomplished efficiently and effectively?"*

A FRAMEWORK FOR EXECUTING STRATEGY

Executing strategy entails figuring out the specific techniques, actions, and behaviors that are needed for a smooth strategy-supportive operation—and then following through to get things done and deliver results. The idea is to make things happen and make them happen right. The first step in implementing strategic change is for management to communicate the case for organizational change so clearly and persuasively to organization members that a determined commitment takes hold throughout the ranks to find ways to put the strategy into place, make it work, and meet performance targets. The ideal condition is for managers to arouse enough enthusiasm for the strategy to turn the implementation process into a companywide crusade. Management's handling of the strategy implementation process can be considered successful if and when the company achieves the targeted strategic and financial performance and shows good progress in making its strategic vision a reality.

The specifics of how to execute a strategy—the exact items that need to be placed on management's action agenda—always need to be customized to fit the particulars of a company's situation. The hot buttons for successfully executing a low-cost provider strategy are different from those for executing a high-end differentiation strategy. Implementing a new strategy for a struggling company in the midst of a financial crisis is a different job from that of making minor improvements to strategy execution in a company that is doing relatively well. Moreover, some managers are more adept than others at using particular approaches to achieving the desired kinds of organizational changes. Hence, there's no definitive managerial recipe for successful strategy execution that cuts across all company situations and all types of strategies or that works for all types of managers. Rather, the specific actions required to implement a strategy—the "to-do list" that constitutes management's action agenda—always represent management's judgment about how best to proceed in light of prevailing circumstances.

The Principal Components of the Strategy Execution Process

Despite the need to tailor a company's strategy-executing approaches to the particulars of its situation, certain managerial bases must be covered no matter what the circumstances. Ten basic managerial tasks crop up repeatedly in company efforts to execute strategy (see Figure 10.1):

1. Staff the organization with managers and employees capable of executing the strategy well.
2. Build the organizational capabilities required for successful strategy execution.
3. Create a strategy-supportive organizational structure.
4. Allocate sufficient budgetary (and other) resources to the strategy execution effort.
5. Institute policies and procedures that facilitate strategy execution.
6. Adopt best practices and business processes that drive continuous improvement in strategy execution activities.
7. Install information and operating systems that enable company personnel to carry out their strategic roles proficiently.
8. Tie rewards and incentives directly to the achievement of strategic and financial targets.
9. Instill a corporate culture that promotes good strategy execution.
10. Exercise the internal leadership needed to propel strategy implementation forward.

How well managers perform these 10 tasks has a decisive impact on whether the outcome of the strategy execution effort is a spectacular success, a colossal failure, or something in between.

Figure 10.1   **The 10 Basic Tasks of the Strategy Execution Process**

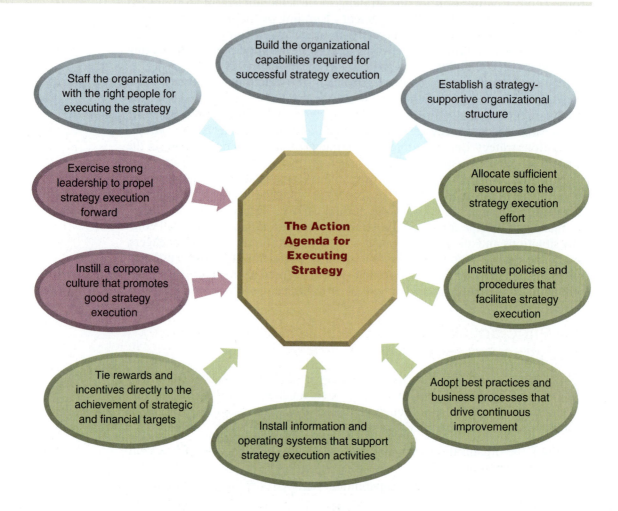

When strategies fail, it is often because of poor execution. Strategy execution is therefore a critical managerial endeavor.

In devising an action agenda for executing strategy, the way for managers to start is with *a probing assessment of what the organization must do differently to carry out the strategy successfully.* They should then consider *precisely how to make the necessary internal changes* as rapidly as possible. Successful strategy implementers have a knack for diagnosing what their organizations need to do to execute the chosen strategy well and figuring out how to get things done cost-efficiently and with all deliberate speed. They are masters in promoting results-oriented behaviors on the part of company personnel and following through on making the right things happen in a timely fashion.[4]

In big organizations with geographically scattered operating units, the action agenda of senior executives mostly involves communicating the case for change, building consensus for how to proceed, installing strong managers to move the process forward in key organizational units, directing resources to the right places, establishing deadlines and measures of progress, rewarding those who achieve implementation milestones, and personally leading the strategic change process. Thus, the bigger the organization, the more that successful strategy execution depends on the cooperation and implementing skills of operating managers who can promote needed changes at the lowest organizational levels and deliver results. In small organizations, top managers can deal directly with frontline managers and employees, personally orchestrating the action steps and implementation sequence, observing firsthand how implementation is progressing, and deciding how hard and how fast to push the process along. Regardless of the organization's size and whether implementation involves sweeping or minor changes, the most important leadership trait is a strong, confident sense of what to do and how to do it. Having a strong grip on these two things comes from understanding the circumstances of the organization and the requirements for effective strategy execution. Then it remains for company personnel in strategy-critical areas to step up to the plate and produce the desired results.

> The two best signs of good strategy execution are whether a company is meeting or beating its performance targets and performing value chain activities in a manner that is conducive to company-wide operating excellence.

What's Covered in Chapters 10, 11, and 12   In the remainder of this chapter and the next two chapters, we will discuss what is involved in performing the 10 key managerial tasks that shape the process of executing strategy. This chapter explores the first three of these tasks (highlighted in blue in Figure 10.1): (1) staffing the organization with people capable of executing the strategy well, (2) building the organizational capabilities needed for successful strategy execution, and (3) creating an organizational structure supportive of the strategy execution process. Chapter 11 concerns the tasks of allocating resources, instituting strategy-facilitating policies and procedures, employing business process management tools and best practices, installing operating and information systems, and tying rewards to the achievement of good results (highlighted in green in Figure 10.1). Chapter 12 deals with the two remaining tasks: creating a strategy-supportive corporate culture and exercising the leadership needed to drive the execution process forward (highlighted in purple in Figure 10.1).

BUILDING AN ORGANIZATION CAPABLE OF GOOD STRATEGY EXECUTION: WHERE TO BEGIN

Building an organization capable of good strategy execution depends foremost on ensuring that the resources and capabilities that are the basis for the strategy are in place, ready to be deployed. Recall from Chapter 4 that these include the skills, talents, experience, and knowledge of the company's human resources (managerial and otherwise). Proficient strategy execution depends heavily on competent personnel of all types, but because of the many managerial tasks involved and the role of leadership in strategy execution, assembling a strong management team is especially important.

If the strategy being implemented is a new strategy, the company may need to add to its resource and capability mix in other respects as well. But renewing, upgrading, and revising the organization's resources and capabilities is a part of the strategy execution process even if the strategy is fundamentally the same, since resources depreciate and conditions are always changing. Thus, augmenting and strengthening the firm's core competencies and seeing that they are suited to the current strategy are also top priorities.

Figure 10.2   **Building an Organization Capable of Proficient Strategy Execution: Three Types of Paramount Actions**

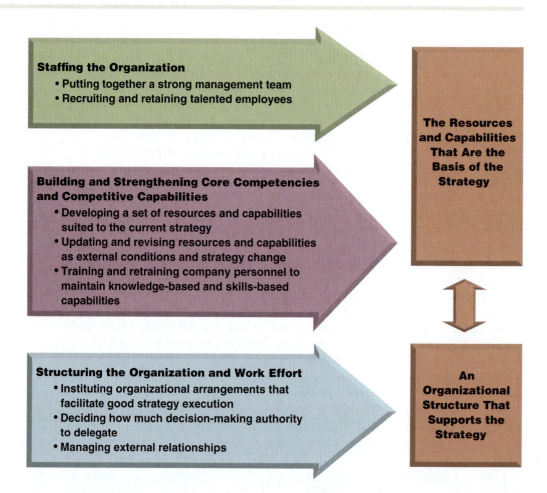

Staffing the Organization
- Putting together a strong management team
- Recruiting and retaining talented employees

Building and Strengthening Core Competencies and Competitive Capabilities
- Developing a set of resources and capabilities suited to the current strategy
- Updating and revising resources and capabilities as external conditions and strategy change
- Training and retraining company personnel to maintain knowledge-based and skills-based capabilities

Structuring the Organization and Work Effort
- Instituting organizational arrangements that facilitate good strategy execution
- Deciding how much decision-making authority to delegate
- Managing external relationships

The Resources and Capabilities That Are the Basis of the Strategy

An Organizational Structure That Supports the Strategy

Structuring the organization and work effort is another critical aspect of building an organization capable of good strategy execution. An organization structure that is well matched to the strategy can help facilitate its implementation; one that is not well suited can lead to higher bureaucratic costs and communication or coordination breakdowns. As shown in Figure 10.2, three types of organization-building actions are paramount:

- *Staffing the organization:* putting together a strong management team, and recruiting and retaining employees with the needed experience, technical skills, and intellectual capital.

- *Building and strengthening core competencies and competitive capabilities:* developing proficiencies in performing strategy-critical value chain activities and updating them to match changing market conditions and customer expectations.

- *Structuring the organization and work effort:* organizing value chain activities and business processes, establishing lines of authority and reporting relationships, deciding how much decision-making authority to delegate to lower-level managers and frontline employees, and managing external relationships.

STAFFING THE ORGANIZATION

No company can hope to perform the activities required for successful strategy execution without attracting and retaining talented managers and employees with suitable skills and intellectual capital.

LO 2

Learn why hiring, training, and retaining the right people constitute a key component of the strategy execution process.

Putting Together a Strong Management Team

Assembling a capable management team is a cornerstone of the organization-building task.[5] While different strategies and company circumstances sometimes call for different mixes of backgrounds, experiences, management styles, and know-how, *the most important consideration is to fill key managerial slots with smart people who are clear thinkers, capable of figuring out what needs to be done, good at managing people, and skilled in delivering good results.*[6] The task of implementing challenging strategic initiatives must be assigned to executives who have the skills and talents to turn their decisions into results that meet or beat the established performance targets. Without a smart, capable, results-oriented management team, the implementation process is likely to be hampered by missed deadlines, misdirected or wasteful efforts, and managerial ineptness.[7] Weak executives are serious impediments to getting optimal results because they are unable to differentiate between ideas that have merit and those that are misguided—the caliber of work done under their supervision usually suffers accordingly.[8] In contrast, managers with strong strategy-implementing capabilities have a talent for asking tough, incisive questions; they know enough about the details of the business to be able to ensure the soundness of the decisions of the people around them, and they can discern whether the resources people are asking for to put the strategy in place make sense. They are good at getting things done through others, partly by making sure they have the right people under them and that these people are put in the right jobs.[9] They consistently follow through on issues, monitor progress carefully, make adjustments when needed, and keep important details from slipping through the cracks. In short, they understand how to drive organizational change, and they have the managerial skills and discipline requisite for first-rate strategy execution.

> Putting together a talented management team with the right mix of experiences, skills, and abilities to get things done is one of the first strategy-implementing steps.

Sometimes a company's existing management team is up to the task; at other times it may need to be strengthened or expanded by promoting qualified people from within or by bringing in outsiders whose experiences, talents, and leadership styles better suit the situation. In turnaround and rapid-growth situations, and in instances when a company doesn't have insiders with the requisite know-how, filling key management slots from the outside is a fairly standard organization-building approach. In addition, it is important to ferret out and replace managers who, for whatever reasons, either do not buy into the case for making organizational changes or do not see ways to make things better.[10] For a management team to be truly effective at strategy execution, it must be composed of managers who recognize that organizational changes are needed and who are ready to get on with the process. Weak executives and die-hard resisters have to be replaced or sidelined, perhaps by shifting them to areas where they cannot hamper new strategy execution initiatives.

The overriding aim in building a management team should be to assemble a *critical mass* of talented managers who can function as agents of change and further the cause of first-rate strategy execution. Every manager's success is enhanced (or limited) by the quality of his or her managerial colleagues and the degree to which they freely exchange ideas, debate ways to make operating improvements, and join forces to tackle issues and solve problems.[11] When a first-rate manager enjoys the help and support of other first-rate managers, it's possible to create a managerial whole that is greater than the sum of individual efforts—talented managers who work well together as a team can produce organizational results that are dramatically better than what one or two star managers acting individually can achieve.[12]

Illustration Capsule 10.1 describes General Electric's widely acclaimed approach to developing a top-caliber management team.

Recruiting, Training, and Retaining Capable Employees

Assembling a capable management team is not enough. Staffing the organization with the right kinds of people must go much deeper than managerial jobs in

> In many industries, adding to a company's talent base and building intellectual capital are more important to good strategy execution than additional investments in capital projects.

order for strategy-critical value chain activities to be performed competently. *The quality of an organization's people is always an essential ingredient of successful strategy execution—knowledgeable, engaged employees are a company's best source of creative ideas for the nuts-and-bolts operating improvements that lead to operating excellence.* Companies like Google, Microsoft, McKinsey & Company, Southwest Airlines, Cisco Systems, Amazon.com, Procter & Gamble, PepsiCo, Nike, Electronic Data Systems (EDS), Goldman Sachs, and Intel make a concerted effort to recruit the best and brightest people they can find and then retain them with excellent compensation packages, opportunities for rapid advancement and professional growth, and interesting assignments. Having a pool of "A players" with strong skill sets and lots of brainpower is essential to their business.

Microsoft makes a point of hiring the very brightest and most talented programmers it can find and motivating them with both good monetary incentives and the challenge of working on cutting-edge software design projects. McKinsey & Company, one of the world's premier management consulting firms, recruits only cream-of-the-crop MBAs at the nation's top-10 business schools; such talent is essential to McKinsey's strategy of performing high-level consulting for the world's top corporations. The leading global accounting firms screen candidates not only on the basis of their accounting expertise but also on whether they possess the people skills needed to relate well with clients and colleagues. Southwest Airlines goes to considerable lengths to hire people who can have fun and be fun on the job; it uses special interviewing and screening methods to gauge whether applicants for customer-contact jobs have outgoing personality traits that match its strategy of creating a high-spirited, fun-loving, in-flight atmosphere for passengers. Southwest Airlines is so selective that only about 3 percent of the people who apply are offered jobs.

In high-tech companies, the challenge is to staff work groups with gifted, imaginative, and energetic people who can bring life to new ideas quickly and inject into the organization what one Dell executive calls "hum."[13] The saying "People are our most important asset" may seem trite, but it fits high-technology companies precisely. Besides checking closely for functional and technical skills, Dell tests

How General Electric Develops a Talented and Deep Management Team

General Electric (GE) is widely considered to be one of the best-managed companies in the world, partly because of its concerted effort to develop outstanding managers. It ranked number one among the best companies for leadership in the most recent global survey conducted by the Hay Group. For starters, GE strives to hire talented people with high potential for executive leadership; it then goes to great lengths to expand the leadership, business, and decision-making capabilities of all its managers. The company spends about $1 billion annually on training and education programs. In 2009, all of its 191 most-senior executives had spent at least 12 months in training and professional development during their first 15 years at GE.

Four key elements undergird GE's efforts to build a talent-rich stable of managers:

1. GE makes a practice of transferring managers across divisional, business, or functional lines for sustained periods of time. Such transfers allow managers to develop relationships with colleagues in other parts of the company, help break down insular thinking in business "silos," promote the sharing of cross-business ideas and best practices, and build a mindset open and adaptive to international markets. There is an enormous emphasis at GE on transferring ideas and best practices from business to business and making GE a "boundaryless" company.

2. In selecting executives for key positions, GE is strongly disposed to candidates who exhibit what are called the four E's—enormous personal *energy,* the ability to *energize* others, *edge* (a GE code word for instinctive competitiveness and the ability to make tough decisions in a timely fashion—saying yes or no, and not maybe), and *execution* (the ability to carry things through to fruition). Considerable attention is also paid to problem-solving ability, experience in multiple functions or businesses, and experience in driving business growth (as indicated by good market instincts, in-depth knowledge of particular markets, customer touch, and technical understanding).

3. All managers are expected to be proficient at what GE calls *workout*—a process in which managers and employees come together to confront issues as soon as they come up, pinpoint the root cause of the issues, and bring about quick resolutions so that the business can move forward. Workout is GE's way of training its managers to diagnose what to do and how to do it.

4. Each year GE sends about 10,000 newly hired and longtime managers to its John F. Welch Leadership Development Center (generally regarded as one of the best corporate training centers in the world) for a three-week course on the company's Six Sigma quality initiative. GE's Leadership Development Center also offers advanced courses for senior managers that may focus on a single management topic for a month. All classes involve managers from different GE businesses and different parts of the world. Some of the most valuable learning comes between formal class sessions when GE managers from different businesses trade ideas about how to improve processes and better serve the customer. This knowledge sharing not only spreads best practices throughout the organization but also improves each GE manager's knowledge.

One of the keys to the success of the management development process at GE is its ability to be adapted to a changing environment: "It's a constant evolution," according to Chief Learning Officer Susan Peters.* Under the leadership of Jack Welch, GE's CEO from 1980 to 2001, training activities were

(Continued)

focused around cost cutting, efficiency, and deal making. His successor, Jeffrey Immelt, adapted the focus of development programs to drive toward new goals of risk taking, innovation, and customer focus. Recently, GE has tackled the ascendancy of emerging markets by increased focus on global capability development, including the development of the China Learning Center in Shanghai. This has had a visible impact on the organization: In the last seven years the proportion of non-U.S. executives has doubled, from 15 percent to more than 30.

As a key part of talent development, talent assessment and feedback are approached with characteristic GE energy. Each of GE's 85,000 managers and professionals is graded in an annual process that divides them into five tiers: the top 10 percent, the next 15 percent, the middle 50 percent, the next 15 percent, and the bottom 10 percent. Everyone in the top tier gets stock awards, nobody in the fourth tier gets shares of stock, and most of those in the fifth tier become candidates for being weeded out. Business heads are pressured to wean out "C" players. CEO Jeffrey Immelt personally reviews the performance reviews of the top-600 employees each year, as part of GE's intensive, months-long performance review process.

* D. Brady, "Can GE Still Manage?" *Bloomberg BusinessWeek*, April 25, 2010, pp. 26–32.

Developed with Jeffrey L. Boyink.

Sources: GE Web site (accessed June 2010); Hewitt Associates, "Managing Leadership in Turbulent Times—Why and How the Global Top Companies for Leaders Optimize Leadership Talent in Emerging Markets" (White Paper), www.hewittassociates.com/_MetaBasicCMAssetCache_/Assets/Articles/2009/Managing_Leadership_Turbulent_Times_033009.pdf; D. Brady, "Can GE Still Manage?" *Bloomberg BusinessWeek*, April 25, 2010, pp. 26–32; "Hay Group Study Identifies Best Companies for Leadership," *Bloomberg BusinessWeek.com,* February 18, 2010, www.greatleadershipbydan.com/2010/02/bloomberg-businessweekcomhay-group.html.

> The best companies make a point of recruiting and retaining talented employees—the objective is to make the company's entire workforce (managers and rank-and-file employees) a genuine competitive asset.

applicants for their tolerance of ambiguity and change, their capacity to work in teams, and their ability to learn on the fly. Companies like Amazon.com, Google, and Cisco Systems have broken new ground in recruiting, hiring, cultivating, developing, and retaining talented employees—almost all of whom are in their 20s and 30s. Cisco goes after the top 10 percent, raiding other companies and endeavoring to retain key people at the companies it acquires. Cisco executives believe that a cadre of star engineers, programmers, managers, salespeople, and support personnel is the backbone of the company's efforts to execute its strategy and remain the world's leading provider of Internet infrastructure products and technology.

The practices listed below are common among companies dedicated to recruiting, training, and retaining the most capable people they can find:

1. Spending considerable effort on screening and evaluating job applicants—selecting only those with suitable skill sets, energy, initiative, judgment, aptitude for learning, and personality traits that mesh well with the company's work environment and culture.

2. Putting employees through training programs that continue throughout their careers.

3. Providing promising employees with challenging, interesting, and skill-stretching assignments.

4. Rotating people through jobs that span functional and geographic boundaries. Providing people with opportunities to gain experience in a variety of international settings is increasingly considered an essential part of career development in multinational or global companies.

5. Making the work environment stimulating and engaging so that employees will consider the company a great place to work. Progressive companies work hard at creating an environment in which employees are made to feel that their views and suggestions count.

6. Striving to retain talented, high-performing employees via promotions, salary increases, performance bonuses, stock options and equity ownership, fringe-benefit packages, and other perks.

7. Coaching average performers to improve their skills and capabilities, while weeding out underperformers and benchwarmers.

BUILDING AND STRENGTHENING CORE COMPETENCIES AND COMPETITIVE CAPABILITIES

High among the organization-building priorities in the strategy execution process is the need to build and strengthen competitively valuable core competences and capabilities. As explained in Chapter 4, a company's ability to perform the value-creating activities that express its strategy derives from its resources and capabilities. In the course of crafting strategy, managers identify the resources and capabilities that will enable the firm's strategy. In executing the strategy, managers deploy those resources and capabilities in the form of value-creating activities. But the first step is to ensure that the necessary resources and capabilities are in place and that they are renewed, upgraded, or augmented, as needed.

> **LO 3**
>
> Understand that good strategy execution requires continuously building and upgrading the organization's resources and capabilities.

If the strategy being implemented is new, company managers may have to acquire new resources, significantly broaden or deepen certain capabilities, or even add entirely new competencies in order to put the strategic initiatives in place and execute them proficiently. But even if the strategy has not changed materially, good strategy execution involves refreshing and strengthening the firm's resources and capabilities to keep them in top form. Moreover, it involves augmenting and modifying them to keep pace with evolving market needs and competitive conditions.

Three Approaches to Building and Strengthening Capabilities

Building core competencies and competitive capabilities is a time-consuming, managerially challenging exercise. While some assistance can be gotten from discovering how best-in-industry or best-in-world companies perform a particular activity, trying to replicate and then improve on the competencies and capabilities of others is, however, much easier said than done—for the same reasons that one is unlikely to ever become a good golfer just by studying what Tiger Woods does.

> Building new competencies and capabilities is a multistage process that occurs over a period of months and years. It is not something that is accomplished overnight.

With deliberate effort, well-orchestrated organizational actions, and continued practice, however, it is possible for a firm to become proficient at capability building despite the difficulty. Indeed, by making capability-building activities a routine part of their strategy execution endeavors, some firms are able to develop *dynamic capabilities* that assist them in managing resource and capability change, as discussed in Chapter 4. The most common approaches to capability building include (1) internal development, (2) acquiring capabilities through mergers and acquisitions, and (3) accessing capabilities via collaborative partnerships.[14]

Developing Capabilities Internally   Capabilities develop incrementally along an evolutionary development path as organizations search for solutions to their problems. The process is a complex one, since capabilities are the product of bundles of skills and know-how that are integrated into organizational routines and deployed within activity systems through the combined efforts of teams and work groups that are often cross-functional in nature, spanning a variety of departments and locations. For instance, the capability of speeding new products to market involves the collaborative efforts of personnel in R&D, engineering and design, purchasing, production, marketing, and distribution. Similarly, the capability to provide superior customer service is a team effort among people in customer call centers (where orders are taken and inquiries are answered), shipping and delivery, billing and accounts receivable, and after-sale support. The process of building a capability begins when managers set an objective of developing a particular capability and organize activity around that objective.[15] Managers can ignite the process by having high aspirations and setting "stretch goals" for the organization.[16]

Because the process is incremental, the first step is to develop the *ability* to do something, however imperfectly or inefficiently. This entails selecting people with the requisite skills and experience, upgrading or expanding individual abilities as needed, and then molding the efforts of individuals into a collaborative effort to create an organizational ability. At this stage, progress can be fitful since it depends on experimentation, active search for alternative solutions, and learning through trial and error.[17]

As experience grows and company personnel learn how to perform the activities consistently well and at an acceptable cost, the ability evolves into a tried-and-true competence or capability. Getting to this point requires a continual investment of resources and systematic efforts to improve processes and solve problems creatively as they arise. Improvements in the functioning of a capability come from task repetition and the resulting learning by doing of individuals and teams.[18] But the process can be accelerated by making learning a more deliberate endeavor and providing the incentives that will motivate company personnel to achieve the desired ends.[19] This can be critical to successful strategy execution when market conditions are changing rapidly.

> A company's capabilities must be continually refreshed and renewed to remain aligned with changing customer expectations, altered competitive conditions, and new strategic initiatives.

It is generally much easier and less time-consuming to update and remodel a company's existing capabilities as external conditions and company strategy change than it is to create them from scratch. Maintaining capabilities in top form may simply require exercising them continually and fine-tuning them as necessary. Refreshing and updating capabilities require only a limited set of modifications to a set of routines that is otherwise in place. Phasing out an existing capability takes significantly less effort than adding a brand-new one. Replicating a company capability, while not an easy process, still begins with an established template.[20] Even the process of augmenting a capability may require less effort if it involves the recombination of well-established company capabilities and draws on existing company resources.[21] Companies like Cray in large computers and Honda in gasoline engines, for example, have leveraged the expertise of their talent pool by frequently re-forming high-intensity teams and reusing key people on special projects designed to augment their capabilities. Canon combined miniaturization capabilities that it developed in producing calculators with its existing capabilities in precision optics to revolutionize the 35-mm camera market.[22] Toyota, en route to overtaking General Motors as the global leader in motor vehicles, has aggressively upgraded its capabilities in fuel-efficient hybrid engine technology and constantly fine-tuned its famed Toyota Production System to enhance its already proficient capabilities in manufacturing top-quality vehicles at relatively low costs—see Illustration Capsule 10.2.

Toyota's Legendary Production System: A Capability That Translates into Competitive Advantage

The heart of Toyota's strategy in motor vehicles is to outcompete rivals by manufacturing world-class, quality vehicles at lower costs and selling them at competitive price levels. Executing this strategy requires top-notch manufacturing capability and super-efficient management of people, equipment, and materials. Toyota began conscious efforts to improve its manufacturing competence over 50 years ago. Through tireless trial and error, the company gradually took what started as a loose collection of techniques and practices and integrated them into a full-fledged process that has come to be known as the Toyota Production System (TPS). The TPS drives all plant operations and the company's supply chain management practices. TPS is grounded in the following principles, practices, and techniques:

- *Use just-in-time delivery of parts and components to the point of vehicle assembly.* The idea here is to cut out all the bits and pieces of transferring materials from place to place and to discontinue all activities on the part of workers that don't add value (particularly activities where nothing ends up being made or assembled).

- *Develop people who can come up with unique ideas for production improvements.* Toyota encourages employees at all levels to question existing ways of doing things—even if this means challenging a boss on the soundness of a directive. Former Toyota president Katsuaki Watanabe encouraged the company's employees to "pick a friendly fight." Also, Toyota doesn't fire its employees who, at first, have little judgment for improving work flows; instead, the company gives them extensive training to become better problem solvers.

- *Emphasize continuous improvement.* Workers are expected to use their heads and develop better ways of doing things, rather than mechanically follow instructions. Toyota managers tout messages such as "Never be satisfied" and "There's got to be a better way." Another mantra at Toyota is that the *T* in TPS also stands for "Thinking." The thesis is that a work environment where people have to think generates the wisdom to spot opportunities for making tasks simpler and easier to perform, increasing the speed and efficiency with which activities are performed, and constantly improving product quality.

- *Empower workers to stop the assembly line when there's a problem or a defect is spotted.* Toyota views worker efforts to purge defects and sort out the problem immediately as critical to the whole concept of building quality into the production process. According to TPS, "If the line doesn't stop, useless defective items will move on to the next stage. If you don't know where the problem occurred, you can't do anything to fix it."

- *Deal with defects only when they occur.* TPS philosophy holds that when things are running smoothly, they should not be subject to control; if attention is directed to fixing problems that are found, quality control along the assembly line can be handled with fewer personnel.

- *Ask yourself "Why?" five times.* While errors need to be fixed whenever they occur, the value of asking "Why?" five times enables identifying the root cause of the error and correcting it so that the error won't recur.

- *Organize all jobs around human motion to create a production/assembly system with no wasted effort.* Work organized in this fashion is called "standardized work" and people are trained to observe standardized work procedures (which include supplying parts to each process on the

(Continued)

assembly line at the proper time, sequencing the work in an optimal manner, and allowing workers to do their jobs continuously in a set sequence of subprocesses).

- *Find where a part is made cheaply, and use that price as a benchmark.*

The TPS utilizes a unique vocabulary of terms (such as *kanban, takt-time, jikoda, kaizen, heijunka, mono-zukuri, poka yoke,* and *muda*) that facilitates precise discussion of specific TPS elements. In 2003, Toyota established its Global Production Center to efficiently train large numbers of shop-floor experts in the latest TPS methods and better operate an increasing number of production sites worldwide. Since then, additional upgrades and refinements have been introduced, some in response to the large number of defects in Toyota vehicles that surfaced in 2009–2010.

There's widespread agreement that Toyota's ongoing effort to refine and improve on its renowned TPS gives it important manufacturing capabilities that are the envy of other motor vehicle manufacturers. Not only have such auto manufacturers as Ford, Daimler, Volkswagen, and General Motors attempted to emulate key elements of TPS, but elements of Toyota's production philosophy have been adopted by hospitals and postal services.

Sources: Information posted at www.toyotageorgetown.com; Hirotaka Takeuchi, Emi Osono, and Norihiko Shimizu, "The Contradictions That Drive Toyota's Success," *Harvard Business Review* 86, no. 6 (June 2008), pp. 96–104; Taiichi Ohno, *Toyota Production System: Beyond Large-Scale Production* (New York: Sheridan, 1988).

Managerial actions to develop core competencies and competitive capabilities generally take one of two forms: either strengthening the company's base of skills, knowledge, and intellect or coordinating and integrating the efforts of the various work groups and departments. Actions of the first sort can be undertaken at all managerial levels, but actions of the second sort are best orchestrated by senior managers who not only appreciate the strategy-executing significance of strong capabilities but also have the clout to enforce the necessary cooperation and coordination among individuals, groups, departments, and external allies.[23]

Acquiring Capabilities through Mergers and Acquisitions

Sometimes a company can refresh and strengthen its competencies by acquiring another company with attractive resources and capabilities.[24] An acquisition aimed at building a stronger portfolio of competencies and capabilities can be every bit as valuable as an acquisition aimed at adding new products or services to the company's lineup of offerings. The advantage of this mode of acquiring new capabilities is primarily one of speed, since developing new capabilities internally can take many years of effort. Capabilities-motivated acquisitions are essential (1) when a market opportunity can slip by faster than a needed capability can be created internally and (2) when industry conditions, technology, or competitors are moving at such a rapid clip that time is of the essence.

At the same time, acquiring capabilities in this way is not without difficulty. Capabilities involve tacit knowledge and complex routines that cannot be transferred readily from one organizational unit to another. This may limit the extent to which the new capability can be utilized. For example, the Newell Company acquired Rubbermaid in part for its famed product innovation capabilities. Transferring these capabilities to other parts of the Newell organization proved easier said than done, however, contributing to a slump in the firm's stock prices that lasted for some time. Integrating the capabilities of two firms involved in a merger or acquisition may pose an additional challenge, particularly if there are underlying incompatibilities in their supporting systems or processes. Moreover, since internal fit is important, there is always the risk that under new management the acquired capabilities may not be as productive as they had been. In a worst-case scenario, the acquisition process may end up damaging or destroying the very capabilities that were the object of the acquisition in the first place.

Accessing Capabilities through Collaborative Partnerships

Another method of acquiring capabilities from an external source is to access them via collaborative partnerships with suppliers, competitors, or other companies having the cutting-edge expertise. There are three basic ways to pursue this course of action:

1. *Outsource the function requiring the capabilities to a key supplier or another provider.* Whether this is a wise move depends on what can be safely delegated to outside suppliers or allies versus what internal capabilities are key to the company's long-term success. As discussed in Chapter 6, outsourcing has the advantage of conserving resources so that the firm can focus its energies on those activities most central to its strategy. It may be a good choice for firms that are too small and resource-constrained to execute all the parts of their strategy internally.

2. *Collaborate with a firm that has complementary resources and capabilities in a joint venture, strategic alliance, or other type of partnership established for the purpose of achieving a shared strategic objective.* This requires launching initiatives to identify the most attractive potential partners and to establish collaborative working relationships. Since the success of the venture will depend on how well the partners work together, potential partners should be selected as much for their management style, culture, and goals as for their resources and capabilities.

3. *Engage in a collaborative partnership for the purpose of learning how the partner does things, internalizing its methods and thereby acquiring its capabilities.* Since this method involves an abuse of trust, it not only puts the cooperative venture at risk but also encourages the firm's partner to treat the firm similarly or refuse further dealings with the firm.

Upgrading Employee Skills and Knowledge Resources

Good strategy execution also requires that employees have the skills and knowledge resources they will need to perform their tasks well. Employee training thus plays an important role in the strategy execution process. Training and retraining are important when a company shifts to a strategy requiring different skills, competitive capabilities, and operating methods. Training is also strategically important in organizational efforts to build skills-based competencies. And it is a key activity in businesses where technical know-how is changing so rapidly that a company loses its ability to compete unless its employees have cutting-edge knowledge and expertise. Successful strategy implementers see to it that the training function is both adequately funded and effective. If the chosen strategy calls for new skills, deeper technological capability, or the building and using of new capabilities, training should be placed near the top of the action agenda.

The strategic importance of training has not gone unnoticed. Over 600 companies have established internal "universities" to lead the training effort, facilitate continuous organizational learning, and help upgrade company capabilities. Many companies conduct orientation sessions for new employees, fund an assortment of competence-building training programs, and reimburse employees for tuition and other expenses associated with obtaining additional college education, attending professional development courses, and earning professional certification of one kind or another. A number of companies offer online, just-in-time training courses to employees around the clock. Increasingly, employees at all levels are expected to take an active role in their own professional development and assume responsibility for keeping their skills up to date and in sync with the company's needs.

Strategy Execution Capabilities and Competitive Advantage

As firms get better at executing their strategies, they develop capabilities in the domain of strategy execution much as they build other organizational capabilities. Superior strategy execution capabilities allow companies to get the most from their organizational resources and competitive capabilities. In this way they contribute to the success of a firm's business model. But excellence in strategy execution can also be a more direct source of competitive advantage, since more efficient and effective strategy execution can lower costs and permit firms to deliver more value to customers. Superior strategy execution capabilities may also enable a company to react more quickly to market changes and beat other firms to the market with new products and services. This can allow a company to profit from a period of uncontested market dominance.

> Superior strategy execution capabilities are the only source of sustainable competitive advantage when strategies are easy for rivals to copy.

Because strategy execution capabilities are socially complex capabilities that develop with experience over long periods of time, they are hard to imitate. And there is no substitute for good strategy execution. (Recall the tests of resource advantage from Chapter 4.) As such, they may be as important a source of sustained competitive advantage as the capabilities that drive a firm's strategies. Indeed, they may be a far more important avenue for securing a competitive edge over rivals in situations where it is relatively easy for rivals to copy promising strategies. In such cases, the only way for firms to achieve lasting competitive advantage is to outexecute their competitors.

ORGANIZING THE WORK EFFORT WITH A SUPPORTIVE ORGANIZATIONAL STRUCTURE

LO 4

Gain command of what issues to consider in establishing a strategy-supportive organizational structure and organizing the work effort.

There are few hard-and-fast rules for organizing the work effort to support good strategy execution. Every firm's organization chart is partly a product of its particular situation, reflecting prior organizational patterns, varying internal circumstances, executive judgments about reporting relationships, and the politics of who gets which assignments. Moreover, every strategy is grounded in its own set of organizational capabilities and value chain activities. But some considerations in organizing the work effort are common to all companies. These are summarized in Figure 10.3 and discussed in the following sections.

Figure 10.3   Structuring the Work Effort to Promote Successful Strategy Execution

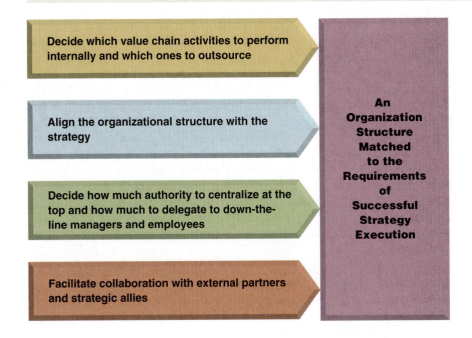

Deciding Which Value Chain Activities to Perform Internally and Which to Outsource

The advantages of a company's having an outsourcing component in its strategy were discussed in Chapter 6, but there is also a need to consider the role of outsourcing in executing the strategy. Aside from the fact that another company (because of its experience, scale of operations, and specialized know-how) may be able to perform certain value chain activities better or cheaper than a company can perform them internally, outsourcing can also sometimes make a positive contribution to better strategy execution. Managers too often spend inordinate amounts of time, mental energy, and resources haggling with functional support groups or other internal bureaucracies over needed services, leaving less time for them to devote to performing strategy-critical activities in the most proficient manner.

One way to reduce such distractions is to outsource the performance of assorted administrative support functions and perhaps even selected primary value chain activities to outside vendors, thereby enabling the company to concentrate its full energies on performing the value chain activities that are at the core of its strategy, where it can create unique value. For example, E. & J. Gallo Winery outsources 95 percent of its grape production, letting farmers take on weather-related and other grape-growing risks while it concentrates its efforts on wine production and sales.[25] Broadcom, a global leader in chips for broadband communication systems, outsources the manufacture of its chips to Taiwan Semiconductor, thus freeing company personnel to focus their full energies on R&D, new chip design, and marketing. Nike concentrates on design, marketing, and distribution while outsourcing virtually all production of its shoes and sporting apparel.

> Wisely choosing which activities to perform internally and which to outsource can lead to several strategy-executing advantages—lower costs, heightened strategic focus, less internal bureaucracy, speedier decision making, and a better arsenal of organizational capabilities.

Such heightened focus on performing strategy-critical activities can yield three important execution-related benefits:

- *The company improves its chances for outclassing rivals in the performance of strategy-critical activities and turning a core competence into a distinctive competence.* At the very least, the heightened focus on performing a select few value chain activities should promote more effective performance of those activities. This could materially enhance competitive capabilities by either lowering costs or improving quality. Whirlpool, ING Insurance, Hugo Boss, Japan Airlines, and Chevron have outsourced their data processing activities to computer service firms, believing that outside specialists can perform the needed services at lower costs and equal or better quality. A relatively large number of companies outsource the operation of their Web sites to Web design and hosting enterprises. Many business that get a lot of inquiries from customers or that have to provide 24/7 technical support to users of their products across the world have found that it is considerably less expensive to outsource these functions to specialists (often located in foreign countries where skilled personnel are readily available and worker compensation costs are much lower) than to operate their own call centers.

- *The streamlining of internal operations that flows from outsourcing often serves to decrease internal bureaucracies, flatten the organizational structure, speed internal decision making, and shorten the time it takes to respond to changing market conditions.*[26] In consumer electronics, where advancing technology drives new product innovation, organizing the work effort in a manner that expedites getting next-generation products to market ahead of rivals is a critical competitive capability. The world's motor vehicle manufacturers have found that they can shorten the cycle time for new models by outsourcing the large majority of their parts and components from independent suppliers and then working closely with their vendors to swiftly incorporate new technology and better integrate individual parts and components to form engine cooling systems, transmission systems, and electrical systems.

- *Partnerships can add to a company's arsenal of capabilities and contribute to better strategy execution.* By building, continually improving, and then leveraging partnerships, a company enhances its overall organizational capabilities and strengthens its competitive assets—assets that deliver more value to customers and consequently pave the way for competitive success. Soft-drink and beer manufacturers cultivate their relationships with their bottlers and distributors to strengthen access to local markets and build loyalty, support, and commitment for corporate marketing programs, without which their own sales and growth are weakened. Similarly, fast-food enterprises like McDonald's and Taco Bell find it essential to work hand in hand with franchisees on outlet cleanliness, consistency of product quality, in-store ambience, courtesy and friendliness of store personnel, and other aspects of store operations. Unless franchisees continuously deliver sufficient customer satisfaction to attract repeat business, a fast-food chain's sales and competitive standing will suffer quickly. Companies like Boeing, Aerospatiale, Verizon Communications, and Dell have learned that their central R&D groups cannot begin to match the innovative capabilities of a well-managed network of supply chain partners.[27]

However, as was emphasized in Chapter 6, a company must guard against going overboard on outsourcing and becoming overly dependent on outside suppliers.

A company cannot be the master of its own destiny unless it maintains expertise and resource depth in performing those value chain activities that underpin its long-term competitive success.[28] As a general rule, therefore, it is the strategically less important activities—like handling customer inquiries and providing technical support, doing the payroll, administering employee benefit programs, providing corporate security, managing stockholder relations, maintaining fleet vehicles, operating the company's Web site, conducting employee training, and managing an assortment of information and data processing functions—for which outsourcing makes the most strategic sense.

Aligning the Firm's Organizational Structure with Its Strategy

The design of the firm's **organizational structure** is a critical aspect of the strategy execution process. The organizational structure comprises the formal and informal arrangement of tasks, responsibilities, and lines of authority and communication by which the firm is administered.[29] It specifies the linkages among parts of the organization, the reporting relationships, the direction of information flows, and the decision-making processes. It is a key factor in strategy implementation since it exerts a strong influence on how well managers can coordinate and control the complex set of activities involved.[30]

> **CORE CONCEPT**
>
> A firm's **organizational structure** comprises the formal and informal arrangement of tasks, responsibilities, lines of authority, and reporting relationships by which the firm is administered.

A well-designed organizational structure is one in which the various parts (e.g., decision-making rights, communication patterns) are aligned with one another and also matched to the requirements of the strategy. With the right structure in place, managers can orchestrate the various aspects of the implementation process with an even hand and a light touch. Without a supportive structure, strategy execution is more likely to become bogged down by administrative confusion, political maneuvering, and bureaucratic waste.

Good organizational design may even contribute to the firm's ability to create value for customers and realize a profit. By enabling lower bureaucratic costs and facilitating operational efficiency, it can lower a firm's operating costs. By facilitating the coordination of activities within the firm, it can improve the capability-building process, leading to greater differentiation and/or lower costs. Moreover, by improving the speed with which information is communicated and activities are coordinated, it can enable the firm to beat rivals to the market and profit from a period of unrivaled advantage.

Making Strategy-Critical Activities the Main Building Blocks of the Organizational Structure
In any business, some activities in the value chain are always more critical to successful strategy execution than others. For instance, a ski apparel manufacturer must be good at styling and design, low-cost manufacturing, distribution (convincing an attractively large number of retailers to stock and promote the company's brand), and marketing and advertising (building a brand image that generates buzz and appeal among ski enthusiasts). In discount stock brokerage, the strategy-critical activities are fast access to information, accurate order execution, efficient record keeping and transactions processing, and good customer service. In specialty chemicals, the critical activities are R&D, product innovation, getting new products onto the market quickly, effective marketing, and expertise in assisting customers.

Where such is the case, it is important for management to build its organizational structure around proficient performance of these activities, making them the centerpieces or main building blocks in the enterprise's organizational structure.

The rationale for making strategy-critical activities the main building blocks in structuring a business is compelling: If activities crucial to strategic success are to have the resources, decision-making influence, and organizational impact they need, they have to be centerpieces in the organizational scheme. Making them the focus of structuring efforts will also facilitate their coordination and promote good internal fit—an essential attribute of a winning strategy, as summarized in Chapter 1. To the extent that implementing a new strategy entails new or altered key activities or capabilities, different organizational arrangements may be required.[31]

Matching Type of Organizational Structure to Strategy Execution Requirements

Organizational structures can be classified into a limited number of standard types. The type that is most suitable for a given firm will depend on the firm's size and complexity as well as its strategy. As firms grow and their needs for structure evolve, their structural form is likely to evolve from one type to another. The four basic types are the *simple structure,* the *functional structure,* the *multidivisional structure,* and the *matrix structure,* as described below.

1. Simple Structure   A **simple structure** is one in which a central executive (often the owner-manager) handles all major decisions and oversees the operations of the organization with the help of a small staff.[32] Simple structures are also known as *line-and-staff structures,* since a central administrative staff supervises line employees who conduct the operations of the firm, or *flat structures,* since there are few levels of hierarchy.[33] It is characterized by limited task specialization; few rules; informal relationships; minimal use of training, planning, and liaison devices; and a lack of sophisticated support systems. It has all the advantages of simplicity, including low administrative costs, ease of coordination, flexibility, quick decision making, adaptability, and responsiveness to change.[34] Its informality and lack of rules may foster creativity and heightened individual responsibility.

Simple organizational structures are typically employed by small firms and entrepreneurial start-ups. The simple structure is the most common type of organizational structure since small firms are the most prevalent type of business. As an organization grows, however, this structural form becomes inadequate to the demands that come with size and complexity. In response, growing firms tend to alter their organizational structure from a simple structure to a functional structure.

2. Functional Structure   A **functional structure** is one that is organized along functional lines, where a function represents a major step in the firm's value chain, such as R&D, engineering and design, manufacturing, sales and marketing, logistics, and customer service. Each functional unit is supervised by functional line managers who report to the chief executive officer and a corporate staff. This arrangement allows functional managers to focus on their area of responsibility, leaving it to the CEO and headquarters to provide direction and ensure that their activities are coordinated and integrated. Functional structures

CORE CONCEPT

A **simple structure** consists of a central executive who handles all major decisions and oversees all operations with the help of a small staff.

Simple structures are also called *line-and-staff* structures or *flat* structures.

CORE CONCEPT

A **functional structure** is organized into functional departments, with departmental managers who report to the CEO and small corporate staff.

are also known as *departmental structures,* since the functional units are commonly called departments, and *unitary structures* or *U-forms,* since a single unit is responsible for each function.

In large organizations, functional structures lighten the load on top management, relative to simple structures, and make for a more efficient use of managerial resources. Their primary advantage, however, is due to greater task specialization, which promotes learning, enables the realization of scale economies, and offers productivity advantages not otherwise available. Their disadvantage is that the departmental boundaries can inhibit the flow of information and limit the opportunities for cross-functional cooperation and coordination.

It is generally agreed that some type of functional structure is the best organizational arrangement when a company is in just one particular business (regardless of which of the five generic competitive strategies it opts to pursue). For instance, a technical instruments manufacturer may be organized around research and development, engineering, supply chain management, assembly, quality control, marketing, and technical services. A discount retailer, such as Dollar General or Kmart, may organize around such functional units as purchasing, warehousing and distribution, store operations, advertising and sales, merchandising, and customer service. Functional structures can also be appropriate for firms with high-volume production, products that are closely related, and a limited degree of vertical integration. For example, General Motors now manages all of its brands (e.g., Cadillac, Oldsmobile, Chevrolet, Buick) under a common functional structure designed to promote technical transfer and capture economies of scale.[35]

> Functional structures are also called *departmental* structures, *unitary* structures, or *U-forms.*

As firms continue to grow, they often become more diversified and complex, placing a greater burden on top management. At some point, the centralized control that characterizes the functional structure becomes a liability, and the advantages of functional specialization begin to break down. To resolve these problems and address a growing need for coordination across functions, firms generally turn to the multidivisional structure.

3. Multidivisional Structure A **multidivisional structure** is a decentralized structure consisting of a set of operating divisions organized along market, customer, product, or geographic lines, and a central corporate headquarters, which monitors divisional activities, allocates resources, performs assorted support functions, and exercises overall control. Since each division is essentially a business, the divisions typically operate as independent profit centers (i.e., with profit/loss responsibility) and are organized internally along functional lines.[36] Division managers oversee day-to-day operations and the development of business-level strategy, while corporate executives attend to overall performance and corporate strategy, the elements of which were described in Chapter 8. Multidivisional structures are also called *divisional structures* or *M-forms,* in contrast with the U-form (functional) structure.

> **CORE CONCEPT**
>
> A **multidivisional structure** is a decentralized structure consisting of a set of operating divisions organized along business, product, customer group, or geographic lines, and a central corporate headquarters that allocates resources, provides support functions, and monitors divisional activities.

Multidivisional structures are common among companies pursuing some form of diversification strategy or global strategy, with operations in a number of businesses or countries. When the strategy is one of unrelated diversification, as in a conglomerate or holding company, the divisions generally represent separate industries. When the strategy is based on related diversification, the divisions may be organized according to markets, customer groups, product lines, geographic regions, or technologies. In this arrangement, the decision about where to draw the divisional lines depends foremost on the nature of the relatedness and the strategy-critical building blocks, in terms of which businesses have key value chain activities in common. For example, a company selling closely related products to business customers as well as two types of end consumers—online buyers and in-store buyers—may organize its divisions according to customer groups since the value chains involved in serving the three groups differ. Another company may organize by product line due to commonalities in product development and production within each product line. Multidivisional structures are also common among vertically integrated firms. There the major building blocks are often divisional units performing one or more of the major processing steps along the value chain (e.g., raw-material production, components manufacture, assembly, wholesale distribution, retail store operations).

Multidivisional structures offer significant advantages over functional structures in terms of facilitating the management of a complex and diverse set of operations.[37] Putting business-level strategy in the hands of division managers while leaving corporate strategy to top executives reduces the potential for information overload and improves the quality of decision making in each domain. This also minimizes the costs of coordinating divisionwide activities while enhancing top management's ability to control a diverse and complex operation. Moreover, multidivisional structures can help align individual incentives with the goals of the corporation and spur productivity by encouraging competition for resources among the different divisions.

But a divisional business-unit structure can also present some problems to a company pursuing related diversification, because having independent business units—each running its own business in its own way—inhibits cross-business collaboration and the capture of cross-business synergies. To solve this type of problem, firms turn to more complex structures, such as the matrix structure.

4. Matrix Structure   A **matrix structure** is a combination structure in which the organization is organized along two or more dimensions at once (e.g., business, geographic area, value chain function) for the purpose of enhancing cross-unit communication, collaboration, and coordination. In essence, it overlays one type of structure onto another type. Matrix structures are managed through multiple reporting relationships, so a middle manager may report to several bosses. For instance, in a matrix structure based on product line, region, and function, a sales manager for plastic containers in Georgia might report to the manager of the plastics division, the head of the southeast sales region, and the head of marketing.

Matrix organizational structures have evolved from the complex, over-formalized structures that were popular in the 60s, 70s and 80s but often produced inefficient, unwieldy bureaucracies. The modern incarnation of the matrix structure is generally a more flexible arrangement, with a single primary reporting relationship that can be overlaid with a temporary secondary reporting relationship as need arises. For example, a software company that is organized into functional departments (software design, quality control, customer relations) may assign employees from those departments to different projects on a temporary basis, so an employee reports to a project manager as well as to his or her primary boss (the functional department head) for the duration of a project.

Matrix structures are also called *composite structures* or *combination structures*. They are often used for project-based, process-based, or team-based management.

Such approaches are common in businesses involving projects of limited duration, such as consulting, architecture, and engineering services. The type of close cross-unit collaboration that a flexible matrix structure supports is also needed to build competitive capabilities in strategically important activities, such as speeding new products to market, that involve employees scattered across several organizational units.[38] Capabilities-based matrix structures that combine process departments (like new product development) with more traditional functional departments provide a solution.

An advantage of matrix structures is that they facilitate the sharing of plant and equipment, specialized knowledge, and other key resources—they lower costs by enabling the realization of economies of scope. They also have the advantage of flexibility in form and may allow for better oversight since supervision is provided from more than one perspective. A disadvantage is that they add an additional layer of management, thereby increasing bureaucratic costs and decreasing response time to new situations.[39] In addition, there is a potential for confusion among employees due to dual reporting relationships and divided loyalties. While there is some controversy over the utility of matrix structures, the modern approach to matrix structures does much to minimize their disadvantages.[40]

> Matrix structures are also called *composite* structures or *combination* structures.

Determining How Much Authority to Delegate

On average, larger companies with more complex organizational structures are more decentralized in their decision making than smaller firms with simple structures—by necessity and by design. Under any organizational structure, however, there is still room for considerable variation in how much authority top managers retain and how much is delegated to down-the-line managers and employees. In executing strategy, then, companies must decide how much authority to delegate to the managers of each organizational unit—especially the heads of divisions, functional departments, and other operating units—and how much decision-making latitude to give individual employees in performing their jobs. The two extremes are to *centralize decision making* at the top (the CEO and a few close lieutenants) or to *decentralize decision making* by giving managers and employees considerable decision-making latitude in their areas of responsibility. As shown in Table 10.1, the two approaches are based on sharply different underlying principles and beliefs, with each having its pros and cons.

LO 5

Become aware of the pros and cons of centralized and decentralized decision making in implementing the chosen strategy.

Centralized Decision Making: Pros and Cons *In a highly centralized organizational structure, top executives retain authority for most strategic and operating decisions and keep a tight rein on business-unit heads, department heads, and the managers of key operating units; comparatively little discretionary authority is granted to frontline supervisors and rank-and-file employees.* The command-and-control paradigm of centralized structures is based on the underlying assumptions that frontline personnel have neither the time nor the inclination to direct and properly control the work they are performing and that they lack the knowledge and judgment to make wise decisions about how best to do it—hence the need for managerially prescribed policies and procedures, close supervision, and tight control. The thesis underlying authoritarian structures is that strict enforcement of detailed procedures backed by rigorous managerial oversight is the most reliable way to keep the daily execution of strategy on track.

One advantage of an authoritarian structure is tight control by the manager in charge—it is easy to know who is accountable when things do not go well.

Table 10.1   **Advantages and Disadvantages of Centralized versus Decentralized Decision Making**

Centralized Organizational Structures	Decentralized Organizational Structures
Basic Tenets	**Basic Tenets**
• Decisions on most matters of importance should be in the hands of top-level managers who have the experience, expertise, and judgment to decide what is the best course of action. • Lower-level personnel have neither the knowledge, the time, nor the inclination to properly manage the tasks they are performing. • Strong control from the top is a more effective means for coordinating company actions.	• Decision-making authority should be put in the hands of the people closest to, and most familiar with, the situation. • Those with decision-making authority should be trained to exercise good judgment. • A company that draws on the combined intellectual capital of all its employees can outperform a command-and-control company.
Chief Advantages	**Chief Advantages**
• Fixes accountability through tight control from the top. • Eliminates goal conflict among those with differing perspectives or interests. • Allows for quick decision making and strong leadership under crisis situations.	• Encourages company employees to exercise initiative and act responsibly. • Promotes greater motivation and involvement in the business on the part of more company personnel. • Spurs new ideas and creative thinking. • Allows fast response to market change. • May entail fewer layers of management.
Primary Disadvantages	**Primary Disadvantages**
• Lengthens response times by those closest to the market conditions because they must seek approval for their actions. • Does not encourage responsibility among lower-level managers and rank-and-file employees. • Discourages lower-level managers and rank-and-file employees from exercising any initiative.	• Top management lacks "full control"—higher-level managers may be unaware of actions taken by empowered personnel under their supervision. • Puts the organization at risk if empowered employees happen to make "bad" decisions. • Can impair cross-unit collaboration.

This structure can also reduce goal conflict among managers from different parts of the organization who may have different perspectives, incentives, and objectives. For example, a manager in charge of an engineering department may be more interested in pursuing a new technology than is a marketing manager who doubts that customers will value the technology as highly. Another advantage of a command-and-control structure is that it can enable a more uniform and swift response to a crisis situation that affects the organization as a whole.

But there are some serious disadvantages as well. Hierarchical command-and-control structures make a large organization with a complex structure sluggish in responding to changing market conditions because of the time it takes for the review/approval process to run up all the layers of the management bureaucracy. Furthermore, to work well, centralized decision making requires top-level managers to gather and process whatever information is relevant to the decision. When the relevant knowledge resides at lower organizational levels (or is technical, detailed, or hard to express in words), it is difficult and time-consuming to get all the facts and nuances in front of a high-level executive located far from the scene of the action—full understanding of the situation cannot be readily copied from one mind to another. Hence, centralized decision making is often impractical—the larger the company and the more scattered its operations, the more that decision-making authority must be delegated to managers closer to the scene of the action.

Decentralized Decision Making: Pros and Cons *In a highly decentralized organization, decision-making authority is pushed down to the lowest organizational level capable of making timely, informed, competent decisions.* The objective is to put adequate decision-making authority in the hands of the people closest to and most familiar with the situation and train them to weigh all the factors and exercise good judgment. Decentralized decision making means, for example, that employees with customer contact are empowered to do what it takes to please customers. At Starbucks, for example, employees are encouraged to exercise initiative in promoting customer satisfaction—there's the oft-repeated story of a store employee who, when the computerized cash register system went offline, enthusiastically offered free coffee to waiting customers.[41]

> The ultimate goal of decentralized decision making is to put authority in the hands of those persons or teams closest to and most knowledgeable about the situation.

The case for empowering down-the-line managers and employees to make decisions regarding daily operations and strategy execution is based on the belief that a company that draws on the combined intellectual capital of all its employees can outperform a command-and-control company.[42] The challenge in a decentralized system is in maintaining adequate control. With decentralized decision making, top management maintains control by determining the limits to authority for each type of position, installing companywide strategic control systems, holding people accountable for their decisions, instituting compensation incentives that reward people for doing their jobs in a manner that contributes to good company performance, and creating a corporate culture where there's strong peer pressure on individuals to act responsibly.[43]

Decentralized organization structures have much to recommend them. Pushing decision-making authority down to subordinate managers, work teams, and individual employees shortens organizational response times and spurs new ideas, creative thinking, innovation, and greater involvement on the part of all company personnel. Moreover, in worker-empowered structures, jobs can be defined more broadly, several tasks can be integrated into a single job, and people can direct their own work. Fewer layers of managers are needed because deciding how to do things becomes part of each person's or team's job. Today's online communication systems and smart phones make it easy and relatively inexpensive for people at all organizational levels to have direct access to data, other employees, managers, suppliers, and customers. They can access information quickly (via the Internet or company network), readily check with superiors or whomever else as needed, and take responsible action. Typically, there are genuine gains in morale and productivity when people are provided with the tools and information they need to operate in a self-directed way.

But decentralization also has some disadvantages. Top managers lose an element of control over what goes on (since empowered subordinates have authority to act on their own) and may thus be unaware of actions being taken by personnel under their supervision. Such lack of control can put a company at risk in the event that empowered employees make unwise decisions. Moreover, because decentralization gives organizational units the authority to act independently, there is risk of too little collaboration and coordination between different organizational units.

Many companies have concluded that the advantages of decentralization outweigh the disadvantages. Over the past 15 to 20 years, there's been a decided shift from authoritarian multilayered hierarchical structures to flatter, more decentralized structures that stress employee empowerment. This shift reflects a strong and growing consensus that authoritarian, hierarchical organizational structures are not well suited to implementing and executing strategies in an era when extensive information and instant communication are the norm and when a big fraction of the organization's most valuable assets consists of intellectual capital and resides in the knowledge and capabilities of its employees.

Capturing Cross-Business Strategic Fit in a Decentralized Structure   Diversified companies striving to capture the benefits of synergy between separate businesses have to beware of giving business-unit heads full rein to operate independently. Cross-business strategic fit typically has to be captured either by enforcing close cross-business collaboration or by centralizing performance of functions requiring close coordination at the corporate level.[44] For example, if businesses with overlapping process and product technologies have their own independent R&D departments— each pursuing its own priorities, projects, and strategic agendas—it's hard for the corporate parent to prevent duplication of effort, capture either economies of scale or economies of scope, or encourage more collaborative R&D efforts. Where the potential for cross-business R&D synergies exist, the best solution is usually to centralize the R&D function and have a coordinated corporate R&D effort that serves the interests of both the individual businesses and the company as a whole. Likewise, centralizing the related activities of separate businesses makes sense when there are opportunities to share a common sales force, use common distribution channels, rely on a common field service organization, use common e-commerce systems, and so on.

> Efforts to decentralize decision making and give company personnel some leeway in conducting operations must be tempered with the need to maintain adequate control and cross-unit coordination.

Facilitating Collaboration with External Partners and Strategic Allies

Organizational mechanisms—whether formal or informal—are also required to ensure effective working relationships with each major outside constituency involved in strategy execution. Strategic alliances, outsourcing arrangements, joint ventures, and cooperative partnerships present immediate opportunities and open the door to future possibilities, but little of value can be realized without active management of the relationship. Unless top management sees that constructive organizational bridge building with strategic partners occurs and that productive working relationships emerge, the value of cooperative relationships is lost and the company's power to execute its strategy is weakened. If close working relationships with suppliers are crucial, then supply chain management must enter into considerations regarding how to create an effective organizational structure. If distributor/dealer/franchisee relationships are important, someone must be assigned the task of nurturing the relationships with forward channel allies. If working in parallel with providers of complementary products and services contributes to enhanced organizational capability, then cooperative organizational arrangements have to be put in place and managed to good effect.

Building organizational bridges with external allies can be accomplished by appointing "relationship managers" with responsibility for making particular strategic partnerships or alliances generate the intended benefits. Relationship managers have many roles and functions: getting the right people together, promoting good rapport, seeing that plans for specific activities are developed and carried out, helping adjust internal organizational procedures and communication systems, ironing out operating dissimilarities, and nurturing interpersonal cooperation. Multiple cross-organization ties have to be established and kept open to ensure proper communication and coordination.[45] There has to be enough information sharing to make the relationship work and periodic frank discussions of conflicts, trouble spots, and changing situations.

Organizing and managing a network structure provides another mechanism for encouraging more effective collaboration and cooperation among external partners. A **network structure** is the arrangement linking a number of independent organizations involved in some common undertaking. A well-managed network structure typically includes one firm in a more central role, with the responsibility of ensuring that the right partners are included and the activities across the network are coordinated. The high-end Italian motorcycle company Ducati operates in this manner, assembling its motorcycles from parts obtained from a hand-picked integrated network of parts suppliers.

> **CORE CONCEPT**
>
> A **network structure** is the arrangement linking a number of independent organizations involved in some common undertaking.

Further Perspectives on Structuring the Work Effort

All organization designs have their strategy-related strengths and weaknesses. To do a good job of matching structure to strategy, strategy implementers first have to pick a basic design and modify it as needed to fit the company's particular business lineup. They must then (1) supplement the design with appropriate coordinating mechanisms (cross-functional task forces, special project teams, self-contained work teams, and so on) and (2) institute whatever networking and communications arrangements it takes to support effective execution of the firm's strategy. Some companies may avoid setting up "ideal" organizational arrangements because they do not want to disturb existing reporting relationships or because they need to accommodate other situational idiosyncrasies, yet they must still work toward the goal of building a competitively capable organization.

The ways and means of developing stronger core competencies and organizational capabilities (or creating altogether new ones) have to fit a company's own circumstances. Not only do different companies and executives tackle the capabilities-building challenge in different ways, but the task of building different capabilities requires different organizing techniques. Thus, generalizing about how to build capabilities has to be done cautiously. What can be said unequivocally is that building a capable organization entails a process of consciously knitting together the efforts of individuals and groups. Organizational capabilities emerge from establishing and nurturing cooperative working relationships among people and groups to perform activities in a more efficient, value-creating fashion. While an appropriate organizational structure can facilitate this, organization building is a task in which senior management must be deeply involved. Indeed, effectively managing both internal organization processes and external collaboration to create and develop competitively valuable organizational capabilities remains a top challenge for senior executives in today's companies.

KEY POINTS

1. Executing strategy is an action-oriented, operations-driven activity revolving around the management of people and business processes. The way for managers to start in implementing a new strategy is with *a probing assessment of what the organization must do differently to carry out the strategy successfully.* They should then consider *precisely how to make the necessary internal changes* as rapidly as possible.

2. Good strategy execution requires a *team effort.* All managers have strategy-executing responsibility in their areas of authority, and all employees are active participants in the strategy execution process.

3. Ten managerial tasks crop up repeatedly in company efforts to execute strategy: (1) staffing the organization well, (2) building the necessary organizational capabilities, (3) creating a supportive organizational structure, (4) allocating sufficient resources, (5) instituting supportive policies and procedures, (6) adopting processes for continuous improvement, (7) installing systems that enable proficient company operations, (8) tying incentives to the achievement of desired targets, (9) instilling the right corporate culture, and (10) exercising internal leadership.

4. The two best signs of good strategy execution are whether a company is meeting or beating its performance targets and performing value chain activities in a manner that is conducive to companywide operating excellence. *Shortfalls in performance signal weak strategy, weak execution, or both.*

5. Building an organization capable of good strategy execution entails three types of organization-building actions: (1) s*taffing the organization*—assembling a talented management team, and recruiting and retaining employees with the needed experience, technical skills, and intellectual capital; (2) *building and strengthening core competencies and competitive capabilities*—developing proficiencies in performing strategy-critical value chain activities and updating them to match changing market conditions and customer expectations; and (3) *structuring the organization and work effort*—instituting organizational arrangements that facilitate good strategy execution, deciding how much decision-making authority to delegate, and managing external relationships.

6. Building core competencies and competitive capabilities is a time-consuming, managerially challenging exercise that can be approached in three ways: (1) developing capabilities internally, (2) acquiring capabilities through mergers and acquisitions, and (3) accessing capabilities via collaborative partnerships.

7. In building capabilities internally, the first step is to develop the *ability* to do something, through experimentation, active search for alternative solutions, and learning by trial and error. As experience grows and company personnel learn how to perform the activities consistently well and at an acceptable cost, the ability evolves into a tried-and-true capability. The process can be accelerated by making learning a more deliberate endeavor and providing the incentives that will motivate company personnel to achieve the desired ends.

8. As firms get better at executing their strategies, they develop capabilities in the domain of strategy execution. Superior strategy execution capabilities allow companies to get the most from their organizational resources and competitive capabilities. But excellence in strategy execution can also be a more direct source of competitive advantage, since more efficient and effective strategy execution can lower costs and permit firms to deliver more value to customers. Superior

strategy execution capabilities are hard to imitate and have no good substitutes. As such, they can be an important source of *sustainable* competitive advantage. Any time rivals can readily duplicate successful strategies, making it impossible to *outstrategize* rivals, the chief way to achieve lasting competitive advantage is to *outexecute* them.

9.   Structuring the organization and organizing the work effort in a strategy-supportive fashion has four aspects: (1) deciding which value chain activities to perform internally and which ones to outsource; (2) aligning the firm's organizational structure with its strategy; (3) deciding how much authority to centralize at the top and how much to delegate to down-the-line managers and employees; and (4) facilitating the necessary collaboration and coordination with external partners and strategic allies.

10.   To align the firm's organizational structure with its strategy, it is important to make strategy-critical activities the main building blocks. There are four basic types of organizational structures: the simple structure, the functional structure, the multidivisional structure, and the matrix structure. Which is most appropriate depends on the firm's size, complexity, and strategy.

ASSURANCE OF LEARNING EXERCISES

LO 2, LO 3

1.   Review the Careers link on L'Oréal's worldwide corporate Web site (go to www.loreal.com and click on the company's worldwide corporate Web site option). The section provides extensive information about personal development, international learning opportunities, integration of new hires into existing teams, and other areas of management development. How do the programs discussed help L'Oréal to hire good people and build core competencies and competitive capabilities? Please use the chapter's discussions of recruiting, training, and retaining capable employees and building core competencies and competitive capabilities as a guide for preparing your answer.

LO 4

2.   Examine the overall corporate organizational structure chart for Exelon Corporation. The chart can be found by going to www.exeloncorp.com and using the Web site search feature to locate "organizational charts." Does it appear that strategy-critical activities are the building blocks of Exelon's organizational arrangement? Is its organizational structure best characterized as a departmental structure tied to functional, process, or geographic departments? Is the company's organizational structure better categorized as a divisional structure? Would you categorize Exelon's organizational structure as a matrix arrangement? Explain your answer.

LO 5

3.   Using Google Scholar or your university library's access to EBSCO, InfoTrac, or other online databases, do a search for recent writings on decentralized decision making and employee empowerment. According to the articles you find in the various management journals, what are the conditions under which decision making should be pushed down to lower levels of management?

EXERCISES FOR SIMULATION PARTICIPANTS

LO 5

1. How would you describe the organization of your company's top management team? Is some decision making decentralized and delegated to individual managers? If so, explain how the decentralization works. Or are decisions made more by consensus, with all co-managers having input? What do you see as the advantages and disadvantages of the decision-making approach your company is employing?

LO 3

2. What specific actions have you and your co-managers taken to develop core competencies or competitive capabilities that can contribute to good strategy execution and potential competitive advantage? If no actions have been taken, explain your rationale for doing nothing.

LO 1, LO 4

3. What value chain activities are most crucial to good execution of your company's strategy? Does your company have the ability to outsource any value chain activities? If so, have you and your co-managers opted to engage in outsourcing? Why or why not?

ENDNOTES

[1] As quoted in Steven W. Floyd and Bill Wooldridge, "Managing Strategic Consensus: The Foundation of Effective Implementation," *Academy of Management Executive* 6, no. 4 (November 1992), p. 27.

[2] As cited in Gary L. Neilson, Karla L. Martin, and Elizabeth Powers, "The Secrets of Successful Strategy Execution," *Harvard Business Review* 86, no. 6 (June 2008), pp. 61–62.

[3] Jack Welch with Suzy Welch, *Winning* (New York: HarperBusiness, 2005), p. 135.

[4] For an excellent and very pragmatic discussion of this point, see Larry Bossidy and Ram Charan, *Execution: The Discipline of Getting Things Done* (New York: Crown Business, 2002), chap. 1.

[5] For an insightful discussion of how important staffing an organization with the right people is, see Christopher A. Bartlett and Sumantra Ghoshal, "Building Competitive Advantage through People," *MIT Sloan Management Review* 43, no. 2 (Winter 2002), pp. 34–41.

[6] The importance of assembling an executive team that has an exceptional ability to gauge what needs to be done and an instinctive talent for figuring out how to get it done is discussed in Justin Menkes, "Hiring for Smarts," *Harvard Business Review* 83, no. 11 (November 2005), pp. 100–9, and Justin Menkes, *Executive Intelligence* (New York: HarperCollins, 2005), especially chaps. 1 to 4.

[7] See Bossidy and Charan, *Execution: The Discipline of Getting Things Done*, chap. 1.

[8] Menkes, *Executive Intelligence*, pp. 68, 76.

[9] Bossidy and Charan, *Execution: The Discipline of Getting Things Done*, chap. 5.

[10] Welch with Welch, *Winning*, pp. 141–42.

[11] Menkes, *Executive Intelligence*, pp. 65–71.

[12] Jim Collins, *Good to Great* (New York: HarperBusiness, 2001), p. 44.

[13] John Byrne, "The Search for the Young and Gifted," *BusinessWeek*, October 4, 1999, p. 108.

[14] See chapters 5 and 6 in Helfat et al., *Dynamic Capabilities: Understanding Strategic Change in Organizations* (Malden, MA: Blackwell, 2007); R. Grant, *Contemporary Strategy Analysis*, 6th ed. (Malden, MA: Blackwell, 2008).

[15] C. Helfat and M. Peteraf, "The Dynamic Resource-Based View: Capability Lifecycles," *Strategic Management Journal*, 24, no. 10 (October 2003), pp. 997–1010.

[16] G. Hamel and C. K. Prahalad, "Strategy as Stretch and Leverage," *Harvard Business Review* 71, no. 2 (March/April 1993), pp. 75–84.

[17] G. Dosi, R. Nelson, and S. Winter (eds.), *The Nature and Dynamics of Organizational Capabilities* (Oxford, England: Oxford University Press, 2001).

[18] C. Helfat and M. Peteraf, "The Dynamic Resource-Based View: Capability Lifecycles."

[19] S. Winter, "The Satisficing Principle in Capability Learning," *Strategic Management Journal* 21, nos. 10/11 (October/November 2000), pp. 981–96; M. Zollo and S. Winter, "Deliberate Learning and the Evolution of Dynamic Capabilities," *Organization Science* 13, no. 3 (May/June 2002), pp. 339–51.

[20] G. Szulanski and S. Winter, "Getting It Right the Second Time," *Harvard Business Review* 80 (January 2002), pp. 62–69; S. Winter and G. Szulanski, "Replication as Strategy," *Organization Science* 12, no. 6 (November/December 2001), pp. 730–43.

[21] B. Kogut and U. Zander, "Knowledge of the Firm, Combinative Capabilities, and the Replication of Technology," *Organization Science* 3, no. 3 (August 1992), pp. 383–97.

[22] C. Helfat and R. Raubitschek, "Product Sequencing: Co-Evolution of Knowledge, Capabilities and Products," *Strategic Management Journal* 21, nos. 10/11 (October/November 2000), pp. 961–80.

[23] Robert H. Hayes, Gary P. Pisano, and David M. Upton, *Strategic Operations: Competing through Capabilities* (New York: Free Press, 1996), pp. 503–7. Also see Jonas Ridderstråle, "Cashing In on Corporate Competencies," *Business Strategy Review* 14, no. 1 (Spring 2003), pp. 27–38; Danny Miller, Russell Eisenstat, and Nathaniel Foote, "Strategy from the Inside Out: Building Capability-Creating Organizations," *California Management Review* 44, no. 3 (Spring 2002), pp. 37–55.

[24] S. Karim and W. Mitchell, "Path-Dependent and Path-Breaking Change: Reconfiguring Business Resources Following Business," *Strategic Management Journal* 21, nos. 10/11 (October/November 2000), pp. 1061–82; L. Capron, P. Dussague, and W. Mitchell,

"Resource Redeployment Following Horizontal Acquisitions in Europe and North America, 1988–1992," *Strategic Management Journal* 19, no. 7 (July 1998), pp. 631–62.

[25] J. B. Quinn, *Intelligent Enterprise* (New York: Free Press, 1992), p. 43.

[26] Ibid., pp. 33 and 89; J. B. Quinn and F. Hilmer, "Strategic Outsourcing," *McKinsey Quarterly* 1 (1995), pp. 48–70; Jussi Heikkilä and Carlos Cordon, "Outsourcing: A Core or Non-core Strategic Management Decision," *Strategic Change* 11, no. 3 (June–July 2002), pp. 183–93; and J. B. Quinn, "Strategic Outsourcing: Leveraging Knowledge Capabilities," *Sloan Management Review* 40, no. 4 (Summer 1999), pp. 9–21. A strong case for outsourcing is presented in C. K. Pralahad, "The Art of Outsourcing," *Wall Street Journal,* June 8, 2005, p. A13. For a discussion of why outsourcing initiatives fall short of expectations, see Jérôme Barthélemy, "The Seven Deadly Sins of Outsourcing," *Academy of Management Executive* 17, no. 2 (May 2003), pp. 87–98.

[27] Quinn, "Strategic Outsourcing: Leveraging Knowledge Capabilities," p. 17.

[28] Quinn, *Intelligent Enterprise,* pp. 39–40; also see Gary P. Pisano and Willy C. Shih, "Restoring American Competitiveness," *Harvard Business Review* 87, nos. 7–8 (July–August 2009), pp. 114–25; Barthélemy, "The Seven Deadly Sins of Outsourcing."

[29] A. Chandler, *Strategy and Structure* (Cambridge, MA: MIT Press, 1962).

[30] E. Olsen, S. Slater, and G. Hult, "The Importance of Structure and Process to Strategy Implementation," *Business Horizons* 48, no. 1 (2005), pp. 47–54; H. Barkema, J. Baum, and E. Mannix, "Management Challenges in a New Time", *Academy of Management Journal* 45, no. 5 (October 2002), pp. 916–30.

[31] The importance of matching organization design and structure to the particular requirements for good strategy execution was first brought to the forefront in a landmark study of 70 large corporations conducted by Professor Alfred Chandler of Harvard University. Chandler's research revealed that changes in an organization's strategy bring about new administrative problems that, in turn, require a new or refashioned structure for the new strategy to be successfully implemented and executed. He found that structure tends to follow the growth strategy of the firm—but often not until inefficiency and internal operating problems provoke a structural adjustment. The experiences of these firms followed a consistent sequential pattern: new strategy creation, emergence of new administrative problems, a decline in profitability and performance, a shift to a more appropriate organizational structure, and then recovery to more profitable levels and improved strategy execution. See Chandler, *Strategy and Structure*.

[32] H. Mintzberg, *The Structuring of Organizations* (Englewood Cliffs, NJ: Prentice Hall, 1979); C. Levicki, *The Interactive Strategy Workout,* 2nd ed. (London: Prentice Hall, 1999).

[33] Chandler, *Strategy and Structure*.

[34] Mintzberg, *The Structuring of Organizations*.

[35] Grant, *Contemporary Strategy Analysis*.

[36] Chandler, *Strategy and Structure*.

[37] O. Williamson, *Market and Hierarchies* (New York: Free Press, 1975); R. M. Burton and B. Obel, "A Computer Simulation Test of the M-Form Hypothesis," *Administrative Science Quarterly* 25 (1980), pp. 457–76.

[38] J. Baum and S. Wally, "Strategic Decision Speed and Firm Performance," *Strategic Management Journal* 24 (2003), pp. 1107–29.

[39] C. Bartlett and S. Ghoshal, "Matrix Management: Not a Structure, a Frame of Mind," *Harvard Business Review,* July–August 1990, pp. 138–45.

[40] M. Goold and A. Campbell, "Structured Networks: Towards the Well Designed Matrix," *Long Range Planning* 36, no. 5 (2003), pp. 427–39.

[41] Iain Somerville and John Edward Mroz, "New Competencies for a New World," in Frances Hesselbein, Marshall Goldsmith, and Richard Beckard (eds.), *The Organization of the Future* (San Francisco: Jossey-Bass, 1997), p. 70.

[42] The importance of empowering workers in executing strategy and the value of creating a great working environment are discussed in Stanley E. Fawcett, Gary K. Rhoads, and Phillip Burnah, "People as the Bridge to Competitiveness: Benchmarking the 'ABCs' of an Empowered Workforce," *Benchmarking: An International Journal* 11, no. 4 (2004), pp. 346–60.

[43] A discussion of the problems of maintaining adequate control over empowered employees and possible solutions is presented in Robert Simons, "Control in an Age of Empowerment," *Harvard Business Review* 73 (March–April 1995), pp. 80–88.

[44] For a discussion of the importance of cross-business coordination, see Jeanne M. Liedtka, "Collaboration across Lines of Business for Competitive Advantage," *Academy of Management Executive* 10, no. 2 (May 1996), pp. 20–34.

[45] Rosabeth Moss Kanter, "Collaborative Advantage: The Art of the Alliance," *Harvard Business Review* 72, no. 4 (July–August 1994), pp. 105–6.

CHAPTER 11

MANAGING INTERNAL OPERATIONS

Actions That Promote Good Strategy Execution

> True motivation comes from achievement, personal development, job satisfaction, and recognition.
>
> **—Frederick Herzberg**
> *Expert on motivation*

> Note to salary setters: Pay your people the least possible and you'll get the same from them.
>
> **—Malcolm Forbes**
> *Late publisher of Forbes Magazine*

> Leadership almost always involves cooperative and collaborative activity that can occur only in a conducive context.
>
> **—Lt. General William G. Pagonis**
> *Retired U.S. Army officer and author*

LEARNING OBJECTIVES

LO 1. Learn why resource allocation should always be based on strategic priorities.

LO 2. Understand how well-designed policies and procedures can facilitate good strategy execution.

LO 3. Learn how process management tools that drive continuous improvement in the performance of value chain activities can help an organization achieve superior strategy execution.

LO 4. Recognize the role of information and operating systems in enabling company personnel to carry out their strategic roles proficiently.

LO 5. Appreciate how and why the use of well-designed incentives and rewards can be management's single most powerful tool for promoting adept strategy execution and operating excellence.

In Chapter 10, we emphasized the importance of building organization capabilities and structuring the work effort so as to perform execution-critical value chain activities in a coordinated and competent manner. In this chapter, we discuss five additional managerial actions that promote good strategy execution:

- Allocating resources to the drive for good strategy execution.
- Instituting policies and procedures that facilitate strategy execution.
- Using process management tools to drive continuous improvement in how value chain activities are performed.
- Installing information and operating systems that enable company personnel to carry out their strategic roles proficiently.
- Using rewards and incentives to promote better strategy execution and the achievement of strategic and financial targets.

ALLOCATING RESOURCES TO THE STRATEGY EXECUTION EFFORT

Early in the process of implementing a new strategy, managers need to determine what resources (in terms of funding, people, etc.) will be required for good strategy execution and how they should be distributed across the various organizational units involved. A company's ability to marshal the resources needed to support new strategic initiatives has a major impact on the strategy execution process. Too little funding slows progress and impedes the efforts of organizational units to execute their pieces of the strategic plan proficiently. Too much funding wastes organizational resources and reduces financial performance. Both outcomes argue for managers to be deeply involved in reviewing budget proposals and directing the proper amounts of resources to strategy-critical organizational units. This includes carefully screening requests for more people and new facilities and equipment, approving those that hold promise for making a contribution to strategy execution and turning down those that don't. Should internal cash flows prove insufficient to fund the planned strategic initiatives, then management must raise additional funds through borrowing or selling additional shares of stock to willing investors.

A change in strategy nearly always calls for budget reallocations and resource shifting. Previously important units having a lesser role in the new strategy may need downsizing. Units that now have a bigger strategic role may need more people, new equipment, additional facilities, and above-average increases in their operating budgets. Implementing a new strategy requires managers to take an active and sometimes forceful role in shifting resources, downsizing some functions and upsizing others, not only to amply fund activities with a critical role in the new strategy but also to avoid inefficiency and achieve profit projections. It requires putting enough resources behind new strategic initiatives to fuel their success and making the tough decisions to kill projects and activities that are no longer justified. Honda's strong support of R&D activities allowed it to develop the first motorcycle airbag, the first low-polluting four-stroke outboard marine engine, a wide range of ultra-low-emission cars, the first hybrid car (Honda Insight) in the U.S. market, and the first hydrogen fuel cell car (Honda Clarity). However, Honda managers had no trouble stopping production of the Honda Insight in 2006 when its sales failed to take off and then shifting resources to the development and manufacture of other promising hybrid models, including a totally redesigned Insight that was launched in the United States in 2009.

Visible actions to reallocate operating funds and move people into new organizational units signal a determined commitment to strategic change and frequently are needed to catalyze the implementation process and give it credibility. Microsoft has made a practice of regularly shifting hundreds of programmers to new high-priority programming initiatives within a matter of weeks or even days. At Harris Corporation, where the strategy was to diffuse research ideas into areas that were commercially viable, top management regularly moved groups of engineers out of low-opportunity activities into its most promising new commercial venture divisions. Fast-moving developments in many markets are prompting companies to abandon traditional annual or semiannual budgeting and resource allocation cycles in favor of resource allocation processes supportive of more rapid adjustments in strategy.

> The funding requirements of good strategy execution must drive how capital allocations are made and the size of each unit's operating budget. Underfunding organizational units and activities pivotal to the strategy impedes successful strategy implementation.

The bigger the change in strategy (or the more obstacles that lie in the path of good strategy execution), the bigger the resource shifts that will likely be required. Merely fine-tuning the execution of a company's existing strategy seldom requires big movements of people and money from one area to another. The desired improvements can usually be accomplished through above-average budget increases to organizational units launching new initiatives and below-average increases (or even small budget cuts) for the remaining organizational units. However, there are times when strategy changes or new execution initiatives need to be made without adding to total company expenses. In such circumstances, managers have to work their way through the existing budget line by line and activity by activity, looking for ways to trim costs and shift resources to higher-priority activities where new execution initiatives are needed. In the event that a

> A company's operating budget must be both *strategy-driven* (in order to amply fund the performance of key value chain activities) and *lean* (in order to operate as cost-efficiently as possible).

company needs to make significant cost cuts during the course of launching new strategic initiatives, then managers have to be especially creative in finding ways to do more with less and execute the strategy more efficiently. Indeed, it is not unusual for strategy changes and the drive for good strategy execution to be conducted in a manner that entails achieving considerably higher levels of operating efficiency and, at the same time, making sure key activities are performed as effectively as possible.

Figure 11.1   **How Policies and Procedures Facilitate Good Strategy Execution**

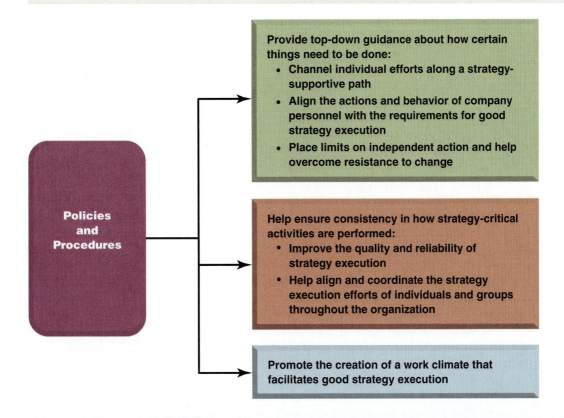

Policies and Procedures

Provide top-down guidance about how certain things need to be done:
- **Channel individual efforts along a strategy-supportive path**
- **Align the actions and behavior of company personnel with the requirements for good strategy execution**
- **Place limits on independent action and help overcome resistance to change**

Help ensure consistency in how strategy-critical activities are performed:
- **Improve the quality and reliability of strategy execution**
- **Help align and coordinate the strategy execution efforts of individuals and groups throughout the organization**

Promote the creation of a work climate that facilitates good strategy execution

INSTITUTING POLICIES AND PROCEDURES THAT FACILITATE STRATEGY EXECUTION

A company's policies and procedures can either support or obstruct good strategy execution. Any time a company moves to put new strategy elements in place or improve its strategy execution capabilities, some changes in work practices and the behavior of company personnel are usually required. Managers are thus well advised to examine whether existing policies and procedures support such changes and to proactively revise or discard those that are out of sync.

As shown in Figure 11.1, well-conceived policies and operating procedures facilitate strategy execution in three ways:

- *They provide top-down guidance regarding how things need to be done.* Policies and procedures provide company personnel with a set of guidelines for how to perform organizational activities, conduct various aspects of operations, solve problems as they arise, and accomplish particular tasks. In essence, they represent a store of organizational or managerial knowledge about efficient and effective ways of doing things. They clarify uncertainty about how to proceed in executing strategy and align the actions and behavior of company personnel

LO 2

Understand how well-designed policies and procedures can facilitate good strategy execution.

Well-conceived policies and procedures aid strategy execution; out-of-sync ones hinder effective execution.

with the requirements for good strategy execution. Moreover, they place limits on ineffective independent action. When they are well matched with the requirements of the strategy implementation plan, they channel the efforts of individuals along a path that supports the plan and facilitates good strategy execution. When existing ways of doing things are misaligned with strategy execution initiatives, actions and behaviors have to be changed. Under these conditions, the managerial role is to establish and enforce new policies and operating practices that are more conducive to executing the strategy appropriately. Policies are a particularly useful way to counteract tendencies for some people to resist change. People generally refrain from violating company policy or going against recommended practices and procedures without gaining clearance and having strong justification.

- *They help ensure consistency in how execution-critical activities are performed.* Policies and procedures serve to standardize the way that activities are performed and encourage strict conformity to the standardized approach. This is important for ensuring the quality and reliability of the strategy execution process. It helps align and coordinate the strategy execution efforts of individuals and groups throughout the organization—a feature that is particularly beneficial when there are geographically scattered operating units. For example, eliminating significant differences in the operating practices of different plants, sales regions, customer service centers, or the individual outlets in a chain operation helps a company deliver consistent product quality and service to customers. Good strategy execution nearly always entails an ability to replicate product quality and the caliber of customer service at every location where the company does business—anything less blurs the company's image and lowers customer satisfaction.

- *They promote the creation of a work climate that facilitates good strategy execution.* A company's policies and procedures help to set the tone of a company's work climate and contribute to a common understanding of "how we do things around here." Because discarding old policies and procedures in favor of new ones invariably alters the internal work climate, managers can use the policy-changing process as a powerful lever for changing the corporate culture in ways that produce a stronger fit with the new strategy. The trick here, obviously, is to come up with new policies or procedures that catch the immediate attention of company personnel, quickly shift their actions and behavior, and then become embedded in how things are done.

To ensure consistency in product quality and service behavior patterns, McDonald's policy manual spells out detailed procedures that personnel in each McDonald's unit are expected to observe. For example, "Cooks must turn, never flip, hamburgers. If they haven't been purchased, Big Macs must be discarded in 10 minutes after being cooked and French fries in 7 minutes. Cashiers must make eye contact with and smile at every customer." Nordstrom has a company policy of promoting only those people whose personnel records contain evidence of "heroic acts" to please customers—especially customers who may have made "unreasonable requests" that require special efforts. This induces store personnel to dedicate themselves to outstanding customer service, consistent with the requirements of executing a strategy based on exceptionally high service quality. To ensure that its R&D activities are responsive to customer needs and expectations, Hewlett-Packard requires its R&D people to make regular visits to customers to learn about their problems and learn their reactions to HP's latest new products.

One of the big policy-making issues concerns what activities need to be rigidly prescribed and what activities ought to allow room for independent action on the part of empowered personnel. Few companies need thick policy manuals to direct the strategy execution process or prescribe exactly how daily operations are to be conducted. Too much policy can be as much of a hindrance as wrong policy and as confusing as no policy. There is wisdom in a middle approach: *Prescribe enough policies to give organization members clear direction and to place reasonable boundaries on their actions; then empower them to act within these boundaries in whatever way they think makes sense.* Allowing company personnel to act with some degree of freedom is especially appropriate when individual creativity and initiative are more essential to good strategy execution than standardization and strict conformity. Instituting policies that facilitate strategy execution can therefore mean more policies, fewer policies, or different policies. It can mean policies that require things be done according to a strictly defined standard or policies that give employees substantial leeway to do activities the way they think best.

USING PROCESS MANAGEMENT TOOLS TO STRIVE FOR CONTINUOUS IMPROVEMENT

Company managers can significantly advance the cause of superior strategy execution by using various process management tools to drive continuous improvement in how internal operations are conducted. One of the most widely used and effective tools for gauging how well a company is executing pieces of its strategy entails benchmarking the company's performance of particular activities and business processes against "best-in-industry" and "best-in-world" performers.[1] It can also be useful to look at "best-in-company" performers of an activity if a company has a number of different organizational units performing much the same function at different locations. Identifying, analyzing, and understanding how top-performing companies or organizational units conduct particular value chain activities and business processes provides useful yardsticks for judging the effectiveness and efficiency of internal operations and setting performance standards for organizational units to meet or beat.

How the Process of Identifying and Incorporating Best Practices Works

A **best practice** is a technique for performing an activity or business process that has been shown to consistently deliver superior results compared to other methods.[2] To qualify as a legitimate best practice, the technique must have a proven record in significantly lowering costs, improving quality or performance, shortening time requirements, enhancing safety, or delivering some other highly positive operating outcome. Best practices thus identify a path to operating excellence. For a best practice to be valuable and transferable, it must demonstrate success over time, deliver quantifiable and highly positive results, and be repeatable.

Figure 11.2 From Benchmarking and Best-Practice Implementation to Operating Excellence

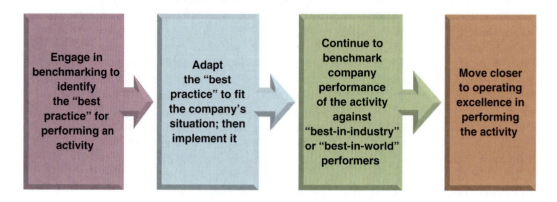

As discussed in Chapter 4, *benchmarking* is the backbone of the process of identifying, studying, and implementing best practices. A company's benchmarking effort looks outward to find best practices and then proceeds to develop the data for measuring how well a company's own performance of an activity stacks up against the best-practice standard. For individual managers, benchmarking involves being humble enough to admit that others have come up with world-class ways to perform particular activities yet wise enough to try to learn how to match, and even surpass, them. But, as shown in Figure 11.2, the payoff of benchmarking comes from adapting the top-notch approaches pioneered by other companies to the company's own operation and thereby boosting, perhaps dramatically, the proficiency with which strategy-critical value chain tasks are performed.

However, benchmarking is more complicated than simply identifying which companies are the best performers of an activity and then trying to imitate their approaches—especially if these companies are in other industries. Normally, the outstanding practices of other organizations have to be *adapted* to fit the specific circumstances of a company's own business, strategy, and operating requirements. Since each organization is unique, the telling part of any best-practice initiative is how well the company puts its own version of the best practice into place and makes it work.

Indeed, a best practice remains little more than another company's interesting success story unless company personnel buy into the task of translating what can be learned from other companies into real action and results. The agents of change must be frontline employees who are convinced of the need to abandon the old ways of doing things and switch to a best-practice mindset. *The more that organizational units use best practices in performing their work, the closer a company moves toward performing its value chain activities as effectively and efficiently as possible.* This is what excellent strategy execution is all about.

> The more that organizational units use best practices in performing their work, the closer a company comes to achieving effective and efficient strategy execution.

Legions of companies across the world now engage in benchmarking to improve their strategy execution efforts. Scores of trade associations and special-interest organizations have undertaken efforts to collect best-practice data relevant to a particular industry or business function and make their databases available online to members. Good examples include The Benchmarking Exchange (**www.benchnet.com**); Best Practices, LLC (www.best-in-class.com); and the American Productivity and Quality Center (www.apqc.org). Benchmarking and best-practice implementation have clearly emerged as legitimate and valuable managerial tools for promoting operational excellence and enhancing strategy execution.

Business Process Reengineering, Total Quality Management, and Six Sigma Quality Programs: Tools for Promoting Operating Excellence

In striving for operating excellence, many companies have also come to rely on three other potent process management tools: business process reengineering, total quality management (TQM), and Six Sigma quality control techniques. Indeed, these three tools have become globally pervasive techniques for implementing strategies keyed to cost reduction, defect-free manufacture, superior product quality, superior customer service, and total customer satisfaction. The following sections describe how business process reengineering, TQM, and Six Sigma programs can contribute to top-notch strategy execution and operating excellence.

Business Process Reengineering   Companies scouring for ways to improve their operations have sometimes discovered that the execution of strategy-critical activities is hindered by an organizational arrangement where pieces of the activity are performed in several different functional departments, with no one manager or group being accountable for optimal performance of the entire activity. This can easily occur in such inherently cross-functional activities as customer service (which can involve personnel in order filling, warehousing and shipping, invoicing, accounts receivable, after-sale repair, and technical support), new product development (which typically involves personnel in R&D, design and engineering, purchasing, manufacturing, and sales and marketing), and supply chain management (which cuts across such areas as purchasing, inventory management, manufacturing and assembly, warehousing, and shipping).

To address the suboptimal performance problems that can arise from this type of situation, many companies have opted to *reengineer the work effort,* pulling the pieces of strategy-critical activities out of different departments and creating a single department or work group to take charge of the whole process and perform it in a better, cheaper, and more strategy-supportive fashion. The use of cross-functional teams has been popularized by the practice of **business process reengineering,** which involves radically redesigning and streamlining the workflow (often enabled by cutting-edge use of online technology and information systems), with the goal of achieving quantum gains in performance of the activity.[3]

> **CORE CONCEPT**
>
> **Business process reengineering** involves radically redesigning and streamlining how an activity is performed, with the intent of achieving dramatic improvements in performance.

When done properly, business process reengineering can produce dramatic operating benefits. Hallmark reengineered its process for developing new greeting cards, creating teams of mixed-occupation personnel (artists, writers, lithographers, merchandisers, and administrators) to work on a single holiday or greeting card theme; the reengineered process speeded development times for new lines of greeting cards by up to 24 months, was more cost-efficient, and increased customer satisfaction.[4] In the order-processing section of General Electric's circuit breaker division, elapsed time from order receipt to delivery was cut from three weeks to three days by consolidating six production units into one, reducing a variety of former inventory and handling steps, automating the design system to replace a human custom-design process, and cutting the organizational layers between managers and workers from three to one. Productivity rose 20 percent in one year, and unit manufacturing costs dropped 30 percent. Northwest Water, a British utility, used process reengineering to eliminate 45 work depots that served as home bases to crews who installed and repaired water and sewage lines and equipment. Under the reengineered arrangement, crews worked directly from their vehicles, receiving assignments and reporting work completion from computer terminals in their trucks. Crew members became contractors to Northwest Water rather than employees, a move that not only eliminated the need for the work depots but also allowed Northwest Water to eliminate a big percentage of the bureaucratic personnel and supervisory organization that managed the crews.[5]

Reengineering of value chain activities has been undertaken at many companies in many industries all over the world, with excellent results at some firms.[6] At companies where it has produced only modest results, this is usually because of ineptness and/or lack of wholehearted commitment from the top. While business process reengineering has been criticized for its use by some companies as an excuse for downsizing, it has nonetheless proved itself as a useful tool for streamlining a company's work effort and moving closer to operational excellence. It has also inspired more technologically based approaches to integrating and streamlining business processes, such as *Enterprise Resource Planning,* a software-based system implemented with the help of consulting companies such as SAP (the leading provider of business software).

Total Quality Management Programs   Total quality management (TQM) is a philosophy of managing a set of business practices that emphasizes continuous improvement in all phases of operations, 100 percent accuracy in per-

forming tasks, involvement and empowerment of employees at all levels, team-based work design, benchmarking, and total customer satisfaction.[7] While TQM concentrates on producing quality goods and fully satisfying customer expectations, it achieves its biggest successes when it is extended to employee efforts in *all departments*—for example, human resources, billing, accounting, and information systems—that may lack pressing, customer-driven incentives to improve. It involves reforming the corporate culture and shifting to a total quality/continuous improvement business philosophy that permeates every facet of the organization.[8] TQM aims at instilling enthusiasm and commitment to doing things right from the top to the bottom of the organization. Management's job is to kindle an organizationwide search for ways to improve, a search that involves all company personnel exercising initiative and using their ingenuity. TQM doctrine preaches that there's no such thing as "good enough" and that everyone has a responsibility to participate in continuous improvement. TQM is thus a race without a finish. Success comes from making little steps forward each day, a process that the Japanese call *kaizen.*

TQM takes a fairly long time to show significant results—very little benefit emerges within the first six months. The long-term payoff of TQM, if it comes, depends heavily on management's success in implanting a culture within which the TQM philosophy and practices can thrive. TQM is a managerial tool that has attracted numerous users and advocates over several decades, and it can deliver good results when used properly.

Six Sigma Quality Programs   Six Sigma programs offer another way to drive continuous improvement in quality and strategy execution. This approach entails the use of advanced statistical methods to identify and remove the causes of defects (errors) and variability in performing an activity or business process. When performance of an activity or process reaches "Six Sigma quality," there are *no more than 3.4 defects per million iterations* (equal to 99.9997 percent accuracy)[9]

There are two important types of Six Sigma programs. DMAIC (define, measure, analyze, improve, and control) is an improvement system for existing processes falling below specification and needing incremental improvement. The DMADV process of define, measure, analyze, design, and verify is used to develop *new* processes or products at Six Sigma quality levels. DMADV is sometimes referred to as a Design for Six Sigma, or DFSS. Both Six Sigma programs are overseen by personnel who have completed Six Sigma "master black belt" training and are executed by personnel who have earned Six Sigma "green belts" and Six Sigma "black belts." According to the Six Sigma Academy, personnel with black belts can save companies approximately $230,000 per project and can complete four to six projects a year.[10]

The statistical thinking underlying Six Sigma is based on the following three principles: All work is a process, all processes have variability, and all processes create data that explain variability.[11] To illustrate how these three principles drive the metrics of DMAIC, consider the case of a hypothetical janitorial company that wants to improve the caliber of work done by its cleaning crews and thereby improve customer satisfaction. The janitorial company's Six Sigma team can pursue quality enhancement and continuous improvement via the DMAIC process as follows:

- *Define.* Because Six Sigma is aimed at reducing defects, the first step is to define what constitutes a defect. Six Sigma team members might decide that leaving streaks on windows is a defect because it is a source of customer dissatisfaction.

- *Measure.* The next step is to collect data to find out why, how, and how often this defect occurs. This might include creating a process flow map of the specific ways that cleaning crews go about the task of cleaning a commercial customer's windows. Other metrics may include recording what tools and cleaning products the crews use to clean windows.

- *Analyze.* After the data are gathered and the statistics analyzed, the company's Six Sigma team may discover that the tools and window-cleaning techniques of certain employees are better than those of other employees because their tools and procedures leave no streaked windows—a "best practice" for avoiding window streaking is thus identified and documented.

- *Improve.* The Six Sigma team implements the documented best practice as a standard way of cleaning windows.

- *Control.* The company teaches new and existing employees the best-practice technique for window cleaning. Over time, there is significant improvement in customer satisfaction and increased business.

Six Sigma's DMAIC process is a particularly good vehicle for improving performance when there are *wide variations* in how well an activity is performed.[12] For instance, airlines striving to improve the on-time performance of their flights have more to gain from actions to curtail the number of flights that are late by more than 30 minutes than from actions to reduce the number of flights that are late by less than 5 minutes. Likewise, FedEx might have a 16-hour average delivery time for its overnight package service operation, but if the actual delivery time varies around the 16-hour average from a low of 12 hours to a high of 26 hours, such that 10 percent of its packages are delivered over 6 hours late, then it has a huge reliability problem of the sort that Six Sigma programs are well suited to address.

Since the mid-1990s, thousands of companies and nonprofit organizations around the world have used Six Sigma programs to promote operating excellence. Such manufacturers as Motorola, Caterpillar, DuPont, Xerox, Alcan Aluminum, BMW, Volkswagen, Nokia, Owens Corning, Boeing, and Emerson Electric have employed Six Sigma techniques to improve their strategy execution and increase production quality. General Electric (GE), one of the most successful companies implementing Six Sigma training and pursuing Six Sigma perfection across the company's entire operations, estimated benefits on the order of $10 billion during the first five years of implementation; its Lighting division, for example, cut invoice defects and disputes by 98 percent, while GE Capital Mortgage improved the chances of a caller reaching a "live" GE person from 76 to 99 percent.[13] Illustration Capsule 11.1 describes Whirlpool's use of Six Sigma in its appliance business.

Six Sigma is, however, not just a quality-enhancing tool for manufacturers. At one company, product sales personnel typically wined and dined customers to close their deals, but the costs of such entertaining were viewed as excessively high.[14] A Six Sigma project that examined sales data found that although face time with customers was important, wining, dining, and other types of entertainment were not. The data showed that regular face time helped close sales, but that time could be spent over a cup of coffee instead of golfing at a resort or taking clients to expensive restaurants. In addition, analysis showed that too much face time with customers was counterproductive. A regularly scheduled customer picnic was found to be detrimental to closing sales because it was held at a busy time of year, when customers preferred not to be away from their offices. Changing the manner in which prospective customers were wooed resulted in a 10 percent increase in sales. Six Sigma has also been used to improve processes in health care. A Milwaukee hospital used Six Sigma to improve the accuracy of administering the proper drug doses to patients. DMAIC analysis of the three-stage process by which prescriptions were written by doctors, filled by the hospital pharmacy, and then administered to patients by nurses revealed that most mistakes came from misreading the doctors' handwriting.[15] The hospital implemented a program requiring doctors to enter the prescription on the hospital's computers, which slashed the number of errors dramatically. Bank of America, Starwood Hotels, Penske Truck Leasing, Jacksonville Electric Authority (JEA), United Heath Group, Amazon.com, and the United States Army, Navy, Air Force, and Marine Corps also have reportedly used Six Sigma techniques successfully in their operations.

While many enterprises have used Six Sigma methods to improve the quality with which activities are performed, there is evidence that Six Sigma techniques can stifle innovation and creativity.[16] The essence of Six Sigma is to reduce variability in processes, but creative processes, by nature, include quite a bit of variability. In many instances, breakthrough innovations occur only after thousands of ideas have been abandoned and promising ideas have gone through multiple iterations and extensive prototyping. Google CEO Eric Schmidt has commented

Whirlpool's Use of Six Sigma to Promote Operating Excellence

Top management at Whirlpool Corporation (with 67 manufacturing and technology centers around the globe and sales in some 170 countries totaling $17 billion in 2009) has a vision of Whirlpool appliances in "Every Home . . . Everywhere with Pride, Passion, and Performance." One of management's chief objectives in pursuing this vision is to build unmatched customer loyalty to the Whirlpool brand. Whirlpool's strategy to win the hearts and minds of appliance buyers the world over has been to produce and market appliances with top-notch quality and innovative features that users will find appealing. In addition, Whirlpool's strategy has been to offer a wide selection of models (recognizing that buyer tastes and needs differ) and to strive for low-cost production efficiency, thereby enabling Whirlpool to price its products very competitively. Executing this strategy at Whirlpool's operations in North America (where it is the market leader), Latin America (where it is also the market leader), Europe (where it ranks third), and Asia (where it is number one in India and has a foothold with huge growth opportunities elsewhere) has involved a strong focus on continuous improvement, lean manufacturing capabilities, and a drive for operating excellence. To marshal the efforts of its 67,000 employees in executing the strategy successfully, management developed a comprehensive Operational Excellence program with Six Sigma as one of the centerpieces.

The Operational Excellence initiative, which began in the 1990s, incorporated Six Sigma techniques to improve the quality of Whirlpool products and, at the same time, lower costs and trim the time it took to get product innovations into the marketplace. The Six Sigma program helped Whirlpool save $175 million in manufacturing costs in its first three years.

To sustain the productivity gains and cost savings, Whirlpool embedded Six Sigma practices within each of its manufacturing facilities worldwide and instilled a culture based on Six Sigma and lean manufacturing skills and capabilities. In 2002, each of Whirlpool's operating units began taking the Six Sigma initiative to a higher level by first placing the needs of the customer at the center of every function—R&D, technology, manufacturing, marketing, and administrative support—and then striving to consistently improve quality levels while eliminating all unnecessary costs. The company systematically went through every aspect of its business with the view that company personnel should perform every activity at every level in a manner that delivers value to the customer and leads to continuous improvement on how things are done.

Whirlpool management believes that the company's Operational Excellence process has been a major contributor in sustaining the company's position as the leading global manufacturer and marketer of home appliances.

Source: www.whirlpool.com, accessed September 25, 2003, November 15, 2005, August 16, 2008, and July 9, 2010; Lexis-Nexis -Edgar Online, exhibit type: exhibit 99 - additional exhibits, filing date: June 21, 2010.

that the innovation process is "anti-Six Sigma" and that applying Six Sigma principles to those performing creative work at Google would choke off innovation at the company.[17]

James McNerney, a GE executive schooled in the constructive use of Six Sigma, became CEO at 3M Corporation and proceeded to institute a series of Six Sigma–based principles. McNerney's dedication to Six Sigma and his elimination of 8 percent of the company's workforce did cause 3M's profits to jump shortly after his arrival, but the application of Six Sigma in 3M's R&D and new product development activities soon proved to stifle innovation and new product introductions, undermining the company's long-standing reputation for innovation. 3M's researchers complained that the innovation process did not lend itself well to the extensive data collection and analysis required under Six Sigma and that too much time was spent completing reports that outlined the market potential and possible manufacturing concerns for projects in all stages of the R&D pipeline. Six Sigma rigidity and a freeze on 3M's R&D budget from McNerney's first year as CEO through 2005 was blamed for the company's drop from first to seventh place on the Boston Consulting Group's Most Innovative Companies list.[18]

A blended approach to Six Sigma implementation that is gaining in popularity pursues incremental improvements in operating efficiency, while R&D and other processes that allow the company to develop new ways of offering value to customers are given freer rein. Managers of these *ambidextrous organizations* are adept at employing continuous improvement in operating processes but allowing R&D to operate under a set of rules that allows for the development of breakthrough innovations. However, the two distinctly different approaches to managing employees must be carried out by tightly integrated senior managers to ensure that the separate and diversely oriented units operate with a common purpose. Ciba Vision, a global leader in contact lenses, has dramatically reduced operating expenses through the use of continuous improvement programs, while simultaneously and harmoniously developing new series of contact lens products that have allowed its revenues to increase by 300 percent over a 10-year period.[19] An enterprise that systematically and wisely applies Six Sigma methods to its value chain, activity by activity, can make major strides in improving the proficiency with which its strategy is executed without sacrificing innovation. As is the case with TQM, obtaining managerial commitment, establishing a quality culture, and fully involving employees are all of critical importance to the successful implementation of Six Sigma quality programs.[20]

The Difference between Business Process Reengineering and Continuous Improvement Programs like Six Sigma and TQM

Business process reengineering and continuous improvement efforts like TQM and Six Sigma both aim at improved productivity and reduced costs, better product quality, and greater customer satisfaction. The essential difference between business process reengineering and continuous improvement programs is that reengineering aims at *quantum gains* on the order of 30 to 50 percent or more, whereas programs like TQM and Six Sigma stress *incremental progress,* striving for inch-by-inch gains again and again in a never-ending stream. The two approaches to improved performance of value chain activities and operating excellence are not mutually exclusive; it makes sense to use them in tandem. Reengineering can be used first to produce a good basic design that yields quick, dramatic improvements in performing a business process. Total quality programs can then be used as a follow-on to reengineering and/or best-practice implementation, delivering gradual improvements over a longer period of time. Such a two-pronged approach to implementing operational excellence is like a marathon race in which you run the first 4 miles as fast as you can and then gradually pick up speed the remainder of the way.

> Business process reengineering aims at one-time quantum improvement, while continuous improvement programs like TQM and Six Sigma aim at ongoing incremental improvements.

Capturing the Benefits of Initiatives to Improve Operations

The biggest beneficiaries of benchmarking and best-practice initiatives, reengineering, TQM, and Six Sigma are companies that view such programs not as ends in themselves but as tools for implementing company strategy more effectively. The skimpiest payoffs occur when company managers seize on them as something worth trying—novel ideas that could improve things. In most such instances, they result in strategy-blind efforts to simply manage better.

There's an important lesson here. Business process management tools all need to be linked to a company's strategic priorities to contribute effectively to improving the strategy's execution. Only strategy can point to which value chain activities matter and what performance targets make the most sense. Without a strategic framework, managers lack the context in which to fix things that really matter to business-unit performance and competitive success.

To get the most from initiatives to execute strategy more proficiently, managers must have a clear idea of what specific outcomes really matter. Is it high on-time delivery, lower overall costs, fewer customer complaints, shorter cycle times, a higher percentage of revenues coming from recently introduced products, or what? Benchmarking best-in-industry and best-in-world performance of most or all value chain activities provides a realistic basis for setting internal performance milestones and longer-range targets.

Once initiatives to improve operations are linked to the company's strategic priorities, then comes the managerial task of building a total quality culture that is genuinely committed to achieving the performance outcomes that strategic success requires.[21] Managers can take the following action steps to realize full value from TQM or Six Sigma initiatives and promote a culture of operating excellence:[22]

1. Visible, unequivocal, and unyielding commitment to total quality and continuous improvement, including a vision concerned with quality and specific, measurable objectives for increasing quality and making continuous improvement.
2. Nudging people toward quality-supportive behaviors by:
    a. Screening job applicants rigorously and hiring only those with attitudes and aptitudes right for quality-based performance.
    b. Providing quality training for most employees.
    c. Using teams and team-building exercises to reinforce and nurture individual effort (the creation of a quality culture is facilitated when teams become more cross-functional, multitask-oriented, and increasingly self-managed).
    d. Recognizing and rewarding individual and team efforts to improve quality regularly and systematically.
    e. Stressing prevention (doing it right the first time), not inspection (instituting ways to correct mistakes).
3. Empowering employees so that authority for delivering great service or improving products is in the hands of the doers rather than the overseers—*improving quality has to be seen as part of everyone's job.*
4. Using online systems to provide all relevant parties with the latest best practices, thereby speeding the diffusion and adoption of best practices throughout the organization. Online systems can also allow company personnel to exchange data and opinions about how to upgrade the prevailing best practices.

5. Emphasizing that performance can, and must, be improved because competitors are not resting on their laurels and customers are always looking for something better.

If the quality initiatives are linked to the strategic objectives and if all organization members buy into a supporting culture of operating excellence, then a company's continuous improvement practices become decidedly more conducive to proficient strategy execution.

The purpose of using benchmarking, best practices, business process reengineering, TQM, and Six Sigma programs is to improve the performance of strategy-critical activities and thereby enhance strategy execution.

In sum, benchmarking, the adoption of best practices, business process reengineering, TQM, and Six Sigma techniques all need to be seen and used as part of a bigger-picture effort to execute strategy proficiently. Used properly, all of these tools are capable of improving the proficiency with which an organization performs its value chain activities. Not only do improvements from such initiatives add up over time and strengthen organizational capabilities, but they also help build a culture of operating excellence. All this lays the groundwork for gaining a competitive advantage.[23] While it is relatively easy for rivals to also implement process management tools, it is much more difficult and time-consuming for them to instill a deeply ingrained culture of operating excellence (as occurs when such techniques are religiously employed and top management exhibits lasting commitment to operational excellence throughout the organization).

INSTALLING INFORMATION AND OPERATING SYSTEMS

LO 4

Recognize the role of information and operating systems in enabling company personnel to carry out their strategic roles proficiently.

Company strategies can't be executed well without a number of internal systems for business operations. Southwest Airlines, Singapore Airlines, Lufthansa, British Airways, and other successful airlines cannot hope to provide passenger-pleasing service without a user-friendly online reservation system, an accurate and speedy baggage handling system, and a strict aircraft maintenance program that minimizes problems requiring at-the-gate service that delay departures. FedEx has internal communication systems that allow it to coordinate its over 80,000 vehicles in handling an average of 8.0 million packages a day. Its leading-edge flight operations systems allow a single controller to direct as many as 200 of FedEx's 664 aircraft simultaneously, overriding their flight plans should weather problems or other special circumstances arise. In addition, FedEx has created a series of e-business tools for customers that allow them to ship and track packages online, create address books, review shipping history, generate custom reports, simplify customer billing, reduce internal warehousing and inventory management costs, purchase goods and services from suppliers, and respond to quickly changing customer demands. All of FedEx's systems support the company's strategy of providing businesses and individuals with a broad array of package delivery services (from premium next-day to economical five-day deliveries) and enhancing its competitiveness against United Parcel Service, DHL, and the U.S. Postal Service.

Otis Elevator, the world's largest manufacturer of elevators, with some 2.3 million elevators and escalators installed worldwide, has a 24-hour remote electronic monitoring system that can detect when an elevator or escalator installed on a customer's site has any of 325 problems.[24] If the monitoring system detects a problem, it analyzes and diagnoses the cause and location, then makes the service call to an Otis mechanic at the nearest location, and helps the mechanic (who is equipped with a Web-enabled cell phone) identify the component causing the problem. The company's maintenance system helps keep outage times under three hours. All trouble-call data are relayed to design and manufacturing personnel, allowing them to quickly alter design specifications or manufacturing procedures when needed to correct recurring problems. All customers have online access to performance data on each of their Otis elevators and escalators.

Amazon.com ships customer orders of books, CDs, toys, and myriad other items from fully computerized warehouses with a capacity of over 17½ million square feet in 2010. The warehouses are so technologically sophisticated that they require about as many lines of code to run as Amazon's Web site does. Using complex picking algorithms, computers initiate the order-picking process by sending signals to workers' wireless receivers, telling them which items to pick off the shelves in which order. Computers also generate data on misboxed items, chute backup times, line speed, worker productivity, and shipping weights on orders. Systems are upgraded regularly, and productivity improvements are aggressively pursued. In 2003 Amazon turned their inventory over 20 times annually in an industry whose average was 15 turns; by 2009 its industry turnover had decreased to an unprecedented 12. Amazon's warehouse efficiency and cost per order filled was so low that one of the fastest-growing and most profitable parts of Amazon's business was using its warehouses to run the e-commerce operations of large retail chains such as Target.

Most telephone companies, electric utilities, and TV broadcasting systems have online monitoring systems to spot transmission problems within seconds and increase the reliability of their services. At eBay, there are systems for real-time monitoring of new listings, bidding activity, Web site traffic, and page views. Kaiser Permanente spent $3 billion to digitize the medical records of its 8.2 million members so that it could manage patient care more efficiently.[25] IBM makes extensive use of social software applications such as Lotus Connections to support its 1,796 online communities, having discovered that many of its employees depend on these tools to do their work.[26] In businesses such as public accounting and management consulting, where large numbers of professional staff need cutting-edge technical know-how, companies have developed systems that identify when it is time for certain employees to attend training programs to update their skills and know-how. Many companies have cataloged best-practice information on their intranets to promote faster transfer and implementation organizationwide.[27]

Well-conceived state-of-the-art operating systems not only enable better strategy execution but also strengthen organizational capabilities—sometimes enough to provide a competitive edge over rivals. For example, a company with a differentiation strategy based on superior quality has added capability if it has systems for training personnel in quality techniques, tracking product quality at each production step, and ensuring that all goods shipped meet quality standards. If the systems it employs are advanced systems that have not yet been adopted by rivals, the systems may provide the company with a competitive advantage as long as the costs of deploying the systems do not outweigh their benefits. Similarly, a company striving to be a low-cost provider is competitively stronger if it has an unrivaled benchmarking system that identifies opportunities to implement best practices and drive costs out of the business. Fast-growing companies get an important assist from having capabilities in place to recruit and train new employees in large numbers and from investing in infrastructure that gives them the capability to handle rapid growth as it occurs. It is nearly always better to put infrastructure and support systems in place before they are actually needed than to have to scramble to catch up to customer demand.

Instituting Adequate Information Systems, Performance Tracking, and Controls

Accurate and timely information about daily operations is essential if managers are to gauge how well the strategy execution process is proceeding. Information systems need to cover five broad areas: (1) customer data, (2) operations data, (3) employee data, (4) supplier/partner/collaborative ally data, and (5) financial performance data. All key strategic performance indicators must be tracked and reported in real time where possible. Long the norm, monthly profit-and-loss statements and monthly statistical summaries are fast being replaced with daily statistical updates and even up-to-the-minute performance monitoring, made possible by online technology. Most retail companies have automated online systems that generate daily sales reports for each store and maintain up-to-the-minute inventory and sales records on each item. Manufacturing plants typically generate daily production reports and track labor productivity on every shift. Many retailers and manufacturers have online data systems connecting them with their suppliers that monitor the status of inventories, track shipments and deliveries, and measure defect rates.

Real-time information systems permit company managers to stay on top of implementation initiatives and daily operations and to intervene if things seem to be drifting off course. Tracking key performance indicators, gathering information from operating personnel, quickly identifying and diagnosing problems, and taking corrective actions are all integral pieces of the process of managing strategy implementation and exercising adequate control over operations. A number of companies have recently begun creating "electronic scorecards" for senior managers that gather daily or weekly statistics from different databases about inventory, sales, costs, and sales trends; such information enables these managers to easily stay abreast of what's happening and make better on-the-spot decisions.[28] Telephone companies have elaborate information systems to measure signal quality, connection times, interrupts, wrong connections, billing errors, and other measures of reliability that affect customer service and satisfaction. British Petroleum (BP) has outfitted rail cars carrying hazardous materials with sensors and global-positioning systems (GPS) so that it can track the status, location, and other information about these shipments via satellite and relay the data to its corporate intranet. Companies that rely on empowered customer-contact personnel to act promptly and creatively in pleasing customers have installed online information systems that make essential customer data accessible to such personnel through a few keystrokes; this enables them to respond more effectively to customer inquiries and deliver personalized customer service.

Statistical information gives managers a feel for the numbers; briefings and meetings provide a feel for the latest developments and emerging issues; and personal contacts add a feel for the people dimension. All are good barometers.

> Having state-of-the-art operating systems, information systems, and real-time data is integral to superior strategy execution and operating excellence.

Managers must identify problem areas and deviations from plans before they can take action to get the organization back on course, by either improving the approaches to strategy execution or fine-tuning the strategy. Jeff Bezos, Amazon's CEO, is an ardent proponent of managing by the numbers. As he puts it, "Math-based decisions always trump opinion and judgment. The trouble with most corporations is that they make judgment-based decisions when data-based decisions could be made."[29]

Monitoring Employee Performance Information systems also provide managers with a means for monitoring the performance of empowered workers to see that they are acting within the specified limits.[30] Leaving empowered employees to their own devices in meeting performance standards without appropriate checks and balances can expose an organization to excessive risk.[31] Instances abound of employees' decisions or behavior having gone awry, sometimes costing a company huge sums or producing lawsuits aside from just generating embarrassing publicity.

Scrutinizing daily and weekly operating statistics is one of the important ways in which managers can monitor the results that flow from the actions of empowered subordinates without resorting to constant over-the-shoulder supervision; if the operating results flowing from the actions of empowered employees look good, then it is reasonable to assume that empowerment is working. But close monitoring of operating performance is only one of the control tools at management's disposal. Another valuable lever of control in companies that rely on empowered employees, especially in those that use self-managed work groups or other such teams, is peer-based control. Because peer evaluation is such a powerful control device, companies organized into teams can remove some layers of the management hierarchy and rely on strong peer pressure to keep team members operating between the white lines. This is especially true when a company has the information systems capability to monitor team performance daily or in real time.

TYING REWARDS AND INCENTIVES TO STRATEGY EXECUTION

It is essential that company personnel be enthusiastically committed to executing strategy successfully and achieving performance targets. Company managers typically use an assortment of motivational techniques and rewards to enlist organizationwide commitment to executing the strategic plan. Indeed, a properly designed reward structure is management's most powerful tool for mobilizing organizational commitment to successful strategy execution. But incentives and rewards do more than just strengthen the resolve of company personnel to succeed—they also focus their attention on the accomplishment of specific strategy execution objectives. Not only do they spur the efforts of individuals to achieve those aims, but they also help to coordinate the activities of individuals throughout the organization by aligning their personal motives with the goals of the organization. In this manner, reward systems serve as an indirect type of control mechanism that conserves on the more costly control mechanism of supervisory oversight.

LO 5

Appreciate how and why the use of well-designed incentives and rewards can be management's single most powerful tool for promoting adept strategy execution and operating excellence.

A properly designed reward structure is management's most powerful tool for mobilizing organizational commitment to successful strategy execution and aligning efforts throughout the organization with strategic priorities.

CORE CONCEPT

Financial rewards provide **high-powered incentives** when rewards are tied to specific outcome objectives.

To win employees' sustained, energetic commitment to the strategy execution process, management must be resourceful in designing and using motivational incentives—both monetary and nonmonetary. The more a manager understands what motivates subordinates and the more he or she relies on motivational incentives as a tool for achieving the targeted strategic and financial results, the greater will be employees' commitment to good day-in, day-out strategy execution and achievement of performance targets.[32]

Incentives and Motivational Practices That Facilitate Good Strategy Execution

Financial incentives generally head the list of motivating tools for gaining wholehearted employee commitment to good strategy execution and focusing attention on strategic priorities. They provide *high-powered* motivation for individuals to increase their efforts when rewards are tied to specific outcome objectives. A company's package of monetary rewards typically includes some combination of base-pay increases, performance bonuses, profit-sharing plans, stock awards, company contributions to employee 401(k) or retirement plans, and piecework incentives (in the case of production workers). But most successful companies and managers also make extensive use of nonmonetary incentives. Some of the most important nonmonetary approaches companies can use to enhance motivation are listed below:[33]

- *Provide attractive perks and fringe benefits.* The various options include full coverage of health insurance premiums, college tuition reimbursement, generous paid vacation time, on-site child care, on-site fitness centers, getaway opportunities at company-owned recreational facilities, personal concierge services, subsidized cafeterias and free lunches, casual dress every day, personal travel services, paid sabbaticals, maternity and paternity leaves, paid leaves to care for ill family members, telecommuting, compressed workweeks (four 10-hour days instead of five 8-hour days), flextime (variable work schedules that accommodate individual needs), college scholarships for children, and relocation services.

- *Give awards and other forms of public recognition to high performers, and celebrate the achievement of organizational goals.* Many companies hold award ceremonies to honor top-performing individuals, teams, and organizational units and to showcase company successes. This can help create healthy competition among units and teams within the company, but it can also create a positive esprit de corps among the organization as a whole. Other examples include special recognition at informal company gatherings or in the company newsletter, tangible tokens of appreciation for jobs well done, and frequent words of praise.

- *Rely on promotion from within whenever possible.* The practice of promoting from within helps bind workers to their employer, and employers to their workers, providing strong incentives for good performance. Moreover, promoting from within helps ensure that people in positions of responsibility have knowledge specific to the business, technology, and operations they are managing.

- *Invite and act on ideas and suggestions from employees.* Many companies find that their best ideas for nuts-and-bolts operating improvements come from the suggestions of employees. Moreover, research indicates that the moves of many companies to push decision making down the line and empower employees increases employees' motivation and satisfaction as well as their productivity. The use of self-managed teams has much the same effect.

• *Create a work atmosphere in which there is genuine caring and mutual respect among workers and between management and employees.* A "family" work environment where people are on a first-name basis and there is strong camaraderie promotes teamwork and cross-unit collaboration.

• *State the strategic vision in inspirational terms so that employees feel they are a part of something very worthwhile in a larger social sense.* There's strong motivating power associated with giving people a chance to be part of something exciting and personally satisfying. Jobs with noble purpose tend to inspire employees to give their all. As described in Chapter 9, this not only increases productivity but reduces turnover and lowers costs for staff recruitment and training as well.

• *Share information with employees about financial performance, strategy, operational measures, market conditions, and competitors' actions.* Broad disclosure and prompt communication send the message that managers trust their workers and regard them as valued partners in the enterprise. Keeping employees in the dark denies them information useful to performing their jobs, prevents them from being intellectually engaged, saps their motivation, and detracts from performance.

• *Maintain attractive office space and facilities.* A workplace environment that is attractive and comfortable usually has decidedly positive effects on employee morale and productivity. An appealing work environment is particularly important when workers are expected to spend long hours at work.

For specific examples of the motivational tactics employed by several prominent companies (many of which appear on *Fortune*'s list of the 100 best companies to work for in America), see Illustration Capsule 11.2.

Striking the Right Balance between Rewards and Punishment

Decisions on salary increases, incentive compensation, promotions, key assignments, and the ways and means of awarding praise and recognition are potent attention-getting, commitment-generating devices. Such decisions seldom escape the closest employee scrutiny, thus saying more about what is expected and who is considered to be doing a good job than virtually any other factor. While most approaches to motivation, compensation, and people management accentuate the positive, companies also combine positive rewards with the risk of punishment. At General Electric, McKinsey & Company, several global public accounting firms, and other companies that look for and expect top-notch individual performance, there's an "up-or-out" policy—managers and professionals whose performance is not good enough to warrant promotion are first denied bonuses and stock awards and eventually weeded out. A number of companies deliberately give employees heavy workloads and tight deadlines—personnel are pushed hard to achieve "stretch" objectives and are expected to put in long hours (nights and weekends if need be). At most companies, senior executives and key personnel in underperforming units are pressured to raise performance to acceptable levels and keep it there or risk being replaced.

What Companies Do to Motivate and Reward Employees

Companies have come up with an impressive variety of motivational and reward practices to help create a work environment that energizes employees and promotes better strategy execution. Here's a sampling of what companies are doing:

- Google has a sprawling 20-building headquarters complex known as the Googleplex where its several thousand employees have access to 19 cafes and 60 snack centers, unlimited ice cream, four gyms, heated swimming pools, ping-pong and pool tables, and community bicycles to go from building to building. Management built the Googleplex to be "a dream workplace" and a showcase for environmentally correct building design and construction.

- Lincoln Electric, widely known for its piecework pay scheme and incentive bonus plan, rewards individual productivity by paying workers for each nondefective piece produced. Workers have to correct quality problems on their own time—defects in products used by customers can be traced back to the worker who caused them. Lincoln's piecework plan motivates workers to pay attention to both quality and volume produced. In addition, the company sets aside a substantial portion of its profits above a specified base for worker bonuses. To determine bonus size, Lincoln Electric rates each worker on four equally important performance measures: (1) dependability, (2) quality, (3) output, and (4) ideas and cooperation. The higher a worker's merit rating, the higher the incentive bonus earned; the highest-rated workers in good profit years receive bonuses of as much as 110 percent of their piecework compensation.

- At JM Family Enterprises, a Toyota distributor in Florida, employees get attractive lease options on new Toyotas and enjoy on-site amenities such as a heated lap pool, a fitness center, a free nail salon, free prescriptions delivered by a "pharmacy concierge," and professionally made take-home dinners. Exceptionally high performers are flown to the Bahamas for cruises on the 172-foot company yacht.

- Wegmans, a family-owned grocer with 75 stores on the East Coast of the United States, provides employees with flexible schedules and benefits that include onsite fitness centers. The company's approach to managing people allows it to provide a very high level of customer service not found in other grocery chains. Employees ranging from cashiers to butchers to store managers are all treated equally and viewed as experts in their jobs. Employees receive 50 hours of formal training per year and are allowed to make decisions that they believe are appropriate for their jobs. The company's 2009 annual turnover rate is only 7 percent, which is less than one-half the 19 percent average turnover rate in the U.S. supermarket industry.

- Nordstrom, widely regarded for its superior in-house customer service experience, typically pays its retail salespeople an hourly wage higher than the prevailing rates paid by other department store chains plus a commission on each sale. Spurred by a culture that encourages salespeople to go all out to satisfy customers and to seek out and promote new fashion ideas, Nordstrom salespeople earn nearly 65 percent more than the average sales employee at competing stores. The typical Nordstrom salesperson earns nearly $38,900 per year, but top performers can earn salaries in the six figures.[34] Nordstrom's rules for employees are simple: "Rule #1: Use your good judgment in all situations. There will be no additional rules."

(Coninued)

- At W. L. Gore (the maker of GORE-TEX), employees get to choose what project/team they work on, and each team member's compensation is based on other team members' rankings of his or her contribution to the enterprise.
- At Ukrop's Super Markets, a family-owned chain, stores stay closed on Sunday; the company pays out 20 percent of pretax profits to employees in the form of quarterly bonuses; and

the company picks up the membership tab for employees if they visit their health club 30 times a quarter.
- At biotech leader Amgen, employees get 16 paid holidays, generous vacation time, tuition reimbursements up to $10,000, on-site massages, discounted car-wash services, and the convenience of shopping at on-site farmers' markets.

Sources: Fortune's lists of the 100 best companies to work for in America, 2002, 2004, 2005, 2008, 2009, and 2010; Jefferson Graham, "The Search Engine That Could," USA Today, August 26, 2003, p. B3; company Web sites (accessed June 2010).

As a general rule, it is unwise to take off the pressure for good individual and group performance or play down the adverse consequences of shortfalls in performance. There is no evidence that a no-pressure/no-adverse-consequences work environment leads to superior strategy execution or operating excellence. As the CEO of a major bank put it, "There's a deliberate policy here to create a level of anxiety. Winners usually play like they're one touchdown behind."[35] High-performing organizations nearly always have a cadre of ambitious people who relish the opportunity to climb the ladder of success, love a challenge, thrive in a performance-oriented environment, and find some competition and pressure useful to satisfy their own drives for personal recognition, accomplishment, and self-satisfaction.

However, if an organization's motivational approaches and reward structure induce too much stress, internal competitiveness, job insecurity, and fear of unpleasant consequences, the impact on workforce morale and strategy execution can be counterproductive. Evidence shows that managerial initiatives to improve strategy execution should incorporate more positive than negative motivational elements because when cooperation is positively enlisted and rewarded, rather than coerced by orders and threats (implicit or explicit), people tend to respond with more enthusiasm, dedication, creativity, and initiative.[36]

Linking Rewards to Strategically Relevant Performance Outcomes

To create a strategy-supportive system of rewards and incentives, a company must reward people for accomplishing results, not for just dutifully performing assigned tasks. To make the work environment results-oriented, managers need to focus jobholders' attention and energy on what to *achieve* as opposed to what to *do*. It is flawed management to tie incentives and rewards to satisfactory performance of duties and activities instead of desired business outcomes and company achievements.[37] In any job, performing assigned tasks is not equivalent to achieving intended outcomes. Diligently showing up for work and attending to one's job assignment does not, by itself, guarantee results. Employee productivity among employees at Best Buy's corporate headquarters rose by 35 percent after the company began to focus on the results of each employee's work rather than on employees' willingness to come to work early and stay late.

> Incentives must be based on accomplishing the right results, not on dutifully performing assigned tasks.

The key to creating a reward system that promotes good strategy execution is to make measures of good business performance and good strategy execution the *dominating basis* for designing incentives, evaluating individual and group efforts, and handing out rewards.

Ideally, performance targets should be set for every organizational unit, every manager, every team or work group, and perhaps every employee—targets that measure whether strategy execution is progressing satisfactorily. If the company's strategy is to be a low-cost provider, the incentive system must reward actions and achievements that result in lower costs. If the company has a differentiation strategy based on superior quality and service, the incentive system must reward such outcomes as Six Sigma defect rates, infrequent need for product repair, low numbers of customer complaints, speedy order processing and delivery, and high levels of customer satisfaction. If a company's growth is predicated on a strategy of new product innovation, incentives should be tied to factors such as the percentages of revenues and profits coming from newly introduced products.

Incentive compensation for top executives is typically tied to such financial measures as revenue and earnings growth, stock price performance, return on investment, and creditworthiness or to strategic measures such as market share growth. However, incentives for department heads, teams, and individual workers may be tied to performance outcomes more closely related to their strategic area of responsibility. In manufacturing, incentive compensation may be tied to unit manufacturing costs, on-time production and shipping, defect rates, the number and extent of work stoppages due to equipment breakdowns, and so on. In sales and marketing, there may be incentives for achieving dollar sales or unit volume targets, market share, sales penetration of each target customer group, the fate of newly introduced products, the frequency of customer complaints, the number of new accounts acquired, and customer satisfaction. Which performance measures to base incentive compensation on depends on the situation—the priority placed on various financial and strategic objectives, the requirements for strategic and competitive success, and what specific results are needed in different facets of the business to keep strategy execution on track.

Illustration Capsule 11.3 provides a vivid example of how one company has designed incentives linked directly to outcomes reflecting good execution.

Guidelines for Designing Effective Incentive Compensation Systems

As explained above, the first principle in designing an effective incentive compensation system is to tie rewards to performance outcomes directly linked to good strategy execution and targeted strategic and financial objectives. But for a company's reward system to truly motivate organization members, inspire their best efforts, and sustain high levels of productivity, it is equally important to observe the following additional guidelines in designing and administering the reward system:

- *Make the financial incentives a major, not minor, piece of the total compensation package.* Performance payoffs must be at least 10 to 12 percent of base salary to have much impact. Incentives that amount to 20 percent or more of total compensation are big attention-getters, likely to really drive individual or team efforts. Incentives amounting to less than 5 percent of total compensation have a comparatively weak motivational impact. Moreover, the payoff for high-performing individuals and teams must be meaningfully greater than the payoff for average performers, and the payoff for average performers meaningfully bigger than that for below-average performers.

- *Have incentives that extend to all managers and all workers, not just top management.* Lower-level managers and employees are just as likely as senior executives to be motivated by the possibility of lucrative rewards.

Nucor Corporation: Tying Incentives Directly to Strategy Execution

The strategy at Nucor Corporation, one of the three largest steel producers in the United States, is to be *the* low-cost producer of steel products. Because labor costs are a significant fraction of total cost in the steel business, successful implementation of Nucor's low-cost leadership strategy entails achieving lower labor costs per ton of steel than competitors' costs. Nucor management uses an incentive system to promote high worker productivity and drive labor costs per ton below rivals'. Each plant's workforce is organized into production teams (each assigned to perform particular functions), and weekly production targets are established for each team. Base-pay scales are set at levels comparable to wages for similar manufacturing jobs in the local areas where Nucor has plants, but workers can earn a 1 percent bonus for each 1 percent that their output exceeds target levels. If a production team exceeds its weekly production target by 10 percent, team members receive a 10 percent bonus in their next paycheck; if a team exceeds its quota by 20 percent, team members earn a 20 percent bonus. Bonuses, paid every two weeks, are based on the prior two weeks' actual production levels measured against the targets.

Nucor's piece-rate incentive plan has produced impressive results. The production teams put forth exceptional effort; it is not uncommon for most teams to beat their weekly production targets anywhere from 20 to 50 percent. When added to their base pay, the bonuses earned by Nucor workers make Nucor's work force among the highest-paid in the U.S. steel industry. From a management perspective, the incentive system has resulted

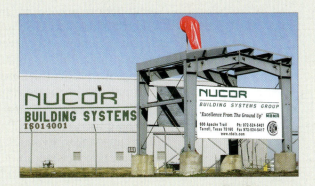

in Nucor having labor productivity levels 10 to 20 percent above the average of the unionized workforces at several of its largest rivals, which in turn has given Nucor a significant labor cost advantage over most rivals.

After years of record-setting profits, Nucor struggled in the economic downturn of 2008–2010, along with the manufacturers and builders who buy its steel. But while bonuses have dwindled, Nucor showed remarkable loyalty to its production workers, avoiding layoffs by having employees get ahead on maintenance, perform work formerly done by contractors, and search for cost savings. Morale at the company has remained high and Nucor's CEO Daniel DiMicco has received thank-you notes from grateful employees by the basketful. As industry growth resumes, Nucor will have a well-trained workforce still in place, more committed than ever to achieving the kind of productivity for which Nucor is justifiably famous. When the turnaround comes, DiMicco has good reason to expect Nucor to be "first out of the box."

Sources: Company Web site (accessed July 2010); N. Byrnes, "Pain, but No Layoffs at Nucor," *Bloomberg Businessweek,* March 26, 2009.

- *Administer the reward system with scrupulous objectivity and fairness.* If performance standards are set unrealistically high or if individual/group performance evaluations are not accurate and well documented, dissatisfaction with the system will overcome any positive benefits.
- *Ensure that the performance targets each individual or team is expected to achieve involve outcomes that the individual or team can personally affect.* The role of incentives is to enhance individual commitment and channel behavior in

beneficial directions. This role is not well served when the performance measures by which company personnel are judged are outside their arena of influence.

- *Keep the time between achieving the targeted performance outcome and the payment of the reward as short as possible.* Companies like Nucor Steel and Continental Airlines have discovered that weekly or monthly payments for good performance work much better than annual payments. Nucor pays weekly bonuses based on prior-week production levels, while Continental pays employees a bonus whenever actual on-time flight performance meets or beats the monthly on-time target. Annual bonus payouts work best for higher-level managers and for situations where the outcome target relates to overall company profitability or stock price performance.

- *Avoid rewarding effort rather than results.* While it is tempting to reward people who have tried hard yet fallen short of achieving performance targets because of circumstances beyond their control, it is ill advised. The problem with making exceptions for unknowable, uncontrollable, or unforeseeable circumstances is that once "good excuses" start to creep into justifying rewards for subpar results, the door is open for all kinds of reasons why actual performance has failed to match targeted performance. A "no excuses" standard is more even-handed, easier to administer, and more conducive to creating a results-oriented work climate.

> The unwavering standard for judging whether individuals, teams, and organizational units have done a good job must be whether they meet or beat performance targets that reflect good strategy execution.

Once an organization's incentive plan is designed, it must be communicated and explained. Everybody needs to understand how his or her incentive compensation is calculated and how individual/group performance targets contribute to organizational performance targets. The pressure to continuously improve strategy execution and achieve performance objectives should be unrelenting, with no loopholes for rewarding shortfalls in performance. People at all levels must be held accountable for carrying out their assigned parts of the strategic plan, and they must understand that their rewards are based on the caliber of results achieved. But with the pressure to perform should come meaningful rewards. Without an ample payoff, the system breaks down, and managers are left with the less workable options of issuing orders, trying to enforce compliance, and depending on the goodwill of employees.

KEY POINTS

1. Implementing and executing a new or different strategy calls for managers to identify the resource requirements of each new strategic initiative and then consider whether the current pattern of resource allocation and the budgets of the various subunits are suitable.

2. Company policies and procedures facilitate strategy execution when they are designed to fit the strategy and its objectives. Anytime a company alters its strategy, managers should review existing policies and operating procedures and replace those that are out of sync. Well conceived policies and procedures aid the task of strategy execution by (1) providing top-down guidance to company personnel regarding how certain things need to be done and what the boundaries are on independent actions and decisions, (2) enforcing

consistency in the performance of strategy-critical activities, thereby improving the quality of the strategy execution effort and aligning the actions of company personnel, however widely dispersed, and (3) promoting the creation of a work climate conducive to good strategy execution.

3. Competent strategy execution entails visible unyielding managerial commitment to best practices and continuous improvement. Benchmarking, best-practice adoption, business process reengineering, total quality management (TQM), and Six Sigma programs are important process management tools for promoting better strategy execution.

4. Company strategies can't be implemented or executed well without a number of support systems to carry on business operations. Real-time information systems and control systems further aid the cause of good strategy execution.

5. Strategy-supportive motivational practices and reward systems are powerful management tools for gaining employee commitment and focusing their attention on the strategy execution goals. The key to creating a reward system that promotes good strategy execution is to make measures of good business performance and good strategy execution the *dominating basis* for designing incentives, evaluating individual and group efforts, and handing out rewards. Positive motivational practices generally work better than negative ones, but there is a place for both. While financial rewards provide high-powered incentives, there's also place for nonmonetary incentives. For an incentive compensation system to work well, (1) the monetary payoff should be a major percentage of the compensation package, (2) the use of incentives should extend to all managers and workers, (3) the system should be administered with care and fairness, (4) each individual's performance targets should involve outcomes the person can personally affect, (5) rewards should promptly follow the determination of good performance, and (6) rewards should be given for results and not just effort.

ASSURANCE OF LEARNING EXERCISES

LO 3

1. Using your favorite search engine, do a search on the term *best practices*. Browse through the search results to identify at least five organizations that have gathered a set of best practices and are making the best-practice library they have assembled available to members.

LO 3

2. Read some of the recent Six Sigma articles posted at isixsigma.com. Prepare a one-page report to your instructor detailing how Six Sigma is being used in various companies and what benefits these companies are reaping from Six Sigma implementation.

LO 3

3. Review the profiles and applications of the latest Malcolm Baldrige National Quality Award recipients at www.baldrige.nist.gov. What are the standout features of the companies' approaches to managing operations? What do you

find impressive about the companies' policies and procedures, use of best practices, emphasis on continuous improvement, and use of rewards and incentives?

LO 5

4. Consult the issue of *Fortune* containing the latest annual "100 Best Companies to Work For" (usually a late-January or early-February issue), or else go to www.fortune.com to access the list, and identify at least five compensation incentives and work practices that these companies use to enhance employee motivation and reward them for good strategic and financial performance. You should identify compensation methods and work practices that are different from those cited in Illustration Capsule 11.2.

LO 5

5. Using Google Scholar or your university library's access to online business periodicals, search for the term *incentive compensation* and prepare a 1- to 2-page report for your instructor discussing the successful (or unsuccessful) use of incentive compensation plans by various companies. Based on the research you found, what factors seem to determine whether incentive compensation plans succeed or fail?

EXERCISES FOR SIMULATION PARTICIPANTS

LO 1

1. Have you and your co-managers allocated ample resources to strategy-critical areas? If so, explain how these investments have contributed to good strategy execution and improved company performance.

LO 3

2. Is benchmarking data available in the simulation exercise in which you are participating? If so, do you and your co-managers regularly study the benchmarking data to see how well your company is doing? Do you consider the benchmarking information provided to be valuable? Why or why not? Cite three recent instances in which your examination of the benchmarking statistics has caused you and your co-managers to take corrective actions to boost company performance.

LO 2, LO 3, LO 4

3. What actions, if any, is your company taking to pursue continuous improvement in how it performs certain value chain activities?

LO 5

4. Does your company have opportunities to use incentive compensation techniques? If so, explain your company's approach to incentive compensation. Is there any hard evidence you can cite that indicates your company's use of incentive compensation techniques has worked? For example, have your company's compensation incentives actually increased productivity? Can you cite

evidence indicating that the productivity gains have resulted in lower labor costs? If the productivity gains have *not* translated into lower labor costs, is it fair to say that your company's use of incentive compensation is a failure?

LO 2, LO 3, LO 4

5. Are you and your co-managers consciously trying to achieve "operating excellence"? What are the indicators of operating excellence at your company? Based on these indicators, how well does your company measure up?

LO 3

6. What hard evidence can you cite that indicates your company's management team is doing a *better* or *worse* job of achieving operating excellence and executing your strategy than are the management teams at rival companies?

ENDNOTES

[1] For a discussion of the value of benchmarking in implementing and executing strategy, see Christopher E. Bogan and Michael J. English, *Benchmarking for Best Practices: Winning through Innovative Adaptation* (New York: McGraw-Hill, 1994) chaps. 2 and 6; Mustafa Ungan, "Factors Affecting the Adoption of Manufacturing Best Practices," *Benchmarking: An International Journal* 11, no. 5 (2004), pp. 504–20; Paul Hyland and Ron Beckett, "Learning to Compete: The Value of Internal Benchmarking," *Benchmarking: An International Journal* 9, no. 3 (2002), pp. 293–304; Yoshinobu Ohinata, "Benchmarking: The Japanese Experience," *Long-Range Planning* 27, no. 4 (August 1994), pp. 48–53.

[2] www.businessdictionary.com/definition/best-practice.html (accessed December 2, 2009).

[3] M. Hammer and J. Champy, *Reengineering the Corporation: A Manifesto for Business Revolution* (New York: Harper Collins Publishers, 1993), pp. 26–27.

[4] Information on the greeting card industry is posted at www.answers.com (accessed July 8, 2009), and "Reengineering: Beyond the Buzzword," *BusinessWeek,* May 24, 1993, www.businessweek.com (accessed July 8, 2009).

[5] Gene Hall, Jim Rosenthal, and Judy Wade, "How to Make Reengineering Really Work," *Harvard Business Review* 71, no. 6 (November–December 1993), pp. 119–31.

[6] For more information on business process reengineering and how well it has worked in various companies, see James Brian Quinn, *Intelligent Enterprise* (New York: Free Press, 1992), p. 162; Ann Majchrzak and Qianwei Wang, "Breaking the Functional Mind-Set in Process Organizations," *Harvard Business Review* 74, no 5 (September–October 1996), pp. 93–99; Stephen L. Walston, Lawton. R. Burns, and John R. Kimberly, "Does Reengineering Really Work? An Examination of the Context and Outcomes of Hospital Reengineering Initiatives," *Health Services Research* 34, no. 6 (February 2000), pp. 1363–88; Allessio Ascari, Melinda Rock, and Soumitra Dutta, "Reengineering and Organizational Change: Lessons from a Comparative Analysis of Company Experiences," *European Management Journal* 13, no. 1 (March 1995), pp. 1–13. For a review of why some company personnel embrace process reengineering and some don't, see Ronald J. Burke, "Process Reengineering: Who Embraces It and Why?" *TQM Magazine* 16, no. 2 (2004), pp. 114–19.

[7] For some of the seminal discussions of what TQM is and how it works, written by ardent enthusiasts of the technique, see M. Walton, *The Deming Management Method* (New York: Pedigree, 1986); J. Juran, *Juran on Quality by Design* (New York: Free Press, 1992); Philip Crosby, *Quality Is Free: The Act of Making Quality Certain* (New York: McGraw-Hill, 1979); S. George, *The Baldrige Quality System* (New York: Wiley, 1992). For a critique of TQM, see Mark J. Zbaracki, "The Rhetoric and Reality of Total Quality Management," *Administrative Science Quarterly* 43, no 3 (September 1998), pp. 602–36.

[8] For a discussion of the shift in work environment and culture that TQM entails, see Robert T. Amsden, Thomas W. Ferratt, and Davida M. Amsden, "TQM: Core Paradigm Changes," *Business Horizons* 39, no. 6 (November–December 1996), pp. 6–14.

[9] For easy-to-understand overviews of what Six Sigma is all about, see Peter S. Pande and Larry Holpp, *What Is Six Sigma?* (New York: McGraw-Hill, 2002); Jiju Antony, "Some Pros and Cons of Six Sigma: An Academic Perspective," *TQM Magazine* 16, no. 4 (2004), pp. 303–6; Peter S. Pande, Robert P. Neuman, and Roland R. Cavanagh, *The Six Sigma Way: How GE, Motorola and Other Top Companies Are Honing Their Performance* (New York: McGraw-Hill, 2000); Joseph Gordon and M. Joseph Gordon, Jr., *Six Sigma Quality for Business and Manufacture* (New York: Elsevier, 2002). For how Six Sigma can be used in smaller companies, see Godecke Wessel and Peter Burcher, "Six Sigma for Small and Medium-Sized Enterprises," *TQM Magazine* 16, no. 4 (2004), pp. 264–72.

[10] Based on information posted at www.isixsigma.com (accessed November 4, 2002).

[11] Kennedy Smith, "Six Sigma for the Service Sector," *Quality Digest Magazine,* May 2003, www.qualitydigest.com (accessed September 28, 2003).

[12] Del Jones, "Taking the Six Sigma Approach," *USA Today,* October 31, 2002, p. 5B.

[13] Pande, Neuman, and Cavanagh, *The Six Sigma Way,* pp. 5–6.

[14] Smith, "Six Sigma for the Service Sector."

[15] Jones, "Taking the Six Sigma Approach," p. 5B.

[16] See, for example, "A Dark Art No More," *Economist* 385, no. 8550 (October 13, 2007), p. 10; Brian Hindo, "At 3M, a Struggle between Efficiency and Creativity," *BusinessWeek,* June 11, 2007, pp. 8–16.

[17] As quoted in "A Dark Art No More."

[18] Hindo, "At 3M, a Struggle between Efficiency and Creativity."

[19] For a discussion of approaches to pursuing radical or disruptive innovations while also seeking incremental gains in efficiency, see Charles A. O'Reilly and Michael L. Tushman, "The Ambidextrous Organization," *Harvard Business Review* 82, no. 4 (April 2004), pp. 74–81.

[20] Terry Nels Lee, Stanley E. Fawcett, and Jason Briscoe, "Benchmarking the Challenge to Quality Program Implementation," *Benchmarking: An International Journal* 9, no. 4 (2002), pp. 374–87.

[21] For a recent study documenting the imperatives of establishing a supportive culture, see Milan Ambrož, "Total Quality System as a Product of the Empowered Corporate Culture," *TQM Magazine* 16, no. 2 (2004), pp. 93–104. Research confirming the factors that are important in making TQM programs successful in both Europe and the United States is

presented in Nick A. Dayton, "The Demise of Total Quality Management," *TQM Magazine* 15, no. 6 (2003), pp. 391–96.

[22] Judy D. Olian and Sara L. Rynes, "Making Total Quality Work: Aligning Organizational Processes, Performance Measures, and Stakeholders," *Human Resource Management* 30, no. 3 (Fall 1991), pp. 310–11; Paul S. Goodman and Eric D. Darr, "Exchanging Best Practices Information through Computer-Aided Systems," *Academy of Management Executive* 10, no. 2 (May 1996), p. 7.

[23] Thomas C. Powell, "Total Quality Management as Competitive Advantage," *Strategic Management Journal* 16 (1995), pp. 15–37. See also Richard M. Hodgetts, "Quality Lessons from America's Baldrige Winners," *Business Horizons* 37, no. 4 (July–August 1994), pp. 74–79; Richard Reed, David J. Lemak, and Joseph C. Montgomery, "Beyond Process: TQM Content and Firm Performance," *Academy of Management Review* 21, no. 1 (January 1996), pp. 173–202.

[24] Based on information at www.otiselevator .com (accessed July 9, 2009).

[25] "The Web Smart 50," *BusinessWeek,* November 21, 2005, pp. 87–88.

[26] Aishah Mustapha, "Net Value: Social Software a New Way to Work," *The Edge Malaysia (Weekly),* February 16, 2009.

[27] Such systems speed organizational learning by providing fast, efficient communication, creating an organizational memory for collecting and retaining best-practice information, and permitting people all across the organization to exchange information and updated solutions. See Goodman and Darr, "Exchanging Best Practices Information through Computer-Aided Systems," pp. 7–17.

[28] "The Web Smart 50," pp. 85–90.

[29] Fred Vogelstein, "Winning the Amazon Way," *Fortune* 147, no. 10 (May 26, 2003), pp. 60–69.

[30] For a discussion of the need for putting appropriate boundaries on the actions of empowered employees and possible control and monitoring systems that can be used, see Robert Simons, "Control in an Age of Empowerment," *Harvard Business Review* 73 (March–April 1995), pp. 80–88.

[31] Ibid. Also see David C. Band and Gerald Scanlan, "Strategic Control through Core Competencies," *Long Range Planning* 28, no. 2 (April 1995), pp. 102–14.

[32] The importance of motivating and empowering workers so as to create a working environment that is highly conducive to good strategy execution is discussed in Stanley E. Fawcett, Gary K. Rhoads, and Phillip Burnah, "People as the Bridge to Competitiveness: Benchmarking the 'ABCs' of an Empowered Workforce," *Benchmarking: An International Journal* 11 no. 4 (2004), pp. 346–60.

[33] Jeffrey Pfeffer and John F. Veiga, "Putting People First for Organizational Success," *Academy of Management Executive* 13, no. 2 (May 1999), pp. 37–45; Linda K. Stroh and Paula M. Caliguiri, "Increasing Global Competitiveness through Effective People Management," *Journal of World Business* 33, no. 1 (Spring 1998), pp. 1–16; articles in *Fortune* on the 100 best companies to work for (various issues).

[34] Jenni Mintz, "Nordstrom Opening in Three Weeks: Company Plans 'Tailgate Party for Women' and Other Events", *Ventura County Star* (California), *McClatchy-Tribune Regional News,* August 12, 2008.

[35] As quoted in John P. Kotter and James L. Heskett, *Corporate Culture and Performance* (New York: Free Press, 1992), p. 91.

[36] Clayton M. Christensen, Matt Marx, and Howard Stevenson, "The Tools of Cooperation and Change," *Harvard Business Review* 84, no. 10 (October 2006), pp. 73–80.

[37] See Steven Kerr, "On the Folly of Rewarding A While Hoping for B," *Academy of Management Executive* 9, no. 1 (February 1995), pp. 7–14; S. Kerr and E. Davies, "Risky Business: The New Pay Game," *Fortune* 134, no. 2 (July 22, 1996) pp. 94–96; and Doran Twer, "Linking Pay to Business Objectives," *Journal of Business Strategy* 15, no. 4 (July–August 1994), pp. 15–18.

CHAPTER 12

CORPORATE CULTURE AND LEADERSHIP

Keys to Good Strategy Execution

> The biggest levers you've got to change a company are strategy, structure, and culture. If I could pick two, I'd pick strategy and culture.
>
> **—Wayne Leonard**
> *Chairman and CEO, Entergy Corporation*

> Success goes to those with a corporate culture that assures the ability to anticipate and meet customer demand.
>
> **—Tadashi Okamura**
> *Former Chairman and CEO of Toshiba Corporation*

> The soft stuff is always harder than the hard stuff.
>
> **—Roger Enrico**
> *Former CEO of PepsiCo*

LEARNING OBJECTIVES

LO 1. Be able to identify the key features of a company's corporate culture and appreciate the role of a company's core values and ethical standards in building corporate culture.

LO 2. Gain an understanding of how and why a company's culture can aid the drive for proficient strategy execution and operating excellence.

LO 3. Learn the kinds of actions management can take to change a problem corporate culture.

LO 4. Understand what constitutes effective managerial leadership in achieving superior strategy execution.

In the previous two chapters, we examined six of the managerial tasks that drive good strategy execution: building a capable organization, marshaling the needed resources and steering them to strategy-critical operating units, establishing appropriate policies and procedures, driving continuous improvement in value chain activities, creating the necessary operating systems, and providing the incentives needed to ensure employee commitment to the strategy execution process. In this chapter, we explore the two remaining managerial tasks that contribute to good strategy execution: creating a strategy-supportive corporate culture and exerting the internal leadership needed to drive the implementation of strategic initiatives forward and achieve higher plateaus of operating excellence.

INSTILLING A CORPORATE CULTURE THAT PROMOTES GOOD STRATEGY EXECUTION

Every company has its own unique culture. The character of a company's culture or work climate is a product of the core values and business principles that executives espouse, the standards of what is ethically acceptable and what is not, the work practices and norms of behavior that define "how we do things around here," the approach to people management and style of operating, the "chemistry" and the "personality" that permeates the work environment, and the stories that get told over and over to illustrate and reinforce the company's values, business practices, and traditions. The meshing together of shared values, beliefs, business principles, and traditions into a style of operating, behavioral norms, ingrained attitudes, and work atmosphere defines a company's **corporate culture.**[1] A company's culture is important because it influences the organization's actions and approaches to conducting business—in a very real sense, the culture is the company's automatic, self-replicating "operating system"—it can be thought of as the organizational DNA.[2] As we learned in Chapter 4, a superior corporate culture can also be a source of sustainable competitive advantage under some circumstances.

Corporate cultures vary widely. For instance, the bedrock of Walmart's culture is dedication to zealous pursuit of low costs and frugal operating practices, a strong work ethic, ritualistic headquarters meetings to exchange ideas and review problems, and company executives' commitment to visiting stores, listening to customers, and soliciting suggestions from employees. General Electric's culture is founded on a hard-driving, results-oriented atmosphere; extensive cross-business sharing of ideas, best practices, and learning; reliance on "workout sessions" to identify, debate, and resolve burning issues; a commitment to Six Sigma quality; and a globalized approach to operations. At Nordstrom, the corporate culture is centered on delivering exceptional service to customers—the company's motto is "Respond to unreasonable customer requests," and each out-of-the-ordinary request is seen as an opportunity for a "heroic" act by an employee that can further the company's reputation for unparalleled customer service. Nordstrom makes a point of promoting employees noted for their heroic acts and dedication to outstanding service; the company motivates its salespeople with a commission-based compensation system that enables Nordstrom's best salespeople to earn more than double what other department stores pay. Illustration Capsule 12.1 relates how Google and Albert-Culver describe their corporate cultures.

> **CORE CONCEPT**
>
> **Corporate culture** refers to the character of a company's internal work climate—as shaped by a system of *shared* values, beliefs, ethical standards, and traditions that define behavioral norms, ingrained attitudes, accepted work practices, and styles of operating.

Identifying the Key Features of a Company's Corporate Culture

> **LO 1**
>
> Be able to identify the key features of a company's corporate culture and appreciate the role of a company's core values and ethical standards in building corporate culture.

A company's corporate culture is mirrored in the character or "personality" of its work environment—the factors that underlie how the company tries to conduct its business and the behaviors that are held in high esteem. Some of these factors are readily apparent, and others operate quite subtly. The chief things to look for include the following:

- The values, business principles, and ethical standards that management preaches and *practices*—these are the key to a company's culture, but actions speak much louder than words here.

- The company's approach to people management and the official policies, procedures, and operating practices that provide guidelines for the behavior of company personnel.

- The atmosphere and spirit that pervades the work climate. Is the workplace vibrant and fun? Methodical and all business? Tense and harried? Highly competitive and politicized? Are people excited about their work and emotionally connected to the company's business, or are they just there to draw a paycheck? Is there an emphasis on empowered worker creativity, or do people have little discretion in how jobs are done?

- The way managers and employees interact and relate to one another—the reliance on teamwork and open communication, the extent to which there is good camaraderie, whether people are called by their first names, whether co-workers spend little or lots of time together outside the workplace, and what the dress codes are (the accepted styles of attire and whether there are casual days).

- The strength of peer pressure to do things in particular ways and conform to expected norms—what actions and behaviors are encouraged on a peer-to-peer basis?

Founded in 1998 by Larry Page and Sergey Brin, two Ph.D. students in computer science at Stanford University, Google has become world-renowned for its search engine technology. Google.com was the most frequently visited Internet site in 2009, attracting over 844 million unique visitors monthly from around the world. Google has some unique ways of operating, and its culture is also rather quirky. The company describes its culture as follows:

Though growing rapidly, Google still maintains a small company feel. At lunchtime, almost everyone eats in the office café, sitting at whatever table has an opening and enjoying conversations with Googlers from different teams. Our commitment to innovation depends on everyone being comfortable sharing ideas and opinions. Every employee is a hands-on contributor, and everyone wears several hats. Because we believe that each Googler is an equally important part of our success, no one hesitates to pose questions directly to Larry or Sergey in our weekly all-hands ("TGIF") meetings—or spike a volleyball across the net at a corporate officer.

We are aggressively inclusive in our hiring, and we favor ability over experience. We have offices around the world and dozens of languages are spoken by Google staffers, from Turkish to Telugu. The result is a team that reflects the global audience Google serves. When not at work, Googlers pursue interests from cross-country cycling to wine tasting, from flying to frisbee.

As we continue to grow, we are always looking for those who share a commitment to creating search perfection and having a great time doing it.

Our corporate headquarters, fondly nicknamed the Googleplex, is located in Mountain View, California. Today it's one of our many offices around the globe. While our offices are not identical, they tend to share some essential elements. Here are a few things you might see in a Google workspace:

- *Local expressions of each location, from a mural in Buenos Aires to ski gondolas in Zurich, showcasing each office's region and personality.*
- *Bicycles or scooters for efficient travel between meetings; dogs; lava lamps; massage chairs; large inflatable balls.*

- *Googlers sharing cubes, yurts and huddle rooms—and very few solo offices.*
- *Laptops everywhere—standard issue for mobile coding, email on the go and note-taking.*
- *Foosball, pool tables, volleyball courts, assorted video games, pianos, ping pong tables, and gyms that offer yoga and dance classes.*
- *Grassroots employee groups for all interests, like meditation, film, wine tasting and salsa dancing.*
- *Healthy lunches and dinners for all staff at a variety of cafés.*
- *Break rooms packed with a variety of snacks and drinks to keep Googlers going.*

The Alberto-Culver Company, with fiscal 2009 revenues of more than $1.4 billion, is the producer and marketer of Alberto VO5, TRESemmé, Motions, Soft & Beautiful, Just for Me, and Nexxus hair care products; St. Ives skin care products; and such brands as Molly McButter, Mrs. Dash, Sugar Twin, and Static Guard. Alberto-Culver brands are sold in more than 120 countries.

At the careers section of its Web site, the company described its culture in the following words:

Building careers is as important to us as building brands. We believe that passionate people create powerful growth. We believe in a workplace built on values and believe our best people display those same values in their families and their communities. We believe in recognizing and rewarding accomplishment and celebrating our victories.

We believe the best ideas work their way—quickly—up an organization, not down. We believe that we should take advantage of every ounce of your talent on teams and cross-functional activities, not just assign you to a box.

We believe in open communication. We believe that you can improve what you measure, so we survey and spot check all the time. For that same reason, everyone has specific goals so that their expectations are in line with their managers' and the company's.

We believe that victory is a team accomplishment. We believe in personal development. We believe if you talk with us you will catch our enthusiasm and want to be a part of the Alberto-Culver team.

Sources: Information posted at www.google.com and www.alberto.com (accessed June 30, 2010); S. McClellan, "Alberto Culver Launches Global Search: The Client's Annual U.S. Ad Spending Alone Touches $100 Mil.," *Adweek,* January 29, 2010, www.adweek.com/aw/content_display/news/account-activity/e3i68e64a3cf2727350dd0013083626e8ae.

- The actions and behaviors that are explicitly encouraged and rewarded by management in the form of compensation and promotion.
- The company's revered traditions and oft-repeated stories about "heroic acts" and "how we do things around here."
- The manner in which the company deals with external stakeholders (particularly vendors and local communities where it has operations)—whether it treats suppliers as business partners or prefers hard-nosed, arm's-length business arrangements, and the strength and genuineness of the commitment to corporate citizenship and environmental sustainability.

The values, beliefs, and practices that undergird a company's culture can come from anywhere in the organizational hierarchy, most often representing the business philosophy and managerial style of influential executives but also resulting from exemplary actions on the part of company personnel and consensus agreement about appropriate norms of behavior.[3] Typically, key elements of the culture originate with a founder or certain strong leaders who articulated them as a set of business principles, company policies, operating approaches, and ways of dealing with employees, customers, vendors, shareholders, and local communities where the company has operations. Over time, these cultural underpinnings take root, become embedded in how the company conducts its business, come to be accepted by company managers and employees alike, and then persist as new employees are encouraged to embrace the company values and adopt the implied attitudes, behaviors, and work practices.

The Role of Core Values and Ethics

The foundation of a company's corporate culture nearly always resides in its dedication to certain core values and the bar it sets for ethical behavior. The culture-shaping significance of core values and ethical behaviors accounts for one reason why so many companies have developed a formal values statement and a code of ethics. Many executives want the work climate at their companies to mirror certain values and ethical standards, partly because they are personally committed to these values and ethical standards but also because they are convinced that adherence to such values and ethical principles will promote better strategy execution, make the company a better performer, and improve its image.[4] And, not incidentally, strongly ingrained values and ethical standards reduce the likelihood of lapses in ethical and socially approved behavior that mar a company's reputation and put its financial performance and market standing at risk, as discussed in Chapter 9.

> A company's culture is grounded in and shaped by its core values and ethical standards.

As depicted in Figure 12.1, a company's stated core values and ethical principles have two roles in the culture-building process. First, a company that works hard at putting its stated core values and ethical principles into practice fosters a work climate in which company personnel share strongly held convictions about how the company's business is to be conducted. Second, the stated values and ethical principles provide company personnel with guidance about the manner in which they are to do their jobs—which behaviors and ways of doing things are approved (and expected) and which are out-of-bounds. These values-based and ethics-based cultural norms serve as yardsticks for gauging the appropriateness of particular actions, decisions, and behaviors, thus helping steer company personnel toward both doing things right and doing the right thing.

Figure 12.1 **The Two Culture-Building Roles of a Company's Core Values and Ethical Standards**

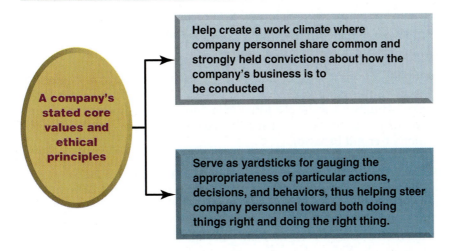

A company's stated core values and ethical principles

Help create a work climate where company personnel share common and strongly held convictions about how the company's business is to be conducted

Serve as yardsticks for gauging the appropriateness of particular actions, decisions, and behaviors, thus helping steer company personnel toward both doing things right and doing the right thing.

Transforming Core Values and Ethical Standards into Cultural Norms   Once values and ethical standards have been formally adopted, they must be institutionalized in the company's policies and practices and embedded in the conduct of company personnel. This can be done in a number of different ways.[5] Tradition-steeped companies with a rich folklore rely heavily on word-of-mouth indoctrination and the power of tradition to instill values and enforce ethical conduct. But most companies employ a variety of techniques, drawing on some or all of the following:

> A company's values statement and code of ethics communicate expectations of how employees should conduct themselves in the workplace.

1. Giving explicit attention to values and ethics in recruiting and hiring to screen out applicants who do not exhibit compatible character traits.

2. Incorporating the statement of values and the code of ethics into orientation programs for new employees and training courses for managers and employees.

3. Having senior executives frequently reiterate the importance and role of company values and ethical principles at company events and in internal communications to employees.

4. Using values statements and codes of ethical conduct as benchmarks for judging the appropriateness of company policies and operating practices.

5. Making the display of core values and ethical principles a big factor in evaluating each person's job performance—there's no better way to win the attention and commitment of company personnel than by using the degree to which individuals observe core values and ethical standards as a basis for compensation increases and promotion.

6. Making sure that managers, from the CEO down to frontline supervisors, are diligent in stressing the importance of ethical conduct and observance of core values. Line managers at all levels must give serious and continuous attention to the task of explaining how the values and ethical code apply in their areas.

7. Encouraging everyone to use his or her influence in helping enforce observance of core values and ethical standards—strong peer pressure to exhibit core values and ethical standards is a deterrent to wayward behavior.

8. Periodically having ceremonial occasions to recognize individuals and groups who display the company values and ethical principles.

9. Instituting ethics enforcement procedures.

To deeply ingrain the stated core values and high ethical standards, companies must turn them into *strictly enforced cultural norms.* They must put a stake in the ground, making it unequivocally clear that living up to the company's values and ethical standards has to be "a way of life" at the company and that there will be little toleration of errant behavior.

The Role of Stories

Frequently, a significant part of a company's culture is captured in the stories that get told over and over again to illustrate to newcomers the importance of certain values and the depth of commitment that various company personnel have displayed. One of the folktales at FedEx, world renowned for the reliability of its next-day package delivery guarantee, is about a deliveryman who had been given the wrong key to a FedEx drop box. Rather than leave the packages in the drop box until the next day when the right key was available, the deliveryman unbolted the drop box from its base, loaded it into the truck, and took it back to the station. There, the box was pried open and the contents removed and sped on their way to their destination the next day. Nordstrom keeps a scrapbook commemorating the heroic acts of its employees and uses it as a regular reminder of the above-and-beyond-the-call-of-duty behaviors that employees are encouraged to display. When a customer was unable to find a shoe she was looking for at Nordstrom, a salesman found the shoe at a competing store and had it shipped to her, at Nordstrom's expense.[6] At Frito-Lay, there are dozens of stories about truck drivers who went to extraordinary lengths in overcoming adverse weather conditions in order to make scheduled deliveries to retail customers and keep store shelves stocked with Frito-Lay products. At Microsoft, there are stories of the long hours programmers put in, the emotional peaks and valleys in encountering and overcoming coding problems, the exhilaration of completing a complex program on schedule, the satisfaction of working on cutting-edge projects, the rewards of being part of a team responsible for a popular new software program, and the tradition of competing aggressively. Such stories serve the valuable purpose of illustrating the kinds of behavior the company reveres and inspiring company personnel to perform similarly. Moreover, each retelling of a legendary story puts a bit more peer pressure on company personnel to display core values and do their part in keeping the company's traditions alive.

Perpetuating the Culture

Once established, company cultures are perpetuated in six important ways: (1) by screening and selecting new employees that will mesh well with the culture, (2) by systematic indoctrination of new members in the culture's fundamentals, (3) by the efforts of senior managers to reiterate core values in daily conversations and pronouncements, (4) by the telling and retelling of company legends, (5) by regular ceremonies honoring employees who display desired cultural behaviors, and (6) by visibly rewarding those who display cultural norms and penalizing those who don't.[7] *The more new employees a company is hiring, the more important it becomes to screen job applicants every bit as much for how well their values, beliefs, and personalities match up with the culture as for their technical skills and experience.* For example, a company that stresses operating with integrity and fairness has to hire people who themselves have integrity and place a high value on fair play. A company whose culture revolves around creativity, product innovation, and leading change has to screen new hires for their ability to think outside the box, generate new ideas, and thrive in a climate of rapid change and ambiguity. Southwest Airlines—whose two core values, "LUV" and fun, permeate the work environment and whose objective is to ensure that passengers have a positive and enjoyable flying experience—goes to considerable lengths to hire flight attendants and gate personnel who are witty, cheery, and outgoing and who display "whistle while you work" attitudes. Fast-growing companies risk creating a culture by chance rather than by design if they rush to hire employees mainly for their talents and credentials and neglect to screen out candidates whose values, philosophies, and personalities aren't a good fit with the organizational character, vision, and strategy being articulated by the company's senior executives.

As a rule, companies are careful to hire people who they believe will fit in and embrace the prevailing culture. And, usually, job seekers lean toward accepting jobs at companies where they feel comfortable with the atmosphere and the people they will be working with. Employees who don't fit in well at a company tend to leave quickly, while employees who thrive and are pleased with the work environment stay on, eventually moving up the ranks to positions of greater responsibility. The longer people stay at an organization, the more that they come to embrace and mirror the corporate culture—their values and beliefs tend to be molded by mentors, co-workers, company training programs, and the reward structure. Normally, employees who have worked at a company for a long time play a major role in indoctrinating new employees into the culture.

Forces That Cause a Company's Culture to Evolve   However, cultures aren't static—just like strategy and organization structure, they evolve. New challenges in the marketplace, revolutionary technologies, and shifting internal conditions—especially eroding business prospects, an internal crisis, or top executive turnover—tend to breed new ways of doing things and, in turn, drive cultural evolution. An incoming CEO who decides to shake up the existing business and take it in new directions often triggers a cultural shift, perhaps one of major proportions. Likewise, diversification into new businesses, expansion into foreign countries, rapid growth that brings an influx of new employees, and merger with or acquisition of another company can all precipitate significant cultural change.

Company Cultures Can Be Strongly or Weakly Embedded

Company cultures vary widely in strength and influence. Some are strongly embedded and have a big influence on a company's operating practices and the behavior of company personnel. Others are weakly ingrained and have little effect on behaviors and how company activities are conducted.

Strong-Culture Companies   The hallmark of a **strong-culture company** is the dominating presence of certain deeply rooted values, behavioral norms, and operating approaches that are widely shared and "regulate" the conduct of a company's business and the climate of its workplace.[8] Strong cultures emerge over a period of years (sometimes decades) and are never an overnight phenomenon. In strong-culture companies, senior managers make a point of reiterating the company's principles and values to organization members and explaining how they relate to its business environment. But, more importantly, the managers make a conscious effort to display these principles in their own actions and behavior—they walk the talk and *insist* that *company values and business principles be reflected in the decisions and actions taken by all company personnel.* An unequivocal expectation that company personnel will act and behave in accordance with the adopted values and ways of doing business leads to two important outcomes: (1) Over time, the values come to be widely shared by rank-and-file employees—people who dislike the culture tend to leave—and (2) individuals encounter strong peer pressure from co-workers to observe the culturally approved norms and behaviors. Hence, a strongly implanted corporate culture ends up having a powerful influence on behavior because so many company personnel are accepting of cultural traditions and because this acceptance is reinforced by both management expectations and co-worker peer pressure to conform to cultural norms.

Two factors contribute to the development of strong cultures: (1) a founder or strong leader who established core values, principles, and practices that are viewed as having contributed to the success of the company, and (2) a sincere, long-standing company commitment to operating the business according to these established traditions and values, thereby creating an internal environment that supports decision making based on cultural norms. Continuity of leadership, low workforce turnover, geographic concentration, and considerable organizational success all contribute to the emergence and sustainability of a strong culture.[9]

In strong-culture companies, values and behavioral norms are so ingrained that they can endure leadership changes at the top—although their strength can erode over time if new CEOs cease to nurture them or move aggressively to institute cultural adjustments. The cultural norms in a strong-culture company typically do not change much as strategy evolves, either because the culture constrains the choice of new strategies or because the dominant traits of the culture are somewhat strategy-neutral and compatible with evolving versions of the company's strategy.

Weak-Culture Companies   In direct contrast to strong-culture companies, weak-culture companies lack values and principles that are consistently preached or widely shared (sometimes because the company has had a series of CEOs with differing values and differing views about how the company's business ought to be conducted). As a consequence, few widely revered traditions and few culture-induced norms are evident in employee behavior or operating practices. Because top executives at a weak-culture company don't repeatedly espouse any particular business philosophy or exhibit long-standing commitment to particular values or behavioral norms, individuals encounter little pressure to do things in particular ways. A weak company culture breeds no strong employee allegiance to what the company stands for or to operating the business in well-defined ways. While individual employees may well have some bonds of identification with and loyalty toward their department, their colleagues, their union, or their immediate boss, there's neither passion about the company nor emotional commitment to what it is trying to accomplish—a condition that often results in many employees viewing their company as just a place to work and their job as just a way to make a living.

As a consequence, *weak cultures provide little or no assistance in executing strategy* because there are no traditions, beliefs, values, common bonds, or behavioral norms that management can use as levers to mobilize commitment to executing the chosen strategy. The only plus of a weak culture is that it does not usually pose a strong barrier to strategy execution, but the negative of not providing any support means that culture building has to be high on management's action agenda. Without a work climate that channels organizational energy in the direction of good strategy execution, managers are left with the options of either using compensation incentives and other motivational devices to mobilize employee commitment, supervising and monitoring employee actions more closely, or trying to establish cultural roots that will in time start to nurture the strategy execution process.

Why Corporate Cultures Matter to the Strategy Execution Process

Unlike weak cultures, strong cultures can have a powerful effect on the strategy execution process. This effect may be *positive or negative* since a company's present culture and work climate may or may not be compatible with what is needed for effective implementation and execution of the chosen strategy. When a company's present culture promotes attitudes, behaviors, and ways of doing things that are conducive to first-rate strategy execution, the culture functions as a valuable ally in the strategy execution process.

For example, a corporate culture characterized by frugality and thrift nurtures employee actions to identify cost-saving opportunities—the very behavior needed for successful execution of a low-cost leadership strategy. A culture built around such business principles as outstanding customer satisfaction, operating excellence, and employee empowerment promotes employee behaviors and an esprit de corps that facilitate execution of strategies keyed to high product quality and superior customer service. A culture in which taking initiative, exhibiting creativity, taking risks, and embracing change are the behavioral norms is conducive to successful execution of product innovation and technological leadership strategies.[10]

A culture that is grounded in actions, behaviors, and work practices that are conducive to good strategy implementation assists the strategy execution effort in three ways:[11]

LO 2

Gain an understanding of how and why a company's culture can aid the drive for proficient strategy execution and operating excellence.

> A strong culture that encourages actions, behaviors, and work practices conducive to good strategy execution adds significantly to the power and effectiveness of a company's strategy execution effort.

1. *A culture that is well matched to the requirements of the strategy execution effort focuses the attention of employees on what is most important to this effort.* Moreover, it directs their behavior and serves as a guide to their decision making. In this manner, it can align the efforts and decisions of employees throughout the firm and minimize the need for direct supervision.

2. *Culture-induced peer pressure further induces company personnel to do things in a manner that aids the cause of good strategy execution.* The stronger the culture (the more widely shared and deeply held the values), the more effective peer pressure is in shaping and supporting the strategy execution effort. Research has shown that strong group norms can shape employee behavior even more powerfully than can financial incentives.[12]

3. *A company culture that is consistent with the requirements for good strategy execution can energize employees, deepen their commitment to execute the*

strategy flawlessly, and enhance worker productivity in the process. When a company's culture is grounded in many of the needed strategy-executing behaviors, employees feel genuinely better about their jobs, the company they work for, and the merits of what the company is trying to accomplish. As a consequence, greater numbers of company personnel exhibit passion in their work and exert their best efforts to execute the strategy and achieve performance targets.

In sharp contrast, when a culture is in conflict with what is required to execute the company's strategy well, a strong culture becomes a hindrance to the success of the implementation effort.[13] Some of the very behaviors needed to execute the strategy successfully run contrary to the attitudes, behaviors, and operating practices embedded in the prevailing culture. Such a clash poses a real dilemma for company personnel. Should they be loyal to the culture and company traditions (to which they are likely to be emotionally attached) and thus resist or be indifferent to actions that will promote better strategy execution—a choice that will certainly weaken the drive for good strategy execution? Alternatively, should they go along with the strategy execution effort and engage in actions that run counter to the culture—a choice that will likely impair morale and lead to a less-than-wholehearted commitment to management's strategy execution efforts? Neither choice leads to desirable outcomes. Culture-bred resistance to the actions and behaviors needed for good strategy execution, particularly if strong and widespread, poses a formidable hurdle that must be cleared for a strategy's execution to get very far.

This says something important about the task of managing the strategy execution process: *Closely aligning corporate culture with the requirements for proficient strategy execution merits the full attention of senior executives.* The culture-building objective is to create a work climate and style of operating that mobilize the energy and behavior of company personnel squarely behind efforts to execute strategy competently. The more deeply that management can embed execution-supportive ways of doing things, the more that management can rely on the culture to automatically steer company personnel toward behaviors and work practices that aid good strategy execution and veer from doing things that impede it. Moreover, culturally astute managers understand that nourishing the right cultural environment not only adds power to their push for proficient strategy execution but also promotes strong employee identification with and commitment to the company's vision, performance targets, and strategy.

> It is in management's best interest to dedicate considerable effort to establishing a corporate culture that encourages behaviors and work practices conducive to good strategy execution.

Healthy Cultures That Aid Good Strategy Execution

A strong culture, provided it embraces execution-supportive attitudes, behaviors, and work practices, is definitely a healthy culture. Two other types of cultures exist that tend to be healthy and largely supportive of good strategy execution: high-performance cultures and adaptive cultures.

High-Performance Cultures   Some companies have so-called high-performance cultures where the standout traits are a "can-do" spirit, pride in doing things right, no-excuses accountability, and a pervasive results-oriented work climate in which people go all out to meet or beat stretch objectives.[14] In high-performance cultures, there's a strong sense of involvement on the part of company personnel and emphasis on individual initiative and effort. Performance expectations are clearly delineated for the company as a whole, for each organizational unit, and for each individual. Issues and problems are promptly addressed; there's a razor-sharp focus on what needs to be done. The clear and unyielding expectation is that all company personnel, from senior executives to frontline employees, will display high-performance behaviors and a passion for making the company successful. Such a culture—supported by constructive pressure to achieve good results—is a valuable contributor to good strategy execution and operating excellence. Results-oriented cultures are permeated with a spirit of achievement and have a good track record in meeting or beating performance targets.[15]

The challenge in creating a high-performance culture is to inspire high loyalty and dedication on the part of employees, such that they are energized to put forth their very best efforts to do things right and be unusually productive. Managers have to take pains to reinforce constructive behavior, reward top performers, and purge habits and behaviors that stand in the way of high productivity and good results. They must work at knowing the strengths and weaknesses of their subordinates, so as to better match talent with task and enable people to make meaningful contributions by doing what they do best.[16] They have to stress learning from mistakes and building on strengths and must put an unrelenting emphasis on moving forward and making good progress—in effect, there has to be a disciplined, performance-focused approach to managing the organization.

Adaptive Cultures   The hallmark of adaptive corporate cultures is willingness on the part of organization members to accept change and take on the challenge of introducing and executing new strategies.[17] Company personnel share a feeling of confidence that the organization can deal with whatever threats and opportunities arise; they are receptive to risk taking, experimentation, innovation, and changing strategies and practices. The work climate is supportive of managers and employees at all ranks who propose or initiate useful change. Internal entrepreneurship on the part of individuals and groups is encouraged and rewarded. Senior executives seek out, support, and promote individuals who exercise initiative, spot opportunities for improvement, and display the skills to implement them. Managers openly evaluate ideas and suggestions, fund initiatives to develop new or better products, and take prudent risks to pursue emerging market opportunities. As in high-performance cultures, the company exhibits a proactive approach to identifying issues, evaluating the implications and options, and moving ahead quickly with workable solutions. Strategies and traditional operating practices are modified as needed to adjust to or take advantage of changes in the business environment.

But why is change so willingly embraced in an adaptive culture? Why are organization members not fearful of how change will affect them? Why does an adaptive culture not break down from the force of ongoing changes in strategy, operating practices, and approaches to strategy execution? The answers lie in two distinctive and dominant traits of an adaptive culture: (1) Any changes in operating practices and behaviors must *not* compromise core values and long-standing business principles (since they are at the root of the culture), and (2) the changes that are instituted must satisfy the legitimate interests of stakeholders—customers, employees, shareowners, suppliers, and the communities where the company operates.[18] In other words, what sustains an adaptive culture is that organization members

As a company's strategy evolves, an adaptive culture is a definite ally in the strategy-implementing, strategy-executing process as compared to cultures that are resistant to change.

perceive the changes that management is trying to institute as *legitimate* and in keeping with the core values and business principles that form the heart and soul of the culture.[19] Not surprisingly, company personnel are usually more receptive to change when their employment security is not threatened and when they view new duties or job assignments as part of the process of adapting to new conditions. Should workforce downsizing be necessary, it is important that layoffs be handled humanely and employee departures be made as painless as possible.

Technology companies, software companies, and Internet-based companies are good illustrations of organizations with adaptive cultures. Such companies thrive on change—driving it, leading it, and capitalizing on it. Companies like Google, Intel, Cisco Systems, eBay, Amazon.com, and Apple cultivate the capability to act and react rapidly. They are avid practitioners of entrepreneurship and innovation, with a demonstrated willingness to take bold risks to create altogether new products, new businesses, and new industries. To create and nurture a culture that can adapt rapidly to shifting business conditions, they make a point of staffing their organizations with people who are flexible, who rise to the challenge of change, and who have an aptitude for adapting well to new circumstances.

In fast-changing business environments, a corporate culture that is receptive to altering organizational practices and behaviors is a virtual necessity. However, adaptive cultures work to the advantage of all companies, not just those in rapid-change environments. Every company operates in a market and business climate that is changing to one degree or another and that, in turn, requires internal operating responses and new behaviors on the part of organization members.

Unhealthy Cultures That Impede Good Strategy Execution

The distinctive characteristic of an unhealthy corporate culture is the presence of counterproductive cultural traits that adversely impact the work climate and company performance.[20] Five particularly unhealthy cultural traits are hostility to change, heavily politicized decision making, insular thinking, behaviors that are driven by greed and a disregard for ethical standards, and the presence of incompatible, clashing subcultures.

Change-Resistant Cultures   In contrast to adaptive cultures, change-resistant cultures—where skepticism about the importance of new developments and a fear of change are the norm—place a premium on not making mistakes, prompting managers to lean toward safe, conservative options intended to maintain the status quo, protect their power base, and guard the interests of their immediate work groups. When such companies encounter business environments with accelerating change, going slow on altering traditional ways of doing things can be a serious liability. Under these conditions, change-resistant cultures encourage a number of undesirable or unhealthy behaviors—viewing circumstances myopically, avoiding risks, not capitalizing on emerging opportunities, taking a lax approach to both product innovation and continuous improvement in performing value chain activities, and responding more slowly than is warranted to market change. In change-resistant cultures, word quickly gets around that proposals to do things differently face an uphill battle and that people who champion them may be seen as something of a nuisance. Executives who don't value managers or employees with initiative and new ideas put a damper on product innovation, experimentation, and efforts to improve. At the same time, change-resistant companies have little appetite for being first movers or fast followers, believing that being in the forefront of change is too risky and that acting too quickly increases vulnerability to costly mistakes. Hostility to change is most often found in companies with multilayered management bureaucracies that have enjoyed considerable market success in years past and that are wedded to the "We have done it this way for years" syndrome. Before filing bankruptcy in 2009, General Motors was a classic example of a company whose change-resistant bureaucracy was slow to adapt to fundamental changes in its markets, preferring to cling to the traditions, operating practices, and business approaches that had at one time made it the global industry leader.

Politicized Cultures   What makes a politicized internal environment so unhealthy is that political infighting consumes a great deal of organizational energy, often with the result that what's best for the company takes a backseat to political maneuvering. In companies where internal politics pervades the work climate, empire-building managers jealously guard their decision-making prerogatives. They have their own agendas and operate the work units under their supervision as autonomous "fiefdoms"; the positions they take on issues are usually aimed at protecting or expanding their own turf. Collaboration with other organizational units is viewed with suspicion, and cross-unit cooperation occurs grudgingly. The support or opposition of politically influential executives and/or coalitions among departments with vested interests in a particular outcome tends to shape what actions the company takes. All this political maneuvering takes away from efforts to execute strategy with real proficiency and frustrates company personnel who are less political and more inclined to do what is in the company's best interests.

Insular, Inwardly Focused Cultures   Sometimes a company reigns as an industry leader or enjoys great market success for so long that its personnel start to believe they have all the answers or can develop them on their own. There is a strong tendency to neglect what customers are saying and how their needs and expectations are changing. Such confidence in the correctness of its approach to business and an unflinching belief in the company's competitive superiority breeds arrogance, prompting company personnel to discount the merits of what outsiders are doing and the payoff from studying best-in-class performers. Insular thinking, internally driven solutions, and a must-be-invented-here mindset come to permeate the corporate culture. An inwardly focused corporate culture gives rise to managerial inbreeding and a failure to recruit people who can offer fresh thinking and outside perspectives. The big risk of insular cultural thinking is that the company can underestimate the capabilities and accomplishments of rival companies and overestimate its own progress—until its loss of market position makes the realities obvious.

Unethical and Greed-Driven Cultures   Companies that have little regard for ethical standards or that are run by executives driven by greed and ego gratification are scandals waiting to happen, as discussed in Chapter 9. Executives exude the negatives of arrogance, ego, greed, and an "ends-justify-the-means" mentality in pursuing stretch revenue and profitability targets.[21] Senior managers wink at unethical behavior and may cross over the line to unethical (and sometimes criminal) behavior themselves. They are prone to adopt accounting principles that make financial performance look better than it really is. Legions of companies have fallen prey to unethical behavior and greed, most notably WorldCom, Enron, Quest, HealthSouth, Adelphia, Tyco, Parmalat, Rite Aid, Hollinger International, Refco, Marsh & McLennan, Siemens, Countrywide Financial, and Stanford Financial Group, with executives being indicted and/or convicted of criminal behavior.

Incompatible Subcultures   Although it is common to speak about corporate culture in the singular, it is not unusual for companies to have multiple cultures (or subcultures).[22] Values, beliefs, and practices within a company sometimes vary significantly by department, geographic location, division, or business unit. As long as the subcultures are compatible with the overarching corporate culture and are supportive of the strategy execution efforts, this is not problematic. Multiple cultures pose an unhealthy situation when they are composed of incompatible subcultures that embrace conflicting business philosophies, support inconsistent approaches to strategy execution, and encourage incompatible methods of people management. Clashing subcultures can prevent a company from coordinating its efforts to craft and execute strategy and can distract company personnel from the business of business. When incompatible subcultures encourage the emergence of warring factions within the company, they are not just unhealthy—they are downright poisonous.

Incompatible subcultures arise most commonly because of important cultural differences between a company's culture and that of a recently acquired company or because of a merger between companies with cultural differences. Companies with M&A experience are quite alert to the importance of cultural compatibility in making acquisitions and the need to integrate the cultures of newly acquired companies—cultural due diligence is often as important as financial due diligence in deciding whether to go forward on an acquisition or merger. On a number of occasions, companies decided to pass on acquiring particular companies because of culture conflicts they believed would be hard to resolve.

Changing a Problem Culture: The Role of Leadership

When a strong culture is unhealthy or otherwise out of sync with the actions and behaviors needed to execute the strategy successfully, the culture must be changed as rapidly as can be managed. While correcting a strategy-culture conflict can occasionally mean revamping a company's approach to strategy execution to better fit the company's culture, more usually it means altering aspects of the mismatched culture to better enable first-rate strategy execution. The more entrenched the mismatched or unhealthy aspects of a company culture, the more likely the culture will impede strategy execution and the greater the need for change.

Changing a problem culture is among the toughest management tasks because of the heavy anchor of ingrained behaviors and attitudes. It is natural for company personnel to cling to familiar practices and to be wary, if not hostile, to new approaches of how things are to be done. Consequently, it takes concerted management action over a period of time to root out unconstructive behaviors and replace them with new ways of doing things deemed more conducive to executing the strategy.

The single most visible factor that distinguishes successful culture-change efforts from failed attempts is competent leadership at the top. Great power is needed to force major cultural change and overcome the "springback" resistance of entrenched cultures—and great power is possessed only by the most senior executives, especially the CEO. However, while top management must be out front leading the effort, marshaling support for a new culture and instilling the desired cultural behaviors is a job for the whole management team. Middle managers and frontline supervisors play a key role in implementing the new work practices and operating approaches, helping win rank-and-file acceptance of and support for the desired behavioral norms.

As shown in Figure 12.2, the first step in fixing a problem culture is for top management to identify those facets of the present culture that are dysfunctional and pose obstacles to executing new strategic initiatives and meeting company performance targets. Second, managers must clearly define the desired new behaviors and features of the culture they want to create. Third, managers have to convince company personnel of why the present culture poses problems and why and how new behaviors and operating approaches will improve company performance—the case for cultural reform has to be persuasive. Fourth, and most important, all the talk about remodeling the present culture has to be followed swiftly by visible, forceful actions to promote the desired new behaviors and work practices—actions that company personnel will interpret as a determined top management commitment to bringing about a different work climate and new ways of operating.

Making a Compelling Case for Culture Change   The way for management to begin a major remodeling of the corporate culture is by selling company personnel on the need for new-style behaviors and work practices. This means making a compelling case for why the culture-remodeling efforts are in the organization's best interests and why company personnel should wholeheartedly join the effort to doing things somewhat differently. Skeptics and opinion leaders have to be convinced that all is not well with the status quo. This can be done by:

- Explaining why and how certain behavioral norms and work practices in the current culture pose obstacles to good execution of strategic initiatives.
- Explaining how new behaviors and work practices will be more advantageous and produce better results. Effective culture-change leaders are good at telling stories to describe the new values and desired behaviors and connect them to everyday practices.
- Citing reasons why the current strategy has to be modified, if the need for cultural change is due to a change in strategy. This includes explaining why the new strategic initiatives will bolster the company's competitiveness and performance and how a change in culture can help in executing the new strategy.

It is essential for the CEO and other top executives to talk personally to company personnel all across the company about the reasons for modifying work practices and culture-related behaviors. Senior officers and department heads have to play a lead role in explaining the need for a change in behavioral norms to those they manage—and the explanations will likely have to be repeated many times. For the culture-change effort to be successful, frontline supervisors and employee opinion leaders must be won over to the cause, which means convincing them of the merits of *practicing* and *enforcing* cultural norms at every level of the organization, from the highest to the lowest. Arguments for new ways of doing things and new work practices tend to be embraced more readily if employees understand how they will benefit company stakeholders (particularly customers, employees, and shareholders).

Figure 12.2   Steps to Take in Changing a Problem Culture

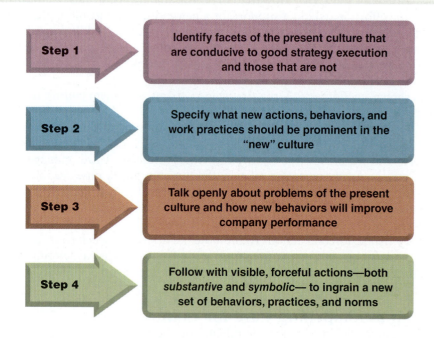

Step 1	Identify facets of the present culture that are conducive to good strategy execution and those that are not
Step 2	Specify what new actions, behaviors, and work practices should be prominent in the "new" culture
Step 3	Talk openly about problems of the present culture and how new behaviors will improve company performance
Step 4	Follow with visible, forceful actions—both *substantive* and *symbolic*— to ingrain a new set of behaviors, practices, and norms

Until a large majority of employees accept the need for a new culture and agree that different work practices and behaviors are called for, there's more work to be done in selling company personnel on the whys and wherefores of culture change. Building widespread organizational support requires taking every opportunity to repeat the message of why the new work practices, operating approaches, and behaviors are good for company stakeholders.

Management's efforts to make a persuasive case for changing what is deemed to be a problem culture must be *followed quickly* by forceful, high-profile actions across several fronts. The actions to implant the new culture must be both substantive and symbolic.

Substantive Culture-Changing Actions   No culture change effort can get very far with just talk about the need for different actions, behaviors, and work practices. Company executives must give the culture-change effort some teeth by initiating *a series of actions* that company personnel will see as credible and unmistakably indicative of the seriousness of management's commitment to cultural change. The strongest signs that management is truly committed to instilling a new culture include:

• Replacing key executives who are stonewalling needed organizational and cultural changes.

• Promoting individuals who have stepped forward to advocate the shift to a different culture and who can serve as role models for the desired cultural behavior.

• Appointing outsiders with the desired cultural attributes to high-profile positions—bringing in new-breed managers sends an unmistakable message that a new era is dawning.

- Screening all candidates for new positions carefully, hiring only those who appear to fit in with the new culture.
- Mandating that all company personnel attend culture-training programs to learn more about the new work practices and to better understand the culture-related actions and behaviors that are expected.
- Designing compensation incentives that boost the pay of teams and individuals who display the desired cultural behaviors. Company personnel are much more inclined to exhibit the desired kinds of actions and behaviors when it is in their financial best interest to do so.
- Revising policies and procedures in ways that will help drive cultural change.

Executives must take care to launch enough companywide culture-change actions at the outset so as to leave no room for doubt that management is dead serious about changing the present culture and that a cultural transformation is inevitable. The series of actions initiated by top management must create lots of hallway talk across the whole company, get the change process off to a fast start, and be followed by unrelenting efforts to firmly establish the new work practices, desired behaviors, and style of operating as "standard."

Symbolic Culture-Changing Actions There's also an important place for symbolic managerial actions to alter a problem culture and tighten the strategy-culture fit. The most important symbolic actions are those that top executives take to *lead by example.* For instance, if the organization's strategy involves a drive to become the industry's low-cost producer, senior managers must display frugality in their own actions and decisions: inexpensive decorations in the executive suite, conservative expense accounts and entertainment allowances, a lean staff in the corporate office, scrutiny of budget requests, few executive perks, and so on. At Walmart, all the executive offices are simply decorated; executives are habitually frugal in their own actions, and they are zealous in their efforts to control costs and promote greater efficiency. At Nucor, one of the world's low-cost producers of steel products, executives fly coach class and use taxis at airports rather than limousines. If the culture-change imperative is to be more responsive to customers' needs and to pleasing customers, the CEO can instill greater customer awareness by requiring all officers and executives to spend a significant portion of each week talking with customers about their needs. Top executives must be alert to the fact that company personnel will be watching their actions and decisions to see if their actions match their rhetoric. Hence, they need to make sure their current decisions and behaviors will be construed as consistent with the new-culture values and norms.[23]

Another category of symbolic actions includes holding ceremonial events to single out and honor people whose actions and performance exemplify what is called for in the new culture. A point is made of holding events to celebrate each culture-change success (and any other outcome that management would like to see happen again). Executives sensitive to their role in promoting strategy-culture fit make a habit of appearing at ceremonial functions to praise individuals and groups that exemplify the desired behaviors. They show up at employee training programs to stress strategic priorities, values, ethical principles, and cultural norms. Every group gathering is seen as an opportunity to repeat and ingrain values, praise good deeds, expound on the merits of the new culture, and cite instances of how the new work practices and operating approaches have worked to good advantage.

The use of symbols in culture building is widespread. Many universities give outstanding teacher awards each year to symbolize their commitment to good teaching and their esteem for instructors who display exceptional classroom talents. Numerous businesses have employee-of-the-month awards. The military has a long-standing custom of awarding ribbons and medals for exemplary actions. Mary Kay Cosmetics awards an array of prizes ceremoniously to its beauty consultants for reaching various sales plateaus.

How Long Does It Take to Change a Problem Culture?   Planting and growing the seeds of a new culture require a determined effort by the chief executive and other senior managers. A sustained and persistent effort to reinforce the culture at every opportunity through both word and deed is required. Changing a problem culture is never a short-term exercise. It takes time for a new culture to emerge and prevail; overnight transformations simply don't occur. And it takes even longer for a new culture to become deeply embedded. The bigger the organization and the greater the cultural shift needed to produce an execution-supportive fit, the longer it takes. In large companies, fixing a problem culture and instilling a new set of attitudes and behaviors can take two to five years. In fact, it is usually tougher to reform an entrenched problematic culture than it is to instill a strategy-supportive culture from scratch in a brand new organization.

Illustration Capsule 12.2 discusses the approaches used at Chrysler in 2009–2010 to change a culture that was grounded in a 1970s view of the automobile industry.

LEADING THE STRATEGY EXECUTION PROCESS

LO 4

Understand what constitutes effective managerial leadership in achieving superior strategy execution.

For an enterprise to execute its strategy in truly proficient fashion and approach operating excellence, top executives have to take the lead in the implementation/execution process and personally drive the pace of progress. The have to be out in the field, seeing for themselves how well operations are going, gathering information firsthand, and gauging the progress being made. Proficient strategy execution requires company managers to be diligent and adept in spotting problems, learning what obstacles lie in the path of good execution, and then clearing the way for progress—the goal must be to produce better results speedily and productively. There has to be constructive, but unrelenting, pressure on organizational units to (1) demonstrate excellence in all dimensions of strategy execution and (2) do so on a consistent basis—ultimately, that's what will enable a well-crafted strategy to achieve the desired performance results.

The strategy execution process must be driven by mandates to get things on the right track and show good results. The specifics of how to implement a strategy and deliver the intended results must start with understanding the requirements for good strategy execution. Afterward comes a diagnosis of the organization's preparedness to execute the strategic initiatives and decisions as to which of several ways to proceed to move forward and achieve the targeted results.[24] In general, leading the drive for good strategy execution and operating excellence calls for three actions on the part of the manager in charge:

• Staying on top of what is happening and closely monitoring progress.

ILLUSTRATION CAPSULE 12.2

Changing the "Old Detroit" Culture at Chrysler

When Chrysler Group LLC emerged from bankruptcy in June 2009, its road to recovery was far from certain. "It was questionable whether they'd survive 2010," said Michelle Krebs, an analyst with auto information provider Edmunds. com. One thing that was holding Chrysler back was its culture—a legacy of "the Old Detroit," which was characterized by finger-pointing and blame shifting whenever problems arose.[a]

Chrysler's management had long been aware of its culture problem. In 2008, Robert Nardelli, Chrysler's autocratic new CEO, placed himself in charge of a wide-ranging culture-change program designed to break the ingrained behaviors that had damaged the company's reputation for quality. Chrysler's slide into bankruptcy was hardly the comeback that the controversial Nardelli envisioned when he was hired for the job by private-equity firm Cerberus Capital Management (which controlled Chrysler from 2007 until 2009).

A strategic partnership ceding management control to Italian automaker Fiat SpA was part of the deal for Chrysler's bankruptcy reorganization, with Fiat's CEO, Sergio Marchionne, becoming Chrysler's CEO as well. In discussing his five-year plan for Chrysler, Marchionne remarked, "What I've learned as a CEO is that culture is not part of the game—it is the game!"[b]

Marchionne put Doug Betts, a veteran of Toyota Motor Corp. and Nissan Motor Co., in charge of a systematic overhaul of Chrysler quality, with cultural change as the fundamental driver. Betts began

by creating new cross-functional teams designed to break down Chrysler's balkanized silos of manufacturing and engineering. Whereas problems were formerly handed off from one department to another, delaying action for an average of 71 days, quality teams are now encouraged to take ownership of solutions.[c] Betts has also taken aim at the climate of fear, replacing concerns over recrimination and retribution with a positive focus on team empowerment and problem solving. By the end of 2009, Betts was saying, "It's different now. People are talking openly about problems now and how to fix [them]."[d] By May 2010, confidence in Chrysler was increasing and sales were up by 33 percent over the same period in the previous year. Analysts were hopeful that Chrysler had finally begun to get it right.

[a] Jerry Hirsch, "Chrysler Performance Exceeds Expectations: The Fiat-Managed Company Cut Its Losses to $197 Million and Recorded a $143-Million Operating Profit in the First Quarter of the Year," *Los Angeles Times,* April 22, 2010, http://articles.latimes.com/2010/apr/22/business/la-fi-chrysler-20100422.

[b] Daniel Howes, "Chrysler's Last Chance to Get It Right," *Detroit News,* Business section, 1-dot edition, p. 4B.

[c] Ibid.

[d] Alisa Priddle, "'Different' Chrysler Zeroes In on Quality," *Detroit News,* Business section, 2-dot edition, p. 1A.

Developed with Amy Florentino.

Sources: Robert Snell, "Chrysler Sales Up 33% for May; Ford, GM Rise 23%, 16.6%," *Detroit News:* last updated June 2, 2010, http://detnews.com/article/20100602/AUTO01/6020390/Chrysler-sales-up-33—for-May—Ford—GM-rise-23—16.6-#ixzz0sNQX7iWR; http://topics.nytimes.com/top/reference/timestopics/people/n/robert_l_nardelli/index.html, updated May 1, 2009; Neal E. Boudette, "Nardelli Tries to Shift Chrysler's Culture," *Wall Street Journal,* June 18, 2008, p. B1.

- Putting constructive pressure on the organization to execute the strategy well and achieve operating excellence.
- Initiating corrective actions to improve strategy execution and achieve the targeted performance results.

Staying on Top of How Well Things Are Going

To stay on top of how well the strategy execution process is going, senior executives have to tap into information from a wide range of sources. In addition to talking with key subordinates and reviewing the latest operating results, watching the competitive reactions of rival firms, and visiting with key customers and suppliers to get their perspectives, they usually make regular visits to various company facilities and talk with many different company personnel at many different organization levels—a technique often labeled **managing by walking around (MBWA).** Most managers attach great importance to spending time with people at company facilities, asking questions, listening to their opinions and concerns, and gathering firsthand information about how well aspects of the strategy execution process are going. Facilities tours and face-to-face contacts with operating-level employees give executives a good grasp of what progress is being made, what problems are being encountered, and whether additional resources or different approaches may be needed. Just as important, MBWA provides opportunities to give encouragement, lift spirits, shift attention from the old to the new priorities, and create some excitement—all of which can boost strategy execution efforts.

> **CORE CONCEPT**
>
> **Management by walking around (MBWA)** is one of the techniques that effective leaders use to stay informed about how well the strategy execution process is progressing.

Jeff Bezos, Amazon.com's CEO, is noted for his practice of MBWA, firing off a battery of questions when he tours facilities and insisting that Amazon managers spend time in the trenches with their people to prevent getting disconnected from the reality of what's happening.[25] Walmart executives have had a long-standing practice of spending two to three days every week visiting Walmart's stores and talking with store managers and employees. Sam Walton, Walmart's founder, insisted, "The key is to get out into the store and listen to what the associates have to say." Jack Welch, the highly effective CEO of General Electric (GE) from 1980 to 2001, not only spent several days each month personally visiting GE operations and talking with major customers but also arranged his schedule so that he could spend time exchanging information and ideas with GE managers from all over the world who were attending classes at the company's leadership development center near GE's headquarters.

Many manufacturing executives make a point of strolling the factory floor to talk with workers and meeting regularly with union officials. Some managers operate out of open cubicles in big spaces populated with open cubicles for other personnel so that they can interact easily and frequently with co-workers. Managers at some companies host weekly get-togethers (often on Friday afternoons) to create a regular opportunity for information to flow freely between down-the-line employees and executives.

Putting Constructive Pressure on Organizational Units to Execute the Strategy Well and Achieve Operating Excellence

Managers have to be out front in mobilizing organizational energy behind the drive for good strategy execution and operating excellence. Part of the leadership task entails nurturing a results-oriented work climate, where performance standards are high and a spirit of achievement is pervasive. Successfully leading the effort to foster a results-oriented, high-performance culture generally entails such leadership actions and managerial practices as:

- *Treating employees as valued partners in the drive for operating excellence and good business performance.* Some companies symbolize the value of individual employees and the importance of their contributions by referring to them as cast members (Disney), crew members (McDonald's), job owners (Graniterock), partners (Starbucks), or associates (Walmart, LensCrafters, W. L. Gore, Edward Jones, Publix Supermarkets, and Marriott International). Very often, there is a strong company commitment to providing thorough training, offering attractive compensation and career opportunities, emphasizing promotion from within, providing a high degree of job security, and otherwise making employees feel well treated and valued.

- *Fostering an esprit de corps that energizes organization members.* The task here is to skillfully use people-management practices calculated to build morale, foster pride in doing things right, promote teamwork, create a strong sense of involvement on the part of company personnel, win their emotional commitment, and inspire them to do their best.[26]

- *Using empowerment to help create a fully engaged workforce.* Top executives must seek to engage the full organization in the strategy execution effort. A fully engaged workforce, one where individuals bring their best to work every day, is necessary to produce great results.[27] So is having a group of dedicated managers committed to making a difference in their organization. The two best things top-level executives can do to create a fully engaged organization are (1) delegate authority to middle and lower-level managers to get the implementation/execution process moving and (2) empower rank-and-file employees to act on their own initiative. Operating excellence requires that everybody contribute ideas, exercise initiative and creativity in performing his or her work, and have a desire to do things in the best possible manner.

- *Making champions out of the people who spearhead new ideas and/or turn in winning performances.* The best champions and change agents are persistent, competitive, tenacious, committed, and fanatical about seeing their ideas through to success. It is particularly important that people who champion an unsuccessful idea not be punished or sidelined but, rather, be encouraged to try again. Encouraging lots of "tries" is important, since many ideas won't pan out.

- *Setting stretch objectives and clearly communicating an expectation that company personnel are to give their best in achieving performance targets.* Stretch objectives—those beyond an organization's current capacities—can sometimes spur organization members to increase their resolve and redouble their efforts to execute the strategy flawlessly and ultimately reach the stretch objectives. When stretch objectives are met, the satisfaction of achievement and boost to employee morale can result in an even higher level of organizational drive.

- *Using the tools of benchmarking best practices, business process reengineering, TQM, and Six Sigma to focus attention on continuous improvement.* These are proven approaches to getting better operating results and facilitating better strategy execution.

- *Using the full range of motivational techniques and compensation incentives to inspire company personnel, nurture a results-oriented work climate, and enforce high-performance standards.* Managers cannot mandate innovative improvements by simply exhorting people to "be creative," nor can they make continuous progress toward operating excellence with directives to "try harder." Rather, they must foster a culture where innovative ideas and experimentation with new ways of doing things can blossom and thrive. Individuals and groups should be strongly encouraged to brainstorm, let their imaginations fly in all directions, and come up with proposals for improving how things are done. This means giving company personnel enough autonomy to stand out, excel, and contribute. And it means that the rewards for successful champions of new ideas and operating improvements should be large and visible.

- *Celebrating individual, group, and company successes.* Top management should miss no opportunity to express respect for individual employees and appreciation of extraordinary individual and group effort.[28] Companies like Mary Kay Cosmetics, Tupperware, and McDonald's actively seek out reasons and opportunities to give pins, ribbons, buttons, badges, and medals for good showings by average performers—the idea being to express appreciation and give a motivational boost to people who stand out in doing ordinary jobs. General Electric and 3M Corporation make a point of ceremoniously honoring individuals who believe so strongly in their ideas that they take it on themselves to hurdle the bureaucracy, maneuver their projects through the system, and turn them into improved services, new products, or even new businesses.

While leadership efforts to instill a results-oriented, high-performance culture usually accentuate the positive, negative reinforcers abound too. Managers whose units consistently perform poorly must be replaced. Low-performing workers and people who reject the results-oriented cultural emphasis must be weeded out or at least employed differently. Average performers should be candidly counseled that they have limited career potential unless they show more progress in the form of additional effort, better skills, and improved ability to execute the strategy well and deliver good results.

Leading the Process of Making Corrective Adjustments

Since strategy execution takes place amid changing environmental and organizational circumstances, there is often a need for corrective adjustments. The process of making corrective adjustments in strategy execution varies according to the situation. In a crisis, taking remedial action fairly quickly is of the essence. But it still takes time to review the situation, examine the available data, identify and evaluate options (crunching whatever numbers may be appropriate to determine which options are likely to generate the best outcomes), and decide what to do. When the situation allows managers to proceed more deliberately in deciding when to make changes and what changes to make, most managers seem to prefer a process of incrementally solidifying commitment to a particular course of action.[29] The process that managers go through in deciding on corrective adjustments is essentially the same for both proactive and reactive changes: They sense needs, gather information, broaden and deepen their understanding of the situation, develop options and explore their pros and cons, put forth action proposals, strive for a consensus, and finally formally adopt an agreed-on course of action.[30] The time frame for deciding what corrective changes to initiate can be a few hours, a few days, a few weeks, or even a few months if the situation is particularly complicated.

Success in making corrective actions hinges on (1) a thorough analysis of the situation, (2) the exercise of good business judgment in deciding what actions to take, and (3) good implementation of the corrective actions that are initiated.

Successful managers are skilled in getting an organization back on track rather quickly. They (and their staffs) are good at discerning what actions to take and in bringing them to a successful conclusion. Managers who struggle to show measurable progress in implementing corrective actions in a timely fashion are often candidates for being replaced.

The challenges of making the right corrective adjustments and leading a successful strategy execution effort are, without question, substantial.[31] Because each instance of executing strategy occurs under different organizational circumstances, the managerial agenda for executing strategy always needs to be situation-specific—there's no generic procedure to follow. But the job is definitely doable. Although there is no prescriptive answer to the question of exactly what to do, any of several courses of action may produce good results. And, as we said at the beginning of Chapter 10, executing strategy is an action-oriented, make-the-right-things-happen task that challenges a manager's ability to lead and direct organizational change, create or reinvent business processes, manage and motivate people, and achieve performance targets.

A FINAL WORD ON LEADING THE PROCESS OF CRAFTING AND EXECUTING STRATEGY

In practice, it is hard to separate leading the process of executing strategy from leading the other pieces of the strategy process. As we emphasized in Chapter 2, the job of crafting, implementing, and executing strategy consists of five inter-related and linked stages, with much looping and recycling to fine-tune and adjust the strategic vision, objectives, strategy, and implementation/execution approaches to fit one another and to fit changing circumstances. The process is continuous, and the conceptually separate acts of crafting and executing strategy blur together in real-world situations. The best tests of good strategic leadership are whether the company has a good strategy and business model, whether the strategy is being competently executed, and whether the enterprise is meeting or beating its performance targets. If these three conditions exist, then there is every reason to conclude that the company has good strategic leadership and is a well managed enterprise.

KEY POINTS

1. Corporate culture is the character of a company's internal work climate—as shaped by a system of *shared* values, beliefs, ethical standards, and traditions that in turn define behavioral norms, ingrained attitudes, accepted work practices, and styles of operating. A company's culture is important because it influences the organization's actions and approaches to conducting business. In a very real sense, the culture is the company's organizational DNA.

2. The key features of a company's culture include the company's values and ethical standards, its approach to people management, its work atmosphere

and company spirit, how its personnel interact, the behaviors awarded through incentives (both financial and symbolic), the traditions and oft-repeated "myths," and its manner of dealing with stakeholders.

3. A company's culture is grounded in and shaped by its core values and ethical standards. Core values and ethical principles serve two roles in the culture-building process: (1) They foster a work climate in which employees share common and strongly held convictions about how company business is to be conducted, and (2) they serve as yardsticks for gauging the appropriateness of particular actions, decisions, and behaviors, thus helping steer company personnel toward both doing things right and doing the right thing.

4. Company cultures vary widely in strength and influence. Some are strongly embedded and have a big impact on a company's practices and behavioral norms. Others are weak and have comparatively little influence on company operations.

5. Strong company cultures can have either positive or negative effects on strategy execution. When they are well matched to the behavioral requirements of the company's strategy implementation plan, they can be a powerful aid to strategy execution. A culture that is grounded in the types of actions and behaviors that are conducive to good strategy execution assists the effort in three ways:

   - By focusing employee attention on the actions that are most important in the strategy execution effort.
   - Through culture-induced peer pressure for employees to contribute to the success of the strategy execution effort.
   - By energizing employees, deepening their commitment to the strategy execution effort, and increasing the productivity of their efforts

6. It is thus in management's best interest to dedicate considerable effort to establishing a strongly implanted corporate culture that encourages behaviors and work practices conducive to good strategy execution.

7. Strong corporate cultures that are conducive to good strategy execution are healthy cultures. So are high-performance cultures and adaptive cultures. The latter are particularly important in dynamic environments. Strong cultures can also be unhealthy. The five types of unhealthy cultures are (1) those that are change-resistant, (2) those that are characterized by heavily politicized decision making, (3) those that are insular and inwardly focused, (4) those that are ethically unprincipled and infused with greed, and (5) those that are composed of incompatible subcultures. All five impede good strategy execution.

8. Changing a company's culture, especially a strong one with traits that don't fit a new strategy's requirements, is a tough and often time-consuming challenge. Changing a culture requires competent leadership at the top. It requires making a compelling case for cultural change and employing both symbolic actions and substantive actions that unmistakably indicate serious commitment on the part of top management. The more that culture-driven actions and behaviors fit what's needed for good strategy execution, the less managers must depend on policies, rules, procedures, and supervision to enforce what people should and should not do.

9. Leading the drive for good strategy execution and operating excellence calls for three actions on the part of the manager in charge:

- Staying on top of what is happening and closely monitoring progress. This is often accomplished through managing by walking around (MBWA).
- Putting constructive pressure on the organization to execute the strategy well and achieve operating excellence.
- Initiating corrective actions to improve strategy execution and achieve the targeted performance results.

ASSURANCE OF LEARNING EXERCISES

LO 1, LO 2

1. Go to www.google.com. Click on the About Google link and then on the Corporate Info link. Under the Culture link, read what Google has to say about its culture. Also, in the "Our Philosophy" section, read "Ten things Google has found to be true." How do the "ten things" and Google's culture aid in management's attempts to execute the company's strategy?

LO 1, LO 2

2. Go to the Jobs section at www.intel.com, and see what Intel has to say about its culture under the links for Careers, Diversity, and The Workplace. Does what's on this Web site appear to be just recruiting propaganda, or does it convey the type of work climate that management is actually trying to create? Explain your answer.

LO 3

3. Using Google Scholar or your university library's access to EBSCO, Lexis-Nexis, or other databases, search for recent articles in business publications on "culture change." Give examples of three companies that have recently undergone culture-change initiatives. What are the key features of each company's culture-change program? What results did management achieve at each company?

LO 1, LO 2

4. Go to www.jnj.com, the Web site of Johnson & Johnson, and read the J&J Credo, which sets forth the company's responsibilities to customers, employees, the community, and shareholders. Then read the "Our Company" section. Why do you think the credo has resulted in numerous awards and accolades that recognize the company as a good corporate citizen?

LO 4

5. In the last couple of years, Liz Claiborne, Inc., has been engaged in efforts to turn around its faltering Mexx chain. Use your favorite browser to search for information on the turnaround plan at Mexx, and read at least two articles or reports on this subject. Describe in 1 to 2 pages the approach being taken to turn around the Mexx chain. In your opinion, have the managers involved been demonstrating the kind of internal leadership needed for superior strategy execution at Mexx? Explain your answer.

EXERCISES FOR SIMULATION PARTICIPANTS

LO 1, LO 2

1. If you were making a speech to company personnel, what would you tell them about the kind of corporate culture you would like to have at your company? What specific cultural traits would you like your company to exhibit? Explain.

LO 1

2. What core values would you want to ingrain in your company's culture? Why?

LO 3, LO 4

3. Following each decision round, do you and your co-managers make corrective adjustments in either your company's strategy or how well the strategy is being executed? List at least three such adjustments you made in the most recent decision round. What hard evidence (in the form of results relating to your company's performance in the most recent year) can you cite that indicates the various corrective adjustments you made either succeeded or failed to improve your company's performance?

LO 4

4. What would happen to your company's performance if you and your co-managers stick with the status quo and fail to make any corrective adjustments after each decision round?

ENDNOTES

[1] Jennifer A. Chatham and Sandra E. Cha, "Leading by Leveraging Culture," *California Management Review* 45, no. 4 (Summer 2003), pp. 20–34.

[2] Joanne Reid and Victoria Hubbell, "Creating a Performance Culture," *Ivey Business Journal* 69, no. 4 (March–April 2005), p. 1.

[3] John P. Kotter and James L. Heskett, *Corporate Culture and Performance* (New York: Free Press, 1992), p. 7. See also Robert Goffee and Gareth Jones, *The Character of a Corporation* (New York: HarperCollins, 1998).

[4] For several perspectives on the role and importance of core values and ethical behavior, see Joseph L. Badaracco, *Defining Moments: When Managers Must Choose between Right and Wrong* (Boston: Harvard Business School Press, 1997); Joe Badaracco and Allen P. Webb. "Business Ethics: A View from the Trenches," *California Management Review* 37, no. 2 (Winter 1995), pp. 8–28; Patrick E. Murphy, "Corporate Ethics Statements: Current Status and Future Prospects," *Journal of Business Ethics* 14 (1995), pp. 727–40; and Lynn Sharp Paine, "Managing for Organizational Integrity," *Harvard Business Review* 72, no. 2 (March–April 1994), pp. 106–17.

[5] For a study of the status of formal codes of ethics in large corporations, see Emily F. Carasco and Jang B. Singh, "The Content and Focus of the Codes of Ethics of the World's Largest Transnational Corporations," *Business and Society Review* 108, no. 1 (January 2003), pp. 71–94, and Patrick E. Murphy, "Corporate Ethics Statements: Current Status and Future Prospects," *Journal of Business Ethics* 14 (1995), pp. 727–40. For a discussion of the strategic benefits of formal statements of corporate values, see John Humble, David Jackson, and Alan Thomson, "The Strategic Power of Corporate Values," *Long Range Planning* 27, no. 6 (December 1994), pp. 28–42. An excellent discussion of whether one should assume that company codes of ethics are always ethical is presented in Mark S. Schwartz, "A Code of Ethics for Corporate Codes of Ethics," *Journal of Business Ethics* 41, nos. 1–2 (November–December 2002), pp. 27–43.

[6] Chatham and Cha, "Leading by Leveraging Culture."

[7] Kotter and Heskett, *Corporate Culture and Performance,* pp. 7–8.

[8] Terrence E. Deal and Allen A. Kennedy, *Corporate Cultures* (Reading, MA: Addison-Wesley, 1982), p. 22. See also Terrence E. Deal and Allen A. Kennedy, *The New Corporate Cultures: Revitalizing the Workplace after Downsizing, Mergers, and Reengineering* (Cambridge, MA: Perseus Publishing, 1999); Chatham and Cha, "Leading by Leveraging Culture."

[9] Vijay Sathe, *Culture and Related Corporate Realities* (Homewood, IL: Irwin, 1985).

[10] Avan R. Jassawalla and Hemant C. Sashittal, "Cultures That Support Product-Innovation Processes," *Academy of Management Executive* 16, no. 3 (August 2002), pp. 42–54.

[11] Kotter and Heskett, *Corporate Culture and Performance,* pp. 15–16. Also see Chatham and Cha, "Leading by Leveraging Culture."

[12] Chatham and Cha, "Leading by Leveraging Culture."

[13] Kotter and Heskett, *Corporate Culture and Performance,* p. 5.

[14] For a discussion of how to build a high-performance culture, see Reid and Hubbell, "Creating a Performance Culture," pp. 1–5.

[15] A strategy-supportive, high-performance culture can contribute to competitive advantage; see Jay B. Barney and Delwyn N. Clark, *Resource-Based Theory: Creating and Sustaining Competitive Advantage* (New York: Oxford University Press, 2007), chap. 4.

[16] Reid and Hubbell, "Creating a Performance Culture," pp. 2 and 5.

[17] This section draws heavily on the discussion of Kotter and Heskett, *Corporate Culture and Performance,* chap. 4.

[18] There's no inherent reason why new strategic initiatives should conflict with core values and business principles. While conflict is always possible, most strategy makers lean toward choosing strategic initiatives that are compatible with the company's character and culture and that don't go against ingrained values and beliefs. After all, the company's culture is usually something that strategy makers have had a hand in building and perpetuating, so they are not often anxious to undermine core values and business principles without serious soul-searching and compelling business reasons.

[19] For a more in-depth discussion of using values as legitimate boundaries, see Rosabeth Moss Kanter, "Transforming Giants," *Harvard Business Review* 86, no. 1 (January 2008), pp. 43–52.

[20] Ibid., chap. 6.

[21] See Kurt Eichenwald, *Conspiracy of Fools: A True Story* (New York: Broadway Books, 2005).

[22] Ibid., p. 5.

[23] Judy D. Olian and Sara L. Rynes, "Making Total Quality Work: Aligning Organizational Processes, Performance Measures, and Stakeholders," *Human Resource Management* 30, no. 3 (Fall 1991), p. 324.

[24] For excellent discussions of the problems and pitfalls in leading the transition to a new strategy and to fundamentally new ways of doing business, see Larry Bossidy and Ram Charan, *Confronting Reality: Doing What Matters to Get Things Right* (New York: Crown Business, 2004); Larry Bossidy and Ram Charan, *Execution: The Discipline of Getting Things Done* (New York: Crown Business, 2002), especially chaps. 3 and 5; John P. Kotter, "Leading Change: Why Transformation Efforts Fail," *Harvard Business Review* 73, no. 2 (March–April 1995), pp. 59–67; Thomas M. Hout and John C. Carter, "Getting It Done: New Roles for Senior Executives," *Harvard Business Review* 73, no. 6 (November–December 1995), pp. 133–45; Sumantra Ghoshal and Christopher A. Bartlett, "Changing the Role of Top Management: Beyond Structure to Processes," *Harvard Business Review* 73, no. 1 (January–February 1995), pp. 86–96.

[25] Fred Vogelstein, "Winning the Amazon Way," *Fortune,* May 26, 2003, p. 64.

[26] For a more in-depth discussion of the leader's role in creating a results-oriented culture that nurtures success, see Benjamin Schneider, Sarah K. Gunnarson, and Kathryn Niles-Jolly, "Creating the Climate and Culture of Success," *Organizational Dynamics,* Summer 1994, pp. 17–29.

[27] Michael T. Kanazawa and Robert H. Miles, *Big Ideas to Big Results* (Upper Saddle River, NJ: FT Press, 2008), p. 96.

[28] Jeffrey Pfeffer, "Producing Sustainable Competitive Advantage through the Effective Management of People," *Academy of Management Executive* 9, no.1 (February 1995), pp. 55–69.

[29] James Brian Quinn, *Strategies for Change: Logical Incrementalism* (Homewood, IL: Richard D. Irwin, 1980), pp. 20–22.

[30] Ibid., p. 146.

[31] For a good discussion of the challenges, see Daniel Goleman, "What Makes a Leader," *Harvard Business Review* 76, no. 6 (November–December 1998), pp. 92–102; Ronald A. Heifetz and Donald L. Laurie, "The Work of Leadership," *Harvard Business Review* 75, no. 1 (January–February 1997), pp. 124–34; Charles M. Farkas and Suzy Wetlaufer, "The Ways Chief Executive Officers Lead," *Harvard Business Review* 74, no. 3 (May–June 1996), pp. 110–22. See also Michael E. Porter, Jay W. Lorsch, and Nitin Nohria, "Seven Surprises for New CEOs," *Harvard Business Review* 82, no. 10 (October 2004), pp. 62–72.

PART 2

Cases in Crafting and Executing Strategy

Mystic Monk Coffee

David L. Turnipseed
University of South Alabama

As Father Daniel Mary, the Prior of the Carmelite Order of monks in Clark, Wyoming, walked to chapel to preside over Mass, he noticed the sun glistening across the four-inch snowfall from the previous evening. Snow in June was not unheard of in Wyoming, but the late snowfall and the bright glow of the rising sun made him consider the opposing forces accompanying change and how he might best prepare his monastery to achieve his vision of creating a new Mount Carmel in the Rocky Mountains. His vision of transforming the small brotherhood of 13 monks living in a small home used as makeshift rectory into a 500-acre monastery that would include accommodations for 30 monks, a Gothic church, a convent for Carmelite nuns, a retreat center for lay visitors, and a hermitage presented a formidable challenge. However, as a former high school football player, boxer, bull rider, and man of great faith, Father Prior Daniel Mary was unaccustomed to shrinking from a challenge.

Father Prior had identified a nearby ranch for sale that met the requirements of his vision perfectly, but its current listing price of $8.9 million presented a financial obstacle to creating a place of prayer, worship, and solitude in the Rockies. The Carmelites had received a $250,000 donation that could be used toward the purchase, and the monastery had earned nearly $75,000 during the first year of its Mystic Monk coffee-roasting operations, but more money would be needed. The coffee roaster used to produce packaged coffee sold to Catholic consumers at the Mystic Monk Coffee website was reaching its capacity, but a larger roaster could be purchased for $35,000. Also, local Cody, Wyoming, business owners had begun a foundation for those wishing to donate to the monks' cause. Father Prior Daniel Mary did not have a great deal of experience in business matters but considered to what extent the monastery could rely on its Mystic Monk Coffee operations to fund the purchase of the ranch. If Mystic Monk Coffee was capable of making the vision a reality, what were the next steps in turning the coffee into land?

THE CARMELITE MONKS OF WYOMING

Carmelites are a religious order of the Catholic Church that was formed by men who came to the Holy Land as pilgrims and crusaders and had chosen to remain near Jerusalem to seek God. The men established their hermitage at Mount Carmel because of its beauty, seclusion, and Biblical importance as the site where Elijah stood against King Ahab and the false prophets of Jezebel to prove Jehovah to be the one true God. The Carmelites led a life of solitude, silence, and prayer at Mount Carmel before eventually returning to Europe and becoming a recognized order of the Catholic Church. The size of the Carmelite Order varied widely throughout the centuries with its peak coming in the 1600s and stood at approximately 2,200 friars living on all inhabited continents at the beginning of the 21st century.

The Wyoming Carmelite monastery was founded by Father Daniel Mary who lived as a Carmelite hermit in Minnesota before moving to Clark, Wyoming, to establish the new monastery. The Wyoming Carmelites were a cloistered order and were allowed to leave the monastery only by permission of the bishop for medical needs or the death of a family member. The Wyoming monastery's abbey bore little resemblance to the great stone cathedrals and monasteries of Europe and was confined to a rectory that had once been a four-bedroom ranch-style home and an adjoining 42 acres of land that had been donated to the monastery.

There were 13 monks dedicated to a life of prayer and worship in the Wyoming Carmelite monastery. Since the founding of the monastery six years ago, there had been more than 500 inquiries from young men considering becoming a Wyoming Carmelite. Father Prior Daniel Mary wished to eventually have 30 monks who would join the brotherhood at age 19 to 30 and live out their lives in the monastery. However, the selection criteria for acceptance into the monastery were rigorous, with the monks making certain that applicants understood the reality of the vows of obedience, chastity, and poverty and the sacrifices associated with living a cloistered religious life.

The Daily Activities of a Carmelite Monk

The Carmelite monks' day began at 4:10 A.M., when they arose and went to chapel for worship wearing traditional brown habits and handmade sandals. At about 6:00 A.M., the monks rested and contemplated in silence for one hour before Father Prior began morning Mass. After Mass, the monks went about their manual labors. In performing their labors, each brother had a special set of skills that enabled the monastery to independently maintain its operations. Brother Joseph Marie was an excellent mechanic, Brother Paul was a carpenter, Brother Peter Joseph (Brother Cook) worked in the kitchen, and five-foot, four-inch Brother Simon Mary (Little Monk) was the secretary to Father Daniel Mary. Brother Elias,

affectionately known as Brother Java, was Mystic Monk Coffee's master roaster, although he was not a coffee drinker.

Each monk worked up to six hours per day; however, the monks' primary focus was spiritual, with eight hours of each day spent in prayer. At 11:40 A.M., the monks stopped work and went to Chapel. Afterward they had lunch, cleaned the dishes, and went back to work. At 3:00 P.M., the hour that Jesus was believed to have died on the cross, work stopped again for prayer and worship. The monks then returned to work until the bell was rung for Vespers (evening prayer). After Vespers, the monks had an hour of silent contemplation, an evening meal, and more prayers before bedtime.

The New Mount Carmel

Soon after arriving in Wyoming, Father Daniel Mary had formed the vision of acquiring a large parcel of land—a new Mount Carmel—and building a monastery with accommodations for 30 monks, a retreat center for lay visitors, a Gothic church, a convent for Carmelite nuns, and a hermitage. In a letter to supporters posted on the monastery's website, Father Daniel Mary succinctly stated his vision: "We beg your prayers, your friendship and your support that this vision, our vision may come to be that Mount Carmel may be refounded in Wyoming's Rockies for the glory of God."

The brothers located a 496-acre ranch for sale that would satisfy all of the requirements to create a new Mount Carmel. The Irma Lake Ranch was located about 21 miles outside Cody, Wyoming, and included a remodeled 17,800-square-foot residence, a 1,700-square-foot caretaker house, a 2,950-square-foot guesthouse, a hunting cabin, a dairy and horse barn, and forested land. The ranch was at the end of a seven-mile-long private gravel road and was bordered on one side by the private Hoodoo Ranch (100,000 acres) and on the other by the Shoshone National Park (2.4 million acres). Although the asking price was $8.9 million, the monks believed they would be able to acquire the property through donations and the profits generated by the monastery's Mystic Monk Coffee operations. The $250,000 donation they had received from an individual wishing to support the Carmelites could be applied toward whatever purpose the monks chose. Additionally, a group of Cody business owners had formed the New Mount Carmel Foundation to help the monks raise funds.

OVERVIEW OF THE COFFEE INDUSTRY

About 150 million consumers in the United States drank coffee, with 89 percent of U.S. coffee drinkers brewing their own coffee at home rather than purchasing ready-to-drink coffee at coffee shops and restaurants such as Starbucks, Dunkin' Donuts, or McDonald's. Packaged coffee for home brewing was easy to find in any grocery store and typically carried a retail price of $4 to $6 for a 12-ounce package. About 30 million coffee drinkers in the United States preferred premium-quality specialty coffees that sold for $7 to $10 per 12-ounce package. Specialty coffees were made from high-quality Arabica beans instead of the mix of low-quality Arabica beans and bitter, less flavorful Robusta beans that makers of value brands used. The wholesale price of Robusta coffee beans averaged $1.15 per pound, while mild Columbian Arabica wholesale prices averaged $1.43 per pound.

Specialty coffees sold under premium brands such as Starbucks, Seattle's Best, Millstone, and Green Mountain Coffee Roasters might also be made from shade-grown or organically grown coffee beans, or have been purchased from a grower belonging to a World Fair Trade Organization (WFTO) cooperative. WFTO cooperative growers were paid above-market prices to better support the cost of operating their farms—for example, WFTO-certified organic wholesale prices averaged $1.55 per pound. Many consumers who purchased specialty coffees were willing to pay a higher price for organic, shade-grown, or fair trade coffee because of their personal health or social concerns—organic coffees were grown without the use of synthetic fertilizers or pesticides, shade-grown coffee plants were allowed to grow beneath the canopies of larger indigenous trees, and fair trade pricing made it easier for farmers in developing countries to pay workers a living wage. The specialty coffee segment of the retail coffee industry had grown dramatically in the United States, with retail sales increasing from $8.3 billion to $13.5 billion during the last seven years. The retail sales of organic coffee accounted for about $1 billion of industry sales and had grown at an annual rate of 32 percent for each of the last seven years.

MYSTIC MONK COFFEE

Mystic Monk Coffee was produced using high-quality fair trade Arabica and fair trade/organic Arabica beans. The monks produced whole-bean and ground caffeinated and decaffeinated varieties in dark, medium, and light roasts and in different flavors. The most popular Mystic Monk flavors were Mystical Chants of Carmel, Cowboy Blend, Royal Rum Pecan, and Mystic Monk Blend. With the exception of sample bags, which carried a retail price of $2.99, all varieties of Mystic Monk Coffee were sold via the monastery's website (www.mysticmonkcoffee.com) in 12-ounce bags at a price of $9.95. All purchases from the website were delivered by United Parcel Service (UPS) or the U.S. Postal Service. Frequent customers were given the option of joining a "coffee club," which offered monthly delivery of one to six bags of preselected coffee. Purchases of three or more bags qualified for free shipping. The Mystic Monk Coffee website also featured T-shirts, gift cards, CDs featuring the monastery's Gregorian chants, and coffee mugs.

Mystic Monk Coffee's target market was the segment of the U.S. Catholic population who drank coffee and wished to support the monastery's mission. More than 69 million Americans were members of the Catholic Church—making it four times larger than the second-largest Christian denomination in the United States. An appeal to Catholics to "use their Catholic coffee dollar for Christ and his Catholic church" was published on the Mystic Monk Coffee website.

Mystic Monk Coffee-Roasting Operations

After the morning religious services and breakfast, Brother Java roasted the green coffee beans delivered each week from a coffee broker in Seattle, Washington. The monks paid the Seattle broker the prevailing wholesale price per pound, which fluctuated daily with global supply and demand. The capacity of Mystic Monk Coffee's roaster limited production to 540 pounds per day; production was also limited by time devoted to prayer, silent meditation, and worship. Demand for Mystic Monk Coffee had not yet exceeded the roaster's capacity, but the monastery planned to purchase a larger, 130-pound-per-hour-roaster when demand further approached the current roaster's capacity. The monks had received a quote of $35,000 for the new larger roaster.

Marketing and Website Operations

Mystic Monk Coffee was promoted primarily by word of mouth among loyal customers in Catholic parishes across the United States. The majority of Mystic Monk's sales were made through its website, but on occasion telephone orders were placed with the monks' secretary, who worked outside the cloistered part of the monastery. Mystic Monk also offered secular website operators commissions on its sales through its Mystic Monk Coffee Affiliate Program, which placed banner ads and text ads on participating websites. Affiliate sites earned an 18 percent commission on sales made to customers who were directed to the Mystic Monk site from their site. The affiliate program's ShareASale participation level allowed affiliates to refer new affiliates to Mystic Monk and earn 56 percent of the new affiliate's commission. The monks had also just recently expanded Mystic Monk's business model to include wholesale sales to churches and local coffee shops.

Mystic Monk's Financial Performance

At the conclusion of Mystic Monk Coffee's first year in operation, its sales of coffee and coffee accessories averaged about $56,500 per month. Its cost of sales averaged about 30 percent of revenues, inbound shipping costs accounted for 19 percent of revenues, and broker fees were 3 percent of revenues—for a total cost of goods sold of 52 percent. Operating expenses such as utilities, supplies, telephone, and website maintenance averaged 37 percent of revenues. Thus, Mystic Monk's net profit margin averaged 11 percent of revenues.

REALIZING THE VISION

During a welcome period of solitude before his evening meal, Father Prior Daniel Mary again contemplated the purchase of the Irma Lake Ranch. He realized that his vision of purchasing the ranch would require careful planning and execution. For the Wyoming Carmelites, coffee sales were a means of support from the outside world that might provide the financial resources to purchase the land. Father Prior understood that the cloistered monastic environment offered unique challenges to operating a business enterprise, but it also provided opportunities that were not available to secular businesses. He resolved to develop an execution plan that would enable Mystic Monk Coffee to minimize the effect of its cloistered monastic constraints, maximize the potential of monastic opportunities, and realize his vision of buying the Irma Lake Ranch.

Whole Foods Market in 2010: Vision, Core Values, and Strategy

Arthur A. Thompson
The University of Alabama

Founded in 1980, Whole Foods Market had evolved from a local supermarket for natural and health foods in Austin, Texas, into the world's largest chain of natural and organic foods supermarkets. The company had 2009 sales revenues of $8 billion and, in early 2010, had 289 stores in the United States, Canada, and Great Britain. Over the course of its 30-year history, Whole Foods Market had emerged as a leader in the natural and organic foods movement across the United States, helping the industry gain acceptance among growing numbers of consumers concerned about the food they ate. The company sought to offer the highest quality, least processed, most flavorful naturally preserved and fresh foods available, and it marketed them in appealing store environments that made shopping at Whole Foods interesting and enjoyable. John Mackey, the company's cofounder and CEO, believed that marketing high-quality natural and organic foods to more and more customers in more and more communities would gradually transform the diets of individuals in a manner that would help them live longer, healthier, more pleasurable lives.

Mackey's vision was for Whole Foods to become an international brand synonymous with carrying the highest quality natural and organic foods available and being the best food retailer in every community in which Whole Foods stores were located. He wanted Whole Foods Market to set the standard for excellence in food retailing. But the company's mission—summarized in the slogan "Whole Foods, Whole People, Whole Planet"—extended well beyond food retailing (see Exhibit 1). Mackey was convinced that Whole Foods' rapid growth and market success had much to do with its having "remained a uniquely mission-driven company—highly selective about what we sell, dedicated to our core values and stringent quality standards, and committed to sustainable agriculture."

While Mackey's growth objectives for Whole Foods had been to have 400 stores and sales of $12 billion by the end of fiscal year 2010, the economic downturn in the United States that accelerated swiftly in 2008 hit Whole Foods hard and forced a number of strategy changes in 2008–2009.

THE NATURAL AND ORGANIC FOODS INDUSTRY

Foods labeled "natural" and "organic" generated estimated retail sales across North America of $30 to $35 billion in 2009. *Natural foods* are defined as foods that are (1) minimally processed; (2) largely or completely free of artificial ingredients, preservatives, and other non–naturally occurring chemicals; and (3) as near to their whole, natural state as possible. The U.S. Department of Agriculture's Food and Safety Inspection Service defines *natural food* as "a product containing no artificial ingredient or added color and that is minimally processed." Organic foods were a special subset of the natural foods category and, to earn the label "organic," had to be grown and processed without the use of pesticides, antibiotics,

Exhibit 1   Whole Foods' Mission: Whole Foods, Whole People, Whole Planet

---

Whole Foods

We obtain our products locally and from all over the world, often from small, uniquely dedicated food artisans. We strive to offer the highest quality, least processed, most flavorful and naturally preserved foods. We believe that food in its purest state, unadulterated by artificial additives, sweeteners, colorings and preservatives, is the best tasting and most nutritious food available.

Whole People

We recruit the best people we can to become part of our team. We empower them to make many operational decisions, creating a respectful workplace where team members are treated fairly and are highly motivated to succeed. We look for team members who are passionate about food, but also well-rounded human beings who can play a critical role in helping to build our Company into a profitable and beneficial part of every community we serve.

Whole Planet

We believe companies, like individuals, must assume their share of responsibility for our planet. We actively support organic farming on a global basis because we believe it is the best method for promoting sustainable agriculture and protecting the environment and farm workers. We also assist our global neighbors through our Whole Planet Foundation's microlending operations. On a local basis, we are actively involved in our communities by supporting food banks, sponsoring neighborhood events, and contributing at least 5% of our after-tax profits in the form of cash or products to not-for-profit organizations.

Source: Whole Foods, 2009 10-K report, p. 5.

---

hormones, synthetic chemicals, artificial fertilizers, preservatives, dyes or additives, or genetic engineering. Organic foods included fresh fruits and vegetables, meats, and processed foods that had been produced using:

1. Agricultural management practices that promoted a healthy and renewable ecosystem that used no genetically engineered seeds or crops; petroleum-based fertilizers; fertilizers made from sewage sludge; or long-lasting pesticides, herbicides, or fungicides.

2. Livestock management practices that involved organically grown feed, fresh air and outdoor access for the animals, and no use of antibiotics or growth hormones.

3. Food-processing practices that protected the integrity of the organic product and disallowed the use of radiation, genetically modified ingredients, or synthetic preservatives.

According to the Nielsen Company's "Healthy Eating Report for 2008," food labeled as "natural" generated $22.3 billion in sales in the United States in 2008, up 10 percent from 2007, and up 37 percent from 2004; UPC-coded organic foods accounted for $4.9 billion in sales, up 16 percent from the year before, and up 132 percent since 2004.[1] A study sponsored by the Organic Trade Association found that U.S. sales of organic food

and nonfood products in 2008 totaled $24.6 billion. *Nutrition Business Journal,* a provider of marketing research data for the nutrition industry, estimated that sales of natural and organic foods in the United States totaled $31 billion in 2009. Organic food sales were said to represent 3.5 percent of total U.S. retail sales of food and beverages and about 1 percent of total retail sales of food and beverages in Canada.[2] Global sales of organic products were estimated to be $52 billion in 2008 and to have grown at a compound rate of 13 percent since 2004.[3]

In 1990, passage of the Organic Food Production Act started the process of establishing national standards for organically grown products in the United States, a movement that included farmers, food activists, conventional food producers, and consumer groups. In October 2002, the U.S. Department of Agriculture (USDA) officially established labeling standards for organic products, overriding both the patchwork of inconsistent state regulations for what could be labeled as organic and the different rules of some 43 agencies for certifying organic products. The new USDA regulations established four categories of food with organic ingredients, with varying levels of organic purity:

1. *100 percent organic products:* Such products were usually whole foods, such as fresh

fruits and vegetables, grown by organic methods—which meant that the product had been grown without the use of synthetic pesticides or sewage-based fertilizers; had not been subjected to irradiation; and had not been genetically modified or injected with bioengineered organisms, growth hormones, or antibiotics. Products that were 100 percent organic could carry the green USDA organic certification seal, provided the merchant could document that the food product had been organically grown (usually by a certified organic producer).

2. *Organic products:* Such products, often processed, had to have at least 95 percent organically certified ingredients. These could also carry the green USDA organic certification seal.

3. *Made with organic ingredients:* Such products had to have at least 70 percent organic ingredients; they could be labeled "made with organic ingredients" but could not display the USDA seal.

4. *All other products with organic ingredients:* Products with less than 70 percent organic ingredients could not use the word *organic* on the front of a package, but organic ingredients could be listed among other ingredients in a less prominent part of the package.

The USDA's labeling standards were intended to enable shoppers who were ingredient-conscious or wanted to buy pesticide-free food or support sustainable agricultural practices to evaluate product labels where the word *organic* appeared. The standards were not meant to imply anything about the health or safety of organic products (because there was no credible scientific evidence that organic products were more nutritious or safer to eat than conventionally grown products). The USDA also issued regulations requiring documentation on the part of growers, processors, exporters, importers, shippers, and merchants to verify that they were certified to grow, process, or handle organic products carrying the USDA's organic seal. In 2003, Whole Foods was designated as the first national "Certified Organic" grocer by Quality Assurance International, a federally recognized, independent third-party certification organization.

Major food-processing companies like Kraft, General Mills, Groupe Danone (the parent of yogurt-maker Dannon), Dean Foods, and Kellogg had all purchased organic food producers in an effort to capitalize on growing consumer interest in organic foods. Heinz had introduced an organic ketchup and bought a 19 percent stake in Hain Celestial Group, one of the largest organic and natural foods producers. Campbell Soup had introduced organic tomato juice. Starbucks, Green Mountain Coffee Roasters, and several other premium coffee marketers were marketing organically grown coffees; Coca-Cola's Odwalla juices were organic; Del Monte and Hunt's were marketing organic canned tomatoes; and Tyson Foods and several other chicken producers had introduced organic chicken products. Producers of organically grown beef were selling all they could produce; in 2009, the market share of natural/organic beef was about 2.7 percent based on dollars and 1.8 percent based on volume.[4]

According to the most recent data from the USDA, there were 4.1 million acres of organic farmland in the United States (about 1.7 million acres of cropland and 2.4 million acres of rangeland and pasture) in 2005, up from a total of 2.1 million acres in 2001.[5] There were approximately 13,000 certified organic producers in the United States in 2007, and perhaps another 9,000 small farmers growing organic products. All 50 states had some certified organic farmland, with California, North Dakota, Montana, Minnesota, Wisconsin, Texas, and Idaho having the largest amount of certified organic cropland.

While less than 1 percent of U.S. farmland was certified organic in 2005, farmers were becoming increasingly interested in and attracted to organic farming, chiefly because of the substantially higher prices they could get for organically grown fruits, vegetables, and meats. Since 2005, health-conscious chefs at many fine restaurants had begun sourcing ingredients for their dishes from local organic farmers and touting the use of organically grown products on their menus. Growing restaurant use of organically grown herbs, vegetables, and fruits, as well as organic cheeses and meats, was spurring the growth of organic farming (since supplying local restaurants gave organic producers a ready market for their crops).

RETAILING OF ORGANIC FOODS

Organic foods and beverages were available in nearly every food category in 2010 and were available in more than 80 percent of U.S. retail food stores. Close to 70 percent of overall organic sales in 2009 were through mainstream supermarkets/grocery stores and leading organic and natural food supermarket chains such as Whole Foods, Trader Joe's, and Fresh Market. Roughly 20 percent of organic sales were through small, independent chain natural grocery stores.

In recent years, mainstream supermarkets had gradually expanded their offerings of natural and organic products for two reasons. One was that mounting consumer enthusiasm for organic products allowed retailers to earn attractively high profit margins on organics (compared with other grocery items, where intense price competition among rival supermarket chains on general food products limited profit margins). The other was that consumer demand for organics was growing at double-digit rates (compared with growth rates of only 2–3 percent for traditional grocery products). Several factors had combined to transform organic foods retailing, once a niche market, into the fastest-growing segment of U.S. food sales:

- A "wellness," or health-consciousness, trend among people of many ages and ethnic groups.
- Heightened awareness of the role that food, nutrition, and good eating patterns played in long-term health. Among those most interested in organic products were aging, affluent people concerned about their health.
- Increasing consumer concerns over the purity and safety of food due to the presence of pesticide residues, growth hormones, artificial ingredients and other chemicals, and genetically engineered ingredients.
- Growing belief that organic farming had positive environmental effects, particularly in contributing to healthier soil and water conditions and to sustainable agricultural practices.

Organic food products were anywhere from to 10 to 40 percent more expensive than non-organic foods, chiefly because of higher production, distribution, and marketing costs for organic products.

Such higher prices were the primary barrier for most consumers in trying or using organic products.

By 2010, most supermarket chains stocked a selection of natural and organic food items—including fresh produce, canned and frozen fruits and vegetables, milk, cheeses, yogurt, vinegars, salad dressings, cereals, pastas, and meats—and the number and variety of organic items on supermarket shelves was growing. Fresh fruits and vegetables accounted for close to 40 percent of total organic food sales, with organic lettuce, spinach, broccoli, cauliflower, celery, carrots, and apples among the biggest sellers. Meat, dairy, bread and grains, and snack foods were among the fastest-growing organic product categories.

Leading supermarket chains like Walmart, Kroger, Publix, Safeway, and Supervalu/Save-a-Lot had created special "organic and health food" sections for nonperishable natural foods and organics in most of their stores. Kroger, Publix, and several other chains also had special sections for fresh organic fruits and vegetables in their produce cases in most all of their stores. Walmart, Target, Safeway, Publix, and Kroger were stocking organic beef and chicken in many of their stores. Whole Foods was struggling to find organic beef and chicken suppliers that were big enough to supply all its stores. Two chains—upscale Harris Teeter in the southeastern United States and Whole Foods Market—had launched their own private-label brands of organics. Exhibit 2 shows the leading supermarket retailers in North America in 2009. Whole Foods Market was ranked 21st in 2009, up from 26th in 2004.

WHOLE FOODS MARKET

Whole Foods Market was founded in Austin, Texas, when John Mackey, the current CEO, and two other local natural foods grocers in Austin decided the natural foods industry was ready for a supermarket format. The original Whole Foods Market opened in 1980 with a staff of only 19. It was an immediate success. At the time, there were less than half a dozen natural foods supermarkets in the United States. By 1991, the company had 10 stores, revenues of $92.5 million, and net income of $1.6 million; over the next 18 years, sales grew at a compound annual rate of approximately 28 percent, to just over $8 billion. Whole Foods

Exhibit 2   Leading North American Supermarket Chains, 2009

Rank/Company	Number of Stores	2009 Estimated Sales of Food and Grocery Products in North America (in billions)	Estimated Share of Total Grocery Sales in North America ($894 billion)
1. Walmart	2,751	$125.3[a]	14.0%
2. Kroger	2,477	77.2[b]	8.6
3. Supervalu	2,491	45.0[c]	5.0
4. Safeway	1,743	44.8	5.0
5. Costco	527	39.1[d]	4.4
6. Loblaw[f]	1,036	31.5	3.5
7. Sam's Club	599	25.7[e]	2.9
8. Publix Supermarkets	990	24.0	2.7
9. Ahold USA[g]	704	21.8	2.4
10. Delhaize America[h]	1,544	19.2	2.1
11. Whole Foods Market	284	8.0	0.9

[a] Sales revenue numbers are an estimate of sales of food, grocery, and supermarket-related items only for all Walmart Discount Stores and Supercenters in the United States; such sales represented about 49 percent of total sales at these stores.

[b] The sales revenue number for Kroger includes sales at all of the company's retail outlets (including fuel centers, drugstores, apparel, and jewelry), not just those at its several supermarket chains (Kroger, City Market, King Sooper, Ralph's, and 11 other small chains).

[c] Sales data for Supervalu include 1,279 conventional supermarkets (including stores recently acquired from Albertson's), 317 corporate-owned Save-A-Lots, 863 licensed Save-A-Lots, and 32 licensed Cub Foods stores.

[d] The sales revenue number for Costco includes only the sales of grocery and supermarket-related items (food, sundries, fresh produce) rather than sales of all products sold at Costco stores.

[e] The sales number for Sam's Club includes only those items related to food and sundries (snack foods, tobacco, alcoholic and nonalcoholic beverages, paper goods, laundry and home care, and other consumables) but is for all Sam's Club stores worldwide; food and sundries items accounted for 67% of total sales of approximately $46.7 billion at all Sam's Club locations worldwide in 2009.

[f] Loblaw is a Canadian chain that operates 628 corporate stores and supplies 408 franchised stores. The sales revenue numbers are in U.S. dollars.

[g] Ahold USA, the U.S. division of Netherlands-based Ahold, includes 376 Stop & Shops, 180 Giant Foods (Landover, Md.), and 148 Giant Foods (Carlisle, Pa.).

[h] Delhaize includes 1,148 Food Lion stores, 167 Hannaford Bros. stores, 108 Sweetbay Supermarkets, 69 Harvey's stores, 61 Bloom units, and 18 Bottom Dollar Food stores.

Source: Wal-Mart's 2009 10-K report, Costco's 2009 10-K report, and Top 75 North American Food Retailers, www.supermarketnews.com, accessed March 29, 2010.

became a public company in 1992, with its stock trading on the NASDAQ. As of March 2010, Whole Foods operated 278 stores in 38 U.S. states and the District of Columbia, 6 stores in Canada, and 5 in Great Britain. Just over 97 percent of Whole Foods' sales were in the United States. Its stores averaged approximately 37,000 square feet in size and $29 million in sales annually.

Core Values

In 1997, when Whole Foods developed the "Whole Foods, Whole People, Whole Planet" slogan to symbolize its mission, John Mackey, known as a

go-getter with a "cowboy way of doing things," said:

> This slogan taps into perhaps the deepest purpose of Whole Foods Market. It's a purpose we seldom talk about because it seems pretentious, but a purpose nevertheless felt by many of our team members and by many of our customers (and hopefully many of our shareholders too). Our deepest purpose as an organization is helping support the health, well-being, and healing of both people (customers and Team Members) and of the planet (sustainable agriculture, organic production and environmental sensitivity). When I peel away the onion of my personal consciousness down to its

core in trying to understand what has driven me to create and grow this company, I come to my desire to promote the general well-being of everyone on earth as well as the earth itself. This is my personal greater purpose with the company and the slogan perfectly reflects it.

Complementing the "Whole Foods, Whole People, Whole Planet" mission was a statement of seven core values that governed how the company endeavored to conduct its business (see Exhibit 3).

Whole Foods' managers and, just as important, employees (referred to as team members) took pride in "walking the talk" when it came to the seven core values. The prevailing philosophy at Whole Foods was that the company's success and long-term profitability depended on its ability to simultaneously satisfy the needs and desires of its customers, team members, investors, and suppliers, while also demonstrating a genuine concern for the communities in which it operated and the environment.

Exhibit 3 Whole Foods Market's Seven Core Values

Our Core Values

The following list of core values reflects what is truly important to us as an organization. These are not values that change from time to time, situation to situation or person to person, but rather they are the underpinning of our company culture. Many people feel Whole Foods is an exciting company of which to be a part and a very special place to work. These core values are the primary reasons for this feeling, and they transcend our size and our growth rate. By maintaining these core values, regardless of how large a company Whole Foods becomes, we can preserve what has always been special about our company. These core values are the soul of our company.

1. Selling the Highest Quality Natural and Organic Products Available

- **Passion for Food**—We appreciate and celebrate the difference natural and organic products can make in the quality of one's life.
- **Quality Standards**—We have high standards and our goal is to sell the highest quality products we possibly can. We define quality by evaluating the ingredients, freshness, safety, taste, nutritive value and appearance of all of the products we carry. We are buying agents for our customers and not the selling agents for the manufacturers.

2. Satisfying and Delighting Our Customers

- **Our Customers**—They are our most important stakeholders in our business and the lifeblood of our business. Only by satisfying our customers first do we have the opportunity to satisfy the needs of our other stakeholders.
- **Extraordinary Customer Service**—We go to extraordinary lengths to satisfy and delight our customers. We want to meet or exceed their expectations on every shopping trip. We know that by doing so we turn customers into advocates for our business. Advocates do more than shop with us, they talk about Whole Foods to their friends and others. We want to serve our customers competently, efficiently, knowledgeably and with flair.
- **Education**—We can generate greater appreciation and loyalty from all of our stakeholders by educating them about natural and organic foods, health, nutrition and the environment.
- **Meaningful Value**—We offer value to our customers by providing them with high quality products, extraordinary service and a competitive price. We are constantly challenged to improve the value proposition to our customers.
- **Retail Innovation**—We value retail experiments. Friendly competition within the company helps us to continually improve our stores. We constantly innovate and raise our retail standards and are not afraid to try new ideas and concepts.
- **Inviting Store Environments**—We create store environments that are inviting and fun, and reflect the communities they serve. We want our stores to become community meeting places where our customers meet their friends and make new ones.

3. Team Member Happiness and Excellence

- **Empowering Work Environments**—Our success is dependent upon the collective energy and intelligence of all of our Team Members. We strive to create a work environment where motivated Team Members can flourish and succeed to their highest potential. We appreciate effort and reward results.
- **Self-Responsibility**—We take responsibility for our own success and failures. We celebrate success and see failures as opportunities for growth. We recognize that we are responsible for our own happiness and success.
- **Self-Directed Teams**—The fundamental work unit of the company is the self-directed Team. Teams meet regularly to discuss issues, solve problems and appreciate each others' contributions. Every Team Member belongs to a Team.

(Continued)

Our Core Values

- **Open & Timely Information**—We believe knowledge is power and we support our Team Members' right to access information that impacts their jobs. Our books are open to our Team Members, including our annual individual compensation report. We also recognize everyone's right to be listened to and heard regardless of their point of view.

- **Incremental Progress**—Our company continually improves through unleashing the collective creativity and intelligence of all of our Team Members. We recognize that everyone has a contribution to make. We keep getting better at what we do.

- **Shared Fate**—We recognize there is a community of interest among all of our stakeholders. There are no entitlements; we share together in our collective fate. To that end we have a salary cap that limits the compensation (wages plus profit incentive bonuses) of any Team Member to nineteen times the average total compensation of all full-time Team Members in the company.

4. Creating Wealth Through Profits & Growth

- **Stewardship**—We are stewards of our shareholders' investments and we take that responsibility very seriously. We are committed to increasing long term shareholder value.

- **Profits**—We earn our profits every day through voluntary exchange with our customers. We recognize that profits are essential to creating capital for growth, prosperity, opportunity, job satisfaction and job security.

5. Caring About Our Communities & Our Environment

- **Sustainable Agriculture**—We support organic farmers, growers and the environment through our commitment to sustainable agriculture and by expanding the market for organic products.

- **Wise Environmental Practices**—We respect our environment and recycle, reuse, and reduce our waste wherever and whenever we can.

- **Community Citizenship**—We recognize our responsibility to be active participants in our local communities. We give a minimum of 5% of our profits every year to a wide variety of community and non-profit organizations.

- **Integrity in All Business Dealings**—Our trade partners are our allies in serving our stakeholders. We treat them with respect, fairness and integrity at all times and expect the same in return.

6. Creating Ongoing Win-Win Partnerships With Our Suppliers

- **Integrity in All Business Dealings**—Our supplier partners are our allies in serving the interests of our other stakeholders in bringing to market the safest highest quality products available. We treat them with respect, fairness and integrity at all times and expect the same in return. We seek supplier partnerships that share our concern for social responsibility and the environment.

- **Honesty and Communication**—We are committed to honesty, timeliness and clarity in communicating with our suppliers and we expect the same in return.

- **Transparency**—We seek to create transparency from "farm to fork" with respect to production, planning, sourcing, ingredients, product safety and efficacy in order to bring to market the safest highest quality products available. We work with our supplier partners in eliminating all unnecessary production and distribution costs to help ensure the best possible price.

- **Education**—We partner with our suppliers to educate, inspire and communicate the outstanding quality and benefits of our products to promote a lifestyle of health, balance and well-being.

- **Innovation/Differentiation**—We foster supplier partnerships that enable us to remain at the forefront of the retail food industry, by creating new, unique and innovative products.

7. Promoting the health of our stakeholders through healthy eating education

These core values speak to our belief in a balanced way of doing business. They very succinctly express the purpose of our business, which is not only to make profits, but to create value for all of our major stakeholders—our customers, team members, suppliers, investors, and the community and environment. All are linked interdependently.

Source: Whole Foods Market, www.wholefoodsmarket.com, accessed March 11, 2010.

Growth Strategy

Since going public in 1991, Whole Foods had maintained a growth strategy of expanding via a combination of opening its own new stores and acquiring small, owner-managed chains that had capable personnel and were located in desirable markets—the company's most significant acquisitions are shown in Exhibit 4. But attractive acquisition candidates were hard to find because

Exhibit 4   Major Acquisitions by Whole Foods Market, 1992–2009

Year	Company Acquired	Location	Number of Stores	Acquisition Costs
1992	Bread & Circus	U.S. Northeast	6	$20 million plus $6.2 million in common stock
1993	Mrs. Gooch's	Southern California	7	2,970,596 shares of common stock
1996	Fresh Fields Markets	East Coast and Chicago area	22	4.8 million shares of stock plus options for 549,000 additional shares
1997	Merchant of Vino	Detroit area	6	Approximately 1 million shares of common stock
1997	Bread of Life	South Florida	2	200,000 shares of common stock
1999	Nature's Heartland	Boston area	4	$24.5 million in cash
2000	Food for Thought (Natural Abilities, Inc)	Sonoma County, California	3	$25.7 million in cash, plus assumption of certain liabilities
2001	Harry's Farmer's Market	Atlanta	3	Approximately $35 million in cash
2004	Fresh & Wild	Great Britain	7	$20 million in cash plus 239,000 shares of common stock
2007	Wild Oats Natural Marketplace	United States and Canada	74 (after sale of 35 stores)	$565 million plus the assumption of $137 million in debt; however, Whole Foods received approximately $166 million for the 35 stores that were subsequently sold (out of the total of 109 stores that were acquired)

Source: Investor relations section of www.wholefoodsmarket.com, accessed November 18, 2004, and March 21, 2008.

most retailers of natural and organic foods were one-store operations or small, regional chains having stores in the 5,000- to 20,000-square-foot range. Starting in 2002, Whole Food's management decided to drive growth by opening 10 to 15 decidedly bigger stores in metropolitan areas each year—stores that ranged from 40,000 square feet to as much as 80,000 square feet and were on the same scale or larger than the conventional supermarkets operated by Kroger, Safeway, Publix, and other chains.

Then, in 2007, Whole Foods began what proved to be a largely successful, but contentious, two-and-a-half-year battle to purchase the struggling Wild Oats Market—Whole Foods' biggest competitor in natural and organic foods—for an acquisition price of $700 million. Wild Oats

operated 109 older and smaller stores (averaging 24,000 square feet in size) in 23 states under the Wild Oats Market, Henry's Farmer's Market, and Sun Harvest brands and had total annual sales of about $1.2 billion. The Federal Trade Commission (FTC) opposed the acquisition on the grounds that competition in the organic foods retailing segment would be weakened; however, a U.S. district court ruled that the FTC's position lacked merit. When the district court's ruling was upheld on appeal, Whole Foods went forward and completed its acquisition of Wild Oats in late August 2007. Acquiring Wild Oats gave Whole Foods entry into 5 new states and 14 new metropolitan markets. Whole Foods then quickly sold 35 Henry's and Sun Harvest stores in California and Texas previously acquired by Wild

Oats, along with a California distribution center, to Los Angeles food retailer Smart & Final, realizing approximately $165 million from the sale and reducing its net purchase price for Wild Oats Market to about $535 million (which included the assumption of $148 million in Wild Oats' debt).[6] In addition, Whole Foods immediately closed nine Wild Oats stores that did not fit with its brand strategy or real estate strategy and began planning to relocate seven smaller Wild Oats stores to existing or soon-to-be-opened Whole Foods locations. In fiscal 2008, Whole Foods launched a program to spend close to $45 million renovating Wild Oats stores and rebranding them as Whole Foods stores.

Then, in a surprising move in July 2008, the U.S. Court of Appeals for the District of Columbia reversed the lower court's order allowing Whole Foods to acquire Wild Oats and directed the U.S. district court to reopen proceedings for further evidentiary hearings. Separately, the FTC reopened its administrative actions challenging the acquisition on antitrust grounds. To resolve the dispute, the FTC and Whole Foods entered into a consent agreement in March 2009 whereby Whole Foods would sell:

- Twelve of the former Wild Oats stores it was currently operating and one Whole Foods store.
- The leases and related fixed assets for 19 former Wild Oats stores (10 of which were closed by Wild Oats prior to the acquisition and 9 of which were closed by Whole Foods Market).
- Wild Oats trademarks and other intellectual property associated with the Wild Oats stores.

The divestiture period was later extended until 2010 to allow for the finalization of good-faith offers for 6 of the 13 operating stores and 2 of the closed stores, as well as Wild Oats' trademark and intellectual property; Whole Foods was allowed to keep the 7 remaining operating stores without further obligation to attempt to divest them. In 2010, there were 51 former Wild Oats stores operating under the Whole Foods name. In his "Letter to Stakeholders" in the company's 2009 annual report, John Mackey expressed confidence that sales and profits at these stores would continue to improve in coming years, enabling the company to realize a solid return for shareholders on the Wild Oats acquisition. However, management stated that, going forward, Whole Foods' growth strategy would be based primarily on opening new stores rather than on making acquisitions.[7]

Store Location Strategy

In March 2010, Whole Foods had 290 stores in 38 states; it planned to open an additional 9 stores by the end of fiscal year 2010, 17 new stores in fiscal year 2011, and 17 new stores in fiscal 2012 (Whole Foods' fiscal year ended the last Sunday in September). Whole Foods favored store locations in the upscale areas of urban metropolitan areas. Most stores were in high-traffic shopping locations on premier real estate sites; some were freestanding, some were in strip centers; and some were in high-density mixed-use projects. The company's "sweet spot" for most markets it had entered during 2001–2009 was a store footprint between 45,000 and 60,000 square feet (the new stores of supermarket chains like Safeway and Kroger averaged around 55,000 square feet). All told, in 2010, Whole Foods had more than 90 stores that were 40,000 square feet or larger—the biggest was a 99,800-square-foot store in London, England. Whole Foods had the two largest supermarkets in New York City: a 58,000-square-foot store on Columbus Circle in Manhattan and a 71,000-square-foot store in the Bowery area. Whole Foods had a 74,500-square-foot store in Columbus, Ohio; a flagship 78,000-square-foot store in Austin, Texas; a 77,000-square-foot store in Pasadena, California; a 75,000-square-foot store in Chicago; and two 75,000-square-foot stores in the suburbs of Atlanta, Georgia. It had more than 13 stores in excess of 65,000 square feet and an additional 4 of that size in development.

But the economic slowdown that began in 2007 and then quickly accelerated into a deep recession in 2008–2009 forced a major overhaul of Whole Foods' store expansion strategy. In November 2007, when Whole Foods had 87 new stores in varying stages of development, the company announced it was scaling back its store expansion program. The leases for 14 of the new stores were downsized by an average of 12,000 square feet each, and planned openings of some stores were delayed, prompting a reduction in the gross square footage of stores in development from 4.5 million in November 2007 to 3.3 million in November 2008 and 2.4 million in 2009. Then in 2008–2009, when the recession in the United States hit full force, management terminated 18 leases for stores in development and downsized others, determining that planned store openings during 2010–2012 would be reduced and that the majority of its new stores would be in the range of 35,000–50,000 square feet. The leases that Whole Foods had for its 51 stores in varying stages of development (some of which were for relocations of existing stores) in February 2010 averaged about 44,000 square feet (down from an average of 56,000 square feet for the 88 stores in development in November 2006). In addition, the construction and store development teams for Whole Foods' new stores adopted a leaner and more disciplined approach to design and building, including plans for smaller stores with simpler decor and smaller, less labor-intensive perishable departments; these moves were expected to result in lower costs on both a per-store and per-square-foot basis. Exhibit 5 provides store-related statistics.

Exhibit 5 **Number of Stores in the Whole Foods Markets Chain, 1991–2007, and Selected Store Operating Statistics, 2000–2007**

Year	Number of Stores at End of Fiscal Year	Year	Number of Stores End of Fiscal Year
1991	10	2001	126
1992	25	2002	135
1993	42	2003	145
1994	49	2004	163
1995	61	2005	175
1996	68	2006	186
1997	75	2007	276
1998	87	2008	275
1999	100	2009	284
2000	117	Jan. 2010	289

	Fiscal Years Ending the Last Sunday in September					
	2000	**2005**	**2006**	**2007**	**2008**	**2009**
Store sales (000s)	$1,838,630	$4,701,289	$5,607,376	$6,591,773	$7,953,912	$ 8,031,620
Average weekly sales	$ 324,710	$ 536,986	$ 593,439	$ 616,706	$ 570,000	$ 549,000
Comparable store sales growth*	8.6%	12.8%	11.0%	7.1%	4.9%	−3.1%
Total square footage of all stores, end of year	3,180,000	5,820,000	6,377,000	9,312,000	9,895,000	10,566,000
Average store size, end of year, in square feet	27,000	33,000	34,000	34,000	36,000	37,000
Gross margin, all-store average	34.5%	34.6%	34.2%	35.1%	34.9%	34.8%
Store contribution, all-store average**	9.4%	9.6%	9.3%	9.6%	9.6%	8.9%

* Defined as average annual sales increases at stores open a full year or more; represents the rate at which sales at existing stores are increasing annually on average.

** Defined as gross profit minus direct store expenses, where gross profit equals store revenues less cost of goods sold.

Sources: Whole Foods Market's 2005 10-K report and 2009 10-K report. Investor relations section of www.wholefoodsmarket.com, accessed November 18, 2004, and March 21, 2008.

The cash investment needed to get a new Whole Foods Market site ready for opening varied with the metropolitan area, store size, amount of work performed by the landlord, and the complexity of site development issues—the average capital cost for new stores was projected to be about $8 million in 2010–2012 (in 2007, capital costs averaged $15.1 million per new store).[8] In addition to the capital cost of a new store, it took about $850,000 to stock a store with inventory, a portion of which was financed by vendors. Pre-opening expenses (including rent) averaged $3 million for the 15 new stores opened or relocated in fiscal 2009.

Whole Foods had its own internally developed model to analyze potential markets according to education levels, population density, and income within certain drive times. After picking a target metropolitan area, the company's store development group did a comprehensive site study and developed sales and profit projections for several potential locations; before entering into a lease for a site, the projections had to pass specified profitability hurdles over and above a return on the capital invested in a store. During the 2007–2009 period, because of both the uncertain economic environment and internally constrained cash flows, Whole Foods' management instituted lease approval requirements for new store sites that entailed conservative sales projections and the expectation of a cumulative profit in five years or less (after deducting a return on Whole Foods' cash investment in the store). New stores opened 12 to 24 months after a lease was signed.

Product Line Strategy

Because Whole Foods stores were different sizes and had different shopper clienteles, the product and brand selections varied from 20,000 items in small stores to 50,000 items in the largest stores. Whole Foods' product line included natural, organic, and gourmet food and nonfood items in the following principal categories:

- Fresh produce—fruits; vegetables; displays of fresh-cut fruits; and a selection of seasonal, exotic, and specialty products like cactus pears, cippolini onions, and Japanese eggplant.
- Meat and poultry—natural and organic meats, house-made sausages, turkey, and chicken products from animals raised on wholesome grains, pastureland, and well water (and not grown with the use of by-products, hormones, or steroids).
- Fresh seafoods, some wild-caught and some farmed using safe and environmentally responsible practices. A portion of the fresh fish selections came from the company's four seafood processing and distribution facilities (Pigeon Cove, Select Fish, South Seafood, and Mid-Atlantic Seafood). Seafood items coming from distant supply sources were flown in to stores to ensure maximum freshness.
- A selection of daily baked goods—breads, cakes, pies, cookies, bagels, muffins, and scones.
- Prepared foods—soups, packaged salads and sandwiches, oven-ready meals, rotisserie meats, hearth-fired pizza, pastas, salad bars, a sandwich station, and a selection of entrées and side foods prepared daily.
- Fine-quality cheeses, olives (up to 40 varieties in some stores), chocolates, and confections.
- Frozen foods, juices, yogurt and dairy products, smoothies, and bottled waters.
- A wide selection of dried fruits, nuts, and spices (either prepackaged or dispensed from bins).
- Beer and wines.
- Coffees and teas. The company's Allegro coffee subsidiary supplied all stores with specialty and organic coffees that spanned the roasting spectrum from light to extra-dark roast. The tea selections included only fine and exotic teas from all the major tea-growing regions of the world.
- Grocery and household products—canned and packaged goods, pastas, soaps, cleaning products, and other conventional household items that helped make Whole Foods' larger stores a one-stop grocery shopping destination where people could get everything on their shopping list.
- A body care and nutrition department with natural and organic body care and cosmetics products, vitamin supplements, homeopathic remedies, and aromatherapy products. All items entailed the use of non-animal testing methods and contained no artificial ingredients.

- A family of private-label offerings led by its "365 Everyday Value" and "365 Organic" brands that spanned many product categories and were less expensive than comparable name brands. Whole Foods had also created private-label branding with consistent logos and packaging for specific departments and product categories (examples included "Whole Body" for personal care and nutrition products; "Whole Baby" for baby foods and baby care products; "Whole Pantry" for herbs, spices, and condiments; and "Whole Catch" for prepackaged fresh and frozen seafood items). In addition, Whole Foods had a grouping of "exclusive" and "control brand" products that outside suppliers produced and packaged exclusively for sale in Whole Foods stores. Altogether, Whole Foods' private-label lineup included 2,400 individual stock-keeping units (SKUs).

- Natural and organic pet foods (including the company's own private-label line), treats, toys, and pest control remedies.

- A floral department with sophisticated flower bouquets and a selection of plants for inside and outside the home.

- Educational materials and books related to healthy eating, cooking, healing and alternative healthcare, and lifestyle.

Whole Foods was the world's biggest seller of organic produce. Prepared foods, fresh produce, and fresh meats and seafood accounted for about 67 percent of Whole Foods' sales in 2007–2009, considerably higher than the 40–50 percent that such perishables represented at conventional supermarkets. The 2001 acquisition of the Harry's Market superstores in Atlanta, where 75 percent of sales were perishables, had provided the company with personnel having valuable intellectual capital in creatively merchandising all major perishables categories. Management believed that the company's emphasis on fresh fruits and vegetables, bakery goods, meats, seafood, and other perishables differentiated Whole Foods stores from other supermarkets and attracted a broader customer base. According to John Mackey:

> First-time visitors to Whole Foods Market are often awed by our perishables. We devote more space to fresh fruits and vegetables, including

an extensive selection of organics, than most of our competitors. Our meat and poultry products are natural—no artificial ingredients, minimal processing, and raised without the use of artificial growth hormones, antibiotics or animal by-products in their feed. Our seafood is either wild-caught or sourced from aquaculture farms where environmental concerns are a priority. Also, our seafood is never treated with chlorine or other chemicals, as is common practice in the food retailing industry. With each new store or renovation, we challenge ourselves to create more entertaining, theatrical, and scintillatingly appetizing prepared foods areas. We bake daily, using whole grains and unbleached, unbromated flour and feature European-style loaves, pastries, cookies and cakes as well as gluten-free baked goods for those allergic to wheat. We also offer many vegetarian and vegan products for our customers seeking to avoid all animal products. Our cheeses are free of artificial flavors, colors, and synthetic preservatives, and we offer an outstanding variety of both organic cheeses and cheeses made using traditional methods.[9]

Whole Foods' three-story showcase Union Square store in Manhattan carried locally made New York offerings, seasonal items from the nearby Greenmarket farmer's market, and numerous exotic and gourmet items. A 28-foot international section featured such items as Lebanese fig jam, preserved lemons from Morocco, Indian curries, Thai rice, stuffed grape leaves from Greece, and goulash from Hungary. The prepared foods section had a Grilling Station where shoppers could get grilled-to-order dishes such as swordfish in red pepper Romesco sauce and steak with a mushroom demi-glace.

One of Whole Foods Market's foremost commitments to its customers was to sell foods that met strict standards and that were of high quality in terms of nutrition, freshness, appearance, and taste—Exhibit 6 shows the company's quality standards. Whole Foods guaranteed 100 percent satisfaction on all items purchased and went to great lengths to live up to its core value of satisfying and delighting customers. Buyers personally visited the facilities of many of the company's suppliers and were very picky about the items they chose and the ingredients they contained. For the benefit of prospective food suppliers, the company maintained a list of ingredients it considered unacceptable in food products.

Exhibit 6   **Whole Foods Market's Product Quality Standards and Customer Commitments**

Our business is to sell the highest quality foods we can find at the most competitive prices possible. We evaluate quality in terms of nutrition, freshness, appearance, and taste. Our search for quality is a never-ending process involving the careful judgment of buyers throughout the company.

- We carefully evaluate each and every product we sell.
- We feature foods that are free of artificial preservatives, colors, flavors, sweeteners, and hydrogenated fats.
- We are passionate about great tasting food and the pleasure of sharing it with others.
- We are committed to foods that are fresh, wholesome and safe to eat.
- We seek out and promote organically grown foods.
- We provide food and nutritional products that support health and well-being.

Whole Foods Market's Quality Standards team maintains an extensive list of unacceptable ingredients (see below). However, creating a product with no unacceptable ingredients does not guarantee that Whole Foods Market will sell it. Our buyers are passionate about seeking out the freshest, most healthful, minimally processed products available. In 2008, there were 81 chemicals on Whole Foods' list of unacceptable ingredients, including artificial colors, artificial flavors, aspartame, bleached flour, cyclamates, hydrogenated fats, irradiated foods, nitrates and nitrites, saccharin, sorbic acid, sucralose, and sulfites (sulfur dioxide).

Source: Whole Foods Market, "Our Quality Standards," **www.wholefoodsmarket.com**, accessed March 24, 2008, and March 16, 2010.

Pricing Strategy

Whole Foods' strategy was to sell at the most competitive prices possible. While the majority of the company's private-label products and some of its other offerings were "value-priced," prices at Whole Foods were normally higher than at conventional supermarkets. This was in part because the costs of growing, distributing, and marketing organic products were 10 to 40 percent more than those of non-organic items and in part because Whole Foods' strategy was to carry the highest-quality natural and organic foods available. Likewise, the earth-friendly detergents, toilet papers, and other household items that Whole Foods merchandised frequently had higher price tags than did the name brands of comparable products found in traditional supermarkets. The higher prices that Whole Foods charged for many of its products had prompted some media critics to dub the stores "Whole Paycheck," a term that resonated with price-sensitive grocery shoppers who had visited a Whole Foods store. Nonetheless, Whole Foods' clientele was sufficiently enchanted with the company's product offerings and shopping experience that they overlooked the pricing and patronized Whole Foods stores in increasing numbers.

Sales revenues at Whole Foods grew a robust 20 percent annually during 2000–2007. Average weekly sales at Whole Foods stores rose steadily from $324,700 in fiscal 2000 to $616,700 in fiscal 2007, a compound increase of 9.6 percent annually. Observers attributed this to several factors. One grocery industry analyst said, "If people believe that the food is healthier and they are doing something good for themselves, they are willing to invest a bit more, particularly as they get older. It's not a fad."[10] Another analyst noted that while Whole Foods served a growing niche, it had managed to attract a new kind of customer, one who was willing to pay a premium to dabble in health food without being totally committed to vegetarianism or an organic lifestyle.[11] Shopping at Whole Foods was also attractive to food lovers and fine-food connoisseurs who saw food as being about pleasurable taste and indulgence and were willing to pay a premium for what they saw as a high-quality gourmet experience.

However, despite all the attractions of a Whole Foods shopping event, sales growth at Whole Foods stores unexpectedly evaporated when the U.S. economy collapsed in the fall of 2008, a deep recession ensued, and concerned consumers cut back on spending. Average weekly sales at Whole Foods stores dropped from $616,700 in fiscal 2007 to $569,700 in fiscal 2008 and to $549,500 in 2009. Annual sales per square foot of store space fell from $879 in fiscal 2006 to $804 in fiscal 2008 and to $760 in fiscal 2009.[12] The company's 1 percent increase in sales revenues from $7.95 billion in fiscal 2008 to just $8.03 billion in fiscal 2009 was far and away the smallest annual revenue gain since Whole Foods became a public company in 1991. According to John Mackey, "We knew that 2009 was going to be a tough year but did not predict just how challenging the economic environment would be. For the first time in 30 years, we experienced a decline in our comparable store sales."[13] As was the case with the company's store expansion strategy, the great recession of 2008–2009 caused Mackey and other Whole Foods executives to act swiftly and decisively to change the company's strategy to better match the economic climate and allay customer concerns about the higher costs of doing their grocery shopping at Whole Foods.

Among the company's early strategic moves was an aggressive campaign to emphasize the number of value-priced items that were available at Whole Foods, to better communicate to customers how Whole Foods' prices stacked up against those of rivals, and to improve the perception of customers about the value of shopping at Whole Foods—or, as Mackey put it, to "stress our 'value' along with our 'values.'" The new pricing strategy campaign to improve shopper perceptions of Whole Foods regarding value had several elements:

- Drawing upon new pricing research capabilities to monitor the prices of its supermarket rivals, Whole Foods trimmed the prices of items it considered as "key" to boosting the value perceptions of shoppers. Signs were placed on store shelves calling attention to items with price reductions and to hundreds of value-priced items, many of which were at such popular price points as $0.99, $1.09, $1.49, $1.99, and $2.99. In a number of areas (like cheeses and packaged nuts), Whole Foods instituted programs to get deals from suppliers that enabled it to provide better values for customers without sacrificing its gross margins. The goal was to strike the right balance between spurring higher sales and maintaining profit margins.

- To help put good value front and center, the company began using aisle displays with accompanying signage to feature weekly hot deals, everyday-low-priced products, budget-priced cheeses and wines, and out-of-the-ordinary products with budget prices; formerly, the practice was to use most aisle displays to promote gourmet cheeses, upscale wines, exotic fresh produce, and novel but premium-priced items. In addition, grocery bags at checkout counters had such printed messages as "365 Everyday Value Products. Cut Costs. Not Quality" and "365 Everyday Value Products. Comparison Shopping Strongly Encouraged."

- Stores began featuring new family-sized prepared food selections for $17.99, prepared food items in "sizes for every budget," and family-sized value packs of fruits, vegetables, meats, and chicken.

- An in-store value guide, *The Whole Deal*, was created that contained cents-off coupons, highlighted products with everyday low prices, and offered low-budget recipes and meal-planning advice to help shoppers stretch their food dollars. *The Whole Deal* proved quite popular among customers, prompting the company to increase its printing from 800,000 copies quarterly to 1.3 million copies bimonthly and to begin a *Whole Deal* e-newsletter (which enabled shoppers to see the specials and print out the coupons before they left home). In the months following its introduction, *The Whole Deal* spurred increased redemption rates for the coupons, along with increases in basket size and number of items per basket. Whole Foods had about 500,000 e-newsletter subscribers as of early 2010.

- The company took advantage of opportunity buys offered by suppliers and lower costs in several product categories, including fresh produce and meat, using those to push strong promotions and pass the savings on to customers in the form of lower prices. In-store signs announced "Great Buys" and "More of the good stuff for less than you think!"

In February 2010, Whole Foods' management was pleased with the results of its new pricing strategy and emphasis on value, believing that it had changed the dialogue about Whole Foods prices and improved customer perceptions about the value of doing their grocery shopping at Whole Foods. Sales growth per store for the first quarter of fiscal 2010 was 3.5 percent (versus −4.0

percent in the first quarter of fiscal 2009), and total revenues were up 7.0 percent over the first quarter of fiscal 2009. John Mackey said,

> Early last year, we made the shift from being fairly reactionary on pricing to being much more strategic. We have seen this strategy successfully play out over the last several quarters, as we produced strong year-over-year improvement in gross margin and comparable store sales growth. While many of our competitors have gone back and forth on their pricing strategies, we remain focused on continuing to strike the right balance between driving sales over the long term by improving our value offerings while maintaining margin.
>
> Our first quarter results exceeded our own expectations on both the top line and bottom line. Given the strong sales momentum we are seeing, there are many reasons to be bullish about our future results.[14]

Management said its outlook for full-year fiscal 2010 was sales growth of 8.5 to 10.5 percent and comparable store sales growth (for stores open at least 12 months) of 3.5 to 5.5 percent. Mackey indicated that the company would continue to press forward on its value-pricing strategy, endeavoring to be aggressive in seeking out good prices from suppliers and keeping its prices on key items as competitive as possible. Mackey indicated that Whole Foods could not match the prices charged by either Walmart or Costco (neither of which stocked many organic products). However, it was Whole Foods' policy for the prices on its 365 private-label products to match the prices of comparable items at Trader Joe's, one of its principal competitors in organic foods, unless there was a significant difference in quality. Many Whole Foods customers also shopped at Trader Joe's in communities where both companies had stores.

New Strategic Moves to Control Expenses in 2008–2009

When the sharp economic downturn began in September 2008, Whole Foods' management also moved swiftly to institute a series of cost-containment measures relating to cost of goods sold, direct store expenses, and general and administrative expenses. Purchases from suppliers were scrutinized for possible cost savings. A hiring and salary freeze was imposed and remained in effect until July 2009. In order to trim back on labor costs at its stores, the company used a set of tools on a daily basis to monitor and adjust the work hours of some store employees according to hourly shopper traffic and sales volumes. The size of the company's overall workforce was reduced by normal attrition (as team members retired or left the company), but there were no involuntary layoffs. Team members joined forces with managers throughout the company to find ways to operate the business more frugally.

Management was pleased with the success of its cost-containment initiatives. Gross profit (sales minus cost of goods sold) as a percentage of sales improved from 34.03 percent in fiscal 2008 to 34.29 percent in fiscal 2009 and 34.34 percent in the first quarter of fiscal 2010. Direct store expenses as a percent of sales held steady at 26.5 percent in fiscal 2008, 26.7 percent in fiscal 2009, and 26.6 percent in the first quarter of fiscal 2010. General and administrative expenses dropped from $270.4 million in fiscal 2008 to $243.7 million in fiscal 2009; in the first quarter of 2010, they were 8.1 percent below the level of the prior-year first quarter.

Merchandising Strategy

The layout of each Whole Foods store was customized to fit the particular site and building configuration and to best show off the particular product mix chosen for that store's target clientele. The driving concept of Whole Foods' merchandising strategy was to create an inviting and interactive store atmosphere that turned shopping for food from a chore into a fun, pleasurable experience. Stores had colorful decor, and products were displayed in an attractive manner that both welcomed close inspection and stimulated purchases (see Exhibit 7). The effect was to project Whole Foods as an authentic retailer of natural and organic products, a lifestyle brand, and a supermarket playground with both a unique environment and unusually appealing food selections (some wholesome and safe to eat, some "must try," and some definitely calorific with mouthwatering eye appeal). According to one industry analyst, Whole Foods had "put together the ideal model for the foodie who's a premium gourmet and the natural foods buyer. When you walk into a Whole Foods store, you're overwhelmed by a desire to look at everything you see."[15]

Exhibit 7   **Scenes from Whole Foods Stores**

Most stores featured hand-stacked produce, appealing displays of fresh seafood and meats, open kitchens with teams of in-store chefs, scratch bakeries, prepared foods stations, salad bars, gourmet food sections with items from around the world, multiple opportunities to sample products, and ever-changing merchandise displays. To further a sense of community and interaction with customers, Whole Foods stores typically included sit-down eating areas, a healthy-eating center where shoppers could speak with trained store personnel about healthy eating choices, customer comment boards, and customer service booths. There were "Take Action" centers for customers who wanted information on such topics as sustainable agriculture, organics, the sustainability of seafood supplies and overfishing problems, food safety, product quality, the environment, and similar issues. Cooking classes were offered at 39 stores, and 30 Whole Foods stores had state-of-the art culinary centers equipped with instructional kitchens that offered hands-on cooking classes, tastings, demonstration dinners, and workshops. A few stores offered valet parking, massages, personal shopping, and home delivery. Management's intent was for Whole Foods stores to play a unique role as a third place, besides the home and office, where its customers could gather, interact, and learn while at the same time discovering the many joys of eating and sharing food.

Whole Foods' 78,000-square-foot flagship Austin store was a top Central Texas tourist destination and downtown Austin landmark; it had an intimate village-style layout; six mini-restaurants within the store; a raw food and juice bar; more than 600 varieties of cheese and 40 varieties of olives; a selection of 1,800 wines; a Candy Island with handmade lollipops and popcorn balls; a hot nut bar with an in-house nut roaster; a world foods section; a walk-in beer cooler with 800 selections; 14 pastry chefs making a variety of items; a natural home section with organic cotton apparel and household linens; an extensive meat department with an in-house smoker and 50 oven-ready items prepared by in-house chefs; and a theater-like seafood department with more than 150 fresh seafood items and on-the-spot shucking, cooking, smoking, slicing, and frying to order. The Columbus Circle store in Manhattan had a 248-seat café

where shoppers could enjoy restaurant-quality prepared foods while relaxing in a comfortable community setting; a Jamba Juice smoothie station that served freshly blended-to-order fruit smoothies and juices; a full-service sushi bar by Genji Express where customers sat on bar stools enjoying fresh-cut sushi wrapped in organic nori; a walk-in greenhouse showcasing fresh-cut and exotic flowers; a wine shop with more than 700 varieties of wine from both large and small vineyards and family estates; and a chocolate enrobing station in the bakery where customers could request just about anything covered in chocolate. The two-story store in Pasadena, California (Whole Foods' largest store west of the Rocky Mountains), had a wine and tapas lounge, a seafood bar, a sandwich bar, an Italian trattoria, 1,200 selections of wine, fresh donuts made hourly, a 6,000-square-foot produce department that featured more than 500 items daily, and free wireless Internet access. The three-floor, 99,800-square-foot store in London, England, had 55 in-store chefs, 13 dining venues (including a tapas bar, a champagne and oyster bar, a pub, and a sushi and dim sum eatery) that accommodated 350 diners, a self-service bulk foods center with 100 selections, and a 12-meter display of fresh seafood (many of the seafood selections were hook-and-line caught off the shores of the UK). Management believed that the extensive and attractive displays of fresh produce, seafood, meats and house-made sausages, baked goods, and prepared foods in its larger stores appealed to a broader customer base and were responsible for the fact that Whole Foods stores bigger than 35,000 square feet had performed better than the company's smaller stores (up until 2008–2009 when the full forces of a deep recession hit the company's largest stores particularly hard).

Whole Foods got very high marks from merchandising experts and customers for its presentation—from the bright colors of the produce displays, to the quality of the foods and customer service, to the wide aisles and cleanliness. Management was continually experimenting with new merchandising concepts to keep stores fresh and exciting for customers. According to a Whole Foods regional manager, "We take the best ideas from each of our stores and try to incorporate them in all our other stores. We're constantly making our stores better."[16] Whole Foods' merchandising skills were said to be a prime factor in its success in luring shoppers back time and again—sales per square foot at Whole Foods stores tended to run about double the sales per square foot of Kroger and Safeway.

Marketing and Customer Service

Whole Foods spent less than other supermarkets on advertising and marketing—about 0.4 percent of its revenues in fiscal 2009—preferring instead to rely primarily on word-of-mouth recommendations and testimonials from customers. The corporate marketing budget was divided among national and regional programs, *The Whole Deal* in-store value guide and e-newsletter, and activities for individual stores. Stores spent most of their marketing budgets on in-store promotional signage and events such as local farmers' markets, taste fairs, classes, store tours, and product samplings. Store personnel were encouraged to extend company efforts to encourage the adoption of a natural and organic lifestyle by going out into the community and conducting a proactive public relations campaign. Each store also had a separate budget for making contributions to philanthropic activities and community outreach programs in an effort to maintain a high profile in the local community.

Since one of its core values was to satisfy and delight customers, Whole Foods Market empowered team members to exert their best efforts to meet or exceed customer expectations on every shopping trip. Store personnel were personable and chatty with shoppers. Customers could get personal attention in every department of the store. When customers asked where an item was located, team members often took them to the spot, making conversation along the way and offering to answer any questions. Team members were quite knowledgeable and enthusiastic about the products in their particular department and tried to take advantage of opportunities to inform and educate customers about natural foods, organics, healthy eating, and food-related environmental issues. They took pride in helping customers navigate the extensive variety to make the best choices. Seafood and meat department personnel provided customers with custom cuts, cooking instructions, and personal recommendations.

Management wanted competent, knowledgeable, and friendly service to be a hallmark of shopping at a Whole Foods Market. The aim was to turn highly satisfied customers into advocates for Whole Foods who talked to close friends and acquaintances about their positive experiences shopping at Whole Foods.

Store Operations and Work Environment

Whole Foods employed a team approach to store operations. Depending on store size and traffic volume, Whole Foods stores employed between 25 and 620 team members, who were organized into as many as 13 self-managed teams per store, each led by a team leader. Each team within a store was responsible for a different product category or aspect of store operations such as customer service, prepared foods, produce, and customer checkout stations. Teams were empowered to make many decisions at the store level pertaining to merchandising, departmental operations, and efforts to please customers. Each year, Whole Foods asked team members to give their leaders constructive feedback by completing a confidential team leader survey.

Whole Foods' commitment to team-based management of store operations stemmed from the conviction that the company's long-term success was dependent on the collective efforts of energetic and intelligent team members who were motivated to (1) go to great lengths to satisfy and delight customers and (2) operate the store as efficiently and profitably as possible. The team approach, complemented by a strong emphasis on empowering employees and tying a part of their compensation to store profitability and stock option awards, was seen as promoting a strong corporate culture and contributing to a work environment where motivated team members could flourish, build a career, and reach their highest potential. Management also believed that team members were further motivated and inspired by the company's strategic vision—many team members felt good about their jobs and had a greater sense of purpose because the work they did contributed to better diets and eating habits on the part of Whole Foods shoppers and to the overall well-being of society at large. Indeed, many job candidates were drawn to interview at Whole

Foods because their personal philosophy and life-style matched well with the company's "Whole Foods, Whole People, Whole Planet" mission of selling natural and organic foods, advancing the cause of long-term sustainable agricultural practices, and promoting a cleaner environment. Management believed that voluntary turnover of full-time team members at Whole Foods, which fell from 23 percent in fiscal year 2008 to 12 percent in fiscal year 2009, was very low for the food retailing industry and helped the company do a better job of satisfying its customers and operating its stores efficiently.

Top executives at Whole Foods were acutely aware that the company's decentralized team approach to store operations—where many personnel, merchandising, and operating decisions were made by teams at the individual store level—made it critical to have an effective store team leader. The store team leader worked with one or more associate store team leaders, as well as with all the department team leaders, to operate the store as efficiently and profitably as possible. Team leaders screened candidates for job openings on their team, but a two-thirds majority of the team had to approve a new hire—approval came only after a 30-day trial for the candidate. Store team leaders reported directly to one of twelve regional presidents.

All the teams at each store were continuously evaluated on measures relating to sales, operations, and morale; the results were made available to team members and to headquarters personnel.[17] Teams competed not only against the goals they had set for themselves but also against other teams at their stores or in their region—competition among teams was encouraged. In addition, stores went through two review processes—a store tour and a "customer snapshot." Each store was toured periodically and subjected to a rigorous evaluation by a group of 40 personnel from another region; the group included region heads, store team leaders, associate team leaders, and leaders from two operating teams. Customer snapshots involved a surprise inspection by a headquarters official or regional president who rated the store on 300 items; each store had 10 surprise inspections annually, with the results distributed to every store and included in the reward system. Rewards were team-based and tied to performance metrics.

Whole Foods promoted from within as much as possible, with team members often moving up to assume positions at stores soon to be opened or at stores in other regions. Whole Foods had created the intranet Whole Foods Market University (WFM-U) to provide team members with information and education on a vast array of topics and better connect them to the company's core values, aspects of the company's operations, and the organic food and supermarket industries. There were self-paced courses available on such subjects as organic products, dietary supplements and the law, the company's numerous quality standards, and how the gain-sharing program worked. All stores had budgets for enhancing team member job skills and performance.

Every year, management gave team members an opportunity to complete a morale survey covering job satisfaction, opportunity and empowerment, pay, training, and benefits. In 2004, the overall participation rate was 63 percent (versus 71 percent in 2003). Of the team members responding in 2004, 86 percent said they almost always or frequently enjoyed their job (the same percentage as in 2003), and 82 percent said they almost always or frequently felt empowered to do their best work at Whole Foods Market (up slightly from 81 percent in 2003). Common responses to the question "What is the best thing about working at Whole Foods Market?" included "my coworkers," "the customers," "flexibility," "the work environment," "growth and learning opportunities," "the products Whole Foods sells," "the employee benefits," "the team concept," and "the culture of empowerment."

A team member at Whole Foods' store in Austin, Texas, said, "I really feel like we're a part of making the world a better place. When I joined the company 17 years ago, we only had four stores. I have always loved—as a customer and now as a Team Member—the camaraderie, support for others, and progressive atmosphere at Whole Foods Market."[18] A team member at a New York store said, "I love working for Whole Foods Market because you have a better chance of advancing and great benefits. I've worked for a lot of companies, and I have to say that this feels more like a family than a group of co-workers. Everyone gets credit for what they do, not just leadership."[19] According to the company's vice president of human resources, "Team members who love to take initiative, while enjoying working as part of a team and being rewarded through shared fate, thrive here."

Whole Foods Market had approximately 52,500 team members in 2009, including approximately 43,000 full-time, 7,500 part-time, and 2,000 temporary team members; 45 percent were minorities and 44 percent were women.[20] None were represented by unions, although there had been a couple of unionization attempts. John Mackey was viewed as fiercely anti-union and had once said: "The union is like having herpes. It doesn't kill you, but it's unpleasant and inconvenient and it stops a lot of people from becoming your lover."[21] When workers at a Whole Foods Market in Madison, Wisconsin, voted to unionize in 2002, John Mackey spent more than nine months going to all of the company's stores to speak with store employees personally, listen to what was on their minds, and gather suggestions for improving working conditions. Unionization efforts had never made any headway at Whole Foods, and the company was widely regarded as very progressive and genuinely committed to creating a positive, satisfying work environment.

Whole Foods had made *Fortune* magazine's "100 Best Companies to Work For" list for 13 consecutive years (1998–2010), one of only 13 companies to make the list every year since its inception. It ranked 18th in 2010, 22nd in 2009, 16th in 2008, 5th in 2007, and 15th in 2006; only in 2000 did it rank lower than 50th on the list. In scoring companies, *Fortune* placed two-thirds weight on responses to a 57-question survey of approximately 400 randomly selected employees and one-third on *Fortune*'s own evaluation of a company's demographic makeup, pay and benefits, and culture.

Compensation, Incentives, Benefits, and the Use of Economic Value Added (EVA) Measures of Performance

Whole Foods' management wanted the company's compensation, incentive and reward programs, and benefits package to be perceived as fair to all stakeholders. Compensation levels were attractive. In early 2010, Whole Foods said its average hourly wage was $16.98.[22] Wages and salary differentials between store employees and executives reflected a philosophy of egalitarianism. Whole Foods had a salary cap that limited the compensation (wages plus profit incentive bonuses) of any team member or officer to 19 times the average total compensation of all full-time team members in the company—a policy mandated in the company's core values. The salary cap was raised from 14 to 19 times the average total compensation in 2007—it had been 8 times in 2003; the increases stemmed from the need to attract and retain key executives. Thus, if the average total compensation of a Whole Foods team member was $35,000, then a cap of 19 times the average meant that an executive could not be paid more than $665,000. All team members had access to the company's financial books, including an annual compensation report listing the gross pay of each team member and company executive. Cofounder and CEO John Mackey had recently set his annual salary at $1 and received no cash bonuses or stock option awards.

In addition, Whole Foods strived to create a "shared-fate consciousness" on the part of team members by uniting the self-interests of team members with those of shareholders. One way management reinforced this concept was through a "gain-sharing program" (which was equivalent to profit-sharing plans that some companies employed) based on an economic value added (EVA) management and incentive system adopted by Whole Foods in 1999. EVA is defined as company net operating profits after taxes minus a charge for the cost of capital necessary to generate that profit. Senior executives managed the company with the goal of improving EVA at the store level and company-wide; they believed that an EVA-based bonus system was the best financial framework for team members to use in helping make decisions that created sustainable shareholder value. At Whole Foods, EVA at the store level was based on store contribution (store revenues minus cost of goods sold minus store operating expenses) relative to store investment over and above a weighted-average cost of capital of 9 percent—average store contribution percentages for 2000–2009 are shown in the last line of Exhibit 5. The teams in all stores were challenged to find ways to boost store contribution and store EVA, and all gain-sharing bonuses for store-level team members (except store leaders and assistant store leaders) were tied to these two measures of store performance. Typically, gain-sharing distributions added 5–7 percent to team member wages.

In 2009, approximately 1,000 senior executives, regional managers, store team leaders, and assistant store team leaders throughout the company were also on an EVA-based incentive compensation plan. The primary measure determining the payout for these officers and team leaders was EVA improvement. The company's overall EVA climbed from a negative $30.4 million in fiscal 2001 to a positive $2.6 million in fiscal 2003, $15.6 million in fiscal 2004, $25.8 million in 2005, and $64.4 million in 2006, but then dropped sharply to $35.4 million in 2007. The company did not publicly report overall EVA data for fiscal years 2008 and 2009. (Note: In addition to using EVA measures for its incentive system, Whole Foods used EVA calculations [1] to determine whether the sales and profit projections for new stores would yield a positive and large enough EVA to justify the investment, [2] to guide decisions on store closings, and [3] to evaluate new acquisitions.) Whole Foods executives believed that the emphasis on empowered teams and EVA-based incentives helped harness the collective energy and intelligence of team members to operate their departments effectively and efficiently—thereby enabling Whole Foods to manage its stores better than rival supermarket chains managed their stores.

A second way that Whole Foods endeavored to link the interests of team members with those of shareholders was through three kinds of stock ownership programs:

1. *A team member stock option plan*—All full-time and part-time team members were eligible to receive stock option grants each year based on their leadership performance and their length of service; the number of shares available for these grants was determined annually by the company's board of directors. Stock-option grants based on outstanding leadership performance were awarded on the basis of the recommendation of a team member's regional president. Stock-option grants based on length of service were made to full- or part-time nonseasonal team members with more than 6,000 service hours. Options were granted at a price equal to the market value of the stock at the grant date and were exercisable over a four-year period beginning one year from the date of the grant. Since the inception of the plan in 1992, approximately 94 percent of the stock options granted were to team members who were not executive officers. The share-based expenses associated with these stock-option awards to team members (which were based on the Black-Scholes multiple option pricing model and were reported on the company's consolidated statement of operations in accordance with generally accepted accounting principles) totaled $12.8 million in fiscal 2009, $10.5 million in 2008, and $13.2 million in 2007.[23] The company had recently instituted a policy limiting the number of shares granted in any one year so that annual earnings-per-share dilution due to share-based payment expenses would not exceed 10 percent.

2. *A team member stock purchase plan*—Through payroll deductions, all full-time team members with a minimum of 400 hours of service could purchase shares of Whole Foods common stock at 95 percent of the market price on the purchase date. Approximately 194,000 shares were purchased by team members in fiscal 2009.

3. *A team member 401(k) retirement savings plan*—Team members with a minimum of 1,000 service hours in any one year were eligible to participate in a "Growing Your Future" 401(k) plan. Team members were automatically enrolled unless they opted out of the plan. In fiscal 2009, Whole Foods made matching contributions totaling $3.7 million to the 401(k) plan. Whole Foods Market stock was one of the investment options in the 401(k) plan.

In fiscal 2009, Whole Foods issued a total of $52.9 million in common stock pursuant to its various stock plans for team members, as compared to $119.5 million in fiscal 2008 and $110.3 million in fiscal 2007.[24]

The Benefits Package for Team Members Starting in 2002, team members across the company were encouraged to actively contribute ideas about the benefits they would like the company to offer. The suggestions were compiled and put into a choice of packages, and the choices were submitted to team members for a vote. The benefits plan that was adopted for 2003 through 2006 was approved by 83 percent of the 79 percent of the team members participating in the benefits vote. Under the adopted plan, team members could select their own benefits package. The resulting health insurance plan that the company put in place in January 2003 involved the company paying 100 percent of the premium for full-time employees and the establishment of company-funded "personal wellness accounts," which team members could use to pay the higher deductibles; any unused balances in a team member's account could roll over and accumulate for future expenses.

A second company-wide benefits vote was held in fiscal 2006 to determine the benefits program that would be in place from 2007 through 2009. One outcome of the second vote, in which approximately 77 percent of eligible team members participated, was that the company again provided health insurance at no cost to eligible full-time employees (defined as those who worked 30 or more hours per week and had worked a minimum of 800 hours); the cost of dependent health insurance premiums was shared between the company and the team member, with the percentage paid by the team member declining as years of service with the company increased.

A third vote, in which 84 percent of Whole Foods employees participated, was taken in fiscal 2009 to establish the benefit package for 2010 through 2012. This vote resulted in a continuation of company-paid health insurance at no cost to eligible full-time team members, defined in this instance as those who worked 30 or more hours per week and had worked a minimum of 10,000 service hours (approximately five years of employment). Team members who had worked a minimum of 800 service hours and less than 10,000 service hours paid a medical insurance premium of $10 per biweekly period. Dependent health insurance premiums were generally shared between the company and the team member, with the percentage paid by the team member declining as years of service with the company increased; dependent premiums for health insurance became 100 percent company-paid when a

team member reached 10,000 service hours. As in the two prior voting periods, the benefits package for 2010–2012 called for Whole Foods to provide each team member with a personal wellness account (from $300 up to $1,800 per year, based on years of service) to help cover the cost of deductibles and other allowable out-of-pocket health care expenses not covered by insurance; unused balances in a team member's personal wellness account rolled forward at the end of the year.

Other key benefits included:

- Paid time off based on hours worked. The paid time off could be used for vacations, holidays, illness, and personal days, as a team member saw fit.
- A 20 percent discount on all purchases at Whole Foods. This benefit became available on a team member's first day of employment.
- Dental and eye care plans. Coverage was available for both team members and their dependents.
- Life insurance and disability insurance plans.
- A dependent care reimbursement plan that allowed team members to contribute pretax funds to pay for anticipated day care expenses incurred while at work.
- Assistance for unforeseeable emergencies. This benefit was funded by voluntary team member paycheck deductions (usually $1), by paid-time-off donations (from team member to team member), and by the company (in situations where there was a major disaster).

Purchasing and Distribution

Whole Foods' buyers purchased most of the items retailed in the company's stores from local, regional, and national wholesale suppliers and vendors. Much of the buying responsibility was located at the regional and national levels in order to put the company in a better position to negotiate volume discounts with major vendors and distributors. Whole Foods Market was the largest account for many suppliers of natural and organic foods. United Natural Foods was the company's biggest supplier, accounting for about 28 percent of Whole Foods' total purchases in fiscal 2009; United was the company's primary supplier of dry grocery and frozen food products.

However, regional and store managers had discretionary authority to source from local organic farmers and suppliers that met the company's quality standards. In 2007–2008, the company's buyers began to place stronger emphasis on buying directly from producers and manufacturers.

Whole Foods owned two produce procurement centers that facilitated the procurement and distribution of the majority of the produce Whole Foods sold. However, where feasible, local store personnel sourced produce items from local organic farmers as part of the company's commitment to promote and support organic farming methods. Recently, Whole Foods had instituted its Local Producer Loan Program, which provided up to $10 million in low-interest loans to small local producers; the purpose of this loan program was to make it easier for small organic farmers and start-up entrepreneurs to bring more locally produced organic foods to market. Loans ranged from $1,000 to $100,000 and could be used for purchasing more animals, investing in new equipment, or converting to organic production. Whole Foods kept the fees, interest rates, and paperwork to a minimum so as not to discourage a small local farm or business from taking steps to expand its operations. Whole Foods hosted farmers' markets in the parking lots of some of its stores.

The company operated 10 regional distribution centers to supply its stores. Eight regional bake houses and five regional commissary kitchens supplied area stores with various prepared foods. A central coffee-roasting operation supplied stores with the company's Allegro brand of coffees.

Whole Foods' Social Responsibility Strategy and Community Citizenship Initiatives

Whole Foods was pursuing a comprehensive social responsibility strategy. Key elements of this strategy included standards relating to animal welfare, support for organic farming and sustainable agriculture, healthy eating education, a loan program to support local producers of organic products, actions to promote responsible and sustainable seafood practices, the Green Action program to implement wise environmental practices,

a policy of donating at least 5 percent of after-tax profits (in cash or products) to nonprofit or educational organizations, the Whole Trade Guarantee program, the activities of the company's Whole Planet Foundation, and a variety of community citizenship activities. The loan program to support small organic farmers was mentioned earlier. Other elements of Whole Foods' social responsibility strategy included the following:

• Whole Foods had implemented a system called Five-Step Animal Welfare Rating, which laid out a set of "animal compassionate" standards expected of Whole Foods' meat and poultry suppliers. These standards entailed a requirement of humane living conditions for animals, prohibited the use antibiotics and growth hormones, prohibited the use of feeds containing animal by-products, and specified other permissible and prohibited production and handling techniques (e.g., prohibitions against raising animals in crates, cages, or crowded facilities). Whole Foods ceased selling live lobsters in 2006 because the process of handling live lobsters throughout the supply chain (from capture to in-store tank conditions) was not in line with the company's commitment to humane treatment. In early 2008, Whole Foods created the Global Animal Partnership, a foundation for the purpose of working with farms, ranches, and others to foster continuous improvement of the environment and conditions for each species that supported the animal's natural physical, emotional, and behavioral well-being. Whole Foods refused to sell commercial veal from tethered calves, foie gras from force-fed geese, and eggs from caged hens.

• Whole Foods' Green Mission Task Force promoted environmentally sound practices for every aspect of store and facility operations, including paperless ordering systems, use of biodegradable supplies for food and wine sampling, composting, use of recycled paper, holding company and community recycling drives for electronics, providing receptacles for glass and plastic recycling in dining areas, the use of Green Seal products for cleaning and maintenance, and installation of flushless urinals (each of which saved an average of 40,000 gallons of water annually). Starting in

2006, Whole Foods began purchasing renewable energy credits from wind farms to offset 100 percent of the electricity used in all of its stores and facilities in the United States and Canada; a growing number of Whole Foods stores had installed solar panels to supply a portion of their electricity requirements. In early 2008, Whole Foods began using all-natural fiber packaging at its salad and food bars. As of Earth Day 2008 (April 22), Whole Foods ended the use of disposable plastic bags at the checkout lanes of all its stores, chiefly because such bags did not break down in landfills. Company officials said the move would eliminate use of 100 million plastic bags annually—customers were instead offered reusable paper bags made of 100 percent recycled paper (at a cost of 10 cents each) and an opportunity to purchase stylish long-life canvas bags for 99 cents (80 percent of the content of the canvas bags came from recycled plastic bottles). Whole Foods' distribution vehicles had been converted to the use of biodiesel fuel.

- In October 2005, Whole Foods established the not-for-profit Whole Planet Foundation, charged with combating poverty and promoting self-sufficiency in third-world countries that supplied Whole Foods with some of the products it sold. Most of the foundation's efforts involved providing loans, training, and other financial services to aspiring entrepreneurs and the self-employed poor. So far, Whole Foods had made grants and microloans in excess of $11 million to more than 60,000 recipients (98 percent of whom were women) in 17 countries; the average loan size was $185, and the loan repayment rate was running about 98 percent.[25] In 2010, the Whole Planet Foundation initiated a $1.5 million campaign to help empower poor women in developing countries to create prosperity for themselves; shoppers could donate $1 to the program at the checkout registers in all Whole Foods stores or make a donation at the company's website. In the days following the January 2010 earthquake disaster in Haiti, the foundation also committed $1 million to enable its partner organization in Haiti, Fonkoze Financial Services, to rebuild its infrastructure and reopen its branch offices; Fonkoze served more than 55,000 women borrowers and 1 million families who received monies from relatives and friends abroad. The funding allowed Fonkoze to be the first bank in Haiti to reopen after the earthquake and get needed cash to customers and make microloans to members to reestablish their businesses.

- In March 2007, Whole Foods launched its Whole Trade Guarantee, a program that committed the company to paying small-scale producers (chiefly in impoverished, low-wage countries where living standards were low) a price for their products that more than covered the producer's costs. The goal was to make sure that the producers of products meeting Whole Foods' quality standards could always afford to create, harvest, or grow their product so that they did not have to abandon their work or jeopardize the well-being of their family to make ends meet. The commitment to paying such producers a premium price was viewed as an investment in them and their communities as well as a way for producers to be able to put money back into their operations, enable them to invest in training and education for their workers, and have sufficient take-home pay to help support a better life. In 2010, the Whole Trade Guarantee label was featured on more than 1,350 items at Whole Foods stores. Whole Foods donated 1 percent of the retail sales of all Whole Trade Guarantee products sold to the Whole Planet Foundation (such donations amounted to $762,000 in fiscal 2009).

- A renewed drive to make customers more aware of healthy-eating choices began in 2009 and was in full force in 2010. The company had partnered with Eat Right America and the creator of the Engine 2 Diet to create Getting Started programs. In addition, there were in-store healthy eating areas, new healthy prepared foods selections, an educational booth where team members dispensed information and provided healthy eating materials, signs and brochures explaining how to use the Aggregate Nutrient Density Index (ANDI) scoring system as a guide to selecting healthy foods, and Health Starts Here logos and signs adjacent to items considered to be good healthy eating choices.

During 2010, John Mackey planned to launch a program to better engage the company's team members in the healthy eating campaign (because they were the ones who interfaced with customers) by giving them a monetary incentive to get healthier. All team members received a standard 20 percent discount on their purchases at Whole Foods. Mackey's plan was for team members who scored well on three of four biomarkers of good health (having a low body mass index, not being a smoker, having a good cholesterol count, and having good blood pressure) to receive a 25 percent silver discount card; team members with acceptable scores on all four markers were to receive a 30 percent gold discount card. Mackey believed that a silver or gold discount card would become a status symbol among team members. He also envisioned instituting competitions for the healthiest team in a store, the healthiest store in each region, and the healthiest region in the company. Mackey said, "I fully expect that I am going to get a gold card. I see in my mind's eye how this is going to play out. I'm into it."[26]

• Team members at every Whole Foods store were heavily involved in such community citizenship activities as sponsoring blood donation drives, preparing meals for seniors and the homeless, holding fund-raisers to help the disadvantaged, growing vegetables for a domestic violence shelter, participating in housing renovation projects, and working as delivery people for Meals on Wheels. Each store donated food to area food banks and shelters. Several times a year, individual Whole Foods stores held events called 5% Days (or CommUnity Giving Days), during which 5 percent of that day's sales were donated to a local nonprofit or educational organization. Each store had latitude in deciding what activities it would undertake to support the local community.

Most Whole Foods stores had signs alerting customers to the company's various social responsibility initiatives; brochures were available at all stores containing more detailed information about the various programs discussed above. Exhibit 8 presents Whole Foods' efforts to support responsible and sustainable seafood practices.

In 2010, Ethisphere Institute named Whole Foods as one of the world's most ethical companies; Ethisphere is a leading research-based international think tank dedicated to the creation, advancement, and sharing of best practices in business ethics, corporate social responsibility, anticorruption, and environmental sustainability.

Mackey's Ethics Are Called into Question.

Business Ethics named Whole Foods Market to its "100 Best Corporate Citizens" list in 2004, 2006, and 2007. However, during 2007, CEO John Mackey was the center of attention in two ethics-related incidents. The first involved a discovery that, over a seven-year period, Mackey had typed out more than 1,100 entries on Yahoo Finance's message board touting his company's stock and occasionally making uncomplimentary remarks about rival Wild Oats Markets. Mackey's postings stopped several months prior to Whole Foods' offer to buy Wild Oats Market. In making his postings, Mackey used the alias Rahodeb—a variation of Deborah, his wife's name. *The Wall Street Journal* reported that in January 2005 Rahodeb posted that no one would buy Wild Oats at its current price of $8 per share and that Whole Foods had nothing to gain by buying Wild Oats because the latter's stores were too small.[27] A *New York Times* article reported that, on March 28, 2006, Rahodeb wrote, "OATS has lost their way and no longer has a sense of mission or even a well-thought-out theory of the business. They lack a viable business model that they can replicate. They are floundering around hoping to find a viable strategy that may stop their erosion. Problem is they lack the time and the capital now."[28] The *New York Times* article quoted Mackey as saying, "I posted on Yahoo! under a pseudonym because I had fun doing it. I never intended any of those postings to be identified with me." Mackey's postings, which came to light in June–July 2007 and spurred calls for his resignation on grounds that he breached his fiduciary responsibility, were first discovered by the Federal Trade Commission in Whole Foods documents that the FTC obtained in the course of challenging the Wild Oats acquisition. According to Mackey, some of the views he expressed in his Rahodeb postings represented his personal beliefs and others represented his playing the role

Exhibit 8   Whole Foods' Position on Seafood Sustainability

It's pretty clear that our oceans are in trouble. The world's fish stocks are disappearing due to overfishing and bad harvesting practices and fish farming is not yet the solution we thought it would be.

The good news is that there's hope, but we all have to pitch in so our favorite seafood remains available for us and for future generations. As a shopper, you have the power to turn the tide. Buying seafood from responsible, certified fisheries is the way to go. You reward their actions and encourage other fisheries to be responsible too. Looking for the blue Marine Stewardship Council sticker on seafood packaging is a good place to start.

As a company, we're committed to responsible seafood practices, including:

- Supporting fishing practices that ensure the ecological health of the ocean and the abundance of marine life.
- Partnering with groups who encourage responsible practices and provide the public with accurate information about the issue.
- Operating our own well-managed seafood facilities.
- Helping educate our customers on the importance of practices that can make a difference now and well into the future.
- Promoting and selling the products of well-managed fisheries.

As the largest retailer of natural and organic food, we want to be able to continue over the long-term to provide our customers with fish to buy. However, at the same time, we want to support ecological health and the abundance of marine life. We believe the Marine Stewardship Council's "Fish Forever" certified sustainably managed seafood program accomplishes both.

A global independent, not-for-profit organization, the Marine Stewardship Council promotes sustainable fisheries and responsible fishing practices world-wide to help preserve fish stocks for future generations. Whole Foods Market Inc. was one of the first American companies to support and participate in the Marine Stewardship Council.

Accredited, independent certifying agencies measure compliance to the principles and criteria of sustainability developed by the Marine Stewardship Council. Certified fisheries are rewarded the right to use the "Fish Forever" eco-label to signify to consumers that the product was caught using environmentally sound, economical and socially responsible management practices.

Source: Whole Foods Market, www.wholefoodsmarket.com, accessed March 24, 2010.

of devil's advocate. He said that no proprietary information about Whole Foods was disclosed.[29] In the days following the media reports of the postings, Mackey expressed remorse for his postings, apologized for his behavior, and asked stakeholders to forgive him for exercising bad judgment. Nonetheless, the content of certain Mackey postings were cited in court documents filed by the FTC as reasons why Whole Foods' acquisition of Wild Oats should be blocked. On July 17, 2007, the Securities and Exchange Commission (SEC) announced that it had begun an investigation of the postings. That same day, Whole Foods announced that the company's board of directors had formed a special committee to investigate the postings and retained legal counsel to advise it during the investigation. Whole Foods said it would cooperate fully with the SEC inquiry.

In October 2007, Whole Foods announced that the special committee had completed its investigation of Mackey's message board postings and that the board of directors affirmed its support of the CEO; the company indicated that

the special committee's findings would be turned over to the SEC and that the company would have no further comment pending the SEC investigation.[30] In April 2008, the SEC closed its investigation into Mackey's online chat activities and took no actions against Mackey or Whole Foods.

A second controversy-stirring incident involved a Mackey-authored blog entitled "Whole Foods, Wild Oats and the FTC" that appeared on the company's website on June 19, 2007. Mackey, who objected strenuously to the grounds on which the Federal Trade Commission was trying to block Whole Foods' acquisition of Wild Oats, dedicated the blog to providing updates and information regarding the FTC proceeding and to making the case for why the company's acquisition of Wild Oats Market should be allowed to go forward. Mackey explained the basis for the blog:

> My blog posting provides a detailed look into Whole Foods Market's decision-making process regarding the merger, as well as our company's experience interacting with the FTC staff assigned to this merger. I provide explanations of

how I think the FTC, to date, has neglected to do its homework appropriately, especially given the statements made regarding prices, quality, and service levels in its complaint. I also provide a glimpse into the bullying tactics used against Whole Foods Market by this taxpayer-funded agency. Finally, I provide answers in my FAQ section to many of the questions that various Team Members have fielded from both the media and company stakeholders. As previously announced, we set an intention as a company to be as transparent as possible throughout this legal process, and this blog entry is my first detailed effort at transparency.

The blog by Mackey included the following post titles:

- Why Whole Foods Market Wants to Buy Wild Oats
- Whole Foods Market's Objections to the FTC's Investigation
- What the FTC Is Claiming in Its Objections to the Merger
- FAQs

Critics of Mackey's blog said it was inappropriate for a CEO to publicly air the company's position, to take issue with the FTC, and to make the company's case for why the acquisition should be allowed to proceed. At the least, some critics opined, the blog should be toned down.[31] When the SEC announced on July 17, 2007, that it would investigate John Mackey's financial message board postings, Mackey put a hold on further blog postings regarding the FTC's actions to try to block the Wild Oats acquisition.

Whole Foods Market's Financial Performance

Since 1991, Whole Foods Market had been profitable every year except 2000, when it reported a net loss of $8.5 million, owing to divestiture of its NatureSmart nutritional supplement business and losses in two affiliated dot-com enterprises in which Whole Foods owned a minority interest. However, the company quickly returned to profitability, with earnings rising from $67.8 million in fiscal year 2001 to a peak of $203.8 million in fiscal year 2006. Even though Whole Foods' revenues grew from $5.6 billion in fiscal 2006 to $8.0 billion in fiscal 2009, profitability suffered because of a combination of three factors:

1. The rising costs associated with opening a larger number of new stores (many of which were also bigger and entailed larger preopening costs) in 2007 and 2008.

2. The expenses associated with acquiring Wild Oats in 2007 and trying to make its stores profitable in 2008. The additional debt to finance the Wild Oats acquisition drove interest expenses up from a mere $32,000 in fiscal 2007 to $36.5 million in fiscal 2008. Store relocations, closures, and lease termination costs (much of was directly related to the Wild Oats stores) jumped from $5.3 million in fiscal 2006 to $10.9 million in fiscal 2007 and to $36.5 million in fiscal 2008.

3. The sudden and deep economic recession in 2008–2009, which prompted a drop in average weekly sales at Whole Foods stores.

Whole Foods' net profits declined to $182.7 million in fiscal 2007 and to $114.5 million in fiscal 2008 before rebounding slightly to $118.8 million in fiscal 2009. Exhibits 9, 10, and 11 present the company's recent statements of operations, consolidated balance sheets, and selected cash flow data.

Whole Foods had very strong cash flows from operations prior to the Wild Oats acquisition, enabling it to fund its capital requirements (which were mainly for new store development and store relocations) and avoid incurring much, if any, long-term debt. The company began paying dividends in January 2004, raising them several times, and paying a special dividend of $1.60 per share in fiscal 2006. But the Wild Oats acquisition triggered a cash flow crunch. To aid in financing the Wild Oats acquisition and continue fast-paced opening of new stores, Whole Foods took on long-term debt of more than $700 million and negotiated a $250 million revolving line of credit with its banks during the last quarter of fiscal 2007; the revolving line of credit was later increased to $350 million. Starting in fiscal 2009, the company's board of directors suspended dividend payments on common shares for the foreseeable future.

In November–December 2008 (the first quarter of Whole Foods' fiscal year 2009), the cash shortage became so severe that Whole Foods negotiated the issuance of 425,000 shares of preferred stock to Leonard Green & Partners for approximately

Exhibit 9   Whole Foods Market, Statement of Operations, Fiscal Years 2005–2009 ($ thousands)

	Fiscal Year 2009	Fiscal Year 2008	Fiscal Year 2007	Fiscal Year 2006	Fiscal Year 2005
Sales	$8,031,620	$7,953,912	$6,591,773	$5,607,376	$4,701,289
Cost of goods sold and occupancy costs	5,277,310	5,247,207	4,295,170	3,647,734	3,052,184
Gross profit	2,754,310	2,706,705	2,296,603	1,959,642	1,649,105
Direct store expenses	2,145,809	2,107,940	1,711,229	1,421,968	1,223,473
Store contribution	608,501	598,765	585,374	537,674	425,632
General and administrative expenses	243,749	270,428	217,743	181,244	158,864
Pre-opening and relocation costs	80,403	92,099	70,180	37,421	37,035
Operating income	284,349	236,238	297,451	319,009	229,733
Interest expense, net	(36,856)	(36,416)	(4,208)	(32)	(2,223)
Investment and other income	3,449	6,697	11,324	20,736	9,623
Income before income taxes	250,942	206,519	304,567	339,713	237,133
Provision for income taxes	104,138	91,995	121,827	135,885	100,782
Net income	$ 146,804	$ 114,524	$ 182,740	$ 203,828	$ 136,351
Basic earnings per share	$0.85	$0.82	$1.30	$1.46	$1.05
Weighted average shares outstanding	140,414	139,886	140,088	139,328	130,090
Diluted earnings per share	$0.85	$0.82	$1.29	$1.41	$0.99
Weighted average shares outstanding, diluted basis	140,414	140,011	141,836	145,082	139,950
Dividends declared per share	—	$0.60	$0.87	$2.45	$0.47

Note: Whole Foods' fiscal year ends the last Sunday in September.
Source: Whole Foods Market, 2009 10-K report, p. 24.

$413.1 million, net of closing and issuance costs of $11.9 million. The preferred shares called for an 8.0 percent annual dividend payment and included a provision restricting Whole Foods' ability to pay cash dividends on its common stock without prior written consent of the holders of a majority of the preferred shares. Two Leonard Green partners were subsequently elected to membership on Whole Foods' board of directors. The agreement also gave Leonard Green the option to convert its shares of preferred stock into shares of Whole Foods common stock at any time prior to November 27, 2009 (the earliest date at which Whole Foods could opt to redeem the 425,000 shares of preferred stock). On October 23, 2009, because of rapidly improving internal cash flows from operations, Whole Foods announced its intention to redeem all 425,000 preferred shares on November 27, 2009. Leonard Green & Partners then proceeded to exercise its conversion option and received 29.7 million shares of Whole Foods common stock in return for its 425,000 preferred shares, which boosted the total number of common shares outstanding to about 170.3 million. At the time of the conversion, Whole Foods' common stock price was trading at about $25.90, making the value of the conversion to Leonard Green & Partners worth approximately $770 million, far above the $425 million redeemable value of the preferred shares. Because of the conversion to common stock, Whole Foods did not have to use any cash to redeem the $425 million in preferred stock.

Exhibit 10   Whole Foods Market, Consolidated Balance Sheet, Fiscal Years 2008–2009 ($ thousands)

	Year Ending Sept. 27, 2009	Year Ending Sept. 28, 2008
Assets		
Current assets:		
Cash and cash equivalents	$ 430,130	$ 30,534
Restricted cash	71,023	617
Accounts receivable	104,731	115,424
Merchandise inventories	310,602	327,452
Deferred income taxes	87,757	80,429
Prepaid expenses and other current assets	51,137	68,150
Total current assets	1,055,380	622,606
Property and equipment, net of accumulated depreciation and amortization	1,897,853	1,900,117
Goodwill	658,254	659,559
Intangible assets, net of accumulated amortization	73,035	78,499
Deferred income taxes	91,000	109,002
Other assets	7,866	10,953
Total assets	$3,783,388	$3,380,736
Liabilities and Shareholders' Equity		
Current liabilities:		
Current installments of long-term debt and capital lease obligations	$ 389	$ 380
Accounts payable	189,597	183,134
Accrued payroll, bonus and other benefits due team members	207,983	196,233
Dividends payable	8,217	—
Other current liabilities	277,838	286,430
Total current liabilities	684,024	666,177
Long-term debt and capital lease obligations, less current installments	738,848	928,790
Deferred lease liabilities	250,326	199,635
Other long-term liabilities	69,262	80,110
Total liabilities	1,742,460	1,874,712
Series A redeemable preferred stock, $0.01 par value, 425 and no shares authorized, issued and outstanding in 2009 and 2008, respectively	413,052	—
Shareholders' equity:		
Common stock, no par value, 300,000 shares authorized; 140,542 and 140,286 shares issued and outstanding in 2009 and 2008, respectively	1,283,028	1,266,141
Accumulated other comprehensive income (loss)	(13,367)	422
Retained earnings	358,215	239,461
Total shareholders' equity	1,627,876	1,506,024
Commitments and contingencies		
Total liabilities and shareholders' equity	$3,783,388	$3,380,736

Source: Whole Foods Market, 2009 10-K report, p. 40.

Exhibit 11 **Whole Foods Market, Selected Cash Flow Data, Fiscal Years 2007–2009 ($ thousands)**

	Fiscal Year ending Sept. 27, 2009	Fiscal Year ending Sept. 28, 2008	Fiscal Year ending Sept. 30, 2007
Net cash provided by operating activities	$ 587,721	$ 334,992	$ 391,486
Cash flows from investing activities			
Development costs of new store locations	(247,999)	(357,520)	(388,759)
Other property, plant and equipment expenditures	(66,616)	(171,952)	(135,772)
Purchase of available-for-sale securities	—	(194,316)	(277,283)
Sale of available-for-sale securities	—	194,316	475,625
Payment for purchase of acquired entities, net of cash acquired	—	(5,480)	(596,236)
Proceeds received from divestiture, net	—	163,913	—
Other items	32,595	(36,167)	32,595
Net cash used in investing activities	$(386,283)	$(372,721)	$(890,373)
Cash flows from financing activities			
Dividends paid	—	$(109,072)	$ (96,742)
Issuance of common stock	4,286	18,019	54,383
Purchase of treasury stock	—	—	(99,997)
Excess tax benefit related to exercise of tem member stock options	42	5,686	12,839
Proceeds from issuance of redeemable preferred stock, net	413,042	—	—
Proceeds form long-term borrowing	123,000	317,000	717,000
Payments on long-term debt and capital lease obligations	(318,370)	(161,151)	(93,360)
Net cash provided by (used in) financing activities	$ 199,455	$ (69,830)	$ 494,123
Other cash flow data			
Cash and cash equivalents at beginning of year	$ 30,534	—	$ 2,252
Cash and cash equivalents at end of year	430,130	30,534	—
Net change in cash and cash equivalents	399,596	30,534	(2,252)
Interest paid	43,685	36,155	4,561
Federal and state income taxes paid	69,701	118,366	152,626

Source: Whole Foods Market, 2009 10-K report, p. 43.

Whole Foods' strategy changes at the beginning of fiscal 2009—particularly the cost-containment and value-pricing initiatives—helped produce very strong cash flows from operations of $587.7 million for fiscal year 2009, well above the $335 million in fiscal 2008 and $391.5 million in fiscal 2007. This allowed Whole Foods to internally fund its development costs for new stores ($248 million) and other capital projects ($66.6 million). Cash flows were sufficient to pay down the company's total long-term debt by $190 million and increase cash and cash equivalents to $430.1 million (versus only $30.5 million at the end of fiscal 2008). Management expressed confidence in being able to cover the long-term debt maturing in 2012. Capital expenditures during fiscal 2010 were expected to be in the range of $350–$400 million, with about 65 percent of this amount being for new-store development. In March 2010, Whole Foods announced that it was forecasting diluted earnings per share of $1.20 to $1.25 for fiscal 2010. As of December 31, 2009, the company had further boosted its cash and short-term investments to $569.6 million; total debt was $734.1 million.[32]

COMPETITORS

The food retailing business was intensely competitive. The degree of competition Whole Foods faced varied from locality to locality, and to some extent from store location to store location within a given locale depending on the proximity of stores of its two closest competitors in the natural foods and organics segment of the food retailing industry, Fresh Market and Trader Joe's. Other competitors included conventional supermarkets, small chains, local independent retailers of natural and health foods, and regional and national supermarkets, a number of which had a growing selection of natural and organic foods. Whole Foods also faced competition in parts of its product line from specialty grocery stores (with upscale delicatessen offerings and prepared foods), small-scale health food stores, and retailers of vitamins and nutritional supplements. Whole Foods' executives had said it was to the company's benefit for conventional supermarkets to offer natural and organic foods for two reasons: first, it helped fulfill the company's mission of improving the health and well-being of people and the planet, and, second, it helped create new customers for Whole Foods by providing a gateway experience. They contended that as more people were exposed to natural and organic products, they were more likely to become a Whole Foods customer because Whole Foods was the category leader for natural and organic products, offered the largest selection at competitive prices, and provided the most-informed customer service.

Fresh Market

Fresh Market, headquartered in Greensboro, North Carolina, was a family-owned 94-store chain operating in 18 states in the Southeast,

Midwest, Mid-Atlantic, and Northeast. Founded by Ray Berry, a former vice president with Southland Corporation who had responsibility over some 3,600 7-Eleven stores, the first Fresh Market store opened in 1982 in Greensboro. Berry's concept was to develop a small neighborhood store with the feel and atmosphere of an open European-style market that was service-oriented and focused on perishable goods (particularly fresh produce and meats and seafood displayed in glass-front refrigerated cases). All fixtures and display pieces were purchased used, as the store was financed entirely with the family's savings. The Greensboro store, which had low-level lighting and classical music playing in the background, was a hit with customers, and Berry began to open similar stores in other locales. During the 1982–2000 period, Fresh Market's sales revenues grew at a 25.2 percent compound rate, reaching $193 million in 2000; revenues were an estimated $655 million in 2009. The company had almost 7,000 employees in early 2010. Management planned to open 9 to 12 new stores annually, gradually expanding into more states. Expansion was funded by internal cash flows and bank debt. Financial data were not available because the company was privately owned, but Fresh Market's profitability was believed to be above the industry average.

Fresh Market stores were typically in the range of 18,000 to 25,000 square feet and were located in neighborhood shopping areas near educated, high-income residents. Newer stores had an open-air design that evoked "old-world European charm, artful sophistication, old-fashioned retail sentiment, and a warm and friendly atmosphere." Warm lights, classical background music, and terra-cotta-colored tiles made Fresh Market stores a cozier place to shop than a typical supermarket. Fresh Market's product line included meats, seafood, 400 fresh produce items (that included a growing organic selection), fresh-baked goods (30 breads, 15 pies, cakes, cookies, and fruit tarts), prepared foods and meals to-go, 30 varieties of coffees, a small selection of grocery and dairy items, bulk products, 200 varieties of domestic and imported cheeses, deli items (including rotisserie meats, sandwiches, wraps, soups, and sandwiches), wine and beer, and a small assortment of cookbooks, gift cards, baskets, cutting boards, and gift baskets. The emphasis was on variety, freshness, and quality.

Aside from inviting store ambience and the atmosphere of an old-world European market, Fresh Market differentiated itself from natural foods stores and traditional supermarkets with what management considered to be superlative service, attractive fresh produce displays, daily product sampling (including freshly brewed coffee for shoppers), and "upscale grocery boutique" items such as pick-and-pack spices; gourmet chocolates; hard-to-get H&H bagels from New York City; Ferrara's New York cheesecake; fresh Orsini parmesan cheese; Acqua della Madonna bottled water; and an extended selection of olive oils, mustards, bulk products (granolas, nuts, beans, dried fruits, spices, and snack mixes), wine, and beer. Each department had at least one employee in the area constantly to help shoppers and answer questions—the idea was to force interaction between store employees and shoppers. From time to time, stores had cooking classes, wine tastings, and food sampling events. Each Fresh Market store had an annual sidewalk sale to raise funds for the Juvenile Diabetes Research Foundation where root beer floats, hot dogs, and gourmet cookies were offered in exchange for a donation.

Stores had 75 to 100 employees, resulting in labor costs that were about double those of supermarket chains. Whenever possible, Fresh Market offered promotions and transfers to people from within the company; all store managers had been promoted from within the company. After 90 days, all full-time employees were eligible to enroll in plans providing medical, prescription medication, dental, vision, life, and disability coverage; coverage could be extended to spouses or domestic partners and children. There were also low-cost medical, prescription, life, dental, and vision insurance plans for new and part-time employees. In addition, there were annual bonus programs for all employees, 20 percent employee discounts on most products, a paid annual leave program, a 401(k) plan with 50 percent company matching of employee contributions, an employee assistance program, and a flexible spending account program.

Trader Joe's

Founded in 1967 and based in Pasadena, California, Trader Joe's was a specialty supermarket chain with more than 339 stores in 25 states as well as Washington, D.C.; about half of the stores were in California. The company had an ongoing strategy to open additional stores. A privately owned company, Trader Joe's had seen its sales increase from an estimated $2.1 billion in 2003 (with 210 stores) to approximately $8.0 billion in 2009, roughly equal to sales at Whole Foods; Trader Joe's was ranked 21st on *Supermarket News'* 2010 list of the top 75 retailers (based on 2009 sales estimates).

Management described the company's mission and business as follows:

> At Trader Joe's, our mission is to bring our customers the best food and beverage values and the information to make informed buying decisions. There are more than 2,000 unique grocery items in our label, all at honest everyday low prices. We work hard at buying things right: Our buyers travel the world searching for new items and we work with a variety of suppliers who make interesting products for us, many of them exclusive to Trader Joe's. All our private label products have their own "angle," i.e., vegetarian, Kosher, organic or just plain decadent, and all have minimally processed ingredients.
>
> Customers tell us, "I never knew food shopping could be so much fun!" Some even call us "The home of cheap thrills!" We like to be part of our neighborhoods and get to know our customers. And where else do you shop that even the CEO, Dan Bane, wears a loud Hawaiian shirt.
>
> Our tasting panel tastes every product before we buy it. If we don't like it, we don't buy it. If customers don't like it, they can bring it back for a no-hassle refund.
>
> We stick to the business we know: good food at the best prices! Whenever possible we buy direct from our suppliers, in large volume. We bargain hard and manage our costs carefully. We pay in cash, and on time, so our suppliers like to do business with us.
>
> Trader Joe's Crew Members are friendly, knowledgeable and happy to see their customers. They taste our items too, so they can discuss them with their customers. All our stores regularly cook up new and interesting products for our customers to sample.[33]

Prices and product offerings varied somewhat by region and state. There were no weekly specials or cents-off coupons or glitzy promotional discounts. Customers could choose from an eclectic and somewhat upscale variety of baked goods, organic foods, fresh fruits and vegetables, imported and domestic cheeses, gourmet chocolates and candies, coffees, fresh salads, meatless entrées and other vegan products, low-fat and low-carbohydrate foods, frozen fish and seafood, heat-and-serve entrées, packaged meats, juices, wine and beer, snack foods, energy bars, vitamins, nuts and trail mixes, and whatever other exotic items the company's buyers had come upon. About 20–25 percent of Trader's Joe's products were imported. There were very few brand-name items; some 2,000 items carried the Trader Joe's label and its other quirky labels for particular foods: Trader Jose's (Mexican food), Trader Ming's (Chinese food), Trader Giotto's (Italian food), Pilgrim Joe's (seafood), Trader Jacques' (imported French soaps), Joe's Diner (certain frozen entrées), and Joe's Kids (children's food); these accounted for about 70 percent of total sales. Items with a Trader Joe's logo contained no artificial flavors, colors, preservatives, trans fats, MSG, or genetically modified ingredients. About 10 to 15 new, seasonal, or one-time-buy items were introduced each week. Products that weren't selling well were dropped. Trader Joe's was the exclusive retailer of Charles Shaw wine, popularly known as "Two Buck Chuck" because of its $1.99 price tag in California (outside California, the price ranged as high as $3 because of higher liquor taxes and transportation costs). In its early days, the company had been built on its large selection of California wines and hard liquors; later, when the company's founder, Joe Coulombe, realized that Trader Joe's stores appealed to the highly educated and to lower-income people, food items sold at low everyday prices were added.[34]

Stores were open, with wide aisles, appealing displays, cedar plank walls, and a nautical decor; employees ("crew members") wore colorful Hawaiian shirts. Given the combination of low prices, an emporium-like atmosphere, intriguing selections, and friendly service, customers viewed shopping at Trader Joe's as an enjoyable experience. The company was able to keep the prices of its unique products attractively low (relative to those at Whole Foods and Fresh Market) because of (1) buyers who were always on the lookout for exotic items they could buy at a discount (all products had to pass a taste test and a cost test), (2) less expensive store locations and decor, (3) lower labor costs (there were fewer employees per store), (4) big private-label sales, and (5) very high sales volumes per square foot of store space (said to be $1,132 in 2003).[35]

Trader Joe's crew members were well paid; wages at the non-union company were said to average $21 per hour in 2004 (versus an average of $17.90 paid to unionized grocery chains); pay for first-year supervisors averaged $40,000 per year and entry-level part-timers earned $8 to $12 per hour.[36] The benefits package for employees was considered quite good and included a company-paid retirement plan; a 10 percent employee discount; flexible work hours; free Trader Joe's shirts (which were required on-the-job attire); disability insurance; an employee assistance program; and medical, dental, and vision insurance. Part-time crew members were eligible for medical, dental, and vision coverage after meeting the eligibility requirements; most crew members qualified after working two to three months.

Full-time employees were scheduled to work 40 or 47.5 hours a week and were supervisors. Full-time positions included three levels of hourly supervisors (Novitiate, Specialist, and Merchant) and two levels of salaried management—First Mate (assistant store manager) and Captain (store manager). About 80 percent of Trader Joe's Novitiates began their employment as part-time crew members; individuals outside the company who had strong retail/grocery experience were also considered for the position of Novitiate (supervisor-in-training). The company had a retail management training program designed to take experienced candidates from the level of Novitiate to Second Mate (assistant manager) in about 15 months. Part-time employees worked up to 40 hours a week and did not supervise other crew members; the performance of part-time crew members was reviewed twice a year. All appointments as Captains and First Mates came from the ranks of crew members currently employed at Trader Joe's, including those chosen for newly opened stores. When a new store was scheduled to open, the store Captain and First Mate were responsible for hiring crew members.

Fresh & Easy Neighborhood Markets

In 2007, a new chain, Fresh & Easy Neighborhood Market, emerged as a competitor in the natural and organic segment of the retail grocery industry. Fresh & Easy was a newly established subsidiary of British supermarket giant

Tesco, the world's third-largest retailer (sales of £59.4 billion for fiscal year ending February 23, 2008, equivalent to about $95 billion). Tesco did extensive research on 60 American families and had numerous focus groups in California provide comments on store prototypes before opening its first 21 stores in Phoenix, followed quickly by an additional 38 stores in Las Vegas, San Diego, and Los Angeles. Some of the stores were located in low-income central-city neighborhoods, while others were adjacent to medium- and upper-income residential areas. Tesco's ambitious growth strategy called for opening Fresh & Easy locations at the rate of 3 stores per week, with 200 stores open by February 2009 and as many as 500 stores by 2011. The company opened an 820,000-square-foot distribution center (big enough to supply about 400 stores) in a Los Angeles suburb that was used both to create and package prepared foods and to supply area stores; a warehouse for northern California was being planned for when store expansion moved northward.

The Fresh & Easy concept called for stores to be in readily accessible neighborhood locations, have about 10,000 square feet of shopping space (about the size of an average Walgreens), stock around 3,500 items (versus about 60,000 at a typical supermarket), and convey a theme of fresh, wholesome, and easy-to-prepare foods in a convenient and pleasant setting. Product offerings ranged from gourmet items to everyday staples and included natural and organic foods; fruits and vegetables; meats, fish, and poultry; and a selection of prepared foods and grab-and-go products—all intended to convey a theme of fresh, wholesome, and easy-to-prepare. About 45 percent of the products on the shelves were house-branded Fresh & Easy items—one of the biggest-selling private-label items was a $1.99 bottle of Fresh & Easy "Big Kahuna" Australian wine (an idea said to be an imitation of Trader Joe's Two-Buck Chuck).[37] Other key features of Fresh & Easy stores included:

- Low prices (around 20–25 percent below traditional supermarkets and on a par with the prices at Walmart Supercenters).
- Locally sourced and mostly packaged fresh produce with expiration dates.
- Wide aisles and simple store layouts.

- Low shelves that allowed shoppers to see all across the store.
- All self-checkout.
- Energy-efficient store designs, lighting, and equipment (and the 820,000-square-foot distribution center had the largest solar panel roof in California).
- Packages, particularly for Fresh & Easy brand prepared foods, that let shoppers see what was inside.
- A taste-before-you-buy policy that encouraged shoppers to take almost any product to the "Kitchen Table" area of the store, where a staff person would open it or cook it and dole out samples.

However, in April 2008, top executives at Fresh & Easy announced that the company would put a three-month hold on further new store openings "to kick the tires, smooth out any wrinkles and make some improvements customers have asked for."[38] Management had already corrected a problem of stores frequently running out of certain items and responded to unexpectedly high demand for prepared foods by adding more than 100 new selections. But there was also thought to be a more fundamental strategic issue about whether the Fresh & Easy concept of offering a limited selection of organic and natural foods at relatively cheap prices was really working. One analyst estimated that weekly sales at Fresh & Easy stores had only been about $170,000 instead of the projected $200,000.[39] A research report by another analyst was considerably more downbeat, suggesting that weekly sales could be averaging as little as $60,000.[40] Skeptics of the Fresh & Easy format believed that health-conscious food shoppers could find a far wider, more appealing selection at Whole Foods stores (and to a lesser extent at Trader Joe's), and the shopping ambience was much superior at both Whole Foods and Trader Joe's. Inexpensive packaged foods were commonplace at supermarkets and full-range superstores.

However, Tesco was widely viewed as a formidable retailer with ample resources to fine-tune Fresh & Easy's business concept and strategy and to eventually generate a return on its $700 million–plus investment in Fresh & Easy. In commenting on the Fresh & Easy venture in the United States, Tesco CEO Sir

Terry Leahy said, "Clearly, it is high risk. If it fails it's embarrassing. . . . If it succeeds then it's transformational."[41] In April 2008, Leahy announced that sales at the 115 Fresh & Easy stores in Arizona, California, and Nevada were "ahead of budget" and that the best-performing stores were exceeding $20 in sales per square foot per week—a typical new grocery store in the U.S. was said to average $9 to $10 in weekly sales per square foot during the first year of operations.[42] He indicated that the company planned to have 200 Fresh & Easy stores open in the United States by mid-2009. However, as of March 2010, Fresh & Easy had only 146 stores in three states (California, Arizona, and Nevada). Tesco reported a loss of approximately $220 million on its Fresh & Easy business for fiscal 2009, up from a loss of about $124 million in fiscal 2008.[43]

Independent and Small Chain Retailers of Natural and Organic Products

In 2009 there were approximately 12,250 independent and small chain retailers of natural and organic foods, vitamins/supplements, and natural personal care products. Combined sales of independent natural and organic product retailers were an estimated $20.9 billion in 2008.[44] There were a number of small regional chains like Sunflower Farmers Market (30 stores in six states) and Sprouts Farmers Markets (53 stores in four states), but the majority were single-store, owner-managed enterprises serving small to medium-size communities and particular neighborhoods in metropolitan areas. Product lines and range of selection at the stores of independent natural and health foods retailers varied from narrow to moderately broad, depending on a store's market focus and the shopper traffic it was able to generate. Two vitamin/supplement chains, General Nutrition and Vitamin World, dominated the $9.3 billion vitamin/supplement segment with about 5,700 store locations; vitamin/supplement chains were an alternative source for many of the products that Whole Foods stocked in the vitamin/supplement section of its stores.

Over half of the independent stores had less than 2,500 square feet of retail sales space and generated revenues of less than $1 million annually; the core product offerings of these retailers were vitamins and mineral/herbal supplements, complemented by a selection of organic and natural foods and certain prepared foods—some 5,000 items in total. But there were roughly 1,000 natural and health foods retailers with store sizes exceeding 6,000 square feet and sales per store of about $10 million annually. Sales of vitamins and mineral/herbal supplements at many small independent stores were beginning to flatten, chiefly because conventional supermarket chains and most large drugstore chains now carried a sizable selection of vitamins/supplements. Sales at small retailers of natural and organic foods were also under pressure because conventional supermarkets had a growing selection of organic and natural foods, while chains like Whole Foods and Trader Joe's had a far wider selection of organic and natural products of all types. One industry expert noted that "shoppers can pick up a bag of mixed organic salad greens, a half-gallon of organic milk, some hormone-free chicken, trans fat–free cookies and crackers, non-dairy beverages and—brace yourself—even gluten-free foods, right in the aisles of their regular supermarkets."[45]

Sunflower Farmers Market Sunflower Farmers Market, headquartered in Boulder, Colorado, began operations in 2003 with four stores—two in Phoenix, one in Albuquerque, and one in Denver.[46] In late 2007, Sunflower raised $30 million in equity financing from PCG Capital Partners (in return for one-third ownership of the company) to fund its store expansion initiative; plans called for opening about eight new locations annually. The founding partner and CEO of Sunflower Farmers Market was Mark Gilliland, formerly a cofounder and president of Wild Oats Market who had been forced out at Wild Oats when his aggressive expansion strategy put the company in dire financial straits. Gilliland's vision was for Sunflower to have 50 locations in 2013 and annual sales of $500 million. By 2010, the company had grown to 30 stores in Arizona, New Mexico, Colorado, California, Nevada, and Utah; it also operated a distribution center in Phoenix. Revenues were roughly $200 million in 2008. About 90 percent of Sunflower's management team was comprised of former Wild Oats managers.

Sunflower's strategic objective was to establish a discount niche in organic and natural foods using a strategy with elements borrowed from Trader Joe's and small farmer's market-type stores. The company's mission statement described its four-pronged strategic approach:

- **We Will Always Offer the Best Quality Food at the Lowest Prices in Town.** "Better-than-supermarket quality at better-than-supermarket prices" is our motto.
- **We Keep Our Overhead Low.** No fancy fixtures or high rent. No corporate headquarters . . . just regular people, like you, looking for the best deals we can find.
- **We Buy Big.** We source directly, we pay our vendors quickly and we buy almost everything by the pallet or truckload. That buying power means big savings for you!
- **We Keep It Simple.** We don't charge our vendors "slotting allowances" or shelf space fees. Just honest-to-goodness negotiating for the lowest possible price and we pass the savings on to you.

Sunflower's tag line was "Serious Food . . . Silly Prices." The company targeted budget-conscious consumers who wanted to eat healthy or were interested in natural and organic foods but were averse to paying premium prices. According to Gilliland, "There's nothing fancy about us. In terms of atmosphere, we're comparable to Trader Joe's, but with a few more bells and whistles and a higher level of finish. For instance, we have a service meat department and offer lots more produce. . . . We try to kill everyone on price, especially on produce. It's our loss leader. We even beat Walmart when it comes to produce prices."[47] The chain had been described as a more-affordable, downsized, no-frills version of Whole Foods.[48] Management strived to locate new stores on recycled real estate sites, keep store build-out costs low, and use basic store fixtures and furnishings, thus enabling a new store to be built and equipped for less than $2 million.

Sunflower's stores had an average footprint of 20,000 square feet and a bright, colorful warehouse-like atmosphere. Stores stocked about 6,000 different items, a number of which were one-of-a-kind products purchased in large lots from brokers. The product focus was on organic, natural, and minimally processed food items. Pallets of goods were placed wherever there was floor space available. Each store stocked fresh produce; meats and seafood; cereals; nutrition bars; canned goods; pastas; frozen meals; premium roasted coffees; gluten-free foods; bulk foods; cheeses; breads; deli selections (sliced meats, soups, salads, sandwiches, sushi, and a fresh olive and antipasto bar); beer and wine; and an assortment of health, wellness, and personal care items. Private-label items accounted for about 20 percent of sales. Each store had a weekly sales flyer (also available by e-mail), and an events calendar for each store could be viewed online at the company's website (www.sfmarkets.com). Stores also served the community by organizing activities, lectures, and events that emphasized the value of good nutrition and a healthy lifestyle.

Sprouts Farmers Market   Founded in 2002, Sprouts was a regional chain with stores in Arizona, Texas, California, and Colorado. It specialized in fresh produce but also offered a large selection of vitamins and supplements, all-natural meats, fresh seafood, 200 bins of bulk food items, a selection of natural and organic grocery products, 1,500 gluten-free products, dairy products (including rBST-free milk), imported cheeses, deli meats, bakery items, and beer and wine. Its mission was "helping America eat healthier, live longer, and spend less." Its vision was to operate stores throughout the United States and "strive to create value for the customer, maintain a fun and unique environment for our customers and employees, be the employer of choice, and create an environment where new ideas and risk taking are encouraged." In 2010, the company, headquartered in Phoenix, had 50 stores in four states (Arizona, California, Colorado, and Texas) and more than 4,000 employees. Twelve new stores were planned for 2010. Revenues were expected to approach $500 million in 2010, up from an estimated $110 million in 2005. Sprouts Farmers Market, owned by the Boney family, was the 13-largest privately held company in Arizona and the seventh-fastest-growing privately held company in the state. The Boney family had sold its Henry's Market chain to Wild Oats in 1999.

Existing Sprouts stores ranged from 23,000 to 37,000 square feet and were bright and cheery, with wide aisles and low shelves that allowed shoppers to see all parts of the store. Each store had weekly specials; Wednesdays were promoted as "Double Ad Day" because the previous week's ad prices overlapped the current week's ad prices (which began on Wednesdays); weekly specials, as well as a calendar of events at each store, could be accessed at the company's website (www.sprouts.com). A magazine issued every two months, *Sprouts Farmers Market,* had feature articles on various subjects, health and wellness information,

recipes, menus, and a news and notes section, as well as ads featuring products available at the company's stores.

The company had been referred to as "Whole Foods Lite" because, while using fresh produce as a primary sales driver, stores carried less organic produce and items were sold at lower price points.[49] It targeted educated, health-oriented, value-conscious grocery shoppers.

ENDNOTES

[1] The Nielsen Company, "Healthy Eating Report for 2008," January 21, 2009, posted at http://blog.nielsen.com/nielsenwire/consumer, accessed March 10, 2010.

[2] Lieberman Research Group, *2009 Organic Industry Survey,* a study conducted for the Organic Trade Association and posted at www.environmentalleader.com/2009/05/06/us-organic-sales-up-by-171/, accessed March 10, 2010; Anne Macey, "Retail Sales of Certified Organic Food Products, in Canada, in 2006," a study commissioned and published by the Organic Agriculture Centre of Canada, May 2007.

[3] Datamonitor, "Food: Global Industry Guide," www.researchandmarkets.com/research/18f9c2/food_global_indus, accessed March 11, 2010.

[4] Based on data in "Organic Beef Profile," Iowa State University Extension, www.agmrc.org, accessed on March 10, 2010.

[5] Economic Research Service, U.S. Department of Agriculture, data accessed at www.ers.usda.gov on March 25, 2008.

[6] Whole Foods Market, 2009 10-K report, p. 51.

[7] Whole Foods Market, 2009 10-K report, p. 10.

[8] Company press releases, February 19, 2008, and February 16, 2010.

[9] Whole Foods Market, "Letter to Shareholders," 2003 annual report.

[10] Hollie Shaw, "Retail-Savvy Whole Foods Opens in Canada," *National Post,* May 1, 2002, p. FP9.

[11] See Karin Schill Rives, "Texas-Based Whole Foods Market Makes Changes to Cary, N.C., Grocery Store," *News and Observer,* March 7, 2002.

[12] Calculated from data in Exhibit 5.

[13] Whole Foods Market, "Letter to Stakeholders," 2009 annual report.

[14] Company press release, February 16, 2010.

[15] As quoted in Marilyn Much, "Whole Foods Markets: Austin, Texas Green Grocer Relishes Atypical Sales," *Investors Business Daily,* September 10, 2002.

[16] As quoted in "Whole Foods Market to Open in Albuquerque, N.M.," *Santa Fe New Mexican,* September 10, 2002.

[17] Information contained in John R. Wells and Travis Haglock, "Whole Foods Market, Inc.," Harvard Business School case study 9-705-476.

[18] Company press release, January 21, 2003.

[19] Company press release announcing Whole Foods Market's inclusion on *Fortune's* "The 100 Best Companies to Work For" list, January 21, 2010.

[20] Whole Foods Market, 2009 10-K report, p. 14, and company press release, January 21, 2010.

[21] As quoted in John K. Wilson, "Going Whole Hog with Whole Foods," Bankrate.com, posted December 23, 1999, and accessed March 21, 2010. Mackey made the statement in 1991 when efforts were being made to unionize the company's store in Berkeley, California.

[22] Company press release, January 21, 2010.

[23] Whole Foods Market, 2009 10-K report, pp. 28 and 34.

[24] Whole Foods Market, 2009 10-K report, p. 42; 2008 10-K report, p. 48; and 2007 10-K report, p. 43.

[25] Slide presentation at Whole Foods Market's annual shareholders meeting, March 8, 2010.

[26] "Frank Talk from Whole Foods' John Mackey," *Wall Street Journal,* August 4, 2009, http://online.wsj.com, accessed March 13, 2010.

[27] David Kesmodel and John. R. Wilke, "Whole Foods Is Hot, Wild Oats a Dud—So Said Rahodeb," *Wall Street Journal,* July 12, 2007, http://online.wsj.com/article/SB118418782959963745.html, accessed April 7, 2007.

[28] Andrew Martin, "Whole Foods Executive Used Alias," *New York Times,* July 12, 2007, http://www.nytimes.com/2007/07/12/business/12foods.html, accessed April 7, 2008.

[29] Ibid.

[30] Company press release, October 5, 2007.

[31] According to a July 13, 2007, posting on a *BusinessWeek* message board, http://www.businessweek.com/careers/managementiq/archives/2007/07/who_advises_joh.html, accessed March 26, 2010.

[32] Company press release, February 16, 2010, p. 1.

[33] Trader Joe's, www.traderjoes.com, accessed December 1, 2005.

[34] In 1977, Coulombe sold the company to German billionaire Theo Albrecht (who had since put the company in a trust); Albrecht was a cofounder of German supermarket chain Aldi.

[35] "Trader Joe's: The Trendy American Cousin," *Business Week,* April 26, 2004, www.businessweek.com, accessed March 29, 2010.

[36] "The American Way of Aldi," *Deutsche Welle,* January 16, 2004, www.dw-world.de, accessed March 29, 2010.

[37] Matthew Boyle, "Tesco Needs a Fresh Start in the U.S.," *Fortune,* December 4, 2007, www.cnnmoney.com, accessed April 7, 2008.

[38] As quoted in Bruce Horovitz, "British Invasion Hits Grocery Stores," *USA Today,* April 7, 2008, p. B2.

[39] Ibid.

[40] Ibid.

[41] As quoted in "Fresh, But Far from Easy," *The Economist,* June 21, 2007, www.economist.com, accessed April 7, 2008.

[42] Company press release, April 15, 2008.

[43] "Tesco Faces Growing Losses in US," *Daily Mail,* April 21, 2009, www.thisismoney.co.uk, accessed March 30, 2010.

[44] *National Foods Merchandiser,* June 2009, p. 12, www.naturalfoodmerchandiser.com, accessed March 31, 2010.

[45] Jay Jacobwitz, "Independent Retailers Need New Customers: The New 'Integrated' Foods Shopper," *Merchandising Insights,* November 2009, http://wfcgreenbook.com, accessed March 30, 2010.

[46] This section is based on information posted at the Sunflower Markets website (www.sunflowermarkets.com) and in Joe Lewandowski, "Naturals Stores Freshen Their Strategies," *Natural Foods Merchandiser,* January 1, 2004, www.naturalfoodsmerchandiser.com, accessed November 19, 2004.

[47] Connie Gentry, Katherine Field, and Marianne Wilson, "Forty Under 40: Small Chains Flourish," *Chain Store Age,* January 2009, www.sfmarkets.com, accessed March 31, 2010.

[48] Ibid.

[49] David Giddens, "Sprouts Growing in Texas," *Dallas Business Journal,* June 10, 2005, www.dallas.bizjournals.com, accessed March 31, 2010.

The O-Fold Innovation for Preventing Wrinkles: A Good Business Opportunity?

A. J. Strickland
The University of Alabama

Jimmy Marquis
The University of Alabama, Faculty Scholar

Alex Richards, a junior at a well-respected university, was double-majoring in finance and accounting. He took his schoolwork very seriously and had maintained a 4.0 grade point average. Richards had always dreamed of becoming a corporate executive and assisting in the strategic direction of an established company. He had been told by friends and professors that starting in public accounting and getting a CPA was a traditional stepping-stone to a corporate executive position. What attracted Richards to his dream job was not just the compensation package but also the fact that he could set the direction of a company and see his strategy unfold before his eyes. Richards's father was a controller at a medium-size private company, and his mother was a homemaker. While Richards grew up in comfort, he by no means could have been considered from "old money."

During the summer between his sophomore and junior years, Richards flew out to Colorado to propose to his fiancée. Now engaged, Richards planned to get married right after graduation but also to hold off on having children for at least seven years. His fiancée had decided to become a physician's assistant, which would require three years of additional school right after her undergraduate degree (she was also a junior).

Before his trip to Colorado, Richards was debating whether to bring a suit to wear. He didn't want to wear it on the airplane or pay to check a suitcase, so he thought about packing the suit in his carry-on bag. In imagining how wrinkled his suit would end up after being stuffed into his carry-on, Richards realized that clothing wrinkled when it came in contact with an edge. That was when he came up with the idea behind O-Fold and created a rough model:

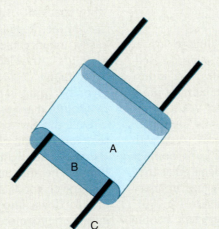

A: A canvas wrapping around a wire skeleton forming a cylindrical tube that the garment is designed to fold around (multiple times). A will be flush with both ends (labeled B).

B: One end will be removable (slides off) allowing the user access to store items inside the tube (such as socks, underwear, belts, valuables).

C: Each is a Velcro strap with one pair designed to be used in the beginning to secure the garment to the "O-Fold" while the other is used after the garment is wrapped around the "O-Fold" as a final securing mechanism.

Suits could be wrapped around the cylindrical O-Fold, secured with straps, packed into tight spaces, and arrive at the destination wrinkle-free. The traveler could store items within the O-Fold's hollow interior and thus would not lose any valuable space. With no edges on the O-Fold, the traveler could pack delicate clothing without the fear of wrinkles.

A couple of days later, Richards got on the computer to perform a preliminary patent search online to see if anyone had already patented such an idea. Not finding anything to discourage him, Richards decided that he might want to consider doing something with his idea. He realized that he might be able to patent the O-Fold and sell the rights to it, or he could start a company with the O-Fold as the flagship product. Richards was aware that creating a company required a tremendous commitment in both time and money; however, he still enjoyed dreaming about raking in the millions.

With a great GPA and a competitive résumé, Richards knew he should be able to get a good job after graduation if he desired it. With the plan of getting married, Richards was unsure whether starting a company right away would be wise. The opportunity cost of starting a company—giving up a likely good job—was steep in both a financial sense and a security sense. While considering his options, Richards decided to do some preliminary research about the luggage industry.

THE LUGGAGE INDUSTRY

The luggage industry evolved over time to answer the needs that different modes of travel presented. With more than $5 billion in sales, the industry expected strong growth as the baby boomer generation reached the peak travel years. Average household luggage spending was highest in households with adults ages 35 to 64. And with the peak age group of 45–54, the baby boomer generation was expected to boost demand as they increased their travel time. The luggage industry took a major hit from the September 11, 2001, terrorist attacks. As might be expected, people who feared traveling were reluctant to replace their existing luggage with new pieces. The industry rebounded nicely within two years as Americans once again began to view traveling as a right.

Prior to 9/11, profit margins in the industry were very healthy and had been improving: Average gross plant profit margins were 28.9 percent in 1990, 41 percent in 1995, and 45.9 percent in 2000. Part of the growth in profits could be attributed to overseas manufacturing. Beginning in the late 1980s, there was a push for American-made products. Yet the luggage industry began importing close to 75 percent of the merchandise while manufacturing 25 percent (often solid-surface suitcases, which are expensive to import) in the United States. As one industry insider put it, "Almost all nylon goods, whether it's Samsonite, American Tourister, Verdi, it's all imported. It has the good old American name, but basically it's an import."

Another important trend in the luggage industry was the emergence of the businesswoman. Back in 1977, only 3 percent of business travelers were women; now that number was 45 percent. With women also making 80 percent of the household purchases, luggage manufacturers had to begin catering their products to a female taste. Luggage colors moved from the traditional blacks to basic colors to hot pink with polka dots as travelers began to use their luggage to make a fashion statement. Luggage began to come in different shapes with different fabrics and new compartments.

Another trend was a premium put on lightweight luggage. With fuel costs rising, airlines began lowering the maximum weight of checked bags while enforcing a financial penalty on those who checked overweight bags. Travelers also needed their luggage to be smaller as well as more easily manageable. With more security checks after 9/11, travelers began to seek ways to save time; many decided to forgo checking bags in favor of using carry-ons. Allison Polish, senior marketing manager for Victorinox (which popularized the Swiss Army brand), noted, "We've seen a reduction of the sales of 30-inch uprights; the move to lightweight luggage has meant a boom. The premium on these has soared."

Travel goods sales for 2000–2005 could be broken down into the following categories: luggage, brief/computer cases, travel/sports bags, handbags, flat goods, and backpacks. Exhibits 1 and 2 show sales of travel goods by sector.

Exhibit 3 shows the market potential for luggage in 2009. Worldwide demand for luggage was dominated by three areas: Asia and the Middle East, Europe, and North America and the Caribbean. Latent demand signified the potential demand if market variables turned out to favor

Exhibit 1   Dollar Volume of Travel Goods by Sector, 2000–2005 ($ millions)

Category	2000	2001	2002	2003	2004	2005
Luggage	$ 2,106.7	$ 1,972.1	$ 1,688.1	$ 1,512.5	$1,780.0	$ 1,811.1
Brief/computer cases	698.2	631.1	518.4	497.5	571.7	593.1
Travel/sports bags	6,371.4	5,817.2	5,354.5	5,207.5	5,818.4	6,146.7
Handbags	3,977.6	3,777.6	4,043.7	4,612.2	5,900.1	6,136.6
Flat goods	2,269.4	2,069.1	2,050.8	2,131.7	2,503.7	2,509.8
Backpacks	950.7	919.7	912.9	942.5	1,044.1	1,049.1
Total	$16,374.0	$15,186.8	$14,568.3	$14,903.8	$17,617.8	$18,246.4

Source: Euromonitor International, from trade sources.

the luggage industry. It was also used to signify market potential.

After researching the luggage industry, Richards went to talk to one of his professors about his idea. His professor recommended looking into early-stage investing and examining what it was like trying to raise money for a new business. Richards's professor mentioned that he might want to specifically look into angel investing due to the infancy of Richards's idea. However, having had experience with angel investors before, his professor quickly warned against making any assumption relating an angel investor to some kind of generous benefactor.

ANGEL INVESTING

Angel investors, in contrast with venture capital firms, typically made investments in the range of $25,000–$50,000. In contrast, venture capi-

tal (VC) firms regularly made investments in the range of $5–$10 million. In 2008, angel investors invested 16 percent of their funds in health care, 13 percent in software, 12 percent in retail, 11 percent in biotech, 8 percent in industrial/energy, and 7 percent in media. Mergers and acquisitions (M&As) made up 70 percent of angel exits in 2008, while 26 percent of exits were bankruptcies and 4 percent were initial public offerings (IPOs). Average annual returns, while quite variable, were 22 percent for M&A and IPO exits. The number of companies that received funding from angel investors had declined steadily from 23 percent in 2005 to 10 percent in 2008.

The angel investing community was made up largely of wealthy individuals who invested in start-up and early-stage companies. The two main criteria in judging a potential investment—the business and the entrepreneur—were weighted according to what stage in the investing

Exhibit 2   Percentage Sales of Travel Goods by Sector, 2000–2005

Sector	2000	2001	2002	2003	2004	2005
Luggage	12.9%	13.0%	11.6%	10.1%	10.1%	9.9%
Brief/computer cases	4.3	4.2	3.6	3.3	3.2	3.3
Travel/sports bags	38.9	38.3	36.8	34.9	33.0	33.7
Handbags	24.3	24.9	27.8	30.9	33.5	33.6
Flat goods	13.9	13.6	14.1	14.3	14.2	13.8
Backpacks	5.8	6.1	6.3	6.3	5.9	5.7
Total	100.0%	100.0%	100.0%	100.0%	100.0%	100.0%

Source: Euromonitor International, from trade sources.

Exhibit 3 Estimated Worldwide Market Potential for Luggage, 2009 ($ millions)

Region	Latent Demand	% of Whole
Asia and the Middle East	$ 4,625	36.0%
Europe	3,407	26.6
North America and the Caribbean	3,045	23.7
Latin America	1,053	8.2
Africa	521	4.1
Oceana	179	1.4
Total	$12,830	100.0%

Source: Philip M. Parker, INSEAD, copyright 2008, www.icongrouponline.com.

process they were in. In the beginning, a group of angel investors looked over the business plan with the goal of determining whether there would be enough demand for the company to survive and eventually thrive. Once a start-up passed this first test, quality of management typically became a very important factor because angel investing was indeed a partnership. Angel investors would be willing to use, and often required, a hands-on approach with the companies in which they invested; they filled an important gap in the funding process for start-up companies where the risk was too high for VC firms and the amount of money needed was too large for many entrepreneurs to raise on their own or from family and friends. Exhibit 4 shows the change in a company's capital needs over time.

The landscape of angel investing had changed along with many other facets of the economy during the 2008–2009 economic downturn. Through the second quarter of 2008, angel investments totaled $12.4 billion, up 4.2 percent from the preceding year. However, only 23,000 ventures received those funds, signifying a 3.8 percent drop. Angel investors were still investing in a shaky economy, but they were not investing in as many ventures as before. Marianne Hudson, executive director of the Angel Capital Association, said, "There's safety in numbers. Angels see syndication not only as a way of reducing risk, but also as a means of ensuring that good companies are properly funded." In the recessionary climate, it was not impossible to receive angel investing; however, entrepreneurs had to be extremely prepared when pitching an idea to angel investors. The rules for pitching to angel investors (be succinct, avoid jargon, have an exit strategy) were

Exhibit 4 Change in Capital Needs

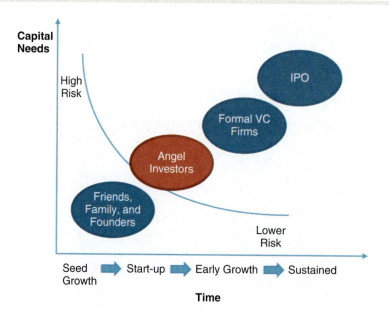

even more important in the recession because a misstep could result in losing a potential investor.

Angel investing in the economic downturn was very much a buyer's market. During a recession, as unemployment went up, the number of would-be start-ups also typically increased as people who had lost their job looked for other ways to make money. Also, investors began to worry about how the recession would endanger their prior investments and prepared to circle the wagons around the companies in which they already had an interest. The increased demand for funds with a decreased supply of funds for new ventures created a shortage of funds for the would-be start-ups. It was not impossible to get funding, but entrepreneurs had to be prepared to give up more control while also accepting a lower valuation. John May, managing partner of New Vantage Group in Vienna, Virginia, stated, "I'm not saying we are going to be angels from hell, but we are not going to be stupid about how to price."

SUBSTITUTES

Fighting wrinkles on the road was not a new problem for business travelers. In the past, airlines had allowed garment bags as a carry-on item. Given new size restrictions on carry-on items, travelers moved to more creative solutions to fight the wrinkling of their business clothes.

Plastic was a unique material in that it combated friction, which could cause wrinkles. With this knowledge, some travelers creatively used dry-cleaning bags when they were traveling. They could minimize wrinkles by placing one article of clothing in a dry-cleaning bag and then rolling it up and placing it in a carry-on. This was obviously an inexpensive solution that many business travelers currently were using.

Samsonite had also responded to the wrinkle problem by offering carry-on luggage with a garment

bag built in. This allowed the convenience of traveling with just a carry-on without having to forgo a garment bag. The Samsonite Silhouette 11, a 22-inch upright garment bag (shown in the photo), retailed at $440.

PRICE POINTS

Alex Richards knew that if the O-Fold was to have any success, the price point would be a key determining factor. Before pricing the O-Fold, Richards decided he needed to know more about the cost of direct materials as well as the pricing of other luggage accessories. Richards remembered hearing in class that retail stores typically had close to a 100 percent price markup, whereas the manufacturing markup was broader, at 50–200 percent. Unsure of how to estimate wholesale material costs, Richards decided to examine a comparable product from a materials and manufacturing standpoint, price out the corresponding markups, and end with a rough direct materials budget per unit. The key here was to pick a product that used about the same amount of material and was similar in manufacturing complexity, so Richards picked a log carrier that retailed at $10.25, measured 36½ inches wide and 17½ inches long, and was made of a heavy-duty canvas similar to the type of material the O-Fold would be made of. Because the log carrier retailed at $10.25, Richards reasoned, the wholesale price to the retailer was probably around $5.25.

All that was left to price out was the manufacturer markup, but Richards was unsure of which percentage to use. Richards took this problem to one of his finance professors to see what she thought. Richards's finance professor asked him, "If you were to begin producing O-Folds tomorrow, do you think you would pay more or less for your materials than an established company?"

Richards responded with "More" because he would have to develop supplier relationships as well as eventually achieve some economies of scale from a production standpoint. The professor agreed with him and then suggested using the 50 percent manufacturing markup so that Richards could initially factor in the markup start-up companies have to fight against when competing with other companies that have achieved greater economies of scale and can buy materials at a deeper discount. Pricing out the manufacturer's 50 percent markup, Richards arrived at a raw material price per unit of around $3.50.

When looking for a retail price comparable, Richards decided to focus on products similar in function and utility to the O-Fold. He began looking at luggage accessories and came across Eagle Creek Pack-It Folders (shown in photo). Eagle Creek Pack-It Folders were designed to fit in a suitcase or briefcase as a supplemental travel accessory. A traveler could place shirts inside the folder for protection while traveling. Although the Pack-It Folder did not offer the wrinkle protection of the O-Fold, it did offer similar utility. Also, the Pack-It Folder came in three widths: 15, 18, and 20 inches. This was important to Richards because it did not limit the potential market by clothing size. The price points for the Pack-It-Folder were $24.00, $27.50, and $30.00 for the 15-, 18-, and 20-inch models, respectively. The price increments were obviously due to the increase in materials required by the larger pieces, a problem that Richards was likely to run into with the O-Fold.

To simplify his business model, Richards decided that he would price all O-Fold sizes the same, at $25.00 retail per unit. Richards knew that $25.00 was just what the ultimate consumer would likely pay for an O-Fold, while he would be

able to sell the items wholesale at around $12.50 a unit (given the already-mentioned 100 percent retail markup). At a wholesale price of $12.50 per unit, with materials costing $3.50 per unit, Richards now had to estimate his manufacturing costs.

Before estimating the costs, Richards purchased materials to make an O-Fold so that he could see how long it would take someone to complete the assembly process. The first step in making an O-Fold was creating the casing for the canvas to be wrapped around; this was achieved by putting together a wire skeleton. Richards spent 10 minutes creating the skeleton, 6 minutes sewing the canvas (with a sewing machine), 3 minutes sewing on the straps (also with a sewing machine), and estimated an additional 5 minutes for packaging. In sum, Richards found that he could produce one O-Fold every 24 minutes, or 2.5 O-Folds per hour. Exhibit 5 shows the O-Fold manufacturing time estimate.

Richards then recruited his brother to work the sewing machine and set up a two-person assembly line. As a team, Richards and his brother were able to complete seven O-Folds per hour. The assembly-line approach increased the per-person output per hour from 2.5 O-Folds to 3.5 O-Folds while still only requiring the use of a single sewing machine. Richards realized that his brother was using the sewing machine almost the entire time; he was therefore unsure whether adding more people per machine would greatly improve the per-person hourly output. For the sake of the business model, Richards decided to set the standard at 3.5 O-Folds per hour per person per machine.

Wanting to keep his options open, Richards figured he should look into what it would cost

Exhibit 5   O-Fold Manufacturing Time, Alex Richards alone (minutes)

Manufacturing Activity	Time (minutes)
Casing assembly	10
Canvas sewing	6
Strap sewing	3
Packaging	5
Total	24

him to hire some people to produce the O-Folds for him. One of his professors suggested that Richards look at possibly hiring some people from the more rural part of the state to help produce the O-Folds. Richards called the Terry County Career Center and spoke with the director, Francine Bassett. Bassett explained to Richards that Terry County was known economically for its quilt barns. A quilt barn was a place—literally a barn—in which some of the older women from around the community produced handmade quilts for sale. Quilters recruited some younger women as well. The quilts could fetch a pretty good price, with some of the nicer ones retailing at more than $2,000. With little education, a lot of the quilters had begun producing quilts at a young age, and they continued quilting professionally well into their 60s and 70s. Bassett offered to take Richards to see one of the quilting barns in action, and Richards happily agreed.

Mama Gee's Quilting has been around for more than 100 years and was one of the original quilt barns in Terry County. Richards met with the current owner, Gladys Smith, the granddaughter of the founder. Smith informed Richards that quilting allowed women of all ages to help make a living and provide for their families. A lot of young girls in the community would come to her and ask to work free so that they could learn the quilt-making trade. Mama Gee's Quilting employed around 30 women and had more than $400,000 in revenue last year, all without owning a single computer. Smith did not pay by the hour; rather, she sold the quilts on consignment, with a worker making money only if her quilt sold. Bassett informed Richards that minimum wage would be very desirable and that Terry County certainly had a sewing background. At a minimum wage of $7.25 per hour, and a production rate of 3.5 O-Folds per hour, each O-Fold will cost $2.10 in labor to make.

The $2.10 per unit in manufacturing cost plus the $3.50 in material cost placed the finished O-Fold in Richards's possession with a per-unit cost of $5.60. Richards could then sell finished O-Folds wholesale at $12.50 per unit, representing a 123 percent markup and a contribution margin of $6.90. Richards was young and new at business, so he reasoned there would be more variable costs that he was not yet aware of, such as shipping and returns. Richards rationalized an additional "cookie-jar" (i.e., contingency) cost estimated at $2.25 per unit for budgeting reasons. This cookie-jar cost would, he hoped, alleviate some of the turmoil caused by unforeseen costs and still leave a healthy per-unit contribution margin of $4.65.

PATENT

While Richards was unsure of the structure of the start-up, he was fairly certain that he would need at least to secure a patent in order to protect the idea behind the O-Fold. After doing some research, Richards budgeted $10,000 for obtaining a patent and related fees. Assuming the $4.65 contribution margin, Richards calculated that he would have to sell 2,000 units to cover the cost of the patent. While a patent was certainly not cheap, Richards believed it to be necessary if the O-Fold was going to have a chance at being successful. Richards didn't have $10,000 sitting in his back pocket, so the need for outside investors began to become more and more unavoidable. While researching patents, Richards came up with an interesting strategy regarding the timeline for obtaining a patent. The U.S. government provided a one-year patent grace period for inventors by allowing the inventors one year to patent their invention. The grace period began when one of four conditions was met:

1. The invention was placed on sale to the public.
2. A description of the invention was published.
3. A detailed description of the product was presented at a public meeting.
4. The invention was placed into the hands of the public.

Richards believed the grace period provided an opportunity for the product to be market-tested before a patent became necessary. Richards assumed that if he could meet one of the four grace-period conditions, he could begin production and see if the market provided signs that the O-Fold was a viable product. Also, making use of the patent grace period would put Richards in a better position with potential investors because he would then have some real market data to provide credibility to his business model and lower the risk for potential investors.

BUSINESS MODELS

Richards now faced the difficult decision of determining how to design a business model that would give the O-Fold the best chance of being profitable. Each business model would be evaluated on its leverage, risk, probability of success, potential profits, and exit strategy. Richards came up with four potential basic business models for the O-Fold: sell the idea, license the idea, outsource production, and use a crawl-walk-run strategy.

Sell the Idea

Richards's first potential business model—sell the idea—provided a clear exit strategy. Theoretically, the only thing needed for this business model was a patent; however, without market data, it was unlikely that anyone would be willing to pay a large premium for the patent. Although this option would get him out of the game quickly with a little money in his pocket, Richards was unsure whether anyone would be willing to pay what he believed the O-Fold idea to be worth. It could be challenging to convince someone to buy something that hadn't been tested or proved in the marketplace. However, although Richards was by no means rich, he believed he would have enough money to go this route on his own without any outside investors. Exhibit 6 shows Richards's costs, and Exhibit 7 includes the break-even quantity.

License the Idea

Richards's second potential business model was to license the idea. While the perceived cost of licensing a product might seem low, Richards believed it would be wise to bring in an angel investor not just for the money but for the business connections as well. The ideal licensing agreement, in Richards's opinion, would be one in which he received some money up front and then a royalty on the back end for each unit sold. Not only did Richards lack the business connections, but he also knew close to nothing about licensing contracts. The know-how and expertise of an angel investor might be worth even more than the loan itself in terms of total value added by the partnership.

Another positive for licensing the idea was that it would take a lot of the operational elements out of Richards's hands, thus freeing him to pursue other opportunities. This would also put the O-Fold into the hands of a more experienced person who would know how to bring a product such as the O-Fold to the marketplace. The feasibility of this strategy relied heavily on Richard's ability to get his foot in the door at a company that would be interested in licensing the O-Fold. Richards, not the best networker by any means, knew that he could not go this path alone and would need outside help to make it work.

A potential negative was that if the O-Fold proved to be a great idea, Richards would likely be leaving some money on the table when compared to producing and selling the product himself. As with just selling the idea, it would certainly be better if Richards had some type of market data to back up his business model. Being an inexperienced entrepreneur, Richard would find that a lot of people would question the legitimacy of his estimates. While Richards could not fix his inexperience in the short term, he could seek out proven comparables to back up his numbers in order to somewhat increase their reliability.

Exhibit 6   Fixed Costs for O-Fold Production

Patent	$10,000.00
Prototype	500.00
Professional fees	1,000.00
Total	$11,500.00

Exhibit 7   Fixed Costs Plus Break-Even Amount for O-Fold Production

Patent	$10,000.00
Prototype	500.00
Professional fees	1,000.00
Total	$11,500.00
Break-even quantity	2,473
($4.65 profit per quantity sold)	

Outsource Production

The third potential business model took a giant leap in terms of Richards's involvement. Richards could outsource the manufacturing of the O-Fold and sell the finished items himself. This would allow Richards to keep a larger portion of the profits while also allowing him to maintain some control over the strategic direction of the O-Fold. Using Terry County as a potential outsourcing location, Richards would be able to produce an O-Fold with direct materials and direct labor totaling $5.60 per unit and overhead totaling $2.25 per unit. Richards believed that this option would almost certainly require the money and expertise of an angel investor. While the risks were greater with the outsourcing option, the idea of running his own company was very appealing to Richards. He likely would have to put some of his own money at stake; he would also probably have to make this his job. Forgoing the more traditional accounting route, Richards would have to factor in the opportunity cost of giving up a steady salary as well as factoring in the uncertainty of future cash flows associated with the O-Fold. If Richards decided to go this route, he would also have to provide more information about what he believed the strategic direction of

the O-Fold should be. Exhibit 8 presents an outsource production strategy break-even analysis for the O-Fold.

Distribution If he chose the outsourcing business model, Richards would have to answer the question of distribution. There were many options here for Richards to consider. First, he could go the traditional retail route by selling in bulk to retailers at the wholesale price. Selling to retail stores was one option where it could be tough to get a foot in the door. Second, he could sell the O-Fold through a website; this represented a cheaper option than the retail route. Richards could post videos about the O-Fold, provide packing tutorials, and take orders all from one website. He would have to work hard at marketing with the online route in order to generate some online traffic. Third, he could advertise the O-Fold in travel magazines and/or airline catalogs. This option would help isolate the target market in terms of marketing effectiveness. Delta's *SkyMall* magazine was placed on all Delta flights, featured merchandise that travelers might be interested in, and provided a way for the customer to place an order. What better way to focus on your market than to advertise a way to

Exhibit 8   Outsource Production Strategy Break-Even Analysis

	Start-up	Year 1	Year 2	Year 3
Fixed Costs				
Patent	$ 10,000			
Prototype	500			
Professional fees	1,000			
Website	1,000			
Computer and software	$ 1,500	$ 500	$ 500	$ 500
Telephone	600	600	600	600
Office supplies	500	500	500	500
Website management	100	100	100	100
Total:	$15,200	$1,700	$1,700	$1,700
Variable Costs				
Direct materials	$ 3.50	$ 3.50	$ 3.50	$ 3.50
Direct labor	2.10	2.10	2.10	2.10
Unexpected costs	2.25	2.25	2.25	2.25
Break-Even Quantity	3,269	366	366	366

pack clothes without wrinkles to people who had just packed clothes themselves? The distribution question was an important one that would have to be answered for the angel investors.

Marketing   Another important question was how to get the word out about the O-Fold. Richards could simply rely on store shelf advertising if he went the retail route, or he could consider online, print, or many other forms of advertising. Working under the assumption that there was a need for the O-Fold out there, Richards would have to find a way to identify, locate, and sell to the customers who would fall in his target market.

Exit Strategy   Angel investors would be very interested to know what Richards envisioned the end game to be for the O-Fold. They would also be interested, even more so, in when they would exit the venture. Companies like this could sometimes have a "market cap" in terms of limiting how much of the market they could control. If an entrepreneur made too much noise, one of the bigger fish in the market would find a way to attack his or her market share, thus limiting how much the new company could grow. One strategy was to grow while staying unnoticed by the major players in the market. There were several options to pursue for the exit strategy all the way from an IPO to selling the company to a competitor. The angel investors would want to know when they would get their money back, how much certainty there was of getting their money back, and what return they could expect on their investment.

Use a Crawl-Walk-Run Strategy

The crawl-walk-run strategy was a three-step process of growing a company.

Crawl   In the crawl stage, Richards would likely recruit his brother and start making some O-Folds. He then would find a way to sell the finished products either online, door to door, or by some other fairly simple means of distribution. While the profits were certainly limited, this part of the strategy would provide Richards with a type of low-risk market research. At the crawl stage, Richards possibly would not need angel investors; beginning on his own could be of benefit to him

later by showing that he bore all the initial risk and garnered some market data to back up the legitimacy of his idea. He could almost certainly get a better valuation with a company that had actually sold something than he could with a company that existed only on paper. Richards would also be able to get a feel for what the day-to-day process of running a business looks like, only on a much smaller scale. This could prove to be beneficial later on when he moved up to the walk stage.

Walk   At this point Richards would likely want to bring in some angel investors to help finance the expansion. As stated above, he could expect a higher valuation once he had some market data to back up his claims. At this stage he would need to move from actually making the O-Folds to outsourcing their production. He would also need to have a patent, a developed distribution channel, and a marketing strategy. These factors would provide a potential early exit strategy for some of the investors if revenues and profits grew accordingly and some other company offered to buy O-Fold.

Run   The run stage was achieved when the company was producing large quantities and enjoying economies of scale. It would be difficult for the start-up to go unnoticed at this stage—new entrants into the market would be attracted—and the entrepreneur would certainly have to have an exit strategy in mind. If Richards could make it to this stage and sold his interest in the company, he could stand to make a fairly large sum of money. Typically, risk followed reward, and failing at this level would result in some people losing a substantial amount of money. Exhibit 9 shows the volume necessary to reach breakeven.

DECISION

Richards met with one of his professors to go over some of the different business models and decide which, if any, he should pursue. The professor told Richards that he could line up a meeting with some angel investors if that was what Richards desired. While Richards had enjoyed researching some ideas about starting a company, now a decision was required of him. Should he meet with the angel investors and, if so, what should his pitch be?

Exhibit 9   **Crawl-Walk-Run Strategy Break-Even Analysis**

	Start-Up	Year 1	Year 2	Year 3
Fixed Costs				
Website	$ 1,000	$ 100	$ 100	$ 100
Patent	10,000			
Professional fees	2,000			
Sewing machine	100			
Computer and software	1,500			
Telephone	600	600	600	600
Office supplies	500	500	500	500
Administrative salary	35,000	40,000	40,000	45,000
Building lease	12,000	12,000	12,000	12,000
Equipment lease	24,000	24,000	24,000	24,000
Total	$86,700	$77,200	$77,200	$82,200
Variable Costs				
Direct materials	$3.50	$3.50	$3.50	$3.50
Direct labor	2.10	2.10	2.10	2.10
Unexpected costs	2.25	2.25	2.25	2.25
Break-Even Quantity	18,645	16,602	16,602	17,677

Competition among the North American Warehouse Clubs: Costco Wholesale versus Sam's Club versus BJ's Wholesale

Arthur A. Thompson
The University of Alabama

In 2010, the nearly $125 billion discount warehouse and wholesale club segment of the North American retailing industry consisted of three principal competitors: Costco Wholesale, Sam's Club (a Walmart subsidiary), and BJ's Wholesale Club. Warehouse clubs operated no-frills, self-service big-box facilities where customers could choose from a relatively narrow assortment of discount-priced merchandise across a wide range of product categories, including food and household supplies, electronics, office supplies, selected appliances and furniture items, apparel, books and DVDs, home furnishings, and tires. Items were typically sold in case lots (cleaning supplies, paper products, office supplies, soft drinks, bottled waters); packaged in large containers (laundry detergents); shrink-wrapped in quantities of 6, 8, or 12 (canned goods); bundled in cartons of 100 or more (trash bags, paper plates, disposable cups), or giant-sized bags (potato chips, pretzels). In order to achieve high sales volumes and rapid inventory turnover, warehouse clubs generally limited merchandise selections to brand-name items that were leaders in their categories and an assortment of private-label items.

Warehouse clubs drew customers away from other wholesale and retail outlets such as supermarkets, department stores, drugstores, office supply stores, consumer electronics stores, and automotive stores chiefly because it was difficult for such sellers to match the low prices of a wholesale club. Costco, Sam's Club, and BJ's Wholesale had substantially lower operating and costs than most retailers because they purchased full truckloads of merchandise directly from manufacturers, displayed items on pallets or inexpensive shelving,

kept extra inventory on high shelving directly on the sales floor rather than in central warehouses, had very low costs for store decor and fixtures, had comparatively low labor costs (because warehouses were open fewer hours than conventional retailers and required comparatively fewer people to operate relative to the sales volumes that a store generated), and spent minimally on advertising and customer service. The low operating costs of warehouse clubs enabled them to charge significantly lower prices than traditional wholesalers, mass merchandisers, supermarkets, and other retailers. Moreover, because of high sales volumes at each store location and consequently rapid inventory turnover, warehouse clubs were able to receive cash for a large portion of their inventory before they had to pay many of their merchandise vendors (even in instances when a club elected to take advantage of early payment discounts offered by vendors rather than delay vendor payment until the standard 30 to 60 days after the merchandise was delivered). Thus, a warehouse club could finance a big percentage of its merchandise inventory through the payment terms provided by vendors rather than by having to maintain sizable working capital (defined as current assets minus current liabilities) to facilitate timely payment of suppliers.

The low prices and broad merchandise selection found at the three leading warehouse clubs were attractive to small-business owners, churches and nonprofit organizations, caterers, small restaurants, and individual households (particularly bargain hunters and those with large families). A significant number of business members shopped wholesale clubs for their personal needs as well as their business needs. Interested shoppers paid an annual membership fee to make purchases at a warehouse club.

There were more than 1,250 warehouse club locations in the United States, Canada, and Mexico; most every major metropolitan area had one, if not several, warehouse club operations. Costco had about a 56 percent share of warehouse club sales in North America (the United States, Canada, and Mexico); Sam's Club had roughly a 36 percent share; and BJ's Wholesale Club and several small warehouse club competitors had an 8 percent share. Competition was based on such factors as price, merchandise quality and selection, location, and member service. However, all three warehouse clubs also competed with a wide range of other types of retailers, including retail discounters like Walmart and Dollar General, general merchandise chains like Target and Kohl's, specialty chains like Office Depot and Staples in office supplies and Best Buy in electronics and DVDs, supermarkets, gasoline stations, and Internet retailers. Not only did Walmart, the world's largest retailer, compete directly with Costco and BJ Wholesale via its Sam's Club subsidiary, but its 3,000+ Walmart Supercenters in the United States, Canada, and Mexico sold many of the same types of merchandise at attractively low prices as well.

INDUSTRY BACKGROUND

The membership warehouse concept was pioneered by discount merchandising sage Sol Price, who opened the first Price Club in a converted airplane hangar on Morena Boulevard in San Diego in 1976. Price Club lost $750,000 in its first year of operation, but by 1979 it had two stores, 900 employees, 200,000 members, and a $1 million profit. Years earlier, Sol Price had experimented with discount retailing at a San Diego store called Fed-Mart. Jim Sinegal, the cofounder and current CEO of Costco Wholesale, got his start in retailing at the San Diego Fed-Mart at the age of 18, loading mattresses for $1.25 an hour while attending San Diego Community College. When Sol Price sold Fed-Mart, Sinegal left with Price to help him start the San Diego Price Club store; within a few years, Sol Price's Price Club emerged

as the unchallenged leader in member warehouse retailing, with stores operating primarily on the West Coast. Although he originally conceived Price Club as a place where small local businesses could obtain needed merchandise at economical prices, Sol Price soon concluded that his fledgling operation could achieve far greater sales volumes and gain buying clout with suppliers by also granting membership to individuals—a conclusion that launched the deep-discount warehouse club industry on a steep growth curve.

When Sinegal was 26, Sol Price made him the manager of the original San Diego store, which had become unprofitable. Price saw that Jim Sinegal had a special knack for discount retailing and for spotting what a store was doing wrong (usually either not being in the right merchandise categories or not selling items at the right price points)—the very things that Sol Price was good at and that were at the root of the Price Club's growing success in the marketplace. Sinegal soon got the San Diego store back into the black. Over the next several years, Sinegal continued to build his prowess and talents for discount merchandising. He mirrored Sol Price's attention to detail and absorbed all the nuances and subtleties of his mentor's style of operating—constantly improving store operations, keeping operating costs and overhead low, stocking items that moved quickly, and charging ultra-low prices that kept customers coming back to shop. Realizing that he had mastered the tricks of running a successful membership warehouse business from Sol Price, Sinegal decided to leave Price Club and form a new warehouse club operation, which he named Costco. His cofounder in the venture was Seattle entrepreneur Jeff Brotman (now chairman of Costco's board of directors).

The first Costco store began operations in Seattle in 1983, the same year that Walmart opened its first Sam's Club warehouses. By the end of 1984, there were nine Costco stores in five states, serving more than 200,000 members. In December 1985, Costco became a public company, selling shares to the public and raising additional capital for expansion. Costco became the first ever U.S. company to reach $1 billion in sales in less than six years. In October 1993, Costco merged with Price Club. Jim Sinegal became CEO of the merged company, presiding over 206 PriceCostco locations, which in total generated

$16 billion in annual sales. Jeff Brotman, who had functioned as Costco's chairman since the company's founding, became vice chairman of PriceCostco in 1993 and was elevated to chairman in December 1994. In January 1997, after the spin-off of most of its nonwarehouse assets to Price Enterprises Inc., PriceCostco changed its name to Costco Companies Inc. When the company reincorporated from Delaware to Washington in August 1999, the name was changed to Costco Wholesale Corporation. The company's headquarters was in Issaquah, Washington, not far from Seattle.

Like Costco, Walmart proceeded to grow its Sam's Club operation at a rapid pace. In 1994, 11 years after opening its first three stores, Walmart had 419 Sam's Club operations open in 48 states, with total sales in fiscal 1993 exceeding $12.3 billion and average sales per store of just over $48 million. Expansion in the following years slowed somewhat. By 2000, Walmart was operating 463 Sam's Clubs warehouses in the United States and 49 warehouses in five countries outside the United States; the domestic Sam's Clubs had total revenues of $24.8 billion (equal to average annual revenues of $53.6 million per store) and total operating income of $759 million (about $1.6 million per domestic store). But store growth and sales at Sam's Club had slowed since 2007, and Costco was extending its leadership position in the industry, especially in foreign markets, where it had more store locations than Sam's Club did (153 versus 121 in early 2010) and plans for additional stores.

BJ's Wholesale Club introduced the warehouse club concept to New England in 1984, one year after Costco and Sam's Club opened their first warehouses. BJ's grew modestly over the next 25 years, gradually expanding its operations to include 187 store locations in 15 states on the East Coast, from Maine to Florida. In 1997, BJ's became an independent, publicly owned Delaware corporation when Waban Inc., BJ's parent company at the time, distributed shares in BJ's Wholesale to all of Waban's stockholders; prior to then, BJ's operated as a division of Waban. BJ's was headquartered in Natick, Massachusetts, on the western outskirts of Boston.

Exhibit 1 presents comparative 2009 data for the three leading warehouse club competitors in North America.

COSTCO WHOLESALE

Costco was the third-largest retailer in the United States and the eighth-largest in the world. As of March 2010, Costco operated 567 warehouses, including 414 in the United States and Puerto Rico, 77 in Canada, 32 in Mexico (via a 50 percent–owned joint venture), 21 in the United Kingdom, 9 in Japan, 7 in Korea, 6 in Taiwan, and 1 in Australia. Plans called for opening four to six additional stores prior to the end of Costco's 2010 fiscal year in August. Costco warehouses averaged just over 1.4 million transactions per day. More than 50 of Costco's warehouses generated sales exceeding $200 million annually, and 2 had sales exceeding $300 million. The company's most profitable store was in Korea, and its second most profitable store was in Taiwan. Sales per store averaged $131 million annually. Some 5.7 million businesses and 31.1 million households had Costco memberships. The membership renewal rate in the United States and Canada was about 87 percent. Exhibit 2 shows Costco's key financial and operating statistics for fiscal years 2000–2009.

Costco's Strategy

Costco's strategy was aimed squarely at selling top-quality merchandise at prices consistently below what other wholesalers or retailers charged. The company stocked only those items that could be priced at bargain levels and thereby provide members with significant cost savings—Costco even refrained from stocking items frequently requested by customers unless it could price them low enough to remain true to its commitment of saving its members money. The philosophy was to keep members coming in to shop by wowing them with low prices and thereby generating big sales volumes. Examples of Costco's 2009 sales volumes in particular product categories included meat sales of $3.7 billion, seafood sales of $708 million, television sales of $2.2 billion, and fresh produce sales of $3.1 billion (sourced from 41 countries); amounts sold included 79,600 carats of diamonds, 47.7 million rotisserie chickens, 2.1 billion gallons of gasoline, 7.3 million tires, 30.4 million prescriptions, 3 million pairs of glasses, and 91 million $1.50 hot dog/soda combinations. Costco was the world's largest seller of fine wines ($597 million out of total 2009 wine sales of $1.1 billion).[1]

Exhibit 1 A Profile of the Leading Wholesale Clubs in North America in 2009

Company	2009 Revenues ($ millions)			2009 Operating Income ($ millions)	2009 Net Income ($ millions)
	Merchandise Sales	Membership Fees	Total		
Costco Wholesale	$69,889	$1,533	$71,422	$1,777	$1,086
Sam's Club	Not available	Not available	46,710[a]	1,512	n.a.[b]
BJ's Wholesale	9,954	182	10,187	224	132

Company	Number of Members 2009	Number of Stores in 2010		Average Annual Net Sales per Store
		United States	Worldwide	
Costco Wholesale	58.8 million[c]	413	566[d]	$132.6 million[e]
Sam's Club	47.0 million[f]	596	729[g]	76.3 million[h] (est., U.S. only)
BJ's Wholesale	9.4 million	187	187	53.2 million

[a]Includes U.S. revenues only; revenues for Sam's Club locations outside the United States are not separately available since they are reported as part of the Walmart International division, which includes all types of Walmart stores located outside the United States.

[b]Walmart does not report net income for subsidiary operations, only for the company as a whole.

[c]Includes 2,800,000 members of Costco Mexico, which was part of a 50% owned joint venture.

[d]Includes 36 warehouses operated in Mexico through a 50% owned joint venture.

[e]Does not include the 36 warehouses operated in Mexico through a 50% owned joint venture because sales for the joint venture were not publicly available.

[f]As of 2008; membership data for 2009 were not reported.

[g]Includes 23 Sam's Club locations in Brazil, 98 Sam's Club locations in Mexico, 9 Sam's Club locations in Puerto Rico, and 3 Sam's Club locations in China.

[h]Based on U.S. stores only and estimated membership fees of $1.2 billion (which are not a part of sales per store).

The key elements of Costco's strategy were ultra-low prices, a limited selection of nationally branded and private-label products, a "treasure hunt" shopping environment, strong emphasis on low operating costs, and a three-pronged growth initiative to boost sales and profits.

Pricing In keeping with Costco's mission, "To continually provide our members with quality goods and services at the lowest possible prices," Costco capped the margins on brand-name merchandise at 14 percent (whereas the markups over cost at other retailers often resulted in 20 to 50 percent margins for the very same items). The margins on Costco's private-label Kirkland Signature items—which included vitamins, juice, bottled water, coffee, spices, olive oil, canned salmon and tuna, nuts, laundry detergent, baby products, dog food, luggage, cookware, trash bags, batteries, wines and spirits, paper towels,

toilet paper, and clothing—were a maximum of 15 percent, but the fractionally higher markups on Costco's private-label items still resulted in its private-label prices being about 20 percent below comparable name-brand items. As a result of these low markups, Costco's prices were just fractionally above break-even levels, producing net sales revenues (not counting membership fees) that barely covered all operating expenses and generated only a modest contribution to operating profits. As can be verified from Exhibit 2, every year during 2005–2009, over 70 percent of the Costco's operating profits were attributable to membership fees and, in fact, membership fees were larger than Costco's net income in every year shown in Exhibit 2 but 2000. (To put it another way, without the revenues from membership fees, Costco's profits would be minuscule due to its strategy of capping the margins on branded goods at 14 percent and private-label goods at 15 percent.)

Exhibit 2   **Selected Financial and Operating Data for Costco Wholesale Corporation, Fiscal Years 2000–2009 ($ millions, except for per share data)**

	Fiscal Years Ending on Sunday Closest to August 31					
	2009	2008	2007	2006	2005	2000
Income Statement Data						
Net sales	$69,889	$70,977	$63,088	$58,963	$51,862	$31,621
Membership fees	1,533	1,506	1,313	1,188	1,073	544
Total revenue	71,422	72,483	64,400	60,151	52,935	32,164
Operating expenses						
Merchandise costs	62,335	63,503	56,450	52,745	46,347	28,322
Selling, general, and administrative	7,252	6,954	6,273	5,732	5,044	2,755
Preopening expenses	41	57	55	43	53	42
Provision for impaired assets and store closing costs	17	0	14	5	16	7
Operating income	1,777	1,969	1,609	1,626	1,474	1,037
Other income (expense)						
Interest expense	(108)	(103)	(64)	(13)	(34)	(39)
Interest income and other	45	133	165	138	109	54
Income before income taxes	1,714	1,999	1,710	1,751	1,549	1,052
Provision for income taxes	628	716	627	648	486	421
Net income	$ 1,086	$ 1,283	$ 1,083	$ 1,103	$ 1,063	$ 631
Diluted net income per share	$2.47	$2.89	$2.37	$2.30	$2.18	$1.35
Dividends per share	$0.68	$0.61	$0.55	$0.49	$0.43	$0.00
Millions of shares used in per share calculations	440.5	444.2	457.6	480.3	492.0	475.7
Balance Sheet Data						
Cash and cash equivalents	$ 3,157	$ 2,619	$ 2,780	$ 1,511	$ 2,063	$ 525
Merchandise inventories	5,405	5,039	4,879	4,561	4,015	2,490
Current assets	10,337	9,462	9,324	8,232	8,238	3,470
Current liabilities	9,281	8,874	8,582	7,819	6,761	3,404
Net property and equipment	10,900	10,355	9,520	8,564	7,790	4,834
Total assets	21,979	20,682	19,607	17,495	16,514	8,634
Short-term borrowings	16	134	54	41	54	10
Long-term debt	2,206	2,206	2,108	215	711	790
Stockholders' equity	10,018	9,192	8,623	9,143	8,881	4,240
Cash Flow Data						
Net cash provided by operating activities	$ 2,092	$ 2,206	$ 2,076	$ 1,831	$ 1,773	$ 1,070
Warehouses in Operation						
Beginning of year	512	488	458	433	417	292
Opened	19	34	30	28	21	25
Closed	(4)	(10)	—	(3)	(5)	(4)
End of year	527	512	488	458	433	313

(Continued)

	Fiscal Years Ending on Sunday Closest to August 31					
	2009	2008	2007	2006	2005	2000
Members at year-end [a]						
Businesses (000s)	5,700	5,600	5,400	5,200	5,000	4,200
Gold Star members (000s)	21,500	20,200	18,600	17,300	16,200	10,500
Add-on cardholders (employees of business members, spouses of members)	28,800	27,700	26,400	25,000	n.a.	n.a.

[a]Membership numbers do not include cardholders of Costco Mexico.
Note: Some totals may not add due to rounding.
Sources: Costco, 10-K reports 2000, 2005, 2007, and 2009.

Costco CEO Jim Sinegal described the company's approach to pricing:

> We always look to see how much of a gulf we can create between ourselves and the competition. So that the competitors eventually say, "These guys are crazy. We'll compete somewhere else." Some years ago, we were selling a hot brand of jeans for $29.99. They were $50 in a department store. We got a great deal on them and could have sold them for a higher price but we went down to $29.99. Why? We knew it would create a riot.[2]

At another time, he explained,

> We're very good merchants, and we offer value. The traditional retailer will say: "I'm selling this for $10. I wonder whether we can get $10.50 or $11." We say: "We're selling this for $9. How do we get it down to $8?" We understand that our members don't come and shop with us because of the window displays or the Santa Claus or the piano player. They come and shop with us because we offer great values.[3]

Indeed, Costco's markups and prices were so fractionally above the level needed to cover operating costs and interest expenses that Wall Street analysts had criticized Costco management for going all out to please customers at the expense of charging prices that would increase profits for shareholders. One retailing analyst said, "They could probably get more money for a lot of the items they sell."[4] Unimpressed with Wall Street's criticism, Sinegal commented, "Those people are in the business of making money between now and next Tuesday. We're trying to build an organization that's going to be here 50 years from now."[5] He went on to explain why Costco's approach to pricing fractionally above levels needed to cover operating expenses would remain unaltered during his tenure:

> When I started, Sears, Roebuck was the Costco of the country, but they allowed someone else to come in under them. We don't want to be one of the casualties. We don't want to turn around and say, "We got so fancy we've raised our prices," and all of a sudden a new competitor comes in and beats our prices.[6]

Product Quality and Selection Most of the merchandise Costco sold was of good-to-excellent quality and was supplied by name-brand manufacturers. The specifications for Costco's private-label Kirkland Signature products were high, often resulting in their being of equal or better quality than those of highly regarded or better-known brands; but it was the company's strategy to purchase and stock only those private-label items that could be sold to members at prices significantly below comparable name-brand items. During the 2006–2009 period, Costco expanded its Kirkland Signature private-label line from some 400 items to nearly 600 items.

The selections of branded and private-label merchandise were deliberately limited in order to keep costs, and thereby prices, low. Whereas typical supermarkets stocked about 45,000 items and a Walmart Supercenter or SuperTarget could have 125,000 to 150,000 items for shoppers to choose from, Costco's merchandising strategy was to provide members with a selection of 3,800 to 4,000 items. Thus, while Costco's product range did cover a broad spectrum—fresh-baked breads and desserts, prime steaks, gourmet cheeses, flat-screen TVs, iPods, fresh flowers, electric toothbrushes, caskets, baby strollers, toys and games, musical instruments, basketballs, sheets and towels, vacuum cleaners, books, DVDs, stainless-steel cookware, seat-cover kits for autos, lightbulbs, washers and dryers, ballpoint pens, vitamins, office products, restaurant supplies, gasoline, one-hour photo finishing—the selection within each product category was restricted, in some cases to a single offering. The approximate percentage of Costco's net sales accounted for by each major category of items is shown in Exhibit 3.

The selections of appliances, equipment, and tools often included commercial and professional models because many of Costco's members were small businesses. Many consumable products like detergents, canned goods, office supplies, and soft drinks were sold only in case, carton, big-container, or multipack quantities. For example, Costco stocked only a 325-count bottle of Advil—a size many shoppers might find too large for their needs; Sinegal explained the reason behind the company's narrow selection strategy:

> If you had ten customers come in to buy Advil, how many are not going to buy any because you just have one size? Maybe one or two. We refer to that as the intelligent loss of sales. We are prepared to give up that one customer. But if we had four or five sizes of Advil, as most grocery stores do, it would make our business more difficult to manage. Our business can only succeed if we are efficient. You can't go on selling at these margins if you are not.[7]

Management believed that its limited selection strategy contributed significantly to lower purchasing, shipping, and in-store handling and merchandising costs.

As a means of giving members reasons to shop at Costco more frequently and make Costco more of a one-stop shopping destination, the company had opened ancillary departments within or next to most Costco warehouses, as shown in the following table:

	2009	2008	2007
Total number of warehouses	527	512	488
Warehouses having stores with			
Food court and hot dog stands	521	506	482
One-hour photo centers	518	504	480
Optical dispensing centers	509	496	472
Pharmacies	464	451	429
Gas stations	323	307	279
Hearing aid centers	303	274	237
Print shops and copy centers	10	8	8

Treasure Hunt Merchandising

Costco's merchandise buyers were constantly on the lookout to make one-time purchases of items that would appeal to the company's clientele and that would sell out quickly. A sizable number of these items were high-end or name-brand products that carried big price tags—like $800 espresso machines, expensive jewelry and diamond rings (priced from $50,000 to $250,000), Movado watches, exotic cheeses, Coach bags, $5,000 necklaces, cashmere sport coats, $1,500 digital pianos,

Exhibit 3   Costco's Sales by Major Product Category, 2003–2009

	2009	2008	2007	2005	2003
Food (fresh produce, meats and fish, bakery and deli products, and dry and institutionally packaged foods)	33%	32%	31%	30%	30%
Sundries (candy, snack foods, tobacco, alcoholic and nonalcoholic beverages, and cleaning and institutional supplies)	23	22	23	25	26
Hardlines (major appliances, electronics, health and beauty aids, hardware, office supplies, garden and patio, sporting goods, furniture, cameras, and automotive supplies)	19	19	21	20	20
Softlines (including apparel, domestics, jewelry, housewares, books, movie DVDs, video games, music, home furnishings, and small appliances)	10	10	11	12	14
Ancillary and other (gasoline, pharmacy, food court, optical, one-hour photo, hearing aids, and travel)	15	17	14	13	10

Source: Costco, 10-K reports, 2005, 2007, and 2009.

and Dom Perignon champagne. Dozens of featured specials came and went quickly, sometimes in several days or a week—like Italian-made Hathaway shirts priced at $29.99 and $800 leather sectional sofas. The strategy was to entice shoppers to spend more than they might by offering irresistible deals on big-ticket items or name-brand specials and, further, to keep the mix of featured and treasure-hunt items constantly changing so that bargain-hunting shoppers would go to Costco more frequently than for periodic "stock-up" trips.

Costco members quickly learned that they needed to go ahead and buy treasure-hunt specials that interested them, because the items would very likely not be available on their next shopping trip. In many cases, Costco did not obtain its luxury offerings directly from high-end manufacturers like Calvin Klein or Waterford (which were unlikely to want their merchandise marketed at deep discounts at places like Costco). Rather, Costco's buyers searched for opportunities to source such items legally on the gray market from other wholesalers or distressed retailers looking to get rid of excess or slow-selling inventory.

Marketing and Advertising
Costco's low prices and its reputation for making shopping at Costco something of a treasure hunt made it unnecessary to engage in extensive advertising or sales campaigns. Marketing and promotional activities were generally limited to regular direct mail programs aimed at existing members, special campaigns for new warehouse openings, and occasional direct mail marketing to help recruit prospective new members. The company's primary direct mail program for members was the Costco Connection, a multipage mailout that contained a host of savings coupons for featured specials over upcoming weeks. For new warehouse openings, marketing teams personally contacted businesses in the area that were potential wholesale members; these contacts were supplemented with direct mailings during the period immediately prior to opening. In addition to using direct mail to recruit more individual members, the company also strove to attract members by working with local employee groups and businesses with large numbers of employees. After a membership base was established in an area, most new memberships came from word of mouth (existing members telling friends and acquaintances about

their shopping experiences at Costco), follow-up messages distributed through regular payroll or other organizational communications to employee groups, and ongoing direct solicitations to prospective business and individual members. Management believed that its emphasis on direct mail advertising kept its marketing expenses low relative to those at typical retailers, discounters, and supermarkets.

Low-Cost Emphasis
Keeping operating costs to a bare minimum was a key element of Costco's strategy and a key to its low pricing; Jim Sinegal explained:

> Costco is able to offer lower prices and better values by eliminating virtually all the frills and costs historically associated with conventional wholesalers and retailers, including salespeople, fancy buildings, delivery, billing, and accounts receivable. We run a tight operation with extremely low overhead, which enables us to pass on dramatic savings to our members.[8]

While Costco management made a point of locating warehouses on high-traffic routes in or near upscale suburbs that were easily accessible by small businesses and residents with above-average incomes, it avoided prime real estate sites in order to contain land costs.

Because shoppers were attracted principally by Costco's low prices and merchandise selection, most warehouses were of a metal preengineered design, with concrete floors and minimal interior decor. Floor plans were designed for economy and efficiency in use of selling space, the handling of merchandise, and the control of inventory. Merchandise was generally stored on racks above the sales floor and displayed on pallets containing large quantities of each item, thereby reducing labor required for handling and stocking. In-store signage was done mostly on laser printers; there were no shopping bags at the checkout counter—merchandise was put directly into the shopping cart or sometimes loaded into empty boxes. Costco warehouses ranged in size from 70,000 to 205,000 square feet; the average size was 141,000 square feet. Newer units were usually in the range of 150,000 to 205,000 square feet. Scenes of Costco's warehouses are shown in Exhibit 4.

Warehouses generally operated on a 7-day, 69-hour week, typically being open between

Exhibit 4   Scenes from Costco's Warehouses

Source: Costco management presentations, May 29, 2008, and March 2010.

10:00 A.M. and 8:30 P.M. weekdays, with earlier closing hours on the weekend; the gasoline operations outside many stores usually had extended hours. The shorter hours of operation—as compared with those of traditional retailers, discount retailers, and supermarkets—resulted in lower labor costs relative to the volume of sales.

Growth Strategy   Costco's strategy to grow sales and profits had three main elements: open more new warehouses; build an ever larger, fiercely loyal membership base; and employ well-executed merchandising techniques to induce members to shop at Costco more often and purchase more per shopping trip. Costco had opened 265 new warehouses since September 2000, a key reason why company revenues climbed from $31.6 billion in fiscal 2000 to $71.4 billion in fiscal 2009. Expansion efforts in the United States were focused on entering cities and states where Costco did not yet have a warehouse (10 states had no Costco stores in 2010) and opening additional warehouses in metropolitan areas big enough to support two or more Costco locations. Expansion was under way internationally as well, with further expansion being planned in all of the company's Asian markets. Costco planned to double its store count in Taiwan from 6 to 12 over the next five years and to open a new distribution center; the company's sales in Taiwan (where it was the only wholesale club) had nearly tripled between 2004 ($250 million) and 2009 ($747 million), a period in which retail sales in Taiwan had grown by only 8.3 percent.[9] Retailing in Taiwan was a $72 billion market. However, less than 10 percent of Costco's operating income came from warehouses located outside the United States and Canada. Exhibit 5 presents selected geographical operating data for Costco's 2005–2009 fiscal years.

Costco's strategy to attract more members and entice members to do a bigger percentage of their shopping at Costco had three components:

- Give members a place to buy supplies of practical, frequently used business and household items at money-saving prices.
- Make shopping at Costco interesting and rewarding because of opportunities to purchase an ever-changing array of big-ticket items and indulgences at rock-bottom prices—in this regard, it was important that

members be able to spot appealing new items on the sales floor each time they shopped at Costco. Costco buyers constantly scanned the manufacturing landscape, looking for one-time opportunities to buy items that would appeal to bargain-hunting members. And warehouse personnel strived to do an effective job of displaying and merchandising the special buys on the sales floor.

- Acclimate members to the merits of visiting Costco weekly or bimonthly so as not to miss out on the special one-time-only merchandise selections that typically sold out in a matter of days.

To further grow its business, Costco operated two websites—**www.costco.com** in the United States and **www.costco.ca** in Canada—as a means of expanding product offerings to include big-ticket items that could not be economically displayed on the warehouse sales floor (e.g., indoor and outdoor furniture, special buys on PCs or other electronic items), and as a convenience to members who were not always able to purchase certain items at the warehouse where they customarily shopped. At Costco's online photo center, members could upload images and pick up the prints at their local warehouse in little over an hour. Costco's e-commerce sales totaled $1.2 billion in fiscal 2007, up from $534 million in fiscal 2005 and $376 million in fiscal 2004 (more recent e-commerce sales data was not reported).

Jim Sinegal—Costco's Cofounder and CEO

Jim Sinegal was the driving force behind Costco's success. He was far from the stereotypical CEO. A grandfatherly 73-year-old, Sinegal dressed casually and unpretentiously, often going to the office or touring Costco stores wearing an open-collared cotton shirt that came from a Costco bargain rack and sporting a standard employee name tag that said, simply, "Jim." His informal dress, mustache, gray hair, and unimposing appearance made it easy for Costco shoppers to mistake him for a store clerk. He answered his own phone, once telling ABC News reporters, "If a customer's calling and they have a gripe, don't you think they kind of enjoy the fact that I picked up the phone and talked to them?"[10]

Exhibit 5 Selected Geographic Operating Data, Costco Wholesale Corporation, Fiscal Years 2005–2009 ($ millions)

	U.S. Operations	Canadian Operations	Other International Operations	Total
Year Ended August 30, 2009				
Total revenue (including membership fees)	$56,548	$9,737	$5,137	$71,442
Operating income	1,273	354	150	1,777
Capital expenditures	904	135	211	1,250
Number of warehouses	406	77	44	527
Year Ended August 31, 2008				
Total revenue (including membership fees)	$56,903	$10,528	$5,052	$72,483
Operating income	1,393	420	156	1,969
Capital expenditures	1,190	246	163	1,599
Number of warehouses	398	75	39	512
Year Ended September 2, 2007				
Total revenue (including membership fees)	$51,532	$8,724	$4,144	$64,400
Operating income	1,217	287	105	1,609
Capital expenditures	1,104	207	74	1,386
Number of warehouses	383	71	34	488
Year Ended September 3, 2006				
Total revenue (including membership fees)	$48,466	$8,122	$3,564	$60,151
Operating income	1,246	293	87	1,626
Capital expenditures	934	188	90	1,213
Number of warehouses	358	68	32	458
Year Ended August 28, 2005				
Total revenue (including membership fees)	$43,064	$6,732	$3,155	$52,952
Operating income	1,168	242	65	1,474
Capital expenditures	734	140	122	995
Number of warehouses	338	65	30	433

Note: The dollar numbers shown for "Other" countries represent only Costco's ownership share, since all foreign operations were joint ventures (although Costco was the majority owner of these ventures); the 32 warehouses operated by Costco Mexico (33 warehouses as of 2009) in which Costco was only a 50% joint venture partner are not included in the data for the "Other" countries.
Source: Costco, 10-K reports, 2009 and 2007.

Sinegal spent much of his time touring Costco stores, using the company plane to fly from location to location and sometimes visiting 8 to 10 stores daily (the record for a single day was 12). Treated like a celebrity when he appeared at a store (the news "Jim's in the store" spread quickly), Sinegal made a point of greeting store employees. He observed, "The employees know that I want to say hello to them, because I like them. We have said from the very beginning: 'We're going to be a company that's on a first-name basis with everyone.'"[11] Employees genuinely seemed to like Sinegal. He talked quietly, in a commonsensical manner that suggested what he was saying was no big deal.[12] He came across as kind yet stern, but he was prone to display irritation when he disagreed sharply with what people were saying to him.

In touring a Costco store with the local store manager, Sinegal was very much the person in charge. He functioned as producer, director, and knowledgeable critic. He cut to the chase quickly, exhibiting intense attention to detail and pricing, wandering through store aisles firing a barrage of questions at store managers about sales volumes and stock levels of particular items, critiquing merchandising displays or the position of certain products in the stores, commenting on any aspect of store operations that caught his eye, and asking managers to do further research and get back to him with more information whenever he found their answers to his questions less than satisfying. It was readily apparent that Sinegal had tremendous merchandising savvy, that he demanded much of store managers and employees, and that his views about discount retailing set the tone for how the company operated. Knowledgeable observers regarded Jim Sinegal's merchandising expertise as being on a par with that of the legendary Sam Walton, the founder of Walmart.

Warehouse Operations

Costco bought the majority of its merchandise directly from manufacturers, routing it either directly to its warehouse stores or to one of nine cross-docking depots that served as distribution points for nearby stores. Depots received container-based shipments from manufacturers and reallocated these goods for combined shipment to individual warehouses, generally in less than 24 hours. This maximized freight volume and handling efficiencies. When merchandise arrived at a warehouse, it was moved directly onto the sales floor; very little was stored in locations off the sales floor, thereby lowering receiving costs by eliminating many of the costs associated with multiple-step handling of merchandise, such as purchasing from distributors as opposed to manufacturers, use of central receiving, operating regional distribution centers for inventory storage and distribution of merchandise to nearby stores, and having storage areas at retail sites where merchandise could be held in reserve off the sales floor.

Costco had direct buying relationships with many producers of national name-brand merchandise (e.g., Canon, Casio, Coca-Cola, Colgate-Palmolive, Dell, Fuji, Hewlett-Packard, Jones of New York, Kimberly-Clark, Kodak, Kitchen Aid, Levi Strauss, Michelin, Nestlé, Panasonic, Procter & Gamble, Samsung, and Sony) and with manufacturers that supplied its Kirkland Signature private-label products. No single manufacturer supplied a significant percentage of the merchandise that Costco stocked. Costco had not experienced any difficulty in obtaining sufficient quantities of merchandise, and management believed that if one or more of its current sources of supply became unavailable, the company could switch its purchases to alternative manufacturers without experiencing a substantial disruption of its business.

Costco warehouses accepted cash, checks, most debit cards, American Express, and a private-label Costco credit card. Costco accepted merchandise returns when members were dissatisfied with their purchases. Losses associated with dishonored checks were minimal because members who bounced checks were prevented from paying by check or cashing checks at the point of sale until restitution was made. The membership format facilitated strictly controlling the entrances and exits of warehouses, resulting in inventory losses of less than two-tenths of 1 percent of net sales—well below those of other retail discounters.

Warehouse Managers Costco's warehouse managers were delegated considerable authority over store operations and, in effect, functioned as entrepreneurs running their own retail operation. They were responsible for effectively merchandising the ever-changing lineup of treasure-hunt products, orchestrating in-store product locations and displays to maximize sales and quick turnover, and coming up with new ideas about what items would sell in their stores. In experimenting with what items to stock and what in-store merchandising techniques to employ, warehouse managers drew on their knowledge of the clientele that patronized their locations—for instance, big-ticket diamonds sold well at some warehouses but not at others. Costco's best managers kept their fingers on the pulse of the members who shopped their warehouse location to stay in sync with what would sell well, and they had a flair for creating a certain element of excitement, hum, and buzz in their warehouses that spurred above-average sales volumes (sales at Costco's top-volume warehouses often exceeded $5 million a week, with sales topping $1 million on many days). Successful managers also thrived on the rat race of running a high-traffic store and solving the inevitable crises of the moment.

Costco's Membership Base and Member Demographics

Costco had two primary types of memberships: Business and Gold Star. Gold Star memberships were for individuals who did not qualify for a Business membership. Businesses, including individuals with a business license, retail sales license, or other evidence of business existence, qualified as Business members. Business members generally paid an annual membership fee of $50 for the primary and spouse membership cards and could purchase add-on membership cards for an annual fee of $40 each for partners or employees (these add-on also included a spouse card). A significant number of Business members also shopped at Costco for their personal needs.

Gold Star members generally paid an annual fee of $50, which included a spouse card. In addition, all members in the United States and Canada could upgrade to an Executive membership for an annual fee of $100; Executive members qualified for 2 percent additional savings on qualified purchases at Costco (redeemable at Costco warehouses), up to a maximum rebate of $500 per year. The Executive membership also offered savings and benefits on various business and consumer services offered by Costco, including merchant credit card processing, small-business loans, auto and home insurance, long-distance telephone service, check printing, and real estate and mortgage services; these services were mostly provided by third parties and varied by state. In 2009, Executive members represented 29 percent of Costco's primary membership base and generated more than 40 percent of consolidated net sales. Members could shop at any Costco warehouse; member renewal rates were about 87 percent.

Compensation and Workforce Practices

In September 2009, Costco had 79,000 full-time employees and 63,000 part-time employees worldwide, not including approximately 9,000 people employed by Costco Mexico, whose operations were not consolidated in Costco's financial and operating results. Approximately 13,500 hourly employees at locations in California, Maryland, New Jersey, and New York and one warehouse in Virginia were represented by the International Brotherhood of Teamsters. All remaining employees were non-union.

Starting wages for new Costco employees were in the $10.50–$11.00 per hour range in 2008. Depending on the job classification, the median pay scales for Costco employees with five or more years' experience were in the $17–$21 per hour range.[13] Warehouse employees received time-and-a-half pay for working on Sundays and were paid double time in the event they were called on to work more than 12 hours in a given shift. Median salaries for managerial positions at Costco warehouses in 2008 were in the $55,000–$75,000 range.[14]

Employees received biannual bonuses and a full spectrum of benefits that were regarded as being quite good in comparison to those of other retailers. Salaried employees were eligible for benefits on the first of the month after the date of hire. Full-time hourly employees were eligible for benefits on the first of the month after working a probationary 90 days; part-time hourly employees became benefit-eligible on the first of the month after working 180 days.

Although admitting that paying good wages and good benefits was contrary to conventional wisdom in discount retailing, Jim Sinegal was convinced that having a well-compensated workforce was very important to executing Costco's strategy successfully: "Paying good wages and keeping your people working with you is very good business."[15] When a reporter asked him about why Costco treated its workers so well compared with other retailers (particularly Walmart, which paid lower wages and had a skimpier benefits package), Sinegal replied: "Why shouldn't employees have the right to good wages and good careers? . . . It absolutely makes good business sense. Most people agree that we're the lowest-cost producer. Yet we pay the highest wages. So it must mean we get better productivity. Its axiomatic in our business—you get what you pay for."[16] In 2007, Sinegal announced his support for raising the minimum wage from $5.15 an hour to $7.25, saying "The more people make, the better lives they are going to have and the better consumers they're going to be."[17]

Selecting People for Open Positions

Costco's top management wanted employees to feel that they could have a long-term career at Costco. It was company policy to fill at least 86 percent of its higher-level opening by promotions from within; in actuality, the percentage ran close to 98 percent, which meant that the majority of Costco's management team (including warehouse, merchandise, administrative, membership, front-end, and receiving managers) were homegrown. Many of the company's vice presidents had started in entry-level jobs; according to Jim Sinegal, "We have guys who started pushing shopping carts out on the parking lot for us who are now vice presidents of our company."[18] However, Costco insisted that candidates for warehouse managers be top-flight merchandisers with a gift for the details of making items fly off the shelves; Sinegal said, "People who have a feel for it just start to get it. Others, you look at them and it's like staring at a blank canvas. I'm not trying to be unduly harsh, but that's the way it works."[19] Most newly appointed warehouse managers at Costco came from the ranks of assistant warehouse managers who had a track record of being shrewd merchandisers tuned into what new or different products might sell well given the clientele that patronized their particular warehouse—just having skills in people management, crisis management, and cost-effective warehouse operations was not enough.

SAM'S CLUB

In early 2010, Sam's Club operated 596 U.S. warehouses in 48 states (the exceptions were Vermont and Oregon), 23 warehouses in Brazil, 98 warehouses in Mexico, 9 warehouses in Puerto Rico, and 3 warehouses in China. Six Sam's Club warehouses in Canada were closed in March 2009, and, in January 2010, Sam's Club CEO Brian Connell announced that 10 underperforming warehouses in the United States (including 4 in California) would be closed. Nonetheless, there were plans in place to open between 5 and 10 new Sam's Club warehouses (including relocations) in 2010. Recently, Sam's Club executives had launched a major warehouse remodeling program; some 52 remodels were completed during fiscal 2010, and another 60 to 80 clubs were targeted for remodeling during fiscal 2011 (February 2010 through January 2011). Selected financial and operating data for Sam's Club is shown in Exhibit 6.

The first Sam's Club opened in 1984, and management had pursued rapid expansion of the membership club format. Going into 2001, there were 475 warehouse locations in the United States and 53 international locations: Brazil, 8; China, 1; Mexico, 38; and Puerto Rico, 6. Over the next nine years, an additional 121 warehouses were opened in the United States and 80 internationally. Many Sam's Club locations were adjacent to Walmart Supercenters. The concept of the Sam's Club format was to sell merchandise at very low profit margins, resulting in low prices to members. The mission of Sam's Club was "to make savings simple for members by providing them with exciting, quality merchandise and a superior shopping experience, all at a great value."[20]

Facility sizes ranged between 71,000 and 190,000 square feet, with an average size of approximately 133,000 square feet. All warehouses had concrete floors; sparse decor; and goods displayed on pallets, simple wooden shelves, or racks (in the case of apparel).

Merchandise Offerings

Sam's Club stocked brand-name merchandise, including hardgoods, some softgoods, institutional-size grocery items, and selected private-label items sold under the brands Member's Mark, Bakers & Chefs, and Sam's Club. Generally, each Sam's Club warehouse also carried software, electronics, jewelry, sporting goods, toys, tires and batteries, books, DVDs, and office supplies; most had fresh-foods departments that included bakery, meat, produce, floral products, and a Sam's Cafe. A significant number of clubs had a one-hour photo processing department, a pharmacy that filled prescriptions, an optical department, and self-service gasoline pumps. Members could shop for a broad assortment of merchandise and services online at www.samsclub.com.

Like Costco Wholesale, Sam's Club stocked about 4,000 items, a big fraction of which

Exhibit 6   **Selected Financial and Operating Data for Sam's Club, Fiscal Years 2000–2010**

Sam's Club	Fiscal Years Ending January 31					
	2010	2009	2008	2007	2006	2001
U.S. sales[a] ($ millions)	$ 46,710	$ 46,899	$ 44,336	$ 41,582	$ 39,798	$ 26,798
Operating income ($ millions)	1,512	1,646	1,648	1,480	1,407	942
Assets ($ millions)	12,073	12,339	11,722	11,448	10,588	3,843
Number of locations at year-end	729	727	713	693	670	564
U.S.	596	602	591	579	567	475
International	133	125	122	114	103	64
Average sales per U.S. location ($ millions)	$78.4	$77.9	$75.1	$71.8	$70.2	$56.8
Sales growth at existing warehouses open more than 12 months:						
Including gasoline sales	−1.4%	4.9%	4.9%	2.5%	5.0%	n.a.
Not including gasoline sales	0.7%	3.7%	4.2%	2.9%	n.a.	n.a.
Average warehouse size (square feet)	133,000	133,000	132,000	132,000	129,400	122,100

[a]The sales figure includes membership fees and is for U.S. warehouses only. For financial reporting purposes, Walmart consolidates the operations of all foreign-based stores into a single "international" segment figure; thus, financial information for foreign-based Sam's Club locations is not separately available.

Source: Walmart, 10-K reports and annual reports, fiscal years 2010, 2008, 2006, and 2001.

were standard and a small fraction of which represented special buys and one-time offerings. The treasure-hunt items at Sam's tended to be less upscale and carry lower price tags than those at Costco. The reported percentage composition of sales at Sam's Club is shown in the table below.

Membership and Hours of Operation

The annual fee for Sam's Club business members was $35 for the primary membership card, with a spouse card available at no additional cost. Business

		Fiscal year ending January 31	
		2010	2009
Food and beverages (dairy, meat, bakery, deli, produce, dry, chilled or frozen packaged foods, alcoholic and nonalcoholic beverages, floral and other grocery items)		39%	39%
Health and wellness (pharmacy and optical services, health and beauty aids, paper goods, laundry and home care, baby care, pet supplies and restaurant supplies)		19	18
Technology, office, and entertainment (electronics, wireless, software, video games, movies, books, music, toys, office supplies, office furniture and photo processing)		10	10
Home and apparel (home improvement Items, outdoor living, grills, gardening, furniture, apparel, jewelry, house wares, seasonal items, mattresses and small appliances)		8	9
Tobacco/candy and fuel/auto (tobacco, snack foods, tools and power equipment, sales of gasoline, and tire and battery centers)		24	24

members could add up to eight business associates for $35 each and could purchase memberships for employees at $30 per membership for 50 to 999 employees and $25 for 1,000 or more employees. The annual membership fee for an Advantage (individual) member was $40, which included a spouse card. A Sam's Club Plus premium membership cost $100 and included an assortment of additional benefits and services, including health insurance; merchant credit card processing; website operation; personal and financial services; and an auto, boat, and recreational vehicle insurance program.

Operating hours for Sam's Clubs were Monday through Friday, 10:00 A.M. to 8:30 P.M.; Saturday, 9:00 A.M. to 8:30 P.M.; and Sunday, 10:00 A.M. to 6:00 P.M. All club locations offered a Gold Key program that permitted business members to shop before the regular operating hours Monday through Saturday, starting at 7:00 A.M. Members could use a variety of payment methods, including debit cards, certain types of credit cards, and a private-label co-branded Discover credit card issued by a third-party provider. The pharmacy and optical departments accepted payments for products and services through members' health insurance plans.

Distribution

Approximately 63 percent of the nonfuel merchandise at Sam's Club was shipped from the division's own distribution facilities and, in the case of perishable items, from some of Walmart's grocery distribution centers; the balance was shipped by suppliers direct to Sam's Club locations. Like Costco, Sam's Club distribution centers employed cross-docking techniques whereby incoming shipments were transferred immediately to outgoing trailers destined for Sam's Club locations; shipments typically spent less than 24 hours at a cross-docking facility and, in some instances less than an hour. The Sam's Club distribution center network consisted of 8 company-owned and operated distribution facilities and 18 third-party-owned and operated facilities. A combination of company-owned trucks and independent trucking companies were used to transport nonperishable merchandise from distribution centers to club locations; Sam's used

independent trucking companies to transport perishable grocery items to distribution centers to its warehouses.

BJ'S WHOLESALE

Since the beginning of 2004, BJ's Wholesale had expanded from 150 warehouse club locations to 187 warehouse clubs; its operations were exclusively in the eastern United States, from Maine to Florida. BJ's planned to open seven to nine new warehouses in 2010 (including one relocation), all in existing geographic markets. BJ's had 167 "full-sized" warehouses, averaging 113,000 square feet, and 20 smaller format warehouses, averaging 72,000 square feet and located in markets too small to support a full-sized warehouse. Approximately 85 percent of BJ's full-sized warehouse clubs had at least one Costco or Sam's Club warehouse operating in their trading areas (within 10 miles). Only one of the smaller BJ's clubs faced competition from a Costco or Sam's Club located within 10 miles. In early 2010, BJ's had approximately 23,500 full- and part-time employees; none of BJ's employees were represented by a union.

Exhibit 7 presents financial and operating data for BJ's Wholesale for 2006–2010.

BJ's Strategy

Like Costco and Sam's, BJ's Wholesale sold high-quality brand-name merchandise at prices that were significantly lower than those at supermarkets, discount retail chains, department stores, drugstores, and specialty retail stores like Best Buy. But BJ's had developed a strategy and operating model that management believed differentiated the company from its two primary competitors:

- It focused on its Inner Circle (individual) members through merchandising strategies that emphasized a customer-friendly shopping experience in several respects:
    - BJ's stocked a broader product assortment than Sam's Club and Costco, approximately 7,000 items.
    - To make shopping easier and more efficient for members, BJ's had aisle markers, express checkout lanes, self-checkout lanes, and low-cost video-based sales aids.

Exhibit 7　Selected Financial and Operating Data, BJ's Wholesale Club, Fiscal Years 2006–2010

	Fiscal Year Ended				
	Jan. 30, 2010	Jan. 31, 2009	Feb. 2, 2008	Feb. 3, 2007 (53 weeks)	Jan. 28, 2006
Selected Income Statement Data ($ millions, except per share data)					
Net sales	$ 9,954	$ 9,802	$ 8,792	$ 8,280	$ 7,725
Membership fees	182	178	176	162	150
Other revenues	51	48	47	54	58
Total revenues	10,187	10,027	9,014	8,497	7,933
Cost of sales, including buying and occupancy costs	9,081	9,004	8,091	7,601	7,064
Selling, general and administrative expenses	875	799	724	740	643
Operating income	224	221	195	144	214
Interest income, net	(1)	1	4	3	3
Provision for income taxes	91	86	78	57	86
Net income	$　132	$　135	$　123	$　72	$　129
Income per common share:					
Basic earnings per share:	$2.47	$2.32	$1.93	$1.10	$1.89
Diluted earnings per share:	2.42	2.28	1.90	1.08	1.87
Balance Sheet and Cash Flow Data ($ millions)					
Cash and cash equivalents	$　59	$　51	$　97	$　56	$　162
Current assets	1,173	1,076	1,145	1,070	1,120
Current liabilities	1,006	909	946	867	862
Working capital	167	167	199	203	258
Merchandise inventories	930	860	877	851	813
Total assets	2,166	2,021	2,047	1,993	1,990
Long-term debt	1	1	2	2	3
Stockholders' equity	1,033	985	980	1,020	1,016
Cash flow from operations	298	224	305	173	192
Capital expenditures	176	138	90	191	123
Selected Operating Data					
Clubs open at end of year	187	180	177	172	163
Number of members (in thousands)	9,400	9,000	8,800	8,700	8,619
Average sales per club location ($ millions)	$53.2	$54.6	$49.7	$48.1	$47.4
Sales growth at existing clubs open more than 12 months	−1.9%	9.4%	3.7%	1.2%	3.6%

Source: BJ's Wholesale Club, 10-K reports for 2010, 2008, and 2007.

- Stores were open more hours than both Costco and Sam's stores; typical hours of operation were 9:00 A.M. to 7:00 P.M. Monday through Friday and 9:00 A.M. to 6:00 P.M. Saturday and Sunday.

- While many items were sold in bulk, BJ's offered some smaller package sizes that were easier to carry home and store, including sizes that were comparable to those offered in supermarkets. Smaller package sizes were typical in a number of fresh-food categories, including dairy, meat, bakery, fish, and produce. Management worked closely with manufacturers to develop packaging and sizes well suited for selling through the warehouse club format in order to economize on handling costs and help keep prices low.

- In some product assortments, BJ's had three price categories for members to choose from—good, deluxe, and luxury.

- BJ's was the only major warehouse club operator to accept manufacturers' coupons, which provided added value for members; it also accepted more credit and debit payment options than its warehouse club competitors.

- BJ's warehouses had a number of specialty services designed to enable members to complete more of their shopping at BJ's and to encourage more frequent trips to the clubs. These services included full-service optical centers, food courts, full-service Verizon Wireless centers, home improvement services, BJ's Vacations, garden and storage sheds, patios and sunrooms, installation of home security systems, a propane-tank-filling service, an automobile-buying service, a car rental service, muffler and brake services operated in conjunction with Monro Muffler Brake, television and home theater installation, and electronics and jewelry protection plans. Most of these services were provided by outside operators in space leased from BJ's. As of January 2010, there were gas station operations at 104 warehouse club locations; like Costco, BJ's sold gasoline at a discounted price as a means of displaying a favorable price image to prospective members and providing added value to existing members. In early 2007, BJ's abandoned prescription filling and closed all of its 46 in-club pharmacies.

- At the BJ's website (www.bjs.com), members could shop from thousands of additional products not found in the company's warehouse clubs. Items sold on the BJ's website included electronics, computers, video games, office equipment, products for the home, health and beauty aids, sporting goods, outdoor living products, baby products, toys and jewelry, and such services as auto and home insurance, home improvement, travel services, and television and home theater installation.

- Club locations were clustered in order to benefit from greater name recognition and maximize the efficiencies of management support, distribution, and marketing activities.

- BJ's strove to establish and maintain the first or second industry leading position in each major market area where it operated.

Food accounted for approximately 65 percent of BJ's merchandise sales in 2009. The remaining 35 percent consisted of a wide variety of general merchandise items. Food categories at BJ's included frozen foods, fresh meat and dairy products, beverages, dry grocery items, fresh produce and flowers, canned goods, and household paper products. General merchandise included consumer electronics, prerecorded media, small appliances, tires, jewelry, health and beauty aids, household needs, chemicals, computer software, books, greeting cards, apparel, furniture, toys and seasonal items. More than 70 percent of the products BJ's sold were items that could also be found in supermarkets.

BJ's private-label products were primarily of premium quality and were generally priced below the top-competing branded product. During the past two years, BJ's had pruned its private-label offerings by about 12 percent, opting to focus on those items having the highest margins and biggest sales volumes. Private-label goods accounted for approximately 10 percent of food and general merchandise sales in 2009, versus 11 percent in 2008 and 13 percent in 2007.

Warehouse Club Operations

BJ's warehouses were located in both freestanding locations and shopping centers. Construction and site development costs for a full-sized owned BJ's club were in the $6–$10 million range; land acquisition costs ranged from $5 to $10 million but could be significantly higher in some locations. Each warehouse generally had an investment of $3.5 to $4.0 million for fixtures and equipment. Pre-opening expenses at a new club ran $1.0 to $1.5 million. Including space for parking, a typical full-sized BJ's club required 13 to 14 acres of land; smaller clubs typically required about 8 acres. During recent years, the company had financed all of its club expansions, as well as all other capital expenditures, with internally generated funds.

Merchandise purchased from manufacturers was routed either to a BJ's cross-docking facility or directly to clubs. Personnel at the cross-docking facilities broke down truckload quantity shipments from manufacturers and reallocated goods for shipment to individual clubs, generally within 24 hours. BJ's worked closely with manufacturers to minimize the amount of handling required once merchandise is received at a club. Merchandise was generally displayed on pallets containing large quantities of each item, thereby reducing labor required for handling, stocking, and restocking. Backup merchandise was generally stored in steel racks above the sales floor. Most merchandise was premarked by the manufacturer so that it did not require ticketing at the club. Full-sized clubs had approximately $2 million in inventory. Management had been able to limit inventory shrinkage to no more than 0.20 percent of net sales in each of the last three fiscal years (a percentage well below those of other types of retailers) by strictly controlling the exits of clubs, by generally limiting customers to members, and by using state-of-the-art electronic article surveillance technology. Exhibit 8 shows interior and exterior scenes at various BJ's locations.

Membership

Since 2006, the number of businesses and individuals with BJ's membership cards had climbed from 8.6 million to 9.4 million. The company charged $45 per year for a primary Inner Circle membership (for individuals and households), which included one free supplemental membership; members in the same household could purchase additional supplemental memberships for $20. A business membership also cost $45 per year, which included one free supplemental membership and the ability to purchase additional supplemental memberships for $20. Since 2003, BJ's had offered a Rewards membership program geared to high-frequency, high-volume members that entailed a 2 percent rebate, capped at $500 per year, on most in-club purchases. In the fiscal year ending January 30, 2010, 5.5 percent of all BJ's members were Rewards members (which entailed an annual fee of $90); these members accounted for 13 percent of BJ's total merchandise and food sales.

BJ's was the only warehouse club that accepted MasterCard, Visa, Discover, and American Express cards at all locations; members could also pay for purchases by cash, check, and debit cards. BJ's accepted returns of most merchandise within 30 days of purchase. Losses associated with payments by check were insignificant; members who bounced checks were restricted to cash-only terms.

Information Systems

Starting in 2007, BJ's management began a large-scale technology initiative to upgrade or replace the company's sales reporting, financial, human resources, and membership systems; the effort was expected to take a minimum of five years to complete. A new warehouse management system, implemented in 2009, enabled the company to more efficiently manage its logistics, inventory, and warehouse replenishment activities. Sales data was analyzed daily for replenishment purposes. Detailed point-of-sale data enabled warehouse managers and buying staff to track changes in members' buying behavior. The company had recently improved the efficiency of its checkout process and implemented an online system to handle merchandise returns and refunds.

Advertising and Public Relations

BJ's Wholesale increased customer awareness of its clubs primarily through a variety of public relations and community involvement

Exhibit 8   Scenes of BJ's Wholesale Clubs

activities, marketing programs for newly opened clubs, social media outreach, and a publication called *BJ's Journal,* which was mailed to members throughout the year. During the holiday season, BJ's engaged in radio and TV advertising, a portion of which was funded by vendors. BJ's employed dedicated marketing personnel to solicit potential business members and to contact selected other organizations to attract new members. BJ's used one-day passes to introduce non-members to its club and, in the fall and spring, the company typically ran free trial membership promotions. Members could sign up for e-mail offers at the company's website.

In addition, BJ's had a co-branded Visa card that was underwritten by a major financial institution on a nonrecourse basis. Purchases made at BJ's with the co-branded Visa card earned a 2 percent rebate; all other purchases with the card earned a 1 percent rebate. Rebates were issued by the financial institution in the form of BJ's Bucks, which were certificates redeemable for merchandise at any BJ's club.

BJ's Charitable Foundation donated to dozens of nonprofit organizations providing basic-need services to children and families in communities where a BJ's Wholesale Club was located; in 2009, these donations amounted to more than $1.6 million.

ENDNOTES

[1] Costco management presentation, March 2010, www.costco.com, accessed April 7, 2010.

[2] As quoted in Matthew Boyle, "Why Costco Is So Damn Addictive," *Fortune,* October 30, 2006, pp. 128–29.

[3] Steven Greenhouse, "How Costco Became the Anti-Wal-Mart," *New York Times,* July 17, 2005, www.wakeupwalmart.com/news, accessed November 28, 2006.

[4] Quoted in Greenhouse, "How Costco Became the Anti-Wal-Mart."

[5] Quoted in Nina Shapiro, "Company for the People," *Seattle Weekly,* December 15, 2004, www.seattleweekly.com, accessed November 14, 2006.

[6] Quoted in Greenhouse, "How Costco Became the Anti-Wal-Mart."

[7] Boyle, "Why Costco Is So Damn Addictive," p. 132.

[8] Costco, 2005 annual report.

[9] Andria Cheng, "Costco Cracks Taiwan Market," *Wall Street Journal,* April 2, 2010, p. B5.

[10] As quoted in Alan B. Goldberg and Bill Ritter, "Costco CEO Finds Pro-Worker Means Profitability," *20/20,* August 2, 2006, http://abcnews.go.com/2020/Business/story?id=1362779, accessed November 15, 2006.

[11] Ibid.

[12] As described in Nina Shapiro, "Company for the People," *Seattle Weekly,* December 15, 2004, www.seattleweekly.com, accessed November 14, 2006.

[13] Based on data for Costco posted at PayScale, www.payscale.com, accessed October 9, 2008.

[14] Ibid.

[15] Quoted in Goldberg and Ritter, "Costco CEO Finds Pro-Worker Means Profitability."

[16] Shapiro, "Company for the People."

[17] Quoted in Lori Montgomery, "Maverick Costco CEO Joins Push to Raise Minimum Wage," *Washington Post,* January 30, 2007, p. D4.

[18] Quoted in Goldberg and Ritter, "Costco CEO Finds Pro-Worker Means Profitability."

[19] Ibid.

[20] Walmart, 2010 annual report, p. 8.

Competition in Energy Drinks, Sports Drinks, and Vitamin-Enhanced Beverages

John E. Gamble
University of South Alabama

Alternative beverages such as energy drinks, sports drinks, and vitamin-enhanced beverages were the stars of the beverage industry during the mid-2000s. Rapid growth in the category, coupled with premium prices and high profit margins made alternative beverages an important part of beverage companies' lineup of brands. Global beverage companies such as Coca-Cola and PepsiCo had relied on such beverages to sustain volume growth in mature markets where consumers were reducing their consumption of carbonated soft drinks. In addition, Coca-Cola, PepsiCo, and other beverage companies were intent on expanding the market for alternative beverages by introducing energy drinks, sports drinks, and vitamin drinks in more and more emerging international markets. Global beverage producers had not been the only ones to benefit from increasing consumer demand for alternative beverage choices. Entrepreneurs such as the founders of Red Bull GmbH, Rockstar, Inc., Hansen Natural Corporation (maker of Monster Energy), Living Essentials (maker of 5-Hour Energy), and Energy Brands (originator of glacéau vitaminwater) had become multimillionaires through their development and sale of alternative beverages.

However, the premium-priced alternative beverage market had been hit especially hard by the lingering economic downturn in the United States. Sales of sports drinks declined by 12.3 percent between 2008 and 2009, and sales of flavored and vitamin-enhanced waters had declined by 12.5 percent over the same period. The sales of energy drinks fared better, but 2009 segment sales exceeded sales in 2008 by only 0.2 percent. Industry analysts were undecided on what percentage of the poor 2009 performance for alternative beverages was related to the overall economy and how much could be attributed to market maturity. Beverage producers had made various attempts at increasing the size of the market for alternative beverages by extending existing product lines and developing altogether new products. For example, PepsiCo had expanded its lineup of Amp Energy drinks to 12 flavors, expanded SoBe vitamin-enhanced beverages to 28 flavors and variations, and increased the Gatorade lineup to include dozens of flavors and variations. Beverage producers were also seeking additional growth by quickly launching concentrated two-ounce energy shots to garner a share of the new beverage category that originated with the development of Living Essentials' 5-Hour Energy. Some beverage producers were also moving to capture demand for new relaxation drinks that were designed to have a calming effect or help those with insomnia.

While attempting to expand the market for alternative beverages and increase sales and market share, beverage producers also were forced to contend with criticism from some that energy drinks, energy shots, and relaxation drinks presented health risks for consumers and that some producers' strategies promoted reckless behavior. Excessive consumption of high-caffeine-content beverages could produce arrhythmias and insomnia, while mixing alcohol with energy drinks could mask the consumer's level of intoxication and lead to increased risk-taking and other serious alcohol-related problems. In addition, many physicians warned consumers against consuming relaxation drinks that contained the potentially harmful ingredients melatonin and kava. But as 2011 approached, the primary concern of most producers of energy drinks, sports drinks, and vitamin-enhanced beverages was how to best improve their competitive standing in the marketplace.

INDUSTRY CONDITIONS IN 2010

The global beverage industry was projected to grow from $1.58 trillion in 2009 to nearly $1.78 trillion in 2014 as beverage producers entered new geographic markets, developed new types of beverages, and continued to create demand for popular drinks. A great deal of industry growth was expected to result from steady growth in the purchasing power of consumers in developing countries, since the saturation rate for all types of beverages was high in developed countries. For example, market maturity and poor economic conditions caused the U.S. beverage industry to decline by 2.1 percent in 2008 and by 3.1 percent in 2009. The 2.3 percent decline in the volume sales of carbonated soft drinks marked the

fifth consecutive year that U.S. consumers had purchased fewer carbonated soft drinks than the year before. Industry analysts believed that while carbonated soft drinks would remain the most-consumed beverage in the United States for some time, annual sales would continue to decline as consumers developed preferences for bottled water, sports drinks, fruit juices, ready-to-drink tea, vitamin-enhanced beverages, energy drinks, ready-to-drink coffee, and other types of beverages.

As consumer preferences shifted during the 2000s, sports drinks, energy drinks, and vitamin-enhanced drinks had grown to become important segments within the industry in 2010. In addition, such alternative beverages tended to carry high price points, which made them attractive to both new entrants and established beverage companies such as the Coca-Cola Company and PepsiCo. Sports drinks and vitamin-enhanced beverages tended to carry retail prices that were 50 to 75 percent higher than similar-size carbonated soft drinks and bottled water, while energy drink pricing by volume might be as much as 400 percent higher than carbonated soft drinks. While the alternative beverage segment of the industry offered opportunities for bottlers, the poor economy had decreased demand for higher-priced beverages, with sales of sports drinks declining by 12.3 percent between 2008 and 2009 and the sales of flavored and vitamin-enhanced waters declining by 12.5 percent over the same period. The economy had also impacted the sales of energy drinks, but only by slowing the growth in volume sales to 0.2 percent between 2008 and 2009. Among all types of beverages, only energy drinks and ready-to-drink tea experienced volume growth between 2008 and 2009. Exhibits 1 and 2 present sales statistics for the global and U.S. beverage industry.

Worldwide dollar sales of alternative beverages (sports drinks, energy drinks, and vitamin-enhanced beverages) grew by more than 13 percent annually between 2005 and 2007 before slowing to about 6 percent annually between 2007 and 2009. Demand in the United States had contributed greatly to the worldwide growth in alternative beverage consumption, with the United States accounting for 42.3 percent of the industry's worldwide sales of $40.2 billion in 2009. In the United States, sports drinks accounted for

Exhibit 1 **Dollar Value and Volume Sales of the Global Beverage Industry, 2005–2009, with Forecasts for 2010–2014**

Year	Dollar Value ($ billions)	Volume Sales (billions of liters)
2005	$1,428.4	391.8
2006	1,469.3	409.1
2007	1,514.1	427.3
2008	1,548.3	442.6
2009	1,581.7	458.3
2010*	1,618.4	474.9
2011*	1,657.6	492.1
2012*	1,696.1	508.4
2013*	1,736.5	525.8
2014*	1,775.3	542.5

*Forecast.

Source: Global Beverages Industry Profile, Datamonitor, March 2010.

Exhibit 2   U.S. Beverage Industry Volume Sales by Segment, 2009

Category	Volume (millions of gallons)	Market Share	Growth	Share Point Change
Carbonated soft drinks	13,919.3	48.2%	−2.3%	+0.4
Bottled water	8,435.3	29.2	−2.7	+0.1
Fruit beverages	3,579.2	12.4	−3.7	−0.1
Sports drinks	1,157.8	4.0	−12.3	+0.4
Ready-to-drink tea	901.4	3.1	1.2	+0.1
Flavored or enhanced water	460.0	1.6	−12.5	−0.2
Energy drinks	354.5	1.2	0.2	0.0
Ready-to-drink coffee	51.5	0.2	−5.4	0.0
Total	28,859.0	100.0%	− 3.1%	0.0

Note: Totals may not match data reported by Datamonitor because of differences in research methods.
Source: Beverage Marketing Corporation, as reported in "A Market in Decline," *Beverage World,* April 2010, p. 52.

nearly 60 percent of alternative beverage sales in 2009, while vitamin-enhanced drinks and energy drinks accounted for about 23 percent and 18 percent of 2009 alternative beverage sales, respectively. Exhibit 3 presents alternative beverage dollar value and volume sales for 2005 through 2009 and forecasts for alternative beverage sales for 2010 through 2014. Exhibits 4–7 present statistics on the relative sizes of the regional markets for alternative beverages.

Exhibit 3   Dollar Value and Volume Sales of the Global Market for Alternative Beverages, 2005–2009, with Forecasts for 2010–2014

Year	Dollar Value ($ billions)	Volume (billions of liters)
2005	$27.7	9.4
2006	31.9	10.3
2007	35.5	11.1
2008	37.8	11.9
2009	40.2	12.7
2010*	42.8	13.5
2011*	45.5	14.4
2012*	48.0	15.1
2013*	50.8	16
2014*	53.5	16.8

*Forecast.
Source: Global Functional Drinks Industry Profile, Datamonitor, April 2010.

Even though energy drinks, sports drinks, and vitamin-enhanced drinks were all categorized as alternative beverages, the consumer profile varied substantially across the three types of beverages. While the profile of an energy drink consumer was a teenage boy, sports drinks were most frequently purchased by those who engaged in sports, fitness, or other strenuous activities such as outdoor manual labor jobs. It was quite common for teens to consume sports drinks after practicing or participating in school sports events and for manual laborers to consume sports drinks on hot days. Vitamin-enhanced beverages could substitute for sports drinks but were frequently purchased by adult consumers interested in increasing their intakes of vitamins. Even though enhanced waters offered potential benefits, there

Exhibit 4   Geographic Share of the Alternative Beverages Market, 2009

Country	Percentage
United States	42.3%
Asia-Pacific	31.5
Europe	22.2
Americas (excluding U.S.)	4.0
Total	100.0%

Source: Global Functional Drinks Industry Profile, Datamonitor, April 2010, and United States Functional Drinks Industry Profile, Datamonitor, April 2010.

Exhibit 5   **Dollar Value and Volume Sales of the U.S. Market for Alternative Beverages, 2005–2009, with Forecasts for 2010–2014**

Year	Dollar Value ($ billions)	Volume (billions of liters)
2005	$9.2	2.8
2006	12.4	3.3
2007	14.8	3.7
2008	15.9	4.0
2009	17.0	4.2
2010*	18.2	4.5
2011*	19.5	4.7
2012*	20.8	5.0
2013*	22.2	5.3
2014*	23.6	5.5

*Forecast.
Source: United States Functional Drinks Industry Profile, Datamonitor, April 2010.

were some features of enhanced waters that might cause consumers to limit their consumption of such products, including the need for sweeteners to disguise the taste of added vitamins and

Exhibit 6   **Volume Sales and Dollar Value of the Asia-Pacific Alternative Beverages Market, 2005–2009, Forecasts for 2010–2014**

Year	Dollar Value ($ billions)	Volume (billions of liters)
2005	$10.2	4.80
2006	10.7	5.10
2007	11.2	5.44
2008	12.0	5.81
2009	12.7	6.20
2010*	13.5	6.63
2011*	14.3	7.09
2012*	14.9	7.41
2013*	15.7	7.82
2014*	16.5	8.23

*Forecast.
Source: Asia-Pacific Functional Drinks Industry Profile, Datamonitor, April 2010.

Exhibit 7   **Volume Sales and Dollar Value of the European Alternative Beverages Market, 2005–2009, with Forecasts for 2010–2014**

Year	Dollar Value ($ billions)	Volume (billions of liters)
2005	$7.4	1.27
2006	7.8	1.34
2007	8.2	1.43
2008	8.6	1.51
2009	9.1	1.60
2010*	9.5	1.69
2011*	9.9	1.78
2012*	10.4	1.88
2013*	10.8	1.98
2014*	11.3	2.08

*Forecast.
Source: Europe Functional Drinks Industry Profile, Datamonitor, April 2010.

supplements. As a result, calorie counts for vitamin-enhanced beverages ranged from 20 calories per 16-ounce serving for Propel to 100 calories per 16-ounce serving for glacéau vitaminwater. In addition, some medical researchers had suggested that consumers would need to drink approximately 10 bottles of enhanced water each day to meet minimum dietary requirements for the vitamins promoted on the waters' labels.

Distribution and Sale of Alternative Beverages

Consumers could purchase most alternative beverages in supermarkets, supercenters, natural foods stores, wholesale clubs, and convenience stores. Convenience stores were a particularly important distribution channel for alternative beverages since sports drinks, vitamin-enriched drinks, and energy drinks were usually purchased for immediate consumption. In fact, convenience stores accounted for about 75 percent of energy drink sales in 2010. Although energy drinks were typically purchased in convenience stores, sports drinks and vitamin-enhanced beverages were also available in most delis and many restaurants, from vending machines, and sometimes at sporting events and other special events like concerts, outdoor festivals, and carnivals.

Pepsi-Cola and Coca-Cola's soft drink businesses aided the two companies in making alternative beverages available in supermarkets, supercenters, wholesale clubs, and convenience stores. Soft drink sales were important to all types of food stores since soft drinks made up a sizable percentage of the store's sales and since food retailers frequently relied on soft drink promotions to generate store traffic. Coca-Cola and Pepsi-Cola were able to encourage their customers to purchase items across its product line to ensure prompt and complete shipment of key soft drink products. Smaller producers typically used third parties like beer and wine distributors or food distributors to make sales and deliveries to supermarkets, convenience store buyers, and restaurants and delis. Most distributors made deliveries of alternative beverages to convenience stores and restaurants along with their regular scheduled deliveries of other foods and beverages.

Because of the difficulty for food service distributors to restock vending machines and provide alternative beverages to special events, Coca-Cola and Pepsi-Cola were able to dominate such channels since they could make deliveries of sports drinks and vitamin-enhanced drinks along with their deliveries of carbonated soft drinks. Coca-Cola and Pepsi-Cola's vast beverage distribution systems made it easy for the two companies to make Gatorade, SoBe, Powerade, and glacéau vitaminwater available anywhere Coke or Pepsi could be purchased.

Convenience stores were aggressive in pressing alternative beverage producers and food distributors for low prices and slotting fees. Most convenience stores carried only two to four brands of alternative beverages beyond what was distributed by Coca-Cola and PepsiCo, and required sellers to pay annual slotting fees in return for providing bottle facings on a cooler shelf. Food and beverage distributors usually allowed alternative beverage producers to negotiate slotting fees and any rebates directly with convenience store buyers.

There was not as much competition among producers of sports drinks and vitamin-enhanced drinks to gain shelf space in delis and restaurants, since volume was relatively low—making per unit distribution costs exceedingly high unless other beverages were delivered along with alternative beverages. PepsiCo and Coca-Cola were among the better-suited alternative beverage producers to economically distribute sports drinks and vitamin-enhanced beverages to restaurants, since they likely provided fountain drinks to such establishments. Exhibit 8 presents worldwide and regional market shares for the three largest producers of alternative beverages in 2009. Distributors for the leading energy drink brands sold in the United States are listed in Exhibit 9.

Suppliers to the Industry

The suppliers to the alternative beverage industry included the makers of such nutritive and non-nutritive ingredients as sugar, aspartame, fructose, glucose, natural and artificial flavoring,

Exhibit 8 Worldwide and Regional Market Shares for the Three Largest Producers of Alternative Beverages, 2009

Company	Worldwide	United States	Asia-Pacific	Europe
PepsiCo	26.5%	47.8%	12.4	12.9%
Coca-Cola	11.5	10.2	13.7	n.a.
Red Bull	7.0	10.6	n.a.	10.1
Others	55.0	31.5	73.9	77.0
Total	100.0%	100.0%	100.0%	100.0%

n.a. = Not available

Sources: Global Functional Drinks Industry Profile, Datamonitor, April 2010; United States Functional Drinks Industry Profile, Datamonitor, April 2010; Asia-Pacific Functional Drinks Industry Profile, Datamonitor, April 2010; and Europe Functional Drinks Industry Profile, Datamonitor, April 2010.

Exhibit 9   Market Shares for the Leading Energy Drink Brands in the United States, 2006–2009

Brand	Distributor	2006 (% of dollar sales)	2007 (% of dollar sales)	2008 (% of dollar sales)	2009 (% of dollar sales)
Red Bull	Independent	43%	35%	40%	40%
Monster	Coca-Cola	15	27	23	27
Rockstar	PepsiCo	11	11	12	8
NOS	Coca-Cola	n.a.	2	2	4
Amp	PepsiCo	4	5	8	3
DoubleShot	PepsiCo	n.a.	n.a.	2	3
Full Throttle	Coca-Cola	7	7	4	2
Others		20	13	9	13
Total		100%	100%	100%	100%

n.a. = Not available.

Sources: "2010 State of the Industry Report," *Beverage World,* April 2010; BevNET.com.

artificial colors, caffeine, taurine, glucuronolactone, niacin, sodium, potassium, chloride, and other nutritional supplements. Suppliers to the industry also included the manufacturers of aluminum cans, plastic bottles and caps, label printers, and secondary packaging suppliers. While unique supplements like taurine might be available from only a few sources, most packaging supplies needed for the production of alternative beverages were readily available for a large number of suppliers. The numerous suppliers of secondary packaging materials (e.g., cardboard boxes, shrink-wrap, six-pack rings, printed film or paper labels) aggressively competed for the business of large alternative beverage producers. All but the largest sellers of alternative beverages contracted procurement and production activities to contract bottlers who produced energy drinks and other alternative beverages to the sellers' specifications.

Key Competitive Capabilities in the Alternative Beverages Market

Product innovation had been among the most important competitive features of the alternative beverage industry since the introduction of Gatorade in 1967. Alternative beverages competed on the basis of differentiation from traditional drinks such as carbonated soft drinks or fruit juices and

were also positioned within their respective segments on the basis of differentiation. For example, all energy drink brands attempted to develop brand loyalty based on taste, the energy-boosting properties of their ingredients, and image. An energy drink's image was a factor of its brand name and packaging, clever ads, endorsements from celebrities and extreme sports athletes, and sponsorships of extreme sports events and music concerts. Differentiation among vitamin-enhanced beverages tended to center on brand name and packaging, advertising, unique flavors, and nutritional properties. Because of the importance of brand recognition, successful sellers of alternative beverages were required to possess well-developed brand-building skills. The industry's largest sellers were global food and beverage companies—having built respected brands in snack foods, soft drinks, and fruit juices prior to entering the alternative beverage industry.

Alternative beverage sellers also needed to have efficient distribution systems to supermarket and convenience store channels to be successful in the industry. It was imperative for alternative beverage distributors (whether direct store delivery by bottlers or delivery by third-parties) to maximize the number of deliveries per driver since distribution included high fixed costs for warehouses, trucks, handheld inventory tracking devices, and labor. It was also critical for distributors and sellers to provide on-time deliveries and offer responsive customer service to large customers. Also, volume and market share were key factors in keeping marketing expenses at an acceptable per-unit level.

Recent Trends in the Alternative Beverage Market

Despite the impact of the ongoing U.S. recession on the entire beverage industry, alternative beverage producers were optimistic about prospects for the industry. Demand was expected to grow worldwide as consumer purchasing power increased, and even though volume was down in the United States for sports drinks and vitamin-enhanced drinks, alternative beverages offered profit margins much higher than those of other beverages. Innovation in brands, flavors, and formulations was expected to be necessary for supporting premium pricing and volume increases. Industry analysts believed that such exotic flavors as cardamom, hibiscus, and cupuacu might prove to be hits in 2011 and 2012.

The emergence of two-ounce energy shots sold on convenience store counters had proved to be an important growth category for the industry. The category was created with the introduction of Living Essentials' 5-Hour Energy in 2004. 5-Hour Energy contained amino acids and taurine plus 2,000 percent of the daily requirement for vitamin B_6, 8,333 percent of the daily requirement for B_{12}, and 100 milligrams of caffeine (the equivalent of a cup of coffee). By comparison, the caffeine content of energy drinks ranged from 160 milligrams for Red Bull to 240 milligrams for Rockstar Punched. Unlike energy drinks that focused on teens, energy shots were targeted to office workers, parents, and other adults who might need a boost of energy during a demanding day. Red Bull, Coca-Cola's NOS, Hansen's Monster, PepsiCo's Amp, and Rockstar had all developed competing energy shots, but none were a serious threat to Living Essentials' 5-Hour Energy in 2010. 5-Hour Energy held an 85 percent market share in the category in 2009. Exhibit 10 presents annual revenues for the top five energy shot brands in the United States in 2009. Analysts believed that Europe, Australia, South America, and the Middle East were attractive markets for the expansion-minded makers of energy shots.

Unlike carbonated soft drinks, the caffeine content of energy shots and energy drinks was

Exhibit 10 Annual Revenues for the Top Five Energy Shot Brands in the United States, 2009

Brand	Revenues ($ millions)	Revenue Growth (2008–2009)
5-Hour Energy	$494.6	+58.6%
Stacker2 6-Hour Power	30.4	+32.9
Red Bull Energy Shot	22.1	n.a.
Monster Hitman	19.7	+611.7
NOS Energy Shot	11.8	−10.4

n.a. = Not available

Source: *Beverage World* 2010 State of the Industry Report, April 2010.

not regulated by the U.S. Food and Drug Administration and could contain as much caffeine as the producer thought appropriate. There was concern among some health professionals over the high caffeine content of energy drinks and the effects of large doses of caffeine on individuals, especially children. The most significant health problems related to high caffeine consumption were heart arrhythmia and insomnia. It was not unheard of for adults with heart arrhythmias to be admitted to emergency rooms after consuming three or more energy drinks in one day. Also, physicians attributed a New Mexico man's appendicitis and gallstones to excessive consumption of energy drinks. Physicians also warned that the combination of energy drinks and over-the-counter drugs such as NoDoz could cause seizures. However, clinical studies had shown that, in moderate doses, caffeine contributed to healthy weight loss, was an effective treatment for asthma and headaches and reduced the risk of Parkinson's disease, depression, colon cancer, and type 2 diabetes. As a precaution, Monster Energy placed the following warning on its labels: "Limit 3 cans per day, not recommended for children, pregnant women or people sensitive to caffeine."[1]

There was also concern over the tendency of some individuals to mix alcohol with energy drinks. It was not uncommon at all for partiers to use energy drinks as a mixer to help offset the depressive effects of alcohol and keep their energy levels high throughout the evening. It was estimated that more than 25 percent of college-age drinkers mixed alcohol with energy drinks. The frequency of the practice led MillerCoors to develop an alcohol energy drink that contained caffeine, taurine, guarana, and ginseng in addition to alcohol. Anheuser-Busch sold two similar drinks called Tilt and Bud Extra. Both companies removed the caffeine from the drinks after attorneys general in several states had written the U.S. Food and Drug Administration (FDA) to ask that the federal government force the removal of the products from the market. The attorneys general argued that the addition of caffeine to alcohol masked a drinker's level of intoxication and could lead to "increased risk-taking and other serious alcohol related problems such as traffic accidents, violence, sexual assault, and suicide."[2]

The relaxation drink niche within the alternative beverage industry also caused some concern among health professionals and members of law enforcement. Relaxation drinks such as Vacation in a Bottle (ViB) and Dream Water contained the hormone melatonin, which was produced by humans, plants, and animals and had many known and unknown effects on the human body. Melatonin had been associated with rapid-eye movement (REM) sleep and was used by some as a supplement to help treat insomnia. A Harvard Medical School sleep expert warned against the consumption of relaxation drinks by stating that hormones "should not be put in beverages, since the amount people drink often depends on thirst and taste rather than being taken only when needed like any other drug."[3] Kava and valerian root were two other common ingredients of relaxation drinks; the FDA warned against the use of kava and had not approved valerian root as a food additive.

Controversy also surrounded some relaxation drinks because of their association with the abuse of prescription cough syrup. The practice of mixing a prescription cough syrup whose ingredients included promethazine and codeine with Sprite or other carbonated soft drinks had become common in some inner-city areas, especially in southern U.S. states. The purple-colored cough syrup drink, which was commonly called "purple drank" or "sizzurp," was said to have been originated by Houston, Texas, disc jockey and rapper DJ Screw, who died from an overdose of purple drank in 2000. Purple drank was frequently

mentioned in hip-hop and rap songs such as those performed by Three 6 Mafia, Eminem, Lil'Wyte, Lil Boosie, Mike Jones, Lil' Wayne, Ludacris, T.I., and Kanye West. The use of sizzurp was also a problem in professional sports, and possession of the controlled substances used to make sizzurp had led to the arrests of a number of professional athletes, including Green Bay Packers defensive lineman Johnny Jolly and former Oakland Raiders quarterback JaMarcus Russell. Legal authorities believed that the purple-colored relaxation drinks Drank and Purple Stuff attempted to exploit the street use of purple drank. Innovative Beverage Group, the maker of Drank, had built its marketing plan on product placements in rap and hip-hop videos and launched a competition in summer 2010 that would award prizes to those who wrote the best new rap songs about the company's product.

PROFILES OF THE LEADING ALTERNATIVE BEVERAGE PRODUCERS

PepsiCo

In 2010, PepsiCo was the world's fourth-largest food and beverage company, with 2009 sales of about $43 billion. The company's brands were sold in more than 200 countries and included such well-known names as Lay's, Tostitos, Cheetos, Mountain Dew, Pepsi, Doritos, Lipton Iced Tea, Tropicana, Aquafina, SoBe, Gatorade, Quaker, and Cracker Jack. The company held commanding market shares in many of the food and beverage categories where it competed. In 2009, it was the number one seller of beverages in the United States and its Frito-Lay division was four times as large as the next-largest seller of snacks in the United States. PepsiCo had upset Coca-Cola to become the largest seller of beverages in the United States, not by selling more carbonated soft drinks than Coke (Coca-Cola was the largest seller of carbonated soft drinks in 2009), but by leading in most other beverage categories. For example, Aquafina was the best-selling brand of water in the United States, Frappuccino was the number one brand of ready-to-drink coffee, Tropicana was ranked first in orange juice sales, and Gatorade held a commanding lead in sports drinks. The company's strength in noncarbonated beverages made it the world's largest seller of alternative beverages, with a global market share in 2009 of 26.5 percent. PepsiCo held more than a 2-to-1 worldwide market-share lead over industry runner-up, Coca-Cola, which had a global market share in alternative beverages of 11.5 percent in 2009. However, PepsiCo's greatest strength was in the United States, where it held a 47.8 percent share of the total alternative beverage market in 2009.

PepsiCo's best-selling alternative beverages included Gatorade (which held a 75 percent share of the $1.57 billion U.S. sports drink market), Propel, SoBe Lifewater, and Amp Energy. PepsiCo produced 12 flavors of Amp Energy drinks and two flavors of No Fear energy drinks. Its SoBe brand included both energy drinks and vitamin-enhanced drinks. In 2010, PepsiCo bottled and marketed 2 varieties of SoBe Adrenaline Rush energy drinks and 28 varieties of SoBe vitamin-enhanced beverages. PespiCo also marketed a line of DoubleShot Energy drinks that complemented its Starbucks Frappuccino drink line.

The company expanded its lineup of alternative drinks in 2009 with the launch of Charge, a lemon-flavored energy drink containing L-carnitine; Rebuild, a black tea drink fortified with amino acids and antioxidants; Defend, a drink fortified with antioxidants and beta-alanine; and Bloodshot, a juice drink containing 150 percent of the daily recommended dosage of vitamins B and C. The company also had a multiyear distribution agreement with Rockstar to distribute Rockstar energy drinks in the United States and Canada.

A summary of PepsiCo's financial performance between 2007 and 2009 is presented in Exhibit 11.

The Coca-Cola Company

The Coca-Cola Company was the world's leading manufacturer, marketer, and distributor of nonalcoholic beverage concentrates, with 2009 revenues of nearly $31 billion and sales in more than 200 countries. The company was best known for Coca-Cola, which had been called the world's most valuable brand. Along with the universal appeal of the Coca-Cola brand, Coca-Cola's vast global distribution system—which included independent bottlers, bottlers partially owned by Coca-Cola, and company-owned bottlers—made

Exhibit 11   **Financial Summary for PepsiCo, 2007–2009 ($ millions, except per share information)**

	2009	2008	2007
Net revenue	$43,232	$43,251	$39,474
Cost of sales	20,099	20,351	18,038
Selling, general and administrative expenses	15,026	15,877	14,196
Amortization of intangible assets	63	64	58
Operating profit	8,044	6,959	7,182
Bottling equity income	365	374	560
Interest expense	(397)	(329)	(224)
Interest income	67	41	125
Income before income taxes	8,079	7,045	7,643
Provision for income taxes	2,100	1,879	1,973
Net income	5,979	5,166	5,670
Less: Net income attributable to noncontrolling interests	33	24	12
Net income attributable to PepsiCo	$5,946	$5,142	$5,658
Net income attributable to PepsiCo per common share			
Basic	$3.81	$3.26	$3.48
Diluted	$3.77	$3.21	$3.41

Source: PepsiCo, 2009 10-K report.

Coke an almost unstoppable international powerhouse. Coca-Cola, Diet Coke, Fanta, and Sprite all ranked among the top five best-selling nonalcoholic beverages worldwide in 2009.

The strength of the Coca-Cola brand also aided the company in gaining distribution for new beverages. In the United States, Coca-Cola produced, marketed, and distributed Minute Maid orange juice products, Dasani purified water, Powerade sports drinks, an assortment of energy drink brands, Fuze vitamin-enhanced beverages, Nestea ready-to-drink teas, and glacéau vitaminwater. The company also produced and sold country- and region-specific beverages such as Bonaqua sparkling water in Europe, Georgia ready-to-drink coffee in Japan, and Hugo fruit and milk protein drinks in Latin America.

Even though Coca-Cola was the worldwide leader in carbonated soft drink sales, it had struggled to build market share in alternative beverages and trailed PepsiCo by a significant margin worldwide in energy drinks, sports drinks, and vitamin-enhanced beverages. Asia was the only geographic market where Coca-Cola's sales of alternative beverages exceeded the sales of PepsiCo's energy drinks, sports drinks, and vitamin-enhanced beverages. As of 2009, Coca-Cola had yet to gain strong demand for its alternative beverages in Europe and, as a result, was not listed among the leading sellers of alternative beverages in that market. In the United States, Coca-Cola was the third-largest seller of alternative beverages, with its combined sales of Powerade, Full Throttle, NOS, Rehab, TaB, and Vault energy drinks; glacéau vitaminwater; and Fuze vitamin-enhanced drinks, falling just short of the sales of Red Bull energy drinks.

Much of the company's efforts to build market share in 2009 and 2010 centered on new-product development and the introduction of existing brands into new country markets. In 2009, Coca-Cola introduced glacéau vitaminwater in South Africa, France, South Korea, Japan, Belgium, Portugal, Hong Kong, China, and Sweden; in that same year it also launched Cascal, a fermented fruit drink, in the United States and Burn energy drink in India. The company had introduced its newly developed Gladiator energy drink in Latin America in 2008. Among Coca-Cola's greatest resources in the energy drink category was its multiyear distribution agreement with Hansen Natural Corporation to distribute Hansen's Monster energy drink in parts of the United States, Canada, and six European countries.

A summary of the Coca-Cola Company's financial performance between 2007 and 2009 is presented in Exhibit 12.

Red Bull GmbH

Red Bull was the world's number one seller of energy drinks, which made it the third-largest producer of alternative beverages worldwide and the number two seller of alternative beverages in the United States and Europe. Red Bull's distinctive taste and formula of vitamins, taurine, and caffeine launched the energy drink market in the Western world in the late 1990s. Energy drinks similar to Red Bull had been produced and marketed in Asia since the 1970s. In fact, Red Bull's formula was modeled after Krating Daeng, a popular energy drink sold in Thailand that was recommended as a jet lag remedy to Austrian businessman Dietrich Mateschitz. Mateschitz had been in Thailand to call on T.C. Pharmaceutical, which was a client of his employer at the time and the manufacturer or Krating Daeng. Mateschitz was so impressed with the flavor and energy-boosting capabilities of Krating Daeng that he left his job and formed a partnership with T.C. Pharmaceutical's founder in 1984 to market the drink in Europe. The energy drink's formula was modified slightly to better appeal to Western palates and was renamed Red Bull, which was the English translation of Krating Daeng. Red Bull was launched in Austria in 1987 and sold more than 1 million cans during the year. The company expanded into Hungary and Slovenia in 1992, Germany and the United Kingdom in 1994, and the United States in 1997. In 2010, the company exported its energy drinks to more than 160 countries and delivered to retailers by independent distributors.

The company's slogan, "Red Bull gives you wings," signaled its energy-boosting properties, and the company's endorsements involved almost every high-energy sport worldwide. In 2010, Red Bull sponsored not only athletes and teams competing in sports ranging from auto racing to freestyle biking to wakeboarding to snowboarding to golf but also a number of music events around the

Exhibit 12 Financial Summary for the Coca-Cola Company, 2007–2009 ($ millions)

	2009	2008	2007
Net operating revenues	$30,990	$31,944	$28,857
Cost of goods sold	11,088	11,374	10,406
Gross profit	19,902	20,570	18,451
Selling, general, and administrative expenses	11,358	11,774	10,945
Other operating charges	313	350	254
Operating income	8,231	8,446	7,252
Interest income	249	333	236
Interest expense	355	438	456
Equity income (loss)—net	781	(874)	668
Other income (loss)—net	40	39	219
Income before income taxes	8,946	7,506	7,919
Income taxes	2,040	1,632	1,892
Consolidated net income	6,906	5,874	6,027
Less: Net income attributable to noncontrolling interests	82	67	46
Net income	$ 6,824	$ 5,807	$ 5,981

Source: Coca-Cola Company, 2009 10-K report.

world featuring hip-hop, rap, and hard rock groups. In addition, Red Bull fielded company-sponsored soccer teams in New York City; Salzburg, Austria; Leipzig, Germany; and São Paulo, Brazil. The company owned the Salzburg, Austria, hockey team that played under the Red Bull name.

Red Bull also promoted a series of Flugtag (flight day) events held around the world, during which participants were encouraged to fly their homemade human-powered flying machines—most of which seemed more comically designed than flightworthy. Teams of five designed and piloted their crafts to the end of a 30-foot-high ramp positioned over a body of water. Each team was scored for flight distance, creativity, and showmanship to determine a winner. The appeal of attending the events for spectators was to watch the vast majority of the flying machines merely crash off the end of the ramp.

In 2010, the company produced Red Bull Energy Drink, Red Bull Sugarfree, Red Bull Cola, Red Bull Energy Shots. The privately held company did not disclose financial information to the public, but it did announce shipments of 3.906 billion cans in 2009 and shipments of 3.921 billion cans in 2008.

Hansen Natural Corporation

Hansen Natural Corporation developed and marketed a variety of alternative beverages including natural sodas, blended fruit juices, energy drinks, sports drinks, fruit juice smoothies, ready-to-drink teas, and vitamin-enhanced drinks. The Corona, California, company was founded in 1935 by Hubert Hansen to produce a line of natural sodas and fruit juices and was acquired by South Africans Rodney Sacks and Hilton Schlosberg in 1992 for $14.5 million. Under the leadership of Sacks and Schlosberg, Hansen's sales steadily grew from about $17 million in 1992 to $80 million in 2001. However, the company's sales skyrocketed after its launch of Monster Energy drinks in 2002. By 2004, the company's revenues had increased to $180 million and its profits had grown from $3 million in 2001 to $20 million in 2004. In 2009, Monster was the second-best-selling energy drink brand in the United States and the company's annual revenues and net earnings had grown to more than $1.3 billion and $208 million, respectively. A summary of the company's financial performance between 2005 and 2009 is presented in Exhibit 13.

Exhibit 13   **Financial Summary for Hansen Natural Corporation, 2005–2009 ($ thousands, except per share information)**

	2009	2008	2007	2006	2005
Gross sales	$1,309,335	$1,182,876	$1,025,795	$696,322	$415,417
Net sales	1,143,299	1,033,780	904,465	605,774	348,886
Gross profit	612,316	538,794	468,013	316,594	182,543
Gross profit as a percentage to net sales	53.6%	52.1%	51.7%	52.3%	52.3%
Operating income	337,309	163,591	230,986	158,579	103,443
Net income	$208,716	$108,032	$149,406	$97,949	$62,775
Net income per common share:					
Basic	$2.32	$1.17	$1.64	$1.09	$0.71
Diluted	$2.21	$1.11	$1.51	$0.99	$0.65
Cash, cash equivalents, and investments	$427,672	$375,513	$302,650	$136,796	$73,515
Total assets	800,070	761,837	544,603	308,372	163,890
Debt	206	959	663	303	525
Stockholders' equity	584,953	436,316	422,167	225,084	125,509

Source: Hansen Natural Corporation, 2009 10-K report.

In 2010, Hansen's energy drink lineup included Monster Energy, X-Presso Monster Hammer, Nitrous Monster Energy, Monster Hitman Energy Shooter, Hansen Energy Pro, and Lost Energy. The company also produced and sold Hansen's natural juices and iced tea; Peace Tea, Rumba, Samba, and Tango energy juices; Blue Sky natural sodas; SELF Beauty Elixir; and Vidration enhanced alternative beverages. Sales of Monster energy drinks accounted for approximately 90 percent of Hansen Natural Corporation's total revenues in 2009.

Hansen Natural's rapid success in the energy drink market came about in large part because of its decision in 2002 to match Red Bull on price while packaging Monster drinks in 16-ounce containers (nearly double the size of Red Bull's 8.3-ounce container). The company also imitated Red Bull's image-building and marketing approaches through eye-catching in-store promotions and point-of-sale materials and extreme sports endorsements in snowboarding, BMX, mountain biking, skiing, snowmobiling, skateboarding, and automobile and motorcycle racing. In addition, Hansen and Vans co-sponsored music festivals featuring hard rock and alternative bands.

Hansen Natural outsourced 100 percent of its production of energy drinks and other beverages to contract bottlers throughout the United States. Distribution of the company's energy drinks and other beverages in the United States was split between Anheuser-Busch and Coca-Cola. Coca-Cola also distributed Monster energy drinks in Great Britain, France, Belgium, the Netherlands, Luxembourg, and Monaco. Hansen Natural had also entered into distribution agreements with beverage producers in Mexico and Australia to make Monster energy drinks available in those countries. While its energy drinks were sold in supermarkets, convenience stores, bars, nightclubs, and restaurants, Hansen's other beverage brands were typically found only in health food stores.

Other Sellers

In addition to the industry's leading sellers of alternative beverages, there were hundreds of regional and specialty brands of energy drinks, sports drinks, and enhanced beverages in the United States and internationally. Most of these companies were privately held bottlers with distribution limited to either small geographic regions or specialty grocers and health food stores. In some cases, regional brands were produced by divisions of large corporations and might have a commanding market share in one particular country but limited distribution outside that market. For example, global pharmaceutical giant GlaxoSmithKline did not sell alternative beverages in North America or Asia, but its sales of Lucozade Energy, Lucozade Sport, and Lucozade Alert energy shot made it the second-largest seller of alternative beverages in Europe, with a 2009 market share of 11.4 percent. GlaxoSmith-Kline's sales of alternative beverages accounted for $1.3 billion of its 2009 annual revenues of $44.2 billion. The majority of the company's revenues came from the sale of prescription drugs and over-the-counter medicines and oral care products such as Contact, Nicorette gum, Tums, and Aquafresh. Japanese pharmaceutical company Otsuka Pharmaceutical was the third-largest seller of energy drinks, sports drinks, and vitamin-enhanced beverages in the Asia-Pacific region, with a 9.4 percent market share in 2009.

Other than Red Bull, Rockstar was the most noteworthy privately held alternative beverage company. The Las Vegas, Nevada–based company entered the energy drink market in 2001 using a strategy that would be imitated by Hansen's Monster brand a year later. Rockstar was packaged in a 16-ounce can and priced comparably to Red Bull's pricing for its 8.3-ounce can. Rockstar's image, like that of Red Bull and Monster, was built on extreme sports endorsements and hard rock promotions. Among the company's

annually sponsored music festivals was the Mayhem Festival, which in 2010 included such musical acts as Rob Zombie, Five Finger Death Punch, Korn, In This Moment, Chimaira, and 3 Inches of Blood. The company also sponsored other hard rock and metal tours such as Taste of Chaos, the Warped Tour, and the Uproar Festival. In 2010, Rockstar energy drinks were available in 11 flavors and Rockstar energy shots were available in two flavors. Rockstar beverages were distributed in the United States and Canada by PepsiCo and were distributed in Australia, New Zealand, Japan, Germany, Switzerland, Finland, Spain, the Netherlands, and the United Kingdom through agreements with beverage distributors in those countries.

The number of brands competing in the sports drinks, energy drinks, and vitamin-enhanced beverage segments of the alternative beverage industry continued to grow each year. In 2009, 231 new vitamin-enhanced beverages were introduced in the United States. The relative maturity of the sports drink segment and the dominant market position held by Gatorade limited the number of new sports drink introductions to 51 in 2009. Launches of new energy drink brands had grown steadily from 172 in 2005 to 380 in 2008, but energy drink introductions fell to 138 in 2009 as the segment matured and financially squeezed consumers became more price conscious. Overall, the relative strength of the energy drink, enhanced beverage, and sports drink beverage segments would likely attract additional entrants over the next several years.

ENDNOTES

[1] Quoted in "Energy Boost a Bummer? Hospital Study Raises Alarm about Drinks," *Chattanooga Times Free Press*, April 9, 2009, p. E6.

[2] Quoted in "FDA Questions Safety of Alcoholic Energy Drinks," Associated Press, November 13, 2009.

[3] Quoted in "These Drinks'll Knock You Out!" *Daily News* (New York), February 7, 2010, p. 6.

Netflix's Business Model and Strategy in Renting Movies and TV Episodes

Arthur A. Thompson
The University of Alabama

In May 2010, Netflix's strategy was producing impressive strategic and financial results. During the past five years, Netflix had emerged as the world's largest subscription service for sending DVDs by mail and streaming movies and TV episodes over the Internet. It had attracted 15 million subscribers as of July 2010, up from 4.2 million at year-end 2007 and 1.6 million at year-end 2004. Netflix was shipping about 2 million DVDs on average daily to subscribers, and some 61 percent of the company's subscribers were now watching movies and TV episodes streamed from Netflix over the Internet, up from 48 percent at year-end 2009 and 38 percent in the first quarter of 2009.

Netflix's revenues grew from $500 million in 2004 to $1.2 billion in 2007 to $1.7 billion in 2009 and were expected to surpass $2.1 billion in 2010. In the second quarter of 2010, revenues were $519.8 million, representing 27 percent year-over-year growth from $408.5 million in the second quarter of 2009 and 5 percent sequential growth from $493.7 million in the first quarter of 2010. The company's net income had increased from $21.6 million in 2004 to $115.8 million in 2009, equal to a compound annual growth rate of nearly 40 percent; top management expected net income for full-year 2010 to be in the range of $141 to $156 million. Netflix's stock price closed at an all-time high of $170.83 on September 29, 2010, up from closing prices of $55.09 on December 31, 2009, and $29.87 on January 2, 2009.

Meanwhile, Netflix's traditional video store competitors were experiencing sharp declines in sales and heavy losses. Blockbuster and Movie Gallery, both of which operated thousands of video stores where customers could rent DVDs, were facing financial disaster. During 2009, Blockbuster's worldwide revenues from rentals of movies and video games declined by nearly $530 million to $2.5 billion; many analysts believed that the downward trend in Blockbuster's rental revenues, which began in 2003 when its rental revenues were $4.5 billion, would be hard to reverse. In September 2010, Blockbuster filed for reorganization under Chapter 11 of the U.S. Bankruptcy Code, owing to declining revenues, net losses of $569 million in 2009 and $385 million in 2008, and the burden of its $963 million debt (including capital lease obligations). Since 2002, Blockbuster had only been profitable one year (earning $39 million) and had lost a total of $3.8 billion. Prior to its bankruptcy filing, Blockbuster was planning to close 500 to 545 of its 5,220 company-owned stores worldwide, after closing or selling 586 stores in 2009 and 1,459 stores in 2005–2008.

Movie Gallery filed for Chapter 11 bankruptcy in February 2010, less than two years after emerging from bankruptcy in the spring of 2008 under new owners. Movie Gallery's troubles began after the company took on too much debt to acquire Hollywood Entertainment Corporation in 2005 for more than $800 million. At the time of its second bankruptcy filing, Movie Gallery had $600 million in debt and was plagued with declining sales and losses. As part of its strategic moves to emerge from its February 2010 bankruptcy filing, Movie Gallery had begun closing 760 of its Movie Gallery, Hollywood Video, and Game

Crazy rental locations across the United States. After these closings, company management was proposing to continue operations at 1,111 Movie Gallery, 545 Hollywood Video, and 250 Game Crazy locations that either generated or were expected to generate positive cash flows. However, in May 2010, Movie Gallery announced that it would begin closing all of its remaining stores and that its entire business would be liquidated.

INDUSTRY ENVIRONMENT

Since 2000, the introduction of new technologies and electronics products had rapidly multiplied consumer opportunities to view movies. It was commonplace in 2010 for people to view movies at theaters, on airline flights, in hotels, from the rear seats of motor vehicles equipped with video consoles, in homes, or most anywhere on a laptop PC or handheld device like an iPad or iPod Touch. Home viewing was possible on PCs, televisions, and video game consoles. The digital video disc (DVD) player was one of the most successful consumer electronic products of all time; as of 2010, more than 85 percent of U.S. households had one or more DVD players and increasing numbers of households had combination DVD players/recorders. Sales of combination DVD players-recorders surpassed sales of play-only DVD players in 2007–2008. Many households had big-screen high-definition televisions (HDTVs), and a much lesser number had upgraded to Blu-ray DVD players or players-recorders; both HDTVs and Blu-ray devices enabled more spectacular pictures and a significantly higher caliber in-home movie-viewing experience compared with standard televisions.

Consumers could obtain or view movie DVDs and TV episodes through a wide variety of distribution channels and providers. The options included:

- Purchasing movie DVDs and TV episodes from such retailers as Walmart, Target, Best Buy, Toys "R" Us, and Amazon.com.
- Renting movie DVDs from DVD outlets and vending machine kiosks such as Blockbuster, Movie Gallery/Hollywood Video, Redbox, and/or a host of locally owned providers.

- Renting movie DVDs online from Netflix, Blockbuster, or any of several other subscription services that either mailed DVDs directly to subscribers' homes or had the capability to stream content to subscribers via high-speed broadband connections to the Internet.
- Watching movies on assorted cable channels included in the TV and entertainment packages provided by traditional cable providers (such as Time Warner and Comcast), direct broadcast satellite providers (such as DirecTV and DISH Network), or telecommunication providers (e.g., AT&T and Verizon) that used fiber-optic technology to provide TV packages along with phone, Internet, and wireless services.
- Subscribing to any of several movie-only channels (such as HBO, Showtime, and Starz) through a cable, satellite, or telecommunications provider.
- Using a cable or satellite TV remotes to order movies instantly streamed directly to their TVs on a pay-per-view basis—generally referred to as video on demand (VOD).
- Using the services of Internet movie and TV content providers, such as Apple's iTunes, Amazon.com, Hulu.com, and Google's YouTube.
- Pirating files of movies and other content from Internet sources via the use of illegal file-sharing software.

Exhibit 1 provides data showing the estimated sizes of selected segments of the market for renting movies, TV episodes, and video games in the United States during 2006–2009.

Traditionally, movie studios released filmed entertainment content for distribution to movie DVD retailers and rental companies three to six months after films were released for showing in theaters. Three to seven months after theatrical release, movie studios usually released their films to pay-per-view and VOD providers. Premium TV channels like HBO, Starz, Cinemax, and Showtime were next in the distribution window, getting access to filmed content one year after theatrical release. Movie studios released films for viewing to basic cable and network TV two to three years after theatrical release. Recently, however, some movie studios had experimented with shortened

Exhibit 1   **Estimated Sizes of Various Segments of the Markets for Rentals and Sales of Movies, TV Episodes, and Video Games in the United States, 2006–2009 ($ millions)**

	2009	2008	2007	2006
In-store rentals of movies and TV episodes on DVDs	$ 5,118	$ 5,674	$ 6,215	$ 7,030
Vending machine rentals	917	486	198	79
By-mail rentals	2,114	1,949	1,797	1,291
Total physical DVD rentals	$ 8,149	$ 8,109	8,210	8,400
Cable video-on-demand (VOD)	$ 1,277	$ 1,094	$ 1,038	$ 977
Digital VOD	142	71	28	12
Subscription VOD	265	200	11	4
Total digital rentals of movies and TV episodes	$ 1,684	$ 1,365	$ 1,077	$993
Total rentals of films and TV episodes	$ 9,833	$9,474	$ 9,287	$ 9,393
Physical DVD sales of movies/TV episodes at retail	$13,008	$14,516	$15,932	$16,460
Digital download sales at retail	617	403	90	20
Total retail sales of movies and TV episodes	$13,625	$14,919	$16,022	$16,480
Video game software (rentals and sales at retail)	$ 9,916	$10,998	$ 6,016	$ 4,864
Total U.S. market for film rentals, film sales, and video game software	**$33,374**	**$35,391**	**$31,325**	**$30,737**

Source: Based on Blockbuster's compilations from reports and information published by Adams Media Research and NPD Group and included in Blockbuster's 2009 10-K report, p. 4, and 2008 10-K report, p. 5.

release periods, including making new-release titles available to VOD providers or for online purchase on the same date as the DVD release. Other movie studios had implemented or announced their intention to implement policies preventing movie rental providers from renting movie DVDs until 30 to 45 days following release of a DVD title for sale by retailers. TV episodes were often made available for Internet viewing shortly after the original airing date. Movie studios and TV networks were expected to continue to experiment with the timing of the releases to various distribution channels and providers, in an ongoing effort to discover how best to maximize revenues.

Market Trends in Home Viewing of Movies

The wave of the future in viewing movies at home was widely thought to be in streaming rented movies directly to big-screen HDTVs. Streaming had the advantage of allowing household members to order and instantly watch the movies they chose to rent. Renting a streamed movie could be done either by using the services of Netflix, Blockbuster Online, Amazon Video-on-Demand, Apple's iTunes, and other streaming video providers or by using a TV remote to place orders with a cable or satellite provider to instantly watch a movie from a list of several hundred selections that changed periodically. Providing VOD had been technically possible and available for many years prior to 2010, but it had not garnered substantial usage because movie studios were leery of the potential for movie-pirating and doubtful of whether they could earn acceptable profits from a VOD business model. However, streaming video was less subject to pirating than downloading movie rentals, and ongoing advances in streaming video technology had improved the likelihood that VOD would emerge as the dominant movie rental channel by 2015.

Several strategic initiatives to promote increased use of streaming video were under way in 2010. The owners of Hulu—NBC Universal; ABC's parent Walt Disney; and Fox Entertainment's parent, News Corp—had announced plans to begin offering a premium service for $10 per month that would provide a bigger library of TV shows to watch. Hulu (www.hulu.com) was a free online video service that offered a number of hit TV shows and movies from the libraries of its owners and several other cable networks and movie studios; Hulu derived its revenues from online advertisers, but it was striving to create a business model based on both advertising and subscriptions. Time Warner and Comcast were promoting a "TV Everywhere" concept whereby consumers could watch TV shows free at any time on any device (computers and such mobile devices as iPads and smart phones) so long as they were paying cable subscribers. Time Warner owned a number of cable channels (TNT, TBS, HBO, CNN, and Cartoon Network); CBS was the only major broadcast network currently participating in the trials, but Comcast was in the process of finalizing its acquisition of NBC Universal, which owned NBC, Universal Studios, and a share of Hulu.

In May 2010, Google announced the availability of beta versions of Google TV, based on Google's Android and Chrome software, that enabled households to combine their regular TV experience with the capability to access music, videos, and photos anywhere on the Internet. Google TV was a search-based feature that allowed users to easily and quickly navigate to television channels, apps, and Internet sites. Google's long-term strategy was to eliminate the need to download and install Google TV software by working with electronics manufacturers to equip their new models of televisions, Blu-ray players, and companion boxes with Google TV software. The first such models were expected to go on sale in the fall of 2010. In 2009, Apple had begun exploring the launch of a subscription television service that would offer a package of broadcast shows for $10 per month, but the effort fizzled when several of the biggest studios rejected Apple's proposed fee arrangement for their content and also its comeback proposal to charge 99 cents per TV episode.

In addition, several other developments were acting to reshape the movie rental marketplace:

- The 2009 requirement that all TV stations in the United States use digital technology and equipment to broadcast all their programs had resulted in far more programs being transmitted in high-definition format.

- Prices for wide-screen HDTVs had been dropping rapidly, and picture quality was exceptionally good, if not stunning, on most all models.

- Increasing numbers of devices were appearing in electronics stores that enabled TVs to be connected to the Internet and receive streamed movies from online providers with no hassle. These devices made it simple for households to order streamed movies with just a few clicks instead of traveling to a video rental store or waiting for a disk to be delivered through the mail.

- Sales of movie DVDs were declining; the chief reasons were said to be the flagging economy and the convenience of online rentals of movie DVDs and VOD. Hollywood movie producers had hoped that next-generation, high-definition optical disc format DVDs that incorporated Blu-ray technology would rejuvenate sales of movie DVDs. But movie rental outlets were renting Blu-ray movie DVDs and, so far, there was little evidence that growing numbers of households with Blu-ray players would spur movie DVD sales, given growing popularity of streaming rented movies directly to TVs, a desktop or laptop computer, or a small handheld device like an iPad or a netbook.

- Cable and satellite TV companies were promoting their VOD services and making more movie titles available to their customers. The Starz Entertainment Group claimed its research showed that Comcast customers who were using the Starz on Demand service tended to reduce their purchases and rentals of movie DVDs due to the ease of using the VOD service.

Competitive Intensity

The movie rental business was intensely competitive in 2010. Netflix was growing rapidly and gaining market share. One of the most attractive appeals of Internet movie providers like Netflix,

Hulu, and iTunes was that they were a cheaper alternative to paying monthly cable fees for premium movie channels like HBO, Starz, Cinemax, and Showtime.

Local movie rental stores were rapidly losing market ground and were desperately looking for ways to stave off further declines in rental revenues. Movie Gallery, the second-largest movie rental chain, was in the process of liquidating its entire movie rental business and closing all of its store locations; Blockbuster was shutting stores by the hundreds and teetering on the edge of filing for bankruptcy. Redbox had recently entered the movie rental business with a vending-machine-based strategy whereby Redbox self-service DVD kiosks were placed in leading supermarkets, drugstores, mass merchants like Walmart, convenience stores, and fast-food restaurants like McDonald's; customers could rent new-release movie DVDs for $1 per day. Retailers with Redbox kiosks were paid a percentage of the rental revenues. In mid-2010, Redbox had deployed more than 22,000 of its vending kiosks in all states in the continental United States, Puerto Rico, and Great Britain and was aggressively pursuing efforts to put Redbox vending machines in 7,000 to 8,000 additional locations by year-end 2010.

VOD—streaming movies directly to in-home devices—seemed on the verge of becoming the fastest-growing movie rental segment. In February 2010, Walmart announced its intention to distribute movies over the Internet and had acquired Vudu, a leading provider of digital technologies that enabled the delivery of entertainment content directly to Internet-connected TVs and Blu-ray players. With Vudu technology, households with broadband Internet access and an Internet-ready TV or Blu-ray player could rent or purchase movies, typically in high definition, without needing a connected computer or cable/satellite service. Vudu had licensing agreements with almost every major movie studio and dozens of independent and international film distributors to offer approximately 16,000 movies, including the largest high-definition library of VOD movies available anywhere.

Cable companies were also going on the offensive to grow their VOD revenues. In March 2010, the Cable and Telecommunications Association for Marketing Co-op—a group that included Comcast, Time Warner, other cable providers, Sony Pictures, and Universal Pictures—announced plans to spend $30 million on an advertising campaign to expand consumer awareness of renting movies on demand and illustrate how easy it was for digital cable customers to make a few clicks on their remotes and have movies instantly streamed to their homes. Both Time Warner and Comcast were in the process of creating an authentication system that enabled subscribers—and only subscribers—to access their TV shows and films online. As a defensive move, HBO (a subsidiary of Time Warner) had recently announced the launch of HBO Go, a video streaming service.

NETFLIX'S BUSINESS MODEL AND STRATEGY

Since launching the company's online movie rental service in 1999, Reed Hastings, founder and CEO of Netflix, had diligently striven to improve on the company's service offerings and better enable the company to outcompete its movie rental competitors. Hastings's goals for Netflix were simple: to build the world's best Internet movie service and to deliver a growing subscriber base and earnings per share every year. He had personally engineered the company's creative but simple subscription-based business model and strategy that had catapulted Netflix into becoming the world's largest online entertainment subscription service and revolutionized the way that many people rented movies.

Netflix's Subscription-Based Business Model

Netflix employed a subscription-based business model. Members could choose from eight "unlimited" subscription plans:

- An $8.99 per month plan that entailed unlimited DVDs each month, one title out at a time, plus unlimited streaming.
- A $13.99 per month plan that entailed unlimited DVDs each month, two titles out at a time, plus unlimited streaming.
- A $16.99 per month plan that entailed unlimited DVDs each month, three titles out at a time, plus unlimited streaming.

- A $23.99 per month plan that entailed unlimited DVDs each month, four titles out at a time, plus unlimited streaming.
- A $29.99 per month plan that entailed unlimited DVDs each month, five titles out at a time, plus unlimited streaming.
- A $35.99 per month plan that entailed unlimited DVDs each month, six titles out at a time, plus unlimited streaming.
- A $41.99 per month plan that entailed unlimited DVDs each month, seven titles out at a time, plus unlimited streaming.
- A $47.99 per month plan that entailed unlimited DVDs each month, eight titles out at a time, plus unlimited streaming.

The company also offered a "limited" plan for $4.99 that entailed a maximum of two DVDs per month with up to two hours of video streaming to a PC or Apple Mac (this plan did not allow members to stream movies to their TV via a Netflix-ready device—as was the case with the eight unlimited plans). All new subscribers were automatically enrolled for a free one-month trial that provided full access to Netflix's whole library of 120,000 movie titles and unlimited streaming to PCs, Apple Macs, or TVs via an Internet-connected Netflix-ready device. At the end of the free trial period, members were automatically enrolled as paying subscribers, unless they canceled their subscription. All paying subscribers were billed monthly in advance. Payments were made by credit card or debit card.

The most popular plans were the $8.99, $13.99, and $16.99 plans with unlimited streaming. Subscribers could cancel at any time. Average monthly revenue per paying subscriber was $14.95 in 2007, $13.75 in 2008, and $13.30 in 2009.

Streaming content was enabled by Netflix-controlled software that could run on a variety of Netflix-ready devices, including Netflix-capable Blu-ray players, increasing numbers of Internet-connected TV models and home theater systems that were Netflix-ready, TiVo DVRs, Nintendo's Wii, Microsoft's Xbox 360, Sony's PlayStation 3, and special Netflix players made by Roku and several other electronics manufacturers. However, Netflix subscribers could enjoy Netflix streaming without the need to buy additional hardware; they could use any Windows PC (XP/Vista/7) or Intel-based Apple Mac with decent video capabilities

to access Netflix streaming directly through a Web browser and then connect a TV to the computer's video output. In mid-2010, Netflix had about 20,000 movie titles available for streaming. Streaming was highly attractive and economical because subscribers got unlimited access to thousands of hours of on-demand programming with no pay-per-view fees (beyond the chosen monthly subscription fee).

Subscribers who opted to receive movie and TV episode DVDs by mail went to Netflix's website, selected one or more movies from its DVD library, and received the movie DVDs by first-class mail generally within one business day—more than 97 percent of Netflix's subscribers lived within one-day delivery of the company 50 distribution centers (plus 50 other shipping points) located throughout the United States. Subscribers could keep a DVD for as long as they wished, with no due dates, no late fees, no shipping fees, and no pay-per-view fees. Subscribers returned DVDs via the U.S. Postal Service in a prepaid return envelope that came with each movie order.

New subscribers were drawn to try Netflix's online movie rental service because of (1) the wide selection; (2) the extensive information Netflix provided about each movie in its rental library (including critic reviews, member reviews, online trailers, and subscriber ratings); (3) the ease with which they could find and order movies; (4) Netflix's policies of no late fees and no due dates (which eliminated the hassle of getting DVDs back to local rental stores by the designated due date); (5) the convenience of being provided a postage-paid return envelope for mailing DVDs back to Netflix; and (6) the convenience of ordering and instantly watching movies streamed to their TVs or computers with no additional pay-per-view charge. Netflix had been highly rated in online retail customer satisfaction by Nielsen Online and ForeSee/FGI Research. Over 90 percent of surveyed subscribers said that they would recommend the Netflix service to a friend.

Management believed that Netflix's subscriber base consisted of three types of customers: those who liked the convenience of home delivery, bargain hunters who were enthused about being able to watch many movies for an economical monthly price, and movie buffs who wanted access to a very wide selection of films.

Exhibit 2 shows trends in Netflix's subscriber growth.

Netflix's Strategy

Netflix had a multipronged strategy to build an ever-growing subscriber base that included:

- Providing subscribers with a comprehensive selection of DVD titles.
- Acquiring new content by building and maintaining mutually beneficial relationships with entertainment video providers.
- Making it easy for subscribers to identify movies they were likely to enjoy.
- Giving subscribers a choice of watching streaming content or receiving quickly delivered DVDs by mail.
- Spending aggressively on marketing to attract subscribers and build widespread awareness of the Netflix brand and service.
- Gradually transitioning subscribers to streaming delivery rather than mail delivery as the popularity of Internet-delivered content grew.

A Comprehensive Library of Movies and TV Episodes   Since Netflix's early days, the company's strategy had been to offer subscribers a large and diverse selection of DVD titles. It was aggressive in seeking out attractive

new titles to add to its offerings. Its library had grown from some 55,000 titles in 2005 to more than 100,000 titles in 2010. The lineup included the latest Hollywood releases, releases several decades old, movie classics, independent films, hard-to-locate documentaries, TV shows, and how-to videos; Netflix's DVD library far outdistanced the selection available in local brick-and-mortar movie rental stores.

In October 2008, Netflix and Starz Entertainment, a premium movie service provider operating in the United States, announced an agreement to make movies from Starz, through its Starz Play broadband subscription movie service, available to be streamed instantly at Netflix. Access to the Starz Play service at Netflix was included with Netflix members' current monthly subscription fee. The agreement with Starz Play gave Netflix members access to an additional 2,500 movies that could be streamed directly to their TVs and boosted Netflix's library of instantly watchable movies from 12,000 to 14,500. In 2009, Netflix expanded the number of titles available for streaming by about 30 percent; management expected that the number of streaming content choices would continue to grow rapidly for the foreseeable future.

New Content Acquisition   Netflix had invested substantial resources in establishing

Exhibit 2   Subscriber Data for Netflix, 2000–2009

	2000	2005	2006	2007	2008	2009
Total subscribers at beginning of period	107,000	2,610,000	4,179,000	6,316,000	7,479,000	9,390,000
Gross subscriber additions during period	515,000	3,729,000	5,250,000	5,340,000	6,859,000	9,322,000
Subscriber cancellations during the period	330,000	2,160,000	3,113,000	4,177,000	4,948,000	6,444,000
Total subscribers at end of period	292,000	4,179,000	6,316,000	7,479,000	9,390,000	12,268,000
Net subscriber additions during the period	185,000	1,569,000	2,137,000	1,163,000	1,911,000	2,878,000
Free trial subscribers at year-end	n.a.	153,000	162,000	153,000	226,000	376,000
Subscriber acquisition cost	$49.96	$38.78	$42.94	$40.86	$29.12	$25.48

n.a. = not available

Sources: Netflix, 2009 10-K report, pp. 26 and 32, and 2003 10-K report, p. 11.

strong ties with various entertainment video providers and leveraging those ties to both expand its content library and gain access to new releases as early as possible. The company acquired new content from movie studios and distributors through direct purchases, revenue-sharing agreements, and licensing. During 2010, Netflix entered into agreements with such content providers as Universal Studios, Twentieth Century Fox, Warner Bros., Indie Films, Relativity Media, and Epix that expanded the number of movie and TV episodes in Netflix's library and, in particular, broadened the company's ability to stream movies and TV shows to subscribers. A free Netflix App for iPads became available at Apple's App Store at www.itunes.com in April 2010, allowing Netflix subscribers to instantly watch an unlimited number of TV episodes and movies streamed from Netflix to their iPads. Netflix management was firmly committed to continuing the company's longstanding strategy to expand the content options offered to subscribers; the emphasis in 2010 had been on acquiring the rights to stream greater numbers of movies and TV episodes and on expanding the number of devices to which content could be streamed. Analysts expected such emphasis would be ongoing.

Netflix acquired many of its new-release movie DVDs from studios for a low up-front fee in exchange for a commitment for a defined period either to share a percentage of its subscription revenues or to pay a fee based on content utilization. After the revenue-sharing period expired for a title, Netflix generally had the option of returning the title to the studio, purchasing the title, or destroying its copies of the title. On occasion, Netflix also purchased DVDs for a fixed fee per disc from various studios, distributors, and other suppliers. In the case of movie titles and TV episodes that were delivered to subscribers via the Internet for instant viewing, Netflix generally paid a fee to license the content for a defined period. Following expiration of the license term, Netflix either removed the content from its library of streamed offerings or negotiated extension or renewal of the license agreement.

The company's December 31, 2009, balance sheet indicated that its content had a net value of $108.8 million (after depreciation). New-release DVDs were amortized over one year; the useful life of back-library titles (some of which qualified

as classics) was amortized over three years (since the personalized movie recommendation software generated significant rentals of older titles). Some directly purchased DVDs could be sold at the end of their useful lives, but most had a salvage value of zero; during 2005–2009, Netflix's losses on the disposal of used DVDs ranged between $2 and $7 million annually.

Netflix's Convenient, Easy-to-Use Movie Selection Software   Netflix had developed proprietary software that enabled it to provide subscribers with detailed information about each title in the Netflix library as well as personalized movie recommendations every time they visited the Netflix website. The information for each title included length, rating, cast and crew, screen formats, movie trailers, plot synopses, and reviews written by Netflix editors, third parties, and subscribers. The personalized recommendations were based on a subscriber's individual likes and dislikes (determined by their rental or streaming history, their personal ratings of movies viewed, and movies on the subscriber's lists for future streamed viewing and/or mail delivery), the ratings of movie critics and other rating services, and the ratings submitted by other Netflix subscribers. Subscribers often began their search for movie titles by starting from a familiar title and then using the recommendations tool to find other titles they might enjoy.

The recommendation software had an Oracle database platform and used proprietary algorithms that organized Netflix's library of movies into clusters of similar movies and then sorted the movies in each cluster from most liked to least liked according to ratings provided by subscribers. In 2010, Netflix had more than 3 billion movie ratings from subscribers in its database and was adding new movie ratings from subscribers at the rate of about 20 million per week. Those subscribers who rated similar movies in similar clusters were categorized as like-minded viewers. When a subscriber was online and browsing through the movie selections, the software was programmed to check the clusters the subscriber had rented/viewed in the past, determine which movies the customer had yet to rent/view in that cluster, and recommend only those movies in the cluster that had been highly rated by viewers. Viewer ratings determined which available titles were displayed to a subscriber and in what order. The recommendations helped subscribers quickly create a list of DVD titles they wanted to receive by mail and/or a list indicating the titles they wished to have streamed; subscribers used these lists to specify the order in which movies would be mailed out or streamed and could alter the lists at any time. They could also reserve a copy of upcoming releases. Netflix management saw the movie recommendation tool as a quick and personalized means of helping subscribers identify titles they were likely to enjoy.

Netflix also used subscriber ratings to determine which titles to feature most prominently on the company's website, to generate lists of similar titles, and to select the promotional trailers that a subscriber would see when using the Previews feature. Netflix management believed that over 50 percent of the titles selected by subscribers came from the recommendations generated by its proprietary software. The software algorithms were thought to be particularly effective in promoting selections of lesser-known, high-quality films to subscribers who otherwise might not have discovered them in the company's massive and ever-changing collection. On average, about 85 percent of the titles in the Netflix library were rented each quarter, an indication of the effectiveness of the company's recommendation software in steering subscribers to movies of interest and achieving broader utilization of the company's entire library of titles. About 70 percent of the DVDs that Netflix shipped to subscribers during 2009 were titles that had been released to movie rental enterprises and available to subscribers for three months or longer.

A Choice of Mail Delivery versus Streaming

Until 2007–2008, when streaming technology had advanced to the point that made providing VOD a viable option, Netflix concentrated its efforts on speeding the time it took to deliver subscriber orders via mail delivery. The strategy was to establish a nationwide network of distribution centers and shipping points with the capability to deliver DVDs ordered by subscribers within one business day. To achieve quick delivery and return capability, Netflix created sophisticated software to track the location of each DVD title in inventory and determine the fastest way of getting the DVD orders to subscribers. When

a subscriber placed an order for a specific DVD, the system first looked for that DVD at the shipping center closest to the customer. If that center didn't have the DVD in stock, the system then checked for availability at the next closest center. The search continued until the DVD was found, at which point the regional distribution center with the ordered DVD in inventory was provided with the information needed to initiate the order fulfillment and shipping process. If the DVD was unavailable anywhere in the system, it was waitlisted. The software system then moved to the customer's next choice and the process started over. And no matter where the DVD was sent from, the system knew to print the return label on the prepaid envelope to send the DVDs to the shipping center closest to the customer to reduce return mail times and permit more efficient use of Netflix's DVD inventory. No subscriber orders were shipped on holidays or weekends.

By early 2007, Netflix had 50 regional distribution centers and another 50 shipping points scattered across the United States, giving it one-business-day delivery capability for 95 percent of its subscribers and, in most cases, also enabling one-day return times. As of 2010, additional improvements in Netflix's distribution and shipping network had resulted in one-business-day delivery capability for 98 percent of Netflix's subscribers.

In 2007, when entertainment studios became more willing to allow Internet delivery of their content (since recent technological advances prevented streamed movies from being pirated), Netflix moved quickly to better compete with the growing numbers of VOD providers by adding the feature of unlimited streaming to its regular monthly subscription plans. The market for Internet delivery of media content consisted of three segments: the rental of Internet-delivered content, the download-to-own segment, and the advertising-supported online delivery segment (mainly YouTube and Hulu). Netflix's objective was to be the clear leader in the rental segment via its Watch Instantly feature.

Giving subscribers the option of watching DVDs delivered by mail or instantly watching movies streamed to subscribers' computers or TVs had considerable strategic appeal to Netflix in two respects. First, giving subscribers the option to order and instantly watch streamed content put Netflix in position to compete head-to-head with the growing numbers of VOD providers. Second, providing streamed content to subscribers had the attraction of being cheaper than (1) paying the postage on DVD orders and returns, (2) having to obtain and manage an ever-larger inventory of DVDs, and (3) covering the labor costs of additional distribution center personnel to fill a growing volume of DVD orders and handle increased numbers of returned DVDs. But streaming content to subscribers was not cost-free; it required server capacity, software to authenticate orders from subscribers, and a system of computers containing copies of the content files placed at various points in a network so as to maximize bandwidth and allow subscribers to access a copy of the file on a server near the subscriber. Having subscribers accessing a central server ran the risk of an Internet transmission bottleneck. Netflix also used third-party content delivery networks to help it efficiently stream movies and TV episodes in high volume to Netflix subscribers over the Internet.

By combining streaming and DVDs-by-mail as part of the Netflix subscription, Netflix was able to offer members a uniquely compelling selection of movies for one low monthly price. Netflix executives believed this created a competitive advantage as compared to a postal-delivery-only or Internet-delivery-only subscription service. Furthermore, management believed that Netflix's combination postal-streaming subscription service delivered compelling customer value and customer satisfaction by eliminating the hassle involved in making trips to local movie rental stores to choose and return rented DVDs.

Marketing and Advertising   Netflix used multiple marketing channels to attract subscribers, including online advertising (paid search listings, banner ads, text on popular sites such as AOL and Yahoo, and permission-based e-mails), radio stations, regional and national television, direct mail, and print ads. It also participated in a variety of cooperative advertising programs with studios through which Netflix received cash consideration in return for featuring a studio's movies in its advertising. Most recently, Netflix had begun working closely with the makers of Netflix-ready electronics devices to help generate new subscribers for its service.

Advertising campaigns of one type or another were under way more or less continuously, with the lure of one-month free trials usually being the prominent ad feature. Advertising expenses totaled approximately $205.9 million in 2009, $181.4 million in 2008, and $207.9 million in 2007. Netflix management believed that its paid advertising efforts were significantly enhanced by the benefits of word-of-mouth advertising, the referrals of satisfied subscribers, and its active public relations programs.

Management had boosted marketing expenditures of all kinds (including paid advertising) from $25.7 million in 2000 (16.8 percent of revenues) to $142.0 million in 2005 (20.8 percent of revenues) to $218.2 million in 2007 (18.1 percent of revenues). When the recession hit in late 2007 and 2008, management trimmed 2008 marketing expenditures to $199.7 million (14.6 percent of revenues) as a cost-containment measure, but in 2009 marketing expenditures resumed their upward trend, climbing to $237.7 million (14.2 percent of revenues).

Transitioning to Internet Delivery of Content   In early 2010, Netflix had two primary strategic objectives: (1) to continue to grow a large subscription business and (2) to gradually migrate subscribers from postal delivery of DVDs to Internet-based delivery of content as the popularity of Internet-delivery grew. Top executives at Netflix expected that Internet delivery of media content would surpass postal delivery within three to seven years and that eventually postal delivery would account for a relatively small fraction of Netflix's business.

NETFLIX'S PERFORMANCE AND PROSPECTS

Recent financial statement data for Netflix are shown in Exhibits 3 and 4. Management's latest forecast called for having between 15.5 million and 16.3 million subscribers by year-end 2010, full-year 2010 revenues of $2.11 billion to $2.16 billion, and diluted earnings per share of $2.41 to $2.63. The company announced a $100 million program to repurchase shares of its common

Exhibit 3   Netflix's Consolidated Statements of Operations, 2000–2009
($ millions, except per share data)

	2000	2005	2006	2007	2008	2009
Revenues	$ 35.9	$682.2	$996.7	$1,205.3	$1,364.7	$1,670.3
Cost of revenues:						
Subscription costs	24.9	393.8	532.6	664.4	761.1	909.5
Fulfillment expenses	10.2	72.0	94.4	121.3	149.1	169.8
Total cost of revenues	35.1	465.8	627.0	786.2	910.2	1,079.3
Gross profit	0.8	216.4	369.7	419.2	454.4	591.0
Operating expenses						
Technology and development	16.8	35.4	48.4	71.0	89.9	114.5
Marketing	25.7	144.6	225.5	218.2	199.7	237.7
General and administrative	7.0	35.5	36.2	52.4	49.7	51.3
Stock-based compensation*	9.7	—	—	—	—	—
Gain (loss) on disposal of DVDs	—	(2.0)	(4.8)	(7.2)	(6.3)	(4.6)
Gain on legal settlement	—	—	—	(7.0)	—	—
Total operating expenses	59.2	213.4	305.3	327.4	332.9	399.1
Operating income	(58.4)	3.0	64.4	91.8	121.5	191.9
Interest and other income (expense)	(0.2)	5.3	15.9	20.1	10.0	0.3
Income before income taxes	—	8.3	80.3	110.9	131.5	192.2
Provision for (benefit from) income taxes	—	(33.7)	31.2	44.3	48.5	76.3
Net income	$(58.5)	$42.0	$49.1	$66.7	$83.0	$115.9
Net income per share:						
Basic	$(20.61)	$0.79	$0.78	$0.99	$1.36	$2.05
Diluted	(20.61)	0.64	0.71	0.97	1.32	1.98
Weighted-average common shares outstanding:						
Basic	2.8	53.5	62.6	67.1	61.0	56.6
Diluted	2.8	65.5	69.1	68.9	62.8	58.4

Note: Totals may not add due to rounding.

*Stock-based compensation costs for 2005–2009 totaled $14.3 million in 2005, $12.7 million in 2006, $12.0 million in 2007, $12.3 million in 2008, and $12.6 million in 2009; these costs were allocated to fulfillment expenses, technology and development, marketing, and general and administrative based on the area of Netflix's business in which the personnel receiving the stock option awards were employed. Thus, the amounts shown in the line-item expenses for fulfillment, technology and development, marketing, and general and administrative for 2005–2009 include their respective allocation of stock-based compensation costs.

Source: Netflix, 10-K reports for 2003, 2006, and 2009.

stock in April 2007. A second stock repurchase program involving the expenditure of $100 million was announced in January 2008, and in March 2008 Netflix's board of directors authorized a third repurchase program to spend an additional $150 million to buy back shares during the remainder of 2008. A fourth program to repurchase shares was announced in January 2009; it resulted in expenditures of $175 million. In August 2009, the company's board of directors authorized expenditures of up to $300 million to

repurchase shares of common stock through the end of 2010. As of early 2010, these programs had resulted in the repurchase of more than 20 million shares; the net reduction in shares outstanding was less than 20 million shares because of the issuance of new shares under the company's stock-based compensation program for executives and employees. In June 2010, Netflix's Board of Directors approved a stock repurchase program authorizing the repurchase of up to $300 million in common stock through the end of 2012.

Exhibit 4 **Selected Balance Sheet and Cash Flow Data for Netflix, 2000–2009 (in millions of $)**

	2000	2005	2006	2007	2008	2009
Selected Balance Sheet Data						
Cash and cash equivalents	$ 14.9	$212.3	$400.4	$177.4	$139.9	$134.2
Short-term investments	—	—	—	207.7	157.4	186.0
Current assets	n.a.	243.7	428.4	432.4	358.9	416.5
Net investment in DVD library	n.a.	57.0	104.9	112.1	98.5	108.8
Total assets	52.5	364.7	608.8	679.0	617.9	679.7
Current liabilities	n.a.	137.6	193.4	208.9	216.0	226.4
Working capital*	(1.7)	106.1	235.0	223.5	142.9	190.1
Stockholders equity	(73.3)	226.3	414.2	429.8	347.2	199.1
Cash Flow Data						
Net cash provided by operating activities	$(22.7)	$ 157.5	$247.9	$277.4	$284.0	$325.1
Net cash used in investing activities	(25.0)	(133.2)	(185.9)	(436.0)	(145.0)	(246.1)
Net cash provided by financing activities	48.4	13.3	126.2	(64.4)	176.6	(84.6)

*Defined as current assets minus current liabilities.

Sources: Netflix, 10-K reports for 2003, 2005, 2007, 2008, and 2009.

BLOCKBUSTER'S SURVIVAL STRATEGY

Despite its troubles, Blockbuster remained the global leader in the movie rental industry in 2010, with nearly 47 million customers served daily in 18 countries. As of January 2010, it provided content to customers via rentals at some 6,500 store locations (1,300 of which were operated by franchisees), mail delivery, online delivery, digital download, and 2,225 vending machine kiosks. In 2009, it had an estimated 37 percent share of the roughly $8.1 billion U.S. market for renting movies for in-home viewing and a globally recognized brand in movie rentals.

Blockbuster recorded net losses of $2.8 billion during the 2003–2005 period; earned a modest $39.2 million after-tax profit in 2006; and lost $85.1 million in 2007, $385.4 million in 2008, and $569.3 million in 2009. Total revenues dropped from $5.1 billion in 2008 to $4.1 billion in 2009, a decline of 19.6 percent. In February 2010, Standard & Poor's downgraded Blockbuster's corporate credit rating to CCC from B–, with a negative outlook; four weeks later, Standard & Poor's

downgraded the company's credit rating again, this time to CC. In March 2010, Moody's downgraded both Blockbuster's probability of default rating and its corporate family rating to Caa3 from Caa1, with a negative outlook.

Blockbuster's financial troubles were in part attributable to the terms of its October 2004 split-off from media conglomerate Viacom (Viacom had acquired Blockbuster in 1994 for $8.4 billion), which entailed Blockbuster paying a special one-time $5 dividend (totaling $905 million) to all shareholders, including Viacom (which owned 81.5 percent of Blockbuster's shares prior to the divestiture deal). The $905 million cash dividend payment and other aspects of the spin-off forced Blockbuster to take on long-term debt of more than $1 billion, drove the company's annual interest expenses up to around $100 million annually, and severely limited the financial resources available for overcoming sluggish sales and eroding movie rentals that Blockbuster was already experiencing at its stores. In July 2007, James F. Keyes, former president and CEO of 7-Eleven, was appointed to replace John F. Antioco, who had served as Blockbuster's CEO since 1997. Keyes quickly initiated a series of efforts to recast Blockbuster's strategy and put the company in better position to improve its dismal bottom-line performance. But Keyes's initial strategy overhaul met with limited success and failed to turn the company's financial performance around.

In a second attempt to stem the bleeding, conserve cash, and get the company back on track, Blockbuster executives launched another round of strategic initiatives in 2009–2010:

- Selling the company's 184-store subsidiary in Ireland during the third quarter of 2009.

- Closing 470 underperforming Blockbuster stores in the first four months of 2010, on the heels of having closed 586 company-owned stores (and 299 franchised stores) in 2009.

- Going forward with plans to close an additional 81 stores by year-end 2010.

- Continuing to increase the size of its library of movie, TV episode, and video game titles. (The library included more than 125,000 titles as of May 2010.)

- Pursuing rapid expansion of the Blockbuster-branded vending machine kiosk network from 2,225 locations to 10,000 locations by the end of 2010. Seeking to expand its revenues from DVD rentals, Blockbuster entered into a strategic alliance with NCR in August 2008 to place vending machines containing a limited selection of movie DVDs in high-traffic locations; the kiosks were owned and operated by NCR, which also controlled the pricing and location of the kiosks. Blockbuster was responsible for providing the DVD titles that were older than 26 weeks past their release dates on a consignment basis and received 50 percent of the rental revenue from these titles. NCR was responsible for providing the DVDs for newer titles and paid Blockbuster a license fee of 1 to 10 percent of net revenues, depending on the monthly revenues of each individual kiosk and the total number of kiosks deployed. Blockbuster's share of the revenues from the vending machine kiosk locations in place during the first three months of 2010 was less than $5 million. In May 2010, NCR had deployed over 4,000 Blockbuster Express kiosks and plans were proceeding to deploy an additional 6,000 kiosks by year-end.

- Instituting new in-store and online merchandising techniques and graphics packages to make it easier for prospective renters to make decisions on their entertainment selections and thereby reduce the store walkout rate and browse-but-don't-rent rate at the Blockbuster website.

- Giving Blockbuster Online subscribers the option of exchanging their DVDs through the mail or returning them to a nearby Blockbuster store in exchange for free in-store movie rentals.

- Instituting a Blockbuster Rewards program that offered in-store benefits to members and encouraged them to rent movies and games only from Blockbuster stores.

- Introducing Direct Access whereby in-store customers could access Blockbuster's by-mail inventory and have DVD titles shipped directly to their homes.

- Increasing store remodeling efforts in select locations. (The remodeling typically entailed brighter paint, lower shelves, and new merchandising displays.)

- Renegotiating the leases for 2,036 stores in the United States in 2009 and the first four months of 2010 to significantly reduce future store occupancy costs.

- Instituting a higher daily rental rate for each day a customer chose to keep a rental following the initial rental period.

- Selling the DVD inventories of titles that were rented infrequently.

- Curtailing non-essential or discretionary capital expenditures in 2010 and lengthening the payment cycle to certain vendors.

- Further reducing selling, general, and administrative expenses in 2010.

- Aggressively exploring options to sell, license, or divest some of the company's international operations.

- Suspending the payment of 7½ percent dividends on the company's Series A convertible preferred stock for five consecutive quarterly periods beginning February 15, 2009, and ending May 14, 2010. Suspension of the dividend payment for further quarters was expected because, under Delaware law (the state where Blockbuster was incorporated),

Blockbuster could only pay preferred stock dividends out of either net profits or a surplus of net assets over the aggregate par value of the outstanding shares of capital stock. As of April 2010, Blockbuster had no net profits and its capital surplus was negative.

So far, the results of these initiatives had done little to brighten Blockbuster's increasingly dismal outlook; however, management believed that the forthcoming Movie Gallery store closings would favorably affect rental revenues at hundreds of Blockbuster locations during the remainder of 2010. In the first quarter of 2010, Blockbuster's total revenues were 13.5 percent below the levels of a year earlier, and the company posted a quarterly net loss of $67.1 million (as compared to a net profit of $24.9 million in the first quarter of 2009)—see Exhibit 5. Blockbuster management attributed the revenue decline

Exhibit 5   Blockbuster's Consolidated Statement of Operations, First Quarter 2010 versus First Quarter 2009 and Fiscal Years 2007–2009 ($ millions, except per share amounts)

	Thirteen Weeks Ended		Fiscal Year Ended		
	April 4, 2010	April 5, 2009	January 3, 2010	January 3, 2009	January 3, 2008
Revenues					
Base rental revenues	$598.7	$704.9	$2,528.0	$3,166.5	$3,353.7
Previously rented product ("PRP") revenues	120.9	138.3	557.9	619.8	649.9
Merchandise sales	215.1	236.7	956.1	1,246.9	1,251.2
Other revenues	4.7	6.0	20.4	32.2	59.2
Total revenues	939.4	1,085.9	4,062.4	5,065.4	5,314.0
Cost of sales					
Cost of rental revenues	270.1	309.9	1,130.6	1,446.7	1,584.0
Cost of merchandise sold	167.1	202.7	753.6	988.4	956.3
Total cost of sales	437.2	512.6	1,884.2	2,435.1	2,540.3
Gross profit	502.2	573.3	2,178.2	2,630.3	2,773.7
Operating expenses					
General and administrative	484.4	477.9	1,928.7	2,235.3	2,454.9
Advertising	21.0	11.5	91.4	117.7	190.5
Depreciation and intangible amortization	26.2	33.7	144.1	146.6	180.3
Impairment of goodwill and other long-lived assets	—		369.2	435.0	2.2
Gain on sale of Gamestation	—		—	—	(81.5)
Total operating expenses	531.6	523.1	2,533.4	2,934.6	2,746.4
Operating income (loss)	(29.4)	50.2	(355.2)	(304.3)	27.3
Interest expense	(33.2)	(17.5)	(111.6)	(72.9)	(88.2)
Loss on extinguishment of debt			(29.9)	—	—
Interest income	—	0.2	1.3	2.4	6.4
Other items, net	(1.6)	(0.8)	(10.4)	16.3	(1.3)
Income (loss) from continuing operations before income taxes	(64.2)	32.1	(505.8)	(358.5)	(55.8)
Provision for income taxes	(1.1)	(5.5)	(11.8)	(24.4)	(28.4)

(Continued)

Exhibit 5   *(Concluded)*

	Thirteen Weeks Ended		Fiscal Year Ended		
	April 4, 2010	April 5, 2009	January 3, 2010	January 3, 2009	January 3, 2008
Income (loss) from continuing operations before income taxes	(65.3)	26.6	(517.6)	(382.9)	(84.2)
Income (loss) from discontinued operations, net of tax	(0.1)	1.1	(40.6)	8.8	10.4
Net income (loss)	(65.4)	27.7	(558.2)	(374.1)	(73.8)
Preferred stock dividends	(1.7)	(2.8)	(11.1)	(11.3)	(11.3)
Net income (loss) applicable to common stockholders	$(67.1)	$24.9	$(569.3)	$(385.4)	$(85.1)
Net income (loss) per common share:					
Basic	$(0.33)	$0.13	$(2.93)	$(2.01)	$(0.45)
Diluted	$(0.33)	$0.12	$(2.93)	$(2.01)	$(0.45)
Weighted-average common shares outstanding (in millions):					
Basic	202.9	192.7	194.1	191.8	190.3
Diluted	202.9	222.8	194.1	191.8	190.3

Source: Blockbuster's 10-Q report, May 14, 2010, and 2009 10-K report, p. 79.

to increased competitive pressures. Long-term debt (including the current portion) as of April 4, 2010, was $895.4 million, resulting in first-quarter 2010 interest expenses of $33.2 million. The company's cash and cash equivalents had dwindled to $109.9 million—see Exhibit 6.

In May 2010, Blockbuster's common stock was trading in the $0.35 to $0.45 range, down from a high of $10 in 2004 and a high of $6.87 in 2007. Because Blockbuster's stock price had remained below $1 per share for well over a month—a violation of New York Stock Exchange

Exhibit 6   Blockbuster's Consolidated Balance Sheets, April 4 and January 3, 2010, and January 4, 2009 ($ millions, except per share amounts)

	April 4, 2010	January 3, 2010	January 4, 2009
Assets			
Current assets:			
Cash and cash equivalents	$ 109.9	$ 188.7	$ 154.9
Receivables, less allowances of $5.1 and $6.0 for 2010 and 2009, respectively	55.6	79.4	117.1
Merchandise inventories	255.2	298.5	432.8
Rental library, net	319.3	340.7	355.8
Deferred income taxes	13.7	13.6	13.4
Prepaid and other current assets	126.9	139.1	184.6
Total current assets	880.6	1,060.0	1,258.6
Property and equipment, net	238.4	249.4	406.0
Deferred income taxes	110.0	114.6	124.3
Intangibles, net	7.5	7.7	11.5

(Continued)

Exhibit 6   *(Concluded)*

	April 4, 2010	January 3, 2010	January 4, 2009
Restricted cash	35.8	58.5	—
Other assets	46.5	48.1	16.0
Total assets	$1,318.8	$1,538.3	$2,154.5
Liabilities and Stockholders' Equity (Deficit)			
Current liabilities:			
Accounts payable	$ 206.6	$ 300.8	$ 427.3
Accrued expenses	390.8	407.7	493.8
Current portion of long-term debt	79.4	101.6	198.0
Current portion of capital lease obligations	5.7	6.1	8.5
Deferred income taxes	114.0	118.6	125.8
Total current liabilities	796.5	934.8	1,253.4
Long-term debt, less current portion	816.0	836.0	538.0
Capital lease obligations, less current portion	18.5	19.9	28.3
Other liabilities	62.0	61.9	75.5
Total liabilities	1,693.0	1,852.6	1,940.2
Stockholders' equity:			
Preferred stock, par value $0.01 per share; 100 shares authorized; .072 and 0.146 shares issued and outstanding for 2010 and 2009, respectively, with a liquidation preference of $1,000 per share	71.7	145.9	150.0
Class A common stock, par value $0.01 per share; 400 shares authorized; 137.7 and 122.4 shares issued and outstanding for 2010 and 2009	1.4	1.3	1.2
Class B common stock, par value $0.01 per share; 500 shares authorized; 72.0 shares issued and outstanding for 2010 and 2009	0.7	0.7	0.7
Additional paid-in capital	5,453.8	5,377.0	5,378.4
Accumulated deficit	(5,852.3)	(5,786.9)	(5,228.7)
Accumulated other comprehensive loss	(49.5)	(52.3)	(87.3)
Total stockholders' equity (deficit)	(374.2)	(314.3)	214.3
Total liabilities and stockholders' equity	$1,318.8	$1,538.3	$2,154.5

Source: Blockbuster's 10-Q report, May 14, 2010, and 2009 10-K report, p. 80.

(NYSE) requirements for listing—the NYSE delisted Blockbuster's stock in June 2010.

As of October 2010, the company was continuing to operate its stores and kiosks in the United States as it reorganized under bankruptcy protection; Blockbuster's operations outside the United States and domestic and international franchisees were not part of the Chapter 11 reorganization. In its September 2010 bankruptcy filing, Blockbuster said that it had reached agreement with its bondholders on a recapitalization plan to reduce its debt from about $1 billion to about $100 million or less by swapping debt for shares of the company's common stock. Blockbuster's largest creditors included the Bank of New York Mellon, Twentieth Century Fox Home Entertainment, Warner Home Video, Sony Pictures Home Entertainment, The Walt Disney Co., Universal Studios Home Entertainment, and other movie studios. Analysts predicted that Blockbuster management would likely be forced to close additional Blockbuster stores beyond the 470 stores closed in early 2010 in order to restore company profitability.

Redbox's Strategy in the Movie Rental Industry

Arthur A. Thompson
The University of Alabama

Spotting what it believed was a promising opportunity in the self-service DVD rental business, Redbox in 2004 began deploying vending machine kiosks containing mostly new release movie DVDs in high-traffic shopping locations. The idea was that people could be easily enticed to rent movies at a place where they shopped regularly rather than making a special trip to a local movie rental store, especially if the rental fee was dirt cheap. Redbox charged a rental fee of $1 per day, and rented DVDs could be returned to Redbox kiosks at any location. Customers could also purchase new and used movie DVDs; Redbox's typical price for a previously rented DVD was $7. As of May 2010, Redbox had deployed 22,400 of its vending kiosks at locations in all states in the continental United States, Puerto Rico, and the United Kingdom. In the late-afternoon and early-evening hours of a typical Friday and Saturday in 2009, Redbox processed 70 to 80 rental transactions per second. It rented more than 365 million DVDs in 2009 and generated revenues of $773.5 million from rentals and sales of DVDs at its kiosks. On New Year's Eve 2009, Redbox rented a record-breaking 2 million DVDs. Redbox estimated that its share of the DVD rental market in the United States was 16.8 percent at the end of 2009, up from about 9 percent at the beginning of the year, with virtually all of the market share gains coming from rentals taken away from Blockbuster, Movie Gallery, and other local video rental outlets.

COMPANY BACKGROUND

Redbox was a wholly owned and operated subsidiary of Coinstar Inc., which, in addition to its Redbox movie rental business, was also a leading provider of money transfer services and self-service coin-counting kiosks where people could convert coins to cash, a gift-card, or e-certificates, among other options. In 2010, Coinstar products and services could be found at more than 80,000 points of presence, including supermarkets, drugstores, mass merchants, financial institutions, convenience stores, restaurants, and money transfer agent locations. Coinstar was incorporated in Delaware in 1993 and maintained its corporate headquarters in Bellevue, Washington; Redbox operated out of offices in Oakbrook Terrace, Illinois.

Redbox Automated Retail LLC began operations in 2004 with funding provided by McDonald's Ventures, a subsidiary of McDonald's Corporation. The initial Redbox vending machines were placed in a number of McDonald's fast-food restaurants. In 2005, Coinstar purchased a 47.3 percent ownership interest in Redbox. In January 2008, Coinstar exercised its option to acquire a majority ownership interest in the voting equity of Redbox Automated Retail, paying $5.1 million to boost its ownership share to 51.0 percent. Then in February 2009, Coinstar purchased the remaining ownership interests in Redbox for approximately $162.4 million.[1] At the time of the February 2009 acquisition, Redbox had some 12,000 kiosks in supermarkets, Walgreens and other drugstores, and select Walmart and McDonald's locations, with plans to add 6,000 to 8,000 kiosk locations during the remainder of 2009. Coinstar's own DVDXpress vending machine business (which was acquired in 2007) had an additional 1,700 kiosk installations. After acquiring full ownership of Redbox, Coinstar continued to operate DVDXpress and Redbox Automated Retail as separate subsidiaries.

Purchasing 100 percent ownership in Redbox, as opposed to remaining a minority owner, appealed to Coinstar executives for five reasons:

- Revenue growth at Redbox kiosks was attractive (reaching an average of $50,000 per kiosk after three years). Although many kiosks had been installed only a short while, sales growth at kiosks installed longer than one year averaged 52 percent in 2008 and 28 percent during 2009.
- The projected return on Coinstar's investment in Redbox was attractively high.
- Feedback from Redbox customers was quite positive.[2] Customers were attracted by the low price of $1 per day, ease of use, convenience, selection, the option of returning a rented DVD to any Redbox kiosk, and the online reservation feature guaranteeing in-stock status for a reserved DVD.
- In two of Redbox's oldest markets—Denver and Houston—there were indications that Redbox could capture as much as a 20 percent share of the DVD rental business in localities with good density of well-located Redbox kiosks.
- Survey data indicated that 80 percent of Redbox customers would recommend the service to a friend.

Coinstar reported 2009 consolidated revenues of $1.14 billion and net income of $53.6 million. Revenues from Redbox's operations accounted for 67.6 percent of Coinstar's 2009 revenues.

Interestingly, Greg Meyer, the cofounder and CEO of DVDXpress prior to its acquisition by Coinstar, had contacted Blockbuster in 2005, offering to partner with Blockbuster in setting up DVD rental machines outside Blockbuster stores. In his proposal, Meyer stated that by his calculations Blockbuster could save $140 million in store operating costs by shortening the number of hours Blockbuster stores were open and having customer get DVDs at vending machines located just outside its stores. Meyer never heard back on his offer. After selling DVDXpress to Coinstar in 2007, Meyer remained as Coinstar's managing director for the DVDXpress division until Coinstar acquired Redbox in 2009. Since leaving Coinstar, Meyer had purchased 645,000 shares of Blockbuster and in early 2010 submitted a proxy notice to Blockbuster shareholders seeking to replace board member James Crystal; Blockbuster's CEO, James Keyes, had expressed his opposition to Meyer's election, stating that stock ownership was insufficient grounds for board membership.

REDBOX'S STRATEGY

Redbox's strategy centered on (1) attracting customers with a combination of low price and convenience and (2) rapidly expanding the number of shopping locations with a Redbox kiosk. Its vending machines supplied the same functionality as a local video rental store, albeit with a smaller selection. But its $1 per day rental price was considerably cheaper than the $4.50 rental fee charged by many movie rental outlets. And the convenience of picking up a rental at a Redbox machine had considerable appeal—in mid-2009 Redbox's CEO, Mitch Lowe, estimated that every week 150 million people walked within 10 feet of one of Redbox's nearly 20,000 locations.[3] Lowe said, "The way we'll grow is by focusing on the customer experience. That's how we have come out of nowhere."[4] If a customer knew what movie title he or she wanted to rent, the rental process could be completed in less than a minute. All a customer had to do was use a touch screen to select a DVD from as many as 200 different titles, swipe a valid credit or debit card, retrieve the DVD from the dispenser slot, and leave. Returns could be completed in 20 seconds or less at an unoccupied machine. The rental and return process was designed to be fast, efficient, and fully automated, with no membership fees. Exhibit 1 shows examples of Redbox kiosks and the features of the company's vending machine rental process.

Exhibit 1   Renting a DVD at Redbox

Redbox machines read bar codes on each DVD to track when it went out on rental and when it was returned. Redbox maintained constant electronic contact with every Redbox machine (primarily via cell phone transmissions) to monitor how many copies of each title were in a given machine at any one time—machines could hold 630 discs representing up to 200 titles. The company's inventory monitoring system enabled it to give customers the option of going to Redbox's website to see what was in stock at nearby Redbox locations and reserve a DVD at a particular machine. In February 2010, Redbox executives said that the free Redbox iPhone app (which enabled customers to use an iPhone to reserve a DVD) had been downloaded more than 1 million times since its launch in November 2009. Renters could keep a DVD for as long as they wished at the $1 per day charge. After 25 days and a charge of $25, they could keep the DVD; in mid-2009, Redbox management indicated that about 10 percent did so.[5]

Since acquiring full ownership of Redbox in early 2009, Coinstar management had been aggressive in continuing to deploy additional vending machine kiosks—see Exhibit 2. The company planned to install 7,000 to 8,000 new kiosks in 2010, of which some 2,400 had been deployed by April 1, 2010. Plans called for capital expenditures of $115 million to $125 million for new kiosk locations.[6] Redbox kiosks were already in place at select store locations of such chains as Walgreens, Walmart, McDonald's, 7-Eleven, Kroger, and Albertson's. Redbox kiosks were also located at select airports and libraries and within such landmark locations as the Pentagon, the Empire State Building in New York City, and the Willis Tower in Chicago. Most recently, Redbox had negotiated arrangements to locate 86 kiosks at navy exchange stores on 48 or more of the naval bases in the continental United States and Hawaii, put kiosks in 100 Schnuck Markets stores in 7 states, and expand its presence to more than 281 of Kum & Go's 430+ convenience stores in 11 states.

Most Redbox kiosks were located in the area between a retail store's cash registers and front entrance. In many instances, retailers had historically generated little revenue from this space, which made it appealing to put a potentially high-traffic Redbox kiosk in that space (perhaps along with a Coinstar self-service coin-counting machine and/or a Coinstar electronic money transfer service) and better optimize revenue per square foot. Inside-the-store Redbox kiosks occupied an area of less than 10 square feet; outside locations were slightly larger.

The ease with which Redbox had, so far, been able to secure additional retail locations for its DVD rental kiosks went beyond just the attractive revenue stream that a Redbox kiosk produced for the retailer and the buzz that Redbox was generating among retailers interested in boosting customer traffic in their stores. It also had to do with Coinstar's ability to capitalize on the relationships it had previously established with many retail chains and its expertise in developing, deploying, and operating kiosks in retail settings. Prior to Coinstar's acquisition of Redbox, Coinstar had been well-known among many multistore retailers because of its track record in supplying them with other proven ways to generate revenues from the area between their cash registers and front entrances and also to boost store traffic. For example, Coinstar had 19,200 self-service coin-counting kiosks and 49,000 automated money transfer service locations at year-end 2009, a substantial fraction of which were in retail establishments. Coinstar had built productive business relationships with many chain retailers in the course of securing these locations, and the data from its coin-counting kiosks and money transfer locations provided valuable insight into which of its current retail partners and which of their locations were likely to be the most revenue-productive places to deploy a Redbox kiosk. The recent deployment

Exhibit 2   **Number of Redbox and DVDXpress Kiosk Locations, 2006–2010**

Time Period	Total Number of Installed Redbox and DVDXpress Kiosks
Year-end 2006	2,200
Year-end 2007	7,000
Year-end 2008	13,700
Year-end 2009	22,400
March 31, 2010	24,800

Source: Coinstar's 10-Q and 10-K reports, various periods.

of Redbox kiosks at the locations of retailers that also had coin-counting and/or money transfer services in some of their stores had made some of its partnerships with retailers of prime importance. For instance, Walmart, Walgreens, Kroger, and Supervalu (the parent company of Albertson's and other grocery chains) accounted for a combined 44.7 percent of Coinstar's total revenues in 2009; McDonald's accounted for an additional 9.0 percent of Coinstar's 2009 revenues.

Redbox management foresaw opportunities to deploy thousands of additional kiosks and to capture a meaningful portion of the customers displaced by the closing of so many Blockbuster, Movie Gallery, Hollywood Video, and other movie rental outlets. The store closures meant that Redbox's growth was not dependent on the DVD rental market continuing to grow or even remain flat—Redbox could grow in a stagnating market by simply getting many DVD rental outlet customers to patronize a Redbox kiosk instead.

KIOSK ECONOMICS

Each Redbox kiosk had an installed cost of about $15,000. Requests from retailers for Redbox installations far exceeded the numbers that Redbox actually installed, chiefly because the estimated rental revenues at some retailer locations were not deemed high enough to cover operating costs and also meet Redbox management's strict internal rate of return (IRR) hurdle. Redbox executives closely monitored the density of kiosk locations in each geographic market where kiosks had been installed. Even in markets with the densest number of kiosk locations, the deployed machines generated internal rates of return on investment well above the company's cost of capital, although high-density geographic markets did have slightly lower IRRs than the average kiosk.[7]

Experience indicated that annual rental revenues at machines installed in a location for three years or more tended to top out at around $50,000. Retailers were paid a percentage of the revenue collected at kiosks located in their stores. Redbox vending machines were assigned a useful life of five years and were depreciated on a straight-line basis.

Redbox paid about $18 for a DVD and rented a DVD about 15 times at an average of $2 per transaction.[8] Redbox sold about 3 percent of its previously rented DVDs to customers for about $7. It typically sold about half of its used DVD copies at the end of their rental life to certain wholesale distributors at a negotiated price; the sell-back prices averaged about $4 per disc in 2009. The rest were destroyed. The DVD discs that Redbox acquired for its library were initially recorded at cost and were amortized over an assumed useful life to their estimated salvage value. Estimated salvage value was based on the amounts that Redbox had historically recovered on selling DVDs at the end of their useful rental lives. The amortization charges were accelerated to reflect higher rentals of the DVD in the first few weeks after release, and substantially all of the amortization expense was recognized within one year of the assumed life of the DVDs.

CONTENT ACQUISITION AND LICENSE AGREEMENTS

Redbox obtained copies of DVD titles through licensing arrangements with movie studios, wholesale distributors, and third-party retailers. Redbox's relationships with several movie studios had been contentious, in some cases resulting in Redbox instituting litigation to combat the refusal of Universal Studios, 20th Century Fox, and Warner Bros. to sell their movie DVDs to Redbox for rental purposes until 30 to 45 days after the release of movie DVDs to retailers. Such delays forced Redbox to try to obtain those DVD titles from alternative sources—including buying copies from retailers at the regular retail price. The delayed rental window imposed on Redbox by these movie studios raised Redbox's title acquisition costs and impaired its ability to stock its vending machines with ample copies of new releases; indeed, some retailers (Walmart, for example) had limited the number of copies of new releases they would sell to Redbox.

Redbox management estimated that during 2009 its inability to secure ample copies of certain titles resulted in lost rental revenues of $15 to $25 million.[9] The revenue loss would have been greater had it not been for Redbox's ability to track disc title inventories in real time at each vending location and use this information to guide Redbox's field staff in moving copies of discs from machine to machine in order to improve title availability rates at particular Redbox locations. In addition to the revenue losses associated with not having enough copies of certain titles, Redbox incurred incremental costs of $1 to $2 per DVD to purchase the disc copies it was able to obtain. However, Redbox had recently succeeded in negotiating license agreements with six prominent movie studios establishing the terms on which Redbox would be entitled to obtain copies of their DVDs:[10]

- *Sony agreement:* In July 2009, Redbox entered into a licensing agreement with Sony Pictures Home Entertainment that called for Redbox to receive deliveries of new releases by the "street date," defined in the agreement as the initial date the titles became available on a rental basis to the general public for in-home entertainment viewing. Under terms of the agreement, Redbox would license specified minimum quantities of each new release and would pay Sony an estimated $487 million during the term of the agreement, which was expected to last from July 1, 2009, until September 30, 2014. However, at Sony's discretion, the agreement was subject to termination as early as September 30, 2011. In addition to the $487 million payment by Redbox over the expected five-year life of the agreement, Coinstar granted 193,348 shares of restricted common stock to Sony. Sony became entitled to 19,335 of these shares on December 31, 2009, and was scheduled to receive additional portions of the 193,348-share total at specified times during the remainder of the agreement.

- *Lionsgate agreement:* In August 2009, Redbox entered into an agreement with Lions Gate Entertainment Corporation (known commonly as Lionsgate) to license minimum quantities of Lionsgate's new releases for rental in each location that Redbox had a DVD kiosk in the United States. Like the Sony agreement, Redbox would receive delivery of Lionsgate's new releases on the initial date the titles became available for rental by the general public for in-home entertainment viewing. Redbox estimated that it would pay Lionsgate approximately $160 million during the term of the agreement, which was expected to last from September 1, 2009, until August 31, 2014. However, Lionsgate had the option of terminating the agreement as early as August 31, 2011.

- *Paramount agreement:* Also in August 2009, Redbox entered into a revenue-sharing licensing agreement with Paramount Home Entertainment that originally ran from August 25, 2009, through December 31, 2009. But in early December 2009, Redbox and Paramount agreed to extend the term of the agreement until June 30, 2010, with the proviso that prior to June 15, 2010, Paramount had the unilateral right to extend the term of the agreement to December 31, 2014. If Paramount exercised its option to extend the agreement through December 2014, Paramount could unilaterally elect to terminate the agreement as early as December 31, 2011. Redbox estimated that it would pay Paramount approximately $56 million during the period August 25, 2009, to June 30, 2010, and approximately $494 million during the period August 25, 2009, to December 31, 2014, for licensing minimum quantities of Paramount's DVDs in each location in the United States where Redbox had a DVD kiosk. Coinstar was required to provide a $28 million letter of credit to Paramount for the period October 1, 2009, through January 31, 2010; during the remainder of the agreement period, the letter of credit was replaced with a Coinstar guarantee to Paramount of up to $25 million. As was the case with the Sony and Lionsgate agreements, Redbox would receive delivery of Paramount's new releases on the initial date the titles were distributed on a rental basis to the general public for home entertainment purposes, whether on a rental or sell-through basis.

- *Warner Bros. agreement:* In February 2010, Redbox entered into a rental revenue-sharing agreement with Warner Home Video, a division of Warner Bros. Home Entertainment Inc., whereby Redbox would license minimum quantities of Warner's DVDs for rental at each location that had a DVD-rental kiosk owned and/or operated by Redbox in the United States. Under the agreement, Redbox could begin renting Warner-released DVDs 28 days after the "street date," defined as the earliest date on which Warner made its new releases available on physical home video formats to consumers, whether on a rental or sell-through basis. The agreement further called for Redbox to dismiss its lawsuit against Warner relating to Redbox's access to Warner titles. Redbox estimated that it would pay Warner approximately $124 million during the term of the agreement, which was expected to last from February 1, 2010, through January 31, 2012.

• *Universal Studios and 20th Century Fox agreements:* In April 2010, Redbox entered into multiyear licensing and distribution agreements with both Universal Studios and 20th Century Fox. The terms on which Redbox would be able to obtain access to rent new DVDs released by these studios were essentially identical to those in the Warner agreement, with Redbox also agreeing to dismiss its lawsuit against Universal and 20th Century Fox.

These recent agreements gave Redbox access to about 90 percent of the DVD content the company needed for 2010.[11]

Redbox's agreements with some of the movie studios called for Redbox to destroy the discs of their titles following their useful life in Redbox's rental kiosk rather than selling them to customers or to wholesale distributors. This was beneficial to the studios because it reduced the number of used movie DVDs in circulation, potentially enhancing retail sales of new DVDs for these titles.

REDBOX'S FINANCIAL PERFORMANCE

Exhibit 3 shows all of the data from Coinstar's financial reports regarding the recent performance of Coinstar's DVD services business, which includes the operations of both Redbox-branded and DVDXpress-branded kiosks. Coinstar reported that $105 million of the $374 million in revenue growth at Redbox and DVD Express in 2009 was due to increased sales at kiosks in operation at least 12 months. Coinstar management said the following about the reasons for the decline in operating income as a percentage of

Exhibit 3   **Financial Performance of Coinstar's DVD Services Business (includes the operations of both Redbox-branded and DVDXpress-branded kiosks), 2007–2009 ($ millions)**

Combined Operations of Redbox-Branded and DVDXpress-Branded Kiosks	Three Months Ending		Years Ended December 31		
	March 31, 2010	March 31, 2009	2009	2008	2007
Revenues	$263.1	$154.7	$773.5	$399.5*	$143.6*
Operating income (before depreciation/amortization and stock-based compensation/share-based payments)	44.8	20.8	128.3	72.3	Not available
Operating income as a percent of revenues	17.0%	13.4%	16.6%	18.6%	—
Total assets	$482.6	$445.2	$491.8	$378.1	Not available

*Includes revenues of $11.0 million for the period January 1, 2008, through January 17, 2008, and revenues of $134.1 million for full-year 2007 when Coinstar did not consolidate the operating results of Redbox, owing to its minority ownership of Redbox.
Sources: Coinstar's 10-K reports for 2008 and 2009.

revenues from 18.6 percent in 2008 to 16.6 percent in 2009:

> The decline in DVD services segment operating income as a percentage of revenue for the year ended December 31, 2009, compared to the prior year was mostly driven by higher product costs, offset in part by the favorable effects of leveraging general and administrative expenses. The higher product costs resulted from the decrease in DVD salvage values, as well as the increased cost associated with purchasing certain DVD titles from alternative procurement sources. Throughout 2009, one movie studio has restricted the distribution of DVDs to our DVD services segment. During October 2009, two additional movie studios began restricting the distribution of DVDs to our DVD services segment. The increased restriction of DVDs has had a negative impact on the operating income margins in our DVD services business, because in these situations we must obtain DVD titles from alternative sources including certain wholesale distributors and third party retailers, often at a higher cost and often not in advantageous quantities.[12]

REDBOX'S FUTURE OUTLOOK

In February 2010, Gregg Kaplan, Coinstar's chief operating officer, said the following:

> The future looks extremely bright for Redbox. We strongly believe that physical DVDs will be the preferred medium of home entertainment for many years to come. As studios continue to develop high content entertainment such as Blu-ray and 3-D movies, Redbox is well positioned to be the delivery mechanism of choice due to our ability to deliver content to a broad base of consumers very inexpensively through our physical kiosk presence. Our kiosks eliminate the challenges of time and bandwidth that would be necessary for consumers to directly access this content in their homes.
>
> We should also point out that Redbox's growth is not dependent upon a flat or growing DVD rental market. We believe that Redbox will continue to take share and be a leader in the DVD rental market, even as that market eventually plateaus and as our competitors continue to close the doors of their retail stores.
>
> Despite our confidence that Redbox's physical DVD rental business will sustain it for quite a long time, we recognize that there will be a gradual shift to digital, and we will not be watching from the sidelines. We believe digital represents a great way for loyal Redbox customers to access a wider variety of titles than we can effectively offer in our kiosks. Over time, Redbox customers have said to us, we love Redbox and usually rent new releases, but there are times when we want to watch an old classic, can you offer that? Digital is a great way for us to offer that alternative. We began testing digital downloads in 2009 and will use 2010 to continue testing.[13]

In his 2009 letter to stockholders, Coinstar CEO Paul Davis said:

> Over the years, we have developed an expertise in kiosk development, deployment, and operations, and in building solid relationships with the best-known retailers in the world. These core competencies combined with our strong market presence will continue to drive our automated retail strategy. Looking ahead we will focus on three areas: delight and engage our customers, strengthen partner relationships, and generate profitable growth.

ENDNOTES

[1] Coinstar, 2009 10-K report, p. 2.
[2] Coinstar, Q4 2008 earnings call transcript, February 13, 2009, www.seekingalpha.com, accessed May 24, 2010.
[3] David Lieberman, "Video Kiosks Have Rivals Seeing Red," *USA Today,* August 12, 2009, p. 3B.
[4] Ibid.
[5] Ibid.
[6] Coinstar, Q4 2009 earnings call transcript, February 11, 2010, www.seekingalpha.com, accessed May 25, 2010.
[7] Ibid.
[8] Lieberman, "Video Kiosks Have Rivals Seeing Red," p. 3B.
[9] Coinstar, Q4 2009 earnings call transcript.
[10] Coinstar, 2009 10-K report, p. 4 and pp. 26–27; Coinstar news releases, April 22, 2010.
[11] Statement by Coinstar CEO Paul Davis in his letter to stockholders, in Coinstar, 2009 annual report.
[12] Coinstar, 2009 10-K report, p. 37.
[13] Coinstar, Q4 2009 earnings call transcript.

Cash Connection: Are Its Payday Lender Strategy and Its Business Model Ethical?

A. J. Strickland
The University of Alabama

Tyler Chapman
The University of Alabama
MBA Candidate

After operating through years where the market growth seemed to have peaked due to the large number of rival companies, Cash Connection's president, Allen Franks, sat at his desk pondering new ideas on how to differentiate his firm from others in the short-term cash-lending business. In addition to rival companies, Cash Connection was also facing the looming influence of a financial czar designed by the federal government to heavily influence the operations of all companies within the financial services industry, primarily those within banking. The costs of audits that accompanied governmental regulations could be quite substantial for financial service companies. Franks believed that additional governmental restrictions would indeed take away from his company's ability to compete. He needed to find a way for Cash Connection to differentiate itself from its competitors so that it could gain the largest amount of market share possible in an attempt to weather the storm of the restrictions being imposed by the financial czar.

Allen Franks was born and raised in Shreveport, Louisiana. The son of a local veterinarian, Franks attended grade school in Shreveport and graduated from Jesuit High School. After high school, he attended Louisiana State University and graduated in 1979 with a degree in business administration.

While attending college, Franks purchased and remodeled rental homes in Shreveport. Upon completion of his degree, he owned and rented approximately 30 units and continued in the real estate industry until 1986, when he opened a check-cashing store in Shreveport. The first store of its kind in Shreveport, Franks's check-cashing store did quite well. After opening two more stores in Shreveport, however, Franks came to understand that the first store in a city was always more profitable than succeeding stores.

After this realization, he decided to open check-cashing stores only in cities that did not yet have one. After establishing stores in Jackson, Mississippi; Montgomery, Alabama; and Toledo, Ohio, Franks left real estate to work full-time in the check-cashing industry; his company became known as Cash Connection. In addition to providing payday advances and check cashing, Cash Connection expanded into offering bill payment services, prepaid phone cards, and money orders; its stores also served as Western Union agents to allow customers to transfer funds.

Throughout the mid to late 1990s, Cash Connection was one of several companies competing in an industry of substantial growth: short-term cash lending. Although the principle of extending short-term loans to borrowers in need has been around since the 18th century, much of the pioneering credit for making microloans to cash-constrained people living at or near the poverty level has been given to Muhammad Yunus, President of Grameen Bank, for his acts in the 1970s in Bangladesh. During this time Yunus began making microloans to impoverished people in Bangladesh to enable them to create their own fledgling business enterprise. Yunus hoped that such microloans for cash-constrained entrepreneurs would allow borrowers to become self-supporting and, ideally, to build sufficient wealth to exit poverty. Over the course of several years, Yunus was said to have loaned approximately $8 billion to some 8 million aspiring entrepreneurs in Bangladesh. As a result of his generous initiative, he was awarded the Nobel Peace Prize in 2006.

Payday advance services emerged in the early 1990s and grew as a result of robust consumer demand and changing conditions in the financial services marketplace, including the following:

1. The exiting of traditional financial institutions from the small-denomination, short-term credit market—a change largely due to the market's high cost structure.

2. The soaring cost of bounced checks and overdraft protection fees, late bill payment penalties, and other informal extensions of short-term credit.

3. The continuing trend toward regulation of the payday advance services, providing customers with important consumer protections.

As of 2010, industry analysts estimated that there were more than 22,000 payday advance locations across the United States, a higher number than the 9,500 banks spread throughout the country. Payday advances extended about $40 billion in short-term credit each year to millions of middle-class households that experienced cash shortfalls between paydays.

PAYDAY LOANS

Payday loans were short-term cash loans intended to cover the borrower's expenses until the borrower's next payday. Although repayment amounts could be very high, the loans were quick and convenient. The borrower typically wrote a postdated check that included the loan fees and was used as "collateral" for the loan; the borrower could also sign an Automated Clearing House (ACH) authorization to debit the borrower's account on payday.

The average payday loan amount was $300 and the term was typically for 14 to 30 days. Fees varied but averaged between $15 and $20 per $100. For a 14-day loan at $20 per $100, the annual percentage rate (APR) was an astounding 520 percent. That APR, as most payday lenders were quick to point out, would apply only if the borrower had the loan for the whole year and paid $20 every two weeks. Payday loan fees were high because such loans carried a lot of risk for the company: many people who took out payday loans did not pay them back.

Throughout the United States, governments on every level were looking at payday loan outlets with increasing concern. Many people thought that they took advantage of low-income people in financial trouble. Some went as far as to say that payday lenders "preyed" on the poor. Those providing the loans argued that they were filling a need and not doing anything illegal.

The following situation illustrates why many people felt that payday loans worked against the

favor of a large number of people: Suppose that you had an unexpected expense one month and took out a short-term loan to provide you with enough capital to solve your problem and allow you to get on with your life. Well, what if your next paycheck, after your budgeted expenses, wasn't enough to allow you to pay back the loan? If you came up short again, you could renew, or extend, your loan. This process was called a "rollover." If you rolled over your loan too many times, however, it could end up costing you a lot of money. Say you borrowed $100 for 14 days until your next payday. You wrote a check to the lender for $115 (the $100 in principal plus a $15 fee). The APR of that loan would be 391 percent! If you couldn't pay back the $115 on the due date, you could roll over the loan for another two weeks. If you rolled over the loan three times, the finances charge would reach $60 for the original $100 loan.

To avoid appearing to roll over the debt, some lenders asked the debtor to take out a "new loan" by paying a new fee and writing another check. Also, in a practice called "touch and go," lenders took a cash "payoff" for the old loan and immediately provided the borrower with funds from the "new loan." Irrespective of whether the repeat transactions were cast as "renewals," "extensions," or "new loans," the result was a continuous flow of interest-only payments at very short intervals that never reduced the principal. Given the high fees and very short terms, borrowers could find themselves owing more than the amount they originally borrowed after just a few rollovers within a single year.

The potential to recognize substantial profits through fees and interest charges, along with strong consumer demand, resulted in heavy saturation of payday lending companies throughout large cities and towns in the United States. Another reason for the high numbers of payday lending firms was that the start-up cost for an individual location was only approximately $130,000.

In addition to providing credit to many consumers, the payday loan industry had made significant contributions to U.S. and state economies (see Exhibit 1). The industry contributed more than $10 billion to the U.S. gross domestic product in 2007 and supported more than 155,000 jobs nationally; some 77,000 people worked in nearly 24,000 retail locations that made payday loans.

In 2007, the payday lending industry provided approximately $44 billion in credit to U.S. consumers. Between 2006 and 2007, there was a decrease of 2.5 percent in the number of payday loan stores in the United States, from 24,189 to 23,586. There was no clear pattern for store closings. Some states experienced double-digit growth, and others experienced large drops in the number of stores per state. States with the highest growth in the number of stores in 2007 were South Dakota, Kansas, and Nevada. States with the biggest drops were Oregon, Indiana, and Minnesota.

Overall, the total labor income impact from the payday loan industry was $6.4 billion in 2007, as the industry helped generate over $2.6 billion in federal, state, and local taxes. Through direct employment, payday loan stores contributed $2.9 billion in labor income, which translated to approximately $37,689 per store employee. Suppliers to the payday lending industry contributed $1.4 billion in labor income as an indirect result of the revenues generated by the payday loan industry. Altogether, $2.1 billion was generated as payday loan store employees and supplier industries' employees spent their wages in local economies. In regard to the size of companies that served as industry players, any company with more than 51 branch locations nationwide was considered a national player. Cash Advance America, Check & Go, and Check America were examples of national players.

Exhibit 1   **Total U.S. Economic Impact of Payday Lending Industry in 2007**

Value Added to GDP	Total Employment	Labor Income (Employee Compensation)	Tax Revenues Generated
$10,212,730,000	155,581	$6,415,800,000	$2,630,000,000

Source: http://www.cfsa.net/downloads/eco_impact.pdf.

THE MARKET FOR PAYDAY LOANS

Policymakers, regulators, and consumer advocates had stakes equal to the industry's in getting a handle on the size and composition of the market for payday loans. If the near-term growth in demand by consumers who had never taken out a payday loan was insufficient to meet the industry's dramatically expanded capacity to originate them, the only way to make up the deficit in new demand was for lenders to encourage existing customers to borrow more frequently. This meant developing marketing and other strategies to convert occasional users of payday loans into routine borrowers.

Considerably less data was available on the aggregate size of the market for payday loans than on the characteristics of borrowers. Analysts who closely followed the industry estimated that about 5 percent of the U.S. population had taken out at least one payday loan at some time. Community Financial Services Association of America, an industry trade organization, reported that more than 24 million Americans (10 percent of the population) said they were somewhat or very likely to obtain a payday advance. Taken together, these estimates suggested that the industry had penetrated about half its potential market and that there were substantial unrealized growth opportunities without having to entice existing customers to borrow more frequently.

Exhibit 2 shows the financial performance of Cash Connection from 2007 to 2009. The company's net income significantly decreased from 2007 to 2008, with additional declines in 2009. A large portion of the decline in performance could likely be attributed to the fast-growing number of firms competing in the payday lending industry while banks and other loan institutions were finding ways to differentiate themselves to be more appealing in attracting customers. Some industry experts felt the decline in income in the industry was due to the saturation of competitors and the overall decline in the economy.

PAYDAY LENDING INDUSTRY CUSTOMERS

Payday lending companies served the heart of America's working- and middle-class population.

Customers came from hardworking families who had relationships with mainstream financial institutions. Although data on the demographics of payday loan borrowers were limited, many borrowers often faced severe credit restraints, had poor credit histories, and had bounced one or more checks in the previous five years. A 2001 study revealed the following demographic facts about payday advance customers:

1. They were of middle income.
   - The majority earned between $25,000 and $50,000.
2. They were of average education.
   - 94 percent had a high school diploma or better.
   - 56 percent had some college or a college degree.
3. They consisted of young families.
   - 68 percent were under 45 years old (only 3.5 percent were 65 or older).
   - The majority were married.
   - 64 percent had children in the household.
4. They were of the stable working class.
   - 42 percent owned homes.
   - 57 percent had major credit cards.
   - 100 percent had steady incomes.

Within these characteristics of customers, Cash Connection had two requirements that customers had to meet before they could receive loans. First, customers had to have a job that provided some source of income. Second, they had to have a checking account.

UNBANKED CUSTOMERS

Other prime users of the services provided by Cash Connection were "unbanked" or "underbanked." Unbanked individuals were those without an account at a bank or other financial institution for one reason or another. Underbanked, or underserved, individuals were those who had poor access to mainstream financial services. A recent study conducted by the Federal Deposit Insurance Corporation (FDIC) estimated that 10 million American households were either unbanked or underbanked. The fact that payday loans produced quick in-hand cash and offered

Exhibit 2   Cash Connection Profit & Loss Statement, 2007–2009

	Jan–Dec 31, 2007	Jan–Dec 31, 2008	Jan 1–Dec 27, 2009
Total Income	$6,348,544	$6,283,860	$5,768,805
Expenses			
Returned Items	389,147	690,003	847,310
401(k) Matching Funds	3,294	3,384	3,074
Advertising	142,160	176,939	187,294
Alarm Monitoring—Security	3,418	5,070	53,497
Armored Car Service	93,029	97,308	99,461
Auto Expense	62,123	72,072	59,545
Bad Debt	5,356	391	0
Check Cashing	4,050	3,885	5,505
Pay Day Loans	0	0	0
Total Bad Debt	9,405	4,276	5,505
Bank Charges	105,437	108,065	93,645
Cashier Errors	34,590	32,618	−3,225
Casual Labor	−52	0	113
Check Verification Expense	8,982	5,409	4,188
Collection Service	188	0	86
Consulting Expense	4,188	0	0
Depreciation	60,159	81,731	0
Donations	44	0	1,253
Dues, Subs & Directories	11,997	10,324	10,519
Employee Benefits	114,857	85,428	100,884
Fees, Permits & Licenses	34,745	30,969	30,570
Insurance			
Insurance—Operations	78,704	49,906	30,540
Insurance—Worker's Comp	13,648	9,522	10,668
Total Insurance	92,352	59,428	41,208
Interest	0	0	5,342
Interest—Investors	0	−1,133	21,594
Interest—Banks	242,574	114,859	111,093
Total Interest	242,574	113,726	138,029
Internet Provider	8,565	2,374	3,941
Management Fees	64,565	146,580	146,580
Meals & Entertainment	6,479	10,760	7,523
Miscellaneous	333	426	6,797
Money Order Expense	19,496	18,272	15,243
Outside Services	251,184	312,108	7,482
Pager	0	366	0
Postage	85,131	72,606	63,203
Professional Services			
Accounting & Audits	227,981	181,857	156,101
Legal	96,391	77,027	32,027
Legal—Collections	5,755	4,321	362
Payroll Service	0	0	10,434
Total Professional Services	330,127	263,205	198,923
Promotions	0	0	18,598

(Continued)

Exhibit 2   *(Concluded)*

	Jan–Dec 31, 2007	Jan–Dec 31, 2008	Jan 1–Dec 27, 2009
Rent			
Equipment	1,514	3,359	2,519
Storage	34,666	31,896	2,249
Building	400,156	417,872	443,285
Total Rent	436,336	453,127	448,053
Total Repairs & Maintenance	85,429	95,919	113,563
Salaries & Wages	0	138	0
District Management	255,959	202,163	209,622
Salaries allocated from CCC/CNI	0	0	251,696
Operations	1,438,701	1,550,049	1,686,903
Total Salaries & Wages	1,694,660	1,752,350	2,148,221
Software and Data Maintenance	0	0	40,592
Supplies	82,186	98,755	96,011
Supplies—Printing	7,296	14,554	3,404
Taxes			
Federal	−110	0	0
Payroll	156,353	160,934	174,544
Property	6,630	2,959	2,763
State	78,830	24,839	25,606
Total Taxes	241,702	188,732	202,912
Telephone	0	0	1,896
Land	148,166	135,562	143,463
Cellular	18,496	20,716	11,321
Total Telephone	166,663	156,279	156,679
Travel & Lodging	34,435	24,516	20,082
Utilities			
Gas & Electric	88,826	97,315	114,323
Water	1,126	3,791	4,332
Total Utilities	89,952	101,106	118,655
Total Expenses	5,017,173	5,488,623	5,569,912
Net Operating Income	1,331,371	795,237	198,893
Other Expenses			
Cherry Creek Ranch Income/Loss	0	344,586	0
Crime Loss	0	30,547	21,813
Monthly Accrued Payroll	0	0	0
Salary Expenses Accrued from Prior Year	−5,487	42,514	−94,880
7050 Settlements	241	34,900	0
Total Other Expenses	−5,246	452,548	−73,068
Net Other Income	5,246	−452,548	73,068
Net Income	$1,336,617	$ 342,689	$ 271,961

Source: Cash Connection.

easy repayment plans were reasons why these loans were so appealing for underbanked individuals. For unbanked individuals, who had no collection of funds in an account of their own and were at higher risk of nonrepayment, Cash Collection and other firms competing in this industry chose to provide only the service of check cashing.

In January 2009, the FDIC sponsored a special survey to collect national, state, and metropolitan area data on the number of U.S. households that were unbanked or underbanked, their demographic characteristics, and their reasons for being unbanked or underbanked (see Exhibit 3). Data for roughly 47,000 participating households were collected. The FDIC undertook this effort to address a gap in reliable data on the number of unbanked and underbanked households in the United States. Access to an account at a federally

Exhibit 3   Reasons Why Households Who Have Never Banked Are Unbanked

Reasons Household Is Unbanked	Number (000s)	Percent of Total
Customer Service Reasons		
Banks have inconvenient hours	158	3.60%
There is no bank near work or home	153	3.49
There are language barriers at banks	293	6.68
Banks do not feel comfortable or welcoming	389	8.87
Banks do not offer needed services	149	3.40
Other/None of the above	3,041	69.37
Don't know/Refused	201	4.58
Total	**4,384**	**100.0%**
Financial Reasons		
Minimum balance requirement is too high	540	11.98%
Service charges are too high	267	5.92
Bounced too many checks/had too many overdrafts	71	1.57
Banks take too long to clear checks	48	1.06
Do not have enough money to need account	1,581	35.06
Credit problems	139	3.08
Other/None of the above	1,606	35.62
Don't know/Refused	257	5.70
Total	**4,509**	**100.0%**
Other Reasons		
Do not write enough checks	765	17.06%
Could not manage or balance account	162	3.61
Do not trust banks	268	5.98
Do not have documents to open account	235	5.24
Do not know how to open account	103	2.30
Do not see value of having account	530	11.82
Other/None of the above	2,105	46.96
Don't know/Refused	315	7.03
Total	**4,483**	**100.0%**

Note: Figures do not always reconcile to totals because of the rounding of household weights to represent the population totals. Households not involved in household finance are excluded from this tabulation. Total percentages may sum to more than 100 because respondents were permitted to choose multiple responses.

Source: FDIC National Survey of Unbanked and Underbanked Households, December 2009, http://www.fdic.gov/householdsurvey/full_report.

insured institution provided households with the opportunity to conduct basic financial transactions, save for emergency and long-term security needs, and access credit on affordable terms. Many people, particularly those in low- to moderate-income households, did not have access to mainstream financial products such as bank accounts and low-cost loans. Other households had access to a bank account but nevertheless relied on more costly financial service providers for a variety of reasons. In addition to paying more for basic transaction and credit financial services, these households could be vulnerable to loss or theft and often struggled to build credit histories and achieve financial security.

COMPETITION IN THE PAYDAY LENDING INDUSTRY

The relaxation of federal restrictions starting in the early 1980s led to increased competition in the payday lending industry. Increasing regulation in the loan servicing industry as well as the financial industry only heightened the ease with which new companies could enter the industry and remain competitive while protecting the revenue and profits of companies that were well established in the industry.

A barrier to entry was the level of industry competition. Large retail banking firms such as Bank of America, Wells Fargo, JPMorgan Chase, and Citigroup were major players in the loan origination industry. These companies had an increased ability to generate a portfolio of serviced loans. It was difficult for new companies to purchase loans from third parties and generate their own loan-servicing portfolios.

Individual company performance relative to other companies within the industry largely depended on the company's cost structure and services relative to other lending companies.

The performance of equity markets had affected both the demand for consumer lending and the quality of lending portfolios. A positive development in the stock market generally resulted in increased lending due to the wealth effect of rising share prices. Investors feeling wealthier felt more confident to undertake projects that

increased their demand for credit. Rising stock prices also affected the quality of the lending portfolios because borrowers had an increased ability to meet repayments. Conversely, a fall in share prices had a negative impact on borrowers' ability to service debt, resulting in increased risk for those who extended the credit.

BANKING SERVICES

A 2008 study of the payday loan industry by Stephens Inc. projected that the payday loan market could encompass 10 percent of U.S. households. The substitute products for payday loans could have undesirable features for some consumers. Overdraft protection on a checking account was perhaps the closest substitute for payday loans, but its fees were on par with payday loan fees. Automated overdraft fees assessed by banks ranged from $10 to $38, with the average fee being $28.35, based on 1,024 banks in 364 cities. This average was an increase of more than $2.00 since the 2003 National Fee Survey was released. About one-fourth of the banks surveyed in the 2008 study also tacked on additional fees for accounts that remained in negative balance status. These fees were in the form of flat fees or interest charged on a percentage basis.

Bank service fees practically doubled in the eight years from 1995 to 2003, increasing from $16.4 to $32.6 billion. Fees from overdraft protection programs, also called nonsufficient funds (NSF) fees, had risen so dramatically that they represented the preponderance of all such fee

Source: http://www.ibisworld.com.libdata.lib.ua.edu/industry/conditions.aspx?indid51304.

income for banks and credit unions. NSF income for banks and/or credit unions could amount to as much as 50 percent of total consumer checking account revenue. One recent analysis estimated that NSF fees accounted for more than half, or roughly $18.8 billion, of the service-fee income derived by America's banks and credit unions. Another analysis estimated that banks collected $22 billion in overdraft fees in 2003.

The large majority of retail banks elected not to serve the needs of individuals who sought services such as payday loans. One recent study showed that 73 percent of banks were aware that significant unbanked and/or underbanked populations were in their market areas, but less than 18 percent of banks identified expanding services to unbanked and/or underbanked individuals as a priority in their business strategy. These depository institutions cited the lack of profitability as a significant barrier to serving unbanked and underbanked individuals. This was because banks tended to directly focus on the risk involved with conducting business with individuals who were not the most creditworthy of borrowers. Compared with that of payday loan companies, the lending structure of modern retail banks operated with loans of higher amounts over more extended terms after a background of credit was conducted on the consumers obtaining the loans. Many banks felt that collecting repayments, late fees, and default fees was highly unlikely in the event that short-term loans were placed in the wrong hands.

Exhibit 4 shows the impact of the recession on the banking industry in 2007 and 2008. Banks in those two years were attempting to increase fees to drive more income but were reluctant to move into new or different business segments. Exhibit 5 illustrates that the primary strategy at that time was building more branches.

CREDIT UNIONS

Credit unions were nonprofit organizations owned by and operated for the benefit of members. They generally were sponsored by an employer or association, so usually only employees or association members were eligible to join. Since there were no shareholders to answer to, they could often offer higher interest rates and lower fees than banks could; however, their services were more limited than those of banks. The size of the credit union could affect the variety of services offered. Smaller credit unions might offer only savings accounts and loans. Some credit unions focused on banking for low-income communities. Just like banks, credit unions collected deposits and made loans to their members. Deposits and loan payments often came from automatic payroll deposits that enabled credit unions to extend loans to their members at relatively low risk. A lower level of risk meant lower fees charged for services offered by credit unions. Since credit unions were nonprofit and paid no state or federal taxes, they often paid higher rates and charged lower fees than banks did. Any profit earned by a credit union was either invested back into the organization or paid out to members as a dividend. See Exhibit 6 for financial trends in federally insured credit unions.

The profile of a payday loan borrower suggested an individual who was capable of making rational decisions yet chose to do business with a payday lender instead of a credit union, for whatever reason. Somewhere between 10 and 20 percent of credit union members opted to do at least some of their business with payday lenders. Why? Perhaps it was the fear of being turned down, which in turn came from the knowledge that they had credit issues. Perhaps the credit union's hours and location weren't convenient when the member needed the loan. But more likely, it was because the credit union didn't have the right product—a small, short-term cash loan that could be accessed quickly and conveniently.

Exhibit 4 Recent Performance of Commercial Banking Industry in the U.S.

	Revenue ($ millions)	Growth Rate(%)
2005	$585.9	7.7%
2006	640.1	9.3
2007	643.0	0.5
2008	542.7	−15.6
2009	489.0	−9.9

Source: http://www.ibisworld.com.libdata.lib.ua.edu/industryus/currentperformance.aspx?indid51288/.

Exhibit 5 Balance Sheet Statistics for U.S. Retail Banks, 2004–2008

	2008	2007	2006	2005	2004
Number of institutions reporting	7,086	7,283	7,401	7,526	7,631
Assets					
Cash from depository institutions	$ 1,041,800,469	$ 482,167,038	$ 433,022,250	$ 400,266,591	$ 387,555,301
Securities	1,746,324,740	1,590,804,716	1,666,232,385	1,572,272,561	1,551,101,104
Federal funds sold	688,071,175	646,116,706	529,562,658	443,397,239	385,239,490
Net loans & leases	6,681,762,460	6,537,222,244	5,912,241,523	5,312,245,715	4,832,865,517
Trading account assets	939,848,184	867,549,217	619,558,531	499,187,288	504,289,109
Bank premises & fixed assets	109,679,684	105,022,132	96,811,538	91,705,731	86,799,336
Other real estate owned	22,914,392	9,790,917	5,467,048	4,026,398	3,852,709
Goodwill and other intangibles	392,526,497	423,216,712	358,508,090	302,933,608	275,726,003
All other assets	685,929,531	514,200,896	470,136,854	414,258,899	388,186,394
Total assets	**$12,308,857,132**	**$11,176,090,578**	**$10,091,540,877**	**$9,040,294,030**	**$8,415,614,963**
Liabilities					
Total deposits	$ 8,082,183,258	$ 7,309,840,803	$6,731,419,422	$6,073,144,887	$5,593,174,725
Federal funds purchased	803,925,770	765,572,423	719,361,004	667,577,176	577,571,016
Trading liabilities	469,787,117	342,666,695	266,349,279	251,710,818	280,474,394
Other borrowed funds	1,275,166,890	1,114,956,388	869,841,343	755,848,619	738,096,866
Subordinated debt	182,987,299	174,904,850	149,794,691	122,236,763	110,137,664
All other liabilities	340,611,084	325,230,537	324,925,231	257,334,811	265,975,308
Total liabilities	**$11,154,661,418**	**$10,033,171,696**	**$9,061,690,970**	**$ 8,127,853,074**	**$7,565,429,973**
Equity Capital					
Perpetual preferred stock	$ 6,391,140	$ 4,999,917	$ 5,122,235	$ 5,263,958	$ 6,237,011
Common stock	45,438,608	35,987,933	33,835,473	32,273,780	29,810,632
Surplus	851,008,910	738,886,871	625,617,888	529,798,223	493,501,576
Undivided profits	251,357,056	363,044,161	365,274,311	345,104,995	320,635,771
Total equity capital	**$1,154,195,714**	**$1,142,918,882**	**$1,029,849,907**	**$912,440,956**	**$850,184,990**

Source: http://www2.fdic.gov/SDI/SOB/

Why had credit unions shied away from payday-like loans? Perhaps credit unions feared that offering such loans placed them in the same category as a payday lender, which could be an unsettling feeling. However, credit unions were beginning to realize they could not ignore what it was costing their members to do business with payday lenders. Credit unions could offer a better-valued product that was both empowering for their members and sustainable for the credit union.

For credit unions, the national average NSF fee was $23.94, based on 519 locations in 253 cities. This represented an increase of nearly $3.00 since 2003. The national average returned-check fee charged by major merchants had risen by $1.44, to $26.64. The national high for bounced-check fees for both merchants and credit unions

Exhibit 6   **Financial Trends in Federally Insured Credit Unions, January 1, 2002–December 31, 2008**

Highlights	Year	Number of Credit Unions Reporting	
		Federal Credit Unions	**State Credit Unions**
Assets increased $58.45 billion, or 7.74%, to $813.44 billion.	2002	5,953	3,735
Net Worth increased $2.80 billion, or 3.26%. The net worth to assets ratio decreased from 11.41% to 10.93%.	2003	5,776	3,593
	2004	5,572	3,442
	2005	5,393	3,302
Earnings as measured by the return on average assets decreased from 0.63% to 0.31%	2006	5,189	3,173
	2007	5,036	3,065
Loans increased $37.43 billion, or 7.08%. The loan-to-share ratio decreased from 83.58% to 83.10%.	2008	4,847	2,959

Source: "Payday Lending: The Credit Union Way," April 2008.

was $50.00. FDIC data suggest that more than 18,000 financial institutions and credit unions collected $32.6 billion annually in service charges from the 56 million checking accounts they serviced. Thus, these institutions annually derived $582 in service charges from an average checking account (see Exhibit 7).

Other sources of credit (e.g., pawnshops, auto title lenders, and subprime home equity) required borrowers to front collateral and were often not viewed by many consumers as suitable alternatives. For this reason, payday loans were often viewed as a valuable alternative source of credit for consumers.

CREDIT CARDS

Of all the instruments consumers used to obtain short term credit, nothing was more commonly used than credit cards. In the fast-paced environ-ment of the 21st century, U.S. consumers used credit cards for nearly 100,000 transactions per minute. Although the credit card industry had produced billions of dollars in profits, it had also produced trillions of dollars worth of debt, as Americans simply had not been able to pay back the amount of debt that had grown over the last 30 years. Throughout this time, banks had constantly changed terms on credit card usage and interest rates on individual consumers to appear as if they were locked in a game with these consumers. The use of credit cards also played a hand in the recent economic meltdown, as many consumers began to refinance their houses in order to help pay off their credit card debt. A large number of these individuals then turned around and quickly used up the amount of credit allotted on their cards.

One credit card company in particular, whose name was synonymous with the tricks and traps that had entangled credit card customers over the

Exhibit 7   **2008 Survey Data Regarding Overdraft or Nonsufficient Funds (NSF) Fees in the United States**

	Number of Vendors	Number of Cities	Average Fee	Increase since 2003
Bank NSF fees	364	1,024	$28.35	more than $2.00
Credit union NSF Fees	253	519	$23.94	$3.00
Merchant returned-check fees	342	—	$26.64	$1.44

Source: http://www.ncua.gov/Resources/Reports/statistics/Yearend2008.pdf.

Source: http://www.superiorpawn.com/gallery/signlg.jpg.

qualified for a credit card—that is, the riskiest of borrowers. Providian viewed these individuals as the ones who would generate the most profit for the company, and it soon began to generate nearly $1 billion per year through penalty fees and high interest rates. Providian's strategy was to get borrowers to pay back their transactions with the minimum payment so that it took longer for them to pay back the initial loan. By doing this, Providian generated larger profits. Borrowers could obtain cards from Providian with no activation fee but high interest rates and high penalty fees for late payments. Although Providian may have been the leading innovator of practices that many people would consider unethical, it was quickly followed by other credit card companies not long after the large profit margins were recognized. Exhibit 8 shows the late fees of credit cards in comparison with other similar late fees.

last 20 years, was Providian. Providian's downspin in reputation was believed to have started when the company began extending credit to the 35 to 40 million unbanked U.S. prospects that had low incomes, were bankrupt, or previously had not

THE REGULATING ENVIRONMENT

The payday loan industry was regulated by a combination of state and federal laws and competitive

Exhibit 8   Late Fees Expressed as an Annual Percentage Rate (APR)

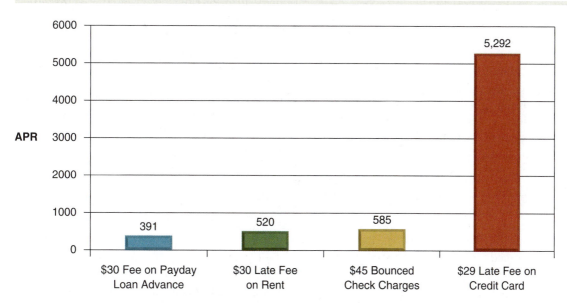

Source: "The Card Game." PBS Frontline. http://www.pbs.org/wgbh/pages/frontline/creditcards/.

market forces. As the payday loan industry matured over the past decade and consumers continued to demonstrate a desire for payday loans, the state and federal regulatory environment evolved along with the industry.

State Laws

Thirty-nine states and the District of Columbia explicitly allowed payday lending. However, via the Internet and telephone, payday lending was a de facto reality in virtually all states. Typically, states excused payday lenders from interest rate limits otherwise applicable to consumer loans in exchange for maximum fees and rollover limits. States also applied licensing regimes and conducted regular examinations. Twenty-two states did not permit immediate rollovers. Five states limited rollovers to three times. Some states allowed rollovers only if debt counseling was available. Only Georgia and Maryland explicitly prohibited payday lending in every form. The vast majority of states that permitted payday loans had established limits on the loan amount; many of those limits were set at approximately $500.

State laws usually prohibited lenders from threatening borrowers with criminal or civil action if the borrowers defaulted. In states where payday lending was authorized, regulatory regimes existed to ensure that lenders were complying with state and federal laws, and that they were not financially vulnerable.

Federal Laws

The following laws regulating payday lending operations are just one example of ways in which the federal government was attempting to heighten its control over the financial services industry:

- *Truth in Lending Act:* This law required lenders to disclose loan APRs and finance charges. The Federal Trade Commission oversaw compliance with this legislation by nonbank payday lenders, and the FDIC generally enforced compliance for its insured banks.
- *Fair Debt Collection Practices Act:* While this legislation applied only to third-party collection, the industry best practices set

out by the Community Financial Services Association (CFSA) suggested that members adhere to the Fair Debt Collection Practices Act.

- *The Federal Deposit Insurance Act:* Under Section 27 of the Federal Deposit Insurance Act, insured state-chartered banks (which were presently the only banks making payday loans) were entitled to charge nationwide the interest rates that applied in their home states. This law (and its analog with respect to national banks, Section 85 of the National Bank Act) had led a number of financial institutions to establish credit card banks in states without interest rate limits. Some payday lenders had agreements with Delaware- and South Dakota–based banks, by which the bank provided the loan by "exporting" the interest-rate laws of its home state. The CFSA's "best practices" placed restrictions on such relationships.
- *Gramm-Leach-Bliley Act:* This act's privacy requirements applied to payday lenders and were enforced by the Federal Trade Commission with respect to nonbank lenders.

Federal and state regulators were also considering mandating interest rates and placing limits on the amount of funds available to be loaned to consumers.

Although a rational belief would be that many restrictions placed on payday loans would favor borrowers, several research studies have found that heavy regulations and bans on payday lending have left borrowers in greater financial distress. These studies found that, since their states eliminated payday lending, consumers in Georgia and North Carolina have bounced more checks, complained more about lenders and debt collectors, and have filed for Chapter 7 bankruptcy at a higher rate than before. In states that have been given some form of loan restriction, the most common option for consumers dealing with a financial constraint has been to pay late or not to pay at all. Of those who paid bills late or not at all, 10 percent had utilities disconnected, went without a prescription medication, or had a damaged credit rating, and 50 percent incurred late fees on charges, including those who said that their bill was turned over to a collection agency or that they faced repossession or bankruptcy.

BUSINESS OBJECTIVE

For companies that operated within the payday loan industry, a desirable main objective was to serve customers in compliance with the rules of the industry and better educate them on financial services and products. Alabama's Council for Fair Lending (CFL) was established in November of 2007 by a group of Alabama-based cash advance and title loan lenders that recognized a need to operate in a parallel style. While they expressed an understanding that the loans they offered served as a short-term solution for many consumers, they made a conscious effort to inform those consumers on the importance of wise borrowing. The CFL's Code of Fair Lending is shown in Exhibit 9.

PAYDAY LENDING NATIONAL CUSTOMER SURVEY

In 2004, a survey was conducted by Cypress Research Group to examine the degree of customer satisfaction for individuals involved with a payday lending process. Two thousand payday advance customers were surveyed in an effort to examine industry performance from the customer's perspective; evaluate the long-term viability of the industry; and assess consumer confidence in, and satisfaction with, the payday advance service. The following (next page) are some of the findings taken from the survey:

Exhibit 9   Alabama Council for Fair Lending's Code of Fair Lending

OUR CODE OF FAIR LENDING......

We, the members of this association, in order to best serve the citizens of this state, recognize and adopt the following operating principles:

1. All customers will be treated with concern in an honest & professional manner.
2. All customers will be fully informed of their borrowing rights & obligations.
3. We will promote the responsible use of credit and strive to educate our customers on their financial choices.
4. Our employees will treat all customers with courtesy, fairness & integrity and will respond to any complaint about our service promptly and directly.
5. We will protect our customer's rights to privacy with respect to personal information.
6. We will honor and respect members of active military & their dependents. The Department of Defense's regulations on loans will be strictly adhered to.
7. We will comply with city, county, state and federal laws and keep our customers informed of the regulations that govern our actions.
8. We will exercise compassion to cash advance customers when warranted by offering repayment options before proceeding with civil collections. Title customers whose vehicles are repossessed will be offered options to retrieve their vehicles.
9. We will offer reasonably affordable loans to customers on fixed incomes.
10. We will not allow customers to roll over a loan unless authorized by state law.
11. We will give our customers the right to rescind, at no cost, a new loan on or before the close of the next business day.
12. We will prominently display the Borrow Smart seal in all of our stores and adhere to the Borrow Smart Alabama Code of Customer Service.

Source: http://www.borrowsmartalabama.com/.

Source: Cash Connection of Tuscaloosa, AL.

- Most of these consumers had other financial options available, but payday advance could sometimes be a better financial decision and was quick and convenient.
- Two-thirds of customers had at least one option that offered quick access to money.
- Half of customers had overdraft protection on their checking accounts.
- Fifty percent of customers had a major credit card(s). Thirty-five percent had a credit card(s) with available credit.
- In comparison to other credit products with which respondents had recent experience, customer overall satisfaction with payday advance (75 percent) was second only to check overdraft protection (83 percent). Payday advance also ranked higher than overall satisfactions with obtaining a home equity line of credit, a major credit card, a loan with a bank or credit union, and a car title loan.
- A large majority of customers cited the following reasons for taking a payday advance:

  1. Cover an unexpected expense (84 percent).
  2. Avoid late charges on bills (73 percent).
  3. Avoid bouncing checks (66 percent).
  4. Bridge a temporary reduction in income (62 percent).

More than three-quarters of customers were satisfied with the repayment schedule, the amount they could borrow and their ability to refinance or renew the loan if they chose to.

The rationale behind the boom in payday loans was perceived to be the high credit card rates and high bank fees for bounced checks charged by companies that operated as alternatives to payday lending firms. The immediate gratification offered by payday loans to the consumer was another driving force in the deferred deposit business, as there was nowhere a consumer could go for a small loan in an emergency. Banks did not offer very small loans, and loan companies were too slow and complicated. When looking at whether lenders or borrowers benefited the most from payday loans, a July 2007 study, "Expanding Credit Access: Using Randomized Supply Decisions to Estimate the Impacts," favored the borrowers. Individuals taking high-interest loans were less likely to be in poverty, less likely to be hungry or malnourished, and less likely to have lost their jobs.

With the federal government acting as a looming financial czar over many businesses in the private sector, especially those in the financial services industry, companies felt that they had to do everything within reasonable limits to give themselves an upper hand over competitors. In difficult times, the decisions of company leaders were crucial to future performance. Given the expected regulation by the federal government and expected moves by competitive firms, what could Allen Franks do to differentiate Cash Connection and make it the top choice for consumers attempting to receive a payday loan?

Blue Nile Inc. in 2010: Will Its Strategy to Remain Number One in Online Diamond Retailing Work?

Arthur A. Thompson
The University of Alabama

Ronald W. Eastburn
Case Western Reserve University

A 2009 issue of *Forbes* cited the experience of a Cleveland couple, Sanjay and Amy Bhargave, who were shopping for an engagement ring.[1] During a trip to New York City, Amy, 33, led Sanjay into a Tiffany store. But while this gave the soon-to-be-married couple a chance to scout diamonds, neither was happy with the service or the inventory. Back at home, they visited several local jewelry stores, but again, quality was a concern. Then one of Sanjay's clients suggested Blue Nile, the world's largest online jeweler. After viewing Blue Nile's extensive diamond inventory and spending six hours over the course of three weeks talking to his diamond consultant, Sanjay placed an order for a 2.2 carat princess cut in a Petite Trellis platinum setting for $20,000.

Once Blue Nile received an online order from a customer such as Sanjay Bhargave, the company secured the selected diamond from one of their exclusive suppliers, who then shipped the diamond overnight to Blue Nile's 27,000-square-foot warehouse in Seattle. There, a bench jeweler created the finished product. The ring was then steam-cleaned and packaged in a Blue Nile signature blue-and-silver box and shipped overnight to the customer. The purchase process typically took just three days. Furthermore, the satisfaction guarantee allowed dissatisfied customers to return items within 30 days of shipment for a full refund. Sanjay's ring arrived in time for his planned New Year's Eve proposal.

Founded in 1999, and taken public in 2004, Blue Nile had grown to become the world's largest online retailer of certified diamonds and fine jewelry, with sales of $302 million in 2009 (up from $169.2 million in 2004). The vast majority of Blue Nile's sales were diamond engagement rings—the company had sold more than 200,000 engagement rings by 2009. Blue Nile was ranked 58th in *Internet Retailer*'s "Top 500 Guide to Retail Web Sites" in 2009 and had been named best online retailer by *Kiplinger Personal Finance* each year between 2006 and 2009 and had been listed as a Forbes Favorite by *Forbes* magazine every year since 2000. In addition, Blue Nile had received the BizRate.com Circle of Excellence Platinum Award, which recognized the best in online customer service as ranked by actual consumers. The only jeweler to have ever received this award, Blue Nile had won it every year since 2002. A March 2008 article in *The Economist* said, "Creating a website that looks good and makes it easy for men to learn about diamonds before buying has turned Blue Nile into the leading online seller of jewelry, confounding predictions that luxury and e-commerce would never mix."[2]

In 2009, jewelry sales in the United States were estimated at $58.8 billion. Industry revenues had grown by approximately 5.5 percent annually since the mid-1980s to reach a peak of $60 billion in 2007 before declining after the onset of the U.S. recession in 2008. Diamond jewelry sales were particularly hard hit by the recession, with industry sales declining from $32.5 billion in 2005 to an estimated $29.5 billion in 2009. Blue Nile's revenues fell by nearly 8 percent between 2007 and 2008 before improving by 2.5 percent between

2008 and 2009. The company's strategy—which was keyed to having a large inventory of high-quality diamonds, exceptional customer service, and low prices—had allowed it to weather the effects of the U.S. recession far better than most of its rivals in the industry.

However, in 2010, Blue Nile management remained concerned about the lingering effects of poor economic conditions in the United States on the diamond jewelry industry, the increasing number of brick-and-mortar jewelers that had begun selling online, and weaknesses in the company's strategy that might limit its growth and competitiveness. Also of concern was how the company might encourage a greater percentage of jewelry consumers to shop online for jewelry purchases, how it should go about increasing its sales of diamond jewelry other than engagement rings, and how aggressively it should pursue expansion in international markets.

BLUE NILE'S BUSINESS MODEL AND STRATEGY

In an industry famous for big markups, frequent "closeout" sales, and a myriad of ill-understood ways of judging the caliber and value of its product offering, online jewelers faced the marketing challenge of convincing understandably skittish shoppers to purchase diamonds and fine jewelry online. It was one thing to shop for diamonds in a reputable jewelry store where one could put on a ring or other jewelry item to see how it looked, perhaps inspect the stones with a magnifying glass or microscope, and have a qualified jeweler explain the caliber of the stones and address concerns about pricing, characteristics of the stones, and jewelry settings. It was quite another thing to commit to buying expensive jewelry sight-unseen on the Internet.

Blue Nile's strategy to attract customers had two core elements. The first was offering high-quality diamonds and fine jewelry at competitively attractive prices. The second entailed providing jewelry shoppers with a host of useful information and trusted guidance throughout their purchasing process. Top management believed that Blue Nile's strategy of providing educational information, in-depth product information, and grading reports, coupled with its wide product selection and attractive prices, were the key drivers of the company's success and, ideally, would lead to customers looking on Blue Nile as their jeweler for life:

> We have established and are continuing to develop a brand based on trust, guidance and value, and we believe our customers view Blue Nile as a trusted authority on diamonds and fine jewelry. Our goal is for consumers to seek out the Blue Nile brand whenever they purchase high quality diamonds and fine jewelry.[3]

Competitive Pricing, Lean Costs, and Supply Chain Efficiency

Blue Nile's websites showcased as many as 60,000 independently certified diamonds and styles of fine jewelry, including rings, wedding bands, earrings, necklaces, pendants, bracelets, and watches. The product offerings ranged from simple classic designs suitable for wearing every day to an impressive signature collection of some of the finest diamonds in the world. Diamonds were the most significant component of Blue Nile's merchandise offerings, but the selection was limited chiefly to high-quality stones in terms of shape, cut, color, clarity, and carat weight. Complementing the large diamond selection was a broad range of diamond, platinum, gold, pearl, and sterling silver jewelry that included settings, rings, wedding bands, earrings, necklaces, pendants, bracelets, and watches.

Blue Nile specialized in the customization of diamond jewelry with a Build Your Own feature that offered customers the ability to customize diamond rings, pendants, and earrings. The company's product offerings included more than 60,000 diamonds and hundreds of settings. Customers could select a diamond and then choose from a variety of ring, earring, and pendant settings that were designed to match the characteristics of each individual diamond.

Blue Nile's economical supply chain and comparatively low operating costs allowed it to sell comparable-quality diamonds, gemstones, and fine jewelry pieces at substantially lower prices than those of reputable local jewelers. The supply chain bypassed the markups of traditional layers of diamond wholesalers and brokers, thus generally allowing Blue Nile to obtain most of its product offerings more cost-efficiently than traditional brick-and-mortar jewelers. The distinctive feature of Blue Nile's supply chain was its set of exclusive arrangements that allowed it to display leading diamond and gem suppliers' products on its website; some of these arrangements entailed multiyear agreements whereby designated diamonds were offered only at Blue Nile. Blue Nile did not actually purchase a diamond or gem from these suppliers until a customer placed an order for it; this enabled Blue Nile to minimize the costs associated with carrying large inventories and limited its risk of potential markdowns. However, Blue Nile did selectively purchase jewelry merchandise (usually bracelets, necklaces, earrings, pendants, wedding bands, and watches), stocking them in its own inventory until they were ordered and delivered to customers. Blue Nile's inventory was $19.4 million at year-end 2009. In contrast, traditional jewelers had far bigger inventories relative to annual sales. For example, Zale Corporation—which not only sold online but also was the parent of Zales Jewelers (700 stores in the United States and Puerto Rico), Zales Outlet, Gordon's Jewelers, Peoples Jewelers (the largest Canadian jeweler), Mappins Jewelers (another Canadian jewelry chain), and Piercing Pagoda—reported year-end inventories of $740.3 million on 2009 sales of $1.8 billion. Luxury jewelry retailer Tiffany & Co. reported year-end inventories of $1.43 billion on 2009 sales of $2.7 billion.

Blue Nile's supply chain savings gave it a significant pricing advantage. In 2009, for every dollar that Blue Nile paid suppliers for stones, settings, and other purchased items, it sold its finished jewelry for a markup of about 28 percent over cost. In contrast, Tiffany sold at an average markup of 130 percent over cost of goods sold and Zale sold at an average markup over cost of goods sold of 88 percent.

While much of Blue Nile's competitiveness was dependent on maintaining favorable arrangements with its suppliers, the company was somewhat protected by having negotiated agreements with a variety of suppliers, thus limiting its dependence on particular suppliers—the top three suppliers accounted for only 22 percent of the company's purchases in 2008 and 24 percent of its purchases in 2009. Moreover, the supply

arrangements were favorable to suppliers, providing them with real-time market intelligence about what items were selling, the potential of high sales volume through a single account, and a way to achieve more inventory turns and otherwise manage their own inventories more efficiently.

Another cost-saving element of Blue Nile's strategy was lean operating costs. The company had only 183 full-time employees, 5 part-time employees, and 1 independent contractor as of early 2010. Operations were conducted via a combination of proprietary and licensed technologies. Blue Nile licensed third-party information technology systems for financial reporting, inventory management, order fulfillment, and merchandising. Redundant Internet carriers were used to minimize service interruptions and downtime at its website. Various operating systems were monitored continuously using third-party software, and an on-call team responded to any emergencies or technology issues. Management continuously explored avenues to improve operating efficiency, refine its supply chain, and leverage its investment in fixed-cost technology. In 2009, Blue Nile's selling, general, and administrative (SG&A) expenses were only 15.2 percent of annual sales; in contrast, SG&A expenses were 40.2 percent of 2009 sales at Tiffany & Co. and 57.4 percent of 2009 sales at Zale Corporation. The strength of Blue Nile's business model and its efficient operations provided a net profit margin of 4.2 percent in 2009, compared to a 2009 net profit margin of 9.8 percent at Tiffany and a 2009 net loss at Zale.

Educational Information and Certification

Blue Nile went to considerable lengths to put to rest any concerns shoppers might have about buying fine jewelry online. It employed an informative sales process, striving to demystify and simplify the process of choosing a diamond or some other gemstone. Blue Nile's website provided a wealth of easy-to-understand information about the five C's (cut shape, cut, color, clarity, and carat weight—see Exhibit 1), allowing shoppers to educate themselves about what characteristics determined the quality and value of various stones. In addition to providing substantial educational information, Blue Nile's website

Exhibit 1 Determining a Diamond's Value: The Five C's

CARAT: Refers to a diamond's weight, not its size. One carat equals one-fifth of a gram. While lighter diamonds often carry a lower price per carat, a 1.0 carat diamond might sparkle more than a 1.25 carat diamond if it is cut differently or has better color and clarity.

CLARITY: Concerns the degree to which a diamond is free of inclusions (i.e., flaws)—blemishes, internal imperfections, scratches, trace minerals, or other tiny characteristics that can detract from a diamond's beauty. Diamonds that are absolutely clear are the most sought-after and therefore the most expensive. The lower the clarity (and the greater the inclusions), the lower the value of the diamond. The naked eye can see flaws in diamonds with very poor clarity, but even using a magnifying glass untrained eyes would have trouble seeing flaws in a high-clarity diamond. There are 11 grades of clarity ranging from "flawless" to "included," based on the number, location, size, and type of inclusions present in a diamond. Inclusions were more visible to the naked eye in lower-grade emerald cuts than in lower-grade round diamonds.

COLOR: Concerns a diamond's transparency. Acting as a prism, a diamond can divide light into a spectrum of colors and reflect this light as colorful flashes called fire. Just as when looking through colored glass, color in a diamond will act as a filter and will diminish the spectrum of color emitted. The less color in a diamond, the more colorful the fire and the better the color grade. A little color in a white diamond could diminish its brilliance. White diamonds with very little color are the most highly valued and are priced accordingly. Color grades range from D (absolutely colorless and extremely rare) to Z. White diamonds with grade of D, E, or F are considered "colorless" grade and very high quality; diamonds with grades of G or H are near-colorless and offer excellent value: diamonds with grades of I or J have slightly detectable color but still represent good value; the color in diamonds graded K–Z detracts from the beauty of a diamond and is especially noticeable in platinum or white gold settings. (Blue Nile only sold diamonds with color grades of J or higher.) Yellow diamonds (some of which were fancy and highly valued) are graded on a different scale than white diamonds are.

CUT: Concerns a diamond's shape (round, square, oval, pear, heart, marquise, and so on) and style (width, depth, symmetry, polish, and number/position of flat surfaces). Most diamonds are cut with 58 facets, or separate flat surfaces; it is the diamond cutter's job, utilizing precise mathematical formulas, to align the facets at precise angles in relation to each other to maximize the reflection and refraction of light. Cut style affects how light travels within a diamond, thus determining its brightness, fire, and face-up appearance. The cutter's goal is to transform a diamond in the rough into a sparkling, polished stone of the largest possible size and greatest optical beauty; a poor or less desirable cut can dull the look and brilliance of diamonds with excellent color and clarity. There is no single measurement of a diamond that defines its cut, but rather a collection of measurements and observations that determine the relationship between a diamond's light performance, dimensions, and finish.

CUT GRADE: This newest of the five C's is perhaps the overall best measure or indicator of a diamond's brilliance, sparkle, and "wow effect." Fewer than 5% of diamonds on the market qualify for the highest cut grade rating. Cut grade is a summary rating that takes into account such measures as the diamond's table size (the flat surface at the top of the diamond) as a percentage of the diamond's girth (the widest part of the diamond), the crown of the diamond (the portion above the girth) and the crown angle, the pavilion (the portion of the diamond below the girth)— the height of the pavilion contributes to its brilliance, the pavilion angle, the depth of the diamond (from the top facet to the culet), culet size, the diamond's polish and symmetry, and several other factors affecting sparkle, radiance, and brilliance.

Source: Compiled from a variety of sources, including the educational information posted at www.bluenile.com and www.diamonds.com, accessed August 23, 2006. The two price tables are from Blue Nile, www.bluenile.com, accessed August 13, 2010.

and its extensively trained customer service representatives provided detailed product information that enabled customers to objectively compare diamonds and fine jewelry products and to make informed decisions in choosing a stone of suitable size/weight, cut, color, clarity, look, and price.

Blue Nile management believed that having reputable industry professionals certify and grade each diamond/gemstone offered for sale had many advantages. The grading reports provided valuable guidance to consumers in

choosing a stone that was right for them and their pocketbook—the carat weight, color, cut, and clarity of a diamond was critical in providing the buyer with the desired sparkle, brilliance, and dazzling or sophisticated look. In addition, a jewelry shopper's ability to immediately review professionally prepared grading reports for a diamond/gemstone of particular interest instilled confidence in shopping for fine jewelry at Blue Nile, typically quelling any fears that the stone(s) might not live up to expectations. Furthermore,

The following table shows price variations in diamonds with varying clarity but the same carat weight and color grade:

Price Comparison: 1 Carat, H-color, Ideal Cut Diamond		
Clarity Grade	**Description**	**Price**
FL	**Flawless** No internal or external finish flaws.	$9,500
IF	**Internally Flawless** No internal flaws.	$8,200
VVS1 VVS2	**Very Very Slightly Included** Very difficult to see inclusions under 10x magnification.	$7,800 $7,300
VS1 VS2	**Very Slightly Included** Difficult to see inclusions under 10x magnification, typically unable to see inclusions with unaided eye.	$6,700 $6,200
SI1 SI2	**Slightly Included** Easy to see inclusions under 10x magnification, may not be able to see inclusions with unaided eye.	$5,800 $5,000

The following table compares the prices of diamonds with varying color grades but the same clarity grade (VS1) and carat weight:

Price Comparison: 1–1.09 Carat VS1 Round Diamond						
Colorless			**Near-Colorless**			
D	**E**	**F**	**G**	**H**	**I**	**J**
Ideal	$10,000	$9,000	$8,500	$7,500	$6,800	$5,500	$4,700
Very Good	$ 9,600	$8,000	$7,500	$6,800	$6,200	$5,000	$4,500
Good	$ 9,200	$7,500	$6,800	$6,000	$5,500	$4,800	$4,000
Fair	$ 8,700	$6,900	$6,200	$5,400	$4,900	$4,300	$3,700

the grading reports that Blue Nile provided facilitated comparison shopping, allowing jewelry shoppers not only to compare alternative Blue Nile diamonds/gems but also to see how Blue Nile's products stacked up against the products they might be considering at competing jewelers.

Customers interested in a particular diamond displayed at Blue Nile's websites could view or print out an accompanying diamond grading or certification report that documented the specific characteristics of the diamond and that was pre-pared by an independent team of professional gemologists—see Exhibit 2. A Diamond Dossier (also called a diamond quality document or diamond grading report) was a report created by a team of gemologists who evaluated, measured, and scrutinized the diamond using trained eyes, a jeweler's loupe, a microscope, and other industry tools. A completed certificate included an analysis of the diamond's dimensions, clarity, color, polish, symmetry, and other characteristics. Many round diamonds had a cut grade on the report.

Exhibit 2   Diamond Characteristics Documented in a GIA Diamond Grading Report

---

Shape and Cutting Style: The diamond shape and cutting style.

Measurement: The diamond's dimensions in millimeters.

Carat Weight: The weight of the diamond listed to the nearest hundredth of a carat.

Color Grade: The absence of color in the diamond.

Clarity Grade: The degree of clarity determined under 10x magnification.

Cut Grade: A grade of cut as determined by a diamond's face-up appearance, design, and craftsmanship. A GIA cut grade was available on round diamonds graded after January 1, 2006.

Finish: The diamond's surface and facet placement.

Polish: The overall smoothness of the diamond's surface.

Symmetry: The shape, alignment, and placement of the diamond's facets in relation to one another as well as the evenness of the outline.

Fluorescence: The color and strength of color when the diamond is viewed under ultraviolet light.

Clarity: The approximate size, type, and position of inclusions as viewed under a microscope.

Proportion: A map of the diamond's actual proportions, typically with information about the following:

- **Culet:** Appearance, or lack thereof, of the culet facet. The culet (pronounced "que-let" or the French-sounding "que-lay") was a tiny flat surface formed by polishing off the tip at the bottom of a diamond. A culet protects the fragile tip of the diamond from chipping during the cutting, handling, and setting of the diamond. However, Asians often prefer diamonds without a culet, so the practice of downgrading diamonds without culets has been discontinued.
- **Table:** The largest facet (or flat surface), located at the top of the diamond.
- **Depth:** The height of the diamond measured from the culet to the table.
- **Girdle:** The range of thickness.

Comments: A description of additional diamond characteristics not already mentioned in the report.

Source: Blue Nile, www.bluenile.com, accessed August 27, 2010.

Every loose diamond sold by Blue Nile was analyzed and graded by either the Gemological Institute of America (GIA) or the American Gem Society Laboratories (AGSL).

- The GIA was regarded as the world's foremost authority in gemology; its mission was to promote public trust in gems and jewelry. In the 1950s, the GIA had created the International Diamond Grading System and established standards that revolutionized the diamond industry. Most recently, the GIA had introduced its new Diamond Cut Grading System, which used computer modeling to assess and predict the cut quality in round brilliant cut diamonds. The GIA's research revealed that there was no single set of proportions that defined a well-cut round brilliant diamond; many different proportions could produce attractive diamonds. The GIA had also developed software that provided a method of estimating a cut grade—and a database that was embedded into a number of leading diamond-measuring devices so that cut grade estimation could be automated. As a result, manufacturers could plan and, in effect, predict cut grades; buyers could compare cut qualities; and retailers could communicate the effects of cut on round brilliant diamonds. In 2006, the GIA Laboratory introduced new versions of the GIA Diamond Grading Report and Diamond Dossier that provided a single, comprehensive cut grade for all standard round brilliant diamonds falling in the GIA D-to-Z color scale and Flawless-to-I3 clarity scale. Diamonds received one of five cut grades, from Excellent to Poor.

- Founded in 1996, the AGSL was the only diamond-grading laboratory to offer a unique 0 to 10 grading system that provided easy-to-read, clear, and accurate information about each diamond it graded. A cut grade of 10 was the lowest quality, and a grade of 000 was the absolute finest or ideal quality, but so far the AGSL had only awarded cut grades to select round and square-cut diamonds (it was considering expanding the grading system to other cuts). AGSL grading reports were based on the gemological industry's highest standards of evaluating the four C's of cut, color, clarity, and carat weight. AGSL grades allowed a shopper to compare the quality of the diamond against the price.

These two laboratories were among the most respected laboratories in the diamond industry and were known for their consistency and unbiased diamond-grading systems. Diamonds that were accompanied by GIA and ASGL grading reports were the most highly valued in the industry.

All diamonds in Blue Nile's signature collection also were certified by the Gem Certification and Appraisal Lab (GCAL) in addition to being graded by the GIA or AGSL. This provided a second authoritative analysis of the diamond. The GCAL verified that a diamond met all the specific quality requirements of the Blue Nile Signature Collection—see Exhibit 3.

Marketing

Blue Nile's marketing strategy was designed to increase Blue Nile brand recognition, generate consumer traffic, acquire customers, build a loyal customer base, and promote repeat purchases. Top executives at Blue Nile believed that jewelry shoppers preferred to seek out high-quality diamonds and fine jewelry from a trusted source in a non-intimidating environment, where information, guidance, reputation, convenience, and value were important characteristics. Hence, a major portion of Blue Nile's marketing effort was focused on making sure that site visitors had a positive, informative experience, one that inspired their confidence to buy diamonds and fine jewelry from the company. One key initiative to provide a good customer experience was the development of a user-friendly interactive search tool that allowed shoppers to customize their search and quickly identify diamonds with the characteristics they were looking for. Blue Nile's website was redesigned in 2009 to improve the site's appeal with women and allow site visitors to more easily search Blue Nile's diamond collection according to any of 12 criteria, including price, carat weight, cut, color, clarity, polish, symmetry, fluorescence, culet, diamond grading report, depth percentage, and table percentage. Blue Nile's redesigned website also included a blog page where customers could write about their proposal stories. Site visitors could browse 1,100 stories (broken down by adventurous, extravagant, romantic, creative, humorous, and so on) to get ideas and inspiration on how others had popped the question.

Exhibit 3   Contents of a Certificate of Authenticity Issued by the Gem Certification and Appraisal Lab (GCAL)

Actual Size Photo: A photo of the diamond at its true size.

Laser Inscription Photo: A close-up shot of the laser inscription on the diamond taken at 50x magnification.

Proportion Diagram: The actual scale and specific measurements of the diamond are noted on a diagram. These measurements are used to determine the cut grade.

Enlarged Photomicrograph: A photo of the diamond viewed from top and bottom.

An Optical Brilliance Analysis: Images of the diamond are captured using a controlled lighting environment and carefully calibrated amounts of light at specific viewing angles. These tests show the amount of light return or brilliance as it exited the diamond's crown.

Optical Symmetry Analysis: A test analyzing the light exiting the diamond and showing the discrepancies in the balance of the diamond. An even and symmetrical pattern shows that the light is well balanced and indicates exceptional diamond quality.

Certification Statement: A statement signed by the GCAL laboratory director verifying the quality of the graded diamond.

Diamond Grading Analysis: Notes on the diamond's shape, measurements, carat weight, and cut grade based on its proportions, polish, symmetry, color, and clarity grades. The analysis also contains any comments regarding the diamond.

Source: Blue Nile, www.bluenile.com, accessed August 27, 2010.

Blue Nile's website also emphasized that the company did not market "blood" or "conflict" diamonds, which were gems that had been traded for money or guns to fight wars in parts of Africa. Blue Nile and all other major sellers of diamond jewelry had entered into partnerships with the United Nations, governments, and nongovernmental organizations to prevent the trade of illegal diamonds through measures such as the Kimberley Process, which tracked diamonds from mine to market. A goal of Blue Nile's communications with its customers was to empower them with knowledge and confidence as they evaluated, selected, and purchased diamonds and fine jewelry.

The company's efforts to draw more shoppers to its site and boost awareness of Blue Nile included both online and offline marketing and advertising efforts. Most of Blue Nile's advertising dollars went for banner ads at Web portals (Yahoo, Google, Facebook, YouTube, and MSN), search engine sites (Google and Bing), and select other sites. As competition for online advertising had increased, the cost for these services had also increased. The company also did some direct online marketing. Advertising expenses were $6.5 million in 2004, growing to $11.9 million in 2007, $12.4 million in 2008, and $11.6 million in 2009.

Customer Service and Support

Blue Nile strove to provide a high level of customer service and was continuously engaged in refining the customer service aspects in every step of the purchase process. Complementing the extensive information resources on its website was a call center staffed with knowledgeable, highly trained support personnel. Blue Nile diamond and jewelry consultants were trained to provide guidance on all steps in the process of buying diamonds and fine jewelry, including the processes for selecting an appropriate item, purchasing that item, financing the purchase, and having the item shipped. The company further boosted service quality by adopting a salary-based compensation plan for sales personnel that did not create incentives to put undue pressure on customers to purchase products that had the highest margins or highest commissions.

Blue Nile customers with questions could call a prominently displayed toll-free number or send an e-mail to service@bluenile.com; most calls to the Blue Nile call center were answered within 10 seconds.[4] Policies relating to privacy, security, product availability, pricing, shipping, refunds, exchanges, and special orders were readily accessed at the company's website. In 2009, Blue Nile released mobile applications for the iPhone and Android-equipped smartphones to make comparison shopping easier when customers were visiting brick-and-mortar jewelry stores operated by its competitors.

Order Fulfillment Operations

Order fulfillment at Blue Nile was designed to enhance customer value and confidence by filling customer orders accurately and delivering them quickly and securely. When an order for a customized diamond jewelry piece was received, the supplier holding the diamond in inventory generally shipped it to Blue Nile (or an independent third-party jeweler with whom Blue Nile maintained an ongoing relationship for assembly) within one business day. Upon receipt at Blue Nile, the diamond was sent to assembly for setting and sizing, tasks performed by either Blue Nile bench jewelers or independent third-party bench jewelers. Each diamond was inspected upon arrival from suppliers; additionally, each finished setting or sizing was inspected prior to shipment to a customer. Prompt and secure delivery was a high priority, and Blue Nile shipped nearly all diamond and fine jewelry products via FedEx. The company had an on-time order delivery rate of 99.96 percent, which it was striving to push to 100 percent.[5] Shipping and handling costs totaled $2.8 million in 2009.

Blue Nile's order fulfillment costs, included as part of SG&A expenses, totaled $3.0 million in 2009, up from $1.6 million in 2004, reflecting the increase in sales. These costs included all expenses associated with operating and staffing the Seattle warehouse and order fulfillment center, including costs attributable to receiving, inspecting, and warehousing inventories and picking, preparing, and packaging customers' orders for shipment.

Product Line Expansion

Blue Nile was selectively expanding its product offerings in terms of both price points and product mix. New product offerings included both customized and noncustomized jewelry items. Management believed that the online nature of Blue Nile's business, coupled with its supply arrangements and just-in-time inventory management, allowed it to readily test shopper response to new diamond and gemstone offerings and to efficiently add promising new merchandise to its overall assortment of fine jewelry.

Expansion into International Markets

Blue Nile was selectively pursuing opportunities in international markets where management believed the company could leverage its existing infrastructure and deliver compelling customer value. Blue Nile's international business began in August 2004, when Blue Nile launched a website in the United Kingdom (www.bluenile.co.uk), offering a limited number of products; in September 2005, Blue Nile began providing customers at its UK website with the ability to customize their diamond jewelry purchases and to buy wedding bands. A website in Canada (www.bluenile.ca) was launched in January 2005. Blue Nile opened a fulfillment center in Dublin, Ireland, to serve the company's UK and European Union customers in 2007. The company launched its Chinese-language site in April 2010, which increased its number of international markets to 40. Customers in 35 international markets could complete transactions in their local currency. Blue Nile revenues generated outside the United States had grown from $8.3 million in 2006 to $33.2 million in 2009. Blue Nile's CEO, Diane Irvine, stated in a 2008 *Forbes* video interview that "over the long term, we believe international will be half or more of our total business."[6]

Other Strategy Elements

Blue Nile's strategy had several other key elements:

- Blue Nile had a 30-day return policy that gave customers plenty of time to consider their purchase and make sure they had made a good decision. If customers were not satisfied for any reason, they could return any item without custom engraving in its original condition within 30 days of the date of shipment for a refund or an exchange. Requests for a refund or a different item were processed within a few days.

- Blue Nile offered free shipping with every order delivered to a U.S. address; orders were shipped via FedEx Express, FedEx Ground, or U.S. Postal Service, depending on order value and destination. All orders under $250 were shipped via FedEx Ground if within the 48 contiguous states or by U.S. Postal Service for destinations in Hawaii and Alaska. Orders between $250 and $1,000 were shipped via FedEx two-day delivery. All orders over $1,000 and all loose diamond orders were shipped via FedEx Priority Overnight. Customers had the option to upgrade the delivery of items under $1,000 to FedEx Priority Overnight for a $15 charge.

- Blue Nile automatically provided an appraisal stating the approximate retail replacement value of the item to customers who bought (1) a preset engagement ring priced under $2,500; (2) a diamond jewelry item priced $1,000 or over (except preset solitaire engagement rings, preset earrings, or preset solitaire pendants priced $2,500 or over, all of which came with International Gemological Institute appraisals); or (3) any custom diamond ring, earring, or pendant. The appraisal value was based on current market data; typical retail prices; the weight of the precious metal included in the item; craftsmanship; and the cut, color, clarity, and carat weight of the gemstone(s). Included with the appraisal was a brief description of the item being appraised; a photograph of the item; and the cut, color, clarity, and either carat weight (for diamonds) or millimeter dimensions (for gemstones). An appraisal represented value-added to customers because it was necessary to obtain insurance coverage and determine what constituted equal replacement in case of loss, theft, or damage.

Blue Nile's Financial Performance

Between 2005 and 2007, Blue Nile's revenues grew from $203 million to $319 million and its earnings increased from $13.1 million to nearly $17.5 million. The company's stellar performance pushed its stock price over the $100 mark just weeks before U.S. consumers began feeling the effects of the deep recession that began in late 2007. The recession caused consumers to rapidly cut back on discretionary spending, which directly affected the sales of almost every business operating in the United States. Blue Nile's revenues and earnings declined to $295 million and $11.6 million, respectively, in 2008 before increasing slightly in 2009.

Despite the poor climate for luxury goods, Blue Nile's business model continued to generate cash 40 to 55 days ahead of the need to pay suppliers; in a very real sense, Blue Nile's business model was self-funding because suppliers financed Blue Nile's sales growth—see Exhibit 4. The company generated $36.7 million in free cash flow in 2009. Since 2001, Blue Nile had generated more than $200 million in cumulative free cash. At year-end 2009, the firm had a cash balance of $93.1 million, total assets of $130.4 million, and minimal debt outstanding. Moreover, the company's business model was readily scalable to substantially higher sales volumes with minimal additional capital investment. Blue Nile's capital expenditures for facilities and equipment were a meager $2.3 million in 2009, $2.0 million in 2008, and $4.9 million in 2007. Exhibit 5 presents

a summary of Blue Nile's financial results from 2005 through 2009.

Stock Issues and Repurchases

Blue Nile became a public company in 2004, selling some 2.3 million shares of common stock at $20.50 per share and realizing proceeds of $42.5 million after expenses. Trading of the company's stock began on May 20, 2004, on the NASDAQ exchange under the symbol NILE. Since trading began, the stock had traded as low as $22.50 (August 2004) and as high as $104.25 (September 2007); the stock price had steadily declined from $65 in January 2010 to near $40 in August 2010.

Blue Nile had not paid any cash dividends on the common stock since the inception of the company and, in February 2006, had authorized the repurchase of $100 million of its common stock over a two-year period. Blue Nile repurchased 438,755 shares for approximately $20 million in 2007 and another 1.6 million shares of stock for approximately $66.5 million in 2008. The company had not reauthorized its repurchase plan beyond 2008 and subsequently did not repurchase any shares in 2009 or 2010.

Blue Nile had several stock-based compensation plans, under which stock options could be

Exhibit 4   The Cash-Generating Capability of Blue Nile's Business Model

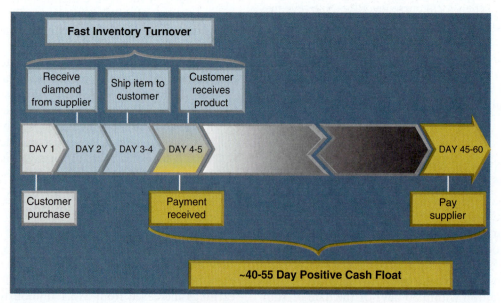

Source: Blue Nile Management Presentation, Goldman Sachs Seventh Annual Internet Conference, May 24, 2006.

Exhibit 5   **Selected Financial Data, Blue Nile Inc., 2005–2009 ($ thousands, except per share data)**

	2009	2008	2007	2006	2005
Income Statement Data					
Revenue	$302,134	$295,329	$319,264	$251,600	$203,169
Cost of goods sold	236,790	235,333	254,060	200,700	158,127
Gross profit	65,344	59,996	65,204	50,900	45,042
Selling, general, and administrative costs	45,997	44,005	42,792	34,300	26,993
Earnings before interest and taxes	19,347	15,991	22,412	16,600	18,049
Interest	—	—	—	—	—
Other items	331	1,865	4,175	3,400	2,500
EBIT	19,678	17,856	26,587	20,000	20,549
Taxes	6,878	6,226	9,128	6,916	7,400
Net income	$ 12,800	$ 11,630	$ 17,459	$ 13,084	$ 13,149
Average shares outstanding (000's)					
Basic	14,534	14,925	15,919	16,563	17,550
Diluted	15,216	15,505	16,814	17,278	18,597
EPS (diluted)	$0.84	$0.75	$1.04	$0.76	$0.71
Dividends/share	—	—	—	—	—
Balance Sheet Data					
Cash and cash equivalents	$ 78,149	$ 54,451	$122,793	$ 78,659	$ 72,040
Short-term investments	15,000	—	—	19,767	42,748
Accounts receivable	1,835	1,709	3,576	1,640	1,877
Inventories	19,434	18,834	20,906	14,616	11,764
Other current assets	1,426	1,739	1,871	1,338	4,067
Total current assets	115,844	76,733	149,146	116,020	132,496
Property and equipment	7,332	7,558	7,601	3,391	3,261
Other assets (including intangibles)	7,239	5,374	3,839	2,697	2,248
Total assets	130,415	89,665	160,586	122,106	138,005
Accounts payable	76,128	62,291	85,866	66,625	50,157
Total current liabilities	86,138	69,103	95,691	74,137	55,630
Long-term financing obligations	964	1,213	1,418	666	863
Retained earnings	48,999	36,199	24,569	7,110	(6,362)
Treasury stock at cost	(161,841)	(161,841)	(95,391)	(75,395)	(18,008)
Stockholders' equity	43,269	19,290	63,477	47,303	81,515
Cash Flow Data					
Net cash provided by operating activities	$ 39,018	($ 2,927)	$ 41,455	$ 40,518	$ 31,272
Net cash used in investing activities	(17,345)	(2,000)	15,016	21,065	(2,053)
Net cash provided (used) in financing activities	1,981	(63,357)	(12,296)	(54,964)	(16,797)

Source: Blue Nile Inc., 10-K reports and annual reports for 2005, 2007, and 2009.

issued to officers, employees, non-employee directors, and consultants. Going into 2010, stock options for just over 2.6 million shares were outstanding; of those, 1.6 million were exercisable in 2010. Blue Nile also had an employee stock purchase plan, but no shares had been issued as of January 2010.

OVERVIEW OF THE JEWELRY INDUSTRY

The worldwide jewelry and watch market was estimated to be between $135 million and $140 billion in 2009 and, according to U.S. Department of Commerce, U.S. jewelry sales totaled $58.8 billion in 2009. Industry revenues had grown by approximately 5.5 percent annually since the mid-1980s before reaching a peak at $60 billion in 2007 and then declining with the onset of the U.S. recession in 2008. Diamond jewelry sales were particularly hard hit by the recession, with industry sales declining from $32.5 billion in 2005 to an estimated $29.5 billion in 2009. The 2008–2009 falloff in sales was the steepest decline in industry revenues since the recession of the early 1980s. In addition to being cyclical, diamond jewelry sales were also somewhat seasonal, with relatively higher sales in February (Valentine's Day), May (Mother's Day), and the October–December holiday shopping season.

The diamond and fine jewelry retail market was intensely competitive, with sales highly fragmented among locally owned jewelry stores, retail jewelry store chains with 100+ stores, numerous chain department stores, online retailers that sold fine jewelry, online auction sites, television shopping retailers, and mass merchants such as discount superstores and wholesale clubs whose merchandise offerings included fine jewelry. The Jewelry Board of Trade estimated that there were some 22,415 specialty jewelry firms in the United States in 2009, down from 26,750 specialty jewelry retailers in 1999. Most specialty retailers operated only one or two stores and recorded annual sales of about $1.7 million. However, while the number of jewelers was in decline, the number of jewelry stores in the United States remained relatively stable at about 27,000. According to the *National Jeweler,* the top 40 jewelry chain stores operated 6,405 stores in 2008, up from 4,537 a decade earlier. For example, Zale Corporation increased its stores from 1,100 to 1,900 and Sterling Jewelers increased its stores from 768 to 1,360 over the decade. The five largest specialty jewelry retailers in the United States had increased their collective share from about 18 percent to about 22 percent of specialty jewelry sales since 1999—reflecting a continuing industry trend toward consolidation.

Nonetheless, independent jewelers, including those with fewer than 100 stores, accounted for about 70 percent of the sales made by specialty jewelry retailers. Exhibit 6 presents revenues and market shares for the top 20 U.S. jewelry retailers in 2008.

Competition in Jewelry Retailing

The principal competitive factors in the fine jewelry market were product selection and quality; price; customer service and support; brand recognition; reputation; reliability and trust; and, in the case of online retailers, website features and functionality, convenience, and speed of delivery. Blue Nile's primary competition came from both online and offline retailers that offered products within the higher value segment of the jewelry market. Many brick-and-mortar jewelry retailers (including market leaders Zale, Sterling, Tiffany, and Helzberg, among many others) had recently begun selling jewelry online at their websites, although the online category represented a small portion of their total sales. For example, only 3.6 percent of Zale Corporation's sales were made online. The U.S. Department of Commerce estimated Internet sales of jewelry in 2009 at $2.7 billion—a 10.7 percent increase from 2008.

Blue Nile's Chief Rivals in Online Jewelry Retailing

There were dozens of online retailers of diamonds in 2010. Most online jewelry retailers employed a business model similar to Blue Nile's, keeping their inventories lean, purchasing stones from suppliers only when an order for a specific stone was received, and delivering the merchandise a few days after the order was placed. The most popular sites, in addition to market leader Blue Nile, included Diamonds.com, Whiteflash.com, Ice.com, JamesAllen.com, Overstock.com, and Amazon.com.

Diamonds.com   Diamonds.com was founded in 2000 and headquartered in Las Vegas; the principal owners had more than 25 years' experience in all areas of the diamond industry. The company's product offering included more than 40,000 loose diamonds sourced from New York City's famed 47th Street diamond district, along with a selection of settings, rings, bracelets,

Exhibit 6   **Revenues and Market Shares for the 20 Largest U.S. Jewelry Retailers, 2008 ($ billions)**

Rank	Marketer	Sales	Market Share (%)
1	Walmart	$ 2.9	4.8%
2	Sterling Jewelers*	2.5	4.3
	Jared	0.7	
	Kays	1.5	
	Regionals	0.3	
3	Zale Corporation (1,900 locations in the United States, Canada, and Puerto Rico)	1.7	4.8
4	Tiffany & Co. (220 stores in the United States and international locations)	1.5	4.3
5	QVC	1.4	2.9
6	Sears	0.9	2.6
7	JCPenney	0.9	2.3
8	Finlay Fine Jewelry**	0.9	1.6
9	Macy's East	0.6	1.5
10	Neiman Marcus	0.6	1.4
11	Costco Wholesale	0.5	0.9
12	Target	0.5	0.9
13	Fred Meyer Jewelers (374 stores in 34 states under the brands Fred Meyer Jewelers, Littman Jewelers, and Barclay Jewelers)	0.4	0.8
14	Helzberg Diamond Shops (270 locations)	0.4	0.8
15	Jewelry Television	0.4	0.7
16	Macy's West	0.4	0.7
17	Tourneau (30 locations in 13 states)***	0.4	0.7
18	Cartier	0.3	0.6
19	Blue Nile	0.3	0.6
20	HSN	0.3	0.6
Subtotal	Top 20 firms	17.8	30.0
Others	22,400 firms (average $1.7 million)	42.2	70.0
Total		$60.0	100.0%

*Sterling was a wholly owned subsidiary of Britain-based Signet Group, plc; Sterling operated 925 Kay's Jewelry stores in 50 states, 175 Jared Galleria of Jewelry showrooms in 26 states, and 260 other regional stores under a variety of brand names in 31 states.

**Finlay New York provided considerable product to department stores.

***Tourneau's sales were heavily concentrated in fine watches.

Source: Company websites and annual reports, and IDEX online.

necklaces, and earrings. There was extensive educational information on the Diamonds.com website; the discussion of the four C's of purchasing a diamond was lucid and informative. There was a search function that allowed site visitors to search the loose diamond inventory based on shape, carat size, cut, color, clarity, and price. Shoppers had the ability to customize their purchase by choosing a stone and a setting. Online shoppers could view diamond grading reports issued by either the Gemological Institute of America or the American Gemological Society Laboratory for all loose diamonds, shipping was free, and orders came with an identifying grading report and a warranty document. Customers could return noncustomized orders for a full refund (excluding shipping, handling, and insurance) for up to 30 days after delivery; returns were not accepted on custom work or special orders unless an error had been made. The staff at Diamonds.com included expert gemologists trained at the world's leading gemological laboratories; shoppers could call a toll-free number to receive assistance or to place a phone order.

Whiteflash.com

About half of Whiteflash's sales involved orders for customized jewelry. Whiteflash could tap a pool of about 50,000 stones, most of which were also available for sale at other online retailers.[7] Of particular interest was a trade-up program that Blue Nile and most other online rivals didn't match: a customer could swap a Whiteflash rock for a higher-priced one at any time, paying the difference between the new diamond and the original purchase price, less shipping. Whiteflash had a policy of not accepting returns on customized jewelry products unless an error had been made in doing the custom work; for loose stones and standard settings Whiteflash offered a risk-free 10-day return policy. The education materials at the Whiteflash website included video tutorials.

Ice.com

More than 500,000 customers had made purchases at Ice.com since the company began online operations in 2001. Its product offerings were all finished products; no customization options were available. The company had a monthly payment option, provided free shipping on orders over $150, and had an unconditional 30-day money-back guarantee. Bridal and engagement rings came with an appraisal certificate. There was no educational information on the company's website, and the information provided about the quality of its diamond jewelry was limited. Customers could make inquiries via a toll-free number or e-mail.

JamesAllen.com

Founded in 1998, JamesAllen.com had grown to be one of the largest online diamond retailers. The firm claimed to offer "the world's most beautiful engagement rings coupled with the finest laboratory graded diamonds, all at an extraordinary value." It had been featured in such trade magazines as *National Jeweler* and profiled by the *Washington Post, U.S. News & World Report,* NBC News, and National Public Radio. While an estimated 3 percent of the round diamonds sold in the United States qualified as "Ideal" under AGSL grading standards, more than 90 percent of the customers shopping at JamesAllen.com chose diamonds from the retailer's Signature Ideal, Ideal, or Premium categories. All stones came with grading reports from either the Gemological Institute of America or the American Gemological Society Laboratory.

The product offerings at JamesAllen.com included 55,000 loose diamonds; preset engagement rings; preset wedding and anniversary rings; diamond studs; other diamond jewelry; and designer jewelry by Amy Levine, Danhov, and Leo Popov. Shoppers could customize their own diamond rings, studs, and pendants. The JamesAllen.com website had a comprehensive Education section that featured an interactive demonstration of the importance of diamond cut, 3D viewing, and tips and search tools. An expert staff answered questions via phone or e-mail. JamesAllen.com provided free overnight shipping via FedEx or UPS on all orders within the United States. Orders outside the United States had to be prepaid via wire transfer and carried a shipping fee of $100. The company had a full 30-day return policy, but loose diamond returns that did not include the original laboratory grading report were subject to a charge of $150.

ENDNOTES

[1] Kiri Blakeley, "Are Diamonds Still a Girl's Best Friend?" *Forbes,* April 17, 2009, http://www.forbes.com/2009/04/17/engagement-weddings-diamonds-forbes-woman-style-retail.html, accessed August 19, 2010.
[2] Quoted in "A Boy's Best Friend: Internet Jewelers," *The Economist* 386, no. 8572 (March 22, 2008), p. 7.

[3] Blue Nile, 2007 10-K report, p. 4.
[4] Sean O'Neill, "Clicks and Stones" *Kiplinger's Personal Finance,* February 2006, www.kiplinger.com/personalfinance/magazine/archives/2006/02/diamonds.html, accessed August 27, 2010.
[5] As cited in "Internet Retailer Best of the Web 2007," *Internet Retailer,* December 2006,

www.internetretailer.com, accessed February 27, 2010.
[6] *Forbes,* http://video.forbes.com/fvn/lifestyle/blue-nile, accessed August 18, 2010.
[7] Kiplinger.com, accessed February 2010.

Apple Inc. in 2010

Lou Marino
The University of Alabama

John E. Gamble
University of South Alabama

Despite the effects of ongoing poor economic conditions in the United States, Apple Inc. celebrated record quarterly revenues and unit sales of computers during its third quarter of 2010. In addition, the company's newly released iPad tablet computer had sold 3.3 million units between its April 3, 2010, launch and the June 26, 2010, quarter end. The company also sold 8.4 million iPhones during the quarter. Most of the smartphone units sold during the third quarter of 2010 were iPhone 3GS models since the new iPhone 4 launched only four days prior to the close of the quarter. Although there had been some criticism of the antenna design of the iPhone 4, more than 3 million iPhone 4 units had been purchased by July 16, 2010, with only 1.7 percent being returned by dissatisfied customers. By comparison, the iPhone 3GS had a 6 percent return rate.

Apple's chief operating officer, Tim Cook, commented to the *Wall Street Journal* that the company was selling iPads and iPhones "as fast as we can make them" and was "working around the clock to try to get supply and demand in balance."[1] Some analysts were projecting that Apple would sell nearly 12 million iPad tablet computers by year-end 2010. However, others were concerned that once Apple aficionados had purchased an iPad to complement their iPhone, iPod, or Mac, further sales growth might be difficult to achieve. A former Apple executive commented, "The first five million will be sold in a heartbeat. But let's see: you can't make a phone call with it, you can't take a picture with it, and you have to buy content that before now you were not willing to pay for. That seems tough to me."[2]

Analysts were also concerned with the general decline in iPod unit sales and worried that Apple might have to struggle to sustain its growth in the smartphone market. The iPod had been important in the company's resurgence in the past decade, but sustained growth in iPhone sales were critical to the company's financial performance, since iPhone sales accounted for $5.33 billion of the company's third-quarter 2010 revenues of $15.7 billion. Research in Motion (RIM) had been known for innovative smartphones since it introduced the BlackBerry in 1999, but Google's development of the Android operating system for smartphones had allowed HTC, LG, Nokia, and Samsung to introduce smartphones that matched many of the iPhone's best features. In addition, Microsoft's Windows Mobile 7 operating system, planned for a late-2010 launch, was expected to surpass some of the capabilities of the iPhone operating system. Google was also a growing threat to Apple, since many computer makers were developing new tablet computers similar to the iPad that would run the Android operating system; the two companies seemed to be headed for a future battle in mobile ads.

COMPANY HISTORY AND FINANCIAL PERFORMANCE

Steven Wozniak and Steven Jobs founded Apple Computer in 1976 when they began selling a crudely designed personal computer called the

Apple I to Silicon Valley computer enthusiasts. Two years later, the partners introduced the first mass-produced personal computer (PC), the Apple II. The Apple II boasted the first color display and eventually sold more than 10,000 units. While the Apple II was relatively successful, the next revision of the product line, the Macintosh (Mac), would dramatically change personal computing through its user-friendly graphical user interface (GUI), which allowed users to interact with screen images rather than merely type text commands.

The Macintosh that was introduced in 1984 was hailed as a breakthrough in personal computing, but it did not have the speed, power, or software availability to compete with the PC that IBM had introduced in 1981. One of the reasons the Macintosh lacked the necessary software was that Apple put very strict restrictions on the Apple Certified Developer Program, which made it difficult for software developers to obtain Macs at a discount and receive informational materials about the operating system.

With the Mac faring poorly in the market, founder Steve Jobs became highly critical of the company's president and CEO, John Sculley, who had been hired by the board in 1983. Finally, in 1985, as Sculley was preparing to visit China, Jobs devised a boardroom coup to replace him. Sculley found out about the plan and canceled his trip. After Apple's board voted unanimously to keep Sculley in his position, Jobs, who was retained as chairman of the company but stripped of all decision-making authority, soon resigned. During the remainder of 1985, Apple continued to encounter problems and laid off one-fifth of its employees while posting its first ever quarterly loss.

Despite these setbacks, Apple kept bringing innovative products to the market, while closely guarding the secrets behind its technology. In 1987, Apple released a revamped Macintosh computer that proved to be a favorite in K–12 schools and with graphic artists and other users needing excellent graphics capabilities. However, by 1990, PCs running Windows 3.0 and Word for Windows were preferred by businesses and consumers and held a commanding 97+ percent share of the market for personal computers.

In 1991, Apple released its first-generation notebook computer, the PowerBook and, in 1993, Apple's board of directors opted to remove Sculley from the position of CEO. The board chose to place the chief operating officer, Michael Spindler, in the vacated spot. Under Spindler, Apple released the PowerMac family of PCs in 1994, the first Macs to incorporate the PowerPC chip, a very fast processor co-developed with Motorola and IBM. Even though the PowerMac family received excellent reviews by technology analysts, Microsoft's Windows 95 matched many of the capabilities of the Mac OS and prevented the PowerMac from gaining significant market share. In January 1996, Apple asked Spindler to resign and chose Gil Amelio, former president of National Semiconductor, to take his place.

During his first 100 days in office, Amelio announced many sweeping changes for the company. He split Apple into seven distinct divisions, each responsible for its own profit or loss, and he tried to better inform the developers and consumers of Apple's products and projects. Amelio acquired NeXT, the company Steve Jobs had founded upon his resignation from Apple in 1985. Steve Jobs was rehired by Apple as part of the acquisition. In 1997, after recording additional quarterly losses, Apple's board terminated Amelio's employment with the company and named Steve Jobs interim CEO.

Apple introduced the limited feature iMac in 1998 and the company's iBook line of notebook computers in 1999. The company was profitable in every quarter during 1998 and 1999, and its share price reached an all-time high in the upper $70 range. Jobs was named permanent CEO of Apple in 2000 and, in 2001, oversaw the release of the iPod. The iPod recorded modest sales until the 2003 launch of iTunes—the online retail store where consumers could legally purchase individual songs. By July 2004, 100 million songs had been sold and iTunes had a 70 percent market share among all legal online music download services. The tremendous success of the iPod helped transform Apple from a struggling computer company into a powerful consumer electronics company.

By 2005, consumers' satisfaction with the iPod had helped renew interest in Apple computers, with its market share in personal computers growing from a negligible share to 4 percent. The company also exploited consumer loyalty and satisfaction with the iPod to enter the market for smartphones with the 2007 launch of the iPhone.

Much of Apple's turnaround could be credited to Steve Jobs, who had idea after idea for how to improve the company and turn its performance around. He not only consistently pushed for innovative new ideas and products but also enforced several structural changes, including ridding the company of unprofitable segments and divisions.

The success of the turnaround could also be attributed to the efforts of Tim Cook, Apple's chief operating officer. While Jobs provided the vision for the organization, Cook and the other members of the executive staff and the board of directors were responsible for ensuring that all operations of Apple ran efficiently and smoothly. Between mid-2008 and mid-2009, when Steve Jobs took a leave of absence to receive a liver transplant, Cook took on the role of acting CEO.

A summary of Apple's financial performance for fiscal years 2005 through 2009 is provided in Exhibit 1. The company's net sales by operating segment and product line and unit sales by product line for 2005 through 2009 are provided in Exhibit 2.

OVERVIEW OF THE PERSONAL COMPUTER INDUSTRY

The personal computer industry was relatively consolidated, with five sellers accounting for 78.5 percent of the U.S. shipments and 60.3 percent of worldwide shipments in 2009—see Exhibit 3. Prior to the onset of the recession that began in 2008, the PC industry was expected to grow at a rate of 5–6 percent, to reach $354 billion by 2012. However, the effects of the recession caused a dramatic decline in industry revenues in 2008 and 2009.

PC industry shipments grew by a healthy 22.4 percent during the second quarter of 2010 as businesses were forced to replace aging computers. The sharp spike in shipments was not expected to continue throughout the year, with analysts expecting a 12.6 percent increase in worldwide shipments for the full year 2010. PC shipments in emerging markets were expected to grow at 18.5 percent to allow demand in emerging markets to overtake demand for PCs in developed countries by the end of 2010. Shipments of PCs

in developed countries were expected to increase by only 7.2 percent in 2010 and were not expected to reach double-digit rates until 2011. Industry revenues were projected to grow more slowly than shipments because average selling prices had declined steadily since 2008.

Both businesses and consumers were tending to replace desktop PCs with portable PCs such as laptops and netbooks. Total shipments of portable PCs grew by 18.4 percent in 2009, with consumer purchases of portable PCs growing by 38 percent during the year. Low-end laptops and netbooks accounted for the majority of consumer portable PC sales in 2009. The sale of desktop computers was expected to decline in all country markets except emerging markets in Asia, which would allow portable PCs to make up 70 percent of industry shipments by 2012.

APPLE'S COMPETITIVE POSITION IN THE PERSONAL COMPUTER INDUSTRY

Even though a larger percentage of Apple's revenues were increasingly coming from noncomputer products, the company still saw computers as its core business. Apple's proprietary operating system and strong graphics-handling capabilities differentiated Macs from PCs, but many consumers and business users who owned PCs were hesitant to purchase a Mac because of Apple's premium pricing and because of the learning curve involved with mastering its proprietary operating system. The company's market share in the United States had improved from 4 percent in 2005 to 8 percent in 2009 primarily because of the success of the iPod and iPhone. These products created a halo effect whereby some consumers (but not business users) switched to Apple computers after purchasing an iPod or iPhone.

Apple's computer product line consisted of several models in various configurations. Its desktop lines included the Mac Pro (aimed at professional and business users); the iMac (targeted toward consumer, educational, and business use); and Mac mini (made specifically for consumer use). Apple had three notebook product

Exhibit 1 **Summary of Apple, Inc.'s Financial Performance, 2005–2009 ($ millions, except share amounts)**

Income Statement Data	2009	2008	2007	2006	2005
Net Sales					
Domestic	$ 19,870	$ 18,469	$ 14,128	$ 11,486	$ 8,334
International	16,667	14,010	9,878	7,829	5,597
Total net sales	36,537	32,479	24,006	19,315	13,931
Costs and Expenses					
Cost of sales	23,397	21,334	15,852	13,717	9,889
Research and development (R&D)	1,333	1,109	782	712	535
Selling, general and administrative (SG&A)	4,149	3,761	2,963	2,433	1,864
Total operating expenses	5,482	4,870	3,745	3,145	2,399
Operating income	7,658	6,275	4,409	2,453	1,643
Other income and expense	326	620	599	365	165
Income before provision for income taxes	7,984	6,895	5,008	2,818	1,808
Provision for income taxes	2,280	2,061	1,512	829	480
Net income	$ 5,704	$ 4,834	$ 3,496	$ 1,989	$ 1,328
Earnings per common share—diluted	$6.29	$5.36	$3.93	$2.27	$1.55
Shares used in computing earnings per share—diluted (in thousands)	907,005	902,139	889,292	877,526	856,878

Balance Sheet Data (as of September 30)					
Cash, cash equivalents, and short-term investments	$ 23,464	$ 24,490	$ 15,386	$ 10,110	$ 8,261
Accounts receivable, net	3,361	2,422	1,637	1,252	895
Inventories	455	509	346	270	165
Property, plant, and equipment, net	2,954	2,455	1,832	1,281	817
Total assets	53,851	39,572	25,347	17,205	11,516
Current liabilities	19,284	14,092	9,299	6,443	3,487
Noncurrent liabilities	6,737	4,450	1,516	778	601
Shareholders' equity	$ 27,832	$ 21,030	$ 14,532	$ 9,984	$ 7,428

Source: Apple Inc., 2007 and 2009 10-K reports.

Exhibit 2 Apple, Inc.'s Net Sales by Operating Segment, Net Sales by Product, and Unit Sales by Product, 2005–2009 ($ millions)

	2009	2008	2007	2006	2005
Net Sales by Operating Segment					
Americas net sales	$16,142	$14,573	$11,596	$ 9,415	$ 6,950
Europe net sales	9,365	7,622	5,460	4,096	3,073
Japan net sales	1,831	1,509	1,082	1,211	920
Retail net sales	6,574	6,315	4,115	3,246	2,350
Other Segments net sales [a]	2,625	2,460	1,753	1,347	998
Total net sales	$36,537	$32,479	$24,006	$19,315	$13,931
Net Sales by Product					
Desktops [b]	$ 4,308	$ 5,603	$ 4,020	$ 3,319	$ 3,436
Portables [c]	9,472	8,673	6,294	4,056	2,839
Total Macintosh net sales	$13,780	$14,276	10,314	7,375	6,275
iPod	8,091	9,153	8,305	7,375	4,540
Other music related products and services [d]	4,036	3,340	2,496	1,885	899
iPhone and related products and services [e]	6,754	1,844	123	—	—
Peripherals and other hardware [f]	1,470	1,659	1,260	1,100	1,126
Software, service, and other sales [g]	2,406	2,207	1,508	1,279	1,091
Total net sales	$36,537	$32,479	$24,006	$19,315	$13,931
Unit Sales by Product:					
Desktops [b]	3,182	3,712	2,714	2,434	2,520
Portables [c]	7,214	6,003	4,337	2,869	2,014
Total Macintosh unit sales	10,396	9,715	7,051	5,303	4,534
Net sales per Macintosh unit sold [h]	$1,326	$1,469	$1,463	$1,391	$1,384
iPod unit sales	54,132	54,828	51,630	39,409	22,497
Net sales per iPod unit sold [i]	$149	$167	$161	$195	$202
iPhone unit sales	20,731	11,627	1,389	—	—

[a] Other segments include Asia Pacific and FileMaker.
[b] Includes iMac, eMac, Mac mini, Power Mac, and Xserve product lines.
[c] Includes MacBook, MacBook Pro, iBook, and PowerBook product lines.
[d] Consists of iTunes Music Store sales, iPod services, and Apple-branded and third-party iPod accessories.
[e] Derived from handset sales, carrier agreements, and Apple-branded and third-party iPhone accessories.
[f] Includes sales of Apple-branded and third-party displays, wireless connectivity and networking solutions, and other hardware accessories.
[g] Includes sales of Apple-branded operating system, application software, third-party software, AppleCare, and Internet services.
[h] Derived by dividing total Macintosh net sales by total Macintosh unit sales.
[i] Derived by dividing total iPod net sales by total iPod unit sales.
Source: Apple Inc., 2007 and 2009 10-K reports.

Exhibit 3   **U.S. and Global Market Shares of Leading PC Vendors, 2000 and 2005–2009**

A. U.S. Market Shares of the Leading PC Vendors, 2000 and 2005–2009

2009 Rank	Vendor	2009		2008		2007		2006		2005		2000	
		Shipments (in 000s)	Market Share	Shipments (in 000s)	Market Share	Shipments (in 000s)	Market Share	Shipments (in 000s)	Market Share	Shipments (in 000s)	Market Share	Shipments (in 000s)	Market Share
1	Hewlett Packard[1]	18,781	26.9%	16,218	24.7%	16,759	23.9%	11,600	21.5%	12,456	19.5%	5,630	11.5%
2	Dell	17,099	24.5	19,276	29.4	19,645	28.0	20,472	31.2	21,466	33.6	9,645	19.7
	Compaq[1]	—	—	—	—	—	—	—	—	—	—	7,761	15.9
3	Acer[1]	7,983	11.4	6,106	9.3	3,860	5.5	1,421	2.2	n.a.	n.a.	n.a.	n.a.
4	Apple	5,579	8.0	5,158	7.9	4,081	5.8	3,109	4.7	2,555	4.0	n.a.	n.a.
5	Toshiba	5,379	7.7	3,788	5.8	3,509	5.0	2,843	4.3	2,327	3.6	n.a.	n.a.
	Others	15,008	21.5	15,026	22.9	22,235	31.7	23,350	35.7	25,070	39.2	18,959	38.8
	All vendors	69,829	100.0%	65,571	100.0%	70,088	100.0%	65,481	100.0%	63,874	100.0%	48,900	100.0%

B. Worldwide Market Shares of the Leading PC Vendors, 2000 and 2005–2009

2009 Rank	Vendor	2009		2008		2007		2006		2005		2000	
		Shipments (in 000s)	Market Share	Shipments (in 000s)	Market Share	Shipments (in 000s)	Market Share	Shipments (in 000s)	Market Share	Shipments (in 000s)	Market Share	Shipments (in 000s)	Market Share
1	Hewlett Packard[1]	59,942	20.3%	54,293	18.9%	50,526	18.8%	38,838	16.5%	32,575	15.7%	10,327	7.4%
2	Dell	38,416	13.1	42,388	14.7	39,993	14.9	39,094	16.6	37,755	18.2	14,801	10.6
	Compaq[1]	—	—	—	—	—	—	—	—	—	—	17,399	12.5
3	Acer[2]	38,377	13.0	31,377	10.9	21,206	7.9	13,594	5.8	9,845	4.7	n.a.	n.a.
4	Lenovo/IBM[3]	24,887	8.5	21,870	7.6	20,224	7.5	16,609	7.1	12,979	6.2	9,308	6.7
5	Toshiba	15,878	5.4	13,727	4.8	10,936	4.1	9,292	3.9	7,234	3.5	n.a.	n.a.
	Others	116,709	39.7	123,910	43.1	126,075	46.9	117,971	50.1	107,450	51.7	80,640	58.0
	All vendors	294,208	100.0%	287,566	100.0%	268,960	100.0%	235,397	100.0%	207,837	100.0%	139,057	100.0%

n.a. = not available; sales and market shares for these companies in the years where n.a. appears are included in the "Others" category because the company was not in the top 5 in shipments or market share.

[1]Compaq was acquired by Hewlett-Packard in May 2002.

[2]Acer acquired Gateway in 2007 and Packard Bell in 2008. Data for Acer includes shipments for Gateway starting in Q4 2007 and shipments for Packard Bell starting in Q1 2008, and only Acer data for prior periods.

[3]Lenovo, a Chinese computer company, completed the acquisition of IBM's PC business in 2005. The numbers for Lenovo/IBM for 2000 reflect sales of IBM branded PCs only; the numbers for 2005–2009 reflect their combined sales beginning in the second quarter of 2005. In 2007, Lenovo rebranded all IBM PCs as Lenovo.

Source: International Data Corp.

lines as well: MacBook Pro (for professional and advanced consumer users), the MacBook (designed for education users and consumers), and the MacBook Air (designed for professional and consumer users).

The MacBook Air was Apple's most recent notebook introduction. The MacBook Air was designed to target users who valued both portability and power. The notebook featured a 13.3-inch screen, a full-size keyboard, a built-in video camera, and cutting-edge wireless connectivity. This sleek notebook measured only 0.76 inches at its maximum height when closed and weighed only three pounds. The MacBook Air had won critical acclaim for both its design and its ease of use, and was one of the products helping Apple gain ground in the competitive computer industry. All Apple computers were priced at a steep premium compared to PCs and laptops offered by Dell, HP, and other rivals. The company lowered the prices of all its computer models by 10 percent or more in June 2009, with the price of the MacBook Pro falling to $1,199 and the MacBook Air getting a $300 price cut, to $1,499.

APPLE'S RIVALS IN THE PERSONAL COMPUTER INDUSTRY

Hewlett-Packard

Hewlett-Packard (HP) was broadly diversified across segments of the computer industry with business divisions focused on information technology consulting services, large enterprise systems, software, personal computers, printers and other imaging devices, and financial services. The company's Personal Systems Group (PSG), which manufactured and marketed HP and Compaq desktop computers and portable computers, was its largest division, accounting for revenues of $35.3 billion in 2009. HP recorded total net revenues of $114.6 billion in 2009, with information technology services contributing nearly $34.7 billion, imaging and printing devices contributing $24 billion, and enterprise systems accounting for about $15.4 billion. The company's financial services and software business units accounted for sales of about $6 billion in 2009.

HP's sales of personal computers declined by 16.5 percent between 2008 and 2009 as the recession forced consumers and businesses to reduce expenditures and capital investments. Handheld computers and workstations were affected most by the recession, with sales declining by 52.2 percent and 33.7 percent, respectively, during 2009. The company's sales of desktop computers were affected not only by the recession but also by business users' and consumers' growing preference for portable computers over desktop models. HP portable computers were harmed least by the recession, with a 10.8 percent decline in sales between 2008 and 2009. HP did sustain some growth in emerging markets despite the recession in developed countries. Exhibit 4 provides the revenue contribution by PSG product line for 2005 through 2009.

Dell Inc.

Dell Inc. was the world's second-largest seller of personal computers, with revenues of $52.9 billion for the fiscal year ending January 29, 2010.

Exhibit 4 Hewlett-Packard Personal Systems Group, Net Revenue ($ millions)

Product	2009	2008	2007	2006	2005
Notebooks	$20,210	$22,657	$17,650	$12,005	$ 9,763
Desktop PCs	12,864	16,626	15,889	14,641	14,406
Workstations	1,261	1,902	1,721	1,368	1,195
Handhelds	172	360	531	650	836
Other	798	750	618	502	541
Total	$35,305	$42,295	$36,409	$29,166	$26,741

Source: Hewlett-Packard, 2007 and 2008 10-K reports.

Exhibit 5   **Dell's Revenues by Product Category, Fiscal 2008–Fiscal 2010 ($ millions)**

| Fiscal Year Ended | January 29, 2010 | | January 30, 2009 | | February 1, 2008 | |
	Dollars	% of Revenue	Dollars	% of Revenue	Dollars	% of Revenue
Servers and networking	$ 6,032	11%	$ 6,512	11%	$ 6,486	11%
Storage	2,192	4	2,667	4	2,429	4
Services	5,622	11	5,351	9	4,980	8
Software and peripherals	9,499	18	10,603	17	9,927	16
Mobility	16,610	31	18,604	30	17,961	29
Desktop PCs	12,947	25	17,364	29	19,350	32
Totals	$52,902	100%	$61,101	100%	$61,133	100%

Source: Dell Inc., 2010 10-K report.

Exhibit 5 presents Dell's revenues by product category for fiscal 2008 through fiscal 2010. The recession significantly affected Dell's financial performance in late 2008, when its fourth-quarter sales declined by 48 percent from the same period in the prior year. The revenue decline was a result of an overall decline in unit sales and strong price competition in both desktop PCs and portables. In addition, Dell's net earnings fell from $2.9 billion in fiscal 2008 to $2.5 billion in fiscal 2009 to $1.4 billion in fiscal 2010. The company offered a wide range of desktop computers and portables, ranging from low-end, low-priced models to state-of-the-art, high-priced models. The company also offered servers; workstations; peripherals such as printers, monitors, and projectors; and Wi-Fi products.

Acer

Taiwan-based Acer was the world's second-largest portable computer provider and third-largest desktop computer manufacturer in 2010. Acer's 2009 consolidated revenues rose by approximately 13 percent from the previous year to reach $18.3 billion, while operating income increased by 17 percent to reach $488 million. Its 40.5 percent annual growth in global PC shipments between 2005 and 2009 ranked first among the industry's leading sellers. The company's largest and one of its fastest-growing geographic segments was the Europe/Middle East/Africa segment, which accounted for 52 percent of the company's PC, desktop, and notebook sales. A summary of the company's financial performance between 2006 and 2009 is presented in Exhibit 6.

Exhibit 6   **Financial Summary for Acer Incorporated, 2006–2009 ($ thousands)**

	2009	2008	2007	2006
Revenue	$18,264,125	$16,186,102	$15,252,801	$10,577,113
Gross profit	1,855,993	1,697,374	1,565,278	1,150,865
Operating income	488,102	416,962	336,211	224,993
Operating margin	2.7%	2.6%	2.2%	2.1%
Income before income taxes	476,759	438,723	498,736	408,481
Net income	$361,248	$347,919	$427,774	$308,080

Source: Acer Incorporated Financial Snapshot, http://www.acer-group.com/public/Investor_Relations/financial_snapshot.htm.

Acer's multibrand strategy—which positioned Acer, Gateway, eMachines, and Packard Bell at distinct price points in the market for PCs—had helped it become one of the fastest-growing vendors in the United States. The company based its competitive strategy on its four pillars of success: a winning business model, competitive products, an innovative marketing strategy, and an efficient operation model. The company's computer offering included desktop and mobile PCs, LCD monitors, servers and storage, and high-definition TVs and projectors. In 2009, the company entered the market for smartphones with the launch of its Liquid line of stylish, high-end smartphones, which used Google's Android operating system.

APPLE'S COMPETITIVE POSITION IN THE PERSONAL MEDIA PLAYER INDUSTRY

Although Apple didn't introduce the first portable digital music player, the company held a 73 percent market share digital music players in 2010 and the name iPod had become a generic term used to describe digital media players. When Apple launched its first iPod, many critics did not give the product much of a chance for success, given its fairly hefty price tag of $399. However, the iPod's sleek styling, ease of use, and eventual price decreases allowed it to develop such high levels of customer satisfaction and loyalty that rivals found it difficult to gain traction in the marketplace.

The most popular portable players in 2010 not only played music but could be connected to Wi-Fi networks to play videos, access the Internet, view photos, or listen to FM high-definition radio. The iPod Touch was the best-selling media player in 2010, but electronics sector reviewers generally agreed that Microsoft's Zune, Archos's Vision models, and Sony's X-series media players compared quite favorably to the iPod Touch. In addition, electronics reviewers found that inexpensive MP3 music players offered by SanDisk, Creative, iRiver, and others generally performed as well as Apple's more basic iPod models. However, none of Apple's key rivals in the media player industry had been able to achieve a market share greater than 5 percent in 2010. Most consumers did not find many convincing reasons to consider any brand of media player other than Apple.

In 2010, Apple offered four basic styles in the iPod product line:

- *The iPod Shuffle*—a basic flash-based player with no screen, FM radio, or voice recorder. The 4 gigabyte (GB) model was capable of storing 1,000 songs, and its rechargeable lithium polymer battery provided up to 10 hours of playback time.

- *The iPod Nano*—a multimedia player offered in 8 GB (8 hours of video or 2,000 songs) and 16 GB (16 hours of video or 4,000 songs) sizes that used a click wheel interface to navigate the player's controls. It allowed users to view photos and videos as well as to listen to music in Apple's Advanced Audio Coding (AAC) format, and it provided up to 24 hours of music playback and 5 hours of video playback on a single charge.

- *The iPod Classic*—a hard-drive-based click-wheel-controlled multimedia player offered with a 160 GB hard drive that, similar to the smaller Nano, played music in Apple's AAC format and showed videos and photos. The 160 GB player held up to 40,000 songs or 200 hours of video and provided up to 36 hours of audio playback or 6 hours of video playback on a single charge.

- *The iPod Touch*—a multimedia flash memory player controlled though an innovative touch screen interface that was a feature of the iPhone. It was offered in 8 GB (1,750 songs, 10 hours of video), 32 GB (7,000 songs, 40 hours of video), and 64 GB (14,000 songs, 80 hours of video) sizes, and provided up to 30 hours of music playback and 6 hours of video playback on a single charge. This multimedia player featured a wide 3.5-inch screen and built-in Wi-Fi, which allowed users to connect to the Internet and access e-mail, buy music from the iTunes store, and surf the Web from wireless hotspots. Touch users also had access to maps, the weather, and stocks, and the ability to write notes to themselves. The Touch featured an accelerometer that detected when the Touch rotated and automatically changed the display from portrait to landscape.

iTunes

Aside from the iPod's stylish design and ease of use, another factor that contributed to the popularity of the iPod was Apple's iPod/iTunes combination. In 2010, more than 50 million customers visited the iTunes Store to purchase and download music, videos, movies, and television shows that could be played on iPods, iPhones, or Apple TV devices. (Apple TV was a device that allowed users to play iTunes content on televisions.) Also in 2010, Apple's iTunes Store recorded its 10-billionth download since its launch in 2003. Additionally, iTunes was the world's most popular online movie store, with customers purchasing and renting more than 50,000 movies each day. Apple did not offer an iTunes subscription service, although a July 2010 survey by research firm NPD Group found that 7 to 8 million iPod owners would have a strong interest in subscribing to a service that would allow them to stream iTunes music and videos.

The success of the iPod/iTunes combination gave iTunes a 69 percent share of the U.S. digital music market in 2010. Since downloads accounted for about 40 percent of all music sales in the United States, iTunes' commanding share of the digital music sales also gave it a 27 percent share of total U.S. music sales. Amazon.com was the second-largest seller of digital music in the United States, with an 8 percent share of the market. Amazon.com and Walmart were tied for second in total U.S. music sales, with 12 percent market shares.

APPLE'S COMPETITIVE POSITION IN THE MOBILE PHONE INDUSTRY

The first version of the iPhone was released on June 29, 2007, and had a multitouch screen with a virtual keyboard, a camera, and a portable media player (equivalent to the iPod) in addition to text messaging and visual voice mail. It also offered Internet services including e-mail, Web browsing (using access to Apple's Safari Web browser), and local Wi-Fi connectivity. More than 270,000 first-generation iPhones were sold during the first 30 hours of the product's launch. The iPhone was named *Time* magazine's Invention of the Year in 2007.

The iPhone 3G was released in 70 countries on July 11, 2008, and was available in the United States exclusively through AT&T Mobility. The iPhone 3G combined the functionality of a wireless phone and an iPod, and allowed users to access the Internet wirelessly at twice the speed of the previous version of the iPhone. Apple's new phone also featured a built-in global positioning system (GPS) and, in an effort to increase adoption by corporate users, was compatible with Microsoft Exchange.

The iPhone 3GS was introduced on June 19, 2009, and included all of the features of the iPhone 3G but could also launch applications and render Web pages twice as fast as the iPhone 3G. The iPhone 3GS also featured a 3-megapixel camera, video recording, voice control, and up to 32 GB of flash memory. The iPhone 4 was launched on June 24, 2010, with the 16 GB model priced at $199 on a two-year AT&T contract and the 32 GB model priced at $299 on a two-year AT&T contract. Upgrades over the 3GS included video-calling capabilities (only over a Wi-Fi network), a higher resolution display, a 5-megapixel camera including flash and zoom, 720p video recording, a longer-lasting battery, and a gyroscopic motion sensor to enable an improved gaming experience. The iPhone 4 sold more than 1.7 million units within three days of its launch.

Similar to the iTunes/iPod partnership, Apple launched the App Store for the iPhone. The App Store allowed developers to build applications for the iPhone and to offer them either for free or for a fee. In January 2010, more than 3 billion apps had been downloaded by iPhone and iPod Touch users. Both Apple and Google had begun to embed ads into mobile apps to both create additional revenue sources and to allow app developers to earn revenues from apps that could be downloaded free of charge.

While worldwide shipments of mobile phones declined from 1.19 billion in 2008 to 1.27 billion in 2009 because of poor economic conditions in the United States and many other major country markets, worldwide sales of mobile phones grew by 21.7 percent during the first quarter of 2010 as economies in most countries began to improve. However, industry analysts did not expect the 21.7 percent year-over-year sales increase during the first quarter of 2010 to continue throughout the year and projected annual sales growth of about 11 percent for 2010. The growth in shipments of smartphones during the first quarter of 2010 outpaced the growth in basic-feature phone shipments by a considerable margin. The shipments of smartphones grew by 56.7 percent during the first quarter of 2010, while shipments of basic-feature phones increased by 18.8 percent between the first quarter of 2009 and the first quarter of 2010. The rapid growth in demand for smartphones during early 2010 allowed Research in Motion (RIM) to become the first company producing only smartphones to become a Top 5 vendor in the industry—see Exhibit 7.

Developing countries such as China offered the greatest growth opportunities but also presented challenges to smartphone producers. For example, there were 700 million mobile phone users in China, but popular-selling models were quickly counterfeited, it was difficult to develop keyboards that included the thousands of commonly used characters in the Chinese language, and most consumers preferred inexpensive feature phones over smartphones. Nevertheless, many analysts expected China to account for 10 percent of worldwide smartphone shipments within the near term. Apple planned to begin selling the iPhone in China in 2010 through a network of 25 flagship stores located in the country's largest cities. The iPhone would be available in 80 countries by year-end 2010.

With the market for smartphones growing rapidly and supporting high average selling prices, competition was becoming more heated. Google's entry into the market with its Android operating system had allowed vendors such as HTC, Motorola, Acer, and Samsung to offer models that matched many of the features of the iPhone. In addition, Microsoft's Windows Mobile 7, which was planned for a late-2010 launch, was expected to exceed the capabilities of the iPhone operating system with live tiles of rotating pictures, e-mail messages, and social-networking feeds. In addition, smartphones operating on Windows Mobile 7 would have all of the functionality of a Zune media player just as the iPhone included all of the functionality of the iPod Touch. While iPhones and Android phones primarily targeted consumers enthralled with clever and helpful Web apps, RIM had built a number one position in the smartphone market by appealing to businesspeople who needed the ability to check e-mail; maintain appointment calendars; receive fax transmissions; and open, edit, and save Microsoft Office and Adobe PDF files. Hewlett-Packard entered the market for smartphones in May 2010 with its $1.2 billion acquisition of Palm. However, Palm had lost its edge in innovation years before and was primarily popular with users who had purchased Palm Pilots in the company's heyday. Exhibit 8 presents market shares for the leading smartphone brands between 2006 and the first quarter of 2010.

APPLE'S ENTRY INTO THE MARKET FOR TABLET COMPUTERS

Apple entered the market for tablet computers with its April 3, 2010, launch of the iPad. Tablet computers such as the iPad allowed users to access the Internet, read and send e-mail, view photos, watch videos, listen to music, read e-books, and play video games. In addition, Apple's iPad could run 11,000 apps developed specifically for the iPad and most of the 225,000-plus apps developed for the iPhone and iPod Touch. Apple sold more than 3 million iPads within the first 90 days the product was on the market. Industry analysts expected that 13 million tablet computers would be sold in 2010, with Apple accounting for almost all shipments of tablet computers. The market for tablet computers was expected to increase to 46 million units by 2014. By comparison, the market for portable PCs was expected to grow to 398 million units by 2014.

Tablet computers had been on the market since the late 1990s, but only Apple's version had gained any significant interest from consumers and business users. Previous-generation tablet computers required the use of a stylus to launch applications and enter information. Most users found the stylus interface to be an annoyance and preferred to use a smartphone or laptop when portability was required. Dell, Acer, Hewlett-Packard, and Nokia were all racing to get touchscreen tablet computers to market but would be unable to do so until very late 2010 or early 2011 because of the technological differences between tablet computers and PCs. Tablet computers were technologically similar to smartphones and

Exhibit 7   Worldwide Market Shares of Leading Mobile Phone Vendors, 2000 and 2005–2009

Q1 2010 Rank	Vendor	Q1 2010		2009		2008		2007	
		Shipments (in millions)	Market Share	Shipments (in millions)	Market Share	Shipments (in millions)	Market Share	Shipments (in millions)	Market Share
1	Nokia	107.8	36.6%	431.8	38.3%	468.4	39.4%	437.1	38.3%
2	Samsung	64.3	21.8	227.2	20.1	196.8	16.5	161.1	14.1
3	LG	27.1	9.2	117.9	10.5	100.8	8.5	80.5	7.1
4	RIM	10.6	3.6	n.a.	n.a.	n.a.	n.a.	n.a.	n.a.
5	Sony Ericsson	10.5	3.6	57.0	5.1	96.6	8.1	103.4	9.1
	Others	74.6	25.3	293.8	26.0	327.7	27.5	358.8	31.4
	All vendors	294.9	100.0%	1,127.8	100.0%	1,190.1	100.0%	1,140.9	100.0%

n.a. = not available; sales and market shares for these companies in the years where n.a. appears are included in the "Others" category because the company was not in the top 5 in shipments or market share.

Source: International Data Corp.

Exhibit 8 **U.S. Smartphone Platform Market Share Rankings, Selected Periods, September 2009–May 2010**

Smartphone Platform	Share of Smartphone Subscribers			
	September 2009	December 2009	February 2010	May 2010
RIM (BlackBerry)	42.6%	41.6%	42.1%	41.7%
Apple iPhone	24.1	25.3	25.4	24.4
Microsoft Windows Mobile	19.0	18.0	15.1	13.2
Google Android	2.5	5.2	9.0	13.0
Palm	8.3	6.1	5.4	4.8
Others	3.5	3.8	3.0	2.9
Total	100.0%	100.0%	100.0%	100.0%

Source: ComScore.com.

shared almost no components with PCs. The primary reason tablet computers could not use PC components was that the small size of tablet computers limited battery size. The small battery size prevented the use of energy-hungry PC components and required that tablet computers run the limited-capability microprocessors and operating systems found in smartphones. This minimal processing capability made tablet computers suitable only for viewing information and prevented the devices from running applications such as Microsoft Word, Excel, or PowerPoint.

Intel's new Atom microprocessor and Microsoft's Windows Mobile 7 would both be suitable for use in tablet computers and were expected to arrive to market in late 2010. PC manufacturers unwilling to wait for the development of the Atom and Windows Mobile 7 were designing tablet computers that used smartphone microprocessors and Google's Android operating system. Analysts believed that HP's 2010 acquisition of Palm was motivated more by the desire to use the Palm operating system in HP tablet computers than the company's interest in entering the smartphone market. Smartphone manufacturer Archos was the only vendor offering a viable competing product to the iPad in mid-2010. E-readers such as Amazon's Kindle were not considered direct competitors to the iPad since dedicated reading devices could not browse the Internet, view videos, play music, or perform other media tasks. In addition, e-readers carried prices in the $99–$189 range, which was considerably lower than the $499–$829 range charged by Apple for various iPad models.

APPLE'S PERFORMANCE GOING INTO THE FOURTH QUARTER OF 2010

Apple set a number of records with its third-quarter 2010 performance. The company's quarterly revenue of 15.7 billion was its highest-ever quarterly sales figure, and the company set a new record for quarterly shipments of computers, with 3.47 million Macs shipped during the quarter. The company also sold 3.3 million iPads by the June 26, 2010, close of the quarter. By comparison, it took the first iPod 20 months to reach 1 million units in sales—the iPad hit the 1-million-unit mark within 30 days of its April 3, 2010, launch. In addition, Apple sold 8.4 million iPhones during the third quarter of 2010, which was 61 percent more than what was sold during the same period in 2009. The increase in iPhone sales came primarily from sales of iPhone 3GS models since the iPhone 4 launched only four days before the quarter end. Unit sales for the iPod declined by 8.6 percent between the third quarter of 2009 and the third quarter of 2010, although iPod revenues increased by 4 percent to reach $1.5 billion as consumers purchased a higher percentage of iPod Touch models rather than lower-priced iPod Shuffle, iPod Nano, and iPod Classic models.

However, the company did face some concerns going into the fourth quarter of 2010. The U.S. Justice Department had launched a preliminary inquiry into the company's tactics in the digital music industry. Specifically, the government was investigating reports that Apple had discouraged music labels from participating in an Amazon promotion by threatening to withdraw marketing support for songs included in Amazon's promotion that were also sold by the iTunes Store. Also, Steve Jobs was called upon to personally intervene in a flap involving the antenna design of the iPhone 4. Shortly after the iPhone 4 launch, the media widely reported that the iPhone 4's antenna design caused calls to be dropped if users touched the lower edges of the phone. The company reported that the company had received fewer returns of iPhone 4s than iPhone 3GS models at its launch. To calm the media frenzy that he dubbed "Antennagate," Steve Jobs called a press conference to announce that the company would provide free bumper cases to iPhone 4 buyers concerned with reception problems caused by touching the metal edge of the phone.

ENDNOTES

[1] Quoted in "New Gadgets Power Apple Sales," *Wall Street Journal Online,* July 21, 2010.

[2] Quoted in "Doing the iPad Math: Utility + Price + Desire," *New York Times,* April 2, 2010, p. B1.

Gap Inc. in 2010: Is the Turnaround Strategy Working?

Annette Lohman
California State University,
Long Beach

In the 1990s, Gap Inc. appeared to be in perfect sync with American pop culture and tastes. The brands represented affordable style and just about everyone—from well-known celebrities to typical American families—was wearing Gap clothing. Many people had to have the latest pair of khakis or a cardigan from Gap. In addition, the company's Old Navy clothing stores had reached $1 billion in annual revenues in 1997 and its Banana Republic chain hit the $1 billion sales mark in 1998. However, the company's rapid expansion during the late 1990s was accompanied by the addition of long-term debt of nearly $3 billion, the quality of its clothing declined, and the popularity of its styling waned. Despite being so perfectly attuned to American fashion and tastes in the 1990s, Gap began a decline in 2000 that had yet to be fully resolved by 2010.

The company had brought in a new CEO in 2002 and then again in 2007, both with turnaround strategies that produced some level of positive results. The 2002 turnaround strategy had successfully eliminated all long-term debt by 2007, while the company's turnaround strategy launched in 2007 was directed at expanding internationally and improving Gap's quality, styling, and overall image. By 2008, Gap had opened dozens of franchised stores the Middle East and Asia and hired well-known designer Patrick Robinson to develop more stylish and fashionable lines for its clothing stores.

Even though the company's profitability had improved through year-end 2009, its annual revenues continued the decline that began in 2005. Particularly disturbing was its rapid decline in comparable-store sales. Comparable-store sales for U.S. and international Gap, Banana Republic, and Old Navy Stores declined on average by 5 percent in 2005, 7 percent in 2006, 4 percent in 2007, 12 percent in 2008, and 3 percent in 2009. Comparable-store sales had improved slightly during the first quarter of 2010, with Gap stores experiencing a 2 percent quarter-over-quarter improvement in comparable-store sales, Banana Republic comparable-store sales improving by 5 percent between the first quarter of 2009 and the first quarter of 2010, and Old Navy comparable-store sales in the first quarter of 2010 improving by 7 percent over the same quarter in 2009. International sales remained unchanged from the first quarter of 2009 to the first quarter of 2010. It was yet to be determined if the slight improvement in comparable-store sales was a signal that Gap's latest turnaround strategy was working as planned or was a result of the gradually improving U.S. economy, which had been in a deep recession since 2008 and grew by 2.7 percent during the first quarter of 2010. Gap's consolidated statements of income for fiscal 2005 through fiscal 2009 are presented in Exhibit 1. Exhibit 2 presents the company's consolidated balance sheets for fiscal 2007 through fiscal 2009.

COMPANY HISTORY AND OVERVIEW

The Gap was founded as a San Francisco blue jeans retailer in 1969 by Doris and Don Fisher.

Exhibit 1   Gap Inc. Consolidated Statements of Earnings, Fiscal 2005–Fiscal 2009 ($ millions, except per share amounts)

	Fiscal Year Ending				
	Jan. 30, 2010	Jan. 31, 2009	Feb. 2, 2008	Feb. 3, 2009	Jan. 28, 2006
Net sales	$14,197	$14,526	$15,763	$15,923	16,023
Cost of goods sold and occupancy expenses	8,473	9.079	10,071	10,266	10,154
Gross profit	5,724	5,447	5,692	5,657	5,869
Operating expenses	3,909	3,899	4,377	4,432	4,124
Operating income	1,815	1,548	1,315	1,225	1,745
Interest expense	6	1	26	41	45
Interest income	(7)	(37)	(117)	(131)	(93)
Earnings from continuing operations before income taxes	1,816	1,584	1,406	1,315	1,793
Income taxes	714	617	539	506	680
Earnings from discontinued operations, net of income tax benefit	—	—	(34)	(31)	—
Net earnings	$ 1,102	$ 967	$ 833	$ 778	1,113
Weighted-average number of shares—basic*	694	716	791	831	881
Weighted-average number of shares—diluted*	699	719	794	836	902
Earnings from continuing operations, net of income taxes	$1.59	$1.35	$1.10	$0.97	$1.26
Loss from discontinued operation, net of income tax benefit	—	—	(0.05)	(0.03)	—
Net earnings per share	$1.59	$1.35	$1.05	$0.94	$1.26
Diluted earnings per share:					
Earnings from continuing operations, net of income taxes	$1.58	$1.34	$1.09	$0.97	$1.24
Loss from discontinued operation, net of income tax benefit	—	—	(0.04)	(0.04)	—
Net earnings per share	$1.58	$1.34	$1.05	$0.93	$1.24

*In millions.

Source: Gap Inc., 2009, 2008, and 2006 annual reports.

The Fishers' vision was to "make it simple to find a pair of jeans" and stocked a wide variety of sizes and styles that appealed primarily to San Francisco's teenagers. The Fishers expanded their product line during the 1970s by adding active wear appealing to a broader range of customers. The company went public in 1976 and began a rapid expansion strategy after the consummate retailer Millard "Mickey" Drexler was hired as the company's president in 1983. Through a combination of acquisitions, new ventures, and strategies designed to produce organic growth, Drexler transformed Gap from a company with annual revenues of $400 million and 450 stores in 1983 to a retailing giant with annual revenues of $14 billion and more than 2,000 stores in 2002. Drexler was largely credited with creating Gap's hip image and making its preppy product line cool, with memorable print ads such as ones depicting iconic photos of Ernest Hemingway, Humphrey Bogart, Jack Kerouac, and Marilyn Monroe wearing khakis similar to those sold by Gap. Under Drexler, Gap also acquired the Banana Republic chain in 1983, opened its first GapKids store in 1986, expanded internationally in 1989, became the second-largest apparel brand in the world in 1992, and launched Old Navy in 1994. Drexler was fired from his position as CEO in 2002 after

Exhibit 2 **Gap Inc. Consolidated Balance Sheets, Fiscal 2007–Fiscal 2009 ($ millions except par value)**

	January 30, 2010	January 31, 2009	February 2, 2008
ASSETS			
Current assets			
Cash and cash equivalents	$2,348	$1,715	$1,724
Short-term investments	225	—	177
Restricted cash	18	41	38
Merchandise inventory	1,477	1,506	1,575
Other current assets	596	743	572
Total current assets	4,664	4,004	4,086
Property and equipment, net	2,628	2,933	3,267
Other long-term assets	693	626	485
Total assets	$7,985	$7,564	$7,838
LIABILITIES AND STOCKHOLDERS' EQUITY			
Current liabilities			
Current maturities of long-term debt	$ —	$ 50	$ 138
Accounts payable	1,027	975	1,006
Accrued expenses and other current liabilities	1,063	1,076	1,259
Income taxes payable	41	57	30
Total current liabilities	$2,131	$2,158	$2,433
Long-term Liabilities			
Long-term debt	—	—	50
Lease incentives and other long-term liabilities	963	1,019	1,081
Total long-term liabilities	963	1,019	1,131
Commitments and contingencies*			
Stockholders' equity			
Common stock $0.05 par value Authorized 2,300 shares: Issued 1,105 and 1,100 shares Outstanding 694 and 734 shares	55	55	55
Additional paid-in capital	2,935	2,895	2,783
Retained earnings	10,815	9,447	9,223
Accumulated other comprehensive earnings	155	123	125
Treasury stock, at cost (411 and 366 shares)	(9,069)	(8,633)	(7,912)
Total stockholders' equity	4,891	4,387	4,274
Total liabilities and stockholders' equity	$7,985	$7,564	$7,838

*Gap Inc. leases most of its facilities and distribution centers. Most are five-year renewable leases that come due at staggered intervals. The company also leases much of its equipment. Total lease commitments are valued at $4,694.

Source: Gap Inc. 2008, 2009, and 2010 annual reports.

Gap's comparable-store sales declined by double digits every quarter between 2000 and 2002.

Paul Pressler replaced Drexler as Gap's CEO in 2002. Pressler launched the Internet-only retailer Piperlime.com and expanded into new markets in Asia and the Middle East in 2006. He resigned in 2007 and was replaced by Glen Murphy. Murphy began franchising Gap and Banana Republic stores in countries located in the Middle East and Asia and acquired the women's activewear company Athleta in 2008. Also under Murphy, Gap.com was reconfigured to allow

Internet customers to shop for Gap, Old Navy, Banana Republic, Piperlime, or Athleta apparel using a single shopping cart. The following list presents an overview of Gap's five brands in 2010:

- *Gap*—Gap offered an extensive selection of "classically styled, high quality casual apparel at moderate price points. Products ranged from wardrobe basics such as khakis and T-shirts to fashion apparel, accessories and personal care products for men and women."[1] GapKids and babyGap brands offered casual apparel for infants and children through preteen. Gap stores also offered a line of maternity apparel and women's underwear, sleepwear, loungewear, and sports and active apparel.

- *Old Navy*—The Old Navy clothing store brand targeted customers seeking value-priced casual family apparel, shoes, and accessories. Old Navy stores also offered a line of maternity wear and personal care items.

- *Banana Republic*—The Banana Republic clothing store brand carried more sophisticated casual and tailored apparel, shoes, accessories and personal care products at price points higher than those at Gap.

- *Athleta*—Athleta offered "stylish and functional high-quality apparel for women for a variety of sports, including running, skiing, snowboarding, surfing and yoga."[2] Advertised as athletic apparel, "designed by women athletes for women athletes" in 2010 this brand was only sold through the company's website and a catalog.

- *Piperlime*—Piperlime.com offered men, women, and children over 200 leading footwear brands from casual to high fashion and nearly 40 handbag brands. Gap Inc. controlled all aspects of the Piperlime.com except product design.

OVERVIEW OF THE U.S. FAMILY CLOTHING STORES INDUSTRY

Gap Inc. was one of the four largest retailers in the U.S. family clothing store industry in 2010. The family clothing store industry was one of six industries that made up the broader U.S. clothing stores sector, which in 2009 accounted for approximately $156 billion in revenues. Sales for the U.S. clothing store sector had declined from $164 billion in 2008, due in large part to the severe worldwide recession that began in 2008. As the largest industry within the sector, the U.S. family clothing store industry accounted for sales of $84.4 billion in 2009, representing more than 54 percent of clothing store sector sales during the year. The remaining 46 percent of clothing store sector sales were made by retailers in the department store industry; the men's clothing store industry; the women's clothing store industry; the children's and infant's clothing store industry; and the lingerie, swimwear, uniform, and bridal store industry. Sales in all industry segments of the clothing store sector were highly seasonal, with the 13 weeks during the back-to-school (August) and holiday (November through December) periods accounting for a substantial proportion of most clothing retailers' business. Exhibit 3 presents selected industry statistics for the U.S. family clothing store industry.[3]

GLOBALIZATION

The level of globalization in the U.S. family clothing stores industry was relatively low. In 2010, the industry was made up of a large number of small, local companies and the major companies selling in the U.S. market were domestically owned. The larger industry rivals such as Gap and TJX Stores generated between 10 and 20 percent of their sales from international operations. However, there had been some entry into the U.S. clothing store market by international companies like Uniqlo from Japan, H&M from Sweden, and Zara from Spain. This group of new entrants focused their market penetration efforts on the youth demographic (people ages 18 to 24), which was particularly well-suited to these companies because of their access to low-cost contract manufacturers and a distinctive competence in developing new designs to cater to mini-trends in as few as two weeks.

Foreign entrants and domestic-based clothing stores both relied on independent third parties to manufacture the majority of their products, with most suppliers located in Asia, the Middle East,

Exhibit 3   Selected Industry Statistics for the U.S. Family Clothing Stores Industry, 2006–2010

	2006	2007	2008	2009*	2010*
Industry Data					
Industry revenue ($ millions)	$88,154	$89,256	$86,410	$83,950	$84,400
Industry gross product ($ millions)	$14,208	$14,999	$12,584	$12,280	$13,166
Number of establishments (units)	35,929	36,595	34,564	32,741	33,760
Number of enterprises (units)	18,398	18,664	17,628	16,063	16,880
Quantity of clothing items (thousands)	573,000	583,737	582,482	543,650	547,104
Annual Percent Change					
Industry revenue	2.6%	1.3%	−3.2%	−2.8%	0.5%
Industry gross product	4.1	5.6	−16.1	−2.4	7.2
Number of establishments	2.4	1.9	−5.5	−5.3	3.1
Number of enterprises	0.8	1.4	−5.6	−8.9	5.1
Quantity of clothing	3.1	1.9	−0.2	−6.7	0.6

*All numbers are estimates.

Source: IBISWorld Inc., "Family Clothing Stores in the US: 44814. Recession Update: January 12, 2009 and Industry Report," January 2010.

and South America. Overseas factories placed retailers at risk for exposure to negative publicity through sourcing partners' illegal or unethical operations, such as using child labor or sweatshop working conditions and low pay. Many companies had developed procedures to monitor and train their partners to minimize these risks. Risk also came from potential shortages of apparel or materials. If significant increases in demand for a product occurred or a company lost a vendor, there was the likelihood that retailers would not have the products needed to meet demand in their stores. Other risks associated with overseas manufacturing included shipment delays and interruptions in supply because of foreign government action.

INDUSTRY SEGMENTATION

The U.S. clothing store industry could be segmented by gender, age, size, and price considerations. Women traditionally spent more on clothes than men did, with women's wear accounting for 50 percent of the product share in this industry, men's wear 37 percent, and children's wear 13 percent.[4] The plus-sized segment had become a $27 billion segment within the industry by 2010,

as the number of obese adults ages 20 and over had grown to 34 percent of the population by 2008. U.S. government statistics indicated that 18 percent of adolescents ages 12 to 19 could be considered obese. The demand for plus-size garments had increased for both genders and consumers of all ages.

The industry was also segmented by price point, with value-priced clothing lines accounting for about 65 percent of industry sales. The remaining 35 percent of industry sales were made up of higher-priced items, which carried higher margins. In the family clothing stores industry, the majority of stores—such as Ross Stores, TJX Companies, and Stein—all targeted price-conscious consumers who still wanted name brands but at a discount and were willing to purchase styles off-season or from the previous year. Fashion- and brand-conscious consumers who shopped at retailers such as Gap and Abercrombie & Fitch tended to be emotionally driven in their purchasing behavior and were influenced by marketing efforts that showcased a store's latest and greatest offerings.[5] The discount segment had withstood the effects of the 2008–2009 recessionary period somewhat better than premium-priced stores as consumers at almost all income levels placed a greater focus on value.[6]

COST/PROFIT STRUCTURE OF THE INDUSTRY

The average cost/profit structure of retailers in the U.S. family clothing store industry, as estimated by IBISWorld, followed the chain of value-adding activities and was made up as follows:

- *Purchases of clothing:* Purchases of clothing from contract manufacturers primarily located offshore made up approximately 68.9 percent of industry revenues. Purchases of clothing were often affected by exchange-rate fluctuations and trade restrictions. Perhaps the most important trade policy affecting U.S. family clothing stores was the World Trade Organization (WTO) agreement on textiles and clothing. Implemented in 1974, the internationally negotiated Multi-Fiber Arrangement (MFA) created a system of quotas that limited the amount of textiles and apparel that could be exported from developing countries to developed ones. This agreement was intended to be a short-term solution that would allow manufacturers of textiles and apparel in developed countries time to adjust to imports from underdeveloped countries.[7] The unintended outcome of these restrictions was a practice known as "chasing quota," in which clothing buyers would satisfy their production needs by scattering orders over numerous countries. On many occasions, this practice created garment industries in countries that otherwise lacked the proximity, infrastructure, workforce, or cost base to compete effectively in the open market.

  - With the ending of the MFA on January 1, 2005, U.S. family clothing stores industry participants anticipated that the ability to develop supply chains with fewer artificial restrictions than they had previously experienced.[8] However, because the United States and China, which in 2008 provided about 37 percent of women's and girls' apparel, agreed to continue with certain restrictions on apparel and textiles through December 2008, there was concern that some restrictions might continue beyond this point.[9] However, as China's minimum wage had increased, imported clothing had become sourced from the Philippines and Vietnam, where labor remained cheap. Industry analysts anticipated that American wholesalers would seek additional contract manufacturing sources from Indonesia, India, and Cambodia.[10]

  - The extensive use of off-shore sourcing had another unintended consequence—the growing bargaining power and leverage of low-cost foreign clothing manufacturers when negotiating with U.S. clothing stores. In response, retail family clothing store companies had tended toward using a "portfolio approach to sourcing," which involved sourcing from various global regions. The portfolio approach allowed companies to diminish some of the risk associated with conducting business with only one or very few suppliers.[11]

- *Wages:* Industry wages in 2009 were estimated at 9.8 percent of U.S. clothing stores' industry sales. Retailing industries were labor-intensive, with staff needed to serve store customers and maintain store inventory levels. While some chains achieved lower labor costs through lower wages and fewer personnel, others used higher-quality personnel and more employees in the stores to make customer service a differentiating feature of the chain. Most retailers used a combination of full- and part-time employees to meet light and peak store traffic requirements. In addition, seasonal factors—particularly summer and holiday sales—required the use of part-time personnel.

- *Other expenses:* Typical other expenses included rent (5 percent), advertising (1.5 percent), depreciation (1.5 percent), and other (10.3 percent).

- *Before-tax profits:* After all expenses, IBISWorld estimated, average before-tax profits for the U.S. clothing store industry were 3.0 percent in 2009—IBISWorld estimated the industry's before-tax profit margin at 3.4 percent in 2008.[12]

FACTORS DETERMINING COMPETITIVE SUCCESS IN THE FAMILY CLOTHING STORE INDUSTRY

Of the competitive elements directly affecting the prosperity of companies in the branded segment of the U.S. family clothing industry, none was more important than the ability to successfully develop new product lines that reflected the latest fashion trends and then quickly bring them to market. Consumer purchasing decisions were also affected by the number of similar stores in the buyer's immediate shopping environment, although strong brand loyalty could cause buyers to extend their shopping range. However, it was generally important for clothing store chains to have a broad network of retail stores located in prime real estate locations. The growth of Internet retailing had made it easier for consumers to find sought-after items if a store was not nearby or if a store was out of stock, but many consumers preferred to visually inspect or try on clothing items that they were unfamiliar with.

It was also critical for rivals in the U.S. family clothing stores industry to build brand loyalty, which acted as a barrier to entry for potential new entrants to the market. Many rival firms dedicated considerable resources to brand building and advertising. Finally, because of the extremely slim profit margins that existed in the industry, it was critical for companies to have excellent financial management and inventory management skills to control cash flow, reduce debt, and keep costs low.[13]

MAJOR RIVALS IN THE U.S. FAMILY CLOTHING STORE INDUSTRY

With the exception of national chains, the U.S. family clothing stores industry was highly fragmented and was made up of thousands of small local or regional retailers that individually held very small market shares. However, the four largest national chains accounted for about 39.4 percent of total market share in 2009. The top four U.S. family clothing stores industry performers were (1) the TJX Companies Inc., with a 13.4 percent market share (up from 11.5 percent in 2006); (2) Gap Inc., with a 15 percent market share (down from 18.6 percent in 2006); (3) Ross Stores Inc., with a 6.9 percent market share (up from 4.0 percent in 2006); and (4) Abercrombie & Fitch, with a 4.1 percent market share (steady since 2006 but up from 3.8 percent in 2005). American Eagle Outfitters was also a notable rival in the industry, with an estimated market share in 2009 of about 1 percent.

TJX Companies

TJX Companies was the leading off-price retailer of clothing and home fashions in the United States in 2010. The company owned and operated 890 T. J. Maxx discount stores, which carried family clothing, women's footwear and apparel, home fashion, beauty items, and jewelry and accessories. T. J. Maxx priced its products at 20–60 percent below department and specialty store pricing. Similarly, TJX operated 813 Marshall's, which was a discount department store chain carrying family clothing, a full line of family footwear, women's apparel, men's apparel, home fashions, and toys. The company also operated 323 HomeGoods off-price home decor stores and 150 A. J. Wright deep-discount family clothing and home fashion stores. In Canada, TJX owned and operated 208 Winners family clothing stores and 79 HomeSense stores. Winners' merchandise mix was similar to that of T. J. Maxx, and HomeSense's was similar to HomeGoods'. In 2008, the company launched Stylesense in Canada, which was an off-price footwear retailer. There were no plans to expand the number of Stylesense stores until the concept was more fully developed.

In 1994, the company opened T. K. Maxx stores in the United Kingdom and had become the seventh-largest UK fashion retailer, with 263 stores, and was the only major off-price retailer in Europe in 2010. The company expanded T. K. Maxx to Germany in 2007 and Poland in 2009. TJX also operated 14 HomeSense stores in the UK in 2010. In 2009, TJX's Canadian and European stores accounted for 10.7 percent and 10.9 percent of total revenues, respectively. For the fiscal year ending January 31, 2010, TJX's comparable-store sales in Canada increased by 3 percent, comparable-store sales in Europe increased by 5 percent, and comparable-store sales at T. J. Maxx and Marshall's stores improved by 7 percent. Comparable-store sales at HomeGoods and A. J. Wright increased by 9 percent during fiscal 2009. Comparable-store sales for all TJX stores for the first quarter of 2010 increased by 9 percent when compared to the same period in 2009. A summary of TJX's financial performance for fiscal 2008 and 2009 is presented in Exhibit 4.

Ross Stores

Ross Stores was the second-largest off-price retailer in the United States, with fiscal 2009 revenues of $7.2 billion. As of January 30, 2010, the company operated a chain of 953 Ross Dress for Less stores in 27 states and Guam—up from 904 stores in 2008. Ross Dress for Less offered name-brand apparel and designer apparel at everyday low prices that were 20 to 60 percent off regular department store prices. In addition, the company operated 52 dd's DISCOUNTS locations in California, Florida, Texas, and Arizona. The dd's DISCOUNTS stores featured a moderately priced assortment of first-quality, in-season, name-brand fashion apparel, accessories, and footwear for the entire family at everyday savings of 20 to 70 percent off moderate department and discount store regular prices. For the fiscal year 2009, ending January 30, 2010, Ross Stores posted record earnings of $442.8 million on revenues of nearly $7.2 billion. Its comparable-store sales were 6 percent greater than in fiscal 2008. The company's comparable store sales for the first quarter of fiscal 2010 were 10 percent greater than the same period in fiscal 2009. A summary of Ross Stores' financial performance for fiscal 2008 and fiscal 2009 are presented in Exhibit 5.

Abercrombie & Fitch

Abercrombie & Fitch (A&F) was a specialty retailer selling upscale, premium-priced casual clothing for men, women, and children. At year-end 2009, A&F operated approximately 1,096 stores in the United States, Canada, and Europe, including 340 Abercrombie & Fitch stores, 205 abercrombie kids stores, 507 Hollister stores, and 16 Gilly Hicks stores. All A&F store brands also operated Internet retailing sites through which consumers could purchase its apparel items. The

Exhibit 4   **Financial Summary for TJX Companies, Fiscal 2009–Fiscal 2010 ($ thousands except per share amounts)**

	52 Weeks Ended January 30, 2010	53 Weeks Ended January 31, 2009
Net sales	$20,288,444	$18,999,505
Cost of sales, including buying and occupancy costs	14,968,429	14,429,185
Selling, general, and administrative expenses	3,328,944	3,135,589
Provision (credit) for Computer Intrusion related costs	—	(30,500)
Interest expense, net	39,509	14,291
Income from continuing operations before provision for income taxes	1,951,562	1,450,940
Provision for income taxes	737,990	536,054
Income from continuing operations	1,213,572	914,886
Income (loss) from discontinued operations, net of income taxes	—	(34,269)
Net income	$ 1,213,572	$ 880,617
Diluted earnings per share:		
Income from continuing operations	$2.84	$2.08
Net income	$2.84	$2.00

Source: TJX Companies, press release, February 24, 2010.

Exhibit 5   Financial Summary for Ross Stores, Fiscal 2009–Fiscal 2010 ($ thousands except per share amounts)

	Twelve Months Ended	
	January 30, 2010	**January 31, 2009**
Sales	$7,184,213	$6,486,139
Costs and expenses		
Costs of goods sold	5,327,278	4,956,576
Selling, general and administrative	1,130,813	1,034,357
Interest expense (income), net	7,593	(157)
Total costs and expenses	6,465,684	5,990,776
Earnings before taxes	718,529	495,363
Provision for taxes on earnings	275,772	189,922
Net earnings	$ 442,757	$ 305,441
Earnings per share		
Basic	$3.60	$2.36
Diluted	$3.54	$2.33
Weighted average shares outstanding (000)		
Basic	122,887	129,235
Diluted	125,014	131,315

Source: Ross Stores, press release, March 18, 2010.

company also operated 6 Abercrombie & Fitch stores, 4 abercrombie kids stores, and 18 Hollister stores internationally. Both Abercrombie & Fitch and abercrombie kids stores developed images and product lines that were inspired by East Coast Ivy League and preparatory schools, while Hollister drew on the Southern California culture for its image and product line. Gilly Hicks was an Australian-themed chain specializing in underwear, swimwear, and casual wear for young women. In 2009, the company discontinued its Ruehl clothing stores business, which had incurred losses of $23.4 million in 2007, $35.9 million in 2008, and $78.7 million in 2009. The closure of the Ruehl clothing stores business resulted in a $56.1 million pretax exit charge against 2009 earnings. The company's Ruehl-branded stores had been launched in 2004 with higher price points than its other stores and were intended to appeal to young professionals. Between 2010 and 2011, the company planned to open new flagship Abercrombie & Fitch stores in Fukuoka, Japan; Copenhagen, Denmark; and Paris, France, and 30 new Hollister stores in Europe and Asia. A comparison of the financial performance of Abercrombie & Fitch's store

brands between 2007 and 2009 is presented in Exhibit 6. A summary of the company's consolidated financial performance for 2009 and 2010 is presented in Exhibit 7.

American Eagle Outfitters

American Eagle Outfitters (AEO) operated 938 stores in the United States and Canada. AEO stores carried trendy, affordably priced casual wear appealing to 15- to 25-year-olds. The company also operated 138 stores under the brand name aerie in the United States and Canada; aerie stores sold underwear and leisure wear for young women. Apparel sold in both American Eagle Outfitters and aerie stores was also available for purchase online at www.ae.com. The company's 77kids by American Eagle brand of clothing for children was available online only at www.ae.com and www.77kids.com. The company had operated 28 Martin + Osa stores, which carried apparel items similar to those sold in American Eagle Outfitters stores but focused on the 30+ age demographic. AEO closed all Martin + Osa stores in March 2010 after the brand lost $44 million in fiscal 2009.

Exhibit 6   Financial Comparison of Abercrombie & Fitch Store Brands, 2007–2009 ($ thousands except per share amounts)

	2009	2008	2007
Net sales	**$2,928,626**	**$3,484,058**	**$3,699,656**
Abercrombie & Fitch	1,272,287	1,531,480	1,638,929
abercrombie kids	343,164	420,518	471,045
Hollister	1,287,241	1,514,204	1,589,452
Gilly Hicks	25,934	17,856	230
Increase (decrease) in net sales from prior year	**(16)%**	**(6)%**	**13%**
Abercrombie & Fitch	(17)	(7)	8
abercrombie kids	(18)	(11)	16
Hollister	(15)	(5)	17
Gilly Hicks	45	NM	NM
Decrease in comparable store sales	**(23)%**	**(13)%**	**(1)%**
Abercrombie & Fitch	(19)	(8)	0
abercrombie kids	(23)	(19)	0
Hollister	(27)	(17)	(2)

Source: Abercrombie & Fitch, 2009 10-K report.

Even though the recession had contributed to an overall comparable-store sales decline of 10 percent in 2008 and 4 percent in 2009, the company's new aerie stores experienced a 25 percent improvement in comparable-store sales between 2008 and 2009. Additionally, the company planned to open seven brick-and-mortar 77kids stores in 2010. A summary of American Eagle Outfitters' financial performance for 2008 and 2009 is presented in Exhibit 8.

Competition from Other Clothing Sector Industries

Consumers purchased apparel not only from family clothing stores but also from sellers competing in the department store industry, big-box store industry, men's clothing store industry, women's clothing store industry, and children's and infant's clothing store industry. Department store companies such as The Federated Group, Sears, and JCPenney as well as big-box mass merchandisers such as Target and Walmart brought competitive pressure on family clothing stores. In addition, consumers who did not need to try on an article of clothing frequently turned to the Internet to find closeouts or other discounts that might not be available locally. Internet retailing

sites also allowed customers who were loyal to a particular brand to purchase desired items even if the retailer did not have a store nearby. Subsequently, most major brick-and-mortar apparel retailers had expanded into Internet retailing as well.

TURNAROUND STRATEGIES AT GAP

With Gap's same-store sales beginning a long-term decline in 2000, the company's first turnaround strategy began with Mickey Drexler's replacement by Paul Pressler as CEO in 2002. Pressler had spent 15 years with the Walt Disney Company before coming to Gap and began his turnaround with a redesign of the company's websites and online presence. A completely new e-commerce platform was developed for Gap.com, BananaRepublic.com, and OldNavy.com, with all three websites redesigned to provide greater functionality and a more convenient shopping experience. The *New York Times* reported that Gap's redesigned websites were "among the best e-commerce sites in retail."[14]

In an effort to expand Gap's brand offerings to women over age 35, Pressler created the Forth &

Exhibit 7   **Financial Summary for Abercrombie & Fitch, 2008–2009 ($ thousands except per share amounts)**

	2009	% of Net Sales	2008	% of Net Sales
Net sales	$2,928,626	100.0%	$3,484,058	100.0%
Cost of goods sold	1,045,028	35.7%	1,152,963	33.1%
Gross profit	1,883,598	64.3%	2,331,095	66.9%
Total stores and distribution expense	1,425,950	48.7%	1,436,363	41.2%
Total marketing, general and administrative expense	353,269	12.1%	405,248	11.6%
Other operating income, net	(13,533)	−0.5%	(8,778)	−0.3%
Operating income	117,912	4.0%	498,262	14.3%
Interest income, net	(1,598)	−0.1%	(11,382)	−0.3%
Income from continuing				
Operation before income taxes	119,510	4.1%	509,644	14.6%
Income tax expense for continuing operations	40,557	1.4%	201,475	5.8%
Net income from continuing operations	78,953	2.7%	308,169	8.8%
Net loss from discontinued operations (net of taxes)	(78,699)	−2.7%	(35,914)	−1.0%
Net income	$ 254	0.0%	$ 272,255	7.8%
Net income per share from continuing operations:				
Basic	$0.90		$3.55	
Diluted	$0.89		$3.45	
Net loss per share from discontinued operations:				
Basic	$(0.90)		$(0.41)	
Diluted	$(0.89)		$(0.40)	
Total net income per share:				
Basic	$0.00		$3.14	
Diluted	$0.00		$3.05	
Weighted-average shares outstanding (000s):				
Basic	87,874		86,816	
Diluted	88,609		89,291	

Source: Abercrombie & Fitch, press release, February 16, 2010.

Towne chain of branded clothing stores in 2005 with the first stores opening in Chicago and New York. However, the concept was short-lived, with mixed reviews on the attractiveness and fit of the clothes—some customers and analysts loved them, and others hated them. It was generally recognized that the company ineffectively launched and marketed the chain. Gap ended up closing all of its Forth & Towne stores in June 2007 following Pressler's departure from the company. Some analysts and customers complained that the concept hadn't been given a chance. Pressler's turnaround strategy also included the 2006 launch of Piperlime.com—an online shoe store offering men, women, and children an assortment of third-party brands.

Under Pressler's leadership, the company also focused on reducing debt, which had reached nearly $2.9 billion in fiscal 2002. Pressler and the company's chief financial managers had successfully reduced the company's outstanding long-term indebtedness to $513 million by the end of fiscal 2005 and had eliminated all long-term debt by the end of fiscal 2007. The elimination of debt allowed Gap to consistently increase dividend payments to shareholders from $0.09 per share in 2002 to $0.32 per share in 2007. In addition, the company executed share repurchase plans that reduced outstanding shares from 887 million shares outstanding in 2002 to 794 million shares outstanding in 2007. However, despite Pressler's success in strengthening the company's balance

Exhibit 8   **Financial Summary for American Eagle Outfitters, 2008–2009 ($ thousands except per share amounts)**

	For the Fiscal Year Ending	
	January 30, 2010	January 31, 2009
Summary of Operations		
Net sales	$2,990,520	$2,988,866
Comparable store sales (decrease) increase	(4)%	(10)%
Gross profit	$1,158,049	$ 1,174,101
Gross profit as a percentage of net sales	38.7%	39.3%
Operating income	$ 238,393	$ 302,140
Operating income as a percentage of net sales	8.0%	10.1%
Income from continuing operations	$ 169,022	$ 179,061
Income from continuing operations as a percentage of net sales	5.7%	6.0%
Per Share Results		
Income from continuing operations per common share—basic	$0.82	$0.87
Income from continuing operations per common share—diluted	$0.81	$0.86
Weighted average common shares outstanding (000s)—basic	206,171	205,169
Weighted average common shares outstanding (000s)—diluted	209,512	207,582

Source: American Eagle Outfitters, 2009 annual report.

sheets, many analysts believed that Pressler had made excessive cuts in expenditures related to design, product development, and marketing. Also, decisions to cut costs in the supply chain led to slowed product-to-market cycle times, which made the company less able to respond to fashion changes.

Analysts also believed that Gap was hindered in the marketplace by constant disagreements between research and design personnel that led to delayed decision making and eventual unwise compromises to merely get something on stores shelves. With a lack of interesting new lines and products, Gap's revenues and earnings began to decline after peaking in fiscal 2004 at $16.2 billion and $1.15 billion, respectively. As the company's revenues began to decline, Pressler began to lose key executives who were frustrated with his approach and lack of understanding of the apparel industry.

The company's weakening financial and strategic performance led to Pressler's replacement by Glenn Murphy in the summer of 2007. Murphy came to Gap with more than 20 years of retail experience in the areas of food, health and beauty, and books. His turnaround strategy for Gap focused on improving the appeal of the

company's product lines and expanding its business internationally. During Murphy's first year as CEO, Gap opened franchised stores in 11 countries, including Saudi Arabia, Bahrain, Indonesia, United Arab Emirates, Kuwait, Qatar, and South Korea. Murphy also opened franchised Banana Republic stores in nine countries during his first year as CEO. By 2008, more than 100 Gap franchised stores were in operation, with additional stores opening in Greece, Russia, Israel, Jordan, Mexico, and Romania in 2008 and 2009. New franchised Banana Republic stores opened in the United Kingdom, Saudi Arabia, Turkey, and the Philippines. The company also expanded its Gap and Banana Republic factory outlet stores to Canada in 2008. Murphy also diversified the company's apparel store variety with the $150 million acquisition of Athleta in 2008. Athleta was a direct marketer of women's athletic apparel, swimwear, and athletic-inspired leisure wear.

Murphy continued many of the cost-cutting measures of his predecessor but found it necessary to allocate resources to restore Gap brands' reputation for style and quality. One of Murphy's first and most important moves was to bring in Patrick Robinson as Gap's design chief. Robinson was well-known in apparel design circles, having worked for Anne Klein, Giorgio Armani, Perry Ellis, and Paco Rabanne. Robinson believed that what ailed the company was targeting a customer that was too young (18 to 24 years old), producing poor-quality clothes, and trying to imitate foreign newcomers Uniqlo (Japan), H&M (Sweden), and Zara (Spain), all of which emphasized "fast fashion," or rapid-fire mini-trends. Robinson commented that he was determined to get Gap off the "trend treadmill" and bring back the classics that had established the brand in its heyday.[15]

By the fall of 2008, some Wall Street analysts were hailing Murphy and Robinson's efforts as being in the right direction. Analysts saw the company's improved merchandise, clearer focus on the 25- to 35-year-old demographic, stronger leadership team, and additional cost-cutting initiatives as strengths of the turnaround strategy. However, the company's revenues and comparable-store sales had not seen a great deal of improvement through year-end 2009. There was some debate concerning to what extent the lingering recession was impeding a financial turnaround of the company.

GAP IN 2010

Store Operations

Gap owned and operated more than 3,100 Gap, Banana Republic, and Old Navy stores worldwide in 2010. This number also included a number of Gap Outlet stores. Store locations outside the United States included Canada, the United Kingdom, France, Ireland, and Japan. In addition to company-owned stores, the company had franchising agreements to operate Gap and Banana Republic stores in Bahrain, Indonesia, Kuwait, Malaysia, the Philippines, Oman, Qatar, Saudi Arabia, Singapore, South Korea, Turkey, the United Arab Emirates, Greece, Romania, Bulgaria, Cyprus, Mexico, Egypt, Jordan, and Croatia. In February 2009, the company announced plans to open stores in Israel under the Gap and Banana Republic brands through an agreement with Elbit Trade and Retail Ltd.

The seasonality of the business required that the company carry a significant amount of inventory, especially before the beginning of a peak selling season. Replenishment inventory was kept not in the stores but at distribution centers from which it could be quickly shipped to stores. The company reviewed its inventories regularly to identify slow-moving merchandise and determine markdown amounts necessary to clear merchandise.[16] One of Pressler's most significant achievements as CEO was the reduction of Gap's inventory carrying costs.

Information Systems and Technology

Gap's information technology systems were critical to maintaining proper inventory and supporting its Internet retailing efforts. The company's website was attractive and easy to navigate for customers wanting to view new styles or purchase products online. Gap had contracted with IBM to operate aspects of its information technology infrastructure, including support for its mainframe computer, servers, network and data center, store operations systems, help desk, customer service support, and some disaster recovery. In January 2009, the company implemented a sophisticated software package for managing the real estate throughout its operations. The software allowed the company to monitor its real estate workflow and forecast the financial impact of real estate decisions, including those of consolidating or expanding or remodeling store locations. In the fall of 2009, in time for the holiday season, the company also successfully transitioned its order processing to a new system acquired from Kiva Systems. The company said that the system would allow its e-commerce division, Gap Inc. Direct, to process orders faster and with greater accuracy. The company planned to leverage its investment in its Kiva Systems software as it expanded its Internet retailing internationally in 2010.

Brand and Product Development

Gap controlled all aspects of brand development from design to distribution in-house. Most of its products were manufactured by approximately 79 independent vendors located in 60 countries. Approximately 3 percent of the company's products were produced domestically, with the remainder produced outside the United States. The company also offered products designed and manufactured by branded third parties for the company's online shoe store, Piperlime.

Gap also initiated a number of collaborations with celebrity designers and other companies to develop products.

- In June 2009, the company announced collaboration with designer Stella McCartney to create a collection for GapKids and babyGap that would be sold in select GapKids and babyGap stores in the United States, Canada, the United Kingdom, France, and Ireland and online in the United States.
- Also in 2009, the company entered into a partnership with the Paris boutique Merci, to create a Merci Gap store in Paris. The store would feature a number of products sourced from all over the world as well as Gap T-shirts with Merci graphics.
- In February 2010, Collective Brands, the parent company of the shoe retailer Keds, announced that it would create an alliance with Gap to create classically inspired lines of sneakers. The collection was expected to be in stores by fall 2010.[17]
- In May 2010, Gap's Banana Republic division announced that it had teamed up with Chan Lau, a renowned jewelry designer, to develop a collection of limited-edition bracelets.

Marketing

Gap allocated considerable resources to store design, customer service, and advertising. The company's primary advertising media included print ads in major metropolitan newspapers, Sunday magazines, and magazines emphasizing lifestyle and fashion. The company also placed ads in various outdoor and indoor venues using transit posters, exterior bus panels, billboards, and mall kiosks. Gap also spent significantly on television and radio advertising with highly recognizable ads. In the fall of 2009, the company introduced an ad campaign for its flagship Gap division that included a Facebook page, video clips, a realistic online fashion show on a virtual catwalk, and an application for the iPhone called the StyleMixer.

The company also hosted a nationwide "simultaneous acoustic concert" in its stores across the country to commemorate its 40th anniversary on August 21, 2009. "Music has always been an integral part of Gap—from musicians participating in our ad campaigns to musicians performing in our stores, to the way music is infused into the very soul of Gap," said Ivy Ross, Gap's executive vice president of marketing.[18] During the 2009 holiday retail season, the company put on a multicity road tour of street performances featuring Gap's Cheer Squad and Drumline, a group of 12 professional dancers and drummers.

The company also donated to arts-related organizations in an effort to boost its image in urban art-oriented communities. A number of art benefit events were planned, including the sponsorship of the Metropolitan Museum of Art's May 2010 exhibition titled *American Woman: A Celebration of Fashion's Role in Defining the Modern Woman*. Working with award-winning designers for the gala, the company sponsored the creation of eight original gowns, which were worn by celebrities from fashion, music, film, television, and Broadway. The company also collaborated with a number of artists in a celebration of the San Francisco Museum of Modern Art's 75th anniversary in 2010.

Corporate Citizenship and Social Responsibility

In March 2010, Gap was recognized for a fourth consecutive year as one of the world's most ethical companies by the Ethisphere Institute. Also in 2010, Gap had been recognized for the fifth time by *Corporate Responsibility Magazine* on its list of "100 Best Corporate Citizens." The company was ranked ninth on the overall list and first among retailers. Gap had achieved such recognition by focusing on corporate citizenship activities such as improving factory conditions and standards for suppliers, investing in various communities and charities, environmental stewardship, and developing diversity and enrichment programs for employees. The company had developed its own Code of Vendor Conduct (COVC), by which it managed its relationships with its vendors. The code was designed to ensure that workers employed by vendors were paid fairly, did not work excessively long hours, and worked in a safe and healthy environment. Exhibit 9 lists selected Gap's social responsibility policies.

Exhibit 9   Selected Social Responsibility Policies at Gap, Inc., 2009

Working with Factories

Because we don't own the factories where our clothes are made, we regularly inspect them to ensure that working conditions meet our standards. But our efforts don't stop there. We recognize that we have a responsibility to work in partnership with factories, as well as other apparel companies and concerned organizations, to improve working conditions across the industry. Together, we are striving to make garment factories around the world safe and fair places to work. Gap Inc. has more than 80 full-time employees around the world who are dedicated to improving the lives of factory workers. In 2007, our Vendor Compliance Officers conducted approximately 4,000 inspections in more than 2,000 garment factories around the world.[22]

Improving our Practices

Through our membership in the Ethical Trading Initiative (ETI), we started working with Women Working Worldwide (WWW), a non-governmental organization, to better understand how our purchasing practices can impact working conditions and how we can improve. WWW met with our employees, factory management and workers to understand our planning and production process and its impact on factories.

Partnerships

Today, we're partnering with many organizations around the world to address industry-wide issues. Our initiatives include helping workers better understand their rights, training factory supervisors how to lead more effectively and encouraging governments to strengthen enforcement of their own labor and environmental laws. Our partners include labor and human rights groups, internationally based non-governmental organizations (NGOs), trade unions and universities.

Our Team

Our Social Responsibility Team represents approximately 25 nationalities and speaks as many languages. Most members are from the region or country they work in.

Source: Gap, http://www.gapinc.com/public/SocialResponsibility/socialres.shtml, accessed March 16, 2009.

The company also supported a number of nonprofit organizations and sponsored various charitable events, including the following:

- In July 2009, Gap joined up with Grammy Award winner John Legend to create a (RED) ZONE seating section for the artist's August 13, 2009, concert at Madison Square Garden in New York City. Sales of tickets from the zone would go to benefit HIV/AIDS treatment programs in Africa.

- In November 2009, Gap announced its Give and Get campaign. Participants in the program were able to donate 5 percent of the purchase price of Gap products to a number of charities, including the Leukemia and Lymphoma Society, during the holiday season.[19]

- Also in November 2009, Gap's Piperlime shoe division unveiled its Holiday Gift List, featuring shopping lists from celebrities Brooke Shields, Rachel Bilson, Rashida Jones, and Kristen Bell. Ten percent of proceeds from items on the celebrities' lists were slotted to go to the Art of Elysium, a nonprofit organization that helps children through music and the arts.[20]

- In March 2010, Cotton Incorporated announced that it would be working with Gap to launch its Cotton: From Blue to Green denim drive. The drive encouraged consumers to bring their used denim clothing to Gap stores; the used items would then be recycled to provide cotton fiber insulation for 540 homes. Consumers who brought in their used denims were given a 30 percent discount on a new pair of Gap jeans.[21]

International Operations

In 2009, international revenues accounted for 18 percent of Gap's total company revenues. The company operated stores in the United States, Canada, the United Kingdom, France, Ireland, and Japan. The company also had entered into franchise agreements with third parties that operated more than 130 franchise stores selling Gap apparel in 20 countries throughout Asia, Europe, Latin America, and the Middle East. Some of the company's international plans included the following:

- *Expansion into China.* The company announced that it planned to open its first Gap store in China during 2010.
- *Online business expansion.* Gap expected to launch online businesses in both Canada and the United Kingdom in 2010.
- *Italy.* In February 2010, Gap announced that it would be opening its first Italian stores in Milan, and an outlet store in Rome was scheduled for a 2011 opening.
- *Thailand.* Minor International plc, a leading distributor of fashion goods, opened its first store in Thailand, selling Gap clothes, in March 2010. The company planned to open three more Gap stores in Bangkok.
- *Australia.* In March 2010, Gap signed a franchise agreement with Brand Republic Pty. Ltd. for exclusive rights to operate Gap brand stores in Australia.

GAP'S FINANCIAL PERFORMANCE IN 2010

The year 2009 had been a difficult one for Gap and its brands as sales continued to decline across all of it chains—see Exhibits 10 and 11. Poor economic conditions in the United States likely contributed to the company's lackluster performance, but improving sales across the retail sector during the first quarter of 2010 were expected to help boost Gap's performance. However, the first-quarter improvement in same-store sales might prove to be short-lived, as U.S. consumer confidence dropped by 10 points between May and June 2010. Lynn Franco, the director of the Conference Board Consumer Research Center, suggested that "until the pace of job growth picks up, consumer confidence is not likely to pick up."[23]

In June 2010, Gap's chief financial officer, Sabrina Simmons, reported, "In May, we continued to deliver on our overarching goal of driving sales growth."[24] May's net sales were up

Exhibit 10   Gap Sales by Quarter and Division, Fiscal 2006–Fiscal 2009 ($ millions)

Fiscal Year 2009 Ending January 30, 2010					
	Q1	**Q2**	**Q3**	**Q4**	**FY2009**
Gap North America	$ 834	$ 878	$ 987	$1,100	$3,799
Banana Republic North America	475	516	541	664	2,196
Old Navy North America	1,180	1,240	1,300	1,600	5,320
International[1]	369	361	378	514	1,622
Other[2]	267	224	298	329	1,110
Total Gap Inc.	$3,125	$3,219	$3,504	$4,207	$14,047
Fiscal Year 2008 Ending January 31, 2009					
	Q1	**Q2**	**Q3**	**Q4**	**FY2008**
Gap North America	$1,052	$1,058	$1,161	$1,231	$4,502
Banana Republic North America	571	629	603	709	2,512
Old Navy North America	1,353	1,390	1,363	1,601	5,707
International[1]	398	412	413	505	1,728
Other[2]	10	10	21	36	77
Total Gap Inc.	$3,384	$3,499	$3,561	$4,082	$14,526
Fiscal Year 2007 Ending February 2, 2008					
	Q1	**Q2**	**Q3**	**Q4**	**FY2007**
Gap North America	$1,086	$1,079	$1,224	$1,429	$ 4,818
Banana Republic North America	559	623	643	809	2,634

(Continued)

Exhibit 10   *(Concluded)*

Fiscal Year 2007 Ending February 2, 2008					
	Q1	**Q2**	**Q3**	**Q4**	**FY2007**
Old Navy North America	1,546	1,603	1,598	1,918	6,665
International[1]	353	373	379	510	1,615
Other[2]	5	7	10	9	31
Total Gap Inc.	$3,549	$3,685	$3,854	$4,675	$15,763
Fiscal Year 2006 Ending February 3, 2007					
	Q1	**Q2**	**Q3**	**Q4**	**FY2006**
Gap North America	$1,121	$1,155	$1,282	$1,576	$5,134
Banana Republic North America	518	571	590	808	2,487
Old Navy North America	1,503	1,649	1,644	2,033	6,829
International[1]	296	339	335	496	1,466
Other[2]	1	—	—	6	7
Total Gap Inc.	$3,439	$3,714	$3,851	$4,919	$15,923

Note: Prior periods subject to adjustments for rounding purposes. Annual amounts agree to 10-K.

[1]Includes wholesale business and franchise business beginning September 2006.

[2]Other includes Piperlime.com beginning October 2006, Athleta beginning September 2008, and Business Direct which ended in July 2006.

Source: Gap, http://www.gapinc.com/public/Investors/inv_financials.shtml, accessed June 7, 2010.

Exhibit 11   Gap Sales by Brand, Region, and Reportable Segment, Fiscal 2006–Fiscal 2009 ($ millions)

Fiscal Year 2009 (Ending January 30, 2010)	GAP	Old Navy	Banana Republic	Other[3]	Total	Percentage of Net Sales
United States[1]	$3,508	$4,949	$2,034	$ —	$10,491	74%
Canada	312	386	162	—	860	6
Europe	683	—	24	36	743	5
Asia	774	—	106	48	928	7
Other regions	—	—	—	57	57	—
Total stores segment	$5,277	$5,335	$2,326	$141	$13,079	92
Direct reportable segment[2]	324	473	134	187	1,118	8
Total	$5,601	$5,808	$2,460	$328	$14,197	100%
Fiscal Year 2008 (Ending January 31, 2009)	**GAP**	**Old Navy**	**Banana Republic**	**Other[3]**	**Total**	**Percentage of Net Sales**
United States[1]	$3,840	$4,840	$2,221	$ —	$10,901	75%
Canada	329	392	146	—	867	6
Europe	724	—	23	33	780	6
Asia	732	—	101	47	880	6
Other regions	—	—	—	68	68	—
Total stores segment	$5,625	$5,232	$2,491	$148	$13,496	$93
Direct reportable segment[2]	333	475	145	77	1,030	7
Total	$5,958	$5,707	$2,636	$225	$14,526	100%

(Continued)

Exhibit 11   *(Concluded)*

Fiscal Year 2007 (Ending February 2, 2008)	GAP	Old Navy	Banana Republic	Other[3]	Total	Percentage of Net Sales
United States[1]	$4,146	$5,776	$2,351	$ —	$12,273	78%
Canada	364	461	147	—	972	6
Europe	822	—	—	5	827	5
Asia	613	—	89	36	738	5
Other regions	—	—	—	50	50	—
Total stores reportable segment	$5,945	$6,237	$2,587	$91	$14,860	94
Direct reportable segment[2]	308	428	136	31	903	6
Total	$6,253	$6,665	$2,723	$122	$15,763	100%

Fiscal Year 2006 (Ending February 3, 2007)	GAP	Old Navy	Banana Republic	Other[3]	Total	Percentage of Net Sales
United States[1]	$4,494	$6,042	$2,251	$ —	$12,787	80%
Canada	379	442	119	—	940	6
Europe	792	—	—	1	793	5
Asia	581	—	61	7	649	4
Other regions	—	—	—	24	24	—
Total stores reportable segment	$6,246	$6,484	$2,431	$32	$15,193	95
Direct reportable segment[2]	261	345	117	7	730	5
Total	$6,507	$6,829	$2,548	$ 39	$15,923	100%

[1]Includes United States and Puerto Rico.
[2]Results of online business. Includes Athleta beginning September 2008.
[3]Other includes wholesale business, franchise business, Piperlime, and, beginning September 2008, Athleta.
Source: Gap, 2008 annual report, p. 63, and 2009 annual report, pp. 65–66.

2 percent, reaching $1.05 billion versus the previous year's May sales of $1.03 billion. Company-wide year-to-date sales for the first quarter of 2010 were also reported up 5 percent, to $4.38 billion versus sales over the same period of 2009 of $4.16 billion.[25] Despite the positive news, not all of Gap's brands had fared equally well. While Banana Republic North America, Old Navy, and the company's international stores reported gains in sales compared to losses in the previous year, Gap North America, the flagship division of the company, continued to lose same-store sales, although the losses slowed to 2 percent compared to the previous year's losses of 11 percent. While Wall Street analysts were generally positive about the company's prospects, many questions about the potential success of the turnaround strategy remained.

ENDNOTES

1 Gap, 2008 annual report, p. 4.
2 Gap, www.gapinc.com/public/Media/Press_Releases/med_pr_Athleta041709.shtml, accessed April 24, 2009.
3 IBISWorld, "Family Clothing Stores in the US: 44814. Recession Update: January 12, 2009," industry report, January 2010.
4 Ibid.
5 Reuters, "(2007) Retail (Apparel): Overview."
6 IBISWorld, "Family Clothing Stores."
7 Wikipedia, "Multi Fibre Agreement," http://en.wikipedia.org/wiki/Multi_Fibre_Agreement, accessed March 30, 2009.
8 Ibid.
9 Gap, 2007 annual report.
10 IBISWorld, "Family Clothing Stores."
11 S. Kusterbeck, "China Appeals to U.S. Buyers with 'Supply Chain Cities,'" *Apparel* 46 (August 2005), pp. 24–28.
12 IBISWorld, "Family Clothing Stores."

13 Ibid.
14 Gap, 2005 annual report.
15 Jane Porter, "A Fashion Guy Gets Gap Back to Basics," *BusinessWeek,* August 18, 2008, p. 56.
16 Gap, 2007 annual report.
17 Bee-Shyuan Chang, "Gap and Keds to Collaborate on Collection of Sneakers," *StyleList,* February 19, 2010.
18 "First Time in Exchange History Traders Wear Jeans on NYSE Trading Floor," *Business Wire,* August 21, 2009.
19 "GAP Inc. Give and Get Campaign Benefits Leukemia and Lymphoma Society," *States News Service,* November 6, 2009.
20 "Piperlime Unveils Celebrity Holiday Favorites," *PR Newswire,* November 24, 2009.
21 "Cotton Incorporated Partners with Gap for Nationwide 'Cotton: From Blue to Green®' Denim Drive," *PR Newswire,* March 4, 2010.

22 Gap, www.gapinc.com/public/documents/SR_India_Fact_Sheet_Update.pdf, accessed March 16, 2009. In response to allegations in 2007 that the company used factories employing child labor to make product for its GapKids brand, the company, on June 12, 2008, announced enhanced monitoring activities of suppliers and canceled the product made by the "unauthorized makeshift factory in India."
23 Quoted in "The Conference Board Consumer Confidence Index Drops Sharply," Conference Board press release, June 29, 2010.
24 Gap, www.gapinc.com/public/Media/Press_Releases/med_pr_May-2010sales06032010.shtm, accessed June 5, 2010.
25 Ibid.

Google's Strategy in 2010

John E. Gamble

University of South Alabama

Google was the leading Internet search firm in 2010, with 60+ percent market shares in both searches performed on computers and searches performed on mobile devices. Google's business model allowed advertisers to bid on search terms that would describe their product or service on a cost-per-impression (CPI) or cost-per-click (CPC) basis. Google's search-based ads were displayed near Google's search results and generated advertising revenues of nearly $22.9 billion in 2009. The company also generated revenues of $761 in 2009 from licensing fees charged to businesses that wished to install Google's search appliance on company intranets and from a variety of new ventures. New ventures were becoming a growing priority with Google management since the company dominated the market for search based ads and sought additional opportunities to sustain its extraordinary growth in revenues, earnings, and net cash provided by operations.

In 2008, Google had launched its Android operating system for mobile phones, which allowed wireless phone manufacturers such as LG, HTC, and Nokia to produce Internet-enabled phones boasting features similar to those available on Apple's iPhone. Widespread use of the Internet-enabled Android phones would not only help Google solidify its lead in mobile search but also allow the company to increase its share of banner ads and video ads displayed on mobile phones. Google had also entered into alliances with Intel, Sony, DISH Network, Logitech, and other firms to develop the technology and products required to launch Google TV. Google TV was scheduled for a fall 2010 launch and would allow users to search live network and cable programming; streaming videos from providers such as Netflix, Amazon Video On Demand, and YouTube; and recorded programs on a DVR. Perhaps the company's most ambitious strategic initiative in 2010 was its desire to change the market for commonly used business productivity applications such as word processing, spreadsheets, and presentation software from the desktop to the Internet. Information technology analysts believed that the market for such applications—collectively called cloud computing—could grow to $95 billion by 2013.

While Google's growth initiatives seemed to take the company into new industries and thrust it into competition with companies ranging from AT&T to Microsoft to Apple, its CEO, Eric Schmidt, saw the new ventures as natural extensions of the company's mission to "organize the world's information and make it universally accessible and useful."[1] In a July 2010 interview with the *Telegraph,* Schmidt commented that Google's new ventures into mobile devices, television search, and cloud computing would allow the company to "organize the world's information on any device and in any way that we can figure out to do it."[2] In July 2010, it was yet to be determined to what extent Google's new initiatives would contribute to the company's growth. Some industry analysts preferred that Google focus on improving its search technology to protect its competitive advantage in search and thereby its key revenue source. There was also a concern among some that, as the company pushed harder to sustain its impressive historical growth rates, it had backed away from its commitment to "make money without doing evil."[3] While free-speech advocates had criticized Google for aiding China in its Internet censorship practices since its 2006 entry into China, authorities in the United States, Canada, Australia, Germany, Italy, the United Kingdom, and Spain were conducting investigations into Google's Street View data collection practices. It had been discovered that while Google's camera cars photographed homes and businesses along city streets, the company also captured personal data from Wi-Fi networks in the photographed homes and businesses. In addition, the U.S. House Oversight Committee was in the first phase of an investigation into Google's lobbying efforts to encourage the Obama administration to institute new policies and regulations that would be favorable to the company and the development of its new ventures.

COMPANY HISTORY

The development of Google's search technology began in January 1996 when Stanford University computer science graduate students Larry Page and Sergey Brin collaborated to develop a new search engine. They named the new search engine BackRub because of its ability to rate websites for relevancy by examining the number of back links pointing to the website. The approach for assessing the relevancy of websites to a particular search query used by other websites at the time was based on examining and counting metatags and keywords included on various websites. By 1997, the search accuracy of BackRub had allowed it to gain a loyal following among Silicon Valley Internet users. Yahoo cofounder David Filo was among the converted, and in 1998 he convinced Brin and Page to leave Stanford to focus on making their search technology the backbone of a new Internet company.

BackRub would be renamed Google, which was a play on the word *googol*—a mathematical term for a number represented by the numeral 1 followed by 100 zeros. Brin and Page's adoption of the new name reflected their mission to organize a seemingly infinite amount of information on the Internet. In August 1998, a Stanford professor arranged for Brin and Page to meet at his home with a potential angel investor to demonstrate the Google search engine. The investor, who had been a founder of Sun Microsystems, was immediately impressed with Google's search capabilities but was too pressed for time to hear much of their informal presentation. The investor stopped the two during the presentation and suggested, "Instead of us discussing all the details, why don't I just write you a check?"[4] The two partners held the investor's $100,000 check, made payable to Google Inc., for two weeks while they scrambled to set up a corporation named Google Inc. and open a corporate bank account. The two officers of the freshly incorporated company went on to raise a total of $1 million in venture capital from family, friends, and other angel investors by the end of September 1998.

Even with a cash reserve of $1 million, the two partners ran Google on a shoestring budget, with its main servers built by Brin and Page from discounted computer components and its four employees operating out of a garage owned by a friend of the founders. By year-end 1998, Google's beta version was handling 10,000 search queries per day and *PC Magazine* had named the company to its list of "Top 100 Web Sites and Search Engines for 1998."

The new company recorded successes at a lightning-fast pace, with the search kernel answering more than 500,000 queries per day and Red Hat agreeing to become the company's first search customer in early 1999. Google attracted an additional $25 million in funding from two leading Silicon Valley venture capital firms by mid-year 1999 to support further growth and enhancements to Google's search technology. The company's innovations in 2000 included wireless search technology, search capabilities in 10 languages, and a Google Toolbar browser plug-in that allowed computer users to search the Internet without first visiting a Google-affiliated Web portal or Google's home page. Features added through 2004 included Google News, Google Product Search, Google Scholar, and Google Local. The company also expanded its index of Web pages to more than 8 billion and increased its country domains to more than 150 by 2004. Google also further expanded its products for mobile phones with a short message service (SMS) feature that allowed mobile phone users to send a search request to Google as a text message. After submitting the search request to 466453 (google), a mobile phone user would receive a text message from Google providing results to his or her query.

The Initial Public Offering

Google's April 29, 2004, initial public offering (IPO) registration became the most talked-about planned offering involving an Internet company since the dot-com bust of 2000. The registration announced Google's intention to raise as much as $3.6 billion from the issue of 25.7 million shares through an unusual Dutch auction. Among the 10 key tenets of Google's philosophy (presented in Exhibit 1) was "You can make money without doing evil."[5] The choice of a Dutch auction stemmed from this philosophy, since Dutch auctions allowed potential investors to place bids for shares regardless of size. The choice of a Dutch auction was also favorable to Google since it involved considerably lower investment banking and underwriting fees and few or no commissions for brokers.

At the conclusion of the first day of trading, Google's shares had appreciated by 18 percent to make Brin and Page each worth approximately $3.8 billion. Also, an estimated 900 to 1,000 Google employees were worth at least $1 million, with 600 to 700 holding at least $2 million in Google stock. On average, each of Google's 2,292 staff members held approximately $1.7 million in company stock, excluding the holdings of the top five executives. Stanford University also enjoyed a $179.5 million windfall from its stock holdings granted for its early investment in Brin and Page's search engine. Some of Google's early contractors and consultants also profited handsomely from forgoing fees in return for stock options in the company. One such contractor was Abbe Patterson, who took options for 4,000 shares rather than a $5,000 fee for preparing a PowerPoint presentation and speaking notes for one of Brin and Page's first presentations to venture capitalists. After two splits and four days of trading, her 16,000 shares were worth $1.7 million.[6] The company executed a second public offering of 14,159,265 shares of common stock in September 2005. The number of shares issued represented the first eight digits to the right of the decimal point for the value of π (pi). The issue added more than $4 billion to Google's liquid assets.

Exhibit 2 tracks the performance of Google's common shares between August 19, 2004, and July 2010.

Google Feature Additions between 2005 and 2010

Google used its vast cash reserves to make strategic acquisitions that might lead to the development of new Internet applications offering advertising opportunities. Google Earth was launched in 2005 after the company acquired Keyhole, a digital mapping company, in 2004. Google Earth and its companion software Google Maps allowed Internet users to search and view satellite images of any location in the world. The feature was enhanced in 2007 with the addition of street-view images taken by traveling Google camera cars. Digital images, webcam feeds, and videos captured by Internet users could be linked to locations displayed by Google Maps. Real estate listings and short personal messages could also be linked to Google Maps locations. In 2010, Google further enhanced Google Maps with the inclusion of an Earth View mode that allowed users to view 3D images of various locations from the ground level. Other search features added to Google between 2005 and 2010 that users found particularly useful included Book Search, Music Search, Video Search, and the expansion of Google News to include archived news articles dating to 1900.

Google also expanded its website features beyond search functionality to include its Gmail software, a Web-based calendar, Web-based document and spreadsheet applications, its Picasa Web photo albums, and a translation feature that accommodated 51 languages. The company also released services for mobile phone uses such as Mobile Web Search, Blogger Mobile, Gmail, Google News, and Maps for Mobile. A complete list of Google services and tools for computers and mobile phones in 2010 is presented in Exhibit 3.

GOOGLE'S BUSINESS MODEL

Google's business model had evolved since the company's inception to include revenue beyond the licensing fees charged to corporations needing search capabilities on company intranets or

Exhibit 1   The 10 Principles of Google's Corporate Philosophy

1. Focus on the user and all else will follow.

From its inception, Google has focused on providing the best user experience possible. While many companies claim to put their customers first, few are able to resist the temptation to make small sacrifices to increase shareholder value. Google has steadfastly refused to make any change that does not offer a benefit to the users who come to the site:

- The interface is clear and simple.
- Pages load instantly.
- Placement in search results is never sold to anyone.
- Advertising on the site must offer relevant content and not be a distraction.

By always placing the interests of the user first, Google has built the most loyal audience on the web. And that growth has come not through TV ad campaigns, but through word of mouth from one satisfied user to another.

2. It's best to do one thing really, really well.

Google does search. With one of the world's largest research groups focused exclusively on solving search problems, we know what we do well, and how we could do it better. Through continued iteration on difficult problems, we've been able to solve complex issues and provide continuous improvements to a service already considered the best on the web at making finding information a fast and seamless experience for millions of users. Our dedication to improving search has also allowed us to apply what we've learned to new products, including Gmail, Google Desktop, and Google Maps.

3. Fast is better than slow.

Google believes in instant gratification. You want answers and you want them right now. Who are we to argue? Google may be the only company in the world whose stated goal is to have users leave its website as quickly as possible. By fanatically obsessing on shaving every excess bit and byte from our pages and increasing the efficiency of our serving environment, Google has broken its own speed records time and again.

4. Democracy on the web works.

Google works because it relies on the millions of individuals posting websites to determine which other sites offer content of value. Instead of relying on a group of editors or solely on the frequency with which certain terms appear, Google ranks every web page using a breakthrough technique called PageRank™. PageRank evaluates all of the sites linking to a web page and assigns them a value, based in part on the sites linking to them. By analyzing the full structure of the web, Google is able to determine which sites have been "voted" the best sources of information by those most interested in the information they offer.

5. You don't need to be at your desk to need an answer.

The world is increasingly mobile and unwilling to be constrained to a fixed location. Whether it's through their PDAs, their wireless phones or even their automobiles, people want information to come to them.

6. You can make money without doing evil.

Google is a business. The revenue the company generates is derived from offering its search technology to companies and from the sale of advertising displayed on Google and on other sites across the web. However, you may have never seen an ad on Google. That's because Google does not allow ads to be displayed on our results pages unless they're relevant to the results page on which they're shown. So, only certain searches produce sponsored links above or to the right of the results. Google firmly believes that ads can provide useful information if, and only if, they are relevant to what you wish to find.

Advertising on Google is always clearly identified as a "Sponsored Link." It is a core value for Google that there be no compromising of the integrity of our results. We never manipulate rankings to put our partners higher in our search results. No one can buy better PageRank. Our users trust Google's objectivity and no short-term gain could ever justify breaching that trust.

7. There's always more information out there.

Once Google had indexed more of the HTML pages on the Internet than any other search service, our engineers turned their attention to information that was not as readily accessible. Sometimes it was just a matter of integrating new databases, such as adding a phone number and address lookup and a business directory. Other efforts required a bit more creativity, like adding the ability to search billions of images and a way to view pages that were originally created as PDF files. The popularity of PDF results led us to expand the list of file types searched to include documents produced in a dozen formats such as Microsoft Word, Excel and PowerPoint. For wireless users, Google developed a unique way to translate HTML formatted files into a format that could be read by mobile devices. The list is not likely to end there as Google's researchers continue looking into ways to bring all the world's information to users seeking answers.

(Continued)

Exhibit 1   *(Concluded)*

8. The need for information crosses all borders.

Though Google is headquartered in California, our mission is to facilitate access to information for the entire world, so we have offices around the globe. To that end we maintain dozens of Internet domains and serve more than half of our results to users living outside the United States. Google search results can be restricted to pages written in more than 35 languages according to a user's preference. We also offer a translation feature to make content available to users regardless of their native tongue and for those who prefer not to search in English, Google's interface can be customized into more than 100 languages.

9. You can be serious without a suit.

Google's founders have often stated that the company is not serious about anything but search. They built a company around the idea that work should be challenging and the challenge should be fun. To that end, Google's culture is unlike any in corporate America, and it's not because of the ubiquitous lava lamps and large rubber balls, or the fact that the company's chef used to cook for the Grateful Dead. In the same way Google puts users first when it comes to our online service, Google Inc. puts employees first when it comes to daily life in our Googleplex headquarters. There is an emphasis on team achievements and pride in individual accomplishments that contribute to the company's overall success. Ideas are traded, tested and put into practice with an alacrity that can be dizzying. Meetings that would take hours elsewhere are frequently little more than a conversation in line for lunch and few walls separate those who write the code from those who write the checks. This highly communicative environment fosters a productivity and camaraderie fueled by the realization that millions of people rely on Google results. Give the proper tools to a group of people who like to make a difference, and they will.

10. Great just isn't good enough.

Always deliver more than expected. Google does not accept being the best as an endpoint, but a starting point. Through innovation and iteration, Google takes something that works well and improves upon it in unexpected ways. Google's point of distinction however, is anticipating needs not yet articulated by our global audience, then meeting them with products and services that set new standards. This constant dissatisfaction with the way things are is ultimately the driving force behind the world's best search engine.

Source: Google.com.

Exhibit 2   **Performance of Google's Stock Price, August 19, 2004, to July 2010**

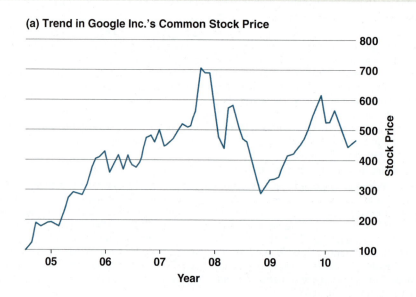

(a) Trend in Google Inc.'s Common Stock Price

(b) Performance of Google Inc.'s Stock Price Versus the S&P 500 Index

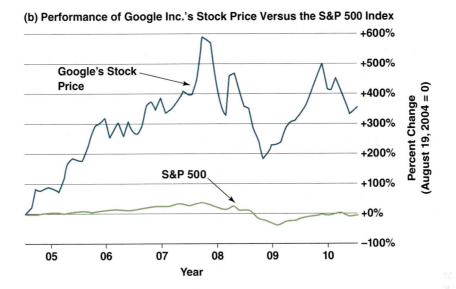

Exhibit 3   Google' Services and Tools in 2010

Search Features	
Alerts Get email updates on the topics of your choice	
Blog Search Find blogs on your favorite topics	
Books Search the full text of books	
Checkout Complete online purchases more quickly and securely	
Google Chrome A browser built for speed, stability and security	
Custom Search Create a customized search experience for your community	
Desktop Search and personalize your computer	
Directory Search the web, organized by topic or category	
Earth Explore the world from your computer	
Finance Business info, news, and interactive charts	

(Continued)

Exhibit 3   *(Continued)*

Search Features	
	GOOG-411 Find and connect with businesses from your phone
	Google Health Organize your medical records online
	iGoogle Add news, games and more to your Google homepage
	Images Search for images on the Web
	Maps View maps and directions
	News Search thousands of news stories
	Patent Search Search the full text of US Patents
	Product Search Search for stuff to buy
	Scholar Search scholarly papers
	Toolbar Add a search box to your browser
	Trends Explore past and present search trends
	Videos Search for videos on the Web
	Web Search Search billions of Web pages

Google Tools and Web Applications	
	Code Developer tools, APIs and resources
	Labs Explore Google's technology playground
	Blogger Share your life online with a blog—it's fast, easy, and free

(Continued)

Exhibit 3 *(Concluded)*

Google Tools and Web Applications

Calendar
Organize your schedule and share events with friends

Docs
Create and share your online documents, presentations, and spreadsheets

Google Mail
Fast, searchable email with less spam

Groups
Create mailing lists and discussion groups

Knol
Share what you know

Orkut
Meet new people and stay in touch with friends

Picasa
Find, edit and share your photos

Reader
Get all your blogs and news feeds fast

Sites
Create Web sites and secure group wikis

SketchUp
Build 3D models quickly and easily

Talk
IM and call your friends through your computer

Translate
View Web pages in other languages

YouTube
Watch, upload and share videos

Google Mobile Applications

Maps for mobile
View maps, your location and get directions on your phone

Search for mobile
Search Google wherever you are

Source: Google.com.

websites. The 2000 development of keyword-targeted advertising expanded its business model to include revenues from the placement of highly targeted text-only sponsor ads adjacent to its search results. Google was able to target its ads to specific users based on the user's browsing history. The addition of advertising-based revenue allowed Google to increase annual revenues from $220,000 in 1999 to more than $86 million in 2001. A summary of Google's financial performance between 2001 and 2009 is presented in Exhibit 4. The company's balance sheets for 2008 and 2009 are presented in Exhibit 5.

Google Search Appliance

Google's search technology could be integrated into a third party's website or intranet if search functionality was important to the customer. Google's Site Search allowed enterprises ranging from small businesses to public companies to license Google's search appliance for use on their websites for as little as $100 per year. The Google Search Appliance was designed for use on corporate intranets to allow employees to search company documents. The Search Appliance included a variety of security features to ensure that only employees with proper authority were able to view restricted documents. The Google Mini Search Appliance was designed for small businesses with 50,000 to 300,000 documents stored on local PCs and servers. The Google Mini hardware and software package could be licensed online (at **www.google.com/enterprise/mini**) at prices ranging from $2,990 to $9,900, depending on document count capability. Google's more robust search appliance had a document count capability of up to 30 million documents and was designed for midsized to global businesses. Licensing fees for the Google Search appliance ranged from $30,000 to $600,000, depending on document count capability.

AdWords

Google AdWords allowed advertisers, either independently through Google's automated tools or with the assistance of Google's marketing teams, to create text-based ads that would appear alongside Google search results. AdWords users could evaluate the effectiveness of their advertising expenditures with Google through the use of performance reports that tracked the effectiveness of each ad. Google also offered a keyword targeting program that suggested synonyms for keywords entered by advertisers, a traffic estimator that helped potential advertisers anticipate charges, and multiple payment options that included charges to credit cards, debit cards, and monthly invoicing.

Larger advertisers were offered additional services to help run large, dynamic advertising campaigns. Such assistance included the availability of specialists with expertise in various industries to offer suggestions for targeting potential customers and identifying relevant keywords. Google's advertising specialists helped develop ads for customers that would increase click-through rates and purchase rates. Google also offered its large advertising customers bulk posting services that helped launch and manage campaigns including ads using hundreds or thousands of keywords.

Google's search-based ads were priced using an auction system that allowed advertisers to bid on keywords that would describe their product or service. Bids could be made on a cost-per-impression (CPI) or cost-per-click (CPC) basis. Most Google advertisers placed bids based on CPC frequency rather than how many times an ad was displayed by Google. Google's auction pricing model assigned each bidder a Quality Score, which was determined by the advertiser's past keyword click-through rate and the relevance of the ad text. Advertisers with high Quality Scores were offered lower minimum bids than advertisers with poor quality scores.

Google allowed users to pay a CPC rate lower than their bid price if their bid was considerably more than the next highest bid. For example, an advertiser who bid $0.75 per click for a particular keyword would be charged only $0.51 per click if the next highest bid was only $0.50. The AdWords discounter ensured that advertisers paid only 1 cent more than the next highest bid, regardless of the actual amount of their bid.

AdSense

Google's AdSense program allowed Web publishers to share in the advertising revenues generated by Google's text ads. The AdSense program served content-relevant Google text ads to pages

Exhibit 4 Financial Summary for Google, 2001–2009 ($ thousands, except per share amounts)

	2009	2008	2007	2006	2005	2004	2003	2002	2001
Revenues	$23,650,563	$21,795,550	$16,593,986	$10,604,917	$6,138,560	$3,189,223	$1,465,934	$439,508	$86,426
Costs and expenses:									
Cost of revenues	8,844,115	8,621,506	6,649,085	4,225,027	2,577,088	1,457,653	625,854	131,510	14,228
Research and development	2,843,027	2,793,192	2,119,985	1,228,589	599,510	225,632	91,228	31,748	16,500
Sales and marketing	1,983,941	1,946,244	1,461,266	849,518	468,152	246,300	120,328	43,849	20,076
General and administrative	1,667,294	1,802,639	1,279,250	751,787	386,532	188,151	286,060	45,935	24,658
Contribution to Google Foundation	—	—	—	—	90,000	—	—	—	—
Non-recurring portion of settlement of disputes with Yahoo	—	—	—	—	—	201,000	—	—	—
Total costs and expenses	15,338,377	15,163,581	11,509,586	7,054,921	4,121,282	2,549,031	1,123,470	253,042	75,462
Income (loss) from operations	8,312,186	6,631,969	5,084,400	3,549,996	2,017,278	640,192	342,464	186,466	10,964
Impairment of equity investments	—	(1,094,757)	—	—	—	—	—	—	—
Interest income (expense) and other, net	69,003	316,384	589,580	461,044	124,399	10,042	4,190	-1,551	-896
Income (loss) before income taxes	8,381,189	5,853,596	5,673,980	4,011,040	2,141,677	650,234	346,654	184,915	10,068
Provision for income taxes	1,860,741	1,626,738	1,470,260	933,594	676,280	251,115	241,006	85,259	3,083
Net income (loss)	$6,520,448	$4,226,858	$4,203,720	$3,077,446	$1,465,397	$399,119	$105,648	$99,656	$6,985
Net income (loss) per share:									
Basic	$20.62	$13.46	$13.53	$10.21	$5.31	$2.07	$0.77	$0.86	$0.07
Diluted	$20.41	$13.31	$13.29	$9.94	$5.02	$1.46	$0.41	$0.45	$0.04
Number of shares used in per share calculations: (in thousands)									
Basic	316,220	314,031	310,806	301,403	275,844	193,176	137,697	115,242	94,523
Diluted	319,473	317,570	316,210	309,548	291,874	272,781	256,638	220,633	186,776
Net cash provided by operating activities	$9,316,198	$7,852,857	$5,775,410	$3,580,508	$2,459,422	$977,044	$395,445	$155,265	n/a
Net proceeds from public offerings	—	—	—	2,063,549	4,287,229	1,161,466	—	—	—
Cash, cash equivalents, and marketable securities	24,484,775	15,845,771	14,218,613	11,243,914	8,034,247	2,132,297	334,718	146,331	n/a
Total assets	40,496,778	31,767,575	25,335,806	18,473,351	10,271,813	3,313,351	871,458	286,892	n/a
Total long-term liabilities	1,745,087	1,226,623	610,525	128,924	107,472	43,927	33,365	n/a	n/a
Total stockholders' equity	36,004,224	28,238,862	22,689,679	17,039,840	9,418,957	2,929,056	588,770	173,953	n/a

Source: Google, Form S-1, filed April 29, 2004; Google, 2009 10-K report.

Exhibit 5   Google's Balance Sheets, 2008–2009 ($ thousands, except per share amounts)

	As of December 31	
	2009	2008
Assets		
Current assets:		
Cash and cash equivalents	$10,197,588	$ 8,656,672
Marketable securities	14,287,187	7,189,099
Accounts receivable, net of allowance of $16,914 and $32,887	3,178,471	2,642,192
Deferred income taxes, net	644,406	286,105
Income taxes receivable	23,244	—
Prepaid revenue share, expenses and other assets	836,062	1,404,114
Total current assets	29,166,958	20,178,182
Prepaid revenue share, expenses and other assets, non-current	416,119	433,846
Deferred income taxes, net, non-current	262,611	—
Non-marketable equity securities	128,977	85,160
Property and equipment, net	4,844,610	5,233,843
Intangible assets, net	4,774,938	996,690
Goodwill	4,902,565	4,839,854
Total assets	$40,496,778	$31,767,575
Liabilities and Stockholders' Equity		
Current liabilities:		
Accounts payable	$ 215,867	$ 178,004
Accrued compensation and benefits	982,482	811,643
Accrued expenses and other current liabilities	570,080	480,263
Accrued revenue share	693,958	532,547
Deferred revenue	285,080	218,084
Income taxes payable, net	—	81,549
Total current liabilities	2,747,467	2,302,090
Deferred revenue, long-term	41,618	29,818
Income taxes payable, long-term	1,392,468	890,115
Deferred income taxes, net, non-current	—	12,515
Other long-term liabilities	311,001	294,175
Commitments and contingencies		
Stockholders' equity:		
Convertible preferred stock, $0.001 par value, 100,000 shares authorized; no shares issued and outstanding	—	—
Class A and Class B common stock, $0.001 par value per share: 9,000,000 shares authorized; 315,114 (Class A 240,073, Class B 75,041) and par value of $315 (Class A $240, Class B $75) and 317,772 (Class A 243,611, Class B 74,161) and par value of $318 (Class A $244, Class B $74) shares issued and outstanding, excluding 26 and zero Class A shares subject to repurchase at December 31, 2008 and 2009	318	315
Additional paid-in capital	15,816,738	14,450,338
Accumulated other comprehensive income	105,090	226,579
Retained earnings	20,082,078	13,561,630
Total stockholders' equity	36,004,224	28,238,862
Total liabilities and stockholders' equity	$40,496,778	$31,767,575

Source: Google, 2009 10-K report.

on Google Network websites. For example, an Internet user reading an article about the state of the economy at Reuters.com would see Google text ads by investment magazines and companies specializing in home business opportunities. Google Network members shared in the advertising revenue whenever a site visitor clicked on a Google ad displayed on their sites. The more than 1 million Google Network members did not pay a fee to participate in the program and received about 60 percent of advertising dollars generated from the ads. Google's AdSense program also allowed mobile phone operators to share in Google revenues if text and image ads were displayed on mobile handsets. Also, owners of dormant domain names, Web-based game sites, video sites, and news feed services could also participate in the AdSense program. The breakdown of Google's revenues by source for 2003 through 2009 is presented in Exhibit 6.

Other Revenue Sources

The company's 2006 acquisition of YouTube allowed it to receive advertising revenues for ads displayed during Internet videos, while its 2008 acquisition of DoubleClick allowed the company to generate advertising revenues through banner ads. The company's 2008 launch of Google Checkout generated fees of as much as 2 percent of the transaction amount for purchases made at participating e-retailer sites. Google's business model was further expanded in 2008 to include licensing fees paid by users of its Web-based Google Apps document and spreadsheet software.

GOOGLE'S STRATEGY AND COMPETITIVE POSITION IN 2010

Google's Strategies to Dominate Internet Advertising

Google's multiple acquisitions since its 2004 IPO, and its research and development activities, were directed at increasing the company's dominance in Internet advertising. The addition of Google Maps, local search, airline travel information, weather, Book Search, Gmail, Blogger, and other features increased traffic to Google sites and gave the company more opportunities to serve ads to Internet users. Also, the acquisition of Double-Click in 2008 allowed Google to diversify its Internet advertising beyond search ads to include banner ads. However, not all of Google's acquisitions and innovations had resulted in meaningful contributions to the company's revenues. Even though more than 12 billion videos were watched on YouTube each month, the online video site's advertising revenues in 2009 were estimated at less than $300 million. Also, the company's internally developed social networking site, Orkut, had failed to match the success of competing social networking sites Facebook.com and MySpace.com.

Google's strategy to dominate Internet advertising also entailed becoming the number one search engine used not only in the United States but also across the world. In 2010, Google's search-based ads could be delivered to Internet users

Exhibit 6   **Google's Revenues by Source, 2003–2009 ($ thousands)**

	2009	2008	2007	2006	2005	2004	2003
Advertising revenues:							
Google websites	$15,722,486	$14,413,826	$10,624,705	$ 6,332,797	$3,377,060	$1,589,032	$ 792,063
Google Network websites	7,166,318	6,714,688	5,787,938	4,159,831	2,687,942	1,554,256	628,600
Total	22,888,804	21,128,514	16,412,643	10,492,628	6,065,002	3,143,288	1,420,663
Licensing and other revenues	761,759	667,036	181,343	112,289	73,558	45,935	45,271
Total revenues	$23,650,563	$21,795,550	$16,593,986	$10,604,917	$6,138,560	$3,189,223	$1,465,934

Source: Google, 2007 and 2009 10-K reports.

in 41 different languages. More than 50 percent of the company's 2009 revenues and traffic were generated from outside the United States, and the percentage of sales from outside the United States was expected to grow as Google entered emerging markets like Russia and China. China was a particularly attractive market for Google since it had more Internet users (300+ million) than any other country in the world. However, Google's 2006 entry into China was accompanied by challenges, including strong competition from local search provider Baidu and requirements by the Chinese government to censor search results that were critical of the government. Google complied with government censorship requirements until early 2010, when cyberattacks originating in China stole proprietary computer code from Google and information from the Gmail accounts of several Chinese human rights activists. Google first responded to the hacking incidents by stating that it would withdraw from the Chinese search market and then shifted to a strategy of redirecting users of its censored Google.cn site in China to its uncensored Hong Kong search site, Google.com.hk. The Chinese government was able to block search results from Google's Hong Kong site, but the new policy ended Google's involvement in China's censorship practices. To avoid breaking Chinese law prohibiting the distribution of information not authorized by the government,

Google agreed in June 2010 to stop the automatic redirects to its Hong Kong site. Instead, it presented Google.cn users with a link to Google.com.hk. In 2009, 64 percent of Internet searches in China were performed by Baidu, while Google held a 31 percent share of searches in that country. A breakdown of Google's revenues and long-lived assets by geographic region for 2006 through 2009 is presented in Exhibit 7.

Mobile Search and Google's Entry into the Market for Smartphones

In 2010, 234 million Americans ages 13 and older owned and used mobile phones. More than 30 percent of mobile phone users accessed the Internet from mobile devices, and a rapidly growing number of mobile phone users were exchanging basic mobile phones for smartphones. Smartphones like Research in Motion's Blackberry and Apple's iPhone could connect to the networks of wireless carriers to make phone calls, access the Internet, or run various Internet applications. Between February 2010 and May 2010, the number of smartphone users had grown by 8.1 percent to reach 49.1 million.

The company's introduction of its Android operating system for smartphones in 2008 was expected to allow it to increase its 60-plus percent

Exhibit 7   **Google's Revenues and Long-Lived Assets by Geographic Region, 2006–2009 (in thousands)**

	Year Ended December 31			
Revenues	**2009**	**2008**	**2007**	**2006**
United States	$11,193,557	$10,635,553	$ 8,698,021	$ 6,030,140
United Kingdom	2,986,040	3,038,488	2,530,916	1,603,842
Rest of the world	9,470,966	8,121,509	5,365,049	2,970,935
Total revenues	$23,650,563	$21,795,550	$16,593,986	$10,604,917

	As of December 31			
Long-Lived Assets	**2009**	**2008**	**2007**	**2006**
United States	$ 9,432,113	$ 9,782,825	$ 7,334,877	$ 5,070,694
Rest of the world	1,897,707	1,806,568	711,791	362,810
Total long-lived assets	$11,329,820	$11,589,393	$ 8,046,668	$ 5,433,504

Source: Google, 2007 and 2009 10-K reports.

Exhibit 8   **U.S. Smartphone Platform Market Share Rankings, Selected Periods, September 2009–May 2010**

Smartphone Platform	Share of Smartphone Subscribers			
	September 2009	December 2009	February 2010	May 2010
RIM (Blackberry)	42.6%	41.6%	42.1%	41.7%
Apple iPhone	24.1	25.3	25.4	24.4
Microsoft Windows Mobile	19.0	18.0	15.1	13.2
Google Android	2.5	5.2	9.0	13.0
Palm	8.3	6.1	5.4	4.8
Others	3.5	3.8	3.0	2.9
Total	100.0%	100.0%	100.0%	100.0%

Source: ComScore.com.

share of mobile searches and expand the market for other types of Internet ads delivered on mobile devices. Android was not a phone, but an operating system that Google made available free of charge to any phone manufacturer wishing to market mobile devices with Internet capability. Android's core applications included Wi-Fi capability, e-mail, a Web-based calendar, Google Earth maps, a browser, and GPS. T-Mobile was the first wireless provider to market an Android phone. Its $179 G1 was launched in September 2008 and included essentially the same features found on the more expensive Apple iPhone. By 2010, all major mobile phone providers had added smartphone models running Android software to its lineup of handsets. In addition, Google marketed its own Nexus One smartphone, which was produced by HTC and was compatible with all major wireless carrier 3G and 4G networks. Google was also collaborating with Verizon to develop a tablet computer similar to Apple's iPad that would run on Verizon's wireless networks.

Google's Android software had achieved remarkable success, despite its late entry into the market, with its market share increasing from zero in 2008 to 13.0 percent in May 2010—see Exhibit 8. Google also allowed mobile apps developers to use the Android operating system free of licensing fees. The worldwide market for mobile apps was expected to increase from $4.1 billion in 2009 to $17.5 billion by 2012. In 2010, more than 10,000 free and paid apps were available at Google's Android Market and more than 60 percent of mobile developers were actively working on new

apps for Android. About 50 percent of mobile developers were developing new apps for the iPhone and phones running Microsoft's Windows Mobile platform. Also in 2010, Google acquired AdMob, which had developed technology to deliver banner ads to smartphones and other mobile phones able to connect to the Internet. The transaction provided AdMob stockholders with Google shares worth $750 million.

Google's Strategic Offensive to Control the Desktop

Google's senior management believed that, in the very near future, most computer software programs used by businesses would move from local hard drives or intranets to the Internet. Many information technology analysts agreed that cloud computing would become a common software platform and could grow to a $95 billion market by 2013. Moving software applications to the cloud offered many possible benefits to corporate users, including lower software acquisition costs, lower computing support costs, and easier collaboration among employees in different locations. The beta version of Google Apps was launched in 2006 as a free word processing and spreadsheet package for individuals, but was relaunched in 2008 as a competing product to Microsoft Office. Google Apps was hosted on computers in Google's data centers and included Gmail, a calendar, instant messaging, word processing, spreadsheets, presentation software, and file storage space. Google Apps could be licensed by corporate customers at $50 per user per year. The licensing fee for the Microsoft Office and Outlook package was typically $350 per user per year. Industry analysts estimated Google Apps users at about 25 million and paid subscribers at about 1.5 million in 2010. Microsoft estimated Microsoft Office users at about 500 million in 2010.

Google's Chrome browser, which was launched in September 2008, and Chrome operating system (OS) launched in July 2009 were developed specifically to accommodate cloud computing applications. The bare-bones Chrome browser was built on a multiprocessor design that would allow users to operate spreadsheets, word processing, video editing, and other applications on separate tabs that could be run simultaneously. Each tab operated independently so that if one tab crashed, other applications running from Google's data centers were not affected. The Chrome browser also provided Google with a defense against moves by Microsoft to make it more difficult for Google to deliver relevant search-based ads to Internet users. Microsoft's Internet Explorer 8 allowed users to hide their Internet address and viewing history, which prevented Google from collecting user-specific information needed for ad targeting. Mozilla's Firefox browser employed a similar feature that prevented third parties from tracking a user's viewing habits. The clean-running Chrome OS was an open source operating system specifically designed as a platform for cloud computing applications.

Late in 2009, Google entered into agreements with Acer, Hewlett-Packard, and Lenovo to begin producing netbooks that would use the Chrome OS and Chrome browser to access the cloud-based Google Apps productivity software. Chrome OS netbooks were expected to be available for purchase by consumers and businesses in late 2010. Worldwide market share statistics for the leading browsers in September 2008 and June 2010 are presented in Exhibit 9.

Google's Initiatives to Expand Search to Television

In mid-2010, Google entered into an alliance with Intel, Sony, Logitech, Best Buy, DISH Network, and Adobe to develop Google TV. Google TV would be built on the Android platform and would run the Chrome browser software to search live network and cable programming; streaming

Exhibit 9   Worldwide Browser Market Share Rankings, September 2008 and June 2010

Browser	September 2008	June 2010
Internet Explorer	74%	60%
Firefox	19	24
Chrome	1	7
Safari	3	5
Opera	2	3
Others	1	1
Total	100%	100%

Source: "Google Rekindles Browser War," *Wall Street Journal Online,* July 7, 2010.

videos from providers such as Netflix, Amazon Video On Demand, and YouTube; and recorded programs on a DVR. Google TV users would also be able to use their televisions to browse the Web and run cloud-based applications such as Google Apps. Google TV was expected to be integrated into DISH Network's satellite service by fall 2010, while Sony was on schedule for fall 2010 shipments of Google TV–compatible high-definition televisions (HDTVs). Logitech was also on track for fall 2010 shipments of Google TV set-top boxes that would be compatible with all brands of HDTVs and Google TV accessories such as HD cameras that could be used for video chats.

Google acquired On2 Technologies, which was the leading developer of video compression technology, in February 2010 in a $124 million stock and cash transaction. The acquisition of On2 was expected to improve the video streaming capabilities of Google TV. Google also lobbied heavily during 2009 and 2010 to encourage the Obama administration to adopt a "Net neutrality" policy that would require Internet providers to manage traffic in a manner that would not restrict high-bandwidth services such as Internet television. The company was also testing an ultrafast broadband network in several cities across the United States that was as much as 100 times faster than what was offered by competing Internet providers. Google management had stated that the company did not intend to launch a nationwide Internet service, but did want to expose consumers to Internet applications and content that would be possible with greater bandwidth and faster transmission speeds.

GOOGLE'S INTERNET RIVALS

Google's ability to sustain its competitive advantage among search companies was a function of its ability to maintain strong relationships with Internet users, advertisers, and websites. In 2010, Google was the world's most-visited Internet site, with nearly 147 million unique Internet users going to Google sites each month to search for information. Google management believed its primary competitors to be Microsoft and Yahoo. A comparison of the percentage of Internet searches among websites offering search capabilities in July 2006, June 2009, and May 2010 is shown in Exhibit 10.

Exhibit 10   **U.S. Search Engine Market Share Rankings, July 2006, June 2009, and May 2010**

	Percent of Searches		
Search Entity	July 2006	June 2009	May 2010
Google Sites	43.7%	65.0%	63.7%
Yahoo Sites	28.8	19.6	18.3
Microsoft Sites	12.8	8.4	12.1
Ask.com	5.4	3.9	3.6
AOL	5.9	3.1	2.3
Others	3.4	n.m.	n.m.
Total	100.0%	100.0%	100.0%

n.m. = not material.

Source: ComScore.com.

Yahoo

Yahoo was founded in 1994 and was the third-most-visited Internet destination worldwide in 2010, with 130.5 million unique visitors each month. Facebook was the second-most-visited website, with 132 million unique visitors each month in 2010. Almost any information available on the Internet could be accessed through Yahoo's Web portal. Visitors could access content categorized by Yahoo or set up an account with Yahoo to maintain a personal calendar and e-mail account, check the latest news, check local weather, obtain maps, check TV listings, watch a movie trailer, track a stock portfolio, maintain a golf handicap, keep an online photo album, or search personal ads or job listings.

Yahoo also hosted websites for small businesses and Internet retailers and had entered into strategic partnerships with 20 mobile phone operators in the United States and Europe to provide mobile search and display ads to their customers. Yahoo accounted for about 35 percent of searches performed on mobile phones in 2010. Yahoo's broad range of services allowed it to generate revenues from numerous sources—it received fees for banner ads displayed at Yahoo.com, Yahoo! Messenger, Yahoo! Mail, Flickr, or mobile phone customers; it received listing fees at Yahoo! Autos, Cars.com, and Yahoo! Real Estate; it received revenues from paid search results at Yahoo! Search; it shared in travel agency booking fees made at Yahoo! Travel; and it received subscription fees from its registered users at Rivals.com, Yahoo! Games, Yahoo! Music, and Yahoo! Personals.

Yahoo's relationship with Google dated to 2000 and, since that time, had oscillated between cooperative and adversarial. Yahoo was among Google's earliest customers for its search appliance, but Yahoo began to distance itself from Google in 2002 when it began acquiring companies with developed search technologies. Yahoo replaced Google with its own search capabilities in February 2004. Yahoo later levied a patent infringement charge against Google that resulted in a settlement that gave Google ownership of the technology rights in return for 2.7 million shares of Google stock. Yahoo attempted to renew its relationship with Google in 2008 in hopes of reversing a decline in profitability and liquidity that began in 2006. After averting a hostile takeover by Microsoft in June 2008, Yahoo reached an agreement with Google that would allow Yahoo to host Google search ads. The partnership would provide Yahoo with an estimated $800 million in additional revenues annually, most of which would go directly to its bottom line. However, Google withdrew from the agreement in November 2008 after receiving notification from the U.S. Justice Department that

the alliance would possibly violate antitrust stat-
utes. Shortly after being notified that Google was
withdrawing from the deal, Yahoo's chief managers told business reporters that the company was
"disappointed that Google has elected to withdraw from the agreement rather than defend it in
court."[7] In July 2009, Microsoft and Yahoo finally
came to an agreement that would make Microsoft
Bing Yahoo's imbedded search engine for a period
of 10 years. A summary of Yahoo's financial performance between 2003 and 2009 is presented in
Exhibit 11.

Microsoft Online Services

Microsoft Corporation recorded fiscal 2009 revenues and net income of approximately $58.4 billion
and $14.6 billion, respectively, through the sales of
computer software, consulting services, video game
hardware, and online services. Windows 7 and
Microsoft Office accounted for more than one-
half of the company's 2009 revenues and nearly
all of its operating profit. The company's online
services business recorded sales of nearly $3.1 bil-
lion and an operating loss of almost $2.3 billion
during fiscal 2009. Microsoft's online services
business generated revenues from banner ads displayed at the company's MSN Web portal and its
affiliated websites, search-based ads displayed with
Bing results, and subscription fees from its MSN

dial-up service. A financial summary for Microsoft
Corporation and its Online Services Division is
provided in Exhibit 12.

Microsoft's search business was launched
in November 2004 as Live Search to compete
directly with Google and slow whatever intentions Google might have to threaten Microsoft in
its core operating system and productivity software businesses. Microsoft's concern with threats
posed by Google arose shortly after Google's
IPO, when Bill Gates noticed that many of the
Google job postings on its site were nearly identical to Microsoft job specifications. Recognizing
that the position announcements had more to do
with operating-system design than search, Gates
e-mailed key Microsoft executives, warning, "We
have to watch these guys. It looks like they are
building something to compete with us."[8] Gates
later commented that Google was "more like us
than anyone else we have ever competed with."[9]

Gates speculated that Google's long-term
strategy involved the development of Web-based
software applications comparable to Word, Excel,
PowerPoint, and other Microsoft products. Microsoft's strategy to compete with Google was keyed to
making Live Search more effective than Google at
providing highly relevant search results. Microsoft
believed that any conversion of Google users to
Live Search would reduce the number of PC users
who might ultimately adopt Google's Web-based

Exhibit 11   **Selected Financial Data for Yahoo, 2003–2009 ($ thousands)**

	2009	2008	2007	2006	2005	2004	2003
Revenues	$ 6,460,315	$ 7,208,502	$ 6,969,274	$ 6,425,679	$ 5,257,668	$3,574,517	$1,625,097
Income from operations	386,692	12,963	695,413	940,966	1,107,725	688,581	295,666
Net income	597,992	418,921	639,155	731,568	1,877,407	839,553	237,879
Cash and cash equivalents	1,275,430	2,292,296	1,513,930	1,569,871	1,429,693	823,723	415,892
Marketable securities	3,242,574	1,229,677	849,542	1,967,414	2,570,155	2,918,539	2,150,323
Working capital	2,877,044	3,040,483	937,274	2,276,148	2,245,481	2,909,768	1,013,913
Total assets	14,936,030	13,689,848	12,229,741	11,513,608	10,831,834	9,178,201	5,931,654
Long-term liabilities	699,666	715,872	384,208	870,948	1,061,367	851,782	822,890
Total stockholders' equity	12,493,320	11,250,942	9,532,831	9,160,610	8,566,415	7,101,446	4,363,490

Source: Yahoo, 2007 and 2009 10-K reports.

Exhibit 12 **Selected Financial Data for Microsoft Corporation and Microsoft's Online Services Business Unit, 2006–2009 ($ millions)**

	Fiscal Year Ended June 30			
Microsoft Corporation	**2009**	**2008**	**2007**	**2006**
Revenue	$58,437	$60,420	$51,122	$44,282
Operating income	20,363	22,492	18,524	16,472
Net income	14,569	17,681	14,065	12,599
Cash, cash equivalents, and short-term investments	$31,447	$23,662	$23,411	$34,161
Total assets	77,888	72,793	63,171	69,597
Long-term obligations	11,296	6,621	8,320	7,051
Stockholders' equity	39,558	36,286	31,097	40,104
Microsoft's Online Services Business Unit	**2009**	**2008**	**2007**	**2006**
Revenue	$ 3,088	$ 3,214	$ 2,441	$ 2,296
Operating income (loss)	(2,253)	(1,233)	(617)	5

Source: Microsoft, 2007 and 2009 annual reports.

word processing, spreadsheet, and presentation software packages. In 2008, Microsoft paid more than $100 million to acquire Powerset, which was the developer of a semantic search engine. Semantic search technology offered the opportunity to surpass the relevancy of Google's search results since semantic search evaluated the meaning of a word or phrase and considered its context when returning search results. Even though semantic search had the capability to answer questions stated in common language, semantic search processing time took several seconds to return results. The amount of time necessary to conduct a search had caused Microsoft to limit Powerset's search index to only articles listed in Wikipedia. Microsoft's developers were focused on increasing the speed of its semantic search capabilities so that its search index could be expanded to a greater number of Internet pages. The company's developers also incorporated some of Powerset's capabilities into its latest-generation search engine, Bing, which was launched in June 2009.

Microsoft's search agreement with Yahoo was engineered to allow the company to increase its Internet search market share and achieve advertising scale necessary to make its online services business profitable. The addition of Yahoo's 130.5 million unique monthly users was expected to double exposure for Microsoft's banner ads to more than 200 million unique monthly users. Banner ads comprised the bulk of Microsoft's online advertising revenues, since its Bing search engine accounted for only 12 percent of online searches in 2010. Even though the market for display ads was only about one-half the size of the search ad market in 2009, the advertising spending on banner ads was expected to double by 2012 to reach $15 billion.

Microsoft was also moving forward with its own approach to cloud computing. The company's 2008 launch of Windows Live allowed Internet users to store files online at its password-protected SkyDrive site. SkyDrive's online file storage allowed users to access and edit files from multiple locations, share files with coworkers who might need editing privileges, or make files available in a public folder for wide distribution. Azure was Microsoft's most ambitious cloud computing initiative in 2010 and was intended to allow businesses to reduce computing costs by allowing Microsoft to host its operating programs and data files. In addition to reducing capital expenditures for software upgrades and added server capacity, Azure's offsite hosting provided data security in the event of natural disasters such as fires or hurricanes.

ISSUES CONCERNING GOOGLE'S PERFORMANCE AND BUSINESS ETHICS IN 2010

During its first quarter of fiscal 2010, Google had been able to achieve year-over-year revenue growth of 23 percent, while most companies in almost every industry struggled as the U.S. economy continued to falter. So far, it appeared that Google's business model and strategy had insulated it from the effects of the recession and it was in position to pursue its growth strategies. The company's strategic priorities in 2010 focused on expanding its share of mobile search and smartphone platforms, pushing forward with its plans to become the dominant provider of cloud computing solutions, increasing search advertising revenues from markets outside the United States, and extending search to television. Some analysts believed the company's priorities should also include the development of semantic search capabilities, while others were concerned that the company had strayed from its 10 Principles—specifically, Principle 6, "You can make money without doing evil."

Free-speech advocates had criticized Google for its complicity in China's censorship of Internet content since it launched its Chinese site in 2006, while privacy advocates complained that Google Map's street view mode violated privacy rights. The New Zealand government addressed privacy rights by requiring Google to blur the faces of all individuals photographed by its camera cars. The most serious issue involving Google's Street View involved Google management's decision to allow the company's camera cars to capture Wi-Fi data emitted from homes and businesses while photographing the route. In May 2010, authorities in the United States, Canada, Australia, Germany, Italy, the United Kingdom, and Spain were conducting investigations into Google's data collection activities to determine if prosecution of company managers was warranted. Google cofounder Sergey Brin said the company "screwed up" by collecting personal data through wireless networks in an attempt to improve its mapping system.[10]

Also, the company's lobbying efforts to encourage the Obama administration to institute policies to promote Net neutrality had drawn the scrutiny of the U.S. House Oversight Committee. The primary concern of the House Oversight Committee involved communications between the company and its former head of public policy and government affairs, Andrew McLaughlin, who had been appointed to the position of White House deputy chief technology officer. Ethics rules created by an executive order signed by President Obama barred all White House officials from communicating with lobbyists or a company potentially affected by pending policy matters. A Freedom of Information Act (FOIA) request by a consumer group found that McLaughlin regularly communicated with Google executives to discuss the administration's push to have the Internet regulated by the Federal Communications Commission to promote Net neutrality. McLaughlin's e-mails could be obtained under the FOIA since all White House e-mail accounts were required to be archived under federal law. The House Oversight Committee was particularly disturbed by McLaughlin's alleged use of a personal Gmail account to avoid having his communications with Google executives archived and subject to FOIA requests.

Some analysts believed that pressure to achieve the revenue and earnings growth necessary to maintain Google's lofty stock price may have caused Google management to make decisions that pushed the bounds of its corporate philosophy. The company's revenues and earnings growth had begun to slow in recent years, and the sluggish U.S. economy seemed unlikely to give Google a dramatic boost in revenues in 2010. It remained to be determined if Google's strategies could sustain its growth and stock performance in a manner that would adhere to the company founders' early beliefs.

ENDNOTES

[1] Google, www.google.com/corporate/, accessed July 13, 2010.

[2] Quoted in "Google's Eric Schmidt: You Can Trust Us with Your Data," *UK Telegraph,* July 1, 2010.

[3] Google, www.google.com/corporate/tenthings.html, accessed July 13, 2010.

[4] Quoted in Google's Corporate Information, www.google.com/corporate/history.html.

[5] Google, "Our Philosophy," www.google.com/corporate/tenthings.html.

[6] "For Some Who Passed on Google Long Ago, Wistful Thinking," *Wall Street Journal Online,* August 23, 2004.

[7] Quoted in "With Google Gone, Will Microsoft Come Back to Yahoo?" *Fortune,* November 5, 2008.

[8] Quoted in "Gates vs. Google," *Fortune,* April 18, 2005.

[9] Ibid.

[10] Quoted in "Google Faces European Probes on Wi-Fi Data," *Wall Street Journal Online,* May 20, 2010.

SkyWest, Inc., and the Regional Airline Industry in 2009

Annette Lohman

California State University,
Long Beach

At the end of June 2009, SkyWest, Inc., the parent holding company of SkyWest Airlines and Atlantic Southeast Airlines (ASA), was the largest independently owned regional airline company in the regional airline subgroup of the airline industry. Its two wholly owned regional airlines' combined operations offered service through approximately 2,400 departures to 208 cities in the United States, Canada, Mexico, and the Caribbean.[1] SkyWest, Inc., and its subsidiary, SkyWest Airlines, had been the darling of airline industry analysts for years, especially since the company surpassed American Eagle, a subsidiary of American Airlines, as the number one regional airline in 2006. The company enjoyed respectable profits even when other airlines produced flat earnings or lost money. Its reputation for being well run had been enhanced by its success in overcoming the operational problems of its Atlantic Southeast Airlines (ASA) subsidiary, which it had acquired from Delta Airlines in late 2005. At that time, ASA was known for its poor performance on baggage delivery and on-time arrival metrics. Within two years, ASA's standing on the Transportation Department's performance list improved from 20th to 10th place.[2] Exhibit 1 shows a map of the destinations served by the airlines of the combined company.

Despite its successes, SkyWest, Inc., was experiencing many challenges in late 2009. Probably foremost was the state of the economy and its overall effect on the airline industry. The airline industry was cyclical and its financial performance was highly correlated to the economy; recessions traditionally sent industry participants' income statements and balance sheets into the red. The most recent recession that had begun in 2007 was no exception. Reports highlighting airline losses, bankruptcies, and consolidations were in the news. An important issue for SkyWest was the state of its relationship with Delta Airlines, one of its two main code-share partners, with which it had a legal dispute over Delta's refusal to pay expenses which SkyWest claimed were due them based on their contract with Delta. The company believed it was owed nearly $25 million in payments, but it was also concerned that suing the much larger airline would dampen Delta's enthusiasm for sending more business their way.

Another important strategic issue was the wind-down of SkyWest's partnership with Midwest Airlines. The partnership had originally been announced with great fanfare in December 2006 and then expanded in January 2008. Midwest's subsequent bankruptcy and purchase by investment group TPG Capital was followed by the announcement on June 23, 2009, that the airline would be purchased by Republic Airways Holdings, a direct competitor of SkyWest.[3] In fact, Republic was purchasing not only Midwest Airlines but also Frontier Airlines, moves that would make Republic a much larger company and extend its operations into flying larger airplanes covering greater distances. These capabilities would make them a much more formidable competitor in the future.

Fuel was another concern for SkyWest. Although SkyWest's contracts with its partners typically included compensation for fuel costs, there was some concern that availability could

Exhibit 1   Route Map for SkyWest Airlines and Atlantic Southeast Airlines, 2009

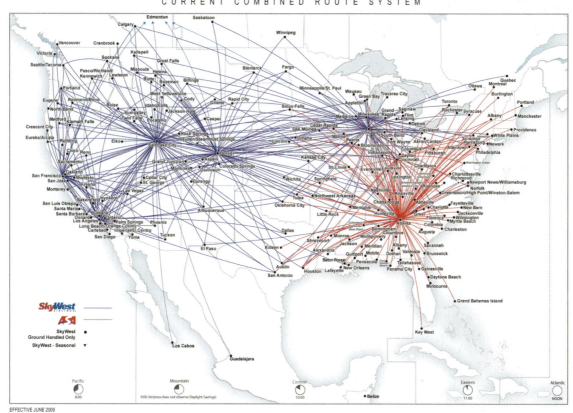

Source: SkyWest.com.

also become a problem, limiting the number of flights the company could support. A further issue involved stipulations in the "scope clauses" in the labor contracts that all airlines had with their pilots' unions that spelled out the maximum size of airplane that an outside partner could operate. Since all of SkyWest, Inc.'s business would be conducted in partnership with United and Delta (since the Midwest business was going away), "scope clauses" would limit the size of aircraft that they could fly in service of these contracts. Delta pilot contracts limited outside companies to 76-seat aircraft and United pilot contracts limited outside companies to 70-seat aircraft. Without these limitations, SkyWest could probably have purchased larger aircraft to take advantage of their efficiencies.

With larger aircraft, the company could have captured more business from its partners.

The effect of the economic downturn on the company's 2008 and 2009 financial performance was readily apparent. Even though overall revenues and income grew in 2008, fourth-quarter results dragged down its overall yearly results. Operating revenues for the quarter ending December 31, 2008, were $743.3 million—down from $854.7 million the previous year—and reported income for the quarter was $53.8 million—down from $83.6 million. In the first quarter of 2009 ending on March 31, the company reported that, compared to the same quarter the previous year, revenues at $672.6 million were down from $868.0 million, and operating income of $40.8 million was down from $68.2 million. In a discussion of these results, the company noted that approximately $18.3 million of the revenue decline was due to reductions in flight schedules made by the company's major partners. Lower fuel costs paid by partners and recorded as revenues accounted for $147 million of SkyWest's revenue decline during the first quarter of 2009. Additionally, ASA experienced significant weather-related cancellations at its Atlanta hub as well as the grounding of 60 regional aircraft in order to perform safety inspections recommended by the manufacturer, reducing revenues another $7.6 million. Finally, as a result of the ongoing negotiations regarding compensation of expenses with partner Delta Airlines, the company suffered a further $5 million reduction in revenues. SkyWest, Inc.'s consolidated statements of income for 2004 through 2008 are provided in Exhibit 2. The company's balance sheets for 2007 and 2008 are presented in Exhibit 3. Selected operating statistics for SkyWest, Inc., between 2004 and 2008 are shown in Exhibit 4.

THE AIRLINE INDUSTRY

The global airline industry comprised firms primarily offering domestic and international air transportation of passengers and/or cargo over regular routes on regular schedules. Airlines operated flights even if they were only partially loaded. Companies whose main business was providing air transportation of mail on a contract basis were included in the industry.[5]

The U.S. Airline Industry

There were three types of domestic airline carriers: (1) network, (2) low-cost, and (3) regional carriers. They operated under three different business models. Network carriers, often referred to as the "majors" or "legacy carriers," operated a significant portion of their flights using what is known as a hub-and-spoke system. In 2009, United, US Airways, Northwest, American, Continental, and Delta Airlines were the largest of this group. The merger of Northwest and Delta Airlines, approved on October 29, 2008, and expected to be completed within 12 to 24 months,[6] would leave this group with five large players.

Low-cost carriers were those that the industry generally recognized as operating under a low-cost

business model most often using point-to-point flights. The largest carriers in this segment were Southwest and JetBlue Airlines. Several major carriers, in an effort to respond to the loss of revenues from low-cost competitors, had started up their own low-cost airlines. Two examples were United's Ted Airlines and Delta's Song Airlines.

Regional carriers provided service from small cities, using primarily regional jets, to support the network carriers' hub-and-spoke systems. Regional airlines were air carriers that specialized in short-haul flights that serviced small communities that had neither the facilities nor frequency of passenger travel to support a larger airport and the accompanying aircraft. The largest regional carriers operated under a business model that relied on contracts with major carriers to generate revenues. The regional carriers painted their airplanes with the colors and logos of the major carriers, and flights were operated under the codes of their major carrier partners.

Turbulence in the Industry

The U.S. airline industry had experienced more than its share of turbulence since the September 11, 2001, terrorist attacks on the World Trade Center and the Pentagon. This disruption, coupled with the major airlines' prior overexpansion and bloated flight schedules, increasing fuel costs, increased competitive pressures from low-cost carriers, and the post-9/11 fear of flying, translated into huge losses for the major carriers. Most major airlines started 2006 in serious financial trouble, if not bankruptcy. United Airlines and US Airways filed for bankruptcy in 2002 (with United emerging to post profits in 2006),[7] followed by ATA in 2004, and Northwest and Delta in September 2005. In the spring of 2008, both ATA and Aloha Airlines indicated that they would cease operations.

Some analysts believed that the U.S. airline industry, as it existed, was not sustainable and that the time was ripe for serious consolidations. In the fall of 2005, the US Airways–America West merger was finalized. In April 2008, Delta announced that a deal had been struck to acquire Northwest Airlines based in Minnesota.[8] The merger was expected to create the world's largest airline once operations were consolidated over the next two years. There had also been rumors

Exhibit 2 **SkyWest, Inc.'s Consolidated Statements of Income (dollars and shares in thousands, except per share amounts)**

	Twelve Months Ended December 31				
	2008	2007	2006	2005	2004
Operating Revenue					
Passenger	$3,466,287	$3,342,131	$3,087,215	$1,938,450	$1,139,580
Ground handling and other	29,962	32,201	27,441	25,598	16,464
Total operating revenues	3,496,249	3,374,332	3,114,656	1,964,048	1,156,044
Operating Expenses:					
Aircraft fuel	1,220,618	1,062,079	1,010,717	590,776	252,556
Salaries, wages and benefits	724,094	726,947	673,961	434,218	282,676
Aircraft maintenance, materials and repair	381,653	297,960	220,705	129,626	77,514
Aircraft rentals	295,784	294,443	281,497	281,496	210,496
Depreciation and amortization	220,195	208,944	189,885	115,275	76,817
Station rentals and landing fees	132,017	135,757	118,990	n.a.*	n.a.*
Ground handling services	106,135	140,374	134,034	n.a.*	n.a.*
Other	160,522	163,304	145,707	263,248	175,686
Total operating expenses	3,241,018	3,029,808	2,775,496	1,743,640	1,011,268
Operating Income	255,231	344,524	339,160	220,408	144,776
Other income (expense):					
Interest income	20,776	31,650	19,953	12,943	10,050
Interest expense	(106,064)	(126,320)	(118,002)	(53,330)	(18,239)
Other	6,240	467	(1,084)	(395)	—
Total other expense(net)	(79,048)	(94,203)	(99,133)	(40,782)	(8,189)
Income before income taxes	176,183	250,321	240,027	179,626	136,587
Provision for income taxes	63,254	91,129	94,221	67,359	54,635
Net income	$ 112,929	$ 159,192	$ 145,806	$ 112,267	$ 81,952
Basic earnings per share	$1.95	$2.54	$2.33	$1.94	$1.42
Diluted earnings per share	$1.93	$2.49	$2.30	$1.90	$1.40
Weighted average common shares:					
Basic	57,790	62,710	62,474	57,851	57,858
Diluted	58,633	64,044	63,382	58,933	58,350

Note: Increases between 2004 and 2005 are due in large part to the acquisition of ASA.

*Changes in reporting categories made these numbers unavailable.

Source: SkyWest, Inc.[5]

of a potential merger between United and Continental Airlines.[9] Analysts viewed mergers from two perspectives. First, they had the potential to take out some of the excess capacity in the industry leading to more stable profits and less devastating price competition. This was viewed as positive. On the other hand, they were likely to be accompanied by higher debt and higher costs associated with merging the operations of two airlines. As many airlines were already struggling under heavy debt loads,[10] increased merger activity leading to higher debt could further destabilize the industry.

The industry was highly sensitive to fluctuations in the economy because a significant portion of travel by both leisure and business travelers was discretionary. The recession in the early 2000s lowered the overall demand for airline services in the United States. As 2009 began, a worldwide recession of a scale not seen since

Exhibit 3   **SkyWest, Inc.'s Consolidated Balance Sheets, 2008 and 2009 ($ thousands)**

Assets		
	December 31, 2008	December 31, 2007
Current Assets		
Cash and cash equivalents	$ 125,892	$ 122,802
Marketable securities	568,567	522,925
Restricted cash	10,728	14,705
Income tax receivable	14,868	23,114
Receivables, net	55,458	81,216
Inventories, net	104,383	105,738
Prepaid aircraft rents	226,474	223,891
Deferred tax assets	76,093	70,523
Other current assets	38,205	45,225
Total current assets	1,220,668	1,210,139
Property and Equipment		
Aircraft and rotable spares	3,273,705	3,146,602
Deposits on aircraft	20,390	23,848
Buildings and ground equipment	239,573	215,466
Total	3,533,668	3,385,916
Less accumulated depreciation and amortization	(824,293)	(685,327)
Total property and equipment, net	2,709,375	2,700,589
Other Assets		
Intangible assets, net	26,247	28,498
Other assets	58,001	51,299
Total other assets	84,248	79,797
Total assets	$4,014,291	$3,990,525

Liabilities and Stockholders' Equity		
	December 31, 2008	December 31, 2007
Current Liabilities		
Current maturities of long-term debt	$ 129,783	$ 118,202
Accounts payable	110,902	133,728
Accrued salaries, wages and benefits	66,663	67,242
Accrued aircraft rents	25,676	26,516
Taxes other than income taxes	16,651	12,433
Other current liabilities	37,039	40,098
Other long-term liabilities	386,604	398,219
Total current liabilities	41,525	40,355
Long-term debt, net of current maturities	1,681,705	1,732,748
Deferred income taxes payable	507,113	445,993
Deferred aircraft credits	121,823	127,203
Commitments and contingencies		
Stockholders' equity	—	—
Preferred stock, 5,000,000 shares authorized; not issued . . .		
Common stock, no par value, 120,000,000 shares authoried; 73,520,292 and 72,272,671 issued respectively	562,395	533,545
Retained earnings	977,736	871,874
Treasury stock, at cost, 17,150,580 and 11,794,056 shares, respectively	(261,174)	(158,542)
Accumulated other comprehensive loss	(3,436)	(870)
Total stockholders' equity	1,275,521	1,246,007
Total liabilities and stockholders' equity	$4,014,291	$3,990,525

Source: SkyWest, Inc., 2008 annual report.

Exhibit 4   **Selected Operating Statistics for SkyWest, Inc.**

Operating Metric	Year Ended December 31					
	2008	2007	% Change 2007–2008	2006	2005	2004
Passengers carried	33,461,819	34,392,755	(2.7)	31,465,552	20,343,975	13,424,520
Revenue passenger miles (000)	17,101,910	17,892,282	(4.4)	15,819,191	9,538,906	5,546,069
Available seat miles (000)	22,020,250	22,968,768	(4.1)	20,209,888	12,718,973	7,546,318
Passenger load factor	77.7%	77.9%	(0.2) pts	78.3%	75.0%	73.5%
Passenger break-even load factor	74.4%	72.9%	1.5 pts	72.9%	68.6%	65.5%
Yield per revenue passenger mile	$0.203	$0.187	8.6	$0.195	$0.203	$0.205
Revenue per available seat mile	15.9¢	14.7¢	8.2	15.4¢	15.4¢	15.3¢
Cost per available seat mile	15.2¢	13.7¢	10.9	14.3¢	14.1¢	13.6¢
Fuel cost per available seat mile	5.5¢	04.6¢	19.6	n.a.	n.a.	n.a.
Average passenger trip length (in miles)	511	520	(1.7)	503	469	413
Number of operating aircraft at end of year	442	436	1.0	410	380	206

n.a. = not available

Source: SkyWest, Inc.[4]

the Great Depression was expected to exacerbate the problems already affecting the industry. In December 2008, new forecasts from the International Air Transport Association (IATA) had predicted that worldwide passenger traffic, in response to the worldwide recession, would fall by 3 percent to $394 billion from $425 billion in 2008 and cargo revenues would fall to $54 billion from $59 billion. In its report, the IATA noted that weak travel markets due to recession had typically lasted three years, so travel was not expected to grow more than 4 percent until 2011.[11] It was well known that the most recent recession had also had a strong impact on credit markets. Airlines needed credit to acquire new aircraft.

Finally, the airline industry was affected by seasonal fluctuations that included increased travel during summer months and flight cancellations and delays owing to inclement weather primarily during the winter.[12] For example, SkyWest, Inc., reported that one storm during December 2006 led to a two-day closing of the Denver International Airport and the subsequent cancellation of 2,850 of its flights. The weather-related flight cancellations resulted in a decrease in SkyWest pretax income of approximately $5.2 million.[13]

Airline Passengers

There were two main types of passengers in the airline industry: business travelers and leisure travelers. Business travelers tended to be more profitable for airlines because they flew more often. Also, a great deal of business travel was not planned very far in advance, forcing business travelers to purchase tickets at a premium. Leisure passengers traveled less and were more price sensitive than business travelers. The regional airlines, primarily through their contracts with the major carriers, serviced both market segments; however, their passenger base had historically been made up of more business travelers than leisure travelers. Business travelers used regional airlines to commute to and from locations that were considered too far to drive.

Traditionally, the major airlines, through their partnerships with regional airlines, serviced almost the entire business market. However, an increasing number of business travelers had begun to travel on low-cost carriers. The major airlines' share of the business market had dropped to 60 percent, while the low-cost carriers had picked up 20 percent. The major airlines were responding to these competitive pressures by offering their own low-cost carrier lines, such as United's Ted and Delta's Song. These moves were expected to potentially lower overall demand for routes traditionally served by the regional carriers.

Safety

The September 11, 2001, terrorist attacks on the United States were a major contributor to the decreased demand in the airline industry in the early 2000s. People were afraid to fly and, in an uncertain economy, this translated into less revenue for the major airlines. This factor likely did not directly affect regional airlines because of the assumption that a smaller regional aircraft wouldn't be a target for terrorism. However, since regionals derived most, if not all, of their revenues from contracts with the majors, they were affected as well. Regional airlines also suffered from the general view that smaller airplanes were less safe than larger airplanes. In reality, regional airlines had a slightly lower accident rate than the major airlines and had increased safety standards in recent years. Two dramatic airline disasters within weeks of each other in early 2009 again focused media attention on safety.

Regulation

The airline industry in the United States was regulated by the Federal Aviation Administration (FAA), the Department of Transportation (DOT), and the Transportation Security Administration (TSA). Post-9/11 fears of terrorist attacks had led to stepped-up government intervention in the industry through increased security regulations, leading to additional costs for the airlines.

Each new government regulation of the industry created additional costs for airlines. For example, the Department of Transportation had considered implementing a regulation (amending the Air Carrier Access Act of 1986) to require airlines to provide oxygen for passengers who needed oxygen. The proposal, if enacted, would have increased regional airlines' costs since equipment would have needed to be purchased and maintained and personnel trained to properly use the equipment. The cost for this regulation had been estimated to be between $262 million and $577 million to the airline industry over 10 years.[14]

Fuel Cost Increases

The increasing price of jet fuel had been a contributing factor to the financial troubles of the major airlines. Before the unprecedented increases in fuel costs experienced by the airline industry in 2008, the costs of fuel had made up 10–20 percent of overall airline costs with 14–16 percent being the average.[15] Although fuel costs during 2008 had receded somewhat by the end of the year, most analysts didn't expect much relief in fuel costs in the foreseeable future. At the beginning of 2009, fuel expenses ranged from 35 to 50 percent of an airline's operating costs.[16] In response to the threat of rising fuel costs, most of the major airlines implemented stringent luggage restrictions, with stiff fees for passengers who exceeded specified limits. Increased fuel costs were also a threat to regional carriers as their major airline partners pressured them for lower fees.[17]

Labor Unions

The airline business had always been highly labor intensive. It was estimated that 40 percent of an airline's expenses comprised pay for airline professionals such as pilots, flight attendants, baggage carriers, customer service personnel, etc.[18] Most airline employees were represented by one of many labor unions including the Airline Pilots Association and the Allied Pilots Association, the Professional Flight Attendants Union, the Transportation Workers Union, the International Association of Machinists, and the Airline Professional Flight Attendants Association. Labor unions and airlines had a history of acrimonious relationships leading to strikes and huge losses for the airlines affected. Some analysts who followed the industry anticipated that labor unions would see any return to profits for the industry as an opportunity to lobby for wage and salary increases.[19]

THE REGIONAL AIRLINE INDUSTRY

The regional airline industry was made up of air carriers that specialized in short-haul flights that serviced small communities which had neither the facilities nor frequency of passenger travel to support a larger airport and the accompanying aircraft. Initially, regional airlines operated small, slow planes in one general geographic area. As the industry grew and regional companies partnered with the major airlines, they began to increase their reach. The introduction of faster, more efficient commuter jets also helped the regional airlines expand their service areas. A major portion of regional airline growth was attributed to the development of smaller regional jets that could be flown on routes that the majors had previously serviced through the use of larger 737s, DC9s, MD80s and A319s. In 2009, the six major U.S. airlines had a significant number of older aircraft of these models. Their potential retirement created opportunities for regional partners to take over the routes that these aircraft previously flew.

Regional airlines primarily operated to serve as feeder airlines bringing passengers to and from small communities to a large hub airport to connect with larger airlines with larger aircraft and greater geographic reach. About 95 percent of regional airlines' business served this purpose.[20] Other regional airlines were formed to serve particular low-use routes and were often most important to small and isolated communities for whom the airline was the only reasonable link to a larger town.

Regional airlines operated mostly through partnerships with the major airlines. Some regional airline companies such as SkyWest, Inc., were independent entities; often, however, regionals were wholly owned subsidiaries of major airlines where the separate corporate structure allowed the subsidiary to operate under different (and lower) pay schedules. Examples of such subsidiaries included American Eagle, Canada Air Jazz, Comair, and Continental Express. When a regional airline entered into a partnership with a major carrier, the major carrier paid the regional airline a contracted fee per departure. The major carriers relied on the regional airlines to make their hubs work efficiently, and the regional airlines gained access to an established customer base and a steady revenue stream. Under these conditions, the revenues of regional airlines were not directly related to ticket sales generated by the regional carrier. A passenger wanting to travel along a route served by a regional airline would book his or her flight with a major carrier that had a partnership with the regional. The passenger was the customer of the major carrier and the identity of the regional airline was not normally of concern or interest to the passenger.[21] A list of partnerships between major air carriers and regional airlines is presented in Exhibit 5.

Regional airlines were subject to a number of operating constraints and problems that their major carrier partners did not face. Regional airlines often fared poorly in periodic releases of the Airline Quality Report, but many of the problems cited were beyond the control of the regional airlines. For example, Atlantic Southeast Airlines, owned by SkyWest, Inc., came in worst for bumping passengers due to overselling seats even though it was Delta Airlines that was responsible for overselling its flights.[22] In one rating in the third quarter of 2006, four of the worst on-time records were held by regional carriers. The six worst carriers in baggage handling were all regionals and six of the seven worst carriers for cancelling flights were also regionals. As the ASA example above illustrates, many of the regionals' problems were caused by their partners. The partners controlled the regionals' scheduling, not allowing enough time to load and unload passengers and luggage. In addition, regional carriers, which were usually limited geographically to one region, were more affected by bad weather. At some hub airports, regional carriers' flights were routinely cancelled to make room on runways for major carrier airplanes when the weather was bad.[23]

The financial troubles of the major airlines during the 2000s created both opportunities and threats for their regional partners. The majors, in an attempt to stop the flow of red ink, rolled back operations and outsourced more of their routes to the regional airlines. This created opportunities for the regional carriers to expand their service areas and often put them into direct competition with the low-cost carriers, such as Southwest and Jet Blue. Increased pressure on the major carriers to cut costs also forced them to put pressure on their regional partners to accept lower fees.

Exhibit 5   Regional Airline Partnerships (as of September 2008)

Mainline Carrier	Regional Brand	Operating Partners
Alaska Airlines	None	Horizon Air Peninsula Airways
America Airlines	American Eagle American Connection	American Eagle American Eagle/Executive Chautauqua Airlines Tran States Airlines
Continental Airlines	Continental Express Continental Connection	Chautauqua Airlines ExpressJet Cape Air Colgan Air Commut Air Gulfstream International Airlines
Delta Air Lines	Delta Connection	Atlantic Southeast Airlines Chautauqua Airlines Comair Freedom Airlines Pinnacle Airlines Shuttle America SkyWest Airlines
Frontier Airlines	None	Great Lakes Lynx Aviation
JetBlue Airways	None	Cape Air
Midwest Airlines	Midwest Connect	SkyWest Airlines Republic Airlines (as of 10/1/2008)
Northwest Airlines	NWA Airlink	Compass Airlines Mesaba Aviation Pinnacle Airlines
United Airlines	United Express	Chautauqua Airlines Colgan Air Gojet Airlines Great Lakes Mesa Airlines Shuttle America SkyWest Airlines Trans States Airlines.
US Airways	US Airways Express	Air Wisconsin Chautauqua Airlines Colgan Air Mesa Airlines Piedmont PSA Republic Airlines Trans States Airlines

Furthermore, the bankruptcy filings of major carriers increased the risk of regionals whose partners were in reorganization. Such regionals found it necessary to expand their base of partnership contracts and develop more revenue sources.

When Northwest Airlines filed for bankruptcy protection on September 14, 2005, its major regional partner, Mesaba Airlines, followed suit on October 13, 2005, citing the $30 million due it in the Northwest Chapter 11 case.[24]

It was expected that the potential mergers of several of the major airlines could also create tougher times for their regional partners. Consolidations would mean more limited growth opportunities for the regionals that moved the majors' passengers to their hubs from smaller cities. Consolidations would allow carriers to shut down some of their hubs around the country, especially some of the smaller ones that depended more on regional airline flights.[25]

Aircraft

There were two major choices of type of aircraft used by regional carriers: the turboprop and the regional jet. The uses for these two aircraft differed and complemented each other. The turboprop was used for short- to medium-haul flights and was able to land on shorter runways. Many travelers were hesitant to ride on turboprops, given the perception that they were loud and uncomfortable. Some of the major turboprops included the Embraer EMB 120, a twin-engine 30-passenger aircraft manufactured by Brazil's Empresa Brasileira de Aeronautica SA, the Jetstream 41, Saab 340, ATR 72, Dornier 328, the de Havilland Dash 8-100 and 8-200, and the Bombardier Q Series turboprop, which was equipped with noise and vibration reduction devices that reduced the noise and vibration levels to those of a regional jet.

Regional jets, on the other hand, had increasingly been used to service longer-haul flights to destinations up to 1,200 miles away. The Bombardier Regional Jet (the CRJ 200, CRJ 700, and CRJ 900) was the main regional jet used in the industry. Its introduction allowed the regional carriers to operate new longer routes and run shorter routes more efficiently.

Competition

Like competition among the majors and low-cost carriers, competition among the regional airlines had become increasingly fierce as the regional airlines competed with each other for partnerships with only a few major airlines. Rivalry was expected to continue to increase as the regional airlines competed for new routes being offered and bid out by the major airlines. To be able to successfully acquire contracts with the majors, a regional airline was required to:

- Develop and maintain high levels of customer service: Airlines had become notorious for providing poor customer service by mishandling baggage and cancelling flights. However, many times regional airlines' baggage problems were attributed to scheduling decisions by partners which did not allow enough time between their flights and the regional's to transfer luggage. As mentioned above, inclement weather could force flight cancellations for regionals when runway priority was given to the majors.

- Develop and maintain a strong safety image: Passengers would not fly with an airline that had an unsafe image.

- Maximize on-time arrivals: To ensure passengers continued to fly with a regional airline, the airline was required to deliver passengers to their destination on time so passengers did not miss their connecting flight.

- Acquire new aircraft: Regional airlines needed capital and financing to increase the size of their fleets to service the longer routes being outsourced by the major airlines. Yet they had to be able to do this without compromising their scope contracts with labor.

SkyWest, Inc., viewed its main rivals in the regional airline industry to be Air Wisconsin Airlines Corporation, American Eagle Airlines (owned by American), Comair (owned by Delta), ExpressJet Holdings, Inc., Horizon Air Industries, Inc. (owned by Alaska Air Group, Inc.), Mesa Air Group, Inc., Pinnacle Airlines Corp., Republic Airways Holdings Inc., and Trans State Airlines, Inc.[26] Selected consolidated operating and financial data for the five largest independent regional airlines in the United States for 2004 through 2008 is presented in Exhibit 6. Exhibit 7 provides operating revenues for each of the five largest regional carriers between 2004 and 2008. Exhibit 8 provides a comparison of operating costs per passenger revenue mile for the five largest regional carriers for 2004 through 2008.

A brief overview of SkyWest, Inc.'s major independent competitors is given below:

Mesa Air Group, a publicly held company, operated 188 aircraft with over 1,100 daily system departures to 173 cities, 46 states, the District of Columbia, Canada, and Mexico.

Exhibit 6   **Selected Consolidated Operating and Financial Data for the Five Largest U.S.Independent Regional Airlines, 2004–2008**

	2008	2007	2006	2005	2004
Passengers (in thousands)	94,389	95,532	85,799	62,775	46,051
Flights (in thousands)	2,462	2,601	2,231	2,206	1,880
Revenue passenger miles (in millions)	47,808	48,323	43,827	33,308	23,956
Available seat miles (in millions)	63,308	63,657	57,186	45,700	33,901
Passenger load factor	75.5%	75.9%	76.6%	72.9%	70.7%
Passenger revenues (in millions)	$8,374	$8,355	$7,968	$6,321	$4,784

Source: Annual reports of SkyWest, Mesa Air Group, ExpressJet Holdings, Republic Airways Holdings, and Pinnacle Airlines Corp., 2004–2008.

Exhibit 7   **Operating Revenues of the Five Largest U.S. Independent Regional Airlines, 2004–2008 ($ millions)**

	2008	2007	2006	2005	2004
SkyWest, Inc.	$3,496	$3,374	$3,115	$1,964	$1,156
Mesa Air Group, Inc.	1,316	1,372	1,183	943	741
ExpressJet Holdings, Inc.	1,318	1,686	1,682	1,563	1,508
Republic Airways Holdings, Inc.	1,480	1,293	1,143	905	646
Pinnacle Airlines Corp.	865	787	825	842	635

On December 22, 2006, the Mesa Air Group signed an agreement with Shenzhen Airlines to create a new regional airline through a joint venture. The new airline was expected to have twenty 50-seat regional jets flying prior to the Beijing Olympic Games in 2008. The company also operated partnerships with United Airlines, US Airways, Midwest Airlines, and Delta Airlines. Wholly owned subsidiaries included:

- **Air Midwest,** doing business as **Mesa Airlines,** primarily served federally subsidized markets across the country through a fleet of twenty 19-passenger, Raytheon 1900D Aircraft.

- **Freedom Airlines, Inc.,** operated Delta Connection services primarily in the southeast.

- **Go! Hawaii Airlines** was a low-cost inter-island airline operated by Mesa Airlines that flew 66 routes per day between the islands of Hawaii.[27]

Republic Airways Holdings, based in Indianapolis, Indiana, was an airline holding company that operated Chautauqua Airlines, Republic Airlines, and Shuttle America. The airlines offered scheduled passenger service on approximately 1,200 flights daily to 119 cities in 38 states, Canada, Mexico, and the U.S. Virgin Islands through airline services agreements with four major U.S. airlines. All of the airlines' flights were operated under their major airline partner's brand, such as American Connection, Delta Connection, Frontier Airlines, United Express, and US Airways Express. As of December 2008, the combined airlines employed over 4,700 people and operated 219 regional jets.[28] However, in June 2009, the company announced plans to acquire both Midwest Airlines (one of its partners) and Frontier Airlines, moves that would significantly increase its size and bring it into direct competition with legacy and low-cost carriers.

Exhibit 8 **Comparative Operating Cost Statistics for Major U.S. Regional Airlines, 2004–2008 (costs per passenger revenue mile in cents)**

Year	Wages and Benefits Compensation	Maintenance	Fleet Rental Costs	Landing Fees and Ground Handling	Fuel	Depreciation and Amortization	Other
SkyWest, Inc.							
2008	4.2¢	2.2¢	1.7¢	1.4¢	7.1¢	1.3¢	0.9¢
2007	4.1	1.7	1.6	1.5	5.9	1.2	0.9
2006	4.3	1.4	1.8	1.6	6.4	1.2	0.9
2005	4.6	1.4	3.0	n.a.	6.2	1.2	2.8
2004	5.1	1.4	3.8	n.a.	4.6	1.4	3.2
ExpressJet Holdings, Inc.							
2008	4.2¢	2.1¢	2.1¢	1.7¢	2.4¢	0.3¢	0.3¢
2007	4.3	2.1	3.4	2.1	3.2	0.3	0.3
2006	3.8	1.9	3.2	2.1	2.2	0.3	1.8
2005	3.9	2.0	3.5	2.2	2.4	0.3	1.8
2004	4.3	2.1	3.8	2.6	2.5	0.3	2.3
Pinnacle Airlines Corp							
2008	4.1¢	1.7¢	2.4¢	3.1¢	0.9¢	0.5¢	2.2¢
2007	4.0	1.8	2.8	3.2	0.8	0.2	2.2
2006	3.3	0.8	6.2	3.0	2.5	0.1	1.5
2005	3.2	0.8	6.7	1.0	2.7	2.2	1.4
2004	3.6	0.8	7.2	1.3	2.9	2.3	1.4
Republic Airways Holdings Inc.							
2008	2.6¢	1.7¢	1.4¢	0.6¢	3.4¢	1.4¢	1.6¢
2007	2.6	1.5	1.4	0.6	3.5	1.2	1.2
2006	2.6	1.6	1.4	0.6	4.9	1.4	1.5
2005	3.2	1.7	1.7	0.7	6.2	1.4	1.7
2004	3.7	2.3	2.4	0.8	5.7	1.1	2.1
Mesa Air Group, Inc.							
2008	n.a.	4.3¢	n.a.	1.3¢	8.6¢	0.6¢	0.9¢
2007	n.a.	3.7	n.a.	1.2	6.3	0.6	2.5
2006	n.a.	3.1	n.a.	1.1	6.5	0.5	0.7
2005	n.a.	3.2	n.a.	1.1	4.9	0.7	1.2
2004	n.a.	3.2	n.a.	1.3	3.9	0.6	1.6

Costs categories are divided by passenger revenue miles reported in annual reports.

n.a. = not available. Some costs not available in annual reports or 10Ks.

Sources: Annual Reports and 10Ks for SkyWest, ExpressJet Holdings, Pinnacle Airlines Corp., Republic Airways Holdings, and Mesa Air Group, Inc. for years 2005, 2006, 2007, and 2008; all fiscal years ending on December 31 except Mesa Air Group fiscal years ending on September 30.

ExpressJet Holdings was a publicly held company with operations in the air transportation sector, including ExpressJet Airlines, Inc. (which operated under the name Continental Express), and ExpressJet Services, LLC, which provided third-party maintenance services. The company was also invested in other entities that permitted it to leverage the management experience, efficiencies, and economies of scale. ExpressJet Airlines operated as Continental Express flying 1,000 departures per day and serving 125 destinations in North America and the Caribbean. It operated hubs in New York/Newark, Cleveland, and Houston. ExpressJet Airlines employed about 8,000 people.[29]

Pinnacle Airlines Corp., headquartered in Memphis, Tennessee, was the parent holding company of Pinnacle Airlines and Colgan Air, Inc. Until 2003 it had been a wholly owned subsidiary of Northwest Airlines. Pinnacle Airlines conducted its operations under the name of Northwest Airlink, providing flights from Northwest hubs in Detroit, Memphis, Minneapolis/St. Paul, and Indianapolis and as Delta Connection. As of December 31, 2008, the airline employed 5,644 people. Pinnacle Airlines flew 142 regional jets and Colgan Air flew an all-turboprop fleet under regional connect contracts for United, Continental, and US Airways to these locations. Colgan Air was involved in one of two airline disasters in early 2009 when its Continental Connect flight 3407 crashed into a home on the ground on the way to the Buffalo, New York, airport killing all 49 people on board and one on the ground. On January 27, 2009, the company announced limited workforce reductions and other cost-cutting measures needed to address the Delta-NWA merger and the economic slowdown.[30]

SKYWEST, INC.

SkyWest, Inc., was founded as SkyWest Airlines in 1972 in St. George, Utah, to facilitate "the connections of passengers to flights of major partners" by partnering with the major airlines to service smaller airports and shorter routes. The struggling airline acquired Palm Springs–based Sun Aire in 1984, entered its first code-share contract with Western Airlines in 1985, and in 1986 went public. With its first stock offering, the company was able to pay off some of the debt on its aircraft. Western was purchased by Delta Airlines later that year, putting SkyWest in a position to compete for more code-share contracts. Since 2002, the company had been named the Regional

Airline Company of the Year by two airline magazines and its subsidiary, SkyWest Airlines, had been named the number one on-time airline by the Department of Transportation several times. In 2005 the company completed the acquisition (from Delta Airlines) of Atlantic Southeast Airlines (ASA), a regional airline based in Atlanta. In June 2007, the company celebrated its 35th anniversary.[31]

At the beginning of 2009, the company continued to operate its SkyWest and ASA operations as separate companies although it was seeking to reduce costs in some parts of its operations through combining activities in finance, treasury, IT, and administrative services to realize economies. The company explained that it maintained separate operations to identify best practices that could be applied to both airlines.

SkyWest, Inc., operated primarily through partnership contracts with United and Delta. The two legacy carriers had both been in bankruptcy protection with United emerging from the proceedings early in 2006 and Delta coming out of bankruptcy in April 2007. SkyWest, Inc., relied almost completely on these carriers for its customers and revenue. Because both United and Delta operated with very similar business models and were exposed to the same types of economic and environmental risks, SkyWest, Inc.'s revenues had become less predictable and more risky.

In an effort to diversify its risk, the company entered into an agreement with Midwest Airlines in December 2006 to fly some of its connector routes, an agreement that was expanded in January 2008 when SkyWest took over all of Midwest Airlines' regional connecting flights.[32] It was intended that these contracts expand and diversify operations and thereby reduce the dependence on United and Delta. However, the relationship was expected to end since Midwest had been acquired by Republic Airways Holdings in 2009.

SkyWest Airlines

At the beginning of January 2009, SkyWest Airlines operations served 158 cities in 42 states, five Canadian provinces, and Mexico. Its hubs were in Chicago O'Hare, Los Angeles, San Francisco, Milwaukee, Portland, Denver, San Francisco, and Salt Lake City; maintenance bases were in Atlanta, Chicago, Colorado Springs, Denver,

Fresno, Los Angeles, Milwaukee, Palm Springs, Portland, Salt Lake City, San Francisco, and Tucson. The airline employed more than 11,000 people, who were not represented by union contracts.[33]

SkyWest Airlines had a good reputation for safety, on-time arrivals, and other factors affecting customer satisfaction. In 2009, SkyWest was tied for first among regional carriers for on-time arrivals, had an average number of mishandled baggage reports, had the second fewest number of involuntary denied boardings, and was fourth among regional carriers in number of complaints per 100,000 passengers. Exhibit 9 provides comparisons among regional airlines on various customer service criteria from 2004 to 2009.

Atlantic Southeast Airlines

Atlantic Southeast Airlines was founded in 1979 in Atlanta. In 1984, ASA was selected by Delta Air Lines as one of the first partners in the Delta Connection program. After 15 years of partnership, ASA was acquired by Delta Airlines in 1999. During the next six years, the company's fleet grew by 100 aircraft. In 2005, the airline was acquired by SkyWest, Inc.

By the end of June 2009, ASA served 130 airports with 155 aircraft in 30 U.S. states, Washington, DC, Canada, Mexico, Belize, the Bahamas, Jamaica, Puerto Rico, and the Turks and Caicos Islands. The carrier had hubs in Atlanta, Salt Lake City, Los Angeles, and Cincinnati. Its maintenance stations were in Atlanta; Macon, Georgia; Salt Lake City; Baton Rouge; Shreveport, Louisiana; Columbia, South Carolina; Fort Walt Beach, Florida; and Montgomery, Alabama. The airline employed 3,700 full-time employees, who were represented by the Air Line Pilots Association, International, the Association of Flight Attendants–CNA, and the Professional Airline Flight Control Association. The airline, despite difficulties it had had with its unions, had never experienced a work stoppage due to a labor dispute and considered its relationship with its employees to be good.[34]

Prior to its being acquired by SkyWest, Inc., ASA, under its ownership by Delta Airlines, had one of the worst customer service records in the industry. In August 2005, ASA flights were on time only 59.6 percent of the time, which was the worst out of all reporting airlines. ASA also cancelled 8 percent of its flights and its rate of luggage mishandling was 19.95 reports out of 1,000. Both rates were the worst in the industry. The airline's performance on measures of customer service had improved significantly since being acquired by SkyWest, Inc., but still ranked last or near last among regional carriers in 2009 (see Exhibit 9).

Partnerships

Partnership contracts with the two airlines were fairly complex and provided for a number of fixed fees and incentives as well as provisions for early cancellation. SkyWest, Inc., operated Delta Connection contracts through both of its airline operations. The combined Delta Connection contracts represented approximately 59.9 percent of the company's capacity. Approximately 40.1 percent of capacity was dedicated to its United Express contracts.

Delta Connection As of December 31, 2008, SkyWest Airlines was operating approximately 430 Delta Connection flights per day between Salt Lake City and designated outlying destinations. Delta was entitled to all passenger, cargo, and other revenues associated with each flight. In exchange for providing the designated number of flights and performing SkyWest Airlines' other obligations under the SkyWest Airlines Delta Connection Agreement, SkyWest Airlines received from Delta on a weekly basis (1) reimbursement for 100 percent of its direct costs related to the Delta Connection flights plus (2) a fixed dollar payment per completed flight block hour, subject to annual escalation at an agreed rate. Costs directly reimbursed by Delta under the SkyWest Airlines Delta Connection Agreement included costs related to fuel, ground handling, and aircraft maintenance and ownership.[35]

Under the Atlantic Southeast Airline Delta Connection Agreement, the company operated more than 775 Delta Connection flights per day between Atlanta, Cincinnati, Salt Lake City, and designated outlying destinations. Under the Agreement, Delta was entitled to all passenger, cargo, and other revenues associated with each flight. Commencing in 2008, ASA was guaranteed to maintain its percentage of total

Exhibit 9   **On-Time Flights, Mishandled Baggage, Denied Boardings, and Passenger Complaints for Major U.S. Regional Airlines, 2004–2009**

Percentage of Scheduled Flights Arriving on Time (Previous 12 Months Ending in May of Each Year)						
Carrier	2004	2005	2006	2007	2008	2009
American Eagle	75.2%	75.3%	74.4%	70.2%	68.8%	76.3%
Atlantic Southeast	78.6	72.5	71.3	64.2	66.4	70.8
Comair	n.a.	77.3	80.9	67.6	69.5	65.7
Expressjet	79.8	76.9	74.0	72.5	73.8	81.6
Mesa	78.2	n.a.	n.a.	71.4	73.1	81.6
Pinnacle	n.a.	n.a.	n.a.	n.a.	74.9	86.8
Skywest	85.3	82.8	80.3	75.3	76.5	86.8

Mishandled Baggage Reports per 1,000 Passenger (In May of Each Year)						
Carrier	2004	2005	2006	2007	2008	2009
American Eagle	8.38	7.89	12.51	11.60	9.06	7.44
Atlantic Southeast	10.94	14.50	11.33	7.74	5.81	6.24
Comair	8.89	8.37	7.73	8.84	5.86	4.63
Expressjet	5.45	5.10	7.15	7.46	5.52	2.86
Mesa	n.a.	n.a.	7.92	9.95	7.61	4.32
Pinnacle	n.a.	n.a.	n.a.	6.30	4.87	4.53
Skywest	7.94	8.11	6.85	9.21	5.76	4.92

Involuntary Denied Boardings per 10,000 Passengers due to Oversold Flights (January Through March of Each Year)						
Carrier	2004	2005	2006	2007	2008	2009
American Eagle	0.38	0.79	2.15	1.19	2.79	3.14
Atlantic Southeast	3.20	2.68	6.89	5.43	5.22	3.94
Comair	4.58	1.08	2.97	3.32	4.48	3.17
Expressjet	n.a.	n.a.	n.a.	n.a.	n.a.	2.39
Mesa	n.a.	n.a.	1.70	1.94	1.19	1.21
Pinnacle	n.a.	n.a.	n.a.	n.a.	4.71	1.60
Skywest	0.00	0.70	1.26	2.73	2.02	1.57

Complaints per 100,000 Passengers Boarded (In May of Each Year)						
Carrier	2004	2005	2006	2007	2008	2009
American Eagle	0.48	0.32	0.88	1.26	0.39	0.71
Atlantic Southeast	0.23	0.28	0.95	0.57	0.27	0.52
Comair	0.36	0.26	0.00	1.22	0.56	0.96
Expressjet	0.00	0.30	0.31	0.35	0.40	0.36
Mesa	n.a.	n.a.	0.69	0.58	0.60	0.63
Pinnacle	n.a.	n.a.	n.a.	0.91	0.97	0.33
Skywest	0.39	0.36	0.36	0.63	0.28	0.57

Note: Atlantic Southeast Airlines and SkyWest Airlines are operating companies of SkyWest, Inc., but are reported separately in this report.
n.a. = not available
Source: Office of Aviation Enforcement and Proceedings, Air Travel Consumer Report, 2004–2009.

Delta Connection flights that it had in 2007, so long as ASA's bid for additional regional flying was competitive with other regional carriers. In exchange for providing the designated number of flights and performing ASA's other obligations under the ASA Delta Connection Agreement, ASA received from Delta on a weekly basis (1) reimbursement for 100 percent of its direct costs related to Delta Connection flights plus (2) if ASA completed a certain minimum percentage of its Delta Connection flights, an amount equal to a certain percentage of the direct costs related to the Delta Connection flights (not including fuel costs). Costs directly reimbursed by Delta under the ASA Delta Connection Agreement included costs related to fuel, ground handling, and aircraft maintenance and ownership.[36] The ASA Delta Connection Agreement was scheduled to terminate on September 8, 2020, unless Delta elected to exercise its option to extend.[37]

United Express   At the end of December 2008, SkyWest Airlines offered approximately 900 scheduled departures for United Airlines under its United Express Agreement. Under the Agreement, SkyWest Airlines received, from United, compensation (subject to an annual adjustment) of a fixed fee per completed block hour, a fixed fee per completed departure, a fixed fee per passenger, a fixed fee for overhead and aircraft costs, and one-time start-up costs for each aircraft delivered. The United Express Agreement provided for incentives based upon SkyWest Airlines' performance, including on-time arrival performance and completion percentage rates. Additionally, certain of SkyWest Airline's operating costs were reimbursed by United, including costs related to fuel and aircraft ownership and maintenance. Expiration of these contracts, unless options for renewals were exercised, was expected to occur incrementally in 2011, 2013, and 2015.[38]

Midwest Connect   Under the terms of its December 21, 2006, agreement, SkyWest Airlines' operations extended to serving markets from Midwest Airlines' hubs in Milwaukee and Kansas City. The agreement provided for an initial term of five years with automatic two-year extensions thereafter. Commenting on the new agreement, Bradford R. Rich, executive vice president, CFO, and treasurer for SkyWest, Inc., said, "SkyWest

and Midwest have similar corporate cultures and great reputations for quality customer service and we believe that our partnership will be beneficial for customers, employees, and shareholders. . . . This transaction also furthers certain of our strategic diversification objectives."[39] In January 2008, SkyWest took over all of Midwest's regional connecting flights.[40] However, with the financial troubles of the airline and takeover by Republic Airways, the contracts were expected to end in the very near term.

Safety and Maintenance

SkyWest, Inc.'s safety department voluntarily participated in the Aviation Safety Action Program, which was a reporting program for pilots designed to determine potential safety hazards. Additionally, the department served as a compliance liaison between SkyWest and the Department of Transportation and the Federal Aviation Administration. SkyWest, Inc., had also implemented Stetson Quality Suite, which was mobile data collection and reporting software used to ensure its companies were meeting or exceeding its safety and quality standards.

The company performed all routine airframe and engine maintenance and periodic inspection of equipment at their respective maintenance facilities. Nonroutine maintenance was handled through contracts with third parties.[41] The company scheduled two hours of maintenance for every one hour in flight. Mechanics conducted line service inspection of each aircraft every fifth day. In addition, the company's proactive safety and maintenance policies required that when a manufacturer of an airplane issued a service bulletin on any component of a plane that impacted safety, the company immediately carried it out ahead of a mandatory directive from the FAA. The airlines also provided the vast majority of training to both company pilots and maintenance personnel at their training facilities. The company's six-week maintenance training program was so comprehensive and respected that it attracted tuition-paying FAA personnel.[42]

Human Resource Policies

Prior to the acquisition of Atlantic Southeast Airlines, the company's workforce was nonunion and its competitive salaries and bonuses, rapid promotion of pilots, retirement plan, and employee stock purchase plan created a level of employee satisfaction that discouraged the unionization of its workforce. The nonunion workforce gave Sky-West Airlines more flexibility in making decisions when compared to its competitors. For example, SkyWest's pilots agreed to operate 70- and 90-seat aircraft at the same rate as 50-seat aircraft. The 2005 acquisition of Atlantic Southeast Airlines changed SkyWest, Inc.'s relationship with its workforce as ASA's employees were represented by the Air Line Pilots Association, International, the Association of Flight Attendants–CNA, and the Professional Airline Flight Control Association. The airline acknowledged that there existed significant risk to the company should the labor unions associated with their ASA operations seek a "single carrier determination" from the National Mediation Board and attempt to unionize Sky-West Airlines' employees. Despite several attempts by the ALPA to unionize SkyWest Airlines, the sister company had remained union free.

Employees of both SkyWest Airlines and Atlantic Southeast Airlines were eligible to participate in company retirement plans where the company matched, up to a certain point, participant contributions. Employees who completed 90 days or more of service were also eligible to participate in the company stock purchase plan.[43] In addition to these programs, the company offered a full array of generous benefits including a credit union; a wellness program; medical, dental, and vision benefits; income protection; travel discounts; an educational savings plan; and a complete package of life and disability insurance programs.[44]

SkyWest, Inc.'s Fleet

At the beginning of January 2009, the airline fielded a fleet of 442 aircraft—a mix of 56 Embraer EMB 120 twin-turboprop aircraft, 374 Bombardier Regional Jets (with 10 more to be acquired in 2009), and 12 ATR 72 twin-turboprop aircraft. To facilitate the company's expansion plans and improve efficiencies, SkyWest Airlines and Atlantic Southeast Airlines had combined firm orders to acquire additional aircraft. The new regional aircraft were expected to be more cost-efficient to operate than older models, which was important given the increasing costs of operating aircraft.[45]

Bombardier Regional Jets   The Bombardier Regional Jets were among the quietest commercial jets available and offered many of the amenities of larger commercial jet aircraft, including flight attendant service, as well as a stand-up cabin, overhead and under-seat storage, lavatories, and in-flight snack and beverage service. The speed of Bombardier Regional Jets was comparable to larger aircraft operated by the major airlines, and they had a range of approximately 1,600 miles. However, because of their smaller size and efficient design, the per-flight cost of operating a Bombardier Regional Jet was generally less than that of a 120-seat or larger jet aircraft. The majority of the company's aircraft were these small jets.

Embraer and ATR Turboprops   The 30-seat Embraer EMB 120 turboprops and 74-seat ATR 72 turboprops were able to operate more economically over short-haul routes than larger jet aircraft. These factors made it economically feasible to provide high frequency service in markets with relatively low volumes of passenger traffic. Passenger comfort features of the Embraer and ATR turboprops included stand-up headroom, a lavatory, overhead baggage compartments, and flight attendant service. The company expected that Delta and United would want them to continue to operate turboprops in markets where passenger load and other factors made the operation of a Bombardier Regional Jet impractical.

The Future

During the five years ending December 31, 2008, SkyWest, Inc., had grown at a compounded annual growth rate of 29.6 percent and the number of flights had increased from about 1,500 to 2,300. The company's growth had primarily come about through the addition of new partnerships and expansion of current ones to include new routes and additional departures. The acquisition of Atlantic Southeast Airlines in 2005 allowed SkyWest to expand geographically. Previously, the company had been mostly based in the western United States and had had little presence on the east coast. The acquisition of ASA gave SkyWest access to the East Coast markets and comprehensive national coverage and greatly expanded the scope of operations by adding regional jets to their fleet and an anticipated $1 billion to operations.

The Chapter 11 filings of United and Delta created growth opportunities for SkyWest, Inc., as the majors began to outsource more of their routes during the restructuring of their operations. However, the bankruptcies also highlighted the risk inherent in contracts with major air carriers.[46] The company had attempted to expand its contractual relationships and had operated a few routes for Continental in the past and had made some overtures into establishing partnerships with low-cost carriers such as US Airways, Southwest, and Jet Blue. As of 2009, SkyWest had yet to attract permanent business from these carriers. Also, SkyWest had attempted an unsuccessful acquisition of ExpressJet in 2008. ExpressJet would have brought a large number of departures for Continental with it.

Considering the company's limited domestic opportunities, SkyWest had been undertaking efforts to expand its operations outside the United States. Internationally, SkyWest, Inc., was working with regional carriers in Europe, Latin America, and China. According to CEO Atkins, "Putting Europe aside since it is a mature market and we have a unique situation with which we are dealing, China, Brazil and Mexico are all high growth, emerging regional aviation markets. We questioned whether we should put in our portfolio some non-U.S. business. We've had people approach us for help in building their airline in Brazil or China. We'd help to train people, and, with our purchasing power, we can help to buy things at a lower rate. We would help organize them from a 10- to 20-aircraft operation to a major regional carrier in countries that really need a major regional carrier.[47] The opportunities afforded by international joint ventures are limited, however, by the 49 percent ownership limits that many foreign governments place on U.S. carriers."[48]

A consideration in further expansion for SkyWest was the "scope" clauses in major airline labor contracts with their pilots, as discussed earlier. Scope contracts placed limitations on the number and size of aircraft or flight activity that could be operated by a major airline's regional airline partners such as SkyWest Airlines or ASA. Since 2001, a number of major airlines (US Airways, Northwest Airlines, Delta, American Airlines, and United Airlines) had sought some removal of restrictions. Approval of scope clause liberalization could create opportunities for regional airlines to increase the numbers of routes flown in contract with major airline partners.[49]

Despite challenges and reduced revenues in the first five months of 2009, management expected that the company's (and the industry's) future was promising. SkyWest's combined revenue passenger miles had increased by 4.9 percent in June 2009, and its load factor had improved from 80.0 percent in June 2008 to 82.3 percent in June 2009.[50] Improved revenues for the second quarter had resulted in profits for JetBlue, US Airways, and Alaska Air Group, an indication that conditions in the industry might be poised to turn around. According to Dave Barger, CEO at JetBlue, June bookings had "started to pick back up."[51] Other observers did not expect a quick turnaround since business travel was still far below historical averages. Some analysts expected further consolidations and bankruptcies if the U.S. economy did not improve by year-end 2009. Such skeptical analysts believed continued bankruptcies would bring more chaos to an already chaotic industry environment.[52]

ENDNOTES

[1] SkyWest, Inc., press release, July 13, 2009.
[2] James Ott, "Humble Mission," *Aviation Week and Space Technology,* March 24, 2008.
[3] Midwest Airlines, press release, June 23, 2009.
[4] SkyWest, Inc., press release, February 11, 2009; 2008, 2007, 2006, and 2005 annual reports.

[5] IBIS World Report on Industry Risk for "Scheduled Domestic Air Transportation in the U.S.," December 30, 2006.
[6] Delta Airlines, http://news.delta.com/article_display.cfm?article_id = 11176, accessed February 9, 2009.
[7] United Airlines website, press releases dated February 1, 2006, and July 31, 2006.

[8] Delta Airlines website, press release April 15, 2008.
[9] Interview with Brian Nelson, airline industry analyst from Morningstar, in James Bernstein, "Industry Analyst Sees More Airline Consolidations on the Radar as Carriers Try to Stay Competitive; Flight Pattern Is Merger," *Newsday,* December 14, 2006.

[10] Susan Carey, "Earnings Digest—Airlines: Return to Profit Has Wings after Massive Losses; Spoilers Could Emerge amid Fragile Recovery; The Merger 'Wild Card,'" *Wall Street Journal,* January 2, 2007, p. C5.

[11] IATA FACT SHEET: Industry Statistics, www.iata.org/ps/publications/9265.htm, accessed February 9, 2009.

[12] Investopedia.com, "The Industry Handbook—The Airline Industry," www.investopedia.com/features/industryhandbook/airline.asp, accessed January 5, 2007; and SkyWest, Inc., 2005 Annual Report.

[13] SkyWest, Inc., news releases dated January 15, 2007, and February 7, 2007.

[14] "Airlines Troubled by DOT's Proposed Oxygen Rules," *Regional Aviation News,* September 25, 2005, p. 1.

[15] Investopedia.com, "The Industry Handbook—The Airline Industry."

[16] Emily Feliz, "Airline Uncertainty," *Avionic Magazine,* January 1, 2009, www.aviationto-day.com/av/categories/commercial/28584.html, accessed February 16, 2009.

[17] Energy Intelligence Group, Inc., "Market Forces: Airlines' Fortunes Look Up," December 1, 2006.

[18] Investopedia.com, "The Industry Handbook—The Airline Industry."

[19] NPR Radio, Morning Edition, "Airline Outlook Improves, While Uncertainties Remain," November 16, 2006.

[20] Roger Cohen, president, Regional Airline Association, letter to the editor of *Wall Street Journal,* January 2, 2007, posted on the RAA website, accessed January 3, 2007.

[21] Wikipedia.com, "Regional Airline," http://en.wikipedia.org/wiki/Regional_airline, accessed January 3, 2007.

[22] *Regional Aviation News,* April 14, 2008.

[23] Scott McCarthy, "The Middle Seat: Flying Gets Rough on Regional Airlines," *Wall Street Journal,* January 2, 2007, p. D1; and Cohen, letter.

[24] Mesaba Airlines' Web pages, accessed January 2, 2007.

[25] Stan Choe, "Regional Airlines May Suffer in Mergers," Forbes.com, December 15, 2006, www.forbes.com/feeds/ap/2006/12/15/ap3259544.html, accessed January 5, 2007.

[26] SkyWest, Inc., 2005 annual report, p. 6.

[27] Mesa Air Group Inc. Web pages, accessed January 1, 2007.

[28] Republic Airlines' website, accessed February 17, 2009.

[29] ExpressJet Holdings' website, accessed February 17, 2009.

[30] Pinnacle Airlines Corp. Web pages, press release, January 27, 2009, accessed February 16, 2009.

[31] Yahoo! Finance, "Airline Continues Coast to Coast Expansion," December 27, 2006, http://biz.yahoo.com/prnews/061227/law038.html?.v = 88, accessed January 5, 2007.

[32] *Regional Aviation News,* January 21, 2008.

[33] SkyWest Airlines' website, accessed February 18, 2009.

[34] SkyWest, Inc., 2008 annual report.

[35] SkyWest, Inc., 2005 annual report.

[36] Ibid.

[37] Ibid.

[38] Ibid.

[39] Sky West, Inc., website, news release, December 21, 2006, accessed January 3, 2007.

[40] *Regional Aviation News,* January 21, 2008.

[41] SkyWest, Inc., 2005 annual report.

[42] Ott, "Humble Mission."

[43] SkyWest, Inc., 2005 annual report.

[44] SkyWest, Inc., website, "Benefits," accessed February 18, 2009.

[45] SkyWest, Inc., press release February 11, 2009.

[46] SkyWest, Inc., 2005 annual report.

[47] *Regional Aviation News,* May 19, 2008.

[48] *Regional Aviation News,* March 10, 2008.

[49] SkyWest, Inc., 2008 annual report.

[50] SkyWest, Inc., press release, July 13, 2009.

[51] Susan Carey, "Airlines Report Some Signs of Stabilizing," *Wall Street Journal,* July 24, 2009, p. 3.

[52] Linda Lloyd, "Airlines Facing Big Economic Trouble in Winter Ahead," *McClatchy-Tribune Business News,* July 23, 2009.

Silver Ships' Strategy in the Military and Workboat Industry

David L. Turnipseed

University of South Alabama

As Mike McCarty walked through the Silver Ships shipyard monitoring the production of several aluminum hull boats in various stages of production, he began to think "What now?" He had seen his shipyard grow from a boatbuilding operation in the garage of his home in 1985 to a large, state-of-the-art company manufacturing 26- to 60-foot aluminum-hull boats in 2010. During its 25 years in business, McCarty's company had sold more than 1,500 boats to the U.S. military, various federal agencies, law enforcement agencies, shipping companies, and others needing custom-designed small to medium-size vessels. Exhibit 1 presents a sample of typical military and workboats produced by Silver Ships.

McCarty built his business by focusing on the highest possible quality and performance and taking care of his employees. His commitment to quality had allowed the company to increase revenues from $5.7 million in 2006 to nearly $11 million in 2009. In addition, the company had a strong balance sheet and had never been forced to lay off a single employee in its 25-year history. An income statement for 2006 through 2009 is presented in Exhibit 2. The company's balance sheets for 2006 through 2009 are presented in Exhibit 3.

As 2011 approached, McCarty was at an age where he could consider retirement and begin shopping the business to potential buyers or continue to drive Silver Ships' growth through various expansion opportunities. The company's most immediate opportunities for growth involved bidding on contracts to produce vessels needed by the U.S. Navy and U.S. Coast Guard that could be used to thwart terrorist activities near shore and in ports and the opportunity to work with General Dynamics–European Land Systems to pursue a contract with the U.S. Army to build a new fleet of bridge erection boats. However, the poor state of the U.S. economy had created a difficult environment for many of Silver Ships' private-sector workboat customers, and the threat of a double-dip recession and a looming tax increase on small businesses had frozen many shipping firms' plans for expansion and further investment. Mike McCarty also understood that economic uncertainty amplified the risk associated with any expansion plans he might have and required that he avoid any miscalculations in forecasting additional demand resulting from new business opportunities he might choose to pursue.

COMPANY BACKGROUND

A bad day fishing is better than a great day at the office. Mike McCarty believed this old adage and transitioned his love of fishing into a career as a commercial fisherman. McCarty began fishing commercially after graduating from high school in Knoxville, Tennessee. Fishing the rivers and lakes around Knoxville provided a good living, and eventually McCarty began buying other fishermen's catch and became "the market." He expanded from wholesale to retail and began buying and reselling ocean fish from the Atlantic and Gulf of Mexico.

Exhibit 1   Typical Military and Workboats Produced by Silver Ships

In 1971, McCarty got out of the wholesale and retail seafood business and moved to coastal Mobile, Alabama, to start up a commercial salt-water fishing enterprise. Always looking for a way to improve his catch, he designed a boat to allow fishing by purse seining, in which a net with a weighted bottom and a buoyant top is run around a school of fish. However, shortly after McCarty completed of his new fishing boat, states along the Gulf of Mexico banned purse seining. McCarty's career seemed over.

However, the end of his fishing career led to the development of his third career. Other fishermen who had seen McCarty's purse seining boat and had been impressed with its fine construction approached him to build strong, high-performance vessels to fit their unique needs. The demand for his boats continued to increase and, in 1985, McCarty founded Silver Ships, named after the color of the aluminum used in the boats' construction. The company progressively outgrew three different rental locations and, in 1996, moved to its present Theodore, Alabama, location. McCarty renamed his obsolete purse seining

boat *Run Aground* and used it for the sign for his new facility. A summary of company milestones is presented in Exhibit 4.

SILVER SHIPS ACQUIRES AMBAR MARINE

Ambar Marine Inc., a New Orleans–based ship-builder producing aluminum boats, began searching in the late 1980s for a subcontractor to build its "survival of life at sea" (SOLAS) boat, a rescue boat for ships and oil platforms. Ambar approached McCarty at a New Orleans workboat show and proposed that Silver Ships build boats for it. After a visit from the Ambar executives to Silver Ships' original, humble facility, Ambar decided that McCarty's facility was not what they wanted to show their customers.

Several years later, after building his new facility in Theodore, Alabama, McCarty again met Ambar executives at a boat show. Ambar was dissatisfied with the subcontract builders for their SOLAS boats, and discussions eventually led to

Exhibit 2 Silver Ships' Statements of Income, 2006–2009

	2009	2008	2007	2006
Net sales	$10,974,028	$10,808,531	$5,869,027	$5,705,890
Cost of goods sold				
Direct labor	2,088,548	2,088,119	1,110,476	948,472
Direct materials	5,229,520	5,453,081	2,822,216	2,297,718
Other direct costs	483,725	545,559	273,840	236,470
Total cost of goods sold	7,801,793	8,086,759	4,206,532	3,482,660
Gross profit	3,172,235	2,721,772	1,662,495	2,223,230
Operating expenses				
Salaries and wages	626,871	486,581	411,356	481,221
Payroll taxes	190,997	206,019	132,655	109,785
Employee benefits	257,908	237,610	132,655	109,785
Amortization and depreciation expense	242,261	133,496	109,572	80,712
Insurance	219,201	308,445	189,849	157,295
Rents	63,042	41,040	41,688	41,040
Repairs and maintenance	39,518	51,107	21,235	51,828
Other operating expenses	493,048	611,627	369,218	336,988
Total operating expenses	2,132,846	2,075,925	1,408,228	1,368,654
Income from operations	1,039,389	645,847	254,267	854,576
Other income (expense)	982	27,448	39,392	21,845
Income before income taxes	1,040,371	673,295	293,659	876,421
Provision for income taxes	365,109	210,026	29,943	325,460
Net income	$ 675,262	$ 463,269	$ 263,716	$ 550,961

Source: Silver Ships Incorporated.

Silver Ships building boats for Ambar. Ambar Marine encountered a period of financial difficulties in the late 1990s and, in 2000, was acquired by Silver Ships.

Silver Ships kept the Ambar Marine name because of its name recognition and reputation for producing high-quality rigid-hull inflatable boats (RHIBs). RHIBs were also known as "collar boats" because of the inflatable collar that surrounded the perimeter of the boat. The collar system used on Ambar's RHIBs, among the best on the market, used a small air bladder between the hull and the foam of the collar that provided extra tension to keep the collar tight when the boat was under way. If the air bladder was punctured, the foam collar remained intact and would not hinder performance of the vessel. Silver Ships retained the Ambar name on its AM series RHIBs. Silver Ships' boats not equipped with a collar system were branded as the Silver Ships SS series. Exhibit 5 presents a cross-sectional

drawing of the collar system used by Silver Ships on its Ambar RHIBs.

Silver Ships' Ambar collar design was totally modular: if a piece needed replacing, the customer purchased only the needed section, which reduced repair and shipping costs.

Silver Ships' Ambar RHIBs were easily adaptable to various applications and were routinely customized to customer specifications. Standard Ambar RHIB options offered by Silver Ships included:

• Diesel or gas propulsion engines.
• Outboard, waterjet, or surface-piercing propulsors.
• Climate control systems.
• Complete navigational electronics.
• Thermal imaging cameras.
• Integrated communication systems.
• Ballistic protection.

Exhibit 3   Silver Ships' Balance Sheets, 2006–2009

	2009	2008	2007	2006
Assets				
Current assets				
Cash	$3,449,334	$1,535,138	$265,973	$1,518,518
Accounts receivable	2,435,277	2,167,502	2,096,447	1,311,266
Notes receivable—current	0	0	0	11,503
Inventory	501,722	890,707	1,378,626	383,406
Prepaid expenses	0	13,980	40,475	31,955
Prepaid corporate income tax	0	103,965	0	3,327
Other current assets	125,693	120,586	113,105	107,864
Total current assets	6,512,026	4,831,878	3,894,626	3,367,839
Property and Equipment				
Leasehold improvements	2,334,934	1,726,178	1,344,717	1,344,717
Shop machinery and equipment	1,019,823	639,448	541,719	479,759
Furniture and fixtures	76,966	126,605	101,696	94,558
Vehicles	105,852	126,097	124,598	124,595
Total	3,537,575	2,618,328	2,112,730	2,043,629
Less accumulated depreciation	(747,921)	(723,528)	(611,522)	(504,989)
Construction in progress	0	480,872	450,329	8,208
Net property and equipment	2,789,654	2,375,672	1,951,537	1,546,848
Other assets	0	0	23,560	26,601
Total	2,789,654	2,375,672	1,975,097	1,573,449
Total assets	$9,301,680	$7,207,550	$5,869,723	$4,941,288
Liabilities and Shareholder Equity				
Current liabilities				
Trade accounts payable	$567,409	$313,794	$335,559	$151,716
Accrued expenses	123,122	107,004	66,106	74,100
Payroll taxes payable	59,722	15,906	6,894	4,387
Deferred revenue	2,095,556	1,350,987	618,208	40,195
Accrued income tax	132,010	0	20,714	0
Total current assets	2,977,819	1,787,691	1,047,481	270,398
Long-term liabilities				
Deferred income tax	470,182	241,436	80,700	158,601
Total liabilities	3,448,001	2,029,127	1,128,181	428,999
Shareholder equity				
Common stock	22,800	22,800	22,800	22,800
Retained earnings	5,830,879	5,155,623	4,718,742	4,489,489
Total shareholder equity	5,853,679	5,178,423	4,741,542	4,512,289
Total liabilities and shareholder equity	$9,301,680	$7,207,550	$5,869,723	$4,941,288

Source: Silver Ships Incorporated.

Since the company's founding in 1985, more than 1,500 AM series and SS series aluminum boats had been produced and shipped to customers throughout the world. Exhibit 6 presents a partial list of customers that had purchased aluminum-hull military and workboats from Silver Ships.

Exhibit 4   Chronology of Important Dates in the History of Silver Ships

1985	Formed to build custom aluminum boats
1990	Built its first aluminum rigid-hull inflatable boat (RHIB)
1996	Moved to a 19,600-square-foot facility on 32 acres in Theodore, Alabama
1997	Began work as a subcontractor to Ambar Marine of New Orleans, Louisiana
2000	Purchased Ambar Marine
2002	Added 8,000 square feet of additional production space
2006	Added 20,000-square-foot building as a "rigging" shop for post-structural assembly (e.g., install electronics, mount motors, radars, lights, collars, seats, steering systems, etc.); also added two 20-ton bridge cranes
2008	Completed 8,500-square-foot paint building with self-contained environment for greater control of the finished product
2009	Added 15,000-square-foot building to house CNC router with 40-foot cutting table and additional 20,000-square-foot final assembly space

Exhibit 5   Cross-Sectional Diagram of Silver Ships' Ambar RHIB Collar System

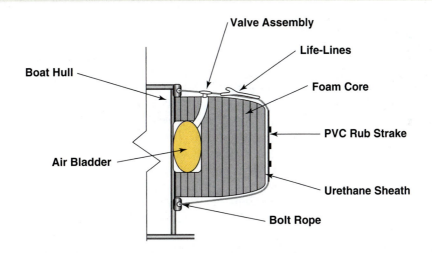

Exhibit 6   List of Silver Ships' Customers for Its Military and Workboats

U.S. Army	City of Jacksonville, FL
U.S. Air Force	City of Orange Beach, Alabama
U.S. Navy	Jamaica Coast Guard
U.S. Coast Guard	Panama Canal
U.S. Border Patrol	Costa Rica
U.S. State Department	National Oceanic and Atmospheric Administration (NOAA)
U.S. Army Corps of Engineers	Mobil Oil
U.S. Environmental Protection Agency	Shell Oil
U.S. Fish and Wildlife Service	Chevron Oil
U.S. National Park Service	Exxon Oil
City and state police, fire and rescue departments	Amoco Oil

(Continued)

Exhibit 6   *(Concluded)*

State fisheries/wildlife protection departments	British Petroleum
State parks and recreation departments	Tidewater Marine
Mississippi Department of Marine Resources	Seacor Marine
New Hampshire Department of Safety	Trico Marine
Alabama Highway Department	Hornbeck
Alabama Power Company	Quality Shipyards
Alabama State Docks	Bollinger Shipbuilding
Alabama Department of Marine Resources	Halter Marine
Contract Drilling and Blasting	Bender Shipbuilding
Ciba Geigy	Levac Shipyards
Oceaneering International	Houma Fabricators
Diamond Offshore Drilling	

McCARTY'S VISION AND APPROACH TO DOING BUSINESS

Mike McCarty's interest in boatbuilding began as a teenager when he built his own wooden fishing boat. He explained, "I wanted to build my own boat. I just didn't feel that other boats were up to my standards. I feel the same way today—I can build a better boat than our competitors." The company's vision statement—"Silver Ships/Ambar Marine exists to design and manufacture the most advanced, life-sustaining, and mission-capable 20- to 65-foot aluminum boats in the world"—reflected McCarty's personal commitment to quality and was prominently displayed in the foyer of the company's office. As Silver Ships grew, McCarty continued to personally oversee the daily operations. He seldom sat in his office, preferring to walk around the various buildings and constantly watch as the boats moved toward completion. Exhibit 7 shows McCarty inspecting an AM series RHIB nearing completion.

McCarty summarized the importance of his attention to details by stating, "If you never let a little problem go, you won't have to deal with a big problem later." He had an open-door policy and ate lunch with employees in the design and engineering department to hear firsthand about possible emerging operating problems. McCarty developed the following seven principles to guide Silver Ships employees:

1. *Uncompromising excellence* in each boat and all processes involved in their design and manufacture.
2. *Mission-driven design* for each vessel that provides the user with a boat customized for his or her specific use.
3. *Exceed customer expectations* in convenience, safety, comfort, reliability, and functionality in each boat we build.
4. *Passion for service and respect for each customer* as his or her job is treated as our most important.
5. *Focus on innovation down to the minute detail,* providing the customer with the most advanced, integrated technology available.
6. *Making each boat better than the last* as we learn from our manufacturing experience and the constant development of our employees.
7. *Vision-directed operations* in which each employee is a valued part of the processes, treated with respect and dignity, and encouraged to advance as far as his or her abilities and desires allow.

PRODUCING THE SILVER SHIPS

Silver Ships' location on 32 acres in Theodore, Alabama, provided adequate land for future growth. Theodore was very close to Mobile, Alabama, which had a large deepwater port and Pascagoula,

Mississippi, which was home to a large navy warship production facility. The maritime industry around Silver Ships provided all the needed raw materials, parts, assemblies, and services. Also, due to the large maritime industry nearby, there was a good supply of well-trained and experienced labor with all types of surface boatbuilding backgrounds; however, the wages were very competitive. Several U.S. Navy, Air Force, and Coast Guard facilities were located in the area, which put Silver Ships close to some of its largest customers.

Silver Ships' location at 45 feet above mean tide level protected the boatbuilding operation from flooding even in the worst hurricanes. The company had never lost a day's work due to flooding, which was a significant threat along the Gulf Coast. Although Mobile Bay, which adjoins the Gulf of Mexico, was only about three miles away, Silver Ships' inland location avoided the corrosion and storm damage of a seaside facility. Being away from the salt water and salt air lengthened the machinery, equipment, and facilities' life span. However, in about 10 minutes, boats could be transported and launched in nearby Fowl River, which provided quick access to Mobile Bay and the Gulf of Mexico for sea trials.

McCarty's focus on excellence extended to his production facility, which was a group of fully enclosed, insulated metal buildings. All work and all storage were done indoors. Although Silver Ships' boats were used primarily in the world's oceans, which were the most corrosive environments on earth, McCarty's attention to quality required that even incoming aluminum shipments be stored inside.

Silver Ships produced two series of boats, ranging from 20 to 65 feet in length. The Ambar AM series was a fast, oceangoing aluminum-hull RHIB with a hybrid air/foam collar. The AM series boats ranged from 20 to 36 feet and were typically employed as fire, rescue, patrol, or research vessels. The collar increased stability and made the boats virtually unsinkable. The second series was the Silver Ships SS series, which ranged from 25 to 60 feet. SS Series boats were custom-built, mission-specific aluminum work boats, such as pilot, patrol, survey, crew, or fire boats. The SS series boats did not have RHIB collars.

Target boats for the U.S. Navy were one of Silver Ships' mainstay products. These were high-speed, 26-foot AM series boats used for marine

Exhibit 7   **Silver Ships Owner Mike McCarty Aboard an AM Series RHIB**

surface targets. In addition to being used as targets, these boats were used for ship perimeter protection and ship support. Exhibit 8 shows a Silver Ships target boat immediately after a near miss by a SeaSparrow missile fired from a U.S. Navy ship.

Silver Ships' boat manufacturing process, from aluminum plate to the finished boat, required an average of seven weeks. Aluminum plate and extrusions were cut and formed both by hand operations and with jigs, then cleaned and welded to fabricate the hull. The company used primarily 1/8-inch to 1/2-inch marine-grade plate aluminum and extrusions to produce their boats.

Over 90 percent of the welds were metal inert gas (MIG). In traditional stick welding, the flux on the welding electrode melted and formed a gas that shielded the electrode puddle from the

Exhibit 8   **Silver Ships Target Boat Being Fired On by a U.S. Navy Ship**

atmosphere. The hydrogen, nitrogen, oxygen, and other gases naturally in the atmosphere could cause weld defects if they got into the weld pool. In MIG welding, an inert gas streamed from the gun and protected the weld puddle from the atmosphere, thus producing better welds.

After all welding was completed, the boats were sandblasted, then acid-washed to remove contaminants and residues. Finally, the boats that were to be painted were coated with the appropriate marine coating in the paint facility. (Aluminum does not need to be painted because it is corrosion-resistant; however, most boats were painted at least on the bottom.) In 2008, the company built an 8,400-square-foot covered paint building, which included a 2,800-square-foot paint booth. The filtering system in the paint booth was capable of moving 250,000 cubic feet of air per minute. All paint residues and toxins were removed by a state-of-the-art filtering system, making Silver Ships' facility environmentally friendly.

Rigging—which included electronics, motors, windshields, handrails, gun mounts, lights, wenches, cranes, and other accessories—was installed in the final assembly building. Although quality assurance was integrated throughout the manufacturing process, the finished products received an in-depth inspection in the rigging shop prior to going to the water for sea trials. Each boat was subjected to rigorous sea trials to ensure its seaworthiness and performance capabilities before delivery to the customer. McCarty stressed, "I build every boat like I'm building it for my own use—that is how exacting we are on getting it right."

MAJOR COST DRIVERS IN THE MILITARY AND WORKBOAT INDUSTRY

Nearly all manufacturers of military and workboats paid about the same prices for engines, lights, seats, deck cleats, radios, and other fittings. Three expense categories accounted for most of the variance in production costs: aluminum, labor, and logistics.

Aluminum

Aluminum had many characteristics that made it ideal for shipbuilding. It was nonmagnetic, lightweight (about one-third as much as steel), did not spark, and had excellent corrosion-resisting properties. Although aluminum was the second-most-abundant metal in the Earth's crust, it had been produced in commercial quantities for just over 100 years.

Silver Ships' boats were made totally of aluminum, and consequently the metal component of the company's cost structure was significant. Aluminum prices varied greatly: in 2003, for example, the price per pound dropped below $0.65; in 2005, it traded in the mid-$0.80 range; and in the three-year period between 2006 and 2008, prices rose above $1.40 per pound. In mid-2010, the price per pound had again dropped to the mid-$0.80 range. The effect of price fluctuations could be managed to varying degrees by hedging, inventory management, and waste control. Silver Ships kept close watch on aluminum prices, and McCarty personally controlled all purchases of aluminum.

Much of the aluminum used in production arrived in large sheets and was cut into smaller pieces used to fabricate the boats and parts used in construction. Although computers were used to plan the most efficient cutting patterns, some scrap was inevitable. There was also scrap from extruded aluminum raw material and reworked parts. However, Silver Ships had recently begun ordering extruded materials in the exact length needed. Silver Ships captured the scrap aluminum and sold it to recyclers to minimize the scrap cost. The scrap price averaged 25 to 30 percent of the price of finished aluminum.

Labor

There was a very large pool of experienced boat-builders, aluminum welders, and other marine construction laborers along the Gulf Coast. Prior to the recession that began in late 2007, the Gulf Coast economy was booming and experienced welders and marine construction workers demanded high salaries. The recession did not hurt shipbuilding along the Gulf Coast as much as it hurt the general manufacturing sector. The largest shipbuilders primarily produced military ships that required several years to complete and continued to work on the ships under construction despite bad economic conditions. Two global companies specializing in defense contracting, Austal USA (an Australian shipbuilding company) and Northrop Grumman Shipbuilding, set the pay scale for maritime construction workers.

Austal USA Located in Mobile, Austal was the builder of the USS *Independence,* a new-generation 418-foot aluminum trimaran littoral combat ship (LCS). The LCS was designed to engage in battle within the littoral zone, which was from the shoreline to 600 feet of water. The keel was laid in 2003, and the ship was commissioned in 2010. Upon the commissioning of the USS *Independence,* Austal began production on a second such ship—the USS *Coronado* (LCS-4). Austal opened a new module manufacturing facility (MMF) in early 2010, and shortly thereafter the company began the *Spearhead,* built on the U.S. Department of Defense's next-generation multiuse platform, the joint high-speed vessel (JHSV), a 10-ship program potentially worth more than $1.6 billion.

The *Spearhead* was a 103-meter aluminum catamaran capable of reaching speeds in excess of 35 knots and was the first of a class of 10 vessels to be operated by both the U.S. Army and the U.S. Navy. These large warships required hundreds of workers, including aluminum welders. Austal regularly advertised for welders and, in 2010, at the depth of the recession and during the BP/Deepwater Horizon oil spill, offered a starting wage of $16.00 per hour for untrained apprentice welders.

Northrop Grumman Ship Building (NGSB)

Located in Pascagoula, Mississippi, Northrop Grumman Shipbuilding (NGSB) built more ships, of more ship classes, than any other U.S. naval shipbuilder. NGSB's Gulf Coast facilities employed more than 18,000 employees, making the company the largest manufacturing employer in Mississippi and Louisiana, and a major contributor to the economic growth of coastal Alabama. The 800-acre Pascagoula, Mississippi, location, which was about 30 miles from Silver Ships' Theodore, Alabama, location, built surface combat ships, amphibious assault and transport vessels, Coast Guard cutters, and fleet support vessels. Like Austal, NGSB offered apprentice welders a starting hourly pay rate of $16.00 per hour.

In 2010, NGSB was building the U.S. Navy's newest class of large-deck amphibious assault ships, with the first in the line, the *USS America* (LHA-6), about 25 percent complete. In June 2010, the Navy awarded a $175 million contract to Northrop Grumman Corporation for advance procurement of long-lead materials and performance of engineering/planning efforts for LHA-7, the second assault ship to be produced by NGSB. Although the national economy had yet to recover from the long-term slump, the continuing military ship construction at Austal USA and NGSB kept shipbuilding wages high on the Alabama and Mississippi Gulf Coast.

Logistics

Silver Ships was located not only near several U.S. Navy, Air Force, and Coast Guard facilities but also near many Gulf Coast municipalities and states that had a need for seagoing boats. Boats were also purchased by inland municipalities and law enforcement agencies for operations on lakes and rivers. Because the majority of Silver Ships' business was secured through bids, cost was a major concern. Boatbuilders were a competitive disadvantage when bidding on boats going to distant locations (versus boats going to nearby locations) not only because of transportation costs but also because of limitations related to road-lane width and bridge and overpass height.

Standardizing the Custom Building Process

The majority of boats that Silver Ships produced were built to unique customer and mission requirements. There were occasional orders for multiple boats with the same specifications (usually military orders), but customization was the norm. Silver Ships standardized the custom boatbuilding process by using specialized production teams that built components such as hulls, decks, wheelhouses, and fuel tanks. These components would later be integrated by highly skilled master boatbuilders. Master boatbuilders were also inserted into the production process at any point the boat under construction required custom parts or features.

Silver Ships' Use of Technology in the Design and Production Process

Silver Ships also relied on computer-aided drafting (CAD) and three-dimensional modeling to improve boat quality, design, and performance, and increase productivity. The program allowed the design to be rotated on three axes, and the operation of any movable part could be simulated, including opening and closing doors and access panels. The three-dimensional modeling program allowed potential customers to see how custom features would look and work on the boat. Having the ability to move an idea to a workable design, inspect the boat in three dimensions, view the simulated operation of movable components, and make immediate design changes or corrections gave Silver Ships an advantage over competitors that did not have such a capability. This three-dimensional modeling also allowed production workers to understand exactly how the boat and its parts should look after assembly and helped reduce manufacturing errors.

In 2009, the company also purchased a computer numerically controlled (CNC) router with a 40-foot cutting table. The router was controlled by Mastercam software, which increased the speed and accuracy of aluminum plate cutting. The software determined the optimal number of cuts to get the maximum number of aluminum pieces with the least amount of scrap. The Mastercam program also determined the fastest tool path through the sheet of aluminum to minimize machine time. The CNC router also cut hull planks and deck plates to higher tolerances than required by standard bid requirements, but exceeding customer bid specifications was consistent with McCarty's business philosophy.

Marketing

Silver Ships' approach to marketing relied on word-of-mouth advertising, bidding on requests for proposals (RFPs) issued by the military and government agencies, and promoting the company at boat shows. Boats shows were a very important tool in selling boats. The boating industry held more than 200 boat shows annually in the United States and many more around the world. Although most boat shows featured a wide range of buyers and boats (ski boats, fishing boats, cruisers, work boats, and commercial boats), others focused more on a specific market niche. Two of the most important boat shows in the military and workboat niches were the International Workboat Show and the Multi-Agency Craft Conference.

The International Workboat Show, held annually in New Orleans, Louisiana, allowed marine manufacturers to promote their products to thousands of targeted customers. Buyers at the 2009 show represented $2.3 billion in purchasing power. Each year the list of exhibitors included about 20 to 30 boat manufacturers and dozens of marine-related manufacturers. Surveys had shown that about 65 percent of attendees in prior years had purchased a workboat within 12 months of attending the show.

The Multi-Agency Craft Conference (MACC) held at the Little Creek Naval Amphibious Base in Norfolk, Virginia, also allowed vendors to promote their boats, meet with government officials, and share new technology. In 2009, the MACC was attended by 179 vendors and more than 1,700 prospective buyers.

SILVER SHIPS' PRIMARY RIVALS IN THE MILITARY AND WORKBOAT INDUSTRY

Competition in the military and workboat industry was based on price, the ability to meet bid specifications, performance and reliability, and the ability to make timely delivery. The industry included several rivals capable of producing high-quality workboats and small military vessels, including SAFE Boats International (www.safeboats.com), based near Seattle, Washington; Aluminum Chambered Boats (www.acbboats.com), located on Puget Sound near Bellingham, Washington; Willard Marine(www.willardmarine.com)of Anaheim, California; SeaArk Marine (www.seaark.com) of Monticello, Arkansas; and Metal Shark Boats (www.metalsharkboats.com) of Jeanerette, Louisiana.

SAFE Boats

SAFE Boats focused on boats similar in size and purpose to those produced by Silver Ships and competed with Silver Ships on a large number of bids. SAFE Boats boasted that its RIB collar system was superior to that used by other manufacturers since its construction could stop small-arms fire from penetrating the boat's hull. SAFE Boats advertised that its RIB collar could withstand rounds as large as 7.62 millimeters if ballistic material was added to the collar.

Aluminum Chambered Boats

Even though the Coast Guard did not require flotation specifications for vessels 20 feet or longer, Aluminum Chambered Boats (ACB) differentiated itself by its chambered hull design that prevented its boats from sinking even if the hull and a chamber were punctured. The company built the only vessel that passed the U.S. Coast Guard upright and level flotation test for boats less than 20 feet without the use of foam. No ACB boat had ever capsized or sunk during hours of testing or during customer opera-

tions. ACB produced a large variety of military boats, including boats for special operations and homeland security.

Willard Marine

Willard Marine was a leading manufacturer of aluminum and fiberglass boats for the U.S. government, the U.S. Coast Guard, and nonmilitary customers. Willard specialized in a versatile class of commercial and military 16- to 54-foot RHIBs, 26- to 40-foot personnel boats, high-speed patrol boats, fire boats, and SOLAS boats. In addition to its operations in Anaheim, California, Willard had recently opened a second manufacturing and reconditioning facility in Virginia Beach, Virginia, to serve East Coast customers. The Virginia Beach facility manufactured 16- to 43-foot aluminum and fiberglass composite boats for the U.S. Coast Guard, U.S. Navy, Department of Homeland Security, and domestic and international law enforcement agencies. The new facility would also serve as the eastern home for the company's Technical Operation Programs, which trained, diagnosed, and assessed problems with Willard's boats all over the world.

SeaArk Marine

SeaArk was founded as MonArk Boat Company in 1959 and began building riveted aluminum flat-bottom Jon boats. The company added to its product line and later began selling riveted and all-welded boats to law enforcement departments, fish and wildlife departments, and governmental agencies. The company operated two divisions—recreational and workboat (commercial). The recreational boat division produced both fiberglass and aluminum-hull boats, and the workboat division focused on all-welded, heavy-duty aluminum boats. The workboat division—which had been renamed SeaArk Marine Inc.—continued to manufacture all-welded patrol boats, fire boats, and workboats up to 65 feet. SeaArk Marine's primary customers included the U.S. military (including the U.S. Army Corps of Engineers), law enforcement agencies, other domestic and international governmental agencies, oil companies, and survey companies.

Metal Shark Boats

Metal Shark Boats was established in 2005 as a producer of aluminum commercial, military, and government boats. In 2009, Metal Shark began a joint venture with Rescue One Connector Boats, a highly respected manufacturer of fire and rescue boats. The joint venture concentrated on 21- to 52-foot boats for firefighting, rescue, dive operations, response, and recovery. Metal Shark designed, engineered, and manufactured the boats, while Rescue One marketed and distributed the vessels. Metal Shark's purpose for the collaborative venture was to take advantage of both companies' core competencies in creating high-quality, technologically advanced boats manufactured specifically to the customer's needs.

Metal Shark was fast to market with its products. In mid-July 2010, during the BP/Deepwater Horizon oil spill in the Gulf of Mexico, the company delivered the 3rd of 20 boats specially designed for oil-spill cleanup in near-shore applications. The 30-foot barge-style oil response boats were in use off the Louisiana coast by late July, and the company planned to build and deliver two boats per week throughout the duration of the oil-spill disaster. Metal Shark's design had a large, flat deck and a low freeboard, which placed workers close to the surface of the water and allowed the boats to operate in water as shallow as eight inches, making it ideal for the cleanup operations in the shallow water along the Louisiana coast.

THE UNCERTAINTIES AHEAD

Mike McCarty tried to balance his desire for growth at Silver Ships with an understanding that growth would bring about increases in fixed costs and that less-than-hoped-for additional demand could jeopardize the company's future profitability. McCarty had identified growth opportunities and external threats to the company's well-being that would require a strategic decision from him. The changing nature of naval warfare, the opportunity to pursue a U.S. Army bridge erection boat contract, the state of the U.S. economy, and the

likelihood of new taxes on small businesses were all strategic issues facing the company.

The U.S. Navy was the strongest navy in the world and was able to gain and maintain sea control anywhere in the oceans of the world. However, the Navy had traditionally been a deepwater force, and its tactics and warships were designed for operations on the high seas. The threat of large-scale conventional warfare was thought to be declining, while small-scale terrorist operations such as the bombing of the USS *Cole* were becoming a larger national security concern. Because of the increasing likelihood of such skirmishes with terrorist organizations, the littoral zone appeared to be the most significant new area in naval warfare. Also, continuing problems related to drug smuggling and illegal immigration had caused the U.S. Navy, Coast Guard, Border Patrol, and other law enforcement agencies to place a greater emphasis on littoral patrol. The small, fast, shallow draft boats manufactured by Silver Ships and its competitors were well suited for operations in littoral and inland waterways. McCarty would have to determine to what extent Silver Ships would engage in the development of armed patrol boats and other combat-capable military vessels.

Another opportunity for Silver Ships involved the planned replacement of the U.S. Army's 20-year-old bridge erection boats. The bridge erection boats used by the Army in 2010 were manufactured by Babcock Marine in the 1980s and had many limitations. The Babcock-built boats would not run on the military's new JP-8 fuel, which was intended to replace diesel; had difficulty operating in shallow water; and had limited maneuverability. The U.S. Army had issued a request for proposals (RFP) to replace the Babcock boats and was considering bids from various vendors in 2010. General Dynamics European Land Systems (GDELS) had submitted a proposal to the Army based on its bridge erection boats used by the German Army and had selected Silver Ships as its U.S. partner to produce the boats, since the RFP required the boats to be built in the United States. Silver Ships and GDELS–Germany had built three prototypes that would be submitted to the Army in February 2011 for evaluation and testing. It was expected that the U.S. Army would evaluate prototypes from several shipbuilders over a 12-month period and select a contractor to produce the new fleet of bridge erection boats in early 2012.

The enduring stagnant economy was a threat to Silver Ships' revenue growth since the company's commercial customers tended to expand only during stable economic times and since government agencies were experiencing severe budget crises. Even though states and municipalities were struggling as tax revenues declined with reduced consumer spending and growing business failures, Silver Ships' military and governmental contracts had remained fairly steady. The economic downturn had also allowed Silver Ships to buy aluminum and other materials and components at decreased prices. However, McCarty realized that if the recovery from the recession continued

at its slow pace, governmental contracts would likely not hold up. In addition, the threat of a dramatic tax increase on small businesses set to take place in January 2011 would damage Silver Ships' ability to expand and maintain employment. Mike McCarty, like many other entrepreneurs and small-business owners, was hesitant to make major financial commitments and hire new employees with the expectation of higher taxes and no sign of a sustained recovery. McCarty was proud that there had never been a layoff at Silver Ships and wanted that record to continue. His company could use additional capacity and could pursue a number of new growth possibilities, but any misstep could produce devastating results for his employees and his family.

Skype versus AT&T and the Future of Telecommunications

A. J. Strickland
The University of Alabama

Matt Zarzour
The University of Alabama
MBA Candidate

Josh Silverman, president of Skype, walked into the boardroom to greet the rest of his executive team. He could not help but smile as he grabbed a seat at the head of the long rectangular conference table. His secretary had just handed him a copy of an e-mail that James Cicconi, AT&T's senior executive vice president of legislative affairs, had sent out to all 300,000+ AT&T employees. The e-mail was asking all employees at AT&T to express their "deep concern" about network (net) neutrality on the website of the Federal Communications Commission (FCC) in hopes of persuading the FCC to vote against the proposed net neutrality law decreasing the power of big telecommunications companies like AT&T. This meant that AT&T was showing signs of fear over Internet telephone. Silverman knew that Skype was finally a big enough player in the telecommunications industry to make a global impact.

However, Silverman's smile quickly dissipated as he remembered why his executive team was meeting. Skype's revenue growth was taking hits. Revenue growth had shrunk from 685 percent in 2006, to 95 percent in 2007, to 37 percent in 2008. Skype needed to better understand the reason for this shrinkage. Moreover, Silverman realized that Skype needed to place more focus on attacking AT&T and other big phone companies. Two big questions for Skype needed to be answered as quickly as possible. Competition in the industry was increasing rapidly, and Skype had to make a move to remain an industry leader.

VoIP

Skype was a little different from AT&T. Skype offered its customers Voice-over Internet Protocol (VoIP), which, defined simply, was the transmission of voice traffic over IP-based networks. In other words, it was telephone via an Internet connection. Exhibit 1 shows a standard VoIP connection. Traditional telephone, which AT&T used, was run through a public switched telephone network (PSTN) and was much more expensive. Whereas telephone calls were billed according to time connected through the PSTN (i.e., by the second or minute), VoIP calls were billed per amount of information (data) sent over the Internet. The reason VoIP had become so popular was that it offered cost advantages compared with traditional telephone networks. Most telephone users paid a flat monthly fee for local telephone calls and a per-minute charge for long-distance calls. In contrast, Skype users could communicate for free with other Skype users and paid only a small fee for long-distance calls to landlines. The following were three methods of connecting to a VoIP network:

- Using a VoIP telephone.
- Using a "normal" telephone with a VoIP adapter (PSTN VoIP providers).
- Using a computer with speakers and a microphone.

Unlike telecommunications carriers such as AT&T, VoIP providers were not required to invest

Exhibit 1 VoIP Connection Diagram

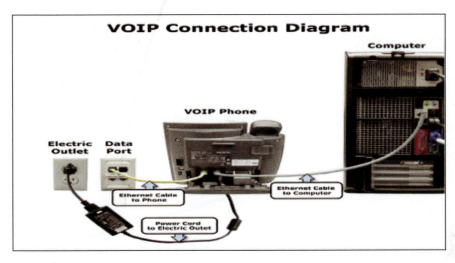

Source: Google, www.google.com.

substantial sums of capital in equipment and infrastructure, given that they utilized what was already in place. VoIP providers were classified as information service providers and therefore fell outside the Telecommunications Act of 1996, which heavily regulated telecommunications carriers. The lack of regulation made it easier for companies to enter the VoIP market than to enter the telecommunications market.

VoIP was expected to show constantly increasing growth rates in the near future. According to a report by Infonetics Research, the global VoIP services market had reached $15.8 billion in 2006, an increase of 66 percent over 2005, and was on track to triple to $48.9 billion by the end of 2010. Projected growth for the decade was in the area of 145–150 percent. However, VoIP's market share in the overall global telecommunications market was still minimal. Led by a few major companies—Comcast, Vonage, Time Warner, and Cox Communications—the telecom industry was worth more than $1 trillion in 2010. With a roughly 5 percent market share by the end of 2010, VoIP was still a small competitor in the industry.

A major opportunity for VoIP providers was to capitalize on the cellular market. Experts predicted that, by 2019, half of all mobile calls would be over IP networks. The IP connections would be available through VoIP applications

that ran through a cellular device. Mobile VoIP applications were expected to reach 278 million users, generating a $32.2 billion profit.

For Andy Abramson, CEO of the marketing firm Communicano Inc., a big part of the attraction of such offerings on a mobile device would be in customers' ability to design services for themselves rather than buy prepackaged sets of features. Eventually phone providers would be forced to allow customers to pick and choose their own services, and many of the current paid services would be offered free of charge in the carrier's VoIP offerings. Abramson said:

> You're talking about eliminating the horror story of dealing with the carriers. . . . I expect that there will be a war among AT&T, AOL (Time Warner), and all the major cable companies to win VoIP users over the next several years, and the extent to which people are given the chance to service themselves will be a differentiator.

Along with the notion that consumers would increasingly look at expanded VoIP services as a motivator for adoption, many experts hinted at the idea that the growth of Internet telephony technologies would signal the demise of the PSTN. Exhibits 2 and 3 show the growth of VoIP and attendant decline of landline use. While most technology providers acknowledged the concept that consumers and businesses would indeed drive continued growth of VoIP systems,

Exhibit 2   Growth of VoIP Subscribers and Decline of Landline Subscribers, 2005–2008*

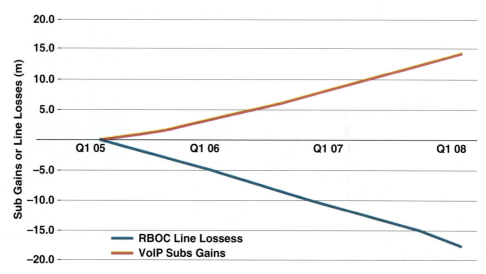

While VoIP services were growing fast, incumbent phone companies, particularly the three Regional Bell Operating Companies (RBOCs)—AT&T, Verizon, and Qwest—were hemorrhaging traditional fixed-line subscribers. Since the start of 2005, the RBOCs had lost 17.3 million residential telephone lines, while VoIP service providers had gained 14.4 million new customers.

Source: TeleGeography, www.telegeography.com.

Exhibit 3   U.S. Local Service Revenues, 2003–2010

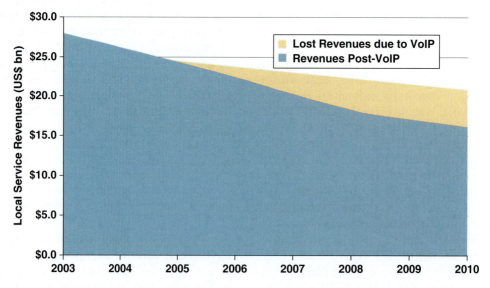

Source: TeleGeography Research, *US VoIP Research Service.*

many agreed that there would always be a mix of traditional and Internet phone services widely used.

There was a clear advantage for VoIP, and the future of VoIP was making big telephone companies like AT&T cringe. They would lose their stranglehold on the industry. That's where the debate over net neutrality came into play.

NET NEUTRALITY

The Internet was a complicated infrastructure with numerous components that together made the cyberspace that users had come to know. It was a massive collection of internetworked computer systems that spanned the entire globe. Communication across those systems depended on sets of rules called protocols. The Internet also relied heavily on a huge infrastructure of routers, servers, and network access points (NAPs). Also, there were satellites, miles of cable, and thousands of wireless devices that transmitted signals between computers and networks. Cables crisscrossed oceans and continents to link some of the most remote places on earth. As far as ownership went, the Internet was technically not owned by anyone. No government or company could claim ownership of the Internet. However, thousands of people and organizations owned the physical aspects of the Internet. Some of those owners could control the quality and level of access an individual had to the Internet. The physical Internet that carried information and data was called the Internet backbone. Several large companies provided the routers and cables that made up that backbone. These companies, called upstream Internet service providers (ISPs), included AT&T, Global Crossing, Level 3 Communications, Qwest, Sprint, and Verizon Business's UUNET. Anyone who wanted to access the Internet ultimately had to work with these companies.

Many individual consumers and businesses subscribed to ISPs that were not part of the Internet backbone. These ISPs negotiated with the upstream ISPs for Internet access. Cable and digital subscriber line (DSL) companies were examples of smaller ISPs.

If the FCC were to pass a net neutrality bill, upstream ISPs and smaller ISPs would not be allowed to restrict what their customers did on the Internet. If the law was not passed and the upstream ISPs and smaller ISPs were allowed to make their own decisions, then they could charge extra for access to certain websites, much like cable television or satellite television packages. Net neutrality was thus a hot topic. Tumblr.com

defined net neutrality as "a principle proposed for user access networks participating in the Internet that advocates no restrictions on content, sites, or platforms, on the kinds of equipment that may be attached, and on the modes of communication allowed, as well as communication that is not unreasonably degraded by other traffic."

THE TELEPHONE

If one were to ask an average person who invented the telephone, the answer would probably be "Alexander Graham Bell." That was what people had been taught to believe. However, the history of the invention of the telephone was a confusing collection of claims and counterclaims, made no less confusing by the numerous lawsuits and disputed patent claims brought by countless individuals.

In 1871, an Italian-born inventor named Antonio Meucci filed a patent caveat with the U.S. Patent Office titled "sound telegraph," describing communication of voice between two people by wire. This patent caveat was basically just an idea and sketches. The idea of a caveat was to reserve something while the inventor was working on it so that no one could beat him or her to the punch. However, a caveat had to be renewed every two years. Unfortunately for Meucci, he ran out of money and was unable to renew his patent, so it expired. The concept of Meucci's sound telegraph had become known among a select group of tinkerers. The most notable were Elisha Gray and Alexander Graham Bell. After a back-and-forth of patent applications, and due to sheer timing and proper networking with the right people, Bell was officially credited with the invention of the telephone on March 10, 1876. The concept was a collection of many different mechanisms created by several people, but Bell got the fame and credit. The telephone was born in controversy and remained hand in hand with it into the present.

SKYPE

Founded by Niklas Zennström and Janus Friis in 2003, Skype was based in Luxembourg and had offices throughout Europe, the United States, and Asia. The company was purchased by eBay in 2005, and a majority share was later sold to an investor group led by Silver Lake, which included individuals like Zennström, Friis, and Andreessen Horowitz, along with eBay, Joltid Limited, and the Canada Pension Plan Investment Board.

Skype offered voice and video calling, as well as instant messaging (IM) and short messaging services (SMS), on a wide range of operating systems and mobile devices. Skype was available 24 hours a day, 7 days a week, worldwide. The company's original mission was "to enable the world's conversations." That mission was tweaked occasionally to focus strategically on a certain goal. CEO Josh Silverman stated, "Skype is a real-time communication platform for the Internet that is leading the communication transition from hardware to software."

In the third quarter of 2009, Skype users made 27.7 billion minutes of Skype-to-Skype calls (more than a third of which were video calls) and 3.1 billion minutes of calls to landlines and mobile phones. During that time, Skype accounted for 8 percent of the world's calling minutes.

For Skype, the main issue internally was mismatch in the relationship between revenue growth rate and company growth rate. Exhibit 4 shows an increasing company growth rate from 2007 to 2008, Exhibit 5 shows that in 2009 Skype traffic grew by more than 60 percent, and Exhibit 6 shows a steady increase in the number of Skype users who were logged in to their accounts in a given day from 2003 to 2009 (with further projected increases for 2010). However, increases in the company's revenue rates had begun to flatten; Exhibits 7, 8, and 9 show recent statistics. Skype executives realized that the main reason for the flattening in revenue rates was the company's

cheap international calling rates and the free user-to-user calls and videos. Exhibit 10 shows Skype's calling plans and prices. A major question for Skype was whether or not rates should be applied to services that currently were free.

Skype was still in the early growth stages of its existence, especially in the United States, where in 2010 the company held a market share in the VoIP industry of around 1 percent. Skype had a major opportunity for growth in the United States, but the question was to how to penetrate the market more substantially.

One of Skype's main success factors had been the buzz created by users. Skype did minimal advertising and relied heavily on word of mouth to market its product. This was highly beneficial for Skype in that it held down operating costs. Ease of use had also been critical for Skype. The company created a website with convenience and functionality in mind. Skype's biggest factor, however, was its low cost for users. This was something that competitors were expected to match soon, so the company knew that a quick strategic move was imperative.

Skype had an accelerated growth plan that laid out the company's strategy for the short term. The plan had three phases, one of which had already been completed:

• Phase 1 (completed): Become operational on at least one platform (PCs), at least one revenue stream (SkypeOut), focus on one market segment (long-distance calling), with one primary service (voice), one primary market (mature Internet markets in Europe and Asia) and one target user (consumers).

Exhibit 4   **Skype Growth Numbers (Global), Third Quarter 2007–Fourth Quarter 2008**

	Q3 07	Q4 07	Q1 08	Q2 08	Q3 08	Q4 08
Registered Users (in millions)	246	276	309	338	370	405
Y/Y Growth	*81%*	*61%*	*58%*	*54%*	*51%*	*47%*
Skype to Skype Minutes (in billions)	9.8	11.9	14.2	14.8	16.0	20.5
Y/Y Growth	*31%*	*26%*	*30%*	*38%*	*63%*	*72%*
Skype Out Minutes (in billions)	1.4	1.6	1.7	1.9	2.2	2.6
Y/Y Growth	*25%*	*7%*	*33%*	*42%*	*54%*	*61%*

Source: www.skypeworld.com.

Exhibit 5   **Skype Growth in Number of Users , 2005–2011 (projected)**

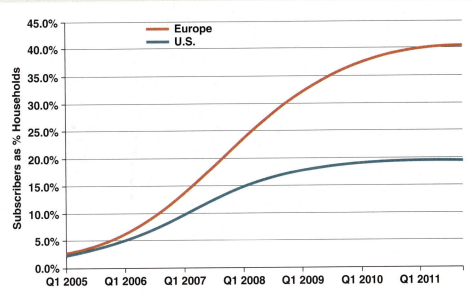

Source: www.share.skype.com.

Exhibit 6   **Skype Dialtone: Peak Number of Accounts Logged in During One Day, 2003–2010**

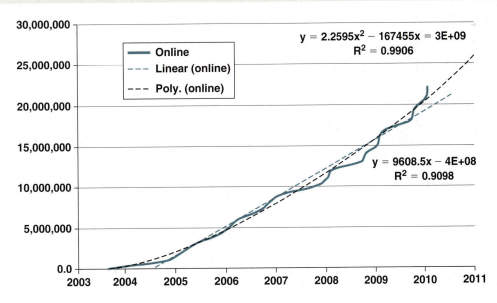

$$y = 2.2595x^2 - 167455x = 3E+09$$
$$R^2 = 0.9906$$

$$y = 9608.5x - 4E+08$$
$$R^2 = 0.9098$$

Source: www.skypejournal.com.

- Phase 2 (2010 to 2011): The key word is *many*. Develop many platforms (PC, mobile, TV, Web); diversified revenue streams (subscriptions, licensing, advertising), including business subscriptions; many conversation modes (voice, video, chat, collaboration tools); and many regions and many target markets.

Exhibit 7   **Skype Revenue, Second Quarter 2008–Third Quarter 2009**

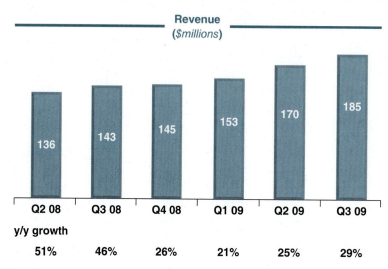

Revenue
($millions)

Q2 08	Q3 08	Q4 08	Q1 09	Q2 09	Q3 09
136	143	145	153	170	185

y/y growth

| 51% | 46% | 26% | 21% | 25% | 29% |

Source: www.skype.world.com.

Exhibit 8   **Net Increase in International Phone and Skype Traffic, 2005–2009**

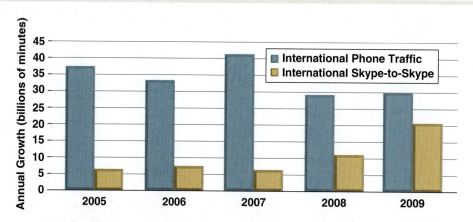

Notes: International phone traffic reflects carrier TDM and VoIP. Skype traffic growth reflects
Skype-to-Skype traffic only. Data for 2009 are projections.

Source: TeleGeography, www.telegeography.com.

• Phase 3 (2012 and beyond): The key word is *any.* Use any mode, any platform, anywhere. Develop multiple market segments, established products, regional ubiquity, and mature target markets.

With regard to "any platform," Skype's strategy for the future could also include a partnership with a major U.S. cellular company to boost usage of its product. This concept had already been initiated somewhat between Skype and AT&T, but the agreement was under dispute due to questionable third-generation (3G) service coverage from AT&T. Phones needed 3G or better coverage in order for Skype to be accessible.

Upon closer examination, Skype's revenue data portrayed phenomenal growth in all sectors. For four years there was little reason to doubt the future of the company due to the steady double-digit growth. Exhibits 11–14 present Skype's

Exhibit 9   **U.S. and International Revenue for Skype, Third Quarter 2006–Second Quarter 2009 ($ millions)**

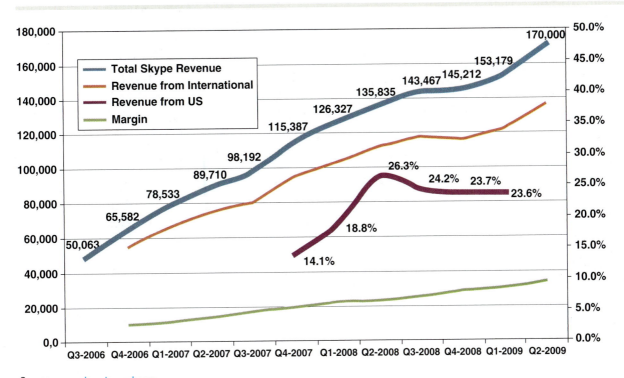

Source: www.skypejournal.com.

operations data, cash flows, balance sheet data, and net revenues for 2005–2009. Skype presented its executive outlook as follows:

> We believe the scale, global distribution and growth of our user base provide us with powerful network effects, whereby Skype becomes more valuable as more people use it, thereby creating an incentive for existing users to encourage new users to join. We believe that these network effects help us to attract new users and provide significant competitive advantages, such as strengthening our brand and enabling us to benefit from "viral" marketing, which provides us with a cost advantage by keeping our user acquisition costs low. In addition, our scale and network effects encourage other companies to form strategic relationships with Skype, creating more value for our users and increasing user engagement. For example, we have recently announced strategic relationships with leading mobile operators such as Verizon Wireless in the United States and with television manufacturers (LG, Panasonic and Samsung) that embed Skype software in their applications and devices.

Strategic relationships like these help us make Skype present in more communications devices, which increases the accessibility and usage of Skype by our large and growing user base.

MAJOR COMPETITORS IN THE VoIP MARKET

Major players in the U.S. VoIP market included Comcast Corporation, Time Warner Cable, Cox Enterprises, and Vonage Holdings. There were also a number of smaller players in the market, including Skype. Exhibit 15 shows the market shares for the major competitors in the VoIP market in the United States in 2009.

Comcast Corporation

In 1963, Comcast was founded solely as a single-system cable operation. By 2009, Comcast was by far the largest cable provider in the United States,

Exhibit 10   Skype Calling Plans and Prices

Free	**Pay As You Go**	**Pay Monthly**
Skype-to-Skype video and voice calls are always free. As are group IMs and conference calls on Skype.	Make calls and send text messages anywhere in the world direct from Skype with pay as you go Skype Credit.	Subscriptions include unlimited calls to landlines¹ and additional benefits. Call any time of the day, any day of the week.
View free features	Buy now	Learn more

🔲 Download Skype

Find out at a glance what's free, what costs a little and what you can save if you get a subscription.

There are many ways in which you can purchase credit and products – check out the ways to pay section for more information.

What do calls cost ❓
See all of our calling rates.

Related
○ Call phones
○ Online number
○ Send SMS
○ Skype Credit

📞 Skype-to-Skype calls	**Free**
📞 Transfer calls to people on Skype	**Free**
📹 Video calls	**Free**
💬 Instant messaging and group IMs	**Free**
📞 Conference calls	**Free**
📞 Forward calls to people on Skype	**Free**
📞 Call phones and mobiles	From $ 0.021 per minute² – See rates Buy Skype Credit · **Save with a subscription**
📞 Receive calls from phones and mobiles with an online number	$ 18 or $ 60 (3 or 12 months) Buy a number · **Save with a subscription**
📞 Send and receive voicemails	$ 6 or $ 20 (3 or 12 months) Get voicemail · **Save with a subscription**
📞 Skype To Go number	Available with any purchase of Skype Credit or a subscription.
📞 Forward calls to phones	From $ 0.021 per minute² – See rates Buy Skype Credit · **Save with a subscription**
📞 Send SMS messages	From $ 0.047 See rates **Buy Skype Credit**
📞 Transfer calls to phones and mobiles	From $ 0.021 per minute² Available with a subscription at no extra cost.

Check out the latest accessories for Skype
Headsets, webcams and phones.
See offers

No emergency calls with Skype. Skype is not a replacement for your ordinary telephone and can't be used for emergency calling.

🌐 Internet   100%

Source: www.skype.com.

Exhibit 11   Summary Statement of Skype's Operations Data, 2005–2009
($ thousands, except per share data)

	Pre-eBay Predecessor			Predecessor			Successor
	January 1 to October 13, 2005	October 14 to December 31, 2005	Year ended December 31, 2006	Year ended December 31, 2007	Year ended December 31, 2008	January 1 to November 18, 2009	November 19 to December 31, 2009
Net revenues	$ 47,076	$ 24,809	$ 193,696	$ 381,551	$ 551,364	$ 626,458	$ 92,445
Cost of net revenues	33,729	17,842	140,107	228,638	290,053	293,533	44,836
Gross profit	13,347	6,967	53,589	152,913	261,311	332,925	47,609
Operating expenses:							
Sales and marketing	14,200	13,097	59,787	67,195	85,630	111,029	17,267
Product development	5,027	6,536	38,900	22,078	31,124	34,993	5,809
General and administrative	11,588	5,787	37,865	41,169	51,863	50,208	113,284
Amortization of acquired intangible assets	—	13,694	60,156	65,514	69,832	55,453	13,284
Litigation settlement	—	—	—	1,390,938	—	343,826	—
Impairment of goodwill	—	—	—	—	—	—	—
Total operating expenses	30,815	39,114	196,708	1,586,894	238,449	595,509	149,644
(Loss)/income from operations	(17,468)	(32,147)	(143,119)	(1,433,981)	22,862	(262,584)	(102,035)
Interest income and other (expense), net	272	493	2,029	5,303	10,297	(2,549)	5,492
Interest expense	—	—	—	—	—	—	(10,387)
(Loss)/income before income taxes	(17,196)	(31,654)	(141,090)	(1,428,678)	33,159	(265,133)	(106,930)
Income tax (benefit)/expense	1,141	(2,380)	(22,044)	(23,342)	(8,447)	3,950	(7,209)
Net income (loss)	$(18,337)	$ (29,274)	$(119,046)	$(1,405,336)	$ 41,606	$(269,083)	$ (99,721)
Basic and diluted net loss per share (Class A through J)							$ (10.59)
Weighted number of shares, basic and diluted (Class A through J)							9,414,600

Source: eBay records.

Exhibit 12   **Summary Cash Flow Data for Skype, 2007–2009 ($ thousands)**

	Predecessor			Successor	Predecessor
	Year ended December 31, 2007	Year ended December 31, 2008	January 1 to November 18, 2009	November 19 to December 31, 2009	Six months ended June 30, 2009
Net cash provided by (used in) operating activities	$ 80,220	$148,801	$ 128,049	$ (150,913)[2]	$93,976
Net cash provided by (used in) investing activities	(536,020)[1]	(4,964)	(11,733)	(1,958,981)[3]	(5,264)
Net cash provided by (used in) financing activities	468,354[5]	13,305	(263,302)	2,082,013[4]	—

[1]This amount primarily reflected a $530.3 million cash payment by eBay pursuant to an earn-out settlement agreement with certain former shareholders of the Pre-eBay Predecessor and the earn-out representative. Financing activities to finance this payment resulted in a corresponding increase in net cash provided by financing activities.

[2]This amount was impacted by outgoing cash payments of $94.4 million in connection with the Joltid litigation settlement as part of the Joltid Transaction. For more information see "Certain Relationships and Related Party Transactions—Acquisition-Related Matters—The Joltid Transaction" and Note 13 to our audited consolidated financial statements included elsewhere in this prospectus. In addition, net cash of $98.7 million was also paid as fees and expenses in connection with the Skype Acquisition.

[3]This amount includes $1.9 billion in cash paid to eBay as a portion of the consideration in the Skype Acquisition. In addition, $34.6 million was paid to acquire intangible assets as part of the Joltid Transaction that was entered into prior to the Skype Acquisition.

[4]This amount includes $681.7 million net proceeds from indebtedness incurred in connection with the Skype Acquisition and $1.4 billion in net cash proceeds from the issuance of common stock in the Skype Acquisition.

[5]This amount primarily reflects the refinancing of the company's Amended Five Year Credit Agreement and the contemporaneous repayment of the entire $125.0 million outstanding payment-in-kind loan agreement with eBay.

Source: eBay records.

Exhibit 13   **Selected Balance Sheet Data for Skype, 2005–2009 ($ thousands)**

	Predecessor				
	As of December 31				As of December 31, 2009
	2005	2006	2007	2008	
Cash and cash equivalents	$ 88,156	$ 92,837	$ 115,884	$ 260,187	$ 114,077
Total current assets	107,352	121,953	154,234	319,804	202,445
Property and equipment, net	1,023	7,123	9,075	6,040	13,238
Goodwill	2,312,359	2,575,931	1,919,341	1,836,562	2,372,779
Intangible assets, net	263,406	235,711	188,204	112,934	788,118
Total assets	2,684,286	2,944,758	2,275,410	2,282,535	3,409,704
Accrued expenses and other current liabilities	20,187	39,658	46,359	65,159	90,852
Deferred revenue and user advances	22,429	56,219	89,419	108,012	142,600
Total current liabilities	52,684	111,740	170,463	219,893	302,246
Long term debt	—	—	—	—	772,220
Total liabilities	115,694	150,730	186,007	222,493	1,172,131
Total invested / shareholders' equity	2,568,592	2,794,028	2,089,403	2,060,042	2,237,573
Total liabilities and invested/ shareholders' equity	$2,684,286	$2,944,758	$2,275,410	$2,282,535	$3,409,704

Source: eBay records.

Exhibit 14   Net Revenues for Skype, 2007–2009 ($ thousands)

	Year ended December 31,					
	Predecessor 2007	Predecessor 2008	Pro Forma 2009	Predecessor Jan. 1– Nov. 18, 2009	Successor Nov. 19–Dec. 31, 2009	Predecessor 2009
Net Revenues by Type						
Communications services	$365,533	$526,341	$665,457	$575,939	$89,517	$299,528
Marketing and other services	16,018	25,023	53,446	50,519	2,928	25,310
Total net revenues	$381,551	$551,364	$718,903	$626,458	$92,445	$324,838
Net Revenues by Geography						
U.S.	$ 55,016	$ 89,395	$116,872	$101,850	$15,022	$ 53,728
Non-U.S.	326,535	461,969	602,031	524,608	77,423	271,110
Total net revenues	$381,551	$551,364	$718,903	$626,548	$92,445	$324,838

Source: eBay records.

Exhibit 15   VoIP Market Share (U.S.), 2009

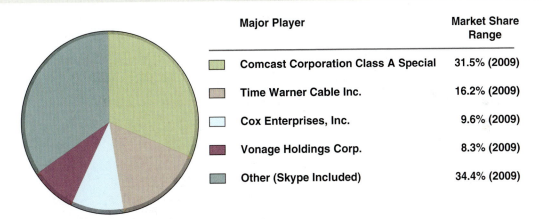

	Major Player	Market Share Range
	Comcast Corporation Class A Special	31.5% (2009)
	Time Warner Cable Inc.	16.2% (2009)
	Cox Enterprises, Inc.	9.6% (2009)
	Vonage Holdings Corp.	8.3% (2009)
	Other (Skype Included)	34.4% (2009)

with roughly 46.5 million subscribers across its different products. Comcast's cable systems simultaneously conveyed high-speed Internet, digital phone, and video services to subscribers. As of September 2009, Comcast had 15.6 million high-speed Internet subscribers, 7.8 million digital voice subscribers, and 23.6 million video cable subscribers. Comcast had mostly eliminated its circuit-switched phone services, with only 2,000 circuit-switched subscribers remaining as of September 2009. Comcast's clear number one earner was the video service segment. Industry experts expected the video segment to generate 55 percent of Comcast's revenue in 2009, followed by the Internet segment, with 22 percent. Comcast also generated revenue from other streams, including phone, advertising, and national programming networks such as VERSUS, the Golf Channel, and E! Entertainment Television.

In 2009, Comcast increased its product offering to the "quadruple play," by offering a mobile service under the brand Comcast High-Speed 2go. Comcast began offering wireless data services following its investment in Clearwire in November 2008 (see Exhibit 16). Comcast's 4G services were provided via the Clearwire network, and its 3G service was provided by Sprint's nationwide 3G network.

Acquisitions of competitors with substantial cable system infrastructure played a major role in

Exhibit 16   **Screen Shot of News Release Regarding the Creation of Clearwire**

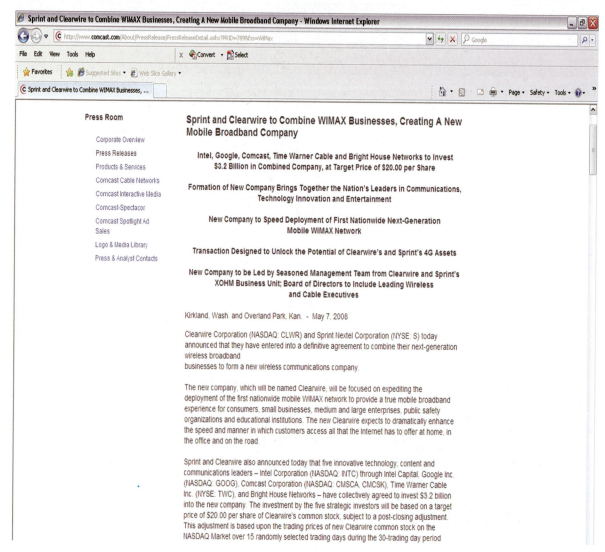

Source: www.comcast.com.

Comcast's expansion. In December 2001, Comcast purchased AT&T's cable operations for $72 billion in stock and assumed debt securities. This major acquisition brought six new U.S. states into the available services market and significantly boosted Comcast's Internet subscriber numbers. In 2006, in association with Time Warner, Comcast purchased the assets of Adelphia, which resulted in 1.7 million new Comcast subscribers.

In 2009, experts expected Comcast's cable division, which included voice, Internet, and video, to generate revenue of $33.3 billion (see Exhibit 17).

That would be a 3.5 percent year-on-year increase and a 14 percent per year increase from $18 billion in 2004. In the preceding two years, the increase in total cable revenue had come from the high-speed Internet and digital voice markets, as video growth had slowed.

VoIP Performance Comcast's revenue from digital voice had skyrocketed in the five years leading up to 2009. VoIP had become a much more widely used means of communication, with revenues increasing 480 percent per annum, from

$500,000 in 2004 to an expected $3.3 billion in 2009 (see Exhibit 18). Comcast's drastic increase in revenue went hand in hand with the growth of VoIP as a communication technology. In 2004, VoIP was a pre-budding technology that had yet to gain mass exposure and penetration. There were a mere 2,000 Comcast VoIP subscribers in the United States. However, consumers began to take notice of the potential cost savings that VoIP offered. In addition to the growing awareness among consumers, the VoIP technology improved and became a closer substitute for the traditional PSTN voice call. As a result, Comcast gained a substantial increase in subscriber base; in the third quarter of 2009, Comcast reported that base to be near 7.7 million consumers.

From 2004 to 2009, cable companies, including Comcast, began to aggressively market the VoIP product. VoIP providers focused on bundled packages as a method to overtake PSTN providers. The strategy proved very successful, as Comcast sub-stantially improved its own cable revenues while also cutting into PSTN providers' subscription numbers. In the first quarter of 2005, Comcast's digital telephone services were available to 1 million homes across the United States. In the third quarter of 2009, Comcast reported that its digital telephone service was available to 48 million homes. The dramatic increase in subscriber numbers was reflected by the corresponding share of cable revenue proportioned to Comcast's digital voice market. In the third quarter of 2009, the digital voice market accounted for 10 percent of total cable revenue, a 6.6 percentage point increase from just 3.4 percent in the first quarter of 2005. Obviously, Comcast had taken advantage of the VoIP boom.

Mobile VoIP   The next challenge for Comcast would be developing mobile VoIP and collaborating with wireless carriers such as AT&T and Verizon. This was the reason Comcast had invested in Clearwire's 4G WiMAX network. In late 2009, Comcast introduced 4G WiMAX services under the brand name High-Speed 2go. The offering bundled Clearwire's 4G WiMAX service with Comcast's own broadband services. It was a direct attempt to win market share from AT&T and Verizon, neither of which offered a comparable bundled product. Success for Clearwire and the cable partners, including Comcast, was expected to depend on their ability to build and market the mobile WiMAX service to new markets before Verizon launched its version of a 4G bundle in late 2010.

Comcast's entry into the wireless industry created endless possibilities for wireless value-added services. For example, Comcast had recently launched its own iPhone and iPod Touch application. The app was tailored for customers who already used the company's available services, including e-mail, VoIP, TV listings, and Comcast On Demand by giving integrated access to all services through the iPhone. This integration could prove to be the ultimate determining factor for mobile VoIP success in the future.

Exhibit 17   Comcast's Cable Segment's Financial Performance, 2005–2009

Year	Revenue ($ millions)	Growth (%)	Operating Income ($ millions)	Growth (%)
2005	$19,987	9.6%	$ 7,939	14.4%
2006	24,042	20.3	9,667	21.8
2007	30,120	25.3	12,246	26.7
2008	32,443	7.7	13,170	7.5
2009	33,681	3.8	13,721	4.2

Source: Annual report, www.ibisworld.com.

Exhibit 18   Comcast's VoIP Segment's Financial Performance, 2005–2009

Year	Revenue ($ millions)	Growth (%)
2005	$ 68.2	13540%
2006	528.0	674
2007	1,619.1	207
2008	2,639.2	63
2009	3,300.0	25

Source: Annual report, www.ibisworld.com.

Time Warner Cable Inc.

Time Warner Cable (TWC) was formed in 1990 through the merger of Time Inc.'s cable television company, American Television and Communications Corporation, and Warner Cable, a division of Warner Communications. Prior to 2009, Time

Warner Inc. (TWI) was the owner of TWC. But in the first quarter of 2009, TWC was spun off from TWI to create a separate entity.

By 2001, TWC had completed a nationwide system upgrade to create a hybrid fiber coaxial (HFC) cable network. In essence, TWC had created its own network of cables to use. That meant no more dealing with upstream ISPs. In addition to the upgraded network, TWC developed new services including digital cable, video on demand, high-definition television (HDTV), high-speed online access via cable modem, digital video recorder (DVR), and digital phone.

By offering what it called Double Play, Triple Play, and Quadruple Play bundles, TWC had been very successful in creating a large subscriber base and achieving large year-on-year revenue gains. The TWC Triple Play included high-speed Internet, digital video, and digital voice services. TWC operated in the VoIP industry through its digital phone offering.

TWC was the second-largest cable TV provider in the United States. As of the third quarter of 2009, TWC had a total of 35 million subscribers, with 4.1 million digital phone subscribers. The market for cable TV had been mature for some time. Like its competitors, TWC began offering bundles that included cable TV/video, high-speed Internet access, and IP-based telephony services. By September 2009, TWC had 3.4 million Triple Play customers.

TWC's digital phone service, launched in 2004, used the company's cable-IP network to allow subscribers to make local, long-distance, and international calls through a voice-enabled cable modem. Calls made to other digital telephone subscribers stayed on the company's VoIP network. However, calls to destinations outside TWC's network were routed through the PSTN.

VoIP Performance   Much like Comcast, TWC recorded extremely strong growth from digital phone revenue between 2004 and 2009. At the end of 2009, TWC digital telephone subscribers had increased by 83 percent per annum to an estimated 4.3 million, a dramatic increase after reporting just 206,000 digital telephone subscribers in 2004. From 2004 to 2009, TWC strongly marketed the VoIP service in bundled packages as a means to attract customers away from traditional telecommunications providers.

The strategy proved to be very successful, and the increased usage of VoIP propelled TWC's VoIP average revenue per user (ARPU) to 25 percent per annum, which resulted in an ARPU of $37.02 by year-end 2009.

Substantial increases in TWC digital phone subscribers and an increasing ARPU combined to substantially increase digital phone revenue. TWC's VoIP revenue was forecast to increase by 130 percent per annum, to $1.9 billion at the end of 2009 (see Exhibit 19). At the end of 2009, VoIP revenue was forecast to account for 10.7 percent of total cable revenue, a 10.4 percentage point increase from 2004 (0.3 percent).

Mobile VoIP   TWC also invested in Clearwire's 4G WiMAX network. In December 2009, TWC launched its Clear-powered mobile WiMAX service in the Dallas/Fort Worth area as a test market. TWC was selling the WiMAX service, dubbed Road Runner Mobile, in bundles and required customers to take at least one other service. TWC planned more city launches in early 2010.

AT&T

AT&T Inc. owned AT&T Mobility, which was, until the 2009 Verizon-Alltel merger, the largest wireless telecommunications carrier in the United States based on total subscribers. AT&T Inc. was an integrated telecommunications provider—offering wireline services such as local, long-distance, and data services—and had exhibited a number of different name changes following various acquisitions. AT&T Mobility was formerly Cingular Wireless, which was formed in 2000 as a joint venture between SBC Communications

Exhibit 19   **Time Warner Cable's VoIP Financial Performance, 2005–2009**

Year	Revenue ($ million)	Growth (%)
2005	$ 282	872.4%
2006	688	144.0
2007	1,159	68.5
2008	1,619	39.7
2009	1,910	18.0

Source: Annual report, www.ibisworld.com.

and BellSouth. These two companies owned 60 percent and 40 percent of the equity in the joint venture, respectively. AT&T's mission and vision statements were as follows:

> *Mission Statement:*
> We aspire to be the most admired and valuable company in the world. Our goal is to enrich our customers' personal lives and to make their businesses more successful by bringing to market exciting and useful communications services, building shareowner value in the process.

> *Vision Statement:*
> Connect people with their world, everywhere they live and work, and do it better than anyone else.

In October 2004, Cingular Wireless completed its merger with AT&T Wireless Services for $41 billion in cash. The biggest upside for Cingular was that AT&T's customer base added a complementary customer mix considering that AT&T's customers tended to generate higher average revenue per user than Cingular's. The new Cingular had 54 million customers and the largest digital voice and data network in the country.

Acquisitions
In 2005, SBC Communications, which owned 60 percent of Cingular Wireless, acquired AT&T Corporation for $16 billion. Following the acquisition, SBC Communications changed its name to AT&T Inc. Then, in 2006, AT&T Inc. acquired BellSouth for $86 billion, the largest takeover in U.S. telecommunications history. AT&T Inc. then acquired the 40 percent of Cingular Wireless that it did not already own. With 100 percent ownership, AT&T Inc. announced that it would rebrand and rename Cingular Wireless to AT&T Mobility. The Cingular Wireless name was eliminated by mid-2007 despite the company having spent billions of dollars on marketing the brand. Unfortunately, management also announced it would reduce AT&T Mobility's workforce by approximately 10,000 people between 2007 and 2009.

AT&T followed up this period of major acquisition activity with a number of small but significant transactions. In 2007, AT&T acquired ninth-placed wireless provider Dobson Communications. Then, in 2008, AT&T purchased Edge Wireless, the 20th-largest wireless company in subscriber terms in the United States. These deals made AT&T the number two player in the industry, behind Verizon.

Business Developments AT&T Mobility claimed to have the largest digital voice and data network in the United States. Revenue growth for the sector had been drastic in the past five years. Projections for 2009 can be found in Exhibit 20. Over the four years leading up to 2009, AT&T Mobility invested billions of dollars in enhancing and upgrading its 3G network. AT&T hoped to boost 3G network capacity and increase data revenues. In perhaps its greatest move to solidify data revenue, AT&T Mobility secured exclusive U.S. distribution rights to Apple's highly anticipated iPhone. Following the iPhone's 2007 release, AT&T benefited from a stronger subscriber base and data revenue growth (see Exhibit 21). Data revenue was forecast to exceed $14.0 billion in 2009, a 49 percent per annum increase from $4.2 billion in 2006.

Exhibit 20 **AT&T Mobility's Financial Performance, 2004–2009**

Year	Revenue ($ million)	Growth (%)	Operating Income ($ million)	Growth (%)
2004	$19,436	25.5%	$ 1,043	–43.5%
2005	34,433	77.2	1,791	71.7
2006	37,506	8.9	4,443	148.1
2007	42,684	13.8	6,838	53.9
2008	49,335	15.6	10,834	58.4
2009	52,759	6.9	12,200	12.6

Source: Annual report, www.ibisworld.com.

Exhibit 21 **AT&T Mobility's Key Performance Indicators, 2004–2009**

Year	Subscribers (thousands)	Growth (%)	Customer Churn (%)
2004	49,109	104.4%	2.7%
2005	54,144	10.3	2.2
2006	61,026	12.7	1.8
2007	70,052	14.8	1.7
2008	77,009	9.9	1.7
2009	82,800	7.5	1.4

Source: Annual report, www.ibisworld.com.

The increase in data use, propelled by the success of the iPod, was a bonus for AT&T in 2008. It not only supported strong wireless revenue growth but also delivered a drastic improvement in the profitability of AT&T's wireless operations. This was because, as a premium service, data services attracted large margins.

Too Much Success The overwhelming success of the iPod created a problem for AT&T. The iPhone was introduced by AT&T with an unlimited data usage plan that was unprecedented in the United States. The unlimited usage created heavy congestion and was downgrading services in some regions.

Experts forecast that global VoIP traffic would quintuple from 2008 to 2013. Overall, IP traffic was expected to achieve a compound annual growth rate of 40 percent. The current pricing method of charging a single rate for all customers regardless of how many bytes they used was unsustainable. As customer usage profiles were diverging dramatically, spreading costs across all subscribers offered poor value for those who used the Internet infrequently. Wireless ISPs, such as AT&T, were expected to implement new pricing structures based on metered bandwidth usage to effectively compete with Skype and the other players.

TIME FOR SKYPE TO MAKE A MOVE

So there Josh Silverman sat, brainstorming about Skype's next move. The company had become a big player in the VoIP industry, and the telecommunications industry was starting to notice the lack of growth from landlines. A fierce competition was brewing, and Skype was log-jammed right in the middle. As a personal adviser to Silverman and the rest of the Skype team, what would you recommend their next move be to continue the growth of Skype? Does it involve collaboration with cell phone providers or restructuring of the pricing model? What about an increase in advertising? Also, how will Skype defend itself against the major powers like AT&T? Is being a first-to-market provider the company's best strategic option?

Sara Lee Corporation in 2011: Has Its Retrenchment Strategy Been Successful?

Arthur A. Thompson
The University of Alabama

John E. Gamble
University of South Alabama

In February 2005, Brenda Barnes, Sara Lee Corporation's newly appointed president and CEO, announced a bold and ambitious multi-year strategic plan to transform Sara Lee into a more tightly focused food, beverage, and household products company. The centerpiece of Barnes's transformation plan was the divestiture of weak-performing business units and product categories accounting for $7.2 billion in sales (37 percent of Sara Lee's annual revenues). While the divestitures would cut Sara Lee's revenues from $19.6 billion to about $12.3 billion, Barnes believed that Sara Lee would be better off concentrating its financial and managerial resources on a smaller number of business segments in which market prospects were promising and Sara Lee's brands were well positioned.[1] Once the retrenchment initiatives were completed, the plan was to drive the company's growth via initiatives to boost the sales, market shares, and profitability of the key remaining brands: Sara Lee breads and bakery products, Ball Park meats, Douwe Egberts coffees, Hillshire Farm meats, Jimmy Dean sausage, and Senseo single-serve coffee products. Company executives believed that the retrenchment would allow revenues to increase to $14 billion by fiscal 2010 and that the company's operating profit margin in 2010 would increase to at least 12 percent (versus an 8.1 percent operating profit margin in fiscal 2004).[2]

By fiscal year-end 2010, it remained unclear to what extent the retrenchment strategy had benefited shareholders. The company had missed both revenue and operating profit margin projections for 2010. Revenues had increased to only $10.8 billion in fiscal 2010, and the company's operating profit margin during the year had improved to only 8.5 percent. During 2010, Sara Lee had engaged in further retrenchment with the divestiture of its International Household and Body Care business, which produced and marketed Kiwi shoe care products, Sanex personal care products, Ambi Pur air fresheners, and various insecticides and cleaning products sold outside North America. The company was also well under way with Project Accelerate, a company-wide cost savings and productivity initiative launched in 2008 that focused on outsourcing, supply chain efficiencies, and overhead reduction. Project Accelerate had produced savings of $180 million by 2010 and was expected to produce cumulative savings of $350 million to $400 million by the end of fiscal 2012. Management also launched a share buyback plan in 2010 that would repurchase $2.5 billion to $3 billion of shares over a three-year period. Also during 2010, Brenda Barnes had been forced to step down as CEO in August after suffering a stroke in May. The company's chief financial officer, Marcel Smits, had been named interim CEO while the board searched for a permanent replacement. Smits's strategies for 2011 focused on increasing share in the company's most powerful brands, pursuing growth in attractive geographic markets, and fully capturing the anticipated benefits of Project Accelerate.

COMPANY BACKGROUND

The origins of Sara Lee Corporation date to 1939, when Nathan Cummins acquired C. D. Kenny Company, a small wholesale distributor of sugar, coffee, and tea that had net sales of $24 million. The purchase of Sprague, Warner & Company in 1942 prompted a name change to Sprague Warner–Kenny Corporation and a shift in the headquarters location from Baltimore to Chicago; the company's shares began trading on the New York Stock Exchange in 1946. In 1954, the company's name was changed to Consolidated Foods Corporation to emphasize its diversified role in food processing, packaging, and distribution. In 1956, Consolidated Foods acquired Kitchens of Sara Lee and also entered the retail food business by acquiring 34 Piggly Wiggly supermarkets (later divested in 1966). The next 40 years were marked by a series of related and unrelated acquisitions:

Year	Acquisitions
1962	Jonker Fris, a Dutch producer of canned goods
1966	Oxford Chemical Corporation
	E. Kahn's Sons Company, a producer of meats
1968	Bryan Foods, a meat products producer
	Electrolux, a direct seller of vacuum cleaners
	Gant, an apparel producer
	Country Set, an apparel producer
	Canadelle, a producer of women's intimate apparel
1969	Aris Gloves (later renamed Aris Isotoner)
1971	Hillshire Farm, a meat producer
	Rudy's Farm, a meat producer
1972	Erdal, a Dutch company that produced and marketed personal care products (later renamed Intradal)
1978	Chef Pierre, a manufacturer/distributor of frozen prepared desserts
	Douwe Egberts, a Dutch coffee and grocery company
1980	Productos Cruz Verde, a Spanish household products company
1982	Standard Meat Company, a processor of meat products
1984	Jimmy Dean Meats, a manufacturer of various meat, food, and leather products
	Nicholas Kiwi Limited, an Australian-based manufacturer and marketer of personal, household, shoe and car care products and home medicines
1987	Bil Mar Foods, a producer of turkey-based products
	Dim, S.A., the leading hosiery brand in France
1988	Adams-Millis Corporation, a manufacturer of hosiery products (provided an entry into the men's basic sock business)
1989	Champion Products, manufacturer of professional-quality knit athletic wear
	Van Nelle, a Dutch company active in coffee and tea
	Hygrade Food Products, a manufacturer of hot dogs, luncheon meats, bacon, and ham (which included the Ball Park and Hygrade hot dog brands)
1990	Henson-Kickernick Inc., a manufacturer of high-quality foundations and daywear
1991	Playtex Apparel Inc., an international manufacturer and marketer of intimate apparel products
	Rinbros, a manufacturer/marketer of men's and boys' underwear in Mexico
1992	BP Nutrition's Consumer Foods Group
	Giltex Hosiery
	Bessin Corporation
	The furniture care businesses of SC Johnson Wax

(Continued)

Year	Acquisitions *(Concluded)*
	A majority interest in Maglificio Bellia SpA
	Select assets of Mark Cross Inc.
1993	SmithKline Beecham's European bath and body care brands
1997	Aoste, a French meats company
	Lovable Italiana SpA, an Italian intimate apparel manufacturer
	Brossard France SA, a French manufacturer of bakery products
1998	NutriMetics
	Café do Ponto
1999	Wechsler Coffee
	Chock full o'Nuts
	Continental Coffee
2000	Hills Bros., MJB, and Chase & Sanborn coffee brands (acquired from Nestlé USA)
	Courtaulds Textiles, UK-based producer of intimate apparel brands Gossard and Berlei
	Café Pilão, the number one coffee company in Brazil
	Sol y Oro, the leading company in women's underwear in Argentina,
2001	The EarthGrains Company, the number two player in the U.S. bakery market
	A major European bakery company

John H. Bryan, former head of Bryan Meats (which the company acquired in 1968), became president and CEO of Consolidated Foods in 1975 and served as CEO until 2000; Bryan was appointed chairman in 1976, a position he held until 2001. Bryan was the chief architect of the company's acquisition strategy during 1975–2000, guiding both its diversification efforts and its emergence as a global corporation. By 1980, sales had reached $5 billion. In 1985, Consolidated Foods changed its name to Sara Lee Corporation. Sales reached $10 billion in 1988, $15 billion in 1994, and $20 billion in 1998. But revenues peaked at the $20 billion level in 1998–1999 as management struggled to manage the company's broadly diversified and geographically scattered operations.

In 2000, C. Steven McMillan succeeded John Bryan as CEO and president of Sara Lee; Bryan remained chairman until he retired a year later, at which time McMillan assumed the additional title. McMillan launched strategic initiatives to narrow Sara Lee's focus on a smaller number of global branded consumer packaged-goods segments—Food and Beverage, Intimates and Underwear, and Household Products. McMillan orchestrated several divestitures to begin the process of sharpening Sara Lee's business focus:

Year	Divestitures
1966	Piggly Wiggly supermarket chains
2000	PYA/Monarch (sold to Royal Ahold's U.S. food service for nearly $1.6 billion)
	Champion Europe
	Coach
	The International Fabrics division of Courtaulds
	The international bakery businesses in France, India, China, and the United Kingdom
2004	Filodoro, an Italian intimate apparel business

Brenda C. Barnes, who had been president of PepsiCola North America from 1996 to 1998, joined Sara Lee as president and chief operating officer in July 2004. At the time of her appointment, Barnes, age 50, was a member of the board of directors at Avon Products, the New York Times Company, Sears Roebuck, and Staples. During her 22-year career at PepsiCo, Barnes had held a number of senior executive positions in operations, general management, manufacturing, sales, and marketing. From November 1999 to March 2000, she served as interim president and chief operating officer of Starwood Hotels & Resorts. Barnes's appointment as president and CEO of Sara Lee was announced on February 10, 2005, the same day as the announcement of the plan to transform Sara Lee into an even more tightly focused company.

SARA LEE'S RETRENCHMENT INITIATIVES

The first phase of Brenda Barnes's transformation plan for Sara Lee was to exit eight businesses that had been targeted as nonstrategic:

- *Direct selling*—a $450 million business that sold cosmetics, skin care products, fragrances, toiletries, household products, apparel, and other products to consumers through a network of independent salespeople in 18 countries around the world, most notably in Mexico, Australia, the Philippines, and Japan. In August 2005, Sara Lee announced a definitive agreement to sell its direct selling business to Tupperware Corporation for $547 million in cash.[3] The sale included products being sold under such brands as Avroy Shlain, House of Fuller, House of Sara Lee, NaturCare, Nutrimetics, Nuvó Cosméticos, and Swissgarde.

- *U.S. retail coffee*—a $213 million business that marketed the well-known Chock full o'Nuts, Hills Bros., MJB, and Chase & Sanborn coffees plus several private-label coffees. Not included in the divestiture plan was the sale of Sara Lee's fast-growing global coffee brand, Senseo, which had sales of approximately $85 million. The U.S. retail coffee business was sold to Italy-based Segafredo Zanetti Group for $82 million in late 2005.[4]

- *European apparel*—a Sara Lee business unit that marketed such well-known brands as Dim, Playtex, Wonderbra, Abanderado, Nur Die, and Unno in France, Germany, Italy, Spain, the United Kingdom, and much of Eastern Europe; it also included Sara Lee Courtaulds, a UK-based maker of private-label clothing for retailers. The branded European apparel business had nearly $1.2 billion in

sales in fiscal year 2005, ending July 2, 2005; the Sara Lee Courtaulds business had fiscal 2005 sales of about $560 million. In November 2005, Sara Lee sold the branded apparel portion of the European apparel business unit to an affiliate of Sun Capital Partners, a U.S. private equity company, based in Boca Raton, Florida, for about $115 million plus possible contingent payments based on future performance.[5] In May 2006, a big fraction of Sara Lee Courtaulds was sold to PD Enterprise Ltd., a global garment producer with nine facilities that produced more than 120 million garments annually, including bras, underwear, nightwear, swim- and beachwear, formal wear, casual wear, jackets and coats, baby clothes, and socks; the deal with PD Enterprise did not include three Sara Lee Courtaulds facilities in Sri Lanka (Sara Lee was continuing its efforts to find a buyer for the Sri Lanka operations). Sara Lee received no material consideration as a result of the sale and remained liable for certain obligations of Sara Lee Courtaulds after the disposition, the most significant of which was the defined benefit pension plans that were underfunded by $483 million at the end of 2005.

- *European nuts and snacks*—a business with approximately €88 million in annual sales in fiscal 2005 that marketed products under the Duyvis brand in the Netherlands and Belgium as well as the Bénénuts brand in France. Sara Lee sold its European nuts and snacks business in the Netherlands, Belgium, and France to PepsiCo for approximately $160 million in November 2005.[6]

- *European rice*—a small business that packaged Lassie brand rice sold in the Netherlands and other European countries. The business unit was sold to Grupo SOS of Spain for $62 million in November 2005.

- *U.S. meat snacks*—a small unit with annual sales of $33 million in fiscal 2005 and $25 million in fiscal 2006. This business was sold in June 2006 for $9 million.[7]

- *European meats*—a $1.1 billion packaged meats business in Europe that had respectable market positions in France, the Benelux region, and Portugal and included such brands as Aoste, Justin Bridou, Cochonou, Nobre, and Imperial. Headquartered in Hoofddorp, the Netherlands, Sara Lee's European meats operation generated $1.1 billion in sales in fiscal 2005, and employed approximately 4,500 people. In June 2006, Sara Lee completed the sale of this unit to Smithfield Foods for $575 million in cash; based in Smithfield, Virginia, Smithfield Foods was the world's largest grower of hogs and producer of pork products and had subsidiaries in France, Poland, Romania, and the United Kingdom that marketed meats under the Krakus and Stefano's brands as well as other brands.[8]

- *Sara Lee branded apparel*—a business that consisted of producing and marketing 10 brands of apparel: Hanes, L'eggs, Champion, Bali, Barely There, Playtex, Wonderbra, Just My Size, Duofold (outdoor apparel), and Outer Banks (golf, corporate, and stylish

sportswear); sales of these brands were chiefly in North America, Latin America, and Asia. Sara Lee's strategy for exiting branded apparel (2004 sales of $4.5 billion) was to spin the entire business off as an independent company named Hanesbrands Inc. Two top executives of the Sara Lee branded apparel business were named to head the new company. The spin-off was completed in September 2006 when Sara Lee distributed 100 percent of the common stock of Hanesbrands to Sara Lee shareholders; shares were traded on the New York Stock Exchange under the symbol HBI.

Sara Lee management expected the retrenchment initiatives to generate combined net after-tax proceeds in excess of $3 billion. Exhibit 1 provides financial data relating to the divested businesses. The next section provides additional details about the Hanesbrands spin-off.

Exhibit 1   Financial Data for Sara Lee's Divested Businesses, Fiscal Years 2004–2006

(a) Sales and Income of Divested Businesses, Fiscal Years 2004–2006 ($ millions)

	Fiscal Years		
	2006	2005	2004
Net Sales of Divested Businesses			
Direct selling	$ 202	$ 473	$ 447
U.S. retail coffee	122	213	206
European branded apparel	641	1,184	1,276
European nuts and snacks	54	64	66
Sara Lee Courtaulds	437	558	536
European rice	n/a	n/a	n/a
U.S. meat snacks	25	30	33
European meats	1,114	1,176	1,111
Total net sales	$2,595	$3,698	$3,675
Pretax Income (Loss) of Divested Businesses			
Direct selling	$ 14	$ 55	$ 55
U.S. retail coffee	(46)	(39)	(2)
European branded apparel	(186)	(302)	67
European nuts and snacks	8	7	12
Sara Lee Courtaulds	(69)	—	14
European rice	n/a	n/a	n/a
U.S. meat snacks	(14)	(1)	(1)
European meats	(57)	90	101
Total pretax income (loss)	$ (350)	$ (190)	$ 246

(Continued)

Exhibit 1   *(Concluded)*

	Fiscal Years		
	2006	2005	2004
After-Tax Income (Loss) of Divested Businesses			
Direct selling	$ 54	$ (12)	$ 34
U.S. retail coffee	(39)	(33)	—
European branded apparel	(153)	(296)	68
European nuts and snacks	3	3	7
Sara Lee Courtaulds	(71)	(1)	26
European rice	n/a	n/a	n/a
U.S. meat snacks	(9)	(1)	—
European meats	(41)	(22)	86
Total after-tax income (loss)	$ (256)	$ (362)	$ 221

(b) Proceeds Realized from the Sales of the Divested Businesses ($ millions)

	Sale Price	Pretax Gain on Sale	Tax Benefit (Charge)	After-Tax Gain
Direct selling	$ 547	$327	$(107)	$220
U.S. retail coffee	82	5	(2)	3
European branded apparel	~115	45	41	86
European nuts and snacks	160	66	4	70
Sara Lee Courtaulds	No material consideration**	22	—	22
European rice	62	n/a	n/a	n/a
U.S. meat snacks	9	1	(1)	—
European meats*	575	42	(2)	40
Totals	$1,550***	$508	$ (67)	$441

*This unit was divested in early fiscal 2007; data regarding the gains from the sale is from a company press release of November 7, 2006, reporting results for the first quarter of fiscal 2007.

**Sara Lee retained liability for unfunded pension benefits of $483 million at Sara Lee Courtaulds and made payments of approximately $93 million to remedy its liability during 2006.

***The actual amount realized from the sales of these businesses was closer to $1.3 billion after taking into account the payments made to remedy unfunded pension liabilities at Sara Lee Courtaulds and other costs incurred in discontinuing the operations of all these businesses.

n/a = not available

Sources: Sara Lee. 2006 10-K report, p. 56, and various company press releases announcing the sale and disposition of the businesses.

THE SPIN-OFF OF HANESBRANDS

Sara Lee management's decision to exit the branded apparel business was driven principally by eroding sales and weak returns on its equity investment in branded apparel—see Exhibit 2. But rather than sell the business, management determined that shareholders would be better served by spinning off the branded apparel business as a stand-alone company. Sara Lee shareholders received one share of Hanesbrands stock for every eight shares owned.

Exhibit 2 Performance of Hanesbrands Prior to Spin-Off by Sara Lee, Fiscal Years 2002–2006 ($ thousands)

	Fiscal Years Ending				
	July 1, 2006	July 3, 2005	July 3, 2004	June 28, 2003	June 29, 2002
Statements of Income Data					
Net sales	$4,472,832	$4,683,683	$4,632,741	$4,669,665	$4,920,840
Cost of sales	2,987,500	3,223,571	3,092,026	3,010,383	3,278,506
Gross profit	1,485,332	1,460,112	1,540,715	1,659,282	1,642,334
Selling, general and administrative expenses	1,051,833	1,053,654	1,087,964	1,126,065	1,146,549
Charges for (income from) exit activities	(101)	46,978	27,466	(14,397)	27,580
Income from operations	433,600	359,480	425,285	547,614	468,205
Interest expense	26,075	35,244	37,411	44,245	2,509
Interest income	(8,795)	(21,280)	(12,998)	(46,631)	(13,753)
Income before income taxes	416,320	345,516	400,872	550,000	479,449
Income tax expense (benefit)	93,827	127,007	(48,680)	121,560	139,488
Net income	$ 322,493	$ 218,509	$ 449,552	$ 428,440	$ 339,961
Balance Sheet Data					
Cash and cash equivalents	$ 298,252	$1,080,799	$ 674,154	$ 289,816	$ 106,250
Total assets	4,891,075	4,237,154	4,402,758	3,915,573	4,064,730
Noncurrent liabilities:					
Noncurrent capital lease obligations	2,786	6,188	7,200	10,054	12,171
Noncurrent deferred tax liabilities	5,014	7,171	—	6,599	10,140
Other noncurrent liabilities	42,187	40,200	28,734	32,598	37,660
Total noncurrent liabilities	49,987	53,559	35,934	49,251	59,971
Total Sara Lee equity investment	3,229,134	2,602,362	2,797,370	2,237,448	1,762,824

Source: Hanesbrands, fiscal 2006 10-K report.

Hanesbrands began independent operations in September 2006 and organized its business around four product/geographic segments, as shown in Exhibit 3.

However, the spin-off of Hanesbrands had some unique financial features. The terms of the spin-off called for Hanesbrands to make a one-time "dividend" payment of $2.4 billion to Sara Lee immediately following the commencement of independent operations. But in order to make the $2.4 billion payment to Sara Lee and to fund its own operations, Hanesbrands borrowed $2.6 billion, thus saddling itself with a huge debt that prompted Standard & Poor's to assign the company a B+ credit rating (which put Hanesbrands in the bottom half of apparel companies from a credit rating stand-

point). The company's debt-to-equity ratio was extraordinarily high, raising some questions about whether the interest expenses associated with the high debt would still leave Hanesbrands with sufficient funds and financial flexibility to invest in revitalizing its brands and growing its business.

A *BusinessWeek* reporter speculated that the reason for the unusually outsized dividend payment to Sara Lee was that the proceeds Sara Lee realized from the sales of the divested units fell far short of the hoped-for $3 billion that was an integral part of the retrenchment strategy and restructuring announced by CEO Brenda Barnes in February 2005.[9] To make up for the shortfall, Sara Lee supposedly opted to get more cash out of the Hanesbrands spin-off.

Exhibit 3 Hanesbrands' Lineup of Products and Brands, 2006

Product/Geographic Segments	Primary Products	Primary Brands
Innerwear	Intimate apparel, such as bras, panties and bodywear	Hanes, Playtex, Bali, barely there, Just My Size, Wonderbra
	Men's underwear and kids' underwear	Hanes, Champion, Polo Ralph Lauren**
	Socks	Hanes, Champion
Outerwear	Activewear, such as performance T-shirts and shorts	Hanes, Champion, Just My Size
	Casual wear, such as T-shirts, fleece and sport shirts	Hanes, Just My Size, Outerbanks, Hanes Beefy-T
Hosiery	Hosiery	L'eggs, Hanes, Just My Size
International	Activewear, men's underwear, kids' underwear, intimate apparel, socks, hosiery and casual wear	Hanes, Wonderbra,* Playtex,* Champion, Rinbros, Bali

*Terms of the February 2006 sale of Sara Lee's European branded apparel business prevented Hanesbrands from selling Wonderbra and Playtex branded products in the European Union, several other European countries, and South Africa.

**Hanesbrands had a license agreement to sell men's underwear and kids' underwear under the Polo Ralph Lauren label.

Source: Hanesbrands, fiscal 2006 10-K report.

SARA LEE'S POSTRETRENCHMENT STRATEGY: INITIATIVES TO REVITALIZE SALES AND BOOST PROFITABILITY

Upon the completion of Sara Lee Corporation's disposition of nonstrategic businesses in September 2006, Sara Lee management turned its full attention to increasing the sales, market shares, and profitability of its remaining businesses. The two chief financial goals were to boost top line sales by 2–4 percent annually to reach $14 billion by 2010 and to achieve a 12 percent operating profit margin by 2010. Sara Lee planned to achieve its objectives by developing three competitive capabilities in all of its remaining businesses. The company's management believed that competitive pricing, innovative new products, and brand-building capabilities were essential to its efforts to please consumers. Category management and leverage through size were also thought to be necessary for the company to win new accounts with supermarket and discount store customers. Operating excellence was the third key element of its corporate strategy, which was critical to competitive pricing. Major operations initiatives at Sara Lee included lean manufacturing, centralized purchasing to achieve economies of scope, and the implementation of a common corporate-wide information systems platform.

While the company was making headway in focusing on consumer needs and category management, its efforts to improve operating efficiency and increase operating margins were showing little progress by year-end 2007. Top management launched Project Accelerate in March 2008 to strengthen the company's ability to meet its objective of achieving an operating profit margin of 12 percent by 2010. Project Accelerate included additional business process outsourcing, operating segment restructuring, new supply chain efficiencies, reductions in corporate overhead, and reductions in employee benefit costs. By the end of fiscal 2010, Project Accelerate had produced total cumulative benefits of $180 million. Management expected cumulative benefits for Project Accelerate to reach $350 million to $400 million by the end of fiscal 2012.

The organizational structure developed by Brenda Barnes and other key Sara Lee managers that would best enable the company's businesses to contribute to corporate goals was a six-division structure built around product similarities, customer types, and geographic regions. The North American Retail division included such products sold in supermarkets and discount stores as lunch meats, breakfast sausage, smoked sausage, frozen desserts, and single-serve coffee; its North American Fresh Bakery division included fresh breads, buns, and bagels sold in supermarkets; and North American Foodservice included the sales of meat products, bakery products, and coffee and tea products sold to food service accounts in North America. The International Beverage division included the sales of coffee and tea products in Europe, while the International Bakery division included sales of bakery goods in Europe. The company's International Household and Body Care division included insecticides, personal hygiene products, and cleaning brands sold outside North America. The Household and Body Care division was discontinued in 2010, with all but shoe care products and cleaning brands divested during the year. In fiscal 2011, Sara Lee was negotiating with a number of potential buyers for the sale of these remaining businesses. Exhibit 4 presents a summary of Sara Lee's financial performance for 2004 through 2010 that includes all businesses operated in each reporting year. A summary of the financial performance between 2006 and 2010 for the company's continuing operations in 2010 is presented in Exhibit 5. Exhibit 6 presents sales and operating profits for Sara Lee's major business segments for 2008 through 2010.

North American Retail

Sara Lee's North American Retail division had limited its product lineup to food categories that offered retailers high margins, were growing faster than the overall industry, and showed consumer preferences for branded products versus private-label brands. In 2010, the division had a number of market-leading brands such as Ball Park franks, Jimmy Dean sausage, Hillshire Farm smoked sausage, State Fair corn dogs, Sara Lee frozen desserts, and Senseo single-serving coffeemakers and coffee pods. Sara Lee was the second-largest seller of lunch meats and frozen desserts in North America. In 2010, Sara Lee North American Retail businesses held market shares of 30 percent in smoked sausage, 23 percent in

hot dogs, 14 percent in lunch meat, 58 percent in breakfast sausage, 22 percent in frozen desserts, and 55 percent in single-serve coffee. Ten of the company's division's 12 core products increased market share in 2010. Between 2008 and 2010, the division's sales had grown faster than the sales of any other processed food company. Also, the operating profit margin for the division improved from 9.2 percent in 2009 to 12.3 percent in 2010. Going into 2011, Sara Lee's North American Retail meats business unit was near completion of a state-of-the art meat-slicing plant and the planned divestiture of its kosher hot dog brands and commodity meat business.

The division's Senseo single-serving coffee pods were also the number one brand in North America, with a 55 percent share of the market for single-serving coffees in 2008. However, the division's Senseo coffeemakers and coffee pods had experienced little growth in the United States and achieved U.S. sales of only $26 million in 2008. Single-serve coffee accounted for less than 6 percent of the global retail coffee market in 2009, but was expected to increase to 8.5 percent of industry sales by 2013.

North American Fresh Bakery

Sara Lee's entry into the fresh bakery business in 2002 had produced phenomenal results, with its sales increasing from $91 million in 2003 to $2.1 billion in 2008. In 2010, Sara Lee was the best-selling brand of packaged bread sold in the United States, with an 8.3 percent market share. Arnold's, Nature's Own, and Pepperidge Farm were the three next best-selling brands in U.S. supermarkets and discount stores. The North American Fresh Bakery division held a number one ranking in hot dog and hamburger buns, and produced and marketed the EarthGrains brand of packaged bread. The company's ability to negotiate with supermarket buyers to increase shelf space allocated for its bakery products accounted for much of the growth in bakery sales. In several cases, Sara Lee's fresh bakery division had been able to increase space on the bread aisle from 1.5 feet to 4.0 feet. Average weekly sales tripled in stores where Sara Lee gained shelf space. Poor economic conditions in the United States had slowed the division's growth in revenues considerably, but the company had been able to improve

Exhibit 4   Summary of Sara Lee Corporation's Annual Financial Performance, 2004–2010 ($ millions, except per share data)

	Years Ended						
	July 3, 2010	June 27, 2009	June 28, 2008	June 30, 2007	July 1, 2006	July 2, 2005	July 3, 2004
Results of Operations							
Continuing and discontinued operations							
Net sales	$10,793	$12,881	$13,212	$12,278	$15,944	$19,254	$19,566
Operating income	918	713	260	566	911	1,120	1,723
Income before income taxes	795	588	160	419	683	934	1,542
Income (loss)	642	364	(41)	426	410	731	1,272
Income (loss) per share of common stock							
Basic	$0.92	$0.52	($0.06)	$0.58	$0.54	$0.93	$1.61
Diluted	$0.92	$0.52	($0.06)	$0.57	$0.53	$0.92	$1.59
Income (loss) from discontinued operations	(199)	—	(14)	62	(256)	(12)	—
Gain (loss) on sale of discontinued operations	84	—	(24)	16	401	—	—
Net income (loss)	527	364	(79)	504	555	719	1,272
Net income (loss) per share of common stock							
Basic	$0.74	$0.52	($0.11)	$0.68	$0.72	$0.91	—
Diluted	$0.73	$0.52	($0.11)	$0.68	$0.72	$0.90	—
Financial Position							
Total assets	$ 8,836	$ 9,417	$10,830	$12,190	$14,522	$14,412	$14,883
Total debt	2,781	2,820	3,188	4,267	5,959	4,754	5,295
Per Common Share							
Dividends declared	$0.44	$0.44	$0.42	$0.40	$0.79	$0.78	$0.75
Book value at year-end	2.25	2.93	3.98	3.61	3.22	3.74	3.71
Market value at year-end	13.99	9.58	12.18	17.4	16.02	19.65	23.17
Shares used in the determination of net income per share							
Basic (in millions)	688	701	715	741	766	789	788
Diluted (in millions)	691	703	715	743	768	796	798
Other Information—Continuing Operations Only							
Net cash flow from operating activities	$631	$900	$596	$492	$1,232	$1,314	$2,042
Depreciation	361	383	398	420	541	563	561
Capital expenditures	375	379	509	631	625	538	530
Number of employees	33,000	41,000	44,000	52,000	109,000	137,000	150,400

Source: Sara Lee Corporation Annual Reports, various years.

Exhibit 5   Financial Summary for Sara Lee Corporation's Continuing Operations, 2006–2010 ($ millions, except per share data)

			Years Ended		
	July 3, 2010	June 27, 2009	June 28, 2008	June 30, 2007	July 1, 2006
Results of Operations, Continuing Operations Only					
Continuing operations only					
Net sales	$10,793	$10,882	$10,949	$ 9,964	$ 9,371
Operating income	918	487	(51)	305	211
Income before income taxes	795	358	(156)	161	(26)
Income (loss)	642	225	(276)	258	(18)
Income (loss) per share of common stock					
Basic	$0.92	$0.31	$(0.39)	$0.35	$(0.02)
Diluted	0.92	0.31	(0.39)	0.34	(0.02)
Income (loss) from discontinued operations	(199)	155	236	228	184
Gain (loss) on sale of discontinued operations	84	—	(24)	16	401
Net income (loss)	527	380	(64)	502	568
Net income (loss) attributable to Sara Lee	506	364	(79)	504	555
Net income (loss) per share of common stock					
Basic	$0.74	$0.52	($0.11)	$0.68	$0.72
Diluted	$0.73	$0.52	($0.11)	$0.68	$0.72
Financial Position					
Total assets	$ 8,836	$ 9,419	$10,831	$11,755	$14,660
Total debt	2,781	2,804	3,164	4,204	5,898
Per Common Share					
Dividends declared	$0.44	$0.44	$0.42	$0.50	$0.59
Book value at year-end	2.25	2.93	3.98	3.51	3.22
Market value at year-end	13.99	9.58	12.18	17.4	16.02
Shares used in the determination of net income per share					
Basic (in millions)	688	701	715	741	766
Diluted (in millions)	691	703	715	743	768
Other Information—Continuing Operations Only					
Net cash flow from operating activities	$631	$640	$385	$268	$122
Depreciation	361	351	367	363	351
Capital expenditures	375	359	490	568	396
Number of employees	33,000	35,000	37,000	38,000	41,000

Source: Sara Lee Corporation 2010 Annual Report.

Exhibit 6   **Net Sales and Operating Profits for Sara Lee Corporation's Business Units, 2008–2010 ($ millions)**

	2010	2009	2008
Net Sales			
North American Retail	$ 2,818	$ 2,767	$ 2,613
North American Fresh Bakery	2,128	2,200	2,028
North American Foodservice	1,873	2,092	2,186
International Beverage	3,221	3,062	3,238
International Bakery	785	795	934
Total business segments	10,825	10,916	10,999
Intersegment sales	(32)	(34)	(50)
Net sales	$10,793	$10,882	$10,949
Income (Loss) from Continuing Operations before Income Taxes			
North American Retail	$346	$ 253	$ 149
North American Fresh Bakery	44	26	55
North American Foodservice	125	36	(324)
International Beverage	592	493	551
International Bakery	(14)	(194)	(346)
Total operating segment income	$ 1,093	$ 614	$ 85

Source: Presentations by Sara Lee, 2010 annual report.

operating income through pricing discipline and Project Accelerate productivity gains.

North American Foodservice

Sara Lee's North American Foodservice division marketed and sold products available to consumers in North American supermarkets to food service distributors such as U.S. Foodservice and Sodexho. North American Foodservice also sold meat, bakery, and coffee products to national restaurant chains like Sonic, Dunkin' Donuts, Waffle House, Quiznos, and Burger King. Most of the division's sales were standard Sara Lee, Jimmy Dean, Hillshire Farm, Ball Park, and State Fair branded products, although the division did customize meat and bakery products for its largest customers. Coffee brands sold to North American food service accounts included Douwe Egberts and Superior Coffee. North American Foodservice also provided commercial-grade coffee machines and espresso makers to food service customers.

The food service industry was expected to be a considerable growth opportunity for Sara Lee as Americans continued to eat a higher percentage of meals away from home. However, the recession that began in late 2007 and resulting reduced consumer spending that continued into 2010 had dramatically decreased spending at restaurants. Even though division sales had declined from nearly $2.2 billion in sales in 2008 to approximately $1.9 billion in sales in 2010, the division had preserved market share in key product categories. North American Foodservice held a 65 percent market share in liquid coffee and tea sold to food service customers, a 52 percent market share in pies, a 19 percent market share in cakes, and a 20 percent share of refrigerated dough sold to food service customers. The division also operated a route sales coffee business and distributed a number of low-margin sauces and dressings sold to restaurants that were both slated for divestiture.

Sara Lee's food service division had benefited from the innovations developed by Sara Lee's retail divisions since the food service trends mirrored those in the grocery industry. For example, presliced deli meats that were intended to satisfy consumers' desire for convenience also made sense for food service accounts. Food service customers had found that it was more cost-effective and more sanitary to purchase presliced meat than to purchase bulk meat for restaurant employees to slice. Sara Lee's dessert and bakery brands like Sara Lee, Bistro Collection, and Chef Pierre also benefited from innovations developed for consumers.

International Beverage

Sara Lee's International Beverage business included teas and coffee products marketed in Europe, Australia, New Zealand, and Brazil. The strength of the company's coffee brands—which included Douwe Egberts, Maison du Café, Marcilla, and Senseo—made it the leader in retail sales of coffee in the Netherlands, Belgium, Hungary, Denmark, and Brazil in 2010. Sara Lee's coffee brands were ranked second in retail coffee sales in France and Spain in 2010. The company was also the number one seller of coffee to food service customers in the United States, the Netherlands, Belgium, Hungary, Denmark, and Norway in 2010.

The global retail coffee market was expected to grow from $51 billion in 2009 to $62 billion in 2013, with instant coffee retail sales projected to increase from $19.6 billion to $23.6 billion, espresso expected to grow from $4.3 billion in 2009 to $9.9 billion in 2013, and single-serving coffee pods expected to increase from $2.9 billion to $5.3 billion between 2009 and 2013. Retail sales of traditional roast and ground coffee were projected to decline from $24.3 billion in 2009 to $23.5 billion in 2013. In 2010, Sara Lee's Senseo single-serving coffeemakers were the best-selling brand of single-serving coffee machines in Europe, with a 40 percent market share, and the sales of its coffee pods had increased from about 15,000 tons in 2004 to approximately 28,000 tons in 2009. The company launched nine new Senseo coffeemaker models in 2009 and expanded its lineup of single-serving coffees to include L'OR Espresso capsules. L'OR Espresso capsules were compatible with Nestlé's Nespresso espresso makers, which were the second-best-selling brand of single-serve coffeemaker in Europe, with a 27 percent market share in 2009.

International Bakery

Sara Lee's International Bakery division primarily consisted of the Bimbo brand of fresh, frozen, and refrigerated bread products. Bimbo fresh bread was sold in Spain and accounted for 63 percent of division sales; Bimbo frozen bread was sold only in Australia and accounted for 12 percent of division sales; and Bimbo refrigerated bread sold in France accounted 25 percent of division sales. Bimbo was the market leader among packaged breads sold in Spain in 2010, with a 37 percent market share—private-label brands collectively ranked as the second-best-selling packaged bread in Spain. Even though Bimbo was the best-selling brand of packaged bread in Spain, the deep long-term economic recession in Spain, which included an unemployment rate higher than 20 percent, had caused division sales declines and operating losses every year since 2007. The division had met with limited success marketing packaged bread in European countries outside of Spain because of a consumer preference for fresh-baked bread. Sara Lee hoped to improve financial performance within the division by introducing new products, adopting an everyday low pricing strategy and increasing bakery capacity utilization from 58 percent in 2009 to more than 80 percent in 2011 and beyond. Increased capacity utilization would be achieved through the sale or closing of underutilized facilities.

International Household & Body Care

Sara Lee's International Household & Body Care unit's Kiwi brand was the number one shoe care brand worldwide, with distribution in 200 countries and a global market share of 30 percent in 2008. Sanex was the number one brand of bath and shower products in Denmark, Spain, and France, and Ambi Pur was the best-selling air freshener in the Netherlands and Spain and the third best-selling air freshener brand in the United Kingdom, Italy, and France. The division also included various insecticide brands sold primarily in India, Malaysia, Spain, and France.

In 2009, Sara Lee announced its intention to divest its entire Household and Body Care business. During 2010, the company sold its household insecticides business in India to Godrej Consumer Products Ltd. for €185 million and its Ambi Pur air care business to Procter & Gamble for €320. Also during fiscal 2010, Sara Lee agreed to sell its global body care and European detergents business to Unilever for €1.275 billion. The transaction was expected to close by the end of the 2010 calendar year. The sale of the company's remaining insecticide brands to S. C. Johnson and Son for €153.5 million was also expected to close by the end of the 2010 calendar year. The company had identified several potential buyers for the remainder of its Household and Body Care unit, which included Kiwi shoe care products sold internationally and Endust and Ty-D-Bol cleaning products sold in the Asia-Pacific region. Analysts believed that Sara Lee could expect $300 million to $400 million from the sale of Kiwi. The amount Sara Lee might receive for the Endust and Ty-D-Bol brands was less definite.

EXPECTATIONS IN EARLY 2011

Sara Lee's top management believed that the company's restructured business lineup and corporate strategy initiatives—both those planned and those under way—would deliver strong increases in shareholder value in 2011 and 2012. Sara Lee's interim CEO, Marcel Smits, expected

that the company's divestiture of its Household and Body Care businesses, the repurchase of $360 million of shares of common stock in 2011, and cumulative Project Accelerate benefits of $350 million to $400 million expected by 2012 would lead to improvements in earnings per share of $0.15 to $0.20. In addition, the company planned to restructure the corporate functions of its International Beverage and Bakery businesses to eliminate 390 positions and reduce overhead by €30 million by fiscal 2013. The company intended for most of its growth to come from the further development and growth of its premium brands such as L' OR Espresso and Senseo as well as its market-leading brands like Ball Park, Hillshire Farm, Jimmy Dean, and Sara Lee. The company also expected that an increased emphasis on wellness and nutrition would allow it to increase sales of its meat and bakery products in North America and Europe. The company expected to contain growth in operating expenses through a continued emphasis on efficiency, focusing on its most promising markets, and by reducing inventories. Smits and his chief lieutenants believed that the company was fully capable of delivering significant gains in shareholder value as the search continued for a permanent CEO.

ENDNOTES

[1] Sara Lee, press release, February 10, 2005.
[2] Sara Lee, press releases on February 10, 2005, and February 25, 2005.
[3] Sara Lee, press release, August 10, 2005.
[4] Sara Lee, press release, October 26, 2005.
[5] Sara Lee, press release, November 14, 2005.
[6] Sara Lee, press release, November 22, 2005.
[7] Sara Lee, fiscal 2006 10-K report.
[8] Sara Lee, press release, June 27, 2006.
[9] Jane Sasseen, "How Sara Lee Left Hanes in Its Skivvies," *BusinessWeek*, September 18, 2006, p. 40.

Smucker's in 2011: Expanding the Business Lineup

John E. Gamble
University of South Alabama

As the first decade of the 21st century began, the J. M. Smucker Company was the leading producer and marketer of jams, jellies, and preserves in the United States, Canada, and Australia; however, the company was quickly becoming less relevant within the global processed foods industry. The company's 2001 annual sales of $651 million paled in comparison to those of such food industry giants as Nestlé, with revenues of 84.7 billion Swiss francs ($61.3 billion); Unilever, with sales of 51.5 billion euros; and Kraft Foods, with revenues of $33.8 billion. In addition, the company's small size and limited product line—which included fruit spreads, natural and organic beverages, ice cream toppings, natural peanut butters, and a few specialty items—put it at a bargaining disadvantage with grocery retailers, which were becoming fewer in number and larger in size as a wave of consolidation had resulted in the top five supermarket chains accounting for 40 percent of all U.S. grocery sales in 2002. Smucker had little ability to bargain for price increases or demand better in-store product placement with chains like Kroger, whose annual grocery sales in 2001 reached nearly $50 billion, or with other leading chains, whose 2001 annual sales reached $20 billion or more.

The larger food producers like Nestlé, Kraft Foods, General Mills, and Campbell Soup had begun acquiring smaller food companies and sometimes merging with equally large food companies to better negotiate with the strengthening supermarket chains. A record number of mergers and acquisitions occurred in the processed food industry between 2000 and 2002, with some mergers involving cash and stock transactions as large as $19 billion. Smucker's fourth generation of family management fully understood that the company would need to pursue its own acquisitions to survive as an independent food company in the rapidly consolidating industry. In 2001, the company identified two business lines slated by Procter & Gamble (P&G) for divestiture that it believed would fit within its range of management skills and allow it to become a larger, stronger competitor in the food industry: Jif and Crisco. In June 2002, Smucker acquired these two brands in a $786 million stock swap. Smucker brothers and co-CEOs Timothy and Richard Smucker believed the merger would allow J. M. Smucker to ultimately grow to $3 billion through a three-legged growth strategy that included organic sales growth of existing brands, new product introductions, and further strategic acquisitions that fit within the company's vision. Richard Smucker said, "Our strategy is to own and market Number 1 brands, sold in the center of the store, in North America. The real money in supermarkets is made in the middle of the store, where processed foods and well-known brands reign supreme."[1]

Smucker's 2004 acquisition of International Multifoods for $840 million gave it two additional center-of-the-store food brands—Pillsbury and Hungry Jack—and its 2008 acquisition of Folgers from P&G for $3.7 billion made it one of North America's largest producers of breakfast foods and beverages. The series of acquisitions gave Smucker the number one brands of coffee, jams and jellies, peanut butter, and cooking oil sold in

North America in 2010. In addition, the strategy had allowed the company's sales to increase from $632 million in 2000 to $4.6 billion in 2010. Its profits over the same 10-year period had increased from $36 million to $494 million, and its stock price had provided shareholders with a 309 percent total return compared to a –15 percent return for the S&P 500 between 2000 and 2010.

However, in early fiscal 2011 there was still concern among some analysts that the company remained much smaller than its rivals in the processed foods industry and may not have gained sufficient bargaining leverage when negotiating with even more powerful retailers. For example, while Smucker's revenues had increased from $651 million in 2001 to $4.6 billion in 2010, Nestlé's revenues had increased from $61.3 billion to nearly $100 billion over the same period. Also, the five largest supermarket chains had consolidated further to account for more than 70 percent of industry sales in 2010. In fact, Walmart had become an even stronger buyer in the industry, with 2010 grocery sales of $154 billion and a 35 percent share of the U.S. supermarket industry's total revenues.

COMPANY HISTORY

The J. M. Smucker Company was founded in 1879 when Jerome Monroe Smucker built a steam-powered cider mill in Orville, Ohio. Smucker soon found that his state-of-the-art mill could produce far more apple cider than he could sell; he used a family recipe for apple butter to expand his product line rather than waste the excess cider. Smucker's apple butter became a hit within the local community, and by 1920 the company began building a complete line of jams, jellies, and preserves to capitalize on the success. Smucker began to distribute its products nationally in 1942, and it expanded its product line again to include ice cream toppings in 1948. The company, which prided itself on meeting or exceeding consumer expectations, introduced reduced-calorie fruit spreads in 1958 as Americans began to become more aware of caloric intake. Smucker went public in 1959 and grew rapidly under the direction of Jerome Smucker's grandson Paul Smucker, who oversaw the introduction of tomato ketchup in 1963, the sale of Smucker's fruit spreads to Kellogg's for Pop-Tarts filling in 1964, the introduction of peanut butter in 1965, and the introduction of Smucker's Goober striped peanut butter and jelly in 1968.

Paul Smucker also led the company to introduce fruit-flavored breakfast syrups, low-sugar preserves, and natural peanut butters during the 1970s and began acquiring other food companies to diversify beyond spreads, peanut butter, and condiments in the 1980s. The company acquired Magic Shell (the maker of an ice cream topping that hardened as soon as it was cooled by the ice cream) in 1982 and Knudsen & Sons (a leading producer of fruit and vegetable juices) in 1984. When Paul Smucker retired from active management of the company in 1987, his two sons, Tim and Richard Smucker, became responsible for the company's day-to-day operations. The two brothers represented the fourth generation of Smucker family management and carried out the acquisitions of Good Morning in 1988 and Henry Jones Foods in 1989. Good Morning was a producer of marmalade and dessert toppings sold in Canada and Henry Jones was the leading manufacturer and marketer of jams and jellies in Australia. The company introduced Simply 100% Fruit in 1987 and Smucker's Light Preserves in 1990. Laura Scudder's Natural Peanut Butter and fruit juice maker After The Fall were acquired in 1994, while Adams Peanut Butter was acquired in 1997. The company introduced Smucker's Snackers (pre-packaged cracker snack kits) in 1997 and Uncrust-ables (crustless prepared peanut butter and jelly sandwiches) in 2000. Smucker had acquired pie-maker Mrs. Smith's from Philip Morris/Kraft in 1997 but divested it two years later. In 2001, Smucker acquired the formulated fruit and vegetable preparation businesses of International Flavors and Fragrances to expand its industrial fruit fillings business, which was among its fastest-growing businesses during the early 2000s. J. M. Smucker Company was listed in the top quartile of *Fortune*'s "100 Best Companies to Work For" every year since the magazine created the ranking in 1997.

THE CREATION OF THE NEW J. M. SMUCKER COMPANY

The 2002 acquisition of P&G brands Jif and Crisco transformed J. M. Smucker. Jams, jellies, and preserves historically made up more than 50 percent of the company's sales; following the transformation, approximately 25 percent of Smucker's revenues came from the sale of fruit spreads, 25 percent from peanut butter sales, 25 percent from the sale of shortening and edible oils, and the remaining 25 percent from the sale of natural beverages, condiments, ice cream toppings, snacks, and sandwiches.

To avoid taxation on the sale of the two brands to Smucker, P&G executed a reverse Morris Trust that called for the assets of Jif and Crisco to be spun off into a new company, whose shares were immediately exchanged for Smucker shares. A traditional spin-off or sale of assets would have left P&G and its shareholders exposed to considerable taxation, since its cost basis in Crisco and Jif would have been based on investments dating from 1911 (in Crisco's case) and 1955 (in the case of Jif). The innovativeness of the transaction was recognized by *Investment Dealers Digest,* which honored the engineers of the merger with its 2002 Best Overall Deal and 2002 M&A Breakthrough Deal Awards. Once the transaction was completed, on June 1, 2002, each P&G shareholder received one share of the new J. M. Smucker Company stock for every 50 shares of P&G he or she held. Smucker shareholders received 0.9451 of a share of the new J. M. Smucker for every 1.0 Smucker share held on May 31, 2002. The new J. M. Smucker Company shares began trading on June 3, 2002. The Smucker family and the company's top management team expected the merger ultimately to boost the company's revenues to $3 billion, while the upper bound of long-term revenues would have been approximately $1 billion without the acquisitions.

The $840 million acquisition of International Multifoods in June 2004 gave Smucker such products as Pillsbury baking mixes and ready-to-spread frostings; Hungry Jack pancake mixes, syrup, and potato side dishes; Martha White baking mixes; and Pet evaporated milk and dry creamer. In Canada, Smucker gained Robin Hood flour and baking mixes and Bick's pickles and condiments, which were both the number one brands in their product categories. The acquisition also gave the J. M. Smucker Company the Golden Temple brand of flour and rice.

Immediately following its acquisition of International Multifoods, Smucker divested businesses and assets that did not fit its strategy of focusing on center-of-the-store brands sold in North America. Between 2004 and 2006, the company divested its Brazilian and Australian jams and jellies businesses, and its industrial ingredients businesses in the United States and Canada. While the businesses operating in Brazil and Australia were divested because of their poor geographic fit with the company's strategic priorities, Smucker exited the industrial ingredients business because of the historically low margins involved with supplying fruit filling to such companies as Kellogg's and Groupe Danone, the producer of Dannon yogurts. The company also divested the Hungry Jack potato side dish product line gained in the International Multifoods acquisition to Basic American Foods in March 2010 for an undisclosed amount.

After divesting businesses with low strategic priority, the company acquired a variety of both small and large businesses. In 2006, Smucker acquired the White Lily Foods Company, which produced all-purpose and specialty flours, cornmeal, muffin mixes, grits, and frozen biscuits. The sales of White Lily totaled approximately $33 million in 2005. In 2007, in a $248 million transaction involving cash and the assumption of debt, the company acquired Eagle Family Foods, which was the largest producer of sweetened condensed and evaporated milk in the United States and Canada. During 2008, Smucker acquired Knott's Berry Farm jams, jellies, and preserves (with annual sales of approximately $40 million) from ConAgra; Carnation brand canned milk products sold in Canada (with annual sales of approximately $50 million) from Nestlé; and privately held Europe's Best brand of frozen fruit sold in Canada and the Eastern and Southern United States (with annual sales of about $70 million). The company made its largest ever acquisition in October 2008 when it bought the Folgers coffee business from P&G for $3.7 billion. Upon completion of the merger, Richard Smucker stated, "We are very pleased with the completion of the Folgers transaction and believe that, as the number-one retail packaged coffee brand in the United States, Folgers clearly aligns with our strategy to own and market number one food brands in North America."[2]

Exhibit 1 presents Smucker's product line and business portfolio prior to its acquisitions made between 2002 and 2008, Exhibit 2 provides a financial summary for Smucker between 2006

Exhibit 1   J. M. Smucker's Business Portfolio in 2001

Product Category	Products
Fruit spreads	Smucker's jams, jellies, and preserves; Smucker's low-sugar and sugar-free preserves; Smucker's Simply 100% Fruit spread; Smucker's cider apple butter and peach butter; Lost Acres preserves; Dickinson's preserves; Glen Ewin fruit spreads (Australia); Allowrie fruit spreads (Australia); Double Fruit spreads (Canada); IXL fruit spreads (Australia); Good Morning fruit spreads (Canada); Shirriff fruit spreads (Canada)
Peanut butter	Smucker's natural peanut butter; Smucker's Goober PB&J; Laura Scudder's peanut butter; Adams peanut butter
Snacks and sandwiches	Smucker's Snackers; Smucker's Uncrustables
Ice cream toppings	Smucker's Magic Shell; Smucker's microwaveable ice cream topping; Smucker's spoonable ice cream topping; Smucker's sugar-free ice cream topping; Smucker's sundae syrup; Smucker's Dove dark chocolate ice cream topping; Smucker's dulce de leche milk caramel ice cream topping
Specialty items	Smucker's fruit syrup; Smucker's Plate Scraper dessert topping; Smucker's sugar-free breakfast syrup; Smucker's strawberry pie glaze; Smucker's tomato ketchup; Taylor's sauces, marinades, and salad dressings (Australia)
Beverages	R. W. Knudsen Family natural fruit beverages, spritzers, celebratory beverages, and sports drinks; Santa Cruz certified organic beverages; After The Fall natural fruit drinks, spritzers, and celebratory beverages; Rocket Juice herbal fruit drinks

Source: J. M. Smucker Company website.

Exhibit 2   Financial Summary for J. M. Smucker Company, 2006–2010 ($ thousands, except per share amounts)

	Year Ended April 30				
	2010	2009	2008	2007	2006
Statements of Income					
Net sales	$4,605,289	$3,757,933	$2,524,774	$2,148,017	$2,154,726
Net income	494,138	265,953	170,379	157,219	143,354
Financial Position					
Total assets	$7,974,853	$8,192,161	$3,129,881	$2,693,823	$2,649,744
Cash and cash equivalents	283,570	456,693	171,541	199,541	71,832
Long-term debt	900,000	910,000	789,684	392,643	428,602
Shareholders' equity	5,326,320	4,939,931	1,799,853	1,795,657	1,728,059
Other Data					
Capital expenditures	$ 136,983	$ 108,907	$ 76,430	$ 57,002	$ 63,580
Weighted-average shares	118,951,434	85,448,592	56,641,810	56,844,151	58,154,704
Weighted-average shares—assuming dilution	119,081,445	85,547,530	56,873,492	57,233,399	58,590,065
Earnings per common share:					
Net income	$4.15	$3.11	$3.01	$2.77	$2.47
Net income—assuming dilution	$4.15	$3.11	$3.00	$2.75	$2.45
Dividends declared per common share	$1.45	$6.31	$1.22	$1.14	$1.09

Source: J. M. Smucker Company, 2010 10-K report.

and 2010, and Exhibit 3 presents the performance of Smucker's stock from September 2000 through October 2010.

OVERVIEW OF THE PROCESSED FOODS INDUSTRY

The processed food industry was composed of many subsectors, each with differing growth expectations, profit margins, competitive intensity, and business risks. Industry participants were constantly challenged to respond to changing consumer preferences and to fend off maneuvers from rival firms to gain market share. Competitive success started with creating a portfolio of attractive products and brands; from there, success depended largely on (1) the ability to achieve organic sales growth for existing brands and improve profit margins and (2) product-line growth through acquisitions (it was generally considered cheaper to buy a successful brand than to build and grow a new one from scratch). Advertising and promotions were considered a key to increasing unit volume and helping drive consumers toward higher margin products; sustained volume growth also usually entailed gaining increased international exposure for a company's

Exhibit 3   **Performance of J. M. Smucker Company's Stock Price, September 2000–October 2010**

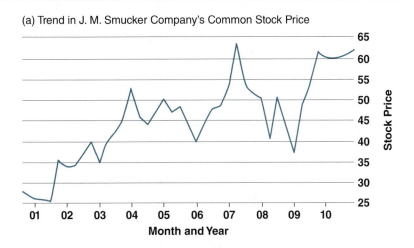

(a) Trend in J. M. Smucker Company's Common Stock Price

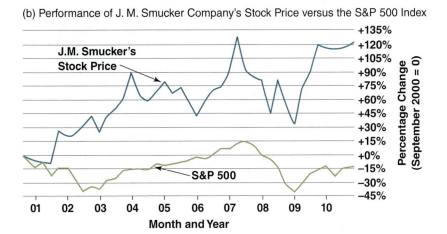

(b) Performance of J. M. Smucker Company's Stock Price versus the S&P 500 Index

brands. Improving a company's profit margins included not only shifting sales to products with higher margins but also boosting efficiency and driving down unit costs.

The processed foods industry was highly consolidated, with manufacturers holding vast brand portfolios. For example, Nestlé was the world's largest food company in 2010, with 2009 worldwide sales of $99.4 billion and thousands of brands sold in more than 140 countries. Similarly, General Mills, the world's sixth-largest processed food company, recorded revenues of $16 billion on the sale of such brands as Cheerios, Yoplait, Fibre One, Progresso, Nature Valley, Hamburger Helper, Green Giant, Old El Paso, and Hägen-Dazs in more than 100 countries. Many of the leading food products companies also had food service divisions that marketed company products to restaurants, cafeterias, and institutions (e.g., schools, hospitals, college student centers, private country clubs, corporate facilities) to gain access to the away-from-home food market. Three factors were driving consolidation pressures in the food industry—slower growth rates in the food sector, rapid consolidation in retail grocery chains (which enhanced the buying power of supermarket chains and enhanced their ability to demand and receive slotting fees for allocating manufacturers favorable shelf space on their grocery aisles), and fierce competition between branded food manufacturers and private-label manufacturers.

Industry Growth Rate

The earnings growth picture for many food companies had been bleak for several years, yet it had improved to some extent in the face of the harsh economic conditions that began in the United States in late 2007. While food companies had been forced to compete more aggressively on price, sales volume had grown on average by 1–2 percent (slightly higher than the 1 percent population growth) as Americans ate more meals at home. Throughout the 1990s, the increase in the number of women working outside the home and the growing number of single-parent households had caused a steady increase in the number of meals eaten away from home—therefore reducing at-home outlays for food and beverages. However, the need for families to cut budgets

during the recession had increased the number of meals prepared and consumed in-home from 817 per year in 2002 to 877 per year in 2010. The growth rate for food and household products across the industrialized countries of Europe was in the 2 percent range, although the recessions in most European countries had ended by 2009. Food industry growth rates in emerging or less-developed countries were more attractive (in the 3–4 percent range), prompting most growth-minded food companies to focus their efforts on markets in Latin America, Asia, Eastern Europe, and Africa.

Consolidation in the Retail Grocery Industry

The consolidation of the $430.3 billion U.S. supermarket industry resulted in approximately 70 percent of industry sales being accounted for by Walmart, Kroger, Safeway, Supervalu/Albertson's, and Ahold USA (Stop & Shop, Giant, and Martin's) in 2010. In 2001, only 40 percent of industry sales were accounted for by the top five grocers and, in 1995, the five largest grocers accounted for just over 25 percent of industry sales. In large part, the consolidation had occurred because of Walmart's entry into the retail grocery industry and attempts by traditional grocers to increase size to counter Walmart's purchasing power. Walmart did not enter the grocery industry until 1988, with the opening of its first Supercenter, but became the co-leader of the supermarket industry in 2001 when its annual grocery sales reached $46.7 billion. Over the next decade, Walmart nearly tripled its number of Supercenters and added new formats such as its smaller Neighborhood Markets to increase revenues to more than $150 billion by 2010. Exhibit 4 presents sales and number of store locations for the 10 largest supermarket chains in the United States for 2001 and 2010.

Increased Price Competition

Growing shopper confidence in the leading supermarket chains had opened the way for retail chains to effectively market their own house-brand versions of name-brand products—provided the house brand was priced attractively below the competing name brands. Indeed, with

Exhibit 4 Estimated Sales and Number of Supermarket Locations for the Top 10 U.S. Grocers, 2001 and 2010

Rank	Company	2010		2001	
		Estimated Sales ($ millions)	Number of Supermarket Locations	Estimated Sales ($ millions)	Number of Supermarket Locations
1	Walmart[1,2]	$154,249	2,906	$28,247	1,103
2	Kroger[1]	62,608	2,470	46,726	2,429
3	Safeway	35,022	1,486	31,451	1,568
4	Supervalu/Albertson's	31,461	1,516	34,347	2,026
5	Ahold USA	24,102	708	24,104	1,245
6	Publix	21,645	1,012	14,624	687
7	Food Lion/Delhaize	18,788	1,604	15,231	1,464
8	H-E-B Grocery	11,641	280	7,057	278
9	Great A&P Tea	9,181	408	8,540	519
10	Meijer[1]	8,624	191	3,939	153

[1]Supercenter statistics reduced to include only traditional supermarket items.

[2]Warehouse clubs such as Sam's Club and Costco represented a substantial volume of food sales, but they have been omitted from the *Progressive Grocer* ranking because of sales to businesses and institutions in institutional packaging not directly competitive with supermarkets.

Source: "The Super 50," *Progressive Grocer* 89, no. 4 (May 2010).

the aid of checkout scanners and computerized inventory systems, retailers knew as well or better (and more quickly) than manufacturers what customers were buying and what price differential it took to induce shoppers to switch from name brands to private-label brands. These developments tilted the balance of power firmly toward retailers. Thus competition between private-label goods and name-brand goods in supermarkets was escalating rapidly, since retailers' margins on private-label goods often exceeded those on name-brand goods. The battle for market share between private-label and name-brand goods was expected to continue as private-label manufacturers improved their capabilities to match the quality of name-brand products, while also gaining the scale economies afforded by a growing market share.

Branded manufacturers were trying to counteract the bargaining power of large supermarket chains and the growth of private-label sales by building a wide-ranging portfolio of strong brands—the thesis being that retailers, fearful of irritating shoppers by not carrying well-known brands, would be forced to stock all of the manufacturer's name-brand products and, in many cases, award them favorable shelf space. At the same time, because they faced pressures on profit margins in negotiating with retailers and combating the competition from rival brands (both name-brand rivals and private-label rivals), manufacturers were trying to squeeze out costs, weed out weak brands, focus their efforts on those items they believed they could develop into global brands, and reduce the number of versions of a product they manufactured wherever local market conditions allowed (to help gain scale economies in production).

SMUCKER'S APPROACH TO BUILDING SHAREHOLDER VALUE IN THE PROCESSED FOODS INDUSTRY

Smucker's corporate strategy was comprised of three main components—(1) growing the market share of its existing brands, (2) introducing new products, and (3) making strategic acquisitions. Long-term, Smucker expected net sales to increase by 6 percent annually through 2–3 percent sales growth from gains in market share, 2–3 percent sales increases resulting from future acquisitions, and a 1 percent increase in sales resulting from new product introductions. In 2010, the company was the market leader in 11 food categories, including fruit spreads and dessert toppings (Smucker's), roasted and ground coffee (Folgers), health and natural beverages (Knudsen), peanut butter (Jif), cooking oil (Crisco), and condensed and evaporated milk (Eagle Brand). Bick's, Europe's Best, Robin Hood, and Carnation were number one brands in their categories in the processed foods industry in Canada.

The company operated four divisions: the U.S. Retail Coffee Market division included Folgers and Millstone coffee products sold in supermarkets in the United States; the U.S. Retail Consumer Market division included Jif, Smucker's, and Hungry Jack brands; the U.S. Retail Oils and Baking Market division included Crisco, Pillsbury, White Lily, Eagle Brand, and Martha White; and the Special Markets division included Knudsen natural beverages, sales of Smucker brands to U.S. food service accounts, and all international sales, including those in Canada. In 2010, Canadian sales accounted for 44 percent of Special Market sales, food service accounted for 36 percent of division sales, natural foods accounted for 14 percent of business unit sales, and international sales outside of Canada accounted for 6 percent of Special Market sales. Revenue contributions for the Smucker's various product categories are presented in Exhibit 5. Selected financial statistics for the company's four business units and geographic segments are provided in Exhibit 6.

The company spent between $50 million and $77 million annually between 2006 and 2009 to advertise its products; in 2010, it increased advertising by 70 percent, to $131 million. Smucker developed more than 15 new commercials in 2010 that were built around its well-known slogans like "With a name like Smucker's, it has to be good," "Choosy moms choose Jif," and "The best part of wakin' up is Folgers in your cup." The company's advertising program also included digital marketing initiatives such as search-based ads,

banner ads on websites and mobile phones, and ads on social networking sites such as Facebook and Twitter.

Smucker's market share and sales growth was also aided in 2010 by the introductions of such new products as Pillsbury sugar-free cake mixes and frostings, Smucker's Orchard's Finest premium fruit preserves, Jif To Go lunchbox snacks, and Smucker's Snack'n Waffles. The company also expanded its lineup of coffee brands by entering into a licensing agreement with Dunkin' Donuts that would allow Smucker to begin sell Dunkin' Donuts branded ground coffee in U.S. supermarkets. Smucker's Dunkin' Donuts branded ground coffee recorded sales of $250 million in 2010. The company also entered into a manufacturing and distribution agreement with Green Coffee Roasters and Keurig that allowed Smucker to introduce Folgers Gourmet Selections and Millstone premium coffees in containers that would be compatible with Keurig's innovative K-Cup coffee system. Folgers and Millstone K-Cup products were launched in U.S. supermarkets in late 2010. The company expected Folgers and Millstone

Exhibit 5   J. M. Smucker Company's Sales Contribution by Product Line, 2008–2010

	Year Ended April 30		
	2010	2009	2008
Coffee	**40%**	25%	—%
Peanut butter	**12**	14	19
Shortening and oils	**8**	11	14
Fruit spreads	**8**	9	13
Baking mixes and frostings	**6**	8	10
Canned milk	**5**	7	10
Flour and baking ingredients	**5**	7	8
Portion control	**3**	4	5
Juices and beverages	**3**	3	5
Uncrustables frozen sandwiches	**3**	3	5
Toppings and syrups	**2**	3	4
Other	**5**	6	7
Total	**100%**	100%	100%

Source: J. M. Smucker Company, 2010 10-K report.

Exhibit 6 **Selected Financial Statistics for J. M. Smucker Company's Domestic and International Segments, 2008–2010 ($ thousands)**

	Year Ended April 30		
	2010	**2009**	**2008**
Net Sales			
U.S. Retail Coffee Market	$1,700,458	$ 855,571	$ —
U.S. Retail Consumer Market	1,125,280	1,103,264	998,556
U.S. Retail Oils and Baking Market	905,719	995,474	875,991
Special Markets	873,832	803,624	650,227
Total net sales	$4,605,289	$3,757,933	$2,524,774
Segment Profit			
U.S. Retail Coffee Market	$ 550,786	$ 240,971	$ —
U.S. Retail Consumer Market	274,969	249,313	233,201
U.S. Retail Oils and Baking Market	142,161	124,150	99,626
Special Markets	148,768	111,741	92,019
Total segment profit	$ 1,116,684	$ 726,175	$ 424,846
Interest income	2,793	6,993	13,259
Interest expense	(65,187)	(62,478)	(42,145)
Amortization	(73,657)	(38,823)	(4,073)
Impairment charges	(11,658)	(1,491)	—
Share-based compensation expense	(20,687)	(14,043)	(11,531)
Restructuring costs	(5,711)	(10,229)	(4,747)
Merger and integration costs	(33,692)	(72,666)	(7,967)
Corporate administrative expenses	(181,132)	(133,313)	(115,618)
Other unallocated income (expense)	3,000	(4,060)	2,764
Income before income taxes	$ 730,753	$ 396,065	$ 254,788
Net Sales			
Domestic	$4,167,042	$3,353,362	$2,199,433
International:			
Canada	$ 385,870	$ 356,300	$ 278,447
All other international	52,377	48,271	46,894
Total international	$ 438,247	$ 404,571	$ 325,341
Total net sales	$4,605,289	$3,757,933	$2,524,774
Assets			
Domestic	$7,591,931	$7,670,192	$2,547,609
International:			
Canada	$ 376,788	$ 514,993	$ 573,829
All other international	6,134	6,976	8,443
Total international	$ 382,922	$ 521,969	$ 582,272
Total assets	$7,974,853	$8,192,161	$3,129,881
Long-lived assets:			
Domestic	$6,543,440	$6,406,085	$1,895,494
International:			
Canada	$ 207,517	$ 386,948	$ 457,345
All other international	266	237	835
Total international	$ 207,783	$ 387,185	$ 458,180
Total long-lived assets	$6,751,223	$6,793,270	$2,353,674

Source: J. M. Smucker Company, 2010 10-K report.

K-Cup coffee sales to achieve success rapidly since single-serve coffee products accounted for 20 percent of the $6.2 billion U.S. at-home coffee market in 2010.

All of the company's coffee products were produced in plants located in New Orleans, Louisiana; Sherman, Texas; and Kansas City, Missouri. For the most part, Smucker's management had been very successful in blending the manufacturing operations of its acquisitions with the operations of its various business segments. The company planned to spend approximately $220 million in 2011 to streamline its coffee and fruit spreads supply chain and to begin construction on a new plant in Orrville, Ohio, for production of fruit spreads, ice cream toppings, and syrup. Smucker planned to close its coffee plant located in Sherman, Texas, in 2011 and its coffee plant in Kansas City, Missouri, in 2012. The new Orrville, Ohio, plant was expected to begin

production in 2012, which would allow the company to close its plants producing fruit spreads, ice cream toppings, and syrup located in Memphis, Tennessee, and Saint Marie, Quebec. Exhibit 7 presents a list of Smucker manufacturing facilities in 2002 and products produced at each plant.

SMUCKER'S PERFORMANCE DURING FISCAL 2011

The company's results looked promising through the first three months of fiscal 2011 despite the lingering effects of the economic downturn in the United States. Its revenues were unchanged from the same period in fiscal 2010, but operating income had grown by 5 percent, from $185 million in the first quarter of fiscal 2010 to $195 million

Exhibit 7   **J. M. Smucker Company's Processing and Manufacturing Locations**

U.S. Locations	Products Produced/Processed
Chico, California	Fruit and vegetable juices, beverages, and natural food products
Cincinnati, Ohio	Shortening and oils
El Paso, Texas	Canned milk
Grandview, Washington	Fruit
Havre de Grace, Maryland	Fruit and vegetable juices, beverages, and natural food products
Kansas City, Missouri	Coffee
Lexington, Kentucky	Peanut butter
Memphis, Tennessee	Fruit spreads, toppings, syrups
New Bethlehem, Pennsylvania	Peanut butter and combination peanut butter and jelly products
New Orleans, Louisiana (two facilities)	Coffee
Orrville, Ohio	Fruit spreads, toppings, syrups
Oxnard, California	Fruit
Ripon, Wisconsin	Fruit spreads, toppings, syrups, condiments
Scottsville, Kentucky	Frozen sandwiches and ready-to-eat waffles
Seneca, Missouri	Canned milk
Sherman, Texas	Coffee
Toledo, Ohio	Baking mixes, frostings, and flour
West Fargo, North Dakota	Frozen sandwiches and ready-to-eat waffles
Canada Locations	**Products Produced/Processed**
Delhi Township, Ontario	Pickles
Dunnville, Ontario	Pickles and relish condiments
Sherbrooke, Quebec	Canned milk
Ste. Marie, Quebec	Fruit spreads, sweet spreads

Source: J. M. Smucker Company, 2010 10-K report.

in the first quarter of fiscal 2011. In addition, the company's operating profit margin had improved from 17.6 percent during the first quarter of fiscal 2010 to 18.7 percent in the first quarter of fiscal 2011. Year-over-year net income had improved by 14 percent between the first quarters of fiscal 2010 and fiscal 2011. The company's strong performance during early 2011 and since 2006 had provided more than $1.3 billion in free cash flow that the company intended to use to fund a $220 million share repurchase plan, $190 in additional dividend payments in 2011, 2011 capital expenditures of $235 million, and acquisitions approximating $150 million annually for the next few years.

The only disappointments for the quarter were that while net sales of coffee products sold in the United States increased by 7 percent during the quarter, sales recorded by the U.S. Retail Consumer Market business unit and U.S. Retail Oils and Baking Market declined by 4 percent and 11 percent, respectively, between the first quarters of fiscal 2010 fiscal 2011. Net sales for the Special Markets business unit remained unchanged between the first quarter of fiscal 2010 and the first quarter of fiscal 2011. Segment operating profit for Special Markets improved by 31 percent between the first quarter of fiscal 2010 and the first quarter of fiscal 2011, while quarterly operating profits improved by 1 percent for the U.S. Retail Coffee Market, improved by 8 percent in the U.S. Consumer Market, and declined by 12 percent for the U.S. Retail Oils and Baking Market. The ability of Smucker's expanded lineup of businesses to defend against competitive forces prevailing in the North American processed foods industry and contribute to gains in shareholder value would become more clear as the strategy further unfolded.

Exhibit 8 presents Smucker's consolidated statements of income for 2008 through 2010. The company balance sheets for 2009 and 2010 are provided in Exhibit 9, and its statements of consolidated cash flows for 2008 through 2010 are presented in Exhibit 10.

Exhibit 8   J. M. Smucker Company Consolidated Statements of Income, 2008–2010 ($ thousands, except per share amounts)

	Year Ended April 30		
	2010	**2009**	**2008**
Net sales	$4,605,289	$3,757,933	$2,524,774
Cost of products sold	2,814,729	2,506,504	1,741,100
Cost of products sold—restructuring	3,870	—	1,510
Gross profit	1,786,690	1,251,429	782,164
Selling, distribution, and administrative expenses	878,221	673,565	486,592
Amortization	73,657	38,823	4,073
Impairment charges	11,658	1,491	—
Merger and integration costs	33,692	72,666	7,967
Other restructuring costs	1,841	10,229	3,237
Other operating (income) expense—net	(2,309)	3,624	(3,879)
Operating income	789,930	451,031	284,174
Interest income	2,793	6,993	13,259
Interest expense	(65,187)	(62,478)	(42,145)
Other income (expense)—net	3,217	519	(500)
Income before income taxes	730,753	396,065	254,788
Income taxes	236,615	130,112	84,409
Net income	$ 494,138	$ 265,953	$ 170,379
Net income per share of common stock (EPS)	$4.15	$3.11	$3.01

Source: J. M. Smucker Company, 2010 10-K report.

Exhibit 9 J. M. Smucker Company's Balance Sheets, 2009–2010 ($ thousands)

	April 30	
	2010	2009
Assets		
Current assets		
Cash and cash equivalents	$ 283,570	$ 456,693
Trade receivables, less allowance for doubtful accounts	238,867	266,037
Inventories:		
Finished products	413,269	441,033
Raw materials	241,670	162,893
	654,939	603,926
Other current assets	46,254	72,235
Total current assets	1,223,630	1,398,891
Property, plant, and equipment		
Land and land improvements	62,982	51,131
Buildings and fixtures	308,358	273,343
Machinery and equipment	997,374	901,614
Construction in progress	31,426	48,593
	1,400,140	1,274,681
Accumulated depreciation	(541,827)	(436,248)
Total property, plant, and equipment	858,313	838,433
Other noncurrent assets		
Goodwill	2,807,730	2,791,391
Other intangible assets, net	3,026,515	3,098,976
Other noncurrent assets	58,665	64,470
Total other noncurrent assets	5,892,910	5,954,837
Total assets	$7,974,853	$8,192,161

	April 30	
	2010	2009
Liabilities and Shareholders Equity		
Current liabilities		
Accounts payable	$ 179,509	$ 198,954
Accrued compensation	60,080	61,251
Accrued trade marketing and merchandising	52,536	54,281
Income taxes	75,977	17,690
Dividends payable	47,648	41,448
Current portion of long-term debt	10,000	276,726
Notes payable	—	350,000
Other current liabilities	53,147	60,886
Total current liabilities	478,897	1,061,236
Noncurrent liabilities		
Long-term debt	900,000	910,000
Defined benefit pensions	86,968	66,401
Postretirement benefits other than pensions	45,592	38,182

(Continued)

Exhibit 9   *(Concluded)*

	April 30	
	2010	2009
Deferred income taxes	1,101,506	1,145,808
Other noncurrent liabilities	35,570	30,603
Total noncurrent liabilities	2,169,636	2,190,994
Shareholders' equity		
Serial preferred shares—no par value:		
Authorized—3,000,000 shares; outstanding—none	—	—
Common shares—no par value:		
Authorized—150,000,000 shares; outstanding—119,119,152 in 2010 and 118,422,123 in 2009 (net of 9,485,013 and 10,179,989 treasury shares, respectively), at stated value	29,780	29,606
Additional capital	4,575,127	4,547,921
Retained income	746,063	424,504
Amount due from ESOP Trust	(4,069)	(4,830)
Accumulated other comprehensive loss	(20,581)	(57,270)
Total shareholders' equity	5,326,320	4,939,931
Total liabilities and shareholder's equity	$7,974,853	$8,192,161

Source: J. M. Smucker Company, 2010 10-K report.

Exhibit 10   J. M. Smucker Company's Statements of Consolidated Cash Flows, 2008–2010 ($ thousands)

	Year Ended April 30		
	2010	2009	2008
Operating Activities			
Net income	$494,138	$265,953	$170,379
Adjustments to reconcile net income to net cash provided by operations:			
Depreciation	108,225	79,450	58,497
Amortization	73,657	38,823	4,073
Impairment charges	11,658	1,491	—
Share-based compensation expense	25,949	22,105	11,531
Restructuring charges	3,870	9,093	1,510
(Gain) loss on sale of assets — net	(7,831)	2,165	1,494
Deferred income tax (benefit) expense	(39,320)	25,525	18,215
Changes in assets and liabilities, net of effect from businesses acquired:			
Trade receivables	31,521	(78,631)	(17,599)
Inventories	(46,160)	34,669	(35,022)
Other current assets	3,461	38,792	(16,208)
Accounts payable and accrued items	(34,620)	67,883	6,988
Defined benefit pension contributions	(4,436)	(34,665)	(3,538)
Income taxes	55,449	22,941	(22,302)
Other—net	37,917	(48,601)	4,900
Net cash provided by operating activities	$713,478	$446,993	$182,918

(Continued)

Exhibit 10   *(Concluded)*

	Year Ended April 30		
	2010	2009	2008
Investing Activities			
Businesses acquired, net of cash acquired	—	$ (77,335)	$(220,949)
Additions to property, plant, and equipment	$(136,983)	(108,907)	(76,430)
Proceeds from sale of businesses	19,554	—	3,407
Purchase of marketable securities	—	—	(229,405)
Sale and maturities of marketable securities	13,519	3,013	257,536
Proceeds from disposal of property, plant, and equipment	205	800	135
Other—net	(738)	5,448	(177)
Net cash used for investing activities	$(104,443)	$(176,981)	$(265,883)
Financing Activities			
Repayment of bank note payable	(350,000)	—	—
Repayments of long-term debt	(275,000)	—	(148,000)
Proceeds from long-term debt	—	400,000	400,000
Quarterly dividends paid	(166,224)	(110,668)	(68,074)
Special dividends paid	—	(274,208)	—
Purchase of treasury shares	(5,569)	(4,025)	(152,521)
Proceeds from stock option exercises	6,413	1,976	17,247
Other—net	1,832	(474)	1,187
Net cash (used for) provided by financing activities	$(788,548)	$ 12,601	$ 49,839
Effect of exchange rate changes on cash	6,390	2,539	5,126
Net (decrease) increase in cash and cash equivalents	(173,123)	285,152	(28,000)
Cash and cash equivalents at beginning of year	456,693	171,541	199,541
Cash and cash equivalents at end of year	$ 283,570	$ 456,693	$ 171,541

Source: J. M. Smucker Company, 2010 10-K report.

ENDNOTES

[1] Quoted in "Smucker's Success: Keep It in the Family," *Fortune Online Edition*, August 4, 2010.

[2] Quoted in J. M. Smucker Company, "The J. M. Smucker Company Announces Completion of Folgers Merger," press release, November 6, 2008.

Robin Hood

Joseph Lampel

New York University

It was in the spring of the second year of his insurrection against the High Sheriff of Nottingham that Robin Hood took a walk in Sherwood Forest. As he walked he pondered the progress of the campaign, the disposition of his forces, the Sheriff's recent moves, and the options that confronted him.

The revolt against the Sheriff had begun as a personal crusade. It erupted out of Robin's conflict with the Sheriff and his administration. However, alone Robin Hood could do little. He therefore sought allies, men with grievances and a deep sense of justice. Later he welcomed all who came, asking few questions and demanding only a willingness to serve. Strength, he believed, lay in numbers.

He spent the first year forging the group into a disciplined band, united in enmity against the Sheriff and willing to live outside the law. The band's organization was simple. Robin ruled supreme, making all important decisions. He delegated specific tasks to his lieutenants. Will Scarlett was in charge of intelligence and scouting. His main job was to shadow the Sheriff and his men, always alert to their next move. He also collected information on the travel plans of rich merchants and tax collectors. Little John kept discipline among the men and saw to it that their archery was at the high peak that their profession demanded. Scarlock took care of the finances, converting loot to cash, paying shares of the take, and finding suitable hiding places for the surplus. Finally, Much the Miller's son had the difficult task of provisioning the ever-increasing band of Merrymen.

The increasing size of the band was a source of satisfaction for Robin, but also a source of concern.

The fame of his Merrymen was spreading, and new recruits were pouring in from every corner of England. As the band grew larger, their small bivouac became a major encampment. Between raids the men milled about, talking and playing games. Vigilance was in decline, and discipline was becoming harder to enforce. "Why," Robin reflected, "I don't know half the men I run into these days."

The growing band was also beginning to exceed the food capacity of the forest. Game was becoming scarce, and supplies had to be obtained from outlying villages. The cost of buying food was beginning to drain the band's financial reserves at the very moment when revenues were in decline. Travelers, especially those with the most to lose, were now giving the forest a wide berth. This was costly and inconvenient to them, but it was preferable to having all their goods confiscated.

Robin believed that the time had come for the Merrymen to change their policy of outright confiscation of goods to one of a fixed transit tax. His lieutenants strongly resisted this idea. They were proud of the Merrymen's famous motto: "Rob the rich and give to the poor." "The farmers and the townspeople," they argued, "are our most important allies. How can we tax them, and still hope for their help in our fight against the Sheriff?"

Robin wondered how long the Merrymen could keep to the ways and methods of their early days. The Sheriff was growing stronger and becoming better organized. He now had the money and the men and was beginning to harass the band, probing for its weaknesses. The tide of events was beginning to turn against the Merrymen. Robin felt that the campaign must be decisively concluded before the Sheriff had a chance to deliver a mortal blow. "But how," he wondered, "could this be done?"

Robin had often entertained the possibility of killing the Sheriff, but the chances for this seemed increasingly remote. Besides, killing the Sheriff might satisfy his personal thirst for revenge, but it would not improve the situation. Robin had hoped that the perpetual state of unrest, and the Sheriff's failure to collect taxes, would lead to his removal from office. Instead, the Sheriff used his political connections to obtain reinforcement. He had powerful friends at court and was well regarded by the regent, Prince John.

Prince John was vicious and volatile. He was consumed by his unpopularity among the people, who wanted the imprisoned King Richard back. He also lived in constant fear of the barons, who had first given him the regency but were now beginning to dispute his claim to the throne. Several of these barons had set out to collect the ransom that would release King Richard the Lionheart from his jail in Austria. Robin was invited to join the conspiracy in return for future amnesty. It was a dangerous proposition. Provincial banditry was one thing, court intrigue another. Prince John had spies everywhere, and he was known for his vindictiveness. If the conspirators' plan failed, the pursuit would be relentless, and retributions swift.

The sound of the supper horn startled Robin from his thoughts. There was the smell of roasting venison in the air. Nothing was resolved or settled. Robin headed for camp promising himself that he would give these problems his utmost attention after tomorrow's raid.

Dilemma at Devil's Den

Allan R. Cohen
Babson College

Kim Johnson
Babson College

My name is Susan, and I'm a business student at Mt. Eagle College. Let me tell you about one of my worst experiences. I had a part-time job in the campus snack bar, The Devil's Den. At the time, I was 21 years old and a junior with a concentration in finance. I originally started working at the Den in order to earn some extra spending money. I had been working there for one semester and became upset with some of the happenings. The Den was managed by contract with an external company, College Food Services (CFS). What bothered me was that many employees were allowing their friends to take free food, and the employees themselves were also taking food in large quantities when leaving their shifts. The policy was that employees could eat whatever they liked free of charge while they were working, but it had become common for employees to leave with food and not to be charged for their snacks while off duty as well.

I felt these problems were occurring for several reasons. For example, employee wages were low, there was easy access to the unlocked storage room door, and inventory was poorly controlled. Also, there was weak supervision by the student managers and no written rules or strict guidelines. It

seemed that most of the employees were enjoying freebies, and it had been going on for so long that it was taken for granted. The problem got so far out of hand that customers who had seen others do it felt free to do it whether they knew the workers or not. The employees who witnessed this never challenged anyone because, in my opinion, they did not care and they feared the loss of friendship or being frowned upon by others. Apparently, speaking up was more costly to the employees than the loss of money to CFS for the unpaid food items. It seemed obvious to me that the employees felt too secure in their jobs and did not feel that their jobs were in jeopardy.

The employees involved were those who worked the night shifts and on the weekends. They were students at the college and were under the supervision of another student, who held the position of manager. There were approximately 30 student employees and 6 student managers on the staff. During the day there were no student managers; instead, a full-time manager was employed by CFS to supervise the Den. The employees and student managers were mostly freshmen and sophomores, probably because of the low wages, inconvenient hours (late weeknights and weekends), and the duties of the job itself. Employees were hard to come by; the high rate of employee turnover indicated that the job qualifications and the selection process were minimal.

The student managers were previous employees chosen by other student managers and the full-time CFS day manager on the basis of their ability to work and on their length of employment. They received no further formal training or written rules beyond what they had already

learned by working there. The student managers were briefed on how to close the snack bar at night but still did not get the job done properly. They received authority and responsibility over events occurring during their shifts as manager, although they were never actually taught how and when to enforce it! Their increase in pay was small, from a starting pay of just over minimum wage to an additional 15 percent for student managers. Regular employees received an additional nickel for each semester of employment.

Although I only worked seven hours per week, I was in the Den often as a customer and saw the problem frequently. I felt the problem was on a large enough scale that action should have been taken, not only to correct any financial loss that the Den might have experienced but also to help give the student employees a true sense of their responsibilities, the limits of their freedom, respect for rules, and pride in their jobs. The issues at hand bothered my conscience, although I was not directly involved. I felt that the employees and customers were taking advantage of the situation whereby they could "steal" food almost whenever they wanted. I believed that I had been brought up correctly and knew right from wrong, and I felt that the happenings in the Den were wrong. It wasn't fair that CFS paid for others' greediness or urges to show what they could get away with in front of their friends.

I was also bothered by the lack of responsibility of the managers to get the employees to do their work. I had seen the morning employees work very hard trying to do their jobs, in addition to the jobs the closing shift should have done. I assumed the night managers did not care or think about who worked the next day. It bothered me to think that the morning employees were suffering because of careless employees and student managers from the night before.

I had never heard of CFS mentioning any problems or taking any corrective action; therefore, I wasn't sure whether they knew what was going on, or if they were ignoring it. I was speaking to a close friend, Mack, a student manager at the Den, and I mentioned the fact that the frequently unlocked door to the storage room was an easy exit through which I had seen different quantities of unpaid goods taken out. I told him about some specific instances and said that I believed that it happened rather frequently.

Nothing was ever said to other employees about this, and the only corrective action was that the door was locked more often, yet the key to the lock was still available upon request to all employees during their shifts.

Another lack of strong corrective action I remembered was when an employee was caught pocketing cash from the register. The student was neither suspended nor threatened with losing his job (nor was the event even mentioned). Instead, he was just told to stay away from the register. I felt that this weak punishment happened not because he was a good worker but because he worked so many hours and it would be difficult to find someone who would work all those hours and remain working for more than a few months. Although a customer reported the incident, I still felt that management should have taken more corrective action.

The attitudes of the student managers seemed to vary. I had noticed that one in particular, Bill, always got the job done. He made a list of each small duty that needed to be done, such as restocking, and he made sure the jobs were divided among the employees and finished before his shift was over. Bill also stared down employees who allowed thefts by their friends or who took freebies themselves; yet I had never heard of an employee being challenged verbally, nor had anyone ever been fired for these actions. My friend Mack was concerned about theft, or so I assumed, because he had taken some action about locking the doors, but he didn't really get after employees to work if they were slacking off.

I didn't think the rest of the student managers were good motivators. I noticed that they did little work themselves and did not show much control over the employees. The student managers allowed their friends to take food for free, thereby setting bad examples for the other workers, and allowed the employees to take what they wanted even when they were not working. I thought their attitudes were shared by most of the other employees: not caring about their jobs or working hard, as long as they got paid and their jobs were not threatened.

I had let the "thefts" continue without mention because I felt that no one else really cared and may even have frowned on me for trying to take action. Management thus far had not reported significant losses to the employees so as to encourage them to watch for theft and prevent it. Management did not threaten employees with job loss, nor did they provide employees with supervision. I felt it was not my place to report the theft to management, because I was just an employee and I would be overstepping the student managers. Also, I was unsure whether management would do anything about it anyway—maybe they did not care. I felt that talking to the student managers or other employees would be useless, because they were either abusing the rules themselves or clearly aware of what was going on and just ignored it. I felt that others may have frowned on me and made it uncomfortable for me to continue working there. This would be very difficult for me, because I wanted to become a student manager the next semester and did not want to create any waves that might have prevented me from doing so. I recognized the student manager position as a chance to gain some managerial and leadership skills, while at the same time adding a great plus to my résumé when I graduated. Besides, as a student manager, I would be in a better position to do something about all the problems at the Den that bothered me so much.

What could I do in the meantime to clear my conscience of the freebies, favors to friends, and employee snacks? What could I do without ruining my chances of becoming a student manager myself someday? I hated just keeping quiet, but I didn't want to make a fool of myself. I was really stuck.

Southwest Airlines in 2010: Culture, Values, and Operating Practices

Arthur A. Thompson
The University of Alabama

John E. Gamble
The University of South Alabama

In 2010, Southwest Airlines was the market share leader in domestic air travel in the United States; it transported more passengers from U.S. airports to U.S. destinations than any other airline, and it offered more regularly scheduled domestic flights than any other airline. Southwest also had the enviable distinction of being the only major U.S. air carrier that was consistently profitable. The U.S. airline industry had lost money in 15 of the 30 years from 1980 through 2009, with combined annual losses exceeding combined annual profits by $43.2 billion. Yet Southwest had reported a profit every year since 1973, chiefly because of its zealous pursuit of low operating costs, low fares, and customer-pleasing service.

From humble beginnings as a quirky but scrappy underdog that flew mainly to secondary airports (rather than high-traffic airports like Chicago O'Hare, Dallas–Fort Worth, Atlanta Hartsfield, and New York's LaGuardia and Kennedy airports), Southwest had climbed up through the industry ranks to become a major competitive force in the domestic segment of the U.S. airline industry. It had weathered industry downturns, dramatic increases in the prices of jet fuel, cataclysmic falloffs in airline traffic due to terrorist attacks and economy-wide recessions, and fare wars and other attempts by rivals to undercut its business, all the while adding more and more flights to more and more airports. Since 2000, the number of passengers flying Southwest had increased by more than 28 million annually, whereas passenger traffic on domestic routes had declined at such carriers as American Airlines, Delta, Continental, United, and US Airways—see Exhibit 1.

COMPANY BACKGROUND

In late 1966, Rollin King, a San Antonio entrepreneur who owned a small commuter air service, marched into Herb Kelleher's law office with a plan to start a low-cost/low-fare airline that would shuttle passengers between San Antonio, Dallas, and Houston.[1] Over the years, King had heard many Texas businesspeople complain about the length of time that it took to drive between the three cities and the expense of flying the airlines currently serving these cities. His business concept for the airline was simple: attract passengers by flying convenient schedules, get passengers to their destination on time, make sure they have a good experience, and charge fares competitive with travel by automobile. Kelleher, skeptical that King's business idea was viable, dug into the possibilities during the next few weeks and concluded that a new airline was feasible; he agreed to handle the necessary legal work and also to invest $10,000 of his own funds in the venture.

In 1967, Kelleher filed papers to incorporate the new airline and submitted an application to the Texas Aeronautics Commission for the new company to begin serving Dallas, Houston, and San Antonio.[2] But rival airlines in Texas pulled every string they could to block the new airline from commencing operations, precipitating a contentious four-year parade of legal and regulatory proceedings. Herb Kelleher led the fight on the company's behalf, eventually prevailing in

Exhibit 1   Total Number of Domestic and International Passengers Traveling on Selected U.S. Airlines, 2000–2009 (in thousands)

Carrier	Total Number of Enplaned Passengers (including both passengers paying for tickets and passengers traveling on frequent flyer awards)						
	2000	2002	2004	2006	2007	2008	2009
American Airlines							
Domestic	68,319	77,489	72,648	76,813	76,581	71,539	66,142
International	17,951	16,580	18,858	21,313	21,562	21,233	19,578
Total	86,270	94,069	91,506	98,126	98,143	92,772	85,720
Continental Air Lines[1]							
Domestic	36,591	31,653	31,529	35,795	37,117	34,501	31,915
International	8,747	8,247	9,146	10,994	11,859	12,418	12,031
Total	45,338	39,900	40,675	46,789	48,976	46,919	43,946
Delta Air Lines[2]							
Domestic	97,965	83,747	79,374	63,496	61,599	59,276	55,627
International	7,596	7,036	7,416	10,020	11,435	12,339	12,118
Total	105,561	90,783	86,790	73,516	73,034	71,615	67,745
JetBlue Airways							
Domestic	1,128	5,672	11,616	18,098	20,528	20,479	20,008
International	—	—	116	408	777	1,345	2,370
Total	1,128	5,672	11,732	18,506	21,305	21,824	22,378
Northwest Airlines[2]							
Domestic	48,462	43,314	45,959	45,141	43,812	38,449	32,542
International	8,228	7,454	7,576	7,831	8,042	10,323	8,323
Total	56,690	50,768	53,535	52,972	51,854	48,772	40,865
Southwest Airlines (Domestic only, has no international flights)	**72,568**	**72,459**	**81,121**	**96,330**	**101,948**	**101,921**	**101,338**
United Air Lines[1]							
Domestic	72,450	57,830	60,081	57,229	56,402	51,661	45,571
International	10,625	9,532	9,490	10,770	11,011	11,409	10,454
Total	83,075	67,362	69,571	67,999	67,413	63,071	56,025
US Airways[3]							
Domestic	56,667	43,480	37,810	31,886	51,895	48,504	44,515
International	3,105	3,679	4,598	4,609	4,978	6,272	6,460
Total	59,772	47,159	42,408	36,495	56,873	54,776	50,975

[1]Continental and United agreed to merge in May 2010; the deal became effective on October 1, 2010.

[2]Delta Air Lines and Northwest Airlines announced their intent to merge in October 2008; however, the merger did not clear all regulatory hurdles until 2010 and combined reporting did not begin until 2010.

[3]US Airways and America West merged in September 2005; beginning in 2007, traffic data for US Airways includes the results of the merger.

Source: U.S. Department of Transportation, Bureau of Transportation Statistics, Air Carrier Statistics, Form T-100.

June 1971 after winning two appeals to the Texas Supreme Court and a favorable ruling from the U.S. Supreme Court. Kelleher recalled, "The constant proceedings had gradually come to enrage me. There was no merit to our competitors' legal assertions. They were simply trying to use their superior economic power to squeeze us dry so we would collapse before we ever got into business. I was bound and determined to show that Southwest Airlines was going to survive and was going into operation."[3]

In January 1971, Lamar Muse was brought in as Southwest's CEO to get operations under way. Muse was an aggressive, self-confident airline veteran who knew the business well and who had the entrepreneurial skills to tackle the challenges of building the airline from scratch and then competing head-on with the major carriers. Through private investors and an initial public offering of stock in June 1971, Muse raised $7 million in new capital to purchase planes and equipment and provide cash for start-up. Boeing agreed to supply three new 737s from its inventory, discounting its price from $5 million to $4 million and financing 90 percent of the $12 million deal. Muse was able to recruit a talented senior staff that included a number of veteran executives from other carriers. He particularly sought out people who were innovative, wouldn't shirk from doing things differently or unconventionally, and were motivated by the challenge of building an airline from scratch. Muse wanted his executive team to be willing to think like mavericks and not be lulled into instituting practices at Southwest that imitated what was done at other airlines.

Southwest's Struggle to Gain a Market Foothold

In June 1971, Southwest initiated its first flights with a schedule that soon included 6 round-trips between Dallas and San Antonio and 12 round-trips between Houston and Dallas. But the introductory $20 one-way fares to fly the Golden Triangle, well below the $27 and $28 fares charged by rivals, attracted disappointingly small numbers of passengers. Southwest's financial resources were stretched so thin that the company bought fuel for several months on Lamar Muse's personal credit card. Money for parts and tools was so tight that, on occasion, company personnel got on the phone with acquaintances at rival airlines operating at the terminal and arranged to borrow what was needed. Nonetheless, morale and enthusiasm remained high; company personnel displayed can-do attitudes and

adeptness at getting by on whatever resources were available.

To try to gain market visibility and drum up more passengers, Southwest decided it had to do more than run ads in the media publicizing its low fares:

- Southwest decided to have its flight hostesses dress in colorful hot pants and white knee-high boots with high heels. Recruiting ads for Southwest's first group of hostesses were headlined "Attention, Raquel Welch: You can have a job if you measure up." Two thousand applicants responded, and those selected for interviews were asked to come dressed in hot pants to show off their legs—the company wanted to hire long-legged beauties with sparkling personalities. More than 30 of Southwest's first graduating class of 40 flight attendants consisted of young women who were cheerleaders and majorettes in high school and thus had experience performing in front of people while skimpily dressed.

- A second attention-getting action was to give passengers free alcoholic beverages during daytime flights. Most passengers on these flights were business travelers. Management's thinking was that many passengers did not drink during the daytime and that with most flights being less than an hour's duration it would be cheaper to simply give the drinks away rather than collect the money.

- Taking a cue from being based at Dallas Love Field, Southwest began using the tag line "Now There's Somebody Else Up There Who Loves You." The routes between Houston, Dallas, and San Antonio became known as the Love Triangle. Southwest's planes were referred to as Love Birds, drinks became Love Potions, peanuts were called Love Bites, drink coupons were Love Stamps, and tickets were printed on Love Machines. The "Love" campaign set the tone for Southwest's approach to its customers and company efforts to make flying Southwest an enjoyable, fun, and differentiating experience. (Later, when the company went public, it chose LUV as its stock-trading symbol.)

- In order to add more flights without buying more planes, the head of Southwest's ground operations came up with a plan for ground crews to off-load passengers and baggage, refuel the plane, clean the cabin and restock the galley, on-load passengers and baggage, do the necessary preflight checks and paperwork, and push away from the gate in 10 minutes. The 10-minute turn became one of Southwest's signatures during the 1970s and 1980s. (In later years, as passenger volume grew and many flights were filled to capacity, the turnaround time gradually expanded to 25 minutes—because it took more time to unload and load a plane with 125 passengers, as compared with a half-full plane with just 60–65 passengers. Even so, the 25-minute average turnaround time at Southwest during the 2000–2009 period was shorter than the 30- to 50-minute turnaround times typical at other major airlines.)

- In late November 1971, Lamar Muse came up with the idea of offering a $10 fare to passengers on the Friday-night Houston–Dallas flight. With no advertising, the 112-seat flight sold out. This led Muse to realize that Southwest was serving two quite distinct types of travelers in the Golden Triangle market: (1) business travelers who were more time-sensitive than price-sensitive and wanted weekday flights at times suitable for conducting business and (2) price-sensitive leisure travelers who wanted lower fares and had more flexibility about when to fly.[4] He came up with a two-tier on-peak/off-peak pricing structure in which all seats on weekday flights departing before 7:00 P.M. were priced at $26 and all seats on other flights were priced at $13. Passenger traffic increased significantly—and system-wide on-peak/off-peak pricing soon became standard across the whole airline industry.

- In 1972, the company decided to move its flights in Houston from the newly opened Houston Intercontinental Airport (where it was losing money and where it took 45 minutes to get to downtown) to the abandoned Houston Hobby Airport located much closer to downtown Houston. Despite being the only carrier to fly into Houston Hobby, the results were spectacular—business travelers who flew to Houston frequently from Dallas and San Antonio found the Houston Hobby location far more convenient, and passenger traffic doubled almost immediately.

- In early 1973, in an attempt to fill empty seats on its San Antonio–Dallas flights, Southwest cut its regular $26 fare to $13 for all seats, all days, and all times. When Braniff International, at that time one of Southwest's major rivals, announced $13 fares of its own, Southwest retaliated with a two-page ad, run in the Dallas newspapers, headlined "Nobody is going to shoot Southwest Airlines out of the sky for a lousy $13" and containing copy saying Braniff was trying to run Southwest out of business. The ad announced that Southwest would not only match Braniff's $13 fare but that it would also give passengers the choice of buying a regular-priced ticket for $26 and receiving a complimentary fifth of Chivas Regal scotch, Crown Royal Canadian whiskey, or Smirnoff vodka (or, for nondrinkers, a leather ice bucket). More than 75 percent of Southwest's Dallas-Houston passengers opted for the $26 fare, although the percentage dropped as the two-month promotion wore on and corporate controllers began insisting that company employees use the $13 fare. The local and national media picked up the story of Southwest's offer, proclaiming the battle as a David-versus-Goliath struggle in which the upstart Southwest did not stand much of a chance against the much larger and well-established Braniff; grassroots sentiment in Texas swung to Southwest's side.

All these moves paid off. The resulting gains in passenger traffic enabled allowed Southwest to report its first-ever annual profit in 1973.

More Legal and Regulatory Hurdles

During the rest of the 1970s, Southwest found itself embroiled in another round of legal and regulatory battles. One involved Southwest's refusal to move its flights from Dallas Love Field, located 10 minutes from downtown, to the newly opened Dallas–Fort Worth (DFW) Regional Airport, which was 30 minutes from downtown Dallas. Local officials were furious because they were counting on fees from Southwest's flights in and out of DFW to help service the debt on the bonds issued to finance the construction of DFW. Southwest's position was that it was not required to move because it had not agreed to do so or been ordered to do so by the Texas Aeronautics Commission—moreover, the company's headquarters were located at Love Field. The courts eventually ruled that Southwest's operations could remain at Love Field.

A second battle ensued when rival airlines protested Southwest's application to begin serving several smaller cities in Texas; their protest was based on arguments that these markets were already well served and that Southwest's entry would result in costly overcapacity. Southwest countered that its low fares would allow more people to fly and grow the market. Again, Southwest prevailed and its views about low fares expanding the market proved accurate. In the year before Southwest initiated service, 123,000 passengers flew from Harlingen Airport in the Rio Grande Valley to Houston, Dallas, or San Antonio; in the 11 months following Southwest's initial flights, 325,000 passengers flew to the same three cities.

Believing that Braniff and Texas International were deliberately engaging in tactics to harass Southwest's operations, Southwest convinced the U.S. government to investigate what it considered predatory tactics by its chief rivals. In February 1975, Braniff and Texas International were indicted by a federal grand jury for conspiring to put Southwest out of business—a violation of the Sherman Antitrust Act. The two airlines pleaded "no contest" to the charges, signed cease-and-desist agreements, and were fined a modest $100,000 each.

When Congress passed the Airline Deregulation Act in 1978, Southwest applied to the Civil Aeronautics Board (now the Federal Aviation Agency) to fly between Houston and New Orleans. The application was vehemently opposed by local government officials and airlines operating out of DFW because of the potential for passenger traffic to be siphoned away from DFW. The opponents solicited the aid of Fort Worth congressman Jim Wright, then the majority leader of the U.S. House of Representatives, who took the matter to the floor of the House of Representatives; a rash of lobbying and maneuvering ensued. What emerged came to be known as the Wright Amendment of 1979: no airline may provide nonstop or through-plane service from Dallas Love Field to any city in any state except for locations in Texas, Louisiana, Arkansas, Oklahoma, and New Mexico. Southwest was prohibited from advertising, publishing schedules or fares, or checking baggage for travel from Dallas Love Field to any city it served outside the five-state "Wright Zone." The Wright Amendment continued in effect until 1997, when Alabama, Mississippi, and Kansas were added to the Wright Zone; in 2005, Missouri was added to the Wright Zone. In 2006, after a heated battle in Congress, legislation was passed and signed into law that repealed the Wright Amendment beginning in 2014.

The Emergence of a Combative Can-Do Culture at Southwest

The legal, regulatory, and competitive battles that Southwest fought in its early years produced a strong esprit de corps among Southwest personnel and a drive to survive and prosper despite the odds. With newspaper and TV stories reporting Southwest's difficulties regularly, employees were fully aware that the airline's existence was constantly on the line. Had the company been forced to move from Love Field, it would most likely have gone under, an outcome that employees, Southwest's rivals, and local government officials understood well. According to Southwest's former president Colleen Barrett, the obstacles thrown in Southwest's path by competitors and local officials were instrumental in building Herb Kelleher's passion for Southwest Airlines and ingraining a combative, can-do spirit into the corporate culture:

> They would put twelve to fifteen lawyers on a case and on our side there was Herb. They almost wore him to the ground. But the more arrogant they were, the more determined Herb got that this airline was going to go into the air—and stay there.
>
> The warrior mentality, the very fight to survive, is truly what created our culture.[5]

When Lamar Muse resigned in 1978, Southwest's board wanted Herb Kelleher to take over as chairman and CEO. But Kelleher enjoyed practicing law and, while he agreed to become chairman of the board, he insisted that someone else be CEO. Southwest's board appointed Howard Putnam, a group vice president of marketing services at United Airlines, as Southwest's president and CEO in July 1978. Putnam asked Kelleher to become more involved in Southwest's day-to-day operations, and over the next three years, Kelleher got to know many of the company's personnel and observe them in action. Putnam announced his resignation in the fall of 1981 to become president and chief operating officer at Braniff International. This time, Southwest's board succeeded in persuading Kelleher to take on the additional duties of CEO and president.

Sustained Growth and the Emergence of a New Industry Leader, 1981–2009

When Herb Kelleher took over in 1981, Southwest was flying 27 planes to 14 destination cities and had $270 million in revenues and 2,100 employees. Over the next 20 years, Southwest Airlines prospered under Kelleher's leadership. When Kelleher stepped down as CEO in mid-2001, the company had 350 planes flying to 58 U.S. airports, annual revenues of $5.6 billion, more than 30,000 employees, and 64 million fare-paying passengers annually. Under the two CEOs who succeeded Kelleher, Southwest continued its march to becoming the market share leader in domestic air travel; by 2009, it was earning annual revenues of $10.4 billion, employing 34,874 people, flying 537 planes to 69 airports in 36 states, and transporting some 86 million fare-paying passengers and some 100 million passengers (including those traveling on frequent flyer awards) annually. In the process, the company won more industry Triple Crown Awards for best on-time record, best baggage handling, and fewest customer complaints than any other U.S. airline.

Exhibit 2 provides a five-year summary of Southwest's financial and operating performance. Exhibit 3 provides selected financial and operating data for major U.S. air carriers during 1995–2009.

Exhibit 2 Summary of Southwest Airlines' Financial and Operating Performance, 2005–2009

	Years Ended December 31				
	2009	**2008**	**2007**	**2006**	**2005**
Financial Data ($ millions, except per share data)					
Operating revenues	$10,350	$11,023	$ 9,861	$ 9,086	$ 7,584
Operating expenses	10,088	10,574	9,070	8,152	6,859
Operating income	262	449	791	934	725
Other expenses (income) net	98	171	(267)	144	(54)
Income before taxes	164	278	1,058	790	779
Provision for income taxes	65	100	413	291	295
Net Income	$ 99	$ 178	$ 645	$ 499	$ 484
Net income per share, basic	$0.13	$0.24	$0.85	$0.63	$0.61
Net income per share, diluted	.13	.24	.84	.61	.60
Cash dividends per common share	$0.018	$0.018	$0.018	$0.018	$0.018
Total assets at period-end	$14,269	$14,068	$16,772	$13,460	$14,003
Long-term obligations at period-end	$ 3,325	$ 3,498	$ 2,050	$ 1,567	$ 1,394
Stockholders' equity at period-end	$ 5,466	$ 4,953	$ 6,941	$ 6,449	$ 6,675

(Continued)

Exhibit 2   *(Concluded)*

	Years Ended December 31				
	2009	2008	2007	2006	2005
Operating Data					
Revenue passengers carried	86,310,229	88,529,234	88,713,472	83,814,823	77,693,875
Enplaned passengers[1]	101,338,228	101,920,598	101,910,809	96,276,907	88,379,900
Revenue passenger miles (RPMs) (000s)	74,456,710	73,491,687	72,318,812	67,691,289	60,223,100
Available seat miles (ASMs) (000s)	98,001,550	103,271,343	99,635,967	92,663,023	85,172,795
Load factor[2]	76.0%	71.2%	72.6%	73.1%	70.7%
Average length of passenger haul (miles)	863	830	815	808	775
Average aircraft stage length (miles)	639	636	629	622	607
Trips flown	1,125,111	1,191,151	1,160,699	1,092,331	1,028,639
Average passenger fare	$114.61	$119.16	$106.60	$104.40	$93.68
Passenger revenue yield per RPM	13.29¢	14.35¢	13.08¢	12.93¢	12.09¢
Operating revenue yield per ASM	10.56¢	10.67¢	9.90¢	9.81¢	8.90¢
Operating expenses per ASM	10.29¢	10.24¢	9.10¢	8.80¢	8.05¢
Fuel costs per gallon (average)	$2.12	$2.44	$1.80	$1.64	$1.13
Fuel consumed, in gallons (millions)	1,428	1,511	1,489	1,389	1,287
Full-time equivalent employees at year-end	34,726	35,499	34,378	32,664	31,729
Size of fleet at year-end[3]	537	537	520	481	445

[1]Includes passengers traveling on free travel award tickets.
[2]Revenue passenger miles divided by available seat miles.
[3]Includes leased aircraft.
Source: Southwest Airlines, 2009 10-K report, p. 23.

HERB KELLEHER: SOUTHWEST'S CELEBRATED CEO

Herb Kelleher majored in philosophy at Wesleyan University in Middletown, Connecticut, graduating with honors. He earned his law degree at New York University, again graduating with honors and also serving as a member of the law review. After graduation, he clerked for a New Jersey Supreme Court justice for two years and then joined a law firm in Newark. Upon marrying a woman from Texas and becoming enamored with Texas, he moved to San Antonio, where he became a successful lawyer and came to represent Rollin King's small aviation company.

When Herb Kelleher took on the role of Southwest's CEO in 1981, he made a point of visiting with maintenance personnel to check on how well the planes were running and of talking with the flight attendants. Kelleher did not do much managing from his office, preferring instead to be out among the troops as much as he could. His style was to listen and observe and to offer

Exhibit 3 **Selected Operating and Financial Data for Major U.S. Airline Carriers, 1995–2009 (selected years)**

	1995	2000	2005	2007	2008	2009
Passengers (in millions)	559.0	666.2	738.3	769.6	743.3	703.9
Flights (in thousands)	8,062	9,035	11,564	11,399	10,841	10,373
Revenue passenger miles (in billions)	603.4	692.8	778.6	829.4	812.4	769.5
Available seat miles (in billions)	807.1	987.9	1,002.7	1,037.7	1,021.3	957.2
Load factor	67.0	72.4	77.7	79.9	79.5	80.4
Passenger revenues (in millions)	$69,470	$93,622	$93,500	$107,678	$111,542	$91,331
Operating profit (loss) (in millions)	$5,852	$6,999	$427	$9,344	($3,348)	$2,409
Net profit (loss) excluding one-time charges and gains (in millions)	$2,283	$2,486	($5,782)	$4,998	($9,464)	($2,799)
Total employees	546,987	679,967	562,467	560,997	556,920	536,200

Sources: Air Transport Association, *2010 Economic Report,* pp. 8, 19, 23, and 30; *2009 Economic Report,* p. 19; Air Transport Association, *2008 Economic Report,* p. 19; and Air Transport Association, *2005 Economic Report,* p. 7.

encouragement. Kelleher attended most graduation ceremonies of flight attendant classes, and he often appeared to help load bags on "Black Wednesday," the busy travel day before Thanksgiving. He was held in the highest regard by Southwest employees and knew thousands of their names. When he attended a Southwest employee function, he was swarmed like a celebrity.

Kelleher had an affinity for bold-print Hawaiian shirts, owned a tricked-out motorcycle, and made no secret of his passion for cigarettes and Wild Turkey whiskey. He loved to make jokes and engage in pranks and corporate antics, prompting some people to refer to him as the "clown prince" of the airline industry. He once appeared at a company gathering dressed in an Elvis costume and had arm-wrestled a South Carolina company executive at a public event in Dallas for rights to use "Just Plane Smart" as an advertising slogan.[6] Kelleher was well known inside and outside the company for his combativeness, particularly when it came to beating back competitors. On one occasion, he reportedly told a group of veteran employees, "If someone says they're going to smack us in the face—knock them out, stomp them out, boot them in the ditch, cover them over, and move on to the next thing. That's the Southwest spirit at work."[7] On another occasion, he said, "I love battles. I think it's part of the Irish in me. It's like what Patton said, 'War is hell and I love it so.' That's how I feel. I've never gotten tired of fighting."[8]

While Southwest was deliberately combative and flamboyant in some aspects of its operations, when it came to the financial side of the business Kelleher insisted on fiscal conservatism, a strong balance sheet, comparatively low levels of debt, and zealous attention to bottom-line profitability. While believing strongly in being prepared for adversity, Kelleher had an aversion to Southwest personnel spending time drawing up all kinds of formal strategic plans, saying, "Reality is chaotic; planning is ordered and logical. The meticulous nit-picking that goes on in most strategic planning processes creates a mental straightjacket that becomes disabling in an industry where things change radically from one day to the next." Kelleher wanted Southwest managers to think ahead, have contingency plans, and be ready to act when it appeared that the future held significant risks or when new conditions suddenly appeared and demanded prompt responses.

Kelleher was a strong believer in the principle that employees—not customers—came first:

> You have to treat your employees like your customers. When you treat them right, then they will treat your outside customers right. That has been a very powerful competitive weapon for us. You've got to take the time to listen to people's ideas. If you just tell somebody no, that's an act of power and, in my opinion, an abuse of power. You don't want to constrain people in their thinking.[9]

Another indication of the importance that Kelleher placed on employees was the message he had penned in 1990 that was prominently displayed in the lobby of Southwest's headquarters in Dallas:

> The people of Southwest Airlines are "the creators" of what we have become—and of what we will be.
>
> Our people transformed an idea into a legend. That legend will continue to grow only so long as it is nourished—by our people's indomitable spirit, boundless energy, immense goodwill, and burning desire to excel.
>
> Our thanks—and our love—to the people of Southwest Airlines for creating a marvelous family and a wondrous airline.

In June 2001, Herb Kelleher stepped down as CEO but continued on in his role as chairman of Southwest's board of directors and the head of the board's executive committee; as chairman, he played a lead role in Southwest's strategy, expansion to new cities and aircraft scheduling, and governmental and industry affairs. In May 2008, after more than 40 years of leadership at Southwest, Kelleher retired as chairman; he was, however, scheduled to remain a full-time Southwest employee until July 2013.

EXECUTIVE LEADERSHIP AT SOUTHWEST, 2001–2010

In June 2001, responding to anxious investor concerns about the company's leadership succession plans, Southwest Airlines began an orderly transfer of power and responsibilities from Herb Kelleher, age 70, to two of his most trusted protégés: James F. Parker, 54, Southwest's general counsel, succeeded Kelleher as Southwest's CEO, and Colleen Barrett, 56, Southwest's executive vice president–customers and self-described keeper of Southwest's pep-rally corporate culture, became president and chief operating officer.

James Parker, CEO from 2001 to 2004

James Parker's association with Herb Kelleher went back 23 years, to the time when they were colleagues at Kelleher's old law firm. Parker moved over to Southwest from the law firm in February 1986. Parker's profile inside the company as Southwest's vice president and general counsel had been relatively low, but he was Southwest's chief labor negotiator, and much of the credit for Southwest's good relations with employee unions belonged to him. Prior to his appointment as CEO, Parker had been a member of the company's executive planning committee; his experiences ranged from properties and facilities to technical services team to the company's alliances with vendors and partners. Parker and Kelleher were said to think much alike, and Parker was regarded as having a good sense of humor, although he did not have as colorful and flamboyant a personality as Kelleher. Parker was seen as an honest, straight-arrow kind of person who had a strong grasp of Southwest's culture and market niche and who could be nice or tough, depending on the situation. When his appointment was announced, Parker said:

> There is going to be no change of course insofar as Southwest is concerned. We have a very experienced leadership team. We've all worked together for a long time. There will be evolutionary changes in Southwest, just as there have always been in our history. We're going to stay true to our business model of being a low-cost, low-fare airline.[10]

Parker retired unexpectedly, for personal reasons, in July 2004, stepping down as CEO and vice chairman of the board and also resigning from the company's board of directors. He was succeeded by Gary C. Kelly.

Colleen Barrett, Southwest's President from 2001 to 2008

Colleen Barrett began working with Kelleher as his legal secretary in 1967 and had been with Southwest since 1978. As executive vice president–customers, Barrett had a high profile among Southwest employees and spent most of her time on culture building, morale building, and customer service; her goal was to ensure that employees felt good about what they were doing and felt empowered to serve the cause of Southwest Airlines.[11] She and Kelleher were regarded as Southwest's guiding lights, and some analysts said she was essentially functioning as the company's chief operating officer (COO) prior to her formal appointment as president. Much of the credit for the company's strong record of customer service and its strong-culture work climate belonged to Barrett.

Barrett had been the driving force behind lining the hallways at Southwest's headquarters with photos of company events and trying to create a family atmosphere at the company. Believing it was important to make employees feel cared about and important, Barrett had put together a network of contacts across the company to help her stay in touch with what was happening with employees and their families. When network members learned about events that were worthy of acknowledgment, the word quickly got to Barrett—the information went into a database, and an appropriate greeting card or gift was sent. Barrett had a remarkable ability to give gifts that were individualized and that connected her to the recipient.[12]

Barrett was the first woman appointed as president and COO of a major U.S. airline. In October 2001, *Fortune* ranked Colleen Barrett 20th on its list of the 50 most powerful women in American business. Barrett retired as president in July 2008, but was scheduled to remain as a full-time Southwest employee until 2013.

Gary C. Kelly, Southwest's CEO from 2004 Onward

Gary Kelly was appointed vice chairman of the board of directors and CEO of Southwest effective July 15, 2004. Prior to that time, Kelly was executive vice president and chief financial officer (CFO) from 2001 to 2004, and vice president–finance and CFO from 1989 to 2001. He joined Southwest in 1986 as its controller. In 2008, effective with the retirement of Kelleher and Barrett, Kelly assumed the titles of chairman of the board, CEO, and president.

When Kelly was named CEO in 2004, Herb Kelleher said:

> Gary Kelly is one of our brightest stars, well respected throughout the industry and well known, over more than a decade, to the media, analyst, and investor communities for his excellence. As part of our Board's succession planning, we had already focused on Gary as Jim Parker's successor, and that process has simply been accelerated by Jim's personal decision to retire. Under Gary's

leadership, Southwest has achieved the strongest balance sheet in the American airline industry; the best fuel hedging position in our industry; and tremendous progress in technology.[13]

During his tenure as CEO, Kelly and other top-level Southwest executives had sharpened and fine-tuned Southwest's strategy in a number of areas, continued to expand operations (adding both more flights and initiating service to new airports), and worked to maintain the company's low-cost advantage over its domestic rivals.

Kelly saw four factors as keys to Southwest's recipe for success:[14]

- Hire great people, treat 'em like family.
- Care for our Customers warmly and personally, like they're guests in our home.
- Keep fares and operating costs lower than anybody else by being safe, efficient, and operationally excellent.
- Stay prepared for bad times with a strong balance sheet, lots of cash, and a stout fuel hedge.

To help Southwest be a standout performer on these four key success factors, Kelly had established five strategic objectives for Southwest:[15]

- Be the best place to work.
- Be the safest, most efficient, and most reliable airline in the world.
- Offer customers a convenient flight schedule with lots of flights to lots of places they want to go.
- Offer customers the best overall travel experience.
- Do all of these things in a way that maintains a low cost structure and the ability to offer low fares.

During 2008–2009, Kelly initiated a slight revision of Southwest's mission statement and also spearheaded a vision statement that called for a steadfast focus on a triple bottom line of Performance, People, and Planet—see Exhibit 4.

SOUTHWEST AIRLINES' STRATEGY

From day one, Southwest had pursued a low-cost/low-price/no-frills strategy. Its signature low

Exhibit 4   Southwest Airline's Mission, Vision, and Triple Bottom Line Commitment to Performance, People, and Planet

---

THE MISSION OF SOUTHWEST AIRLINES

The mission of Southwest Airlines is dedication to the highest quality of Customer Service delivered with a sense of warmth, friendliness, individual pride, and Company Spirit.

TO OUR EMPLOYEES

We are committed to provide our Employees a stable work environment with equal opportunity for learning and personal growth. Creativity and innovation are encouraged for improving the effectiveness of Southwest Airlines. Above all, Employees will be provided the same concern, respect, and caring attitude within the organization that they are expected to share externally with every Southwest Customer.

TO OUR COMMUNITIES

Our goal is to be the hometown airline of every community we serve, and because those communities sustain and nurture us with their support and loyalty, it is vital that we, as individuals and in groups, embrace each community with the SOUTHWEST SPIRIT of involvement, service, and caring to make those communities better places to live and work.

TO OUR PLANET

We strive to be a good environmental steward across our system in all of our hometowns, and one component of our stewardship is efficiency, which by its very nature, translates to eliminating waste and conserving resources. Using cost-effective and environmentally beneficial operating procedures (including facilities and equipment), allows us to reduce the amount of materials we use and, when combined with our ability to reuse and recycle material, preserves these environmental resources.

TO OUR STAKEHOLDERS

Southwest's vision for a sustainable future is one where there will be a balance in our business model between Employees and Community, the Environment, and our Financial Viability. In order to protect our world for future generations, while meeting our commitments to our Employees, Customers, and Stakeholders, we will strive to lead our industry in innovative efficiency that conserves natural resources, maintains a creative and innovative workforce, and gives back to the Communities in which we live and work.

Source: Southwest Airlines, "One Report, 2009," www.southwest.com, accessed August 20, 2010.

fares made air travel affordable to a wide segment of the U.S. population—giving substance to its tag line "The Freedom to Fly." It employed a relatively simple fare structure, with all of the fare options plainly displayed at the company's website. The lowest fares were usually nonrefundable but could be applied to future travel on Southwest Airlines without incurring a change fee (rival airlines charged a change fee of $100 to $175), and the company's advance purchase requirements on tickets were more lenient than those of its rivals. Many Southwest flights had some seats available at deeply discounted fares, provided they were purchased online at the company's website.

In November 2007, Southwest introduced a new Business Select fare to attract economy-minded business travelers; Business Select customers had early boarding privileges, received extra Rapid Rewards (frequent flyer credits), and a free cocktail. In 2008, rival airlines instituted a

series of add-on fees—including a fuel surcharge for each flight, fees for checking bags, fees for processing frequent flyer travel awards, fees for buying a ticket in person at the airport or calling a toll-free number to speak with a ticket agent to make a reservation, fees for changing a previously purchased ticket to a different flight, and fees for in-flight snacks and beverages—to help defray skyrocketing costs for jet fuel (which had climbed from about 15 percent of operating expenses in 2000 to 40 percent of operating expenses in mid-2008). Southwest, however, choose to forgo à la carte pricing and stuck with an all-inclusive fare price. During 2009, Southwest ran an ad campaign called "Bags Fly Free" to publicize the cost savings of flying Southwest rather than paying the $20 to $50 fees that rival airlines charged for a first or second checked bag.

When advance reservations were weak for particular weeks or times of the day or on certain routes, Southwest made a regular practice of initiating special fare promotions to stimulate ticket sales on flights that otherwise would have had numerous empty seats. For instance, the company had used fare sales to combat slack air travel during much of the recession of 2008–2009.

The combined effect of Southwest's "Bags Fly Free" ads and periodic fare sales resulted in company-record load factors for every month from July through December 2009. (A load factor was the percentage of all available seats on all flights that were occupied by fare-paying passengers.) Southwest continued to run the "Bags Fly Free" ads during the first half of 2010. In June 2010, to celebrate its 39 years of flying, Southwest instituted a two-day special promotion of $39 one-way fares for travel up to 450 miles, $79 one-way fares for travel between 451 and 1,000 miles, and $119 one-way fares for travel between 1,001 and 1,500 miles; the fares were good for travel from September 8, 2010, through November 17, 2010 to select destinations.

Southwest was a shrewd practitioner of the concept of price elasticity, proving in one market after another that the revenue gains from increased ticket sales and the volume of passenger traffic would more than compensate for the revenue erosion associated with low fares. When Southwest entered the Florida market with an introductory $17 fare from Tampa to Fort Lauderdale, the number of annual passengers flying that route jumped 50 percent, to more than 330,000. In Manchester, New Hampshire, passenger counts went from 1.1 million in 1997, the year prior to Southwest's entry, to 3.5 million in 2000, and average one-way fares dropped from just over $300 to $129. Southwest's success in stimulating higher passenger traffic at airports across the United States via low fares and frequent flights had been coined the "Southwest effect" by personnel at the U.S. Department of Transportation. Exhibit 5 shows the cities and airports Southwest served in May 2010. Southwest began service to Boston, New York (LaGuardia), Minneapolis–St. Paul, and Milwaukee in 2009. Management had announced plans for Southwest to begin service to Newark, New Jersey and two South Carolina airports—Charleston and Greenville-Spartanburg—in 2011.

Unlike the hub-and-spoke route systems of rival airlines (where operations were concentrated at a limited number of hub cities and most destinations were served via connections through the hub), Southwest's route system had been carefully designed to concentrate on flights between pairs of cities 150 to 700 miles apart that handled enough passenger traffic to allow Southwest to offer a sizable number of daily flights. As a general rule, Southwest did not initiate service to an airport unless it envisioned the potential for originating at least 8 flights a day there and saw opportunities to add more flights over time—in Denver, for example, Southwest had boosted the number of daily departures from 13 in January 2006 (the month in which service to and from Denver was initiated) to 79 daily departures in May 2008 and to 129 departures in May 2010. Southwest's point-to-point route system minimized connections, delays, and total trip time—its emphasis on nonstop flights between pairs of cities allowed about 75 percent of Southwest's passengers to fly nonstop to their destination. While a majority of Southwest's flights involved actual in-air flight times of less than 90 minutes, in recent years the company had added a significant number of nonstop flights to more distant airports where its low fares could generate profitable amounts of passenger traffic.

Southwest's frequent flyer program, Rapid Rewards, was based on trips flown rather than mileage. Rapid Rewards customers received one credit for each one-way trip or two credits for each round-trip flown and could also earn credits by using the services of Southwest's car rental, hotel, and credit card partners. There were two principal types of travel awards:

- *Standard Awards*—these were for Rapid Rewards members who accumulated one free round-trip after the accumulation of 16 credits within 24 consecutive months. Standard Awards were valid for one free round-trip to any destination available on Southwest Airlines, had to be used within 12 months, and were subject to seat restrictions and blackout dates around certain major holidays.

- *Companion Passes*—these were for Rapid Rewards members who accumulated 100 credits within a 12-month period; these passes provided unlimited free round-trip travel to any destination available on Southwest for a designated companion of a qualifying Rapid Rewards Member who purchased a ticket or

Exhibit 5   Airports and Cities Served by Southwest Airlines, May 2010

	Southwest's Top 10 Airports		
	Daily Departures	Number of Gates	Nonstop Cities Served
Chicago Midway	224	29	51
Las Vegas	223	19	57
Baltimore/Washington	181	20	44
Phoenix	177	24	44
Houston (Hobby)	135	17	30
Dallas (Love Field)	131	15	15
Denver	129	14	42
Los Angeles (LAX)	116	11	20
Oakland	114	13	20
Orlando	104	12	33

Other Airports Served by Southwest Airlines			
Albany	Fort Myers/Naples	Minneapolis/St. Paul	Reno/Tahoe
Albuquerque	Harlingen/South Padre	Nashville	Sacramento
Amarillo	Island	New Orleans	St. Louis
Austin	Hartford/Springfield	New York (LaGuardia)	Salt Lake City
Birmingham	Indianapolis	Norfolk	San Antonio
Boise	Long Island (MacArthur)	Oklahoma City	San Francisco
Boston Logan	Jackson, MS	Omaha	San Jose
Buffalo	Jacksonville	Ontario, CA	Seattle/Tacoma
Burbank, CA	Kansas City	Orange County, CA	Spokane
Cleveland	Little Rock	Panama City, FL	Tampa
Columbus, OH	Louisville	Philadelphia	Tucson
Corpus Christi, TX	Lubbock	Pittsburgh	Tulsa
Detroit Metro	Manchester, NH	Portland, OR	Washington, DC (Dulles)
El Paso	Midland/Odessa, TX	Providence	West Palm Beach
Fort Lauderdale	Milwaukee	Raleigh-Durham	

Source: Southwest Airlines, www.southwest.com, accessed August 5, 2010.

used a free travel award ticket. The Rapid Rewards member and designated companion had to travel together on the same flight. Companion Passes were valid for 12 months after issuance and were not subject to seat restrictions or blackout dates.

In addition, Rapid Rewards members who flew 32 qualifying flights within a 12-month period received priority boarding privileges for a year. Southwest customers redeemed 2.4 million free ticket awards during 2009 and 2.8 million free ticket awards in both 2007 and 2008. Free travel award usage accounted for about 8 percent of

Southwest's total revenue passenger miles flown during 2007–2009. Since the inception of Rapid Rewards in 1987, approximately 16 percent of all fully earned awards had expired without being used.

Customer Service and Customer Satisfaction

Southwest's approach to delivering good customer service and creating customer satisfaction was predicated on presenting a happy face to passengers, displaying a fun-loving attitude, and doing things in a manner calculated to make sure passengers had a positive flying experience. The company made a special effort to employ gate personnel who enjoyed interacting with customers, had good interpersonal skills, and displayed cheery, outgoing personalities. A number of Southwest's gate personnel let their wit and sense of humor show by sometimes entertaining those in the gate area with trivia questions or contests such as "Who has the biggest hole in their sock?" Apart from greeting passengers coming onto planes and assisting them in finding open seats and stowing baggage, flight attendants were encouraged to be engaging, converse and joke with passengers, and go about their tasks in ways that made passengers smile. On some flights, attendants sang announcements to passengers on takeoff and landing. On one flight while passengers were boarding, an attendant with bunny ears popped out of an overhead bin exclaiming "Surprise!" The repertoires to amuse passengers varied from flight crew to flight crew.

During their tenure, both Herb Kelleher and Colleen Barrett had made a point of sending congratulatory notes to employees when the company received letters from customers complimenting particular Southwest employees; complaint letters were seen as learning opportunities for employees and reasons to consider making adjustments. Employees were provided the following policy guidance regarding how far to go in trying to please customers:

> No Employee will ever be punished for using good judgment and good old common sense when trying to accommodate a Customer—no matter what our rules are.[16]
>
> When you empower People to make a positive difference every day, you allow them to decide. Most guidelines are written to be broken as long as the Employee is leaning toward the Customer. We follow the Golden Rule and try to do the right thing and think about our Customer.[17]

Southwest executives believed that conveying a friendly, fun-loving spirit to customers was the key to competitive advantage. As one Southwest manager put it, "Our fares can be matched; our airplanes and routes can be copied. But we pride ourselves on our customer service."[18]

In 2007, Southwest did an "extreme gate makeover" to improve the airport experience of customers. The makeover included adding (1) a business-focused area with padded seats, tables with power outlets, power stations with stools, and a flat-screen TV with news programming, and (2) a family-focused area with smaller tables and chairs, power stations for charging electrical devices, and kid-friendly programming on a flat-screen TV.

Marketing and Promotion

Southwest was continually on the lookout for novel ways to tell its story, make its distinctive persona come alive, and strike a chord in the minds of air travelers. Many of its print ads and billboards were deliberately unconventional and attention-getting so as to create and reinforce the company's maverick, fun-loving, and combative image. Some previous campaigns had used the slogans "The Low-Fare Airline" and "The All-Time On-Time Airline"; others had touted the company's Triple Crown Awards. One of the company's billboard campaigns highlighted the frequency of the company's flights with such headlines as "Austin Auften," "Phoenix Phrequently," and "L.A. A.S.A.P." Each holiday season since 1985, Southwest had run a "Christmas Card" ad on TV featuring children and their families from the Ronald McDonald Houses and Southwest employees. Fresh advertising campaigns were launched periodically—Exhibit 6 shows four representative ads.

In 2002, Southwest began changing the look of its planes, updating its somewhat drab gold-orange-red scheme to a much fresher and brighter canyon blue/red/gold/orange scheme—see Exhibit 7.

Southwest tended to advertise far more heavily than any other U.S. carrier. According to The Nielsen Company, during the first six months of 2009, Southwest boosted its ad spending by 20 percent, to $112.6 million, to hammer home its "Bags Fly Free" message. Passenger traffic at Southwest subsequently rose, while passenger volumes went in the opposite direction at Southwest's five largest competitors—Delta, American, United, Continental, and US Airways, all of which had recently introduced or increased fees for checked baggage. Passenger travel on Southwest's domestic flights rose by more than 28 million passengers annually from 2000 through 2009, whereas passenger volume on domestic flights

Exhibit 6   Four Samples of Southwest's Ads

Exhibit 7   Southwest's New Look and Aircraft Equipped with Winglets

Old Color Scheme
(Plane without winglets)

New Color Scheme
(plane with winglets)

was down by 88 million passengers annually at Delta, American, United, Continental, and US Airways during this same period.

Other Strategy Elements

Southwest's strategy included several other elements:

- *Gradual expansion into new geographic markets.* Southwest generally added one or two new cities to its route schedule annually, preferring to saturate the market for daily flights to the cities/airports it currently served before entering new markets. In selecting new cities, Southwest looked for city pairs that could generate substantial amounts of both business and leisure traffic. Management believed that having numerous flights flying the same routes appealed to business travelers looking for convenient flight times and the ability to catch a later flight if they unexpectedly ran late.

- *Adding flights in areas where rivals were cutting back service.* When rivals cut back flights to cities that Southwest served, Southwest often moved in with more flights of its own, believing its lower fares would attract more passengers. When Midway Airlines ceased operations in November 1990, Southwest moved in overnight and quickly instituted flights to Chicago's Midway Airport. Southwest was a first-mover in adding flights on routes where rivals had cut their offerings following the terrorist attacks of September 11, 2001 (9/11).

When American Airlines closed its hubs in Nashville and San Jose, Southwest immediately increased the number of its flights into and out of both locations. When US Airways trimmed its flight schedule for Philadelphia and Pittsburgh, Southwest promptly boosted its flights into and out of those airports. Southwest initiated service to Denver when United, beset with financial difficulties, cut back operations at its big Denver hub.

- *Curtailing flights on marginally profitable routes where numerous seats often went unfilled and shifting planes to routes with good growth opportunities.* Management was attracted to this strategy element because it enabled Southwest to grow revenues and profits without having to add so many new planes to its fleet. This strategy was aggressively pursued in 2008–2009 as a means of coping with industry-wide declines in passenger air travel during the recession. Management canceled the planned additions to the size of its aircraft fleet in 2009, cut the number of flights in markets where ticket bookings were weak, and redeployed the capacity to support entry into four new markets with promising long-term growth potential: New York's LaGuardia Airport, Minneapolis–St. Paul International Airport, Boston's Logan International Airport, and Milwaukee's General Mitchell International Airport.

- *Putting strong emphasis on safety, high-quality maintenance, and reliable operations.*

Southwest management believed the company's low-fare strategy, coupled with frequent flights and friendly service, delivered "more value for less money" to customers rather than "less value for less money." Kelleher said, "Everybody values a very good service provided at a very reasonable price."[19]

SOUTHWEST'S EFFORTS TO EXECUTE ITS LOW-FARE STRATEGY

Southwest management fully understood that low fares necessitated zealous pursuit of low operating costs and had, over the years, instituted a number of practices to keep its costs below those of rival carriers:

- The company operated only one type of aircraft—Boeing 737s—to minimize the size of spare parts inventories, simplify the training of maintenance and repair personnel, improve the proficiency and speed with which maintenance routines could be done, and simplify the task of scheduling planes for particular flights. Furthermore, as the launch

customer for Boeing's 737-300, 737-500, and 737-700 models, Southwest acquired its new aircraft at favorable prices. See Exhibit 8 for statistics on Southwest's aircraft fleet.

- Southwest was the first major airline to introduce ticketless travel (eliminating the need to print and process paper tickets) and also the first to allow customers to make reservations and purchase tickets at the company's website (thus bypassing the need to pay commissions to travel agents for handling the ticketing process and reducing staffing requirements at Southwest's reservation centers). Selling a ticket on its website cost Southwest roughly $1, versus $3 to $4 for a ticket booked through its own internal reservation system and as much as $15 for tickets for business travelers purchased through travel agents and professional business travel partners. Ticketless travel accounted for more than 95 percent of all sales in 2007, and nearly 74 percent of Southwest's revenues were generated through sales at its website.

- The company stressed flights into and out of airports in medium-sized cities and less congested airports in major metropolitan areas (Chicago Midway, Detroit Metro, Houston

Exhibit 8   Southwest's Aircraft Fleet as of March 31, 2010

Type of Aircraft	Number	Seats	Comments
Boeing 737–300	173	137	Southwest was Boeing's launch customer for this model.
Boeing 737–500	25	122	Southwest was Boeing's launch customer for this model.
Boeing 737–700	343	137	Southwest was Boeing's launch customer for this model.
	541		

Other Fleet-Related Facts
Average age of aircraft fleet—10.5 years
Average aircraft trip length—633 miles, with an average duration of 1 hour and 54 minutes
Average aircraft utilization—6.5 flights per day and 12 hours and 15 minutes of flight time
Fleet size—1990: 106   1995: 224   2000: 344   2009: 537
Firm orders for new aircraft—2010: 10   2011: 10   2012: 13   2013–2016: 58

Source: Southwest Airlines, www.southwest.com, accessed August 5, 2010, and 2009 10-K report, p. 18.

Hobby, and Dallas Love Field). This strategy helped produce better-than-average on-time performance and reduce the fuel costs associated with planes sitting in line on crowded taxiways or circling airports waiting for clearance to land. It further allowed the company to avoid paying the higher landing fees and terminal gate costs at such high-traffic airports as Atlanta's Hartsfield International, Chicago's O'Hare, and Dallas–Fort Worth (DFW) where landing slots were controlled and rationed to those airlines willing to pay the high fees. Southwest's strategy of serving less congested airports also helped minimize total travel time for passengers—driving to the airport, parking, ticketing, boarding, and flight time. However, in recent years, to help sustain growth in passenger traffic and revenues, Southwest had initiated service to airports in several large metropolitan cities where air traffic congestion was a frequent problem—such as Los Angeles (LAX), Boston (Logan International, beginning in 2009), New York (LaGuardia), Denver, San Francisco, and Philadelphia.

- Southwest's point-to-point scheduling of flights was more cost-efficient than the hub-and-spoke systems used by rival airlines. Hub-and-spoke systems involved passengers on many different flights coming in from spoke locations (or perhaps another hub) to a central airport or hub within a short span of time and then connecting to an outgoing flight to their destination—a spoke location or another hub). Most flights arrived at and departed from a hub across a two-hour window, creating big peak-valley swings in airport personnel workloads and gate utilization—airport personnel and gate areas were very busy when hub operations were in full swing and then were underutilized in the interval awaiting the next round of inbound/outbound flights. In contrast, Southwest's point-to-point routes permitted scheduling aircraft so as to minimize the time aircraft were at the gate, currently approximately 25 minutes, thereby reducing the number of aircraft and gate facilities that would otherwise be required. Furthermore, with a relatively even flow of incoming/outgoing flights and gate

traffic, Southwest could staff its terminal operations to handle a fairly steady workload across a day, whereas hub-and-spoke operators had to staff their operations to serve three to four daily peak periods.

- To economize on the amount of time it took terminal personnel to check passengers in and to simplify the whole task of making reservations, Southwest dispensed with the practice of assigning each passenger a reserved seat. Instead, for many years, passengers were given color-coded plastic cards with the letters A, B, or C when they checked in at the boarding gate. Passengers then boarded in groups, according to the color/letter on their card, sitting in whatever seat was open when they got on the plane—a procedure described by some as a "cattle call." Passengers who were particular about where they sat had to arrive at the gate early to get boarding cards and then had to position themselves near the front when it was their group's turn to board. In 2002, Southwest abandoned the use of plastic cards and began printing a big, bold A, B, or C on the boarding pass when the passenger checked in at the ticket counter; passengers then boarded in groups according to their assigned letter. In 2007–2008, in order to significantly reduce the time that passengers spent standing in line waiting for their group to board, Southwest introduced an enhanced boarding method that automatically assigned each passenger a specific number within the passenger's boarding group at the time of check-in; passengers then boarded the aircraft in that numerical order. All passengers could check in online up to 24 hours before departure time and print out a boarding pass, thus bypassing counter check-in (unless they wished to check baggage).

- Southwest flight attendants were responsible for cleaning up trash left by deplaning passengers and otherwise getting the plane presentable for passengers to board for the next flight. Rival carriers had cleaning crews come on board to perform this function until they incurred heavy losses in 2001–2005 and were forced to institute stringent cost-cutting measures that included abandoning use of cleaning crews and copying Southwest's practice.

- Southwest did not have a first-class section on any of its planes and had no fancy frequent flyer clubs at terminals.

- Southwest offered passengers no baggage transfer services to other carriers—passengers with checked baggage who were connecting to other carriers to reach their destination were responsible for picking up their luggage at Southwest's baggage claim and then getting it to the check-in facilities of the connecting carrier. (Southwest only booked tickets involving its own flights; customers connecting to flights on other carriers had to book such tickets either through travel agents or the connecting airline.)

- Starting in 2001, Southwest began converting from cloth to leather seats; the team of Southwest employees who investigated the economics of the conversion concluded that an all-leather interior would be more durable and easier to maintain, more than justifying the higher initial costs.

- Southwest was a first-mover among major U.S. airlines in employing fuel hedging and derivative contracts to counteract rising prices for crude oil and jet fuel. From 1998 through 2008, the company's fuel hedging activities produced fuel savings of about $4 billion over what it would have spent had it paid the industry's average price for jet fuel. But unexpectedly large declines in jet fuel prices in late 2008 and 2009 resulted in reported losses of $408 million on the fuel hedging contracts that the company had in place during 2009. Southwest's fuel hedging strategy involved modifying the amount of its future fuel requirements that were hedged based on management's judgments about the forward market prices of crude oil and jet fuel.

- To enhance the performance and efficiency of its aircraft fleet, Southwest had recently added vertical winglets on the wing tips of most all its planes and begun ordering new planes equipped with winglets (see Exhibit 7). These winglets reduced lift drag, allowed aircraft to climb more steeply and reach higher flight levels quicker, improved cruising performance, helped extend engine life and reduce maintenance costs, and reduced

fuel burn. In 2007, Southwest entered into an agreement with Naverus, the worldwide leader in performance-based navigation systems, to develop and implement new flight procedures for Southwest planes that would result in lower fuel consumption and greenhouse gas emissions, better on-time reliability, and increased safety in bad weather and at airports situated in mountainous terrain.

- Southwest regularly upgraded and enhanced its management information systems to speed data flows, improve operating efficiency, lower costs, and upgrade its customer service capabilities. In 2001, Southwest implemented use of new software that significantly decreased the time required to generate optimal crew schedules and help improve on-time performance. In 2007–2008, Southwest invested in next-generation technology and software to improve its ticketless system and its back-office accounting, payroll, and human resource information systems. During 2009, the company replaced or enhanced its point of sale, electronic ticketing and boarding, and revenue accounting systems. During 2010, it completed an initiative to convert to a new SAP enterprise resource planning application that would replace its general ledger, accounts payable, accounts receivable, payroll, benefits, cash management, and fixed asset systems; the conversion was designed to increase data accuracy and consistency, and to lower administrative support costs.

For many decades, Southwest's operating costs had been lower than those of American, Continental, Delta, Northwest, United, US Airways, and other major U.S. airline carriers. Recently, JetBlue, an airline that began operations in 2000 and had grown rapidly with a low-cost, low-fare strategy that was similar to Southwest's strategy, had been able to achieve operating costs that were below those of Southwest—see Exhibit 9 for cost comparisons among the major U.S. airlines during the 1995–2010 period. Exhibit 10 shows a detailed breakdown of Southwest's operating costs based on the number of available seats rather than the number of passenger-occupied seats.

Exhibit 9 Comparative Operating Cost Statistics, Major U.S. Airlines, 1995–First Quarter 2010 (selected years)

	Salaries/Fringe Benefits		Fuel and Oil	Maintenance	Rentals	Landing Fees	Advertising	General and Administrative	Other Operating Expenses	Total Operating Expenses
	Pilots/Copilots	All Employees								
American Airlines										
1995	0.94¢	5.59¢	1.53¢	1.34¢	0.59¢	0.22¢	0.19¢	1.14¢	3.65¢	14.25¢
2000	1.16	5.77	2.04	1.90	0.48	0.23	0.18	0.58	3.30	14.48
2005	0.90	4.65	3.67	1.42	0.41	0.32	0.10	0.95	3.66	15.18
2008	0.87	4.81	6.19	1.72	0.37	0.31	0.12	1.91	4.12	19.54
2009	0.91	5.30	4.10	1.88	0.42	0.35	0.13	1.56	3.47	17.20
Q1 2010	0.98	5.63	4.64	2.16	0.46	0.38	0.14	1.50	3.85	18.76
Continental Air Lines										
1995	0.95¢	3.69¢	1.67¢	1.50¢	1.25¢	0.27¢	0.25¢	0.56¢	3.68¢	12.87¢
2000	1.25	4.43	2.18	1.42	1.17	0.24	0.09	0.59	3.57	13.70
2005	0.79	3.85	3.42	1.18	0.91	0.34	0.13	0.82	5.74	16.38
2008	0.77	3.63	5.90	1.26	0.81	0.33	0.11	1.06	6.04	19.14
2009	0.82	3.89	3.43	1.37	0.79	0.33	0.13	0.98	5.25	16.16
Q1 2010	0.90	4.21	3.75	1.40	0.83	0.35	0.14	1.03	5.80	17.49
Delta Air Lines (merged with Northwest Airlines in 2009 and began combined reporting in January 2010)										
1995	1.27¢	4.97¢	1.70¢	1.16¢	0.71¢	0.30¢	0.18¢	0.43¢	4.07¢	13.53¢
2000	1.27	5.08	1.73	1.41	0.54	0.22	0.12	0.74	3.03	12.85
2005	0.93	4.31	3.68	1.10	0.38	0.22	0.16	0.84	6.01	16.68
2008	0.76	3.55	5.99	1.08	0.20	0.21	0.10	0.82	7.85	19.79
2009	0.86	4.04	4.72	1.28	0.19	0.25	0.14	1.10	6.78	18.52
Q1 2010	1.02	4.46	4.60	1.48	0.13	0.31	0.09	0.52	6.96	18.54
JetBlue Airways										
2005	0.51¢	2.31¢	2.42¢	0.68¢	0.38¢	0.25¢	0.16¢	0.51¢	1.44¢	8.13¢
2008	0.74	2.86	5.35	0.86	0.49	0.33	0.18	0.53	2.06	12.67
2009	0.86	3.20	3.64	0.98	0.48	0.40	0.19	0.62	2.13	11.64
Q1 2010	0.97	3.62	3.93	1.04	0.48	0.40	0.14	0.88	2.30	12.80

Costs Incurred per Revenue Passenger Mile (in cents)*

(Continued)

Exhibit 9   (Concluded)

Costs Incurred per Revenue Passenger Mile (in cents)*

	Salaries/Fringe Benefits		Fuel and Oil	Maintenance	Rentals	Landing Fees	Advertising	General and Administrative	Other Operating Expenses	Total Operating Expenses
	Pilots/Copilots	All Employees								
Northwest Airlines (merged with Delta and began combined reporting in January 2010)										
1995	1.21¢	4.84¢	1.73¢	1.39¢	0.58¢	0.37¢	0.20¢	0.52¢	3.14¢	12.77¢
2000	1.01	4.76	2.35	1.55	0.53	0.31	0.17	0.55	2.77	12.99
2005	0.94	5.07	4.01	1.54	0.57	0.38	0.12	0.58	5.13	17.40
2008	0.73	3.77	7.33	1.30	0.26	0.34	0.08	0.86	6.49	20.43
2009	0.98	4.34	3.79	1.18	0.18	0.32	0.06	1.41	5.22	16.49
Southwest Airlines										
1995	0.92¢	3.94¢	1.56¢	1.21¢	0.79¢	0.35¢	0.41¢	1.09¢	1.56¢	10.91¢
2000	0.86	4.22	1.95	1.22	0.48	0.31	0.35	1.42	0.96	10.91
2005	1.18	4.70	2.44	1.17	0.31	0.34	0.29	0.73	1.23	11.21
2008	1.31	4.81	5.04	1.45	0.26	0.39	0.27	0.84	1.30	14.36
2009	1.33	4.88	4.08	1.43	0.30	0.41	0.27	0.84	1.30	13.53
Q1 2010	1.46	5.27	4.78	1.45	0.34	0.48	0.26	0.95	1.47	14.98
United Air Lines										
1995	0.86¢	4.73¢	1.51¢	1.51¢	0.90¢	0.29¢	0.17¢	0.53¢	2.92¢	12.58¢
2000	1.15	5.75	1.98	1.84	0.73	0.28	0.21	0.76	3.09	14.65
2005	0.62	3.72	3.53	1.60	0.35	0.30	0.16	0.60	5.09	15.35
2008	0.69	4.18	7.02	1.88	0.37	0.31	0.06	1.16	5.00	19.97
2009	0.70	4.06	3.39	1.87	0.35	0.37	0.04	0.90	5.06	16.03
Q1 2010	0.73	4.59	4.15	1.92	0.35	0.41	0.05	0.97	5.52	17.95
US Airways (merged with America West in September 2005 and began combined reporting in 2007)										
1995	1.55¢	7.53¢	1.59¢	2.09¢	1.05¢	0.29¢	0.13¢	0.73¢	4.32¢	17.73¢
2000	1.36	7.59	2.44	2.30	0.97	0.28	0.19	1.10	4.81	19.68
2005	0.78	3.74	3.89	1.50	1.06	0.31	0.06	0.66	7.27	18.49
2008	0.80	3.92	5.94	1.94	1.22	0.24	0.02	2.63	7.59	23.50
2009	0.78	3.97	3.20	1.90	1.23	0.27	0.03	1.06	6.77	18.42
Q1 2010	0.84	4.49	4.07	1.99	1.35	0.28	0.03	1.26	7.48	20.94

*Costs per passenger revenue mile represent the costs per ticketed passenger per mile flown; the figures are derived by dividing the company's total expenses in each of the cost categories by the total number of miles flown by all ticketed passengers—thus, if there are 100 ticketed passengers on a flight that travels 500 miles, the number of passenger revenue miles for that flight is 100 × 500, or 50,000).

Source: U.S. Department of Transportation, Bureau of Transportation Statistics, Air Carrier Statistics Form 298C Summary Data and Form 41, Schedules P-6, P-12, P-51, and P-52.

Exhibit 10   **Southwest Airline's Operating Expenses per Available Seat Mile, 1995–2009 (selected years)**

Expense Category	Costs per Available Seat Mile (in cents)								
	2009	2008	2007	2006	2005	2004	2002	2000	1995
Salaries, wages, bonuses, and benefits	3.54¢	3.23¢	3.22¢	3.29¢	3.27¢	3.18	2.89¢	2.81¢	2.40¢
Fuel and oil	3.11	3.60	2.70	2.31	1.58	1.30	1.11	1.34	1.01
Maintenance materials and repairs	0.73	0.70	0.62	0.51	0.52	0.60	0.57	0.63	0.60
Aircraft rentals	0.19	0.15	0.16	0.17	0.19	0.23	0.27	0.33	0.47
Landing fees and other rentals	0.73	0.64	0.56	0.53	0.53	0.53	0.50	0.44	0.44
Depreciation	0.63	0.58	0.56	0.56	0.55	0.56	0.52	0.47	0.43
Other expenses	1.36	1.34	1.28	1.43	1.41	1.37	1.55	1.71	1.72
Total	**10.29¢**	**10.24¢**	**9.10¢**	**8.80¢**	**8.05¢**	**7.70¢**	**7.41¢**	**7.73¢**	**7.07¢**

Note: Figures in this exhibit differ from those for Southwest in Exhibit 9 because the cost figures in Exhibit 9 are based on *cost per passenger revenue mile,* whereas the cost figures in this exhibit are based on *costs per available seat mile.* Costs per revenue passenger mile represent the costs per ticketed passenger per mile flown, whereas costs per available seat mile are the *costs per seat per mile flown (irrespective of whether the seat was occupied or not).*

Source: Southwest Airlines, 10-K reports and annual reports, various years.

SOUTHWEST'S PEOPLE MANAGEMENT PRACTICES AND CULTURE

Whereas the litany at many companies was that customers come first, at Southwest the operative principle was that "employees come first and customers come second." The high strategic priority placed on employees reflected management's belief that delivering superior service required employees who not only were passionate about their jobs but also knew that the company was genuinely concerned for their well-being and committed to providing them with job security. Southwest's thesis was simple: Keep employees happy—then they will keep customers happy.

In Southwest's 2000 annual report, senior management explained why employees were the company's greatest asset:

> Our people are warm, caring and compassionate and willing to do whatever it takes to bring the Freedom to Fly to their fellow Americans. They take pride in doing well for themselves by doing good for others. They have built a unique and powerful culture that demonstrates that the only way to accomplish our mission to make air travel affordable for others, while ensuring ample profitability, job security, and plentiful Profitsharing for ourselves, is to keep our costs low and Customer Service quality high.
>
> At Southwest, our People are our greatest assets, which is why we devote so much time and energy to hiring great People with winning attitudes. Because we are well known as an excellent place to work with great career opportunities and a secure future, lots of People want to work for Southwest. . . . Once hired, we provide a nurturing and supportive work environment that gives our Employees the freedom to be creative, have fun, and make a positive difference. Although we offer competitive compensation packages, it's our Employees' sense of ownership, pride in team accomplishments, and enhanced job satisfaction that keep our Culture and Southwest Spirit alive and why we continue to produce winning seasons.

Gary Kelly, the company's current CEO, echoed the views of his predecessors: "Our People are our single greatest strength and our most enduring long term competitive advantage."[20]

The company changed the Personnel Department's name to the People Department in 1989. Later, it was renamed the People and Leadership Development Department.

Recruiting, Screening, and Hiring

Southwest hired employees for attitude and trained for skills. Herb Kelleher explained:

> We can train people to do things where skills are concerned. But there is one capability we do not have and that is to change a person's attitude. So we prefer an unskilled person with a good attitude . . . [to] a highly skilled person with a bad attitude.[21]

Southwest recruited employees by means of newspaper ads, career fairs, and Internet job listings; a number of candidates applied because of Southwest's reputation as one of the best companies to work for in America and because they were impressed by their experiences as a customer on Southwest flights. Recruitment ads were designed to capture the attention of people thought to possess Southwest's "personality profile." For instance, one ad showed Herb Kelleher impersonating Elvis Presley and had the following copy:

> Work In A Place Where Elvis Has Been Spotted. The qualifications? It helps to be outgoing. Maybe even a bit off center. And be prepared to stay for a while. After all, we have the lowest employee turnover rate in the industry. If this sounds good to you, just phone our jobline or send your resume. Attention Elvis.[22]

Colleen Barrett elaborated on what the company looked for in screening candidates for job openings:

> We hire People to live the Southwest Way. They must possess a Warrior Spirit, lead with a Servant's Heart, and have a Fun-LUVing attitude. We hire People who fight to win, work hard, are dedicated, and have a passion for Customer Service. We won't hire People if something about their behavior won't be a Cultural fit. We hire the best. When our new hires walk through the door, our message to them is you are starting the flight of your life.[23]

All job applications were processed through the People and Leadership Development Department. Exhibit 11 details what the company called the "Southwest Way."

In hiring for jobs that involved personal contact with passengers, the company looked for people-oriented applicants who were extroverted and had a good sense of humor. It tried to identify candidates with a knack for reading peoples' emotions and responding in a genuinely caring, empathetic manner. Southwest wanted employees to deliver the kind of service that showed they truly enjoyed meeting people, being around passengers, and doing their job, as opposed to delivering the kind of service that came across as being forced or taught. Kelleher elaborated: "We are interested in people who externalize, who focus on other people, who are

---

Exhibit 11   **Personal Traits, Attitudes, and Behaviors That Southwest Wanted Employees to Possess and Display**

Living the Southwest Way		
Warrior Spirit	**Servant's Heart**	**Fun-LUVing Attitude**
• Work hard	• Follow the Golden Rule	• Have FUN
• Desire to be the best	• Adhere to the Basic Principles	• Don't take yourself too seriously
• Be courageous	• Treat others with respect	• Maintain perspective (balance)
• Display a sense of urgency	• Put others first	• Celebrate successes
• Persevere	• Be egalitarian	• Enjoy your work
• Innovate	• Demonstrate proactive Customer Service	• Be a passionate team player
	• Embrace the SWA Family	

Source: Southwest Airlines, www.southwest.com, accessed August 18, 2010.

motivated to help other people. We are not interested in navel gazers."[24] In addition to a "whistle while you work" attitude, Southwest was drawn to candidates who it thought would be likely to exercise initiative, work harmoniously with fellow employees, and be community-spirited.

Southwest did not use personality tests to screen job applicants, nor did it ask them what they would or should do in certain hypothetical situations. Rather, the hiring staff at Southwest analyzed each job category to determine the specific behaviors, knowledge, and motivations that job holders needed and then tried to find candidates with the desired traits—a process called targeted selection. A trait common to all job categories was teamwork; a trait deemed critical for pilots and flight attendants was judgment. In exploring an applicant's aptitude for teamwork, interviewers often asked applicants to tell them about a time in a prior job when they went out of their way to help a coworker or to explain how they had handled conflict with a coworker. Another frequent question was "What was your most embarrassing moment?" The thesis here was that having applicants talk about their past behaviors provided good clues about their future behaviors.

To test for unselfishness, Southwest interviewing teams typically gave a group of potential employees ample time to prepare five-minute presentations about themselves; during the presentations in an informal conversational setting, interviewers watched the audience to see who was absorbed in polishing their presentations and who was listening attentively, enjoying the stories being told, and applauding the efforts of the presenters. Those who were emotionally engaged in hearing the presenters and giving encouragement were deemed more apt to be team players than those who were focused on looking good themselves. All applicants for flight attendant positions were put through such a presentation exercise before an interview panel consisting of customers, experienced flight attendants, and members of the People and Leadership Department. Flight attendant candidates that got through the group presentation interviews then had to complete a three-on-one interview conducted by a recruiter, a supervisor from the hiring section of the People and Leadership Department, and a Southwest flight attendant; following this interview, the three-person panel tried to reach a consensus on whether to recommend or drop the candidate.

Southwest received 90,043 résumés and hired 831 new employees in 2009. In 2007, prior to the onset of the recession, Southwest received 329,200 résumés and hired 4,200 new employees.

Training

Apart from the FAA-mandated training for certain employees, training activities at Southwest were designed and conducted by Southwest's University for People. The curriculum included courses for new recruits, employees, and managers. Learning was viewed as a never-ending process for all company personnel; the expectation was that each employee should be an "intentional learner," looking to grow and develop not just from occasional classes taken at Southwest's festive University for People learning center but also from their everyday on-the-job experiences.

Southwest's University for People conducted a variety of courses offered to maintenance personnel and other employees to meet the training and safety requirements of the Federal Aviation Administration, the U.S. Department of Transportation, the Occupational Safety and Health Administration, and other government agencies. And there were courses on written communications, public speaking, stress management, career development, performance appraisal, decision making, leadership, customer service, corporate culture, and employee relations to help employees advance their careers.

Employees wanting to explore whether a management career was for them could take Leadership 101 and 201. One of the keystone course offerings for new frontline managers was a four-session "Leadership Southwest Style" course, which made extensive use of the Myers-Briggs personality assessment to help managers understand the "why" behind coworkers' behaviors and to learn how to build trust, empathize, resolve conflicts, and do a better job of communicating. There was a special "manager-in-training" course for high-potential employees wanting to pursue a long-term career at Southwest. Leadership courses for people already in supervisory or managerial positions emphasized a management style based on coaching, empowering, and encouraging, rather than supervising or enforcing rules and regulations. From time to time, supervisors and executives attended courses on corporate culture, intended to help instill, ingrain, and nurture such cultural themes as teamwork, trust, harmony, and diversity.

All employees who came into contact with customers, including pilots, received customer care training. Southwest's latest customer-related training initiative involved a course called "Every Customer Matters"; by the end of 2009, 14,225 employees had completed the course. Altogether, Southwest employees spent more than 720,000 hours in training sessions of one kind or another in 2009:[25]

Job Category	Amount of Training
Maintenance and support personnel	81,633 hours
Customer support and services personnel	106,480 hours
Flight attendants	109,450 hours
Pilots	199,500 hours
Ground operations personnel	224,799 hours

The OnBoarding Program for Newly Hired Employees   Southwest had a program called OnBoarding "to welcome New Hires into the Southwest Family" and provide information and assistance from the time they were selected until the end of their first year. Orientation for new employees included a one-day orientation session, videos on Southwest's history, an overview of the airline industry and the competitive challenges that Southwest faced, and an introduction to Southwest's culture and management practices. The culture introduction included a video called the *Southwest Shuffle,* which featured hundreds of Southwest employees rapping about the fun they had on their jobs (at many Southwest gatherings, it was common for a group of employees to do the Southwest Shuffle, with the remaining attendees cheering and clapping). There were also exercises that demonstrated the role of creativity and teamwork and a scavenger hunt in which new hires were given a timeline with specific dates in Southwest's history and were asked to fill in the missing details by viewing the memorabilia decorating the corridors of the Dallas headquarters and getting information from people working in various offices. During their first 30 days at Southwest,

new employees could access an interactive online tool—OnBoarding Online Orientation—to learn about the company.

An additional element of the Onboarding Program involved assigning each new employee to an existing Southwest employee who had volunteered to sponsor a new hire and be of assistance in acclimating the new employee to his or her job and the Southwest Way; each volunteer sponsor received training from Southwest's Onboarding Team in what was expected of a sponsor. Much of the indoctrination of new employees into the company's culture was done by the volunteer sponsor, coworkers, and the new employee's supervisor. Southwest made active use of a one-year probationary employment period to help ensure that new employees fit in with the company's culture and adequately embraced its cultural values.

Promotion

Approximately 80 to 90 percent of Southwest's supervisory positions were filled internally, reflecting management's belief that people who had "been there and done that" would be more likely to appreciate and understand the demands that people under them were experiencing and, also, more likely to enjoy the respect of their peers and higher-level managers. Employees could either apply for supervisory positions or be recommended by their present supervisor. New appointees for supervisor, team leader, and manager attended a three-day class called Leading with Integrity and aimed at developing leadership and communication skills. Employees being considered for managerial positions of large operations (Up and Coming Leaders) received training in every department of the company over a six-month period in which they continued to perform their current job. At the end of the six-month period, candidates were provided with 360-degree feedback from department heads, peers, and subordinates; representatives of the People and Leadership Department analyzed the feedback in deciding on the specific assignment of each candidate.[26]

Compensation

Southwest's pay scales compared quite favorably with other major U.S. airlines (see Exhibit 12).

Exhibit 12 **Estimated Employee Compensation and Benefits at Selected U.S. Airlines, 2008 and 2009**

	Southwest Airlines	American Airlines	Delta	Continental Airlines	JetBlue	United Airlines	US Airways
Average Pilot Wage/Salary							
2008	$172,800	$138,800	$125,600	$136,300	$112,000	$119,500	$113,900
2009	176,200	137,500	137,900	150,200	124,700	125,500	111,300
Average Flight Attendant Wage/Salary							
2008	$ 53,000	$ 49,800	$ 37,000	$ 49,100	$ 33,000	$ 40,100	$ 39,700
2009	46,800	50,900	39,200	51,200	33,800	40,600	40,600
All-Employee Average Wage/Salary							
2008	$ 72,100	$ 60,900	$ 56,100	$ 54,400	$ 54,400	$ 58,100	$ 53,800
2009	75,600	63,000	59,600	56,800	58,600	58,200	55,500
Average Benefits per Employee							
2008	$ 24,200	$ 24,300	$ 45,100	$ 15,800	$ 13,800	$ 25,600	$ 14,500
2009	23,800	30,500	30,100	19,900	14,800	22,700	13,500

Note: The compensation and benefits numbers are estimated from compensation cost and workforce size data reported by the airlines to the Bureau of Transportation Statistics. The number of employees at year-end were used to calculate the averages, which may cause distortions in the event of significant changes in a company's workforce size during the year. In addition, several companies were engaged in mergers and/or major cost restructuring initiatives during 2008–2009, which in some instances (notably Delta) resulted in significant within-company changes from 2008 to 2009.

Source: Derived from data in various airline industry reports published by the Bureau of Transportation Statistics and from information posted at www.airlinefinancials.com.

Southwest's average pay for pilots and its all-employee average compensation were the highest of all the major U.S. airlines—sometimes even at or near the top of the industry—and its benefit packages were quite competitive.

Southwest introduced a profit-sharing plan for senior employees in 1973, the first such plan in the airline industry. By the mid-1990s, the plan had been extended to cover most Southwest employees. As of 2010, Southwest had stock option programs for various employee groups (including those covered by collective bargaining agreements), a 401(k) employee savings plans that included company-matching contributions, an employee stock purchase plan, and a profit-sharing plan covering virtually all employees that consisted of a money purchase defined-contribution plan to which Southwest contributed 15 percent of eligible pretax profits. Company contributions to employee 410(k) and profit-sharing plans totaled

$1.3 billion during 2005–2009; in recent years, the annual contribution had represented 6 to 12 percent of base pay. Employees participating in stock purchases via payroll deduction bought 1.3 million shares in 2007, 1.3 million shares in 2008, and 2.2 million shares in 2009 at prices equal to 90 percent of the market value at the end of each monthly purchase period. Southwest employees owned about 10 percent of Southwest's outstanding shares and, as of December 31, 2009, held options to buy some 78.2 million additional shares.

Employee Relations

About 82 percent of Southwest's 34,700 employees belonged to a union, making Southwest one of the most highly unionized U.S. airlines. An in-house union—the Southwest Airline Pilots Association—represented the company's pilots. The Teamsters Union represented Southwest's stock clerks and flight simulator technicians; a local of the Transportation Workers of America represented flight attendants; another local of the Transportation Workers of America represented baggage handlers, ground crews, and provisioning employees; the International Association of Machinists and Aerospace Workers represented customer service and reservation employees; and the Aircraft Mechanics Fraternal Association represented the company's mechanics.

Management encouraged union members and negotiators to research their pressing issues and to conduct employee surveys before each contract negotiation. Southwest's contracts with the unions representing its employees were relatively free of restrictive work rules and narrow job classifications that might impede worker productivity. All of the contracts allowed any qualified employee to perform any function—thus pilots, ticket agents, and gate personnel could help load and unload baggage when needed and flight attendants could pick up trash and make flight cabins more presentable for passengers boarding the next flight.

Except for one brief strike by machinists in the early 1980s and some unusually difficult negotiations in 2000–2001, Southwest's relationships with the unions representing its employee groups were harmonious and nonadversarial for the most part—even though there were sometimes spirited disagreements over particular issues.

In 2000–2001, the company had contentious negotiations with Local 555 of the Transportation Workers of America (TWU) over a new wage and benefits package for Southwest's ramp, baggage operations, provisioning, and freight personnel; the previous contract had become open for renegotiation in December 1999, and a tentative agreement reached at the end of 2000 was rejected by 64 percent of the union members who voted. A memo from Kelleher to TWU representatives said, "The cost and structure of the TWU 555 negotiating committee's proposal would seriously undermine the competitive strength of Southwest Airlines; endanger our ability to grow; threaten the value of our employees' profit-sharing; require us to contract out work in order to remain competitive; and threaten our 29-year history of job security for our employees." In a union newsletter in early 2001, the president of the TWU local said, "We asked for a decent living wage and benefits to support our families, and were told of how unworthy and how greedy we were." The ongoing dispute resulted in informational picket lines in March 2001 at several Southwest locations, the first picketing since 1980. Later in 2001, with the help of the National Mediation Board, Southwest and the TWU reached an agreement covering Southwest's ramp, operations, and provisioning employees.

Prior to 9/11, Southwest's pilots were somewhat restive about their base pay relative to pilots at other U.S. airlines. The maximum pay for Southwest's 3,700+ pilots (before profit-sharing bonuses) was $148,000, versus maximums of $290,000 for United's pilots, $262,000 for Delta's pilots, $206,000 for American's pilots, and $199,000 for Continental's pilots.[27] Moreover, some veteran Southwest employees were grumbling about staff shortages in certain locations (to hold down labor costs) and cracks in the company's close-knit family culture due to the influx of so many new employees over the past several years. A number of employees who had accepted lower pay because of Southwest's underdog status were said to feel entitled to "big airline" pay now that Southwest had emerged as a major U.S. carrier.[28] However, when airline traffic dropped precipitously following 9/11, Southwest's major airline rivals won big wage and salary concessions from unions representing pilots and other airline workers; moreover, about 1 in 5 airline jobs—some 120,000 in all—were eliminated. In 2006, a senior Boeing 737 pilot at Delta Air Lines working a normal 65-hour month made $116,200 annually, down 26 percent from pre-9/11 wages. A comparable pilot at United Airlines earned $102,200, down 34 percent from before 9/11, and at American Airlines such a pilot made $122,500, 18 percent less than in the days before 9/11.

In 2004, 2007, and 2009, in an attempt to contain rising labor costs and better match workforce size to its operating requirements, Southwest offered voluntary buyout or early retirement packages to selected groups of employees. The 2004 buyout package was offered to approximately 8,700 flight attendants, ramp workers, customer service employees, and those in reservations, operations, and freight who had reached a specific pay scale; the buyout consisted of a $25,000 payment and medical and dental benefits for a specified period. About

1,000 employees accepted the 2004 buyout offer. In 2009, Southwest announced Freedom '09, a one-time voluntary early retirement program offered to older employees, in which the company offered cash bonuses, medical/dental coverage for a specified period of time, and travel privileges based on work group and years of service; some 1,400 employees elected to participate in Freedom '09, resulting in payouts of $66 million.

The No-Layoff Policy

Southwest Airlines had never laid off or furloughed any of its employees since the company began operations in 1971. The company's no-layoff policy was seen as integral to how the company treated its employees and management efforts to sustain and nurture the culture. According to Kelleher:

> Nothing kills your company's culture like layoffs. Nobody has ever been furloughed here, and that is unprecedented in the airline industry. It's been a huge strength of ours. It's certainly helped negotiate our union contracts. . . . We could have furloughed at various times and been more profitable, but I always thought that was shortsighted. You want to show your people you value them and you're not going to hurt them just to get a little more money in the short term. Not furloughing people breeds loyalty. It breeds a sense of security. It breeds a sense of trust.[29]

Southwest had built up considerable goodwill with its employees and unions over the years by avoiding layoffs. Both senior management and Southwest employees regarded the three recent buyout offers as a better approach to workforce reduction than involuntary layoffs.

Operation Kick Tail

In 2007, Southwest management launched an internal initiative called Operation Kick Tail, a multiyear call to action for employees to focus even more attention on providing high-quality customer service, maintaining low costs, and nurturing the Southwest culture. One component of Operation Kick Tail involved singling out employees for special recognition when they did something to make a positive difference in a customer's travel experience or in the life of a coworker.

Gary Kelly saw this aspect of Operation Kick Tail as a way to foster the employee attitudes and commitment needed to provide "Positively Outrageous Customer Service." He explained:

> One of Southwest's rituals is finding and developing People who are "built to serve." That allows us to provide a personal, warm level of service that is unmatched in the airline industry.

Southwest management viewed Operation Kick Tail as a means to better engage and incentivize employees to strengthen their display of the traits included in the Southwest Way and achieve a competitive edge keyed to superior customer service.

Management Style

At Southwest, management strove to do things in a manner that would make Southwest employees proud of the company they worked for and its workforce practices. Managers were expected to spend at least one-third of their time walking around the facilities under their supervision, observing firsthand what was going on, listening to employees, and being responsive to their concerns. A former director of people development at Southwest told of a conversation he had with one of Southwest's terminal managers:

> While I was out in the field visiting one of our stations, one of our managers mentioned to me that he wanted to put up a suggestion box. I responded by saying, "Sure—why don't you put up a suggestion box right here on this wall and then admit you are a failure as a manager?" Our theory is, if you have to put up a box so people can write down their ideas and toss them in, it means you are not doing what you are supposed to be doing. You are supposed to be setting your people up to be winners. To do that, you should be there listening to them and available to them in person, not via a suggestion box. For the most part, I think we have a very good sense of this at Southwest. I think that most people employed here know that they can call any one of our vice presidents on the telephone and get heard, almost immediately.
> The suggestion box gives managers an out; it relinquishes their responsibility to be accessible to their people, and that's when we have gotten in trouble at Southwest—when we can no longer be responsive to our flight attendants or customer service agents, when they can't gain access to somebody who can give them resources and answers.[30]

Company executives were very approachable, insisting on being called by their first names. At new employee orientations, people were told, "We do not call the company chairman and CEO Mr. Kelly, we call him Gary." Managers and executives had an open-door policy, actively listening to employee concerns, opinions, and suggestions for reducing costs and improving efficiency.

Employee-led initiatives were common. Southwest's pilots had been instrumental in developing new protocols for takeoffs and landings that conserved fuel. Another frontline employee had suggested not putting the company logos on trash bags, saving an estimated $250,000 annually. Rather than buy 800 computers for a new reservations center in Albuquerque, company employees determined that they could buy the parts and assemble the PCs themselves for half the price of a new PC, saving the company $1 million. It was Southwest clerks who came up with the idea of doing away with paper tickets and shifting to e-tickets.

There were only four layers of management between a frontline supervisor and the CEO. Southwest's employees enjoyed substantial authority and decision-making power. According to Kelleher:

> We've tried to create an environment where people are able to, in effect, bypass even the fairly lean structures that we have so that they don't have to convene a meeting of the sages in order to get something done. In many cases, they can just go ahead and do it on their own. They can take individual responsibility for it and know they will not be crucified if it doesn't work out. Our leanness requires people to be comfortable in making their own decisions and undertaking their own efforts.[31]

From time to time, there were candid meetings of frontline employees and managers where operating problems and issues between/among workers and departments were acknowledged, openly discussed, and resolved.[32] Informal problem avoidance and rapid problem resolution were seen as managerial virtues.

Southwest's Two Big Core Values—LUV and Fun

Two core values—LUV and fun—permeated the work environment at Southwest. LUV was much more than the company's ticker symbol and a recurring theme in Southwest's advertising

campaigns. Over the years, LUV grew into Southwest's code word for treating individuals—fellow employees and customers—with dignity and respect and demonstrating a caring, loving attitude. The code word *LUV* and red hearts commonly appeared on banners and posters at company facilities, as reminders of the compassion that was expected toward customers and other employees. Practicing the Golden Rule, internally and externally, was expected of all employees. Employees who struggled to live up to these expectations were subjected to considerable peer pressure and usually were asked to seek employment elsewhere if they did not soon leave on their own volition.

Fun at Southwest was exactly what the word implies—and it occurred throughout the company in the form of the generally entertaining behavior of employees in performing their jobs, the ongoing pranks and jokes, and frequent company-sponsored parties and celebrations (which typically included the Southwest Shuffle). On holidays, employees were encouraged to dress in costumes. There were charity benefit games, chili cook-offs, Halloween parties, new Ronald McDonald House dedications, and other special events of one kind or another at one location or another almost every week. According to one manager, "We're kind of a big family here, and family members have fun together."

Culture Building

Southwest executives believed that the company's growth was primarily a function of the rate at which it could hire and train people to fit into its culture and consistently display the desired traits and behaviors. CEO Gary Kelly said, "Some things at Southwest won't change. We will continue to expect our people to live what we describe as the 'Southwest Way,' which is to have a Warrior Spirit, Servant's Heart, and Fun-Loving Attitude. Those three things have defined our culture for 36 years."[33]

The Corporate Culture Committee

Southwest formed its Corporate Culture Committee in 1990 to promote "Positively Outrageous Service" and devise tributes, contests, and celebrations intended to nurture and perpetuate the Southwest Spirit and Living the Southwest Way. The committee, chaired by Colleen Barrett until mid-2008 and then by Ginger Hardage (who was given lead executive responsibility for cultural aspects at Southwest when Barrett retired), was composed of 100 employees who had demonstrated their commitment to Southwest's mission and values and zeal in exhibiting the Southwest Spirit and Living the Southwest Way. Members came from a cross-section of departments and locations and functioned as cultural ambassadors, missionaries, and storytellers during their two-year term.

The Corporate Culture Committee had four all-day meetings annually; ad hoc subcommittees formed throughout the year met more frequently. Over the years, the committee had sponsored and supported hundreds of ways to promote and ingrain the traits and behaviors embedded in Living the Southwest Way—examples included promoting the use of red hearts and LUV to embody the spirit of Southwest employees caring about each other and Southwest's customers, showing up at a facility to serve pizza or ice cream to employees or to remodel and decorate an employee break room. Kelleher indicated, "We're not big on Committees at Southwest, but of the committees we do have, the Culture Committee is the most important."[34]

Efforts to Nurture and Sustain the Southwest Culture

Apart from the efforts of the Corporate Culture Committee, Southwest management had sought to reinforce the company's core values and culture via its annual Heros of the Heart Award, its CoHearts mentoring program, its Day in the Field program in which employees spent time working in another area of the company's operations, its Helping Hands program in which volunteers from around the system traveled to work two weekend shifts at other Southwest facilities that were temporarily shorthanded or experiencing heavy work-loads, and periodic Culture Exchange meetings to celebrate the Southwest Spirit and company milestones. Almost every event at Southwest was videotaped, which provided footage for creating multipurpose videos, such as *Keepin' the Spirit Alive,* that could be shown at company events all over the system and used in training courses. The concepts of LUV and fun were spotlighted in all of the company's training manuals and videos.

Southwest's monthly employee newsletter often spotlighted the experiences and deeds of particular employees, reprinted letters of praise from customers, and reported company celebrations of milestones. A quarterly news video, *As the Plane Turns,* was sent to all facilities to keep employees up to date on company happenings, provide clips of special events, and share messages from customers, employees, and executives. The company had published a book for employees describing "outrageous" acts of service.

Employee Productivity

Management was convinced the company's strategy, culture, esprit de corps, and people management practices fostered high labor productivity and contributed to Southwest's having low labor costs in comparison to the labor costs at its principal domestic rivals. When a Southwest flight pulled up to the gate, ground crews, gate personnel, and flight attendants hustled to perform all the tasks requisite to turn the plane quickly—employees took pride in doing their part to achieve good on-time performance. Southwest's turnaround times were in the range of 25 to 30 minutes, versus an industry average of around 45 minutes. In 2009, Southwest's labor productivity compared quite favorably with its chief domestic competitors (as shown below):

	Productivity Measure	
	Passengers Enplaned per Employee, 2009	**Employees per Plane, 2009**
Southwest Airlines	2,475	65
American Airlines	1,289	109
Continental	1,177	115
Delta	1,430	103
JetBlue	2,121	70
United	1,204	129
US Airways	1,628	90

Source: Calculated from data in Southwest Airlines' 10-K reports.

System Operations

Under Herb Kelleher, instituting practices, procedures, and support systems that promoted operating excellence had become a tradition and a source of company pride. Much time and effort over the years had gone into finding the most effective ways to do aircraft maintenance, to operate safely, to make baggage handling more efficient and baggage transfers more accurate, and to improve the percentage of on-time arrivals and departures. Believing that air travelers were more likely to fly Southwest if its flights were reliable and on time, Southwest's managers constantly monitored on-time arrivals and departures, making inquiries when many flights ran behind and searching for ways to improve on-time performance. One initiative to help minimize weather and operational delays involved the development of a state-of-the-art flight dispatch system.

Southwest's current CEO, Gary Kelly, had followed Kelleher's lead in pushing for operating excellence. One of Kelly's strategic objectives for Southwest was "to be the safest, most efficient, and most reliable airline in the world." Southwest managers and employees in all positions and ranks were proactive in offering suggestions for improving Southwest's practices and procedures; those with merit were quickly implemented. Southwest was considered to have one of the most competent and thorough aircraft maintenance programs in the commercial airline industry and, going into 2008, was widely regarded as the best operator among U.S. airlines. Its recent record vis-à-vis rival airlines on four important measures of operating performance was commendable—see Exhibit 13.

The First Significant Blemish on Southwest's Safety Record
While no Southwest plane had ever crashed and there had never been a passenger fatality, there was an incident in 2005 in which a Southwest plane landing in a snow storm with a strong tailwind at Chicago's Midway airport was unable to stop before overrunning a shorter-than-usual runway, rolling onto a highway, crashing into a car, killing one of the occupants, and injuring 22 of the passengers on the plane. A National Traffic Safety Board investigation concluded that "the pilot's failure to use available reverse thrust in a timely manner to safely slow or stop the airplane after landing" was the probable cause.

Belated Aircraft Inspections Further Tarnish Southwest's Reputation
In early 2008, various media reported that Southwest Airlines over a period of several months in 2006 and 2007 had knowingly failed to conduct required inspections for early detection of fuselage fatigue cracking on 46 of its older Boeing 737-300 jets. The company had voluntarily notified the Federal Aviation Administration about the lapse in checks for fuselage cracks but continued to fly the planes until the work was done—about eight days. The belated inspections revealed tiny cracks in the bodies of six planes, with the largest measuring four inches; none of the cracks impaired flight safety. According to CEO Gary Kelly, "Southwest Airlines discovered the missed inspection area, disclosed it to the FAA, and promptly re-inspected all potentially affected aircraft in March 2007. The FAA approved our actions and considered the matter closed as of April 2007." Nonetheless, on March 12, 2008, shortly after the reports in the media surfaced about Southwest's failure to meet inspection deadlines, Southwest canceled 4 percent of its flights and grounded 44 of its Boeing 737-300s until it verified that the aircraft had undergone required inspections. Gary Kelly then initiated an internal review of the company's maintenance practices; the investigation raised "concerns" about the company's aircraft maintenance procedures, prompting Southwest to put three employees on leave. The FAA subsequently fined Southwest $10.2 million for its transgressions. In an effort to help restore customer confidence, Kelly publicly apologized for the company's wrongdoing, promised that such a lapse would not occur again, and reasserted the company's commitment to safety. He said:

> From our inception, Southwest Airlines has maintained a rigorous Culture of Safety—and has maintained that same dedication for more than 37 years. It is and always has been our number one priority to ensure safety.
>
> We've got a 37-year history of very safe operations, one of the safest operations in the world, and we're safer today than we've ever been.

Exhibit 13 **Comparative Statistics on On-Time Flights, Mishandled Baggage, Boarding Denials Due to Oversold Flights, and Passenger Complaints for Eight Major U.S. Airlines, 2000 through Quarter 1 of 2010**

Percentage of Scheduled Flights Arriving within 15 Minutes of the Scheduled Time (during the previous 12 months ending in May of each year)							
Airline	**2000**	**2005**	**2006**	**2007**	**2008**	**2009**	**Q1 2010**
American Airlines	75.8%	78.0%	75.6%	72.4%	66.9%	75.2%	77.5%
Continental Air Lines	76.7	78.7	74.8	73.5	74.1	75.6	80.4
Delta Air Lines	78.3	76.4	76.2	76.6	75.7	76.3	79.3
JetBlue Airways	n.a.	76.3	73.1	69.4	73.3	74.0	77.3
Northwest Airlines*	80.7	79.3	75.1	71.4	71.1	80.5	—
Southwest Airlines	**78.7**	**79.9**	**80.3**	**80.7**	**78.5**	**83.3**	**81.5**
United Air Lines	71.6	79.8	75.7	73.0	69.1	76.2	82.5
US Airways	72.7	76.0	78.9	69.7	75.5	79.9	81.9

Mishandled Baggage Reports per 1,000 Passengers (in May of each year)							
Airline	**2000**	**2005**	**2006**	**2007**	**2008**	**2009**	**Q1 2010**
American Airlines	5.44	4.58	4.91	6.40	5.82	4.32	3.87
Continental Air Lines	4.11	3.30	3.85	5.02	3.78	2.32	2.27
Delta Air Lines	3.64	6.21	4.75	5.26	3.81	4.33	3.50
JetBlue Airways	n.a.	3.16	2.88	4.38	3.23	2.26	2.15
Northwest Airlines*	4.98	3.58	3.11	3.80	2.97	2.11	—
Southwest Airlines	**4.14**	**3.46**	**3.66**	**5.54**	**4.41**	**3.30**	**3.09**
United Air Lines	6.71	4.00	3.89	4.83	4.76	3.67	3.05
US Airways	4.57	9.73	5.69	7.17	3.86	2.91	2.27

Involuntary Denied Boardings per 10,000 Passengers Due to Oversold Flights (January through March of each year)							
Airline	**2000**	**2005**	**2006**	**2007**	**2008**	**2009**	**Q1 2010**
American Airlines	0.59	0.72	1.16	1.06	0.98	0.43	1.28
Continental Air Lines	0.50	3.01	2.60	1.93	1.57	1.42	2.73
Delta Air Lines	0.44	1.06	2.68	3.47	1.80	1.64	0.63
JetBlue Airways	n.a.	0.00	0.01	0.04	0.02	0.00	0.01
Northwest Airlines*	0.12	1.70	1.00	1.25	1.15	0.68	—
Southwest Airlines	**1.70**	**0.74**	**1.81**	**1.25**	**1.68**	**1.42**	**2.59**
United Air Lines	1.61	0.42	0.88	0.4	0.89	1.30	1.92
US Airways	0.80	1.01	1.07	1.68	2.01	1.50	2.96

Complaints per 100,000 Passengers Boarded (in May of each year)							
Airline	**2000**	**2005**	**2006**	**2007**	**2008**	**2009**	**Q1 2010**
American Airlines	2.77	1.01	1.22	1.44	1.30	1.18	1.61
Continental Air Lines	2.25	0.89	0.85	0.75	1.03	1.03	1.36
Delta Air Lines	1.60	0.91	0.93	1.50	2.10	1.85	1.57
JetBlue Airways	n.a.	0.00	0.22	0.40	0.56	0.93	1.72
Northwest Airlines*	2.17	0.83	0.69	1.13	0.94	0.88	—
Southwest Airlines	**0.41**	**0.17**	**0.18**	**0.19**	**0.32**	**0.13**	**0.26**
United Air Lines	5.07	0.87	1.19	2.00	1.61	1.16	1.67
US Airways	1.63	0.99	1.22	2.65	1.94	1.34	1.19

*Effective January 2010, data of the merged operations of Delta Air Lines and Northwest Airlines were combined and reported as Delta for Q1 2010.

Source: Office of Aviation Enforcement and Proceedings, Air Travel Consumer Report, various years.

In the days following the public revelation of Southwest's maintenance lapse and the tarnishing of its reputation, an industry-wide audit by the FAA revealed similar failures to conduct timely inspections for early signs of fuselage fatigue at five other airlines—American, Continental, Delta, United, and Northwest. An air travel snafu ensued, with more than a thousand flights subsequently being canceled due to FAA-mandated grounding of the affected aircraft while the overdue safety inspections were performed. Further public scrutiny, including a congressional investigation, turned up documents indicating that, in some cases, planes flew for 30 months after the inspection deadlines had passed. Moreover, high-level FAA officials were apparently aware of the failure of Southwest and other airlines to perform the inspections for fuselage cracks at the scheduled times and chose not to strictly enforce the inspection deadlines—according to some commentators, because of allegedly cozy relationships with personnel at Southwest and the other affected airlines. Disgruntled FAA safety supervisors in charge of monitoring the inspections conducted by airline carriers testified before Congress that senior FAA officials frequently ignored their reports that certain routine safety inspections were not being conducted in accordance with prescribed FAA procedures. Shortly thereafter, the FAA issued more stringent procedures to ensure that aircraft safety inspections were properly conducted.

A SUDDEN SHIFT IN STRATEGY

In September 2010, Southwest announced that it had entered into a definitive agreement to acquire all of the outstanding common stock of AirTran Holdings, Inc. (NYSE: AAI), the parent company of AirTran Airways (AirTran), for a combination of cash and Southwest Airlines' common stock. The transaction was valued at about $1.4 billion; Southwest planned to fund approximately $670 million of the acquisition cost out of cash on hand.[35] For the twelve months ending June 30, 2010, AirTran had revenues of $2.5 billion and operating income (excluding special items) of $128 million. Like Southwest, AirTran was also a low-fare, low-cost airline. AirTran served 70 airports in the United States, Mexico, and the Caribbean; nineteen of these coincided with airports already served by Southwest. AirTran's hub was Atlanta's Hartsfield-Jackson International Airport, the busiest airport in the United States and the largest domestic airport not served by Southwest; AirTran had 202 daily departures out of Atlanta.[36] Some analysts believed that Southwest's entry into the Atlanta market alone could translate into 2 million additional passengers for Southwest annually. AirTran had 8,033 employees, 138 aircraft, and 177 nonstop routes; in 2009 AirTran transported 24.0 million passengers, the seventh largest number of all U.S. airlines. Based on current operations, the combined organization would have nearly 43,000 employees and serve more than 100 million passengers annually. In addition, the combined carriers' all-Boeing fleet consisting of 685 active aircraft would include 401 Boeing 737-700s, 173 Boeing 737-300s, 25 Boeing 737-500s, and 86 Boeing 717s, with an average age of approximately 10 years, one of the youngest fleets in the industry. The companies hoped to close the merger deal in early 2011 and then begin integration of AirTran into the Southwest Airlines brand—a process which Southwest management said might take as long as two years in order to maintain Southwest's standards for customer service.

ENDNOTES

[1] Kevin Freiberg and Jackie Freiberg, *NUTS! Southwest Airlines' Crazy Recipe for Business and Personal Success* (New York: Broadway Books, 1998), p.15.
[2] Ibid., pp. 16–18.
[3] Katrina Brooker, "The Chairman of the Board Looks Back," *Fortune,* May 28, 2001, p. 66.
[4] Freiberg and Freiberg, *NUTS,* p. 31.

[5] Ibid., pp. 26–27.
[6] Ibid., pp. 246–47.
[7] Quoted in the *Dallas Morning News,* March 20, 2001.
[8] Quoted in Brooker, "The Chairman of the Board Looks Back," p. 64.
[9] Ibid., p. 72.

[10] Quoted in *Seattle Times,* March 20, 2001, p. C3.
[11] Speech at Texas Christian University, September 13, 2007; accessed at www.southwest.com on September 8, 2008.
[12] Freiberg and Freiberg, *NUTS!,* p. 163.
[13] Company press release, July 15, 2004.

[14] Speech to Greater Boston Chamber of Commerce, April 23, 2008, www.southwest.com, accessed September 5, 2008.
[15] Speech to Business Today International Conference, November 20, 2007, www.southwest.com, accessed September 8, 2008.
[16] As cited in Freiberg and Freiberg, *NUTS!*, p. 288.
[17] Speech by Colleen Barrett on January 22, 2007 and posted at www.southwest.com; accessed on September 5, 2008.
[18] Brenda Paik Sunoo, "How Fun Flies at Southwest Airlines," *Personnel Journal* 74, no. 6 (June 1995), p. 70.
[19] Statement made in a 1993 Harvard Business School video and quoted in Roger Hallowell, "Southwest Airlines: A Case Study Linking Employee Needs Satisfaction and Organizational Capabilities to Competitive Advantage," *Human Resource Management* 35, no. 4 (Winter 1996), p. 517.

[20] Statement posted in the Careers section at www.southwest.com, accessed August 18, 2010.
[21] Quoted in James Campbell Quick, "Crafting an Organizational Structure: Herb's Hand at Southwest Airlines," *Organizational Dynamics* 21, no. 2 (Autumn 1992), p. 51.
[22] Southwest's ad entitled "Work in a Place Where Elvis Has Been Spotted," and Sunoo, "How Fun Flies at Southwest Airlines," pp. 64–65.
[23] Speech to the Paso Del Norte Group in El Paso Texas, January 22, 2007, www.southwest.com, accessed September 5, 2008.
[24] Quick, "Crafting an Organizational Structure," p. 52.
[25] Southwest's "2009 One Report," p. 20, www.southwest.com, accessed August 19, 2010.
[26] Sunoo, "How Fun Flies at Southwest Airlines," p. 72.

[27] Shawn Tully, "From Bad to Worse," *Fortune*, October 15, 2001, p. 124.
[28] Melanie Trottman, "Amid Crippled Rivals, Southwest Tries to Spread Its Wings," *Wall Street Journal*, October 11, 2001, p. A10.
[29] Brooker, "The Chairman of the Board Looks Back," p. 72.
[30] Freiberg and Freiberg, *NUTS!*, p. 273.
[31] Ibid., p. 76.
[32] Hallowell, "Southwest Airlines," p. 524.
[33] Speech to Business Today International Conference, November 20, 2007; accessed at www.southwest.com on September 8, 2008.
[34] Freiberg and Freiberg, *NUTS!*, p. 165.
[35] Southwest Airlines press release, September 27, 2010.
[36] Rhonda Cook and Kelly Yamanouchi, "Southwest Buying AirTran for $1.4 Billion," *Atlanta Journal-Constitution*, September 27, 2010, accessed at www.ajc.com on October 26, 2010.

Namasté Solar

Anne T. Lawrence
San José State University

Anthony I. Mathews
University of California, San Diego

On a warm day in July 2008, Namasté Solar president and chief executive officer (CEO) Blake Jones gathered the company's employee-owners for an all-hands meeting in a warehouse behind their headquarters in Boulder, Colorado. Photovoltaic panels, installation tools, and a discarded wooden sign displaying an image of the sun were piled haphazardly around the edge of the space. A window above the industrial-sized garage door threw a shaft of light across the concrete floor. The group, which had been temporarily displaced while their offices were undergoing a green renovation, had assembled an odd assortment of thrift-shop furniture to create makeshift seating. At the front of the room, they had set up easels, poster boards, and markets to record their deliberations.

The group—made up of more than three dozen installers, designers, salespeople, and office staff (most of whom were under the age of 40)—

had come together to consider a potentially game-changing decision for the young firm. Namasté Solar's business was designing and installing solar electric systems for residential, commercial, nonprofit, and government customers. Despite the emerging recession, the company had been growing at breakneck speed: incentives for the purchase of renewable energy had created a market for solar electric systems in Colorado and beyond, and investors had become increasingly interested in opportunities in the new green economy. Over the past few months, Jones had been fielding a number of inquiries from private equity and venture capital firms, as well as from other strategic players interested in buying the company. Two investors in particular had put serious offers on the table. The company needed to decide whether to sell and, if so, to sell in whole or in part.

From the time of its founding, Namasté Solar had been committed to building a democratic, employee-owned and high-engagement culture. All employees, whether or not they held equity, were encouraged to participate in strategic decisions facing the firm. This decision was certainly the most momentous one the group had faced, and various conflicting interests and perspectives were in play. A series of half-day retreats over the previous month had narrowed the choice to three possible options, which the group had started calling Path A, Path B, and Path C. The group had yet to choose among them, and the decision-making process seemed to be at an impasse. Nerves were frayed and tension was high as people gathered in the warehouse to try to reach a consensus on how best to move forward.

BLAKE JONES

Jones and two partners had founded Namasté Solar in late 2004. Jones, then 30, had trained as a civil engineer. After college, he went to work for the engineering and construction firm Brown & Root, then a subsidiary of Halliburton, where he worked on many oil and gas projects including a large gas field development project in Egypt. Although he was fascinated by energy and enjoyed working in a developing country, Jones was beginning to have concerns about the environmental impact of fossil fuels. He recalled:

> My older brother was a big influence on me. He was saying, "Hey, you shouldn't be in oil and gas, you should be in renewable energy instead." I hadn't thought much about environmental issues and society's over-dependence on fossil fuels until he started sharing those ideas with me. As I started to see these things for myself, I began to have a gradual awakening that I wanted to get out of oil and gas and into renewable energy. In particular, I wanted to work with renewables in a developing country.

Jones left Brown & Root in 2001 and took a position with a 120-person renewable energy company in Nepal. A small, mountainous country wedged between India and China, Nepal had no fossil fuels; however, it did have a fast-growing demand for electricity and many sources of renewable energy. Jones described the opportunities and challenges he faced there:

> Nepal was a playground for clean energy technologies, not just solar, but electric vehicles, biogas, hydro, wind, and more. You're talking about harsh and remote environments in the hills and mountains where the design and installation has to be perfect. You can't afford to have things break down. We learned to do things right the first time.

Although Jones was happy in Nepal, events converged to draw him back to the United States. While living abroad, Jones had returned periodically to visit his brother and sister-in-law in Boulder, Colorado. He met and fell in love with a woman there who was not interested in a permanent move to Nepal. Jones laughed: "Colorado was where I wanted to come back to, because that was part of the deal for getting my wife to agree to marry me!"

NAMASTÉ SOLAR

An opportunity soon presented itself. In November 2004, voters in Colorado passed a ballot initiative that established a renewable electricity standard (RES). The RES required large, investor-owned electric utilities in the state to purchase at least 10 percent of their supply of electricity by 2015 from renewable sources such as solar, wind, biomass, or geothermal. This figure was to rise over time to 20 percent by 2020. The standard also included a "solar carve-out" that mandated that at least 4 percent of the renewable energy come from solar (sun-produced) electricity. Of this, half had to be generated on-site by customers, such as individual homeowners or businesses. The utilities were required to provide whatever incentives were necessary in order to get enough homeowners and business owners to purchase and install solar electric systems. For the first time, the RES created a real economic incentive for the installation of solar systems in newly constructed buildings and retrofits in Colorado. Jones immediately saw an opportunity to apply the skills he had learned in Nepal—and, at the same time, to follow his heart to Boulder.

Back in Colorado, Jones got married and brought in two partners to start a new business. Wes Kennedy, a friend of a friend, had experience in solar installations and was looking for an employment change. Ray Tuomey, a friend of Jones's wife, had a longtime association with community organizations in Boulder and many local contacts. The three men found they had much in common, as well as complementary talents: they decided that Jones would handle business planning, Kennedy would lead the technical design and installation activities, and Tuomey would head up marketing.

Just as important, the three founders also shared a vision of the kind of company they wanted to build. To some extent, their views were shaped by negative experiences in prior jobs. Jones explained:

> Wes had worked for a sole proprietor who never shared anything with his employees. Then, the owner sold out and made a lot of money—without sharing any of it, and all the employees were stuck in an acquisition they didn't choose to be a part of. In Nepal, the company I worked for

had a problem with very high turnover. I learned from that how *not* to treat people. So, we had all these ideas for what we did *and* didn't want to do.

At the same time, they knew they wanted to build a business in which risk and reward were shared, and decision-making was decentralized. In an effort to understand how to do this, they began reading and discussing books, including Jack Stack's *Great Game of Business* and *A Stake in the Outcome* and his co-author Bo Burlingham's *Small Giants,* as well as books and research about companies such as New Belgium Brewing Company, South Mountain Company, Chroma Technology Corp., ClifBar, Equal Exchange, Patagonia, and others that provided ideas and possible models.

To fund their fledgling venture, Jones, Kennedy, and Tuomey each contributed significant portions of their own savings, but it was not enough. When they approached local banks for a loan, however, they ran into resistance. Jones recalled:

> The banks basically didn't want to lend to the company. They were willing to lend to us as individuals, but not to the company. Furthermore, they wouldn't do a non-recourse loan. They had to have a personal guarantee. But for our structure, we didn't want anybody to give a personal guarantee because that meant that person was putting in significantly more risk than others, and we wanted to decentralize everything, share ownership, share the risks, share the reward. So that didn't work for us.
>
> Eventually we decided that if people wanted to loan the company money, they could get a personal bank loan, for example, and then they could turn around and loan these funds to the company. We figured out a way to compensate people for taking that additional risk in a way that still kept the structure intact. Because those loans were non-equity, they didn't affect the ownership structure.

The founders incorporated their business in February 2005, selecting the name Namasté, a traditional Sanskrit greeting that Jones used on daily basis while living in Nepal and that Kennedy used on a daily basis in his yoga practice. To them, the word's meaning was significant: "A greeting of great respect that celebrates the interdependence of all living things."

BUILDING A TEAM

Recruiting employees was a challenge: at the time, the fledgling solar electric industry was growing by leaps and bounds, and competition for experienced or skilled workers was intense. Jones commented:

> In a fast-growing industry like solar, people are being pirated left and right. And it's a relatively new field, so if you've got a year of experience, you're considered a veteran. All of these companies are trying to grow fast and keep pace with the booming market. It's very expensive and time-consuming to train people on your own. It's much cheaper to go and pirate employees from other companies.

Namasté Solar's strategy was to recruit very carefully and to hire people who were a good fit with the company, both in terms of skills and philosophy, and who were prepared to make a long-term commitment. Jones explained:

> We're hiring business partners. When we hire people, we tell them, things in life can change, but we want your ideal situation to be staying with the company for five years or more. We want people who are here for the long-term, because the company's business model depends on long-term thinking. If you have people thinking short-term, but the company's got a long-term vision, it won't work out. So, we have a very lengthy interview process. At the beginning, we were worried that we wouldn't be able to find any like-minded folks who wanted to join our hare-brained venture, but in the end, we were happily surprised. Our business model has attracted an amazing group of people.

During its first four years, Namasté Solar's staff grew to 55 people. The company's retention rate was extraordinarily high: by 2008, Namasté Solar had only three unplanned departures, out of more than 50 hires. One of these departures was Kennedy, who left in early 2008 to take a position with a larger solar company.

The company had an unusually non-hierarchical salary structure for its employees. At first, it had a two-tier salary structure. In 2008, this changed to a 10-tier wage scale, with an average of 5 percent between tiers. No one, including the CEO, made more than two times the salary of the lowest-paid person.

EMPLOYEE OWNERSHIP

A critical part of the founders' vision for Namasté Solar—and a strategy for attracting and retaining employees—was a commitment to employee ownership. Under the terms of a carefully crafted restricted stock plan, all employees had an equal opportunity (but not obligation) to buy shares in the company at any time, at the then-current value. Full vesting occurred over a period of five years. Jones explained the founders' logic:

> Some companies make employees wait five years before they are even able to buy stock. We wanted people to be able to enjoy the benefits of ownership from day one. So at Namasté Solar, you can buy stock on your first day at the company, and you get to enjoy the benefits of ownership, including dividends if they're paid. But, we want our employees to be here for the long run. Since we've been growing so fast, our stock price has been increasing at a similar rate. If you come and join the company and then leave six months later with significant stock price appreciation, we don't want you to be able to take advantage of that kind of short-term plan.

Employees who left the company were required to sell back their shares. Vested shares were bought back at their fully appreciated (or depreciated) value; nonvested shares at their original purchase price (or the depreciated price, whichever was lower). The restricted stock plan contained provisions designed to strike a balance between the redeeming stockholder and the company in terms of how quickly the company had to pay out the value of the redemption. The goal was to pay out departing stockholders as quickly as possible without harming the company, which was achieved by setting annual redemption payments according to a percentage of annual revenue.

As a privately held firm in a dynamic industry, Namasté Solar had considerable difficulty valuing its stock. Jones explained:

> It is one of our biggest challenges. We use multiple methods, primarily market-comparable multiples, based on what other companies have sold for. But, in the solar industry, those multiples are so high, they are ridiculous. So we add a huge dose of conservative caution. One of the charges of our finance committee is to continually talk with investment bankers and other solar companies to find out what other companies have been acquired for. They also look at what normal multiples are for, say, electrical contractors or HVAC (heating, ventilation, and air conditioning) contractors. At the end of the day, our goal is to share long-term ownership using a conservatively and fairly determined stock price.

In 2008, 37 employees (about two-thirds of the total) held equity in the firm. No single shareholder owned more than 50 percent, not even the two remaining founders combined. Most of the co-owners owned between 1 and 3 percent of the company, depending on when they joined the company and how many shares they decided to purchase. Over time, everyone's ownership percentage, including the founders', was declining through dilution, as was their intention.

ORGANIZATIONAL MISSION, VALUES, AND CULTURE

Namasté Solar's started mission was "to propagate the responsible use of solar energy, pioneer conscientious business practices and create holistic wealth for our community." According to the company's brochure, holistic wealth was wealth that "benefits all stakeholders equally—customers, employees, investors, communities and the environment—as opposed to inequitably benefiting any stakeholders at the expense of any others" (see Exhibit 1).

With respect to *care for the earth,* the company's core activity was designing and installing solar energy systems. In 2008, it remodelled its

Exhibit 1   Namasté Solar: Our Values

1. Care for the Earth: Leave the environment a better place than we found it.
2. Care for our customers: Provide the best products, services, and overall customer experience.
3. Care for our community: Be a good neighbor and actively engage with our community.
4. Care for our company: Cultivate a collaborative, equitable, and fun company culture.
5. Care for ourselves: Strive to live balanced, healthy, and fulfilling lives.

building in Boulder to be LEED-gold certified (indicating energy and environmental excellence in design), including—of course—a solar electric system. The company pursued zero-waste operations by recycling all of its waste materials, and its installers used a fleet of hybrid and biodiesel vehicles. The firm provided everyone with annual bus passes, encouraged carpooling and biking to work, and maintained showers and locker rooms in the building.

With respect to *care for the customer,* the company committed to "the best possible" customer experience. It offered a 10-year warranty on all residential installations, and reimbursed customers for lost energy production when equipment was out of service for repairs.

With respect to *care for the community,* Namasté Solar annually donated 1 percent of its revenues in the form of solar system installations to community nonprofits. It also employed one person whose sole job was to perform educational outreach in the community about solar energy. Jones and other employee-owners were actively involved in policy discussions at the local and state levels, particularly regarding energy legislation.

With respect to *care for the company,* Namasté Solar was committed to creating a collaborative and equitable culture. It supported open-book management, democratic decision-making, and a meritocratic system in which employees assumed responsibility based on demonstrated competence.

Finally, with respect to *care for ourselves,* the company strove to "create a work environment where we can be healthy, learn continuously, laugh, have fun and LOVE what we do," according to the firm's brochure.

BIG PICTURE MEETINGS

Soon after establishing Namasté Solar, the founders initiated a process called the "big picture meeting" (BPM). Held weekly, BPMs brought together all employees for a full discussion of the issues facing the company, both large and small. These meetings were typically held on Wednesday mornings in a large, open conference room in the headquarters building. Every employee, whatever their role—and whether or not they owned stock—was expected to attend the BPM and encouraged to participate. Jones stated the rationale:

When you put amazing people in a room, the more diverse perspectives you have, the better chance you have [of finding] the optimal solution. I have a little plaque on my desk that my grandfather originally had on his desk that reads, "No one of us is as smart as all of us." The more people you bring in, the more creativity you get. Through our group discussions, we look under rocks and in nooks and crannies, and find amazing new ideas. It builds on itself, and it ends up being something way beyond what you ever could have thought of by yourself.

At all times, and especially at the BPMs, the company strove for "frank, open and honest" communication—or, as it was known among Namasté Solar employees, "FOH." This meant that "one person provides a frank and honest opinion, [and] the other [person] is open to receiving that opinion." Jones commented:

FOH is something that we take very, very seriously. It's a verb. It's a noun. It's a regular part of our vocabulary. We want everyone to truly speak their minds, and we have to create a culture where people feel comfortable to do so. We also have to trust that when a fellow co-owner FOH's you, they're doing so with good intentions and aren't trying to hurt you. At the end of the day, FOH is a critically important part of our company's culture—and, I might add, it works very, very well. It reduces the potential for grudges, harmful gossip, and wasted energy as a result of not being able to get things off your chest.

Although democratic decision-making was time-consuming, Jones believed that people who had participated in making a decision would be more committed to implementing it:

Making these decisions in a big picture meeting can often be more laborious and time-consuming than they would otherwise be if you were just a sole proprietor or had a small ownership group or management team. But once you decide which direction the ship is going to head, everybody rows with full fervor and intensity because they've bought into the decision. Changing directions can take time, but once you change the direction, you can reach top speed faster and go longer distances.

FROM CONSENSUS TO DELEGATION

As the company grew and its operations became more complex, it gradually moved away from direct to more delegated forms of democracy. Initially, decision-making worked by consensus: Namasté Solar could move forward only when everyone agreed with a particular course of action. Referring to the company's early period, Jones explained: "We used to make our decisions by consensus, absolute consensus. To us, consensus means everybody must give a 'thumbs up.' They must actively say 'yes.'"

Later, when the group grew beyond 20 people, Namasté Solar changed to a process they called "consent," meaning the company could proceed as long as no one voted "thumbs down." Individuals could consent—or acquiesce—to decisions they did not feel strongly about one way or the other.

In early 2008, the company faced an issue for which neither consensus nor consent seemed to work. Namasté Solar's new director of marketing and communications, Heather Leanne Nangle, along with several other employee-owners, felt that the firm needed to rebrand itself, including choosing a new logo. The company commissioned several designs and needed to choose among them. The group became completely bogged down. Jones recalled:

> For three, three and a half years, through hundreds of difficult, painful subjects, we had always reached consensus or consent. It was miraculous. And then to have something come up where it didn't work—it was like, "Whoa!" It was all because the logo decision was so subjective. It was similar to, "Do you like this painting?" Trying to get 50 people to agree on their favorite logo design out of a dozen possibilities seemed impossible.

The marketing director and her team asked the BPM—and received permission—to make the logo decision on their own, without BPM review, and the company was able to proceed with its rebranding campaign. This process gradually became a model for other issues that came before the company.

From early on, the company was organized into functional teams whose members were determined by job role; for example, there were sales, installation, project management, operations, and strategy teams. For everything else, the company was organized into committees, which differed from teams in that members were volunteers with a wide variety of daily job roles. Committees were empowered via BPM votes to address certain issues. These included, for example, marketing, human resources, finance, fun (social events), harmony (resolving interpersonal conflicts), education (of employees and the community) and canine (many Namasté Solar employees brought dogs to the office, which required that policies be created). The BPM continued to deal with some issues as a group: it delegated others to specific teams or committees. The empowered team or committee would then research the issue, deliberate, and report back to the BPM with recommendations to be voted on; alternatively, it might be empowered by a BPM vote to make a decision on its own (as had happened with the logo decision, which prompted the evolution of this alternative). Through trial and error, the group continually developed expectations about what kinds of issues were appropriate for the BPM, for the teams and committees or for individual roles.

Namasté Solar was formally governed by a five-person board of directors. All directors were required to be employees, but not necessarily owners. Each year, three directors were elected (or reelected), so board turnover was rapid. All shareholders were eligible to vote for members of the board. Co-owners were allocated votes based on the number of shares they owned and how many positions on the board were open. They could then cast their votes any way they wished, including casting all their votes for a single candidate. This variation on a cumulative voting method was intended to allow minority groups to pool their votes and allocate them to a single seat, to make sure they had at least one representative on the board. Throughout the company's history, shareholder votes had been rare—mostly for board elections; however, the BPM undertook its discussion of a potential sale of the company knowing that the ultimate decision to sell would require the approval of a supermajority of at least 60 percent of the shareholders.

INVESTMENT OFFERS

By 2008, Namasté Solar had become the largest solar electricity company in Colorado. The firm had installed more than 750 solar systems, more than any other company in the state, with a total capacity of 4,000 kilowatts. The company had a share of between 20 and 25 percent of the state's residential and small commercial solar photovoltaic markets, and had been profitable in every year except its first, with revenue growth of more than 2,250 percent. More than half of its sales came through customer referrals and repeat customers. In 2008, the company was on target to earn revenue of more than $14 million.

At the same time, the industry itself was growing at a breakneck pace. In 2007, installations of photovoltaic solar systems tied to the electrical grid in the United States grew by 45 percent. Colorado ranked fourth in installed capacity (after California, New Jersey, and Nevada). Growth was also brisk in the related areas of solar water heating and concentrating solar power (a technology used by utilities to generate solar electric power on a large scale). Much of the growth was driven by state-level public policies that incentivized renewable energy generation.[1] In Colorado, Namasté Solar faced competition from both national and local firms: these included REC Solar, Standard Renewable Energy, Real Goods Solar, SolSource, Bella Energy, and Akeena Solar.

As the industry grew, it attracted the attention of investors. Venture capital and private equity firms had acquired stakes in a number of Namasté Solar's competitors, and several solar companies had gone public. Jones felt considerable pressure: "I was thinking, Oh crap, our competitors have millions of dollars in their coffers, and they've got huge growth mandates from their investors. They'll probably be willing to lowball and drive prices down and buy up competitors."

At the same time, Jones himself was getting telephone calls:

> I was getting multiple phone calls every week. It's so-and-so from such-and-such private equity firm. It's so-and-so from such-and-such investment bank. It's so-and-so angel investor saying, Can I take you out to lunch? It's so-and-so saying, Hey, how would you like to be a part of our company? How would you like to join the next Starbucks of solar? It was ridiculous how many phone calls we were getting.
>
> Eventually, we starting thinking, Let's listen to what these folks have to say. Part of our motivation was we wanted new perspectives to help us with our stock valuations. So we thought, Let's never hang up on someone who thinks they're interested in investing in us. Let's hear what they've got to say. We had lots to learn from them, including what kind of prices they paid or bid for other companies.

But, as we started to talk to them, we started to take some of those conversations more seriously. The numbers we were hearing—it was like, wow, that's five times what we were internally valuing our company at. That's a lot of money.

At the same time, we were all exhausted from multiple years of nonstop, breakneck growth. At this particular time, we were going through an intense turn on our ongoing roller-coaster ride and many of us were approaching burnout and overload. We all had our life savings in the company and were feeling more scared than normal that summer about the financial risks we were all taking. Our only exit strategy was to sell internally, but we didn't know if that would work. So the end seemed nowhere in sight and we kept having to double-down on our bets.

Last but not least, one of our founders had just left the company. Wes, who everyone looked up to as a founder and a steward of our company vision, had just decided to leave the company, which came as a surprise to all of us. So, you combine all of this together and we were in a very vulnerable place from a morale perspective.

As Jones began fielding inquiries, he shared them immediately in the BPM, so employees were fully briefed on these conversations.

In mid-2008, two particular firms emerged as serious bidders. Jones considered both entities the best candidates among all of the rest, and they were both offering a range of opportunities from a sale of a minority equity stake all the way to a complete acquisition.

"SITTING IN THE CRUCIBLE"[2]

Over the course of the next two months, the company held a series of Wednesday-morning mini-retreats to consider these two offers, and had narrowed its possible response to three options. Now, sitting in thrift-shop chairs and couches in the midsummer heat, the group felt it needed to move to some closure. Both firms wanted to take the next steps, and the company perceived their window of opportunity to be limited in duration.

Path A was, in Jones's words, to "sell the whole kit and caboodle." Path B was a hybrid, involving the sale of a portion of the company, with employees retaining partial ownership. Path C was to recommit to Namasté Solar's original vision of being a privately held, 100 percent employee-owned firm, with or without some changes in strategy.

The discussion of the pros and cons of the three paths was frank and wide-ranging. Path A and Path B would both bring a fresh infusion of capital into the company. The company had been growing faster than it was able to generate capital internally, and found it difficult to obtain non-recourse bank loans. "We were growing so fast, we kept needing more money. Where's the money going to come from? Investors could supply that."

Others agreed, saying the company needed to grow at least as fast as the market, and that they could not do so without accepting external capital.

> We were worried that it was against the natural laws of business. Is it true that "you're either growing or you're dying"? If your market is growing 100 percent a year, and you're only growing at 10 percent a year, is that sustainable?
>
> It was the fear of big fish gobbling up the small fish. People said we're going to get clobbered unless we do something. We'd better take on some money. We'd better keep growing. We'd better keep the triple-digit percentage growth every year.

Selling the company appealed to some, who wanted to spread the "gospel" of solar power as widely as possible. Additional capital would enable the firm to hire more people, reach more customers, and install more solar panels. Nangle, Namasté Solar's director of marketing and communications, later recalled this view: "Some people work here because they want to propagate solar as much as possible and therefore have a greater global effect. It's all about impact. Some people said, Think of all the solar we could do all over the world."

Chris Fox, an installer, recalled, "There was this sense that bringing in investor capital was necessary at the time. Some people were very persuasive, saying we have a great opportunity in this fast-growing market. Let's talk about trying to maximize our profit and our growth curve in order to reap the benefits of that."

For some employee-owners who were vested or close to vested, the matter was more personal: the offers provided an opportunity for a handsome return on their investment in the company. "[To some people], the offers were tempting. As much as we like to say 'It's not about the money,' when you get a stack of hundreds slapped in your face, you're kind of like, 'Hmm, yeah, that's a lot of money.' The numbers we were looking at were five times what we were valuing the company at internally."

Another personal factor was burnout. Many of the employees sitting around the warehouse that day felt tired and overworked. The buyout offered a chance to take the money and move on to a less stressful job.

> That summer was really hard. We had triple-digit growth for several years in a row. We had just opened a new office in Denver, the building here in Boulder was being renovated, and we were all spread out. It was crazy. People felt really burned out, against the ropes. Their idea seemed to be that if we sold the company, we wouldn't have everybody's life savings on the line. We could take our chips off the table, and we wouldn't have to be on the hook anymore.

On the other hand, many expressed grave reservations about the impact of an acquisition on Namasté Solar's carefully crafted culture. "There was the problem of complete loss of control. Culture was just out the window with Path A, unless we felt we could really trust [the acquiring company]. What do we think it's going to be like to work for this company? Are they going to respect our culture? No one has the same values as we do."

Nangle pointed out: "I'm passionate about our grant program. We have an incredible grant program where we give 1 percent of revenue, regardless of our profit, to the community. To me, that makes us one of the coolest companies on the planet, let alone in Colorado. I felt a private investor would say, 'What the heck are you doing that for? Stop that. Don't give your money away.'"

She also expressed concern about a possible loss of the family feeling at the company:

> I was a strong voice for wanting to keep the family quality that we have. I want to be able to sit in a big picture meeting and know every single person there. I don't need to know every detail, but I want to be able to sit next to someone and ask, "How's your child? . . . How's this or that?" If I'm sitting in a room with 500 people, there's no way you're going to know me, or I'm going to know you. The family element would be lost.

Others expressed the concern that a private equity investor would be unlikely to support the firm's concept of "holistic profit."

The appeal of Path B, to some, was that it seemed to offer a way to bring in external capital to support growth, while maintaining control over the culture. Nangle recalled:

Some people passionately advocated for Path B. They thought we could bring a private equity investor on board, and still be in complete control and stay true to our values. Because they [equity investors] don't have majority ownership, we would still be in control. Other people said, "No, they'll want warrants for eventually purchasing the majority of the company."

The supporters of Path C, for their part, argued that it was the only path consistent with the company's values.

Our founding vision was to be a 100 percent employee-owned company, with no external investors, where we're in complete control. Some people

were like, "What? I came into this company thinking that Path C was the only path, what the heck are we doing even discussing Path A and Path B? What's going on here? I wouldn't have joined this company if I thought you guys were thinking of doing this."

Fox recalled that others called Path C "too idealistic."

Jones recalled the scene:

I just remember that the decision was taking such a long time. I kept thinking, Let's not succumb to this frustrated feeling. Let's just sit in the crucible, sit in the fire a little bit longer until we're able to make the right decision. We might just be caught in the perfect storm of stress, fear, doubt, burnout and low morale . . . and somehow we need to allow ourselves to make a decision that we'll be happy with . . . and that we won't look back on and regret.

ENDNOTES

[1] Solar Energy Industries Association, "US Solar Industry Year in Review, 2007," www.seia.org/galleries/pdf/Year_in_Review_2007_sm.pdf, accessed June 3, 2010.

[2] All quotations in this section are from Blake Jones, in a discussion of his recollection of various views expressed at the meeting (not necessarily his own), unless otherwise noted.

Herman Miller Inc.: The Reinvention and Renewal of an Iconic Manufacturer of Office Furniture[1]

Frank Shipper
Salisbury University

Steven B. Adams
Salisbury University

Karen Manz
Author and Researcher

Charles C. Manz
University of Massachusetts—
Amherst

Knowledgeable observers have long regarded Herman Miller Inc. as more than just a large manufacturer of office furniture. The company began developing a reputation for innovative products and production processes in the 1920s, when Dirk Jan De Pree became president. Herman Miller was one of only four companies and the only non-high-technology enterprise named to *Fortune*'s "Most Admired Companies" and "The 100 Best Companies to Work For" lists and also to *FastCompany*'s "Most Innovative Companies" list in both 2008 and 2010. The three high-technology organizations selected for these lists were Microsoft, Cisco, and Google. Unlike most firms, especially those in mature industries and most of its office furniture rivals, Herman Miller had pursued a path distinctively marked by reinvention and renewal.

This path had served it well over the decades. It survived the Great Depression early in its history and multiple recessions in the 20th century. In the early part of the 21st century, it recovered from the dot-com bust. As it entered 2010, Herman Miller once again was facing turbulent and uncertain economic conditions. Would its propensity for using innovation to reinvent and renew its business once again allow the company to flourish and grow? How far and how fast might the company be able to push its annual revenues above the 2009 level of $1.3 billion?

COMPANY BACKGROUND

Herman Miller's roots went back to 1905 and the Star Furniture Company, a manufacturer of traditional-style bedroom suites in Zeeland, Michigan. In 1909, it was renamed Michigan Star Furniture Company and hired Dirk Jan De Pree as a clerk. De Pree became president in 1919 and four years later convinced his father-in-law, Herman Miller, to purchase the majority of shares; De Pree renamed the company Herman Miller Furniture Company in recognition of Miller's support.

In 1927, De Pree committed himself to treating "all workers as individuals with special talents and potential." This occurred after he visited the family of a millwright who had died unexpectedly. During the visit, the widow read some poetry. Upon asking the widow who the poet was, De Pree was surprised to learn it was the millwright. This led him to wonder whether the millwright was a worker who wrote poetry or a poet who worked as a millwright. This story was part of Herman Miller's corporate culture, which continued to generate respect for all employees and fueled the quest to tap the diversity of gifts and skills held by all.

In 1930, the United States was in the Great Depression and Herman Miller was in financial trouble. As De Pree was looking for a way to save the company, Gilbert Rhode, a designer from New York, approached him and told him about his design philosophy. Rhode then asked for an opportunity to design a bedroom suite for a fee of $1,000. When De Pree reacted negatively to such a fee, Rhode suggested an alternative payment plan—a 3 percent royalty on the furniture sold—to which De Pree agreed, figuring that there was nothing to lose.

A few weeks later, De Pree received the first designs from Rhode. Again, he reacted negatively. In response, Rhode wrote De Pree a letter explaining his design philosophy: "[First,] utter simplicity: no surface enrichment, no carvings, no moldings, [and second,] furniture should be anonymous. People are important, not furniture. Furniture should be useful." Rhode's designs were antithetical to traditional designs, but De Pree saw merit in them and set Herman Miller on a course of designing and selling furniture that reflected a way of life.

In 1942, Herman Miller produced its first office furniture—a Gilbert Rhode design referred to as the Executive Office Group. Rhode died two years later, and De Pree began a search for a new design leader. After reading an article in *Life* magazine about designer George Nelson, De Pree hired Nelson as Herman Miller's first design director.

In 1946, De Pree hired Charles and Ray Eames, a husband-and-wife design team based in Los Angeles. In the same year, Charles Eames's designs were featured in the first one-man furniture exhibit at New York's Museum of Modern Art. Some of his designs became part of the museum's permanent collection.

In 1950, Herman Miller, under the guidance of Dr. Carl Frost, a professor at Michigan State University, became the first company in the state of Michigan to implement a Scanlon Plan, a productivity incentive program devised by labor expert Joseph N. Scanlon. Underlying the Scanlon Plan were the "principles of equity and justice for everyone in the company." Two major functional elements of Scanlon Plans were the use of committees for sharing ideas on improvements and a structure for sharing increased profitability. The relationship between Frost and Herman Miller continued for at least four decades.

During the 1950s, Herman Miller introduced a number of new furniture designs, including those by Alexander Girard, Charles and Ray Eames, and George Nelson. Specifically, the company introduced the first molded fiberglass chairs and the Eames lounge chair and ottoman (see Exhibit 1). The Eames designs were introduced on NBC's *Home Show* with Arlene Francis, a precursor to the *Today Show*. Also in the 1950s, Herman Miller began its first overseas foray, selling its products in the European market.

In 1962, D. J. De Pree became chairman of the board and his son, Hugh De Pree, became president and chief executive officer. D. J. De Pree had served for more than 40 years as the president of Herman Miller.

During the 1960s, Herman Miller introduced many new designs for both home and office. The most notable design was the Action Office System, the world's first open-plan modular office arrangement of movable panels and attachments. By the end of the 1960s, Herman Miller had formed a subsidiary in England with sales and marketing responsibility throughout England and the Scandinavian countries. The company also established dealers in South and Central America, Australia, Canada, Europe, Africa, the Near East, and Japan.

In 1970, Herman Miller went public and made its first stock offering. The stock certificate was designed by the Eames office staff. The company entered the health/science market in 1971 and introduced the Ergon chair, its first design based on scientific observation and ergonomic principles, in 1976. In 1979, in conjunction with the University of Michigan, Herman Miller established the Facility Management Institute, which pioneered the profession of facility management. The company continued to expand overseas and introduce new designs throughout the 1970s.

By 1977, more than half of Herman Miller's 2,500 employees worked outside the production area. The Scanlon Plan therefore needed to be overhauled, since it had been designed originally for a production workforce. In addition, employees worked at multiple U.S. and overseas locations. In 1978, an ad hoc committee of 54 people from nearly every segment of the company was elected to examine the need for changes and to make recommendations. By January 1979, the committee had developed a final draft. The plan established a new organization structure based on work teams, caucuses, and councils. All employees were given an opportunity to discuss the new plan in small group settings. On January 26, 1979, 96 percent of the employees voted to accept the new plan.

After 18 years as president and CEO, Hugh De Pree stepped down; his younger brother, Max De Pree, became chairman and chief executive officer in 1980. In 1981, Herman Miller took a major initiative to become more efficient and environmentally friendly. Its Energy Center generated both electrical and steam power to run its 1-million-square-foot facility by burning waste.

In 1983, Herman Miller established a plan whereby all employees became shareholders. This initiative occurred approximately 10 years before congressional incentives fueled employee stock ownership plan (ESOP) growth.

In 1984, Herman Miller introduced the Equa chair, a second chair based on ergonomic principles; many other designs followed in the 1980s. In 1987, the first non–De Pree family member, Dick Ruch, became chief executive officer.

By the end of the decade, *Time* magazine had recognized the Equa chair as a Design of the Decade. Also, in 1989, Herman Miller established its Environmental Quality Action Team, whose purpose was to "coordinate environmental programs worldwide and involve as many employees as possible."

In 1990, Herman Miller became a founding member of the Tropical Forest Foundation and was the only furniture manufacturer to belong. That same year, it discontinued using endangered rosewood in its award-winning Eames lounge chair and ottoman, and substituted cherry and walnut from sustainable sources. It also became a founding member of the U.S. Green Building Council in 1994. Some of the buildings at Herman Miller were used to establish Leadership in Energy and Environmental Design (LEED) standards. Because of its environmental efforts, Herman Miller received awards from *Fortune* magazine and the National Wildlife Federation in the 1990s.

Also in the 1990s, Herman Miller again introduced some groundbreaking designs. In 1994, it introduced the Aeron chair (see Exhibit 2), which almost immediately was added to the New York Museum of Modern Art's permanent design

Exhibit 1   Eames Lounge Chair and Ottoman

Exhibit 2   The Herman Miller Aeron Chair

collection. In 1999, the Aeron chair won the Design of the Decade Award from *BusinessWeek* and the Industrial Designers Society of America.

In 1992, J. Kermit Campbell became Herman Miller's fifth CEO and president. He was the first person from outside the company to hold either position. In 1995, Campbell resigned and Mike Volkema was promoted to CEO. Volkema, just 39 years old, had been with a company called Meridian for seven years before Herman Miller acquired it in 1990, so when he became CEO he had been with either Herman Miller or its subsidiary for

12 years. At the time the industry was in a slump and Herman Miller was being restructured. Sales were approximately $1 billion annually.

In 1994, the company launched a product line called Herman Miller for the Home to focus on the residential market. It reintroduced some of its modern classic designs from the 1940s, 1950s, and 1960s as well as new designs. In 1998, it set up a specific website (www.hmhome.com) to tap this market.

The company took additional marketing initiatives to focus on small and midsize businesses. It established a network of 180 retailers to focus on small businesses and made a 3-D design computer program available to midsize customers. In addition, its order entry system was digitally linked among itself and its suppliers, distributors, and customers to expedite orders and improve their accuracy.

THE FIRST DECADE OF THE 21ST CENTURY

The first decade of the 21st century started off spectacularly for Herman Miller, with record profits and sales in 2000 and 2001. The company offered an employee stock option plan (ESOP) in July 2000, and *Time* magazine selected the Eames molded plywood chair as a Design of the Century. Sales had more than doubled in the six years that Mike Volkema had been CEO.

Then the dot-com bubble burst and the terrorist attacks of September 11, 2001, shook the U.S. economy. Herman Miller's sales dropped by 34 percent, from more than $2.2 billion in 2001 to less than $1.5 billion in 2002. In the same two years, the company saw a decline in profits from a positive $144 million to a negative $56 million. In an interview for *FastCompany* magazine in 2007, Volkema said, "One night I went to bed a genius and woke up the town idiot."

Although sales continued to drop in 2003, Herman Miller returned to profitability in that year. To do so, Herman Miller had to drop its long-held tradition of lifelong employment; approximately 38 percent of the workforce was laid off, and an entire plant in Georgia was closed. Mike Volkema and Brian Walker, then president of Herman Miller North America, met with all the workers to tell them what was happening and why it had to be done. One of the workers being laid off was so moved by Volkema and Walker's presentation that she told them she felt sorry for them having to personally lay off workers.

To replace the tradition of lifelong employment, Volkema, with input from many others, developed what the company referred to as "the new social contract." He explained it as follows:

> We are a commercial enterprise, and the customer has to be on center stage, so we have to first figure out whether your gifts and talents have a match with the needs and wants of this commercial enterprise. If they don't, then we want to wish you the best, but we do need to tell you that I don't have a job for you right now.

As part of the implementation of the social contract, the company redesigned benefit plans such as educational reimbursement and 401K plans to be more portable. This was done to decrease the cost of changing jobs for employees whose gifts and talents no longer matched customer needs.

Herman Miller's sales and profits began to climb from 2003 to 2008. In 2008, even though sales were not at an all-time high, profits were. Walker became president in 2003 and CEO in 2004. Volkema became chairman of the board in 2004.

Then Herman Miller was hit by the recession of 2009. Sales dropped by 19 percent, from approximatey $2.0 billion in 2008 to approximately $1.6 billion in 2009. In the same years, profits dropped from $152 million to $68 million. In March 2009, Mark Schurman, director of external communications at Herman Miller, predicted that the changes made to recover from the 2001–2003 recession would help the company weather the recession that began in late 2007.

HERMAN MILLER ENTERING 2010

Herman Miller had codified its long-practiced organizational values and published them on its website in 2005 on a page titled "What We Believe." Those beliefs, listed as follows, were intended as a basis for uniting all employees, building relationships, and contributing to communities:

- **Curiosity & Exploration:** These are two of our greatest strengths. They lie behind our heritage of research-driven design. How do we keep our curiosity? By respecting and encouraging risk, and by practicing forgiveness. You can't be curious and infallible. In one sense, if you never make a mistake, you're not exploring new ideas often enough. Everybody makes mistakes: we ought to celebrate honest mistakes, learn from them, and move on.

- **Engagement:** For us, it is about being owners—actively committed to the life of this community called Herman Miller, sharing in its success and risk. Stock ownership is an important ingredient, but it's not enough. The strength and the payoff really come when engaged people own problems, solutions, and behavior. Acknowledge responsibility, choose to step forward and be counted. Care about this community and make a difference in it.

- **Performance:** Performance is required for leadership. We want to be leaders, so we are committed to performing at the highest level possible. Performance isn't a choice. It's up to everybody at Herman Miller to perform at his or her best. Our own high performance—however we measure it—enriches our lives as employees, delights our customers, and creates real value for our shareholders

- **Inclusiveness:** To succeed as a company, we must include all the expressions of human talent and potential that society offers. We value the whole person and everything each of us has to offer, obvious or not so obvious. We believe that every person should have the chance to realize his or her potential regardless of color, gender, age, sexual orientation, educational background, weight, height, family status, skill level—the list goes on and on. When we are truly inclusive, we go beyond toleration to understanding all the qualities that make people who they are, that make us unique, and most important, that unite us.

- **Design:** Design for us is a way of looking at the world and how it works—or doesn't. It is a method for getting something done, for solving a problem. To design a solution, rather than simply devising one, requires research, thought, sometimes starting over, listening, and humility. Sometimes design results in memorable occasions, timeless chairs, or really fun parties. Design isn't just the way something looks; it isn't just the way something works, either.

- **Foundations:** The past can be a tricky thing—an anchor or a sail, a tether or a launching pad. We value and respect our past without being ruled by it. The stories, people, and experiences in Herman Miller's past form a unique foundation. Our past teaches us about design, human compassion, leadership, risk taking, seeking out change and working together. From that foundation, we can move forward together with a common language, a set of owned beliefs and understandings. We value our rich legacy more for what it shows us we might become than as a picture of what we've been.

- **A Better World:** This is at the heart of Herman Miller and the real reason why many of us come to work every day. We contribute to a better world by pursuing sustainability and environmental wisdom. Environmental advocacy is part of our heritage and a responsibility we gladly bear for future generations. We reach for a better world by giving time and money to our communities and causes outside the company; through becoming a good corporate citizen worldwide; and even in the (not so) simple act of adding beauty to the world. By participating in the effort, we lift our spirits and the spirits of those around us.

- **Transparency:** Transparency begins with letting people see how decisions are made and owning the decisions we make. So when you make a decision, own it. Confidentiality has a place at Herman Miller, but if you can't tell anybody about a decision you've made, you've probably made a poor choice. Without transparency, it's impossible to have trust and integrity. Without trust and integrity, it's impossible to be transparent

All employees were expected to live these values.

Management

Mike Volkema remained chairman of the board in 2010, and Brian Walker was president and CEO. Walker's compensation was listed by *Bloomberg*

Businessweek as $668,685. The magazine listed compensation for CEOs at four competitors as ranging from $792,000 to $1,100,000. Walker and four other top executives at Herman Miller took a 10 percent pay cut in January 2009 and, along with all salaried workers, another 10 percent cut in March 2009. The production workers were placed on a work schedule that consisted of nine days in two weeks, effectively cutting their pay by 10 percent as well. That the executives would take a pay cut before salaried workers, and one twice as much as that required by workers, was just one way human compassion was practiced at Herman Miller.

By U.S. Securities and Exchange Commission (SEC) regulations, a publicly traded company had to have a board of directors. By Herman Miller's corporate policy, the majority of the 14 members of the board had to be independent. To be judged independent, the individual as a minimum had to meet the NASDAQ National Market requirements for independent directors (NASDAQ Stock Market Rule 4200). In addition, the individual could not have any "other material relationship with the company or its affiliates or with any executive officer of the company or his or her affiliates." Moreover, according to company documents, any "transaction between the Company and any executive officer or director of the Company (including that person's spouse, children, stepchildren, parents, stepparents, siblings, parents-in-law, children-in-law, siblings-in-law and persons sharing the same residence) must be disclosed to the Board of Directors and is subject to the approval of the Board of Directors or the Nominating and Governance Committee unless the proposed transaction is part of a general program available to all directors or employees equally under an existing policy or is a purchase of Company products consistent with the price and terms of other transactions of similar size with other purchasers." Furthermore, "It is the policy of the Board that all directors, consistent with their responsibilities to the stockholders of the company as a whole, hold an equity interest in the company. Toward this end, the Board requires that each director will have an equity interest after one year on the Board, and within five years the Board encourages the directors to have shares of common stock of the company with a value of at least three times the amount of the annual retainer paid to each director." In other words, board members were held to

standards consistent with Herman Miller's corporate beliefs and its ESOP program.

Although Herman Miller had departments, the most frequently referenced work unit was the team. Paul Murray, director of environmental health and safety, explained the relationship between the team and the department as follows:

> At Herman Miller, *team* has just been the term that has been used since the Scanlon Plan and the De Prees brought that into Herman Miller. And so I think that's why we use that almost exclusively. The department—as a department, we help facilitate the other teams. And so they aren't just department driven.

Teams were often cross-functional. Membership on a team was based on the employee's ability to contribute to that team. As Gabe Wing, lead chemical engineer for the company's Design for the Environment division, described it,

> You grab the appropriate representative who can best help your team achieve its goal. It doesn't seem to be driven based on title. It's based on who has the ability to help us drive our initiatives towards our goal.

Teams were often based on product development. When the product had been developed, the members of that team were redistributed to new projects. New projects could come from any level in the organization. One way in which leadership was shared at Herman Miller was through the concept of "talking up and down the ladder." Workers at all levels were encouraged to put forth new ideas. Herman Miller environmental specialist Rudy Bartels said,

> If they try something . . . they have folks there that will help them and be there for them. . . . That requires a presence of one of us or an e-mail or just to say, "Yeah, I think that's a great idea." That's how a lot . . . in the organization works.

Because Herman Miller workers felt empowered, a new manager could run into some startling behavior. Paul Murray recalled,

> I can remember my first day on the job. I took my safety glasses off . . . and an employee stepped forward and said, "Get your safety glasses back on." At [Company X, Company Y],[2] there was no way would they have ever talked to a supervisor like that, much less their supervisor's manager. It's been a fun journey when the workforce is that empowered.

The company's beliefs were also reinforced through the Employee Gifts Committee and the Environmental Quality Action Team. True to Herman Miller's practice of shared leadership, the Employee Gifts Committee distributed funds and other resources based on employee involvement. Jay Link, manager of corporate giving, explained the program as follows:

Our first priority is to honor organizations where our employees are involved. We believe that it's important that we engender kind of a giving spirit in our employees, so if we know they're involved in organizations, which is going to be where we have a manufacturing presence, then our giving kind of comes alongside organizations that they're involved with. So that's our first priority.

In addition, all Herman Miller employees could work 16 paid hours a year with a charitable organization of their choice. The company set goals for the number of employee volunteer hours contributed annually to its communities. Progress toward meeting those goals was reported to the CEO.

The Environmental Affairs Team, formed in 1988 with the authorization of Max De Pree, had responsibility for such activities as recycling solid waste and designing products from sustainable resources. One of the team's successes was in the reduction of solid waste taken to landfills. In 1991, Herman Miller was sending 41 million pounds of solid waste to landfills. That figure was down to 24 million pounds by 1994 and to 3.6 million pounds by 2008. Such improvements were both environmentally friendly and cost-effective.

Herman Miller's beliefs carried over to the family and the community. Gabe Wing related, "I've got the worst lawn in my neighborhood. That's because I don't spread pesticides on it, and I don't put fertilizer down." He went on to say that he and his wife had to make a difficult decision in the summer of 2009 because Herman Miller had a policy "to avoid PVC [polyvinyl chloride] wherever possible." In restoring their home, they chose fiber cement board over PVC siding even though the fiber cement board was considerably more costly. Wing said, "Seven years ago, I didn't really think about it."

Rudy Bartels was involved in a youth soccer association that raised money to buy uniforms by collecting newspapers and aluminum cans.

Bartels said, "When I'll speak they'll say, 'Yeah, that's Rudy. He's Herman Miller. You should—you know we're gonna have to do this.' "

The company's beliefs carried over to all functional areas of the business. Some of them were obviously beneficial, and some were simply the way Herman Miller chose to conduct its business.

Marketing

Herman Miller products were sold internationally through wholly owned subsidiaries in countries including Canada, France, Germany, Italy, Japan, Mexico, Australia, Singapore, China, India, and the Netherlands. Its products were offered through independent dealerships. The customer base was spread over 100 countries.

Herman Miller used so-called green marketing to sell its products. For example, the Mirra chair—introduced in 2003 with PostureFit Technology (see Exhibit 3)—was developed from its inception to be environmentally friendly. The Mirra was made of 45 percent recycled materi-

Exhibit 3   **An Example of Cooperative Advertising**

als, and 96 percent of its materials were, in turn, recyclable. In addition, assembly of the chairs used 100 percent renewable energy. Builders who used Herman Miller products in their buildings could earn points toward Leadership in Energy and Environmental Design (LEED) certification.

In addition, Herman Miller engaged in cooperative advertising with strategic partners. For example, at Hilton Garden Inns, some rooms were equipped with Herman Miller's Mirra chairs. On the desk in the room was a card that explained how to adjust the chair for comfort and listed a Hilton Garden Inn website where the chair could be purchased.

Production/Operations

Herman Miller was globally positioned in terms of manufacturing operations. In the United States, its manufacturing operations were located in Michigan, Georgia, and Washington. In Europe, it had considerable manufacturing presence in the United Kingdom, its largest market outside the United States. In Asia, it had manufacturing operations in Ningbo, China.

Herman Miller used a system of lean manufacturing techniques collectively referred to as the Herman Miller Production System (HMPS)—see Exhibit 4. The HMPS strove to maintain efficiencies and cost savings by minimizing the amount of inventory on hand through a just-in-time process. Some suppliers delivered parts to Herman Miller production facilities five or six times per day.

Production was order-driven, with direct materials and components purchased as needed to meet demand. The standard lead time for the majority of the company's products was 10 to 20 days. As a result, the rate of inventory turnover was high. These combined factors could cause inventory levels to appear relatively low in relation to sales volume. A key element of Herman Miller's manufacturing strategy was to limit fixed production costs by outsourcing component parts from strategic suppliers. This strategy had allowed the company to increase the variable nature of its cost structure while retaining proprietary control over those production processes that it believed to provide a competitive advantage. Because of this strategy, manufacturing operations were largely assembly-based.

The success of the HMPS was the result of much hard work. For example, in 1996, business at the Herman Miller subsidiary Integrated Metals Technology (IMT), which supplied the parent company with pedestals, was not going well. IMT's prices were high, its lead time was long, and its quality was in the 70 percent range. Leaders at IMT decided to hire the Toyota Supplier Support Center, the consulting arm of automaker Toyota. By inquiring, analyzing, and "enlisting help and ideas of everyone," IMT made significant improvements. For example, quality defects in parts per million decreased from approximately 9,000 in 2000 to 1,500 in 2006. Concurrently, on-time shipments improved from 80 percent to 100 percent, and safety incidents per 100 employees dropped from 10 to 3 per year.

Herman Miller's organizational values were incorporated into the environmentally friendly design of the Greenhouse, Herman Miller's main production facility in Michigan. For example, the Greenhouse took advantage of natural light and landscaping to grow native plants without the use of fertilizers, pesticides, or irrigation. After the facility was opened, aggressive paper wasps found the design to their liking. Employees and guests were stung, frequently. Rather than using pesticides to kill the wasps, the company sought a solution that would be in keeping with its beliefs. Through research, it learned that honeybees and paper wasps were incompatible. Therefore, the company located 600,000 honeybees in 12 hives on the property. In addition to driving away the wasps, the introduction of the honeybees resulted (via pollination) in a profusion of wildflowers around the facility and, subsequently, the production of a large amount of honey. Guests to the home office were given a four-ounce bottle of the honey, symbolizing Herman Miller's corporate beliefs.

Human Resource Management

Human resource management was considered a strength for Herman Miller. It was routinely listed on *Fortune*'s "100 Best Companies to Work For" list, including in 2010, and it had approximately 278 applicants for every job opening. In 2009, during the ongoing economic downturn, Herman Miller cut its workforce by more than 15 percent, reduced pay of the remaining workforce by at least 10 percent, and suspended 401(k) contributions. According to the February 8, 2010, issue of *Fortune,* employees praised management for "handling the downturn with class and doing what is best for the collective whole." *Fortune* also estimated voluntary turnover at Herman Miller to be less than 2 percent. On June 1, 2010, the 10 percent time and pay cuts that the company began in the spring of 2009 were discontinued due to Herman Miller's quick turnaround.

Herman Miller practiced what Hugh De Pree had once called "Business as Unusual." That policy appeared to pay off in both good times and tough ones. Herman Miller shared the gains as well as the pains with its employees, especially in regard to compensation.

Pay was geared to firm performance and took many forms at Herman Miller. All employees received a base pay and, in addition, participated in a profit-sharing program whereby they received stock according to the company's annual financial performance. Employees were immediately enrolled in this plan upon joining Herman Miller, and immediately vested. Profit sharing was based on corporate performance; as one employee explained:

> The problem we see is you get to situations where project X corporately had a greater opportunity for the entirety of the business, but it was difficult to tell these folks that they needed to sacrifice in order to support the entirety of the business when they were being compensated specifically on their portion of the business. So you would get into some turf situations. So we ended up moving to a broader corporate EVA [economic value added] compensation to prevent those types of turf battles.

The company offered an employee stock purchase plan (ESPP) through payroll deductions at a 15 percent discount from the market price. Also, all employees were offered a 401(k) plan; until it was suspended in 2009 due to the recession, the company had offered a matching plan in which employees received a 50 percent match for the first 6 percent of their salaries they contributed to the 401(k). Through the profit-sharing plan and the ESPP, the employees owned approximately 8 percent of the outstanding stock.

Furthermore, all employees were offered a retirement income plan whereby the company

Exhibit 4 **The Herman Miller Production System**

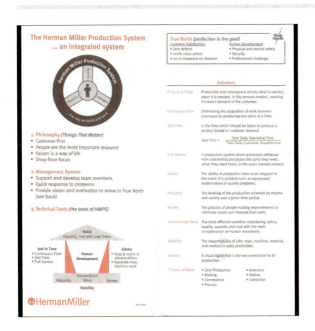

deposited into an account 4 percent of compensation, on which interest was paid quarterly. Employees were immediately eligible to participate in this plan upon joining Herman Miller, but were required to participate for five years before being vested. Additionally, a length-of-service bonus was paid after five years of employment. Finally, the company paid a universal annual bonus to all employees based on the company's performance against economic value added (EVA) objectives. EVA was a calculation of the company's net operating profits, after tax, minus a charge for the cost of shareholder capital. The annual EVA bonus came in addition to the other compensation programs, including profit sharing, with the same calculation used to determine both employee and executive bonus potential.

Thus, most forms of compensation at Herman Miller were at least partially, if not wholly, contingent on corporate performance. One employee summed up pay as follows, "You can dip into Herman Miller's pocket several times based on the performance of the company."

Other benefits also took many forms at Herman Miller. As in many other organizations, employees were given a range of benefits. Standard benefits included health insurance, dental insurance, vision care plans, prescription plans, flexible spending accounts, short- and long-term disability plan, life insurance, accidental death and disability insurance, and critical illness/personal accident/long-term care. The company also offered extensive wellness benefits, including fitness facilities or subsidized gym memberships, health services, employee assistance programs, wellness programs/classes, and health risk assessments. Some benefits, however, were quite different from those found in other organizations. For example, the company offered a $100 rebate on a bike purchase, which it justified as "part of our comprehensive program designed for a better world around you." Other benefits included the following:

- 100 percent tuition reimbursement.
- Employee product purchase discounts.
- Flexible schedules, including job-sharing, compressed workweek, and telecommuting options.
- Concierge services, including directions to travel locations, dry cleaning, greeting cards, and take-home meals.
- On-site services, including massage therapy, cafeterias, banking, health services, fitness centers, fitness classes, and personal trainers.

All benefits were available also to domestic partners.

When appropriate, Herman Miller promoted people within the organization. Education and training were seen as key to preparing employees to take on new responsibilities. For example, environmental specialist Rudy Bartels, as well as multiple vice presidents, began their careers at Herman Miller on the production floor.

Three other benefits were unique to Herman Miller. First, every family that gave birth to or adopted a child received a Herman Miller rocking chair. Second, every employee who retired after 25 years with the company and was 55 or older received an Eames lounge chair. Third, Herman Miller had no executive retreat, but it did have an employee retreat, the Marigold Lodge, on Lake Michigan. This retreat was available to employees for corporate-related events, such as retirement parties and other celebrations, and some of those events included invited family and guests.

Finance

During normal economic times, financial management at Herman Miller would have been considered conservative. Through 2006, the company's leverage ratio was below the industry average and its times-interest-earned ratio was over twice the industry average. Due to the drop-off in business during the recession, the debt-to-equity ratio rose precipitously, from 1.18 in 2006 to 47.66 in 2008. To improve this ratio, the company sold more than 3 million shares of stock in fiscal 2009.[3] In the four previous fiscal years, Herman Miller had been repurchasing shares. The debt-to-equity ratio was reduced to 3.81 by the end of 2009. To improve short-term assets, dividends per share were cut by approximately 70 percent and capital expenditures were reduced to zero in 2009. Exhibits 5 and 6 show the company's financial statements for fiscal years 2006–2010.

For fiscal 2008, 15 percent of Herman Miller's revenues and 10 percent of its profits were from non–North American countries. In 2007, non–North American countries accounted for 16.5 percent of revenues and approximately 20 percent of Herman Miller's profits.

Financially, Herman Miller held true to its beliefs. Even in downturns, it invested in research and development (R&D). In the dot-com downturn, it invested tens of millions of dollars in R&D. Inside Herman Miller this investment project was code-named Purple.

In the December 19, 2007, issue of *FastCompany* magazine, Clayton Christensen, Harvard Business School professor and author of *The Innovator's Dilemma,* commented on the Purple project, saying, "Barely one out of 1,000 companies would do what [Herman Miller] did. It was a daring bet in terms of increasing spending for the sake of tomorrow while cutting back to survive today."

The Accessories Team

Herman Miller's Accessories Team was an outgrowth of project Purple. One of the goals of this project was to stretch beyond the normal business boundaries. Office accessories was one area in which Herman Miller had not been historically involved, even though office accessories were a big part of what independent dealers sold. According

Exhibit 5   Herman Miller's Consolidated Balance Sheets, Fiscal Years 2006–2010 ($ millions, except share and per share data)

	Fiscal Years Ending				
	May 29, 2010	**May 30, 2009**	**May 31, 2008**	**June 2, 2007**	**June 3, 2006**
Assets					
Current assets:					
Cash and cash equivalents	$134.8	$192.9	$155.4	$ 76.4	$106.8
Short-term investments (Note1)	—	—	15.7	15.9	15.2
Marketable securities	12.1	11.3	—	—	—
Accounts receivable	144.7	148.9	209.0	188.1	173.2
Less allowances in each year	4.4	7.3	5.6	4.9	5.0
Inventories, net	57.9	37.3	55.1	56.0	47.1
Prepaid expenses and other	45.2	60.5	58.0	48.3	47.9
Total current assets	394.7	450.9	493.2	384.7	390.2
Property and equipment:					
Land and improvements	19.4	18.8	19.0	18.9	20.9
Buildings and improvements	147.6	137.4	139.4	137.2	139.1
Machinery and equipment	546.4	552.0	547.4	543.3	523.8
Construction in progress	10.7	9.8	17.4	17.6	23.5
	724.1	718.0	723.2	717,0	707.3
Less: accumulated depreciation	(548.9)	(538.8)	(526.9)	(520.4)	(504.0)
Net property and equipment	175.2	179.2	196.3	196.6	203.3
Goodwill and indefinite-lived intangibles	132.6	72.7	40.2	39.1	39.1
Other amortizable intangibles, net	25.0	11.3	—	—	—
Other assets	43.1	53.2	53.5	45.8	35.4
Total assets	$770.6	$767.3	$783.2	$666.2	$668.0
Liabilities and Shareholders' Equity					
Current liabilities:					
Unfunded checks	$ 4.3	$ 3.9	$ 8.5	$ 7.4	$ 6.5
Current maturities of long-term debt	100.0	75.0	—	3.0	3.0
Accounts payable	96.3	79.1	117.9	110.5	112.3
Accrued liabilities	112.4	124.2	184.1	163.6	177.6
Total current liabilities	313.0	282.2	310.5	284.5	299.4
Long-term debt, less current maturities	201.2	302.4	375.5	173.2	175.8
Other liabilities	176.3	174.7	73.8	52.9	54.2
Total liabilities	690.5	759.3	759.8	510.6	529.4
Minority interest	—	—	—	.3	.2
Shareholders' equity:					
Preferred stock, no par value (10,000,000 shares authorized, none issued)	—	—	—	—	—
Common stock, $0.20 par value (240,000,000 shares authorized, 57,002,733 and 53,826,061 shares issued and outstanding in 2010 and 2009, respectively)	11.4	10.8	11.1	12.6	13.2

(Continued)

Exhibit 5   *(Concluded)*

	Fiscal Years Ending				
	May 29, 2010	May 30, 2009	May 31, 2008	June 2, 2007	June 3, 2006
Additional paid-in capital	55.9	5.9	—	—	—
Retained earnings	152.4	129.2	76.7	197.8	192.2
Accumulated other comprehensive loss	(136.2)	(134.1)	(60.1)	(51.6)	(63.3)
Key executive deferred compensation	(3.4)	(3.8)	(4.3)	(3.5)	(3.7)
Total shareholders' equity	80.1	8.0	23.4	155.3	138.4
Total liabilities and shareholders' equity	$770.6	$767.3	$783.2	$666.2	$668.0

Source: Herman Miller, 10-K reports, various years.

Exhibit 6   Herman Miller's Consolidated Statements of Operations, Fiscal Years 2006–2010 ($ millions, except per share data)

	Fiscal Years Ending				
	May 29, 2010	May 30, 2009	May 31, 2008	June 2, 2007	June 3, 2006
Net sales	$1,318.8	$1,630.0	$2,012.1	$1,918.9	$1,737.2
Cost of sales	890.3	1,102.3	1,313.4	1,273.0	1,162.4
Gross margin	428.5	527.7	698.7	645.9	574.8
Operating expenses:					
Selling, general, and administrative	317.7	330.8	395.8	395.8	371.7
Restructuring expenses	16.7	28.4	5.1	—	
Design and research	40.5	45.7	51.2	52.0	45.4
Total operating expenses	374.9	404.9	452.1	447.8	417.1
Operating earnings	53.6	122.8	246.6	198.1	157.7
Other expenses (income):					
Interest expense	21.7	25.6	18.8	13.7	14.0
Interest and other investment income	(4.6)	(2.6)	(3.8)	(4.1)	(4.9)
Other, net	1.7	.9	1.2	1.5	1.0
Net other expenses	18.8	23.9	16.2	1	10.1
Earnings before income taxes and minority interest	34.8	98.9	230.4	187.0	147.6
Income tax expense	6.5	31.0	78.2	57.9	47.7
Minority interest, net of income tax	—	(.1)	(0.1)	—	0.7
Net earnings	$28.3	$68.0	$152.3	$129.1	$99.2
Earnings per share—basic	$0.51	$1.26	$2.58	$2.01	$1.40
Earnings per share—diluted	$0.43	$1.25	$2.56	$1.98	$1.45

Source: Herman Miller, 10-K reports, various years.

to Mark Schurman, director of external communications at Herman Miller, once the company identified accessories as a potential growth area, "Robyn [Hofmeyer] was tapped to put together a team to really explore this as a product segment that we could get more involved with."

In 2006, Hofmeyer established the Accessories Team by recruiting Larry Kallio to be the head engineer and Wayne Baxter to lead sales and marketing. Together, they assembled a flexible team to launch a new product in 16 months. They recruited people with different disciplines needed to support that goal. Over the next two years, they remained a group of six. Some people started with the team to develop a particular product and, as it got through that piece of work, then went on to different roles within the company. During its first eight months, the Accessories Team met twice a week for half a day. Twenty months out, it met only once a week.

The group acted with a fair amount of autonomy, but it did not want complete autonomy. "We don't want to be out there completely on our own because we have such awesome resources here at Herman Miller," Robyn Hofmeyer explained. When different disciplines were needed for a particular product, the group reached out to other areas in the company and found people who could allocate some of their time to support that product.

Wayne Baxter described what happened on the team as follows:

> We all seem to have a very strong voice regarding almost any topic; it's actually quite fun and quite dynamic. We all have kind of our roles on the team, but I think other than maybe true engineering, we've all kind of tapped into other roles and still filled in to help each other as much as we could.

Another member of the Accessories Team described the group's decision making as follows:

> If we wanted to debate and research and get very scientific, we would not be sitting here talking about the things that we've done, we'd still be researching them. In a sense, we rely upon our gut a lot, which I think is, at the end of the day just fine because we have enough experience. We're not experts, but we're also willing to take risks and we're also willing to evolve.

Thus, leadership and decision making was shared both within the Accessories Team and across the organization. Ideas and other contributions to the success of the team were accepted from all sources.

Out of this process grew Herman Miller's Thrive Collection. The name was chosen to indicate the focus on the individual and the idea of personal comfort, control, and ergonomic health. Thrive Collection products included the Ardea Personal Light, the Leaf Personal Light, the Flo Monitor Arm, and C2 Climate Control. All of these were designed for improving the individual's working environment. Continuing Herman Miller's tradition of innovative design, the Ardea Personal Light earned both Gold and Silver honors from the International Design Excellence Awards (IDEA) in June 2010.

THE INDUSTRY

Office equipment (classified by Standard & Poor's Research Insight as Office Services & Supplies) was an economically volatile industry. The office furniture segment of the industry was hit hard by the recession. Sales were expected to drop by 26.5 percent from 2008 to 2009. Herman Miller's sales dropped 19 percent. Herman Miller's stock market value of more than $1 billion at the end of 2009 represented 7.3 percent of the total stock market value of the industry. According to Hoover's, Herman Miller's top three competitors were Haworth, Steelcase, and HNI Corporation.

The industry had been impacted by a couple of trends. First, telecommuting had decreased the need of large companies to have office equipment for all employees. At some companies, such as Oracle, a substantial percentage of employees telecommuted; for example, the majority of Jet-Blue reservation clerks telecommuted. Second, more employees were spending more hours in front of computer screens than ever before. Due to this trend, the need for ergonomically correct office furniture had increased. Such furniture helped decrease fatigue and injuries such as carpal tunnel syndrome. Finally, as with most industries, the cost of raw materials and competition from overseas had had an impact on office furniture.

These trends tended to impact low-cost office furniture producers more than they impacted the high-quality producers.

THE FUTURE

In a June 24, 2010, press release, Herman Miller's CEO, Brian Walker, stated:

> One of the hallmarks of our company's history has been the ability to emerge from challenging periods with transformational products and processes. I believe our commitment to new products and market development over the past two years has put us in a position to do this once again. Throughout this period, we remained focused on maintaining near-term profitability while at the same time investing for the future. The award-winning new products we introduced last week at the NeoCon tradeshow are a testament to that focus, and I am incredibly proud of the collective spirit it has taken at Herman Miller to make this happen.

Looking into the future, executives at Herman Miller faced two particular questions: Will the strategies that have made Herman Miller an outstanding and award-winning company continue to provide it with the ability to reinvent and renew itself? Will disruptive global, economic, and competitive forces compel it to change its business model?

ENDNOTES

[1] Many sources were helpful in providing material for this case, most particularly employees at Herman Miller who generously shared their time and viewpoints about the company to help ensure that the case accurately reflected the company's practices and culture. They provided many resources, including internal documents and stories of their personal experiences.

[2] The names of the two Fortune 500 companies were deleted by the authors.

[3] Herman Miller's fiscal year ends on May 30 of the following calendar year.

Starbucks' Strategy and Internal Initiatives to Return to Profitable Growth

Arthur A. Thompson
The University of Alabama

Amit J. Shah
Frostburg State University

Since its founding in 1987 as a modest nine-store operation in Seattle, Washington, Starbucks had become the world's premier roaster and retailer of specialty coffees, with 8,812 company-owned stores and 7,852 licensed stores in more than 50 countries as of April 2010 and annual sales of about $10 billion. But the company's 2008–2009 fiscal years were challenging. Sales at company-owned Starbucks stores open 13 months or longer declined an average of 3 percent in 2008 and another 5 percent in 2009. Company-wide revenues declined from $10.4 billion in fiscal year 2008 to $9.8 billion in fiscal year 2009. During fiscal 2009, Starbucks closed 800 underperforming company-operated stores in the United States and an additional 100 stores in other countries, restructured its entire operations in Australia (including the closure of 61 stores), and reduced the number of planned new store openings by more than 200. Starbucks' global workforce was trimmed by about 6,700 employees. The company's cost-reduction and labor-efficiency initiatives resulted in savings of about $580 million. Exhibit 1 shows the performance of Starbucks' company-operated retail stores for the most recent five fiscal years.

In his November 2009 letter to company shareholders, Howard Schultz, Starbucks' founder, chairman of the board, and chief executive officer, said:

> Two years ago, I expressed concern over challenges confronting our business of a breadth and magnitude unlike anything I had ever seen before. For the first time, we were beginning to see traffic in our U.S. stores slow. Strong competitors were entering our business. And perhaps most troublesome, where in the past Starbucks had always been forward-thinking and nimble in its decision-making and execution, like many fast-growing companies before us, we had allowed our success to make us complacent.
>
> It was obvious to me, and to our leadership team, that Starbucks needed nothing less than a full-fledged transformation to return to profitable growth. Our blueprint for change was the transformation agenda: improving the state of our business through better training, tools, and products; renewing our attention to store-level economics and operating efficiency; reigniting our emotional attachment with customers; and realigning Starbucks' organization for the long term.
>
> Since then, we have worked through the multitude of challenges required to revitalize our brand and transform our company—all in the face of the worst global economic environment of our generation. Today, I am pleased to report that we have made and continue to make significant progress in transforming Starbucks and returning the company to sustainable, profitable growth while preserving our values and guiding principles.
>
> With our progress over the past two years, we are now in a position to take advantage of the global opportunities for Starbucks.[1]

COMPANY BACKGROUND

Starbucks Coffee, Tea, and Spice

Starbucks got its start in 1971 when three academics, English teacher Jerry Baldwin, history

Exhibit 1   Selected Operating Statistics for Starbucks Stores, Fiscal Years 2005–2009

	Fiscal Years Ending				
	Sept. 27, 2009	Sept. 28, 2008	Sept. 30, 2007	Oct. 1, 2006	Oct. 2, 2005
Net Revenues at Company-Operated Retail Stores ($ millions)					
United States	$ 6,572.1	$ 6,997.7	$ 6,560.9	$ 5,495.2	$ 4,539.5
International	1,608.0	1,774.2	1,437.4	1,087.9	852.5
Operating Income at Company-Operated Retail Stores ($ millions)					
United States	$ 531.8	$ 454.2	$ 1,005.2	$ 955.2	$ 818.5
International	92.9	110.0	137.7	108.5	82.3
Percentage Change in Sales at Company-Operated Stores Open 13 Months or Longer					
United States	−6%	−5%	4%	7%	9%
International	−2%	2%	7%	8%	6%
Worldwide average	−5%	−3%	5%	7%	8%
Average Sales Revenues at Company-Operated Retail Stores					
United States	$938,000	$970,000	$1,048,000	$1,049,000	$1,004,000
United Kingdom and Ireland	$870,000	$924,000	$ 958,000	$ 925,000	$ 853,000
Canada	$835,000	$910,000	$ 918,000	$ 870,000	$ 829,000
China	$549,000	$537,000	$ 508,000	$ 460,000	$ 447,000
All other international locations	$678,000	$681,000	$ 663,000	$ 633,000	$ 605,000
Stores Opened during the Year (net of closures)					
United States					
Company-operated stores	(474)	445	1,065	810	580
Licensed stores	35	438	723	733	596
International					
Company-operated stores	89	236	286	240	177
Licensed stores	305	550	497	416	319
Total store openings (net of closures)	(45)	1,669	2,571	2,199	1,672

Sources: Management Presentation at Barclays Capital Retail and Restaurants Conference on April 28, 2010, www.starbucks.com, accessed June 8, 2010; 2009 10-K report, p. 19 and p. 76; and 2007 10-K report, p. 70.

teacher Zev Siegel, and writer Gordon Bowker—all coffee aficionados—opened Starbucks Coffee, Tea, and Spice in the touristy Pikes Place Market in Seattle. Sharing a love for fine coffees and exotic teas, the three partners believed they could build a clientele in Seattle that would appreciate the best coffees and teas, much like what had already emerged in the San Francisco Bay area. They each invested $1,350 and borrowed another $5,000 from a bank to open the Pikes Place store. The inspiration and mentor for the Starbucks venture in Seattle was a Dutch immigrant named Alfred Peet who had opened Peet's Coffee and Tea in Berkeley, California, in 1966. Peet's store specialized in importing fine coffees and teas and dark-roasting its own beans the European way to bring out the full flavors of the beans. Customers were encouraged to learn how to grind the beans and make their own freshly brewed coffee at home. Baldwin, Siegel, and Bowker were well acquainted with Peet's expertise, having visited his store on numerous occasions and listened to him expound on quality coffees and the importance of proper bean-roasting techniques.

The Pikes Place store featured modest, hand-built, classic nautical fixtures. One wall was devoted to whole bean coffees, while another had shelves of coffee products. The store did not offer fresh-brewed coffee sold by the cup, but tasting samples were sometimes available. Initially, Siegel was the only paid employee. He wore a grocer's apron, scooped out beans for customers, extolled the virtues of fine, dark-roasted coffees, and functioned as the partnership's retail expert. The other two partners kept their day jobs but came by at lunch or after work to help out. During the start-up period, Baldwin kept the books and developed a growing knowledge of coffee; Bowker served as the "magic, mystery, and romance man."[2] The store was an immediate success, with sales exceeding expectations, partly because of interest stirred by a favorable article in the *Seattle Times*. For most of the first year, Starbucks ordered its coffee beans from Peet's, but then the partners purchased a used roaster from Holland, set up roasting operations in a nearby ramshackle building, and came up with their own blends and flavors.

By the early 1980s, the company had four Starbucks stores in the Seattle area and had been profitable every year since opening its doors. But then Zev Siegel experienced burnout and left the company to pursue other interests. Jerry Baldwin took over day-to-day management of the company and functioned as chief executive officer; Gordon Bowker remained involved as an owner but devoted most of his time to his advertising and design firm, a weekly newspaper he had founded, and a microbrewery that he was launching known as the Redhook Ale Brewery.

Howard Schultz Enters the Picture

In 1981, Howard Schultz, vice president and general manager of U.S. operations for a Swedish maker of stylish kitchen equipment and coffeemakers, decided to pay Starbucks a visit—he was curious about why Starbucks was selling so many of his company's products. When he arrived at the Pikes Place store, a solo violinist was playing Mozart at the door (his violin case open for donations). Schultz was immediately taken by the powerful and pleasing aroma of the coffees, the wall displaying coffee beans, and the rows of coffeemakers on the shelves. As he talked with the clerk behind the counter, the clerk scooped out some Sumatran coffee beans, ground them, put the grounds in a cone filter, poured hot water over the cone, and shortly handed Schultz a porcelain mug filled with freshly brewed coffee. After taking only three sips of the brew, Schultz was hooked. He began asking questions about the company, the coffees from different parts of the world, and the different ways of roasting coffee.

Later, when he met with Jerry Baldwin and Gordon Bowker, Schultz was struck by their knowledge of coffee, their commitment to providing customers with quality coffees, and their passion for educating customers about the merits of dark-roasted coffees. Baldwin told Schultz, "We don't manage the business to maximize anything other than the quality of the coffee."[3] The company purchased only the finest arabica coffees and put them through a meticulous dark-roasting process to bring out their full flavors. Baldwin explained that the cheap robusta coffees used in supermarket blends burned when subjected to dark-roasting. He also noted that the makers of supermarket blends preferred lighter roasts because it allowed higher yields (the longer a coffee was roasted, the more weight it lost).

Schultz was also struck by the business philosophy of the two partners. It was clear that Starbucks stood not just for good coffee but also for the dark-roasted flavor profiles that the founders were passionate about. Top-quality, fresh-roasted, whole-bean coffee was the company's differentiating feature and a bedrock value. It was also clear to Schultz that Starbucks was strongly committed to educating its customers to appreciate the qualities of fine coffees. The company depended mainly on word of mouth to get more people into its stores, then built customer loyalty cup by cup as buyers gained a sense of discovery and excitement about the taste of fine coffee.

On his return trip to New York, Howard Schultz could not stop thinking about Starbucks and what it would be like to be a part of the Starbucks enterprise. Schultz recalled, "There was something magic about it, a passion and authenticity I had never experienced in business."[4] The appeal of living in the Seattle area was another strong plus. By the time he landed at Kennedy Airport, he knew in his heart he wanted to go to work for Starbucks. At the first opportunity, Schultz asked Baldwin whether there was any way he could fit into Starbucks. While he and Baldwin had established an easy, comfortable personal rapport, it still took a year, numerous meetings at which Schultz presented his ideas, and a lot of convincing to get Baldwin, Bowker, and their silent partner from San Francisco to agree to hire him. Schultz pursued a job at Starbucks far more vigorously than Starbucks pursued hiring Schultz. The owners were nervous about bringing in an outsider, especially a high-powered New Yorker who had not grown up with the values of the company. Nonetheless, Schultz continued to press his ideas about the tremendous potential of expanding the Starbucks enterprise outside Seattle and exposing people all over America to Starbucks coffee.

At a meeting with the three owners in San Francisco in the spring of 1982, Schultz once again presented his ideas and vision for opening Starbucks stores across the United States and Canada. He thought the meeting went well and flew back to New York, believing a job offer was in the bag. However, the next day Jerry Baldwin called Schultz and indicated that the owners had decided against hiring him because geographic expansion was too risky and they did not share Schultz's vision for Starbucks. Schultz was despondent, seeing his dreams of being a part of Starbucks' future go up in smoke. Still, he believed so deeply in Starbucks' potential that he decided to make a last-ditch appeal; he called Baldwin the next day and made an impassioned, reasoned case for why the decision was a mistake. Baldwin agreed to reconsider. The next morning Baldwin called Schultz and told him the job of heading marketing and overseeing the retail stores was his. In September 1982, Howard Schultz took over his new responsibilities at Starbucks.

Starbucks and Howard Schultz, 1982–1985

In his first few months at Starbucks, Schultz spent most of his waking hours in the four Seattle stores—working behind the counters, tasting different kinds of coffee, talking with customers, getting to know store personnel, and learning the retail aspects of the coffee business. By December, Jerry Baldwin concluded that Schultz was ready for the final part of his training: actually roasting the coffee. Schultz spent a week getting an education about the colors of different coffee beans, listening for the telltale second pop of the beans during the roasting process, learning to taste the subtle differences among the various roasts, and familiarizing himself with the roasting techniques for different beans.

Schultz made a point of acclimating himself to the informal dress code at Starbucks, gaining credibility and building trust with colleagues, and making the transition from the high-energy, coat-and-tie style of New York to the more casual, low-key ambience of the Pacific Northwest. Schultz made real headway in gaining the acceptance and respect of company personnel while working at the Pike Place store one day during the busy Christmas season that first year. The store was packed and Schultz was behind the counter ringing up sales of coffee when someone shouted that a shopper had just headed out the door with two coffeemakers. Without thinking, Schultz leaped over the counter and chased the thief, yelling, "Drop that stuff! Drop it!" The thief dropped both pieces and ran. Schultz returned to the store, holding the coffeemakers up like trophies. Everyone applauded. When Schultz returned to his office later that afternoon, his staff had strung up a banner that read: "Make my day."[5]

Schultz was overflowing with ideas for the company. Early on, he noticed that first-time customers sometimes felt uneasy in the stores because of their lack of knowledge about fine coffees and because store employees sometimes came across as a little arrogant or superior to coffee novices. Schultz worked with store employees on customer-friendly sales skills and developed brochures that made it easy for customers to learn about fine coffees. However, Schultz's biggest inspiration and vision for Starbucks' future came during the spring of 1983 when the company sent him to Milan, Italy, to attend an international housewares show. While walking from his hotel to the convention center, he spotted an espresso bar and went inside to look around. The cashier beside the door nodded and smiled. The barista behind the counter greeted Schultz cheerfully and began pulling a shot of espresso for one customer and handcrafting a foamy cappuccino for another, all the while conversing merrily with patrons standing at the counter. Schultz thought the barista's performance was great theater. Just down the way on a side street, he entered an even more crowded espresso bar, where the barista, which he surmised to be the owner, was greeting customers by name; people were laughing and talking in an atmosphere that plainly was comfortable and familiar. In the next few blocks, he saw two more espresso bars. That afternoon when the trade show concluded for the day, Schultz walked the streets of Milan to explore more espresso bars. Some were stylish and upscale; others attracted a blue-collar clientele. Most had few chairs, and it was common for Italian opera to be playing in the background. What struck Schultz was how popular and vibrant the Italian coffee bars were. They seemed to function as an integral community gathering place, and energy levels were typically high. Each bar had its own unique character, but they all had a barista that performed with flair and established a camaraderie with the customers.

Schultz remained in Milan for a week, exploring coffee bars and learning as much as he could about the Italian passion for coffee drinks. Schultz was particularly struck by the fact that there were 1,500 coffee bars in Milan, a city about the size of Philadelphia, and a total of 200,000 in all of Italy. In one bar, he heard a customer order a *caffelatte* and decided to try one himself—the barista made a shot of espresso, steamed a frothy pitcher of milk, poured the two together in a cup, and put a dollop of foam on the top. Schultz liked it immediately, concluding that lattes should be a feature item on any coffee bar menu even though none of the coffee experts he had talked to had ever mentioned them.

Schultz's 1983 trip to Milan produced a revelation: the Starbucks stores in Seattle completely missed the point. There was much more to the coffee business than just selling beans and getting people to appreciate grinding their own beans and brewing fine coffee in their homes. What Starbucks needed to do was serve fresh-brewed coffee, espressos and cappuccinos in its stores (in addition to beans and coffee equipment) and try to create an American version of the Italian

coffee bar culture. Going to Starbucks should be an experience, a special treat, a place to meet friends and visit. Re-creating the authentic Italian coffee bar culture in the United States could be Starbucks' differentiating factor.

Schultz Becomes Frustrated

On Schultz's return from Italy, he shared his revelation and ideas for modifying the format of Starbucks' stores with Baldwin and Bowker. But instead of winning their approval for trying out some of his ideas, Schultz encountered strong resistance. Baldwin and Bowker argued that Starbucks was a retailer, not a restaurant or coffee bar. They feared that serving drinks would put them in the beverage business and diminish the integrity of Starbucks' mission as a purveyor of fine coffees. They pointed out that Starbucks had been profitable every year and there was no reason to rock the boat in a small, private company like Starbucks. But a more pressing reason not to pursue Schultz's coffee bar concept emerged shortly—Baldwin and Bowker were excited by an opportunity to purchase Peet's Coffee and Tea. The acquisition was finalized in early 1984, and to fund it Starbucks had to take on considerable debt, leaving little in the way of financial flexibility to support Schultz's ideas for entering the beverage part of the coffee business or expanding the number of Starbucks stores. For most of 1984, Starbucks managers were dividing their time between operations in Seattle and the Peet's enterprise in San Francisco. Schultz found himself in San Francisco every other week supervising the marketing and operations of the five Peet stores. Starbucks employees began to feel neglected and, in one quarter, did not receive their usual bonus due to tight financial conditions. Employee discontent escalated to the point where a union election was called. The union won by three votes. Baldwin was shocked at the results, concluding that employees no longer trusted him. In the months that followed, he began to spend more of his energy on the Peet's operation in San Francisco.

It took Howard Schultz nearly a year to convince Jerry Baldwin to let him test an espresso bar. Baldwin relented when Starbucks opened its sixth store in April 1984. It was the first Starbucks store designed to sell beverages, and it was the first located in downtown Seattle. Schultz asked for a 1,500-square-foot space to set up a full-scale Italian-style espresso bar, but Baldwin agreed to allocating only 300 square feet in a corner of the new store. The store opened with no fanfare as a deliberate experiment to see what would happen. By closing time on the first day, some 400 customers had been served, well above the 250-customer average of Starbucks' best-performing stores. Within two months, the store was serving 800 customers per day. The two baristas could not keep up with orders during the early-morning hours, resulting in lines outside the door onto the sidewalk. Most of the business was at the espresso counter, while sales at the regular retail counter were only adequate.

Schultz was elated at the test results, expecting that Baldwin's doubts about entering the beverage side of the business would be dispelled and that he would gain approval to pursue the opportunity to take Starbucks to a new level. Every day he went into Baldwin's office to show him the sales figures and customer counts at the new downtown store. But Baldwin was not comfortable with the success of the new store, believing that it felt wrong and that espresso drinks were a distraction from the core business of marketing fine arabica coffees at retail. Baldwin rebelled at the thought that people would see Starbucks as a place to get a quick cup of coffee to go. He adamantly told Schultz, "We're coffee roasters. I don't want to be in the restaurant business. . . . Besides, we're too deeply in debt to consider pursuing this idea."[6] While he didn't deny that the experiment was succeeding, he didn't want to go forward with introducing beverages in other Starbucks stores. Schultz's efforts to persuade Baldwin to change his mind continued to meet strong resistance, although to avoid a total impasse Baldwin finally did agree to let Schultz put espresso machines in the back of one or two other Starbucks stores.

Over the next several months, Schultz made up his mind to leave Starbucks and start his own company. His plan was to open espresso bars in high-traffic downtown locations, serve espresso drinks and coffee by the cup, and try to emulate the friendly, energetic atmosphere he had encountered in Italian espresso bars. Baldwin and Bowker, knowing how frustrated Schultz had become, supported his efforts to go out on his own and agreed to let him stay in his current

job and office until definitive plans were in place. Schultz left Starbucks in late 1985.

Schultz's Il Giornale Venture

With the aid of a lawyer friend who helped companies raise venture capital and go public, Schultz began seeking out investors for the kind of company he had in mind. Ironically, Jerry Baldwin committed to investing $150,000 of Starbucks' money in Schultz's coffee bar enterprise, thus becoming Schultz's first investor. Baldwin accepted Schultz's invitation to be a director of the new company, and Gordon Bowker agreed to be a part-time consultant for six months. Bowker, pumped up about the new venture, urged Schultz to make sure that everything about the new stores—the name, the presentation, the care taken in preparing the coffee—was calculated to elevate customer expectations and lead them to expect something better than competitors offered. Bowker proposed that the new company be named Il Giornale Coffee Company (pronounced *il jor NAHL ee*), a suggestion that Howard accepted. In December 1985, Bowker and Schultz made a trip to Italy, where they visited some 500 espresso bars in Milan and Verona, observing local habits, taking notes about decor and menus, snapping photographs, and videotaping baristas in action.

About $400,000 in seed capital was raised by the end of January 1986, enough to rent an office, hire a couple of key employees, develop a store design, and open the first store. But it took until the end of 1986 to raise the remaining $1.25 million needed to launch at least eight espresso bars and prove that Schultz's strategy and business model were viable. Schultz made presentations to 242 potential investors, 217 of whom said no. Many who heard Schultz's hourlong presentation saw coffee as a commodity business and thought that Schultz's espresso bar concept lacked any basis for sustainable competitive advantage (no patent on dark roast, no advantage in purchasing coffee beans, no ways to bar the entry of imitative competitors). Some noted that coffee couldn't be turned into a growth business—consumption of coffee had been declining since the mid-1960s. Others were skeptical that people would pay $1.50 or more for a cup of coffee, and the company's hard-to-pronounce name turned some off. Being rejected by so many potential investors was disheartening—some who listened to Schultz's presentation didn't even bother to call him back; others refused to take his calls. Nonetheless, Schultz maintained an upbeat attitude and displayed passion and enthusiasm in making his pitch. He ended up raising $1.65 million from about 30 investors; most of the money came from 9 people, 5 of whom became directors.

The first Il Giornale store opened in April 1986. It had 700 square feet and was located near the entrance of Seattle's tallest building. The decor was Italian, and there were Italian words on the menu. Italian opera music played in the background. The baristas wore white shirts and bow ties. All service was stand-up; there were no chairs. National and international papers were hung on rods on the wall. By closing time on the first day, 300 customers had been served—mostly in the morning hours.

But while the core idea worked well, it soon became apparent that several aspects of the format were not appropriate for Seattle. Some customers objected to the incessant opera music, others wanted a place to sit down, and many did not understand the Italian words on the menu. These "mistakes" were quickly fixed, but an effort was made not to compromise the style and elegance of the store. Within six months, the store was serving more than 1,000 customers a day. Regular customers had learned how to pronounce the company's name. Because most customers were in a hurry, it became apparent that speedy service was essential.

Six months after the first Il Giornale opened, a second store was opened in another downtown building. In April 1987, a third store was opened in Vancouver, British Columbia, to test the transferability of the company's business concept outside Seattle. Schultz's goal was to open 50 stores in five years, and he needed to dispel his investors' doubts about geographic expansion early on to achieve his growth objective. By mid-1987, sales at the three stores were running at a rate equal to $1.5 million annually.

Il Giornale Acquires Starbucks

In March 1987, Jerry Baldwin and Gordon Bowker decided to sell the whole Starbucks operation in Seattle—the stores, the roasting plant, and the Starbucks name. Bowker wanted to cash out his coffee business investment to concentrate on his other enterprises; Baldwin, who was tired of commuting between Seattle and San Francisco, wanted to concentrate on the Peet's operation. As he recalls, "My wife and I had a 30-second conversation and decided to keep Peet's. It was the original and it was better."[7]

Schultz knew immediately that he had to buy Starbucks; his board of directors agreed. Schultz and his newly hired finance and accounting manager drew up a set of financial projections for the combined operations and a financing package that included a stock offering to Il Giornale's original investors and a line of credit with local banks. While a rival plan to acquire Starbucks was put together by another Il Giornale investor, Schultz's proposal prevailed and within weeks Schultz had raised the $3.8 million needed to buy Starbucks. The acquisition was completed in August 1987. The new name of the combined companies was Starbucks Corporation. Howard Schultz, at the age of 34, became Starbucks' president and CEO.

STARBUCKS AS A PRIVATE COMPANY, 1987–1992

The following Monday morning, Howard returned to the Starbucks offices at the roasting plant, greeted all the familiar faces, and accepted their congratulations. Then he called the staff together for a meeting on the roasting plant floor:

> All my life I have wanted to be part of a company and a group of people who share a common vision. . . . I'm here today because I love this company. I love what it represents. . . . I know you're concerned. . . . I promise you I will not let you down. I promise you I will not leave anyone behind. . . . In five years, I want you to look back at this day and say "I was there when it started. I helped build this company into something great."[8]

Schultz told the group that his vision was for Starbucks to become a national company with values and guiding principles that employees could be proud of. He indicated that he wanted to include people in the decision-making process and that he would be open and honest with them.

Schultz believed that building a company that valued and respected its people, that inspired them, and that shared the fruits of success with those who contributed to the company's long-term value was essential, not just an intriguing option. His aspiration was for Starbucks to become the most respected brand name in coffee and for the company to be admired for its corporate responsibility. In the next few days and weeks, Schultz came to see that the unity and morale at Starbucks had deteriorated badly in the 20 months he had been at Il Giornale. Some employees were cynical and felt unappreciated. There was a feeling that prior management had abandoned them and a wariness about what the new regime would bring. Schultz decided to make building a new relationship of mutual respect between employees and management a priority.

The business plan Schultz had presented investors called for the new 9-store company to open 125 stores in the next five years—15 the first year, 20 the second, 25 the third, 30 the fourth, and 35 the fifth. Revenues were projected to reach $60 million in 1992. But the company lacked experienced management. Schultz had never led a growth effort of such magnitude and was just learning what the job of CEO was all about, having been the president of a small company for barely two years. Dave Olsen, a Seattle coffee bar owner whom Schultz had recruited to direct store operations at Il Giornale, was still learning the ropes in managing a multistore operation. Ron Lawrence, the company's controller, had worked as a controller for several organizations. Other Starbucks employees had only the experience of managing or being a part of a six-store organization. When Starbucks' key roaster and coffee buyer resigned, Schultz put Dave Olsen in charge of buying and roasting coffee. Lawrence Maltz, who had 20 years' experience in business and 8 years' experience as president of a profitable public beverage company, was hired as executive vice president and charged with heading operations, finance, and human resources.

In the next several months, a number of changes were instituted. To symbolize the merging of the two companies and the two cultures, a new logo was created that melded the designs of the Starbucks logo and the Il Giornale logo. The Starbucks stores were equipped with espresso machines and remodeled to look more Italian than Old World nautical. Il Giornale green replaced the traditional Starbucks brown. The result was a new type of store—a cross between a retail coffee bean store and an espresso bar/café—that became Starbucks' signature.

By December 1987, the mood of the employees at Starbucks had turned upbeat. They were buying into the changes that Schultz was making, and trust began to build between management and employees. New stores were on the verge of opening in Vancouver and Chicago. One Starbucks store employee, Daryl Moore, who had started working at Starbucks in 1981 and who had voted against unionization in 1985, began to question the need for a union with his fellow employees. Over the next few weeks, Moore began a move to decertify the union. He carried a decertification letter around to Starbucks' stores securing the signatures of employees who no longer wished to be represented by the union. He got a majority of store employees to sign the letter and presented it to the National Labor Relations Board. The union representing store employees was decertified. Later, in 1992, the union representing Starbucks' roasting plant and warehouse employees was also decertified.

Market Expansion Outside the Pacific Northwest

Starbucks' entry into Chicago proved far more troublesome than management anticipated. The first Chicago store opened in October 1987, and three more stores were opened over the next six months. Customer counts at the stores were substantially below expectations. Chicagoans did not take to dark-roasted coffee as fast as Schultz had anticipated. The first downtown store opened onto the street rather than into the lobby of the building where it was located; in the winter months, customers were hesitant to go out in the wind and cold to acquire a cup of coffee. It was expensive to supply fresh coffee to the Chicago stores out of the Seattle warehouse (the company solved the problem of freshness and quality assurance by putting freshly roasted beans in special FlavorLock bags that used vacuum packaging techniques with a one-way valve to allow carbon dioxide to escape without allowing air and moisture in). Rents were higher in Chicago than in Seattle, and so were wage rates. The result was a squeeze on store profit margins. Gradually, customer counts improved, but Starbucks lost money on its Chicago stores until, in 1990, prices were raised to reflect higher rents and labor costs, more experienced store mangers were hired, and a critical mass of customers caught on to the taste of Starbucks products.

Portland, Oregon, was the next market entered, and Portland coffee drinkers took to Starbucks products quickly. By 1991, the Chicago stores had become profitable and the company was ready for its next big market entry. Management decided on California because of its host of neighborhood centers and the receptiveness of Californians to innovative, high-quality food. Los Angeles was chosen as the first California market to enter, principally because of its status as a trendsetter and its cultural ties to the rest of the country. L.A. consumers embraced Starbucks quickly, and the *Los Angeles Times* named Starbucks as the best coffee in America before the first store opened. The entry into San Francisco proved more troublesome because San Francisco had an ordinance against converting stores to restaurant-related uses in certain prime urban neighborhoods; Starbucks could sell beverages and pastries to customers at stand-up counters but could not offer seating in stores that had formerly been used for general retailing. However, the city council was soon convinced by café owners and real estate brokers to change the code. Still, Starbucks faced strong competition from Peet's and local espresso bars in the San Francisco market.

Starbucks' store expansion targets proved easier to meet than Schultz had originally anticipated, and he upped the numbers to keep challenging the organization. Starbucks opened 15 new stores in fiscal 1988, 20 in 1989, 30 in 1990, 32 in 1991, and 53 in 1992—producing a total of 161 stores, significantly above his original 1992 target of 125 stores.

From the outset, the strategy was to open only company-owned stores; franchising was avoided so as to keep the company in full control of the quality of its products and the character and location of its stores. But company owner-ship of all stores required Starbucks to raise new venture capital to cover the cost of new store expansion. In 1988, the company raised $3.9 million; in 1990, venture capitalists provided an additional $13.5 million; and, in 1991, another round of venture capital financing generated $15 million. Starbucks was able to raise the needed funds despite posting losses of $330,000 in 1987, $764,000 in 1988, and $1.2 million in 1989. While the losses were troubling to Starbucks' board of directors and investors, Schultz's business plan had forecast losses during the early years of expansion. At a particularly tense board meeting where directors sharply questioned him about the lack of profitability, Schultz said:

> Look, we're going to keep losing money until we can do three things. We have to attract a management team well beyond our expansion needs. We have to build a world-class roasting facility. And we need a computer information system sophisticated enough to keep track of sales in hundreds and hundreds of stores.[9]

Schultz argued for patience as the company invested in the infrastructure to support continued growth well into the 1990s. He contended that hiring experienced executives ahead of the growth curve, building facilities far beyond current needs, and installing support systems laid a strong foundation for rapid, profitable growth down the road. His arguments carried the day with the board and with investors, especially since revenues were growing by approximately 80 percent annually and customer traffic at the stores was meeting or exceeding expectations.

Starbucks became profitable in 1990. Profits had increased every year since 1990 except for fiscal year 2000 (because of a $58.8 million in investment write-offs in four dot-com enterprises) and for fiscal year 2008 (when the sharp global economic downturn hit the company's bottom line very hard). Because of the economic downturn in 2008–2009, Howard Schultz believed that new strategic initiatives and rejuvenated strategy execution efforts were very much needed at Starbucks. Exhibit 2 provides a summary of the company's financial performance for fiscal years 2005–2009. Exhibit 3 shows the long-term performance of the company's stock price; the stock had split 2-for-1 five times.

Exhibit 2 Financial Summary for Starbucks Corporation, Fiscal Years 2005–2009 ($ billions, except for per share amounts)

	Fiscal Years Ending*				
	Sept. 27, 2009	Sept. 28, 2008	Sept. 30, 2007	Oct. 1, 2006	Oct. 2, 2005
Results of Operations Data					
Net revenues:					
Company-operated retail store revenues	$8,180.1	$ 8,771.9	$7,998.3	$6,583.1	$5,391.9
Specialty revenues:					
Licensing	1,222.3	1,171.6	1,026.3	860.6	673
Foodservice and other	372.2	439.5	386.9	343.2	304.4
Total specialty revenues	1,594.5	1,611.1	1,413.2	1,203.8	977.4
Total net revenues	$9,774.6	$10,383.0	$ 9,411.5	$7,786.9	$6,369.3
Cost of sales, including occupancy costs	4,324.9	4,645.3	3,999.1	3,178.8	2,605.2
Store operating expenses	3,425.1	3,745.3	3,215.9	2,687.8	2,165.9
Other operating expenses	264.4	330.1	294.2	253.7	192.5
Depreciation and amortization expenses	534.7	549.3	467.2	387.2	340.2
General and administrative expenses	453.0	456.0	489.2	479.4	361.6
Restructuring charges	332.4	266.9	—	—	—
Total operating expenses	9,334.5	9,992.7	8,465.6	6,986.9	5,665.4
Income from equity investees	121.9	113.6	108.0	93.9	76.6
Operating income	$ 562.0	$ 503.9	$1,053.9	$ 894.0	$ 780.5
Earnings before cumulative effect of change in accounting principle	390.8	315.5	672.6	581.5	494.4
Cumulative effect of accounting change for asset retirement obligations, net of taxes	—	—	—	17.2	—
Net earnings	$ 390.8	$ 315.5	$ 672.6	$ 564.3	$ 494.4
Net earnings per common share—diluted	$0.52	$0.43	$0.87	$0.71	$0.61
Balance Sheet Data					
Current assets	$2,035.8	$ 1,748.0	$1,696.5	$1,529.8	$1,209.3
Current liabilities	1,581.0	2,189.7	2,155.6	1,935.6	1,227.0
Total assets	5,576.8	5,672.6	5,343.9	4,428.9	3,513.7
Short-term borrowings	—	713	710.3	700	277
Long-term debt (including current portion)	549.5	550.3	550.9	2.7	3.6
Shareholders' equity	$3,045.7	$ 2,490.9	$2,284.1	$2,228.5	$2,090.3
Cash Flow Data					
Net cash provided by operating activities	$1,389.0	$1,258.7	$ 1,331.2	$ 1,131.6	$922.9
Capital expenditures (net additions to property, plant and equipment)	$445.6	$984.5	$1,080.3	$771.2	$643.3

*The company's fiscal year ended on the Sunday closest to September 30.

Source: Starbucks, 2009, 2007 and 2005 10-K reports.

Exhibit 3   The Performance of Starbucks' Stock, 1993–2010

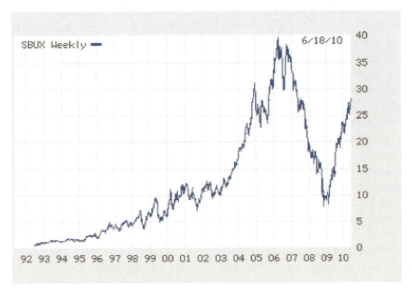

Source: Wall Street Journal, http://online.wsj.com, accessed June 18, 2010.

STARBUCKS STORES: DESIGN, AMBIENCE, AND EXPANSION OF LOCATIONS

Store Design

Starting in 1991, Starbucks created its own in-house team of architects and designers to ensure that each store would convey the right image and character. Stores had to be custom-designed because the company didn't buy real estate or build its own freestanding structures; rather, each space was leased in an existing structure, making each store differ in size and shape. Most stores ranged in size from 1,000 to 1,500 square feet and were located in office buildings, downtown and suburban retail centers, airport terminals, university campus areas, and busy neighborhood shopping areas convenient for pedestrian foot traffic and/or drivers. Only a select few were in suburban malls.

A "stores of the future" project team was formed in 1995 to raise Starbucks' store design to a still higher level and come up with the next generation of Starbucks stores. The team came up with four store designs—one for each of the four stages of coffeemaking: growing, roasting, brewing, and aroma—each with its own color combinations, lighting scheme, and component materials. Within each of the four basic store templates, Starbucks could vary the materials and details to adapt to different store sizes and settings (downtown buildings, college campuses, neighborhood shopping areas). In late 1996, Starbucks began opening new stores based on one of four formats and color schemes.

But as the number of stores increased rapidly between 2000 and 2003, greater store diversity and layout quickly became necessary. Some stores had special seating areas to help make Starbucks a desirable gathering place where customers could meet and chat or simply enjoy a peaceful interlude in their day. Flagship stores in high-traffic, high-visibility locations had fireplaces, leather chairs, newspapers, couches, and lots of ambience. The company also experimented with drive-through windows in locations where speed and convenience were important to customers and with kiosks in supermarkets, building lobbies, and other public places. In recent years, Starbucks had begun emphasizing drive-through retail stores in order to provide a greater degree of access and convenience for nonpedestrian customers. At the end of fiscal 2009, Starbucks had around 2,650 drive-through locations.[10]

In June 2009, Starbucks announced a new global store design strategy. Each new store was to be a reflection of the environment in which it operated and was to be environmentally friendly. In 2010, Starbucks began an effort to achieve Leadership in Energy and Environmental Design (LEED) certification for all new company-owned stores. (LEED certification was a program that used independent third parties to certify that a building incorporated green building design, construction, operations, and maintenance solutions.)[11] Core characteristics of each new store included celebration of local materials and craftsmanship, a focus on reused and recycled elements, exposure of structural integrity and authentic roots, elevation of coffee and removal of unnecessary distractions, storytelling and customer engagement through all five senses, and flexibility to meet the needs of many customer types.[12] Exhibit 4 shows the diverse nature of Starbucks stores.

To better control average store opening costs, the company centralized buying, developed standard contracts and fixed fees for certain items, and consolidated work under those contractors who displayed good cost-control practices. The retail operations group outlined exactly the minimum amount of equipment each core store needed so that standard items could be ordered in volume from vendors at 20 to 30 percent discounts, then delivered just in time to the store site either from company warehouses or the vendor. Modular designs for display cases were developed. The layouts for new and remodeled stores were developed on a computer, with software that allowed the costs to be estimated as the design evolved. All this cut store opening and remodeling costs significantly and shortened the process to about 18 weeks.

Store Ambience

Starbucks management viewed each store as a billboard for the company and as a contributor to building the company's brand and image. The company went to great lengths to make sure that store fixtures, merchandise displays, colors, artwork, banners, music, and aromas all blended to create a consistent, inviting, stimulating environment

that evoked the romance of coffee; that signaled the company's passion for coffee; that enhanced the mood and ambience of the store; and that rewarded customers with ceremony, stories, surprise, and a satisfying experience. The thesis was that every detail mattered in making Starbucks stores a welcoming and pleasant "third place" (apart from home and work) where people could meet friends and family, enjoy a quiet moment alone with a newspaper or book, or simply spend quality time relaxing.

To try to keep the coffee aromas in the stores pure, Starbucks banned smoking and asked employees to refrain from wearing perfumes or colognes. Prepared foods were kept covered so that customers would smell coffee only. Colorful banners and posters were used to keep the look of Starbucks stores fresh and to highlight seasons and holidays. Company designers came up with artwork for commuter mugs and T-shirts in different cities that were in keeping with each city's personality (peach-shaped coffee mugs for Atlanta, pictures of Paul Revere for Boston and the Statue of Liberty for New York).

In August 2002, Starbucks teamed up with T-Mobile USA to experiment with providing Internet access and enhanced digital entertainment to patrons at more than 1,200 Starbucks locations. The objective was to heighten the "third place" Starbucks experience, entice customers into perhaps buying a second latte or espresso while they caught up on e-mail, listened to digital music, put the finishing touches on a presentation, or surfed the Internet. Since the August 2002 introduction of Wi-Fi at Starbucks, wireless Internet service had been added at most company-operated stores in the United States. In an effort to better bridge Starbucks' "third place" coffeehouse experience with digital and social media, Starbucks announced that, beginning July 1, 2010, it would provide free Wi-Fi one-click Internet service through AT&T in all company-operated stores in the United States. There were also plans for a new online customer experience called the Starbucks Digital Network, in partnership with Yahoo, to debut in the fall of 2010 in U.S. company-operated Starbucks stores. This online experience would provide customers with free unrestricted access—via laptop, e-reader, or smartphone—to various paid sites and services such as the *Wall Street Journal*'s site

Exhibit 4 Scenes from Starbucks Stores

(www.wsj.com), exclusive content and previews, free downloads, and local community news and activities.

Store Expansion Strategy

In 1992 and 1993, Starbucks developed a three-year geographic expansion strategy to target areas that not only had favorable demographic profiles but also could be serviced and supported by the company's operations infrastructure. For each targeted region, Starbucks selected a large city to serve as a "hub"; teams of professionals were located in hub cities to support the goal of opening 20 or more stores in the hub in the first two years. Once a number of stores were opened in a hub, then additional stores were opened in smaller, surrounding "spoke" areas in the region. To oversee the expansion process, Starbucks had zone vice presidents who oversaw the store expansion process in a geographic region and instilled the Starbucks culture in the newly opened stores.

In recent years, Starbucks' strategy in major metropolitan cities had been to blanket major cities with stores, even if some stores cannibalized a nearby store's business. While a new store might draw 30 percent of the business of an existing store two or so blocks away, management believed that a "Starbucks everywhere" strategy cut down on delivery and management costs, shortened customer lines at individual stores, and increased foot traffic for all the stores in an area. In 2002, new stores generated an average of $1.2 million in first-year revenues, compared with $700,000 in 1995 and only $427,000 in 1990. The steady increases in new-store revenues were due partly to growing popularity of premium coffee drinks, partly to Starbucks' growing reputation, and partly to expanded product offerings. But the strategy of blanketing metropolitan areas with stores had cannibalized sales of existing stores to such an extent that average sales per store in the United States had dropped to around $1 million annually. Starbucks' long-term profitability target for its retail stores in the United States was an operating profit margin in the high teens—the operating margin was 14.3 percent in fiscal 2007, but declining store sales and depressed economic conditions had driven the margins down to 6.0 percent in fiscal 2008 and 7.5 percent in fiscal 2009.

One of Starbucks' core competencies was identifying good retailing sites for its new stores. The company was regarded as having the best real estate team in the coffee bar industry and a sophisticated system for identifying not only the most attractive individual city blocks but also the exact store location that was best; it also worked hard at building good relationships with local real estate representatives in areas where it was opening multiple store locations.

Licensed Retail Stores In 1995, Starbucks began entering into licensing agreements for store locations in areas where it did not have ability to locate its own outlets. Two early licensing agreements were with Marriott Host International to operate Starbucks retail stores in airport locations and with Aramark Food and Services to put Starbucks stores on university campuses and other locations operated by Aramark. Very quickly, Starbucks began to make increased use of licensing, both domestically and internationally. Starbucks preferred licensing to franchising because licensing permitted tighter controls over the operations of licensees.

Starbucks received a license fee and a royalty on sales at all licensed locations and supplied the coffee for resale at these locations. All licensed stores had to follow Starbucks' detailed operating procedures, and all managers and employees who worked in these stores received the same training given to managers and employees in company-operated Starbucks stores. As of 2009, there were 4,364 licensed stores in the United States and 3,439 licensed stores internationally.

International Expansion In markets outside the continental United States (including Hawaii), Starbucks had a two-pronged store expansion: either open company-owned and -operated stores or else license a reputable and capable local company with retailing know-how in the target host country to develop and operate new Starbucks stores. In most countries, Starbucks used a local partner/licensee to help it recruit talented individuals, set up supplier relationships, locate suitable store sites, and cater to local market conditions. Starbucks looked for partners/licensees that had strong retail/restaurant experience, had values and a corporate culture compatible with Starbucks, were committed to good customer service, possessed talented management and strong financial resources, and had demonstrated brand-building skills. In those foreign countries where business risks were deemed relatively high, most if not all Starbucks stores were licensed rather than being company-owned and operated. As of September 2009, Starbucks had company-operated and licensed stores in 50 countries (see Exhibit 5) and expected to open 200 new stores internationally in fiscal 2010.

Starbucks' long-term profitability target for its international operations was an operating profit margin in the mid-to-high teens. But the margins in recent years had been far below the

Exhibit 5   Company-Operated and Franchised Starbucks Stores

A. Number of Starbucks Store Locations Worldwide, 1987–March 2010 (selected years)

End of Fiscal Year*	Company-Operated Store Locations		Licensed Store Locations		Worldwide Total
	United States	International	United States	International	
1987	17	0	0	0	17
1990	84	0	0	0	84
1995	627	0	49	0	676
2000	2,446	530	173	352	3,501
2005	4,918	1,217	2,435	1,671	10,241
2006	5,728	1,457	3,168	2,087	12,440
2007	6,793	1,743	3,891	2,584	15,011
2008	7,238	1,979	4,329	3,134	16,680
2009	6,764	2,068	4,364	3,439	16,635
March 28, 2010	6,736	2,076	4,385	3,467	16,664

B. International Starbucks Store Locations at End of Fiscal Year 2009

International Locations of Company-Operated Starbucks Stores		International Locations of Licensed Starbucks Stores					
		Americas		Asia-Pacific		Europe/Africa/Middle East	
Canada	775	Canada	262	Japan	875	Turkey	123
United Kingdom	666	Mexico	261	South Korea	288	United Arab Emirates	91
China	191	Other	69	China	283	Spain	76
Germany	144			Taiwan	222	Greece	69
Thailand	131			Philippines	160	Saudi Arabia	68
Singapore	64			Malaysia	118	Kuwait	62
Australia	23			Indonesia	74	France	52
Other	74			New Zealand	42	Switzerland	47
Total	2,068					United Kingdom	46
						Other	151
						Licensed total worldwide	3,439

*Starbucks' fiscal year ended on the Sunday closest to September 30.

Source: Starbucks, 10-K reports, various years, and company records.

target: 8.1 percent in fiscal 2007, 5.2 percent in fiscal 2008, and 4.5 percent in fiscal 2009.

STARBUCKS' STRATEGY TO EXPAND ITS PRODUCT OFFERINGS AND ENTER NEW MARKET SEGMENTS

In the mid-1990s, thinking it was time for Starbucks to move out into mainstream markets, Howard Schultz led what proved to be an ongoing series of initiatives to expand Starbucks' product offerings beyond its retail stores and to pursue sales of Starbucks products in a wider variety of distribution channels and market segments. The strategy was to make Starbucks products more accessible to both existing and new customers where they worked, traveled, shopped, and dined and to find and promote new occasions for enjoying Starbucks products. The strategic objectives were to capitalize on Starbucks' growing brand awareness and brand-name strength and create a broader foundation for sustained long-term growth in revenues and profits.

The first initiative involved the establishment of an in-house specialty sales group to begin marketing Starbucks coffee products to restaurants, airlines, hotels, universities, hospitals, business offices, country clubs, and select retailers. Early users of Starbucks coffee included Horizon Airlines, a regional carrier based in Seattle, and United Airlines. There was much internal debate at Starbucks about whether it made sense for Starbucks coffee to be served on all United flights (since there was different coffeemaking equipment on different planes) and the possible damage to the integrity of the Starbucks brand if the quality of the coffee served did not measure up. It took seven months of negotiations for Starbucks and United to arrive at a mutually agreeable way to handle quality control on United's various types of planes. The specialty sales group also won accounts at Hyatt, Hilton, Sheraton, Radisson, and Westin hotels, resulting in packets of Starbucks coffee being in each room with coffeemaking equipment. Starbucks entered into an agreement with Wells Fargo to provide coffee service at some of the bank's locations in California. Later, the specialty sales group began working with leading institutional foodservice distributors, including Sysco Corporation and US Foodservice, to handle the distribution of Starbucks products to hotels, restaurants, office coffee distributors, educational and health care institutions, and other such enterprises. In fiscal 2009, Starbucks generated revenues of $372.2 million from providing whole bean and ground coffees and assorted other Starbucks products to some 21,000 food service accounts.

The second initiative came in 1994 when PepsiCo and Starbucks entered into a joint venture (now called the North American Coffee Partnership) to create new coffee-related products in bottles or cans for mass distribution through Pepsi channels. Howard Schultz saw the venture with PepsiCo as a major paradigm shift with the potential to cause Starbucks' business to evolve in heretofore unimaginable directions. The joint venture's first new product, Mazagran, a lightly flavored carbonated coffee drink, was a failure. Then, at a meeting with Pepsi executives, Schultz suggested developing a bottled version of Frappuccino, a new cold coffee drink that Starbucks had begun serving at its retail stores in the summer of 1995 and that quickly became a big hot-weather seller. Pepsi executives were enthusiastic. After months of experimentation, the joint venture product research team came up with a shelf-stable version of Frappuccino that tasted quite good. It was tested in West Coast supermarkets in the summer of 1996; sales ran 10 times projections, with 70 percent being repeat business. Sales of Frappuccino ready-to-drink beverages reached $125 million in 1997 and achieved national supermarket penetration of 80 percent. Starbucks' management believed that the market for Frappuccino would ultimately exceed $1 billion. The company began selling ready-to-drink Frappuccino products in Japan, Taiwan, and South Korea in 2005 chiefly through agreements with leading local distributors; the ready-to-drink beverage market in these countries represented more than $10 billion in annual sales.[13] In 2007, the PepsiCo-Starbucks partnership introduced a line of chilled Starbucks Doubleshot espresso drinks in the United States. Also in 2007, PepsiCo and Starbucks entered into a second joint venture called the International Coffee Partnership (ICP) for the purpose of introducing Starbucks-related beverages in country markets outside North America; one of the ICP's early moves was to begin marketing Frappuccino in China.[14] As of 2010, sales of Frappuccino products worldwide had reached $2 billion annually.[15]

In 2008, Starbucks partnered with Suntory to begin selling chilled ready-to-drink Doubleshot drinks in Japan. In 2010, Starbucks partnered with Arla Foods to begin selling Doubleshot products and Starbucks Discoveries chilled cup coffees in retail stores (as well as in Starbucks retail stores) across the United Kingdom.

In October 1995, Starbucks partnered with Dreyer's Grand Ice Cream to supply coffee extract for a new line of coffee ice cream made and distributed by Dreyer's under the Starbucks brand. By July 1996, Starbucks coffee-flavored ice cream was the number-one-selling superpremium brand in the coffee segment. In 2008, Starbucks discontinued its arrangement with Dreyer's and entered into an exclusive agreement with Unilever to manufacture, market, and distribute Starbucks-branded ice creams in the United States and Canada. Unilever was considered the global leader in ice cream, with annual sales of about $6 billion; its ice cream brands included Ben & Jerry's, Breyers, and Good Humor. Seven flavors of Starbucks ice cream and two flavors of novelty bars were marketed in 2010. Pints were available in the freezer sections at supermarkets for a suggested retail price of $3.99; the novelty bars sold for a suggested retail price of $2.49 and were also available in many convenience stores.

In 1997, a Starbucks store manager who had worked in the music industry and selected the music Starbucks played as background in its stores suggested that Starbucks begin selling the background music on tapes (and later on CDs as they become the preferred format). The manager had gotten compliments from customers wanting to buy the music they heard and suggested to senior executives that there was a market for the company's handpicked music. Research through two years of comment cards turned up hundreds asking Starbucks to sell the music it played in its stores. The Starbucks tapes/CDs proved a significant seller as an addition to the company's product line. In 2000, Starbucks acquired Hear Music, a San Francisco–based company, to give it added capability in enhancing its music CD offerings. In

2004, Starbucks introduced Hear Music media bars, a service that offered custom CD burning at select Starbucks stores. Later, Starbucks began offering customers the option of downloading music from the company's 200,000+ song library and, if they wished, having the downloaded songs burned onto a CD for purchase.

In the spring of 2008, Starbucks, in partnership with Apple's iTunes, began offering a Pick of the Week music card at its 7,000 stores in the United States that allowed customers to download each week's music selection at iTunes.[16] In 2010, Starbucks was continuing to offer CDs with handpicked music and new CDs featuring particular artists, all managed by Starbucks Entertainment in conjunction with Concord Music Group (which began managing the Hear Music Record Label in 2008); the CDs were typically priced at $12.95. Starbucks also had established a relationship with the William Morris Agency to identify books that it could offer for sale in its stores. Over the years, Starbucks' successes in music and books had included eight Grammy Awards and three number one books on the *New York Times* best-seller list.

In 1998, Starbucks licensed Kraft Foods to market and distribute Starbucks whole bean and ground coffees in grocery and mass-merchandise channels across the United States. Kraft managed all distribution, marketing, advertising, and promotions and paid a royalty to Starbucks based on a percentage of net sales. Product freshness was guaranteed by Starbucks' FlavorLock packaging, and the price per pound paralleled the prices in Starbucks' retail stores. Flavor selections in supermarkets were more limited than the varieties at Starbucks stores. The licensing relationship with Kraft was later expanded to include the marketing and distribution of Starbucks coffees in the United Kingdom and Europe. Going into 2010, Starbucks coffees were available in some 33,500 grocery and warehouse clubs in the United States and 5,500 retail outlets outside the United States; Starbucks' revenues from these sales were approximately $370 million in fiscal 2009.[17]

In 1999, Starbucks purchased Tazo Tea for $8.1 million. Tazo Tea, a tea manufacturer and distributor based in Portland, Oregon, was founded in 1994 and marketed its teas to restaurants, food stores, and tea houses. Starbucks proceeded to introduce hot and iced Tazo Tea drinks in its retail stores. As part of a long-term campaign to expand the distribution of its line of superpremium Tazo teas, Starbucks expanded its agreement with Kraft to market and distribute Tazo teas worldwide. In August 2008, Starbucks entered into an agreement with PepsiCo and Unilever (Lipton Tea was one of Unilever's leading brands) to manufacture, market, and distribute Starbucks' superpremium Tazo Tea ready-to-drink beverages (including iced teas, juiced teas, and herbal-infused teas) in the United States and Canada. The Tazo line of ready-to-drink beverages was to become part of an existing venture between PepsiCo and Unilever (the Pepsi/Lipton Tea partnership) that was the leading North American distributor of ready-to-drink teas.

In 2001, Starbucks introduced the Starbucks Card, a reloadable card that allowed customers to pay for their purchases with a quick swipe at the cash register and also to earn and redeem rewards. In 2009, about 15 percent of customer purchases at Starbucks stores were made on Starbucks cards.

In 2003, Starbucks acquired Seattle's Best Coffee, an operator of Seattle's Best coffee shops and marketer of Seattle's Best whole bean and ground coffees, for $70 million. Starbucks continued to operate Seattle's Best as a separate subsidiary. As of May 2008, there were more than 540 Seattle's Best cafés in the United States (a number of which were in Borders book and music stores) and 86 Seattle's Best Coffee Express espresso bars. The Seattle's Best product line included more than 30 whole bean and ground coffees (including flavored, organic, and Fair Trade Certified coffees), espresso beverages, signature handcrafted JavaKula blended beverages, OvenSong bakery food and sandwiches, and select merchandise. Shortly after the acquisition, Starbucks expanded its licensing arrangement with Kraft Foods to include marketing and distributing Seattle's Best whole bean and ground coffees in grocery and mass merchandise channels in North America, with Starbucks to receive a royalty on all such sales. In 2009, Seattle's Best whole bean and ground coffee blends were available nationwide in supermarkets and were being served at more than 15,000 food service locations (college campuses, restaurants, hotels, airlines, and cruise lines). A new Seattle's Best line of ready-to-drink iced lattes was introduced in April 2010 in major grocery and convenience stores in the western United States; the manufacture, marketing, and distribution of the new Seattle's Best beverages was managed by PepsiCo as part of the long-standing Starbucks-PepsiCo joint venture for ready-to-drink Frappuccino products. In May 2010, Starbucks announced that it would relaunch Seattle's Best Coffee with new distinctive red packaging and a red logo, boost efforts to open more franchised Seattle's Best cafés, and expand the availability of Seattle's Best coffees to 30,000 distribution points by October 2010. By July 2010, freshly brewed and iced Seattle's Best Coffee drinks were being sold at 7,250 Burger King outlets in the United States, 9,000 Subway locations, and some 299 AMC movie theaters in five countries.

In 2004 Starbucks teamed with Jim Beam Brands to invent a Starbucks Coffee Liqueur that would be sold be sold in bars, liquor stores, and restaurants; projections were for systemwide gross sales of more than $8 million annually. Launched in February 2005, Starbucks Coffee Liqueur was the number-one-selling new spirit product year-to-date through August 2005, according to Nielsen. In October 2005, again collaborating with Jim Beam Brands, Starbucks introduced Starbucks Cream Liqueur, a blend of cream, spirits, and a hint of Starbucks coffee. There were an estimated 22 million cordial consumers in the U.S. market, making the cream liqueur category nearly three times the size of coffee liqueur category. Both Starbucks Coffee Liqueur and Starbucks Cream Liqueur were packaged in 750 milliliter bottles priced at $22.99.

In April 2005, Starbucks acquired Ethos Water for $8 million in cash. The acquisition was made to expand the line of beverages in Starbucks stores in the United States. Following the acquisition, the brand also became known for its campaign to raise $10 million by donating $0.05 of the retail price of each bottle sold to a charitable organization working to increase access to clean drinking water and conduct sanitation and hygiene education programs in developing countries in Africa and Asia; in 2010, more than $6 million had been raised.[18] The production, distribution, and marketing of Ethos water products was handled by PepsiCo, as part of its long-standing joint venture with Starbucks.

In response to customer requests for more wholesome food and beverage options and also to bring in business from non–coffee drinkers, Starbucks in 2008 began offering fruit cups, yogurt parfaits, skinny lattes, banana walnut bread (that was nearly 30 percent real banana), a 300-calorie farmer's market salad with all-natural dressing, and a line of "better-for-you" smoothies called Vivanno Nourishing Blends. Each Vivanno smoothie averaged 250 calories and consisted of one serving of fruit, 16 grams of protein, and 5 grams of fiber.[19] Additionally, in 2009, healthier, lower-calorie selections were included in the bakery cases at Starbucks stores, and the recipes for several other food items on the menu at Starbucks stores were reformulated to include whole grains and dried fruits and to cut back on or eliminate the use of artificial flavorings, dyes, high-fructose corn syrup, and artificial preservatives.[20]

In 2008, Starbucks introduced a new coffee blend called Pike Place Roast that would be brewed every day, all day in every Starbucks store.[21] Before then, Starbucks rotated coffees through its brewed lineup, sometimes switching them weekly, sometimes daily. While some customers liked the ever-changing variety, the feedback from a majority of customers indicated a preference for a consistent brew that customers could count on when they came into a Starbucks store. This reinvention of brewed coffee returned the company to the practice of grinding the beans in the store. Pike Place Roast was brewed in small batches in 30-minute intervals to ensure that customers were provided the freshest coffee possible. The Pike Place Roast was created by Starbucks' master blenders and coffee quality team using input from nearly 1,000 customers—it was smoother than any other Starbucks coffee and tasted great either black or with cream and sugar.

In the fall of 2009, Starbucks introduced Starbucks VIA Ready Brew—packets of roasted coffee in an instant form. VIA was made with a proprietary microground technology that Starbucks claimed represented a breakthrough.[22] Simply adding a packet of VIA to a cup of hot or cold water produced an instant coffee with a rich, full-bodied taste that closely replicated the taste, quality, and flavor of traditional freshly brewed coffee. Initially, VIA was introduced in Starbucks stores in the United States and Canada and select food service accounts; Starbucks stores held a four-day Starbucks VIA Taste Challenge

promotional during which customers were invited to compare the difference between Starbucks VIA and fresh-brewed Starbucks coffee. During the 2009 holiday season, Starbucks VIA Ready Brew was one of the top-selling coffee products at Amazon.com. Encouraged by favorable customer response, in mid-2010 Starbucks expanded the distribution of VIA to include 25,000 grocery store, mass-merchandise store, and drugstore accounts, including Kroger, Safeway, Walmart, Target, Costco, and CVS. VIA was available in three roasts—Colombian, Italian Roast, and Decaffeinated Italian Roast; the suggested retail price for Starbucks VIA was $2.95 for three servings and $7.49 for eight servings. Starbucks executives saw VIA as a promising vehicle for entering the instant coffee market and attracting a bigger fraction of on-the-go and at-home coffee drinkers. Instant coffee made up a significant fraction of the coffee purchases in the United Kingdom (80 percent), Japan (53 percent), Russia (85 percent), and other countries where Starbucks stores were located—in both the UK and Japan, sales of instant coffee exceeded $4 billion annually. Globally, the instant and single-serve coffee category was a $23 billion market. In March 2010, Starbucks made VIA available in all of its Starbucks stores in the UK. In April 2010, Starbucks introduced VIA in all of Japan's 870 Starbucks stores under the name Starbucks VIA Coffee Essence.[23]

The company's overall retail sales mix in 2009 was 76 percent beverages, 18 percent food items, 3 percent coffeemaking equipment and other merchandise, and 3 percent whole bean coffees.[24] However, the product mix in each store varied, depending on the size and location of each outlet. Larger stores carried a greater variety of whole coffee beans, gourmet food items, teas, coffee mugs, coffee grinders, coffeemaking equipment, filters, storage containers, and other accessories. Smaller stores and kiosks typically sold a full line of coffee beverages, a limited selection of whole bean and ground coffees and Tazo teas, and a few coffee-drinking accessories. Moreover, menu offerings at Starbucks stores were typically adapted to local cultures; for instance, the menu offerings at stores in North America included a selection of muffins, but stores in France had no muffins and instead featured locally made French pastries.

Starbucks' Consumer Products Group

All distribution channels for Starbucks products outside both licensed and company-operated retail stores were collectively referred to by Starbucks executives as "specialty operations." In 2010, Starbucks formed its Consumer Products Group (CPG) to manage all specialty operations activities. CPG was responsible for selling a selection of whole bean and ground coffees as well as a selection of premium Tazo teas outside Starbucks retail stores through licensing and distribution arrangements with Kraft, PepsiCo, Unilever, and others that covered both the United States and international markets. CPG also oversaw production and sales of ready-to-drink beverages (including bottled Frappuccino beverages, Starbucks Doubleshot espresso drinks, and Discoveries chilled cup coffee) as well as Starbucks superpremium ice creams and Starbucks liqueurs through the company's marketing and distribution agreements and joint ventures with PepsiCo, Unilever, and others. And it managed the sales of various Starbucks products to both food service accounts and the vast majority of the company's partnerships and licensing arrangements with prominent third parties.

Exhibit 6 shows the recent performance of the Consumer Products Group. Starbucks executives considered CPG's specialty operations attractive from the standpoint of both long-term growth and profitability. In fiscal 2007–2009, the company's operating profit margins from specialty operations were higher than the long-term target of 35 percent and vastly superior to the operating profit margins for the company's U.S. and international operations, as the following table shows:

	Operating Profit Margins		
	FY 2009	**FY 2008**	**FY 2007**
Consumer Products Group	39.6%	37.3%	35.9%
U.S. operations	7.5	6.0	14.3
International operations	4.8	5.2	8.1

Advertising

So far, Starbucks had spent relatively little money on advertising, preferring instead to build the brand cup by cup with customers and depend on word of mouth and the appeal of its storefronts. Advertising expenditures were $126.3 million in fiscal 2009, versus $129.0 million in fiscal 2008, $103.5 million in 2007, and $107.5 million in 2006. Starbucks stepped up advertising efforts in 2008 to combat the strategic initiatives of McDonald's and several other fast-food chains to begin offering premium coffees and coffee drinks at prices below those charged by Starbucks. In 2009, McDonald's reportedly spent more than $100 million on television, print, radio, billboard, and online ads promoting its new line of McCafé coffee drinks. Starbucks countered with the

Exhibit 6 **Performance of Starbuck's Consumer Products Group, Fiscal Years 2007–2009**

	Fiscal Year		
Consumer Product Group Operations	**2009**	**2008**	**2007**
Licensing revenues	$427.2	$392.6	$366.3
Foodservice revenues	322.4	355.0	326.1
Total revenues	$749.6	$747.6	$692.4
Operating income	$296.3	$279.2	$248.9
Operating income as a percent of total revenues	39.5%	37.3%	35.9%

Source: Starbucks, 2009 10-K report, p. 76.

biggest advertising campaign the company had ever undertaken.[25]

Vertical Integration

Howard Schultz saw Starbucks as having a unique strategy compared to the strategies pursued by its many coffeehouse competitors. He observed:

> People sometimes fail to realize that almost unlike any retailer or restaurant, we are completely vertically integrated. We source coffee from 30 countries. We have a proprietary roasting process. We distribute to company owned stores, and finally serve the coffee. Others are resellers of commodity-based coffees.[26]

HOWARD SCHULTZ'S EFFORTS TO MAKE STARBUCKS A GREAT PLACE TO WORK

Howard Schultz deeply believed that Starbucks' success was heavily dependent on customers having a very positive experience in its stores. This meant having store employees who were knowledgeable about the company's products, who paid attention to detail in preparing the company's espresso drinks, who eagerly communicated the company's passion for coffee, and who possessed the skills and personality to deliver consistent, pleasing customer service. Many of the baristas were in their 20s and worked part-time, going to college on the side or pursuing other career activities. The challenge to Starbucks, in Schultz's view, was how to attract, motivate, and reward store employees in a manner that would make Starbucks a company that people would want to work for and that would generate enthusiastic commitment and higher levels of customer service. Moreover, Schultz wanted to send all Starbucks employees a message that would cement the trust that had been building between management and the company's workforce.

Instituting Health Care Coverage for All Employees

One of the requests that employees had made to the prior owners of Starbucks was to extend health insurance benefits to part-time workers. Their request had been turned down, but Schultz believed that expanding health insurance coverage to include part-timers was something the company needed to do. His father had recently passed away from cancer and he knew from having grown up in a family that struggled to make ends meet how difficult it was to cope with rising medical costs. In 1988, Schultz went to the board of directors with his plan to expand the company's health insurance plans to include part-timers who worked at least 20 hours per week. He saw the proposal not as a generous gesture but as a core strategy to win employee loyalty and commitment to the company's mission. Board members resisted because the company was unprofitable and the added costs of the extended coverage would only worsen the company's bottom line. But Schultz argued passionately that it was the right thing to do and wouldn't be as expensive as it seemed. He observed that if the new benefit reduced turnover, which he believed was likely, then it would reduce the costs of hiring and training—which equaled about $3,000 per new hire; he further pointed out that it cost $1,500 a year to provide an employee with full benefits. Part-timers, he argued, were vital to Starbucks, constituting two-thirds of the company's workforce. Many were baristas who knew the favorite drinks of regular customers; if the barista left, that connection with the customer was broken. Moreover, many part-time employees were called on to open the stores early, sometimes at 5:30 or 6:00 a.m.; others had to work until closing, usually 9:00 p.m. or later. Providing these employees with health insurance benefits, he argued, would signal that the company honored their value and contribution.

The board approved Schultz's plan, and starting in late 1988, part-timers working 20 or more hours were offered the same health coverage as full-time employees. Starbucks paid 75 percent of an employee's health insurance premium; the employee paid 25 percent. Over the years, Starbucks extended its health coverage to include preventive care, prescription drugs, dental care, eye care, mental health, and chemical dependency. Coverage was also offered for unmarried partners in a committed relationship. Since most Starbucks employees were young and comparatively healthy, the company had been able to provide broader coverage while keeping monthly payments relatively low. Even when the company fell on lean times in 2008–2009, Starbucks refrained from making cuts in employee health insurance benefits; company expenditures for employee health insurance were $300 million in fiscal 2009, more than the company spent on its purchases of coffee beans.[27]

A Stock Option Plan for Employees

By 1991, the company's profitability had improved to the point where Schultz could pursue a stock option plan for all employees, a program he believed would have a positive, long-term effect on the success of Starbucks.[28] Schultz wanted to turn all Starbucks employees into partners, give them a chance to share in the success of the company, and make clear the connection between their contributions and the company's market value. Even though Starbucks was still a private company, the plan that emerged called for granting stock options to every full-time and part-time employee in proportion to his or her base pay. In May 1991, the plan, dubbed Bean Stock, was presented to the board. Though board members were concerned that increasing the number of shares might unduly dilute the value of the shares of investors who had put up hard cash, the plan received unanimous approval. The first grant was made in October 1991, just after the end of the company's fiscal year in September; each partner was granted stock options worth 12 percent of base pay. When the Bean Stock program was initiated, Starbucks dropped the term *employee* and began referring to all of its people as *partners* because every member of Starbucks' workforce became eligible for stock option awards after six months of employment and 500 paid work hours.

Starbucks went public in June 1992, selling its initial offering at a price of $17 per share. Starting in October 1992 and continuing through October 2004, Starbucks granted each eligible employee a stock option award with a value equal to 14 percent of base pay. Beginning in 2005, the plan was modified to tie the size of each employee's stock option awards to three factors: (1) Starbucks' success and profitability for the fiscal year, (2) the size of an employee's base wages, and (3) the price at which the stock option could be exercised. The value of the stock options exercised by

Starbucks partners was $44 million in fiscal 2009, $50 million in fiscal 2008, and $274 million in fiscal 2007. As of September 27, 2009, Starbucks partners held 63.6 million shares in stock option awards that had a weighted-average contractual life of 6.7 years; these shares had a weighted-average exercise price of $14.75 and an aggregate value of $442.4 million.[29]

Starbucks Stock Purchase Plan for Employees

In 1995, Starbucks implemented an employee stock purchase plan that gave partners who had been employed for at least 90 days an opportunity to purchase company stock through regular payroll deductions. Partners who enrolled could devote anywhere from 1 to 10 percent of their base earnings (up to a maximum of $25,000) to purchasing shares of Starbucks stock. After the end of each calendar quarter, each participant's contributions were used to buy Starbucks stock at a discount of 5 percent of the closing price on the last business day of the each calendar quarter (the discount was 15 percent until March 2009).

Since inception of the plan, some 23.5 million shares had been purchased by partners; roughly one-third of Starbucks partners participated in the stock purchase plan during the 2000–2009 period.

The Workplace Environment

Starbucks' management believed that the company's competitive pay scales and comprehensive benefits for both full-time and part-time partners allowed it to attract motivated people with above-average skills and good work habits. An employee's base pay was determined by the pay scales prevailing in the geographic region where an employee worked and by the person's job skills, experience, and job performance. About 90 percent of Starbucks' partners were full-time or part-time baristas, paid on an hourly basis. After six months of employment, baristas could expect to earn $8.50 to $9.50 per hour. In 2009, experienced full-time baristas in the company's U.S. stores earned an average of about $37,800; store managers earned an average of $44,400.[30] Voluntary turnover at Starbucks was 13 percent in 2009.[31] Starbucks executives believed that efforts to make the company an attractive, caring place to work were responsible for its relatively low turnover rates. Starbucks received 225,000 job applications in 2008 and 150,000 job applications in 2009.

Surveys of Starbucks partners conducted by *Fortune* magazine in the course of selecting companies for inclusion on its annual list "100 Best Companies to Work For" indicated that full-time baristas liked working at Starbucks because of the camaraderie, while part-timers were particularly pleased with the health insurance benefits (those who enrolled in Starbucks' most economical plan for just routine health care paid only $6.25 per week).[32] Starbucks had been named to *Fortune*'s list in 1998, 1999, 2000, and every year from 2002 through 2010. In 2010, Starbucks was ranked 93rd, down from 24th in 2009 and 7th in 2008.

Starbucks' management used annual Partner View surveys to solicit feedback from its workforce, learn their concerns, and measure job satisfaction. The 2002 survey revealed that many employees viewed the benefits package as only "average," prompting the company to increase its match of 401(k) contributions for those who had

been with the company more than three years and to have these contributions vest immediately. In a survey conducted in fiscal 2008, 80 percent of Starbucks partners reported being satisfied.[33]

Schultz's approach to offering employees good compensation and a comprehensive benefits package was driven by his belief that sharing the company's success with the people who made it happen helped everyone think and act like an owner, build positive long-term relationships with customers, and do things efficiently. Schultz's rationale, based on his father's experience of going from one low-wage, no-benefits job to another, was that if you treated your employees well, they in turn would treat customers well.

Exhibit 7 contains a summary of Starbucks' fringe benefit program.

Employee Training and Recognition

To accommodate its strategy of rapid store expansion, Starbucks put in systems to recruit, hire,

Exhibit 7   Starbucks' Fringe Benefit Program, 2010

- Medical insurance
- Sick time
- Dental and vision care
- Paid vacations (up to 120 hours annually for hourly workers with five or more years of service at retail stores and up to 200 hours annually for salaried and nonretail hourly employees with five or more years of service)
- Six paid holidays
- One paid personal day every six months for salaried and nonretail hourly partners
- A 30 percent discount on purchases of beverages, food, and merchandise at Starbucks stores
- Mental health and chemical dependency coverage
- 401(k) retirement savings plan—the company matched from 25% to 150%, based on length of service, of each employee's contributions up to the first 4% of compensation
- Short- and long-term disability
- Stock purchase plan—eligible employees could buy shares at a discounted price through regular payroll deductions
- Life insurance
- Short- and long-term disability insurance
- Accidental death and dismemberment insurance
- Adoption assistance
- Financial assistance program for partners that experience a financial crisis
- Stock option plan (Bean stock)
- Pre-tax payroll deductions for commuter expenses
- Free coffee and tea products each week
- Tuition reimbursement program

Source: Starbucks, "Careers," www.starbucks.com, accessed June 7, 2010.

and train baristas and store managers. Starbucks' vice president for human resources used some simple guidelines in screening candidates for new positions: "We want passionate people who love coffee. . . . We're looking for a diverse workforce, which reflects our community. We want people who enjoy what they're doing and for whom work is an extension of themselves."[34]

All partners/baristas hired for a retail job in a Starbucks store received at least 24 hours training in their first two to four weeks. The topics included classes on coffee history, drink preparation, coffee knowledge (four hours), customer service (four hours), and retail skills, plus a four-hour workshop called "Brewing the Perfect Cup." Baristas spent considerable time learning about beverage preparation—grinding the beans, steaming milk, learning to pull perfect (18- to 23-second) shots of espresso, memorizing the recipes of all the different drinks, practicing making the different drinks, and learning how to customize drinks to customer specifications. There were sessions on cash register operations, how to clean the milk wand on the espresso machine, explaining the Italian drink names to customers, selling home espresso machines, making eye contact with customers and interacting with them, and taking personal responsibility for the cleanliness of the store. And there were rules to be memorized: milk must be steamed to at least 150 degrees Fahrenheit but never more than 170 degrees; every espresso shot not pulled within 23 seconds must be tossed; never let coffee sit in the pot more than 20 minutes; always compensate dissatisfied customers with a Starbucks coupon that entitled them to a free drink.

Management trainees attended classes for 8 to 12 weeks. Their training went much deeper, covering not only coffee knowledge and information imparted to baristas but also details of store operations, practices and procedures as set forth in the company's operating manual, information systems, and the basics of managing people. Starbucks' trainers were all store managers and district managers with on-site experience. One of their major objectives was to ingrain the company's values, principles, and culture and to pass on their knowledge about coffee and their passion about Starbucks.

When Starbucks opened stores in a new market, it sent a Star Team of experienced managers and baristas to the area to lead the store opening effort and to conduct one-on-one training following the company's formal classes and basic orientation sessions at the Starbucks Coffee School in San Francisco. From time to time, Starbucks conducted special training programs, including a coffee masters program for store employees, leadership training for store managers, and career programs for partners in all types of jobs.

To recognize partner contributions, Starbucks had created a partner recognition program consisting of 18 different awards and programs. Examples included Coffee Master awards, Certified Barista awards, Spirit of Starbucks awards for exceptional achievement by a partner, a Manager of the Quarter for store manager leadership, Green Apron Awards for helping create a positive and welcoming store environment, Green Bean Awards for exceptional support for company's environmental mission, and Bravo! Awards for exceeding the standards of Starbucks customer service, significantly increasing sales, or reducing costs.

STARBUCKS' VALUES, BUSINESS PRINCIPLES, AND MISSION

During the early building years, Howard Schultz and other Starbucks senior executives worked to instill some key values and guiding principles into the Starbucks culture. The cornerstone value in their effort "to build a company with soul" was that the company would never stop pursuing the perfect cup of coffee by buying the best beans and roasting them to perfection. Schultz was adamant about controlling the quality of Starbucks products and building a culture common to all stores. He was rigidly opposed to selling artificially flavored coffee beans, saying that "we will not pollute our high-quality beans with chemicals"; if a customer wanted hazelnut-flavored coffee, Starbucks would provide it by adding hazelnut syrup to the drink rather than by adding hazelnut flavoring to the beans during roasting. Running flavored beans through the grinders would result in chemical residues being left behind to alter the flavor of beans ground afterward; plus, the chemical smell given off by artificially flavored beans was absorbed by other beans in the store.

Starbucks' management was also emphatic about the importance of employees paying attention to what pleased customers. Employees were trained to go out of their way and to take heroic measures, if necessary, to make sure customers were fully satisfied. The theme was "just say yes" to customer requests. Further, employees were encouraged to speak their minds without fear of retribution from upper management—senior executives wanted employees to be straight with them, being vocal about what Starbucks was doing right, what it was doing wrong, and what changes were needed. The intent was for employees to be involved in and contribute to the process of making Starbucks a better company.

Starbucks' Mission Statement

In early 1990, the senior executive team at Starbucks went to an off-site retreat to debate the company's values and beliefs and draft a mission statement. Schultz wanted the mission statement to convey a strong sense of organizational purpose and to articulate the company's fundamental beliefs and guiding principles. The draft was submitted to all employees for review, and several changes were made based on employee comments. The resulting mission statement and guiding principles are shown in Exhibit 8. In 2008, Starbucks partners from all across the company met for several months to refresh the mission statement and rephrase the underlying guiding principles; the revised mission statement and guiding principles are also shown in Exhibit 8.

STARBUCKS' COFFEE PURCHASING STRATEGY

Coffee beans were grown in 70 tropical countries and were the second-most-traded commodity in the world after petroleum. Most of the world's coffee was grown by some 25 million small farmers, most of whom lived on the edge of poverty. Starbucks personnel traveled regularly to coffee-producing countries, building relationships with growers and exporters, checking on agricultural conditions and crop yields, and searching out varieties and sources that would meet Starbucks' exacting standards of quality and flavor. The coffee-purchasing group, working with Starbucks personnel in roasting operations, tested new varieties and blends of green coffee beans from different sources. Sourcing from multiple geographic areas not only allowed Starbucks to offer a greater range of coffee varieties to customers but also spread the company's risks regarding weather, price volatility, and changing economic and political conditions in coffee-growing countries.

Starbucks' coffee sourcing strategy had three key elements:

- Make sure that the prices Starbucks paid for green (unroasted) coffee beans were high enough to ensure that small farmers were able to cover their production costs and provide for their families.
- Use purchasing arrangements that limited Starbucks' exposure to sudden price jumps due to weather, economic and political conditions in the growing countries, new agreements establishing export quotas, and periodic efforts to bolster prices by restricting coffee supplies.
- Work directly with small coffee growers, local coffee-growing cooperatives, and other types of coffee suppliers to promote coffee cultivation methods that protected biodiversity and were environmentally sustainable.

Pricing and Purchasing Arrangements

Commodity-grade coffee was traded in a highly competitive market as an undifferentiated product. However, high-altitude arabica coffees of the quality purchased by Starbucks were bought on a negotiated basis at a substantial premium above commodity coffee. The prices of the top-quality coffees sourced by Starbucks depended on supply and demand conditions at the time of the purchase and were subject to considerable volatility due to weather, economic and political conditions in the growing countries, new agreements establishing export quotas, and periodic efforts to bolster prices by restricting coffee supplies.

Starbucks typically used fixed-price purchase commitments to limit its exposure to fluctuating coffee prices in upcoming periods and, on occasion, purchased coffee futures contracts to provide price protection. In years past, there had been times when unexpected jumps in coffee

Exhibit 8   Starbucks' Mission Statement, Values, and Business Principles

Mission Statement, 1990–October 2008

Establish Starbucks as the premier purveyor of the finest coffee in the world while maintaining our uncompromising principles as we grow.

The following six guiding principles will help us measure the appropriateness of our decisions:

- Provide a great work environment and treat each other with respect and dignity.
- Embrace diversity as an essential component in the way we do business.
- Apply the highest standards of excellence to the purchasing, roasting, and fresh delivery of our coffee.
- Develop enthusiastically satisfied customers all of the time.
- Contribute positively to our communities and our environment.
- Recognize that profitability is essential to our future success.

Mission Statement, October 2008 Forward

Our Mission: To inspire and nurture the human spirit—one person, one cup, and one neighborhood at a time.

Here are the principles of how we live that every day:

Our Coffee

It has always been, and will always be, about quality. We're passionate about ethically sourcing the finest coffee beans, roasting them with great care, and improving the lives of people who grow them. We care deeply about all of this; our work is never done.

Our Partners

We're called partners, because it's not just a job, it's our passion. Together, we embrace diversity to create a place where each of us can be ourselves. We always treat each other with respect and dignity. And we hold each other to that standard.

Our Customers

When we are fully engaged, we connect with, laugh with, and uplift the lives of our customers—even if just for a few moments. Sure, it starts with the promise of a perfectly made beverage, but our work goes far beyond that. It's really about human connection.

Our Stores

When our customers feel this sense of belonging, our stores become a haven, a break from the worries outside, a place where you can meet with friends. It's about enjoyment at the speed of life—sometimes slow and savored, sometimes faster. Always full of humanity.

Our Neighborhood

Every store is part of a community, and we take our responsibility to be good neighbors seriously. We want to be invited in wherever we do business. We can be a force for positive action— bringing together our partners, customers, and the community to contribute every day. Now we see that our responsibility—and our potential for good—is even larger. The world is looking to Starbucks to set the new standard, yet again. We will lead.

Our Shareholders

We know that as we deliver in each of these areas, we enjoy the kind of success that rewards our shareholders. We are fully accountable to get each of these elements right so that Starbucks—and everyone it touches—can endure and thrive.

Source: Starbucks, "Our Starbucks Mission," www.starbucks.com, accessed March 7, 2010.

prices had put a squeeze on Starbucks' margins, forcing an increase in the prices of the beverages and beans sold at retail. During fiscal 2008, Starbucks more than doubled its volume of its fixed-price purchase commitments compared with fiscal 2007 because of the risk of rising prices for green coffee beans. Starbucks bought 367 million pounds of green coffee beans in fiscal 2009, paying an average of $1.47 per pound. At the end of fiscal 2009, the company had purchase commitments totaling $238 million, which, together with existing inventory, were expected to provide an adequate supply of green coffee through fiscal 2010.[35]

Starbucks and Fair Trade Certified Coffee

A growing number of small coffee growers were members of democratically run cooperatives that were registered with the Fair Trade Labeling Organizations International; these growers could sell their beans directly to importers, roasters, and retailers at favorable guaranteed fair trade prices. The idea behind guaranteed prices for fair trade coffees was to boost earnings for small coffee growers enough to allow them to invest in their farms and communities, develop the business skills needed to compete in the global market for coffee, and afford basic health care, education, and home improvements.

Starbucks began purchasing Fair Trade Certified coffee in 2000, steadily increasing its purchasing and marketing of such coffees in line with growing awareness of what Fair Trade Certified coffees were all about and consumer willingness to pay the typically higher prices for fair trade coffees. In 2008, Starbucks announced that it would double its purchases of Fair Trade Certified coffees in 2009, resulting in total purchases of 39 million pounds in 2009 (versus 19 million pounds in 2008 and 10 million pounds in 2005) and making Starbucks the largest purchaser of Fair Trade Certified coffee in the world. Starbucks marketed Fair Trade Certified coffees at most of its retail stores and through other locations that sold Starbucks coffees.

Best-Practice Coffee Cultivation and Environmental Sustainability

Since 1998, Starbucks had partnered with Conservation International's Center for Environmental Leadership to promote environmentally sustainable best practices in coffee cultivation methods and to develop specific guidelines—called Coffee and Farmer Equity (C.A.F.E.) Practices—to help farmers grow high-quality coffees in ways that were good for the planet. The C.A.F.E. Practices covered four areas: product quality, the price received by farmers/growers, safe and humane working conditions (including compliance with minimum wage requirements and child labor

provisions), and environmental responsibility.[36] In addition, Starbucks operated Farmer Support Centers in Costa Rica and Rwanda that were staffed with agronomists and experts on environmentally responsible coffee growing methods; staff members at these two centers worked with coffee farming communities to promote best practices in coffee production and improve both coffee quality and production yields. During 2008–2009, approximately 80 percent of the coffee beans purchased by Starbucks came from suppliers whose coffee-growing methods met C.A.F.E. standards. In those instances where Starbucks sourced its coffee beans from non-grower C.A.F.E. Practices suppliers, it required suppliers to submit evidence of payments made through the coffee supply chain to demonstrate how much of the price Starbucks paid for green coffee beans got to the farmer/grower.

A growing percentage of the coffees that Starbucks purchased were grown organically (i.e., without the use of pesticides, herbicides, or chemical fertilizers); organic cultivation methods resulted in clean ground water and helped protect against degrading of local ecosystems, many of which were fragile or in areas where biodiversity was under severe threat. Starbucks purchased 14 million pounds of certified organic coffee in fiscal 2009.

COFFEE ROASTING OPERATIONS

Starbucks considered the roasting of its coffee beans to be something of an art form, entailing trial-and-error testing of different combinations of time and temperature to get the most out of each type of bean and blend. Recipes were put together by the coffee department, once all the components had been tested. Computerized roasters guaranteed consistency. Highly trained and experienced roasting personnel monitored the process, using both smell and hearing, to help check when the beans were perfectly done—coffee beans make a popping sound when ready. Starbucks' standards were so exacting that roasters tested the color of the beans in a blood-cell analyzer and discarded the entire batch if the reading wasn't on target. After roasting and cooling, the coffee was immediately vacuum-sealed in bags that preserved freshness for up to 26 weeks. As a matter of policy, however, Starbucks removed coffees on its shelves after three months and, in the case of coffee used to prepare beverages in stores, the shelf life was limited to seven days after the bag was opened.

Starbucks had roasting plants in Kent, Washington; York, Pennsylvania; Minden, Nevada; Charleston, South Carolina; and The Netherlands. In addition to roasting capability, these plants also had additional space for warehousing and shipping coffees. In keeping with Starbucks' corporate commitment to reduce its environmental footprint, the new state-of-the-art roasting plant in South Carolina had been awarded LEED Silver certification for New Construction by the U.S. Green Building Council. Twenty percent of materials used in the construction of the building were from recycled content and more than 75 percent of the waste generated during construction was recycled. In addition, the facility used state-of-the-art light and water fixtures and was partly powered by wind energy. Some of the green elements in the South Carolina plant were being implemented in the other roasting plants as part of the company's initiative to achieve LEED certification for all company-operated facilities by the end of 2010.[37] In May 2010, Starbucks announced the opening of its first LEED-certified store in Asia. Located in Fukuoka, Japan, the new store was designed to serve as an extension of the existing landscape and to preserve the surrounding trees.[38]

STARBUCKS' CORPORATE SOCIAL RESPONSIBILITY STRATEGY

Howard Schultz's effort to "build a company with soul" included a long history of doing business in ways that were socially and environmentally responsible. A commitment to do the right thing had been central to how Starbucks operated as a company since Howard Schultz first became CEO in 1987. The specific actions comprising Starbucks' social responsibility strategy had varied over the years, but the intent of the strategy was consistently one of contributing positively to the communities in which Starbucks had stores, being a good environmental steward, and conducting its business in ways that earned the trust and respect of customers, partners/employees, suppliers, and the general public.

The Starbucks Foundation was set up in 1997 to orchestrate the company's philanthropic activities. Starbucks stores participated regularly in local charitable projects and community improvement activities. For years, the company had engaged in efforts to reduce, reuse, and recycle waste, conserve on water and energy usage, and generate less solid waste. Customers who brought their own mugs to stores were given a $0.10 discount on beverage purchases—in 2009, some 26 million beverages were served in customers' mugs. Coffee grounds, which were a big portion of the waste stream in stores, were packaged and given to customers, parks, schools, and plant nurseries as a soil amendment. Company personnel purchased paper products with high levels of recycled content and unbleached fiber. Stores participated in Earth Day activities each year with in-store promotions and volunteer efforts to educate employees and customers about the impacts their actions had on the environment. Suppliers were encouraged to provide the most energy-efficient products within their category and eliminate excessive packaging; Starbucks had recently instituted a set of Supplier Social Responsibility Standards covering the suppliers of all the manufactured goods and services used in the company's operations. No genetically modified ingredients were used in any food or beverage products that Starbucks served, with the exception of milk (U.S. labeling requirements do not require milk producers to disclose the use of hormones aimed at increasing the milk production of dairy herds). In 2005, Starbucks made a $5 million, five-year commitment to long-term relief and recovery efforts for victims of hurricanes Rita and Katrina and committed $5 million to support educational programs in China. In 2010, the Starbucks Foundation donated $1 million to the American Red Cross efforts to provide aid to those suffering the devastating effects of the earthquake in Haiti; in addition, Starbucks customers were invited to make cash donations to the Haitian relief effort at store registers.[39]

In 2008–2010, Starbucks' corporate social responsibility strategy had four main elements:

1. *Ethically sourcing all of the company's products.* This included promoting responsible growing practices for the company's coffees, teas, and cocoa and striving to buy the manufactured products and services it needed from suppliers that had a demonstrated commitment to social and environmental responsibility. Starbucks had a 2015 goal of purchasing 100 percent of its coffees through sources there were either Fair Trade Certified or met C.A.F.E. Practices guidelines.

2. *Community involvement.* This included engaging in a wide variety of community service activities, Starbucks Youth Action Grants to engage young people in community improvement projects (in fiscal 2009, Starbucks made 71 grants totaling $2.1 million), a program to provide medicine to people in Africa with HIV, the Ethos Water Fund, and donations by the Starbucks Foundation. The company had a goal of getting Starbucks partners and customers to contribute more than 1 million hours of community service annually by 2015; service contributions totaled 246,000 hours in 2008 and 186,000 hours in 2009.

3. *Environmental stewardship.* Initiatives here included a wide variety of actions to increase recycling, reduce waste, be more energy-efficient and use renewable energy sources, conserve water resources, make all company facilities as green as possible by using environmentally friendly building materials and energy-efficient designs, and engage in more efforts to address climate change. The company had immediate objectives of achieving LEED certification globally for all new company-operated stores beginning in late 2010, reducing energy consumption in company-owned stores by 25 percent by the end of fiscal 2010, and purchasing renewable energy equivalent to 50 percent of the electricity used in company-owned stores by the end of fiscal 2010. Management believed that the company was on track to achieve all three targets.

In 2009, Starbucks became a member of the Business for Innovative Climate Change and Energy Policy coalition, which sought to spur a clean energy economy and mitigate global warming by advocating strong legislation by the U.S. Congress. Starbucks was also collaborating with Earthwatch Institute on replanting rain forests, mapping water resources and biodiversity indicators, and sharing sustainable agriculture practices with coffee growers. Starbucks had goals to implement front-of-store recycling in all company-owned stores by 2015, to ensure that 100 percent of its cups were reusable or recyclable by 2015, to serve 25 percent of the beverages made in its stores in reusable containers by 2015, and to reduce water consumption in company-owned stores by 25 percent by 2015. In 2009 the company made progress toward achieving all these goals but still faced significant challenges in implementing recycling at its more than 16,000 stores worldwide because of wide variations in municipal recycling capabilities.

4. *Farmer loans.* Because many of the tens of thousands of small family farms with less than 30 acres that grew coffees purchased by Starbucks often lacked the money to make farming improvements and/or cover all expenses until they sold their crops, Starbucks provided funding to organizations that made loans to small coffee growers. Over the years, Starbucks had committed more than $15 million to a variety of coffee farmer loan funds. The company boosted its farmer loan commitments from $12.5 million to $14.5 million in 2009 and had a goal to commit a total of $20 million by 2015.

In 2010, Starbucks was named to *Corporate Responsibility Magazine*'s list "The 100 Best Corporate Citizens" for the 10th time. The "100 Best Corporate Citizens" list was based on more than 360 data points of publicly available information in seven categories: Environment, Climate Change, Human Rights, Philanthropy, Employee Relations, Financial Performance, and Governance. In addition, Starbucks had received over 25 awards from a diverse group of organizations for its philanthropic, community service, and environmental activities.

TOP MANAGEMENT CHANGES: CHANGING ROLES FOR HOWARD SCHULTZ

In 2000, Howard Schultz decided to relinquish his role as CEO, retain his position as chairman of the company's board of directors, and assume the newly created role of chief strategic officer. Orin Smith, a Starbucks executive who had been with the company since its early days, was named CEO. Smith retired in 2005 and was replaced as CEO by Jim Donald, who had been president of Starbucks' North American division. In 2006, Donald proceeded to set a long-term objective of having 40,000 stores worldwide and launched a program of rapid store expansion in an effort to achieve that goal.

But investors and members of Starbucks' board of directors (including Howard Schultz) became uneasy about Donald's leadership of the company when customer traffic in Starbucks' U.S. stores began to erode in 2007, new store openings worldwide were continuing at the rate of six per day, and Donald kept pressing for increased efficiency in store operations at the expense of good customer service. Investors were distressed with the company's steadily declining stock price during 2007. Schultz had lamented in a 2007 internal company e-mail (which was leaked to the public) that the company's aggressive growth had led to "a watering down of the Starbucks experience."[40] In January 2008, Starbucks' board asked Howard Schultz to return to his role as CEO and lead a major restructuring and revitalization initiative.

HOWARD SCHULTZ'S TRANSFORMATION AGENDA FOR STARBUCKS, 2008–2010

Immediately upon his return as Starbucks CEO, Schultz undertook a series of moves to revamp the company's executive leadership team and change the roles and responsibilities of several key executives.[41] A former Starbucks executive was hired for the newly created role of chief creative officer responsible for elevating the in-store experience of customers and achieving new levels of innovation and differentiation.

Because he believed that Starbucks in recent years had become less passionate about customer relationships and the coffee experience that had fueled the company's success, Schultz further decided to launch a major campaign to retransform Starbucks into the company he had envisioned it ought to be and to push the company to new plateaus of differentiation and innovation—the transformation effort instantly became the centerpiece of his return as company CEO. Schultz's transformation agenda for Starbucks had three main themes: strengthen the core, elevate the experience, and invest and grow. Specific near-term actions that Schultz implemented to drive his transformation of Starbucks in 2008–2010 included the following:

- Slowing the pace of new store openings in the United States and opening a net of 75 new stores internationally.
- Closing 900 underperforming company-operated stores in the United States, nearly 75 percent of which were within three miles of an existing Starbucks store. It was expected that these closings would boost sales and traffic at many nearby stores.
- Raising the projected return on capital requirements for proposed new store locations.
- Restructuring the company's store operations in Australia to focus on three key cities and surrounding areas—Brisbane, Melbourne, and Sydney—and to close 61 underperforming store locations (mostly located in other parts of Australia).
- Coming up with new designs for future Starbucks stores. The global store design strategy was aimed at promoting a reinvigorated customer experience by reflecting the character of each store's surrounding neighborhood and making customers feel truly at home when visiting their local store. All of the designs had to incorporate environmentally friendly materials and furnishings.
- Enhancing the customer experience at Starbucks stores, including the discontinuance of serving warmed breakfast sandwiches in North American stores (because the scent of

warmed sandwiches interfered with the coffee aroma) and a program to develop best-in-class baked goods and other new menu items that would make Starbucks a good source of a healthy breakfast for people on the go and better complement its coffee and espresso beverages. These efforts to improve the menu offerings at Starbucks stores were directly responsible for (1) the recent additions of fruit cups, yogurt parfaits, skinny lattes, the farmer's market salad, Vivanno smoothies, and healthier bakery selections, (2) the reformulated recipes to cut back on or eliminate the use of artificial flavorings, dyes, high-fructose corn syrup, and artificial preservatives, and (3) all-day brewing of Pikes Place Roast.

- A program to share best practices across all stores worldwide.

- Additional resources and tools for store employees, including laptops, an Internet-based software for scheduling work hours for store employees, and a new point-of-sale system for all stores in the United States, Canada, and the United Kingdom.

- Rigorous cost-containment initiatives to improve the company's bottom line, including a 1,000-person reduction in the staffing of the company's organizational support infrastructure to trim administrative expenses at the company's headquarters and regional offices.

- Renewed attention to employee training and reigniting enthusiasm on the part of store employees to please customers. In February 2008, Schultz ordered that 7,100 U.S. stores be temporarily closed for three regularly operating business hours (at 5:30 p.m. local time) for the purpose of conducting a special training session for store employees. The objectives were to give baristas hands-on training to improve the quality of the drinks they made, help reignite the emotional attachment of store employees to customers (a long-standing tradition at Starbucks stores), and refocus the attention of store employees on pleasing customers. Schultz viewed the training session as a way to help the company regain its "soul of the past" and improve the in-store Starbucks experience for customers.[42] When several major shareholders called Schultz to get his take on why he was closing 7,100 stores for three hours, he told them, "I am doing the right thing. We are retraining our people because we have forgotten what we stand for, and that is the pursuit of an unequivocal, absolute commitment to quality."[43]

Schultz's insistence on more innovation had also spurred the recent introduction of the Starbucks VIA instant coffees.

Howard Schultz believed that the turning point in his effort to transform Starbucks came when he decided to hold a leadership conference for 10,000 store managers in New Orleans in early 2008. According to Schultz:

> I knew that if I could remind people of our character and values, we could make a difference. The conference was about galvanizing the entire leadership of the company—being vulnerable and transparent with our employees about how desperate the situation was, and how we had to understand that everyone must be personally accountable and responsible for every single customer interaction. We started the conference with community service. Our efforts represent the largest single block of community support in the history of New Orleans, contributing more than 54,000 volunteer hours and investing more than $1 million in local projects like painting, landscaping, and building playgrounds.
>
> If we had not had New Orleans, we wouldn't have turned things around. It was real, it was truthful, and it was about leadership. An outside CEO would have come into Starbucks and invariably done what was expected, which was cut the thing to the bone. We didn't do that. Now we did cut $581 million of costs out of the company. The cuts targeted all areas of the business, from supply chain efficiencies to waste reduction to rightsizing our support structure. But 99 percent were not consumer-facing, and in fact, our customer satisfaction scores began to rise at this time and have continued to reach unprecedented levels. We reinvested in our people, we reinvested in innovation, and we reinvested in the values of the company.

In 2010, as part of Schultz's "invest and grow" aspect of transforming Starbucks, the company was formulating plans to open "thousands of new stores" in China over time.[44] Japan had long been Starbucks' biggest foreign market outside North America, but Howard Schultz said that "Asia clearly represents the most significant growth opportunity on a go-forward basis."[45]

Schultz also indicated that Starbucks was anxious to begin opening stores in India and Vietnam, two country markets that Starbucks believed were potentially lucrative.

Exhibit 9 is a letter that Howard Schultz sent to customers on the day he reassumed the position of Starbucks' chief executive officer. Exhibit 10 is a letter that Howard Schultz sent to all Starbucks partners three weeks after he returned as company CEO.

STARBUCKS' FUTURE PROSPECTS

In April 2010, halfway through the fiscal year, Howard Schultz continued to be pleased with the company's progress in returning to a path of profitable, long-term growth. Following five consecutive quarters of declining sales at stores open 13 months or longer (beginning with the first quarter of fiscal 2008), sales at Starbucks' company-operated stores worldwide had improved in each of the most recent five consecutive quarters—see Exhibit 11. Moreover, traffic (as measured by the number of cash register transactions) increased by 3 percent in the company's U.S. stores in the second quarter of fiscal 2010, the first positive increase in the last 13 quarters. Net revenues increased 8.6 percent in the second quarter of fiscal 2010 compared with the same quarter in fiscal 2009, while net income jumped from $25.0 million in the second quarter of fiscal 2009 to $217.3 million in the second quarter of fiscal 2010.

Exhibit 9   **Letter from Howard Schultz to Starbucks Customers, January 7, 2008**

To Our Customers:

Twenty-five years ago, I walked into Starbucks' first store and I fell in love with the coffee I tasted, with the passion of the people working there, and with how it looked, smelled and felt. From that day, I had a vision that a store can offer a welcoming experience for customers, be part of their community, and become a warm "third place" that is part of their lives everyday and that it can provide a truly superior cup of coffee.

Based on that vision, I, along with a very talented group of people, brought Starbucks to life. We did it by being creative, innovative and courageous in offering coffee products that very few in America had ever tasted; by celebrating the interaction between us and our customers; by developing a store design unlike any that existed before; and by bringing on board an exceptionally engaged group of partners (employees) who shared our excitement about building a different kind of company.

In doing this, we developed a culture based on treating each other, our customers and our coffee growers with respect and dignity. This includes embracing diversity, committing ourselves to ethical sourcing practices, providing health care and stock options to all of our eligible full- and part-time partners, supporting the communities we serve, and, most of all, ensuring that we are a company you can be proud to support.

I am writing today to thank you for the trust you have placed in us and to share with you my personal commitment to ensuring that every time you visit our stores you get the distinctive Starbucks Experience that you have come to expect, marked by the consistent delivery of the finest coffee in the world. To ensure this happens, in addition to my role as chairman, I am returning to the position of chief executive officer to help our partners build upon our heritage and our special relationship with you, and lead our company into the future.

We have enormous opportunity and exciting plans in place to make the Starbucks Experience as good as it has ever been and even better. In the coming months, you will see this come to life in the way our stores look, in the way our people serve you, in the new beverages and products we will offer. That is my promise to you. Everyone at Starbucks looks forward to sharing these initiatives with you.

Onward,

Howard Schultz

Source: Starbucks, press release, January 7, 2008, www.starbucks.com, accessed June 17, 2010.

Exhibit 10   Communication from Howard Schultz to All Starbucks Partners, February 4, 2008

What I Know to Be True

Dear Partners,

As I sit down to write this note (6:30 a.m. Sunday morning) I am enjoying a spectacular cup of Sumatra, brewed my favorite way—in a French press.

It has been three weeks since I returned to my role as CEO of the company I love. We have made much progress as we begin to transform and innovate and there is much more to come. But this is not a sprint—it is a marathon—it always has been. I assure you that when all is said and done, we will, as we always have, succeed at our highest potential. We will not be deterred from our course—we are and will be a great, enduring company, known for inspiring and nurturing the human spirit.

During this time, I have heard from so many of you; in fact, I have received more than 2,000 emails. I can feel your passion and commitment to the company, to our customers and to one another. I also thank you for all your ideas and suggestions . . . keep them coming. No one knows our business and our customers better than you. I have visited with you in many of your stores, as well as stopping by to see what our competitors are doing as well.

It's been just a few days since my last communications to you, but I wanted to share with you

what I know to be true:

- Since 1971, we have been ethically sourcing and roasting the highest quality *Arabica* coffee in the world, and today there is not a coffee company on earth providing higher quality coffee to their customers than we are. Period!

- We are in the people business and always have been. What does that mean? It means you make the difference. You are the Starbucks brand. We succeed in the marketplace and distinguish ourselves by each and every partner embracing the values, guiding principles and culture of our company and bringing it to life one customer at a time.

  Our stores have become the Third Place in our communities—a destination where human connections happen tens of thousands of times a day. We are not in the coffee business serving people. We are in the people business serving coffee. You are the best people serving the best coffee and I am proud to be your partner. There is no other place I would rather be than with you right here, right now!

- We have a renewed clarity of purpose and we are laser-focused on the customer experience. We have returned to our core to reaffirm our coffee authority and we will have some fun doing it. We are not going to embrace the status quo. Instead, we will be curious, bold and innovative in our actions and, in doing so, we will exceed the expectation of our customers.

- There will be cynics and critics along the way, all of whom will have an opinion and a point of view. This is not about them or our competitors, although we must humbly respect the changing landscape and the many choices facing every consumer. We will be steadfast in our approach and in our commitment to the *Starbucks Experience*—what we know to be true. However, this is about us and our customers. We are in control of our destiny. Trust the coffee and trust one another.

- I will lead us back to the place where we belong, but I need your help and support every step of the way. My expectations of you are high, but higher of myself.

- I want to hear from you. I want to hear about your ideas, your wins, your concerns, and how we can collectively continue to improve. Please feel free to reach out to me. I have been flooded with emails, but believe me, I am reading and responding to all of them.

As I said, I am proud to be your partner. I know this to be true.

Onward . . .

Howard

P.S. Everything that we do, from this point on (from the most simple and basic), matters.

Master the fundamentals. Experience Starbucks.

Source: Starbucks, press release, February 4, 2008, www.starbucks.com, accessed June 17, 2010.

Exhibit 11   **Quarterly Sales Trends at Starbucks Company-Operated Stores, Quarter 1 of Fiscal 2008 through Quarter 2 of Fiscal 2010**

Sales at Company-Operated Starbucks Stores	Five Quarters of Deteriorating Sales				
	Q1 2008	Q2 2008	Q3 2008	Q4 2008	Q1 2009
United States	(1%)	(4%)	(5%)	(8%)	(10%)
International	5%	3%	2%	0%	(3%)

Sales at Company-Operated Starbucks Stores	Five Quarters of Improving Sales				
	Q2 2009	Q3 2009	Q4 2009	Q1 2010	Q2 2010
United States	(8%)	(6%)	(1%)	4%	7%
International	(3%)	(2%)	0%	4%	7%

In commenting on the company's earnings for the second quarter of fiscal 2010, Schultz said:

> Starbucks second quarter results demonstrate the impact of innovation and the success of our efforts to dramatically transform our business over the last two years. Much credit goes to our partners all around the world who continue to deliver an improved experience to our customers. In addition, new products like Starbucks VIA, the opening of exciting new stores in Asia, Europe and the U.S., and expanded distribution outside our retail stores all represent opportunities for future growth.[46]

In March 2010, Starbucks announced its first-ever cash dividend of $0.10 per share to be paid quarterly starting with the second quarter of fiscal 2010.

The company's updated targets for full-year 2010 were as follows:

- Mid-single-digit revenue growth world-wide, driven by mid-single-digit sales growth at company-operated stores open at least 13 months.
- Opening approximately 100 net new stores in the United States and approximately 200 net new stores in international markets. Both the U.S. and international net new additions were expected to be primarily licensed stores.
- Earnings per share in the range of $1.19 to $1.22.
- Non-GAAP earnings per share in the range of $1.19 to $1.22, excluding approximately $0.03 of expected restructuring charges and including approximately $0.04 from the extra week in the fiscal fourth quarter, as fiscal 2010 was a 53-week year for Starbucks.
- Capital expenditures are expected to be approximately $500 million for the full year.
- Cash flow from operations of at least $1.5 billion, and free cash flow of more than $1 billion.

Long term, the company's objective was to maintain Starbucks' standing as one of the most recognized and respected brands in the world. To achieve this, Starbucks executives planned to continue disciplined global expansion of its company-operated and licensed retail store base, introduce relevant new products in all its channels, and selectively develop new channels of distribution.

Schultz's long-term vision for Starbucks had seven key elements:

- Be the undisputed coffee authority.
- Engage and inspire Starbucks partners.
- Ignite the emotional attachment with our customers.
- Expand our global presence—while making each store the heart of the local neighborhood.
- Be a leader in ethical sourcing and environmental impact.
- Create innovative growth platforms worthy of our coffee.
- Deliver a sustainable economic model.

Schultz believed that Starbucks still had enormous growth potential. In the United States, Starbucks had only a 3 percent share of the estimated

37 billion cups of coffee served to on-the-go coffee drinkers, only a 4 percent share of the 25 billion cups of coffee served at home, and only a 13 percent share of the 3.7 billion cups of coffee served in restaurants and coffeehouses.[47] Internationally, Starbucks' shares of these same segments were smaller. According to Schultz:

> The size of the prize is still huge. We sell less than 10 percent of the coffee consumed in the U.S. and less than 1 percent outside the U.S. The momentum will come from international. Slower growth in the U.S., accelerating growth overseas. The response to the Starbucks brand has been phenomenal in our international markets.[48]

Nonetheless, since his return as CEO in January 2008, Schultz had been mum about whether and when the company would aggressively pursue former CEO Jim Donald's lofty goal of having 40,000 stores worldwide.

ENDNOTES

[1] Starbucks, 2009 annual report, "Letter to Shareholders," p.1.

[2] Howard Schultz and Dori Jones Yang, *Pour Your Heart into It* (New York: Hyperion, 1997), p. 33.

[3] Ibid., p. 34.

[4] Ibid., p. 36.

[5] As told in ibid., p. 48.

[6] Ibid., pp. 61–62.

[7] As quoted in Jennifer Reese, "Starbucks: Inside the Coffee Cult," *Fortune,* December 9, 1996, p.193.

[8] Schultz and Yang, *Pour Your Heart Into It*, pp. 101–2.

[9] Ibid., p. 142.

[10] Starbucks, 2009 annual report, p. 3.

[11] Starbucks, "Global Responsibility Report," 2009, p. 13.

[12] "Starbucks Plans New Global Store Design," *Restaurants and Institutions,* June 25, 2009, www.rimag.com, accessed December 29, 2009.

[13] Starbucks, press releases, May 31, 2005, and October 25, 2005.

[14] Starbucks, press release, November 1, 2007.

[15] As stated by Howard Schultz in an interview with *Harvard Business Review* editor-in-chief Adi Ignatius; the interview was published in the July–August 2010 of the *Harvard Business Review*, pp. 108–15.

[16] Starbucks, "Starbucks and iTunes Bring Complimentary Digital Music and Video Offerings with Starbucks Pick of the Week," April 15, 2008, http://news.starbucks.com/article_display.cfm?article_id=93, accessed June 8, 2010.

[17] Starbucks, 2009 annual report, p. 5.

[18] Starbucks, "Starbucks Foundation," www.starbucks.com, accessed June 18, 2010.

[19] Starbucks, press release, July 14, 2008.

[20] Starbucks, press release, June 30, 2009.

[21] Starbucks, press release, April 7, 2008.

[22] Starbucks, press release, February 19, 2009.

[23] Starbucks, press release, April 13, 2010.

[24] Starbucks, 2009 annual report, p. 4.

[25] Claire Cain Miller, "New Starbucks Ads Seek to Recruit Online Fans," *New York Times,* May 18, 2009, www.nytimes.com, accessed January 3, 2010.

[26] Andy Server, "Schultz' Plan to Fix Starbucks," *Fortune,* January 18, 2008, www.fortune.com, accessed June 21, 2010.

[27] Beth Cowitt, "Starbucks CEO: We Spend More on Healthcare Than Coffee," *Fortune,* June 7, 2010, http://money.cnn.com/2010/06/07/news/companies/starbucks_schultz_healthcare.fortune/index.html, accessed June 8, 2010.

[28] As related in Schultz and Yang, *Pour Your Heart Into It*, pp. 131–36.

[29] Starbucks, 2009 10-K report, p. 68.

[30] "100 Best Companies to Work For," *Fortune,* http://money.cnn.com/magazines/fortune/bestcompanies/2010/snapshots/93.html, accessed June 9, 2010.

[31] Ibid.

[32] Starbucks, press release, May 21, 2009, www.starbucks.com, accessed June 14, 2010.

[33] Starbucks, "Global Responsibility Report," 2008.

[34] Kate Rounds, "Starbucks Coffee," *Incentive* 167, no. 7, p. 22.

[35] Starbucks, 2009 10-K report, p. 6.

[36] Starbucks, "Corporate Responsibility," www.starbucks.com, accessed June 18, 2010.

[37] Starbucks, press release, February 19, 2009.

[38] Starbucks, press release, May 26, 2010.

[39] Starbucks, press release, January 18, 2010.

[40] "Shakeup at Starbucks," January 7, 2008, www.cbsnews.com, accessed June 16, 2010.

[41] Transcript of Starbucks Earnings Conference Call for Quarters 1 and 3 of fiscal year 2008, http://seekingalpha.com, accessed June 16, 2010.

[42] "Coffee Break for Starbucks' 135,000 Baristas," CNN, http://money.cnn.com, February 26, 2008, accessed December 28, 2009, and "Starbucks Takes a 3-Hour Coffee Break," *New York Times,* February 27, 2008, www.nytimes.com, accessed June 15, 2010.

[43] Quoted in Adi Ignatius, "We Had to Own the Mistakes," *Harvard Business Review* 88, no. 7/8 (July–August 2010), p. 111.

[44] Mariko Sanchanta, "Starbucks Plans Major China Expansion," *Wall Street Journal,* April 13, 2010, http://online.wsj.com, accessed June 10, 2010.

[45] Ibid.

[46] Starbucks, press release, April 21, 2010.

[47] Management presentation to Barclays Capital Retail and Restaurants Conference, April 28, 2010, www.starbucks.com, accessed June 21, 2010.

[48] Server, "Schultz' Plan to Fix Starbucks."

Norton Lilly International: Implementing Transformational Change in the Shipping Industry

James Burton
Norton Lilly International

John E. Gamble
University of South Alabama

At a mid-2010 executive committee meeting, Norton Lilly International's chief financial officer (CFO) and chief operating officer (COO), James (Jim) Burton, introduced the meeting's theme: emphasizing growth. He then shared with the executive committee that the company's top line had grown by only 4 percent since 2006, yet the bottom line had improved by 251 percent since 2007 (2006 had produced a loss). In addition, the company's revenue per full-time employee had increased from $91,000 in 2007 to nearly $113,000 by June 2010.

Norton Lilly was an international shipping agency with 37 regional offices that provided services to ships in 70 ports located in North America, the Caribbean, the Pacific, and the Middle East. Typical services provided by Norton Lilly to the operators of oceangoing cargo ships included booking freight for export, clearing inbound cargo with U.S. Customs, fueling vessels, restocking vessels with supplies and provisions, and arranging cargo handling services. The company's dramatic turnaround since 2006 had come about after Burton, a certified public accountant (CPA) and former management consultant with Ernst & Young, Capgemini, and AlixPartners, arrived on scene to transform Norton Lilly's culture and operating practices from those that sprang from an entrepreneurial mind-set to one focused on execution and value added growth.

At the conclusion of the two-day meeting, Burton worried that after more than three years of restructuring, he was still uncertain whether the execution platform was indeed solidly in place. In addition, he was concerned that the company might not be fully prepared to pursue the disciplined growth that would allow bottom-line performance to match top-line growth. Also, Burton had lingering concerns from the meeting that the company's culture change was incomplete, that some managers were not sufficiently focused on customer needs, and that the company might have trouble developing new solutions around evolving customer needs. During a short debriefing with Larry Baldwin, Norton Lilly's vice president of human resources, Burton summed up his concerns: "Our key executives and managers are looking for revenue growth. Do you think that our foundation is strong enough to support the addition of new business without eroding operational effectiveness? Is our culture ready for disciplined growth? Do our business unit leaders truly understand our value creating processes? Do we have the right team in place? Just how complete is our transformation?"

COMPANY HISTORY AND OVERVIEW

Norton Lilly International was well-known and respected within the shipping industry; its operations in 2010 included 37 regional offices that provided services to ships in 70 ports located in North America, the Caribbean, the Pacific, and the Middle East. The company's ship services first began in 1841, when John Norton booked a shipment of kerosene aboard a small sailing ship bound for South America. The company's ownership expanded in 1907 to include the Lilly family, and in 1925 the company expanded internationally with the opening of a Norton Lilly office in Panama. Panama became an important port in the company's growth over the next several decades, with Norton Lilly remaining the market share leader in handling Panama Canal transits in 2010.

The company grew rapidly after the development of cargo containerization in the early 1970s, with its business shifting almost exclusively to providing services to container vessels. The company was acquired in 1999 by two Mobile, Alabama, entrepreneurs, H. W. (Win) Thurber III and John Rutherford Sr. While Rutherford's previous business experience was in insurance and timber management, Thurber had considerable experience in the shipping industry—so much so that he was inducted in the Maritime Hall of Fame in 2005. Under the leadership of Thurber and Rutherford, Norton Lilly expanded into additional international ports during the early 2000s through a combination of acquisitions, joint ventures, and internal development. By 2005, the company provided cargo handling and other services to nearly 22,000 vessels in ports around the world and was the largest privately held shipping agency based in North America.

SETBACKS AT NORTON LILLY

After five years of steady growth, Norton Lilly found itself handicapped by a number of problems in 2006 that led to a $2.6 million net loss for the year. The series of acquisitions, joint ventures, and internal expansion initiatives led by Thurber and Rutherford had allowed annual revenues to increase to more than $41 million, but acquisitions outside the company's core business, a failure to effectively integrate acquired shipping agencies, an inadequate attention to operational performance, and too little focus on bottom-line performance had put the company in a rather precarious situation.

Realizing the company was in need of a dramatic turnaround and likely in need of fresh ideas from an outsider, Thurber and Rutherford launched a search for an operations-oriented leader who could restore the company's profitability. In February 2007, the two partners settled on Jim Burton to take on the roles of CFO and COO and lead the transformation program. During Burton's 25-year career in public accounting and consulting, he had advised such companies as Exxon, Kellogg's, Sprint, Henkel, and Warner Home Video, but his selection as Norton Lilly's CFO and COO was his first major involvement with a privately held business.

In establishing their expectations for Burton, Rutherford and Thurber stated that their desire was to see the development of a sustainable business platform that would be capable of doubling the company's size, while generating an attractive return on investment. A second objective for Burton was to assist with the gradual handoff of the business to a new generation of family members.

NORTON LILLY INTERNATIONAL'S SCOPE OF BUSINESS OPERATIONS IN 2007

When Burton arrived at Norton Lilly International, the company operated three different business units—Liner, Ship Services, and Overseas. The Liner business unit was headed by Steve Haverstock, an industry veteran with more than 30 years' experience who was supported by H. W. (Winchester) Thurber IV, the eldest son of Win Thurber. The younger Thurber was being groomed to one day take over the Liner unit as Rutherford, Win Thurber, and Haverstock stepped aside. Norton Lilly's Liner business unit provided various services to container ships that carried dry cargo in and out of U.S. ports of call. These container ships were sometimes referred to the industry's "bus service" since the oceangoing liners maintained regularly scheduled routes between ports and carried containers of whatever goods had been booked for a particular transportation date.

Norton Lilly's Liner business unit customers were typically foreign-based companies with established ocean trade routes to and from the United States that chose not to set up their own administrative offices within the United States. It was frequently less expensive for foreign shipping firms to outsource support services to a shipping agent. Services performed by Norton Lilly for its outbound liner customers included booking freight, preparing and transmitting bills of lading, and completing shipping manifests for outgoing vessels. Norton Lilly also provided services for inbound ships such as notifying U.S. Customs and consignees of an impending cargo arrival, collecting freight charges from consignees, and clearing all cargo with U.S. Customs before its release from the port. Finally, Norton Lilly arranged truck and/or rail services to move cargo inland.

Norton Lilly's Ship Services business unit was headed by Flemming Buhl, an industry veteran who had more than 20 years' experience and was backed by John Wade Thurber, the youngest son of Win Thurber. Like his older brother, John Wade Thurber was learning at the side of an experienced industry veteran and was expected to one day assume control of the business unit. While the Liner business unit was known as a "bus service," the Ship Services unit was referred to as a "taxi service." Customers of Norton Lilly's Ship Services unit operated car carriers, tankers, and bulk cargo vessels that scheduled shipments to and from U.S. ports based on demand rather than a defined timetable. Therefore, operators of such vessels were on call to pick up shipments of goods when requested and deliver the goods to whatever port the shipper desired. Typical ship services offered by Norton Lilly included fueling vessels, providing crew transport to and from vessels, arranging crew medical services, restocking vessels with supplies and provisions, handling cargo, and arranging tugs to navigate vessels in and out of port. The main difference in the services provided by the Liner and Ship Services divisions was that the Liner unit focused on the cargo whereas the Ship Services unit focused more on the vessel.

The company's Overseas division was managed by Dwain Denniston, another industry veteran with more than 30 years' experience. The Overseas division offered both liner and ship services to vessels entering and departing ports serviced by Norton Lilly that were outside the United States. Norton Lilly's Overseas division operated offices in ports throughout the Caribbean, including Panama, Trinidad, Puerto Rico, and Mexico. The Overseas division also operated offices in ports located in the Middle East,

including ports in Dubai, United Arab Emirates; Amman, Jordan; and Umm Qasr, Basra, and Baghdad, Iraq.

PHASE 1 OF THE TURNAROUND: BUILDING THE FOUNDATION

Understanding his mandate and the company's recent performance, Jim Burton set about analyzing the business with an emphasis on quick wins that would contribute to developing the long-term "execution" foundation. As an industry outsider and former consultant, Burton knew he was dealing with seasoned industry veterans, each with deeply held beliefs and paradigms about the business—how it had been and should be run. In an effort to build confidence and gain acceptance among his senior peers, Burton knew he had to introduce ideas the group would be willing to accept and build on. It had to be an incremental approach.

With encouragement and support of the owners, Burton first formed an executive committee of nine, including the five business unit executives; the two owners, Win Thurber and John Rutherford; the chief administrative officer, Sumner Adams (the son-in-law of John Rutherford), who had joined the company in 2006 after having worked a number of years at a marine terminal; and himself. The objective in forming an executive committee was to begin decentralizing the decision-making process away from the two owners. While they would be members of the committee, the owners would not actively participate in committee sessions, but would instead attend summary reviews, at the conclusion of each meeting, to provide counsel and advice.

Burton knew if he was to transform the company and build the sustainable growth platform the owners wanted, it would be through the executive committee. In consultation with the owners, it was understood that bold action was needed, given the company's 2006 performance; however, long-term success would best be achieved through logical, step-change fundamentals wherein results could be both visible and tangible. As the committee saw improved results, their confidence in the approach would grow and help ensure their continued buy-in to even newer ways of running the business.

Identifying and Understanding Value-Creating Processes

Rather than rapidly changing the company's strategy, Burton focused on its execution and on helping Norton Lilly's executives understand the key processes that enabled good strategy execution and value creation. Burton explained, "We followed the executive committee formation by introducing process mapping, in hopes of helping everyone understand exactly how we delivered our services." Upon arrival, one of the things Burton first heard among employees at all levels was "Well, we've always done it this way." He continued to explain, "The challenge was to instill a mind-set that would allow for a critical examination of how the work was being done and developing better ways of working in the future." This change in mind-set would act as the foundation for a culture of operational discipline and continuous improvement.

Burton first launched process mapping in the Liner group, which operated in eight different U.S. offices. At the time, the Liner division offered a fragmented mix of services across its eight locations, with each location performing some activities more effectively than other locations and all locations failing to provide adequate service in some regard. The intended end-to-end service delivery model—from bill of lading preparation, cargo release, to freight collections—was not coordinated and consisted of nonstandard processes, leading to rework and, more important, financial penalties within the context of existing contracts.

By late 2007, mapping the key processes involved in delivering each type of service had helped management and key employees understand the underlying causes of service failures and begin to close performance gaps. In addition, management and employee understanding of processes led to improved process standardization, ended administrative procedures that duplicated work, improved customer satisfaction, and reduced fines and penalties from $325,000 to $283,000, by December 2007. (Fines and penalties had been reduced to $28,000 by 2010.) The success of process mapping in the Liner business unit created buy-in among executive committee members and helped Burton move the company toward the concept of continuous improvement.

Another early-2007 foundation-building step involved clarifying accountability, as it was unclear who was accountable for what. Burton recalled, "Everyone was accountable, yet no one really was." Using the results from process mapping, Burton identified operating-level objectives for each process; he called those objectives key performance indicators (KPIs). By the end of 2007, Burton had assigned responsibility for achieving KPI goals to individual managers and supervisors overseeing specific value-creating processes within the Liner division.

Implementing a Balanced Scorecard Performance Measurement System

Accompanying the KPI rollout was a balanced scorecard, which further focused managerial employees' attention on the performance of value-creating processes. Metrics included in the balanced scorecard system used at Norton Lilly included process KPIs, customer satisfaction, and financial performance. In terms of integrating customer satisfaction as a performance metric for the first time at Norton Lilly, Burton commented, "I remember asking one of our guys 'How do you know you're meeting customer expectations?' He said, 'If we're not, they'll tell me.' Well, that seemed a little too open-ended. The company needed a more consistent discipline (process mapping) for defining what we did [and] how we did it, and a proactive approach for engaging the customer to ensure what and how we did things aligned with the contract and their expectations of us."

In late 2007, Norton Lilly's balanced scorecard system was expanded to include a "dashboard" of performance indicators that could provide a quick overview of operational and financial performance at the business unit level. The dashboard indicators were first established for the Liner business. The initial dashboards contained a fairly limited collection of KPIs, such as revenue compared to budget, expense groupings compared to budget, capital expenditures compared to budget, and Top 10 customer profitability. Top 10 customer profitability listed the 10 most profitable customer accounts at any given time. The addition of KPIs to Norton Lilly's process mapping better enabled each business unit leader to understand cause-and-effect relationships between day-to-day activities and operating and financial performance.

By the end of 2007, Norton Lilly's business unit leaders were holding monthly meetings to review KPI status and propose corrective actions to resolve differences between expectations and actual performance. In late 2007, John Wade Thurber stated, "When these dashboards and KPIs were first introduced, I admit, I was skeptical. I didn't see how they would add value. Now, having worked with them and having seen them assist in our improved performance, I now see the dashboard as one of the most, if not the most, important management tools at my disposal."

Resource Allocation Policies

Other foundation-building actions undertaken in 2007 included the initiation of various policy changes. One such policy change involved the company's capital outlay policy, which was the first new policy established by the executive committee and required that all projects or investments be considered only after satisfactory due diligence had been performed and proposals evaluated by the executive committee. All project or investment funding would be granted only if solid evidence had been presented demonstrating the projected financial value. For non-project-related expenditures, an authorization for expenditure (AFE) system was implemented to ensure that each business unit leader saw and signed off all capital expenditure requests and understood the impact of the expenditure on the KPI targets.

The capital outlay policy came about after Burton discovered that the company had previously launched into a number of ventures without much success. In probing how those decisions came about, he found that no formalized due diligence existed. For example, Norton Lilly made a decision to buy into a warehouse in

Long Beach, California. While warehousing was a logical extension of the company's business model, the company had no expertise in the area. Moreover, no single executive owned the business, the company overpaid for the warehouse, and within 18 months it had lost over $1 million operating the warehouse. Implementing the capital outlay policy created a formal process for evaluating proposed projects or investments greater than $10,000. The policy called for a nine-step due diligence process, thereby ensuring consistency in proposals coming before the executive committee. The nine steps were as follows:

1. Description of the opportunity.
2. Description of how the opportunity fit with Norton Lilly International's objectives.
3. Assessment of the competitive threats.
4. Assessment of the competitive landscape.
5. How success would be ensured.
6. Proposed exit strategy.
7. Business case.
8. Financial pro forma.
9. List of major assumptions and risks.

The capital outlay policy would ensure that decisions to enter into any business venture would be fully vetted, based on facts, not opinions. As Flemming Buhl stated after signing off on the capital outlay policy, "I guess this means we all must do our homework, together."

Building Managerial Talent

Throughout 2007, Norton Lilly focused on another important foundation-building element—management development. Burton introduced a leadership development program that matched a person's profile to a job. The program was based on the fundamental premise that managerial employees could be classified into one of four basic profiles: strategist, project director, networker (i.e., account manager), or external qualifier (i.e., salesperson). An individual's profile was determined by how the person responded on a survey containing items related to dominance (the need to be in charge); influencing (introvert versus extrovert); steadiness (ability to multitask versus working in linear fashion); compliance (ability to comply with rules versus being a rebel); motivators (e.g., knowledge, status, or money); and cognitive style. The results of the survey determined a person's profile and suggested how he or she might fit or perform within the context of a given job. For example, a project director who was highly focused on "how" might not fare well within a sales job.

After being tested and profiled, the 20 highest-ranking employees at Norton Lilly entered into workshops directed at helping members of the management team interpret each profile and respect and deal effectively with differing profiles. The process aided basic understanding of the strengths of each executive committee member and ensured better communication within the committee. By late 2007, the prior approach of assigning a friend or former colleague to a given role had been replaced by recruitment based on the managerial profiles.

PHASE II OF THE TURNAROUND: REINFORCING THE FOUNDATION

The efforts undertaken during Phase I of Norton Lilly's turnaround had produced a profitable fiscal 2007, which was the company's first profitable year since 2003. The annual net profit provided Jim Burton with the momentum to continue to push the turnaround forward and build on his early execution-related successes. During 2008, the company extended process mapping across other business units, including administrative and accounting units. In addition, information gathered from process maps helped Norton Lilly's management determine break-even pricing and proper staffing levels for various-sized cargo ships.

Improving Information Used for Decision Making

Dashboards were also expanded to all of Norton Lilly's business units—Liner, Ship Services, and Overseas—as well as the addition of financial measures such as cash flow and accounts receivable KPIs. The inclusion of financial KPIs on management dashboards helped the percentage of accounts more than 60 days past due in the Liner business unit decline from 7 percent in December 2008 to less than 1 percent in June 2010.

In early 2008, Sumner Adams assumed the treasurer role and became the process owner for all collection and cash management functions. Using his process maps, Sumner examined the disbursement accounts (essentially customer billings for services rendered) and collection processes and established a service-based cash conversion cycle KPI. Adams's philosophy behind developing the cash conversion KPIs was "The faster we invoice, the faster we collect, therefore improving our cash and liquidity positions." The baseline cash conversion cycle was 24 days in late 2008. By May 2010, the cash conversion KPI was 16 days and tracking toward a stated goal of 15 days. The company's current ratio improved from 0.88:1 to 1.51:1 over the same period.

Changing Financial Performance Expectations

Burton initiated another policy change in 2008, although less a stated policy than a mind-set. The concept of value creation was introduced at an executive committee meeting in late 2007 and became the basis for all 2008 budgeting. As part of the 2008 budget process, Burton determined Norton Lilly's internal cost of capital and established it as the proxy for value creation. Before this point, the collective view at Norton Lilly was that any positive budget or set of results was a good thing. In fact, the 2007 budget called for the company to make $163,000 on $41 million in revenue. At the time, Win Thurber stated, "If you can assure me we can make this, I'll call it a year right now."

The concept of earning a fair rate of return based on assumed risk didn't exist at Norton Lilly, so, as part of the 2008 budgeting exercise, each business unit leader was given a margin target. As the behavioral shift toward value creation and away from budget negotiation began to take hold, each business unit was given greater decision autonomy, but with clear accountability to achieve its assigned margin targets.

A New Approach to Forecasting Financial Performance

Norton Lilly examined its relative performance against budget and found that the company missed its budgeted performance in 2007 and 2008 by 90 percent and 63 percent, respectively. Because of general economic uncertainty that could not be fully factored into a static budget, the company decided to adopt a 12-month rolling forecast. This would (1) provide continual refreshing of the assumptions underlying the forecast and (2) provide the company a continual look at its next 12 months, regardless of how many months were left in the calendar year. The move to rolling forecasts helped managers improve forecasting accuracy to the extent that the company missed its financial projections by only 9 percent in 2009 and was on track to achieve 94 percent of projected financial performance in 2010.

THE STATE OF THE TURNAROUND GOING INTO 2011

By the close of 2009, Norton Lilly International had seen steady improvement in its performance. Despite the general decline in the industry, 2009 proved to be the company's most profitable year, and 2010 showed signs of being even better. The company was on track in 2010 to generate revenues of about $45.7 million (up 4 percent over 2006) and net income of $3.3 million (up 251 percent over 2007). Exhibit 1 presents Norton Lilly International's income statements for 2006 through 2009. The company's balance sheets for 2008 and 2009 are presented in Exhibit 2. Its financial projections for 2010 are presented in Exhibit 3.

Exhibit 1   **Norton Lilly International's Consolidated Statements of Income, 2006–2009 ($ thousands)**

	2009	2008	2007	2006
Revenues	$44,680	$53,576	$55,692	$43,902
Cost of revenues	2,684	2,761	2,755	2,740
Gross profit	41,996	50,815	52,937	41,161
Expenses				
General and administrative expenses	37,435	46,383	49,042	40,659
Depreciation and amortization	704	797	827	858
Total expenses	38,139	47,180	49,869	41,516
Operating income (loss)	3,858	3,635	3,068	(355)
Other income and expenses				
Interest and dividend income	120	162	203	205
Loss on disposal of assets and investments	(49)	(261)	(347)	(68)
Foreign currency transaction gain (loss)	0	(1)	(1)	2
Investment income (loss)	210	383	(412)	(776)
Interest expense	(494)	(541)	(758)	(585)
Total other income and expenses	(212)	(259)	(1,315)	(1,223)
Net income (loss) before income taxes and controlling interests	3,645	3,376	1,753	−1,577
Provision of income taxes	514	560	501	564
Net income (loss) before noncontrolling interests	3,131	2,816	1,252	(2,141)
Noncontrolling interests in subsidiaries earnings	(102)	(185)	(313)	(459)
Net income (loss)	$ 3,030	$ 2,631	$ 939	($ 2,600)

Source: Norton Lilly International.

Exhibit 2 Norton Lilly International's Consolidated Balance Sheets, 2008–2009 ($ thousands)

Assets	2009	2008
Current assets		
Cash	$ 549	$ 1,407
Time deposit pledges	1,758	1,130
Accounts receivable	9,929	11,438
Notes receivable	0	2
Other nontrade receivables	0	203
Deferred tax assets	18	18
Prepaid income taxes	314	34
Prepaid expenses	765	903
Total current assets	13,334	15,135
Property and equipment (net)	1,340	1,835
Intangible assets (net)	9,095	8,767
Deferred tax assets	245	418
Loans to stockholders	663	599
Other assets	1,434	1,038
Total assets	$26,112	$27,792

Liabilities and Stockholders' Equity		
Current liabilities		
Bank overdraft	$ 392	$ 5
Accounts payable	8,699	8,046
Current portion of long-term debt	4,415	215
Current portion of capital lease obligations	78	173
Due to principals	13,377	21,793
Accrued expenses	1,669	3,005
Deferred income taxes	71	38
Deferred revenues	70	60
Seniority premium	188	179
Income taxes payable	72	182
Total current liabilities	29,031	33,694
Long-term debt (net)	1,577	1,582
Capital lease obligations (net)	10	88
Deferred income taxes	956	939
Noncontrolling interests	76	73
Stockholders equity (deficit)	(5,538)	(8,585)
Total liabilities and stockholders equity	$26,112	$27,792

Source: Norton Lilly International.

Exhibit 3 Norton Lilly International's Projected Consolidated Statement of Income, 2010 ($ thousands)*

	2010
Revenues	$47,845
Operating and general expenses	40,103
Contribution margin	7,743
Depreciation and amortization	(496)
Interest income/expense (net)	(982)
Noncontrolling interest earnings (losses)	407
Total other income (expenses)	(1,071)
Operating income	6,672
Provision for taxes	(351)
Net income (loss)	$ 6,320

*Projection is 8 months actual plus 4-month forecast.
Source: Norton Lilly International.

The overall improvement in Norton Lilly's financial performance could largely be traced to the foundation that was begun in 2007, consisting of the following:

- Continuous improvement had become an accepted discipline throughout the company.
- Accountability for achieving KPIs assigned to a unit had become mainstream.
- Dashboards were included in the monthly financial summary package, which was distributed to each executive committee member.
- Value creation and use of a 12-month rolling forecast had also become mainstream. The budget process had been eliminated, and decision making had been decentralized to business unit leaders, with full decision authority but also with accountability for achieving margin and growth targets.
- The use of management development based on the proper matching of people to jobs.
- Policies had been clarified and/or created that ensured decision-making rigor. In addition, resources allocation policies helped ensure that resources would be committed to opportunities that were best in line with the company's strategic priorities.

Despite this foundation, Jim Burton told the company's vice president of human resources,

Larry Baldwin, that he still had concern about the company's ability to execute its strategy with the highest level of proficiency. The company's compensation system had yet to be retooled to closely link rewards for employees at all levels to organizational KPIs, and there were questions about to what extent the culture change had been fully ingrained in the managerial mind-set. During the conversation, Baldwin had noted a deeply entrenched philosophy of managers "knowing only one way to grow—sell, sell, sell. They now need to understand the tools of growth beyond simple expansion. Someone will need to provide that creativity and leadership." The challenge going forward was to find ways of improving growth while maintaining the discipline to produce improved bottom-line results. Burton knew that revenue growth would be a high priority for Norton Lilly International's executive committee members in 2011 since projected revenues for 2010 still remained considerably below the company's peak revenues of nearly $53 million in 2007.

Good Hotel: Doing Good, Doing Well?

Armand Gilinsky, Jr.
Sonoma State University

S. Noorein Inamdar
San José State University

Employees who feel transformed by what they are doing are far more likely to be enthusiastic about their jobs. The hotel industry has become far more expert in retaining its hangers than its employees. The turnover in the hotel business is 70–100 percent; ours is closer to 30 percent. Shouldn't a company want to offer its employees the same opportunities for self-actualization? I call this "karmic capitalism."
—Chip Conley, founder and CEO, Joie de Vivre Hotels, speech to Association of Fundraising Professionals, Commonwealth Club, San Francisco, January 22, 2010

All of our hotels are non-conventional and have a philanthropic community vision. This is one of the main reasons why I plan to stay with Joie de Vivre for a very long time.
—Pam Janusz, General Manager, Joie de Vivre SoMa Hotels, personal interview, March 5, 2010

When Pam Janusz, general manager of Good Hotel, arrived at work on Thursday, April 15, 2010, she found some disquieting news in her e-mail in-box. Janusz worked for Joie de Vivre (JdV), a San Francisco–based hotel management company with 16 properties in the city. Earlier that morning, Ingrid Summerfield, JdV's president, had sent an e-mail message marked "urgent." The message confirmed rumors that the owners of Good Hotel and the two other properties that Janusz managed since November 2009, Best Western Americania and Best Western Carriage Inn, had foreclosed on their holdings and sold the three properties—all of which were in JdV's South of Market Street (SoMa) group—to a new ownership group. The new group planned to run the three hotels themselves and terminate JdV's management contract at the end of May 2010, barring any unforeseen issues related to the sale. Meanwhile, Janusz would be reassigned to another, as yet unknown position at JdV. The remainder of the e-mail message was a request to evaluate the performance of Good Hotel to prepare for its transition to new ownership.

After renovating Best Western Hotel Britton and Best Western Flamingo, JdV had relaunched the two as one new hotel, Good Hotel, in November 2008. Good Hotel was known in the industry as the first to be branded a "hotel with a conscience"—encompassing a positive attitude, environmental sensitivity, and philanthropy. Exhibit 1 presents marketing information about Good Hotel.

After reading the e-mail, Janusz exclaimed,

Wow! I've been trying to get to know our staff, guests, and neighborhood over the last six months. We have a great staff in place. We were able to beat our financial forecasts for the first quarter of 2010. Our guest service has been steadily rising over the last few months. There have not been any major surprises until today.

Janusz thought about her and Good Hotel's accomplishments during the past six months and her priorities for the remaining six weeks. She wondered what she would say about the change in ownership and possible future direction of Good Hotel to her 130 part- and full-time staff members, who serviced 308 rooms among the three

Exhibit 1   The Good Hotel

Philosophy and Customer Experience

The Good Hotel is intended to be the first hotel with a conscience. Our philanthropic and positive approach is designed to inspire the "good in us all."

The Good Hotel is a hip San Francisco hotel that practices philanthropy and believes in doing good for the planet. The eco-friendly hotel décor features reclaimed and recycled construction materials.

Vending machines in the lobby are stocked with wallets made from FedEx envelopes and are one example of our inventive ideas to promote a good lifestyle.

We are also as fun as we are inventive. You'll find humorous touches like "Be Good" written on walls of your room.

What does "good" mean to you? For some, the word may inspire visions of helping a homeless person find shelter for a night. Others may think of global warming and chant the mantra, "reduce, re-use, recycle." Or, maybe your mission isn't to save the world, and it simply connotes a positive fun attitude.

Joie de Vivre Hotels' identity as a socially conscious company inspired us to design this SOMA hotel with all these good intentions. From beds and headboards made from locally reclaimed wood to glow in the dark messages, our guests will discover that we are good with a lighthearted twist.

Hotel Services

- Parking available at $20 per night (plus tax). Hybrid cars receive complimentary parking
- Good Pizza serving artisan-style pizzas using only fresh and local ingredients is located adjacent to the hotel lobby
- Business stations located in the lobby
- High-speed internet access
- Pet friendly hotel offering complimentary treats and water/food bowls upon check-in (additional $25/pet fee applies)
- Access to outdoor, heated pool located across the street
- Bicycles available on loan when you stay with us.

Guestroom Amenities

- "Good" Amenities: bed frame made of 100% reclaimed wood, light fixture made of glass water bottles and toilet top sink
- 26-inch flat screen TV
- iPod docking station
- Hairdryer
- Iron & ironing board
- Coffee/tea maker
- High-speed wireless internet access
- Fold-down writing desk
- Curved shower rod

Source: The Good Hotel, guest brochure.

properties, including 117 rooms at Good Hotel. Hotel staff was to remain with the three properties under the new ownership.

Janusz had spent a good deal of her time training the management team in an effort to increase the standards of service at the hotel and, in turn, guest loyalty. Employee satisfaction was on the rise. Online reviews of the hotel were increasingly frequent and positive. While she anticipated that the new owners would maintain Good Hotel as a theme-based property, she needed within the next six weeks to prepare her evaluation and recommendation to the new ownership group as

to whether to continue, expand, or discontinue the Good Hotel concept.

THE U.S. LODGING INDUSTRY

Large, branded hotel chains dominated the U.S. lodging industry. Twelve leading hotel chains and their brands are profiled in Exhibit 2. The lodging business was cyclical: hoteliers tended to begin building capacity during the upturns, and that capacity came online just in time for the downturns, according to Standard & Poor's. As a result, the industry suffered from chronic overcapacity: as of October 2009, the U.S. lodging industry comprised approximately 4.8 million

Exhibit 2 Selected Financial and Operating Statistics for 12 Major Hotel Chains, 2007–2009

Company Name	Number of Properties	Number of Rooms	Number of Employees	Key Brands
Accor SA	4,000	500,000	158,162	Sofitel, Novotel, Mercure, Suitehotel, Motel 6
Best Western	4,000	303,827	1,059	Best Western
Choice Hotels International	6,021	487,410	1,560	Comfort Inn, Quality Inn, Econo Lodge, Clarion, Rodeway Inn, Sleep Inn
Four Seasons Hotels	80		33,185	Four Seasons, Regent
Hilton Worldwide*	3,500	545,000	130,000	Hilton, Conrad, Doubletree, Embassy Suites, Hampton
Hyatt Hotels Corp	431	119,857	45,000	Hyatt Regency, Grand Hyatt, Park Hyatt, Hyatt Place, Hyatt Summerfield Suites, Hyatt Resorts, Andaz
InterContinental Hotel Group	4,438	646,679	7,556	InterContinental, Holiday Inn Express, Crowne Plaza, Indigo, Staybridge Suites, Candlewood Suites
Kimpton Hotel Group	40 *(all)*	9,322	6,000	Monaco, Palomar
Marriott International	3,420	595,461	137,000	Marriott, Courtyard, Fairfield Inn, Ritz-Carlton
Red Lions Hotels	47	8,910	2,860	Red Lion
Starwood Hotels & Resorts Worldwide	979 *(30)*	292,000	145,000	Four Points, Sheraton, Westin, St. Regis, Luxury Collection, W Hotels, Le Méridien, Aloft, Element
Wyndham Worldwide	7,000	588,000	24,600	Days Inn, Howard Johnson, Ramada, Super 8

Company Name	Fiscal Years Ending December 31 ($ millions)					
	2009		2008		2007	
	Total Revenue	Net Income	Total Revenue	Net Income	Total Revenue	Net Income
Accor SA	$10,726.3	$864.0	$11,812.0	$1,342.4	$9,938.3	$567.3
Best Western						
Choice Hotels International	4,140.0	98.3	4,936.0	100.2	4,692.0	111.3
Four Seasons Hotels	21.0					
Hilton Worldwide*			7,770.0		8,162.0	572.0
Hyatt Hotels Corp	3,332.0	(43.6)	3,837.0	168.0	3,738.0	270.0
InterContinental Hotel Group	1,538.0	214.0	1,854.0	262.0	883.0	231.0
Kimpton Hotel Group	600.0					
Marriott International	10,908.0	(346.0)	12,879.0	362.0	12,990.0	696.0
Red Lions Hotels Corp	165.4	(6.6)	187.6	(1.7)	186.9	6.1
Starwood Hotels & Resorts Worldwide	4,712.0	71.0	5,907.0	329.0	6,153.0	542.0
Wyndham Worldwide Corp	3,750.0	293.0	4,281.0	(1,074.0)	4,360.0	403.0

*Acquired by the Blackstone Group in September 2007.

Sources: Mergent OnLine and Hoover's/Dun & Bradstreet (ProQuest), and individual company websites, accessed April 24 and 25, 2010.

rooms at more than 50,000 properties—about one hotel room for every 64 U.S. residents.

Recent Performance

Beginning in the second half of 2008 and continuing through the first quarter of 2010, the lodging industry experienced one of its longest downturns since industry data first became available in the late 1960s. Headline unemployment, declining business and conference travel, relatively unchanged real GDP, and rampant foreclosures were lead contributors to low occupancy rates of 2008 and 2009. Standard and Poor's projected that 2010 would represent a further decline in hotel industry performance. The prolonged industry downturn was expected to drop occupancy levels by 55 to 56 percent, representing the worst rate since the Great Depression, according to Standard & Poor's. In December 2009, Smith Travel Research estimated that U.S. hotel rates for the year had declined by 8.9 percent, and would fall another 3.4 percent in 2010. Hotel occupancy had declined by 8.8 percent in 2009, and was forecast to drop by a further 0.2 percent in 2010. After ending 2009 down 6 percent, demand was forecast to grow by 1.6 percent in 2010, mostly driven by recovering demand in the second half of the year.

A key industry statistic, revenue per available room (RevPAR), declined by 17 percent in 2009 and was forecast to drop a further 3.6 percent in 2010, according to Smith Travel Research. RevPAR was a ratio commonly used to measure financial performance in the hospitality industry. The metric, which was a function of both room rates and occupancy, was one of the most important gauges of health among hotel operators. There were two ways to calculate RevPAR. The first formula was to divide total room revenue in a given period (net of discounts, sales tax, and meals) by the number of available rooms in the same period. Alternatively, RevPAR could be calculated as the average daily room rate times the occupancy rate. RevPAR was arguably the most important of all ratios used in the hotel industry. Because the measure incorporated both room rates and occupancy, it provided a convenient snapshot of a how well a company was filling its rooms, as well as how much it was able to charge. RevPAR, by definition, was calculated on a per-room basis. Therefore, one company might have a higher RevPAR than another but still have lower total revenues if the second firm managed more rooms.

In a lodging industry review of 2009 and preview for 2010, Jeri Clausing of *Travel Weekly,* a popular trade publication, noted:

> Meetings and business travel will be a big factor in the recovery. Already stung by the slowdown in travel that accompanies any recession, hoteliers were hit with a double whammy in 2009 when luxury and meetings became dirty words. Toward the end of 2009, hotel executives said they were starting to see signs of life again in these markets. The bad news for hoteliers is that most of the corporate rates have already been negotiated, so even if travel picks up more than expected next year, it probably won't show in rates and RevPAR until 2011.

The Greening of the Hotel Industry

The growing interest in and investments made to support sustainability in the hospitality industry had, by late 2009, moved beyond hotel recycling programs and energy-efficient lighting. According to a 2009 article in *Hotels* magazine, hotels seeking new customers and growth in difficult economic times could benefit over the long term with investments in sustainability initiatives, including retrofitting existing properties to achieve Leadership in Energy and Environmental Design (LEED) certification and building new properties to LEED standards. A late-2008 Travel Industry Association study reported that nearly half of U.S. leisure travelers expressed a willingness to pay higher rates for services provided by environmentally friendly travel providers, and of those willing to pay more for "green" lodging, 60 percent said they would pay up to a 9 percent premium. A Deloitte survey from 2008 reported that 28 percent of U.S. business travelers were willing to pay a 10 percent premium to stay in a green lodging facility.

Emerging Demographic Segment

A major driver of the growing demand for green lodging came from an emerging demographic segment that consisted of consumers identified as "Cultural Creatives" by American sociologist Paul Ray and also known as "Lifestyles of Health and

Sustainability" (LOHAS). This segment sought a better world for themselves and their children. They were savvy, sophisticated, ecologically and economically aware customers who believed that society had reached a watershed moment in history owing to increasing public scrutiny of corporations' environmental and ethical practices. The LOHAS consumer focused on health and fitness, the environment, personal development, sustainable living, and social justice. This segment was estimated by the Natural Marketing Institute (NMI) to consist of about 38 million people, or 17 percent of the U.S. adult population, with spending power of $209 billion annually. Among all ages of consumers, younger consumers, ages 14 to 24, were reported to be most concerned about issues such as climate change and environmental protection, and were the major drivers of growth in the LOHAS segment. See Exhibit 3 for a profile of the LOHAS demographic.

The NMI identified a subsegment of the LOHAS demographic as tourists; this subsegment comprised 5 percent of the overall U.S. travel and tourism market and represented a $77 billion market. Major hotel companies like Ritz-Carlton and Starwood were known to be creating eco-branded properties. Hospitality designers and architects increasingly were being asked to "green" facilities across the board, from budget properties to high-end resorts.

San Francisco Tourism and Lodging Patterns

Of the estimated 15.4 million visitors to the city and county of San Francisco in 2009, more than 4.5 million overnight visitors stayed in commercial accommodations, comprising 32,976 hotel rooms and 215 hotels. Visitors paid a 14 percent occupancy tax, which generated about $210 million for San Francisco city and county services, including schools, police, affordable housing, and arts programs. Most tourists in San Francisco took day trips beyond city limits or extended their visit throughout Northern California by taking side trips to other area locales and attractions, such as the Napa/Sonoma wine country (23 percent), Sausalito (14 percent), and the Monterey peninsula (about 10 percent). Exhibit 4 presents San Francisco tourism data and Exhibit 5 shows comparative statistics on the San Francisco hospitality industry for the periods ending March 31, 2008, 2009, and 2010.

The San Francisco Convention and Visitors Bureau forecast that room supply would remain relatively unchanged out to 2015, while demand for rooms would remain flat, in stark contrast to 2004–2008, which represented five consecutive years of growth in both room supply and tourism demand. The bureau also projected that hotel occupancy rates, average daily rates (ADR), and RevPAR would not begin to recover until 2011–2012. One major factor was that the Moscone Convention Center, San Francisco's largest convention and meetings site, was expected to have a weak convention year in 2010 compared with five of the prior six years. Convention center bookings—at places such as the Moscone Center—greatly influenced hotel projections. Nearly 20,000 hotel rooms were in walking distance of the Moscone Center (including Good Hotel, which was five blocks away), and convention travel represented 35 percent of the annual demand for hotel rooms, according to the Convention and Visitor's Bureau. Although eight new hotels were on the drawing board, those new properties were unlikely to alter local room supply in the near term.

Exhibit 3 Comparative Demographics; All Consumers versus "Green" Consumers

	All Consumers	"Green" Consumers
Average age	44	40
Gender		
Female	51%	54%
Male	49%	46%
Ethnicity		
Caucasian/other	75%	62%
Hispanic	13%	21%
African American	11%	16%
College educated	25%	31%
Median household income	$58,700	$65,700

Source: S. Brooks, "The Green Consumer," *Restaurant Business,* September 2009, pp. 20–21.

Exhibit 4   San Francisco Hotel Guest Profile in 2009

Average annual household income:	$93,900
Average spending in SF (per-person, per-day):	$244.33
First-time San Francisco visitors:	17.5%
Traveling with children:	8.7%
Gender:	Male = 53.5% Female = 46.5%
Average age:	46 years old
Average nights in SF hotels:	3.6 nights
Average total length of current trip:	4.6 nights
People per room:	1.77
Used Internet in planning trip:	53.9%
Rental car in San Francisco:	25.8%
Arrived by air:	80.2%
Top five feeder markets of hotel guests [by Designated Market Areas (DMAs)]	Los Angeles—12.7% San Francisco/Oakland/San Jose—7.7% Sacramento/Stockton/Modesto—7% New York City—5.7% Washington, DC—3.5%
Primary reason for visit (% of all hotel guests):	39.7% Leisure 35.3% Convention 22.1% Transient business 2.9% Other

Source: San Francisco Convention and Visitors Bureau, www.sfcvb.org/research/, accessed April 28, 2010.

Exhibit 5   San Francisco Hospitality Statistics, 2008–2010

	March 2008	March 2009	March 2010
Average Daily Room Rate ($)			
Civic Center/Van Ness	$114.16	$92.45	$90.67
Financial District	230.21	189.47	181.93
Fisherman's Wharf	155.52	116.61	111.48
Union Square/Nob Hill/Moscone Center	200.00	176.57	161.99
Occupancy Rate (%)			
Civic Center/Van Ness	79.6%	69.4%	74.3%
Financial District	76.7	69.0	77.0
Fisherman's Wharf	84.0	74.5	86.0
Union Square/Nob Hill/Moscone Center	73.6	66.8	75.2

Sources: San Francisco Convention and Visitors Bureau, www.sfcvb.org/research/, accessed April 28, 2010. Hospitality statistics from PKF Consulting.

JOIE DE VIVRE

Since its founding in 1987, Joie de Vivre had grown to manage 36 boutique hotel properties in California. By 2010, JdV was the second-largest U.S. boutique hotel operator after the Kimpton Hotel & Restaurant Group, which had pioneered the boutique concept in San Francisco in 1981.

Boutique Hotels

Boutique hotels differentiated themselves from branded chain hotels and motels by providing personalized accommodation and services and facilities. Sometimes known as "design hotels" or "lifestyle hotels," boutique hotels began appearing in the 1980s in major cities like London,

New York, and San Francisco. Boutique hotels were furnished in a themed, stylish, and/or aspirational manner. They typically were unique properties operated by individuals or companies with a small collection. In time, their successes prompted several multinational hotel companies to try to establish their own brands in order to capture a market share. The most notable example was Starwood's W Hotels, ranging from large boutique hotels, such as the W Times Square in New York City, to the W "boutique resorts" in the Maldives, to true luxury boutique hotel collections, such as the Bulgari collection, SLS Hotels, Thompson Hotels, the Keating Hotel, and the O Hotel, among others.

Strategy

Chip Conley, JdV's founder and CEO, said:

> I went into hospitality because I enjoyed commercial real estate but hated the transactional part. If you get it right and your customer sees the product as an extension of themselves, you've refreshed the identity of the customers because they feel that by using the product they're becoming more of that aspirational self, according to Abraham Maslow's "Hierarchy of Needs."[1]

In 2007, Conley related JdV's branding strategy to *Travel Weekly:*

> We know California better than anybody else. We are the largest hotelier in the state. About 40 percent of our customers come from within the state. We went through a whole branding process, and what we heard from our customers was that they loved the fact that we create original hotels. We come up with a personality for the hotel by thinking of magazines. It is sort of like a good touchstone for personality. Each [hotel] is its own unique product. You can be geographically diverse, but that means you have to be product-line focused. Or you can be geographically focused and the product line diverse. Holiday Inn is geographically diverse and product-line focused. We are the opposite of Holiday Inn.[2]

Among JdV's most recently opened San Francisco Bay Area properties, the Tomo in Japantown was based on two Japanese pop-culture magazines, *Lucky* (a popular women's magazine) and *Giant Robot* (a magazine devoted to anime, manga, and technology-based art).

Other properties included the Vitale (*Dwell + Real Simple*), Galleria Park (*Vanity Fair + BusinessWeek*), Kabuki (*Travel & Leisure*), and downtown Berkeley's Durant (*Sports Illustrated + Economist*). The Good Hotel concept was based on *Ode + ReadyMade,* and according to Janusz, embodied five key words: hip, happy, humble, conscious, and inventive.

Marketing

JdV spent very little on marketing, preferring to rely mostly on word of mouth and social media promotion on the Internet to attract guests to its hotels. According to industry analysts, social media use among travelers continued to grow faster than the travel industry itself.

Unique monthly visitors to social travel websites such as TripAdvisor.com and Yelp.com rose by 34 percent between the first half of 2008 and the last half of 2009, to 15.9 million, representing year-over-year growth of more than 30 percent in the first half of 2009 and 45 percent in the second half of 2009. By comparison, U.S. travel gross bookings had declined by 16 percent in 2009.[3]

Joie de Vivre's Green Programs

In 2009, JdV's senior vice president of operations and green committee chair, Karlene Holloman, launched the company's Green Dreams portal, a dedicated page on its website (www.jdvhotels.com/greendreams/) where consumers could track the company's ongoing efforts to preserve the environment. Holloman said at the time:

> We want to be transparent and share the progress we've made and the efforts that continue as we strive to have all our hotels green-certified in the near term. In essence, our guests can be green cheerleaders, watching from the sidelines as more of our hotels reach their goals. We hope Joie de Vivre Green Dreams will become a useful tool and resource for our guests and any consumer evaluating green travel programs.[4]

To demonstrate its ongoing commitment to the environment, JdV was working toward a goal of having its hotels certified green by their local city or county while using the San Francisco Green Business Certification standards, as these were the most stringent in the state. Some hotels, like Hotel Carlton, went beyond this goal by investing in solar power and achieving LEED Gold certification, making it San Francisco's first hotel to do so. Exhibit 6 presents a definition of LEED and a listing of Northern California hotel properties carrying this certification as of April 2010.

Financial Performance

In 2009, JdV's hotels, restaurants, and spas generated an estimated $250 million in revenues, at properties ranging from the high-end Ventana Inn in Big Sur, California, with rooms at $700 per night, to Good Hotel, at $70 per night. JdV's room revenues had dropped by 18–20 percent

Exhibit 6   LEED Certified Hotels in Northern California

LEED was an acronym for Leadership in Energy and Environmental Design. Buildings attained LEED certification from the U.S. Green Business Council by earning points in six categories: sustainable sites, water efficiency, energy and atmosphere, materials and resources, indoor environmental air quality, and innovation/design process. Based on the total number of points, a business would then receive a silver, gold or platinum designation. Lower operation costs were typically associated with a LEED building: approximately 30 to 40 percent less energy use and 40 percent less water. Application for LEED certification of an existing property could cost upwards of $10,000, depending upon the size of the property, the number of rooms, and the level of certification sought. Most hotels tried for certification of new construction, which was much easier and potentially less costly to earn than from retrofitting an existing building.

As of March 2010, there were 12 LEED-certified hotels in America, of which four were in San Francisco [Hotel Carlton (Gold), Orchard, Orchard Garden, and W Hotel (Silver)], with more than 100 proposals in the works. See table below. Other reputable certifications by Green Seal and the Green Tourism Business Scheme in the United Kingdom have led to confusion, with no universal stamp of approval available.

Hotel Name and Location	LEED Rating System and Certification Level*	Building Type
San Francisco		
Hotel Carlton	LEED EBOM **Gold**	Commercial
Orchard Garden Hotel	LEED NC Certified (v2.1)	Commercial
Orchard Hotel	LEED EB Certified (v2.0)	Commercial
W Hotel	LEED EBOM Silver	Commercial
Outside San Francisco		
Gaia Napa Valley Hotel, American Canyon	LEED NC **Gold** (v2.1)	Commercial
Gaia Shasta Hotel, Anderson	LEED NC Silver (v2.1)	Commercial

Rating Systems:
LEED CI = LEED for Commercial Interiors
LEED CS = LEED for Core & Shell
LEED EB = LEED for Existing Buildings
LEED EBOM = LEED for Existing Buildings: Operations & Maintenance
LEED H = LEED for Homes
LEED NC = LEED for New Construction (and Major Renovations)
LEED ND = LEED for Neighborhood Development

LEED Certification Levels:
Certified, Silver, Gold, Platinum

Sources: M. Landman, www.mlandman.com/gbuildinginfo/leedbuildings.shtml, accessed April 25, 2010, and *Executive Travel Magazine,* "What Is an LEED Hotel and Where Are They?" www.executivetravelmagazine.com/page/What+is+an+LEED+hotel+--+and+where+are+they%3F, accessed April 25, 2010.

in 2008–2009 but appeared to be rising at about the same rate in the first quarter of 2010, according to Conley. JdV was privately held and did not release information regarding individual hotel revenues or profits. Nevertheless, Conley publicly stated that JdV had remained profitable throughout the downturn. According to an April 9, 2010, report in the *San Francisco Business Times,* Conley was actively seeking a strategic capital partner for JdV, a partner that could provide an investment of $150 million or more to expand the number of properties under JdV's management.

GOOD HOTEL

Operations

Formerly managed by JdV as a Best Western motel and an adjacent property, the Hotel Britton, the Good Hotel was refurbished in 2008 and reopened in November of that year. It was located at the corner of Mission and Seventh Streets—a gritty but slowly revitalizing corner of SoMa, as the area south of Market Street in San Francisco was known. In the immediate vicinity were buildings with single-room-occupancy housing, the futuristic-looking San Francisco Federal Building, and a sleek plaza lined with cafés. Mass transit—including bus, light rail, cable car, and subway—was all within walking distance.

Good Hotel's lobby showcased many environmentally and socially conscious features, including a bench made of recycled felt blankets, a vending machine branded by *ReadyMade* magazine that dispensed wallets fashioned out of FedEx envelopes ($15) and other goodies; wall art by developmentally disabled artists; and an orange phone that connected to a "philanthropy concierge" who arranged volunteer stints through One Brick, a local nonprofit. There was also a photo booth in the lobby ($3 for two prints); the hotel encouraged visitors to add to the photo collage of guests prominently displayed in the lobby. The hotel's 38 motel-style rooms opened onto a courtyard parking lot, and the remaining 79 rooms were located in a five-story brick building.

In the rooms, which had the feel of a slightly upscale youth hostel, platform beds made of reclaimed pine were draped with fleece blankets made of recycled soda bottles. The pillows were made from old bedspreads salvaged from the previous hotel, a Best Western. Each room had a chandelier made of empty Voss water bottles, a recycling bin, a fold-down metal desk just big enough for a laptop and, overhead, a secret message from the hotel that glowed in the dark. Bathrooms featured a Japanese-style toilet-top sink: the gray water from the sink was collected in the toilet tank, saving water. Each room provided free Wi-Fi, an iPod docking station, and a 26-inch flat-screen television. A spacious fitness center and an outdoor heated pool were available across the street, at the recently renovated Best Western Americania. At checkout, guests could donate $1.50 per day to One Brick (donations were automatically added to each room night stay), offset their carbon footprint through Carbonfund.org, or go online on one of the iMacs in the small business center with an option to give a $200 computer through One Laptop per Child.

Writing in the *San Francisco Chronicle* in December 2008, just after the hotel opened, John Flinn described his experience: "San Francisco's new Good Hotel doesn't miss many tricks in its bid to be the greenest, do-goodingest, most politically correct hotel in America. But even Hummer drivers and spotted owl stranglers will appreciate the gratifyingly low room rates, which start at $67 a night."

Leadership

Pam Janusz received an MBA from the University of Texas at Austin in 2004. She initially was responsible for management of three of JdV's smallest boutique hotels. In 2006, she served as the general manager of special projects relating to transitional hotels, a role in which she was responsible for assisting new JdV hotels and restaurants in acclimating to the culture, processes, and operational standards of the company.

In 2007, Janusz was promoted to the general manager role at Hotel Carlton, certified by the city of San Francisco as a green business. In this role she became involved in many JdV-wide initiatives, including the Safety Task Force, the Green Committee, and the Advisory Panel. Janusz led the process at Hotel Carlton to install solar panels that provided 9 percent of the energy used on property, and spearheaded the hotel's application process to become certified by the U.S. Green Building Council at the Gold level for LEED-EB (existing building). As a member of the JdV Green Committee, Janusz also contributed greatly to the new JdV Green Dreams website, which outlined and rated the company's environmental initiatives in four main focus areas: recycling and waste reduction, energy conservation, water conservation, and pollution prevention.

While conducting a tour of Good Hotel in March 2010, Janusz remarked that part of her job entailed educating staff members to ensure that they were aware of JdV's safety and green programs, could explain them to guests, and could answer guests' questions about them. Nearly all guests at Good Hotel were leisure travelers or tourists on a budget. Janusz said:

> Recently, we find travelers are more last minute when reserving their hotel accommodations. We see a lot of walk-in and Internet "on the day of" reservations which drive occupancy. There is a fine line when setting room rates, so we are competitively priced but not too low so we attract clientele that we do not want at our hotels. We've also had to focus a lot on service and safety training due to the fact that this neighborhood is still transitional. Our Green Dreams website and personal contact together provide the most effective means of attracting and keeping guests who are concerned about the environment. I was hoping that

we could convince the owners of the Good Hotel to apply for LEED certification, like we did at the Hotel Carlton, but they were not in a position to immediately move forward on new investments when I arrived at the hotel.

Financial Performance

Smith Travel Research collected monthly operating statistics for hotels. Statistics for the Hotel Britton (the previous property) and the Good Hotel from March 2008 to the end of March 2010 are shown in Exhibit 7, providing comparisons of occupancy rates, average daily rate, and RevPAR with five selected peer group competitors in its neighborhood, size, and class. Exhibit 8 provides monthly operating data for the Good Hotel from its opening in November 2008 to the end of March 2010.

MAKING THE TRANSITION

As Janusz went through her in-box, she saw another message marked "urgent." This one had been sent by the organizer of a Norwegian tour group requesting immediate cancellation of 100 rooms booked at the Good Hotel for the week of

Exhibit 7   **Operating Statistics: Good Hotel versus San Francisco Peer Group, March 2008–March 2010**

March 31, 2008					
Occupancy (%)		ADR ($)		RevPAR ($)	
Hotel Britton*	Peer Group**	Hotel Britton*	Peer Group**	Hotel Britton*	Peer Group**
Current Month	45.4%	67.9%	$79.38	$83.68	$36.07	$56.79
Year-to-Date	39.3	59.2	73.61	76.76	28.92	45.46
Running 3 Month	39.3	59.2	73.61	76.76	28.92	45.46
Running 12 Month	63.3	69.0	80.23	86.02	50.82	59.38

March 2008 vs. 2007 Percent Change (%)					
Occupancy		ADR		RevPAR	
Hotel Britton*	Peer Group**	Hotel Britton*	Peer Group**	Hotel Britton*	Peer Group**
Current Month	−18.5%	−1.1%	28.2%	26.9%	2.8%	25.6%
Year-to-Date	0.3	2.9	9.4	14.7	9.7	18.0

(Continued)

Exhibit 7 *(Continued)*

	March 2008 vs. 2007 Percent Change (%)					
	Occupancy		ADR		RevPAR	
	Hotel Britton*	Peer Group**	Hotel Britton*	Peer Group**	Hotel Britton*	Peer Group**
Running 3 Month	0.3	2.9	9.4	14.7	9.7	18.0
Running 12 Month	1.1	8.4	6.8	7.8	8.0	16.9

	March 31, 2009***					
	Occupancy (%)		ADR ($)		RevPAR ($)	
	Good Hotel	Peer Group**	Good Hotel	Peer Group**	Good Hotel	Peer Group**
Current Month	70.3%	59.3%	$65.82	$66.51	$46.85	$39.90
Year-to-Date	55.3	53.4	62.95	63.88	34.36	34.25
Running 3 Month	55.3	53.4	62.95	63.88	34.36	34.25
Running 12 Month	29.7	67.9	85.23	90.22	31.49	60.10

	March 2009 vs. 2008 Percent Change (%)***					
	Occupancy		ADR		RevPAR	
	Good Hotel	Peer Group**	Good Hotel	Peer Group**	Good Hotel	Peer Group**
Current Month	54.9%	−12.7%	−17.1%	−20.5%	29.9%	−29.7%
Year-to-Date	40.6	−9.8	−14.5	−16.8	18.8	−24.7
Running 3 Month	40.6	−9.8	−14.5	−16.8	18.8	−24.7
Running 12 Month	−53.1	−1.6	6.2	4.9	−38.0	1.2

	March 31, 2010					
	Occupancy (%)		ADR ($)		RevPAR ($)	
	Good Hotel	Peer Group**	Good Hotel	Peer Group**	Good Hotel	Peer Group**
Current Month	66.2%	56.1%	$73.30	$73.66	$48.50	$41.30
Year-to-Date	57.8	51.7	71.94	67.74	41.60	35.02
Running 3 Month	57.8	51.7	71.94	67.74	41.60	35.02
Running 12 Month	76.7	61.8	78.55	80.27	60.21	49.63

	March 2010 vs. 2009 Percent Change (%)					
	Occupancy		ADR		RevPAR	
	Good Hotel	Peer Group**	Good Hotel	Peer Group**	Good Hotel	Peer Group**
Current Month	−6.2%	−5.7%	10.2%	9.7%	3.4%	3.4%
Year-to-Date	4.4	−3.3	12.5	5.7	17.4	2.2

(Continued)

Exhibit 7   (Concluded)

March 2010 vs. 2009 Percent Change (%)					
Occupancy		ADR		RevPAR	
Good Hotel	Peer Group**	Good Hotel	Peer Group**	Good Hotel	Peer Group**
Running 3 Month					
4.4	−3.3	12.5	5.7	17.4	2.2
Running 12 Month					
61.3	−9.9	−8.5	−12.4	47.7	−21.1

*JdV's Hotel Britton was refurbished and reopened as the Good Hotel in November 2008.

**The peer group is comprised of competitive hotels selected by hotel management to benchmark the subject property's performance. The peer group set consisted of five San Francisco hotels near Market Street, with a total of 602 rooms, and included: Knights Inn Downtown San Francisco (68 rooms), The Opal Hotel (164 rooms), Hotel Metropolis (105 rooms), Renoir Hotel (130 rooms), and The Powell Hotel (135 rooms).

***Good Hotel was closed for a few months in 2008 during renovation. This closure affects the running 12 month averages from the 2009 reports.

Source: Smith Travel Research, March 2008 and March 2010.

Exhibit 8   Monthly Operating Statistics: Good Hotel, November 2008–March 2010

	2008	
	November	December
Number of rooms	117	117
Occupancy	26.87%	55.53%
RevPAR	$20.53	$48.93
Total Revenue	$2,402	$5,725

	2009											
	Jan	Feb	Mar	Apr	May	Jun	Jul	Aug	Sep	Oct	Nov	Dec
Number of rooms	117	117	117	117	117	117	117	117	117	117	117	117
Occupancy	40.1%	55.5%	70.5%	77.4%	78.2%	87.5%	92.0%	95.0%	92.3%	90.7%	62.3%	69.8%
RevPAR	$26.57	$32.50	$46.91	$56.29	$68.65	$68.72	$77.01	$79.63	$80.02	$83.33	$43.48	$39.06
Total revenue	$3,109	$3,802	$5,488	$6,586	$8,033	$8,040	$9,011	$9,317	$9,362	$9,750	$5,087	$4,570

	2010		
	Jan	Feb	Mar
Number of rooms	117	117	117
Occupancy (%)	56.96	49.54	66.17
RevPAR ($)	40.31	35.39	48.50
Total revenue	$4,716	$4,141	$5,675

Source: Smith Travel Research, March 2010.

April 18, 2010. Disruption of all air travel and indefinite closure of nearly all airports in Europe had forced cancellation of the tour, due to the huge plume of ash generated by the unexpected eruption of the Eyjafjallajökull volcano in Iceland. Loss of the Norwegian tour group's business meant that many of the 117 rooms would be empty unless last-minute or walk-in bookings showed up. This came at a time when the hotel industry in general was counting on a recovery from the long economic recession in 2008 and 2009, not to mention the normally soft travel bookings during the winter months.

In addition to the canceled bookings, Janusz wondered about how to inform and transition the current Good Hotel staff to the new ownership group. She pondered how her recommendation would impact their commitment to the original intent of Good Hotel.

Janusz's number one task was how best to prepare Good Hotel and its current staff for the transition to new ownership in six weeks' time. She had several weeks remaining to work with her staff to complete a review of Good Hotel, containing her evaluation of the Good Hotel concept.

ENDNOTES

[1] Speech to Association of Fundraising Professionals, Commonwealth Club, San Francisco, January 22, 2010. See also Chip Conley's book on the subject of applying Maslow's hierarchy of needs to business: *Peak: How Great Companies Get Their Mojo from Maslow.* San Francisco: Jossey-Bass, 2007.

[2] M. Milligan, "Joie de Vivre Finds Inspiration for Properties in Pop Culture," *Travel Weekly,* May 1, 2007, www.travelweekly.com/article3_ektid92480.aspx?terms=*joie+de+vivre*, accessed May 1, 2010.

[3] PhoCusWright, "Social Media in Travel: Traffic & Activity," April 2010.

[4] In D. Gale, "The Green Guests Are Coming," *Hotels* 43 (January 2009), p. 33.

REFERENCES

Barrett, S. "Operations Key in Green Effort." *Hotel and Motel Management* 223, no. 5 (2008), p. 1.

Brooks, S. "The Green Consumer." *Restaurant Business,* September 2009, pp. 20–21.

Chan, W. W. "Environmental Measures for Hotels' Environmental Management Systems." *International Journal for Contemporary Hospitality Management* 21, no. 5 (2009), pp. 542–560.

"Chip Conley." *Marketing News* 43, no. 3 (2009), p. 62.

Clark, R. A.; M. D. Hartline; and K. C. Jones. "Effects of Leadership Style on Hotel Employees' Commitment to Service Quality." *Cornell Hospitality Quarterly* 50, no. 2 (March 2009), pp. 209–31.

Clausing, J. "Preview 2010: The Supply Side: Hotels." *Travel Weekly,* December 29, 2009, www.travelweekly.com/article3_ektid208196.aspx?terms=*clausing*&page=6, accessed May 1, 2010.

———. "Hotels Struggle to Harness the Power of Social Media." *Travel Weekly,* April 21, 2010, www.travelweekly.com/article3_ektid213392.aspx?terms=*clausing*, accessed May 1, 2010.

Conley, C. *Peak: How Great Companies Get Their Mojo from Maslow.* San Francisco: Jossey-Bass, 2007.

Dahle, C. "Weathering the Perfect Storm." *Fast Company* 84 (2004), p. 29.

Duxbury, S. "Joie de Vivre Hospitality Seeking $150M, New Investor." *San Francisco Business Times,* April 9, 2010, www.bizjournals.com/sanfrancisco/stories/2010/04/05/story4.html?b=1270440000%5E3130821&s=industry&i=travel, accessed May 1, 2010.

Flinn, J. "The Good Hotel." *San Francisco Chronicle,* December 18, 2008, p. G-33, www.sfgate.com/cgi-bin/article.cgi?f=/c/a/2008/12/18/NS1R14IARP.DTL\ixzz0mmgSnBY8, accessed May 1, 2010.

Gale, D. "The Green Guests Are Coming." *Hotels* 43 (January 2009), p. 33.

Henning, M. "Success Comes from Developed Leadership." *Hotel & Motel Management* 223, no. 2 (March 11, 2008), p. 12.

"Joie de Vivre Looks to Grow by Growing Up." *Hotels* 39, no. 3 (March 2005), p. 18.

Milligan, M. "Joie de Vivre Finds Inspiration for Properties in Pop Culture." *Travel Weekly,* May 1, 2007, www.travelweekly.com/article3_ektid92480.aspx?terms=*joie+de+vivre*, accessed May 1, 2010.

Mount, I. "Open-Book Survival." *Fortune Small Business* 15, no. 5 (June 2005), p. 29.

"Perspectives: Green." *Hospitality Design* 32, no. 2 (March 2010), p. 44.

PhoCusWright. "Social Media in Travel: Traffic & Activity," April 2010.

San Francisco Convention and Visitor's Bureau website, 2010, www.sfcvb.org/research/.

Speer, J. "Reaching the Top of the Pyramid." *Apparel Magazine,* June 2009, p. 2.

Standard & Poor's. "Current Environment: Lodging & Gaming." *Standard & Poor's Industry Surveys,* November 19, 2009, pp. 1–23.

Weinstein, J. "Brands vs. Independents." *Hotels* 40 (July 2006), p. 7.

Woodward, M. "Average Growth Rate Leads Cities Out of Recession." *Hotel & Motel Management* 225, no. 2 (February 1, 2010), p. 14.

Woodworth, R. M., and A. Walls. "Thoughts While Waiting for RevPar to Grow." *Cornell Hospitality Quarterly* 50, no. 3 (August 2009), pp. 289–91.

W. L. Gore & Associates: Developing Global Teams to Meet 21st-Century Challenges[1]

Frank Shipper
Salisbury University

Greg L. Stewart
University of Iowa

Charles C. Manz
University of Massachusetts–Amherst

In 2010, W. L. Gore & Associates celebrated its 52nd year in business. Founded in 1958 by Bill and Vieve Gore in the basement of their home, Gore had grown into a global enterprise famous for its high performance fabrics, medical products, and next-generation electronic products, as well as its use of self-empowered teams of employees (called associates at Gore). In its earlier years, the company had endeavored to restrict the size of its different corporate facilities to 200 associates or fewer, a practice that helped keep the number of teams at a given facility to a manageable number and facilitated cross-team coordination. More recently, however, to better cope with the challenges of a global marketplace, increasing numbers of teams were composed of associates in different facilities, sometimes facilities that were spread across three continents; the coordination of team members working in different facilities was enabled by online communication.

In 2010, Gore's products were sold on six continents and used on all seven continents, as well as under the ocean and in space. The company global operations required teams of associates to tightly coordinate their activities in developing, producing, and marketing products to customers across the world. Currently teams were organized primarily along product lines, with only a few teams consisting of members working in the same Gore facility. As a consequence, it was common for team members to be separated by thousands of miles, work in multiple time zones, speak different languages, and live in quite different cultures. The diversity among team members, combined with the company's emphasis on growth and globalized operations, presented significant challenges for W. L. Gore as it strove to maintain a family-like, entrepreneurial culture. According to Terri Kelly, the president of Gore and a 25-year associate:[2]

> In the early days, our business was largely conducted at the local level. There were global operations, but most relationships were built regionally, and most decisions were made regionally. That picture has evolved dramatically over the last 20 years, as businesses can no longer be defined by brick and mortar. Today, most of our teams are spread across regions and continents. Therefore, the decision-making process is much more global and virtual in nature, and there's a growing need to build strong relationships across geographical boundaries. The globalization of our business has been one of the biggest changes I've seen in the last 25 years.

Elements of the culture at Gore are captured in Exhibit 1. The core belief in the need to take the long-term view in business situations, and to make and keep commitments, drove cooperation among individuals and small teams. This was supported by key practices that replaced traditional, hierarchical structure with flexible relationships and a sense that all workers were in the same boat.

Exhibit 1   W. L. Gore & Associates' Culture

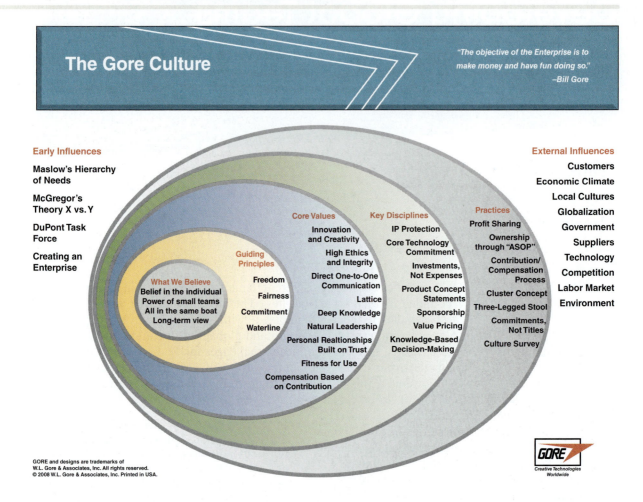

The ultimate focus was on empowering talented associates to deliver highly innovative products.

Despite substantial growth, the core values had not changed at Gore. The objective of the company set forth by the founder Wilbert L. (Bill) Gore, "To make money and have fun," was still part of the Gore culture. Associates around the world were asked to follow the company's four guiding principles:

1. Try to be fair.
2. Encourage, help, and allow other associates to grow in knowledge, skill, and scope of activity and responsibility.
3. Make your own commitments, and keep them.
4. Consult with other associates before taking actions that may be "below the waterline."

The four principles were referred to as *fairness, freedom, commitment,* and *waterline.* The waterline principle was drawn from an analogy to ships. If someone poked a hole in a boat above the waterline, the boat would be in relatively little real danger. If, however, someone poked a hole below the waterline, the boat would be in immediate danger of sinking. The expectation was that "waterline" issues would be discussed across teams, plants, and continents as appropriate before any decisions about them were made. Gore still emphasized this principle even though team members who needed to share in the decision-making process were now spread across the globe.

Commitment was spoken of frequently at Gore. The commitment principle's primary emphasis was on the freedom associates had to make their own commitments, rather than having others assign them to projects or tasks. But commitment could also be viewed as a mutual commitment between associates and the enterprise. Associates worldwide committed to making contributions to the company's success. In return, the company was committed to providing a challenging, opportunity-rich work environment that was responsive to associate needs and concerns.

BACKGROUND

Gore was formed by Wilbert L. (Bill) Gore and his wife, Genevieve (Vieve) Gore, in 1958. The idea for the business sprang from Bill Gore's personal, technical, and organizational experiences at E. I. du Pont de Nemours & Co. and, particularly, his involvement in the characterization of a chemical compound with unique properties. The compound, called polytetrafluorethylene (PTFE), had come to be marketed by DuPont under the Teflon brand name. Gore saw a wide variety of potential applications for this unique new material, and when DuPont showed little interest in pursuing most of them directly, he decided to form his own company and start pursuing the concepts himself. Thus, Gore became one of DuPont's first customers for this new material.

Since then, W. L. Gore & Associates had evolved into a global enterprise, with annual revenues of more than $2.5 billion, supported by more than 8,500 associates worldwide. This placed Gore at number 180 on *Forbes* magazine's 2008 list of the 500 largest private companies in the United States. The enterprise's unique, and now famous, culture and leadership practices had helped make Gore one of only a select few companies to appear on all of the U.S. "100 Best Companies to Work For" rankings since they were introduced in 1984.

Bill Gore was born in Meridian, Idaho, in 1912. By age six, according to his own account, he was an avid hiker in Utah. Later, at a church camp in 1935, he met Genevieve Walton, his future wife. In their eyes, the marriage was a partnership. He would make breakfast and Vieve, as everyone called her, would make lunch. The partnership lasted a lifetime.

Bill Gore attended the University of Utah; he earned a bachelor of science in chemical engineering in 1933 and a master of science in physical chemistry in 1935. He began his professional career at American Smelting and Refining in 1936; moved to Remington Arms, a DuPont subsidiary, in 1941; and then moved to DuPont's headquarters in 1945. He held positions as research supervisor and head of operations research. While at DuPont, he felt a sense of excited commitment, personal fulfillment, and self-direction while working with a task force to develop applications for PTFE.

Having followed the development of the electronics industry, he felt that PTFE had ideal insulating characteristics for use with such equipment. He tried many ways to make a PTFE-coated ribbon cable, but with no success until a breakthrough in his home basement laboratory. One night, while Bill was explaining the problem to his 19-year-old son, Bob, the young Gore saw some PTFE sealant tape and asked his father, "Why don't you try this tape?" Bill explained that everyone knew that you could not bond PTFE to itself. After Bob went to bed, however, Bill remained in the basement lab and proceeded to try what conventional wisdom said could not be done. At about 5:00 a.m., Bill woke up Bob, waving a small piece of cable around and saying excitedly, "It works, it works." The following night father and son returned to the basement lab to make ribbon cable insulated with PTFE. Because the idea came from Bob, the patent for the cable was issued in his name.

After a while, Bill Gore came to realize that DuPont wanted to remain a supplier of raw materials for industrial buyers and not a manufacturer of high-tech products for end-use markets. Bill and Vieve began discussing the possibility of starting their own insulated wire and cable business. On January 1, 1958, their wedding anniversary, they founded W. L. Gore. The basement of their home served as their first facility. After finishing breakfast, Vieve turned to her husband of 23 years and said, "Well, let's clear up the dishes, go downstairs, and get to work."

When Bill Gore (a 45-year-old with five children to support) left DuPont, he put aside a career of 17 years and a good, secure salary. To finance the first two years of their new business, he and Vieve mortgaged their house and took $4,000 from savings. All their friends cautioned them against taking on such a big financial risk.

The first few years were challenging. Some of the young company's associates accepted stock in the company in lieu of salary. Family members who came to help with the business lived in the home as well. At one point, 11 associates were living and working under one roof. One afternoon, while sifting PTFE powder, Vieve received a call from the City of Denver's water department. The caller wanted to ask some technical questions about the ribbon cable and asked for the product manager. Vieve explained that he was not in at the moment. (Bill and two other key associates were out of town.) The caller asked next for the sales manager and then for the president. Vieve explained that "they" were also not in. The caller finally shouted, "What kind of company is this anyway?" With a little diplomacy the Gores were eventually able to secure an order from Denver's water department for around $100,000. This order put the company over the start-up hump and onto a profitable footing. Sales began to take off.

During the decades that followed, W. L. Gore developed a number of new products derived from PTFE, the best known of which was GORE-TEX fabric. The development of GORE-TEX fabric, one of hundreds of new products that followed a key discovery by Bob Gore, was an example of the power of innovation. In 1969, Gore's Wire and Cable Division was facing increased competition. Bill Gore began to look for a way to expand PTFE: "I figured out that if we could ever unfold those molecules, get them to stretch out straight, we'd have a tremendous new kind of material." The new PTFE material would have more volume per pound of raw material with no adverse effect on performance. Thus, fabricating costs would be reduced and profit margins increased. Bob Gore took on the project; he heated rods of PTFE to various temperatures and then slowly stretched them. Regardless of the temperature or how carefully he stretched them, the rods broke. Working alone late one night after countless failures, Bob in frustration stretched one of the rods violently. To his surprise, it did not break. He tried it again and again with the same results. The next morning, Bill Gore recalled, "Bob wanted to surprise me so he took a rod and stretched it slowly. Naturally, it broke. Then he pretended to get mad. He grabbed another rod and said, 'Oh, the hell with this,' and gave it a pull. It didn't break—he'd done

it." The new arrangement of molecules not only changed the Wire and Cable Division but also led to the development of GORE-TEX fabric and many other products.

In 1986, Bill Gore died while backpacking in the Wind River Mountains of Wyoming. Vieve Gore continued to be involved actively in the company and served on the board of directors until her death at 91 in 2005.

W. L. Gore had only four presidents in its 50-year history. Bill Gore served as the president from the enterprise's founding in 1958 until 1976. At that point, his son Bob became president and CEO. Bob had been an active member of the firm from the time of its founding, most recently as chairman of the board of directors. He served as president until 2000, when Chuck Carroll was selected as the third president. In 2005, Terri Kelly succeeded Carroll. As with all the presidents after Bill Gore, Kelly was a longtime employee: she had been with Gore for 22 years before becoming president.

The Gore family established a unique culture that continued to be an inspiration for associates. For example, Dave Gioconda, a current product specialist, recounted meeting Bob Gore for the first time—an experience that reinforced the company's egalitarian culture:

> Two weeks after I joined Gore, I traveled to Phoenix for training. . . . I told the guy next to me on the plane where I worked, and he said, "I work for Gore, too." "No kidding?" I asked. "Where do you work?" He said, "Oh, I work over at the Cherry Hill plant." . . .
>
> I spent two and a half hours on this plane having a conversation with this gentleman who described himself as a technologist and shared some of his experiences. As I got out of the plane, I shook his hand and said, "I'm Dave Gioconda, nice to meet you." He replied, "Oh, I'm Bob Gore." That experience has had a profound influence on the decisions that I make.

Due to the leadership of Bill, Vieve, Bob, and many others, W. L. Gore was selected as one of the "100 Best Companies to Work For" in 2009 by *Fortune* magazine for the 12th consecutive year. In addition, the company was included in all three *100 Best Companies to Work For in America* books (1984, 1985 and 1993). It was one of only a select few companies to appear on all 15 lists. Gore had been selected also as one of the best companies to work for in France, Germany, Italy, Spain, Sweden, and the United Kingdom.

In 2009 Gore had annual revenues of about $2.5 billion and approximately 9,000 employees located in 30 countries worldwide.[3] It was one of the 200 largest privately held U.S. companies; the company's common stock was owned by members of the Gore family and by associates. Because of its privately held status, Gore did not make its financial results public. It did share, however, financial results with all associates on a monthly basis. Gore executives believed that private ownership reinforced its strongly-ingrained cultural emphasis on "taking a long term view" when assessing business situations and making decisions.

COMPETITIVE STRATEGY AT W. L. GORE

For product management, Gore was divided into four divisions: Electronics, Fabrics, Industrial, and Medical. The Electronic Products Division (EPD) developed and manufactured high-performance cables and assemblies as well as specialty materials for electronic devices. The Fabrics Division (FD) developed and provided fabric to the outdoor clothing industry as well as the military, law enforcement, and fire protection industries. Gore fabrics marketed under the GORE-TEX, WINDSTOPPER, CROSS-TECH, and GORE CHEMPAK brands provided the wearer protection while remaining comfortable. The Industrial Products Division (IPD) made filtration, sealant, and other products. These products met diverse contamination and process challenges in many industries. The Medical Products Division (MPD) provided products such as synthetic vascular grafts, interventional devices, endovascular stent-grafts, surgical patches for hernia repair, and sutures for use in vascular, cardiac, general surgery and oral procedures. Although they were recognized as separate divisions, the EPD, FD, IPD, and MPD frequently worked together.

Since it had four divisions that served different industries, Gore could be viewed as a diversified conglomerate. Bob Winterling, a financial associate, described how the four divisions worked together financially as follows:

The thing I love about Gore is that we have four very diverse divisions. During my time here, I've noticed that when one or two divisions are down, you always have one, two or three that are up. I call them cylinders. Sometimes all four cylinders are working really well; not all the time though. Normally it's two or three, but that's the luxury that we have. When one is down—it's good to know that another is up.

At the end of 2007, all four divisions were performing well. Having four diversified divisions not only protected against swings in any one industry, but it also provided multiple investment opportunities. Entering 2008, Gore was investing in a large number of areas, with the heaviest area of investment in the Medical Products Division. This was a conscious choice, as these opportunities were judged to be the largest intersection between Gore's unique capabilities and some very large, attractive market needs. As Brad Jones, an enterprise leader, said, "All opportunities aren't created equal, and there's an awful lot of opportunity that's screaming for resources in the medical environment." At the same time, the leadership at Gore scrutinized large investments so that those in what Brad Jones referred to as "big burn" projects were not made unless there was a reasonable expectation of a payoff.

Developing Quality Products by Creating and Protecting Core Technology

The competitive objective of Gore was to use core technology derived from PTFE and ePTFE to create highly differentiated and unique products. In every product line, the goal was not to produce the lowest-cost goods but rather to create the highest-quality goods that met and exceeded the needs of customers. Of course, Gore worked hard to maintain competitive pricing, but the source of competitive advantage was clearly quality and differentiation. Gore was a company built on technological innovations.

Leaders at Gore often referred to a three-legged stool to explain how they integrated operations. As shown in Exhibit 2, the three legs of the stool were technology, manufacturing, and sales. For each product, the legs of the stool were tied together by a product specialist. For instance, a product specialist might coordinate efforts to

Exhibit 2   Coordinating Technology, Manufacturing, and Sales at Gore

design, make, and sell a vascular graft. Another product specialist would coordinate efforts related to the creation and marketing of fabric for use in winter parkas. Support functions such as human resources, IT, and finance also helped tie together various aspects of technology, manufacturing, and sales.

Gore's Fabrics Division practiced cooperative marketing with the users of its fabrics. In most cases, Gore did not make the finished goods from its fabrics; rather, it supplied the fabrics to manufacturers such as North Face, Marmot, L. L. Bean, Salomon, Adidas, and Puma. On each garment was a tag indicating that it was made using GORE-TEX fabric. According to a former president of Cotton Inc., Gore was a leader in secondary branding. For example, a salesman in a golf pro shop related how he initially tried to explain that he had GORE-TEX fabric rain suits made by various manufacturers. After realizing that his customers did not care who manufactured a given suit, only that it was made from GORE-TEX fabric, he gave up and just directed customers to GORE-TEX fabric rain suits.

Because of its commitment to producing superior goods, Gore emphasized product integrity. For example, only certified and licensed manufacturers were supplied with Gore's fabrics. Gore maintained "rain-rooms" in which to test new garment designs. Shoes with GORE-TEX fabric in them were flexed in water approximately 300,000 times to ensure that they were waterproof.

After all the preventive measures, Gore stood behind its products regardless of who the manufacturer was and even if the defect was cosmetic. Susan Bartley, a Gore manufacturing associate, recounted a recent recall:

A cosmetic flaw, not a fitness-for-use flaw, was found in finished garments, so we bought back the garments from the manufacturer, because we didn't want those garments out on the market.

Such recalls due to either cosmetic or fitness for use flaws happened infrequently. One associate estimated that the last one happened 10 years before the most recent one. Gore was, however, committed to quality of its products and stood behind them.

Gore's Fabrics Division sales and marketing associates believed that positive buyer experiences with one GORE-TEX product (for instance, a ski parka) carried over to purchases of other GORE-TEX products (gloves, pants, rain suits, boots, and jackets). Also, they believed that positive experiences with their products would be shared among customers and potential customers, leading to more sales.

The sharing and enhancing of knowledge were seen as key to the development of current and future products. Great emphasis was placed on sharing knowledge. According to Terri Kelly,

There's a real willingness and openness to share knowledge. That's something I experienced 25 years ago, and it's not changed today. This is a healthy thing. We want to make sure folks understand the need to connect more dots in the lattice.

Gore associates made a conscious effort to share technical knowledge. For example, a core leadership team consisting of eight technical associates got together every other month, reviewed one another's plans, and looked for connections among the upcoming products. According to Jack Kramer, an enterprise leader, "We put a lot of effort into trying to make sure that we connect informally and formally across a lot of boundaries." One way associates connected formally to share knowledge was through monthly technical meetings. At the monthly meetings, scientists and engineers from different divisions presented information to other associates and colleagues. Attended regularly by most technical associates in the area, these presentations were often described as "passionate" and "exciting."

Even though Gore shared knowledge within the organization, much of its highly technical know-how had to be protected for competitive reasons. In a global environment, protection of specialized knowledge was a challenge. Some of the technology was protected by patents. In fact, some of the products were protected by an umbrella of patents. Normally, under U.S. law, patents expired 20 years from the earliest claimed filing date. Thus, the original patents had expired on GORE-TEX fabric and some other Gore products. Globally, patent procedures, protection, and enforcement varied. Both products and processes were patentable. To protect its knowledge base, Gore had sought and been granted more than 2,000 patents worldwide in all areas in which it competed, including electronics, medical devices, and polymer processing. However, patents could sometimes be difficult or expensive to enforce, especially globally. Therefore, many companies protected some of their technology internally. Such knowledge was commonly referred to as proprietary.

Within Gore, proprietary knowledge was shared on a need-to-know basis. Associates were encouraged to closely guard such information. This principle could lead to some awkward moments. Terri Kelly was visiting Shenzhen, China, and was curious about a new laminate that was being commercialized. The development engineer leader kept dodging her questions. Finally, the engineer smiled and said, "Now, Terri, do you have a need to know?" Kelly laughed and said, "You're right. I'm just being nosy."

When Kelly retold the incident, she added, "He played back exactly what he was supposed to, which is: don't share with someone, even if it's a CEO, something that they have no need to know." Kelly continued, "And everyone's—I could see the look in their eyes—thinking, 'Is he going to get fired?' He had taken a great personal risk, certainly for that local culture. We laughed, and we joked and for the next week, it became the running joke." Through stories like this the culture was shared with others in Gore.

Gore's sharing and enhancing of its technology brought recognition from many sources. From the United Kingdom, Gore received the Pollution Abatement Technology Award in 1989 and the Prince Philip Award for Polymers in the Service of Mankind in 1985. In addition, Gore received or shared in receiving the prestigious Plunkett Award from DuPont—for innovative uses of DuPont fluoropolymers—nine times between 1988 and 2006. Bill and Vieve Gore, as well as Bob Gore, received numerous honors for both their business and technical leadership.

Continuing Globalization and Deliberate Growth

From the time W. L. Gore was founded, it recognized the need for globalization. Gore established its first international venture in 1964, only six years after its founding. By 2010, it had facilities in 30 countries and manufacturing facilities in the United States, Germany, Scotland, Japan, and China (see Exhibit 3). One example of Gore's global reach was the fact that it was the dominant supplier of artificial vascular grafts to the global medical community. Gore's Fabrics Division also generated most of its sales outside the United States.

In addition to globalization, Gore had a strategy of continued growth. Growth was expected to come from two sources. One source was Gore associates' innovation. The Gore culture was designed to foster such innovation and allow ideas to be energetically pursued, developed, and evaluated. These ideas were expected to lead to new products and processes. Within Gore, this form of growth was referred to as organic. Gore encouraged both new products and extensions of existing products. To encourage innovation, all associates were allowed to ask for and receive raw material to try out their ideas. Through this process multiple products had come from unexpected areas. For example, the idea for dental floss came from the Industrial Products Division, not the Medical Products Division. Two associates who were fabricating space suits took to flossing their teeth with scraps. Thus, Gore's highly successful GLIDE dental floss was born. GORE RIDE ON bike cables came from a couple of passionate mountain bikers in the MPD. ELIXIR guitar strings also came from the MPD, specifically from an associate who was also a musician. Due to Gore's track record of developing innovative products, *Fast Company* magazine called it "pound for pound, the most innovative company in America."

A second but much less significant source of growth was external acquisitions. Gore evaluated opportunities to acquire technologies and even companies based on whether a given technology or company offered a unique capability that could

Exhibit 3 Locations of Gore's Global Facilities

W. L. Gore & Associates – Worldwide Locations

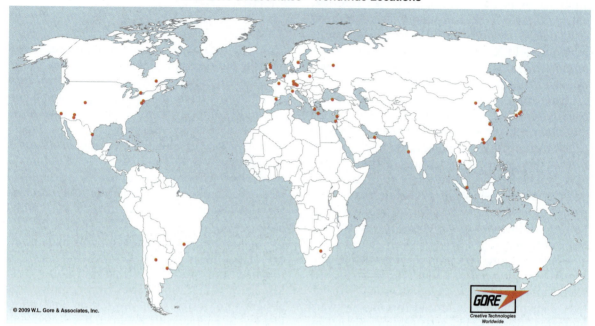

© 2009 W.L. Gore & Associates, Inc.

complement an existing, successful business. The leadership at Gore considered this strategy a way to stack the probability deck in its favor by moving into market spaces its associates already knew very well. To facilitate this growth strategy, Gore had a few associates who evaluated acquisition opportunities at the enterprise level. They did this not in isolation, but in concert with leaders within each division.

By a multibillion-dollar corporate standard, the acquisitions made by Gore were small. To date, the largest company acquired by Gore employed approximately 100 people. Another attribute of these acquisitions was that no stock swap occurred. Since Gore was a privately held company, stock swaps were not an option; acquisitions were made with cash.

A clear issue to any acquisition that Gore considered was cultural compatibility. Gore considered the leadership style in a target company. According to Brad Jones, "If you're acquiring a couple patents and maybe an inventor, that's not a big issue, although if he's a prima donna inventor, it will be an issue." When acquiring a company, Gore closely examined the culture that made the

company successful. Integrating the acquired company's culture with Gore's and making sure that Gore's culture would add value to the acquired company were just two of many cultural considerations. Gore wanted to be able to expand when necessary by buying complementary organizations and their associated technologies, but not at the expense of its culture of 50 years.

Occasionally, Gore had to divest itself of a product. One example was GLIDE dental floss. The product, developed by Gore, was well received by consumers due to its smooth texture, shred resistance, and ability to slide easily between teeth. To meet demand when the product took off, leaders were processing credit cards; human resource people and accountants were out on the manufacturing floor packaging GLIDE floss, and everybody else in the facility pitched in to make sure that the product got out the door. One associate observed that by rolling up their sleeves and pitching in, leaders built credibility with other associates.

Not long after its introduction, mint-flavored GLIDE floss became the biggest selling dental floss in the United States. That attracted the attention of the traditional dental floss manufacturers. Eventually, Procter & Gamble (P&G) and Gore reached an agreement whereby P&G bought the rights to market GLIDE floss, while Gore continued to manufacture it.

Gore made this agreement with the understanding that none of its associates would be laid off. The announcement of the agreement was made to all the GLIDE floss team members on a Thursday. It did come as a shock to some. By Monday, however, the same team was working on a transition plan. Associates who were not needed in the manufacturing or selling of GLIDE floss were absorbed into other fast-growing Gore businesses. In addition, everybody in the enterprise received a share of the profit from the P&G purchase.

LEADERSHIP AT GORE

Competitive strategy at Gore was supported by a unique approach to leadership. Many people stepped forward to take on a variety of leadership roles, but those roles were not part of a hierarchical structure and traditional authority was not vested in them. Leadership at Gore was a dynamic and fluid process in which leaders were defined by "followership." Future leaders emerged because they gained credibility with other associates. Gore referred to this process as "Natural Leadership." Associates gained credibility by demonstrating special knowledge, skill, or experience that advanced a business objective; by achieving a series of successes; and by involving others in significant decisions.

Associates stepped forward to lead when they had the expertise to do so. Within Gore this practice was referred to as "knowledge-based decision making." According to Terri Kelly, decisions were "made by the most knowledgeable person, not [necessarily] the person in charge." This form of decision making flowed naturally from the four guiding principles established by Bill Gore.

Leadership responsibilities could take many forms at Gore. In an internal memo, Bill Gore once described the following kinds of leaders and their roles:

1. *The Associate who is recognized by a team as having a special knowledge, or experience* (for example, this could be a chemist, computer expert, machine operator, salesman, engineer, lawyer). This kind of leader gives the team *guidance in a special area.*

2. *The Associate the team looks to for coordination of individual activities in order to achieve the agreed on objectives of the team.* The role of this leader is to persuade team members to *make the commitments* necessary for success (commitment seeker).

3. *The Associate who proposes necessary objectives and activities and seeks agreement and team consensus on objectives.* This leader is perceived by the team membership as having a good grasp of how the objectives of the team fit in with the broader objectives of the enterprise. This kind of leader is often also a "commitment seeking" leader.

4. *The leader who evaluates the relative contribution of team members (in consultation with other sponsors) and reports these contribution evaluations to a compensation committee.* This leader may also participate in the compensation committee on relative contribution and pay and *reports changes in compensation* to individual Associates. This leader is then also a compensation sponsor.

5. *The leader who coordinates the research, manufacturing, and marketing of one product type within a business, interacting with team leaders and individual Associates who have commitments to the product type.* These leaders are usually called *product specialists.* They are respected for their knowledge and dedication to their products.

6. *Plant leaders* who help coordinate activities of people within a plant.

7. *Business leaders* who help coordinate activities of people in a business.

8. *Functional leaders* who help coordinate activities of people in a "functional" area.

9. *Corporate leaders* who help coordinate activities of people in different businesses and functions and who try to promote communication and cooperation among all Associates.

10. *Intrapreneuring Associates who organize new teams* for new businesses, new products, new processes, new devices, new marketing efforts, or new or better methods of all kinds. These leaders invite other Associates to "sign up" for their project.

Developing a Unique and Flexible Leadership Structure

W. L. Gore had possibly the world's shortest organizational pyramid for a company of its size. Gore was a company largely without titles, hierarchical organization charts, or any other conventional structural arrangement typically employed by enterprises with billions of dollars in sales revenues and thousands of employees.

There were few positions at Gore with formal titles presented to the public. Due to laws of incorporation, the company had a president, Terri Kelly, who also functioned as CEO. Kelly was one of four members of the cross-functional Enterprise Leadership Team, which was responsible for the overall health and growth of the company.

The real key to the egalitarian culture of Gore was the use of a unique lattice rather than a hierarchical structure (see Exhibit 4). The features of Gore's lattice structure included the following:

1. Direct lines of communication—person to person—with no intermediary.
2. No fixed or assigned authority.
3. Sponsors, not bosses.

4. Natural leadership as evidenced by the willingness of others to follow.
5. Objectives set by those who must "make them happen."
6. Tasks and functions organized through commitments.

The lattice structure, as described by the people at Gore, was complex and depended on interpersonal interactions, self-commitment to group-known responsibilities, natural leadership, and group-imposed discipline. Bill Gore once said, "Every successful organization has an underground lattice. It's where the news spreads like lightning, where people can go around the organization to get things done."

One potential disadvantage of such a lattice structure could be a lack of quick response times and decisive action. Gore associates said adamantly that this was not the case, and they distinguished between two types of decisions. First, for time-critical decisions, they maintained that the lattice structure was faster in response than traditional structures because interaction was not hampered by bureaucracy. The leader who had responsibility assembled a knowledge-based team to examine and resolve the issue.

Exhibit 4   Gore's Lattice Structure

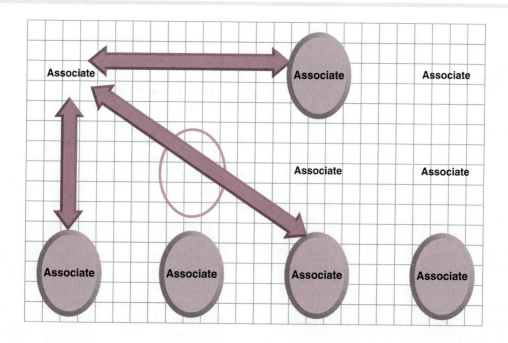

The team members could be recruited by the leader from any area of the company if their expertise was needed. Once the issue was resolved, the team ceased to exist and its members returned to their respective areas. Associate Bob Winterling asserted, "We have no trouble making crisis decisions, and we do it very swiftly and very quickly."

The other response was for critical issues that would have a significant impact on the enterprise's long-term operations. Associates admitted that such decisions could sometimes take a little longer than they would like. Chrissy Lyness, another financial associate, stated:

> We get the buy-in up front instead of creating and implementing the solution and putting something out there that doesn't work for everybody. That can be frustrating to new associates, because they're used to a few people putting their heads together, saying, "This is what we're going to do. This is a solution." That's not the way it works at Gore.
>
> Here, you spend a lot of time at the beginning of the decision-making process gaining feedback, so that when you come out of that process, you have something that's going to work, and the implementation is actually pretty easy.

The associates at Gore believed that time spent in the beginning, tapping into the best ideas and gaining consensus, paid off in the implementation. They further believed that authoritarian decision-making could save time initially but that the quality of the decision would not be as good as one made by consensus. In addition, they believed that authoritarian decisions would take longer to implement than those made by consensus.

Gore's egalitarian culture was supported also informally. For example, all associates were referred to and addressed by their first names. This was as true for the president as for any other associate.

Gore's leaders believed that the company's unique organization structure and culture were significant contributors to associate satisfaction and retention. *Fortune* magazine reported an employee turnover rate of 5 percent for Gore. In addition, it reported 19,108 applicants for 276 new jobs in 2008. In other words, it was harder to get a job at Gore than to get accepted at an elite university.

GLOBAL HUMAN RESOURCE PRACTICES

Globally, Gore's competitive strategy of using cutting-edge technology, empowered teams, and collaborative leadership to create high-quality goods was supported by a number of innovative human resources (HR) practices. Many HR initiatives were designed to support the concept that all associates were stakeholders in the enterprise and had a shared responsibility for its success. Parking lots had no reserved parking spaces for leaders. Dining areas—only one in each plant—were set up as focal points for associate interaction. As an associate in Arizona explained, "The design is no accident. The lunchroom in Flagstaff has a fireplace in the middle. We want people to like to be here." The location of a plant was also no accident. Sites were selected on the basis of transportation access, nearby universities, beautiful surroundings, and climate appeal. To preserve the natural beauty of the site on which a production facility was built in 1982, Vieve Gore insisted that the large trees be preserved, much to the dismay of the construction crews. The Arizona associate explained the company's emphasis on selecting attractive plant sites, stating, "Expanding is not costly in the long run. Losses are what you make happen by stymieing people and putting them into a box."

Getting the Right People on Board

Gore received numerous applicants for every position. Applicants were first screened by personnel specialists. Each candidate who passed the initial screening was interviewed by a group of associates from the team in which the person would work. Finally, personnel specialists contacted multiple references before issuing a job offer. Recruitment was described by Donna Frey, leader of Gore's global human resources function and one of four members of the Enterprise Leadership Team (ELT), as a two-way process. She explained:

> Our recruiting process is very much about us getting to know the applicants and them getting to know us. We are very open and honest about who we are, the kind of organization we have, the kind

of commitments we want and whether or not we think that the applicant's values are aligned with ours. Applicants talk to a number of people that they'll be working directly with if hired. We work very hard in the recruiting process to really build a relationship, get to know people and make sure that we're bringing people in who are going to fit this enterprise.

Whenever someone was hired at Gore, an experienced associate made a commitment to be the applicant's sponsor. The sponsor's role was to take a personal interest in the new associate's contributions, interests, and goals, acting as both a coach and an advocate. The sponsor tracked the new associate's progress, offered help and encouragement, pointed out weaknesses and suggested ways to correct them, and concentrated on how the associate could better make use of his or her strengths. Sponsoring was not a short-term commitment. New hires were likely to have a sponsor in their immediate work area. As associates changed or grew in their commitments, they normally changed sponsors or, in some cases, added a second sponsor. For instance, an associate who moved to a new job in another area of the company could gain a sponsor there and then decide whether to keep his or her former sponsor. Because sponsorship was built on the personal relationship between two people, the relationship most often continued even if the official sponsorship role did not.

New associates were expected to focus on building relationships during the first three to six months of their careers. Donna Frey described the first months for a new associate at Gore as follows:

When new associates join the enterprise, they participate in an orientation program. Then, each new associate works with a starting sponsor to get acclimated and begin building relationships within Gore. The starting sponsor provides the new hire with a list of key associates he/she should meet with during the next few months.

We encourage the new hire to meet with these associates one-on-one. It's not a phone conversation, but a chance to sit down with them face-to-face and get to know them.

This process helps demonstrate the importance of relationships. When you're hiring really good people, they want to have quick wins and make contributions, and building relationships

without a clear goal can be difficult. Often, new associates will say, "I don't feel like I'm contributing. I've spent three months just getting to know people." However, after a year they begin to realize how important this process was.

To ensure that new associates were not overwhelmed by what was probably their first experience in a nonhierarchical organization, Gore developed a two-day orientation program it called Building on the Best. New associates were brought together with other new associates after two or three months to participate in the program, which addressed who Bill Gore was, what his key concepts were, and how the enterprise worked. The program included group activities and interactive presentations given by leaders and other longtime associates.

Helping Associates Build and Maintain Relationships

W. L. Gore recognized the need to strike up initial relationships, continuously develop new ones, and cement ongoing ones. One way this was fostered was through the company's digital voice exchange, called Gorecom. According to Terri Kelly, "Gorecom is the preferred media if you want a quick response." The company wanted to foster an oral culture because it encouraged direct communication.

To further foster the oral culture, team members and leaders were expected to meet face-to-face regularly. For team members and especially leaders, this could mean lots of travel. As one technical associate joked, "Probably, in the last 12 years, I spent 3 years traveling internationally, a couple weeks at a time."

Another way that Gore facilitated the development of teams and individuals was through training. An associate in Newark noted that Gore "works with associates who want to develop themselves and their talents." Associates were offered a variety of in-house training opportunities, not only in technical and engineering areas but also in leadership development. In addition, the company had established cooperative education programs with universities and other outside providers.

In many ways, Gore could feel like an extended family for its associates and the communities in which they lived. Based on their own interests and initiatives, associates gave back to their communities through schools, sports clubs, universities, and other local organizations. Recently, Gore had encouraged its U.S. associates' community outreach activities by providing up to eight hours of paid time off for such efforts. Through this program, associates worked nearly 7,800 hours at nonprofit organizations in a recent fiscal year. In reality, Gore associates volunteered much more of their personal time than eight hours. The associates individually or in teams decided how and where to commit their volunteer time.

Rewarding Associates for Contributions

Compensation at Gore had both short- and long-term equity sharing components. The company's compensation goal was to ensure internal fairness and external competitiveness. To ensure fairness, associates were asked to rank their team members each year in order of contribution to the enterprise. In addition, team members were asked to comment on their rationale behind the ranking, as well as on particular strengths or potential areas of improvement for the associates. To ensure competitiveness, each year Gore benchmarked its associates' pay against a variety of functions and roles with their peers at other companies.

Gore also used profit sharing as a form of short-term compensation. Profits remaining after business requirements were met were distributed among associates as profit sharing. Profit shares were distributed when established financial goals were reached. Every month, the business results were reviewed with associates, who knew whether they were on track to meet forecasts. The first profit sharing occurred in 1960, only two years after the founding of the company.

Beyond short-term equity sharing, Gore had an associates' stock ownership program (ASOP). Each year, Gore contributed up to 12 percent of pay to an account that purchased Gore stock for associates with more than one year of service. Associates had ownership of the account after three years of service, when they became 100 percent vested. Gore also had a 401(k) plan, which provided a contribution of up to 3 percent of pay

to each associate's personal investment accounts. Associates were eligible for the 401(k) after one month of service and were 100 percent vested immediately.

A particular area where Gore's practices differed from traditional practices at other organizations was in how the majority of the sales force was compensated. Salespeople did not work on commission but were paid with a salary, with stock through the company's ASOP, and with profit sharing with all the other associates.[4] When a sales associate was asked to explain this practice, he responded as follows:

> The people who are just concerned with making their sales numbers in other companies usually struggle when they come to Gore. We encourage folks to help others. For example, when we hire new sales associates, we ask experienced sales associates to take some time to help get them acclimated to Gore and how we do things. In other companies where I've worked, that would have been seen as something that would detract from your potential to make your number, so you probably wouldn't be asked to do such a thing.

In other words, the company saw individual sales commissions as detracting from mentoring and sharing what was at the core of the Gore culture.

The entire package of compensation extended beyond direct monetary payments. As with most companies, associates received a range of benefits, such as medical and dental insurance. Another benefit extended to associates was onsite child care. In addition, in *Fortune* magazine's 2008 story that accompanied its "100 Best Companies to Work For" list, Gore's on-site fitness centers were listed as benefits. Gore did have such benefits, but they were not driven from the top down. The company supported multiple wellness programs, but there was not one enterprise-wide program. In keeping with its principles and philosophy, Gore looked for an associate or a group of associates to initiate a program. For example, in the Fabrics Division an associate who was a committed runner might champion a group at lunchtime. Gore would then support such activities with fitness centers, softball fields, volleyball courts, and running trails. Pockets of associates all over Gore pursued these and other wellness activities.

GORE RIDE ON BIKE CABLES: AN EXAMPLE OF STRATEGY, LEADERSHIP, AND HR IN ACTION

A good example of strategy, leadership, and effective talent deployment was the development of GORE RIDE ON bike cables. Initially, the cables were derailleur and brake cables for trail bikes. They were developed by some trail bike enthusiasts at Gore's Medical Product Division in Flagstaff, Arizona, in the 1990s. When the trail bike market declined, the product was withdrawn from the market. In 2006, a group of young engineers went to Jack Kramer, a technical leader at Gore, and said that they wanted to learn what it took to develop a new product by reviving the cables. His response was, "You need someone who has some experience before you go off and try to do that."

One of the young engineers approached Lois Mabon, a product specialist who had about 16 years of experience at Gore and worked in the same facility, and asked her to be the group's coach. Mabon went back to Kramer and talked to him. He was still not sold on the idea, but he allowed Mabon to find out what had happened to the bike cables and explore with the group what it would take to bring a new product to market. Within Gore, associates were encourage to set aside some "dabble time," in which they had the freedom to develop new products and evaluate their viability. After some exploration of what happened to the cables, Mabon led a group that made a presentation to Kramer and some others in the company, and even though they still were not sure, they said, "All right, keep working on it."

After about 9 or 10 months of exploring the possibility, a team of excited and passionate associates developed a set of GORE RIDE ON products. In their exploration, the team learned that the road bike market was larger than the trail bike market and that there might potentially be a product for the racing market.

The team prepared a presentation, referred to within Gore as a "real win-worth" one, for the Industrial Products Division (IPD) leadership team. "Real win-worth" was a rigorous metric that Gore used to help hone the most promising new opportunities. The three issues that had to be addressed in "real win-worth" were: (1) Is the idea real? (2) Can Gore win in the market? and (3) Is it worth pursuing? After listening to and questioning the presenters of the GORE RIDE ON idea, the IPD leadership team responded, "You know what? You do have some really good ideas. Let's do a market study on it. Let's see if the market is interested."

Some samples of the new product were made and taken to 200 top bike stores across the United States. They were handed out to the store owners, and in turn, the store owners were asked to fill out a survey. The survey focused on three questions: (1) Is this a product you would buy? (2) Is it a product you would recommend to your customers? (2) How would you compare this to the other products out in the industry?

An analysis of the surveys showed that 65 to 75 percent of all respondents would either definitely buy the product or were interested in it. Based on these results, the team concluded that people would really want to buy the product.

So with that data in hand, another presentation was made to the IPD leadership team in August 2006. The response was "Okay, go launch it." The product team had 12 months to improve the mountain bike cables, develop the new road bike cables, redesign the packaging, redesign the logo, set up production, and do everything else that was associated with a new product introduction.

Every Gore division was involved in producing the cables. The product was overseen by a team in the Industrial Products Division. The GORE BIKE WEAR products team in the Fabrics Division served as the sales team. The Medical Products Division made a component of the bike cables, and the Electronics Products Division coated the cables.

In September 2007, the product was officially launched at two bike shows. The first one was Euro-Bike on Labor Day, and the other was the Interbike show held in Las Vegas at the end of the month. The top 100 GORE BIKE WEAR product customers and shops were invited to these shows.

In fewer than three months Gore had sold approximately 8,000 pairs of cables. In addition, Gore had teamed with one of the top shifter manufacturers to co-market their products. The shift manufacturer used the Gore cables in its best-selling shifter line, introduced in November 2007.

FACING THE FUTURE TOGETHER

Associates at Gore believed that their unique organizational culture would allow the company to continue maximizing individual potential while cultivating an environment where creativity could flourish. The unique culture resulted from an unwavering commitment to the use of cutting-edge technology for developing high-quality products. This strategy was carried out through a unique approach to leadership and human resource management. The record of success was demonstrated not only by high financial profitability but also by the creation of a highly desirable workplace. Nevertheless, past success did not ensure future success. Brad Jones of Gore's Enterprise Leadership Team said:

Twenty or thirty years ago, markets in different parts of the world were still somewhat distinct and isolated from one another. At that time, we could have pretty much the entire global business team for a particular market niche located in a building. Today, as our markets become more global in nature, we are increasingly seeing the need to support our customers with global virtual teams. How do our paradigms and practices have to change to accommodate those changing realities? Those are active discussions that apply across these many different businesses.

The answer to how Gore would evolve to meet these challenges was not something that would be decided by an isolated CEO or an elite group of executives. Critical decisions, those below the waterline, had never been made that way at Gore, and there was no expectation that this would change.

ENDNOTES

[1] Many sources were helpful in providing material for this case, most particularly associates at Gore who generously shared their time and viewpoints about the company to help ensure that the case accurately reflected the company's practices and culture. They provided many resources, including internal documents and stories of their personal experiences.

[2] Throughout this case the word *associate* is used because Gore always uses the word *associate* instead of *employee*. In fact, the casewriters were told that the term *associates* evolved early in the company's history because it expressed the belief that everyone had a stake in the success of the enterprise.

[3] Information posted at www.gore.com, accessed November 1, 2010.

[4] Gore's ASOP was similar legally to an employee stock ownership plan (ESOP). Again, Gore simply had never allowed the word *employee* in any of its documentation.

Rhino Capture in Kruger National Park

A. J. Strickland
The University of Alabama

William E. Mixon
The University of Alabama
MBA Candidate

Dr. Markus Hofmeyr, head of Veterinary Wildlife Services for South African National Parks (SANParks), returned from another rhino capture with his team. They had captured their 252nd rhino for the year before the rainy season set in, with heat and rain making it almost impossible to continue the capture program. As Hofmeyr and his team were winding down another successful year, given that each rhino was worth between $30,000 and $35,000,[1] he began to reflect on next year's game capture. Hofmeyr faced the daunting question of how to continue to supplement the funding for SANParks' Park Development Fund. Over the years, the budget for his unit had been reduced, and pressure for self-funding of SANParks was increasing.

Some of the funding for SANParks' operations had long been provided by the South African national government in the form of an annual grant. That began to change in 2010, however, when a budget shortfall forced the government to initiate the removal of the grant over three years. The South African government shifted its strategy toward building a new South Africa, focused on providing additional funds for education, job creation through infrastructure expansions, better health care for all South Africans, and economic prosperity. Funding cuts outside of these priority areas threatened the ability of SANParks' Veterinary Wildlife Services to continue delivering normal veterinary and operational services—services that were beneficial to all SANParks wildlife and the habitat in which the wildlife had roamed for centuries. SANParks' budget allocation is shown in Exhibit 1.

KRUGER NATIONAL PARK

Kruger National Park was established in South Africa in 1898 to protect the nation's fast-dwindling wildlife areas. By the turn of that century, it was estimated that white rhinos were extinct in Kruger. The first translocation of white rhinos to Kruger National Park occurred in 1961, and a total of 345 white rhinos had been relocated from the parks in Kwa Zulu Natal by the mid-1970s. In 2007, an assessment by the African Rhino Specialist Group estimated that 15,000 white rhinos and 1,500 black rhinos existed in South Africa. As of 2009, research indicated that 10,000 white rhinos and 500 black rhinos existed within Kruger National Park, making it home to the largest rhino population in the world. Population estimates for rhinos in South Africa are shown in Exhibit 2.

Kruger National Park covered 7,722 square miles (20,000 square kilometers) of conservation area, with eight gates that controlled the flow of

Exhibit 1 **SANParks Budget Allocation (in U.S. dollars)**

Kruger National Park Budget	$4,951,900
Poaching	$ 275,100
Infrastructure	$ 275,100

unauthorized traffic into the park. Since its establishment, it had become known for its unrivaled wildlife diversity and easy viewing and for its world leadership in advanced environmental management techniques, research, and policies. Many viewed Kruger as the best national park in all of Africa in all aspects—management, infrastructure, and, of course, biodiversity. The flagship of South Africa's 22 national parks, Kruger held a variety of species: 336 trees, 49 fish, 34 amphibians, 114 reptiles, 507 birds, and 147 mammals. Over time, the park had developed into a tourist attraction because of the wildlife and the beautiful scenery, which was representative of South Africa's Lowveld region. (The Lowveld consisted of areas around the eastern part of the country where the altitude was about 1,000 feet.)

Tourist operations at Kruger were quite large, with the park offering 21 rest camps, 7 private lodge concessions, and 11 private safari lodges. Lodges that previously had been private were operated in partnership between communities and private companies, which provided concessions for parcels of land. The concessions were placed on tender, and areas were allocated for 25- to 30-year leases, during which operational activities linked with tourism were allowed. At the end of the period, the fixed assets became the property of SANParks, which could decide to extend the lease or retender the concession. An integral part of Kruger National Park's conservation effort was game capture. Traditionally, capturing game allowed Kruger to reintroduce certain species to previously uninhabited areas of the park, as well as to introduce rhino to the other national parks in South Africa and neighboring countries.

Game capture also enabled the park to better manage rare species by placing them in breeding enclosures. In some instances, game capture was used to reduce populations where that goal was impeded by natural regulatory mechanisms.

Exhibit 2   Rhino Population in South Africa

	2007	2010
White rhinos	15,000	17,500
Black rhinos	1,500	4,200

Traditional game capture evolved into an income-generating operation as the demand for rhinos increased.

INCOME GENERATION FROM GAME CAPTURE

The sale of wildlife for income generation was accepted and supported by South Africa's National Environmental Management Act (2004). SANParks maximized income from wildlife sales by concentrating on selling high-value species. The two species sold without clearly required ecological reasons for their sale were white rhinos from Kruger National Park and disease-free buffalos from other parks. The only condition required when an animal was sold was that its removal could not negatively impact the populations from which it came. In 2009, 500 rhinos were sold in South Africa. Kruger National Park claimed 252 of these transactions; the others were sold from provincial parks and the private sector. A flow chart of sales transactions is shown in Exhibit 3. The average selling price for a white rhino was $30,300. Many wildlife biologists and other experts feared that these rhinos would eventually fall into the hands of private game hunters. Rhino hunting and rhino breeding for future sales or hunting were driving up the price for a rhino. SANParks accepted hunting as a legal form of wildlife utilization but did not support unethical put-and-take hunting practices because it was very difficult to determine what happened to a rhino after leaving SANParks. SANParks was not responsible for enforcing hunting regulations on wildlife; instead, this responsibility was passed on to each respective South African province. However, many provinces were understaffed, which weakened the regulation of hunting activities.

The most common method for selling rhinos outside Kruger National Park was through provincial and private-sector auctions. In 2009, 45 auctions accounted for most rhino sales outside SANParks. During that year, 252 rhinos on a direct tender were captured in the bush and sold at three auctions held by SANParks. The revenue generated from rhino sales in 2009 totaled $7,033,400. These revenue sales supplemented the conservation budget for SANParks' Park

Exhibit 3   Flow Chart of Sales Transactions

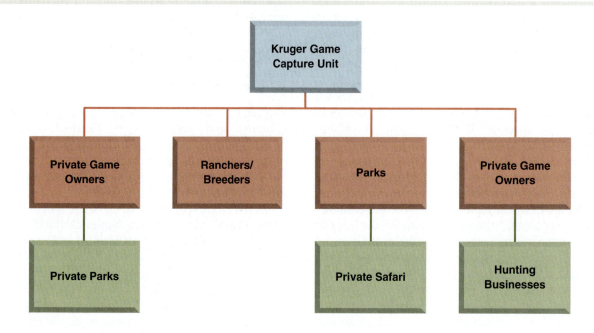

Development Fund. The buyers of the live rhinos were dealers who specialized in wild game or private owners who bought directly from SANParks. Rhinos were typically sold to a private game reserve for either tourist viewing or hunting. Rhinos were also sold or donated by SANParks to neighboring countries. Rhinos purchased in the private sector were sometimes sold internationally to zoos or to buyers who dealt in wild game.

Typically, white rhinos were sold more often than black rhinos, since black rhinos were rarer and much more aggressive. SANParks had sold only two black rhino bulls; the other black rhinos moved from Kruger were donated as part of conservation efforts to reestablish them in countries where they had gone extinct. The private sector bought black rhinos from Kwa Zulu Natal Wildlife, where the remaining black rhinos survived with white rhinos at the turn of the twentieth century. Kwa Zulu Natal moved from completely selling black rhinos to retaining full ownership of the adults and partial ownership of the offspring. Offspring were placed into a custodianship program that split the rights between two or more parties. North West Province sold black rhinos, as did the private sector. Compared with white rhi-

nos, black rhinos were more difficult to introduce and had a higher intraspecies mortality rate from fighting. The tendency to fight made black rhinos a riskier investment than white rhinos, which bred and coexisted much better than black rhinos. The majority of white rhinos were purchased in cow/calf combinations, which were not hunted. White rhino bulls were much more likely than white rhino cows to be purchased for hunting. However, most provinces had regulations that limited the number of rhinos eligible to be hunted. Before a rhino was killed, it had to have lived on the current property for more than two years; however, this regulation was very difficult to enforce. Park Services was a critical component of conservation for rhinos and other animals within the park.

PARK SERVICES

Veterinary Wildlife Services (VWS) offered a variety of operational and veterinary services for Kruger National Park. Veterinarian operations were critical to the conservation of wildlife within and outside the park. The service's operations included wildlife capture, holding, and translocation; park development; species conservation management; wildlife sales; animal exchanges and contractual commitments; regional cooperation; and research. VWS's aims and objectives and responsibilities are shown in Exhibit 4. Game capture operations began in the 1980s for Kruger National Park; Kruger had also operated game capture in other parks. In the 1990s, a second unit was established for operations outside Kruger. Both units were combined to form VWS in 2002, ensuring that the service was serving SANParks' objectives and not just those of Kruger. Kruger aimed for VWS to "provide ethical and professional services relating to capture, holding, translocation and research pertaining to wildlife."[2] Some of the values and functions associated with VWS are shown in Exhibit 5.

SANPARKS' GAME CAPTURE UNIT

SANParks' game capture unit had branch offices in three locations in South Africa: Kruger, Kimberley, and Port Elizabeth. The capture, translocation and reestablishment functions of SANParks' Veterinary Wildlife Services are shown in Exhibit 6.

Population growth, sex and age structure, spatial use, natural dispersal, resource distribution, and population dynamics were considered when making the decision to sell an animal to a private buyer. According to SANParks' chief executive officer, Dr. David Mabunda, "SANParks, by selling or donating rhino, is assisting in the process of recolonization of the range in the country and outside. It should be noted that it would be foolhardy if South Africa were to have its only rhino population residing in the Kruger, because we run the danger of losing them should there be a major outbreak of disease or rampant poaching. We would be sitting ducks." Bovine tuberculosis and anthrax were two diseases being monitored by VWS in efforts to better understand how to contain them, which in turn would lead to better decisions about disease management where required. Intervention was not always needed in wildlife populations, but an understanding of how a disease influenced population dynamics was. VWS disease management services are shown in Exhibit 7. In addition to these issues, SANParks concerned itself with Kru-

ger National Park's capability to assess and evaluate financial implications and the risks imposed to its white rhino population by intense localized removals and emerging diseases.[3]

CAPTURING A RHINO

The rhino capture process involved the use of state-of-the-art equipment accompanied by a team of experts. A game capture team included a helicopter pilot, a veterinarian, an operational coordinator, a veterinary technician, five capture staff personnel, and two drivers for the translocation and crane trucks. Selected operating expenses of a rhino capture are shown in Exhibit 8.

Once a rhino was located, the capture process consisted of darting it with a drug combination from a helicopter. The fast-acting drug combination made the whole capture process less dangerous to the capture unit by rendering the rhino unconscious for evaluation before relocation. Once the rhino was unconscious, a team from the game capture unit moved in to examine it. The game capture unit conducted a medical examination of the rhino by taking blood samples to test for any signs of disease. At this point in the game capture process, three radio-frequency identification (RFID) microchips were tagged on the rhino for identification purposes. Inserting an RFID microchip involved drilling into the horn, which is made of keratin, a material similar to that which human hair and fingernails are composed of. Photos of the game capture process are shown in Exhibit 9.

Park officials used tagging as a method to better understand the rhinos' movement within their landscape. South African law mandated the tagging of any rhino darted as well. Park services were also looking at ways to place tracking devices on rhinos to increase the capability of understanding rhino movements within their landscape. Prevention was the main emphasis of the rhino poaching counteroffensive in Kruger. It was thought that these potential tracking devices would help deter poaching, but the main deterrent was gaining information from informants on possible plans for rhino poaching.

After the evaluation and tagging process, a partial antidote was administered to partially wake up the rhino but keep it in a semi-anesthetized state. Partial antidotes were necessary to protect

Exhibit 4   **Aims, Objectives, and Responsibilities of SANParks' Veterinary Wildlife Services**

The SANParks Strategic Organizational Objectives Framework

Prioritization of services according to resources, ethical and legal constraints

Optimal utilization of resources

Development and training of the wildlife profession

Recognition that SANParks concerns itself with populations rather than individuals

The leveraging of information and skills developed in SANParks to the benefit of the SADC region

The recognition of the importance of the wildlife and ecological socio-interfaces

Coordination of research on wildlife diseases and their impact on human livelihoods, wildlife itself, and livestock

Implementation of wildlife capture and translocation programs

Reintroducing populations into national parks

Enhancing the conservation status of rare and threatened species

Controlling over-abundant wildlife populations to avert the threats of habitat degradation and loss of biodiversity

Generating revenue for SANParks through wildlife sales

Enhancing breeding projects involving valuable and rare species

Building capacity in the veterinary and wildlife capture fields, particularly in persons from historically disadvantaged population groups

Exhibit 5   Veterinary Wildlife Services' Values and Functions

Veterinary Wildlife Values

VWS is a service delivery department for SANParks, providing specialist veterinary and wildlife handling and translocation support.

The SANParks strategic organizational objectives framework of bio-diversity, balancing, people and enabling systems will guide these services.

The resource, ethical, and legal constraints as well as other drivers will make it necessary to prioritize the services that can be delivered. (Guided by the Wildlife Management Commitee recommendations)

Optimal utilitization of resources.

The leveraging of information and skills developed in SANParks to the benefit of the SADEC region, particularly in SANParks TFC involment.

Development and training of the wildlife profession.

The recognition of the importance of wildlife and ecological and diagnostic test development.

Veterinary Wildlife Functions

Service to scientific services and park management with regard to implementing veterinary aspects of removals and introductions into our parks, collar fitting, sample taking and any other activities that require handling of wildlife.

Disease monitoring, management and surveillance (including sample taking, storing and distribution aid research).

Development of current veterinary aspects of capture, translocation and animal husbandry techniques.

Veterinary support to special species management related to approved plans (e.g., predator management plans).

Conservation medicine (implementing and integrating disease and ecological principles in our function).

Veterinary research relevant to the service delivery component of VWS.

Liaison and education at the appropriate national and international level.

Exhibit 6   **The Capture, Translocation and Reestablishment Functions of SANParks' Veterinary Wildlife Services**

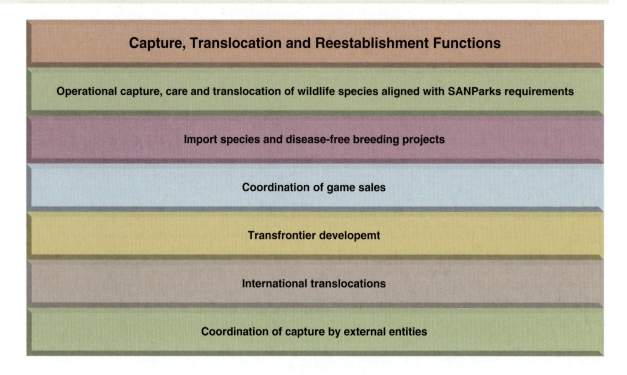

Capture, Translocation and Reestablishment Functions

Operational capture, care and translocation of wildlife species aligned with SANParks requirements

Import species and disease-free breeding projects

Coordination of game sales

Transfrontier developemt

International translocations

Coordination of capture by external entities

Exhibit 7   **Veterinary Wildlife Service's Disease Management Services**

Disease Management Services

BTB monitoring in Buffalo and Lion within Kruger

Monitoring in all parks when opportunities arise

Sarcoid research in Mountain Zebra in Bontebok NP

Disease prevention principles applied to animal movements and quarantine facilities both in Kruger and Kimberely

Exhibit 8   Selected Operating Expenses of Rhino Capture

Game Capture Operating Expenses	Cost per Rhino	Cost per Hour	Cost per Day	Cost per Year	Unit Cost
Helicopter	N/A	$800	N/A	N/A	N/A
Transportation of rhino	$300	N/A	N/A	$11,000	N/A
Truck	N/A	N/A	$ 300	N/A	N/A
Boom	N/A	N/A	$ 300	N/A	N/A
Capture team	N/A	$200	$1,400	N/A	N/A
RFID microchip	$ 50	N/A	N/A	N/A	$17

the game capture team while walking the rhino into the transportation crate. After the rhino was successfully loaded into a transportation crate, a boom truck lifted the crate onto the translocation truck. A boom truck was needed since an average rhino weighed 3,300 pounds (1,500 kilograms). Typically, the average distance traveled by a rhino captured from Kruger National Park was 50 miles (80 kilometers), at a cost of $300 per rhino per 16 miles. The next translocation process was maintenance in holding facilities (see Exhibit 10). Rhinos were placed in *bomas* (holding pens). *Bomas* allowed a rhino to become accustomed to a new habitat by slowly facilitating a passive release. Once released, the rhino was typically still confined to a larger pen or fenced-in area, depending on the buyer's intentions. It was estimated that 50 percent of the bulls transferred to private hunting companies were killed within two years, at a price of $2,800 per inch of rhino horn.

RHINO HUNTING

A typical rhino hunt could cost $82,400 per hunter. In 2009, South Africa generated an estimated $6.9 billion in revenues from tourist attractions; of that amount, hunting accounted for about 70 percent, or about $4.8 billion.[2] The cost of booking a rhino hunt varied depending on the safari company, as detailed in Exhibit 11. Most safari companies required a deposit of 50 percent of the basic cost of a safari, which was fully refundable until within three months of the contracted safari date. Accommodations varied according to packages offered by each safari company and were considered comparable to those of

any other tourist attraction in the world. Some safari companies offered photo safaris and wedding packages, in addition to hunting services, to further generate revenue for operations.

Typically, each safari company recommended certain equipment and clothing for hunters to bring along with them. This list varied by season, since temperatures could range between 30°F (low) in the winter and 90°F (high) in the wet summer season. Expenses also varied according to the specific details of a trip such as length of stay, trophy fees, number of hunters and observers, and the daily rate charged per hunter. Airfare to and from South Africa also varied depending on how far in advance travel arrangements were made and whether the flight was direct. Typically, coach seating ranged from $800 to $1,100, whereas first-class price ranges easily approached $3,000. Rifles, bows, and darting weapons were offered in some packages, but rifles could be imported into South Africa under strict guidelines and regulations. However, hunters were not allowed to import automatic or semiautomatic weapons.

Some companies charged high trophy fees and low daily rates, in contrast to low trophy fees and high daily rates. Trophy fees varied according to the specific animal wounded or killed and were typically not paid until the end of the safari. Daily rates depended on the services offered and could include or exclude a number of amenities necessary to hunt in South Africa. In general, some safari companies offered a lower daily rate as a marketing tool to increase their customer base; a large trophy fee reflected the fact that a safari company's profits depended on a successful hunt by the customer. As Zingeli Safaris stated

Exhibit 9 The Game Capture Process

The game capture unit follows the helicopter in pursuit of a rhino.

The dart shot from the helicopter is inspected by game capture personnel.

Game capture unit personnel inspect the sedated rhino.

Game capture personnel drill a hole in the rhino's horn to insert the RFID microchip.

Game capture personnel inspect the sedated rhino.

Boom trucks are needed to load the rhino.

After the antidote is given, the staff helps the rhino stand up.

in its brochure, "If you don't get your animal we lose; this is your guarantee that we will do our best to find you your dream trophy!" Customers incurred taxidermist fees, in addition to trophy fees, if they desired to have something tangible to take home.

POACHING

Demand for rhino horn in emerging markets such as Asia and India made rhino poaching highly profitable. In 2009, rhino horn was sold on the black market at $3,600 per pound, but by 2010 the price was reported to be $7,200 per pound. An average rhino horn weighed six to eight pounds. Businesses with ties to political insiders were entering the market to supply and sell rhino horn as wealth creation resulted from the growth of Asia's and India's economies.

Exhibit 10 **Dr. Markus Hofmeyr Standing above Several Bomas (Holding Pens)**

Exhibit 11 **Selected Company Safari Expenses and Trip Details**

Africa Sport Hunting Safaris
Services Offered
– First-class rifle and bow hunting
– Ethical, professional hunters
– Personal attention to all our clients
– Family and photographic tours
– Specialized, well-maintained vehicles
– Luxury accommodation
– Excellent cuisine
– Dedicated staff
Firearms and Calibers
– Rhino legal minimum .375 caliber and 3-9 × 40 variable-power telescope
– Ammunition recommended minimum of 40 full metal jacket/solids in addition to soft point bullets
Travel Information
– Valid passport required
Trophy Handling
– All animals will be skinned by our very experienced skinners, as well as marked, salted, and dried prior to being sent to a taxidermist. All documentation will be handled by Africa Sport Hunting Safaris.
Clothing and Other Requirements
– Three sets of hunting clothing: long pants (zip-offs), long-sleeve shirts, socks, and underwear
– Hunting boots/shoes—comfortable
– Casual/running shoes
– Sweater/warm jacket
– Flip flops/sweat suit

(Continued)

Exhibit 11   *(Continued)*

Africa Sport Hunting Safaris	
– Cap/wide-brimmed hat	
– Casual clothes	
– Adjust your clothing to the time of year your hunt takes place.	
– Winter May–August (35–70°F)	
– Summer September–April (50–90°F)	

Personal

– Personal medical kit

– Sunblock—minimum 30 SPF

– Mosquito repellent

– Pair of sunglasses

– Toiletries

Additional Equipment

– Small day pack

– Flashlight with spare batteries

– Binoculars

– Camera with spare film and batteries

– Pocket knife

Accommodation: Luxury Thatched Chalets with a True African Ambience

– Private rooms with ensuite bathrooms

– Running hot and cold water

– Electricity with converters

– Flush toilets

Food and Beverages

– Traditional South African cuisine. For dietary requirements such as diabetes and high cholesterol, please make arrangements on booking of the safari.

Additional Services

– Facials and full body massages

– Manicures and pedicures

– Day excursions

South African Hunting Areas Price List Limpopo Province 2010	
– White Rhino	$45,000
– White Rhino (Green-Hunt)	$13,000
Daily Rate: South Africa	
– Dangerous Game	$ 800
– Plains Game	
– 1 Hunter × 1 Professional Hunter:	$ 400
– 2 Hunters × 1 Professional Hunter:	$ 300
– All non-hunters are welcome at:	$ 200
Included in Daily Rate	
– Pick up and drop off at Polokwane International Airport	

– Hunting licenses and fees

– Transportation to and from hunting concessions

– Field preparation of trophies

– Professional hunters, trackers, skinners, and camp staff

– Fully equipped hunting vehicles

– Luxury accommodation and meals

– Drinks and beverages in moderation

– Daily laundry services

Excluded from Daily Rates

– Flights: international and domestic

– Charter flights where applicable

– All animals shot and wounded will be charged per price list

– Dipping, packing, taxidermy cost

– Non-hunting, traveling days at $150 per day

– Accommodation before and after hunt

– Any additional tours or excursions

Methods of Payment Accepted

– U.S. currency

– Traveler's checks

– Wire transfers

– Credit cards

– Personal checks with prior approval

Members Of:

– Professional Hunters Association South Africa

– Accredited Tour Guides

– Safari Club International

– North American Hunters Association

– National Rifle Association

Chattaronga Safaris	

Daily Fees Hunter

1	$400
2	$350
3	$300
4	$300
Observer	$200

Included Tariffs

– Accommodation including full board

– Liquor and beverages served in camp

– Full-time service of experienced professional hunter.

– Trained staff

– Trackers

– Skinners

(Continued)

Exhibit 11   *(Continued)*

Chattaronga Safaris

- Field preparation of trophies
- All transportation within hunting areas
- All hunting licenses
- Pickup and drop-off at international airport: Limpopo-Polokwane, Kwa-Zulu Natal-Johannesburg, Mpumalanga-Johannesburg

Excluded Tariffs

- International and domestic flights
- Traveling day (non-hunting days) at $180 per day
- Trophy fees of animal shot or wounded
- Rifle hire (firearms may be rented at $80 per day)
- Ammunition is available at cost
- Dipping, packing, taxidermy, and shipping
- Air charters and accommodation before and after safari
- Tips for staff, telephone calls, and curio purchases

Rhino Safari

7 Day 1 × 1	$60,000

Includes representative 20" fake horn (because it is not standard practice to cut off the horn of a rhino).

Dumukwa

Daily Rates

1 hunter/1 professional hunter	$ 400
2 hunters/1 professional hunter	$ 300
Non-hunters/observers	$ 200
Rhino dart	$ 8,500

5 day 1 × 1 Hunt

Included in Daily Rates

- Full accommodation, meals, and use of camp facilities
- All liquid refreshments including wine, beer, bottled water, and sodas
- Daily laundry
- Service of professional hunter with his team of skinners and trackers
- Field preparation of trophies
- Transport of raw trophies to local taxidermist for the area you in hunt in
- All transportation during the safari including from and to the airport
- 14 percent value added tax (VAT) on all packages

Excluded in Daily Rates

- Internet, faxes, and telephone calls
- Airfare
- Hotel accommodation before and after the contracted safari
- Dipping and packing or mounting of trophies
- Shipping of trophies back to your country
- Optional hire of firearms

Zingeli Safaris

Included in Daily Rates

– Full board and lodging with traditional catering

– South African wines and beer in moderation, and soft drinks

– Experienced professional hunter and trained staff

– Trackers and skinners

– Field preparation, salting and packing

– Transportation of trophies to reliable and qualified taxidermist who will follow your instructions and fulfill the necessary requirements

– Use of hunting vehicle

– Laundry services

– Transportation to the ranch and return to Johannesburg International Airport or charter plane

Excluded in Daily Rates

– Air travel before, during and after the contracted period of the safari

– Accommodation and travel charges incurred before and after the contracted period of the safari

– Trophy fees for animals taken or wounded

– Value added tax (VAT) 14 percent on daily rates

– Air charters

– Gratuities to professional hunters and staff

– Preparation, packing, documentation, and export of trophies from South Africa

The market for raw rhino horn was mainly driven by demand in China and Vietnam. Cultural beliefs, combined with increasing wealth, were creating a strong foundation for the demand of rhino horn. Asians believed that rhino horn was a very beneficial aphrodisiac, and Indians desired rhino horn daggers. These beliefs and desires were strong enough to produce enough capital to entice the illegal killing of rhinos without regard to law enforcers such as the SANParks Environmental Crimes Unit, South African Police Service, and park rangers.

Poachers were well equipped with highly sophisticated transportation such as helicopters and the latest military weaponry available in the region. They were able to strike fast within even the most protected game conservation areas. Poaching was even a problem in Kruger National Park, home to what some considered the best antipoaching unit in South Africa. In 2006, two rhinos were even poached by staff members employed by SANParks. In 2009 alone, there were about 50 rhinos poached in Kruger and 100 poached in South Africa as a whole. As of January 22, 2010, poachers had killed 14 rhinos in Kruger National Park as well.

Poachers were ruthless in the slaughtering of rhinos. They typically cut off the rhino's horns after darting it with a deadly poison (see Exhibit 12). Poachers also darted rhinos with an immobilizing antidote that sometimes left the rhino helpless in the wild to be eaten by other game. SANParks' CEO, Dr. David Mabunda, described poachers as "dangerous criminals." Their exploits were not limited to killing rhinos, but also included human trafficking, arms smuggling, prostitution, and drug trafficking.

"Poachers must beware," Mabunda said in a statement announcing a $250,000 funding boost, in addition to the $5.2 million allocated to train and prepare the SANParks Environmental Crimes Unit and South African Police Service. Fifty-seven rangers equipped with night vision goggles and high-powered motorbikes had been dispatched to guard highly poached areas of the park day and night. Said Mabunda, "This war we plan on winning." In addition to the funding boost, plans were considered to guard the porous border near Kruger National Park with military personnel. Elisabeth McLellan, a species expert with the World Wildlife Foundation (WWF), was quoted as saying, "The situation is bad for rhino worldwide, in terms of poaching." Conservationists were facing an environment that had evolved into an industry, as world trade had reached a 15-year high for illegal rhino horn trading.

Kenyan authorities at Jomo Kenyatta International Airport had seized a 662-pound load of elephant tusk and rhino horn believed to have come from South Africa. It was speculated that the load, valued at approximately $1 million, was destined for China. Industry experts suggested that the high value placed on elephant tusk and rhino horn by consumers was driving the demand for both substances.

ANIMAL SUPERMARKET

Kruger National Park was determined to win the war against poaching, but determination alone wasn't enough to protect the rhino. Primary-market transactions involved buyers that protected the rhino—such as other national parks, private game farms, game dealers, and photography safari business owners—but secondary markets from the sale of captured rhinos had also developed. Hunters had become the most numerous buyers in the secondary market, which wasn't aligned with Kruger National Park's mission. Animal rights activists dubbed the sale of animals at Kruger National Park an "animal supermarket." Many believed that the commercial trade posed a greater threat than poaching did. Many also felt it was fundamentally wrong to herd animals from a popular wildlife reserve and sell them in efforts at "conservation." Wildlife activists accused SANParks of misusing the park by serving as nothing more than a private game breeder, and experts feared that the vast majority of the rhinos sold by SANParks would fall into the hands of private hunters.

SANPARKS' JUSTIFICATION

SANParks was guided in its decision to sell wildlife by Clause 55(2)(b) of the Protected

Exhibit 12   **Rhino Left to Die after Poachers Cut Off Horn**

Areas Act No. 57 of 2003 (as amended), which stated that "SANParks may, in managing national parks, sell, exchange or donate any animal, plant, or other organism occurring in a park, or purchase, exchange or otherwise acquire any indigenous species which it may consider desirable to reintroduce into a specific park." SANParks believed that it was critical to its conservation efforts to maintain the sale of animals to private entities. For years, SANParks had sold animals to fund conservation efforts, and in many cases the park had traded animals to obtain other species. Also, SANParks screened animals and buyers to ensure that animals were released not arbitrarily, but to buyers with the proper permits and intentions. Decisions to sell or donate wildlife were scientifically determined according to population dynamics, sex and age structure, spatial use, natural dispersal, and resource distribution.

SANParks' strategy was informed by the following objectives: population control, broadening of the range for populations, spreading the risk of managing wildlife, making the populations more resilient and viable, and fund-raising for specific conservation and land-expansion programs. The responsibilities of SANParks' conservation biologists are shown in Exhibit 13. The challenge facing SANParks was how to effectively communicate that selling rhinos was for the greater good.

Exhibit 13   Responsibilities of Conservation Biologists

Identify key research themes necessary for national parks to achieve their conservation objectives.

Conduct research on key themes.

Coordinating research projects conducted by external scientific institutions in national parks.

Integrating best available biodiversity data into park management through interactions with external researchers and research institutions.

Maintaining inventories of biodiversity in national parks, including species checklists for vertebrates and higher plants and the mapping of landscape. Geology, soil and vegetation.

Identifying and averting threats to biodiversity in national parks, including overabundance of certain wildlife populations, invasive alien plant and animal species, pollutants, human development, excessive resource exploitation or other factors.

Ensuring that development within parks takes place in a manner that does not compromise biodiversity conservation.

Conservation for rare and threatened species.

Provide scientific inputs on the rehabilitation of degraded landscapes.

Providing scientific inputs on biodiversity aspects of park management plans and activities.

Building capacity in conservation biology and related sciences, particularly in persons from historically disadvantaged population groups.

ENDNOTES

[1] All monetary amounts in this case are in U.S. dollars.
[2] *Wildlife Research Magazine.*
[3] Sam Ferreira & Travis Smith Scientific Services, SANParks, Skukuza, South Africa.

Countrywide Financial Corporation and the Subprime Mortgage Debacle

Ronald W. Eastburn
Case Western Reserve University

Angelo Mozilo, founder and chairman of Countrywide Financial Corporation, was the driving force behind the company's efforts to become the largest real estate mortgage originator in the United States and, according to some, was also the driving force behind the company's eventual collapse. Mozilo and his partner, David Loeb, founded Countrywide in 1969 in New York with the strategic intent of creating a nationwide mortgage lending firm. The company opened a retail branch in California in 1974 and, by 1980, had 40 offices in eight states. Mozilo and Loeb launched a securities subsidiary in 1981 that specialized in the sale of mortgage-backed securities (MBSs).[1] The company's annual loan production exceeded $1 billion in 1985 and began to grow at dramatic annual rates on the back of the U.S. housing market bubble that began in 1994 and ended in 2006. The company's greatest number of annual loan originations had occurred by the time of David Loeb's death in 2003, with more than 2.5 million mortgage originations that year. Countrywide Financial Corporation originated more than 2.2 million loans, totaling $408 billion, in 2006. By 2007, the company had 661 branches in 48 states and, in July 2008, was acquired by Bank of America (BoA) for $4 billion in an all-stock transaction. The market value of the company had reached $24 billion in 2006 but fell rapidly in 2007 when it became evident that many of the mortgages Countrywide made during the housing boom were overly risky and likely to go into default.

Problems with Countrywide's loan portfolio and lending practices were evident to BoA management even before the acquisition was consummated, with BoA investing more than $2 billion in Countrywide in return for a 16 percent stake in the company in August 2007 to stabilize the troubled mortgage firm's balance sheet. Shortly after the acquisition, BoA management agreed to enter into an $8.7 billion settlement with a group of state attorneys general over Countrywide Financial Corporation's predatory lending practices. BoA allowed Mozilo to retire from Countrywide's management team and, in June 2009, the Securities and Exchange Commission (SEC) indicted Mozilo and two other key Countrywide executives for fraudulent misrepresentation of the credit and market risk inherent in Countrywide's loan portfolio.

Investigation of Countrywide's business practices disclosed how the real estate market supported by U.S. federal legislative and regulatory decisions fostered an environment that resulted in the collapse of Fannie Mae and Freddie Mac, major banking institutions, Wall Street investment firms, and mortgage brokerage firms. The financial crisis of 2008 had at its foundation subprime mortgages, mortgage-backed securities, and capital markets activity, and as the nation's largest mortgage lender, Countrywide was a significant contributor to the subprime mortgage debacle. As the financial and credit crisis continued to play out into 2009, BoA executives would need to ensure that lending practices at all of its subsidiaries would promote homeownership in a manner that was in the best interest of borrowers, investors in the secondary mortgage market, and the company's own long-term financial interests.

HISTORY OF MORTGAGE LENDING IN THE UNITED STATES

Before the Great Depression, home mortgage instruments in the United States were typically of short term (3–10 years) with loan-to-value (LTV) ratios of about 60 percent. Loans at the time were nonamortizing and required a balloon payment at the expiration of the term. Mortgages were available to a limited client base, with homeownership representing about 40 percent of U.S. households. Many of these short-term mortgages went into default during the Great Depression as homeowners became unable to make regular payments or find new financing to pay off balloon payments that became due.

The U.S. government intervened in the housing market in 1932 with the creation of the Federal Home Loan Bank (FHLB). The FHLB provided short-term lending to financial institutions (primarily savings and loans) to create additional funds for home mortgages. Congress passed the National Housing Act of 1934 to further promote homeownership by providing a system of insured loans that protected lenders against default by borrowers. The mortgage insurance program established by the National Housing Act and administered by the Federal Housing Administration (FHA) reimbursed lenders for any loss associated with a foreclosure up to 80 percent of the appraised value of the home. With the risk associated with default on FHA-backed mortgage loans reduced, lenders extended mortgage loan terms to as long as 20 years and LTVs of 80 percent.

In 1938, the Federal National Mortgage Association (FNMA) was established as a government corporation to facilitate a secondary market for mortgages issued under FHA program guidelines. FNMA allowed private lenders to make a greater number of FHA loans since loans could be sold in the secondary market and did not have to be held for the duration of the loan term. New loans could be generated each time the lender sold large bundles of loans to investors in the secondary market. The FNMA also purchased conventional conforming mortgages from lenders. Conventional conforming loans, unlike FHA mortgages, were neither guaranteed nor insured by the federal government. In 1968, FNMA was reconstituted as Fannie Mae and became a publicly traded government sponsored enterprise (GSE). This move allowed the financial activity of Fannie Mae to be excluded from the U.S. federal budget and transferred its portfolio of government-insured FHA mortgages to a wholly owned government corporation, the Government National Mortgage Association (Ginnie Mae). Fannie Mae's portfolio of conforming loans remained on its balance sheet.

In 1970, the Federal Home Loan Mortgage Corporation (Freddie Mac) was chartered as a GSE and operated in a manner similar to Fannie Mae (although its shares were not traded until 1989). Freddie Mac pooled conforming loans and created mortgage-backed securities (MBSs) that were sold as shares of the pooled loans to investors. The interest yield for these agency securities was between AAA corporate and U.S. Treasury obligations, reflecting the low risk of the securities. The development of MBSs vastly expanded the secondary market for mortgage loans since investors could purchase shares of a loan portfolio rather than purchase an entire portfolio of intact loans.

The value of Freddie Mac and Fannie Mae to the capital market was related to the implicit U.S. government guarantee of their debt and MBS obligations. Their federal charter required them to support the secondary market for residential mortgages, to assist mortgage funding for low- and moderate-income families, and to consider the geographic distribution of mortgage funding, including mortgage finance for underserved geographic sectors. An ancillary benefit of the MBS product required national standardization of underwriting procedures: appraisals, borrower credit histories, and guidelines for determining borrowers' financial capacity to meet debt obligations. This provided the foundation for real growth in the mortgage market. The mortgage market in the United States was also bolstered by the Veterans Administration loan program, which provided zero-down-payment and low-interest loans to veterans.

Mortgage Loan Originators

Prior to 1980, the vast majority of residential home mortgage loans were made by savings and

loans institutions (S&Ls). These institutions originated, serviced (collected payments and managed escrow accounts for insurance and property
taxes), and retained the loans in their own portfolios. S&Ls used the interest earned from their
portfolios of 30-year fixed-rate home mortgages
to pay interest to savings account holders—the
yield spread between interest earned on mortgages
and interest paid on savings allowed S&Ls to earn
consistent profits for decades. The business model
used by S&Ls collapsed when the Federal Reserve
began to raise short-term rates in the late 1970s to
combat inflation pressures, with interest paid on
savings accounts now being greater than interest
earned on the low-rate mortgages originated in
the 1960s and early 1970s. The inverted yield curve
led to the failure of S&Ls across the United States
and an ensuing government bailout under the auspices of the Resolution Trust Corporation (RTC).

The S&L crisis also led to the unbundling of
the mortgage business. Mortgage originations and
loan servicing became separate functions, which
pushed most new mortgage originations into the
secondary market as MBSs or collateralized debt
obligations (CDOs). The ability for mortgage
originators to sell newly recorded mortgages as
MBSs and keep balance sheets uncluttered with
large loan portfolios allowed the number of mortgage originators to increase from 7,000 in 1987 to
nearly 53,000 in 2006. The largest mortgage loan
originators and their relative shares in 2007 are
presented in Exhibit 1.

Expanding Home Ownership and the American Dream

Beginning in the 1970s, social activist groups
began to point to statistics that indicated lenders
and the FHA were engaged in systematic racial
discrimination against minority consumers living
in low-income neighborhoods (a practice called
"redlining"). Such activists mobilized the U.S.
Congress and the Carter administration to enact
the Community Reinvestment Act (CRA) and
the Home Mortgage Disclosure Act (HMDA) to
remedy social injustices in housing and lending.
In part, these acts required financial institutions
to provide greater support to low-income areas
and provide more detailed disclosures regarding
mortgage terms.

Lenders whose disclosures uncovered redlining of low-income neighborhoods defended their

Exhibit 1 **Originations and Market Shares for the Largest U.S. Mortgage Loan Originators, 2007 (dollar amounts in billions)**

Rank	Originator	2007 Originations (In Billions)	Market Share
1	Countrywide	$ 408	15.5%
2	CitiMortgage	272	10.3
3	Wells Fargo Mortgage	210	7.9
4	Chase Mortgage	198	7.5
5	Bank of America	190	7.2
	Others	1,278	48.6
	Total	**$2,628**	**100.0%**

Source: As estimated by Countrywide Financial Corporation in its 2007 10-K report.

practices by pointing to the added risk associated
with making loans to those with lower incomes,
unstable employment histories, high debt-to-
income levels, or inadequate funds for down payments. The Depository Institution Deregulation
and Monetary Control Act of 1980 addressed
such concerns by eliminating interest rate caps
and allowing lenders to charge higher, or subprime, rates to higher-risk borrowers. The Housing and Community Development Act of 1981
created targets for lenders serving low-income
borrowers and allowed FHA borrowers with
imperfect credit records to obtain mortgage loans
with LTVs of 90 to 95 percent. In 1995 the Clinton administration expanded high-LTV subprime
loans under the CRA to further expand homeownership for Americans who were unable to
qualify for mortgage loans using conventional
underwriting criteria.

THE RESIDENTIAL MORTGAGE MARKET IN THE UNITED STATES IN THE 2000s

The effects of the 60 years of federal legislation promoting homeownership allowed nearly
70 percent of Americans to own a home by 2004.

The value of new loan originations had increased from $733 billion in 1994 to an all-time high of $3.12 trillion in 2005, with large spikes in loan origination values occurring in 2001 and 2003 before declining in 2004. Mortgage originations had declined again in 2006 to $2.98 trillion. Exhibit 2 presents the value of total U.S. mortgage originations and the percentage of prime and subprime mortgage loan originations for 1994–2006. A graph representing the percentage of American families owning their own homes for the years 1944 through 2007 is presented in Exhibit 3.

The Subprime Mortgage Market

A subprime mortgage was generally classified as a mortgage loan to a borrower with a low credit score, with a small down payment, or a high debt-to-income ratio. In 1994, the subprime market in the United States was approximately $40 billion and represented approximately 6 percent of total mortgage loans originated. The market for subprime mortgages grew rapidly and by year-end 2005 reached 37.6 percent of total mortgage originations.

At the core of the growth of the subprime market were relaxed underwriting standards.

As the appetite for MBSs on Wall Street rose, mortgage brokers widened their sales net to include relaxed documentation requirements and impaired or limited credit histories. Many loans were provided as "stated income loans," whereby the borrower did not have to prove income (such loans became known among mortgage underwriters as "liar loans"). The most popular mortgage products with consumers tended to be adjustable-rate mortgages (ARMs), which often included introductory below-market rates. Below-market "teaser" rates allowed for a low monthly payment in the first few years of the loan and then were adjusted in line with market rates thereafter. Some real estate investors and homeowners exploited teaser rates to get into a home and flip the property for a profit before the rate was adjusted. Even if homeowners did not purchase a home with the intention of flipping the house for a profit, the rapid appreciation in home values during the early and mid-2000s allowed overleveraged homeowners to sell their homes and get out of high mortgage payments without great difficulty. However, once the housing market slowed, the excesses of the subprime mortgage market were exposed with resultant increase in delinquencies, defaults, and foreclosures. In fact, in March 2007, the Mortgage Bankers Association

Exhibit 2   **Value of U.S. Home Mortgage Originations and Percentage of Prime versus Subprime Mortgage Originations, 1994–2006 ($ billions)**

Year	Total U.S. Originations (In Billions)	Prime Mortgage Originations (Percent of Total)	Subprime Mortgage Originations (Percent of Total)
1994	$773	94.0%	6.0%
1995	639	86.9	13.1
1996	785	83.2	16.8
1997	859	78.3	21.7
1998	1,450	84.0	15.0
1999	1,310	83.2	16.8
2000	1,048	81.5	18.5
2001	2,215	87.9	12.1
2002	2,885	88.4	11.6
2003	3,945	86.5	13.5
2004	2,920	68.1	31.9
2005	3,120	62.4	37.6
2006	2,980	63.7	36.3

Source: The 2007 Mortgage Market Statistical Annual, *Inside Mortgage Finance.*

Exhibit 3   Rate of Home Ownership in the United States, 1944–2007

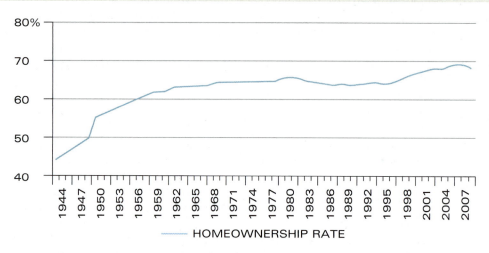

——— HOMEOWNERSHIP RATE

Source: U.S. Census data, 2007.

reported that 13 percent of subprime borrowers were delinquent on their payments by 60 days or more.

The Housing Bubble of the Mid-2000s

The expansion of homeownership increased demand for both new and existing homes and forced prices upward, creating a housing bubble that began in 1994 and peaked in 2006. In 2006, housing values had increased on average some 16 percent over the previous year. In addition to opportunities to make quick profits from buying and selling houses, rapid appreciation in home prices allowed many homeowners to refinance or take out home equity loans to make improvements to their homes, purchase automobiles, or make other general purchases.

The housing bubble burst in 2007 when the U.S. economy began to weaken, with declining demand for housing causing home prices to plummet. With appreciation in home prices coming to an end, many consumers found their properties underwater (a negative equity position caused by the mortgage balance being greater than the fair market value of the property). Homeowners who had lost jobs or income during the recession or who had seen their payments on ARMs rise were faced with foreclosure since they had no hope of

selling their home at a price great enough to pay off their mortgage balance. It was estimated that 10 to 14 percent of all single-family homes in the United States in 2007, regardless of when they were purchased, had negative equity, making one in seven single-family homes in the United States underwater.[2] Exhibit 4 presents a graph of percentage increases and decreases in home prices as measured across major U.S. cities for January 1988 through May 2008.

The U.S. Financial Crisis of 2008

With record numbers of mortgages in default, a general liquidity crisis began to unfold which led to an overall loss of confidence in the U.S. financial system. The system unraveled in 2008 when losses at Fannie Mae and Freddie Mac began to mount and American International Group (AIG) announced it was unable to back the insurance guarantees that had supported the Aaa to B bond ratings assigned to MBSs. Wall Street firms had been packaging loans for sale to investors across the world and now found themselves holding securities with little value. As financial institutions were forced to mark their assets to market value, many, including Bear Stearns, Lehman Brothers, Merrill Lynch, Washington Mutual, and Wachovia, were either forced to declare

Exhibit 4   **S&P/Case-Shiller Home Price Indexes for Major U.S Cities, January 1988–May 2008**

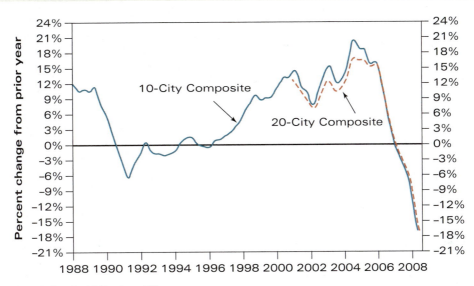

Source: Standard & Poor's and Fiserv.

bankruptcy or acquired by stronger institutions. In September 2008, the U.S. Treasury provided a bailout to AIG[3] and placed Freddie Mac and Fannie Mae into conservatorships.

COUNTRYWIDE FINANCIAL CORPORATION

Countrywide was founded in 1969 and on July 2, 2008, was sold to Bank of America for $4 billion in an all-stock transaction. Countrywide's market value in late 2006 was $24 billion, but mounting mortgage defaults and rumors of impending bankruptcy had slashed the company's market value by the time it negotiated its buyout by BoA in January 2008. Angelo Mozilo, the founder and chairman of Countrywide retired and received a substantial severance package reported at $80 million to $115 million. In June 2009, the Securities and Exchange (SEC) indicted Mozilo for fraudulent misrepresentation of credit and market risk inherent in the Countrywide mortgage portfolio. Exhibit 5 provides key milestones and events in Countrywide's corporate history.

Countrywide's Business Segments

Countrywide was a diversified financial services provider engaged in mortgage lending and other real estate finance–related businesses. At its apex in 2006, Countrywide had $2.6 billion in net earnings and $200 billion in total assets. The business was managed through five business segments: mortgage banking, banking, capital markets, insurance, and global operations.

- *Mortgage banking.* The origination, purchase, sale, and servicing of noncommercial mortgage loans nationwide.
- *Banking.* Gathered retail deposits used to invest in mortgage loans and home equity lines of credit, sourced primarily through the mortgage banking operation as well as through purchases from nonaffiliates.
- *Capital markets.* The institutional broker-dealer business which specialized in trading and underwriting mortgage-backed securities. The business unit also traded derivative products and U.S. Treasury securities, provided asset management services, and originated loans secured by commercial real estate.

Exhibit 5   Key Milestones and Events in Countrywide Financial Corporation's History

1969	Angelo Mozilo and David Loeb launch Countrywide Credit Industries in New York with the aim to one day provide home loans nationwide. Countrywide goes public in September, trading at less than $1 per share. Mozilo and Loeb relocate Countrywide to Los Angeles.
1974	Countrywide opens first retail office in Whittier, Califiornia.
1980	Countrywide has 40 retail offices across eight states.
1981	Mozilo and Loeb launch subsidiary Countrywide Securities Corporation to sell mortgage-backed securities.
1985	Countrywide's ticker symbol, CCR, opens on the New York Stock Exchange on October 7. Stock closes at $2 a share.
1984	The value of loans serviced by Countrywide hits $1 billion. The company begins using computers to originate home loans.
1986	Loan production tops $1 billion.
1987	Loan production soars to $3.1 billion. Countrywide begins servicing loans originated by mortgage lenders.
1993	Countrywide's mortgage-lending reach grows amid a housing and mortgage refinancing boom. Originations increase by 265 percent from 1992.
1996	Company launches business units focused on home equity line of credit (HELOC) and home loans to borrowers with weak credit histories (subprime).
1998	Mozilo named chief executive in February.
1999	Mozilo named chairman in March.
2000–2005	Countrywide benefits from another housing and refinancing boom coupled with historically low interest rates.
2001	Countrywide acquires Treasury Bank N.A. It goes on to become Countrywide Bank FSB.
2002	Company becomes Countrywide Financial Corporation on November 13, with new stock ticker: Countrywide.
2006	Countrywide reports fourth-quarter earnings soar 73 percent to $638.9 million on January 31, as profits climb 29 percent to $2.59 billion.
2007–Jan. 31	Countrywide's fourth-quarter profits fall 2.7 percent and revenue slips 6 percent. The lender blames falling home prices and fewer home sales for a drop in new mortgage loans.
2007–April 26	Countrywide's first-quarter profits tumble 37 percent; revenue shrinks by 15 percent. Mounting mortgage defaults force Countrywide to increase loan reserve $81 million and take a $119 million write-down for declining value of some loans on its books. Mozilo blames deteriorating credit in the subprime mortgage market.
2007–July 24	Countrywide's second-quarter profit declines by nearly a third and revenue dips 15 percent.
2007–Aug. 16	A worsening credit crisis sparked by the collapse of the subprime mortgage market and ongoing housing woes force Countrywide to draw down $11.5 billion from its credit lines.
2007–Aug. 22	Countrywide raises $2 billion by selling a 16 percent stake to Bank of America.
2007–Sept. 9	Under pressure to reduce costs, Countrywide reports it will cut as many as 12,000 jobs. Management takes steps to shift lending activity through its banking arm and stop selling subprime loans.
2007–Sept. 18	Speaking at an investor conference, Mozilo declares the company will "come out stronger in the long run, just as we have often done in the past."
2007–Oct. 23	Countrywide outlines stepped-up efforts to help borrowers in trouble avoid foreclosures.
2007–Oct. 26	Countrywide reports a third-quarter $1.2 billion loss, the first quarterly loss for the company in 25 years. Still, Mozilo says he's "bullish" about the long-term prospects of the company and says it expects to be profitable in the fourth quarter and in 2008.
2007–Nov. 20	Rumors surface that Countrywide may seek bankruptcy protection. Countrywide issues statement declaring it has ample capital and access to cash, and is well positioned to benefit from the financial turmoil rocking the mortgage sector.
2008–Jan. 11	BofA announces acquisition of Countrywide, subject to shareholder and government approvals, for $4 billion in an all stock transaction.
July 2, 2008	Countrywide officially becomes a wholly owned subsidiary of Bank of America.

Source: Countrywide Financial Corporation, SEC filings, annual reports, and press releases.

Within this segment countrywide managed the acquisition and disposition of mortgage loans on behalf of the mortgage banking segment.

- *Insurance.* The property, casualty, life, and disability insurance underwriting provider. The business unit also included reinsurance coverage to primary mortgage insurers.
- *Global operations.* Licensed proprietary technology to mortgage lenders in the United Kingdom and handled some of the company's administrative and loan servicing functions through operations in India.

Mortgage banking was Countrywide's core business, generating 48 percent of its 2006 pretax earnings. A summary of Countrywide's mortgage loan production for 2003 through 2007 is presented in Exhibit 6.

Countrywide Loan Originations and Market Share

Countrywide held the largest market share among U.S. mortgage originators in 2007, with

15.5 percent of all originations, up considerably from 2001, when Countrywide held a 6.6 percent share. As shown Exhibit 7, Countrywide originated 35,000 loans in 1990; those loans were more or less evenly split between conventional and VHA/VA loans. It was not until the 1995–1996 period that Countrywide began to underwrite home equity and subprime loans. The company's loan originations peaked in 2003, with over 2.5 million loans being originated. In 2005, approximately 11 percent of Countrywide's loan originations were subprime and Countrywide home equity line of credit (HELOC) loans reached a peak in 2006. Many of Countrywide's HELOCs were part of so-called 80/20 purchase loans that provided borrowers with 100 percent financing. Countrywide's no-down-payment loans allowed borrowers to piggyback a 20 percent LTV HELOC loan on top of a conventional nonconforming 80 percent LTV mortgage. Countrywide's originations of conventional nonconforming loans began in 2002 and closely matched the company's origination of HELOCs. A significant portion of Countrywide's mortgage loan originations

Exhibit 6   **Countrywide Financial Corporation's Loan Production by Segment and Product, 2003–2007 ($ millions)**

| | Mortgage Loan Production | | | | |
| | Years Ended December 31, | | | | |
	2007	2006	2005	2004	2003
Segment:					
Mortgage banking	$385,141	$421,084	$427,916	$317,811	$398,310
Banking operations	18,090	23,759	46,432	27,116	14,354
Capital markets—conduit acquisitions from nonaffiliates	5,003	17,658	21,028	18,079	22,200
Total residential mortgage loans	408,234	462,501	495,376	363,006	434,864
Commercial real estate	7,400	5,671	3,925	358	—
Total mortgage loans	$415,634	$468,172	$499,301	$363,364	$434,864
Product:					
Prime mortgage	$356,842	$374,029	$405,889	$292,672	$396,934
Prime home equity	34,399	47,876	44,850	30,893	18,103
Nonprime mortgage*	16,993	40,596	44,637	39,441	19,827
Commercial real estate	7,400	5,671	3,925	358	—
Total mortgage loans	$415,634	$468,172	$499,301	$363,364	$434,864

* Countrywide Financial Corporation did not use the term *subprime*. The term *nonprime* was used to categorize subprime mortgages in the company's financial filings.

Source: Countrywide Financial Corporation, 2007 10-K report.

Exhibit 7 **Countrywide Loan Originations, 1990–2007 ($ thousands)**

Year	Conventional Conforming	Conventional Nonconforming	Fha/Va	Heloc	Subprime	Total Loan Originations
1990	19		16			35
1991	23		17			40
1992	64		24			88
1993	192		42			234
1994	316		67			383
1995	176		72	2		250
1996	192		125	8	2	327
1997	190		144	20	9	363
1998	232		162	41	16	451
1999	529		191	54	25	799
2000	359		132	91	43	625
2001	327		119	119	52	617
2002	994	266	157	290	44	1751
2003	1510	493	196	292	95	2586
2004	822	430	102	392	219	1965
2005	767	712	80	493	254	2306
2006	709	649	90	581	227	2256
2007	1088	313	138	330	85	1954

Source: Countrywide, 10-K reports, various years.

were sold into the secondary mortgage markets as MBSs.

Countrywide's Financial and Strategic Performance

Between 2002 and 2007, Countrywide's assets grew from $58 million to $211 million, and its revenues rose from $4.3 billion to $11.4 billion. The mortgage firm's operating earnings grew from $1.3 million in 2002 to $4.3 million in 2006. After recording record-breaking financial results for five consecutive years, Countrywide reported its first-ever loss in 2007. The dramatic reversal in Countrywide's financial performance was largely a result of its strategy keyed to the origination of subprime mortgages and no-down-payment loans. The hidden risk of default, foreclosures, and downgrades of such high-risk loans was masked while real estate values rose through 2006. Exhibit 8 presents selected financial data for Countrywide Financial Corporation for 2003 through 2007.

Incentive Compensation at Countrywide

Compensation expense represented approximately 55–60 percent of Countrywide's total expenses between 2003 and 2007. Compensation included employees' base salary, benefits expense, payroll taxes, and incentive pay. Countrywide's compensation system based incentive pay on loan originations and did not include loan defaults as a performance compensation metric. Many lending institutions frowned on incentive plans linked only to loan originations since loan performance ultimately determined the strength of a loan portfolio. Exhibit 9 provides a graph of incentive pay as a percentage of base pay for all Countrywide employees during 1992 through 2007.

Executive Compensation at Countrywide

The compensation for Mozilo for 2006 and 2007 is shown in Exhibit 10. Mozilo's compensation

Exhibit 8 **Selected Consolidated Financial Data for Countrywide Financial Corporation, 2003–2007 ($ thousands, except per share data)**

	Years Ended December 31				
	2007	2006	2005	2004	2003
Statement of Operations Data					
Revenues:					
Gain on sale of loans and securities	$2,434,723	$5,681,847	$4,861,780	$4,842,082	$5,887,436
Net interest income after provision for loan losses	587,882	2,688,514	2,237,935	1,965,541	1,359,390
Net loan servicing fees and other income (loss) from MSRs and retained interests	909,749	1,300,655	1,493,167	465,650	(463,050)
Net insurance premiums earned	1,523,534	1,171,433	953,647	782,685	732,816
Other	605,549	574,679	470,179	510,669	462,050
Total revenues	6,061,437	11,417,128	10,016,708	8,566,627	7,978,642
Expenses:					
Compensation	4,165,023	4,373,985	3,615,483	3,137,045	2,590,936
Occupancy and other office	1,126,226	1,030,164	879,680	643,378	525,192
Insurance claims	525,045	449,138	441,584	390,203	360,046
Advertising and promotion	321,766	260,652	229,183	171,585	103,902
Other	1,233,651	969,054	703,012	628,543	552,794
Total expenses	7,371,711	7,082,993	5,868,942	4,970,754	4,132,870
(Loss) earnings before income taxes	(1,310,274)	4,334,135	4,147,766	3,595,873	3,845,772
(Benefit) provision for income taxes	(606,736)	1,659,289	1,619,676	1,398,299	1,472,822
Net (loss) earnings	$ (703,538)	$2,674,846	$2,528,090	$2,197,574	$2,372,950
Per Share Data					
(Loss) earnings					
Basic	$(2.03)	$4.42	$4.28	$3.90	$4.44
Diluted	$(2.03)	$4.30	$4.11	$3.63	$4.18
Cash dividends declared	$0.60	$0.60	$0.59	$0.37	$0.15
Stock price at end of period	$8.94	$42.45	$34.19	$37.01	$25.28
Selected Financial Ratios:					
Return on average assets	(0.30%)	1.28%	1.46%	1.80%	2.65%
Return on average equity	(4.57%)	18.81%	22.67%	23.53%	34.25%
Dividend payout ratio	N/M	13.49%	13.81%	9.53%	3.39%
Selected Operating Data (in millions)					
Loan servicing portfolio[1]	$1,476,203	$1,298,394	$1,111,090	$838,322	$644,855
Volume of loans originated	$415,634	$468,172	$499,301	$363,364	$434,864
Volume of Mortgage Banking loans sold	$375,937	$403,035	$411,848	$326,313	$374,245

[1] Includes warehoused loans and loans under subservicing agreements.

(Continued)

Exhibit 8   *(Concluded)*

	Years Ended December 31				
	2007	**2006**	**2005**	**2004**	**2003**
Selected Balance Sheet Data at End of Period:					
Loans:					
Held for sale	$ 11,681,274	$ 31,272,630	$ 36,808,185	$ 37,347,326	$24,103,625
Held for investment	98,000,713	78,019,994	69,865,447	39,661,191	26,375,958
	109,681,987	109,292,624	106,673,632	77,008,517	50,479,583
Securities purchased under agreements to resell, securities borrowed and federal funds sold	9,640,879	27,269,897	23,317,361	13,456,448	10,448,102
Investments in other financial instruments	28,173,281	12,769,451	11,260,725	9,834,214	12,647,213
Mortgage servicing rights, at fair value	18,958,180	16,172,064	—	—	—
Mortgage servicing rights, net	—	—	12,610,839	8,729,929	6,863,625
Other assets	45,275,734	34,442,194	21,222,813	19,466,597	17,539,150
Total assets	$211,730,061	$199,946,230	$175,085,370	$128,495,705	$97,977,673
Deposit liabilities	$ 60,200,599	$ 55,578,682	$ 39,438,916	$ 20,013,208	$ 9,327,671
Securities sold under agreements to repurchase	18,218,162	42,113,501	34,153,205	20,465,123	32,013,412
Notes payable	97,227,413	71,487,584	76,187,886	66,613,671	39,948,461
Other liabilities	21,428,016	16,448,617	12,489,503	11,093,627	8,603,413
Shareholders' equity	14,655,871	14,317,846	12,815,860	10,310,076	8,084,716
Total liabilities and shareholders' equity	$211,730,061	$199,946,230	$175,085,370	$128,495,705	$97,977,673

The 2007 capital ratios reflect the conversion of Countrywide Bank's charter from a national bank to a federal savings bank. Accordingly, the ratios for 2007 are for Countrywide Bank calculated using OTS guidelines and the ratios for the prior periods are calculated for Countrywide Financial Corporation in compliance with the guidelines of the Board of Governors of the Federal Reserve Bank.

Source: Countrywide Financial Corporation, 2007 10-K report.

listed in the table does not include perquisites, which amounted to approximately $108,000 per year and included company cars, country club memberships, the personal use of corporate aircraft, insurance, and a financial planning program. Mozilo also exercised $121 million of stock options in 2007 and reportedly stood to collect a reported windfall of $80 million to $115 million on the $4 billion sale of the company to BofA as part of his severance package. However, after facing heavy criticism from lawmakers, Mozilo said he would forfeit $37.5 million tied to the deal.

Charges of Predatory Lending Practices at Countrywide

Predatory loans were generally considered to be any loan that a borrower would have rejected with full knowledge and understanding of the terms of the loan and the terms of alternatives available to him or her. Predatory lenders typically relied on a range of practices, including deception, fraud, and manipulation to convince borrowers to agree to loan terms that were unethical or illegal. Countrywide Financial Corporation (CFC) was charged with engaging in predatory

Exhibit 9   **Incentive Pay as Percentage of Base Pay for All Employees of Countrywide, 1992–2007**

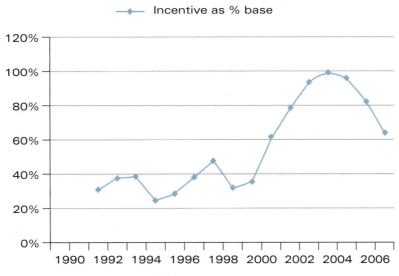

Source: Countrywide, 10-K reports, various years.

lending practices in the case *Department of Legal Affairs (Florida) v. Countrywide Financial Corp. et al.,* filed June 30, 2008. Specific illegal practices alleged in the case included:

1. CFC did not follow its own underwriting standards.
2. CFC did not follow industry underwriting standards.

3. CFC placed borrowers into loans they knew they could not afford.
4. CFC failed to properly disclose loan terms including
   a. Misrepresenting duration of "teaser rates."
   b. Misrepresenting adjustable rates as fixed rates.

Exhibit 10   **Angelo Mozilo's Comensation at Countrywide Financial Corporation, 2006–2007**

Compensation Components	2006	2007	% Change
Base salary	$ 2,900,000	$ 1,900,000	(34%)
Annual incentive	20,461,473	0	(100%)
Equity awards	19,012,000	10,000,036	(47%)
Total	$42,373,473	$ 11,900,036	(72%)
Exercised options	—	$121,502,318	n/a

Note: n/a = not applicable.
Source: Countrywide Financial Corporation 2007 10-K.

    c. Misrepresenting the manner and degree of payment increases after initial fixed rate period.

    d. Not disclosing that low teaser rates would expire and dramatically increase resulting payments that might be far beyond borrower's means.

5. CFC knowingly placed borrowers in inappropriate mortgages.

6. CFC provided underwriters with bonuses based upon volume of mortgages approved.

Countrywide portrayed itself as underwriting mainly prime quality mortgages using rigorous underwriting standards. Concealed from shareholders was the true Countrywide, an increasingly reckless lender assuming greater and greater risk. From 2005 to 2007, Countrywide engaged in an unprecedented expansion of its underwriting guidelines and was writing riskier and riskier loans, according to the SEC. A series of internal e-mails confirmed that senior executives knew that defaults and delinquencies would rise. In particular, the SEC pointed to Countrywide's increased origination of pay-option mortgages, which allow borrowers to choose their monthly payments even if they did not cover the entire interest amount. While Countrywide maintained that these loans were prudently underwritten, the SEC stated that Mozilo wrote in an e-mail that there was evidence that borrowers were lying on their applications and many would be unable to handle the eventual higher payments.

Angelo Mozilo's Internal E-mails at Countrywide Financial Corporation

In June 2009, the SEC filed civil-fraud charges against three former Countrywide executives, including Angelo Mozilo. The complaint cited e-mails sent by Mozilo as evidence of fraudulent behavior at Countrywide. The statements below are from excerpts of Mozilo e-mails released by the SEC.

    April 13, 2006: To Sambol (Countrywide Financial Corporation president) and others to address issues relating to 100 percent-

age financed loans, after Countrywide had to buy back mortgages sold to HSBC because HSBC contended they were defective:

Loans had been originated . . . throughout channels with disregard for process and compliance with guidelines.

April 17, 2006: To Sambol concerning Countrywide's subprime 100 percent financing 80/20 loans. (The term *FICO* refers to credit scores used to assess a borrower's creditworthiness.)

In all my years in business I have never seen a more toxic product. It's not only subordinated to the first, but the first is subprime. In addition, the FICOs are below 600, below 500 and some below 400. With real estate values coming down . . . the product will become increasingly worse. There has to be major changes in this program, including substantial increases in the minimum FICO. . . . Whether you consider the business milk or not, I am prepared to go without milk irrespective of the consequences to our production.

Sept. 26, 2006: Following a meeting with Sambol the previous day about Pay-Option ARM loan portfolio:

We have no way, with any reasonable certainty, to assess the real risk of holding these loans on our balance sheet. . . . The bottom line is that we are flying blind on how these loans will perform in a stressed environment of high unemployment, reduced values and slowing home sales . . . timing is right . . . to . . . sell all newly originated pay option and begin rolling off the bank balance sheet, in an orderly manner.

Countrywide's VIP Loan Program

Countrywide maintained a VIP program that waived points, lender fees, and company borrowing rules for "FOAs"—Friends of Angelo, a reference to Countrywide's chief executive, Angelo Mozilo. While the VIP program also serviced friends and contacts of other Countrywide executives, it is believed the FOAs made up the biggest subset. Some FOAs were individuals who might have been in position to aid the company through regulatory and compliance matters or who may have been able to keep the subprime market viable through favorable legislation. Countrywide's ethics code barred directors, officers, and employees from "improperly influencing the decisions of government employees or contractors by offering or promising to give money, gifts, loans, rewards, favors, or anything else of value." Also, federal employees were prohibited from receiving gifts offered because of their official position, including loans on terms not generally available to the public. Senate rules prohibited members from knowingly receiving gifts worth $100 or more in a calendar year from private entities that, like Countrywide, employed a registered lobbyist.

Countrywide granted VIP loans to 153 employees at Fannie Mae, including several top officials at the GSE. The company also made VIP loans for 20 Freddie Mac Employees. Among the most noteworthy recipients of Countrywide VIP loans were two prominent U.S. senators, two former cabinet members, and a former ambassador to the United Nations. In 2003 and 2004, Senators Christopher Dodd, a Democrat from Connecticut and chairman of the Senate Banking Committee,[4] and Kent Conrad, a Democrat from North Dakota, chairman of the Senate Budget Committee and a member of the Senate Finance Committee, refinanced properties through Countrywide's VIP program.

Other participants in the VIP program included former secretary of Housing and Urban Development (HUD) Alphonso Jackson, former secretary of Health and Human Services Donna Shalala, and former UN ambassador and assistant secretary of state Richard Holbrooke. Jackson was deputy HUD secretary in the Bush administration when he received the loans in 2003. Shalala, who received two loans in 2002, had by then left the Clinton administration for her current position as president of the University of Miami. Holbrooke, whose stint as UN ambassador ended in 2001, was also working in the private sector when he and his family received VIP loans. Holbrooke was an adviser to Hillary Clinton's presidential 2008 campaign. James Johnson, who had been advising presidential candidate Barack Obama on the selection of a running mate in 2008, resigned from the Obama campaign after the *Wall Street Journal* reported

that he received Countrywide loans at below-market rates.

BANK OF AMERICA'S ATTEMPTS TO SALVAGE ITS ACQUISITION OF COUNTRYWIDE FINANCIAL CORPORATION

Almost as soon as the acquisition closed, BofA entered into an $8.7 billion settlement agreement with a group of state attorneys general over Countrywide's lending practices. BofA also agreed to modify the loans of certain Countrywide borrowers with subprime and pay-option mortgages. In the first four months following the settlement agreement, BofA contacted more than 100,000 potentially eligible borrowers, twice the requirement in the agreement, and completed modifications for more than 50,000 of them. The settlement was the largest predatory lending settlement in U.S. history as of 2009.

In March 2009, American International Group (AIG) sued BoA over Countrywide's business practices, alleging the company misrepresented the risk associated with the sale of mortgages totaling over $1 billion. AIG claimed that Countrywide had falsely represented that its mortgages were in compliance with its AIG underwriting standards.

BofA retired the Countrywide brand name in 2009 as it worked to distance itself from the brand and Countrywide's business practices. According to California attorney general Edmund Brown, "CFC lending practices turned the American dream into a nightmare for tens of thousands of families by putting them into loans they could not understand or ultimately could not afford."[5] Going forward, Bank of America senior managers would need to develop a strategic approach to ensure that BoA's mortgage lending practices promoted homeownership in a manner that was in the best interest of borrowers and investors in the secondary mortgage market, as well as in the company's own long-term financial interests.

ENDNOTES

1 These products were developed following the savings and loan (S&L) crisis of the 1980s and converted the actual mortgage into pools of mortgages, which enabled institutions to invest and trade a marketable security. MBSs were also known as collateralized debt obligations.

2 Moody's Economy.com.

3 AIG's core business as the world's largest general insurer was sound. However, AIG's CDO insurance business, while a very small part of the company's overall business, brought the firm close to bankruptcy. As for AIG's global reach, it was far too extensive and a default would have brought down other financial institutions across the world markets.

4 Countrywide had contributed a total of $21,000 to Dodd's campaigns since 1997.

5 Quoted in Frank D. Russo, "Attorney General Brown Announces Largest Predatory Lending Settlement in History," *California Progress Report,* accessed at www.californiaprogress-report.com/2008/10/attorney_genera_3.html, accessed September 5, 2009.

PHOTO CREDITS

Chapter 1:

Page 7, © Yu Chu Di/Redlink/Redlink/Corbis; Page 13, Getty Images

Chapter 2:

Page 25, The Coca-Cola Company; Page 29, Jared McMillen/Aurora Photo/Corbis; Page 32, © RICK WILKING/Reuters/Corbis; Page 42, © Jason Reed/Reuters/Corbis; Page 42, Bloomberg via Getty Images

Chapter 4:

Page 112, Just Coffee Cooperative

Chapter 5:

Page 143, Courtesy of Walmart; Page 155, Pichi Chuang/Reuters/Corbis; Page 156, Joe Robbins/Getty Images; Page 159, 2010 Toyota Motor Sales, USA, Inc.

Chapter 6:

Page 176, Amazon.com, Inc.; Page 188, Courtesy of American Apparel

Chapter 7:

Page 236, MARK/epa/Corbis; Page 239, Bloomberg Via Getty Images

Chapter 8:

Page 283, AP Photo/Mike Derer

Chapter 9:

Page 295, Courtesy of Apple; Page 304, Aaron M. Sprecher/Corbis; Page 307, CLARO CORTESIV/Reuters/Corbis

Chapter 10:

Page 337, AFP/Getty Images; Page 341, Courtesy of Toyota

Chapter 11:

Page 371, Paulo Fridman/Corbis; Page 380, Courtesy of Lincoln Electric; Page 383, Bloomberg Via Getty Images

Chapter 12:

Page 409, AP Photo/Carlos Osorio

ORGANIZATION INDEX

NAME INDEX

SUBJECT INDEX

O